MW00388464

W. E. Vine's
Greek Grammar and Dictionary

Other Works by W. E. Vine

Christ

Classic Reflections on Scripture

Prophecy

Reflections on Words of the New Testament

Vine's Complete Expository Dictionary of Old and New Testament Words with Topical Index

Vine's Concise Dictionary of Old and New Testament Words

W. E. Vine's

Greek Grammar and Dictionary

W. E. Vine, M.A.

THOMAS NELSON
Since 1798

NASHVILLE DALLAS MEXICO CITY RIO DE JANEIRO

© 2012 by W. E. Vine Copyright.

All rights reserved. No portion of this book may be reproduced, stored in a retrieval system, or transmitted in any form or by any means—electronic, mechanical, photocopy, recording, scanning, or other—except for brief quotations in critical reviews or articles, without the prior written permission of the publisher.

Published in Nashville, Tennessee, by Thomas Nelson. Thomas Nelson is a registered trademark of Thomas Nelson, Inc.

Book design and composition by Upper Case Textual Services, Lawrence, Massachusetts.

Thomas Nelson, Inc., titles may be purchased in bulk for educational, business, fund-raising, or sales promotional use. For information, please e-mail SpecialMarkets@ThomasNelson.com.

The material in this book originally was published in other forms in *Vine's Expository Dictionary of Old and New Testament Words*, © 1996, *Vine's You Can Learn New Testament Greek: Course of Self Help for the Layman*, © 1996, all rights reserved.

Unless otherwise noted, Scripture quotations are taken from THE NEW KING JAMES VERSION. © 1982 by Thomas Nelson, Inc. Used by permission. All rights reserved.

Verses marked KJV are taken from the HOLY BIBLE: KING JAMES VERSION

ISBN: 978-1-4185-4643-4

Printed in the United States of America

12 13 14 15 16 QG 1 2 3 4 5 6

Contents

Part 1

Grammar

Preface

THE production of this Grammar is the outcome of a Class held many years ago in Exeter, for students desirous of acquiring a knowledge of the Greek Testament to avail themselves freely of a course of instruction in it. The method adopted was somewhat of a departure from the rigid order prevailing in the School Grammars. From the beginning, use was made of the Greek New Testament, the simpler sentences and phrases being brought into use by way of exercises, with a gradual extension according as progress was made in the Grammar itself. The method proved both practicable and interesting.

More recently, some of the Lessons in this volume appeared monthly in a Magazine, and it became evident that there is a fairly widespread desire to acquire the knowledge of the New Testament in the original tongue. The provision of Lessons in a Magazine involved their length being adjusted to circumstances of the space required for Magazine articles, and this meant a certain amount of overlapping (without repetition of subject matter from one Lesson to another), it not being possible to divide the subjects so as to put them completely into one Lesson. This, however, did not prove an interference in the course of the study. After some twenty-three lessons had been thus inserted, the Magazine was discontinued, and circumstances, over which the author had no control, have necessitated the publication of the Lessons according to the division previously adopted, but no hindrance to the study is thus presented.

Another result of Magazine work is the somewhat conversational style of guiding the studies and providing explanations, and this again is not without advantage. The student should study the Lessons patiently and thoroughly, and follow closely the advice given as to memorizing, and as to repeating certain parts of the Lessons. The Latin proverb "*Festina lente*" ("Hasten slowly") is of great importance in this respect, and though constant review is a laborious task, the ability to read certain parts of the Greek New Testament almost from the commencement of the studies provides interest for those who delight in the Word of God, and makes the task well worthwhile. The author is hopeful that, in spite of defects, some real contribution may have been made towards this important means of knowing the mind of the Lord.

W. E. Vine, M.A.
Bath

Foreword

THERE are many excellent translations of the New Testament from the original Greek into our English tongue, but it is admitted that the student of New Testament Greek has the advantage over the ordinary reader.

The author of this little text book has done a signal service to all who have the linguistic gift. Indeed, under its guidance that talent will be discovered and improved. Mr. Vine has long experience in teaching this subject and his Grammar is no mere echo of other text books. His progressive method and the direct use of the Greek New Testament are his own. No better book can be put into the hands of those who have no previous knowledge of learning languages. It is worthy of a place in any "Teach Yourself" series, especially in this revised edition. Designed for the lay reader, it will also find a place in the equipment of others, who wish to feed first-hand upon the Word of God, and give themselves to its glorious ministry.

Francis Davidson

Introduction

It has been well said that the Greek language is "the most subtle and powerful language that ever flowed from the tongue of man." Yet, comparatively speaking, it is easy, and particularly Biblical Greek. The language of the New Testament Greek was much simpler than what is known as Classical Greek, and is to be distinguished from the writings of men who aspire to literary fame. As the late Dr. J. H. Moulton wrote, "The New Testament writers had little idea that they were writing literature. The Holy Ghost spoke absolutely in the language of the people.... The very grammar and dictionary cry out against men who would allow the Scriptures to appear in any other form than that 'understanded of the people.'" The language spoken throughout the Roman Empire in the first century of this era was Hellenistic Greek, otherwise called the *Koiné,* or the common dialect of the people. How it came about that such a language became universal is described in the writer's manual "B.C. and A.D." or "How the world was prepared for the Gospel," one of the *Witness* manuals. The hand of God is strikingly seen in the national movements which eventually made it possible for the message of eternal life to be conveyed to all nations by means of the natural, yet powerful tongue which it is our privilege to study. The study indeed is important as it opens up the mind of God to us as no translation could ever do. Patience and perseverance are required, but the student who has a few hours to spare in the course of a month will soon make progress, and find that he is experiencing a new delight in the intelligent reading of the actual words by which "Men spake from God, being moved by the Holy Ghost" (2 Pet. 1:21).

Lesson 1

The Alphabet and Notes Thereon

The Alphabet

The student should familiarize himself with the alphabet, capital and small letters, and their names, and should observe carefully the notes given below. Learn the alphabet by heart; to know the order of the letters is useful for concordance work.

Capitals	**Small**	**Name**	**Equivalent**
Α	α	alpha	a
Β	β	beta	b
Γ	γ	gamma	g
Δ	δ	delta	d
Ε	ε	epsilon	e (short)
Ζ	ζ	zeta	z (dz)
Η	η	eta	e (long)
Θ	θ	theta	th
Ι	ι	iota	i
Κ	κ	kappa	k

Λ	λ	lambda	l
Μ	μ	mu	m
Ν	ν	nu	n
Ξ	ξ	xi	x
Ο	ο	omicron	o (short)
Π	π	pi	p
Ρ	ρ	rho	r
Σ	σ (ς)	sigma	s
Τ	τ	tau	t
Υ	υ	upsilon	u
Φ	φ	phi	ph
Χ	χ	chi	ch (hard)
Ψ	ψ	psi	ps
Ω	ω	omega	o (long)

Notes on the Alphabet

(1) There are two forms of the letter E, the short, *epsilon,* pronounced as in "met," the long, *eta,* pronounced as in "mate."

(2) Distinguish the shape of the small letter *eta* from the English "n"; the Greek letter has a long stroke on the right. On the other hand, distinguish the small letter *nu* (the English "n") from the English letter "v." The "v" shape in English is a Greek small "n." The capital *eta* (English long "e") must be distinguished from the English capital H.

(3) There are two forms of the letter O, the short, *omicron,* as in "dot," the long, *omega,* as in "dote" (o and ō).

(4) Distinguish the *xi* (English "x") from the *chi* (English "ch"), sounded hard, as in "Christ." The latter, though it looks like the English "x," combines the two letters c and h.

(5) Distinguish the Greek letter *rho* (English "r") from the English "p." The capital R in Greek is just like the English "P," and the small is somewhat similar. Familiarize the eye in looking at the Greek capital as an "R" not a "P."

(6) There are two forms of the letter "s." One is similar in shape to the English "s," but it is reserved for the end of a word and is never found elsewhere. Greek words ending in the letter "s" must end with the "s" of that shape. Where "s" occurs in the part of a word other than the final letter, the other form must be used. It is like an "o" with a horizontal stroke stretching from the top on the right hand side.

(7) There is no dot over the iota.

(8) In writing *upsilon* keep the letter curved, as if it is made like a "v" it will be confounded with the small *nu.*

(9) The small *gamma* must be distinguished from the English "y." The Greek *gamma* is always hard as in "go," not as in "gem."

(10) The student will observe that there is no "h," or rough breathing in the alphabet. Its place is taken by an inverted comma over a letter, thus— ὃς (who). The soft breathing is signified by a comma over the initial vowel, and denotes an absence of the h sound, thus— ἦν ("was"). Therefore the rough breathing or the soft comes over every vowel or diphthong that begins a word. Every word that begins with ρ (*rho*)must have the "h," or rough breathing, over it: thus ῥῆμα ("a word "). When a word begins with two vowels the breathings come over the second letter thus— υἱός ("a son," pronounced *hweos*) and αὐτός ("he," pronounced *owtos*). Double *rho* in the body of a word is written ῤῥ (the first with the smooth breathing, the second with the rough).

(11) Occasionally a vowel has a small iota underneath it, called the iota subscript. This iota is not pronounced but it is a very important mark to notice, as it often serves to distinguish different forms of the same word.

(12) The *omega* (signifying "great O") is the last letter in the alphabet. Thus when the Lord says "I am the Alpha and the Omega" (Rev. 22:13), our English equivalent (though we must not translate it so) would be "I am the A and the Z."

A Table of some Vowel Sounds

α = long and short, as in ah and fat.

ε = short only, as in set.

η = long only, as in pain (or aim).

ο = short only, as in pot.

ω = long only, as in bone.

ι = long and short, as in police and fit.

υ = long and short, as in true and put.

The student should obtain *Nestle's Greek Testament* (small edition) published by the British and Foreign Bible Society, 146 Queen Victoria Street, London, E.C.4. That is the text which will be used in this course. [This edition of Vine's *New Testament Greek Grammar* uses the Fourth Revised Edition of the United Bible Societies' *The Greek New Testament*, which is available from the American Bible Society, Grand Central Station, New York, NY.]

Lesson 2

Consonants. Pronunciation. Punctuation. Inflections. Numbers. Genders. Cases. The Article. The First Declension

Consonants

The following three classes of consonants should be noted particularly,

(1) Labials: π, β, φ.

(2) Gutturals, or palatals: κ, γ, χ.

(3) Dentals: τ, δ, θ.

(*a*) A labial with s (πς, βς, φς) makes ψ.

(*b*) A guttural with s (κς, γς, χς) makes ξ.

(*c*) The dental with s is dropped, but in the case of δς, makes ζ.

(*d*) The letter ν becomes μ before labials; thus σύνφημι (lit. together to say, i.e., to agree) becomes σύμφημι. It becomes γ before gutturals; thus συνχαίρω (to rejoice with) becomes συγχαίρω. It is dropped before ς or ζ; thus συνστρατιώτης (fellow soldier) becomes συστρατιώτης; σύνζυγος (yokefellow) becomes σύζυγος. Before λ, μ, ρ, (which, with ν itself, are called liquids) ν is changed into the same letter; thus συνλαλέω (to talk with) becomes συλλαλέω; συνμαρτυρέω (to witness with) becomes συμμαρτυρέω.

Further Pronunciations

The guttural γ followed by another guttural, κ, γ, χ, is pronounced like the English "ng." Thus ἄγγελος (angel) is pronounced angelos (hard g, not as in the English word "angel," and ἄγκυρα (anchor) is pronounced ang-kura. In the following double vowels pronounce αυ as in "out"; ει as in "eight"; ου as in "boot", αι as in "by"; ευ as in "beauty."

Punctuation

There are four punctuation marks:— the comma (,); the semicolon or colon, expressed by a point above the line (·); the full stop or period, as in English; the note of interrogation (;). This latter is the same in form as the English semi-colon, but must be distinguished from it. The Greek ; is the English ?.

Exercise

Write the following in Greek characters, without the aid of the Greek text, and correct the result from the text. A good deal of practice can be obtained this way. Avoid trying to learn the meanings of the words. The practice will facilitate progress afterwards. All the vowels are short unless marked long.

John 1:4–11— 4 en autō zōē ēn, kai hē zōē ēn to phōs tōn anthrōpōn; 5 kai to phōs en tē
skotia phainei, kai hē skotia auto ou katelaben.

6 Egeneto anthrōpos, apestalmenos para theou, onoma autō Iōannēs; 7 houtos ēlthen eis
marturian hina marturēsē peri tou phōtos, hina pantes pisteusōsin di' autou. 8 ouk ēn ekeinos
to phōs, all' hina marturēsē peri tou phōtos. 9 En to phōs to alēthinon, ho phōtizei panta
anthrōpon, erchomenon eis ton kosmon. 10 en to kosmō ēn, kai ho kosmos di' autou egeneto,
kai ho kosmos auton ouk egnō. 11 eis ta idia ēlthen, kai hoi idioi auton ou parelabon.

[Practice transcribing further from the Greek text into English letters and transcribing the latter back into the Greek text.]

INFLECTION signifies the change in the form of words to express variation in meaning. Declension is the system of change in the terminations of nouns, adjectives and pronouns to express different relations, as follows:—

GENDERS—There are three genders: Masculine, Feminine, Neuter. These are not determined as in English by conditions of sex. Names of inanimate objects are of different genders. The terminations of the words are a considerable guide.

NUMBERS—These are two, singular and plural. There is a dual (signifying two) in Greek but it does not occur in the Greek Testament.

CASES—There are five cases: (1) The Nominative, expressing the subject; (2) the Vocative, used in direct address; (3) the Genitive, which originally signified motion from and hence separation but afterwards came largely to denote possession. Accordingly it is convenient to associate the preposition "of" with it. Its range is very wide; (4), the Dative signifying the remote object; hence the preposition "to" is associated with it. It also has a large range of meaning, however, such as rest in, conjunction with, etc.; (5) the Accusative, expressing the object of a verb, and used after certain prepositions to express motion towards, etc.; These details will be considered later.

The Article

We are now in a position to consider the forms of the definite article "the" (there is no indefinite article "a").

The following must be learnt by heart, horizontally (masculine, feminine, neuter), and case by case in the order given. The forms largely provide a model to the endings of certain noun, adjective, and pronoun cases, as will be seen later.

Singular

	Masc.	**Fem.**	**Neut.**	
Nom.	ὁ	ἡ	τό	(the)
Gen.	τοῦ	τῆς	τοῦ	(of the)
Dat.	τῷ	τῇ	τῷ	(to the)
Acc.	τόν	τήν	τό	(the)

Plural

	Masc.	**Fem.**	**Neut.**	
Nom.	οἱ	αἱ	τά	(the)
Gen.	τῶν	τῶν	τῶν	(of the)
Dat.	τοῖς	ταῖς	τοῖς	(to the)
Acc.	τούς	τάς	τά	(the)

Note 1—The iota under the vowels in the dative singular must be observed carefully; it is very important. It is called iota subscript.

Note 2—The nominative and accusative are always the same in the neuter.

Note 3—The genitive plural always ends in ων.

Note 4—Masculine and neuter dative forms are always alike.

The First Declension

Nouns

There are three types of inflection of nouns. These are called the Three Declensions. The endings of the First, in the noun form first given, correspond with the feminine form of the article.

First Declension

(1) *Feminine nouns in -η*

πύλη, a gate

	Singular			**Plural**	
Nom.	πύλη	a gate.	Nom.	πύλαι	gates.
Voc.	πύλη	O gate!	Voc.	πύλαι	O gates!
Gen.	πύλης	of a gate.	Gen.	πυλῶν	of gates.
Dat.	πύλῃ	to a gate.	Dat.	πύλαις	to gates.
Acc.	πύλην	a gate.	Acc.	πύλας	gates.

(Learn the above paradigm by heart, putting the feminine of the article with each case, thus: ἡ πύλη, the gate; τὴν πύλην the gate; τῆς πύλης of the gate; etc.)

Declined like πύλη are the following, which should be learned by heart:

τιμή honor

φωνή a voice

ψυχή soul, or life

στολή garment

νύμφη bride

βροχή rain

παιδίσκη a damsel, maid, or bondwoman

ὀφειλή a debt

δίκη justice

σελήνη moon

ὀργή wrath, anger

εἰρήνη peace

ἐπιστολή letter

κεφαλή head

ἀδελφή sister

ἀρχή beginning, rule

προσευχή prayer

ὑπακοή obedience

παρακοή disobedience

ἀγαθωσύνη goodness

ἁγιωσύνη holiness

καταλλαγή reconciliation

ὑπερβολή abundance, excellence

ὑπομονή patience

(Write a few of these out in full, on the model of πύλη.)

Lesson 3

First Declension Nouns (continued). Second Declension and the Verb "To be," Present and Imperfect Tenses

First Declension Nouns in -α

(*These are feminine*)

Note 1—When a noun has the stem-ending - α preceded by a vowel or ρ, the singular retains α throughout, as follows:—

βασιλεία, a kingdom

	Singular	**Plural**
N. & V.	βασιλεία	βασιλεῖαι
Gen.	βασιλείας	βασιλειῶν
Dat.	βασιλείᾳ	βασιλείαις
Acc.	βασιλείαν	βασιλείας

On the model of this, write out in full ἡμέρα, a day

Note 2—When a noun has the stem-ending -α preceded by a consonant, the α becomes η in the genitive and dative singular (α being kept in the other cases), as follows:—

γλῶσσα, a tongue

	Singular	**Plural**
N. & V.	γλῶσσα	γλῶσσαι
Gen.	γλώσσης	γλωσσῶν
Dat.	γλώσσῃ	γλώσσαις
Acc.	γλῶσσαν	γλώσσας

Like βασιλεία and ἡμέρα, are the following, which should be committed to memory:—

ἀλήθεια, truth
ἀδικία, unrighteousness
ἄγνοια, ignorance
ἀνομία, iniquity (lit., lawlessness)
ἐργασία, work, diligence, or gain
ἐριθεία, contention, strife
ἐξουσία, power, authority
μαρτυρία, a witness
σκία, a shadow
οἰκία, a house
λυχνία, a lampstand
σοφία, wisdom
πέτρα, a rock
θύρα, a door

Like γλῶσσα are:—

δόξα, glory
μέριμνα, a care
θάλασσα, a sea
ῥίζα, a root

Write out in full, with their different cases and numbers, οἰκία, μέριμνα, and ῥίζα, putting the feminine article with its appropriate cases, singular and plural, before each, and giving the meanings of each case. Do this without referring to the printed lessons and correct your results therefrom: thus, ἡ οἰκία, the house; τὴν οἰκίαν, the house; τῆς οἰκίας, of the house, etc.

First Declension Nouns in -ης and -ας

(*These are masculine*)

Note 1—Masculine nouns of the first declension in -ης form the genitive singular in -ου and the vocative in -α. In the other cases they are declined just like πύλη (Lesson 2).

Note 2—Masculine nouns of the first declension in -ας also form the genitive singular in -ου and the vocative in -α. In other cases they are like βασιλεία (see above).

Note 3—The plural is the same throughout in all first declension nouns. Commit the following to memory:—

μαθητής, a disciple

	Singular	**Plural**
Nom.	μαθητής	μαθηταί
Voc.	μαθητά	μαθηταί
Gen.	μαθητοῦ	μαθητῶν
Dat.	μαθητῇ	μαθηταῖς
Acc.	μαθητήν	μαθητάς

νεανίας, a young man

	Singular	**Plural**
Nom.	νεανίας	νεανίαι
Voc.	νεανία	νεανίαι
Gen.	νεανίου	νεανιῶν
Dat.	νεανίᾳ	νεανίαις
Acc.	νεανίαν	νεανίας

Write these out putting the masculine article ὁ, with its appropriate cases, singular and plural, before each, and the meanings. Correct the result from the above.

Like μαθητὴς are the following, which should be learned:

προφήτης, a prophet

τελώνης, a publican (tax collector)

κριτής, a judge

ἐργάτης, a laborer

ὀφειλέτης, a debtor

ὑπηρέτης, an attendant, a servant

The Second Declension—Stem ending -ο

Masculine nouns, and a few feminine, in this declension end in -ος. Neuter nouns end in -ον. Learn the following thoroughly. Write them out in full by memory, with the article ὁ for λόγος and τὸ for ἔργον and with the meanings.

λόγος, a word

	Singular		**Plural**	
Nom.	λόγος	a word	λόγοι	words
Voc.	λόγε	O word	λόγοι	O words
Gen.	λόγου	of a word	λόγων	of words
Dat.	λόγῳ	to a word	λόγους	to words
Acc.	λόγον	a word	λόγοις	words

ἔργον, a work

	Singular	**Plural**
Nom.	ἔργον	ἔργα
Voc.	ἔργον	ἔργα
Gen.	ἔργου	ἔργων
Dat.	ἔργῳ	ἔργοις
Acc.	ἔργον	ἔργα

Note 1—All neuter nouns have the same form in the nominative, vocative, and accusative.

Note 2—Observe the iota subscript under the dative singular.

Note 3—The masculine article ὁ must go with masculine nouns when "the" comes before, and the neuter τό with neuter nouns.

With the help of a few extra words, some forms, and some simple principles, we shall be able at once to read some sentences from the New Testament. The third declension will be reserved till later.

Memorize the following:—

The verb "to be"

Present Tense

Singular

1st person	εἰμί	I am
2nd person	εἶ	thou art
3rd person	ἐστί(ν)	he (she, it, or there) is

Plural

1st person	ἐσμέν	we are
2nd person	ἐστέ	ye are
3rd person	εἰσί(ν)	they (or there) are

Note—In English, "thou" is singular and "ye" is plural.

Note—The ν at the end of the 3rd person is used before a vowel, or at the end of a sentence.

Imperfect Tense

Singular

1st person	ἦν	I was
2nd person	ἦσθα	thou wast
3rd person	ἦν	he (she, it, or there) was

Plural

1st person	ἦμεν	we were
2nd person	ἦτε	ye were
3rd person	ἦσαν	they (or there) were

Note—The personal pronouns are included in the verb forms; they are expressed by separate words only when the pronouns require emphasis. These will be given later. When there is another subject of the verb the pronoun is, of course, omitted; thus, ἦν ὁ λόγος is "was the Word."

Learn the following words:— ἐν, in (this preposition is always followed by the dative case; thus ἐν ἀρχῇ, "in (the) beginning"—the omission of the Greek article here will be explained later, it must be rendered in English in this phrase; πρός, towards or with (this is followed by the accusative thus, πρὸς τὸν θεόν, "with God," the article is often used with proper names, but must not be rendered in English); ἐκ, of, or out of; καί, and; οὗτος, this (masculine); αὕτη, this (feminine); τοῦτο, this (neuter); οὐ, not (οὐ has two other forms, οὐκ and οὐχ; οὐκ is used when the next word begins with a vowel, and some consonants; οὐχ when the next word begins with an aspirate ʽ); δέ, but, or and.

υἱός a son	ἄμπελος a vine (fem.)
ἄνθρωπος a man	κόσμος a world
ὁδός a way (fem.)	καθώς even as
ἐγώ I	οὗτος this (masc.)
σύ thou	αὕτη this (fem.)

Translate into English without referring to the texts (these are supplied to enable students to make their own corrections from the New Testament). For the meaning of the words see above.

Ἐν ἀρχῇ ἦν ὁ λόγος, καὶ ὁ λόγος ἦν πρὸς τὸν θεόν, καὶ θεὸς ἦν ὁ λόγος. οὗτος ἦν ἐν ἀρχῇ πρὸς τὸν θεόν. (John 1:1–2).

Καὶ αὕτη ἐστὶν ἡ μαρτυρία τοῦ Ἰωάννου (John 1:19).

οὗτός ἐστιν ὁ υἱὸς τοῦ θεοῦ (John 1:34).

σὺ εἶ ὁ υἱὸς τοῦ θεοῦ (John 1:49).

Ἦν δὲ ἄνθρωπος ἐκ τῶν φαρισαίων (John 3:1).

Ἐγώ εἰμι ἡ ὁδὸς καὶ ἡ ἀλήθεια καὶ ἡ ζωή (John 14:6).

ἐγώ εἰμι ἡ ἄμπελος (John 15:5).

ἐκ τοῦ κόσμου οὐκ εἰσὶν καθὼς ἐγὼ οὐκ εἰμὶ ἐκ τοῦ κόσμου (John 17:16).

Οὗτός ἐστιν ὁ μαθητής (John 21:24).

After writing out the English correctly, retranslate the above sentences into Greek, correcting your results from the texts.

Lesson 4

Adjectives, and Pronouns corresponding to the First and Second Declensions

Adjectives and Pronouns Corresponding to the First and Second Declensions

Note—The masculine and neuter endings correspond to the nouns of the second declension (see λόγος and ἔργον, Lesson 3); the feminine endings correspond to nouns of the first declension (see πύλη, Lesson 2). If the noun forms have been learned thoroughly, the adjectives are easily committed to memory.

First Form

ἀγαθός, good

Singular

	Masc.	**Fem.**	**Neut.**
Nom.	ἀγαθός	ἀγαθή	ἀγαθόν
Voc.	ἀγαθέ	ἀγαθή	ἀγαθόν
Gen.	ἀγαθοῦ	ἀγαθῆς	ἀγαθοῦ
Dat.	ἀγαθῷ	ἀγαθῇ	ἀγαθῷ
Acc.	ἀγαθόν	ἀγαθήν	ἀγαθόν

Plural

N. & V.	ἀγαθοί	ἀγαθαί	ἀγαθά
Gen.	ἀγαθῶν	ἀγαθῶν	ἀγαθῶν
Dat.	ἀγαθοῖς	ἀγαθαῖς	ἀγαθοῖς
Acc.	ἀγαθοῦς	ἀγαθάς	ἀγαθά

As with the nouns, if the -ος of the masculine is preceded by a vowel or ρ, the feminine ends -α instead of -η and retains it throughout (see βασιλεία, Lesson 3). Thus:—

Second Form

ἅγιος, holy

Singular

	Masc.	**Fem.**	**Neut.**
Nom.	ἅγιος	ἁγία	ἅγιον
Voc.	ἅγιε	ἁγία	ἅγιον
Gen.	ἁγίου	ἁγίας	ἁγίου
Dat.	ἁγίῳ	ἁγίᾳ	ἁγίῳ
Acc.	ἅγιον	ἁγίαν	ἅγιον

The plural is like that of ἀγαθός

Write out from memory μικρός, μικρά, μικρόν, "little," remembering the rule about the feminine ending -α after ρ, and correct the result from ἅγιος, ἁγία, ἅγιον above.

Rule—An adjective agrees with the noun which it qualifies in number, gender and case.

Write out in full, from memory, all the cases and genders, singular and plural, with the meanings, of ὁ δίκαιος ἄνθρωπος, "the just man," and correct the results from the paradigms above. Do the same with ἡ καλὴ ἀγγελία, "the good message," and τὸ καλὸν ἔργον, "the beautiful work."

Demonstrative Adjectives and Pronouns

οὗτος, "this"; ἐκεῖνος, "that."

Note 1—The endings, masculine, feminine, and neuter, are practically the same as those of the article, ὁ, ἡ, τό.

Note 2—It is important to observe the aspirate over the second vowel in the nominative of the masculine and feminine, singular and plural.

Note 3—

-*αυ*- runs through the feminine *except in the genitive plural, which has*

-*ου*-; the neuter plural has -*αυ*- in the nominative and accusative.

Singular: "this"

	Masc.	**Fem.**	**Neut.**
Nom.	οὗτος	αὕτη	τοῦτο
Gen.	τούτου	ταύτης	τούτου
Dat.	τούτῳ	ταύτῃ	τούτῳ
Acc.	τοῦτον	ταύτην	τοῦτο

Plural: "these"

	Masc.	**Fem.**	**Neut.**
Nom.	οὗτοι	αὕται	ταῦτα
Gen.	τούτων	τούτων	τούτων
Dat.	τούτοις	ταύταις	τούτοις
Acc.	τούτους	ταύτας	ταῦτα

Singular: "that"

Nom.	ἐκεῖνος	ἐκείνη	ἐκεῖνο

(*Remaining case endings as above*)

Plural: "those"

Nom.	ἐκεῖνοι	ἐκεῖναι	ἐκεῖνα

(*and so on as above*)

Rule 1—οὗτος and ἐκεῖνος agree, in number, gender, case, with the noun which they qualify, and the noun always has the article, which, however, is not translated. Thus οὗτος ὁ ἄνθρωπος is "this man"; οὗτος ὁ υἱὸς "this Son"; ταύτην τὴν ἐντολήν "this commandment"; ἐν ἐκείνῃ τῇ ὥρᾳ "in that hour."

Rule 2—The noun with its article may come first and the adjective οὗτος or ἐκεῖνος after it, without altering the meaning. Thus: either ἡ φωνὴ αὕτη or αὕτη ἡ φωνή is "this voice" ("this sound"). "This Scripture" is either ἡ γραφὴ αὕτη or αὕτη ἡ γραφή. "That disciple" is either ἐκεῖνος ὁ μαθητής or ὁ μαθητὴς ἐκεῖνος.

Rule 3—When οὗτος and ἐκεῖνος stand alone, without a noun, they are demonstrative pronouns. Thus οὗτος means "this man," αὕτη "this woman," τοῦτο "this thing," ταῦτα "these things," ἐκεῖνος "that man," ἐκείνη "that woman," ἐκεῖνο "that thing."

Or again they may simply denote "this," "that," "these," "those," when they stand, for instance, as the subject or object of a verb. Thus οὗτός ἐστιν ὁ μαθητής is "this is the disciple" (John 21:24); καὶ αὕτη ἐστὶν ἡ μαρτυρία is "And this is the witness" (John 1:19).

Learn this vocabulary before doing the exercise, and revise the verb εἰμί (p. 20).

ὥρα an hour	ἡμέρα a day
ζωή an hour life	ἐντολή a commandment
ἄνθρωπος a man	δοῦλος a servant
δικαιοσύνη righteousness	δίκαιος righteous
κριτής a judge	στέφανος a crown
ἐκ from (followed by the genitive case)	ἐν in (takes the dative case)
εἰς unto or among (takes the accusative case)	

Exercise

Translate the following sentences, without referring to the New Testament, unless necessary. When the English has been written out, translate it back into Greek, correcting the result from the Greek Testament.

> Σῶσόν (save) με (me) ἐκ (from) τῆς ὥρας ταύτης ... ἦλθον (I came) εἰς (unto) τὴν ὥραν ταύτην (John 12:27).

αὕτη ἐστὶν ὑμῶν (your) ἡ ὥρα (Luke 22:53).

ἐν ταῖς ἡμέραις ταύταις (Luke 24:18).

ἐξῆλθεν (went forth) οὖν (therefore) οὗτος ὁ λόγος εἰς (among) τοὺς ἀδελφοὺς ὅτι (that) ὁ μαθητὴς ἐκεῖνος οὐκ (not) ἀποθνήσκει (dies) (John 21:23).

Οἴδαμεν (we know) ὅτι (that) οὗτός ἐστιν ὁ υἱὸς ἡμῶν (our) (John 9:20).

αὕτη δέ ἐστιν ἡ αἰώνιος (eternal) ζωή (John 17:3), αἰώνιος has the same form in the feminine as the masculine.

ἐν ἐκείνῃ τῇ ἡμέρᾳ (John 14:20).

Οὐχ οὗτός ἐστιν Ἰησοῦς ὁ υἱὸς Ἰωσήφ; [note the question mark] (John 6:42).

Οὗτοι οἱ λόγοι πιστοὶ καὶ ἀληθινοί (Rev. 22:6, the verb εἰσίν "are" is omitted).

Οὗτοι οἱ λόγοι ἀληθινοὶ τοῦ θεοῦ εἰσιν (Rev. 19:9).

καὶ αὕτη ἐστὶν ἡ ἐντολὴ αὐτοῦ (His) (1 John 3:32).

ἐν τούτῳ ἡ ἀγάπη τοῦ θεοῦ τετελείωται (has been perfected) (1 John 2:5).

Οὗτοι οἱ ἄνθρωποι δοῦλοι τοῦ θεοῦ τοῦ ὑψίστου (Most High) εἰσίν (Acts 16:17).

ὁ τῆς* δικαιοσύνης στέφανος, ὃν (which) ἀποδώσει (shall give) μοι (to me) ὁ κύριος ἐν ἐκείνῃ τῇ ἡμέρᾳ (2 Tim. 4:8).

* This article is not to be translated, as it occurs with an abstract noun. The order, "the of righteousness crown" is common in Greek. Note that the subject of a verb (here ὁ κύριος) often comes after it. This has the effect of stressing the subject.

Lesson 5

Demonstrative Pronouns (continued). Personal and Relative Pronouns

Demonstrative Pronouns (Continued)

There is another demonstrative pronoun, the meaning of which is similar to that of οὗτος (Lesson 4). It is ὅδε, ἥδε, τόδε "this" (this one here). It consists simply of the article ὁ, ἡ, τό with -δε added.

The following demonstrative pronouns should also be noted, all declined like οὗτος:—

(a) of quality: τοιοῦτος, τοιαύτη, τοιοῦτο, "such."

(b) of quantity: τοσοῦτος, τοσαύτη, τοσοῦτο, "so great."

(*c*) of number: τοσοῦτοι etc., "so many." This is simply the plural of (*b*).

(*d*) of degree: τηλικοῦτος etc., "so very great." This occurs only in 2 Cor. 1:10; Heb. 2:3; Jas. 3:4; Rev. 16:18.

The Personal Pronoun, Third Person

For the third person, "he, she, it," the Greeks used the adjectival pronoun αὐτός, αὐτή, αὐτό. This is given here because its endings are those of the 1st and 2nd declensions. The student should become thoroughly familiar with the meanings.

Singular

	Masc.	**Fem.**	**Neut.**
N.	αὐτός he	αὐτή she	αὐτό it
G.	αὐτοῦ of him (or his)	αὐτῆς of her (or hers)	αὐτοῦ of it (or its)
D.	αὐτῷ to him	αὐτῇ to her	αὐτῷ to it
A.	αὐτόν him	αὐτήν her	αὐτό it

Plural

N.	αὐτοί, they	αὐταί, they	αὐται, them
G.	αὐτῶν, of them (their)	αὐτῶν, of them (their)	αὐτῶν, of them (their)
D.	αὐτοῖς, to them	αὐταῖς, to them	αὐτοῖς, to them
A.	αὐτούς, them	αὐτάς, them	αὐτά, of them

Note—Distinguish between αὕτη, this (fem.) and αὐτή, she; between αὗται, these (fem.) and αὐταί, they (fem.).

Rule—When αὐτός in all its cases is connected with a noun, it becomes a reflexive pronoun and denotes "himself, herself, itself." Thus, Ἰησοῦς αὐτὸς οὐκ ἐβάπτιζεν, "Jesus Himself baptized not."

Rule—When preceded by the article, αὐτό·, in all its cases, means "the same." Thus, ἐν τῇ αὐτῇ γνώμῃ is "in the same judgment" (1 Cor. 1:10); τὸ αὐτό means "the same thing."

Note—We must carefully note the order in which αὐτός occurs with a noun and article, and distinguish the two meanings of the pronoun as for example, in the two rules just mentioned: αὐτὸ τὸ πνεῦμα is "the Spirit Himself," but τὸ αὐτὸ πνεῦμα is "the same Spirit." When αὐτός comes after the article it denotes "the same."

Before doing the exercise below, learn the following vocabulary and review all preceding vocabularies. Also review the verb "to be" (Lesson 3).

χάρις thanks or grace	ἄρτος loaf
σπουδή zeal	οὖν therefore
καρδία heart	ἄλλος other

οὐρανός heaven

πόθεν whence

ἐρημία wilderness

ἔσω within

ὑπό by (takes the genitive)

γάρ for (never begins a sentence; usually the second word)

μετά with (takes the genitive; it is shortened to μετ' before a vowel)

δέ but (never comes first word in the sentence)

Exercise

Translate the following, with the help of the meaning given. Correct your result from the English Testament. Then rewrite your corrected rendering back into Greek, without looking at the Exercise, and correct your Greek from the Exercise afterwards.

εἶπον (they said) οὖν αὐτῷ· Μὴ (not) καὶ (also) σὺ (thou) ἐκ τῶν μαθητῶν αὐτοῦ εἶ; (John 18:25).

ἔλεγον (said) οὖν αὐτῷ οἱ ἄλλοι μαθηταί (John 20:25).

ἦσαν ἔσω οἱ μαθηταὶ αὐτοῦ καὶ Θωμᾶς (Thomas) μετ' αὐτῶν (John 20:26) (this word is not "of them" here, but "them," after the preposition μετά. as it takes the genitive).

Σίμων καὶ (also) αὐτὸς ἐπίστευσεν (believed) (Acts 8:13).

Δημητρίῳ (to Demetrius) μεμαρτύρηται (it hath been witnessed) ὑπὸ πάντων (all) καὶ ὑπὸ αὐτῆς τῆς ἀληθείας· (3 John 12).

καὶ (both) κύριον αὐτὸν καὶ Χριστὸν ἐποίησεν (hath made) ὁ θεός, τοῦτον τὸν Ἰησοῦν (Jesus), for the two preceding words see Rule 1 under οὗτος, Lesson 4; note that the subject of this sentence is ὁ θεός (Acts 2:36).

Χάρις δὲ τῷ θεῷ τῷ δόντι (the One giving, or putting) τὴν αὐτὴν σπουδὴν ... ἐν τῇ καρδίᾳ Τίτου (2 Cor. 8:16).

τῶν γὰρ τοιούτων ἐστὶν ἡ βασιλεία τῶν οὐρανῶν (Matt. 19:14).

οἱ γὰρ τοιοῦτοι τῷ κυρίῳ ἡμῶν (our) Χριστῷ οὐ δουλεύουσιν (serve—takes the dative) (Rom. 16:18).

καὶ λέγουσιν (say) αὐτῷ οἱ μαθηταί, Πόθεν ἡμῖν (to us) ἐν ἐρημίᾳ ἄρτοι τοσοῦτοι ... ; (Matt. 15:33).

The Relative Pronoun

Note 1—The relative pronoun ὅς, ἥ, ὅ, "who, which," has the same form as the endings of οὗτος, αὕτη, τοῦτο (see last Lesson), and therefore as those of the 1st and 2nd declensions.

Note 2—Each form has the rough breathing.

Note 3—There are certain forms of this pronoun which look exactly like those of the article ὁ, ἡ, τό, but which always have an accent (turning to the left in the text, though turning to the right when put by themselves as below); these must be distinguished; the forms are as follows:—in the singular, the nom., fem. and neut., and the acc. neut.; in the plural, the nom., masc. and fem. For example, ὁ is "the" but ὅ is "which."

Singular

	Masc.	**Fem.**	**Neut.**
N.	ὅς, who or that	ἥ, ditto	ὅ, which
G.	οὗ, of whom, or whose	ἧς, "	οὗ, of which
D.	ᾧ, to whom	ᾗ, "	ᾧ, to which
A.	ὅν, whom or that	ἥν, "	ὅ, which

Plural

(*Meanings are the same as in the singular*)

N.	οἵ	ἥ	ἅ
G.	ὧν	ὧν	ὧν
D.	οἷς	αἷς	οἷς
A.	οὕς	ἅς	ἅ

Rule 1—The Relative Pronoun refers back to some noun or pronoun in another clause, and this latter noun or pronoun is called its antecedent. Thus in οὐδείς (no one) γάρ (for) δύναται (is able) ταῦτα τα σημεῖα (these signs) ποιεῖν (to do) ἅ (which) σύ (thou) ποιεῖς (doest) (John 3:2), ἅ, the relative, refers back to σημεῖα, the antecedent.

Rule 2—Relative pronouns agree with their antecedents in number and usually in gender, but not in case. Thus in ὁ ἀστήρ (the star) ὅν εἶδον (which they saw) … προῆγεν (went before) αὐτούς (them) (Matt. 2:9), ὅν is singular and masculine, in agreement with the antecedent ἀστήρ, but the case differs.

Rule 3—The case of a relative pronoun depends (with certain exceptions) upon the part it plays in the clause in which it stands. Thus in the following:—λειτουργός (a minister) … τῆς σκηνῆς (of the tabernacle) τῆς ἀληθινῆς (the true) ἣν (which) ἔτηξεν (pitched) ὁ κύριος (the Lord) (Heb. 8:2), ἥν is in the accusative case because it is the object of the verb ἔπηξεν. Again, in παντὶ (to everyone,) … ᾧ (to whom) ἐδόθη (has been given) πολύ (much) (Luke 12:48), ᾧ is necessarily in the dative.

Lesson 6

Possessive Pronouns and Regular Verb, Indicative Mood

Possessive Pronouns

These are declined just like adjectives of the first and second declensions (see ἀγαθός, Lesson 4). They are :—

	Masc.	**Fem.**	**Neut.**	
1st Pers.	ἐμός	ἐμή	ἐμόν	my
	ἡμέτερος	ἡμετέρα	ἡμέτερον	our
2nd Pers.	σός	σή	σόν	thy
	ὑμέτερος	ὑμετέρα	ὑμέτερον	your

For the third person, his, hers, its, theirs, the genitive case (sing. and plur.) of αὐτός, αὐτή, αὐτό, he, she, it, is used (see Lesson 5), or the genitive case of the reflexive pronoun ἑαυτοῦ (see below), which signifies "his own," "her own," etc. As to the former, αὐτοῦ ("of him") is "his," and so with the feminine and neuter. Thus, "on his shoulders" is ἐπὶ τοὺς ὤμους αὐτοῦ, lit. "on the shoulders of him" (ὦμος, a shoulder).

Rule—When a noun is qualified by a possessive pronoun or the genitive of a personal pronoun, it has the article. The pronoun αὐτοῦ, αὐτῆς, αὐτοῦ (his, hers, its), or αὐτῶν (their), comes either before the article and noun or after them. Thus "his son" would be either ὁ υἱός αὐτοῦ or αὐτοῦ ὁ υἱός. With other possessive pronouns the article may be repeated (see sentences 4 and 5, in the exercise below).

Vocabulary

νεκρός, -ά, -όν dead

πρεσβύτερος elder

ἀγρός a field

ὀφθαλμός an eye

καρδία a heart

ἕτοιμος, -η, -ον ready

καιρός a time

οὔπω not yet

πάντοτε always

Exercise

Translate the following sentences after learning the vocabulary. Correct the result from the English Version (preferably the Revised [or the New Revised Standard or New King James]). Then retranslate from the English into Greek, without referring to the Greek unless necessary, and correct your result from it afterwards.

(1) ὅτι (for) οὗτος ὁ υἱός μου νεκρὸς ἦν (Luke 15:24).

(2) Ἦν δὲ (but, or now) ὁ υἱὸς αὐτοῦ ὁ πρεσβύτερος ἐν ἀγρῷ (Luke 15:25. Note that this sentence begins with the verb "was," the subject "his son" coming after).

(3) Τετύφλωκεν (He hath blinded) αὐτῶν τοὺς ὀφθαλμοὺς καὶ ἐπώρωσεν (He hath hardened) αὐτῶν τὴν καρδίαν (John 12:40).

(4) καὶ ἡ κοινωνία (fellowship) δὲ (indeed) ἡ ἡμετέρα … μετὰ (with—takes the genitive) τοῦ υἱοῦ αὐτοῦ Ἰησοῦ Χριστοῦ ("is" is omitted) (1 John 1:3).

(5) λέγει (saith) οὖν (therefore) αὐτοῖς ὁ Ἰησοῦς, Ὁ καιρὸς ὁ ἐμὸς οὔπω πάρεστιν (is come), ὁ δὲ καιρὸς ὁ ὑμέτερος πάντοτέ ἐστιν ἕτοιμος (John 7:6).

The Regular Verb

Before taking the third declension nouns, adjectives and pronouns, we shall study the simpler parts of the Regular Verb. A few introductory notes will serve here.

Note 1—There are in Greek three *Voices*—(1) *the Active Voice* (as in English), signifying that a person, or thing, does something; e.g., λύω, I loose: (2) *the Middle Voice* (not used in English, signifying that a person, or thing, does something for or upon himself, or itself (i.e., in self-interest); e.g., λύομαι, I loose for myself: (3) *the Passive Voice* (as in English), signifying that an action is done upon a person, or thing; e.g., λύομαι, I am loosed. This form is the same as the middle in many respects.

Note 2—There are five *Moods* (1) *the Indicative,* which is used to make an assertion, absolutely, e.g., "I loose": (2) *the Imperative,* which is used to make a command, e.g., "loose thou": (3) *the Subjunctive,* which asserts a supposition or condition, e.g., "I may loose": (4) *the Optative,* used in expressing wishes, and in other ways to be explained later: (5) *the Infinitive,* expressing an act or state, usually rendered by the preposition "to," e.g., "to loose," but often used as a verbal noun, e.g., "the act of loosing."

Note 3—There is also a set of verbal adjectives called *Participles.* These are also used as nouns. They will be treated separately.

Note 4—There are six *Tenses* in the Active Voice, signifying the present, past, or future. Most of these six run through all the Moods and Participles. In the Indicative Mood the tenses run as follows:—

1 *Present,*

λύω, I loose, or I am loosing

2 *Future,*

λύσω, I shall loose

3 *Imperfect,*

ἔλυον, I was loosing

4 *Aorist,*

ἔλυσα, I loosed

5 *Perfect,*

λέλυκα, I have loosed

6 *Pluperfect,*

ἐλελύκειν, I had loosed

Note 5—There are two sorts of verbs, which come under the heading of *Conjugations.* We shall for some time be occupied only with the First Conjugation, the verbs of which end in x, and we shall take the Indicative Mood, completing the others after studying the remaining class of nouns and pronouns. The purpose of this order is to enable the student the more readily to read certain passages of Scripture.

Conjugation of the Verb in -ω-Active Voice

Indicative Mood

Introductory Notes

(1) The endings after the stem λυ- should be written out separately and memorized. Then memorize the whole form of the specimen verb.

(2) The characteristic letter of the future tense is the -σ- before the endings, which otherwise are the same as those of the present tense.

(3) The vowel ἐ- which precedes the imperfect, first aorist and pluperfect forms is called the *Augment* and characterizes these tenses as past, or historic.

(4) The initial syllable λε- which begins the perfect and pluperfect forms is called a *reduplication,* i.e., a doubling of the syllable.

(5) Note the -σ- in the first aorist, and the characteristic vowel -α- except in the 3rd person singular.

(6) Note the -κ- in the perfect and pluperfect. The endings of the perfect are the same as those of the first aorist (except for the 3rd person plural).

	Singular	Plural	
Present Tense			
λύω	I loose	λύομεν	we loose
λύεις	thou loosest	λύετε	ye loose
λύει	he looses	λύουσι	they loose
Future Tense			
λύσω	I shall loose	λύσομεν	we shall loose
λύσεις	thou wilt loose	λύσετε	ye will loose
λύσει	he will loose	λύσουσι	they will loose
Imperfect Tense			
ἔλυον	I was loosing	ἐλύομεν	we were loosing
ἔλυες	thou wast loosing	ἐλύετε	ye were loosing

ἔλυε	he was loosing	ἔλυον	they were loosing

First Aorist Tense

ἔλυσα	I loosed	ἐλύσαμεν	we loosed
ἔλυσας	thou loosedst	ἐλύσατε	ye loosed
ἔλυσε	he loosed	ἔλυσαν	they loosed

Perfect Tense

λέλυκα	I have loosed	λελύκαμεν	we have loosed
λέλυκας	thou hast loosed	λελύκατε	ye have loosed
λέλυκε	he has loosed	λελύκασι	they have loosed

Pluperfect Tense

ἐλελύκειν	I had loosed	ἐλελύκειμεν	we had loosed
ἐλελύκεις	thou hadst loosed	ἐλελύκειτε	ye had loosed
ἐλελύκει	he had loosed	ἐλελύκεσαν	they had loosed

Additional Notes

Note 1—Some verbs have a second aorist tense, with tense-endings like those of the imperfect. The meaning is the same as the first aorist.

Note 2—As we have observed in ἐστί (or ἐστιν), the letter -ν is added to the 3rd person singular when the word comes last in a sentence, or when the next word begins with a vowel. This -ν is likewise added to the 3rd person plural when it ends in -σι.

Lesson 7

Indicative Mood (continued). Contracted Nouns and Adjectives of the Second Declensions. The Third Declension

Indicative Mood(Continued)

Like λύω are πιστεύω, to believe; δουλεύω, to serve; προφητεύω, to prophesy, νηστεύω, to fast, κελεύω, to command; βασιλεύω, to reign; παύω, to cause to cease; κλείω, to shut, and others.

The student, who should have learnt the indicative mood of λύω by heart, should write out all *the tenses* of that mood of "I believe" in English, in all the persons, singular and plural, and put the Greek against them from memory, so as to become thoroughly familiar with the forms; this thoroughness will make progress easy. As an example of what to do we will give the present and 1st aorist:—

Present Indicative

I believe	πιστεύω	We believe	πιστεύομεν
Thou believest	πιστεύεις	You believe	πιστεύετε
He believes	πιστεύει	They believe	πιστεύουσι

First Aorist Indicative

I believed	ἐπίστευσα	We believed	ἐπιστεύσαμεν
Thou believedst	ἐπίστευσας	Ye believed	ἐπιστεύσατε
He believed	ἐπίστευσε	They believed	ἐπίστευσαν

(*Write out the whole mood this way, in the right order of the Tenses*)

The following verbs consist of λύω combined with a preposition:— ἀπολύω to loose, release, put away; καταλύω to destroy. In forming the augment ἐ- for the imperfect, aorist and pluperfect tenses of such compound verbs, the final vowel of the preposition is simply changed to -ε-. Thus the imperfect of ἀπολύω is ἀπέλυον and the aorist is ἀπέλυσα.

Before doing the exercise below, memorize the following vocabulary, and the verbs above at the beginning of this Lesson.

Vocabulary

κύριος a lord

δοῦλος a servant

νῦν now

ναός a temple

μαθητής a disciple

μέχρι until

θάνατος death

ἀλλά but

ἀπό from

Exercise

Write out a translation of the following without reference to the English Version. Correct your results from the English Testament. Rewrite the sentences from the English back into the Greek, without referring to the Greek. Correct your results from the exercise now given.

(1) ὁ κύριος τοῦ δούλου ἐκείνου (see Lesson 4, Rule 1) ἀπέλυσεν (1st aorist) αὐτόν (Matt. 18:27).

(2) Νῦν ἀπολύεις τὸν δοῦλόν σου (Luke 2:29).

(3) Ἐγὼ καταλύσω τὸν ναὸν τοῦτον (Mark 14:58).

(4) ἐπίστευσαν εἰς (on) αὐτὸν οἱ μαθηταὶ αὐτοῦ (John 2:11).

(5) πεπιστεύκατε ὅτι (that) ἐγὼ παρὰ (from) τοῦ θεοῦ ἐξῆλθον (came out) (John 16:27).

(6) ἐγὼ πεπίστευκα (perfect tense, as in R.V.) ὅτι σὺ εἶ (see verb "to be") ὁ Χριστὸς ὁ υἱὸς τοῦ θεοῦ (John 11:27).

(7) ἀλλὰ ἐβασίλευσεν ὁ θάνατος ἀπὸ Ἀδὰμ μέχρι Μωϋσέως (Moses) (Rom. 5:14)—(the article before θάνατος must not be translated; an abstract noun often has the article).

(8) καὶ ἐβασίλευσαν μετὰ (with) τοῦ Χριστοῦ (Rev. 20:4) (the subject of the sentence is "they" and is included in the verb).

(9) βασιλεύσουσιν (future) μετ' αὐτοῦ (Rev. 20:6).

Before proceeding further with the other moods of the verb, we shall make easiest headway in the reading of the Testament by taking the remainder of the nouns, adjectives and pronouns.

Previously to learning these, the student should thoroughly review the nouns of the first and second declensions, πύλη (Lesson 2), βασιλεία, γλῶσσα, μαθητής, νεανίας, λόγος and ἔργον (Lesson 3), the adjectives ἀγαθός and ἅγιος (Lesson 3), and the pronouns οὗτος, ἐκεῖνος, αὐτός (Lesson 3), memorizing all that may have been forgotten. This is necessary in order to keep distinct in the mind the forms that follow, and especially the third declension.

Contracted Nouns and Adjectives of the Second Declension

Note—Contraction means the combining of two distinct vowels to form one vowel sound. There are very few contracted nouns and adjectives, but they must be noted.

Rule 1—When the vowel ο-, in the final syllable, is preceded by ε or ο in the stem, the two vowels generally contract, forming one vowel sound -ου (to be pronounced as in "boot "). Thus νόος (νό-ος), the mind, becomes νοῦς; ὀστέον a bone, becomes ὀστοῦν.

Rule 2—When Omega is preceded by ε or ο, they combine to form simply -ω. Thus νόῳ becomes νῷ.

Rule 3—The vowels -εη combine to form -η, and the vowels -εα combine to form -η or -α. These are illustrated in the adjectives below.

νοῦς, mind

	Singular	**Plural**
Nom.	(νόος)νοῦς	(νόοι) νοῖ
Voc.	(νόε) νοῦ	(νόοι) νοῖ
Gen.	(νόου) νοῦ	(νόων) νῶν
Dat.	(νόῳ)νῷ	(νόοις)νοῖς
Acc.	(νόον) νοῦν	(νόους)νοῦς

Note—This contraction does not by any means invariably take place. Thus, while ὀστοῦν, a bone, is contracted thus from ὀστέον in John 19:36, we find ὀστέων instead of ὀστῶν in Heb. 11:22. (There is no need to learn the neuter paradigm ὀστοῦν).

Contracted Adjectives

χρύσεος, χρυσέα, χρύσεον, golden, becomes χρυσοῦς, χρυσῆ, χρυσοῦν, etc., according to the rules above.

	Singular			**Plural**		
	M.	**F.**	**N.**	**M.**	**F.**	**N.**
N.	χρυσοῦς	χρυσῆ	χρυσοῦν	χρυσοῖ	-αῖ	-ᾶ
V.	χρύσεε	χρυσῆ	χρυσοῦν	χρυσοῖ	-αῖ	-ᾶ
G.	χρυσοῦ	χρυσῆς	χρυσοῦ	χρυσῶν	-ῶν	-ῶν
D.	χρυσῷ	χρυσῇ	χρυσῷ	χρυσοῖς	-αῖς	-οῖς
A.	χρυσοῦν	χρυσῆν	χρυσοῦν	χρυσοῦς	-ᾶς	-ᾶ

Two Irregular Adjectives

Note—The following adjectives are important, as they are of very frequent occurrence; they should be committed to memory. They are irregular only in the masculine and neuter singular, which present shortened forms.

μέγας, great

Singular

	Masc.	**Fem.**	**Neut.**
Nom.	μέγας	μεγάλη	μέγα
Gen.	μεγάλου	μεγάλης	μεγάλου
Dat.	μεγάλῳ	μεγάλῃ	μεγάλῳ
Acc.	μέγαν	μεγάλην	μέγα

Plural

The plural is regular, as if from μεγάλος, and runs μεγάλοι, μεγάλαι, μεγάλα, etc.

πολύς, many

Singular

Masc.	**Fem.**	**Neut.**	
Nom.	πολύς	πολλή	πολύ
Gen.	πολλοῦ	πολλῆς	πολλοῦ
Dat.	πολλῷ	πολλῇ	πολλῷ
Acc.	πολύν	πολλήν	πολύ

Plural

The plural is regular as if from πολλός, and runs πολλοί, πολλαί, πολλά, etc.

The Third Declension

Introductory Note—Nouns in this declension are of all three genders. There is a considerable variety and hence a number of paradigms are necessary, but all follow a simple form which presents little or no difficulty.

The essential thing is to know the *stem,* i.e., the elementary part of the word apart from the endings, or inflections. The stem can always be found from the genitive singular by taking away the inflection ending. Note that the genitive singular in the third declension usually ends in -ος. Take away the -ος and you have the stem. The stem will be a guide to the nominative case.

We will begin with two simple forms, one of a masculine noun (the feminine would be the same) and one of a neuter noun. When these are learned, the rest will follow easily.

αἰών, an age (masc.)

stem, αἰών-

	Singular		**Plural**	
N.	αἰών	an age	αἰῶνες	ages
V.	αἰών	O age	αἰῶνες	ages
G.	αἰῶνος	of an age	αἰώνων	of ages
D.	αἰῶνι	to an age	αἰῶσι(ν)	to ages
A.	αἰῶνα	an age	αἰῶνας	ages

ῥῆμα, a word (neut.) stem, ῥηματ-

	Singular	Plural
Nom.	ῥῆμα	ῥήματα
Voc.	ῥῆμα	ῥήματα
Gen.	ῥήματος	ῥημάτων
Dat.	ῥήματι	ῥήμασι(ν)
Acc.	ῥῆμα	ῥήματα

Notes

(1) The nominative and vocative are alike, and in the neuter the accusative also, as in the first and second declensions.

(2) The accusative singular ending -α was originally -ν, as in the other declensions, and the -ν is retained in several third declension nouns, the stems of which end in a vowel. These will be illustrated later. The -α ending should, however, be regarded as normal.

(3) The genitive singular ending is -ος, added to the stem.

(4) The dative singular ending is -ι, added to the stem.

(5) The nominative plural, in masculine and feminine nouns, ends in -ες, added to the stem. Neuter plurals always end in -α in the nominative, vocative, and accusative.

(6) The accusative plural masculine ends in -ας.

(7) The genitive plural ends in -ων, added to the stem. All genitive plurals end -ων.

(8) The dative plural ends in -σι, added to the stem, with various modifications. The -ν in brackets in the dative plural does not belong to the word; it is added at the close of a sentence, or when the next word begins with a vowel; this is simply for the sake of the sound.

Lesson 8

The Third Declension (continued)

Third Declension(Continued)

Rule 1—The usual ending of the nominative singular is ς, added to the stem. The nominative endings provide a considerable variety and present a difference in form from that of the stem seen in the other cases. There are certain principles which govern the formation of the nominative, but these need not be learned. They simply serve to show that the variety of the third declension nouns is based on one form of case ending. The student should become familiar with the actual examples given and should keep in memory the other case endings, namely, -α, -ος, -ι, of the singular, and -ας, -ων, -σι, of the plural, as already learned in the noun αἰών.

We will first take the noun κῆρυξ, a herald. The paradigm is as follows:—

	Singular	Plural
Nom.	κῆρυξ	κήρυκες
Voc.	κῆρυξ	κήρυκες
Gen.	κήρυκος	κηρύκων
Dat.	κήρυκι	κῆρυξι
Acc.	κήρυκα	κήρυκας

The question arises as to why the nominative, vocative singular, and dative plural have an ξ, whereas the rest of the cases have a κ. The explanation is as follows:—

When the stem (here κήρυκ-) ends in κ, or γ, or χ (which letters are called *gutturals*), the addition of the ς to the stem produces the letter ξ in the nominative and vocative singular and the dative plural. Thus κῆρυκ with ς, makes not κῆρυκς but κῆρυξ. The other cases retain the κ-.

Take another noun with a guttural stem:—

In Heb. 1:8 the student will see the word φλογός. This is a genitive case. Take away the -ος and the stem is φλογ-. The Concordance shows that the nominative is φλόξ. The ξ is due to the combination of the letters γ and ς. So νυκτός (Mark 5:5) is the genitive of νύξ "night." Write out in full, on the model of κήρυξ above, φλόξ, φλόγα, etc. (dat. plur. φλοξί) and νύξ, νύκτα, etc.

We will next take the noun Ἄραψ, an Arab. The paradigm is as follows:—

	Singular	**Plural**
Nom.	Ἄραψ	Ἄραβες
Voc.	Ἄραψ	Ἄραβες
Gen.	Ἄραβος	Ἀράβων
Dat.	Ἄραβι	Ἄραψι
Acc.	Ἄραβα	Ἄραβας

The stem is seen to be Ἄραβ-. When a stem ends in π, or β, or φ (which letters are called *labials*) the addition of the ς to the stem produces the letter ψ. Thus Ἄραβ- with ς makes, not Ἄραβς, but Ἄραψ.

Now for a third specimen:—In Acts 4:25, the word παιδός occurs (a genitive case). The Concordance shows that the nominative is παῖς. Take away the -ος and we get the stem παιδ-. The paradigm is as follows:—

	Singular	**Plural**
Nom.	παῖς	παῖδες
Voc.	παῖ	παῖδες
Gen.	παιδός	παίδων
Dat.	παιδί	παισί
Acc.	παῖδα	παῖδας

We observe that the stem is παιδ-. Now whenever a stem ends in τ, or δ, or θ (which letters are called *dentals*) the addition of ς causes the dropping of the τ, δ, or θ. Hence παιδς becomes παῖς and παιδσι becomes παισί. Similarly ἐλπιδ- is the stem of ἐλπίς, hope. The student should write out ἐλπίς in all its cases from memory, on the model of παῖς.

Note—Nouns in the third declension whose nominative ends in -ις, -υς, -αυς, and -ους usually have, in the accusative singular, a shortened form, ending in -ν. Thus while the stem of χάρις, grace (or thanks) is χαριτ-, and hence the genitive is χάριτος, and the dative χάριτι, the accusative is χάριν, but χάριτα exceptionally in Acts 24:27.

To take a fourth variety, ἰχθύος is "of a fish." Take away the -ος and we get the stem ἰχθυ-. This stem ends, then, in a vowel. When a stem ends in a vowel the nominative is formed by simply adding the ς; "a fish" is ἰχθύς.

Bearing in mind the note just given, that the accusative of nouns ending in -υς etc. end, not in -α, but in -ν, we have the following paradigm for ἰχθύς:—

	Singular	**Plural**
Nom.	ἰχθύς	ἰχθύες
Voc.	ἰχθύ	ἰχθύες
Gen.	ἰχθύος	ἰχθύων
Dat.	ἰχθύϊ	ἰχθυσί
Acc.	ἰχθύν	ἰχθῦς

Rule 2 (not to be committed to memory)—When a stem ends in -ν, or -ντ, or -ς the nominative is formed by lengthening the preceding vowel. The same is usually the case with a stem ending in -ρ.

Take for example, ποιμεν-, the stem of the word for "a shepherd." The nominative is ποιμήν (note the η instead of ε); the accusative is ποιμένα, the genitive ποιμένος, etc. Note that the dative plural is ποιμέσι (not ποιμένσι—the ν was dropped before ς); again, λέων a lion (stem λεοντ-) has accusative λέοντα, genitive λέοντος, etc. The dative plural is λέουσι not λέοντσι—a combination too awkward for Greek ears; note the ω in the nominative instead of ο. So again with ῥήτωρ, an orator (stem ῥήτορ-), it has accus. ῥήτορα, etc. The dative plural is ῥήτορσι.

Write out the declension of ποιμήν, λέων, and ῥήτωρ in full.

Note—One or two nouns ending in ρ are a little irregular. The two following must be memorized:—

πατήρ, a father

	Singular	**Plural**
Nom.	πατήρ	πατέρες
Voc.	πάτερ	πατέρες
Gen.	πατρός	πατέρων
Dat.	πατρί	πατράσι
Acc.	πατέρα	πατέρας

* (*Note short* ε)

Note—μήτηρ, a mother, and θυγάτηρ, a daughter, are declined in the same way. Write them out in full from memory, not forgetting the shortened form in the gen. and dat. sing., and the gen. plur., and the α in the dat. plural.

ἀνήρ, a man

	Singular	**Plural**
Nom.	ἀνήρ	ἄνδρες
Voc.	ἄνερ	ἄνδρες
Gen.	ἀνδρός	ἀνδρῶν
Dat.	ἀνδρί	ἀνδράσι
Acc.	ἄνδρα	ἄνδρας

Note—ἀστήρ, a star, keeps the ε throughout (e.g., gen. ἀστέρος), except that the dative plural is ἀστράσι.

Exercise

Learn the following vocabulary before doing the exercise, and review the indicative mood of λύω.

λέγω I say	ἑπτά seven
τηρέω I keep	ἀστήρ star

ποιέω I do

πιστεύω I believe

φανερόω I manifest

κόσμος world

ἐπιθυμία lust

σάρξ flesh (gen. σαρκός)

διάκονος a servant

καλός, -ή, -όν good

οἶνος wine

ἕως until

ἄρτι now

ὀφθαλμός eye

βίος life

ἀρχή beginning

σημεῖον sign

δόξα glory

μαθητής disciple

νύξ night

φυλακή a guard, or watch

λυχνία lampstand

ἀλαζονεία vainglory

Translate, correcting the result from the English Bible, and then re-translate into the Greek:

(1) λέγει ἡ μήτηρ αὐτοῦ τοῖς διακόνοις (John 2:5).

(2) σὺ τετήρηκας (see τηρέω in the vocabulary above. What tense is indicated by the reduplicating syllable τε- ?) τὸν καλὸν οἶνον ἕως ἄρτι. Ταύτην ἐποίησεν (1st aorist of ποιέω—note the augment ἐ-) ἀρχὴν τῶν σημείων ὁ Ἰησοῦς ἐν Κανὰ τῆς Γαλιλαίας καὶ ἐφανέρωσεν (1st aorist of φανερόω) τὴν δόξαν αὐτοῦ καὶ ἐπίστευσαν εἰς (on) αὐτὸν οἱ μαθηταὶ αὐτοῦ (John 2: end of verse 10 and 11).

(3) τετάρτῃ ("at the fourth") δὲ φυλακῇ (this is a dative of time—hence the whole phrase is "at [not "to"] the fourth watch") τῆς νυκτὸς ἦλθεν (He came) πρὸς (to) αὐτούς (Matt. 14:25).

(4) οἱ ἑπτὰ ἀστέρες ἄγγελοι τῶν ἑπτὰ ἐκκλησιῶν εἰσιν καὶ αἱ λυχνίαι αἱ ἑπτὰ ἑπτὰ ἐκκλησίαι εἰσίν (Rev. 1:20, end, R.V.).

(5) πεπιστεύκαμεν τὴν ἀγάπην ἥ ν ἔχει ὁ θεὸς ἐν ἡμῖν (us) (1 John 4:16).

(6) ὅτι πᾶν τὸ ἐν τῷ κόσμῳ, ἡ ἐπιθυμία τῆς σαρκὸς καὶ ἡ ἐπιθυμία τῶν ὀφθαλμῶν καὶ ἡ ἀλαζονεία τοῦ βίου, οὐκ ἔστιν ἐκ τοῦ πατρὸς ἀλλ᾽ ἐκ τοῦ κόσμου ἐστίν. (1 John 2:16) Bear in mind that ὅτι is "for"; πᾶν τό is "all the," i.e., "all that is."

(7) Πέτρος δὲ καὶ Ἰωάννης ἀνέβαινον εἰς τὸ ἱερὸν ἐπὶ τὴν ὥραν τῆς προσευχῆς τὴν ἐνάτην. (Acts 3:1) ἀνέβαινον is the 3rd person plural, imperfect tense of ἀναβαίνω, I go up: the augment is formed by changing the final vowel of the preposition ἀνα "up" to -ε: βαίνω is "I go"; the

augment must come immediately before it. This is always the case where a preposition is combined with a verb. ἱερόν, "temple"; ἐπί, "at"; προσευχή, prayer; ἔνατος, "ninth."

(8) εὑρίσκει Φίλιππος τὸν Ναθαναὴλ καὶ λέγει αὐτῷ, Ὃν ἔγραψεν Μωϋσῆς ἐν τῷ νόμῳ καὶ οἱ προφῆται εὑρήκαμεν, Ἰησοῦν υἱὸν τοῦ Ἰωσὴφ τὸν ἀπὸ Ναζαρέτ. (John 1:45) ἔγραψεν is the 3rd pers. sing. 1st aorist of γράφω, "I write"; εὑρήκαμεν is the 1st pers. plur. of the perfect of εὑρίσκω, "I find."

Lesson 9

The Third Declension (continued). Adjectives and Participles

The Third Declension(Continued)

Rule 3—Some nouns ending in -ις and -ευς have a genitive ending with -εως instead of -ος. The two following should be memorized:—

πόλις, a city (feminine)

(stem πολι-)

	Singular	**Plural**	
Nom.	πόλις	πόλεις	(for πόλεες)
Voc.	πόλι	πόλεις	(")
Gen.	πόλεως	πόλεων	
Dat.	πόλει	πόλεσι	
Acc.	πόλιν	πόλεις	(for πόλεας)

(Note the accusative in -ιν; see note in Lesson 8)

Like πόλις are δύναμις, power; κρίσις, judgment; ὄφις, a serpent, and others.

βασιλεύς, a king (masculine)

	Singular	Plural	
Nom.	βασιλεύς	βασιλεῖς	(for βασιλέες)
Voc.	βασιλεῦ	βασιλεῖς	(")
Gen.	βασιλέως	βασιλέων	
Dat.	βασιλεῖ	βασιλεῦσι	
Acc.	βασιλέα	βασιλεῖς(for βασιλέας)	

Note (1) the ordinary accusative ending -εα, (2) the nom., voc. and acc. plural in -εες and -εες; contract these double vowels to ει (for the sake of sound).

Like βασιλεύς are γραμματεύς, a scribe; γονεύς, a parent.

Neuter Nouns of the Third Declension

These are important, and are of two chief kinds. Remember that all neuters have the same form for the nominative, vocative and accusative cases.

(1) Most conform to the example ῥῆμα on p. 48.

Learn the following :—

αἷμα blood

γράμμα a letter

θέλημα a will

κρίμα a judgment

ὄνομα a name

πνεῦμα a spirit

στόμα a mouth

σῶμα a body

There are a few words not ending in -μα which are neuter and come here, such as πῦρ, fire (genitive πυρός); φῶς, light (genitive: φωτός); τέρας, a wonder (genitive τέρατος).

(2) Other neuters ending in -ος have some contracted endings. The following model must be memorized:—

γένος, a race, generation

	Singular	Plural
Nom.	γένος (γένεα)	γένη
Voc.	γένος (γένεα)	γένη

Gen.	(γένεος) γένους	(γενέων) γενῶν
Dat.	γένει	γένεσι
Acc.	γένος (γένεα)	γένη

Note 1—The genitive singular γένεος contracts to γένους; the nominative, vocative and accusative γένεα contract to γένη; the genitive plural γενέων to γενῶν.

Note 2—These neuters in -ος, must be distinguished from second declension masculine nouns ending in -ος like λόγος (Lesson 3).

The student will soon become accustomed to the two varieties as found in the New Testament.

Note 3—These neuter plurals in -η (for -εα) must be distinguished from first declension feminines ending in -η, like πύλη (Lesson 2). The context generally helps to distinguish.

Adjectives Containing Third Declension Forms

These are of two kinds: (1) Those which contain endings of the first declension as well as the third. (2) Those which have the same form in the masculine and feminine.

(*1*) These adjectives are of great importance; the verbal adjectives, called participles, are formed on these models. As the participles run parallel to the adjectives now to be learned we shall take them together.

Adjectives

Form I: ἑκών, -οῦσα, -όν willing

Singular

	Masculine	**Feminine**	**Neuter**
Nom.	ἑκών	ἑκοῦσα	ἑκόν
Voc.	ἑκών	ἑκοῦσα	ἑκόν
Gen.	ἑκόντος	ἑκούσης	ἑκόντος
Dat.	ἑκόντι	ἑκούσῃ	ἑκόντι
Acc.	ἑκόντα	ἑκοῦσαν	ἑκόν

Plural

	Masculine	**Feminine**	**Neuter**
Nom.	ἑκόντες	ἑκοῦσαι	ἑκόντα
Voc.	ἑκόντες	ἑκοῦσαι	ἑκόντα
Gen.	ἑκόντων	ἑκουσῶν	ἑκόντων
Dat.	ἑκοῦσι	ἑκούσαις	ἑκοῦσι
Acc.	ἑκόντας	ἑκούσας	ἑκόντα

Note—The feminine conforms to the first declension (see γλῶσσα, Lesson 3), the masculine and neuter to the third declension.

Form II: πᾶς, πᾶσα, πᾶν, all, every

Singular	**Plural**					
	M.	**F.**	**N.**	**M.**	**F.**	**N.**
Nom.	πᾶς	πᾶσα	πᾶν	πάντες	πᾶσαι	πάντα
Voc.	πᾶς	πᾶσα	πᾶν	πάντες	πᾶσαι	πάντα
Gen.	παντός	πάσης	παντός	πάντων	πασῶν	πάντων
Dat.	παντί	πάσῃ	παντί	πᾶσι	πάσαις	πᾶσι
Acc.	πάντα	πᾶσαν	πᾶν	πάντας	πάσας	πάντα

Participles

Present Participles

Present participles of the active voice of the verb are formed exactly like the above. They are verbal adjectives, and qualify nouns just as adjectives do. In Greek, the present participle of εἰμί (see Lesson 3) is, in its three genders, ὤν, οὖσα, ὄν. Notice that, if we take away the ἑκ- of ἑκών above, we have the participial forms in full. Thus ὤν, "being," is declined as follows:—

	Singular			Plural		
	M.	**F.**	**N.**	**M.**	**F.**	**N.**
Nom.	ὤν	οὖσα	ὄν	ὄντες	οὖσαι	ὄντα
Voc.	ὤν	οὖσα	ὄν	ὄντες	οὖσαι	ὄντα
Gen.	ὄντος	οὔσης	ὄντος	ὄντων	οὐσῶν	ὄντων
Dat.	ὄντι	οὔσῃ	ὄντι	οὖσι	οὔσαις	οὖσι
Acc.	ὄντα	οὖσαν	ὄν	ὄντας	οὔσας	ὄντα

Coming now again to the verb λύω, the present participle is λύων, λύουσα, λῦον, and signifies "loosing." These various forms may qualify some noun or pronoun or may simply qualify the definite article. In every case there is agreement in case, number and gender. Thus in Heb. 1:7, ὁ ποιῶν is literally "The (One) making," translated "Who maketh." Again, in 1 Cor. 15:57, τῷ δὲ θεῷ χάρις τῷ διδόντι literally is "But to God thanks, the (One) giving" ἡμῖν, to us, τὸ νῖκος, the victory (for νῖκος see γένος, above); in Jas. 1:5, παρὰ τοῦ διδόντος θεοῦ is "from the giving God." In the following sentence note the feminine participle λέγουσαν "saying," in agreement with the fem. φωνήν, "a voice": ἤκουσεν (he heard, 1st aorist of ἀκούω, I hear) φωνὴν λέγουσαν αὐτῷ· Σαοὺλ Σαούλ, (Saul, Saul), τί (why) με διώκεις; "persecutest thou" (Acts 9:4).

Exercise

Translate the following (after learning the vocabulary), correcting your result from the English version. Then retranslate into Greek, correcting your result from the Greek text.

Ἴδε Behold
ἀμνός a lamb
αἴρω I bear, take away
ποιέω I do
διάβολος Devil
ἀπ᾽ ἀρχῆς from (the) beginning
ἔχω I have
ἁμαρτάνω I sin
ἀγάπη love
μένω I abide
μαρτυρία witness
μή not
αἰώνιος, -ος, -ον eternal

(1) Τῇ ἐπαύριον βλέπει τὸν Ἰησοῦν ἐρχόμενον πρὸς αὐτὸν καὶ λέγει, Ἴδε ὁ ἀμνὸς τοῦ θεοῦ ὁ αἴρων τὴν ἁμαρτίαν τοῦ κόσμου. (John 1:29)—note the article ὁ and the participle αἴρων agreeing with it; this is literally "the (One) bearing."

(2) ὁ ποιῶν τὴν ἁμαρτίαν ἐκ τοῦ διαβόλου ἐστίν, ὅτι ἀπ᾽ ἀρχῆς ὁ διάβολος ἁμαρτάνει. (1 John 3:8a).

(3) Ὁ θεὸς ἀγάπη ἐστίν, καὶ ὁ μένων ἐν τῇ ἀγάπῃ ἐν τῷ θεῷ μένει καὶ ὁ θεὸς ἐν αὐτῷ μένει. (1 John 4:16b).

(4) ὁ πιστεύων εἰς τὸν υἱὸν τοῦ θεοῦ ἔχει τὴν μαρτυρίαν ἐν ἑαυτῷ (in himself), (1 John 5:10a).

(5) 11 καὶ αὕτη ἐστὶν ἡ μαρτυρία, ὅτι ζωὴν αἰώνιον ἔδωκεν ἡμῖν ὁ θεός, καὶ αὕτη ἡ ζωὴ ἐν τῷ υἱῷ αὐτοῦ ἐστιν. 12 ὁ ἔχων τὸν υἱὸν ἔχει τὴν ζωήν· ὁ μὴ ἔχων τὸν υἱὸν τοῦ θεοῦ τὴν ζωὴν οὐκ ἔχει. (1 John 5:11-12)—note that αἰώνιος has the same form in the feminine as the masculine—hence αἰώνιον is feminine agreeing with ζωήν, though the form looks like a masculine.

ἔδωκεν is "gave"; its subject is ὁ θεός.

Lesson 10

Participles (continued)

The Participles of the Active Voice (Continued)

As the present participle, ending in -ων, -ουσα, -ον (e.g., λύων, "loosing ") corresponds to the present tense, indicative (λύω, "I loose") and is really an adjective (see last Lesson), so *the future participle* (e.g., λύσων, "being about to loose") corresponds to the future tense, indicative (λύσω, "I will loose"; see the verb λύω, Lesson 6). This future participle is declined in exactly the same way as the present participle in all cases, numbers and genders. Hence this participle of λύω is λύσων, λύσουσα, λῦσον (Review the present participle in Lesson 9 and form this on the model with the added ς in the middle of the word). The use of the future participle is rare.

There is no participle corresponding to the imperfect tense indicative (ἔλυον, Lesson 6).

The *first aorist participle* ends in -ας, -ασα, -αν and is declined exactly like the adjective πᾶς, πᾶσα, πᾶν (see Lesson 9). This participle corresponds to the first aorist indicative (e.g., ἔλυσα, "I loosed," see Lesson 6). Thus the aorist participle of λύω is λύσας, λύσασα, λῦσαν (three genders). Notice that the augment, ἐ- (in ἔλυσα) is dropped; that is to say, the participle is not ἔλυσας but λύσας. There is no augment outside the indicative mood.

The student should write out the singular and plural, in all genders and cases, of λύσας, λύσασα, λῦσαν, from memory, on the model of πᾶς, πᾶσα, πᾶν.

The first aorist participle is very common. Study the following passages:—

(*a*) ὁ πέμψας με is "The (One) having sent me": πέμψας is the nom. sing. masc., first aorist participle of πέμπω, "I send" (future πέμψω, "I will send," i.e., for πέμπσω, -πς becoming ψ): it agrees in case, number and gender with the article ὁ.

(*b*) ἵνα ("in order that") ἀπόκρισιν ("an answer"—accusative of ἀπόκρισις) δῶμεν ("we may give") τοῖς ("to the [ones]") πέμψασιν ("having sent") ἡμᾶς ("us"). Note that πέμψασιν is the dative plural masc., in agreement with τοῖς. This use of the participle in agreement with the article is very frequent.

Corresponding to the perfect indicative (e.g., λέλυκα "I have loosed," see Lesson 6) is *the perfect participle*, which ends in -ως, -υια, -ος. Thus, the perfect participle of λύω is λελυκώς, λελυκυῖα, λελυκός (three genders). The accusative is λελυκότα, λελυκυῖαν, λελυκός; the masculine and neuter have third declension endings, and the feminine has first declension endings, with -α- throughout, because the preceding letter is a vowel, -ι-, and not a consonant (see Lesson 3, Note 1). The indicative mood tenses and participles thus far learned may be set out as follows:—

Indicative Mood

		Participles		
(1st Person)	**(Nominative)**			
Present	λύω	λύων	λύουσα	λῦον
Imperfect	ἔλυον		none	
Future	λύσω	λύσων	λύσουσα	λῦσον
First Aorist	ἔλυσα	λύσας	λύσασα	λῦσαν
Perfect	λέλυκα	λελυκώς	λελυκυῖα	λελυκός
Pluperfect	ἐλελύκειν		none	

Exercise

The student who has gone carefully through the Lessons up to this point will now be able, with a vocabulary and the translation of a few words here and there (to be explained later), to render considerable portions of the New Testament. We will take the first seven lines (1:1-3a) of the Epistle to the Hebrews. Learn the meanings given in brackets and refer to the various places in the past Lessons as mentioned. Study the passage again and again. Retranslate it. If time permits learn it by heart.

Πολυμερῶς (an adverb meaning "by many portions") καὶ πολυτρόπως ("in many ways") πάλαι ("formerly" or "of old") ὁ θεὸς λαλήσας (1st aorist participle of λαλέω, I speak—see λύσας above—"having spoken") τοῖς πατράσιν (dative plural of πατήρ—see Lesson 8) ἐν ("by"—ἐν often has this meaning instead of "in") τοῖς προφήταις (see under μαθητής, Note 3, Lesson 3), ἐπ' (for ἐπί, a preposition which, when followed by the genitive case, means "at": the ι is omitted before the ἐ- of the next word) ἐσχάτου (ἔσχατος, -η, -ον, "last" "the" is understood: "at the last" or "at the end") τῶν ἡμερῶν τούτων (ἡμέρα, "a day"; for τούτων see Lesson 4, and Rule 2; note that the order here is the same as in ἡ φωνὴ αὕτη, i.e., article noun, demonstrative adjective) ἐλάλησεν (3rd person singular 1st aorist of λαλέω) ἡμῖν (to us) ἐν υἱῷ, ὃν (Lesson 5, here accusative as the object of ἔθηκεν) ἔθηκεν ("He appointed") κληρονόμον ("heir"—accus. sing., agreeing in case and gender with ὅν) πάντων, ("of all things"—gen. plur. neut. of πᾶς—lit. "of all") δι' (for διά, which, when followed by the genitive, means "by") οὗ (see Lesson 5—genitive case "whom") καὶ ("also") ἐποίησεν (1st aorist of ποιέω, I make) τοὺς αἰῶνας· (Lesson 5) ὃς ὢν (present participle of εἰμί—"being") ἀπαύγασμα (an effulgence, or shining forth—the article "the" is not here expressed in Greek, but must be inserted in English) τῆς δόξης (Lesson 3, Note 2, and Vocab.—here the article signifies "the glory (of Him)," i.e., "His glory") καὶ χαρακτὴρ ("impress" or "very image"—our word "character" is a transliteration of it, but not here a translation) τῆς ὑποστάσεως (ὑπόστασις "substance"—like πόλις, Lesson 9) αὐτοῦ, (lit. "of Him," i.e., His—see αὐτός, Lesson 5), φέρων (pres. participle of φέρω, I bear, uphold) τε ("and"—always comes second in the clause) τὰ πάντα ("all things"—acc. plur. neut.—the article τά is not to be translated) τῷ ("by the"—the dative case here expresses the instrument, and is called the instrumental dative; hence we must translate by "by") ῥήματι (dative of ῥῆμα, see Lesson 7, page 48) τῆς δυνάμεως (gen. case of δύναμις, power, like πόλις) αὐτοῦ, ("His").

Translate verses 7 and 8 of the same chapter, with the help of the following vocabulary:—

εὐθύτης uprightness	ῥάβδος a scepter
πῦρ fire	πρός to
φλόξ a flame	μέν indeed
λειτουργός a minister	λέγω I say

Hebrews 1:7 καὶ πρὸς μὲν τοὺς ἀγγέλους λέγει, Ὁ ποιῶν τοὺς ἀγγέλους αὐτοῦ πνεύματα καὶ τοὺς λειτουργοὺς αὐτοῦ πυρὸς φλόγα, 8 πρὸς δὲ τὸν υἱόν, Ὁ θρόνος σου, ὁ θεός, εἰς τὸν αἰῶνα τοῦ αἰῶνος, καὶ ἡ ῥάβδος τῆς εὐθύτητος ῥάβδος τῆς βασιλείας σου.

Note that ὁ ποιῶν is "the (One) making" (present participle—we must render by "who maketh"): ὁ θεός is "O God": the next phrase is literally "unto the age of the age," but its English equivalent is "for ever and ever" and it must be so translated.

Third Declension Adjectives of Two Terminations

These have no separate form for the feminine. There are two kinds. The first kind consists of a simple form ending in -ων, with stem ending -ον, and therefore with genitive ending in -ονος, etc. This must be distinguished from the adjectives ending in -ων (with genitive ending -οντος) which have three forms for the three genders (see ἑκών, ἑκοῦσα, ἑκόν, Lesson 9).

The following is an example:—

σώφρων, sober minded (stem, σωφρον-)

	Singular		**Plural**	
	M. & F.	**Neut.**	**M. & F.**	**Neut.**
Nom.	σώφρων	σῶφρον	σώφρονες	σώφρονα
Voc.	σῶφρον	σῶφρον	σώφρονες	σώφρονα
Gen.	σώφρονος	σώφρονος	σωφρόνων	σωφρόνων
Dat.	σώφρονι	σώφρονι	σώφροσι	σώφροσι
Acc.	σώφρονα	σῶφρον	σώφρονας	σώφρονα

The second kind ends in -ης (neut. -ες). It contracts double vowels into a single sound. *This is a large and important class of adjective.* The contracted forms in the following paradigm must be memorized thoroughly (the uncontracted forms in brackets are quite regular and the endings will already be known).

ἀληθής, -ές, true

Singular

	Masc. & Fem.		**Neut.**
Nom.	ἀληθής		ἀληθές
Voc.	ἀληθές		ἀληθές
Gen.	(ἀληθέος)	ἀληθοῦς	ἀληθοῦς
Dat.	(ἀληθέϊ)	ἀληθεῖ	ἀληθεῖ
Acc.	(ἀληθέα)	ἀληθῆ	ἀληθές

Plural

	Masc. & Fem.		**Neut.**	
Nom.	(ἀληθέες)	ἀληθεῖς	(ἀληθέα)	ἀληθῆ
Voc.	(")	ἀληθεῖς	(")	ἀληθῆ
Gen.	(ἀληθέων)	ἀληθῶν	(ἀληθέων)	ἀληθῶν
Dat.		ἀληθέσι		ἀληθέσι
Acc.	(ἀληθέας)	ἀληθεῖς	(")	ἀληθῆ

Lesson 11

Pronouns

Personal Pronouns

Commit the following to memory:—

First Person

	Singular		**Plural**	
Nom.	ἐγώ		ἡμεῖς	we
Gen.	ἐμοῦ or μου	of me	ἡμῶν	of us
Dat.	ἐμοί or μοι	to me	ἡμῖν	to us
Acc.	ἐμέ or με	me	ἡμᾶς	us

Second Person

	Singular		**Plural**	
Nom.	σύ	thou	ὑμεῖς	you or ye
Gen.	σοῦ	of thee	ὑμῶν	of you
Dat.	σοί	to thee	ὑμῖν	to you
Acc.	σέ	thee	ὑμᾶς	you

For the *Third Person,* "he, she, it," αὐτός, αὐτή, αὐτό, see Lesson 5.

Reflexive Pronouns

In English these end in "-self," "-selves." They are used when the object of a sentence or clause refers to the same person or thing as the subject.

Forms occurring in the New Testament include the following:—

ἐμαυτόν myself	ἑαυτῶν of yourselves,
σεαυτοῦ of thyself, of themselves	
σεαυτόν thyself	ἑαυτοῖς to yourselves
ἑαυτόν (or αὑτόν) himself	ἑαυταῖς same (fem.)
ἑαυτήν (or αὑτήν) herself	ἑαυτούς, ἑαυτάς,etc.

Note 1—When αὐτός, -ή, -ό immediately follows a noun or pronoun with which it is connected it means "self." Thus ὁ ἄνθρωπος αὐτός is "the man himself"; ὁ αὐτός ἄνθρωπος is "the same man."

Note 2—This use of αὐτός as a reflexive must carefully be distinguished from the personal use "he." When used in the nominative for the third person, it is always emphatic: e.g., αὐτὸς ἐγὼ … δουλεύω, I myself serve (Rom. 7:25): αὐτοὶ γὰρ ὑμεῖς θεοδίδακτοί ἐστε, for ye yourselves are taught of God (lit. God-taught) (1 Thess. 4:9).

Note 3—The ε- of ἑαυτόν, etc., is often dropped and the word contracted to αὑτόν, etc. In that case αὑτός, "himself," and the other forms must be distinguished from αὐτός, "he," etc.

Note 4—This third person reflexive pronoun is also used for the first and second persons, when there would be no ambiguity. Thus ἑαυτοῖς is "in ourselves," (Rom. 8:23) instead of ἐν ἡμῖν αὐτοῖς. Again, τὴν ἑαυτῶν σωτηρίαν is "your own salvation," lit., "the salvation of yourselves" (Phil. 2:12) instead of τὴν ὑμῶν αὐτῶν σωτηρίαν.

Other examples are: βλέπετε δὲ ὑμεῖς ἑαυτούς, "But take ye heed to yourselves" (Mark 13:9; cp. 2 John 8); προσέχετε ἑαυτοῖς "take heed to yourselves" (Luke 12:1).

(*Review the demonstrative pronouns, Lesson 4, and the personal and relative pronouns, Lesson 4*)

Indefinite Pronouns

The pronoun τις (masc. and fem.), τι (neut.) one, means "someone," "anyone," "a certain," "some," "any." It is declined as follows, the masculine and feminine being the same, and the endings those of the third declension:—

	Singular		Plural	
	M. & F.	**Neut.**	**M. & F.**	**Neut.**
Nom.	τις	τι	τινές	τινά
Gen.	τινός	τινός	τινῶν	τινῶν
Dat.	τινί	τινί	τισί	τισί
Acc.	τινά	τι	τινάς	τινά

Examples

εἰσίν τινες ὧδε there are some here (Mark 9:1); Ἑκατοντάρχου δέ τινος (and of a certain centurion) δοῦλος (a servant), (Luke 7:2); Ἄνθρωπός τις ἦν πλούσιος, "(there) was a certain rich man," lit., "a certain man was rich" (Luke 16:1); οὔτε (nor) ὕψωμα (height) οὔτε (nor) βάθος (depth) οὔτε (nor) τις (any) κτίσις (creature) ἑτέρα (other) (Rom. 8:39).

Note 1—The indefinite pronoun τις never stands first in a sentence.

Note 2—If used with a noun it generally follows the noun.

Note 3—Other indefinite pronouns are οὔτις and μήτις, each of which means "no one." They are formed by the addition of τις to the negatives οὐ and μή, "not."

Interrogative Pronouns

The simple interrogative pronoun is τίς, τί, who? what? In form it is exactly like the indefinite pronoun τις, τι, the only difference being that it has an accent pointing from left to right. The two must be carefully distinguished.

Examples

Τίς ἐστιν ἡ μήτηρ μου καὶ τίνες εἰσὶν οἱ ἀδελφοί μου; Who is My mother, and who are My brethren? (Matt. 12:48); τίνα σεαυτὸν ποιεῖς; Whom makest Thou Thyself? (John 8:53).

There is an adjectival use of τίς in agreement with a noun, e.g., Τί σημεῖον (What sign) δεικνύεις (showest Thou) ἡμῖν (to us); (John 2:18).

The following interrogative pronouns should also be memorized; they correspond to the relative pronouns οἷος and ὅσος given below. They are all of 1st and 2nd declension endings.

Qualitative, ποῖος, -α, -ον, of what kind?

Quantitative, πόσος, -η, -ον, how great?

The plural πόσοι, -αι, -α signifies "how many?"

There is a relative pronoun, ὁποῖος, "of what kind," corresponding to ποῖος, and occurring five times in the New Testament. In Acts 26:29, it is rendered "such as"; in 1 Cor. 3, 13 "of what sort"; in Gal. 2:6 "whatsoever"; in 1 Thess. 1:9 and Jas. 1:24 "what manner of."

An indefinite relative, "whoever," "whatever," is formed by combining τις, τι, with ὅς, ἥ, ὅ, both parts being declined as follows:—

Singular

	Masc.	**Fem.**	**Neut.**
Nom.	ὅστις	ἥτις	ὅ,τι
Gen.	οὗτινος	ἧστινος	οὗτινος
Dat.	ᾧτινι	ᾗτινι	ᾧτινι
Acc.	ὅντινα	ἥντινα	ὅ,τι

Plural

	Masc.	**Fem.**	**Neut.**
Nom.	οἵτινες	αἵτινες	ἅτινα
Gen.	ὧντινων	ὧντινων	ὧντινων
Dat.	οἷστισι	αἷστισι	οἷστισι
Acc.	οὕστινας	ἅστινας	ἅτινα

Note—The genitive singular masculine is shortened to ὅτου in the phrase ἕως ὅτου "as long as," "until," lit., "until whatever (time)" (See Matt. 5:25).

Other relative pronouns are as follows:—

Qualitative, οἷος, -α, -ον, such as.

Quantitative, ὅσος, -η, -ον, so great as, and its plural ὅσοι, -αι, α, so many as.

Compare the interrogatives above, ποῖος and πόσος.

The following table will sum up the chief pronouns which correspond to one another:—

Demonstrative οὗτος (this)	Relative ὅς (who)	Interrogative τίς (who?)	Indefinite τις (someone)
τοιοῦτος(such an one)	οἷος(such as)	ποῖος(of what sort?)	——
τοσοῦτος(so great)	ὅσος(so great as)	πόσος(how great?)	——
τοσοῦτοι(so many)	ὅσοι(so many as)	τόσοι(how many?)	——

Distributive Pronouns

(1) ἄλλος, ἄλλη, ἄλλο, another (i.e., another of the same sort, of like kind). The plural of this denotes "others." It is declined like ὅς, ἥ, ὅ.

(2) ἕτερος, ἑτέρα, ἕτερον, another (i.e., another of a different kind).

(3) ἀλλήλων, ἀλλήλοις, ἀλλήλους, of each other, to each other, each other; this is used only in the genitive, dative, and accusative plural.

(4) ἕκαστος, -η, -ον, each; this is used only in the singular.

Vocabulary and Exercise

Learn the following words and translate the passages below, correcting your rendering from the English Revised Version; retranslate the English into the Greek without referring to the exercise, and correct your Greek from the exercise.

οἰκοδομέω I build
οἰκία a house
πέτρα a rock
πρός to (followed by the accusative)
ἀληθινός true
σπείρω I sow
θερίζω I reap
ποῦ where?
γογγυσμός a murmuring
περί concerning
ὄχλος a multitude
μέν indeed

δέ but
κύριος lord
φυτεύω I plant
ποτίζω I water
οὖν therefore
διάκονος a minister
ὡς as
ὥστε so then, or so that
ποιέω I do
ἀκούω I hear
οὔτε neither, nor
φρόνιμος prudent

Translate with the help of the accompanying notes:—

(1) Ἐγὼ μέν εἰμι Παύλου, ἕτερος δέ, Ἐγὼ Ἀπολλῶ, οὐκ ἄνθρωποί ἐστε; 5 τί οὖν ἐστιν Ἀπολλῶς;
τί δέ ἐστιν Παῦλος; διάκονοι δι᾽ ὧν ἐπιστεύσατε, καὶ ἑκάστῳ ὡς ὁ κύριος ἔδωκεν. 6 ἐγὼ ἐφύτευσα,
Ἀπολλῶς ἐπότισεν, ἀλλὰ ὁ θεὸς ηὔξανεν· 7 ὥστε οὔτε ὁ φυτεύων ἐστίν τι οὔτε
ὁ ποτίζων ἀλλ᾽ ὁ αὐξάνων θεός. 8 ὁ φυτεύων δὲ καὶ ὁ ποτίζων ἕν εἰσιν, (1 Cor. 3:4b-8a): Note the special significance of ἕτερος, "another" of a different character, not another of the same sort (ἄλλος): δι᾽ is for διά, which with the genitive (ὧν) denotes "by means of": ἐπιστεύσατε, 2nd pers. plural, 1st aor. of πιστεύω: ἔδωκεν "gave" (to be explained later): note that τί is "what" (neut. of τίς—so in R.V., not "who" as in A.V.), but τι, without the accent in verse 7, is "anything." What is the ἐ- in ἐφύτευσα, and in ἐπότισεν [see Lesson 6, Note 3]? Verbs like ποτίζω ending in -ίζω in the present tense change the ζ to ς in the 1st aorist: ηὔξανεν is the imperfect tense of αὐξάνω "was giving the increase": note that ἀ- makes the augment ἠ- not ἐα-: ἕν is "one," it is the neuter of εἷς, μία, ἕν (masc., fem., neut.) and is to be distinguished from ἐν, "in." It might be rendered "one thing." Note the four occurrences of the article ὁ with the present participle, (lit., "the one planting," etc.), this must be rendered by "he that planteth," etc.

(2) Πᾶς οὖν ὅστις ἀκούει μου τους λόγους τούτους καὶ ποιεῖ αὐτούς, ὁμοιωθήσεται ἀνδρὶ φρονίμῳ, ὅστις ᾠκοδόμησεν αὐτοῦ τὴν οἰκίαν ἐπὶ τὴν πέτραν· (Matt. 7:24): Πᾶς is "every one," for μου see beginning of this Lesson. For τούτους see beginning of this Lesson, Rule 2, ὁμοιωθήσεται "shall be likened." ᾠκοδόμησεν is the 3rd pers. sing. of the 1st aorist of οἰκοδομέω; note that the augment of verbs beginning in οἰ is formed by turning the οἰ- into ᾠ- with the iota underneath. The future of verbs ending in -έω ends in -ήσω, and the 1st aorist in -ήσα.

(3) ἦσαν δέ τινες ἐξ αὐτῶν ἄνδρες Κύπριοι καὶ Κυρηναῖοι, οἵτινες ἐλθόντες εἰς Ἀντιόχειαν ἐλάλουν καὶ πρὸς τοὺς Ἑλληνιστάς εὐαγγελιζόμενοι τὸν κύριον Ἰησοῦν (Acts 11:20). Translate ἦσαν "there were"; ἐξ is for ἐκ "of" or "out of"; Κύπριοι Cyprians; ἐλθόντες "having come" (see later); ἐλάλουν is the 3rd pers. plur. imperf. tense of λαλέω, "I speak"—the -ουν is for -εον; εὐαγγελιζόμενοι "preaching" (see later).

(4) ἐν γὰρ τούτῳ ὁ λόγος ἐστὶν ἀληθινὸς ὅτι ἄλλος ἐστὶν ὁ σπείρων καὶ ἄλλος ὁ θερίζων (John 4:37), Ἄλλος ... ἄλλος is "one ... another."

(5) καὶ γογγυσμὸς περὶ αὐτοῦ ἦν πολὺς ἐν τοῖς ὄχλοις· οἱ μὲν ἔλεγον ὅτι Ἀγαθός ἐστιν, ἄλλοι [δὲ] ἔλεγον, Οὔ, ἀλλὰ πλανᾷ τὸν ὄχλον. John 7:12, οἱ μέν is "some indeed"—the "indeed" should be omitted in translating; Οὔ is "No"; πλανᾷ "He deceiveth."

Lesson 12

The Verb (continued). The Imperative Mood. The Subjunctive Mood

The Verb(Continued)

The Imperative Mood

Having learned the Indicative Mood (which makes assertions) and the Participles (or Verbal Adjectives), which correspond to the tenses of Indicative, we have now to consider the Imperative Mood (which makes commands).

There are only three tenses, the Present, which gives a command indicating continuous action, or repeated action (e.g., λῦε, "loose thou, and continue to do so"), the First Aorist, which gives a command without reference to its continuance or frequency (e.g., λῦσον, "loose thou"—a single act), and the Perfect, λέλυκε, "do thou have had loosed, and let it remain so"; this last is rarely used. There is no Future Imperative. There are two persons, the second and the third.

The following specimen should be committed to memory and then should be written out in a column parallel to the tenses of the Indicative Mood, tense against tense where they correspond.

Present Tense (continuous actions)

	Singular	
2nd pers.	λῦε	loose thou
3rd pers.	λυέτω	let him loosen
	Plural	
2nd pers.	λύετε	loose ye
3rd pers.	λυέτωσαν or λυόντων	let them loosen

First Aorist (momentary action)

	Singular	
2nd pers.	λῦσον	loose thou
3rd pers.	λυσάτω	let him loosen
	Plural	
2nd pers.	λύσατε	loose ye
3rd pers.	λυσάτωσαν or λυσάντων	let them loosen

Perfect

	Singular	**Plural**
2nd pers.	λέλυκε	λελύκετε
3rd pers.	λελυκέτω	λελυκέτωσαν or λελυκόντων

(the meanings are "do thou have had loosed," "let him have had loosed," "do ye have had loosed," "let them have had loosed.")

Note 1—There is no augment (ἐ-) in the 1st Aorist of the Imperative, nor indeed does the augment occur outside the Indicative Mood.

Note 2—Observe the characteristic -σ- of the 1st Aorist, and the characteristic reduplication λε- of the Perfect, as in the Indicative Mood.

Note 3—The Aorist Imperative is very frequent in the New Testament and must be carefully noted.

The following vocabulary will be a guide to the exercise below. The student should learn the list, if time permits, at all events the verbs. Then translate the six passages given in the exercise, correcting the result from the English version. Retranslate from the English into Greek, correcting from the Greek version.

ναός a temple ἄνω the brim

ἀπολύω I let go ἀντλέω I draw out, (used of water etc.— future ἀντλήσω)

ἐκεῖνος (see Lesson 4, plural "these")

——————— φέρω I bear

ὅθεν wherefore ἀρχιτρίκλινος a governor of a feast

ἅγιος, -α, -ον holy ———————

κλῆσις a calling (gen. κλήσεως) μή not (always used instead of οὐ with the Imperative)

ἐπουράνιος, -α, -ον heavenly

μέτοχος a partaker θησαυρίζω I lay up treasure

κατανοέω I consider θησαυρός a treasure

Ἀρχιερεύς High Priest (see Lesson 9) ἐπί upon (when used with a genitive)

πιστὸς, -ή, -όν faithful γή earth

ὅλος, -η, -ον all ὅπου where

οἶκος a house σής a moth

——————— βρῶσις rust

γεμίζω I fill (the future is γεμίσω) ἀφανίζω I corrupt

ὑδρία a water pot κλέπτης a thief

ὕδωρ water (gen. ὕδατος— to be explained later) διορύσσω I break through

κλέπτω I steal

ἕως up to καρδία a heart

Exercise on the Imperative Mood

Translate:—

(1) Λύσατε (λύω here means "to destroy") τὸν ναὸν τοῦτον (John 2:19). Note the 1st Aorist, 2nd person plur., "destroy ye."

(2) Ἀπόλυσον τοὺς ἀνθρώπους ἐκείνους (Acts 16:35).

(3) Ὑμεῖς (ye) οὖν (therefore) ἀκούσατε την παραβολήν (Matt. 13:18—the Ὑμεῖς is emphatic).

(4) Ὅθεν, ἀδελφοὶ ἅγιοι, κλήσεως ἐπουρανίου μέτοχοι, κατανοήσατε τὸν ἀπόστολον καὶ ἀρχιερέα τῆς ὁμολογίας ἡμῶν Ἰησοῦν, 2 πιστὸν ὄντα τῷ ποιήσαντι αὐτὸν ὡς καὶ Μωϋσῆς ἐν ὅλῳ τῷ οἴκῳ αὐτοῦ (Heb. 3:1, 2, with the aid of the vocab). Note 1— κατανοήσατε is the 1st Aorist Imperative, 2nd person plural of κατανοέω—verbs ending in -έω make the future end in -ήσω, lengthening the ε to η and so in the 1st Aorist: so ποιέω makes the future ποιήσω; 2— ὄντα is accus. sing. masc. pres. participle of εἰμί: 3 —ποιήσαντι is dat. sing. 1st Aorist Participle of ποιέω, I make.

(5) λέγει αὐτοῖς ὁ Ἰησοῦς, Γεμίσατε τὰς ὑδρίας ὕδατος. καὶ ἐγέμισαν αὐτὰς ἕως ἄνω. 8 καὶ λέγει αὐτοῖς, Ἀντλήσατε νῦν καὶ φέρετε τῷ ἀρχιτρικλίνῳ (John 2:7, 8a). The genitive ὕδατος here signifies "with water" (the genitive must be rendered "with," after a verb denoting "to fill"). Note carefully the difference in the tenses of the Imperative Mood verbs in this verse: Γεμίσατε and Ἀντλήσατε are 1st aorists "fill ye up," "draw out," a single act in each instance; but φέρετε is a present tense, "be carrying" (there is, in this change of tense, a peculiarly delicate suggestion of politeness with regard to the recognition of the place of honor held by the governor of the feast).

(6) Μὴ θησαυρίζετε ὑμῖν θησαυροὺς ἐπὶ τῆς γῆς, ὅπου σὴς καὶ βρῶσις ἀφανίζει καὶ ὅπου κλέπται διορύσσουσιν καὶ κλέπτουσιν· 20 θησαυρίζετε δὲ ὑμῖν θησαυροὺς ἐν οὐρανῷ, ὅπου οὔτε σὴς οὔτε βρῶσις ἀφανίζει καὶ ὅπου κλέπται οὐ διορύσσουσιν οὐδὲ κλέπτουσιν· 21 ὅπου γάρ ἐστιν

ὁ θησαυρός σου, ἐκεῖ ἔσται καὶ ἡ καρδία σου (Matt. 6:19-21). *Note 1*—ὑμῖν (dative plural) "for yourselves," lit., "for you"; the dative signifies "for" as well as "to," and the personal pronoun here stands for the reflexive pronoun, which in full would be ὑμῖν αὐτοῖς (see Lesson 11, Note 4): *2*—ἀφανίζει is singular number "doth corrupt," although it has two subjects "moth and rust," the two being regarded as one subject: *3*—for κλέπται compare μαθητής (Lesson 3): *4*—σοῦ (verse 21) is lit. "of thee," i.e., "thy": *5*—ἔσται is "shall be," this will be learned later.

The Subjunctive Mood

In English the Subjunctive Mood expresses supposition, doubt or uncertainty, and follows the conjunctions if, lest, though, etc. In Greek the scope of the Subjunctive is much wider.

There is no future or imperfect tense and no perfect in the Active Voice save in one irregular verb. Accordingly, the following are the only two Subjunctive tenses in the verb λύω and similar verbs. Note the *iota subscript* (i.e., written under) in the 2nd and 3rd persons singular, and the long vowels η or ω in all the persons.

Present Subjunctive

λύω	I may loose	λύωμεν	we may loose
λύῃς	thou mayest loose	λύητε	ye may loose
λύῃ	he may loose	λύωσι	they may loose

First Aorist Subjunctive

The meaning is either "I may loose" or "I may have loosed," etc.

λύσω	λύσωμεν
λύσῃς	λύσητε
λύσῃ	λύσωσι

Note 1—The endings are the same in each tense, save for the characteristic ς in the First Aorist.

Note 2—There is a Second Aorist in some verbs, with the same meaning as the First. This will be noticed later.

First Aorist Participles in the Active Voice have terminations corresponding to these. See the paragraphs dealing with the Aorist Participle in Lesson 10.

Lesson 13

Subjunctive Mood (continued)

The Subjunctive Mood (Continued)

The following is the present tense of the Subjunctive Mood of εἰμί, the verb "to be,"of which it is the only Subjunctive tense. The student will observe that the words are precisely the same as the endings of the present Subjunctive of λύω (Lesson 12).

Singular	**Plural**
ὦ I may be	ὦμεν we may be
ᾖς thou mayst be	ἦτε you may be
ᾖ he may be	ὦσι(ν) they may be

The following are the principal uses of the Subjunctive Mood in the New Testament:—

I—It is used in *clauses expressing purpose.* These are known as *Final Clauses* (i.e., as having an end or object in view). They are introduced by such conjunctions as ἵνα and ὅπως, each of which means "in order that," or simply "that," and negatively by ἵνα μή or ὅπως μή, "in order that not" or "lest," or even by μή alone, which when so used means the same thing.

Examples

The following sentences give examples of purpose expressed positively:—

John 10:10b, ἐγὼ (I) ἦλθον (came) ἵνα (in order that) ζωὴν (life—the accusative of the object of the verb following) ἔχωσιν (they may have 3rd person plural, pres. subjunctive of ἔχω, I have) καὶ (and) περισσὸν (abundance) ἔχωσιν (they may have).

Matt. 6:4, ὅπως (in order that) ᾖ (may be) σου ἡ ἐλεημοσύνη (thine alms—lit., of thee the alms) ἐν τῷ κρυπτῷ (in secret—τῷ not to be translated).

In the following sentence note that the tenses are *1st Aorist Subjunctive:*

John 1:7, οὗτος (This one, i.e., He) ἦλθεν (came) εἰς (for or unto) μαρτυρίαν (a witness), ἵνα (that) μαρτυρήσῃ (he might bear witness—3rd pers. sing. 1st aor. subjunc. of μαρτυρέω, I bear, witness—the future is μαρτυρήσω, I shall bear witness, the -ε- of the present ending being lengthened to -η-) περὶ (concerning) τοῦ φωτός (the light genitive of φῶς—the preposition περί takes the genitive), ἵνα (that) πάντες (all) πιστεύσωσιν (might believe—3rd pers. plur., 1st aor. subjunc.) δι' (by means of—short for διά, is followed by the genitive) αὐτοῦ (him).

Translate the 8th verse and note the emphatic ἐκεῖνος, "he" ("that one"): οὐκ ἦν ἐκεῖνος τὸ φῶς, ἀλλ' ἵνα μαρτυρήσῃ περὶ τοῦ φωτός.

The question arises What is the difference in meaning between the present subjunctive and the 1st aorist, seeing that both are rendered by "may, etc."? The answer is that the present signifies continuous or repeated action (as, for example, ἔχωσιν in John 10:10 above): the aorist signifies either single action or action undefined in point of time. Thus in the last instance μαρτυρήσῃ speaks of John's witness without reference to its continuity, and πιστεύσωσιν points to the single act of faith in believing.

Exercise

Translate, with the help of the accompanying notes, 1 Cor. 1:10: —Παρακαλῶ δὲ ὑμᾶς, ἀδελφοί, διὰ τοῦ ὀνόματος τοῦ κυρίου ἡμῶν Ἰησοῦ Χριστοῦ, ἵνα τὸ αὐτὸ λέγητε πάντες καὶ μὴ ᾖ ἐν ὑμῖν σχίσματα, ἦτε δὲ κατηρτισμένοι ἐν τῷ αὐτῷ νοῒ καὶ ἐν τῇ αὐτῇ γνώμῃ.

Παρακαλῶ, "I exhort": διὰ, "by": ὀνόματος (genitive of ὄνομα, a name—genitive after διά): τὸ αὐτὸ, "the same [thing]" (see Lesson 5)—this is the accusative, as object of λέγητε (pres. subjunctive of λέγω, "I speak," subjunctive after ἵνα): μὴ ᾖ, "[there] may not be"—note the negative μή (not οὐ) with the subjunctive: ἐν, "among" (takes the dative): σχίσματα, "schisms" (note that in Greek a neuter plural subject of a verb takes the verb in the singular; thus σχίσματα is the subject of ᾖ [singular] "schisms may not be"): ἦτε (subjunc. of εἰμί—-see above): κατηρτισμένοι, "joined" (explained later): νοῒ, dative of νοῦς, "mind" (see Lesson 7): γνώμῃ, "judgment."

(*After becoming thoroughly familiarized with this verse, retranslate it, correcting your result.*)

II—The subjunctive is used in certain *Conditional Clauses* (these are introduced in English by "if"), which imply either possibility or uncertainty with the prospect of decision. In these cases, ἐάν ("if") is used to introduce the subjunctive. Where the supposition assumes a fact, εἰ (which also means "if") is used, followed by the *indicative*. See also p. 113.

Examples

Thus in Matt. 4:3, Εἰ υἱὸς εἶ τοῦ θεοῦ, "if Thou art (the) Son of God," does not express uncertainty or possibility, but signifies "assuming that Thou art the Son of God" (εἶ, "thou art," is the 2nd pers. sing. of the pres. indic. of εἰμί—see Lesson 3). But in Matt. 17:20, ἐὰν ἔχητε πίστιν ὡς κόκκον σινάπεως, "if ye have faith as a grain of mustard seed" (ἔχητε being the pres. *subjunctive* of ἔχω, I have) does not assume that they have faith, but suggests an uncertainty with the prospect of fulfillment, hence the subjunctive is used.

Note:

ἐάν is really εἰ ἄν and the ἄν determines the use of the subjunctive.

Exercise

Translate with the help of notes and, after thoroughly learning the texts, retranslate from the English into Greek.

(1) ἐὰν οὖν θεωρῆτε τὸν υἱὸν τοῦ ἀνθρώπου ἀναβαίνοντα ὅπου ἦν τὸ πρότερον (John 6:62). The "what then" is not expressed in Greek, it is understood; the Greek sentence simply begins with "if": θεωρῆτε is pres. subjunc. of θεωρέω, I behold; ἀναβαίνοντα is acc. sing. masc. of pres. participle of ἀναβαίνω, I ascend; τὸ πρότερον, lit. "the former," is an adverbial phrase meaning "before."

(2) ἐὰν τὰς ἐντολάς μου τηρήσητε, μενεῖτε ἐν τῇ ἀγάπῃ μου, καθὼς ἐγὼ τὰς ἐντολὰς τοῦ πατρός μου τετήρηκα καὶ μένω αὐτοῦ ἐν τῇ ἀγάπῃ (John 15:10). ἐντολάς is acc. plur. of ἐντολή, a commandment, and is the object of the verb τηρήσητε, which is the 1st aor. subj. of τηρέω, I keep; μενεῖτε is the future indic. 2nd pers. plur. of μένω, I abide, and will be explained later. Note the reduplication in τετήρηκα (what tense is this? See λέλυκα, Lesson 6).

(3) περιτομὴ μὲν γὰρ ὠφελεῖ ἐὰν νόμον πράσσῃς· ἐὰν δὲ παραβάτης νόμου ᾖς, ἡ περιτομή σου ἀκροβυστία γέγονεν (Rom 2:25). περιτομὴ, circumcision; μὲν, indeed; ὠφελεῖ "profiteth"—3rd pers. sing. pres. indic. of ὠφελέω, I profit; νόμον, "the Law"—the object of πράσσῃς, "thou doest"

(pres. subjunc. of πράσσω; δὲ, but: παραβάτης, a transgressor; ᾖς, "thou art"—pres. subjunc. of εἰμί (see above); ἀκροβυστία, uncircumcision; γέγονεν, "has become" (to be explained later).

III—The subjunctive is used in *clauses beginning with a relative pronoun or adverb, like* "whoever," "whenever," or "wherever," *which do not refer to a definite person or thing;* in other words, when the word "ever" can be used after the relative.

Note that ἄν or ἐάν follows the relative. This ἄν is not translatable, it simply has a generalizing effect in these clauses. The ἄν is joined to ὅτε "when," making ὅταν "whenever." Two other relatives to be memorized are ὅπου, "where," and ἕως, "until."

Examples

(1) Matt. 18:6: Ὃς δ' ἂν ("but whosoever"—the relative pronoun ὅς with ἄν makes "whosoever": δ' is for δέ, "but"; it never comes first in the sentence) σκανδαλίσῃ (shall cause to stumble—3rd pers. sing. 1st aorist, subjunc. of σκανδαλίζω—ζ in the present tense becomes ς in the future and 1st aorist) ἕνα ("one" accus. masc. of εἷς—the numerals will be given later) τῶν μικρῶν τούτων (of these little [ones]) τῶν πιστευόντων (the [ones] believing) εἰς ἐμέ (on Me).

(2) John 2:5: Ὅ τι ἂν (ὅστις is "whosoever" and the neuter ὅτι is written separately, ὅ τι, or with a comma between, ὅ, τι) λέγῃ (He saith—pres. subjunc.) ὑμῖν (to you) ποιήσατε (do ye—2nd pers. plur. 1st aorist imperative of ποιέω).

(3) Matt. 6:2: Ὅταν (whensoever—a relative adverb, for ὅτε ἄν) οὖν (therefore) ποιῇς (thou doest —pres. subjunc.) ἐλεημοσύνην (alms), μὴ σαλπίσῃς (do not sound a trumpet—1st aor. subjunc. of σαλπίζω—μή with the 1st aor. subjunc. stands for the imperative) ἔμπροσθέν (before—takes the genitive) σου (thee).

Translate: ὅταν ἐν τῷ κόσμῳ ὦ, φῶς εἰμι τοῦ κόσμου (John 9:5). ὅταν, "when" (see R.V.); ὦ, "I am" (pres. subjunc. of εἰμί, see above).

IV—The Subjunctive is used in *Deliberative Questions*, i.e., when persons are deliberating as to what is to be done. This is known as the Deliberate Subjunctive. Thus, "Shall we continue in sin?" is ἐπιμένωμεν τῇ ἁμαρτίᾳ; (Rom. 6:1): ἐπιμένωμεν (note the long ω) is 1st pers. plur. pres. subjunc. of ἐπιμένω, a compound of ἐπί and μένω, "I abide"; the article τῇ is not to be translated, as it is used with abstract nouns such as ἁμαρτία, i.e., when it denotes sin in general. The dative case must here be translated "in sin." The dative case has several significances, which must be rendered appropriately in English according to the word which governs the noun. This will be explained later.

V—The Subjunctive is used in *certain forms of exhortation.* This is called *the Hortatory Subjunctive.* In English it is introduced by "let." Thus 1 Thess. 5:6, γρηγορῶμεν καὶ νήφωμεν is "let us watch and let us be sober"; note the long ω in distinction from the pres. indicative; the first verb is the present subjunctive, first person plural of γρηγορέω, "I watch," and the second verb is the same tense and person of νήφω, "I am sober."

The student should become thoroughly familiar with the whole of this lesson before taking up the next. The use of the Subjunctive is very important. The examples given should be read again and again until the student can easily retranslate them from English into Greek. For further treatment of the Subjunctive, see the additional rules of Syntax.

Lesson 14

Negative Commands or Prohibitions. The Optative Mood

Extra Note on Negative Commands or Prohibitions

For these the Imperative Mood is used, or in certain instances the Subjunctive. The student should review the Imperative Mood of λύω (Lesson 12) and learn now the Imperative of εἰμί, which is as follows:—

ἴσθι be thou	ἔστε be ye
ἔστω or ἤτω let him (or her, or it) be, or let there be	ἔστωσαν let them be

Note—The negative in prohibitions is always μή.

I—The *Present Imperative* with μή most frequently denotes a command to cease to do something, or not to do what is already being done. Thus μὴ κλαίετε is "do not weep," and in Matt. 6:19, μὴ θησαυρίζετε is "do not treasure" ὑμῖν (for yourselves) θησαυροὺς ἐπὶ τῆς γῆς (on the earth).

II—When a command is given not to do something at all, not to begin to do something, μή with the *Aorist Subjunctive* is used. As an example study again the sentence in *III*, (3), Lesson 13 from Matt. 6:2, noticing the latter part of the verse:—Ὅταν οὖν ποιῇς ἐλεημοσύνην, μὴ σαλπίσῃς (do not sound a trumpet—σαλπίσῃς is the 2nd pers. sing. 1st Aorist Subjunctive). Here the command is not to begin that practice.

Exercise

(1) The student should now be able to translate the whole of Matt. 6:19-23. Some of this has already been given. Write out a translation with the help of the following vocabulary. If any noun is forgotten, turn to the English Version (preferably the R.V. [NRSV or NKJV]), but try to translate without doing this. Retranslate the passage into Greek.

ἀφανίζω I consume
διορύσσω I dig through
κλέπτω I steal
ἐκεῖ there
ἔσται 3rd sing. fut. of εἰμί
καὶ also (verse 21)
καρδία heart
λύχνος lamp
σῶμα body
ὀφθαλμός eye
ἁπλοῦς single
ὅλος, -η, -ον all or (the) whole
φωτεινὸς, -ή, -όν full of light
πονηρὸς evil
σκοτεινὸς full of darkness
πόσος how great

6:19 Μὴ θησαυρίζετε ὑμῖν θησαυροὺς ἐπὶ τῆς γῆς, ὅπου σὴς καὶ βρῶσις ἀφανίζει καὶ ὅπου
κλέπται διορύσσουσιν καὶ κλέπτουσιν· 20 θησαυρίζετε δὲ ὑμῖν θησαυροὺς ἐν οὐρανῷ, ὅπου οὔτε
σὴς οὔτε βρῶσις ἀφανίζει καὶ ὅπου κλέπται οὐ διορύσσουσιν οὐδὲ κλέπτουσιν· 21 ὅπου γάρ ἐστιν
ὁ θησαυρός σου, ἐκεῖ ἔσται καὶ ἡ καρδία σου. 22 Ὁ λύχνος τοῦ σώματός ἐστιν ὁ ὀφθαλμός. ἐὰν οὖν
ᾖ ὁ ὀφθαλμός σου ἁπλοῦς, ὅλον τὸ σῶμά σου φωτεινὸν ἔσται· 23 ἐὰν δὲ ὁ ὀφθαλμός σου πονηρὸς ᾖ,
ὅλον τὸ σῶμά σου σκοτεινὸν ἔσται. εἰ οὖν τὸ φῶς τὸ ἐν σοὶ σκότος ἐστίν, τὸ σκότος πόσον. (Matt. 6:19-23)

(2) ἡ πίστις (faith) σου (of thee—i.e., "thy faith") σέσωκέν (perf. of σώζω I save) σε· ὕπαγε (go) εἰς εἰρήνην (peace) καὶ ἴσθι (see Imperative of εἰμί above) ὑγιὴς (whole) ἀπὸ (from, with genitive) τῆς μάστιγός σου (μάστιξ, a scourge, plague—genitive μάστιγος), Mark 5:34.

(3) ἔστω (let be) δὲ ὁ λόγος (speech) ὑμῶν ναὶ (yea) ναί, οὒ οὔ. For ἔστω, see Imperative of εἰμί above, Matt. 5:37a.

(4) Jas. 5:12b (middle of verse)—μὴ ὀμνύετε (ὀμνύω, I swear) ... ἤτω ("let be"—see the Imperative of εἰμί) δὲ ὑμῶν τὸ Ναὶ (lit., "the nay of you") ναὶ καὶ τὸ Οὒ οὔ.

The Optative Mood

This Mood is used either (*a*) in expressing wishes or (*b*) in what are called dependent questions, or (*c*) in deliberative questions. Further details are given later. The use of the Optative is not frequent in New Testament.

Memorize the following:—

The Optative Mood of εἰμί

"I might be," etc.

Singular	**Plural**
εἴην	εἴημεν or εἶμεν
εἴης	εἴητε or εἶτε
εἴη	εἴησαν or εἶεν

The Optative Mood of λύω.

Present

"I might loose," etc. (*The precise meaning is determined by the context.*)

Singular	**Plural**
λύοιμι	λύοιμεν
λύοις	λύοιτε
λύοι	λύοιεν

Future

"I should loose," etc.

Singular	**Plural**
λύσοιμι	λύσοιμεν
λύσοις	λύσοιτε
λύσοι	λύσοιεν

First Aorist

"I might loose," etc. (according to context)

Singular	**Plural**
λύσαιμι	λύσαιμεν
λύσαις	λύσαιτε
λύσαι or λέσειε	λύσαιεν or λύσειαν

Examples of the Optative Mood

(*a*) The following are examples of the expression of a wish:—

(1) Τὸ ἀργύριόν σου σὺν σοὶ εἴη εἰς ἀπώλειαν (Acts 8:20). This is literally "Thy money with thee be unto destruction" (εἴη, 3rd sing. opt. of εἰμί, here simply means '"be," i.e., "may [it] be").

(2) 1 Thess. 3:12: ὑμᾶς ("you"—the accus. object of the two succeeding verbs) δὲ ὁ κύριος (the Lord) πλεονάσαι (make to increase—3rd sing. 1st aor. opt. of πλεονάζω, i.e., may He make to increase) καὶ περισσεύσαι (make to abound—same tense of περισσεύω) τῇ ἀγάπῃ (in love—dative of the point in which the verb is applied; hence we must translate by "in" though there is no preposition in the Greek; the article is used because the noun is abstract) εἰς ἀλλήλους (to one another).

(*b*) The following are examples of dependent questions, i.e., questions which are not asked directly, but depend upon some preceding statement:—

(1) Ὡς (as, or while) δὲ ἐν ἑαυτῷ (in himself) διηπόρει (was doubting—3rd pers. sing. imperf. indic. of διαπορέω—for διηπόρεε, the -εε contracting to -ει—the change from α to η is due to the fact that when a preposition, here διά, is joined to a verb, here ἀπορέω the augment, which must come before the verb, joins with the vowel of the preposition, α and η combining to form η thus, not διαηπόρει but διηπόρει) ὁ Πέτρος (Peter—the article is used with proper names) τί (what) ἂν εἴη (might be—the ἄν is not translated) τὸ ὅραμα (the vision). Note that εἴη is in the optative as the question is not asked directly "What is the vision?" but indirectly, depending on the statement "Peter doubted in himself" (Acts 10:17).

(2) ἀνακρίνοντες (searching—pres. participle, nom. plur. of ἀνακρίνω, I search) τὰς γραφὰς (the Scriptures) εἰ ἔχοι ταῦτα οὕτως (literally, if these [things] had thus—ταῦτα is the neuter plur. "these [things]" and is the subject of ἔχοι—*neuter plurals take the verb in the singular*—

ἔχοι is the optative of ἔχω, I have, and the optative is used because instead of the direct question "Are these things so?" it is put in an indirect way, "searching if these things were so." The use of ἔχω is idiomatic. That is, whereas the Greek is "if these things had so," we must say "if these things were so" (Acts 17:11).

(c) The following is an example of a deliberative question, i.e., a direct question asked not simply for the sake of information but in a rhetorical way:—

καί τινες ἔλεγον (and some were saying), Τί ἂν θέλοι (What would—optative of θέλω, I will, I wish) ὁ σπερμολόγος οὗτος (this babbler) λέγειν (say—infinitive mood, see below), Acts 17:18.

Exercise

Translate, with the help of the accompanying notes:—

(1) Ὁ δὲ κύριος κατευθύναι ὑμῶν τὰς καρδίας εἰς τὴν ἀγάπην τοῦ θεοῦ καὶ εἰς τὴν ὑπομονὴν τοῦ Χριστοῦ. (2 Thess. 3:5) κατευθύναι is the 1st aorist, optative of κατευθύνω, I direct (the omission of the -σ-, which marks the future and 1st aorist tenses, will be explained later): καρδία heart: ὑπομονή patience (note "the patience of Christ"—not as in the A.V.).

(2) Ἐπηρώτων δὲ αὐτὸν οἱ μαθηταὶ αὐτοῦ τίς αὕτη εἴη ἡ παραβολή (Luke 8:9). Ἐπηρώτων is "were asking" (for this form see later): μαθητής, a disciple: τίς, "what" (feminine, agreeing with παραβολή a parable), this is the subject of εἴη (optative, "might be").

(3) ζητεῖν τὸν θεόν, εἰ ἄρα γε ψηλαφήσειαν αὐτὸν (Acts 17:27a). ζητεῖν to seek (infin.—translated in our Version "that-they-should-seek"); ἄρα γε, to be translated together "haply": ψηλαφήσειαν is 3rd pers. plur. 1st aor. optative of ψηλαφάω, I feel after.

Lesson 15

The Infinitive Mood

The Infinitive Mood

The Infinitive (in English expressed by "to," e.g., "to be," "to loose ") is a verbal noun, that is to say, it partakes of the nature both of a verb and a noun.

It has no different forms for cases and persons and is therefore indeclinable.

It is always neuter, and as a noun it may be used with different cases of the neuter article.

As a noun, it may stand as the subject or as the object of another verb or be governed by a preposition.

As a verb, it may itself have a subject or an object. All these points are illustrated below.

Memorize the following:

Infinitive Mood of εἰμί

Present Infinitive	εἶναι	to be.
Future Infinitive	ἔσεσθαι	to be about to be.

Infinitive Mood, Active, of λύω

Present Infinitive	λύειν	to loose.
Future Infinitive	λύσειν	to be about to loose.
1st Aor. Infinitive	λῦσαι	to loose at once.
Perfect Infinitive	λελυκέναι	to have loosed.

Some Examples of The Infinitive Mood

(1) Where the Infinitive, as a noun, is the subject of another verb:

καλὸν ἀνθρώπῳ τὸ οὕτως εἶναι, "(it is) good for a man thus to be" (1 Cor. 7:26). In this sentence the verb ἐστί, "it is," is understood; i.e., καλόν ἐστί "it is good." Now the subject of this is τὸ οὕτως εἶναι lit., "the thus to be," i.e., "the thus to be is good": ἀνθρώπῳ is "for a man."

The article may be omitted: e.g., αἰσχρὸν γάρ ἐστιν (for it is shameful) γυναικὶ (for a woman) λαλεῖν (to speak) ἐν ἐκκλησίᾳ (in church), 1 Cor. 14:35.

Rule—In such instances, when the Infinitive has a subject, the subject, if expressed, is put in the accusative Case.

Thus, in Matt. 17:4, καλόν ἐστιν (it is good) ἡμᾶς (us) ὧδε (here) εἶναι (to be), i.e. "it is good that we should be here" ἡμᾶς is the accusative subject of the Infinitive.

But if the subject of the Infinitive is the same person or thing as the subject of the preceding verb, the subject of the Infinitive is generally omitted, and any words qualifying the omitted subject are put in the nominative. Thus in Rom. 1:22, φάσκοντες εἶναι σοφοί, "professing (themselves) to be wise"; if this were fully expressed it would be φάσκοντες (professing) ἑαυτοὺς εἶναι σοφοί, (themselves to be wise); but the same persons are the subject both of "professing" and "to be"; accordingly ἑαυτούς is omitted and σοφοί is put in the nominative.

Note the omission of the subject in the following, from Jas. 2:14: ἐὰν πίστιν λέγῃ τις ἔχειν, lit., "if anyone saith to have faith," i.e., saith he hath faith. Here τις, "anyone," is the subject of λέγῃ (pres. subjunc. after ἐάν, if), and the same person is the unexpressed subject of ἔχειν "(himself) to have." If it were expressed in full it would have to be ἐὰν πίστιν λέγῃ τις ἑαυτὸν ἔχειν ("himself to have")—(not αὐτὸν ἔχειν ["him to have," which would mean some other person]). Because the person is the same subject for both verbs λέγῃ and ἔχειν, the accusative subject of ἔχειν is omitted. We must, however, insert it in English and say, "If anyone saith he hath" (πίστιν is the accus. object of ἔχειν).

(2) The following is an example of the Infinitive as the object of the verb:—

2 Cor. 8:11, νυνὶ δὲ (but now) καὶ (also) τὸ ποιῆσαι (the doing) ἐπιτελέσατε (complete). What tense of the Infinitive of ποιέω, I do, is ποιῆσαι? Note its noun character with the article; τὸ ποιῆσαι form together the object of the verb ἐπιτελέσατε: this is the 2nd pers. plur., 1st Aorist Imperative of ἐπιτελέω, I complete or fulfill. What is the force of the Aorist Imperative as distinct from the present? (See Lesson 12, 2nd paragraph).

(3) In the following instances the Infinitive is governed by a preposition:—

Matt. 13:5a, 6b: διὰ τὸ μὴ ἔχειν βάθος γῆς … διὰ τὸ μὴ ἔχειν ῥίζαν "on-account-of the not having (lit., to have) depth … on-account-of the not having root." In each clause ἔχειν (the pres. Infinitive of ἔχω) is a verbal noun, used with the article τό. In English the verbal noun is "having"; so τὸ ἔχειν is "the having." When the preposition διά means "on account of" the noun governed by it is in the accusative case. Hence τὸ ἔχειν here is accusative. But ἔχειν is not only a noun, it is also a verb, and as such it governs its object βάθος in the accusative case (for the neuter noun βάθος see γένος, Lesson 9). The negative with the Infinitive is μή (not οὐ).

So also in the second clause, διά governs τὸ ἔχειν as a noun in the accusative case, and τὸ ἔχειν as a verb governs its object ῥίζαν, "a root," in the accusative case.

Matt. 20:19: εἰς τὸ ἐμπαῖξαι καὶ μαστιγῶσαι καὶ σταυρῶσαι, "to mock and scourge and crucify." The three verbs are, respectively, the first aorist Infinitive (see λῦσαι above) of ἐμπαίζω (future ἐμπαίξω), I mock, μαστιγόω (fut. μαστιγώσω), I scourge, and σταυρόω (fut. σταυρώσω), I crucify. The article τό goes with all three, and the article and the three infinitives are all governed in the accusative case by the preposition εἰς: literally "unto the to mock and to scourge and to crucify." The εἰς really signifies "with a view to," or "with the object of (mocking, etc.)."

(*Other uses of the Infinitive will be explained later. The above are sufficient to illustrate the force of this Mood.*)

The student should go over very thoroughly the above examples of the Infinitive. After studying the notes, write out the English translations in a list, and then translate them back into the Greek text. This will help to overcome the difficulties of the Infinitive.

Exercise

Translate the following, with the help of the accompanying notes, learning first the words and their meanings.

(1) νυνὶ δὲ καὶ τὸ ποιῆσαι ἐπιτελέσατε, ὅπως καθάπερ ἡ προθυμία τοῦ θέλειν, οὕτως καὶ τὸ ἐπιτελέσαι ἐκ τοῦ ἔχειν. (2 Cor. 8:11) νυνί, now: ὅπως, in order that: καθάπερ, just as: προθυμία, readiness: θέλω, I will.

Notes

τοῦ θέλειν is lit. "of the to will," i.e., "of the being willing": this follows προθυμία and so the translation is "readiness to will," the genitive of the Infinitive signifying intention or purpose.

(2) πλὴν τοὺς ἐχθρούς μου τούτους τοὺς μὴ θελήσαντάς με βασιλεῦσαι ἐπ' αὐτοὺς ἀγάγετε ὧδε καὶ κατασφάξατε αὐτοὺς ἔμπροσθέν μου. (Luke 19:27) πλὴν, howbeit: ἐχθρός, an enemy: θελήσαντας, accus. plur. masc., 1st aorist participle of θέλω, I wish, am willing, lit. "having been willing":—accus. in agreement with ἐχθρούς: βασιλεῦσαι, 1st aorist Infin. of βασιλεύω, I reign, lit. "me to reign": ἐπ' for ἐπί over: ἀγάγετε, 2nd pers. plur. Imperative of a 2nd aor. (see later) doubled syllable form of ἄγω, I bring: ὧδε, hither: κατασφάξατε 1st aor. Imperative of κατασφάζω, I slay: ἔμπροσθέν, before (takes the genitive case).

(3) οἷς ἠθέλησεν ὁ θεὸς γνωρίσαι τί τὸ πλοῦτος τῆς δόξης τοῦ μυστηρίου τούτου ἐν τοῖς ἔθνεσιν, ὅ ἐστιν Χριστὸς ἐν ὑμῖν, ἡ ἐλπὶς τῆς δόξης· 28 ὃν ἡμεῖς καταγγέλλομεν νουθετοῦντες πάντα ἄνθρωπον καὶ διδάσκοντες πάντα ἄνθρωπον ἐν πάσῃ σοφίᾳ, ἵνα παραστήσωμεν πάντα ἄνθρωπον τέλειον ἐν Χριστῷ: (Col. 1:27, 28) ἠθέλησεν, 3rd pers. sing., 1st aor. Indic. of θέλω, I am willing, I am pleased (this verb takes η for augment instead of ε): γνωρίσαι, 1st aor. Infin. of γνωρίζω, I make known: πλοῦτος, wealth, riches (a neut. noun like γένος): ἔθνεσιν, (dat. plur. of ἔθνος, a nation—here "Gentiles" another neut. noun like γένος—dative case after ἐν): ἐλπὶς, hope (genit. ἐλπίδος): καταγγέλλομεν, I proclaim (pronounced katangello): νουθετοῦντες, nom. plur. masc. pres. participle of νουθετέω, I admonish—the ending -ουντες is contracted for -εοντες (see later): διδάσκω, I teach: παραστήσωμεν, "we may present," subjunctive (for the form see later): τέλειος, perfect.

(4) ὁ δὲ θεὸς τῆς ἐλπίδος πληρώσαι ὑμᾶς πάσης χαρᾶς καὶ εἰρήνης ἐν τῷ πιστεύειν, εἰς τὸ περισσεύειν ὑμᾶς ἐν τῇ ἐλπίδι ἐν δυνάμει πνεύματος ἁγίου. (Rom. 15:13) ἐλπίδος [see under (3)]: πληρώσαι, 3rd pers. sing. 1st aor. optative of πληρόω, I fill (the optative of a wish): χαρᾶς, genit. of χαρά, joy (genitive is used after words of filling to signify "with"): πιστεύειν, Infin. as verbal noun, dative after ἐν—"in believing" (τῷ not to be translated): περισσεύειν, to abound—accus. of the Infin. verbal noun governed by εἰς: ὑμᾶς is the accus. subject of the Infin. (lit. "unto the you to abound"—i.e., "that ye may abound"): δύναμις, power: ἅγιος, holy.

Retranslate the above four passages from English into Greek, correcting your result from the original.

The Second Aorist Active

Some verbs have a Second Aorist tense. Its meaning is the same as the First Aorist: it differs only in form. Very few verbs have both a First and Second Aorist: λύω has only the first. We shall therefore take as an example the verb τύπτω, I strike.

Note 1—The endings of the Second Aorist Indicative are the same as those of the Imperfect, and as it is a past tense the augment is used. There is this difference in form, however, that the endings are added to the simple stem (see below).

Note 2—In the other moods, the endings are the same as those of the present tenses. Here again, the endings are added to the simple stem.

If the Present and Imperfect tenses have been thoroughly learned there is no need to write out the Second Aorist forms in all the persons, save for the sake of practice. Remember that there is no augment except in the Indicative mood.

Second Aorist of τύπτω, I strike

Indicative, ἔτυπον, I struck

(etc., see the Imperfect endings)

Imperative, τύπε, strike thou

(etc., see the Present endings)

Subjunctive, τύπω, I (may) strike

(etc., see the Present endings)

Optative, τύποιμι, I (might) strike

(etc., see the Present endings)

Infinitive, τυπεῖν, to strike

Participle, τυπών, -οῦσα, -όν, having struck

It will be observed that the stem of the Present tense of τύπτω is τυπτ- but the stem of the second Aorist is τυπ-.

The Second Perfect

This tense is rare. It occurs only in the Active Voice and is simply a modified form of the Perfect. Thus, whereas the Perfect of τύπτω is τέτυφα, the 2nd Perfect is τέτυπα. Note the reduplication τε-, characteristic of all Perfect tenses.

Lesson 16

Passive Voice of the Verb.
The Indicative and Imperative Moods

Note for Review—A complete paradigm of the Active Voice should be drawn up by the student from preceding Lessons, putting the Moods as headings of parallel columns, in the following order: Indicative, Imperative, Subjunctive, Optative, Infinitive, Participles: and the names of the tenses down the left side—Present, Imperfect, Future, 1st Aorist, Perfect, Pluperfect, 2nd Aorist, remembering that the Imperfect and Pluperfect Tenses are found only in the Indicative Mood, and that there is no Future in the Imperative and Subjunctive.

The Passive Voice of the Verb

Whereas a verb is in the Active Voice when its subject is spoken of as acting or doing something, the Passive Voice signifies that the subject is acted upon. In English the Passive is formed by the use of the verb "to be" with the Passive Participle. Thus the Passive of "I loose" is "I am loosed" (always to be distinguished from the continuous tense of the Active Voice, formed by the verb "to be" with the Present Participle active, e.g., "I am loosing"). In Greek, the Passive is formed (save in certain Perfect Tenses) simply by the addition of a different set of endings to the stem from those in the Active Voice.

The following are the Indicative Mood Tenses of the Passive Voice of λύω. The student must memorize them; but only after being thoroughly familiar with the Active Voice forms.

The Passive Voice of λύω

Indicative Mood

Present Tense

"I am being loosed"

Singular

1st p.	λύομαι	(I am, etc.)
2nd p.	λύῃ or λύει	(thou art, etc.)
3rd p.	λύεται	(he is, etc.)

Plural

1st p.	λυόμεθα	(we are, etc.)
2nd p.	λύεσθε	(ye are, etc.)
3rd p.	λύονται	(they are, etc.)

Note the iota in the 2nd pers. sing. This form, λύῃ, is the same as the 3rd pers. sing., pres. subjunctive active. There is no difficulty in distinguishing them as to the meaning. The context makes that clear. The Active is "he may loose," the Passive "thou art being loosed."

Note that λυ- is the stem. The endings should be learned apart from the stem.

Imperfect Tense

"I was being loosed," etc.

	Singular	**Plural**
1st p.	ἐλυόμην	ἐλυόμεθα
2nd p.	ἐλύου	ἐλύεσθε
3rd p.	ἐλύετο	ἐλύοντο

Future Tense

"I shall be loosed"

	Singular	Plural
1st p.	λυθήσομαι	λυθησόμεθα
2nd p.	λυθήσῃ	λυθήσεσθε
3rd p.	λυθήσεται	λυθήσονται

First Aorist
"I was loosed"

	Singular	Plural
1st p.	ἐλύθην	ἐλύθημεν
2nd p.	ἐλύθης	ἐλύθητε
3rd p.	ἐλύθη	ἐλύθησαν

(Note—The endings of the First Aorist Passive resemble the Imperfect of εἰμί except in the 2nd and 3rd pers. sing.—see Lesson 3. Observe the -θ- characteristic of the Passive Voice, and the Augment)

Perfect Tense
"I have been loosed"

	Singular	Plural
1st p.	λέλυμαι	λελύμεθα
2nd p.	λέλυσαι	λέλυσθε
3rd p.	λέλυται	λέλυνται

Pluperfect Tense
"I had been loosed"

Singular	Plural	
1st p.	ἐλελύμην	ἐλελύμεθα
2nd p.	ἐλέλυσο	ἐλέλυσθε
3rd p.	ἐλέλυτο	ἐλέλυντο

Exercise on the Indicative Mood of the Passive Voice

Translate the following sentences and passages, after learning the vocabulary. Correct your rendering from the R.V. [or NRSV or NKJV] text and retranslate from the English into Greek.

Vocabulary

μαρτύριον witness	πτωχός, -ή, -όν poor
ἄνομος lawless	οὐρανός heaven
τότε then	πραΰς meek
σάρξ (gen. σαρκός) flesh	δικαιοσύνη righteousness
ἐντολή commandment	ἐλεήμων (neut. -ον) merciful
μακάριος, -α, -ον blessed	

(1) ὅτι (because) ἐπιστεύθη (1st aor. indic. passive of πιστεύω, I believe) τὸ μαρτύριον ἡμῶν ἐφ' ὑμᾶς (2 Thess. 1:10). The subject of the verb is τὸ μαρτύριον ἡμῶν. Note that ἐφ' is for ἐπί, "unto" (not "among," as A.V.): the ι is dropped before the υ of ὑμᾶς and then the π becomes φ because of the rough breathing, the ʽ. To say ἐπʽ ὑμᾶς would be awkward: hence the π becomes aspirated to φ.

(2) καὶ τότε ἀποκαλυφθήσεται (future passive of ἀποκαλύπτω, I reveal) ὁ ἄνομος (2 Thess. 2:8).

(3) οἳ οὐκ ἐξ αἱμάτων οὐδὲ ἐκ θελήματος σαρκὸς οὐδὲ ἐκ θελήματος ἀνδρὸς ἀλλ' ἐκ θεοῦ ἐγεννήθησαν. (John 1:13) ἐξ is for ἐκ, "of," the κ becoming ξ before the αἱ of αἱμάτων). Note this gen. plur., lit., "bloods": αἷμα and θέλημα are declined like πνεῦμα (Lesson 9). For ἀνδρός see Lesson 9. ἐγεννήθησαν is 3rd plur. 1st aor. pass. of γεννάω, I beget (passive "am born"). The change from α in γεννάω to η will be explained later.

(4) ὁ ἔχων τὰς ἐντολάς μου καὶ τηρῶν αὐτὰς ἐκεῖνός ἐστιν ὁ ἀγαπῶν με· ὁ δὲ ἀγαπῶν με ἀγαπηθήσεται ὑπὸ τοῦ πατρός μου, κἀγὼ ἀγαπήσω αὐτὸν καὶ ἐμφανίσω αὐτῷ ἐμαυτόν. (John 14:21) Note the pres. participles of ἔχω, I have, τηρέω, I keep, ἀγαπάω, I love. Note the difference between the future passive ἀγαπηθήσεται (3rd pers.) and the future active ἀγαπήσω (1st pers.): ὑπό is "by"—it takes the genitive: κἀγώ is short for καὶ ἐγώ : ἐμφανίσω is the future of ἐμφανίζω, I manifest. It would be well to commit this verse to memory.

(5) Μακάριοι οἱ πτωχοὶ τῷ πνεύματι, ὅτι αὐτῶν ἐστιν ἡ βασιλεία τῶν οὐρανῶν. 4 μακάριοι οἱ πενθοῦντες, ὅτι αὐτοὶ παρακληθήσονται. 5 μακάριοι οἱ πραεῖς, ὅτι αὐτοὶ κληρονομήσουσιν τὴν γῆν. 6 μακάριοι οἱ πεινῶντες καὶ διψῶντες τὴν δικαιοσύνην, ὅτι αὐτοὶ χορτασθήσονται. 7 μακάριοι οἱ ἐλεήμονες, ὅτι αὐτοὶ ἐλεηθήσονται. (Matt. 5:3-7) Study carefully the following notes. The verb "to be" is often omitted; εἰσίν, "are," is to be understood after μακάριοι: τῷ πνεύματι is dative of the point in which an adjective (here πτωχοί, poor) is applied; hence we must say "poor in spirit" (the article must not be translated): αὐτῶν, "of them," i.e., "theirs", πενθοῦντες is the pres. participle, nom. plur. masc. of πενθέω, I mourn, for πενθέοντες, the εο contracting to ου: παρακληθήσονται is 3rd pers. plur., future, indic. passive of παρακαλέω, I comfort: κληρονομήσουσιν is the fut. active of κληρονομέω, I inherit: πεινῶντες is the nom. plur., masc., pres. participle of πεινάω, I hunger, for πεινάοντες the αο contracting to ω: so διψῶντες is from διψάω, I thirst: χορτασθήσονται is 3rd plur. fut. passive of χορτάζω, I fill, satisfy (verbs in -ζω take ς in fut. and 1st aor.): ἐλεηθήσονται is fut. passive of ἐλεέω, I show mercy.

Imperative Mood—Passive Voice

Present Tense

	Singular	Plural
2nd p.	λύου be thou loosed	λύεσθε be ye loosed
3rd p.	λυέσθω let him (her, it) be loosed	λυέσθωσαν or λυέσθων let them be loosed

Aorist Tense

"Be thou loosed (at once)"

	Singular	Plural
2nd p.	λύθητι	λύθητε
3rd p.	λυθήτω	λυθήτωσαν

Perfect Tense (expressing continuance of a past act)

	Singular	Plural
2nd p.	λέλυσο	λέλυσθε
3rd p.	λελύσθω	λελύσθωσαν or λελύσθων

Students should now obtain a copy of the little Greek-English Lexicon to the New Testament, by A. Souter. This is published by The Clarendon Press, Oxford. It is one of the best books of reference published in connection with Greek Testament study, and forms a good companion to Nestle's Text. Being small in size it is handy for taking about. In the course of the next few lessons, this book will be substituted for the vocabularies given in the exercises. [More up to date and informative is the *Shorter Lexicon of the Greek New Testament* by Gingrich and Danker, available from Zondervan Publishing House and the University of Chicago Press.]

Lesson 17

The Passive Voice (continued). The Subjunctive Mood

Exercise on the Imperative Mood

Learn the following vocabulary. Then translate the passages with the help of the notes. Re-translate into the Greek, correcting your result.

Vocabulary

κόκκος grain

θάλασσα sea

σίναπι (gen. -εως) mustard (declined like πόλις, Lesson 9)

καρδία heart

περισσῶς exceedingly

(1) εἶπεν δὲ ὁ κύριος, Εἰ ἔχετε πίστιν ὡς κόκκον σινάπεως, ἐλέγετε ἂν τῇ συκαμίνῳ [ταύτῃ], Ἐκριζώθητι καὶ φυτεύθητι ἐν τῇ θαλάσσῃ· καὶ ὑπήκουσεν ἂν ὑμῖν. (Luke 17:6) ἔχετε is 2nd pers., plur., pres. indic. of ἔχω: ἐλέγετε ἂν is "ye would say" (this construction of the imperfect with ἂν is explained later): Ἐκριζώθητι 2nd per., sing., 1st aor. imperative passive of ἐκριζόω I root up; φυτεύθητι, the same form from φυτεύω, I plant: ὑπήκουσεν ἄν, "it would obey"—1st aor. active of ὑπακούω, note that the augment is formed by the change of the α of ἀκούω into η, ὑπ being for ὑπό, a preposition compounded with the verb ἀκούω. The preposition does not augment, the main verb does. Note the datives in this verse, one after λέγω, the other after ἐν.

(2) Μὴ ταρασσέσθω ὑμῶν ἡ καρδία· πιστεύετε εἰς τὸν θεόν καὶ εἰς ἐμὲ πιστεύετε. (John 14:1) ταρασσέσθω is 3rd pers., sing., pres. imperative, passive of ταράσσω, I trouble: πιστεύετε may be 2nd pers. plur. of either the pres. indic. active or the pres. imperative active of πιστεύω, i.e., either "believe ye" or "ye believe."

(3) λέγουσιν πάντες, Σταυρωθήτω. This verb is the 1st aor. imperative of σταυρόω, I crucify, i.e., "let Him be crucified" (see λυθήτω, above). This sentence is from Matt. 27:22 (end of verse); translate verse 23: ὁ δὲ ἔφη, Τί γὰρ κακὸν ἐποίησεν; οἱ δὲ περισσῶς ἔκραζον λέγοντες, Σταυρωθήτω. ὁ δὲ is "but he," ἔφη, "said." What tense of ποιέω is ἐποίησεν? ἔκραζον is 3rd pers., plur., imperf. indic. active of κράζω, I cry out, "they kept on crying out."

(4) εἰ γὰρ οὐ κατακαλύπτεται γυνή, καὶ κειράσθω· εἰ δὲ αἰσχρὸν γυναικὶ τὸ κείρασθαι ἢ ξυρᾶσθαι, κατακαλυπτέσθω. 7 ἀνὴρ μὲν γὰρ οὐκ ὀφείλει κατακαλύπτεσθαι τὴν κεφαλὴν εἰκὼν καὶ δόξα θεοῦ ὑπάρχων· ἡ γυνὴ δὲ δόξα ἀνδρός ἐστιν. 8 οὐ γάρ ἐστιν ἀνὴρ ἐκ γυναικός ἀλλὰ γυνὴ ἐξ ἀνδρός. (1 Cor. 11:6-8) κατακαλύπτεται 3rd pers., sing., pres. indic., passive of κατακαλύπτω, I cover up, veil (for the form see λύομαι): γυνή, "a woman," an irregular noun of the 3rd declension (its gen., dat., acc., sing. are γυναικός, γυναικί, γυναῖκα, and the plural cases are γυναῖκες, γυναικῶν, γυναιξί, γυναῖκας): κειράσθω, 3rd pers., sing., aor. imperative, middle, of κείρω, I shear, "let her be shorn."

The Subjunctive Mood, Passive Voice

Present Tense

"I may be loosed" (a process)

1st p.	λύωμαι	λυώμεθα
2nd p.	λύῃ	λύησθε
3rd p.	λύηται	λύωνται

Note the long vowel, characteristic of the subjunctive present, etc. Also the iota subscript in the 2nd pers. sing.

First Aorist

"I may be loosed" (a definite act)

1st p.	λυθῶ	λυθῶμεν
2nd p.	λυθῇς	λυθῆτε
3rd p.	λυθῇ	λυθῶσι(ν)

Note the endings, like the subjunctive of εἰμί; see Lesson 13.

Perfect Tense

"I may have been loosed."

This tense is formed by the perfect participle (see later), with the subjunctive of the verb εἰμί; thus the literal meaning would be "(that) I may be having been loosed," but the literal meaning must not be pressed.

1st p.	λελυμένος ὦ	λελυμένοι ὦμεν
2nd p.	λελυμένος ᾖς	λελυμένοι ἦτε
3rd p.	λελυμένος ᾖ	λελυμένοι ὦσι(ν)

Note—The λελυμένος, being a participle, is also an adjective, and therefore must agree in gender and number with the subject: λελυμένος, -η, -ον is declined like a 2nd declension adjective. Note, e.g., the -οι of the plural. This would be -αι if women were spoken of.

Exercise on the Subjunctive Mood of the Passive Voice.

Before doing this exercise, it will be necessary for the student to review the five principal uses of the Subjunctive mood as given in Lesson 13.

Translate the passages with the help of the notes, learning the meanings of new words. Retranslate into the Greek and correct from the Text.

I—Containing instances of the Subjunctive, Passive, in clauses of *Purpose* (see Lesson 13, *I*).

(1) ἔπεμψα δὲ τοὺς ἀδελφούς, ἵνα μὴ τὸ καύχημα ἡμῶν τὸ ὑπὲρ ὑμῶν κενωθῇ ἐν τῷ μέρει τούτῳ, ἵνα καθὼς ἔλεγον παρεσκευασμένοι ἦτε. (2 Cor. 9:3) ἔπεμψα, 1st aor. indic., active of πέμπω, I send: ἵνα μή, "in order that … not": τὸ καύχημα ἡμῶν τὸ ὑπὲρ ὑμῶν, lit., "the boasting of us (i.e., our boasting) the (i.e., the [boasting]) on behalf of you"; we may render by "our boasting, that, namely, on your behalf": κενωθῇ (1st aor. subjunc., passive of κενόω, I make void), "may (not) be made void": ἔλεγον (1st per. sing., imperf. indic., active of λέγω) "I was saying": παρεσκευασμένοι ἦτε, 2nd pers., plur., perf. subjunc., passive, of παρασκευάζω, I prepare; this is composed of the preposition παρά and the verb σκευάζω; verbs beginning with two consonants (except a mute and a liquid) reduplicate by a simple ε; hence παρα becomes παρε- as with the ordinary augment when a preposition is prefixed to a verb.

(2) ὅπως ἂν ἀποκαλυφθῶσιν ἐκ πολλῶν καρδιῶν διαλογισμοί. (Luke 2:35b) ὅπως, "in order that"; ἄν not to be translated; ἀποκαλυφθῶσιν, 3rd pers., plur., 1st aor. subjunc., passive of

ἀποκαλύπτω, I reveal, agreeing with its subject διαλογισμοί, thoughts; ἐκ can simply be rendered "of"; it takes the genitive, πολλῶν (see Lesson 7).

II—Containing instances of the Subjunctive Passive in *Conditional Clauses* (see Lesson 13, *II*).

(1) 31 νῦν κρίσις ἐστὶν τοῦ κόσμου τούτου, νῦν ὁ ἄρχων τοῦ κόσμου τούτου ἐκβληθήσεται ἔξω· 32 κἀγὼ ἐὰν ὑψωθῶ ἐκ τῆς γῆς, πάντας ἑλκύσω πρὸς ἐμαυτόν. (John 12:31-32) κρίσις, judgment; κόσμος, world; ἄρχων, prince, ruler; ἐκβληθήσεται, 3rd pers., sing., fut. indic., passive of ἐκβάλλω, I cast out (an irregular verb); ἔξω, out (an adverb); κἀγώ for καὶ ἐγώ; ὑψωθῶ 1st aor. subjunc., passive of ὑψόω, I lift up; ἕλκω, I draw; πρός, to.

(2) Οἴδαμεν γὰρ ὅτι ἐὰν ἡ ἐπίγειος ἡμῶν οἰκία τοῦ σκήνους καταλυθῇ, οἰκοδομὴν ἐκ θεοῦ ἔχομεν, οἰκίαν ἀχειροποίητον αἰώνιον ἐν τοῖς οὐρανοῖς. (2 Cor. 5:1) οἴδαμεν, we know (irregular): ἐπίγειος, -α, -ον, earthly; οἰκία, house; σκήνος, tabernacle, tent (3rd declension, neut. like γένος, genit. -ους): καταλυθῇ, 1st aor. subjunc., pass. of καταλύω, I loosen down, take down (of a tent), dissolve; οἰκοδομή, a building; ἀχειροποίητος, not-hand-made (the prefix ἀ- signifies a negative; χείρ, the hand; ποιητός, a verbal adjective, "made"—hence "not made with hands").

III—Containing an instance of the Subjunctive Passive in *Relative Clauses* (see Lesson 13, *III*).

ἀμὴν δὲ λέγω ὑμῖν, ὅπου ἐὰν κηρυχθῇ τὸ εὐαγγέλιον εἰς ὅλον τὸν κόσμον, καὶ ὃ ἐποίησεν αὕτη λαληθήσεται εἰς μνημόσυνον αὐτῆς. (Mark 14:9)ὅπου, "where"—ὅπου ἐάν together make "wherever," introducing an indefinite relative clause, i.e., a relative clause expressing indefiniteness—the ἐάν must not be translated here by "if," it simply adds the idea of indefinite locality to ὅπου; κηρυχθῇ, 3rd pers. sing., 1st aor. subjunc., passive of κηρύσσω, I preach—translate by "is preached" (not "was preached"; the aorist in the subjunctive mood is not necessarily a past tense, here it points to the preaching as a precise announcement)—note the subjunctive in a relative clause with ἐάν, "wherever the gospel is preached": καί, also; λαληθήσεται fut. indic., passive of λαλέω, I speak; εἰς, "unto" or "for"; μνημόσυνον, a memorial.

IV—Containing an instance of the *Deliberative Subjunctive* (see Lesson 13, *IV*).

πῶς οὖν πληρωθῶσιν αἱ γραφαὶ ὅτι οὕτως δεῖ γενέσθαι. (Matt. 26:54) πῶς, how; οὖν, therefore; πληρωθῶσιν, 3rd pers. plur., 1st aor. subjunc., passive of πληρόω, I fulfill, agreeing with its subject γραφαί; γραφή, a writing, scripture; οὕτως, thus; δεῖ, it is necessary; γενέσθαι, "to become" (an irregular verb—see later).

V—The use of the Subjunctive Passive in *Exhortations* is very rare (see Lesson 13, *V*)

Lesson 18

The Passive Voice, Optative Mood.
The Middle Voice

Optative Mood, Passive Voice

Present Tense

"I might be loosed," etc.

	Singular	**Plural**
1st p.	λυοίμην	λυοίμεθα
2nd p.	λύοιο	λύοισθε
3rd p.	λύοιτο	λύοιντο

Future Tense

"I should be loosed"

	Singular	**Plural**
1st p.	λυθησοίμην	λυθησοίμεθα
2nd p.	λυθήσοιο	λυθήσοισθε
3rd p.	λυθήσοιτο	λυθήσοιντο

First Aorist

"I might be (or am to be) loosed"

	Singular	Plural
1st p.	λυθείην	λυθείημεν
2nd p.	λυθείης	λυθείητε
3rd p.	λυθείη	λυθεῖεν

Perfect

"I might have been loosed"

	Singular	Plural
1st p.	λελυμένος εἴην	λελυμένοι εἴημεν
2nd p.	λελυμένος εἴης	λελυμένοι εἴητε
3rd p.	λελυμένος εἴη	λελυμένοι εἴησαν

The Optative Passive is very rare. No exercise therefore will be given upon it.

The Infinitive Mood, Passive Voice

Pres. Infin.	λύεσθαι	to be loosed
Future	λυθήσεσθαι	to be about to be loosed
First Aor.	λυθῆναι	to be loosed (at once)
Perfect	λελύσθαι	to have been loosed

Exercise on the Infinitive Passive

Before doing this exercise review the Notes on the Infinitive Mood at the end of Lesson 14.

Study the accompanying notes, and learn the meanings of new words; after translating, retranslate as usual.

(1) πιστὸς δὲ ὁ θεός, ὃς οὐκ ἐάσει ὑμᾶς πειρασθῆναι ὑπὲρ ὃ δύνασθε ἀλλὰ ποιήσει σὺν τῷ πειρασμῷ καὶ τὴν ἔκβασιν. (1 Cor. 10:13b) πιστός, faithful; ἐάσει, 3rd pers. sing., fut. indic., of ἐάω, I permit, allow; πειρασθῆναι, 1st aor. infin., passive, of πειράζω, I tempt; ὑπέρ, above; ὅ, acc., neut., sing., of ὅς; δύνασθε, ye are able; πειρασμός, a temptation; ἔκβασις, a way of escape.

(2) ἀλλὰ μετὰ τὸ ἐγερθῆναί με προάξω ὑμᾶς εἰς τὴν Γαλιλαίαν. (Mark 14:28) Note particularly the phrase μετα τὸ ἐγερθῆναί με—the preposition μετά is "after," it governs the whole of the rest of the phrase in the accusative case; the article τό describes the phrase ἐγερθῆναί με, which, literally, is "me to be raised," the verb being the 1st aor. infin., passive, of ἐγείρω, I raise. These two words form the construction known as the Accusative with the Infinitive, which will be explained later. Accordingly, τὸ ἐγερθῆναί με is "the me to be raised." Literally, then, the whole phrase is "after the Me to be raised," i.e., "after the [event] that I am raised," and hence we must translate by "after I am raised," for that is the corresponding idiom in English; προάξω fut. of προάγω, I go before.

(3) ὁ δὲ Ἰωάννης διεκώλυεν αὐτὸν λέγων, Ἐγὼ χρείαν ἔχω ὑπὸ σοῦ βαπτισθῆναι, καὶ σὺ ἔρχῃ πρός με; (Matt. 3:14) διεκώλυεν, 3rd pers. sing., imperf. indic., of διακωλύω, I hinder—"he was hindering" (note the augment, the compounded preposition διά changing to διε); βαπτισθῆναι, 1st aor., infin. passive of βαπτίζω; ἔρχῃ, comest (an irregular verb).

(4) οὗτος ἤκουσεν τοῦ Παύλου λαλοῦντος· ὃς ἀτενίσας αὐτῷ καὶ ἰδὼν ὅτι ἔχει πίστιν τοῦ σωθῆναι. (Acts 14:9) ἤκουσεν, imperfect of ἀκούω, I hear, which takes the genitive case (τοῦ Παύλου)—note that ἀ- make augment ἡ-. The τοῦ is not to be translated; the article often goes with a proper name; λαλοῦντος, gen., sing., masc., pres. participle of λαλέω, I speak—for λαλέοντος (εο becomes ου); ἀτενίσας, nom., sing., masc., 1st aor. partic. of ἀτενίζω, I look steadfastly; ἰδών, seeing (explained later); σωθῆναι, 1st aor. infin., pass. of σώζω, I save: the τοῦ is not to be translated—τοῦ σωθῆναι is a genitive construction after πίστιν, faith, lit., "faith of the to be saved," i.e., "faith to be saved."

The Participles of the Passive Voice

Note—These are verbal adjectives, like those of the active voice. They are declined like adjectives, the particular form agreeing in case, number and gender with the noun or pronoun to which the participle refers.

Present Participle: "being loosed"

Masc. λυόμενος Fem. λυομένη Neut. λυόμενον

This is declined, singular and plural, like ἀγαθός (see Lesson 4).

Future Participle: "about to be loosed"

Masc. λυθησόμενος Fem. λυθησομένη Neut. λυθησόμενον

First Aorist Participle: "having been loosed"

Masc. λυθείς Fem. λυθεῖσα Neut. λυθέν

This is declined like ἑκών, ἑκοῦσα, ἑκόν (Lesson 9), -ε- taking the place of -ο- in the masc. and neut. in all cases except the nom. sing. masc., and dat. plur., and -ει- taking the place of -ου- in the fem. and in all genders in the dat. plural.

Thus the genitive singular is λυθέντος, λυθείσης, λυθέντος, the accusative singular is λυθέντα, λυθεῖσαν, λυθέν, and the dat. plural is λυθεῖσι, λυθείσαις, λυθεῖσι.

Perfect Participle: "having been loosened"

Masc. λελυμένος Fem. λελυμένη Neut. λελυμένον

Exercise

Translate the following passages, with the help of the accompanying notes, learning the meaning of new words and retranslating into the Greek.

(1) τῇ γὰρ ἐλπίδι ἐσώθημεν· ἐλπὶς δὲ βλεπομένη οὐκ ἔστιν ἐλπίς· ὃ γὰρ βλέπει τίς ἐλπίζει; (Rom. 8:24) τῇ ... ἐλπίδι is dat. of instrument, "by hope"; ἐσώθημεν, 1st pers. plur., 1st aor., indic. passive, of σώζω, I save; βλεπομένη, nom., sing., fem., pres. partic., passive, of βλέπω, I see, "being seen"; ὃ neut. of ὅς; τις, anyone.

(2) καὶ ἐπέθηκαν ἐπάνω τῆς κεφαλῆς αὐτοῦ τὴν αἰτίαν αὐτοῦ γεγραμμένην· Οὗτός ἐστιν Ἰησοῦς ὁ βασιλεῦς τῶν Ἰουδαίων. (Matt. 27:37) ἐπέθηκαν, they put up (a form explained later); ἐπάνω, above (a preposition taking the genitive); κεφαλή, a head; αἰτία, an accusation (here the accus. object of the verb ἐπέθηκαν); γεγραμμένην, acc., sing., fem., perf. partic., passive, of γράφω, I write, "having been written," or simply "written" (the root of γράφω is γραπ-, and γεγραπμένην becomes γεγραμμένην, the π assimilating to the μ for the sake of sound).

(3) καὶ γὰρ ἐγὼ ἄνθρωπός εἰμι ὑπὸ ἐξουσίαν τασσόμενος ἔχων ὑπ᾽ ἐμαυτὸν στρατιώτας. (Luke 7:8a) καί, also; ὑπό, under; ἐξουσία, authority; τασσόμενος, nom., sing., masc., pres. partic., passive, of τάσσω, I set, "being set"; στρατιώτης, a soldier (like μαθητής, Lesson 3).

(4) 14 ὁ δὲ ἐγερθεὶς παρέλαβεν τὸ παιδίον καὶ τὴν μητέρα αὐτοῦ νυκτὸς καὶ ἀνεχώρησεν εἰς Αἴγυπτον, 15 καὶ ἦν ἐκεῖ ἕως τῆς τελευτῆς Ἡρῴδου· ἵνα πληρωθῇ τὸ ῥηθὲν ὑπὸ κυρίου διὰ τοῦ προφήτου λέγοντος, Ἐξ Αἰγύπτου ἐκάλεσα τὸν υἱόν μου. (Matt. 2:14-15) ὁ δέ, but he; ἐγερθείς, nom., sing., masc., 1st aor., partic. passive, of ἐγείρω, I arouse, awake, lit., "having been aroused," παρέλαβεν "took" (an irregular verb); παιδίον, a little child; νυκτός, by night, genitive of νύξ

(genitive of time); ἀνεχώρησεν, 3rd pers. sing., 1st aor. indic., active, of ἀνα χωρέω, I depart (note the augment -ε- in the preposition ἀνε); ἐκεῖ, there; ἕως, until; τελευτή, an end, or death; πληρωθῇ, 3rd pers. sing., 1st aor. subj., passive, of πληρόω, I fulfill; ῥηθέν, nom., sing., neut., 1st aor. partic., passive, of ρέω, I utter, speak (see λυθείς, λυθεῖσα, λυθέν, above); διά, by means of (takes the genitive).

The Second Aorist Passive

The tense endings are the same as those of the first aorist throughout the moods (save in one ending) but the ending is added to the simple root and without the -θ-. Thus, whereas the first aorist indic. passive of τύπτω, I strike, is ἐτύφθην, etc., the second aorist is ἐτύπην, etc. The only exception is in the 2nd pers. sing., imperative, where -θι is found instead of -τι.

The following will be sufficient. The student who has learned the first aorist tenses will readily supply the full second aorist from memory. They should at all events be written out in full. The meanings are the same.

Indicative ἐτύπην

Imperative τύπηθι (3rd p. s. τυπήτω)

Subjunctive τύπω

Optative τυπείην

Infinitive τυπῆναι

Participle τυπείς, -εῖσα, έν

The Middle Voice

Whereas in English there are only two voices, active and passive, the Greek language has three. The Middle Voice chiefly signifies that a person has a special interest in the effects of his action, that he is acting either upon, or for, himself, or that when he is acting for others he has a personal interest in their condition or welfare. Sometimes, however, it is scarcely possible to distinguish in meaning between the middle and the active. Examples are given below.

In four tenses of the middle voice, the forms are the same as those of the passive. These are the present, imperfect, perfect and pluperfect. Accordingly, for the paradigm of these the student is referred to the passive voice (Lesson 16). The future and aorist tenses are different.

Middle Voice—Indicative Mood

For the four following tenses, see the passive voice: *Present*, λύομαι, etc., "I am loosing myself (or, for myself)"; *Imperfect*, ἐλυόμην, etc., "I was loosing myself (or for myself)"; *Perfect*, λέλυμαι, etc., "I have loosed myself (or for myself)"; *Pluperfect*, ἐλελύμην, etc., "I had, etc."

Future: "I will loose myself (or for, etc.)"

	Singular	**Plural**
1st p.	λύσομαι	λυσόμεθα
2nd p.	λύσῃ	λύσεσθε
3rd p.	λύσεται	λύσονται

First Aorist: "I loosed myself (or for, etc.)"

	Singular	**Plural**
1st p.	ἐλυσάμην	ἐλυσάμεθα
2nd p.	ἐλύσω	ἐλύσασθε
3rd p.	ἐλύσατο	ἐλύσαντο

Imperative Mood

For the two following tenses, see the Passive Voice: *Present,*
λύου, etc., "loose thyself (or for thyself)"; *Perfect,*
λέλυσο, etc., "have loosed thyself (or for thyself)," etc. There is no imperfect or pluperfect outside the indicative, nor any future in the imperative and subjunctive.

First Aorist: "loose thyself (or for thyself)

	Singular	**Plural**
2nd p.	λῦσαι	λύσασθε
3rd p.	λυσάσθω	λυσάσθωσαν or λυσάσθων

Subjunctive Mood

For the two following tenses, see the Passive Voice: *Present,* λύωμαι, etc., "I may loose myself (or for myself)"; *Perfect,* λελυμένος ὦ, etc., "I may have loosed myself (or for myself)."

First Aorist: "I may loose myself (or for myself)"

	Singular	**Plural**
1st p.	λύσωμαι	λυσώμεθα
2nd p.	λύσῃ	λύσησθε
3rd p.	λύσηται	λύσωνται

Lesson 19

The Middle Voice (continued). Deponent Verbs

Middle Voice—Optative Mood

For the two following tenses, see the Passive Voice: Present, λυοίμην, etc., "I might loose myself (or for myself)"; Perfect λελυμένος εἴην, etc., "I might have loosed myself (or for myself)."

Future: "I should loose myself (or for myself)"

	Singular	Plural
1st p.	λυσοίμην	λυσοίμεθα
2nd p.	λύσοιο	λύσοισθε
3rd p.	λύσοιτο	λύσοιντο

First Aorist: "I might loose myself (or for myself)"

	Singular	Plural
1st p.	λυσαίμην	λυσαίμεθα
2nd p.	λύσαιο	λύσαισθε
3rd p.	λύσαιτο	λύσαιντο

Infinitive Mood

Present (like the Passive), λύεσθαι, "to loose oneself (or for oneself)"; *Perfect* (like the Passive), λελύσθαι, "to have loosed oneself (or for oneself)."

Future, λύσεσθαι, "to be about to loose oneself (or for oneself)."

First Aorist, λύσασθαι, "to loose oneself (or for oneself) immediately."

Participles

Present (like the Passive), λυόμενος, -η, --ον, etc., "loosing oneself (or for oneself)"; *Perfect* (like the Passive) λελυμένος, -η, -ον, etc., "having loosed oneself (or for oneself)." *Future*, λυσόμενος, -η, -ον, "being about to loose oneself (etc.)." *First Aorist*, λυσάμενος, -η, -ον, "having loosed oneself (or for oneself) immediately."

The student should compare and contrast the above Futures and First Aorists in the various Moods with those of the Passive Voice, noting carefully the differences. They should be written out in parallel columns from memory.

Exercise on the Middle Voice

Translate the following passages with the help of the accompanying notes, learning new words and retranslating into Greek.

(1) αἰτεῖτε καὶ οὐ λαμβάνετε διότι κακῶς αἰτεῖσθε, ἵνα ἐν ταῖς ἡδοναῖς ὑμῶν δαπανήσητε. (Jas. 4:3) αἰτεῖτε, 2nd pers. plur., pres. indic., active of αἰτέω, I ask (for αἰτέετε: -εε- contracts to -ει-); λαμβάνω, I receive; διότι, because; κακῶς, evilly, amiss; αἰτεῖσθε, (for αἰτέεσθε), same person, number, tense and mood as αἰτεῖτε, but middle voice, "ye ask for yourselves" (note the purposive change, stressing the selfishness); ἡδονή, pleasure; δαπανήσητε, 1st aor. subjunc., of δαπανάω, I spend.

(2) καὶ νῦν τί μέλλεις; ἀναστὰς βάπτισαι καὶ ἀπόλουσαι τὰς ἁμαρτίας σου ἐπικαλεσάμενος τὸ ὄνομα αὐτοῦ. (Acts 22:16) τί, why? μέλλεις, 2nd sing., pres. indic., of μέλλω, I delay, tarry; ἀναστάς, "having arisen" (an aor. partic., explained later); βάπτισαι, 2nd pers. sing., 1st aor., imperative, middle, of βαπτίζω, lit., "get thyself baptized"; ἀπόλουσαι, same tense and voice of ἀπολούω, I wash away, "get (thy sins) washed away"; ἐπικαλεσάμενος, 1st aor. participle, middle, of ἐπικαλέω, I call upon, "calling for thyself upon ..." Note the force of all these aorists, implying decisive and immediate action, the middle voice signifying, in the first two instances, that Saul was to arrange for the thing to be done.

(3) οἱ γὰρ Φαρισαῖοι καὶ πάντες οἱ Ἰουδαῖοι ἐὰν μὴ πυγμῇ νίψωνται τὰς χεῖρας οὐκ ἐσθίουσιν, κρατοῦντες τὴν παράδοσιν τῶν πρεσβυτέρων, 4 καὶ ἀπ' ἀγορᾶς ἐὰν μὴ βαπτίσωνται [in earlier editions of Nestle: ῥαντίσωνται] οὐκ ἐσθίουσιν, καὶ ἄλλα πολλά ἐστιν ἃ παρέλαβον κρατεῖν, βαπτισμοὺς ποτηρίων καὶ ξεστῶν καὶ χαλκίων [καὶ κλινῶν]. (Mark 7:3, 4) πυγμή, a fist (the dative here signifies "with the fist," an idiom used of washing; to wash with the fist was to wash "diligently"); νίψωνται, 3rd pers. plur., 1st aor. subjunc., middle, of νίπτω, I wash—conditional subjunctive after ἐὰν μή, "if not," i.e., unless; χείρ, a hand (fem.); ἐσθίω, I eat; κρατοῦντες, for κρατέοντες, nom., plur., masc., pres. partic., of κρατέω, I hold fast; παράδοσις, a tradition (declined like πόλις); πρεσβύτερος, an elder; ἀπ', for ἀπό (with genit.); ἀγορά, a market place; ῥαντίσωνται, 1st aor. subjunc., middle, of ῥαντίζω, I sprinkle (note the force of the middle voice in each case, intimating zealous self-interest in washing and sprinkling), ἄλλα, neut. plur., of ἄλλος, other, "other things" (distinguish this from ἀλλά, "but"); ἐστιν though singular, must be translated "are," owing to the rule that *when the subject of a verb is in the neuter plural the verb is put in the singular*. Here we must render by "there are"; παρέλαβον, "they received" (an irregular verb); κρατεῖν, pres. infin.; for ποτήριον, ξέστης and χαλκίον see Souter's or another lexicon.

(4) Ὁμοία γάρ ἐστιν ἡ βασιλεία τῶν οὐρανῶν ἀνθρώπῳ οἰκοδεσπότῃ, ὅστις ἐξῆλθεν ἅμα πρωῒ μισθώσασθαι ἐργάτας εἰς τὸν ἀμπελῶνα αὐτοῦ. (Matt. 20:1) ὅμοιος, -α, -ον, like; for βασιλεία and οἰκοδεσπότης, see Souter; ὅστις, who; ἐξῆλθεν, "went out" (an irregular verb); ἅμα πρωῒ, lit. "together early," i.e., "early in the morning", μισθώσασθαι, 1st aor. infin., middle, of μισθόω, I hire (infinitive of purpose), "to hire for himself."

(5) Ἐν σοφίᾳ περιπατεῖτε πρὸς τοὺς ἔξω τὸν καιρὸν ἐξαγοραζόμενοι. (Col. 4:5) περιπατεῖτε, (for περιπατέετε), 2nd pers. plur., pres. imperative, active of περιπατέω, I walk; ἔξω, without; ἐξαγοραζόμενοι, nom., plur., masc., pres. participle, middle, of ἐξαγοράζω, I buy up, "buying up for yourselves."

(6) καὶ ἐξάπινα περιβλεψάμενοι οὐκέτι οὐδένα εἶδον ἀλλὰ τὸν Ἰησοῦν μόνον μεθ' ἑαυτῶν. (Mark 9:8) ἐξάπινα, suddenly, περιβλεψάμενοι, 1st aor. participle, middle, of περιβλέπω, I look around (περί, around, βλέπω, I look)—"having looked around"—the middle voice expresses, in a way that cannot well be brought out in English, their deep interest: οὐκέτι, no longer; οὐδένα, accus. of οὐδείς, nobody; εἶδον, "they saw" (an irregular verb); μόνον, alone; μεθ' for μετά (when this preposition takes the genitive it denotes "with").

Note—The student should become familiar with the whole of the regular verb λύω in the three voices, Active, Middle and Passive. This will greatly facilitate the reading of the Greek Testament. To help towards the thorough acquisition of the regular verb it will be well to write out in full from memory (correcting the result if necessary) the various tense endings of the following regular verb on the model of λύω:—βουλεύω, I advise (the meaning of this in the middle voice is "to advise oneself," that is, "to deliberate").

Deponent Verbs

These are the verbs which have no active voice, but are either middle or passive in form, though they are active in meaning. They were called Deponent from the Latin verb "*deponere*," to lay aside, as they are considered to lay aside passive meanings.

The following are very common and should be committed to memory, especially the various irregular forms of the tenses mentioned.

βούλομαι, I will, wish, purpose; imperf. ἐβουλόμην; 1st aor. ἐβουλήθην.

ἀποκρίνομαι, I answer; for the past tense "I answered," either the 1st aor. passive, ἀπεκρίθην, is used (and this is the usual form), or the 1st aor. middle, ἀπεκρινάμην. Thus "he answered" is usually ἀπεκρίθη, but in seven places we find ἀπεκρίνατο.

γίνομαι, I become; imperf. ἐγινόμην; fut. γενήσομαι; 1st aor. (passive in form) ἐγενήθην; perfect γεγένημαι. There is a perfect with an active form, γέγονα, and with the same meaning, "I have become"; there is also a 2nd aor., ἐγενόμην, "I became," with the same endings as in the imperfect. This 2nd aor. is common in the 3rd pers. sing., optative, γένοιτο, in the phrase μὴ γένοιτο, "let it not be," translated "God forbid."

δέχομαι, I receive; 1st aor. ἐδεξάμην; perf. δέδεγμαι.

λογίζομαι, I reckon; 1st aor. ἐλογισάμην, I reckoned; 1st aor. pass ἐλογίσθην, I was reckoned.

ἄρχομαι, I begin; fut. ἄρξομαι; 1st aor. ἠρξάμην.

ἔρχομαι, I come; imperf. ἠρχόμην; other forms are irregular, as follows:—future ἐλεύσομαι; perfect ἐλήλυθα; 2nd aor. ἦλθον.

Exercise on the Deponent Verbs

(1) Translate: Ἐν ἀρχῇ ἦν ὁ λόγος, καὶ ὁ λόγος ἦν πρὸς τὸν θεόν, καὶ θεὸς ἦν ὁ λόγος. 2 οὗτος
ἦν ἐν ἀρχῇ πρὸς τὸν θεόν. 3 πάντα δι' αὐτοῦ ἐγένετο, καὶ χωρὶς αὐτοῦ ἐγένετο οὐδὲ ἕν. ὃ γέγονεν 4
ἐν αὐτῷ ζωὴ ἦν, καὶ ἡ ζωὴ ἦν τὸ φῶς τῶν ἀνθρώπων· 5 καὶ τὸ φῶς ἐν τῇ σκοτίᾳ φαίνει, καὶ ἡ σκοτία

αὐτὸ οὐ κατέλαβεν. 6 Ἐγένετο ἄνθρωπος ἀπεσταλμένος παρὰ θεοῦ, ὄνομα αὐτῷ Ἰωάννης· 7 οὗτος ἦλθεν εἰς μαρτυρίαν, ἵνα μαρτυρήσῃ περὶ τοῦ φωτός, ἵνα πάντες πιστεύσωσιν δι' αὐτοῦ. 8 οὐκ ἦν ἐκεῖνος τὸ φῶς, ἀλλ' ἵνα μαρτυρήσῃ περὶ τοῦ φωτός. 9 ἦν τὸ φῶς τὸ ἀληθινόν, ὃ φωτίζει πάντα ἄνθρωπον, ἐρχόμενον εἰς τὸν κόσμον. (John 1:1-9) In ver. 3, δι' is for διά, by; ἐγένετο is 3rd pers. sing., 2nd aor. of γίνομαι (see list above), and, though plural in meaning is singular, as it has a neuter plural subject πάντα, all things—"all things became (or came to be)." The next ἐγένετο is singular, in agreement with ἕν, one thing (ἕν is the neut. of the numeral εἷς, μία, ἕν, masc., fem., neut., "one"); οὐδέ is not even."—ἐγένετο οὐδὲ ἕν, "not even one thing came to be" (distinguish the numeral ἕν from the preposition ἐν, in); ὅ, neut. of the rel. pron. ὅς, which; γέγονεν 3rd pers. sing., perf., of γίνομαι, hath come to be; in ver. 5 κατέλαβεν, comprehended, is an irregular verb, to be learned later. In ver. 6 translate Ἐγένετο by "there was"; ἀπεσταλμένος, sent (for this perfect participle see later); παρά with genit., "from." In ver. 7 ἦλθεν is 3rd pers. sing., 2nd aor. of ἔρχομαι (see above); εἰς, unto (i.e., "for "); μαρτυρήσῃ, 1st aor. subjunc. of μαρτυρέω; περὶ, concerning; πιστεύσωσιν, 1st aor. subj. In ver. 9 πάντα is acc., sing., masc., "every"; ἐρχόμενον, nom., sing., neut., pres. partic., "coming" this agrees and goes with φῶς (neut.), not with ἄνθρωπον.

(2) Translate: εἶδεν ὁ Ἰησοῦς τὸν Ναθαναὴλ ἐρχόμενον πρὸς αὐτὸν καὶ λέγει περὶ αὐτοῦ, Ἴδε ἀληθῶς Ἰσραηλίτης ἐν ᾧ δόλος οὐκ ἔστιν. 48 λέγει αὐτῷ Ναθαναήλ, Πόθεν με γινώσκεις; ἀπεκρίθη Ἰησοῦς καὶ εἶπεν αὐτῷ, Πρὸ τοῦ σε Φίλιππον φωνῆσαι ὄντα ὑπὸ τὴν συκῆν εἶδόν σε. 49 ἀπεκρίθη αὐτῷ Ναθαναήλ, Ῥαββί, σὺ εἶ ὁ υἱὸς τοῦ θεοῦ, σὺ βασιλεὺς εἶ τοῦ Ἰσραήλ. (John 1:47-49) εἶδεν, saw—an irregular 2nd aorist (see later), Ἴδε, behold; ἀληθῶς, truly; Πόθεν, whence? γινώσκεις, 2nd pers. sing., pres. indic. of γινώσκω, I know; ἀπεκρίθη, 3rd pers. sing., 1st aor. indic. (passive in form) of ἀποκρίνομαι (see list above); this takes the dative "(answered) to him." Study carefully the phrase Πρὸ τοῦ σε Φίλιππον φωνῆσαι with the help of the following remarks, and see notes on the Infinitive, Lesson 15—πρό, before (a preposition taking the genitive); τοῦ (this article, genitive case after πρό, is not to be translated; it qualifies the whole phrase that follows); σε, thee, is the object of φωνῆσαι ("called thee"); φωνῆσαι is the 1st aor., infin. of φωνέω, I call, lit. "to have called"; the subject of the infinitive is Φίλιππον (for this construction of the accus. with the infin. see Lesson 18, p. 123); this phrase σε φωνῆσαι Φίλιππον is, lit., "Philip to have called thee"; this whole phrase, with its article τοῦ, is governed by πρό; literally, therefore, we have "Before Philip to have called thee." The only way to translate this concise idiomatic phrase is "Before Philip called thee"; ὄντα is acc. sing., masc., of ὤν the pres. partic. of εἰμί (see Lesson 9) "being" (i.e., "when thou wast"); ὑπό, under; εἶδον, I saw. In ver. 49 the τοῦ before Ἰσραήλ is not to be translated, as the article is generally used with a proper noun.

Lesson 20

Verbs with Contracted Vowel Endings

Verbs with Contracted Vowel Endings

Note—Contractions take place only in the present and imperfect tenses. All other tenses, since they have no two vowels coming together, are formed regularly, taking, however, a long vowel in the last syllable but one (see below).

When α, ε, ο precede a vowel, whether long or short, it is generally contracted into one syllable. This has been illustrated in nouns and adjectives with contracted vowels (see Lesson 7). There are three forms of verbs, those with α—stems, e.g., τιμάω (τιμῶ), stem τιμα–,I honor; those with ε—stems, e.g., φιλέω (φιλῶ), stem φιλε–I love; those with ο—stems, e.g., ε— δηλόω (δηλῶ), stem δηλο–I manifest.

In the following paradigms, the uncontracted forms are given in brackets. The contracted forms should be memorized.

(τιμάω) τιμῶ, I honor

Contracted Verbs With –ε– Stems

Active Voice—Indicative Mood

Present Tense

1st p.	(τιμάω)	τιμῶ	(τιμάομεν)	τιμῶμεν
2nd p.	(τιμάεις)	τιμαῖς	(τιμάετε)	τιμᾶτε
3rd p.	(τιμάει)	τιμαῖ	(τιμάουσι)	τιμῶσι

Imperfect Tense

1st p.	(ἐτίμαον)	ἐτίμων	(——ομεν)	ἐτιμῶμεν
2nd p.	(——ες)	ἐτίμας	(——ετε)	ἐτιμᾶτε
3rd p.	(——ε)	ἐτίμα	(——ον)	ἐτίμων

Active Voice—Imperative Mood

Present Tense

2nd p.	(τίμαε)	τίμα	(τιμάετε)	τιμᾶτε
3rd p.	(——έτω)	τιμάτω	(——έτωσαν)	τιμάτωσαν

Active Voice—Subjunctive Mood

The present tense is exactly like the indicative present, owing to the contractions.
Optative Mood

Active Voice—Present Tense

1st p.	(τιμάοιμι)	τιμῷμι	(——οιμεν)	τιμῷμεν
2nd p.	(——οις)	τιμῷς	(——οιτε)	τιμῷτε
3rd p.	(——οι)	τιμῷ	(——οιεν)	τιμῷεν

Note that the iota becomes subscript in each person. There is an alternative and more usual form for this tense, as follows:—

1st p.	τιμῴμην	——ημεν
2nd p.	——ης	——ητε
3rd p.	——η	——ησαν

Active Voice—Infinitive Mood (Present)

(τιμάειν) τιμαῖν

Participle (Present)

Masc.	**Fem.**	**Neut.**
(τιμάων) τιμῶν	(τιμάουσα) τιμῶσα	(τιμάον) τιμῶν

Passive and Middle Voices—Indicative Mood

Present Tense

1st p.	(τιμάομαι)	τιμῶμαι	(——όμεθα)	τιμώμεθα
2nd p.	(——ῃ)	τιμαῖ	(——εσθε)	τιμᾶσθε
3rd p.	(——εται)	τιμᾶται	(——ονται)	τιμῶνται

Imperfect Tense

1st p.	(ἐτιμάομην)	ἐτιμώμην	(——όμεθα)	ἐτιμώμεθα
2nd p.	(——ου)	ἐτιμῶ	(——εσθε)	ἐτιμᾶσθε
3rd p.	(——ετο)	ἐτιμᾶτω	(——ονται)	ἐτιμῶντο

Passive and Middle Voices—Imperative Mood

Present Tense

2nd p.	(τιμάου)	τιμῶ	(——εσθε)	τιμᾶσθε
3rd p.	(——έσθω)	τιμάσθω	(——έσθωσαν)	τιμάσθωσαν
	(or —έσθων)		τιμάσθων	

Passive and Middle Voices—Subjunctive Mood

Like the Indicative

Passive and Middle Voices—Optative Mood

Present Tense

1st p.	(τιμαοίμην)	τιμῴμην	(——οίμεθα)	τιμῴμεθα
2nd p.	(——οιο)	τιμῷο	(——οισθε)	τιμῷσθε
3rd p.	(——οιτο)	τιμῷτο	(——ονται)	τιμῷντο

Passive and Middle Voices—Infinitive Mood

Present Tense

(τιμάεσθαι) τιμᾶσθαι

Participle

Masc.	**Fem.**	**Neut.**
(τιμαόμενος) τιμώμενος	(—ομένη) τιμωμένη	(—όμενον) τιμώμενον

Exercise on Contracted Verbs in -αω

Translate and retranslate, as in previous exercises:

(1) ἐγὼ δὲ λέγω ὑμῖν, ἀγαπᾶτε τοὺς ἐχθροὺς ὑμῶν καὶ προσεύχεσθε ὑπὲρ τῶν διωκόντων ὑμᾶς. (Matt. 5:44) ἀγαπᾶτε, pres., imperative active of ἀγαπάω; προσεύχεσθε pres., imperative of προσεύχομαι (see Deponent Verbs, last Lesson); ὑπέρ, for, on behalf of (takes the genitive); διωκόντων, gen., plur., pres. partic. of διώκω.

(2) καὶ τὸ ἀγαπᾶν αὐτὸν ἐξ ὅλης τῆς καρδίας καὶ ἐξ ὅλης τῆς συνέσεως καὶ ἐξ ὅλης τῆς ἰσχύος καὶ τὸ ἀγαπᾶν τὸν πλησίον ὡς ἑαυτὸν περισσότερόν ἐστιν πάντων τῶν ὁλοκαυτωμάτων καὶ θυσιῶν. (Mark 12:33) ἀγαπᾶν, pres. infinitive—the article is not translatable, it indicates the noun character of the infinitive verb, and thus τὸ ἀγαπᾶν are together the subject of ἐστιν; ἐξ (i.e., ἐκ) "out of" (or "with"); συνέσεως, genit. of συνέσις; περισσότερον, a comparative degree, "more." The comparative, which in English is followed by the word "than," is in Greek simply followed by the genitive case. Thus περισσότερον πάντων is not "more of all" but "more than all"; θυσιῶν, gen., plur. of θυσία.

(3) 15 Ὅτε οὖν ἠρίστησαν λέγει τῷ Σίμωνι Πέτρῳ ὁ Ἰησοῦς, Σίμων Ἰωάννου, ἀγαπᾷς με
πλέον τούτων; λέγει αὐτῷ, Ναί, κύριε, σὺ οἶδας ὅτι φιλῶ σε. λέγει αὐτῷ, Βόσκε τὰ ἀρνία μου. 16

λέγει αὐτῷ πάλιν δεύτερον, Σίμων Ἰωάννου, ἀγαπᾷς με; λέγει αὐτῷ, Ναί, κύριε, σὺ οἶδας ὅτι φιλῶ σε. λέγει αὐτῷ, Ποίμαινε τὰ πρόβατά μου. ἠρίστησαν, 3rd pers. plur., 1st aorist active, of ἀριστέω; (John 21:15-16) Σίμων Ἰωάννου, "Simon, son of John"; the word υἱός, son, was omitted in this phrase; πλέον, more, a comparative followed by the genitive, i.e., "more than these," see above in (2); σύ, note the emphasis on this pronoun; οἶδας, knowest (an irregular verb).

(4) μακάριοι οἱ πεινῶντες καὶ διψῶντες τὴν δικαιοσύνην, ὅτι αὐτοὶ χορτασθήσονται. (Matt. 5:6) πεινῶντες and διψῶντες (for πεινάοντες and διψάοντες), nom., plur., pres. partic. of, πεινάω and διψάω; χορτασθήσονται, 3rd pers. plur., fut. indic., passive, of χορτάζω.

Contracted Verbs With –ε– Stems

These present little difficulty. The -ε- drops out before a long vowel, or vowel combination like -οι- or -ου-. Besides this, -εε- becomes -ει-, and -εο- becomes -ου-. A few tenses will be sufficient to illustrate this. The student should write out the whole of the verb φιλέω in the same way as τιμάω, observing the contractions now mentioned.

(φιλέω), φιλῶ, I love (stem φιλε-)

Active Voice—Indicative Mood

Present Tense

1st p.	(φιλάω)	φιλῶ	(——έομεν)	φιλοῦμεν
2nd p.	(——έεις)	φιλεῖς	(——έετε)	φιλεῖτε
3rd p.	(——έει)	φιλεῖ	(——έουσι)	φιλοῦσι

Imperfect Tense

1st p.	(ἐφίλεον)	ἐφίλουν	(——έομεν)	ἐφιλοῦμεν
2nd p.	(——εες)	ἐφίλεις	(——έετε)	ἐφιλεῖτε
3rd p.	(——εε)	ἐφίλει	(——εον)	ἐφίλουν

The remainder of the active and the middle and passive tenses can be formed easily. Here the present participle active contracts as follows:

(φιλέων) φιλῶν (φιλέουσα) φιλοῦσα (φιλέον) φιλοῦν.

The infinitive passive is φιλεῖσθαι (for φιλέεσθαι)

Contracted Verbs in —οω.

In this third class, the following rules should be noted:—

ο followed by a long vowel becomes ω.

ο followed by a short vowel becomes ου.

ο followed by a vowel combination containing ι becomes οι (except in the pres. infin. active, where —οειν becomes —ουν).

(δηλόω) δηλῶ, I manifest (stem δηλο—)

Active Voice—Indicative Mood

Present Tense

1st p.	(δηλόω)	δηλῶ	(δηλόομεν)	δηλοῦμεν
2nd p.	(—όεις)	—οῖς	(—όετε)	—οῦτε
3rd p.	(—όει)	—οῖ	(—όουσι)	—οῦσι(ν)

Imperfect Tense

This has —ου— throughout: ἐδήλουν (for ἐδήλοον), —ους, —ου, —οῦμεν, etc.

Active Voice—Imperative Mood

Present Tense

This has —ου— throughout: δήλου (for δηλοε), δηλούτω, etc.

Active Voice—Subjunctive Mood

Present Tense

1st p.	(δηλόω)	δηλῶ	(δηλόωμεν)	δηλῶμεν
2nd p.	(—όῃς)	—οῖς	(—όητε)	—ῶτε
3rd p.	(—όῃ)	—οῖ	(—όωσι)	—ῶσι(ν)

Active Voice—Optative Mood

Present Tense

This has —οειν throughout and is like φιλοίμι.
Infinitive—Present: (δηλόειν) δηλοῦν
Participle—Present: δηλῶν, δηλοῦσα, δηλοῦν

Passvie and Middle Voices—Indicative Mood

Present Tense

δηλοῦμαι, —οῖ, —οῦται (the plur. has —ου— in all persons)

Imperfect Tense

ἐδηλούμην, etc. (—ου— throughout)

Passvie and Middle Voices—Imperative Mood

Present Tense

δηλοῦ, —ούσθω, etc. (—ου— throughout)

Passvie and Middle Voices—Subjunctive Mood

Present Tense

δηλῶμαι, δηλοῖ, δηλῶται, etc. (—ω— in plural)

Passvie and Middle Voices—Optative Mood

Present Tense

δηλοίμην, etc. (—οι— throughout)

Infinitive—Present:—δηλοῦσθαι

Participle—Present:—δηλούμενος, —η, —ον

Note—The future active of the three contracted verbs is τιμήσω, φιλήσω, δηλώσω; the perfect is τετίμηκα, πεφίληκα, δεδήλωκα; the first aorist passive, ἐτιμήθην, ἐφιλήθην, ἐδηλώθην; the perfect middle and passive, τετίμημαι, πεφίλημαι, δεδήλωμαι.

Exercise on Contracted Verbs in —εω and —οω

Translate and retranslate the following:—

(1) Ὁ φιλῶν πατέρα ἢ μητέρα ὑπὲρ ἐμὲ οὐκ ἔστιν μου ἄξιος, καὶ ὁ φιλῶν υἱὸν ἢ θυγατέρα ὑπὲρ ἐμὲ οὐκ ἔστιν μου ἄξιος· 38 καὶ ὃς οὐ λαμβάνει τὸν σταυρὸν αὐτοῦ καὶ ἀκολουθεῖ ὀπίσω μου, οὐκ ἔστιν μου ἄξιος. (Matt. 10:37-38: 37) Ὁ φιλῶν is lit. "the one loving" (pres. partic.), i.e., "he that loveth", ὑπέρ, above, i.e., "more than"; θυγατέρα acc. of θυγάτηρ.

(2) 16 λέγει αὐτῷ πάλιν δεύτερον, Σίμων Ἰωάννου, ἀγαπᾷς με; λέγει αὐτῷ, Ναί, κύριε, σὺ οἶδας ὅτι φιλῶ σε. λέγει αὐτῷ, Ποίμαινε τὰ πρόβατά μου. 17 λέγει αὐτῷ τὸ τρίτον, Σίμων Ἰωάννου, φιλεῖς με; ἐλυπήθη ὁ Πέτρος ὅτι εἶπεν αὐτῷ τὸ τρίτον, Φιλεῖς με; καὶ λέγει αὐτῷ, Κύριε, πάντα σὺ οἶδας, σὺ γινώσκεις ὅτι φιλῶ σε. λέγει αὐτῷ [ὁ Ἰησοῦς], Βόσκε τὰ πρόβατά μου. (John 21:16-17) οἶδας, thou knowest (an irregular verb): Ποίμαινε pres. imperative; τὸ τρίτον, the third time; ἐλυπήθη, 3rd pers. sing., 1st aorist passive of λυπέω; εἶπεν, 3rd pers. sing., of an irregular 2nd aor. form of λέγω, he said.

(3) ἐραυνῶντες εἰς τίνα ἢ ποῖον καιρὸν ἐδήλου τὸ ἐν αὐτοῖς πνεῦμα Χριστοῦ προμαρτυρόμενον τὰ εἰς Χριστὸν παθήματα καὶ τὰς μετὰ ταῦτα δόξας. (1 Pet. 1:11) ἐραυνῶντες, nom. plur., pres. participle, active, of ἐραυνάω; εἰς τίνα ἢ ποῖον, "unto what or what sort of"; ἐδήλου, 3rd pers. sing., imperf., indic., of δηλόω; προμαρτυρόμενον, nom. sing., neut., pres. partic. of a deponent verb, agreeing with πνεῦμα (neuter simply in grammatical gender); μετὰ ταῦτα, after these things.

(4) Κατα δὲ ἑορτην ἀπέλυεν αὐτοῖς ἕνα δέσμιον ὃ ν παρῃτοῦντο. (Mark 15:6) Κατά, at; ἀπέλυεν, 3rd pers. sing., imperf. indic. of ἀπολύω (the imperfect signifying a custom "he used to," etc.—note the augment at the end of the prefixed preposition ἀπε–; ἕνα, one; παρῃτοῦντο, 3rd pers. plur., imperf. indic. of the deponent contracted verb παραιτέομαι (a verb with several meanings, here "to ask").

Note—Among the contracted verbs, the verb ζάω, I live, which is a little irregular, is important. The present indicative is ζῶ (or ζάω), ζῇς, ζῇ, ζῶμεν, ζῆτε, ζῶσι; future, ζήσω, or ζήσομαι; 1st aor. ἔζησα. The present participle ζῶν, ζῶσα, ζῶν, (genitive, ζῶντος, ζώσης, ζῶντος) is very frequent in the New Testament and is found in most of its cases.

Exercise

Translate and retranslate: ἐγώ εἰμι ὁ ἄρτος ὁ ζῶν ὁ ἐκ τοῦ οὐρανοῦ καταβάς· ἐάν τις φάγῃ ἐκ τούτου τοῦ ἄρτου ζήσει εἰς τὸν αἰῶνα, καὶ ὁ ἄρτος δὲ ὃν ἐγὼ δώσω ἡ σάρξ μού ἐστιν ὑπὲρ τῆς τοῦ κόσμου ζωῆς. (John 6:51) καταβάς, 1st aor. partic. of καταβαίνω, "having come down": φάγῃ, 2nd aor. subjunc. of an irregular verb ἐσθίω, "I eat" (2nd aor., ἔφαγον—formed from another root); εἰς τὸν αἰῶνα, lit. "unto the age," signifies "for ever," and must be so translated; δώσω, I will give (see later).

Lesson 21

Verbs with Liquid Stem Endings. The Second Conjugation, Active Voice

Verbs With Stem Ending in λ, μ, ν, ρ

Since the consonants λ, μ, ν, ρ are known as liquids, verbs with stems ending in these letters are called Liquid Verbs. The personal endings are regular throughout, but certain simple changes occur in the preceding syllable or stem ending, as follows:—

(1) While the future tense keeps the verbal stem, which has a short vowel, the present tense stem usually has a long vowel, or, in the case of stems ending in λ the λ is doubled. Originally the future ended in -σω, as in the regular verb, but the ς dropped.

Thus the stem of the verb αἴρω, I raise, or take up, is ἀρ-, and the future is ἀρῶ. The stem of ἀποκτείνω, I kill, is ἀποκτεν-, and the future is ἀποκτενῶ. Again the stem of ἀγγέλλω (pronounced angellō), I renounce, is ἀγγελ-, and the future is ἀγγελῶ.

Note that the future, active and middle, of liquid verbs is declined like the present of contracted verbs in -εω.

(2) The first aorist, active and middle, omits the ς like the future, but lengthens the vowel in the preceding syllable by way of compensation.

Thus φαίνω (stem φαν-), I shine, has fut. φανῶ and 1st aor. ἔφηνα; ἀγγέλλω has 1st aor. ἤγγειλα (note the long -ει-).

(3) In the perfect, μ and ν cannot come before κ. One or the other is dropped. So we get κρίνω, I judge, perfect κέκρικα (not κέκρινκα); while, φαίνω has perfect πέφηνα (not πέφηνκα) and μένω and has μεμένηκα, lengthening the vowel.

(4) In the perfect passive, ν is changed into ς or into μ before the ending -μαι, or else is dropped. Thus φαίνω makes πέφασμαι instead of πέφανμαι; κρίνω makes κέκριμαι instead of κέκρινμαι.

Exercise on Liquid Verbs

Translate and retranslate the following passages:—

(1) Μετὰ δέ τινας ἡμέρας εἶπεν πρὸς Βαρναβᾶν Παῦλος, Ἐπιστρέψαντες δὴ ἐπισκεψώμεθα τοὺς ἀδελφοὺς κατὰ πόλιν πᾶσαν ἐν αἷς κατηγγείλαμεν τὸν λόγον τοῦ κυρίου πῶς ἔχουσιν. (Acts 15:36) Μετά, after; εἶπεν, said (an irregular aorist of λέγω); Ἐπιστρέψαντες, nom., plur., masc., 1st aorist participle of ἐπιστρέφω, I return (future -ψω) lit. "returning" (the aorist indicating decisive and immediate action); ἐπισκεψώμεθα, 1st pers. plur., 1st aor. subjunc. of the deponent verb ἐπισκέπτομαι, I visit, "let us visit" (the 1st pers. plur. of the subjunc. present and 1st aor. is often used in a hortatory way, "let us," etc.), κατά, throughout; κατηγγείλαμεν, 1st pers. plur., 1st aor., indic. of καταγγέλλω, I preach (note the position of the augment η, and the long vowel combination a lengthened from ε after the dropping of the ς in the liquid verb); πῶς ἔχουσιν, how they do (lit. "how they have," i.e., "how they are getting on").

(2) πολλοὶ μὲν οὖν ἐξ αὐτῶν ἐπίστευσαν καὶ τῶν Ἑλληνίδων γυναικῶν τῶν εὐσχημόνων καὶ ἀνδρῶν οὐκ ὀλίγοι. 13 Ὡς δὲ ἔγνωσαν οἱ ἀπὸ τῆς Θεσσαλονίκης Ἰουδαῖοι ὅτι καὶ ἐν τῇ Βεροίᾳ κατηγγέλη ὑπὸ τοῦ Παύλου ὁ λόγος τοῦ θεοῦ, ἦλθον κἀκεῖ σαλεύοντες καὶ ταράσσον τες τοὺς ὄχλους. 14 εὐθέως δὲ τότε τὸν Παῦλον ἐξαπέστειλαν οἱ ἀδελφοὶ πορεύεσθαι ἕως ἐπὶ τὴν θάλασσαν, ὑπέμεινάν τε ὅ τε Σιλᾶς καὶ ὁ Τιμόθεος ἐκεῖ. (Acts 17:12-14) γυναικῶν, gen. plur. of γυνή (irregular); ἔγνωσαν, 3rd pers. plur., 2nd aor. of γινώσκω, "I know" (irregular); κατηγγέλη, 3rd pers. sing., 2nd aor. passive of καταγγέλλω, "was preached," agreeing with its subject λόγος (the 1st aor. passive is κατηγγέλθην—the 2nd aor. is simply an alternative form); ἦλθον, 3rd pers. plur., 2nd aor. of ἔρχομαι, I come (see Lesson 19); κἀκεῖ, for καὶ ἐκεῖ, also there; ἐξαπέστειλαν, 3rd pers. plur., 1st aor. indic. active of ἐχαποστέλλω, "I send away" (note the augment ε after the second preposition ἀπο, and the long ει before the single λ); πορεύεσθαι, pres. infin. of πορεύομαι (deponent); ἕως, as far as, ἐπί, to; ὑπέμειναν, 3rd pers. plur., 1st aor. of ὑπομένω.

(3) Ὅταν δὲ νηστεύητε, μὴ γίνεσθε ὡς οἱ ὑποκριταὶ σκυθρωποί, ἀφανίζουσιν γὰρ τὰ πρόςωπα αὐτῶν ὅπως φανῶσιν τοῖς ἀνθρώποις νηστεύοντες· ἀμὴν λέγω ὑμῖν, ἀπέχουσιν τὸν μισθὸν αὐτῶν. 17 σὺ δὲ νηστεύων ἄλειψαί σου τὴν κεφαλὴν καὶ τὸ πρόσωπόν σου νίψαι, 18 ὅπως μὴ φανῇς τοῖς ἀνθρώποις νηστεύων ἀλλὰ τῷ πατρί σου τῷ ἐν τῷ κρυφαίῳ· καὶ ὁ πατήρ σου ὁ βλέπων ἐν τῷ κρυφαίῳ ἀποδώσει σοι. (Matt. 6:16-18) νηστεύητε, pres. subjunc., after the indefinite Ὅταν, whenever; γίνεσθε, 2nd pers. plur., pres. imperat. of γίνομαι (deponent); φανῶσιν, 1st aor. subjunc. of φαίνω, I appear (subjunc. of purpose after ὅπως); νηστεύων, pres. partic.; ἄλειψαι, 2nd pers. sing., 1st aor. imperat., middle of ἀλείφω, "anoint for thyself"; νίψαι, ditto of νίπτω; ἀποδώσει, shall reward (see later).

The Second Conjugation, or Verbs in -μι

The student should thoroughly review the First Conjugation verb before learning the following. The endings of the second conjugation differ from the first only in the present and imperfect tenses, and, in several verbs, in the second aorist active and middle. The other tenses are like those of the First Conjugation, with certain exceptions.

There are two classes, (I) those that double the stem, the reduplication being especially by means of the vowel ι. Thus in δίδωμι, I give, the stem, δο-, is doubled by the prefix δι-; in τίθημι, I put, the stem, θε-, is doubled by τι-; in ἵστημι I place, or stand, the stem, στα-, makes ἱ (for σι): (II) those that add the syllable -νυ- or -ννυ- to the stem, before the person endings. Thus in δείκνυμι, I show, the stem is δεικ- and -νυ- is inserted before the ending -μι; in κεράννυμι, I mix (stem κερα-), -ννυ- is inserted.

Second Conjugation, Class I

There are three regular forms, viz., with stems ending in α-, ε-, ω-. The following model paradigms should be memorized, the persons, I, thou, he (she, it), we, you, they, being borne in mind.

ἵστημι, I stand	τίθημι, I put	δίδωμι, I give
(stem στα-)	(stem θε-)	(stem δο-)

Note—Thefollowing important details must be remembered as to the meanings of the tenses of ἵστημι:—

(1) The present, imperfect, future and 1st aorist of the active voices are transitive, and signify "I cause to stand," "I place," etc.

(2) The perfect and pluperfect are intransitive and are used in a present and imperfect sense, signifying "I stand," "I take my stand," "I was standing." That is to say, these are not to be rendered by "I have stood," "I had stood." These two tenses have a continuous significance and hence we must render by present and imperfect meanings.

(3) The 2nd aorist is also intransitive, and means "I stood."

Active Voice—Indicative Mood

Present Tense

Sing.

ἵστημι	τίθημι	δίδωμι
ἵστης	τίθης	δίδως
ἵστησι(ν)	τίθησι(ν)	δίδωσι(ν)

Plur.

ἵσταμεν	τίθεμεν	δίδομεν
ἵστατε	τίθετε	δίδοτε
ἱστᾶσι(ν)	τιθέασι(ν)	διδόασι(ν)

Imperfect Tense

I was standing, putting, giving, etc.

Sing.

ἵστην	ἐτίθην	ἐδίδουν
ἵστης	ἐτίθεις	ἐδίδους
ἵστη	ἐτίθει	ἐδίδου

Plur.

ἵσταμεν	ἐτίθεμεν	ἐδίδομεν
ἵστατε	ἐτίθετε	ἐδίδοτε
ἵστασαν	ἐτίθεσαν	ἐδίδοσαν

2nd Aorist
I stood
ἔστην
ἔστης
ἔστη

Sing. (No Singular)

Plur.
(*we gave*)

ἔστημεν	ἔθεμεν	ἔδομεν
ἔστητε	ἔθετε	ἔδετε
ἔστησαν	ἔθεσαν	ἔδοσαν

Note—The place of the singular in the *two* last tenses is taken by the 1st aorist ἔδωκα, -κας, -κε.

Active Voice—Imperative Mood

Present Tense (continuous action)
stand thou, put thou, etc.

Sing.

ἵστη	τίθει	δίδου
ἱστάτω	τιθέτω	διδότω

Plur.

ἵστατε	τίθετε	δίδοτε
ἱστάτωσαν	τιθέτωσαν	διδότωσαν

2nd Aorist (immediate action)
(same meaning, but decisive)

Sing.

στῆθι or στα*	θές	δός
στήτω	θέτω	δότω

Plur.

στῆτε	θέτε	δότε
στήτωσαν	θέτωσαν	δότωσαν

* *Note*—

στα is used only in compound verbs, as ἀνάστα (Acts 12:7: Eph. 5:14).

Active Voice—Subjunctive Mood

Present Tense

That I, etc., may stand, put, give

Sing.

ἱστῶ	τιθῶ	διδῶ
ἱστῇς	τιθῇς	διδῷς
ἱστῇ	τιθῇ	διδῷ

Plur.

ἱστῶμεν	τιθῶμεν	διδῶμεν
ἱστῆτε	τιθῆτε	διδῶτε
ἱστῶσι(ν)	τιθῶσι(ν)	διδῶσι(ν)

2nd Aorist

στῶ	θῶ	δῶ
etc.	etc.	etc.

(*Like the present in each verb*)

Active Voice—Optative Mood

Present Tense

that I, etc., might stand, put, give

Sing.

ἱσταίην	τιθείην	διδοίην
ἱσταίης	τιθείης	διδοίης
ἱσταίη	τιθείη	διδοίη

Plur.

ἱσταῖμεν	τιθεῖμεν	διδοῖμεν
ἱσταῖτε	τιθεῖτε	διδοῖτε
ἱσταῖεν	τιθεῖεν	διδοῖεν

2nd Aorist
(*same meaning, but decisive*)

Sing.

σταίην	θείην	δοίην (δῴην)
σταίης	θείης	δοίης (δῴης)
σταίη	θείη	δοίη (δῴη)

Plur.

σταίημεν	θείημεν	δοίημεν
σταίητε	θείητε	δοίητε
σταῖεν	θεῖεν	δοῖεν

Active Voice—Infinitive Mood

to stand, to put, to give

Present	ἱστάναι	τιθέναι	διδόναι
2nd Aor.	στῆναι	θεῖναι	δοῦναι

Participles

Present Tense
standing, putting, giving

ἱστάς, -ᾶσα, -άν　　τιθείς, -εῖσα, -έν　　διδούς, -οῦσα, -όν

2nd Aorist
standing, putting, giving

στάς, -ᾶσα, -άν　　θείς, -εῖσα, -έν　　δούς, -οῦσα, -όν

Exercise on the above Tenses of the Active Voice of Verbs in -μι

Translate and retranslate:—

(1) αὐτὸς δὲ ᾔδει τοὺς διαλογισμοὺς αὐτῶν, εἶπεν δὲ τῷ ἀνδρὶ τῷ ξηρὰν ἔχοντι τὴν χεῖρα, Ἔγειρε καὶ στῆθι εἰς τὸ μέσον· καὶ ἀναστὰς ἔστη. (Luke 6:8) ᾔδει, knew (see later); εἶπεν, he said; ἔχοντι dat., sing., masc., pres. partic. of ἔχω, agreeing with ἀνδρί (dat. of ἀνήρ); στῆθι 2nd aor. imperative; ἀναστάς, 2nd aor. partic. of ἀνίστημι, I arise, "having arisen"; ἔστη, 2nd aor. indic. of ἵστημι.

(2) Βλέπετε, ἀδελφοί, μήποτε ἔσται ἔν τινι ὑμῶν καρδία πονηρὰ ἀπιστίας ἐν τῷ ἀποστῆναι ἀπὸ θεοῦ ζῶντος. (Heb. 3:12) Βλέπετε, 2nd pers. plur., pres. imperat.; μήποτε lest at any time; ἔσται fut. of εἰμί; ἐν τῷ ἀποστῆναι, lit., "in the to depart from," the verb is the 2nd aor. infin. of ἀφίστημι (a compound of ἀπό and ἵστημι); the infinitive is a verbal noun, and is governed by the preposition ἐν, which takes the dative; hence we must translate by "in departing," the article τῷ not being translated.

(3) οὐδὲ καίουσιν λύχνον καὶ τιθέασιν αὐτὸν ὑπὸ τὸν μόδιον ἀλλ' ἐπὶ τὴν λυχνίαν, καὶ λάμπει πᾶσιν τοῖς ἐν τῇ οἰκίᾳ. (Matt. 5:15) τιθέασιν, see the pres. indic. of τίθημι; πᾶσιν, dat. plur. of πᾶς, dative after λάμπει, "it giveth light to."

(4) τίς δὲ ἐξ ὑμῶν μεριμνῶν δύναται ἐπὶ τὴν ἡλικίαν αὐτοῦ προσθεῖναι πῆχυν; (Luke 12:25) μεριμνῶν, nom. sing., masc., pres. partic. of μεριμνάω, "I am anxious"; δύναται, 3rd pers. sing., pres. indic. of δύναμαι, (a deponent verb); ἐπί, to; προσθεῖναι, 2nd aor. infin. of προστίθημι, I put to (πρός and τίθημι).

(5) Αἰτεῖτε καὶ δοθήσεται ὑμῖν, ζητεῖτε καὶ εὑρήσετε, κρούετε καὶ ἀνοιγήσεται ὑμῖν· 8 πᾶς γὰρ ὁ αἰτῶν λαμβάνει καὶ ὁ ζητῶν εὑρίσκει καὶ τῷ κρούοντι ἀνοιγήσεται. 9 ἢ τίς ἐστιν ἐξ ὑμῶν ἄνθρωπος, ὃν αἰτήσει ὁ υἱὸς αὐτοῦ ἄρτον, μὴ λίθον ἐπι δώσει αὐτῷ; 10 ἢ καὶ ἰχθὺν αἰ τήσει, μὴ

ὄφιν ἐπιδώσει αὐτῷ; 11 εἰ οὖν ὑμεῖς πονηροὶ ὄντες οἴδατε δόματα ἀγαθὰ διδόναι τοῖς τέκνοις ὑμῶν, πόσῳ μᾶλλον ὁ πατὴρ ὑμῶν ὁ ἐν τοῖς οὐρανοῖς δώσει ἀγαθὰ τοῖς αἰτοῦσιν αὐτόν. (Matt. 7:7-11)
Αἰτεῖτε, 2nd pers. plur., pres. imperat. of the contracted verb αἰτέω; δοθήσεται, it shall be given (passive of δίδωμι, see later); εὑρήσετε, fut. of εὑρίσκω; ἀνοιγήσεται, fut. passive of ἀνοίγω; πᾶς ὁ αἰτῶν lit., "everyone the (one) asking," to be rendered "everyone that asketh"; αἰτήσει, fut., lit., "whom his son shall ask a loaf"; μή, this is not to be translated, it simply indicates that a negative answer to the question is expected: ἐπιδώσει fut. of ἐπιδίδω μι; οἴδατε, know (see later); διδόναι, pres. infin.; πόσῳ, how much, dat. of degree, "by how much"; αἰτοῦσιν, dat., plur., pres. participle, lit., "to the (ones) asking."

Lesson 22

The Second Conjugation. The Middle Voice

Passive and Middle Voices of Verbs in —μι

Note 1—ThePassive, Indicative, Present of the verb ἵστημι has the meaning of "I am caused to stand," "I am placed," etc., and hence it simply denotes "I stand," etc. Almost the only passive tense used in the New Testament is the 1st aorist.

Passive and Middle—Indicative Mood

I take my stand; am put; am given

Sing.

ἵσταμαι	τίθεμαι	δίδομαι
—σαι	—σαι (or τιθῇ)	—σαι
—ται	—ται	—ται

Plur.

—μεθα	—μεθα	—μεθα
—σθε	—σθε	—σθε
—νται	—νται	—νται

Imperfect

I was taking my stand; was putting; was giving

Sing.

ἱστάμην	ἐτίθεμην	ἐδιδόμην
—σο	—σο (or ἐτίθου)	—σο (or ἐδίδου)
—το	—το	—το

Plur.

—μεθα	—μεθα	—μεθα
—σθε	—σθε	—σθε
—ντο	—ντο	—ντο

2nd Aorist (Middle only)

Sing.

I put	I gave	
(None)	ἐθέμην	ἐδόμην
ἔθου	ἔδου	
—ετο	—ετο	

Plur.

—έμεθα	—όμεθα
—εσθε	—οσθε
—εντο	—οντο

Passive and Middle—Imperative Mood

Present Tense: be stood, or stand; be put, or put; be given, or give

Sing.

ἵστασο, or ἵστω	τίθεσο, or τίθου	δίδοσο, or δίδου
ἱστάσθω	τιθέσθω	διδόσθω

Plur.

ἵστασθε	τίθεσθε	δίδοσθε
ἱστάσθωσαν	τιθέσθωσαν	διδόσθωσαν

2nd Aorist (Middle only)

Sing.

put thou	give thou	
(None)	θοῦ	δοῦ
θέσθω	δόσθω	

Plur.

θέσθε	δόσθε
θέσθωσαν	δόσθωσαν

Passive and Middle—Subjunctive Mood

that I might be stood, stand, etc.

Sing.

ἱστῶμαι	τιθῶμαι	διδῶμαι
——ῇ	——ῇ	——ῷ
——ῆται	——ῆται	——ῶται

Plur.

——ώμεθα	——ώμεθα	——ώμεθα
——ῆσθε	——ῆσθε	——ῶσθε
——ῶνται	——ῶνται	——ῶνται

2nd Aorist (Middle only)

Sing.

(None)	θῶμαι	δῶμαι
θῇ	δῷ	
θῆται	δῶται	

Plur.

θώμεθα	δώμεθα
θῆσθε	δῶσθε
θῶνται	δῶνται

Passive and Middle—Optative Mood

Present Tense: that I might be stood, stand, etc.

Sing.

ἱσαίμην	τιθείμην	διοίμην
—αῖο	—εῖο	—οῖο
—αῖτο	—εῖτο	—οῖτο

Plur.

—αίμεθα	—είμεθα	—οίμεθα
—αῖσθε	—εῖσθε	—οῖσθε
—αῖντο	—εῖντο	—οῖντο

2nd Aorist (Middle only)

Sing.

(None)	θείμην	δοίμην
θεῖο	δοῖο	
θεῖτο	δοῖτο	

Plur.

θείμεθα	δοίμεθα
θεῖσθε	δοῖσθε
θεῖντο	δοῖντο

Passive and Middle—Infinitive Mood

Present Tense
to be stood, to stand (for oneself), etc.

ἵστασθαι	τίθεσθαι	δίδοσθαι

2nd Aorist (Middle only)
to put for oneself, etc.

(None)	θέσθαι	δόσθαι

Participles (Passive and Middle)

Present Tense
being stood, or standing for oneself, etc.

ἱστάμενος, -η, -ον	τιθέμενος, -η, -ον	διδόμενος, -η, -ον

2nd Aorist (Middle only)
having been stood or having stood for oneself, etc.

(None)	θέμενος, -η, -ον	δόμενος, -η, -ον

Perfect: ἑστάμενος, τεθείμενος, δεδομένος

Exercise on the above Tenses of the Passive and Middle Voices in Verbs in -μι

(1) καὶ ἡ γλῶσσα πῦρ· ὁ κόσμος τῆς ἀδικίας ἡ γλῶσσα καθίσταται ἐν τοῖς μέλεσιν ἡμῶν, ἡ σπιλοῦσα ὅλον τὸ σῶμα καὶ φλογίζουσα τὸν τροχὸν τῆς γενέσεως καὶ φλογιζομένη ὑπὸ τῆς γεέννης. (Jas. 3:6) ἐστίν is to be understood in the first clause; the verb "to be" is often omitted; τῆς, not to be translated, being simply the article with an abstract noun; καθίσταται, is set, pres. indic. pass. of καθίστημι; σπιλοῦσα, nom., sing., fem., pres. partic. of σπιλέω, lit. "the (one) defiling"; φλογίζουσα, pres. partic. pass.; ὑπό, by (takes the genit.).

(2) ἔδοξεν γὰρ τῷ πνεύματι τῷ ἁγίῳ καὶ ἡμῖν μηδὲν πλέον ἐπιτίθεσθαι ὑμῖν βάρος πλὴν τούτων τῶν ἐπάναγκες. (Acts 15:28) ἔδοξεν, 3rd pers. sing., 1st aor. of δοκέω, "it seemed good"; from μηδέν to βάρος *is the accusative with the infinitive construction*, lit. "no greater burden to be put upon, etc."; πλέον, acc. neut. of πλέων; ἐπιτίθεσθαι, pres. infin. pass.; βάρος, acc. case (as βάρος is a neut. noun, μηδέν is neut. to agree with it); πλήν, except (takes the genit.); ἐπάναγκες (here only in New Testament).

(3) Διαιρέσεις δὲ χαρισμάτων εἰσίν, τὸ δὲ αὐτὸ πνεῦμα· 5 καὶ διαιρέσεις διακονιῶν εἰσιν, καὶ ὁ
αὐτὸς κύριος· 6 καὶ διαιρέσεις ἐνεργημάτων εἰσίν, ὁ δὲ αὐτὸς θεός ὁ ἐνεργῶν τὰ πάντα ἐν πᾶσιν. 7
ἑκάστῳ δὲ δίδοται ἡ φανέρωσις τοῦ πνεύματος πρὸς τὸ συμφέρον. 8 ᾧ μὲν γὰρ διὰ τοῦ πνεύματος
δίδοται λόγος σοφίας, ἄλλῳ δὲ λόγος γνώσεως κατὰ τὸ αὐτὸ πνεῦμα, 9 ἑτέρῳ πίστις ἐν τῷ αὐτῷ
πνεύματι, ἄλλῳ δὲ χαρίσματα ἰαμάτων ἐν τῷ ἑνὶ πνεύματι, 10 ἄλλῳ δὲ ἐνεργήματα δυνάμεων,
ἄλλῳ [δὲ] προφητεία, ἄλλῳ [δὲ] διακρίσεις πνευμάτων, ἑτέρῳ γένη γλωσσῶν, ἄλλῳ δὲ ἑρμηνεία
γλωσσῶν. (1 Cor. 12:4-10) τὸ αὐτό (see Lesson 5); ὁ ἐνεργῶν, the (one) energizing (working in), i.e., "who worketh in"; πᾶσιν, dat. plur., masc.; δίδοται, pres. passive (pres. of constant action "is given"); πρὸς, with a view to; συμφέρον, acc., neut., pres. partic. of συμφέρω, lit. "profiting" (i.e., "with a view to the profiting"); ᾧ, to the one (this is the meaning of the relative pronoun ὅς when followed by ἄλλος, another, in the next clause); κατὰ, according to; ἑτέρῳ, to another; ἑνί, dat. of εἷς, "one."

Note—The other tenses, active, passive and middle, of these three verb forms of the 2nd conjugation are formed like those of the 1st conjugation. The indicative mood and the 1st person of the tenses are given; the other moods and tenses can be formed on the model of λύω. The meanings are regular, save in ἵστημι (see below). Forms not given are not in New Testament.

Other Tenses of Verbs in –μι

Fut. Active

στήσω	θήσω	δώσω
(I shall cause to stand)	(I shall put)	(I shall give)

1st Aor. Act.

ἔστησα	ἔθηκα	ἔδωκα
(I caused to stand)	(I put)	(I gave)

Perf. Act.

ἕστηκα	τέθεικα	δέδωκα	
(I stand)	(I have put)	(I have given)	

Pluperf.

ἱστήκειν or εἱστήκειν		——	——
(I was standing)			

Fut. Passive

σταθήσομαι	τεθήσομαι	δοθήσομαι	
(I shall stand)		(I shall be put)	etc.

1st Aor. Pass.

ἐστάθην	ἐτέθην	ἐδόθην	
(I stood)	(I was put)	etc.	

Fut. Mid.

στήσομαι	θήσομαι	δώσομαι	
(I shall stand)		(I shall put)	etc.

Perf. Mid. or Pass.

——	τέθειμαι	δέδομαι	

Note the rough breathings on the perf. and pluperf. of ἵστημι. There are two forms of the perf. partic. act., ἑστηκώς and ἑστώς.

Note that the ending of the 1st aor. active of τίθημι and δίδωμι is -κα and not -σα as in λύω.

Exercise on the above Tenses of the Three Verbs

Translate and retranslate:—

(1) εἱστήκεισαν δὲ οἱ δοῦλοι καὶ οἱ ὑπηρέται ἀνθρακιὰν πεποιηκότες, ὅτι ψῦχος ἦν, καὶ ἐθερμαίνοντο· ἦν δὲ καὶ ὁ Πέτρος μετ' αὐτῶν ἑστὼς καὶ θερμαινόμενος. (John 18:18) εἱστήκεισαν, pluperf. tense, "they were standing" (not "they had stood," as in ordinary pluperfects); πεποιηκότες, nom., plur., masc., perf. partic. act. of ποιέω, "having made"; ἐθερμαίνοντο, imperf. middle, "were warming themselves"; ἑστώς, perf. partic., "standing."

(2) ὁ ἔχων τὴν νύμφην νυμφίος ἐστίν· ὁ δὲ φίλος τοῦ νυμφίου ὁ ἑστηκὼς καὶ ἀκούων αὐτοῦ χαρᾷ χαίρει διὰ τὴν φωνὴν τοῦ νυμφίου. αὕτη οὖν ἡ χαρὰ ἡ ἐμὴ πεπλήρωται. (John 3:29) ὁ ἔχων the (one) having, i.e., "he that hath"; ὁ ἑστηκώς, perf. partic. with present meaning, "the (one) standing," i.e., "who standeth"; ἀκούω takes the genit.; χαρᾷ, this dative has the meaning "with joy"; διά, because of; αὕτη ἡ χαρά (see Lesson 5, Personal Pronoun).

(3) 41 ἦν δὲ ἐν τῷ τόπῳ ὅπου ἐσταυρώθη κῆπος, καὶ ἐν τῷ κήπῳ μνημεῖον καινὸν ἐν ᾧ οὐδέπω οὐδεὶς ἦν τεθειμένος· 42 ἐκεῖ οὖν διὰ τὴν παρασκευὴν τῶν Ἰουδαίων, ὅτι ἐγγὺς ἦν τὸ μνημεῖον, ἔθηκαν τὸν Ἰησοῦν. (John 19:41-42) ἐσταυρώθη, 1st aor. passive of σταυρόω; οὐδέπω οὐδείς, lit. "not yet no one," but we must translate by "no one yet"; in Greek two negatives do not, as in English, make a positive, hence the οὐδέπω ("not yet") must be rendered by "yet"; τεθειμένος, perf. partic. passive; ἔθηκαν, 3rd pers. plur., 1st aor. indic.

(4) 31 οἱ πατέρες ἡμῶν τὸ μάννα ἔφαγον ἐν τῇ ἐρήμῳ, καθώς ἐστιν γεγραμμένον, Ἄρτον ἐκ τοῦ
οὐρανοῦ ἔδωκεν αὐτοῖς φαγεῖν. 32 εἶπεν οὖν αὐτοῖς ὁ Ἰησοῦς, Ἀμὴν ἀμὴν λέγω ὑμῖν, οὐ Μωϋσῆς
δέδωκεν ὑμῖν τὸν ἄρτον ἐκ τοῦ οὐρανοῦ, ἀλλ' ὁ πατήρ μου δίδωσιν ὑμῖν τὸν ἄρτον ἐκ τοῦ οὐρανοῦ
τὸν ἀληθινόν· 33 ὁ γὰρ ἄρτος τοῦ θεοῦ ἐστιν ὁ καταβαίνων ἐκ τοῦ οὐρανοῦ καὶ ζωὴν διδοὺς τῷ
κόσμῳ. 34 Εἶπον οὖν πρὸς αὐτόν, Κύριε, πάντοτε δὸς ἡμῖν τὸν ἄρτον τοῦτον. 35 εἶπεν αὐτοῖς ὁ
Ἰησοῦς, Ἐγώ εἰμι ὁ ἄρτος τῆς ζωῆς· ὁ ἐρχόμενος πρός ἐμὲ οὐ μὴ πεινάσῃ, καὶ ὁ πιστεύων εἰς ἐμὲ οὐ
μὴ διψήσει πώποτε. 36 ἀλλ' εἶπον ὑμῖν ὅτι καὶ ἑωράκατέ [με] καὶ οὐ πιστεύετε. 37 Πᾶν ὃ δίδωσίν
μοι ὁ πατὴρ πρὸς ἐμὲ ἥξει, καὶ τὸν ἐρχόμενον πρὸς ἐμὲ οὐ μὴ ἐκβάλω ἔξω, 38 ὅτι καταβέβηκα
ἀπὸ τοῦ οὐρανοῦ οὐχ ἵνα ποιῶ τὸ θέλημα τὸ ἐμὸν ἀλλὰ τὸ θέλημα τοῦ πέμψαντός με. 39 τοῦτο δέ
ἐστιν τὸ θέλημα τοῦ πέμψαντός με, ἵνα πᾶν ὃ δέδωκέν μοι μὴ ἀπολέσω ἐξ αὐτοῦ, ἀλλὰ ἀναστήσω
αὐτὸ [ἐν] τῇ ἐσχάτῃ ἡμέρᾳ. (John 6:31-39) ἔφαγον, 3rd pers. plur., 2nd aor. of ἐσθίω (irregular, see later); γεγραμμένον, perf. partic. passive of γράφω; note the different tenses of δίδωμι here, διδούς is pres. part., δός is 2nd aor. imperat.; in verse 35 ὁ ἐρχόμενος (pres. partic. of ἔρχομαι) is "he that cometh" (lit. "the (one) coming"—deponent); οὐ μὴ πεινάσῃ, this 1st aor. subjunc. with οὐ μή is an idiomatic construction used to express a strong negative assurance, "shall by no means," etc. Here again, the two negatives make a strong negative; the construction of οὐ μή with 1st aor. subjunc. is very important, and is a curious instance of the use of the 1st aor. with a future meaning; οὐ μὴ διψήσει (fut. of διψάω) has the same negative assurance, only now the fut. indic. is used, which is according to the usual meaning of that tense; εἶπον I said (2nd aor. of λέγω irregular); ἑωράκατε 2nd pers. plur., perf. indic. of ὁράω (irregular); in ver. 37 note ὅ with the accent, neut. of ὅς, which; ἥξει, fut. of ἥκω, I come (a different verb from ἔρχομαι); οὐ μὴ ἐκβάλω, another instance of οὐ μή with the fut. (see above, and for ἐκβάλω see on Liquid Verbs,

Lesson 21); καταβέβηκα perf. of καταβαίνω; ποιῶ, subjunc. of purpose after ἵνα; πέμψαντος, gen., sing., 1st aor. partic. of πέμπω, "of the (one) having sent"; ἀπολέσω 1st aor. subjunc. of ἀπόλλυμι "I loose," subjunc. of purpose after ἵνα; ἐξ αὐτοῦ, of it (ἐξ is for ἐκ, out of); ἀναστήσω fut. of ἀνίστημι.

Lesson 23

Special Verbs of the Second Conjugation

Special Verbs Belonging to Class I of -μι Conjugation

The following are conjugated like ἵστημι:—

ὀνίνημι, I benefit, once only in the New Testament, in Phil. 20, where ὀναίμην is 2nd aor. optat., middle, "mayI benefit."

πίμπρημι, I burn, once only in the New Testament, Acts 28:6, where πίμπρασθαι is pres. infin. passive.

φημί, I say; besides this 1st pers., only the following are in the New Testament—3rd pers. sing., φησί(ν); 3rd pers. plur., φασί, they say; 3rd pers. sing., imperfect, ἔφη, said he (very frequent).

Deponent Verbs:—

δύναμαι, I am able, -σαι, -ται, etc., as in ἵσταμαι; imper. ἐδυνάμην or ἠδυνάμην; infin. δύνασθαι; partic. δυνάμενος; fut. δυνήσομαι; 1st aor. ἐδυνήθην (or ἠδυνήθην)

ἐπίσταμαι, I know, feel sure (only in present tenses in the New Testament).

καθῆμαι, I sit; 2nd pers. sing. καθῇ (for καθῆσαι); imperf. ἐκαθήμην; imperat. κάθου; infin. καθῆσθαι; partic. καθήμενος.

κεῖμαι, I lie down (this and the preceding verb are really perfects).

ἀφίημι, I send away, let go, forgive

This is a compound of ἀπό (from) and ἵημι (I send) only used in the New Testament compounded with a preposition. The forms below (many of which are irregular) are those most frequent in the New Testament and should be memorized.

Present Indicative

1st p.	ἀφίημι	ἀθίεμεν (or -ομεν)
2nd p.	ἀφεῖς	ἀφίετε
3rd p.	ἀφίησι	ἀφιοῦσι

Imperf. 3rd pers. sing., ἤφιε: note that, contrary to the rule for the augment (that in a verb compounded with a preposition the verb itself receives the augment and not the preposition) the preposition is augmented here (see Mark 1:34; 11:16). Pres. imperat. 3rd pers. sing., ἀφιέτω; pres. infin. ἀφιέναι; fut. indic. ἀφήσω (regular); 1st aor. ἀφηκα; 2nd aor. imperat., 2nd pers. sing., ἄφες; 2nd pers. plur. ἄφετε; 2nd aor. subjunc. ἀφῶ, etc.; 2nd aor. partic. ἀφείς, ἀφεῖσα, ἀφέν; pres. indic. pass., 3rd pers. plur. ἀφίενται; perf. ἀφέωνται; fut. indic. pass. ἀφεθήσομαι (chiefly in 3rd sing. ἀπεθήσεται); 1st aor. pass. ἀφέθην.

Exercise on special verbs in Class I

Translate and re-translate:—

(1) καὶ ὁ Κορνήλιος ἔφη, Ἀπὸ τετάρτης ἡμέρας μέχρι ταύτης τῆς ὥρας ἤμην τὴν ἐνάτην προσευχόμενος ἐν τῷ οἴκῳ μου, καὶ ἰδοὺ ἀνὴρ ἔστη ἐνώπιόν μου ἐν ἐσθῆτι λαμπρᾷ 31 καὶ φησίν, Κορνήλιε, εἰσηκούσθη σου ἡ προσευχὴ καὶ αἱ ἐλεημοσύναι σου ἐμνήσθησαν ἐνώπιον τοῦ θεοῦ. (Acts 10:30-31) ἔφη, (see under φημί); Ἀπό, from (takes the genit.); μέχρι, until (takes the genit.); ἤμην, an alternative form of ἦν, I was (imperf. of εἰμί); τὴν ἐνάτην, the ninth (ὥραν, "hour" understood), accusative of time, "at the ninth hour", προσευχόμενος, pres. partic. (deponent): ἔστη, (see ἵστημι); ἐνώπιον before (takes the genit.); φησίν, (see φημί); εἰςηκούσθη 3rd pers. sing., 1st aor. pass. of εἰσακούω; ἐμνήσθησαν 3rd pers. plur., 1st aor. pass. of μιμνήσκομαι.

(2) Καὶ ἔρχεται εἰς οἶκον· καὶ συνέρχεται πάλιν [ὁ] ὄχλος, ὥστε μὴ δύνασθαι αὐτοὺς μηδὲ ἄρτον φαγεῖν. 21 καὶ ἀκούσαντες οἱ παρ' αὐτοῦ ἐξῆλθον κρατῆσαι αὐτόν· ἔλεγον γὰρ ὅτι ἐξέστη. 22 καὶ οἱ γραμματεῖς οἱ ἀπὸ Ἱεροσολύμων καταβάντες ἔλεγον ὅτι Βεελζεβοὺλ ἔχει καὶ ὅτι ἐν τῷ ἄρχοντι τῶν δαιμονίων ἐκβάλλει τὰ δαιμόνια. 23 καὶ προσκαλεσάμενος αὐτοὺς ἐν παραβολαῖς ἔλεγεν αὐτοῖς, Πῶς δύναται Σατανᾶς Σατανᾶν ἐκβάλλειν; 24 καὶ ἐὰν βασιλεία ἐφ' ἑαυτὴν μερισθῇ, οὐ δύναται σταθῆναι ἡ βασιλεία ἐκείνη· 25 καὶ ἐὰν οἰκία ἐφ' ἑαυτὴν μερισθῇ, οὐ δυνήσεται ἡ οἰκία ἐκείνη σταθῆναι [in earlier editions of Nestle: στῆναι]. (Mark 3:20-25) Notice the construction ὥστε μὴ δύνασθαι αὐτούς; the particle ὥστε, so that, is followed by the accusative with the infinitive to express result; here αὐτούς is the accusative subject of δύνασθαι, lit., "them to be able,"

the whole clause being, lit., "so that them not to be able," i.e., "so that they were not able" (cp. ὥστε, etc., in Matt. 8:24, and in Matt. 13:32, where ἐλθεῖν is 2nd aor. infin. of ἔρχομαι); ἄρτον is the object of φαγεῖν, which is 2nd aor. infin. of ἐσθίω (irreg.). In ver. 21 οἱ παρ' αὐτοῦ is "the (ones) beside Him," translated freely in A.V., "His friends"; ἀκούσαντες, 1st aor. partic., "having heard"; ἐξῆλθον, 3rd pers. plur. 2nd aor. of ἐξέρχομαι; κρατῆσαι, 1st aor. indic. of κρατέω, to lay hold (decisively); ἐξέστη, 2nd aor. indic. of ἐξίστημι, lit., "I stand out," and hence "am insane"; καταβάντες, nom., plur., masc., 2nd aor. partic. of καταβαίνω (a liquid verb, see Lesson 21); ἔλεγον, imperf. "were saying"; ἐν, by; προσκαλεσάμενος, 1st aor. partic. of the deponent προσκαλέομαι, "I call to myself." In verse 24 ἐφ' is for ἐπί, against; μερισθῇ, 1st aor. subjunc. pass. of μερίζω; σταθῆναι, 1st aor. infin. pass. of ἵστημι, to stand (not "to be stood"); στῆναι, 2nd aor. infin. active (here equivalent to the passive in meaning).

(3) Ἐὰν γὰρ ἀφῆτε τοῖς ἀνθρώποις τὰ παραπτώματα αὐτῶν, ἀφήσει καὶ ὑμῖν ὁ πατὴρ ὑμῶν ὁ οὐράνιος· 15 ἐὰν δὲ μὴ ἀφῆτε τοῖς ἀνθρώποις, οὐδὲ ὁ πατὴρ ὑμῶν ἀφήσει τὰ παραπτώματα ὑμῶν. (Matt. 6:14-15) ἀφῆτε, 2nd pers. plur., 2nd aor. subj. of ἀφίημι (the aor. expressing completeness and decision); ἀφήσει, fut. indic.

The Second Class of Verbs in -μι

Verbs in -νυμι or -ννυμι

Note—Most of these have a second form in the present and imperfect like λύω. Thus δείκνυμι, I show, has another form δεικνύω,

and ζώννυμι, I gird, has ζωννύω. All other tenses are formed without the -νυ- and follow the endings of the regular verb.

δείκνυμι, I show

Act. indic. pres.	δείκνυμι, -νυς, -νυσι (etc. throughout) or δεικνύω, -εις, -ει (like λύω)
Act. indic. imperf.	ἐδείκνυν, -νυς, -νυ, etc.
Act. imperat. pres.	δείκνυ (or -νυε), -νύτω, etc.
Act. subj. pres.	δεικνύω, -ῃς, ῃ, etc.
Act. opt. pres.	δεικνύοιμι, etc.
Act. infin. pres.	δεικνύναι

Act. partic. pres.	δεικνύς, -νῦσα, -νύν (or -νύων, etc.)
Pass. & Mid. indic. pres.	δείκνυμαι, etc.
Pass. & Mid. indic. imperf.	δεικνύμην, etc.
Pass. & Mid. imperat.	δείκνυσο, etc.
Pass. & Mid. subjunc.	δεικνύωμαι, etc.
Pass. & Mid. opt.	δεικνυοίμην, etc.
Pass. & Mid. infin.	δείκνυσθαι (or -νύεσθαι)
Pass. & Mid. partic.	δεικνύμενος, etc.

Other tenses: Act fut. δείξω; perf. δέδειχα; pass. and mid. perf. δέδειγμαι, etc.

Note that the stem of δείκνυμι ends in a consonant, δεικ-; the stem of ζώννυμι ends in a vowel, ζω-. This determines the fut. and 1st aor. endings, the vowel stems simply taking -σ-; e.g., ζώσω, ἔζωσα, etc.

Verbs Like δείκνυμι

μίγνυμι, I mix; 1st aor. ἔμιξα; perf. past pass. μεμίγμενος.

ἀπόλλυμι, I destroy (ἀπό and ὄλλυμι, the simple verb not being in the New Testament); fut. ἀπολέσω (or ἀπολῶ); 1st aor. ἀπώλεσα (note the ω augment); perfect, with intransitive meaning "I perish," ἀπολώλα; partic. ἀπολώλως; pres. partic. mid. ἀπολλύμενος (plur. "the perishing"); fut. mid. ἀπολοῦμαι (for -έσομαι, liquid verb); 2nd aor. ἀπωλόμην.

ὀμνύω (or ὄμνυμι), I swear; 1st aor. ὤμοσα; 1st aor. infin. ὀμόσαι.

ῥήγνυμι, I tear (also ῥήσσω); fut. ῥήξω; 1st aor. ἔῤῥηξα.

ἀμφιέννυμι, I clothe; perf. partic. ἠμφιεσμένον (Matt. 11:8: Luke 7:25).

σβέννυμι, I quench; fut. σβέσω; fut. pass. σβεσθήσομαι.

στρώννυμι, or στρωννύω, I strew, spread; 1st aor. ἔστρωσα; perf. partic. pass. ἐστρωμένος.

For κεράννυμι, I mix, κορέννυμι, I satisfy, ῥώννυμι, I strengthen, see the Lexicon.

Exercise on 2nd Class of Verbs in -μι

Translate and re-translate:—

(1) Ἄνδρες Ἰσραηλῖται, ἀκούσατε τοὺς λόγους τούτους· Ἰησοῦν τὸν Ναζωραῖον, ἄνδρα ἀποδεδειγμένον ἀπὸ τοῦ θεοῦ εἰς ὑμᾶς δυνάμεσι καὶ τέρασι καὶ σημείοις οἷς ἐποίησεν δι' αὐτοῦ ὁ

θεὸς ἐν μέσῳ ὑμῶν καθὼς αὐτοὶ οἴδατε. (Acts 2:22) ἀκούσατε, 1st aor. imperat.; ἀποδεδειγμένον, perf. partic. pass. of ἀποδείκνυμι (see δείκνυμι above); δυνάμεσι, dat. plur. of δύναμις; οἷς, note that this dative plural is attracted to the case of the preceding dative nouns; the strict grammatical construction would be ἅ, acc. plur. as the direct object of ἐποίησεν ("which He did"), but the ἅ becomes οἷς by attraction of the relative pronoun to the preceding noun.

(2) Τίς ἄνθρωπος ἐξ ὑμῶν ἔχων ἑκατὸν πρόβατα καὶ ἀπολέσας ἐξ αὐτῶν ἓν οὐ καταλείπει τὰ ἐνενήκοντα ἐννέα ἐν τῇ ἐρήμῳ καὶ πορεύεται ἐπὶ τὸ ἀπολωλὸς ἕως εὕρῃ αὐτό; (Luke 15:4) ἑκατόν, a hundred, is indeclinable; ἀπολέσας, 1st aor. partic. of ἀπόλλυμι (see above), having lost; ἐπί, after; ἀπολωλός, acc. sing., neut., perf. partic. (see above); εὕρῃ, 2nd aor. subjunc. of εὑρίσκω.

(3) Καὶ καθ᾽ ὅσον οὐ χωρὶς ὁρκωμοσίας· οἱ μὲν γὰρ χωρὶς ὁρκωμοσίας εἰσὶν ἱερεῖς γεγονότες, 21 ὁ δὲ μετὰ ὁρκωμοσίας διὰ τοῦ λέγοντος πρὸς αὐτόν· Ὤμοσεν κύριος, καὶ οὐ μεταμεληθήσεται· Σὺ ἱερεὺς εἰς τὸν αἰῶνα. (Heb. 7:20, 21) καθ᾽ ὅσον, according as, χωρὶς, apart from (takes genit.); οἱ μέν, they indeed (note this use of the article alone, as a personal pronoun, so ὁ δέ, but He, in the next clause); γεγονότες, nom., plur., masc., perf. partic. of γίνομαι, I become (see later) with εἰσίν this means "they have become"; μετά, with; λέγοντος, gen. sing., masc., pres. partic.; Ὤμοσεν, 1st aor. of ὄμνυμι; μεταμεληθήσεται, fut. of the deponent verb μεταμέλομαι, "I repent."

(4) κἀκεῖνος ὑμῖν δείξει ἀνάγαιον μέγα ἐστρωμένον· ἐκεῖ ἑτοιμάσατε. (Luke 22:12) δείξει, (see δείκνυμι); ἐστρωμένον, perf. partic. of στρώννυμι; ἑτοιμάσατε, 2nd pers. plur., 1st aor. imperat. of ἑτοιμάζω.

Lesson 24

Irregular and Defective Verbs

Irregular and Defective Verbs

(1) Some Irregular Futures and 1st Aorists

(*a*) Whereas verbs in -εω make future in -ήσω, the following have -έσω:—ἀρκέω I suffice; ἐπαινέω, I praise (1st aor. ἐπήνεσα); καλέω, I call; τελέω, I finish; φορέω, I carry. The following makes future and 1st aor. in -ευ-:—πνέω, I blow, 1st aor. ἔπνευσα. So καίω, I burn, makes καύσω, and κλαίω, I weep, makes κλαύσω.

(*b*) Some verbs in -ίζω make fut. in -ιῶ instead of -ίσω:—ἀφορίζω, I separate; ἐλπίζω, I hope; κομίζω, carry. In these the first aorist resumes the -ς, e.g., ἀφώρισα.

(*c*) Several active verbs have their future in middle form. The following are common and should be memorized:—

ἀκούω	I hear,	fut.	ἀκούσομαι
ζάω	I live,	"	ζήσομαι
λαμβάνω	I take,	"	λήμψομαι
φεύγω	I flee,	"	φεύξομαι
πίνω	I drink,	"	πίομαι

(*d*) Some liquid verbs in λ transpose the vowel and the λ in the fut., 1st aor. and perf. passive:—βάλλω, I throw, has fut. pass. βληθήσομαι; 1st aor. ἐβλήθην; perf. βέβλημαι: καλέω, I call, has κληθήσομαι, ἐκλήθην, κέκλημαι.

(2) Some Irregular Perfects and Pluperfects

(*a*) Some verbs, instead of reduplicating by the consonant, like λέλυκα, do so by the vowel ε, where the consonant would not sound well: thus ξηραίνω, I wither, has perf. pass. ἐξήραμμαι.

(*b*) Some have a double reduplication, i.e., by both the consonant and a vowel:—ἀκούω, I hear, has perf. ἀκήκοα; ἔρχομαι, I come, has perf. ἐλήλυθα.

(*c*) Verbs beginning with θ reduplicate by τ, sometimes changing the vowel:—τρέφω, I nourish, makes perf. τέτροφα, and perf. pass. τέθραμμαι; θραύω, I crush, makes perf. pass. τέθραυσμαι (inserting a ς, see Luke 4:18).

Irregular and Defective Verbs (continued)

The following list of irregular verbs should be memorized thoroughly. Only the first person singular of the irregular tenses, Indicative, is given; the other person endings are according to the regular verb. If the following are committed to memory, the irregular forms, with which the reader constantly meets in the New Testament, provide no difficulty.

Note—The verbs marked with a dagger are those which derive their forms from different verbal stems. The tenses are thus made up of different verb roots with the same meaning.

Principle Parts of Irregular Verbs

Present	**Future**	**1st Aorist**	**Perfect**	**2nd Aorist**	**1st Aorist Passive**	
ἄγω (lead)	ἄξω	ἦξα		ἤγαγον		
†	αἱρέω (take)	αἱρήσω		ἥρηκα	εἷλον	ἡρέθην
ἀποθνήσκω (die)		ἀποθανοῦμαι			ἀπέθανον	
ἀναβαίνω (go up)		ἀναβήσομαι		ἀναβέβηκα	ἀνέβην	
γινώσκω (know)		γνώσομαι		ἔγνωκα	ἔγνων	ἐγνώσθην
γίνομαι (become)		γενήσομαι		γέγονα	ἐγενόμην	ἐγενήθην
or			passive			

γίγνομαι			γεγένημαι			
ἐγείρω (arouse)		ἐγερῶ	ἤγειρα	ἐγήγερκα		ἠγέρθην
†	ἔρχομαι (come)		ἐλεύσομαι		ἐλήλυθα	ἦλθον
†	ἐσθίω (eat)	φάγομαι			ἔφαγον	
ἔχω (have)	ἕξω		ἔσχηκα	ἔσχον		
λαμβάνω (receive)		λή(μ)ψομαι		εἴληφα	ἔλαβον	ἐλήφθην
			passive			
			εἴλημμαι			
†	λέγω (say)	λέξω	ἔλεξα	passive	εἶπον	ἐλέχθην or
	or		λέλεγμαι		ἐρρέθην or	
	ἐρῶ		εἴρηκα		ἐρρήθην	
			εἴρημαι			
μανθάνω (learn)		μαθήσομαι		μεμάθηκα	ἔμαθον	
†	ὁράω (see)	ὄψομαι		ἑώρακα	* εἶδον	ὤφθην
πάσχω (suffer)				πέπονθα	ἔπαθον	
πίπτω (fall)	πεσοῦμαι		πέπτωκα	ἔπεσον		
†	τρέχω (run)	δραμοῦμαι			ἔδραμον	
τυγχάνω (happen)		τεύξομαι			ἔτυχον	
†	φέρω (bear)	οἴσω	ἤνεγκα	ἐνήνοχα	ἤνεγκον	ᾘνέχθην

* *Note*— οἶδα, I know, is a perfect with a present meaning; it is connected with εἶδον, I saw; the pluperfect is ᾔδειν, I knew; the 2nd aorist infin. is ἰδεῖν and the 2nd perfect infin. εἰδέναι.

Exercise on Irregular Verbs

Translate and retranslate:—

(1) τί με ἐρωτᾷς; ἐρώτησον τοὺς ἀκηκοότας τί ἐλάλησα αὐτοῖς· ἴδε οὗτοι οἴδασιν ἃ εἶπον ἐγώ. 22 ταῦτα δὲ αὐτοῦ εἰπόντος εἷς παρεστηκὼς τῶν ὑπηρετῶν ἔδωκεν ῥάπισμα τῷ Ἰησοῦ εἰπών, Οὕτως ἀποκρίνῃ τῷ ἀρχιερεῖ; (John 18:21, 22) τί, why?; ἐρωτᾷς, 2nd pers. sing., pres. indic. of ἐρωτάω;

ἐρώτησον, 1st aor. imperat.; ἀκηκοότας, acc., plur., masc. of ἀκηκοώς, -υῖα, -ός (gen. -οοτος), perf. partic. of ἀκούω (for the declension of the participle see Lesson 10); τί, what; οἴδασιν, 3rd pers. plur. (see note at foot of above list); εἶπον, (see λέγω above); note the emphatic position of ἐγώ. In ver. 22 note αὐτοῦ εἰπόντος; these genitives (i.e., a pronoun or noun, with the participle of a verb each in the genitive case) form what is known as the genitive absolute construction; it cannot be put literally in English; the actual English equivalent is "he having said", it is best rendered by "when he had said"; this construction is sometimes used when the main sentence has a different subject (here εἷς, one); παρεστηκώς, perf. partic. of παρίστημι, I stand by ("one standing by of the attendants"); ἔδωκεν, 1st aor. ("gave"); εἰπών, 2nd aor. partic. of λέγω ("saying"); ἀποκρίνῃ, 2nd pers. sing., pres. indic. (takes the dative).

(2) Μετὰ ταῦτα ἀπῆλθεν ὁ Ἰησοῦς πέραν τῆς θαλάσσης τῆς Γαλιλαίας τῆς Τιβεριάδος. 2 ἠκολούθει δὲ αὐτῷ ὄχλος πολύς, ὅτι ἐθεώρουν [In earlier editions of Nestle: ἑώρων] τὰ σημεῖα ἃ ἐποίει ἐπὶ τῶν ἀσθενούντων. (John 6:1, 2) Μετὰ, after; ἀπῆλθεν 2nd aor. of ἀπέρχομαι (see list); ἠκολούθει, 3rd pers. sing., imperf. of ἀκολουθέω (takes dat.); ἑώρων, 3rd pers. plur., imperf. of ὁράω; ἐπὶ upon (with gen.); ἀσθενούντων, gen., plur., pres. partic. of ἀσθενέω.

(3) καὶ εὐθὺς ἀποστείλας ὁ βασιλεὺς σπεκουλάτορα ἐπέταξεν ἐνέγκαι τὴν κεφαλὴν αὐτοῦ. καὶ ἀπελθὼν ἀπεκεφάλισεν αὐτὸν ἐν τῇ φυλακῇ 28 καὶ ἤνεγκεν τὴν κεφαλὴν αὐτοῦ ἐπὶ πίνακι καὶ ἔδωκεν αὐτὴν τῷ κορασίῳ, καὶ τὸ κοράσιον ἔδωκεν αὐτὴν τῇ μητρὶ αὐτῆς. (Mark 6:27, 28) ἀποστείλας, 1st aor. partic. of ἀποστέλλω; ἐπέταξεν, 3rd pers. sing., 1st aor. of ἐπιτάσσω; ἐνέγκαι, 1st aor. infin. of φέρω (see list); ἀπελθών, 2nd aor. partic. of ἀπέρχομαι; ἀπεκεφάλισεν, 1st aor. of ἀποκεφαλίζω; ἤνεγκεν (see φέρω).

(4) καὶ ἰδοὺ εἷς τῶν μετὰ Ἰησοῦ ἐκτείνας τὴν χεῖρα ἀπέσπασεν τὴν μάχαιραν αὐτοῦ καὶ πατάξας τὸν δοῦλον τοῦ ἀρχιερέως ἀφεῖλεν αὐτοῦ τὸ ὠτίον. (Matt. 26:51) τῶν μετὰ, of the (ones) with; ἐκτείνας, 1st aor. partic. of ἐκτείνω, "having stretched out"; ἀπέσπασεν, 1st aor. of ἀπο σπάω; πατάξας, 1st aor. partic. of πατάσσω; ἀφεῖλεν, 2nd aor. of ἀφαιρέω (see αἱρέω).

(5) ἐγὼ ἐλήλυθα ἐν τῷ ὀνόματι τοῦ πατρός μου, καὶ οὐ λαμβάνετέ με· ἐὰν ἄλλος ἔλθῃ ἐν τῷ ὀνόματι τῷ ἰδίῳ, ἐκεῖνον λήμψεσθε. (John 5:43) ἐλήλυθα (see ἔρχομαι, above); ἔλθῃ, 2nd aor. subjunc. of the same; τῷ ἰδίῳ, his own; λήμψεσθε, fut. of λαμβάνω.

(6) πειρασμὸς ὑμᾶς οὐκ εἴληφεν εἰ μὴ ἀνθρώπινος· πιστὸς δὲ ὁ θεός, ὃς οὐκ ἐάσει ὑμᾶς πειρασθῆναι ὑπὲρ ὃ δύνασθε ἀλλὰ ποιήσει σὺν τῷ πειρασμῷ καὶ τὴν ἔκβασιν τοῦ δύνασθαι ὑπενεγκεῖν. (1 Cor. 10:13) εἴληφεν, 3rd pers. sing., perf. of λαμβάνω; εἰ μὴ, except (lit. "if not"). In the next sentence, ἐστί is purposely omitted; ἐάσει, fut. of ἐάω; πειρασθῆναι, 1st aor. infin. pass. of πειράζω; τοῦ δύνασθαι, this construction of the genit. of the article with the infinitive is

used to signify purpose, lit., "(in order to) the being able"; ὑπενεγκεῖν, 2nd aor. infin. of ὑποφέρω (see above).

(7) ἀπελθόντες δὲ εὗρον καθὼς εἰρήκει αὐτοῖς καὶ ἡτοίμασαν τὸ πάσχα. (Luke 22:13) ἀπελθόντες, 2nd aor. partic. of ἀπέρχομαι, "having gone away"; εὗρον, 3rd pers. plur., 2nd aor. indic. of εὑρίσκω; εἰρήκει, 3rd pers. sing., plupf. of λέγω, "He had said"; ἡτοίμασαν, 1st aor. indic. of ἑτοιμάζω.

Impersonal Verbs

These are used only in the 3rd pers. sing., and in English are translated with the pronoun "it."

The chief impersonal verbs are:—

δεῖ, it is necessary, one ought; imperf. ἔδει; subjunc. δέῃ; infin. δεῖν.

δοκεῖ, it seems (from δοκέω).

μέλει, it is a care.

πρέπει, it becomes; imperf. ἔπρεπε; pres. partic. πρέπον, becoming. χρή, it is expedient, fitting (only in Jas. 3:10).

Exercise on Impersonal Verbs

Translate and retranslate:—

(1) τὸ γεγεννημένον ἐκ τῆς σαρκὸς σάρξ ἐστιν, καὶ τὸ γεγεννημένον ἐκ τοῦ πνεύματος πνεῦμά ἐστιν. 7 μὴ θαυμάσῃς ὅτι εἶπόν σοι, Δεῖ ὑμᾶς γεννηθῆναι ἄνωθεν. (John 3:6,7) γεγεννημένον, nom., sing., neut., perf. partic. pass. of γεννάω. With the article, τὸ, this, lit., is "the (thing) having been born," i.e., "that which has been born"; θαυμάσῃς, 2nd pers. sing., 1st aor. subjunc. of θαυμάζω; *this tense of the subjunc. with μή is used to express a negative command and this is a substitute for the imperative mood*— "do not marvel"; Δεῖ, it is necessary, is followed by the accusative with the infinitive construction, ὑμᾶς (the accusative) with γεννηθῆναι, 1st aor. infin. passive of γεννάω, lit. "you to be born"; accordingly the whole phrase "it is necessary you to be born" is to be rendered by "ye must be born." See the same construction in verse 30, "it is necessary Him to increase, but me decrease" (ἐλαττοῦσθαι, contracted for —όεσθαι, is pres. infin. of ἐλαττόμαι). See again 4:4, where ἔδει is imperfect, "it was necessary"; διέρχεσθαι, to go through (διά and ἔρχομαι compounded), "it was necessary Him to go through" is "He must needs go through."

(2) δεῖ γὰρ τὸν ἐπίσκοπον ἀνέγκλητον εἶναι ὡς θεοῦ οἰκονόμον, μὴ αὐθάδη, μὴ ὀργίλον, μὴ πάροινον, μὴ πλήκτην, μὴ αἰσχροκερδῆ, 8 ἀλλὰ φιλόξενον φιλάγαθον σώφρονα δίκαιον ὅσιον

ἐγκρατῆ, 9 ἀντεχόμενον τοῦ κατὰ τὴν διδαχὴν πιστοῦ λόγου, ἵνα δυνατὸς ᾖ καὶ παρακαλεῖν ἐν τῇ διδασκαλίᾳ τῇ ὑγιαινούσῃ καὶ τοὺς ἀντιλέγοντας ἐλέγχειν. (Tit. 1:7-9) This accus. with the infin. after δεῖ should be clear, and the rest of the verse can be translated with the help of the Lexicon; note that αὐθάδη is accus., sing., masc. of αὐθάδης, -ης, -ες (see ἀλήθης Lesson 10); ἀντεχόμενον, is pres. partic. of the deponent verb ἀντέχομαι (it takes the genit.); καί … καί, both … and; ἀντιλέγοντας, acc., plur., pres. partic.

(3) λέγει, Ναί. καὶ ἐλθόντα εἰς τὴν οἰκίαν προέφθασεν αὐτὸν ὁ Ἰησοῦς λέγων, Τί σοι δοκεῖ, Σίμων; οἱ βασιλεῖς τῆς γῆς ἀπὸ τίνων λαμβάνουσιν τέλη ἢ κῆνσον; ἀπὸ τῶν υἱῶν αὐτῶν ἢ ἀπὸ τῶν ἀλλοτρίων; (Matt. 17:25) ἐλθόντα, acc., sing., 2nd aor. partic. of ἔρχομαι, agreeing with αὐτόν, "him coming. Jesus anticipated" (προέφθασεν, 1st aor. of προφθάνω, rendered "prevented" in A.V. and "spake first" in R.V.); Τί σοι δοκεῖ, what seems it to thee? (impersonal).

Lesson 25

Notes on the Cases

Notes on the Cases

The Genitive

(1) The genitive is used (*a*) *with several verbs expressive of sense* or *mental affections,* e.g., ἀκούω, I hear; γεύομαι, I taste; θιγγάνω, I touch; ἐπιθυμέω, I desire; μνημονεύω, I remember; λανθάνω, I forget; (*b*) *with verbs of accusing, and condemning, etc.,* whether of the person accused or of the charge. See, e.g., ἐγκαλέω in Acts 19:40, and κατηγορέω in John 5:45; (*c*) *with verbs and adjectives of filling, lacking, etc.,* e.g., ἐμπίπλημι in Luke 1:53, γεμίζω in John 2:7, ὑστερέω in Rom. 3:23, and λείπω in Jas. 1:5; (*d*) *with verbs of separations, difference, hindrance,* e.g., μεθίστημι in Luke 16:4, κωλύω in Acts 27:43, παύω in 1 Pet. 4:1, ἀπαλλοτριοῦμαι in Eph. 2:12, ἀστοχέω in 1 Tim. 1:6, διαφέρω in 1 Cor. 15:41, and in Matt. 10:31, where the meaning is "to be superior"; (*e*) *with verbs of ruling,* e.g., ἄρχειν, etc., in Mark 10:42.

(2) For the genitive after adjectives in the *comparative degree* see later.

(3) *Adverbs of time* take the genitive, e.g., ὀψέ, late (Matt 28:1) λίαν πρωΐ, very early, τῆς μιᾶς σαββάτων, an idiom for "the first day of the week" (Mark 16:2); ἅπαξ, once (Heb. 9:7).

(4) The following *genitive phrases* are used instead of prepositions with a noun: νυκτός, by night (Matt. 2:14); ἡμέρας, by day (Luke 18:7); τοῦ λοιποῦ, for the rest (Gal. 6:17); ποίας (ὁδοῦ), by what (way) (Luke 5:19).

(5) The *objective genitive* expresses the object of a feeling or action, and must be distinguished from the ordinary subjective genitive expressing possession. Thus προσευχῇ τοῦ θεοῦ in Luke 6:12, is "prayer to God" (the preceding article is not to be translated); in Rom. 10:2, ζῆλον θεοῦ is "zeal towards God"; in 2 Cor. 10:5, τοῦ Χριστοῦ is "to Christ"; so with εἰδώλου in 1 Cor. 8:7; and τοῦ υἱοῦ in Gal. 2:20, "in the Son."

(6) The genitive is used in expressing *price, penalty, equivalence, etc.,*

ἀσσαρίου in Matt. 10:29, is "for a farthing"; cp. τοσούτου, for so much (Acts 5:8), and δηναρίου, for a penny (Rev. 6:6).

(7) *The genitive absolute.* The genitive of a noun in agreement with a participle is frequently used in a subordinate sentence without being dependent on any other words, and the genitive refers to some other person or thing than subject of the principal sentence. In translation, this construction is rendered in various ways, e.g., Matt. 17:9, καταβαινόντων αὐτῶν is, lit., "they descending (from the mountain)," i.e., "as they were coming down, etc." The principal sentence has another subject, viz., ὁ Ἰησοῦς. The construction is called "absolute," because it is disconnected from the main sentence. Thus, again, in Matt. 9:33, ἐκβληθέντος τοῦ δαιμονίου is "the demon having being cast out" (gen. of 1st aor. pass. of ἐκβάλλω), and the main sentence is ἐλάλησεν ὁ κωφός, the dumb man spake.

Exercise

Translate and re-translate:—

(1) Ἐγένετο δέ μοι ὑποστρέψαντι εἰς Ἰερουσαλὴμ καὶ προσευχομένου μου ἐν τῷ ἱερῷ γενέσθαι με ἐν ἐκστάσει. 18 καὶ ἰδεῖν αὐτὸν λέγοντά μοι. (Acts 22:17, 18a) Ἐγένετο, it came to pass; προσευχομένου μου, gen. absolute, "while I was praying"; γενέσθαι με, acc. with the infin., lit., "me to become," i.e., "that I became" or "that I fell"; so ἰδεῖν, lit., "(me) to see," i.e., "that I saw." This acc. with infin. construction follows the impersonal verb "it came to pass" (see later).

(2) ζητούντων τε αὐτὸν ἀποκτεῖναι ἀνέβη φάσις τῷ χιλιάρχῳ τῆς σπείρης ὅτι ὅλη συγχύννεται Ἰερουσαλήμ. (Acts 21:31) ζητούντων is the gen. absolute with the pronoun αὐτῶν not expressed but understood, lit., "(they) seeking (to kill him)," i.e., "as they were seeking to kill him"; ἀνέβη, 2nd aor. of ἀναβαίνω; συγχύννεται is present tense but in English must be rendered by the past, "was in an uproar" (for this construction see Lesson 32).

(3) καὶ ὑμεῖς ὅμοιοι ἀνθρώποις προσδεχομένοις τὸν κύριον ἑαυτῶν πότε ἀναλύσῃ ἐκ τῶν γάμων, ἵνα ἐλθόντος καὶ κρούσαντος εὐθέως ἀνοίξωσιν αὐτῷ. (Luke 12:36) ἐλθόντος and κρούσαντος

are gen. absolute participles agreeing with αὐτοῦ, understood, lit. "he coming and knocking"; ἀνοίξωσιν, 1st aor. subjunc. of ἀνοίγω, subjunc. of purpose after ἵνα.

(4) Ἀναχωρησάντων δὲ αὐτῶν ἰδοὺ ἄγγελος κυρίου φαίνεται κατ' ὄναρ τῷ Ἰωσὴφ λέγων, Ἐγερθεὶς παράλαβε τὸ παιδίον καὶ τὴν μητέρα αὐτοῦ καὶ φεῦγε εἰς Αἴγυπτον καὶ ἴσθι ἐκεῖ ἕως ἂν εἴπω σοι· μέλλει γὰρ Ἡρῴδης ζητεῖν τὸ παιδίον τοῦ ἀπολέσαι αὐτό. (Matt. 2:13) Note the opening gen. absolute phrase, lit., "they having departed"; Ἐγερθείς, nom., sing., masc., 1st aor. partic. pass. of ἐγείρω; παράλαβε, 2nd aor. imperat. of παραλαμβάνω; εἴπω, 2nd aor. subjunc. of λέγω (the ἂν expresses indefiniteness, but is not to be translated); τοῦ ἀπολέσαι, 1st aor. infin. of ἀπόλλυμι, with the article, a phrase of purpose, "to destroy," the infin. being a noun in the genitive case, gen. of intention.

The Dative

(1) Verbs denoting *intercourse, companionship, etc.,* take the dative. See the dative after ἀκολουθέω in Matt. 9:9; after κολλάω in Luke 15:15; after ὁμιλέω in Acts 24:26.

(2) After the verbs "to be," "to become," the dative often denotes *possession.* Thus in Matt. 18:12, ἐὰν γένηταί τινι ἀνθρώπῳ is lit. "if there be to any man," i.e., "if any man have."

(3) Verbs denoting *assistance* take the dative. See Matt. 4:11 (διηκόνουν, "they were ministering αὐτῷ, to Him"); also 15:25.

(4) Also verbs expressing *mental affections;* e.g., ὀργίζομαι, I am angry (Matt. 5:22); ἀρέσκω, I please (Gal. 1:10); πιστεύω, I believe (Matt. 21:25); πείθομαι and ὑπακούω, I obey (Acts 5:36-37; Rom. 10:16); προσκυνέω, I worship (Matt. 2:2).

(5) The dative expresses *the mode of an action, or the circumstance attending it.* See, e.g., τῇ προθέσει (Acts 11:23); χάριτι (1 Cor. 10:30); παντὶ τρόπῳ, in every way, etc. (Phil. 1:18); προσυχῇ, with prayer (James 5:17).

(6) The dative expresses *cause or motive.* See, e.g., τῇ ἀπιστίᾳ, through unbelief, and τῇ πίστει, through faith (Rom. 4:20).

(7) The dative expresses *instrument.* See, e.g., πυρί, with fire (Matt. 3:12); ἀδικίᾳ, etc., by (all) iniquity, etc. (Rom. 1:29); χάριτι, by grace, (Eph. 2:5-8); ἰδίᾳ δόξῃ καὶ ἀρετῇ, by His own glory and virtue (2 Pet. 1:3). So χράομαι, I use, takes this dative; see παρρησίᾳ (2 Cor. 3:12).

(8) The dative sometimes is used to express *the agent.* Note αὐτῷ, by Him (Luke 23:15); ὑμῖν, by you (2 Cor. 12:20); αὐτοῖς, by them (Luke 24:35).

(9) The dative expresses *the sphere in which a quality exists.* See τῷ πνεύματι, in spirit (Matt. 5:3); τοῖς ποσίν, in his feet (Acts 14:8); φύσει, in nature (Eph. 2:3).

(10) The dative is used in some expressions of time, either a period or a point. For the period see ἔτεσι, for (about 450) years (Acts 13:20); for the point see τοῖς γενεσίοις αὐτοῦ, on his birthday (Mark 6:21); τῇ τρίτῃ ἡμέρᾳ, on the third day (Matt. 20:19).

The Accusative

(1) A verb sometimes takes a noun in the accus. case which is akin to it in meaning, and so the meaning of the verb is extended. This is known as the *cognate accusative.* Thus, in Matt. 2:10, ἐχάρησαν χαρὰν μεγάλην is, lit., "they rejoiced a great joy," i.e., "they rejoiced exceedingly." So in Luke 2:8, φυλάσσοντες φυλακάς, "watching watches," is "keeping watch." In Col. 2:19, αὔξει τὴν αὔξησιν is "with the increase."

(2) An accusative sometimes defines the verb more closely; this is called *the accusative of closer definition.* It must be rendered in English by a prepositional phrase. Thus in John 6:10, τὸν ἀριθμόν is "in number"; in Phil. 1:11, καρπόν is "with the fruit."

(3) *Relations of time and space* are frequently expressed by the accusative, e.g., Luke 22:41, λίθου βολήν, a stone's throw; so σταδίους in John 6:19; in Rev. 3:3, ποίαν ὥραν, what hour, is acc. of time; see ἔτη, years (acc., plur., neut.) in Luke 15:29.

(4) The accusative is sometimes *irregular,* some word or phrase being understood to complete the sense. See, e.g., ὁδόν in Matt. 4:15; γνώστην in Acts 26:3; τὸ ἀδύνατον, the impossibility, in Rom. 8:3.

Exercise

Translate and retranslate:—

(1) Ταπεινώθητε οὖν ὑπὸ τὴν κραταιὰν χεῖρα τοῦ θεοῦ, ἵνα ὑμᾶς ὑψώσῃ ἐν καιρῷ, 7 πᾶσαν τὴν μέριμναν ὑμῶν ἐπιρίψαντες ἐπ' αὐτόν, ὅτι αὐτῷ μέλει περὶ ὑμῶν. 8 Νήψατε, γρηγορήσατε. ὁ ἀντίδικος ὑμῶν διάβολος ὡς λέων ὠρυόμενος περιπατεῖ ζητῶν [τινα] καταπιεῖν· 9 ᾧ ἀντίστητε στερεοὶ τῇ πίστει εἰδότες τὰ αὐτὰ τῶν παθημάτων τῇ ἐν [τῷ] κόσμῳ ὑμῶν ἀδελφότητι ἐπιτελεῖσθαι. (1 Pet. 5:6-9) αὐτῷ μέλει, lit., "it-is-a-care to Him" (the verb is impersonal), i.e., "He careth"; ἀντίστητε, 2nd aor. imperat. of ἀνθίστημι, governing the dative ᾧ; τὰ αὐτὰ ... ἐπιτελεῖσθαι, accus. with the infin., after εἰδότες, "knowing the same things to be accomplished"; τῇ ... ἀδελφότητι, in the brotherhood (see Rule 9 under the Dative).

(2) πᾶσα γὰρ φύσις θηρίων τε καὶ πετεινῶν, ἑρπετῶν τε καὶ ἐναλίων δαμάζεται καὶ δεδάμασται τῇ φύσει τῇ ἀνθρωπίνῃ, 8 τὴν δὲ γλῶσσαν οὐδεὶς δαμάσαι δύναται ἀνθρώπων, ἀκατάστα τον κακόν, μεστὴ ἰοῦ θανατηφόρου. 9 ἐν αὐτῇ εὐλογοῦμεν τὸν κύριον καὶ πατέρα καὶ ἐν αὐτῇ καταρώμεθα τοὺς ἀνθρώπους τοὺς καθ᾽ ὁμοίωσιν θεοῦ γεγονότας, 10 ἐκ τοῦ αὐτοῦ στόματος ἐξέρχεται εὐλογία καὶ κατάρα. οὐ χρή, ἀδελφοί μου, ταῦτα οὕτως γίνεσθαι. (James 3:7-10) τῇ φύσει, etc., dat. of the agent (see Rule 8) "by human nature."

(3) Μὴ οὖν τις ὑμᾶς κρινέτω ἐν βρώσει καὶ ἐν πόσει ἢ ἐν μέρει ἑορτῆς ἢ νεομηνίας ἢ σαββάτων· 17 ἅ ἐστιν σκιὰ τῶν μελλόντων, τὸ δὲ σῶμα τοῦ Χριστοῦ. 18 μηδεὶς ὑμᾶς καταβραβευέτω θέλων ἐν ταπεινοφροσύνῃ καὶ θρησκείᾳ τῶν ἀγγέλων, ἃ ἑόρακεν ἐμβατεύων, εἰκῇ φυσιούμενος ὑπὸ τοῦ νοὸς τῆς σαρκὸς αὐτοῦ, 19 καὶ οὐ κρατῶν τὴν κεφαλήν, ἐξ οὗ πᾶν τὸ σῶμα διὰ τῶν ἁφῶν καὶ συνδέσμων ἐπιχορηγούμενον καὶ συμβιβαζόμενον αὔξει τὴν αὔξησιν τοῦ θεοῦ. (Col. 2:16-19) κρινέτω and καταβραβευέτω are 3rd pers. sing., pres. imperat.; ἑόρακεν, 3rd pers. sing., perf. indic. of ὁράω.

Lesson 26

The Comparison of Adjectives

The Comparison of Adjectives

There are three degrees of comparison—Positive, Comparative, Superlative.

The regular method of forming the comparative and superlative degrees is by adding -τερος and -τατος to the stem of adjectives of the 2nd declension in -ος, and to the stem of those of the 3rd declension in -ης.

Examples

ἰσχυρός, -ά, -όν, strong (stem ἰσχυρο-); ἰσχυρότερος, -α, -ον, stronger; ἰσχυρότατος, -η, -ον, strongest.

ἀληθής, -ής, -ές, true (stem ἀληθεσ-); ἀληθέστερος, -α, -ον, truer; ἀληθέστατος, -η, -ον, truest.

Note—When the last vowel but one of the adjective is short, the final ο of the stem is lengthened to -ω. Thus σοφός, wise, σοφώτερος, σοφώτατος; νέος, new, νεώτερος, νεώτατος.

The following form their degrees of comparison irregularly:—

Positive	**Comparative**	**Superlative**
ἀγαθός, good	κρείσσων, (or -ττων), better	κράτιστος, best
κακός, bad	χείρων, or ἥσσων, or ἥττων, worse	χείριστος, worst
πολύς, much or many	πλείων, or πλέων, more	πλεῖστος, most

μικρός, little	μικρότερος or ἐλάσσων, less	ἐλάχιστος, least
μέγας, great	μείζων, greater	μέγιστος, greatest

Note 1—These comparatives in -ων are declined like σώφρων (acc. -ονα, gen. -ονος, etc., see Lesson 10); μείζων has an alternative acc. sing. μείζω (i.e., besides μείζονα), and alternative nom. and acc. plural forms, masc. and fem. μείζους (instead of μείζονες and -ονας), neut. μείζω (instead of μείζονα).

Note 2—Adjectives and adverbs in the comparative degree are followed in one or two ways, either (*a*) by ἤ, than, and a noun or pronoun in the same case as the noun or pronoun with which the adjective agrees, or (*b*) simply by the noun or pronoun in the genitive case without ἤ.

Thus (a) John 3:19, μᾶλλον τὸ σκότος ἢ τὸ φῶς, rather the darkness than the light.

(b) John 1:50: μείζω ("greater things," neut. plur. for μείζονα) τούτων ("than these," gen. of comparison) ὄψῃ ("thou shalt see," fut. of ὁράω).

Exercise on the Comparison of Adjectives

Translate and retranslate:

(1) ἐγὼ δὲ ἔχω τὴν μαρτυρίαν μείζω τοῦ Ἰωάννου· τὰ γὰρ ἔργα ἃ δέδωκέν μοι ὁ πατὴρ ἵνα τελειώσω αὐτά, αὐτὰ τὰ ἔργα ἃ ποιῶ μαρτυρεῖ περὶ ἐμοῦ ὅτι ὁ πατήρ με ἀπέσταλκεν· (John 5:36) μείζω, acc., sing., fem.; τελειώσω 1st aor. subjunc. after ἵνα; μαρτυρεῖ, sing. after a neut. plur. subject αὐτὰ τὰ ἔργα, "the very works"; ἀπέσταλκεν, perf. of ἀποστέλλω.

(2) αὐτοῖς δὲ τοῖς κλητοῖς, Ἰουδαίοις τε καὶ Ἕλλησιν, Χριστὸν θεοῦ δύναμιν καὶ θεοῦ σοφίαν. (1 Cor. 1:24)

(3) Καὶ ἔλεγεν, Πῶς ὁμοιώσωμεν τὴν βασιλείαν τοῦ θεοῦ ἢ ἐν τίνι αὐτὴν παραβολῇ θῶμεν; 31 ὡς κόκκῳ σινάπεως, ὃς ὅταν σπαρῇ ἐπὶ τῆς γῆς, μικρότερον ὂν πάντων τῶν σπερμάτων τῶν ἐπὶ τῆς γῆς, 32 καὶ ὅταν σπαρῇ, ἀναβαίνει καὶ γίνεται μεῖζον πάντων τῶν λαχάνων καὶ ποιεῖ κλάδους μεγάλους, ὥστε δύνασθαι ὑπὸ τὴν σκιὰν αὐτοῦ τὰ πετεινὰ τοῦ οὐρανοῦ κατασκηνοῦν. (Mark 4:30-32) ὁμοιώσωμεν, 1st aor. subjunc. (the deliberative subjunctive, "how are we to liken"); θῶμεν, 2nd aor. subjunc. of τίθημι; σπαρῇ, 3rd pers. sing., 1st aor. subjunc. pass. of σπείρω, "I sow" (a liquid verb, see Lesson 21); ὄν, nom., sing., neut., pres. partic. of εἰμί, "being"; ὥστε δύνασθαι … τὰ πετεινά, the acc. with the infin. after ὥστε, "so that," expresses result, lit., "so that the birds to be able," i.e., "so that the birds are able"; κατασκηνοῦν, pres. infin.

(4) τοσούτῳ κρείττων γενόμενος τῶν ἀγγέλων ὅσῳ διαφορώτερον παρ' αὐτοὺς κεκληρονόμηκεν ὄνομα. (Heb. 1:4) τοσούτῳ, by so much (dat. of degree); γενόμενος, 2nd aor. partic. of γίνομαι; ὅσῳ, by how much; παρ' αὐτούς, "in-comparison-with them."

(5) τότε πορεύεται καὶ παραλαμβάνει μεθ' ἑαυτοῦ ἑπτὰ ἕτερα πνεύματα πονηρότερα ἑαυτοῦ καὶ εἰσελθόντα κατοικεῖ ἐκεῖ· καὶ γίνεται τὰ ἔσχατα τοῦ ἀνθρώπου ἐκείνου χείρονα τῶν πρώτων. οὕτως ἔσται καὶ τῇ γενεᾷ ταύτῃ τῇ πονηρᾷ. (Matt. 12:45) εἰσελθόντα, nom., plur., neut., 2nd aor. partic. of εἰσέρχομαι, "having entered" (note the verb in the sing. following); τὰ ἔσχατα, the last things, i.e., "the last state"; with this the neut. plur. χείρονα agrees.

Lesson 27

Adverbs

Adverbs

Adverbs are formed from adjectives by changing the ν of the gen. plur. masc. to ς. Thus the gen. plur. of ἀληθής, true, is ἀληθῶν, and the adverb is ἀληθῶς, truly, verily.

The comparative and superlative degrees of adverbs are formed by using the neut. sing. of the comparative degree of the adjective and the neut. plur. of the superlative of the adjective respectively.

Thus ταχέως is "quickly"; τάχιον, more quickly; τάχιστα, most quickly (Acts 17:15). Note ὡς with the superlative is idiomatic—ὡς τάχιστα is "as quickly as possible," lit., "as most quickly."

The comparative adverb περισσοτέρως, more abundantly, is formed in the same way as in the positive degree, and not by the neut. sing. (2 Cor. 11:23).

Note the adverb ὄντως, truly; it is formed from the pres. partic. of εἰμί.

The following irregular comparisons should be memorized:—

Positive	**Comparative**	**Superlative**
εὖ, well	βέλτιον or κρείσσον, better	
καλῶς, well	κάλλιον, better	
κακῶς, badly	ἧσσον (or -ττον), worse	
πολύ, much	μᾶλλον, more	μάλιστα, most
	πλεῖον or πλέον, more	

Forms omitted in the above are not found in the New Testament.

Exercise on Adverbs

Translate and retranslate:—

(1) Διὰ τοῦτο δεῖ περισσοτέρως προσέχειν ἡμᾶς τοῖς ἀκουσθεῖσιν, μήποτε παραρυῶμεν. (Heb. 2:1) δεῖ, impersonal, "it is necessary"; this is followed by the acc. with the infin. προσέχειν ἡμᾶς lit., "us to give heed," i.e., "that we should give heed", περισσοτέρως, more abundantly, i.e., "more earnestly"; ἀκουσθεῖσιν, dat., plur., neut., 1st aor. partic. pass. "to the (things) having been heard."

(2) δῴη αὐτῷ ὁ κύριος εὑρεῖν ἔλεος παρὰ κυρίου ἐν ἐκείνῃ τῇ ἡμέρᾳ. καὶ ὅσα ἐν Ἐφέσῳ διηκόνησεν, βέλτιον σὺ γινώσκεις. (2 Tim. 1:18) δῴη, 3rd pers. sing., 2nd aor. subjunc. of δίδωμι, the subjunc. of a wish, "may He give"; εὑρεῖν, 2nd aor. infin. of εὑρίσκω; βέλτιον, lit. "better," the comparative being here equivalent to the superlative "very well."

(3) ἔτρεχον δὲ οἱ δύο ὁμοῦ· καὶ ὁ ἄλλος μαθητὴς προέδραμεν τάχιον τοῦ Πέτρου καὶ ἦλθεν πρῶτος εἰς τὸ μνημεῖον. (John 20:4) ἔτρεχον, imperf.; προέδραμεν, 2nd aor. of προτρέχω, "I run before."

(4) Καὶ διὰ τοῦτο καὶ ἡμεῖς εὐχαριστοῦμεν τῷ θεῷ ἀδιαλείπτως, ὅτι παραλαβόντες λόγον ἀκοῆς παρ' ἡμῶν τοῦ θεοῦ ἐδέξασθε οὐ λόγον ἀνθρώπων ἀλλὰ καθώς ἐστιν ἀληθῶς λόγον θεοῦ, ὃς καὶ ἐνεργεῖται ἐν ὑμῖν τοῖς πιστεύουσιν. (1 Thess. 2:13) παραλαβόντες, 2nd aor. partic. of παραλαμβάνω; ἐδέξασθε, 1st aor. of δέχομαι.

Note to Students—The Lesson on "Some Additional Rules of Syntax" may be taken next, the intervening Lessons being postponed.

Lesson 28

Prepositions (Part I)

Prepositions (Part I)

The special significance of the cases in nouns, etc., was pointed out in Lesson 2. The relations broadly stated there, and a variety of others, are expressed also by means of prepositions. Thus, while the accusative itself chiefly signifies motion towards, this relation may be expressed by such a preposition as πρός, with the accusative of the following noun. Again, one of the meanings of the genitive case is motion from, and this is likewise conveyed by ἀπό, with that case of the following noun. The dative may signify rest in a place, or the instrument of an action, etc., and each of these is expressed, e.g., by ἐν with the dative of the noun; a useful example of ἐν in this way is ἐν μαχαίρᾳ, with a sword (Luke 22:49).

Sometimes the use of the preposition is merely emphatic. The case of the noun alone would have expressed the same meaning, but with less force. In most instances, however, the preposition denotes a relation which the noun itself would be insufficient to indicate.

Some prepositions govern one case only; others govern two cases with different meanings; a few are used with three cases, the meanings differing in each case.

Again, the same preposition may have a considerable variety of meanings, and the actual sense must be gathered largely from the context.

Certain prepositions are closely allied in some of their meanings. They express much the same relationship but from different points of view. In English, for instance, we use the prepositions "by" and "through"to signify the same transaction, yet there is a real distinction. We say that something is done by a person, or through him. These prepositions are not, however, synonymous or interchangeable, and in Greek it is specially necessary to observe the distinction.

It is important for the student to become thoroughly acquainted with all the prepositions. The list should be committed to memory.

(a) Prepositions Governing One Case Only

(1) *Those used with the accusative only*

ἀνά and εἰς

ἀνά, up. This is frequently compounded with verbs. Separately with a noun it has a special meaning, as ἀνὰ μέσον, in the midst of (Mark 7:31; Rev. 7:17); ἀνὰ μέρος, by turn (1 Cor. 14:27); with numerals, ἀνὰ δύο, two by two (Luke 10:1); with measures, signifying "apiece," ἀνὰ δηνάριον, a denarius, apiece (Matt. 20:9,10); ἀνὰ μετρητάς, measures apiece (John 2:6); in Rev. 21:21

ἀνὰ εἷς ἕκαστος is each one separately.

εἰς, to, unto, into, towards. This is used (*a*) of place, and the proper meaning is to be gathered from the context; (*b*) of persons, "towards" or "with reference to," as in Rom. 12:16; Acts 2:25, or "over against," as in Luke 12:10; εἰς Χριστόν is "unto Christ" (Rom. 6:3); (*c*) "of purpose," "with a view to," "in order to," "for"; εἰς τὸ σταυρωθῆναι, lit. "unto the to-be-crucified," i.e., "in order to be crucified" (Matt. 26:2); cp. 1 Cor. 11:24; (*d*) to express equivalence (Rom. 4:3); (*e*) with the meaning of ἐν, e.g., εἰς τὸν ἀγρόν in the field (Mark 13:16), cp. Acts 8:40: 21:13.

(2) *Those used with the genitive only*

ἀντί, ἀπό, ἐκ, πρό

ἀντί, over against, instead of, for; the idea is that of an equivalent, often with the sense of opposition. Note the phrase ἀνθ᾽ ὧν, lit. "in return for which things," i.e., "because," Luke 1:20; 12:3; 19:44; 2 Thess. 2:10.

ἀπό, from (from the exterior); sometimes this is equivalent to "on account of," as in Matt. 18:7.

Note the phrases with adverbs ἀπὸ τότε, from then (Matt. 4:17); ἀπ᾽ ἄρτι, henceforth, (Matt. 23:39); ἀπὸ τοῦ νῦν, from now (Luke 1:48, etc.), and others.

ἐκ or ἐξ, from (the interior); this is used of place, origin, source, cause. Note the use signifying belonging to a class, e.g., ὁ ὢν ἐκ τῆς ἀληθείας, he who is of the truth, cp. Rom. 2:8; 4:12-14; Gal. 3:9; also those referring to time, e.g., ἐκ τούτου, from this time (John 6:66); ἐξ ἐτῶν ὀκτώ, for eight years (Acts 9:33).

πρό, before, used of time or place, and in the phrase πρὸ πάντων, before all things, of superiority.

(3) *Those used with the dative only*

ἐν and σύν

ἐν, in, used of time or place. Like ἐκ, this may be used to denote "on," as in ἐν τῷ θρόνῳ μου (Rev. 3:21); cp. Heb. 1:3. It signifies "among" in Matt. 2:6; Acts 2:29; 1 Pet. 5:1-2, and with numbers, e.g., ἐν δέκα χιλιάσιν, among ten thousands.

It is also used to denote *accompaniment*, or even *instrument*, 1 Tim. 1:18; Heb. 9:25; Eph. 6:2; Luke 22:49; Matt. 5:34: 9:34.

Note its use with a noun adverbially, e.g., ἐν τάχει, speedily (Rev. 1:1).

Also its use with the infinitive as a noun, where it signifies "while." Thus in Matt. 13:4, ἐν τῷ σπείρειν αὐτόν, lit., "in the him to sow," i.e., "while he was sowing" (an acc. with the infin., both with the article, and all governed by the preposition). With relative pronouns it denotes "while"; see ἐν ᾧ, in Mark 2:19; so ἐν οἷς in Luke 12:1 is "while."

σύν, together with. Occasionally this denotes "besides." Thus in Luke 24:21, ἀλλά γε καὶ (lit. "but indeed also," i.e., "moreover") σὺν πᾶσιν τούτοις, beside all this (lit. "these things").

Exercise

Translate and retranslate:—

(1) καὶ αὐτὸ τοῦτο δὲ σπουδὴν πᾶσαν παρεισενέγκαντες ἐπιχορηγήσατε ἐν τῇ πίστει ὑμῶν τὴν ἀρετήν, ἐν δὲ τῇ ἀρετῇ τὴν γνῶσιν, 6 ἐν δὲ τῇ γνώσει τὴν ἐγκράτειαν, ἐν δὲ τῇ ἐγκρατείᾳ τὴν ὑπομονήν, ἐν δὲ τῇ ὑπομονῇ τὴν εὐσέβειαν, 7 ἐν δὲ τῇ εὐσεβείᾳ τὴν φιλαδελφίαν, ἐν δὲ τῇ φιλαδελφίᾳ τὴν ἀγάπην. 8 ταῦτα γὰρ ὑμῖν ὑπάρχοντα καὶ πλεονάζοντα οὐκ ἀργοὺς οὐδὲ ἀκάρπους καθίστησιν εἰς τὴν τοῦ κυρίου ἡμῶν Ἰησοῦ Χριστοῦ ἐπίγνωσιν. (2 Pet. 1:5-8) αὐτὸ τοῦτο, this phrase, lit., "itself this," is an adverbial accusative and must be translated "for this very (cause)"; παρεισενέγκαντες, nom., plur., 1st aor. partic. of παρεισφέρω (see φέρω in list of irregular verbs, Lesson 24); καθίστησιν, note this 3rd pers. sing. after the neut. plur. subject ταῦτα.

(2) Εὐλογητὸς ὁ θεὸς καὶ πατὴρ τοῦ κυρίου ἡμῶν Ἰησοῦ Χριστοῦ, ὁ εὐλογήσας ἡμᾶς ἐν
πάσῃ εὐλογίᾳ πνευματικῇ ἐν τοῖς ἐπουρανίοις ἐν Χριστῷ, 4 καθὼς ἐξελέξατο ἡμᾶς ἐν αὐτῷ πρὸ
καταβολῆς κόσμου εἶναι ἡμᾶς ἁγίους καὶ ἀμώμους κατενώπιον αὐτοῦ ἐν ἀγάπη, 5 προ ορίσας ἡμᾶς
εἰς υἱοθεσίαν διὰ Ἰησοῦ Χριστοῦ εἰς αὐτόν, κατὰ τὴν εὐδοκίαν τοῦ θελήματος αὐτοῦ, 6 εἰς ἔπαινον
δόξης τῆς χάριτος αὐτοῦ ἧς ἐχαρίτωσεν ἡμᾶς ἐν τῷ ἠγαπημένῳ. 7 ἐν ᾧ ἔχομεν τὴν ἀπολύτρωσιν
διὰ τοῦ αἵματος αὐτοῦ, τὴν ἄφεσιν τῶν παραπτωμάτων, κατὰ τὸ πλοῦτος τῆς χάριτος αὐτοῦ 8 ἧς
ἐπερίσσευσεν εἰς ἡμᾶς, ἐν πάσῃ σοφίᾳ καὶ φρονήσει. (Eph. 1:3-8) ἐξελέξατο 1st aor. mid. ἐκλέγω; ἧς in verse 6 is an example of attraction from the acc., as the object of following verb, to the genitive of the word but one, χάριτος; we must not translate "of which" but by "which"; "freely-bestowed" is one word.

Lesson 29

Prepositions (Part II)

Prepositions (Part II)

Prepositions Used With the Accusative and Genitive Cases

διά, κατά, μετά, περί, ὑπέρ, ὑπό.

διά with the accusative means "on account of," "because of."

διά with the genitive has three chief meanings:—

(1) of *place,* signifying "through" (John 4:4; 1 Cor. 13:12).

(2) of *instrument,* signifying "by means of," "through" (2 Thess. 2:2).

(3) of *time,* signifying (*a*) "during" (Heb. 2:15; διὰ νυκτός is "by night" (i.e., during, without reference to a particular time), Acts 5:19; (*b*) "after"(Matt. 26:61).

κατά with the accusative means:—

(1) of *place,* either (*a*) "throughout" (Luke 8:39), or (*b*) "before" (Luke 2:31), or distributively, e.g., διώδευεν ("He was journeying"—impf. of διοδεύω) κατὰ πόλιν, from city to city (Luke 8:1).

(2) of *time,* (*a*) "in" or "at" (Matt. 1:20), (*b*) distributively, κατ' ἔτος, year by year (Luke 2:41), καθ' ἡμέραν, daily (Matt. 26:55); καθ' εἷς (or καθεῖς), one by one (John 8:9).

(3) of *comparison,* "according to." Note κατὰ πίστιν, according to faith (Heb. 11:13); also the idioms κατ' ἰδίαν, alone (Matt. 14:13), καθ' ἑαυτόν, by himself (Acts 28:16).

κατά with the genitive means either (*a*) "down" (Matt. 8:32) or (*b*) "against" (Mark 11:25) or (*c*) "throughout" (Luke 4:14).

μετά with the accusative means "after" (Matt. 26:2); in Luke 22:20, μετὰ τὸ δειπνῆσαι is "after supper" (the verb in the aor. infin. being equivalent to a noun).

μετά with the genitive means "with" (Matt. 1:23).

περί with the accusative means (1) of *place,* "around" (Matt. 8:18); (2) of *time,* "about" (Matt. 20: 3); (3) of *an object of thought,* "about" (Luke 10: 40) or "with reference to" (1 Tim. 1:19).

περί with the genitive means "about" or "concerning" (Acts 8:12), sometimes almost like ὑπέρ, for (Rom. 8:3; 1 Thess. 5:25).

ὑπέρ with the accusative means "above" and is used in comparison (Matt. 10:24); note the use after a comparative adjective for the sake of emphasis where the meaning is "than" (Luke 16: 8; Heb. 4:12).

ὑπέρ with the genitive means "on behalf of," "for" (1 Cor. 15:3; 2 Cor. 5:14-15).

ὑπό with the accusative means "under" (Matt. 5:15); note the phrase in Acts 5:21, ὑπὸ τὸν ὄρθρον, under (i.e., close upon) the dawn, i.e., very early in the morning.

ὑπό with the genitive means "by" (Matt. 4:1).

Prepositions Used With the Accusative, Genitive and Dative

ἐπί, παρά, πρός.

ἐπί with the accusative has the following meanings:—

(1) of *place,* "upon," with the idea of motion (Matt. 5:15); note the use after the verb "to hope" (1 Tim. 5:5, and ch. 4:10, where the preposition is used with the dative, "upon" of rest rather than motion—see below).

(2) of *authority,* "over" (Luke 1:33).

(3) of *intention,* "for" or "against" (Matt. 3:7: 26:55).

(4) of *direction,* "towards," "with regard to" (Luke 6:35; Mark 9:12).

(5) of *quantity,* "up to," e.g., ἐπὶ πλεῖον, to a further point, i.e., any further (Acts 4:17). Note the phrase ἐφ' ὅσον, "inasmuch as," also used of time, "as long as" (Matt. 9:15).

(6) of *time,* "during," "for" (Luke 10:35; 18:4). Note the phrase ἐπὶ τὸ αὐτό, "at the same place," or "at the same time," i.e., "together" (Luke 17:35; Acts 2:1, etc.).

ἐπί with the genitive has the following meanings:—

(1) of *place,* "upon"(Matt. 6:10) so figuratively (John 6:2); or "before" (1 Tim. 5:19), or "on the basis of,"e.g., ἐπ' ἀληθείας, in truth (Mark 12:14); cp. 2 Cor. 13:1.

(2) of *authority,* "over"(Acts 6:3).

(3) of *time,* "in the time of" (Luke 3:2; Rom. 1:10; Heb. 1, 2).

ἐπὶ with the dative has the following meanings:—

(1) of *place,* "upon," with rest implied (Luke 21:6).

(2) of *superintendence,* "over" (Luke 12:44).

(3) of *condition, ground, etc.,* "on" or "at" (Matt. 4:4; Mark 9:37; Acts 11:19). Note the phrase ἐφ' ᾧ, "on condition that," "wherefore," "because" (Rom. 5:1-2, etc.).

(4) of *quantity,* "beside,""in addition to" (Luke 3:20).

παρὰ with the accusative has the following meanings:—

(1) of *place,* "by," "near" (Matt. 13:4; Acts 10: 6).

(2) of *contradistinction,* "contrary to," "rather than" (Rom. 1:25-26, 4:18).

(3) of *comparison,* "above," "than"(Luke 13: 2; Heb. 9:23).

Note the phrase παρὰ τοῦτο, "therefore," in 1 Cor. 12:15-16, where the idea is that of consequence through comparison.

παρά with the genitive means "from" ("beside and proceeding from"); it is used of persons (Matt. 2:4; John 16:27). Note the phrase οἱ παρ' αὐτοῦ, lit., "those from Him," i.e., "His friends."

παρά with the dative means "with," whether of *nearness,* as in John 14:17; 19:25; Acts 10:6; or of *estimation* or *ability,* as in Matt. 19:26; Rom. 2:13. Note the phrase παρ' ἑαυτοῖς, lit., "with yourselves," i.e., "in your own conceits."

πρός with the accusative has the following meanings:—

(1) of *direction,* "to"(1 Cor. 13:12): δεῦτε πρός με is "hitherto me" (Matt. 11:28)

(2) of *company* with the thought of attitude towards, "with" (John 1:1; Matt. 13:56).

(3) of *mental direction,* either "towards" or "against" (Luke 23:12; Acts 6:1). Note the meaning "in regard to" in Heb. 1:7.

(4) of *estimation,* "in consideration of" (Matt. 19:8; Luke 12:47; Rom. 8:18).

(5) of *purpose,* "for," "in order to" (Matt. 6: 1; 1 Cor. 10:11).

πρός with the genitive occurs once only in the New Testament, in Acts 27:34, where the idea is "belonging to" or "for."

πρός with the dative means "near," "at," or "about" (Luke 19:37; John 20:12).

Exercise

Translate and retranslate:—

(1) οὐ γὰρ εἰς χειροποίητα εἰσῆλθεν ἅγια Χριστός, ἀντίτυπα τῶν ἀληθινῶν, ἀλλ᾽ εἰς αὐτὸν τὸν οὐρανόν, νῦν ἐμφανισθῆναι τῷ προσώπῳ τοῦ θεοῦ ὑπὲρ ἡμῶν· 25 οὐδ᾽ ἵνα πολλάκις προσφέρῃ ἑαυτόν, ὥσπερ ὁ ἀρχιερεὺς εἰσέρχεται εἰς τὰ ἅγια κατ᾽ ἐνιαυτὸν ἐν αἵματι ἀλλοτρίῳ, 26 ἐπεὶ ἔδει αὐτὸν πολλάκις παθεῖν ἀπὸ καταβολῆς κόσμου· νυνὶ δὲ ἅπαξ ἐπὶ συντελείᾳ τῶν αἰώνων εἰς ἀθέτησιν [τῆς] ἁμαρτίας διὰ τῆς θυσίας αὐτοῦ πεφανέρωται. 27 καὶ καθ᾽ ὅσον ἀπόκειται τοῖς ἀνθρώποις ἅπαξ ἀποθανεῖν, μετὰ δὲ τοῦτο κρίσις. (Heb. 9:24-27) Note κατ᾽ ἐνιαυτόν, "year by year" (verse 25); in verse 26 note the acc. with the infin. αὐτὸν ... παθεῖν (from πάσχω), after the impersonal ἔδει, it was necessary Him to suffer; in verse 27 καθ᾽ ὅσον is "according as" (lit., "according to how much").

(2) καὶ ἐπὶ τὴν αὔριον ἐκβαλὼν ἔδωκεν δύο δηνάρια τῷ πανδοχεῖ καὶ εἶπεν, Ἐπιμελήθητι αὐτοῦ, καὶ ὅ τι ἂν προσδαπανήσῃς ἐγὼ ἐν τῷ ἐπανέρχεσθαί με ἀποδώσω σοι. 36 τίς τούτων τῶν τριῶν πλησίον δοκεῖ σοι γεγονέναι τοῦ ἐμπεσόντος εἰς τοὺς λῃστάς; 37 ὁ δὲ εἶπεν, Ὁ ποιήσας τὸ ἔλεος μετ᾽ αὐτοῦ. εἶπεν δὲ αὐτῷ ὁ Ἰησοῦς, Πορεύου καὶ σὺ ποίει ὁμοίως. (Luke 10:35-37) Note the acc. and infin. after ἐν τῷ ..., lit., "in the me to come back," where the phrase "me to come back" is a noun clause agreeing with τῷ, the whole governed by ἐν; δοκεῖ σοι, does it seem to thee; ἐμπεσόντος, gen. of 2nd aor. partic. of ἐμπίπτω; μετ᾽ αὐτοῦ, lit., "with him."

Lesson 30

Interrogative Particles. Numerals

Interrogative Particles and Numerals

(*a*) Sometimes εἰ, if, is used elliptically, i.e., without any preceding clause such as "Tell us" or "Say." Thus in Matt. 12:10

εἰ ἔξεστι is "is it lawful?" In Acts 19:2

εἰ ... ἐλάβετε is "did ye receive" (for "tell me if ye received"). See also Acts 7:1: 21:37: 22:25.

(*b*) ἤ is occasionally used to introduce a question; in this case, too, a former clause is to be understood. See Rom. 3:29: 6:3: 7:1.

(*c*) ἆρα introduces a question in three places, Luke 18:8; Acts 8:30; Gal. 2:17. It is not to be translated. It is to be distinguished from ἄρα with the acute accent, which means "then" or "accordingly," as in Gal. 2:21.

Exercise on the Particles

Translate and retranslate:—

(1) καὶ ἀτενίσαντες εἰς αὐτὸν πάντες οἱ καθεζόμενοι ἐν τῷ συνεδρίῳ εἶδον τὸ πρόσωπον αὐτοῦ ὡσεὶ πρόσωπον ἀγγέλου. 1 Εἶπεν δὲ ὁ ἀρχιερεύς, Εἰ ταῦτα οὕτως ἔχει; (Acts 6:15–7:1) Εἰ is not to be translated; οὕτως ἔχει, is, lit., "have thus" (sing. verb after neut. plur. subject), i.e., "have these things thus," is "are these things so?"

(2) ἢ ἀγνοεῖτε ὅτι, ὅσοι ἐβαπτίσθημεν εἰς Χριστὸν Ἰησοῦν, εἰς τὸν θάνατον αὐτοῦ ἐβαπτίσθημεν; 4 συνετάφημεν οὖν αὐτῷ διὰ τοῦ βαπτίσματος εἰς τὸν θάνατον, ἵνα ὥσπερ ἠγέρθη Χριστὸς ἐκ νεκρῶν διὰ τῆς δόξης τοῦ πατρός, οὕτως καὶ ἡμεῖς ἐν καινότητι ζωῆς περιπατήσωμεν. (Rom. 6:3-4) ὅσοι followed by the 1st pers. plur. of the verb is "as many (of us) as were, etc.," i.e., "all we who were ..."; συνετάφημεν, 1st pers. plur., 2nd aor. indic., passive of συνθάπτω (note the irregular formation and the regular augment after the preposition).

(3) Ἢ ἀγνοεῖτε, ἀδελφοί, γινώσκουσιν γὰρ νόμον λαλῶ, ὅτι ὁ νόμος κυριεύει τοῦ ἀνθρώπου ἐφ' ὅσον χρόνον ζῇ; (Rom. 7:1) γινώσκουσιν, dat., plur., masc., pres. partic. (not 3rd pers. plur., pres. indic.), lit., "to the (ones) knowing," i.e., "to them that know."

(4) εἰ δὲ ζητοῦντες δικαιωθῆναι ἐν Χριστῷ εὑρέθημεν καὶ αὐτοὶ ἁμαρτωλοί, ἄρα Χριστὸς ἁμαρτίας διάκονος; μὴ γένοιτο. (Gal. 2:17) εὑρέθημεν, 2nd aor. indic. pass.; in the sentence beginning with ἄρα, the verb ἐστί is understood. The verb "to be" is frequently omitted.

Numerals

The Cardinal Numerals

The numbers εἷς, one; δύο, two; τρεῖς, three, τέσσαρες, four, are declined as follows:—

	Masc.	**Fem.**	**Neut.**
Nom.	εἷς	μία	ἕν
Gen.	ἑνί	μιᾷ	ἑνί
Acc.	ἕνα	μίαν	ἕν

Nom., Gen., Acc., δύο; Dat., δυσί(ν).

Nom. and Acc., Masc. and Fem., τρεῖς, Neut., τρία.

Gen. in all three genders, τριῶν.

Dat. in all three genders, τρισί.

Nom. and Acc. Masc. and Fem., τέσσαρες, Neut., τέσσαρα.

Gen. in all three genders, τεσσάρων.

Dat. in all three genders, τέσσαρσι(ν).

Like εἷς are declined its negative compounds οὐδείς and μηδείς, no one.

The rest of the cardinal numerals in the New Testament are to be found in the Lexicon.

The signs for numerals are not numbers but letters with an accent: 1 is α'; 2 is β'; the letters after θ' go in tens: ι' is 20; κ' is 30; but this goes only to π', 80; after this the letters go in hundreds: ρ' is 100; χ' is 600. Thus 666 is χξς' (Rev. 13:18). ς' is 6; Ϛ' is 90; ϡ' is 900.

The Ordinal Numerals

For "first" the superlative πρῶτος is used. Succeeding numbers are formed from the stems of their cardinal numbers and are declined like adjectives of the first two declensions—in -ος, etc. Cardinal numbers are sometimes used instead of ordinals in reckoning the days of the week.

Distributive Numerals

These are formed either by repeating the number or by a preposition with the number. Thus, "two and two" is either δύο δύο (Mark 6:7) or ἀνὰ δύο (Luke 10:1). "One by one" is εἷς καθ' εἷς in Mark 14:19 and John 8:9.

Lesson 31

Some Additional Rules of Syntax. Negative Questions. Subjunctive Mood Uses. Optative Mood Uses

Some Additional Rules of Syntax

Several rules of Syntax have been noted in the exercises. A few of the most important are given here.

(a) Negative Questions

(1) When οὐ is used in a negative question, an affirmative reply is expected. See, e.g., 1 Cor. 9:1.

(2) When μή is used, a negative answer is expected, but the μή is not to be translated. Thus μὴ ἀδικία παρὰ τῷ θεῷ, Is there unrighteousness with God? (Rom. 9:14). The negative may be brought out in this way, "There is not unrighteousness with God, is there?" But that is not a translation.

(3) μήτι more strongly suggests a negative answer. See Matt. 7:16; 26:22, 25.

(b) Some Uses of the Subjunctive Mood

(1) In *exhortations* in the 1st person (the negative is always μή). Thus in John 19:24, μὴ σχίσωμεν, "let us not rend," the verb is 1st aor. subjunc. of σχίζω, and λάχωμεν, "let us cast lots," is the 2nd aor. subjunc. of λαγχάνω.

(2) In *prohibitions*, the subjunctive aorist is used with μή as an alternative to the imperative. See ἐνδύσησθε in Matt. 6:25, and note the imperative μεριμνᾶτε preceding.

(3) Similarly in *requests*. See εἰσενέγκῃς in Matt. 6:13, the 1st aor. subjunc. of εἰσφέρω.

(4) In *deliberative questions* or those expressing doubt. In 1 Cor. 11:22, εἴπω is 2nd aor. subjunc. of λέγω, and ἐπαινέσω is 1st aor. subjunc. of ἐπαινέω.

(5) *Strong denials* take the aorist subjunctive with the double negative οὐ μή. See Matt. 5:18-20; 24:2; 24:35; Luke 6:37; John 6:37; 8:51; 10:28; 13:8; Heb. 13:5; where ἀνῶ is 2nd aor. subjunc. of ἀνίημι.

Exercise

Translate and re-translate:—

(1) διόπερ εἰ βρῶμα σκανδαλίζει τὸν ἀδελφόν μου, οὐ μὴ φάγω κρέα εἰς τὸν αἰῶνα, ἵνα μὴ τὸν ἀδελφόν μου σκανδαλίσω. (1 Cor. 8:13)

(2) Τοῦτο γὰρ ὑμῖν λέγομεν ἐν λόγῳ κυρίου, ὅτι ἡμεῖς οἱ ζῶντες οἱ περι λειπόμενοι εἰς τὴν παρουσίαν τοῦ κυρίου οὐ μὴ φθάσωμεν τοὺς κοιμηθέντας. (1 Thess. 4:15) φθάσωμεν, 1st aor. subjunc. of φθάνω.

(3) ἄρα οὖν μὴ καθεύδωμεν ὡς οἱ λοιποί ἀλλὰ γρηγορῶμεν καὶ νήφωμεν. (1 Thess. 5:6)

(4) ἢ δοκεῖς ὅτι οὐ δύναμαι παρακαλέσαι τὸν πατέρα μου, καὶ παραστήσει μοι ἄρτι πλείω δώδεκα λεγιῶνας ἀγγέλων; 54 πῶς οὖν πληρωθῶσιν αἱ γραφαὶ ὅτι οὕτως δεῖ γενέσθαι; (Matt. 26:53, 54)

(c) The Optative Mood

(1) This expresses wishes. See, e.g., 1 Thess. 3:11-12, where all the optatives are 1st aorists. The negative is μή. See, e.g., Mark 11:14; φάγοι is 2nd aor. opt. of ἐσθίω.

(2) With ἄν there is a potential sense, expressing possibility; ἄν is never translatable. See, e.g., Acts 8:31.

Exercise

Translate and retranslate:—

(1) Πέτρος δὲ εἶπεν πρὸς αὐτόν, Τὸ ἀργύριόν σου σὺν σοὶ εἴη εἰς ἀπώλειαν ὅτι τὴν δωρεὰν τοῦ θεοῦ ἐνόμισας διὰ χρημάτων κτᾶσθαι. (Acts 8:20) εἴη εἰς ἀπώλειαν is "may it be unto destruction," i.e., "may it perish."

(2) Ὁ δὲ κύριος κατευθύναι ὑμῶν τὰς καρδίας εἰς τὴν ἀγάπην τοῦ θεοῦ καὶ εἰς τὴν ὑπο μονὴν τοῦ Χριστοῦ. (2 Thess. 3:5)

(3) ὁ δὲ Παῦλος, Εὐξαίμην ἂν τῷ θεῷ καὶ ἐν ὀλίγῳ καὶ ἐν μεγάλῳ οὐ μόνον σὲ ἀλλὰ καὶ πάντας τοὺς ἀκούοντάς μου σήμερον γενέσθαι τοιούτους ὁποῖος καὶ ἐγώ εἰμι παρεκτὸς τῶν δεσμῶν τούτων. (Acts 26:29)

Lesson 32

Some Rules of Syntax (continued). Dependent Clauses

Rules of Syntax (Continued)

(d) Dependent Clauses

Note—Sentences containing dependent clauses consist of a principal clause containing the main subject and its predicate or verb, and one or more subordinate or dependent clauses. These latter may be formed in a variety of ways, as follows:—

(I) Object Clauses. Here the subordinate clause is itself the object of the verb in the principal clause. Thus in Matt. 9:28, Πιστεύετε ὅτι δύναμαι τοῦτο ποιῆσαι, the clause from ὅτι to ποιῆσαι is the object of Πιστεύετε.

(*a*) If the verb in the principal clause is in the past tense, the verb in the dependent clause is usually in the present indicative (sometimes the optative), but must be translated in English by the past tense. Thus in John 11:13, ἐκεῖνοι δὲ ἔδοξαν ὅτι ... λέγει is, lit., "but they thought that He is speaking." We must render by "that He was speaking." Cp. John 20:14; Mark 5:29.

(*b*) Sometimes ὅτι serves to introduce a *quotation:* it is not to be translated in that case. See, e.g., Matt. 7:23; Luke 8:49.

(*c*) *In indirect questions* the verb in the object clause. is found either in the indicative, or the subjunctive or the optative.

The indicative intimates that the object of inquiry concerns a matter of fact. See, e.g., Luke 23:6, ἐπηρώτησεν εἰ … ἐστιν, "he asked if he were…" (here also the verb in the dependent clause goes into the present tense); cp. Acts 10:18.

The subjunctive expresses future possibility. See, e.g., Matt. 6:25, and Luke 19:48, where ποιήσωσιν is 1st aor. subjunc.

The optative expresses the possibility of what may be thought to exist or to have existed. See, e.g., Luke 1:29; Acts 17:11; 17:27 (εὕροιεν is 2nd aor. opt.). See both indic. and opt. in Acts 21:33.

(II) Conditional Clauses. The dependent clause begins with "if." There are four kinds of supposition:—

(*a*) The supposition of a fact. Here the dependent or εἰ clause has the indicative. See, e.g., Matt. 4:3; Rom. 4:2.

(*b*) The supposition of a possibility, or uncertainty with the prospect of decision. Here ἐάν (i.e., εἰ ἄν) is used with the subjunctive (rarely εἰ). See, e.g., Matt. 17:20; John 3:3-5; 2 Tim. 2:5.

(*c*) The supposition of an uncertainty. Here the optative is used, and always with εἰ. See, e.g., I Pet. 3:14; Acts 24:19.

(*d*) The supposition of an unfulfilled condition. Here the indicative is used with εἰ in the dependent clause, and the main clause takes ἄν. Two tenses are chiefly used in this main clause, the imperfect and the aorist.

When the imperfect is used with ἄν, present time is indicated, e.g., "If this were so (which is not the case), something else would be taking place (but it is not so)." Thus in John 8:42, Εἰ ὁ θεὸς πατὴρ ὑμῶν ἦν ἠγαπᾶτε ἂν ἐμέ, If God were your Father (which is not the case), ye would love Me (but ye do not). Note the imperfect tense with ἄν. See, e.g., Luke 7:39; John 5:46; Heb. 4:8.

When the aorist is used with ἄν, past time is indicated, e.g., "If this had been so (which was not the case) something else would have occurred (but it did not)." Thus, in 1 Cor. 2:8, εἰ γὰρ ἔγνωσαν, οὐκ ἂν … ἐσταύρωσαν, For if they had known (which was not the case) they would not have crucified … (but they did so). See, e.g., John 14:28; Luke 12:39 (where ἀφῆκεν is 1st aor. of ἀφίημι). Sometimes the pluperfect is used with ἄν. See John 11:21; 14:7.

Exercise on Object and Conditional Clauses

Translate and re-translate:—

(1) εἷς δὲ ἐξ αὐτῶν, ἰδὼν ὅτι ἰάθη, ὑπέστρεψεν μετὰ φωνῆς μεγάλης δοξάζων τὸν θεόν. (Luke 17:15) ἰάθη, 1st aor. indic. pass. of ἰάομαι; ὑπέστρεψεν 1st aor. of ὑποστρέφω.

(2) ὁ δὲ Πιλᾶτος ἐθαύμασεν εἰ ἤδη τέθνηκεν καὶ προσκαλεσάμενος τὸν κεντυρίωνα ἐπηρώτησεν αὐτὸν εἰ πάλαι ἀπέθανεν. (Mark 15:44) τέθνηκεν, perf. of θνήσκω; προσκαλεσάμενος, 1st aor. partic. middle; ἀπέθανεν, 2nd aor. of ἀποθνήσκω.

(3) καὶ εἰ μὲν ἐκείνης ἐμνημόνευον ἀφ᾽ ἧς ἐξέβησαν, εἶχον ἂν καιρὸν ἀνακάμψαι. (Heb. 11:15) ἐξέβησαν, 1st aor. of ἐκβαίνω (note the change of κ to ξ before the ε augment); εἶχον, imperf. of ἔχω; ἀνα κάμψαι, 1st aor. infin. of ἀνα κάμπτω.

(4) καὶ εἰ μὴ ἐκολόβωσεν κύριος τὰς ἡμέρας, οὐκ ἂν ἐσώθη πᾶσα σάρξ· ἀλλὰ διὰτοὺς ἐκλεκτοὺς οὓς ἐξελέξατο ἐκολόβωσεν τὰς ἡμέρας. (Mark 13:20) ἐκολόβωσεν, 1st aor. of κολοβόω; ἐξελέξατο, 1st aor. mid. of ἐκλέγω.

(5) καὶ λέγετε, Εἰ ἤμεθα ἐν ταῖς ἡμέραις τῶν πατέρων ἡμῶν, οὐκ ἂν ἤμεθα αὐτῶν κοινωνοὶ ἐν τῷ αἵματι τῶν προφητῶν. (Matt. 23:30)

(III) Final Clauses or Clauses of Purpose. These are introduced either by ἵνα, to the end that (with stress on the result) or ὅπως (with stress on the method) or μή (signifying "lest"or "that ... not"). See also Lesson 13.

(*a*) The verb in the dependent clause is usually in the subjunctive. See, e.g., Matt. 2:8: 6:16; Luke 6:34. The negative is always μή. See, e.g., Matt. 18:10; Heb. 12:15, 16. After verbs of fearing μή is rendered by "lest" or "that." See, e.g., 2 Cor. 12:20-21.

(*b*) Sometimes the future indicative is used, but never after ὅπως. Thus ἔσται in Heb. 3:12. Other tenses of the indicative are occasionally found.

Exercise on Final or Purpose Clauses

Translate and retranslate:—

(1) Τότε προσηνέχθησαν αὐτῷ παιδία ἵνα τὰς χεῖρας ἐπιθῇ αὐτοῖς καὶ προς εὔξηται· οἱ δὲ μαθηταὶ ἐπετίμησαν αὐτοῖς. (Matt. 19:13) προσηνέχθησαν, 1st aor. pass. of προσφέρω; ἐπιθῇ, 2nd aor. subjunc. of ἐπιτίθημι; προσεύξηται, 1st aor. subjunc. of προσεύχομαι.

(2) Ταῦτα ἐλάλησεν Ἰησοῦς, καὶ ἐπάρας τοὺς ὀφθαλμοὺς αὐτοῦ εἰς τὸν οὐρανὸν εἶπεν, Πάτερ, ἐλήλυθεν ἡ ὥρα· δόξασόν σου τὸν υἱόν, ἵνα ὁ υἱὸς δοξάσῃ σέ, 2 καθὼς ἔδωκας αὐτῷ ἐξουσίαν πάσης σαρκός, ἵνα πᾶν ὃ δέδωκας αὐτῷ δώσῃ αὐτοῖς ζωὴν αἰώνιον. 3 αὕτη δέ ἐστιν ἡ αἰώνιος ζωή ἵνα γινώσκωσιν σὲ τὸν μόνον ἀληθινὸν θεὸν καὶ ὃν ἀπέστειλας Ἰησοῦν Χριστόν. 4 ἐγώ σε ἐδόξασα ἐπὶ

τῆς γῆς τὸ ἔργον τελειώσας ὃ δέδωκάς μοι ἵνα ποιήσω. (John 17:1-4) For ἐλήλυθεν see ἔρχομαι. In all cases after ἵνα here the 1st aor. subjunc. is used.

(3) Ταῦτα δέ, ἀδελφοί, μετεσχημάτισα εἰς ἐμαυτὸν καὶ Ἀπολλῶν δι᾽ ὑμᾶς, ἵνα ἐν ἡμῖν μάθητε τὸ μὴ ὑπὲρ ἃ γέγραπται, ἵνα μὴ εἷς ὑπὲρ τοῦ ἑνὸς φυσιοῦσθε κατὰ τοῦ ἑτέρου. (1 Cor. 4:6) While μάθητε is 2nd aor. subjunc. (of μανθάνω) yet φυσιοῦσθε is pres. indic.

Lesson 33

Some Rules of Syntax (continued). The Infinitive Mood and Participles

Some Rules of Syntax(Continued)

(e) The Infinitive Mood

This mood partakes of the character of both verb and noun. Hence it may itself be a subject or an object of another verb, or may have a subject or an object. See Lesson 15.

(1) For an example of the infinitive as the subject of a verb, see Rom. 7:18.

(2) For an example of the infinitive as an object, see Phil. 2:6, where εἶναι is used as a noun with the article τό, both being the object of ἡγήσατο.

(3) *When the subject of the infinitive is expressed, it is always in the accusative case.* The English rendering is usually by a clause beginning with "that." Thus, in Acts 14:19, νομίζοντες αὐτὸν τεθνηκέναι is, lit., "thinking him to have died," i.e., "thinking that he had died." In Luke 24:23, λέγουσιν αὐτὸν ζῆν is, lit., "who say Him to live," i.e., "who say that He is alive."

But when the subject of the infinitive is the same as that of the preceding verb, it is not expressed, except for emphasis, and any words in agreement with it are put in the nominative. Thus, in Rom. 15:24, ἐλπίζω γὰρ διαπορευόμενος θεάσασθαι ὑμᾶς, I hope passing through to see you, if the subject of θεάσασθαι were expressed it would be με, but the same person is the subject of both verbs, and hence it is omitted and the participle agreeing is in the nominative. Cp. Rom. 1:22.

(4) The infinitive may be in various cases. For the genitive, see Luke 10:19, where τοῦ πατεῖν is, lit.," (power) of treading," i.e., "power to tread." So in Acts 27:20, where ἡμᾶς is the acc. subject. In 2 Cor. 1:8, there is an example both of the acc. with the infin., and of the genit. of the infin. The genitive often expresses purpose (Matt. 2:13; 3:13; 21:32), or even result (Acts 7:19).

For the dative, see 2 Cor. 2:13. Here τῷ ... εὑρεῖν is dative of cause "through (my not) finding"; με is the acc. subject; Τίτον is the object.

(5) These cases of the infinitive often come after prepositions. See Matt. 13:5,6, where each διά governs all that follows. In Matt. 24:12, note that τὴν ἀνομίαν is the subject of the infin. Cp. Mark 5:4. In Matt. 13:25, the acc. with the infinitive is governed by ἐν; in 26:32, the article with the acc. and infin. are all governed by μετά. In Matt. 6:1, αὐτοῖς is "by them."

(6) ὥστε with the infin., or with the acc. and infin., expresses result. See Luke 9:52, and Matt. 24:13, 32; Acts 16:26.

(7) The infinitive is occasionally used as an imperative (Phil. 3:16, στοιχεῖν; Rom. 12:15).

(8) The negative with the infinitive may be either οὐ or μή; οὐ denies as a matter of fact; in all other cases and generally speaking, μή is used. Note οὐδ᾽ (not μηδ᾽) in John 21:25: οἶμαι is "I suppose," but the οὐ intimates the certainty that the world would not contain, etc.

Exercise on the Infinitive

Translate and retranslate:—

(1) δέομαι δὲ τὸ μὴ παρὼν θαρρῆσαι τῇ πεποιθήσει ᾗ λογίζομαι τολμῆσαι ἐπί τινας τοὺς λογιζομένους ἡμᾶς ὡς κατὰ σάρκα περιπατοῦντας. (2 Cor. 10:2) τὸ μὴ ... θαρρῆσαι, lit., "the not ... to be bold" is the object of δέομαι; παρών, is nom. pres. partic. of πάρειμι.

(2) ἐν δὲ τῷ πορεύεσθαι ἐγένετο αὐτὸν ἐγγίζειν τῇ Δαμασκῷ, ἐξαίφνης τε αὐτὸν περιήστραψεν φῶς ἐκ τοῦ οὐρανοῦ 4 καὶ πεσὼν ἐπὶ τὴν γῆν ἤκουσεν φωνὴν λέγουσαν αὐτῷ, Σαοὺλ Σαούλ, τί με διώκεις; (Acts 9:3-4) ἐγένετο is "it came to pass" (see γίνομαι); this is followed by the acc. with the infin.; πεσών aor. partic. of πίπτω.

(3) Ἔλεγεν δὲ παραβολὴν αὐτοῖς πρὸς τὸ δεῖν πάντοτε προσεύχεσθαι αὐτοὺς καὶ μὴ ἐγκακεῖν. (Luke 18:1) πρὸς τὸ δεῖν, lit., "unto the to be necessary"; then follows the acc. with the infin., "them to pray," i.e., "that they ought always to pray."

(4) λέγει αὐτῷ Ναθαναήλ, Πόθεν με γινώσκεις; ἀπεκρίθη Ἰησοῦς καὶ εἶπεν αὐτῷ, Πρὸ τοῦ σε Φίλιππον φωνῆσαι ὄντα ὑπὸ τὴν συκῆν εἶδόν σε. (John 1:48) φωνῆσαι, 1st aor. infin. with Φίλιππον as subject and σε as object.

(5) νυνὶ δὲ καὶ τὸ ποιῆσαι ἐπιτελέσατε, ὅπως καθάπερ ἡ προθυμία τοῦ θέλειν, οὕτως καὶ τὸ ἐπιτελέσαι ἐκ τοῦ ἔχειν. (2 Cor. 8:11) ποιῆσαι, 1st aor. infin.; ἐκ τοῦ ἔχειν, lit., "out of the having."

(6) πάντα ὑπέταξας ὑποκάτω τῶν ποδῶν αὐτοῦ. ἐν τῷ γὰρ ὑποτάξαι [αὐτῷ] τὰ πάντα οὐδὲν ἀφῆκεν αὐτῷ ἀνυπότακτον. νῦν δὲ οὔπω ὁρῶμεν αὐτῷ τὰ πάντα ὑποτεταγμένα.... 15 καὶ ἀπαλλάξῃ τούτους, ὅσοι φόβῳ θανάτου διὰ παντὸς τοῦ ζῆν ἔνοχοι ἦσαν δουλείας. (Heb. 2:8, 15)

(f) Participles

These are verbal adjectives. Hence they agree with nouns expressed or understood.

(1) The present and perfect participles are often used with the verb "to be," making compound tense forms. See καιομένη ἦν, was burning, in Luke 24:32; also Gal. 4:24, "are allegorized." Literalism must not be pressed. Thus, in Matt. 18:20, εἰσιν ... συνηγμένοι is not "are having been gathered together," but "are gathered together." In Luke 3:23, ἦν ... ἀρχόμενος is "was beginning (His ministry)," not "began to be (about thirty)."

(2) A participle may simply be an adjective, as in τῇ ἐχομένῃ ἡμέρᾳ (Acts 21:26), on the next day, where the verb is a partic. middle of ἔχω. So in 1 Tim. 1:10, ὑφιαινούσῃ is "healthful," but is a present participle.

(3) The participle with the article is often equivalent to a noun: in 1 Thess. 1:10, τὸν ῥυόμενον ἡμᾶς, lit. "the (One) delivering us," is "Our Deliverer." In Mark 4:14, ὁ σπείρων is "the sower."

(4) The participle is frequently explanatory. Thus, in Phil. 2:7, λαβών explains the sentence "He emptied Himself"; in verse 8 γενόμενος explains "He humbled Himself." In Rom. 12:9, etc., the participles show how the command in verse 8 is to be carried out. So in 1 Pet. 2:8, and in 3:1 and 7, the participles show the mode of the fulfillment of the commands in verse 17.

Exercise in Participles

Translate and retranslate:—

(1) Ἀλλὰ τότε μὲν οὐκ εἰδότες θεὸν ἐδουλεύσατε τοῖς φύσει μὴ οὖσιν θεοῖς· 9 νῦν δὲ γνόντες θεόν, μᾶλλον δὲ γνωσθέντες ὑπὸ θεοῦ, πῶς ἐπιστρέφετε πάλιν ἐπὶ τὰ ἀσθενῆ καὶ πτωχὰ στοιχεῖα οἷς πάλιν ἄνωθεν δουλεύειν θέλετε; (Gal. 4:8-9) εἰδότες (see οἶδα); οὖσιν, dat., plur., masc., pres. partic. of εἰμί, to (those) not being gods.

(2) οὐχὶ μένον σοὶ ἔμενεν καὶ πραθὲν ἐν τῇ σῇ ἐξουσίᾳ ὑπῆρχεν; τί ὅτι ἔθου ἐν τῇ καρδίᾳ σου τὸ πρᾶγμα τοῦτο; οὐκ ἐψεύσω ἀνθρώποις ἀλλὰ τῷ θεῷ. (Acts 5:4) μένον, nom., sing., neut., pres.

partic. of μένω, lit., "remaining (did it not remain to thee)?"; πραθέν, nom., sing., neut., 2nd aor. partic. pass. of πιπράσκω.

(3) ὑμεῖς γὰρ μιμηταὶ ἐγενήθητε, ἀδελφοί, τῶν ἐκκλησιῶν τοῦ θεοῦ τῶν οὐσῶν ἐν τῇ Ἰουδαίᾳ ἐν
Χριστῷ Ἰησοῦ, ὅτι τὰ αὐτὰ ἐπάθετε καὶ ὑμεῖς ὑπὸ τῶν ἰδίων συμφυλετῶν καθὼς καὶ αὐτοὶ ὑπὸ τῶν
Ἰουδαίων, 15 τῶν καὶ τὸν κύριον ἀποκτεινάντων Ἰησοῦν καὶ τοὺς προφήτας καὶ ἡμᾶς ἐκδιωξάντων
καὶ θεῷ μὴ ἀρεσκόντων καὶ πᾶσιν ἀνθρώποις ἐναντίων, 16 κωλυόντων ἡμᾶς τοῖς ἔθνεσιν λαλῆσαι
ἵνα σωθῶσιν, εἰς τὸ ἀναπληρῶσαι αὐτῶν τὰς ἁμαρτίας πάντοτε. ἔφθασεν δὲ ἐπ᾽ αὐτοὺς ἡ ὀργὴ εἰς
τέλος. (1 Thess. 2:14-16) ἐπάθετε, 2nd aor. of πάσχω; ἔφθασεν, 1st aor. of φθάνω.

Lesson 34

Accents

Accents

(1) The accents were used originally to give the correct pitch or tone to a syllable. There are three—the acute (ʹ), the grave (ˋ), the circumflex (˜). The acute stands only on one of the last three syllables of a word, the circumflex only on one of the last two, the grave only on the last. An accent is marked only on vowels; in diphthongs on the second vowel, as in οὕτως, οὖν. The acute and the grave are put after the aspirate or breathing, whether the rough breathing (ʽ), as in ἕξω, or the soft breathing (ʼ), as in ἔχω. The circumflex is put over the breathing, as in οὗτος.

(2) A word that has the acute on the last syllable, as in βασιλεύς, is called *oxytone* (sharp-toned). When the acute is on the last syllable but one (the penult), as in οὕτως, it is called *paroxytone.* When the acute is on the last but two (the ante-penult), as in ἄνθρωπος, it is called *proparoxytone.* The antepenult, if accented, always has the acute.

(3) If the last syllable of a word contains a long vowel, the acute accent must be on the last or last but one, the circumflex on the last only. If, therefore, the last syllable of a proparoxytone is lengthened by declension the accent is thrown forward, so that the word becomes paroxytone, e.g., ἄνθρωπος, but ἀνθρώπων.

(4) When the circumflex comes on the last syllable, as in αὐτοῦ, it is called *perispomenon:* when on the penult, as in οὗτος, it is called *properispomenon.* This pronoun provides an example of the fact that a penult has the circumflex when it is long by *nature,* when the last syllable

is short by nature. Otherwise, it takes the acute, e.g., λόγος. A syllable is long by *nature* when it has a long vowel, e.g., τιμή, or a diphthong, e.g., κτείνω; it is long by *position* when it is followed by two consonants, e.g., ἵσταντες, or by one of the double consonants, ζ (δ and ς), ξ (κ and ς), ψ (π and ς), e.g., ἰσόψυχος.

(5) Final αι and οι are regarded as short in determining the accent, as in ἄνθρωποι, νῆποι, but as long in the optative; thus ποιήσοι (not ποίησοι).

(6) Genitives in -εως and -εων from nouns in -ις and -υς of the third declension have the acute on the antepenult, e.g., πόλεως (genitive of πόλις), but βασιλέως (gen. of βασιλεύς). So with all in -εύς.

(7) An oxytone changes its acute to a grave accent before other words in the sentence, e.g., θεὸς ἦν.

Contracted syllables

(8) A contracted syllable is accented if either of the original syllables had an accent. A contracted penult or antepenult is accented regularly. A contracted final syllable is circumflexed, e.g., τιμῶ, from τιμάω. But if the original word was oxytone the acute is retained, e.g., βεβώς, from βεβαώς. If neither of the original syllables had an accent, the contracted form is accented without regard to the contraction. Thus τίμαε becomes τίμα.

Accents Regarding Enclitics and Proclitics

(9) An enclitic is a word which loses its accent and is pronounced as part of the preceding word. The following are enclitics:—(*a*) the indefinite pronoun τις in all its forms; (*b*) the personal pronouns μοῦ, μοί, μέ, σοῦ, σοί, σέ;(*c*) the pres. indic. of εἰμί (except the 2nd sing. εἶ); (*d*) φημί, φησίν, φασίν; (*e*) the particles γε, τε, and the inseparable δε in ὅδε, etc.; (*f*) the indefinite adverbs ποτέ, που, περ, πω, πως.

If a word is proparoxytone, it receives from the enclitic an acute on the last syllable as a second accent, e.g., ἄνθρωπός τις, and so if a word is properispomenon, e.g., δεῖξόν μοι.

(10) Enclitics lose their accent when the preceding word is (*a*) oxytone, e.g., αὐτόν τινας (Mark 12:13); (*b*) paroxytone, e.g., Ἰουδαίων τε (Acts 14:1); (*c*) perispomenon, e.g., ἀγαπῶν με (John 14:21).

(11) Enclitics retain their accent (*a*) if they begin or end a sentence, e.g., φησίν in John 18:29; (*b*) if they are dissyllables after a paroxytone (to avoid three successive unaccented syllables),

e.g., λόγου ἐστίν (Jas. 1:23); (*c*) when the preceding syllable is elided, e.g., δι' ἐμοῦ, John 14:6; (*d*) if a dissyllable after a proclitic (see below), e.g., οὐκ εἰμί, John 3:28; (*e*) the personal pronouns μοῦ, μοῖ, etc., keep their accent after an accented preposition, e.g., περὶ ἐμοὺ, John 15:26 (except after πρός in πρός με, John 6:65).

(12) Ἐστί (ἐστίν) at the beginning of a sentence retains its accent, and after οὐκ, μή, εἰ, καί, ἀλλά and τοῦτο, or a paroxytone syllable, e.g., Ἰουδαίων ἐστίν (John 4:22), or in mild emphasis, e.g., νῦν ἐστίν (John 4:23). Again, ἔστι, denoting existence or possibility, retains its accent, e.g., ἅγιον ἔστιν (Acts 19:2).

(13) Some monosyllables have no accent, and are closely attached to the following word. They lose their accent in it. These are called *proclitics.* Such are the articles ὁ, ἡ, οἱ, αἱ, the prepositions εἰς, ἐξ (ἐκ), ἐν, the conjunctions εἰ and ὡς and the negative οὐ (οὐκ, οὐχ). But οὐ takes the acute when it stands alone, as οὔ, no! A proclitic followed by an enclitic is oxytoned, as οὔτις (which may be written as one word).

(14) Examples of change of words by accents: ἡ, the (fem.), ἤ, or, than, ἥ, who (fem.); τίς, who? τις, someone; οὐ, not, οὗ, where; ποῦ, where?, που, somewhere; αὐται, they (fem. plur.), αὗται, these (fem.).

Part 2

Dictionary

Publisher's Preface

THIS new edition of W. E. Vine's *An Expository Dictionary of New Testament Words* includes many new features and provides the Bible student with a number of significnt additional benefits. The new typesetting has allowed for numberous factual and typographical errors to be corrected, for British spellings to be changed to their more familiar American counterparts, and for a new two-column format that is easier to use than the previous edition. Additionally, the numbering system foiund in the Greek lexicon of *The New Strong's Exhaustive Concordance of the Bible* (1984) is included immediately following the Greek word in each entry, as well as in the Index. The reader is encouraged to read the following instructions to gain the fullest benefit of this added feature.

1. Words not listed in *Strong's* Greek lexicon but which are simple compounds of other words that are listed are indicated by a combinaiton of numbers (for instance, *diachleuazo*, 1223 and 5512).

2. Phrases of two or more words (for instance, *men oun, ei me*) are not numbered in the main text of *Vine's* unless there is a separate entry for them in *Strong's*.

3. Irregular verbs that are listed separately in *Vine's*, but not in *Strong's*, are indicated as a tnese of the verb (for instance, *eipon*, aorist of 3004.)

4. Intensives, diminuitives, comparatives, or similar forms of other words not listed in *Strong's* are indicated with a single asterisk (for instance, *eleeinoteros*, from *eleeinos* is 1652*).

5. Differing gender, number, or verb forms (for instance, infinitive or participle) of other words not listed in *Strong's* are indicated with a double asterisk (for instance, *opsia*, from *opsion*, is 3798**).

6. Variant spellings of forms of other words not listed in *Strong's* are indicated with a "v" following the number (for instance, *ektromos*, a variant of *entromos*, is 1790v).

7. Derivatives or roots of other words not listed in *Strong's* are indicated with with a "d" following the number (for instance, *genema*, a derivative of *Ginomai*, is 1096d).

8. Words not listed in *Strong's* are indicated with an "a" following the number of the word that would preceed them alphabetically if they were included in *Strong's*.

Character	**Name**	**Transliteration**
α	alpha	a
β	beta	b
γ	gamma	g
δ	delta	d
ε	epsilon	e
ζ	zeta	z
η	eta	ē
θ	theta	th
ι	iota	i
κ	kappa	k
λ	lamda	l
μ	mu	m
ν	nu	n
ξ	xi	x
ο	omicron	o
π	pi	p
ρ	rho	t
σ, ς	sigma	s
τ	tau	t
υ	upsilon	u or y
φ	phi	ph
χ	chi	ch
ψ	psi	ps
ω	omega	ō
ʽ	rough breathing mark	h

Publisher's Preface

We are pleased to add this new and corrected edition of *Vine's* to our list. We therefore send it forth with the same intention Professor Vine expressed in 1939, that it might benefit those who study and teach the Bible "in their knowledge of God and His Word and in helping to equip them in their use and ministry of the Holy Scriptures."

The Publishers

Foreword to the Original Edition

ANYONE who makes a serious and substantial contribution to the understanding of the New Testament, renders a public service, for if religion is the foundation of morality, by the knowledge of God is the welfare of the people. As a book the New Testament stands alone and supreme, simple in its profoundness, and profound in its simplicity. It is the record, in twenty-seven Writings, of the origin, nature and progress of Christianity, and in the quality of its influence it has done more for the world than all other books together.

We are more than fortunate to have this Book in a Version made immortal by William Tyndale, and we are grateful to have it also in the Revised Versions of 1611, and 1881-1885. But the fact remains that they who are entirely dependent upon a Version must miss very much of the glory and richness of these Writings. Provided there is spiritual appreciation, he who can read the New Testament in the language in which it was written stands to get the most out of it. But, of course, all cannot do this; although the accomplishment is by no means the preserve of the linguistic scholar. Yet the average reader is not wholly cut off from the treasures which lie in the Greek of the New Testament, for these have been put within our reach by means of Grammars and Lexicons, the special purpose of which has been to aid the English reader. So far as my acquaintance with these works goes, I do not hesitate to say that this Expository Dictionary more completely fulfils this design than any other such effort, in that it is at once a Concordance, a Dictionary, and a Commentary, produced in the light of the best available scholarship.

Without encumbering his work with philological technicalities and extra-biblical references, Mr. Vine puts at the disposal of the English reader the labours of a lifetime bestowed devoutly upon the New Testament.

To several of the features of this Dictionary I would like to call attention.

First, it shows how rich is the language of the New Testament in words which present shades of the meaning of some common idea.

A good illustration of this is found on pages 203-207, under *Come,* and its related thoughts (e.g., *Appear,* pp. 64-67). Here, including the compounds, upwards of fifty words are employed to express one general thought, and the employment of any one of these, in any given passage, has precise historical or spiritual significance. If this root idea is followed out, for example, in its bearing on Christ's Second Advent, it is profoundly important to apprehend the significance respectively of *erchomai, hēkō, phainō, parousia, apokalupsis,* and *epiphaneia,*

Second, this Dictionary indicates the doctrinal bearing which the use of chosen words has. A case in point will be found on page 60. under *Another.* The use of *allos* and *heteros* in the New Testament should be carefully examined, for *another numerically* must not be confounded with *another generically.* Mr. Vine points this out in John 14:16. When Christ said, "I will make request of the Father, and He shall give you another Helper (*allon Paraklēton*)," He made a tremendous claim both for Himself and for the Spirit, for *allos* here implies the personality of the Spirit, and the equality of both Jesus and the Spirit with the Father. See also Mr. Vine's reference to the use of these words in Galatians 1:6 and 7. For an illustration of how one word can have a variety of meanings see pages 270-271, under *Day.* Unless such expressions as "man's day", "day of the Lord", and "day of Christ", are distinguished, one cannot understand the dispensational teaching of the New Testament. In this connection, the R.V. must be followed in 2 Thess. 2:2.

Third, this Dictionary shows how very many New Testament words are compounds, and how important are prepositional prefixes.

I think it was Bishop Westcott who said that New Testament doctrine is largely based on its prepositions; in any case the importance of them can scarcely be exaggerated. These added to a word either emphasise or extend its meaning, and many such words have become Anglicized. For illustration take the three words *anabolism, katabolism,* and *metabolism.* These words are used in relation to biology and physiology. The root word in each is *ballō,* to cast, or throw, and each has a prepositional prefix; in the first, *ana,* up; in the second, *kata,* down; and in the third, *meta,* with. *Metabolism* tells of the chemical changes in living cells, by which the energy is provided for the vital processes and activities, and new material is assimilated to repair the waste; by a proper *metabolism* or *throwing-together* of the substances of the body, health is promoted. This building up of the nutritive substances into the more complex living protoplasm is *anabolism,* or *throwing-up;* and the want of this results in *katabolism,* or *throwing-down* of protoplasm. Now, two of the three words occur in the New Testament. For *metaballō* see p. 180; and for *kataballō,* p. 172, in both cases all the references are given (see Preface, p. 8, par. 4).

For the possible range of prefixes to one word, see pages 203, 204; *Come,* with *eis,* and *ek,* and *epi,* and *dia,* and *kata,* and *para,* and *pros,* and *sun;* and two of the eleven compounds are double, No. 4 with *epi* and *ana;* and No. 8 with pars and *eis.* These illustrations are sufficient to show the scope and simplicity of this work and consequently its immense usefulness to the English reader.

Fourth, this Dictionary is compiled in the light of the new knowledge which has come to us by the discovery of the papyri. During the last fifty years this light has been brought to bear upon the New Testament with precious and priceless results. In olden days in Egypt it was a custom not to burn waste paper, but to dump it outside the town, and the sands of the desert swept over it, and buried it, and for centuries a vast mass of such rubbish has lain there. However, in 1896-1897 Dr. Grenfell and Dr. Hunt began digging at Oxyrhynchus and discovered a number of papyri, among which was a crumpled leaf, written on both sides in uncial characters, which proved to be a collection of Sayings attributed to Jesus, Logia which Dr. J. Hope Moulton believed to be genuine. These and very many other papyri were classified and edited and one day when Dr. Deissmann was casually looking at a volume of these in the University Library at Heidelberg, he was impressed by the likeness of the language to that with which he was familiar in his study of the Greek New Testament. By further study the great discovery was made that New Testament Greek is not the Attic of the Classics, nor is it "a language of the Holy Ghost" as one scholar called it, but it is the ordinary vernacular Greek of that period, the language of everyday life, as it was spoken and written by the ordinary men and women of the day, tradesmen, soldiers, schoolboys, lovers, clerks, and so on that is, the *koinē,* or "Common" Greek of the great Græco-Roman world.

In illustration of this, look at Col. 2:14, which has several words which are found in the papyri; and take one of these, *Cheirographon,* handwriting. This means a memorandum of debt, 'a writing by hand' used in public and private contracts, and it is a technical word in the Greek papyri. A large number of ancient notes of hand have been published and of these Dr. Deissmann says, "a stereotyped formula in these documents is the promise to pay back the borrowed money, 'I will repay'; and they all are in the debtor's own hand, or, if he could not write, in the handwriting of another acting for him, with the express remark, 'I have written for him' ". In such a note-of-hand, belonging to the first century, and with reference to a hundred silver drachmae, one named Papus wrote on behalf of two people who could not write, "which we will also repay, with any other that we may owe, I Papus wrote for him who is not able to write."

Now, this expression occurs in the New Testament twice, in the parable of "The Lord and his Servants", "have patience with me, and I will pay thee all", and in Paul's note to Philemon concerning Onesimus, "if he hath wronged thee, or oweth thee ought, put that on mine account. I Paul have written it with mine own hand, I will repay it."

In the famous Florentine papyrus of A.D. 85, the governor of Egypt gives this order in the course of a trial—"Let the hand-writing be crossed out," which corresponds to the "blotting out the hand-writing" of Col. 2:14. Many such illustrations might be given, from which we see that the papyri have a distinct expository value.

In Lexicons previous to this discovery are to be found lists of what are called *hapax-legomena,* words which occur once only, and many of which, it was supposed, were created by the Holy Spirit for the conveyance of Christian truth, but now all or nearly all such words have been found in the papyri. The Holy Spirit did not create a special language for Christianity, but used the colloquial tongue of the time; He employed the cosmopolitan Greek. This fact has radically affected our approach to the New Testament, and although, in view of the magnitude of this Dictionary, it has been impossible to do more than make a reference here and there to this learning (e.g., pp. 7, 8, 59), yet the whole is produced in the light of it, and so represents present day scholarship.

I might have made reference also to etymological, cross-reference and other values in this work, but perhaps enough has been said to indicate its scope and usefulness. Mr. Vine has done a great service to the non-academic reader of the New Testament, and those also who are most familiar with the original tongue may learn much from these pages.

W. Graham Scroggie, D.D.
(Edin.)

Foreword to One-Volume Edition

NEARLY twelve years have gone by since the first edition of this *Expository Dictionary* was completed. During these years the work has had ample opportunity to prove its worth as a handbook for serious students of the English Bible. And the high hopes with which the enterprise was launched have been justified not only by the warm welcome each volume of the first edition received as it appeared but also by the increasing sense of indebtedness which Bible students all over the world have felt as they have come to know its value by daily use. Mr. Vine himself has passed from our midst in the meantime, but his Biblical ministry survives in a wide range of published works, at the head of which stands his *Expository Dictionary.* It is a welcome token of its continued usefulness that the publishers have now decided to reissue it in a one-volume edition.

There is no work just like this. The English reader with little or no Greek has, of course, the standard concordances, notably Wigram's *Englishman's Greek Concordance;* the student of Greek has his Grimm-Thayer, Moulton-Milligan, and Bauer. These works provide the lexical skeleton; Mr. Vine's work clothes that skeleton with the flesh and sinews of living exposition, and makes available for the ordinary reader the expert knowledge contained in the more advanced works. In fact, this *Expository Dictionary* comes as near as possible to doing for the non-specialist what is being done for the specialist by Kittel's encyclopaedic *Theological Dictionary to the New Testament,* a German work in several volumes, not yet completed.

A work of this kind, of course, cannot be expected to record every occurrence of each word in the New Testament. But all important and significant occurrences are mentioned, and many of the entries in fact are exhaustive, especially those dealing with words which do not occur very often. By the helpful system of cross-references the reader can see at a glance not only which Greek words are represented by one English word, but also which other English words, if any, are used to translate each Greek word. It is a further advantage that both A.V. and R.V. renderings are listed.

Mr. Vine's Greek scholarship was wide, accurate and up-to-date, and withal unobtrusive. Casual readers will hardly realise the wealth of ripe learning, the years of hard work, of which they may reap the fruit in this work. To his thorough mastery of the classical idiom the author added a close acquaintance with the Hellenistic vernacular, and used his knowledge of both to illustrate the meaning of New Testament words. And bearing in mind the New Testament writers' familiarity with the Septuagint and its influence on their language, he has enhanced the value of his work by giving select references to Septuagint usages.

There are few human pursuits more fascinating than the study of words. As vehicles for conveying the thoughts, feelings and desires of men, they have an abiding interest; how supremely interesting, then, should be the study of those "healthful words" in which the revelation of God Himself has been conveyed!

Yet words, divorced from their meanings, are but empty sounds; instead of being a vehicle of thought, they become a substitute for it. "Words", said Thomas Hobbes, "are wise men's counters; they do but reckon by them: but they are the money of fools." We must know what values to attach to them if we are to profit by them.

Words are not static things. They change their meanings with the passage of time. Many words used in the A.V. no longer possess in current English the meanings they had in 1611. We do not now use "prevent" in the sense of "precede", or "carriage" in the sense of "baggage". These changes of meaning may be inferred from the context, but there are other changes which might not be so readily noticed. An important example is the word "atonement", one of the great technical terms of theology. When this word retained its etymological sense of "at-one-ment", it was an appropriate rendering for Gk. *katallage,* and is so used in the A.V. of Rom. 5:11. But "atonement" has long since ceased to be an English equivalent of "reconciliation", and its continued use leads to confusion of thought on a theme of the utmost importance. A study of the articles on PROPITIATE, RANSOM and RECONCILE in this work will greatly clarify the reader's understanding of the Biblical presentation of what is commonly called "the doctrine of the atonement".

Not only in recent English, but in ancient Greek as well, we find words changing their meanings. Biblical exegetes of an earlier day were at a disadvantage in having to read New

Testament words in the light of their classical usage of four or five centuries earlier. But they recognised certain marked differences between classical and New Testament Greek, and knowing no other Greek quite like that of the New Testament, they concluded that it must be a specially devised "language of the Holy Ghost". During the last seventy or eighty years, however, many documents have been found in the Near East written in this same Greek, from which we have learned the very salutary lesson that the "language of the Holy Ghost" is nothing other than the language of the common people. (One example of a change in the meaning of a Greek word between classical and New Testament times is pointed out in a note at the end of the entry on PUNISHMENT.)

There can be no true Biblical theology unless it is based on sound Biblical exegesis, and there can be no sound Biblical exegesis unless a firm textual and grammatical foundation has been laid for it. Such a foundation is laid in this *Expository Dictionary,* but it provides much more than a foundation. The work is full of careful exegesis, and the student or teacher who makes it his constant companion in the study of Scripture will find that he can afford to dispense with a large number of lesser aids. In fact, it is so valuable a handbook to the study of the New Testament that many of us who have learned to use it regularly wonder how we ever got on without it. It has established a well-deserved reputation for itself and really needs no special commendation such as this, but it is a pleasure to commend it afresh, and to wish it a long term of service in its new format.

F. F. Bruce
Head of the Department
of Biblical History and
Literature in the
University of Sheffield.
September, 1952

Preface

To ascertain the exact meaning of the words and phraseology of the originals of the Holy Scriptures is of great importance, particularly those which have a variety of meanings in English. The research work of the past fifty years, with the discovery of a large number of inscriptions and documents, and especially of the non-literary writings in the tombs and dust heaps of Egypt, has yielded much light upon the use and meaning of the language of the originals. The importance of the Egyptian papyri writings etc. lies in the fact that they were written during the period in which the writers of the New Testament lived. Proof has thus been provided that the language of the New Testament was not a debased form of literary Greek corrupted by Hebrew idioms, but that in the main it was the vernacular, the speech of the everyday life of the people in the countries which came under Greek influence through the conquests of Alexander the Great. As the result of those conquests, the ancient Greek dialects became merged into one common speech, the *Koinē* or 'common' Greek. In one form this language became the literary *Koinē,* or Hellenistic, of such writers as Josephus. In its spoken form it was the everyday speech of millions of people throughout the Græco-Roman world, and in the providence of God it was under these conditions and in this world-language that the New Testament was written.

The fruit of these researches has been provided in such volumes as the "Vocabulary of the Greek Testament," by J. H. Moulton and G. Milligan, the "Grammar of the New Testament Greek" by the former and the book entitled "New Testament Documents" by the latter, "Bible Studies" by G. A. Deissmann, "Light from the Ancient East" by A. Deissmann, and similarly well-known works by W. M. Ramsay. References will be found to some of these in the following pages.

The present volumes are produced especially for the help of those who do not study Greek, though it is hoped that those who are familiar with the original will find them useful.

The work is of an expository character, comments being given on various passages referred to under the different headings. The doctrines of Scripture are dealt with at some length, and notes are provided on matters historical, technical and etymological.

In cases where an English word translates a variety of Greek words the latter are given in English form. Where there are no such variations, each word is dealt with according to its occurrences and usage in the New Testament, reference being made to the differences between the Authorised and Revised Versions.

The method of the Dictionary provides an exhaustive presentation of synonymous words. Where a word in the original has a variety of English renderings, a list is given of these at the close of the note on each word. The list provides in this way a comprehensive study of the use of any given word in the original. In cases where a list has already been given, only the first of these meanings is usually mentioned. There is thus a twofold presentation, firstly, of the different Greek words for one English word, secondly, of the different English meanings attaching to a single Greek word.

The subject-matter is also analysed under the various parts of speech. To take an example, DILIGENCE, DILIGENT, DILIGENTLY, are associated in one heading, and the forms in the original are divided respectively under the sections, Nouns, Verbs, Adjectives, Adverbs. The parts of speech are not given in the same order in every case. The order is largely dependent upon the greater prominence which a word receives in the original. Other considerations have made a variety in this respect advisable.

In many cases the student is referred to the occurrences in the Septuagint Version, especially where that Version presents a comparatively small number of occurrences or contains only one instance of the use. Reference to the Apocryphal books of the Old Testament is omitted.

In many instances all the occurrences and usages of a word are analysed in a list, showing the different meanings as indicated by the context in each passage of the New Testament.

Considerable use has been made of the two Commentaries, written jointly by Mr. C. F. Hogg of London and the present writer, upon the Epistle to the Galatians and the two Epistles to the Thessalonians. I have also made use of Hastings' Dictionary of the Bible, Abbott-Smith's Manual Greek Lexicon of the New Testament, the larger works by Cremer and by Thayer's Grimm, and of A. T. Robertson's Grammar of the Greek New Testament in the Light of Historical Research; also of such works as Trench's New Testament Synonyms.

Preface

A criticism may be raised in regard to a work like this that it would provide students who know little or nothing of the original with an opportunity of airing some knowledge of Greek. Even supposing that such a criticism were valid, the general advantage of the method adopted should outweigh the danger of such proclivities.

I wish to express my great indebtedness to, and appreciation of, the kind assistance of the Rev. H. E. Guillebaud, M.A., of Cambridge, and T. W. Rhodes, Esqre., M.A., recently of Madrid, who have made copious and useful suggestions and emendations, and have co-operated in going through the proofs.

It is with a sense of deep gratitude that I express my indebtedness to my friend Mr. F. F. Bruce, for his wholehearted assistance in going through the typescript and making corrections and valuable suggestions previous to its being printed, and in proof-reading subsequently, whose efficiency, as a classical scholar, and whose knowledge of the originals, have enhanced the value of the work.

I trust that notwithstanding imperfections and limitations of treatment the work may afford assistance to Bible students in enabling them to increase in their knowledge of God and His Word and in helping to equip them in their use and ministry of the Holy Scriptures.

W. E. Vine, M.A.
Bath

ABASE

tapeinoō (ταπεινόω, 5013) signifies "to make low, bring low," (a) of bringing to the ground, making level, reducing to a plain, as in Luke 3:5; (b) metaphorically in the active voice, to bring to a humble condition, "to abase," 2 Cor. 11:7, and in the passive, "to be abased," Phil. 4:12; in Matt. 23:12; Luke 14:11; 18:14, the KJV has "shall be abased," the RV "shall be humbled." It is translated "humble yourselves" in the middle voice sense in Jas. 4:10; 1 Pet. 5:6; "humble," in Matt. 18:4; 2 Cor. 12:21 and Phil. 2:8. See HUMBLE, LOW. Cf., *tapeinos*, "lowly," *tapeinōsis*, "humiliation," and *tapeinophrosunē*, "humility."

ABBA

abba (ἀββά, 5) is an Aramaic word, found in Mark 14:36; Rom. 8:15 and Gal. 4:6. In the Gemara (a Rabbinical commentary on the Mishna, the traditional teaching of the Jews) it is stated that slaves were forbidden to address the head of the family by this title. It approximates to a personal name, in contrast to "Father," with which it is always joined in the NT. This is probably due to the fact that, *abba* having practically become a proper name, Greek-speaking Jews added the Greek word *patēr*, "father," from the language they used. *Abba* is the word framed by the lips of infants, and betokens unreasoning trust; "father" expresses an intelligent apprehension of the relationship. The two together express the love and intelligent confidence of the child.

ABHOR

1. *apostugeō* (ἀποστυγέω, 655) denotes "to shudder" (*apo*, "from," here used intensively, *stugeō*, "to hate") hence, "to abhor," Rom. 12:9.

2. *bdelussō* (βδελύσσω, 948), "to render foul" (from *bdeō*, "to stink"), "to cause to be abhorred" (in the Sept. in Exod. 5:21; Lev. 11:43; 20:25, etc.), is used in the middle voice, signifying "to turn oneself away from" (as if from a stench); hence, "to detest," Rom. 2:22. In Rev. 21:8 it denotes "to be abominable." See ABOMINABLE.

ABILITY, ABLE

A. Nouns.

1. *dunamis* (δύναμις, 1411) is (a) "power, ability," physical or moral, as residing in a person or thing; (b) "power in action," as, e.g., when put forth in performing miracles. It occurs 118 times in the NT. It is sometimes used of the miracle or sign itself, the effect being put for the cause, e.g., Mark 6:5, frequently in the Gospels and Acts. In 1 Cor. 14:11 it is rendered "meaning"; "force" would be more accurate. Cf., the corresponding verbs, B, 1, 2, 3 and the adjective C. 1, below. See ABUNDANCE, DEED, MIGHT, POWER, STRENGTH, VIOLENCE, VIRTUE.

2. *ischus* (ἰσχύς, 2479), connected with *ischō* and *echō*, "to have, to hold" (from the root *ech-*, signifying "holding"), denotes "ability, force, strength"; "ability" in 1 Pet. 4:11, KJV (RV, "strength"). In Eph. 1:19 and 6:10, it is said of the strength of God bestowed upon believers, the phrase "the power of His might" indicating strength afforded by power. In 2 Thess. 1:9, "the glory of His might" signifies the visible expression of the inherent personal power of the Lord Jesus. It is said of angels in 2 Pet. 2:11 (cf., Rev. 18:2, KJV, "mightily"). It is ascribed to God in Rev. 5:12 and 7:12. In Mark 12:30, 33, and Luke 10:27 it describes the full extent of the power wherewith we are to love God. See MIGHT, POWER, STRENGTH.

B. Verbs.

1. *dunamai* (δύναμαι, 1410), "to be able, to have power," whether by virtue of one's own ability and resources, e.g., Rom. 15:14; or through a state of mind, or through favorable circumstances, e.g., 1 Thess. 2:6; or by permission of law or custom, e.g., Acts 24:8, 11; or simply "to be able, powerful," Matt. 3:9; 2 Tim. 3:15, etc. See POWER.

2. *dunamoō* (δυναμόω, 1412), "to make strong, confirm," occurs in Col. 1:11 (some authorities have the 1st aorist or momentary tense, in Heb. 11:34 also). Cf. *endunamoō*, "to enable, strengthen."

3. *dunateō* (δυνατέω, 1414) signifies "to be mighty, to show oneself powerful," Rom. 4:14; 2 Cor. 9:8; 13:3. See A, No. 1.

4. *ischuō* (ἰσχύω, 2480), akin to A, No. 2, "to be strong, to prevail," indicates a more forceful strength or ability than *dunamai*, e.g., Jas. 5:16, where it is rendered "availeth much" (i.e., "prevails greatly"). See PREVAIL, STRENGTH.

Note: Still stronger forms are *exischuō*, "to be thoroughly strong," Eph. 3:18, "may be strong" (not simply "may be able," KJV); *katischuō*, Matt. 16:18, and Luke 23:23, in the former, of the powerlessness of the gates of Hades to prevail against the Church; in the latter, of the power of a fierce mob to prevail over a weak ruler (see *Notes on Galatians*, by Hogg and Vine, p. 251); also Luke 21:36. The prefixed prepositions are intensive in each case.

5. *echō* (ἔχω, 2192), "to have," is translated "your ability" in 2 Cor. 8:11, and "ye may be able" in 2 Pet. 1:15, and is equivalent to the phrase "to have the means of." See HAVE.

6. *euporeō* (εὐπορέω, 2141), lit., "to journey well" (*eu*, "well," *poreō*, "to journey"), hence, "to prosper," is translated "according to (his) ability," in Acts 11:29.

Note: Hikanoō, corresponding to the adjective *hikanos* (see below) signifies "to make competent, qualify, make sufficient"; in 2 Cor. 3:6, KJV, "hath made (us) able"; RV, "hath made us sufficient"; in Col. 1:12, "hath made (us) meet."

C. Adjectives.

1. *dunatos* (δυνατός, 1415), corresponding to A, No. 1, signifies "powerful." See, e.g., Rom. 4:21; 9:22; 11:23; 12:18; 15:1; 1 Cor. 1:26; 2 Cor. 9:8. See MIGHTY, POWER, STRONG.

2. *hikanos* (ἱκανός, 2425), translated "able," is to be distinguished from *dunatos* While *dunatos* means "possessing power," *hikanos*, primarily, "reaching to," has accordingly the meaning "sufficient." When said of things it signifies "enough," e.g., Luke 22:38; when said of persons, it means "competent," "worthy," e.g., 2 Cor. 2:6, 16; 3:5; 2 Tim. 2:2. See CONTENT, GOOD, GREAT, LONG, SECURITY, WORTHY.

Note: Ischuros denotes "strong, mighty"; in an active sense, "mighty," in having inherent and moral power, e.g., Matt. 12:29; 1 Cor. 4:10; Heb. 6:18.

ABOLISH

katargeō (καταργέω, 2673), lit., "to reduce to inactivity" (*kata*, "down," *argos*, "inactive"), is translated "abolish" in Eph. 2:15 and 2 Tim. 1:10, in the RV only in 1 Cor. 15:24, 26. It is rendered "is abolished" in the KJV of 2 Cor. 3:13, the RV corrects to "was passing away" (marg., "was being done away"). In this and similar words not loss of being is implied, but loss of well being.

The barren tree was cumbering the ground, making it useless for the purpose of its existence, Luke 13:7, the unbelief of the Jews could not "make of none effect" the faithfulness of God, Rom. 3:3; the preaching of the gospel could not "make of none effect" the moral enactments of the Law, 3:31; the Law could not make the promise of "none effect," 4:14; Gal. 3:17; the effect of the identification of the believer with Christ in His death is to render inactive his body in regard to sin, Rom. 6:6; the death of a woman's first husband discharges her from the law of the husband, that is, it makes void her status as his wife in the eyes of the law, 7:2; in that sense the believer has been discharged from the Law, 7:6; God has chosen things that are not "to bring to nought things that are," i.e., to render them useless for practical purposes, 1 Cor. 1:28; the princes of this world are "brought to nought," i.e., their wisdom becomes ineffective, 2:6; the use for which the human stomach exists ceases with man's death, 6:13; knowledge, prophesyings, and that which was in part were to be "done away," 1 Cor. 13:8, 10, i.e., they were to be rendered of no effect after their temporary use was fulfilled; when the apostle became a man he did away with the ways of a child, v. 11; God is going to abolish all rule and authority and power, i.e., He is going to render them inactive, 1 Cor. 15:24; the last enemy that shall be abolished, or reduced to inactivity, is death, v. 26; the glory shining in the face of Moses, "was passing away," 2 Cor. 3:7, the transitoriness of its character being of a special significance; so in vv. 11, 13; the veil upon the heart of Israel is "done away" in Christ, v. 14; those who seek justification by the Law are "severed" from Christ, they are rendered inactive in relation to Him, Gal. 5:4; the essential effect of the preaching of the Cross would become inoperative by the preaching of circumcision, 5:11; by the death of Christ the barrier between Jew and Gentile is rendered inoperative as such, Eph. 2:15; the Man of Sin is to be reduced to inactivity by the manifestation of the Lord's *Parousia* with His people, 2 Thess. 2:8; Christ has rendered death inactive for the believer, 2 Tim. 1:10, death becoming the means of a more glorious life, with Christ; the Devil is to be reduced to inactivity through the death of Christ, Heb. 2:14. See CUMBER, DESTROY, NOUGHT, VOID.

ABOMINABLE, ABOMINATION

A. Adjectives.

1. *athemitos* (ἀθέμιτος, 111) occurs in Acts 10:28, "unlawful," and 1 Pet. 4:3, "abominable" (*a*, negative, *themitos*, an adjective from *themis*, "law"), hence, "unlawful." See UNLAWFUL.

2. *bdeluktos* (βδελυκτός, 947), Titus 1:16, is said of deceivers who profess to know God, but deny Him by their works.

B. Verb.

bdelussō (βδελύσσω, 948): see ABHOR, No. 2.

C. Noun.

bdelugma (βδέλυγμα, 946), akin to A, No. 2 and B, denotes an "object of disgust, an abomination." This is said of the image to be set up by Antichrist, Matt. 24:15; Mark 13:14; of that which is highly esteemed amongst men, in contrast to its real character in the sight of God, Luke 16:15. The constant association with idolatry suggests that what is highly esteemed among men constitutes an idol in the human heart. In Rev. 21:27, entrance is forbidden into the Holy City on the part of the unclean, or one who "maketh an abomination and a lie." It is also used of the contents of the golden cup in the hand of the evil woman described in Rev. 17:4, and of the name ascribed to her in the following verse.

For **ABOUND** see ABUNDANCE

ABOVE

The following adverbs have this meaning (prepositions are omitted here):—

1. *anō* (ἄνω, 507) denotes "above, in a higher place," Acts 2:19 (the opposite to *katō*, "below"). With the article it means "that which is above," Gal. 4:26; Phil. 3:14, "the high calling" (RV marg., "upward"); with the plural article, "the things above," John 8:23, lit., "from the things above"; Col. 3:1-2. With *heōs*, "as far as," it is translated "up to the brim," in John 2:7. It has the meaning "upwards" in John 11:41 and Heb. 12:15. See HIGH.

2. *anōteron* (ἀνώτερος, 511), the comparative degree of No. 1, is the neuter of the adjective *anōteros*. It is used (a) of motion to a higher place, "higher," Luke 14:10; (b) of location in a higher place, i.e., in the preceding part of a passage, "above" Heb. 10:8. See HIGHER.

3. *epanō* (ἐπάνω, 1883), *epi*, "over," *anō*, "above," is used frequently as a preposition with a noun; adverbially, of number, e.g., Mark 14:5, RV; 1 Cor. 15:6.

Note: In Acts 4:22, KJV, the adjective *pleion*, "more," is translated "above," the RV corrects to "more than (forty years)."

4. *anōthen* (ἄνωθεν, 509), "from above," is used of place, (a) with the meaning "from the top," Matt. 27:51; Mark 15:38, of the temple veil; in John 19:23, of the garment of Christ, lit., "from the upper parts" (plural); (b) of things which come from heaven, or from God in Heaven, John 3:31; 19:11; Jas. 1:17; 3:15, 17. It is also used in the sense of "again."

For **ABROAD**, see the verbs with which it is used, DISPERSE, SCATTER

ABSENCE, ABSENT

A. Noun.

apousia (ἀπουσία, 666), lit., "a being away from," is used in Phil. 2:12, of the apostle's absence from Philippi, in contrast to his parousia, his presence with the saints there "parousia" does not signify merely "a coming," it includes or suggests "the presence" which follows the arrival.

B. Verbs.

1. *apeimi* (ἄπειμι, 548), "to be absent" (*apo*, "from," *eimi*, "to be"), is found in 1 Cor. 5:3; 2 Cor. 10:1, 11; 13:2, 10; Phil. 1:27; Col. 2:5. See GO.

2. *ekdēmeo* (ἐκδημέω, 1553), lit., "to be away from people" (*ek*, "from," or "out of," *dēmos*, "people"), came to mean either (a) "to go abroad, depart"; the apostle Paul uses it to speak of departing from the body as the earthly abode of the spirit, 2 Cor. 5:8; or (b) "to be away"; in the same passage, of being here in the body and absent from the Lord (v. 6), or being absent from the body and present with the Lord (v. 8). Its other occurrence is in v. 9.

ABSTAIN, ABSTINENCE

apechō (ἀπέχω, 568), "to hold oneself from" (*apo*, "from," *echomai*, the middle voice of *echō*, "to have," i.e., to keep oneself from), in the NT, invariably refers to evil practices, moral and ceremonial, Acts 15:20, 29; 1 Thess. 4:3; 5:22; 1 Tim. 4:3; 1 Pet. 2:11; so in the Sept. in Job 1:1; 2:3.

Note: The noun "abstinence" in Acts 27:21, KJV, translates *asitia*, "without food," RV (*a*, negative, *sitos*, "food"). Cf. *asitos*, "fasting," v. 33.

ABUNDANCE, ABUNDANT, ABUNDANTLY, ABOUND

A. Nouns.

1. *hadrotēs* (ἁδρότης, 100), which, in 2 Cor. 8:20, in reference to the gifts from the church at Corinth for poor saints in Judea, the RV renders "bounty" (KJV, "abundance"), is derived from *hadros*, "thick, fat, full-grown, rich" (in the Sept. it is used chiefly of rich and great men, e.g., Jer. 5:5). In regard, therefore, to the offering in 2 Cor. 8:20 the thought is that of bountiful giving, a fat offering, not mere "abundance."

2. *perisseia* (περισσεία, 4050), "an exceeding measure, something above the ordinary," is used four times; Rom. 5:17, "of abundance of grace"; 2 Cor. 8:2, "of abundance of joy"; 2 Cor. 10:15, of the extension of the apostle's sphere of service through the practical fellowship of the saints at Corinth; in Jas. 1:21 it is rendered, metaphorically, "overflowing," KJV "superfluity," with reference to wickedness. Some would render it "residuum," or "what remains." See No. 3.

3. *perisseuma* (περίσσευμα, 4051) denotes "abundance" in a slightly more concrete form, 2 Cor. 8:13-14, where it stands for the gifts in kind supplied by the saints. In Matt. 12:34 and Luke 6:45 it is used of the "abundance" of the heart; in Mark 8:8, of the broken pieces left after feeding the multitude "that remained over" (KJV "that was left"). In the Sept., Eccl. 2:15.

4. *huperbolē* (ὑπερβολή, 5236), lit., "a throwing beyond" (*huper*, "over," *ballō*, "to throw"), denotes "excellence, exceeding greatness," of the power of God in His servants, 2 Cor. 4:7; of the revelations given to Paul, 12:7; with the preposition *kata*, the phrase signifies "exceeding," Rom. 7:13; "still more excellent," 1 Cor. 12:31; "exceedingly," 2 Cor. 1:8; "beyond measure," Gal. 1:13; and, in a more extended phrase, "more and more exceedingly," 2 Cor. 4:17. See EXCELLENCY, EXCELLENT.

B. Verbs.

1. *perisseuō* (περισσεύω, 4052), akin to A, Nos. 2 and 3, is used intransitively (a) "of exceeding a certain number, or

measure, to be over, to remain," of the fragments after feeding the multitude (cf. *perisseuma*), Luke 9:17; John 6:12-13; "to exist in abundance"; as of wealth, Luke 12:15; 21:4; of food, 15:17. In this sense it is used also of consolation, 2 Cor. 1:5, of the effect of a gift sent to meet the need of saints, 2 Cor. 9:12; of rejoicing, Phil. 1:26; of what comes or falls to the lot of a person in large measure, as of the grace of God and the gift by the grace of Christ, Rom. 5:15, of the sufferings of Christ, 2 Cor. 1:5. In Mark 12:44 and Luke 21:4, the RV has "superfluity."

(b) "to redound to, or to turn out abundantly for something," as of the liberal effects of poverty, 2 Cor. 8:2; in Rom. 3:7, argumentatively of the effects of the truth of God, as to whether God's truthfulness becomes more conspicuous and His glory is increased through man's untruthfulness; of numerical increase, Acts 16:5.

(c) "to be abundantly furnished, to abound in a thing," as of material benefits, Luke 12:15; Phil. 4:18 of spiritual gifts; 1 Cor. 14:12, or "to be pre-eminent, to excel, to be morally better off," as regards partaking of certain meats; 1 Cor. 8:8, "are we the better," "to abound" in hope, Rom. 15:13; the work of the Lord, 1 Cor. 15:58; faith and grace, 2 Cor. 8:7; thanksgiving, Col. 2:7; walking so as to please God, Phil. 1:9; 1 Thess. 4:1, 10; of righteousness, Matt. 5:20; of the Gospel, as the ministration of righteousness 2 Cor. 3:9, "exceed."

It is used transitively, in the sense of "to make to abound," e.g., to provide a person richly so that he has "abundance," as of spiritual truth, Matt. 13:12; the right use of what God has entrusted to us, 25:29; the power of God in conferring grace, 2 Cor. 9:8; Eph. 1:8; to "make abundant" or to cause to excel, as of the effect of grace in regard to thanksgiving, 2 Cor. 4:15; His power to make us "to abound" in love, 1 Thess. 3:12. See BETTER, EXCEED, EXCEL, REDOUND.

2. *huperperisseuō* (ὑπερπερισσεύω, 5248), a strengthened form of No. 1, signifies "to abound exceedingly," Rom. 5:20, of the operation of grace; 2 Cor. 7:4, in the middle voice, of the apostle's joy in the saints. See JOYFUL.

3. *pleonazō* (πλεονάζω, 4121), from *pleion*, or *pleon*, "more" (greater in quantity), akin to *pleō*, "to fill," signifies, (a) intransitively, "to superabound," of a trespass or sin, Rom. 5:20; of grace, Rom. 6:1; 2 Cor. 4:15; of spiritual fruit, Phil. 4:17; of love, 2 Thess. 1:3; of various fruits, 2 Pet. 1:8; of the gathering of the manna, 2 Cor. 8:15, "had ... over"; (b) transitively, "to make to increase," 1 Thess. 3:12.

4. *huperpleonazō* (ὑπερπλεονάζω, 5250), a strengthened form of No. 3, signifying "to abound exceedingly," is used in 1 Tim. 1:14, of the grace of God.

5. *plēthunō* (πληθύνω, 4129), a lengthened form of *plēthō*, "to fill," akin to No. 3, and to *plēthos*, "a multitude," signifies "to increase, to multiply," and, in the passive voice, "to be multiplied," e.g., of iniquity, Matt. 24:12, RV. See MULTIPLY.

Note: Huperballō, akin to A, No. 4, "to exceed, excel," is translated "passeth" in Eph. 3:19. See also 2 Cor. 3:10 (RV, "surpasseth"; KJV, "excelleth"); 9:14, "exceeding"; Eph. 1:19; 2:7. See EXCEED, EXCEL.

C. Adjectives.

1. *perissos* (περισσός, 4053), akin to B, No. 1, "abundant," is translated "advantage" in Rom. 3:1, "superfluous" in 2 Cor. 9:1.

2. *perissoteros* (περισσότερος, 4055), the comparative degree of No. 1, is translated as follows: in Matt. 11:9, and Luke 7:26, RV, "much more" (KJV, "more"); in Mark 12:40, "greater"; in Luke 12:4, 48, "more"; in 1 Cor. 12:23-24, "more abundant"; in 2 Cor. 2:7, "overmuch"; in 2 Cor. 10:8, RV, "abundantly"; KJV, "more." See GREATER.

D. Adverbs.

1. *perissōs* (περισσῶς, 4057), corresponding to Adjective No. 1 above, is found in Matt. 27:23, RV, "exceedingly," KJV, "the more"; Mark 10:26, RV, "exceedingly," KJV, "out of measure"; 15:14; Acts 26:11, "exceedingly." See EXCEEDINGLY, B, No. 4.

2. *perissoterōs* (περισσοτέρως, 4056), the adverbial form of No. 2, above, means "more abundantly"; in Heb. 2:1, lit., "we ought to give heed more abundantly." It is most frequent in 2 Cor. In 11:23, see the RV. See EARNEST, EXCEEDINGLY.

3. *huperperissōs* (ὑπερπερισσῶς, 5249), a strengthened form of No. 1, signifies "exceeding abundantly," Mark 7:37.

4. *huperekperissou* (ὑπερεκπερισσοῦ) (ὑπέρ, 5228, ἐκ, 1537, and περισσός, 4053), a still further strengthened form, is translated "exceeding abundantly" in Eph. 3:20; "exceedingly" in 1 Thess. 3:10; 5:13. See EXCEEDINGLY.

Note: Huperballontōs, akin to A, No. 4, denotes "above measure," 2 Cor. 11:23.

5. *plousiōs* (πλουσίως, 4146), connected with *ploutos*, "riches," is rendered "abundantly," Titus 3:6 and 2 Pet. 1:11; "richly," Col. 3:16 and 1 Tim. 6:17. It is used of (a) the gift of the Holy Spirit; (b) entrance into the coming kingdom; (c) the indwelling of the Word of Christ; (d) material benefits. See RICHLY.

Notes: (1) *Dunamis*, "power," is translated "abundance" in the KJV of Rev. 18:3 (RV and KJV marg., "power").

(2) *Polus*, "much, many," is rendered "abundant" in 1 Pet. 1:3, KJV (marg., "much"), RV, "great."

(3) For the verbs *plouteō* and *ploutizō*, see RICH AND ENRICH.

(4) For *ploutos*, "wealth, riches," and *plousios*, "rich," see RICH.

ABUSE, ABUSERS

A. Verb.

katachraomai (καταχράομαι, 2710), lit., "to use overmuch" (*kata,* "down," intensive, *chraomai,* "to use"), is found in 1 Cor. 7:31, with reference to the believer's use of the world (marg., "use to the full"), and 1 Cor. 9:18, KJV, "abuse," RV, "use to the full."

B. Noun.

For the noun *arsenokoitēs,* see 1 Cor. 6:9, and 1 Tim. 1:10.

For **ABYSS** see BOTTOM

ACCESS

prosagōgē (προσαγωγή, 4318), lit., "a leading or bringing into the presence of" (*pros,* "to," *agō,* "to lead"), denotes "access," with which is associated the thought of freedom to enter through the assistance or favor of another. It is used three times, (a) Rom. 5:2, of the "access" which we have by faith, through our Lord Jesus Christ, into grace; (b) Eph. 2:18, of our "access" in one Spirit through Christ, unto the Father; (c) Eph. 3:12, of the same "access," there said to be "in Christ," and which we have "in confidence through our faith in Him." This "access" involves the acceptance which we have in Christ with God, and the privilege of His favor towards us. Some advocate the meaning "introduction."

ACCOMPANY

A. Verbs.

1. *sunepomai* (συνέπομαι, 4902), lit., "to follow with" (*sun,* "with," *hepomai,* "to follow"), came to mean simply "to accompany," Acts 20:4.

2. *sunerchomai* (συνέρχομαι, 4905), chiefly used of "assembling together," signifies "to accompany," in Luke 23:55; John 11:33; Acts 9:39; 10:45; 11:12; 15:38; 21:16. In Acts 1:21 it is said of men who had "companied with" the apostles all the time the Lord Jesus was with them. See ASSEMBLE, COMPANY, GO.

3. *echō* (ἔχω, 2192), "to have," is rendered "accompany," in Heb. 6:9, "things that accompany salvation." The margin gives perhaps the better sense, "things that are near to salvation."

4. *propempō* (προπέμπω, 4311), translated "accompanied," in Acts 20:38, KJV, lit. means "to send forward"; hence of assisting a person on a journey either (a) in the sense of fitting him out with the requisites for it, or (b) actually "accompanying" him for part of the way. The former seems to be indicated in Rom. 15:24 and 1 Cor. 16:6, and v. 11, where the RV has "set him forward." So in 2 Cor. 1:16 and Titus 3:13, and of John's exhortation to Gaius concerning traveling evangelists, "whom thou wilt do well to set forward on their journey worthily of God," 3 John 6, RV. While personal "accompaniment" is not excluded, practical assistance seems to be generally in view, as indicated by Paul's word to Titus to set forward Zenas and Apollos on their journey and to see "that nothing be wanting unto them." In regard to the parting of Paul from the elders of Ephesus at Miletus, personal "accompaniment" is especially in view, perhaps not without the suggestion of assistance, Acts 20:38, RV "brought him on his way"; "accompaniment" is also indicated in 21:5; "they all with wives and children brought us on our way, till we were out of the city." In Acts 15:3, both ideas perhaps are suggested. See CONDUCT.

ACCORD

A. Adverb.

homothumadon (ὁμοθυμαδόν, 3661), "of one accord" (from *homos,* "same," *thumos,* "mind"), occurs eleven times, ten in the Acts, 1:14; 2:46; 4:24; 5:12; 7:57; 8:6; 12:20; 15:25; 18:12, 19:29, and the other in Rom. 15:6, where, for KJV, "with one mind," the RV has "with one accord," as throughout the Acts. See MIND.

Note: In Acts 2:1, the adverb *homou,* "together," is so rendered in the RV, for KJV, "of one accord."

B. Adjectives.

"Of one's own accord."

1. *authairetos* (αὐθαίρετος, 830), from autos, "self," and *haireomai,* "to choose, self-chosen, voluntary, of one's own accord," occurs in 2 Cor. 8:3 and 17, of the churches of Macedonia as to their gifts for the poor saints in Judea, and of Titus in his willingness to go and exhort the church in Corinth concerning the matter. In 8:3 the RV translates it "(gave) of their own accord," consistently with the rendering in v. 17. See WILLING.

2. *automatos* (αὐτόματος, 844), from *autos,* "self," and a root *ma-,* signifying "desire," denotes of oneself, moved by one's own impulse. It occurs in Mark 4:28, of the power of the earth to produce plants and fruits of itself; Acts 12:10, of the door which opened of its own accord. In the Sept., Lev. 25:5, "spontaneous produce"; v. 11, "produce that comes of itself"; Josh. 6:5; 2 Kings 19:29, "(that which groweth) of itself"; Job 24:24, of an ear of corn "(falling off) of itself (from the stalk)."

3. *sumpsuchos* (σύμψυχος, 4861), lit., "fellow-souled or minded" (*sun,* "with," *psuchē,* "the soul"), occurs in Phil. 2:2, "of one accord."

For **ACCURSED** see CURSE, A, No. 3

ACCUSATION, ACCUSE

A. Nouns.

1. *aitia* (αἰτία, 156) probably has the primary meaning of "a cause, especially an occasion of something evil, hence a charge, an accusation." It is used in a forensic sense, of (a) an accusation, Acts 25:18 (RV, "charge"), 27; (b) a crime, Matt. 27:37; Mark 15:26, John 18:38; 19:4, 6; Acts 13:28; 23:28; 28:18. See FAULT.

2. *aitiōma* (αἰτιώμα, 157), "an accusation," expressing No. 1 more concretely, is found in Acts 25:7, RV, "charges," for KJV, "complaints." See COMPLAINT.

3. *enklēma* (ἔγκλημα, 1462) is "an accusation made in public," but not necessarily before a tribunal. That is the case in Acts 23:29, "laid to his charge." In 25:16 it signifies a matter of complaint; hence, the RV has "the matter laid against him" (KJV, "crime").

4. *katēgoria* (κατηγορία, 2724), "an accusation," is found in John 18:29; 1 Tim. 5:19 and Titus 1:6, lit., "not under accusation." This and the verb *katēgoreō*, "to accuse," and the noun *katēgorōs*, "an accuser" (see below), all have chiefly to do with judicial procedure, as distinct from *diaballō*, "to slander." It is derived from *agora*, "a place of public speaking," prefixed by *kata*, "against"; hence, it signifies a speaking against a person before a public tribunal. It is the opposite to *apologia*, "a defense."

Note: Krisis, which has been translated "accusation," in the KJV of 2 Pet. 2:11 and Jude 9 (RV, "judgement"), does not come under this category. It signifies "a judgment, a decision given concerning anything."

B. Verbs.

1. *diaballō* (διαβάλλω, 1225), used in Luke 16:1, in the passive voice, lit. signifies "to hurl across" (*dia*, "through," *ballō*, "to throw"), and suggests a verbal assault. It stresses the act rather than the author, as in the case of *aitia* and *katēgoria*. *Diabolos* is connected.

2. *enkaleō* (ἐγκαλέω, 1458),—see A, No. 3, "to bring a charge against, or to come forward as an accuser against," lit. denotes "to call in" (*en*, "in," *kaleō*, "to call"), i.e., "to call (something) in or against (someone)"; hence, "to call to account, to accuse," Acts 19:38, RV (KJV, "implead"); in v. 40, "accused" (KJV, "call in question"). It is used in four other places in the Acts, 23:28-29; 26:2, 7, and elsewhere in Rom. 8:33, "shall lay to the charge." See CALL, IMPLEAD.

3. *epēreazō* (ἐπηρεάζω, 1908), besides its more ordinary meaning, "to insult, treat abusively, despitefully," Luke 6:28, has the forensic significance "to accuse falsely," and is used with this meaning in 1 Pet. 3:16, RV, "revile." See DESPITEFULLY, REVILE.

4. *katēgoreō* (κατηγορέω, 2723), "to speak against, accuse" (cf. A, No. 4), is used (a) in a general way, "to accuse," e.g., Luke 6:7, RV, "how to accuse"; Rom. 2:15; Rev. 12:10; (b) before a judge, e.g., Matt. 12:10; Mark 15:4 (RV, "witness against"); Acts 22:30; 25:16. In Acts 24:19, RV renders it "make accusation," for the KJV, "object." See WITNESS.

5. *sukophanteō* (συκοφαντέω, 4811), (Eng., "sycophant") means (a) "to accuse wrongfully"; Luke 3:14 (KJV and RV, margin); RV, "exact wrongfully"; (b) "to exact money wrongfully, to take anything by false accusation," Luke 19:8, and the RV text of 3:14. It is more frequently found in the Sept.; see Gen. 43:18, "to inform against"; Lev. 19:11, "neither shall each falsely accuse his neighbor"; Job 35:9, "they that are oppressed by false accusation"; Ps. 119:122, "let not the proud accuse me falsely"; Prov. 14:31 and 22:16, "he that oppresses the needy by false accusation."

The word is derived from *sukon*, "a fig," and *phainō*, "to show." At Athens a man whose business it was to give information against anyone who might be detected exporting figs out of the province, is said to have been called a *sukophantēs* (see Note (2) below). Probably, however, the word was used to denote one who brings figs to light by shaking the tree, and then in a metaphorical sense one who makes rich men yield up their fruit by "false accusation." Hence in general parlance it was used to designate "a malignant informer," one who accused from love of gain. See EXACT.

Note: Proaitiaomai denotes "to bring a previous charge against," Rom. 3:9, RV.

ACCUSER

1. *diabolos* (διάβολος, 1228), "an accuser" (cf. ACCUSE, B, No. 1), is used 34 times as a title of Satan, the Devil (the English word is derived from the Greek); once of Judas, John 6:70, who, in his opposition to God, acted the part of the Devil. Apart from John 6:70, men are never spoken of as devils. It is always to be distinguished from *daimōn*, "a demon." It is found three times, 1 Tim. 3:11; 2 Tim. 3:3; Titus 2:3, of false accusers, slanderers.

2. *katēgoros* (κατήγορος, 2725), "an accuser," is used in John 8:10; Acts 23:30, 35; 24:8; 25:16, 18. In Rev. 12:10, it is used of Satan. In the Sept., Prov. 18:17.

Notes: (1) *Sukophantia*, "a false accusation or oppression," is used in Eccl. 5:7; 7:8; Ps. 119:134 and Amos 2:8 (not in the NT). See No. 5, above.

(2) *Sukophantēs*, "a false accuser, or oppressor," occurs in Ps. 72:4; Prov. 28:16 (not in the NT).

ACKNOWLEDGE (-MENT)

A. Verb.

epiginōskō (ἐπιγινώσκω, 1921) signifies (a) "to know thoroughly" (*epi* "intensive," *ginōskō*, "to know"); (b) "to recognize a thing to be what it really is, to acknowledge," 1 Cor. 14:37 (RV, "take knowledge of"); 16:18; 2 Cor. 1:13-14. See KNOW, KNOWLEDGE.

Note: In 1 John 2:23, "acknowledgeth" translates the verb *homologeō*, "to confess," RV, "confesseth."

B. Noun.

epignōsis (ἐπίγνωσις, 1922), akin to A, "full, or thorough knowledge, discernment, recognition," is translated "acknowledging" in the KJV of 2 Tim. 2:25; Titus 1:1 and Philem. 6 (in all three, RV, "knowledge," properly, "thorough knowledge"). In Col. 2:2, KJV, "acknowledgement," RV, "that they may know" (i.e., "unto the full knowledge). See KNOWLEDGE.

ACQUAINTANCE

1. *gnōstos* (γνωστός, 1110), from *ginōskō*, "to know," signifies "known, or knowable"; hence, "one's acquaintance"; it is used in this sense, in the plural, in Luke 2:44 and 23:49. See KNOWN, NOTABLE.

2. *idios* (ἴδιος, 2398), "one's own," is translated "acquaintance" in the KJV of Acts 24:23, "friends" (RV). See COMPANY.

ACT

1. *epautophōrō* (ἐπαυτοφώρῳ, 1888) primarily signifies "caught in the act of theft" (*epi*, "upon," intensive, *autos*, "self," *phōr*, "a thief"); then, "caught in the act" of any other crime, John 8:4. In some texts the preposition *epi* is detached from the remainder of the adjective, and appears as *ep' autophōrō*.

2. *dikaiōma* (δικαίωμα, 1345) signifies "an act of righteousness, a concrete expression of righteousness," as in the RV of Rom. 5:18, in reference to the death of Christ; the KJV wrongly renders it "the righteousness of One." The contrast is between the one trespass by Adam and the one act of Christ in His atoning Death. In Rev. 15:4 and 19:8, the word is used in the plural to signify, as in the RV, "righteous acts," respectively, of God, and of the saints. See JUDGMENT, JUSTIFICATION, ORDINANCE, RIGHTEOUSNESS.

3. *prassō* (πράσσω, 4238), "to do, to practice," is translated "act" in the RV of Acts 17:7 (KJV, "do"). See EXACT, KEEP.

ACTIVE

energēs (ἐνεργής, 1756), lit., "in work" (cf. Eng., "energetic"), is used (a) of the Word of God, Heb. 4:12 (RV, "active," KJV, "powerful"); (b) of a door for the Gospel, 1 Cor. 16:9, "effectual"; (c) of faith, Philem. 6, "effectual." See POWERFUL. Cf. the synonymous words *dunatos* and *ischuros* (see ABLE).

ADJURE

1. *horkizō* (ὁρκίζω, 3726), "to cause to swear, to lay under the obligation of an oath" (*horkos*, Mark 5:7; Acts 19:13), is connected with the Heb. word for a thigh, cf. Gen. 24:2, 9; 47:29. Some mss. have this word in 1 Thess. 5:27. The most authentic have No. 3 (below).

2. *exorkizō* (ἐνορκίζω, 3726), an intensive form of No. 1, signifies "to appeal by an oath, to adjure," Matt. 26:63. In the Sept., Gen. 24:3; Judg. 17:2; 1 Kings 22:16.

3. *enorkizō* (ἐνορκίζω, 3726), "to put under (or bind by) an oath," is translated "adjure" in the RV of 1 Thess. 5:27 (KJV, "charge"). In the Sept., Neh. 13:25.

Note: The synonymous verb *omnumi* signifies "to make an oath, to declare or promise with an oath." See, e.g., Mark 6:23, in contrast to 5:7 (*horkizō*).| See OATH and SWEAR.

For the KJV **ADMINISTER and ADMINISTRATION** see MINISTER and MINISTRATION, SERVE, and SERVICE

For the KJV **ADMIRATION and ADMIRE** see WONDER and MARVEL

ADMONITION, ADMONISH

A. Noun.

nouthesia (νουθεσία, 3559), lit., "a putting in mind" (*nous*, "mind," *tithēmi*, "to put"), is used in 1 Cor. 10:11, of the purpose of the Scriptures; in Eph. 6:4, of that which is ministered by the Lord; and in Titus 3:10, of that which is to be administered for the correction of one who creates trouble in the church. *Nouthesia* is "the training by word," whether of encouragement, or, if necessary, by reproof or remonstrance. In contrast to this, the synonymous word *paideia* stresses training by act, though both words are used in each respect.

B. Verbs.

1. *noutheteō* (νουθετέω, 3560), cf. the noun above, means "to put in mind, admonish," Acts 20:31 (KJV, "warn"); Rom. 15:14; 1 Cor. 4:14 (KJV, "warn"); Col. 1:28 (KJV, "warning"); Col. 3:16; 1 Thess. 5:12, 14 (KJV, "warn"); 2 Thess. 3:15.

It is used, (a) of instruction, (b) of warning. It is thus distinguished from *paideuō*, "to correct by discipline, to train by act," Heb. 12:6; cf. Eph. 6:4.

"The difference between 'admonish' and 'teach' seems to be that, whereas the former has mainly in view the things that are wrong and call for warning, the latter has to do chiefly with the impartation of positive truth, cf. Col. 3:16; they were to let the Word of Christ dwell richly in them, so that they might be able (1) to teach and 'admonish' one another, and (2) to abound in the praises of God.

"Admonition differs from remonstrance, in that the former is warning based on instruction; the latter may be little more than expostulation. For example, though Eli remonstrated with his sons, 1 Sam. 2:24, he failed to admonish them, 3:13, LXX. Pastors and teachers in the churches are thus themselves admonished, i.e., instructed and warned, by the Scriptures, 1 Cor. 10:11, so to minister the Word of God to the saints, that, naming the Name of the Lord, they shall depart from unrighteousness, 2 Tim. 2:19." See WARN.

2. *paraineō* (παραινέω, 3867), "to admonish by way of exhorting or advising," is found in Acts 27:9 ("Paul admonished them") and v. 22 ("and now I exhort you"). See EXHORT.

3. *chrēmatizō* (χρηματίζω, 5537), primarily, "to transact business," then, "to give advice to enquirers" (especially of official pronouncements of magistrates), or "a response to those consulting an oracle," came to signify the giving of a divine "admonition" or instruction or warning, in a general way; "admonished" in Heb. 8:5, KJV (RV, "warned"). Elsewhere it is translated by the verb "to warn."

The word is derived from *chrēma*, "an affair, business." Names were given to men from the nature of their business (see the same word in Acts 11:26; Rom. 7:3); hence, the idea of dealing with a person and receiving instruction. In the case of oracular responses, the word is derived from *chrēsmos*, "an oracle." See CALL, REVEAL, WARN.

ADO

thorubeō (θορυβέω, 2350), "to make an uproar, to throw into confusion, or to wail tumultuously," is rendered "make ... ado," in Mark 5:39; elsewhere in Matt. 9:23; Acts 17:5; 20:10. See TROUBLE, UPROAR.

Note: For the corresponding noun, *thorubos*, see TUMULT, UPROAR.

ADOPTION

huiothesia (υἱοθεσία, 5206), from *huios*, "a son," and *thesis*, "a placing," akin to *tithēmi*, "to place," signifies the place and condition of a son given to one to whom it does not naturally belong. The word is used by the apostle Paul only.

In Rom. 8:15, believers are said to have received "the Spirit of adoption," that is, the Holy Spirit who, given as the Firstfruits of all that is to be theirs, produces in them the realization of sonship and the attitude belonging to sons. In Gal. 4:5 they are said to receive "the adoption of sons," i.e., sonship bestowed in distinction from a relationship consequent merely upon birth; here two contrasts are presented, (1) between the sonship of the believer and the unoriginated sonship of Christ, (2) between the freedom enjoyed by the believer and bondage, whether of Gentile natural condition, or of Israel under the Law. In Eph. 1:5 they are said to have been foreordained unto "adoption as sons" through Jesus Christ, RV; the KJV, "adoption of children" is a mistranslation and misleading. God does not "adopt" believers as children; they are begotten as such by His Holy Spirit through faith. "Adoption" is a term involving the dignity of the relationship of believers as sons; it is not a putting into the family by spiritual birth, but a putting into the position of sons. In Rom. 8:23 the "adoption" of the believer is set forth as still future, as it there includes the redemption of the body, when the living will be changed and those who have fallen asleep will be raised. In Rom. 9:4 "adoption" is spoken of as belonging to Israel, in accordance with the statement in Exod. 4:12, "Israel is My Son." Cf. Hos. 11:1. Israel was brought into a special relation with God, a collective relationship, not enjoyed by other nations, Deut. 14:1; Jer. 31:9, etc.

ADORN, ADORNING

A. Verb.

kosmeō (κοσμέω, 2885), primarily "to arrange, to put in order" (Eng., "cosmetic"), is used of furnishing a room, Matt. 12:44; Luke 11:25, and of trimming lamps, Matt. 25:7. Hence, "to adorn, to ornament," as of garnishing tombs, Matt. 23:29; buildings, Luke 21:5; Rev. 21:19; one's person, 1 Tim. 2:9; 1 Pet. 3:5; Rev. 21:2; metaphorically, of "adorning a doctrine, Titus 2:10.

B. Noun.

kosmos (κόσμος, 2889), "a harmonious arrangement or order," then, "adornment, decoration," came to denote "the world, or the universe, as that which is divinely arranged." The meaning "adorning" is found in 1 Pet. 3:3. Elsewhere it signifies "the world." Cf. *kosmios*, decent, modest, 1 Tim. 2:9; 3:2. See WORLD.

ADULTERER (-ESS), ADULTEROUS, ADULTERY

A. Nouns.

1. *moichos* (μοιχός, 3432) denotes one "who has unlawful intercourse with the spouse of another," Luke 18:11; 1 Cor. 6:9; Heb. 13:4. As to Jas. 4:4, see below.

2. *moichalis* (μοιχαλίς, 3428), "an adulteress," is used (a) in the natural sense, 2 Pet. 2:14; Rom. 7:3; (b) in the spiritual sense, Jas. 4:4; here the RV rightly omits the word "adulterers." It was added by a copyist. As in Israel the breach of their relationship with God through their idolatry, was described as "adultery" or "harlotry" (e.g., Ezek. 16:15, etc.; 23:43), so believers who cultivate friendship with the world, thus breaking their spiritual union with Christ, are spiritual "adulteresses," having been spiritually united to Him as wife to husband, Rom. 7:4. It is used adjectivally to describe the Jewish people in transferring their affections from God, Matt. 12:39; 16:4; Mark 8:38. In 2 Pet. 2:14, the lit. translation is "full of an adulteress" (RV, marg.).

3. *moicheia* (μοιχεία, 3430), "adultery," is found in Matt. 15:19; Mark 7:21; John 8:3 (KJV only).

B. Verbs.

1. *moichaō* (μοιχάω, 3429), used in the middle voice in the NT, is said of men in Matt. 5:32; 19:9; Mark 10:11; of women in Mark 10:12.

2. *moicheuō* (μοιχεύω, 3431) is used in Matt. 5:27-28, 32 (in v. 32 some texts have No. 1); 19:18; Mark 10:19; Luke 16:18; 18:20; John 8:4; Rom. 2:22; 13:9; Jas. 2:11; in Rev. 2:22, metaphorically, of those who are by a Jezebel's solicitations drawn away to idolatry.

ADVERSARY

A. Noun.

antidikos (ἀντίδικος, 476), firstly, "an opponent in a lawsuit," Matt. 5:25 (twice); Luke 12:58; 18:3, is also used to denote "an adversary or an enemy," without reference to legal affairs, and this is perhaps its meaning in 1 Pet. 5:8, where it is used of the Devil. Some would regard the word as there used in a legal sense, since the Devil accuses men before God.

B. Verb.

antikeimai (ἀντίκειμαι, 480) is, lit., "to lie opposite to, to be set over against." In addition to its legal sense it signifies "to withstand"; the present participle of the verb with the article, which is equivalent to a noun, signifies "an adversary," e.g., Luke 13:17; 21:15; 1 Cor. 16:9; Phil. 1:28; 1 Tim. 5:14. This construction is used of the Man of Sin, in 2 Thess. 2:4, and is translated "He that opposeth," where, adopting the noun form, we might render by "the opponent and self-exalter against ...." In Gal. 5:17 it is used of the antagonism between the Holy Spirit and the flesh in the believer; in 1 Tim. 1:10, of anything, in addition to persons, that is opposed to the doctrine of Christ. In these two places the word is rendered "contrary to." In the Sept. it is used of Satan, Zech. 3:1, and of men, Job 13:24; Isa. 66:6. See OPPOSE.

C. Adjective.

hupenantios (ὑπεναντίος, 5227), "contrary, opposed," is a strengthened form of *enantios* (*en*, "in," and *antios*, "set against"). The intensive force is due to the preposition *hupo*. It is translated "contrary to," in Col. 2:14, of ordinances; in Heb. 10:27, "adversaries." In each place a more violent form of opposition is suggested than in the case of *enantios*.

For **ADVERSITY**, in Heb. 13:3, where the verb *kakoucheomai* is translated in the KJV, "suffer adversity," see SUFFER, (b), No. 6.

ADVICE, ADVISE

1. *gnōmē* (γνώμη, 1106), connected with *ginōskō*, "to know, perceive," firstly means "the faculty or knowledge, reason"; then, "that which is thought or known, one's mind." Under this heading there are various meanings: (1) a view, judgment, opinion, 1 Cor. 1:10; Philem. 14; Rev. 17:13, 17; (2) an opinion as to what ought to be done, either (a) by oneself, and so a resolve, or purpose, Acts 20:3; or (b) by others, and so, judgment, advice, 1 Cor. 7:25, 40; 2 Cor. 8:10. See JUDGMENT, MIND, WILL.

2. *boulē* (βουλή, 1012), from a root meaning "a will," hence "a counsel, a piece of advice," is to be distinguished from *gnōmē*; *boulē* is the result of determination, *gnōmē* is the result of knowledge. *Boulē* is everywhere rendered by "counsel" in the RV except in Acts 27:12, "advised," lit., "gave counsel." In Acts 13:36 the KJV wrongly has "by the will of God fell on sleep"; the RV, "after he had served the counsel of God, fell on sleep." The word is used of the counsel of God, in Luke 7:30; Acts 2:23; 4:28; 13:36; 20:27; Eph. 1:11; Heb. 6:17; in other passages, of the counsel of men, Luke 23:51; Acts 27:12, 42; 1 Cor. 4:5. See COUNSEL, WILL.

For **ADVOCATE** see COMFORTER

AFFECT

kakoō (κακόω, 2559), from *kakos*, "evil, to treat badly, to hurt," also means "to make evil affected, to embitter," Acts 14:2. See EVIL, HARM, HURT.

Note: Zēloō, akin to *zeō*, "to boil" (Eng., "zeal"), means (a) "to be jealous," Acts 7:9; 17:5; "to envy," 1 Cor. 13:4; "to covet," Jas. 4:2; in a good sense ("jealous over"), in 2 Cor. 11:2; (b) "to desire earnestly," 1 Cor. 12:31; 14:1, 39; "to take a warm interest in, to seek zealously," Gal. 4:17-18, KJV, "zealously affect," "to be zealously affected." The RV corrects this to "zealously seek," etc. See COVET, DESIRE, ENVY, JEALOUS, ZEALOUS.

AFFECTION (-S), AFFECTED

A. Nouns.

1. *pathos* (πάθος, 3806), from *paschō*, "to suffer," primarily denotes whatever one suffers or experiences in any way; hence, "an affection of the mind, a passionate desire." Used by the Greeks of either good or bad desires, it is always used in the NT of the latter, Rom. 1:26 (KJV, "affections," RV, "passions"); Col. 3:5 (KJV, "inordinate affection," RV, "passion"); 1 Thess. 4:5 (KJV, "lust," RV, "passion"). See LUST.

2. *splanchna* (σπλάγχνον, 4698), lit., "the bowels," which were regarded by the Greeks as the seat of the more violent passions, by the Hebrews as the seat of the tender "affections"; hence the word denotes "tender mercies" and is rendered "affections" in 2 Cor. 6:12 (KJV, "bowels"); "inward affection," 2 Cor. 7:15. See BOWELS, COMPASSION, HEART, MERCY. Cf. *epithumia*, "desire."

3. *pathēma* (πάθημα, 3804), akin to No. 1, translated "affections" in Gal. 5:24, KJV, is corrected to "passions" in the RV. See AFFLICTION, B, No. 3.

B. Adjectives.

1. *astorgos* (ἄστοργος, 794) signifies "without natural affection" (*a*, negative, and *storgē*, "love of kindred," especially of parents for children and children for parents; a fanciful etymology associates with this the "stork"), Rom. 1:31; 2 Tim. 3:3.

2. *philostorgos* (φιλόστοργος, 5387), "tenderly loving" (from *philos*, "friendly," *storgē*, see No. 1), is used in Rom. 12:10, RV, "tenderly affectioned" (KJV, "kindly affectioned").

Notes: (1) *Phroneō*, "to think, to set the mind on," implying moral interest and reflection, is translated "set your affection on" in Col. 3:2, KJV (RV, "set your mind on"). See MIND, REGARD.

(2) For *homeiromai* (or *himeiromai*), "to be affectionately desirous of," 1 Thess. 2:8, see DESIRE.

AFFLICT (-ED), AFFLICTION

A. Verbs.

1. *kakoō* (κακόω, 2559) is translated "afflict, in Acts 12:1, RV (KJV, "vex"). See AFFECT.

2. *kakoucheō* (κακουχέω, 2558), from *kakos*, "evil," and *echō*, "to have," signifies, in the passive voice, "to suffer ill, to be maltreated, tormented," Heb. 11:37 (KJV, "tormented," RV, "afflicted"); 13:3, KJV, "suffer adversity," RV, evil entreated. See TORMENT. In the Sept., 1 Kings, 2:26; 11:39.

Note: Sunkakoucheō (*sun*, "with," and No. 1), "to be evil entreated with," is used in Heb. 11:25.

3. *kakopatheō* (κακοπαθέω, 2553), from *kakos*, "evil," *pathos*, "suffering," signifies "to suffer hardship." So the RV in 2 Tim. 2:9; and 4:5; in Jas. 5:13, "suffer" (KJV, "afflicted). See ENDURE, SUFFER.

Note: For *sunkakopatheō*, 2 Tim. 1:8, see HARDSHIP.

4. *thlibō* (θλίβω, 2346), "to suffer affliction, to be troubled," has reference to sufferings due to the pressure of circumstances, or the antagonism of persons, 1 Thess. 3:4; 2 Thess. 1:6-7; "straitened," in Matt. 7:14 (RV); "throng," Mark 3:9; "afflicted," 2 Cor. 1:6; 7:5 (RV); 1 Tim. 5:10; Heb. 11:37; "pressed," 2 Cor. 4:8. Both the verb and the noun (see B, No. 4), when used of the present experience of believers, refer almost invariably to that which comes upon them from without. See NARROW, PRESS, TRIBULATION, TROUBLE.

5. *talaipōreō* (ταλαιπωρέω, 5003), "to be afflicted," is used in Jas. 4:9, in the middle voice ("afflict yourselves"). It is derived from *tlaō*, "to bear, undergo," and *pōros*, "a hard substance, a callus," which metaphorically came to signify that which is miserable.

Note: Talaipōria (akin to No. 5) denotes "misery, hardship," Rom. 3:16; Jas. 5:1. The corresponding adjective is *talaiporos*, "wretched," Rom. 7:24; Rev. 3:17.

B. Nouns.

1. *kakopatheia* (κακοπάθεια, 2552), from *kakos*, "evil," and *paschō*, "to suffer" is rendered "suffering" in Jas. 5:10, RV (KJV, "suffering affliction"). In Sept., Mal. 1:13.

2. *kakōsis* (κάκωσις, 2561), "affliction, ill treatment," is used in Acts 7:34.

3. *pathēma* (πάθημα, 3804), from *pathos*, "suffering," signifies "affliction." The word is frequent in Paul's epistles and is found three times in Hebrews, four in 1 Peter; it is used (a) of "afflictions," Rom. 8:18, etc.; of Christ's "sufferings," 1 Pet. 1:11; 5:1; Heb. 2:9; of those as shared by believers, 2 Cor. 1:5; Phil. 3:10; 1 Pet. 4:13; 5:1; (b) of "an evil emotion, passion," Rom. 7:5; Gal. 5:24. The connection between the two meanings is that the emotions, whether good or evil, were regarded as consequent upon external influences exerted on the mind (cf. the two meanings of the English "passion"). It is more concrete than No. 1, and expresses in sense (b) the uncontrolled nature of evil desires, in contrast to *epithumia*, the general and comprehensive term, lit., "what you set your heart upon" (Trench, *Syn.* Sec. LXXXVII). Its concrete character is seen in Heb. 2:9. See AFFECTION, PASSION, SUFFERING.

Note: The corresponding verbal form *pathētos*, used in Acts 26:23 or the sufferings of Christ, signifies "destined to suffer.

4. *thlipsis* (θλίψις, 2347) primarily means "a pressing, pressure" (see A, No. 4), anything which burdens the spirit. In two passages in Paul's Epistles it is used of future retribution, in the way of "affliction," Rom. 2:9; 2 Thess. 1:6. In Matt. 24:9, the KJV renders it as a verb, "to be afflicted," (RV, "unto tribulation"). It is coupled with *stenochōria*, "anguish," in Rom. 2:9; 8:35; with *anankē*, "distress," 1 Thess. 3:7; with *diōgmos*, "persecution," Matt. 13:21; Mark 4:17; 2 Thess. 1:4. It is used of the calamities of war, Matt. 24:21, 29; Mark 13:19, 24; of want, 2 Cor. 8:13, lit., "distress for you"; Phil. 4:14 (cf. 1:16); Jas. 1:27; of the distress of woman in childbirth, John 16:21; of persecution, Acts 11:19; 14:22; 20:23; 1 Thess. 3:3, 7; Heb. 10:33; Rev. 2:10; 7:14; of the "afflictions" of Christ, from which (His vicarious sufferings apart) his followers must not shrink, whether sufferings of body or mind, Col. 1:24; of sufferings in general, 1 Cor. 7:28; 1 Thess. 1:6, etc. See ANGUISH, DISTRESS, PERSECUTION, TRIBULATION, TROUBLE.

AFFRIGHTED

A. Adjective.

emphobos (ἔμφοβος, 1719), lit., "in fear" (*en*, "in," *phobos*, "fear"), means "affrighted," Luke 24:5, RV (KJV "afraid");

24:37; Acts 10:4, RV (KJV, "afraid"); Rev. 11:13. The RV omits it in Acts 22:9. See TREMBLE.

B. Verbs.

1. *pturō* (πτύρω, 4426), "to frighten, scare," is used in the passive voice in Phil. 1:28, "be affrighted," RV, "be terrified," KJV. See TERRIFY.

2. *ekthambeō* (ἐκθαμβέω, 1568), "to throw into terror," is used in the passive sense, "to be amazed, affrighted," Mark 16:5-6, KJV (RV, "amazed"); Mark 9:15, "were greatly amazed"; 14:33, "to be greatly amazed" (RV), "to be sore amazed" (KJV). See AMAZE, B, No. 4.

For **AFOOT** see FOOT

AFOREPROMISED

proepangellomai (προεπαγγέλλομαι, 4279), "to promise before" (*pro*, "before," *epangellomai*, "to promise"), is translated by the one word "aforepromised," in the RV of 2 Cor. 9:5; in Rom. 1:2, "promised afore."

For **AFRAID** see AFFRIGHTED, A, FEAR, A, No. 2, B, No. 3, D

For **AFRESH** see CROSS, CRUCIFY, B

AGE

A. Nouns.

1. *aiōn* (αἰών, 165), "an age, era" (to be connected with *aei*, "ever," rather than with *aō*, "to breathe"), signifies a period of indefinite duration, or time viewed in relation to what takes place in the period.

The force attaching to the word is not so much that of the actual length of a period, but that of a period marked by spiritual or moral characteristics. This is illustrated in the use of the adjective [see Note (1) below] in the phrase "life eternal," in John 17:3, in respect of the increasing knowledge of God.

The phrases containing this word should not be rendered literally, but consistently with its sense of indefinite duration. Thus *eis ton aiōna* does not mean "unto the age" but "for ever" (see, e.g., Heb. 5:6). The Greeks contrasted that which came to an end with that which was expressed by this phrase, which shows that they conceived of it as expressing interminable duration.

The word occurs most frequently in the Gospel of John, the Hebrews and Revelation. It is sometimes wrongly rendered "world." See ETERNAL, WORLD. It is a characteristic word of John's gospel.

Notes: (1) *Aiōnios*, the adjective corresponding, denoting "eternal," is set in contrast with *proskairos*, lit., "for a season," 2 Cor. 4:18. It is used of that which in nature is endless, as, e.g., of God, Rom. 16:26, His power, 1 Tim. 6:16, His glory, 1 Pet. 5:10, the Holy Spirit, Heb. 9:14, redemption, Heb. 9:12, salvation, 5:9, life in Christ, John 3:16, the resurrection body, 2 Cor. 5:1, the future rule of Christ, 2 Pet. 1:11, which is declared to be without end, Luke 1:33, of sin that never has forgiveness, Mark 3:29, the judgment of God, Heb. 6:2, and of fire, one of its instruments, Matt. 18:8; 25:41; Jude 7. See ETERNAL, EVERLASTING.

(2) In Rev. 15:3, the RV has "King of the ages," according to the texts which have *aiōnōn*, the KJV has "of saints" (*hagiōn*, in inferior mss.). There is good ms. evidence for *ethnōn*, "nations," (KJV, marg.), probably a quotation from Jer. 10:7.

2. *genea* (γενεά, 1074), connected with *ginomai*, "to become," primarily signifies "a begetting, or birth"; hence, that which has been begotten, a family; or successive members of a genealogy, Matt. 1:17, or of a race of people, possessed of similar characteristics, pursuits, etc., (of a bad character) Matt. 17:17; Mark 9:19; Luke 9:41; 16:8; Acts 2:40; or of the whole multitude of men living at the same time, Matt. 24:34; Mark 13:30; Luke 1:48; 21:32; Phil. 2:15, and especially of those of the Jewish race living at the same period, Matt. 11:16, etc. Transferred from people to the time in which they lived, the word came to mean "an age," i.e., a period ordinarily occupied by each successive generation, say, of thirty or forty years, Acts 14:16; 15:21; Eph. 3:5; Col. 1:26; see also, e.g., Gen. 15:16. In Eph. 3:21 *genea* is combined with *aiōn* in a remarkable phrase in a doxology: "Unto Him be the glory in the church and in Christ Jesus, unto all generations for ever and ever (wrongly in KJV 'all ages, world without end')." The word *genea* is to be distinguished from *aiōn*, as not denoting a period of unlimited duration. See GENERATION, NATION.

3. *hēlikia* (ἡλικία, 2244), primarily "an age," as a certain length of life, came to mean (a) "a particular time of life," as when a person is said to be "of age," John 9:21, 23, or beyond a certain stage of life, Heb. 11:11; (b) elsewhere only "of stature," e.g., Matt. 6:27; Luke 2:52; 12:25; 19:3; Eph. 4:13. Some regard Matt. 6:27 and Luke 12:25 as coming under (a). It is to be distinguished from *aiōn* and *genea*, since it has to do simply with matters relating to an individual, either his time of life or his height. See STATURE.

4. *hēmera* (ἡμέρα, 2250), "a day," is rendered "age" in Luke 2:36, "of a great age" (lit., "advanced in many days"). In Luke 3:23 there is no word in the original corresponding to age. The phrase is simply "about thirty years." See DAY, JUDGMENT.

B. Adjectives.

1. *huperakmos* (ὑπέρακμος, 5230) in 1 Cor. 7:36 is rendered "past the flower of her age"; more lit., "beyond the bloom or flower (*acmē*) of life."

2. *teleios* (τέλειος, 5046), "complete, perfect," from *telos*, "an end," is translated "of full age" in Heb. 5:14, KJV (RV, "full-grown man").

Note: In Mark 5:42, RV, "old," KJV, "of the age of," is, lit., "of twelve years." For "of great age," Luke 2:36, see STRICKEN.

AGED

A. Nouns.

1. *presbutēs* (πρεσβύτης, 4246), "an elderly man," is a longer form of *presbus*, the comparative degree of which is *presbuteros*, "a senior, elder," both of which, as also the verb *presbeuō*, "to be elder, to be an ambassador," are derived from *proeisbainō*, "to be far advanced." The noun is found in Luke 1:18, "an old man"; Titus 2:2, "aged men," and Philem. 9, where the RV marg., "Paul an ambassador," is to be accepted, the original almost certainly being *presbeutēs* (not *presbutēs*), "an ambassador." So he describes himself in Eph. 6:20. As Lightfoot points out, he is hardly likely to have made his age a ground of appeal to Philemon, who, if he was the father of Archippus, cannot have been much younger than Paul himself See OLD.

2. *presbutis* (πρεσβύτις, 4247), the feminine of No. 1, "an aged woman," is found in Titus 2:3.

B. Verb.

gēraskō (γηράσκω, 1095), from *gēras*, "old age," signifies "to grow old," John 21:18 ("when thou shalt be old") and Heb. 8:13 (RV, "that which ... waxeth aged," KJV, "old"). See OLD.

For **AGO** see LONG, A, No. 5, and in combination with other words

AGONY

agōnia (ἀγωνία, 74), Eng., "agony," was used among the Greeks as an alternative to *agōn*, "a place of assembly"; then for the contests or games which took place there, and then to denote intense emotion. It was more frequently used eventually in this last respect, to denote severe emotional strain and anguish. So in Luke 22:44, of the Lord's "agony" in Gethsemane.

AH!

1. *oua* (οὐά, 3758), an interjection of derision and insult, is translated "Ha!" in Mark 15:29, RV.

2. *ea* (ἔα, 1436), an interjection of surprise, fear and anger, was the ejaculation of the man with the spirit of an unclean demon, Luke 4:34, RV; the KJV renders it "Let us alone" (see RV, marg.).

AIM

philotimeomai (φιλοτιμέομαι, 5389), lit., "to be fond of honor" (*phileō*, "to love," *timē*, "honor"), and so, actuated by this motive, "to strive to bring something to pass"; hence, "to be ambitious, to make it one's aim," Rom. 15:20, of Paul's "aim" in gospel pioneering, RV (KJV, "strive"); 2 Cor. 5:9, of the "aim" of believers "to be well-pleasing" unto the Lord, RV (KJV, "labor"); in 1 Thess. 4:11, of the "aim" of believers to be quiet, do their own business and work with their own hands; both versions translate it "study." Some would render it, "strive restlessly"; perhaps "strive earnestly" is nearer the mark, but "make it one's aim" is a good translation in all three places. See LABOR, STRIVE, STUDY.

AIR

1. *aēr* (ἀήρ, 109), Eng., "air," signifies "the atmosphere," certainly in five of the seven occurrences Acts 22:23; 1 Cor. 9:26; 14:9; Rev. 9:2; 16:11, and almost certainly in the other two, Eph. 2:2 and 1 Thess. 4:17.

2. *ouranos* (οὐρανός, 3772) denotes "the heaven." The RV always renders it "heaven." The KJV translates it "air" in Matt. 8:20. In the phrase "the fowls (or birds) of the heaven" the KJV always has "air"; "sky" in Matt. 16:2-3; Luke 12:56; in all other instances "heaven." The word is probably derived from a root meaning to cover or encompass. See HEAVEN, SKY.

For **ALAS!** see WOE

ALIEN

allotrios (ἀλλότριος, 245), primarily, "belonging to another" (the opposite to *idios*, "one's own"), came to mean "foreign, strange, not of one's own family, alien, an enemy"; "aliens" in, Heb. 11:34, elsewhere "strange," etc. See STRANGE, STRANGER.

ALIENATE

apallotrioō (ἀπαλλοτριόω, 526) consists of *apo*, "from," and the above; it signifies "to be rendered an alien, to be alienated." In Eph. 2:12 the RV corrects to the verbal form "alienated," for the noun "aliens"; elsewhere in Eph. 4:18 and Col. 1:21; the condition of the unbeliever is presented in a threefold state of "alienation," (a) from the commonwealth of Israel, (b) from the life of God, (c) from God Himself. The word is used of Israelites in the Sept. of Ezek. 14:5 ("estranged") and of the wicked in general, Ps. 58:3.

ALIKE

Note: In Rom. 14:5, this word is in italics. This addition is not needed in the translation.

For **ALIVE** see LIFE, C, LIVE, No. 6

ALLEGORY

allegoreō (ἀλληγορέω, 238), translated in Gal. 4:24 "contain an allegory" (KJV, "are an allegory"), formed from *allos*, "other," and *agoreuō*, "to speak in a place of assembly" (*agora*, "the market-place"), came to signify "to speak," not according to the primary sense of the word, but so that the facts stated are applied to illustrate principles. The "allegorical" meaning does not do away with the literal meaning of the narrative. There may be more than one "allegorical" meaning though, of course, only one literal meaning. Scripture histories represent or embody spiritual principles, and these are ascertained, not by the play of the imagination, but by the rightful application of the doctrines of Scripture.

For **ALLELUIA** (which has been robbed of its initial aspirate) see HALLELUJAH

ALLOW

1. *dokimazō* (δοκιμάζω, 1381), "to prove with a view to approving," is twice translated by the verb "to allow" in the KJV; the RV corrects to "approveth" in Rom. 14:22, and "have been approved," 1 Thess. 2:4, of being qualified to be entrusted with the gospel; in Rom. 1:28, with the negative, the RV has "refused," for KJV, did not like.

2. *ginōskō* (γινώσκω, 1097), "to know," is rendered "allow" in Rom. 7:15 (KJV); the RV has "that which I do I know not"; i.e., "I do not recognize, as a thing for which I am responsible." See FEEL, KNOW, RESOLVE.

3. *suneudokeō* (συνευδοκέω, 4909), "to consent or fully approve" (*sun*, "with," *eu*, "well," *dokeō*, "to think"), is translated "allow" in Luke 11:48; "was consenting" in Acts 8:1; 22:20. See CONSENT.

4. *prosdechomai* (προσδέχομαι, 4327), mistranslated "allow" in Acts 24:15, KJV, means "to wait for," in contrast to rejection, there said of entertaining a hope; hence the RV, "look for."

For **ALLURE** see BEGUILE, No. 4, ENTICE

ALMIGHTY

pantokratōr (παντοκράτωρ, 3841), "almighty, or ruler of all" (*pas*, "all," *krateō*, "to hold, or to have strength"), is used of God only, and is found, in the Epistles, only in 2 Cor. 6:18, where the title is suggestive in connection with the context; elsewhere only in the Apocalypse, nine times. In one place, 19:6, the KJV has "omnipotent"; RV, "(the Lord our God,) the Almighty." The word is introduced in the Sept. as a translation of "Lord (or God) of hosts," e.g., Jer. 5:14 and Amos 4:13.

ALMS, ALMSDEEDS

eleēmosunē (ἐλεημοσύνη, 1654), connected with *eleēmōn*, "merciful," signifies (a) "mercy, pity, particularly in giving alms," Matt. 6:1 (see below), 2-4; Acts 10:2; 24:17; (b) the benefaction itself, the "alms" (the effect for the cause), Luke 11:41; 12:33; Acts 3:2-3, 10; 9:36, "alms-deeds"; 10:2, 4, 31.

Note: In Matt. 6:1, the RV, translating *dikaiosunē*, according to the most authentic texts, has "righteousness," for KJV, "alms."

ALONE (LET ALONE)

A. Adjective.

monos (μόνος, 3441) denotes "single, alone, solitary," Matt. 4:4, etc.

B. Adverbs.

1. *monon* (μόνος, 3441), the neuter of A, meaning "only, exclusively," e.g., Rom. 4:23; Acts 19:26, is translated "alone" in the KJV of John 17:20; RV, "only."

2. *katamonas* (καταμόνας, 2651) signifies "apart, in private, alone," Mark 4:10; Luke 9:18. Some texts have the phrase as one word.

C. Verb.

aphiēmi (ἀφίημι, 863) signifies "to send away, set free"; also "to let alone," Matt. 15:14; Mark 14:6; Luke 13:8; John 11:48; 12:7 (RV, "suffer her"); in Acts 5:38 some texts have *easate* from *eaō*, "to permit." See CRY, FORGIVE, FORSAKE, REMIT, SEND, SUFFER, YIELD.

Notes: (1) The phrase *kath' heautēn* means "by (or in) itself," Jas. 2:17, RV, for KJV, "being alone" (see KJV, marg.).

(2) The phrase *kat' idian*, Mark 4:34, signifies "in private," "privately," RV (KJV, "when they were alone").

(3) For "let us alone" see AH !

For **ALONG** see the RV of Acts 17:23 and 27:13

For **ALOUD** see CRY, B, No. 2

ALTAR

1. *thusiastērion* (θυσιαστήριον, 2379), probably the neuter of the adjective *thusiatērios*, is derived from *thusiazō*, "to sacrifice." Accordingly it denotes an "altar" for the sacrifice of victims, though it was also used for the "altar" of incense, e.g., Luke 1:11. In the NT this word is reserved for the "altar" of the true God, Matt. 5:23-24; 23:18-20, 35; Luke 11:51; 1 Cor. 9:13; 10:18, in contrast to *bōmos*, No. 2, below. In the Sept. *thusiastērion* is mostly, but not entirely, used for the divinely appointed altar; it is used for idol "altars," e.g., in Judg. 2:2; 6:25; 2 Kings 16:10.

2. *bōmos* (βῶμος, 1041), properly, "an elevated place," always denotes either a pagan "altar" or an "altar" reared without divine appointment. In the NT the only place where this is found is Acts 17:23, as this is the only mention of such. Three times in the Sept., but only in the Apocrypha, *bōmos* is used for the divine altar. In Josh. 22 the Sept. translators have carefully observed the distinction, using *bōmos* for the altar which the two and a half tribes erected, vv. 10-11, 16, 19, 23, 26,

34, no divine injunction being given for this; in vv. 19, 28- 29, where the altar ordained of God is mentioned, *thusiastērion* is used.

ALWAY, ALWAYS

1. *aei* (ἀεί, 104) has two meanings: (a) "perpetually, incessantly," Acts 7:51; 2 Cor. 4:11; 6:10; Titus 1:12; Heb. 3:10; (b) "invariably, at any and every time," of successive occurrences, when some thing is to be repeated, according to the circumstances, 1 Pet. 3:15; 2 Pet. 1:12. See EVER.

2. *hekastote* (ἑκάστοτε, 1539), from *hekastos,* "each," is used in 2 Pet. 1:15, RV, "at every time" (KJV, "always").

3. *diapantos* (διαπαντός, 1275) is, lit., "through all," i.e., through all time, (*dia,* "through," *pas,* "all"). In the best texts the words are separated. The phrase, which is used of the time throughout which a thing is done, is sometimes rendered "continually," sometimes "always"; "always" or "alway" in Mark 5:5; Acts 10:2; 24:16; Rom. 11:10; "continually" in Luke 24:53; Heb. 9:6; 13:15, the idea being that of a continuous practice carried on without being abandoned. See CONTINUALLY.

4 and 5. *pantē* (πάντη, 3839), and *pantote* (πάντοτε, 3842) are derived from *pas,* "all." The former is found in Acts 24:3. The latter is the usual word for "always." See EVER.

Note: Two phrases, rendered "always" or "alway" in the KJV, are *en panti kairō* (lit., "in every season"), Luke 21:36, RV, "at every season," Eph. 6:18, RV, "at all seasons," and *pasas tas hēmeras,* (lit., "all the days"), Matt. 28:20, KJV and RV, "alway."

AMAZE, AMAZEMENT

A. Nouns.

1. *ekstasis* (ἔκστασις, 1611) is, lit., "a standing out" (*ek,* "out of," *stasis,* "a standing"). Eng. "ecstasy" is a transliteration. It is translated "amazement" in Acts 3:10. It was said of any displacement, and especially, with reference to the mind, of that alteration of the normal condition by which the person is thrown into a state of surprise or fear, or both; or again, in which a person is so transported out of his natural state that he falls into a trance, Acts 10:10; 11:5; 22:17. As to the other meaning, the RV has "amazement" in Mark 5:42 and Luke 5:26, but "astonishment" in Mark 16:8. See TRANCE.

2. *thambos* (θάμβος, 2285), "amazement, wonder," is probably connected with a root signifying "to render immovable"; it is frequently associated with terror as well as astonishment, as with the verb (No. 3, below) in Acts 9:6. It occurs in Luke 4:36; 5:9; Acts 3:10. See WONDER.

Note: Ptoēsis signifies "terror," not "amazement," 1 Pet. 3:6, RV.

B. Verbs.

1. *existēmi* (ἐξίστημι, 1839), akin to A, No. 1, lit. means "to stand out from." Like the noun, this is used with two distinct meanings: (a) in the sense of amazement, the word should be invariably rendered "amazed," as in the RV, e.g., in the case of Simon Magus (for KJV, "bewitched"), Acts 8:9 and 11. It is used, in the passive voice, of Simon himself in the 13th v., RV, "he was amazed," for KJV, "wondered." "Amaze" is preferable to "astonish" throughout; (b) in Mark 3:21 and 2 Cor. 5:13 it is used with its other meaning of being beside oneself. See BESIDE ONESELF (TO BE), BEWITCH, WONDER.

2. *ekplēssō* (ἐκπλήσσω, 1605), from *ek,* "out of," *plēssō,* "to strike," lit., "to strike out," signifies "to be exceedingly struck in mind, to be astonished" (*ek,* intensive). The English "astonish" should be used for this verb, and "amaze" for *existēmi,* as in the RV; see Matt. 19:25; Luke 2:48; 9:43.

3. *thambeō* (θαμβέω, 2284), akin to A, No. 2, is used in Mark 1:27; 10:24, 32 (and Acts 9:6, KJV). The RV has "amazed" in each place; KJV "astonished," in Mark 10:24.

4. *ekthambeō* (ἐκθαμβέω, 1568), an intensive form of No. 3, is found in Mark's gospel only; in 9:15, "were greatly amazed"; in 14:33, KJV, "were sore amazed"; in 16:5, RV, "were amazed," KJV, "were affrighted"; in v. 6, RV, "be not amazed," KJV, "be not affrighted." See AFFRIGHTED.

C. Adjective.

ekthambos (ἔκθαμβος, 1569), a strengthened form of A, No. 2, is found in Acts 3:11. The intensive force of the word is brought out by the rendering "greatly wondering. See WONDER.

AMBASSADOR, AMBASSAGE

A. Verb.

presbeuō (πρεσβεύω, 4243) denotes (a) "to be elder or eldest, prior in birth or age"; (b) "to be an ambassador," 2 Cor. 5:20, and Eph. 6:20; for Philem. 9 see under AGED. There is a suggestion that to be an "ambassador" for Christ involves the experience suggested by the word "elder." Elder men were chosen as "ambassadors."

B. Noun.

presbeia (πρεσβεία, 4242), primarily, "age, eldership, rank," hence, "an embassy or ambassage," is used in Luke 14:32; in 19:14, RV, "ambassage," for KJV, "message."

AMEN

amēn (ἀμήν, 281) is transliterated from Hebrew into both Greek and English. "Its meanings may be seen in such passages as Deut. 7:9, 'the faithful (the Amen) God,' Isa. 49:7, 'Jehovah that is faithful.' 65:16, 'the God of truth,' marg., 'the God of Amen.' And if God is faithful His testimonies and precepts are "sure (*amēn*)," Ps. 19:7; 111:7, as are also His warnings, Hos. 5:9, and promises, Isa. 33:16; 55:3. 'Amen' is used of men also, e.g., Prov. 25:13.

"There are cases where the people used it to express their assent to a law and their willingness to submit to the penalty attached to the breach of it, Deut. 27:15, cf. Neh. 5:13. It is also used to express acquiescence in another's prayer, 1 Kings 1:36, where it is defined as "(let) God say so too," or in another's thanksgiving, 1 Chron. 16:36, whether by an individual, Jer. 11:5, or by the congregation, Ps. 106:48.

"Thus 'Amen' said by God 'it is and shall be so,' and by men, 'so let it be.'"

"Once in the NT 'Amen' is a title of Christ, Rev. 3:14, because through Him the purposes of God are established, 2 Cor. 1:20.

"The early Christian churches followed the example of Israel in associating themselves audibly with the prayers and thanksgivings offered on their behalf, 1 Cor. 14:16, where the article 'the' points to a common practice. Moreover this custom conforms to the pattern of things in the Heavens, see Rev. 5:14, etc.

"The individual also said 'Amen' to express his 'let it be so' in response to the Divine 'thus it shall be,' Rev. 22:20. Frequently the speaker adds 'Amen' to his own prayers and doxologies, as is the case at Eph. 3:21, e.g.

"The Lord Jesus often used 'Amen,' translated 'verily,' to introduce new revelations of the mind of God. In John's Gospel it is always repeated, 'Amen, Amen,' but not elsewhere. Luke does not use it at all, but where Matthew, 16:28, and Mark, 9:1, have 'Amen,' Luke has 'of a truth'; thus by varying the translation of what the Lord said, Luke throws light on His meaning." See VERILY.

AMISS

A. Adjective.

atopos (ἄτοπος, 824), lit., "out of place" (*a*, negative, *topos*, "a place"), denotes unbecoming, not befitting. It is used four times in the NT, and is rendered "amiss" three times in the RV; in the malefactor's testimony of Christ, Luke 23:41; in Festus' words concerning Paul, Acts 25:5, "if there is anything amiss in the man" (KJV, "wickedness"); in Acts 28:6, of the expected effect of the viper's attack upon Paul (KJV, "harm"); in 2 Thess. 3:2, of men capable of outrageous conduct, "unreasonable." See HARM, UNREASONABLE.

B. Adverb.

kakōs (κακῶς, 2560), akin to *kakos*, "evil," is translated "amiss" in Jas. 4:3; elsewhere in various ways. See EVIL, GRIEVOUS, MISERABLE.

For **ANATHEMA** see CURSE

ANGEL

angelos (ἄγγελος, 32), "a messenger" (from *angellō*, "to deliver a message"), sent whether by God or by man or by Satan, "is also used of a guardian or representative in Rev. 1:20, cf. Matt. 18:10; Acts 12:15 (where it is better understood as 'ghost'), but most frequently of an order of created beings, superior to man, Heb. 2:7; Ps. 8:5, belonging to Heaven, Matt. 24:36; Mark 12:25, and to God, Luke 12:8, and engaged in His service, Ps. 103:20. "Angels" are spirits, Heb. 1:14, i.e., they have not material bodies as men have; they are either human in form, or can assume the human form when necessary, cf. Luke 24:4, with v. 23, Acts 10:3 with v. 30.

"They are called 'holy' in Mark 8:38, and 'elect,' 1 Tim. 5:21, in contrast with some of their original number, Matt. 25:41, who 'sinned,' 2 Pet. 2:4, 'left their proper habitation,' Jude 6, *oikētērion*, a word which occurs again, in the NT, only in 2 Cor. 5:2. Angels are always spoken of in the masculine gender, the feminine form of the word does not occur."

Note: Isangelos, "equal to the angels," occurs in Luke 20:36.

ANGER, ANGRY (to be)

A. Noun.

orgē (ὀργή, 3709), originally any "natural impulse, or desire, or disposition," came to signify "anger," as the strongest of all passions. It is used of the wrath of man, Eph. 4:31; Col. 3:8; 1 Tim. 2:8; Jas. 1:19-20; the displeasure of human governments, Rom. 13:4-5; the sufferings of the Jews at the hands of the Gentiles, Luke 21:23; the terrors of the Law, Rom. 4:15; "the anger" of the Lord Jesus, Mark 3:5; God's "anger" with Israel in the wilderness, in a quotation from the OT, Heb. 3:11; 4:3; God's present "anger" with the Jews nationally, Rom. 9:22; 1 Thess. 2:16; His present "anger" with those who disobey the Lord Jesus in His gospel, John 3:36; God's purposes in judgment, Matt. 3:7; Luke 3:7; Rom. 1:18; 2:5, 8; 3:5; 5:9; 12:19; Eph. 2:3; 5:6; Col. 3:6; 1 Thess. 1:10; 5:9. See INDIGNATION, VENGEANCE, WRATH.

Notes: (1) *Thumos*, "wrath" (not translated "anger"), is to be distinguished from *orgē*, in this respect, that *thumos* indicates a more agitated condition of the feelings, an outburst of wrath from inward indignation, while *orgē* suggests a more settled or abiding condition of mind, frequently with a view to taking revenge. *Orgē* is less sudden in its rise than *thumos*, but more lasting in its nature. *Thumos* expresses more the inward feeling, *orgē* the more active emotion. *Thumos* may issue in revenge, though it does not necessarily include it. It is characteristic that it quickly blazes up and quickly subsides, though that is not necessarily implied in each case.

(2) *Parorgismos*, a strengthened form of *orge*, and used in Eph. 4:26, RV margin, "provocation," points especially to

that which provokes the wrath, and suggests a less continued state than No. (1). "The first keenness of the sense of provocation must not be cherished, though righteous resentment may remain" (Westcott). The preceding verb, *orgizo*, in this verse implies a just occasion for the feeling. This is confirmed by the fact that it is a quotation from Ps. 4:4 (Sept.), where the Hebrew word signifies to quiver with strong emotion.

Thumos is found eighteen times in the NT, ten of which are in the Apocalypse, in seven of which the reference is to the wrath of God; so in Rom. 2:8, RV, "wrath (*thumos*) and indignation" (*orgē*); the order in the KJV is inaccurate. Everywhere else the word *thumos* is used in a bad sense. In Gal. 5:20, it follows the word "jealousies," which when smoldering in the heart break out in wrath. *Thumos* and *orgē* are coupled in two places in the Apocalypse, 16:19, "the fierceness (*thumos*) of His wrath" (*orgē*); and 19:15, "the fierceness of the wrath of Almighty God." See WROTH (BE).

(3) *Aganaktēsis* originally signified "physical pain or irritation" (probably from *agan*, "very much," and *achomai*, "to grieve"), hence, "annoyance, vexation," and is used in 2 Cor. 7:11, "indignation."

B. Verbs.

1. *orgizō* (ὀργίζω, 3710), "to provoke, to arouse to anger," is used in the middle voice in the eight places where it is found, and signifies "to be angry, wroth." It is said of individuals, in Matt. 5:22; 18:34; 22:7; Luke 14:21; 15:28, and Eph. 4:26 (where a possible meaning is "be ye angry with yourselves"); of nations, Rev. 11:18; of Satan as the Dragon, 12:17 See WRATH.

2. *parorgizō* (παροργίζω, 3949) is "to arouse to wrath, provoke" (*para*, used intensively, and No. 1); Rom. 10:19, "will I anger"; Eph. 6:4, "provoke to wrath." See PROVOKE.

3. *cholaō* (χολάω, 5520), connected with *cholē*, "gall, bile," which became used metaphorically to signify bitter anger, means "to be enraged," John 7:23, "wroth," RV, in the Lord's remonstrance with the Jews on account of their indignation at His having made a man whole on the Sabbath Day.

Notes: (1) *Thumomacheō* (from *thumos*, "wrath," *machomai*, "to fight") originally denoted to fight with great animosity, and hence came to mean "to be very angry, to be exasperated," Acts 12:20, of the anger of Herod, "was highly displeased.

(2) *Thumoō*, the corresponding verb, signifies "to provoke to anger," but in the passive voice "to be wroth," as in Matt. 2:16, of the wrath of Herod, "was exceeding wroth."

(3) *Aganakteō*, see A, *Note* (3), is rendered in various ways in the seven places where it is used; "moved with indignation," Matt. 20:24 and 21:15, RV (KJV, "sore displeased"); "had indignation," Matt. 26:8; Mark 14:4. In Mark 10:14 the RV has "was moved with indignation" (KJV, "was much displeased"), said of the Lord Jesus. The same renderings are given in v. 41. In Luke 13:14 (KJV, "with indignation"), the RV rightly puts "being moved with indignation." These words more particularly point to the cause of the vexation. See DISPLEASED, INDIGNATION.

(4) In Col. 3:21, *erethizō* signifies "to provoke." The RV correctly omits "to anger."

C. Adjective.

orgilos (ὀργίλος, 3711), "angry, prone to anger, irascible" (see B, Nos. 1, 2), is rendered "soon angry" in Titus 1:7.

ANGUISH

A. Nouns.

1. *thlipsis* (θλῖψις, 2347), see AFFLICTION (No. 4).

2. *stenochōria* (στενοχωρία, 4730), lit., "narrowness of place" (*stenos*, "narrow," *chōra*, "a place"), metaphorically came to mean the "distress arising from that condition, anguish." It is used in the plural, of various forms of distress, 2 Cor. 6:4 and 12:10, and of "anguish" or distress in general, Rom. 2:9; 8:35, RV, "anguish" for KJV, "distress." The opposite state, of being in a large place, and so metaphorically in a state of joy, is represented by the word *platusmos* in certain Psalms as, e.g., Ps. 118:5; see also 2 Sam. 22:20. See DISTRESS.

3. *sunochē* (συνόχη, 4928), lit., "a holding together, or compressing" (*sun*, "together," *echō*, "to hold"), was used of the narrowing of a way. It is found only in its metaphorical sense, of "straits, distress, anguish," Luke 21:25, "distress of nations," and 2 Cor. 2:4, "anguish of heart." See DISTRESS.

Note: Anankē is associated with *thlipsis*, and signifies a condition of necessity arising from some form of compulsion. It is therefore used not only of necessity but of distress, Luke 21:23; 1 Thess. 3:7, and in the plural in 2 Cor. 6:4; 12:10.

B. Verbs.

1. *stenochōreō* (στενοχωρέω, 4729), akin to A, No. 2, lit., "to crowd into a narrow space," or, in the passive voice "to be pressed for room," hence, metaphorically, "to be straitened," 2 Cor. 4:8 and 6:12 (twice), is found in its literal sense in two places in the Sept., in Josh. 17:15 and Isa. 49:19, and in two places in its metaphorical sense, in Judg. 16:16, where Delilah is said to have pressed Samson sore with her words continually, and to have "straitened him," and in Isa. 28:20. See DISTRESS.

2. *sunechō* (συνέχω, 4912), akin to A, No. 3, lit., "to hold together," is used physically of being held, or thronged, Luke 8:45; 19:43; 22:63; of being taken with a malady, Matt. 4:24; Luke 4:38; Acts 28:8; with fear, Luke 8:37; of being straitened or pressed in spirit with desire, Luke 12:50; Acts 18:5; Phil. 1:23; with the love of Christ, 2 Cor. 5:14. In one place it is used

of the stopping of their ears by those who killed Stephen. See CONSTRAIN, HOLD, KEEP, PRESS, SICK (LIE).

3. *odunaō* (ὀδυνάω, 3600), in the middle and passive voices, signifies "to suffer pain, be in anguish, be greatly distressed" (akin to *odunē*, "pain, distress"); it is rendered "sorrowing" in Luke 2:48; in 16:24-25, RV, "in anguish," for KJV, "tormented"; in Acts 20:38, "sorrowing." See SORROW, TORMENT.

For **ANIMALS** (2 Pet. 2:12, RV), see NATURAL

ANNOUNCE

anangellō (ἀναγγέλλω, 312), "to declare, announce" (*ana*, "up," *angellō*, "to report"), is used especially of heavenly messages, and is translated "announced" in the RV of 1 Pet. 1:12, for KJV "reported," and in 1 John 1:5, RV, "announce," for KJV, "declare." See DECLARE, REHEARSE, REPORT, SHOW.

ANOINT, ANOINTING

A. Verbs.

1 *aleiphō* (ἀλείφω, 218) is a general term used for "an anointing" of any kind, whether of physical refreshment after washing, e.g., in the Sept. of Ruth 3:3; 2 Sam. 12:20; Dan. 10:3; Micah 6:15; in the NT, Matt. 6:17; Luke 7:38, 46; John 11:2; 12:3; or of the sick, Mark 6:13; Jas. 5:14; or a dead body, Mark 16:1. The material used was either oil, or ointment, as in Luke 7:38, 46. In the Sept. it is also used of "anointing" a pillar, Gen. 31:13, or captives, 2 Chron. 28:15, or of daubing a wall with mortar, Ezek. 13:10-12, 14-15; and, in the sacred sense, of "anointing" priests, in Exod. 40:15 (twice), and Num. 3:3.

2. *chriō* (χρίω, 5548) is more limited in its use than No. 1; it is confined to "sacred and symbolical anointings"; of Christ as the "Anointed" of God, Luke 4:18; Acts 4:27; 10:38, and Heb. 1:9, where it is used metaphorically in connection with "the oil of gladness." The title Christ signifies "The Anointed One," The word (*Christos*) is rendered "(His) Anointed" in Acts 4:26, RV. Once it is said of believers, 2 Cor. 1:21. *Chriō* is very frequent in the Sept., and is used of kings, 1 Sam. 10:1, and priests, Ex. 28:41, and prophets, 1 Kings 19:16. Among the Greeks it was used in other senses than the ceremonial, but in the Scriptures it is not found in connection with secular matters.

Note: The distinction referred to by Trench (*Syn.* Sec. XXXVIII), that *aleiphō* is the mundane and profane, *chriō*, the sacred and religious word, is not borne out by evidence. In a papyrus document *chrisis* is used of "a lotion for a sick horse" (Moulton and Milligan, *Vocab. of Greek Test*).

3. *enchriō* (ἐγχρίω, 1472), primarily, "to rub in," hence, "to besmear, to anoint," is used metaphorically in the command to the church in Laodicea to "anoint" their eyes with eyesalve, Rev. 3:18. In the Sept., Jer. 4:30, it is used of the "anointing" of the eyes with a view to beautifying them.

4. *epichriō* (ἐπιχρίω, 2025), primarily, "to rub on" (*epi*, "upon"), is used of the blind man whose eyes Christ "anointed," and indicates the manner in which the "anointing" was done, John 9:6, 11.

5. *murizō* (μυρίζω, 3462), is used of "anointing" the body for burial, in Mark 14:8.

B. Noun.

chrisma (χρίσμα, 5545), the corresponding noun to No. 2, above, signifies "an unguent, or an anointing." It was prepared from oil and aromatic herbs. It is used only metaphorically in the NT; by metonymy, of the Holy Spirit, 1 John 2:20, 27, twice. The RV translates it "anointing" in all three places, instead of the KJV "unction" and "anointing."

That believers have "an anointing from the Holy One" indicates that this anointing renders them holy, separating them to God. The passage teaches that the gift of the Holy Spirit is the allefficient means of enabling believers to possess a knowledge of the truth. In the Sept., it is used of the oil for "anointing" the high priest, e.g., Exod. 29:7, lit., "Thou shalt take of the oil of the anointing." In Exod. 30:25, etc., it is spoken of as "a holy anointing oil." In Dan. 9:26 *chrisma* stands for the "anointed" one, "Christ," the noun standing by metonymy for the person Himself, as for the Holy Spirit in 1 John 2.

Notes: (1) *Aleimma*, akin to A, No. 1 (not in the NT), occurs three times in the Sept., Exod. 30:31, of the "anointing" of the priests; Isa. 61:3, metaphorically, of the oil of joy; Dan. 10:3, of physical refreshment.

(2) *Muron*, a word akin to A, No. 5, denotes "ointment." The distinction between this and *elaion*, "oil," is observable in Christ's reproof of the Pharisee who, while desiring Him to eat with him, failed in the ordinary marks of courtesy; "My head with oil (*elaion*) thou didst not anoint, but she hath anointed My feet with ointment" (*muron*), Luke 7:46.

ANOTHER

allos (ἄλλος, 243) and *heteros* (ἕτερος, 2087) have a difference in meaning, which despite a tendency to be lost, is to be observed in numerous passages. *Allos* expresses a numerical difference and denotes "another of the same sort"; *heteros* expresses a qualitative difference and denotes "another of a different sort." Christ promised to send "another Comforter" (*allos*, "another like Himself," not *heteros*), John 14:16. Paul says "I see a different (KJV, "another") law," *heteros*, a law different from that of the spirit of life (not *allos*, "a law of the same sort"), Rom. 7:23. After Joseph's death "another king arose," *heteros*, one of quite a different character, Acts 7:18. Paul speaks of "a different gospel (*heteros*), which is not another" (*allos*, another like the one he preached), Gal. 1:6-7. See *heteros* (not *allos*) in Matt. 11:3, and Acts 27:1; in Luke 23:32 *heteroi* is used of the two malefactors crucified with Christ. The two words are only apparently interchanged in 1 Cor. 1:16 and 6:1; 12:8-10; 14:17 and 19, e.g., the difference being present, though not so readily discernible.

They are not interchangeable in 1 Cor. 15:39-41; here *heteros* is used to distinguish the heavenly glory from the earthly, for these differ in genus, and *allos* to distinguish the flesh of men, birds, and fishes, which in each case is flesh differing not in genus but in species. *Allos* is used again to distinguish between the glories of the heavenly bodies, for these also differ not in kind but in degree only. For *heteros*, see STRANGE.

Note: The distinction comes out in the compounds of *heteros*, viz., *heteroglōssos*, "strange tongues," 1 Cor. 14:21;; *heterodidaskaleō*, "to teach a different doctrine," 1 Tim. 1:3; 6:3;; *heterozugō*, "to be unequally yoked" (i.e., with those of a different character), 2 Cor. 6:14.

ANSWER

A. Nouns.

1. *apokrisis* (ἀπόκρισις, 612), lit., "a separation or distinction," is the regular word for "answer," Luke 2:47; 20:26; John 1:22 and 19:9.

2. *apokrima* (ἀπόκριμα, 610), akin to No. 1, denotes a judicial "sentence," 2 Cor. 1:9, KJV, and RV, margin, or an "answer" (RV, text), an answer of God to the apostle's appeal, giving him strong confidence. In an ancient inscription it is used of an official decision. In a papyrus document it is used of a reply to a deputation. See SENTENCE.

3. *chrēmatismos* (χρηματισμός, 5538), "a divine response, an oracle," is used in Rom. 11:4, of the answer given by God to Elijah's complaint against Israel. See the verb under CALL.

4. *apologia* (ἀπολογία, 627), a "verbal defense, a speech in defense," is sometimes translated "answer," in the KJV, Acts 25:16; 1 Cor. 9:3; 2 Tim. 4:16, all which the RV corrects to "defense." See Acts 22:1; Phil. 1:7, 16; 2 Cor. 7:11, "clearing." Once it signifies an "answer," 1 Pet. 3:15. Cf. B, No. 4. See CLEARING, DEFENSE.

Note: Eperōtēma, 1 Pet. 3:21, is not, as in the KJV, an "answer." It was used by the Greeks in a legal sense, as a" demand or appeal." Baptism is therefore the ground of an "appeal" by a good conscience against wrong doing.

B. Verbs.

1. *apokrinomai* (ἀποκρίνομαι, 611), akin to A, No. 1, above, signifies either "to give an answer to a question" (its more frequent use) or "to begin to speak," but always where something has preceded, either statement or act to which the remarks refer, e.g., Matt. 11:25; Luke 14:3; John 2:18. The RV translates by "answered," e.g., Matt. 28:5; Mark 12:35; Luke 3:16, where some have suggested "began to say" or "uttered solemnly," whereas the speaker is replying to the unuttered thought or feeling of those addressed by him.

2. *antapokrinomai* (ἀνταποκρίνομαι, 470), *anti*, "against," and No. 1, a strengthened form, "to answer by contradiction, to reply against," is found in Luke 14:6 and Rom. 9:20.

3. *hupolambanō* (ὑπολαμβάνω, 5274) signifies (a) "to take or bear up from beneath," Acts 1:9; (b) "to receive," 3 John 8; (c) "to suppose," Luke 7:43; Acts 2:15; (d) "to catch up (in speech), to answer," Luke 10:30; in sense (d) it indicates that a person follows what another has said, either by controverting or supplementing it.

4. *apologeomai* (ἀπολογέομαι, 626), cf. A, No. 4, lit., "to talk oneself off from" (*apo*, "from," *legō*, "to speak"), "to answer by way of making a defense for oneself" (besides its meaning "to excuse," Rom. 2:15; 2 Cor. 12:19), is translated "answer" in Luke 12:11; 21:14; in Acts 19:33, KJV and RV both have "made defense"; in Acts 24:10; 25:8; 26:1-2, the RV has the verb to make a defense, for the KJV, "to answer," and in 26:24 for the KJV, "spake for himself." See DEFENSE, EXCUSE.

5. *antilegō* (ἀντίλεγω, 483), "to speak against," is rendered "answering again" in the KJV of Titus 2:9 (RV, "gainsaying"). See CONTRADICT.

6. *sustoicheō* (συστοιχέω, 4960), lit., "to be in the same line or row with" (*sun*, "with," *stoichos*, "a row"), is translated "answereth to" in Gal. 4:25.

Note: Cf. *stoicheō*, "to walk" (in line), 5:25; 6:16. For *hupakouō*, rendered to answer in Acts 12:13, RV, see HEARKEN, No. 1, *Note.*

ANTICHRIST

antichristos (ἀντίχριστος, 500) can mean either "against Christ" or "instead of Christ," or perhaps, combining the two, "one who, assuming the guise of Christ, opposes Christ" (Westcott). The word is found only in John's epistles, (a) of the many "antichrists" who are forerunners of the "Antichrist" himself, 1 John 2:18, 22; 2 John 7; (b) of the evil power which already operates anticipatively of the "Antichrist," 1 John 4:3.

What the apostle says of him so closely resembles what he says of the first beast in Rev. 13, and what the apostle Paul says of the Man of Sin in 2 Thess. 2, that the same person seems to be in view in all these passages, rather than the second beast in Rev. 13, the false prophet; for the latter supports the former in all his Antichristian assumptions.

Note: The term *pseudochristos*, "a false Christ," is to be distinguished from the above; it is found in Matt. 24:24 and Mark 13:22. The false Christ does not deny the existence of Christ, he trades upon the expectation of His appearance, affirming that he is the Christ. The Antichrist denies the existence of the true God (Trench, *Syn.* Sec. XXX).

APOSTLE, APOSTLESHIP

1. *apostolos* (ἀπόστολος, 652) is, lit., "one sent forth" (*apo*, "from," *stellō*, "to send"). "The word is used of the Lord Jesus to describe His relation to God, Heb. 3:1; see John 17:3. The twelve disciples chosen by the Lord for special training were so called, Luke 6:13; 9:10. Paul, though he had seen the Lord Jesus, 1 Cor. 9:1; 15:8, had not 'companied with' the Twelve 'all the time' of His earthly ministry, and hence was not eligible for a place among them, according to Peter's description of the necessary qualifications, Acts 1:22. Paul was commissioned directly, by the Lord Himself, after His Ascension, to carry the gospel to the Gentiles.

"The word has also a wider reference. In Acts 14:4, 14, it is used of Barnabas as well as of Paul; in Rom. 16:7 of Andronicus and Junias. In 2 Cor. 8:23 (RV, margin) two unnamed brethren are called 'apostles of the churches'; in Phil. 2:25 (RV, margin) Epaphroditus is referred to as 'your apostle.' It is used in 1 Thess. 2:6 of Paul, Silas and Timothy, to define their relation to Christ."

2. *apostolē* (ἀποστολή, 651), "a sending, a mission," signifies an apostleship, Acts 1:25; Rom. 1:5; 1 Cor. 9:2; Gal. 2:8.

Note: Pseudapostoloi, "false apostles," occurs in 2 Cor. 11:13.

APPARITION

phantasma (φάντασμα, 5326), "a phantasm or phantom" (from *phaino*, "to appear"), is translated "apparition" in the RV of Matt. 14:26 and Mark 6:49 (KJV, "spirit"). In the Sept., Job 20:8; Isa. 28:7.

APPEAR, APPEARING

A. Verbs.

1. *phainō* (φαίνω, 5316) signifies, in the active voice, "to shine"; in the passive, "to be brought forth into light, to become evident, to appear." In Rom. 7:13, concerning sin, the RV has "might be shewn to be," for KJV, "appear."

It is used of the "appearance" of Christ to the disciples, Mark 16:9; of His future "appearing" in glory as the Son of Man, spoken of as a sign to the world, Matt. 24:30; there the genitive is subjective, the sign being the "appearing" of Christ Himself; of Christ as the light, John 1:5; of John the Baptist, 5:35; of the "appearing" of an angel of the Lord, either visibly, Matt. 1:20, or in a dream, 2:13; of a star, 2:7; of men who make an outward show, Matt. 6:5; 6:18 (see the RV); 23:27-28; 2 Cor. 13:7; of tares, Matt. 13:26; of a vapor, Jas. 4:14; of things physical in general, Heb. 11:3; used impersonally in Matt. 9:33, "it was never so seen"; also of what appears to the mind, and so in the sense of to think, Mark 14:64, or to seem, Luke 24:11 (RV, appeared). See SEEM, SHINE.

2. *epiphainō* (ἐπιφαίνω, 2014), a strengthened form of No. 1 but differing in meaning, *epi* signifying "upon," is used in the active voice with the meaning "to give light," Luke 1:79; in the passive voice, "to appear, become visible." It is said of heavenly bodies, e.g., the stars, Acts 27:20 (RV, "shone"); metaphorically, of things spiritual, the grace of God, Titus 2:11; the kindness and the love of God, 3:4. See LIGHT. Cf. *epiphaneia*, B, No. 2.

3. *anaphainō* (ἀναφαίνω, 398), *ana*, "forth, or up," perhaps originally a nautical term, "to come up into view," hence, in general, "to appear suddenly," is used in the passive voice, in Luke 19:11, of the Kingdom of God; active voice, in Acts 21:3, "to come in sight of," RV; "having sighted" would be a suitable rendering (KJV, "having discovered).

4. *phaneroō* (φανερόω, 5319), akin to No. 1, signifies, in the active voice, "to manifest"; in the passive voice, "to be manifested"; so,regularly, in the RV, instead of "to appear." See 2 Cor. 7:12; Col. 3:4; Heb. 9:26; 1 Pet. 5:4; 1 John 2:28; 3:2; Rev. 3:18. To be manifested, in the Scriptural sense of the word, is more than to "appear." A person may "appear" in a false guise or without a disclosure of what he truly is; to be manifested is to be revealed in one's true character; this is especially the meaning of *phaneroō*, see, e.g., John 3:21; 1 Cor. 4:5; 2 Cor. 5:10-11; Eph. 5:13.

5. *emphanizō* (ἐμφανίζω, 1718), from *en*, "in," intensive, and *phainō*, "to shine," is used, either of "physical manifestation," Matt. 27:53; Heb. 9:24; cf. John 14:22, or, metaphorically, of "the manifestation of Christ" by the Holy Spirit in the spiritual experience of believers who abide in His love, John 14:21. It has another, secondary meaning, "to make known, signify, inform." This is confined to the Acts, where it is used five times, 23:15, 22; 24:1; 25:2, 15. There is perhaps a combination of the two meanings in Heb. 11:14, i.e., to declare by oral testimony and to "manifest" by the witness of the life. See INFORM, MANIFEST, SIGNIFY.

6. *optomai* (ὄπτομαι, 3700), "to see" (from *ōps*, "the eye"; cf. Eng. "optical," etc.), in the passive sense, "to be seen, to appear," is used (a) objectively, with reference to the person or thing seen, e.g., 1 Cor. 15:5-8, RV "appeared," for KJV, "was seen"; (b) subjectively, with reference to an inward impression or a spiritual experience, John 3:36, or a mental occupation, Acts 18:15, "look to it"; cf. Matt. 27:4, 24, "see (thou) to it," "see (ye) to it," throwing responsibility on others. *Optomai* is to be found in dictionaries under the word *horaō*, "to see"; it supplies some forms that are lacking in that verb.

These last three words, *emphanizō*, *phaneroō* and *optomai* are used with reference to the "appearances" of Christ in the closing verses of Heb. 9; *emphanizō* in v. 24, of His presence before the face of God for us; *phaneroō* in v. 26, of His past manifestation for "the sacrifice of Himself"; *optomai* in v. 28, of His future "appearance" for His saints.

7. *optanō* (ὀπτάνω, 3700), in the middle voice signifies "to allow oneself to be seen." It is rendered "appearing" in Acts 1:3, RV, for KJV, "being seen," of the Lord's "appearances" after His resurrection; the middle voice expresses the personal interest the Lord took in this.

Note: In Acts 22:30 *sunerchomai* (in its aorist form), "to come together," is translated "appear," KJV; RV, "come together."

B. Nouns.

1. *apokalupsis* (ἀποκάλυψις, 602), lit., "an uncovering, unveiling" (*apo*, "from," *kaluptō*, "to hide, cover"), denotes "a revelation, or appearing" (Eng., apocalypse). It is translated "the appearing" in 1 Pet. 1:7, KJV (RV, "revelation"). See COMING, MANIFESTATION, REVELATION.

2. *epiphaneia* (ἐπιφάνεια, 2015), "epiphany," lit., "a shining forth," was used of the "appearance" of a god to men, and of an enemy to an army in the field, etc. In the NT it occurs of (a) the advent of the Savior when the Word became flesh, 2 Tim. 1:10; (b) the coming of the Lord Jesus into the air to the meeting with His saints, 1 Tim. 6:14; 2 Tim. 4:1, 8; (c) the shining forth of the glory of the Lord Jesus "as the lightning cometh forth from the east, and is seen even unto the west," Matt. 24:27, immediately consequent on the unveiling, *apokalupsis*, of His *Parousia* in the air with His saints, 2 Thess. 2:8; Titus 2:13.

Notes: (1) *Phanerōsis*, akin to A No. 4, "a manifestation," is used in 1 Cor. 12:2 and 2 Cor. 4:2.

(2) For *phaneros*, wrongly translated "may appear," in 1 Tim. 4:15, KJV (RV, "may be manifest," not mere appearance), see MANIFEST.

(3) *Emphanēs*, akin to A, No. 5, "manifest," is used in Acts 10:40 and Rom. 10:20. See MANIFEST, OPENLY.

(4) For *adēlos*, "which appear not," Luke 11:44, see UNCERTAIN.

APPEARANCE

A. Nouns.

1. *eidos* (εἶδος, 1491), properly "that which strikes the eye, that which is exposed to view," signifies the "external appearance, form, or shape," and in this sense is used of the Holy Spirit in taking bodily form, as a dove, Luke 3:22; of Christ, 9:29, "the fashion of His countenance." Christ used it, negatively, of God the Father, when He said "Ye have neither heard His voice at any time, nor seen His form," John 5:37. Thus it is used with reference to each person of the Trinity. Probably the same meaning attaches to the word in the apostle's statement, "We walk by faith, not by sight (*eidos*)," 2 Cor. 5:7, where *eidos* can scarcely mean the act of beholding, but the visible "appearance" of things which are set in contrast to that which directs faith. The believer is guided, then, not only by what he beholds but by what he knows to be true though it is invisible.

It has a somewhat different significance in 1 Thess. 5:22, in the exhortation, "Abstain from every form of evil," i.e., every sort or kind of evil (not "appearance," KJV). This meaning was common in the papyri, the Greek writings of the closing centuries, B.C., and the New Testament era. See FASHION, SHAPE, SIGHT. Cf. No. 4.

2. *prosōpon* (πρόσωπον, 4383), pros, "towards," *ōps*, "an eye," lit., "the part round the eye, the face," in a secondary sense "the look, the countenance," as being the index of the inward thoughts and feelings (cf. 1 Pet. 3:12, there used of the face of the Lord), came to signify the presentation of the whole person (translated "person," e.g., in Matt. 22:16). Cf. the expression in OT passages, as Gen. 19:21 (KJV marg., "thy face"), where it is said by God of Lot, and 33:10, where it is said by Jacob of Esau; see also Deut. 10:17 ("persons"), Lev. 19:15 ("person"). It also signifies the presence of a person, Acts 3:13; 1 Thess. 2:17; or the presence of a company, Acts 5:41. In this sense it is sometimes rendered "appearance," 2 Cor. 5:12. In 2 Cor. 10:7, KJV, "appearance," the RV corrects to face. See COUNTENANCE, FACE, FASHION, PERSON, PRESENCE.

3. *opsis* (ὄψις, 3799), from *ōps*, "the eye," connected with *horaō*, "to see" (cf. No. 2), primarily denotes "seeing, sight"; hence, "the face, the countenance," John 11:44 ("face"); Rev. 1:16 ("countenance"); the outward "appearance," the look, John 7:24, only here, of the outward aspect of a person. See COUNTENANCE, FACE.

4. *eidea* (εἰδέα, 2397), "an aspect, appearance," is used in Matt. 28:3, RV, "appearance"; KJV, "countenance."

B. Verb.

phantazō (φαντάζω, 5324), "to make visible," is used in its participial form (middle voice), with the neuter article, as equivalent to a noun, and is translated "appearance," RV, for KJV, "sight," Heb. 12:21.

APPEASE

katastellō (καταστέλλω, 2687), "to quiet" (lit., "to send down," *kata*, "down," *stellō*, "to send"), in the passive voice, "to be quiet, or to be quieted," is used in Acts 19:35 and 36, in the former verse in the active voice, KJV, "appeased"; RV, "quieted"; in the latter, the passive, "to be quiet" (lit., 'to be quieted') See QUIET.

APPOINT, APPOINTED

1. *histēmi* (ἵστημι, 2476), "to make to stand," means "to appoint," in Acts 17:31, of the day in which God will judge the world by Christ. In Acts 1:23, with reference to Joseph and Barnabas, the RV has "put forward"; for these were not both "appointed" in the accepted sense of the term, but simply singled out, in order that it might be made known which of them the Lord had chosen.

2. *kathistēmi* (καθίστημι, 2525), a strengthened form of No. 1, usually signifies "to appoint a person to a position." In this sense the verb is often translated "to make" or "to set," in appointing a person to a place of authority, e.g., a servant over a household, Matt. 24:45, 47; 25:21, 23; Luke 12:42, 44; a judge, Luke 12:14; Acts 7:27, 35; a governor, Acts 7:10; man by God over the work of His hands, Heb. 2:7. It is rendered "appoint," with reference to the so-called seven deacons in Acts 6:3. The RV translates it by "appoint" in Titus 1:5, instead of "ordain," of the elders whom Titus was to "appoint" in every city in Crete. Not a formal ecclesiastical ordination is in view, but the "appointment," for the recognition of the churches, of those who had already been raised up and qualified by the Holy Spirit, and had given evidence of this in their life and service (see No. 11). It is used of the priests of old, Heb. 5:1; 7:28; 8:3 (RV, "appointed"). See CONDUCT, ORDAIN.

3. *tithēmi* (τίθημι, 5087), "to put," is used of "appointment" to any form of service. Christ used it of His followers, John 15:16 (RV, "appointed" for KJV, "ordained"). "I set you" would be more in keeping with the metaphor of grafting. The verb is used by Paul of his service in the ministry of the gospel, 1 Tim. 1:12 (RV, "appointing" for "putting"); 2:7 (RV, "appointed" for "ordained"); and 2 Tim. 1:11 (RV, "appointing" for "putting"); of the overseers, or bishops, in the local church at Ephesus, as those "appointed" by the Holy Ghost, to tend the church of God, Acts 20:28 ("hath made"); of the Son of God, as appointed Heir of all things, Heb. 1:2. It is also used of "appointment" to punishment, as of the unfaithful servant, Matt. 24:51; Luke 12:46; of unbelieving Israel, 1 Pet. 2:8. Cf. 2 Pet. 2:6. See BOW, CONCEIVE, ORDAIN, SINK.

Note: Akin to *tithēmi* is the latter part of the noun *prothesmia*, Gal. 4:2, of a term or period "appointed."

4. *diatithēmi* (διατίθημι, 1303), a strengthened form of No. 3 (*dia*, "through," intensive), is used in the middle voice only. The Lord used it of His disciples with reference to the kingdom which is to be theirs hereafter, and of Himself in the same respect, as that which has been "appointed" for Him by His Father, Luke 22:29. For its use in connection with a covenant, see TESTATOR.

5. *tassō* (τάσσω, 5021), "to place in order, arrange," signifies "to appoint," e.g., of the place where Christ had "appointed" a meeting with His disciples after His resurrection, Matt. 28:16; of positions of military and civil authority over others, whether "appointed" by men, Luke 7:8, or by God, Rom. 13:1, "ordained." It is said of those who, having believed the gospel, "were ordained to eternal life," Acts 13:48. The house of Stephanas at Corinth had "set themselves" to the ministry of the saints (KJV, "addicted"), 1 Cor. 16:15. Other instances of the arranging of special details occur in Acts 15:2; 22:10; 28:23. See ORDAIN.

6. *diatassō* (διατάσσω, 1299), a strengthened form of No. 5 (*dia*, "through," intensive), frequently denotes "to arrange, appoint, prescribe," e.g., of what was "appointed" for tax collectors to collect, Luke 3:13; of the tabernacle, as "appointed" by God for Moses to make, Acts 7:44; of the arrangements "appointed" by Paul with regard to himself and his travelling companions, Acts 20:13; of what the apostle "ordained" in all the churches in regard to marital conditions, 1 Cor. 7:17; of what the Lord "ordained" in regard to the support of those who proclaimed the gospel, 1 Cor. 9:14; of the Law as divinely "ordained," or administered, through angels, by Moses, Gal. 3:19.

In Titus 1:5, KJV, "had appointed thee," the sense is rather that of commanding, RV, "gave thee charge. See COMMAND, No. 1, ORDAIN.

7. *suntassō* (συντάσσω, 4929), *sun*, "with," and No. 5, lit., "to arrange together with," hence "to appoint, prescribe," is used twice, in Matt. 26:19 of what the Lord "appointed" for His disciples, and in 27:10, in a quotation concerning the price of the potter's field.

8. *protassō* (προτάσσω, 4384), *pro*, "before," and No. 5, "to appoint before," is used in Acts 17:26 (RV, "appointed"), of the seasons arranged by God for nations, and the bounds of their habitation.

9. *keimai* (κεῖμαι, 2749), "to lie," is used in 1 Thess. 3:3 of the "appointment" of affliction for faithful believers. It is rendered "set" in Luke 2:34 and Phil. 1:16, RV, where the sense is the same. The verb is a perfect tense, used for the perfect passive of *tithēmi*, "to place," "I have been placed," i.e., "I lie." See LIE.

10. *apokeimai* (ἀπόκειμαι, 606), *apo*, "from," and No. 9, signifies "to be laid, reserved," Luke 19:20; Col. 1:5; 2 Tim. 4:8; "appointed," in Heb. 9:27, where it is said of death and the judgment following (RV, marg., "laid up").

11. *cheirotoneō* (χειροτονέω, 5500), primarily used of voting in the Athenian legislative assembly and meaning "to stretch forth the hands" (*cheir*, "the hand," *teinō*, "to stretch"), is not to be taken in its literal sense; it could not be so taken in its compound *procheirotoneō*, "to choose before," since it is said of God, Acts 10:41. *Cheirotoneō* is said of "the appointment" of elders by apostolic missionaries in the various churches which they revisited, Acts 14:23, RV, "had

appointed," i.e., by the recognition of those who had been manifesting themselves as gifted of God to discharge the functions of elders (see No. 2). It is also said of those who were "appointed" (not by voting, but with general approbation) by the churches in Greece to accompany the apostle in conveying their gifts to the poor saints in Judea, 2 Cor. 8:19. See CHOOSE, ORDAIN.

12. *procheirizō* (προχειρίζω, 4400), from *procheiros*, "at hand," signifies (a) "to deliver up, appoint," Acts 3:20 (RV, "appointed"); (b) in the middle voice, "to take into one's hand, to determine, appoint beforehand," translated "appointed" in Acts 22:14, RV (for KJV, "hath chosen"), and "to appoint" in 26:16 (for KJV, "to make").

13. *horizō* (ὁρίζω, 3724), (Eng., "horizon"), lit., "to mark by a limit," hence, "to determine, ordain," is used of Christ as ordained of God to be a judge of the living and the dead, Acts 17:31; of His being "marked out" as the Son of God, Rom. 1:4; of divinely appointed seasons, Acts 17:26, "having determined." See DEFINE.

14. *anadeiknumi* (ἀναδείκνυμι, 322), lit., "to show up, to show clearly," also signifies "to appoint to a position or a service"; it is used in this sense of the 70 disciples, Luke 10:1; for the meaning "show," see Acts 1:24.

15. *poieō* (ποιέω, 4160), "to do, to make," is rendered "appointed" in Heb. 3:2, of Christ. For Mark 3:14, RV, see ORDAIN, *Note* (2).

Note: Epithanatios, "appointed to death," doomed to it by condemnation, 1 Cor. 4:9, KJV, is corrected to "doomed to death" in the RV (*epi*, "for," *thanatos*, "death").

APPREHEND

1. *katalambanō* (καταλαμβάνω, 2638) properly signifies "to lay hold of"; then, "to lay hold of so as to possess as one's own, to appropriate." Hence it has the same twofold meaning as the Eng. "to apprehend"; (a), "to seize upon, take possession of," (1) with a beneficial effect, as of "laying hold" of the righteousness which is of faith, Rom. 9:30 (not there a matter of attainment, as in the Eng. versions, but of appropriation); of the obtaining of a prize, 1 Cor. 9:24 (RV, "attain"); of the apostle's desire "to apprehend," or "lay hold of," that for which he was apprehended by Christ, Phil. 3:12-13; (2) with a detrimental effect, e.g., of demon power, Mark 9:18; of human action in seizing upon a person, John 8:3-4; metaphorically, with the added idea of overtaking, of spiritual darkness in coming upon people, John 12:35; of the Day of the Lord, in suddenly coming upon unbelievers as a thief, 1 Thess. 5:4; (b), "to lay hold of" with the mind, to understand, perceive, e.g., metaphorically, of darkness with regard to light, John 1:5, though possibly here the sense is that of (a) as in 12:35; of mental perception, Acts 4:13; 10:34; 25:25; Eph. 3:18. See OVERTAKE.

Note: Cf. *epilambanō*, "to take hold of," always in the middle voice in the NT. See HOLD.

2. *piazō* (πιάζω, 4084), "to lay hold of," with the suggestion of firm pressure or force, is used in the Gospels only in John, six times of efforts to seize Christ and is always rendered "take" in the RV, 7:30, 32, 44; 8:20; 10:39; 11:57. The KJV has "laid hands on" in 8:20. In Acts 12:4 and 2 Cor. 11:32 (KJV), it is translated respectively "apprehended" and "apprehend" (RV, "had taken," and "take"). In Rev. 19:20 it is used of the seizure of the Beast and the False Prophet. In John 21:3, 10 it is used of catching fish. Elsewhere in Acts 3:7. In the Sept., Song of Sol. 2:15.

APPROACH

A. Verb.

engizō (ἐγγίζω, 1448), "to draw near, to approach," from *engus*, "near," is used (a) of place and position, literally and physically, Matt. 21:1; Mark 11:1; Luke 12:33; 15:25; figuratively, of drawing near to God, Matt. 15:8; Heb. 7:19; Jas. 4:8; (b) of time, with reference to things that are imminent, as the kingdom of heaven, Matt. 3:2; 4:17; 10:7; the kingdom of God, Mark 1:15; Luke 10:9, 11; the time of fruit, Matt. 21:34; the desolation of Jerusalem, Luke 21:8; redemption, 21:28; the fulfillment of a promise, Acts 7:17; the Day of Christ in contrast to the present night of the world's spiritual darkness, Rom. 13:12; Heb. 10:25; the coming of the Lord, Jas. 5:8; the end of all things, 1 Pet. 4:7. It is also said of one who was drawing near to death, Phil. 2:30. See HAND (AT).

B. Adjective.

aprositos (ἀπρόσιτος, 676), "unapproachable, inaccessible" (a), negative, and an adjective formed from *proseimi*, "to go to"), is used, in 1 Tim. 6:16, of the light in which God dwells (KJV, "which no man can approach unto"; RV, "unapproachable").

For **APT** see TEACH, B

ARCHANGEL

archangelos (ἀρχάγγελος, 743) "is not found in the OT, and in the NT only in 1 Thess. 4:16 and Jude 9, where it is used of Michael, who in Daniel is called 'one of the chief princes,' and 'the great prince' (Sept., 'the great angel'), 10:13, 21; 12:1. Cf. also Rev. 12:7 .... Whether there are other beings of this exalted rank in the heavenly hosts, Scripture does not say, though the description 'one of the chief princes' suggests that this may be the case; cf. also Rom. 8:38; Eph. 1:21; Col. 1:16, where the word translated 'principalities' is *archē*, the prefix in archangel." In 1 Thess. 4:16 the meaning seems to be that the voice of the Lord Jesus will be of the character of an "archangelic" shout.

ARISE, AROSE, AROUSE, RAISE, RISE, ROUSE

1. *anistēmi* (ἀνίστημι, 450), "to stand up or to make to stand up," according as its use is intransitive or transitive (*ana*, "up," *histēmi*, "to stand"), is used (a) of a physical change of position, e.g., of "rising" from sleep, Mark 1:35; from a meeting in a synagogue, Luke 4:29; of the illegal "rising" of the high priest in the tribunal in Matt. 26:62; of an invalid "rising" from his couch, Luke 5:25; the "rising" up of a disciple from his vocation to follow Christ, Luke 5:28; cf. John 11:31; "rising" up from prayer, Luke 22:45; of a whole company, Acts 26:30; 1 Cor. 10:7; (b) metaphorically, of "rising" up antagonistically against persons, e.g. of officials against people, Acts 5:17; of a seditious leader, 5:36, of the "rising" up of Satan, Mark 3:26; of false teachers, Acts 20:30; (c) of "rising" to a position of preeminence or power; e.g., of Christ as a prophet, Acts 3:22; 7:37; as God's servant in the midst of the nation of Israel, Acts 3:26; as the Son of God in the midst of the nation, 13:33 (not here of resurrection, but with reference to the Incarnation: the KJV "again" has nothing corresponding to it in the original, it was added as a misinterpretation: the mention of His resurrection is in the next verse, in which it is stressed by way of contrast and by the addition, "from the dead"); as a priest, Heb. 7:11, 15; as king over the nations, Rom. 15:12; (d) of a spiritual awakening from lethargy, Eph. 5:14; (e) of resurrection from the dead: (1) of the resurrection of Christ, Matt. 17:9; 20:19; Mark 8:31; 9:9-10, 31; 10:34; Luke 18:33; 24:7, 46; John 20:9; Acts 2:24, 32; 10:41; 13:34; 17:3, 31; 1 Thess. 4:14; (2) of believers, John 6:39-40, 44, 54; 11:24; 1 Thess. 4:16; of unbelievers, Matt. 12:41.

2. *exanistēmi* (ἐξανίστημι, 1817), a strengthened form of No. 1 (*ex*, i.e., *ek*, intensive), signifies "to raise up," Mark 12:19; Luke 20:28; intransitively, "to rise up, Acts 15:5.

3. *egeirō* (ἐγείρω, 1453) is frequently used in the NT in the sense of "raising" (active voice), or "rising" (middle and passive voices): (a) from sitting, lying, sickness, e.g., Matt. 2:14; 9:5, 7, 19; Jas. 5:15; Rev. 11:1; (b) of causing to appear, or, in the passive, appearing, or raising up so as to occupy a place in the midst of people, Matt. 3:9; 11:11; Mark 13:22; Acts 13:22. It is thus said of Christ in Acts 13:23; cf. No. 1, (c); (c) of rousing, stirring up, or "rising" against, Matt. 24:7; Mark 13:8; (d) of "raising buildings," John 2:19-20; (e) of "raising or rising" from the dead; (1) of Christ, Matt. 16:21; and frequently elsewhere (but not in Phil., 2 Thess., 1 Tim., Titus, Jas., 2 Pet., 1, 2, 3 John, and Jude); (2) of Christ's "raising" the dead, Matt. 11:5; Mark 5:41; Luke 7:14; John 12:1, 9, 17; (3) of the act of the disciples, Matt. 10:8; (4) of the resurrection of believers, Matt. 27:52; John 5:21; 1 Cor. 15:15-16, 29, 32, 35, 42-44 52; 2 Cor. 1:9; 4:14; of unbelievers, Matt. 12:42 (cf. v. 41, No. 1).

Egeiro stands in contrast to *anistēmi* (when used with reference to resurrection) in this respect, that *egeiro* is frequently used both in the transitive sense of "raising up" and the intransitive of "rising," whereas *anistēmi* is comparatively infrequent in the transitive use. See AWAKE.

4. *diegeirō* (διεγείρω, 1326), a strengthened form of No. 3 (*dia*, "through," intensive), signifies "to rouse, to awaken from sleep." The active voice is not used intransitively. In Matt. 1:24, RV, "Joseph arose from his sleep," the passive participle is, lit., "being aroused." In Mark 4:39 (KJV, "he arose," RV, "he awoke"), the lit. rendering is "he being awakened." In John 6:18 the imperfect tense of the passive voice is used, and the rendering should be, "the sea was being aroused. See AWAKE, No. 2.

5. *ginomai* (γίνομαι, 1096), "to become, to take place," is sometimes suitably translated "arise"; e.g., Matt. 8:24; Mark 4:37, "there arose a great tempest." So of the arising of persecution, Matt. 13:21; Mark 4:17; this might be translated "taketh place"; of a tumult, Matt. 27:24, RV, "arising," for KJV, "made"; of a flood, Luke 6:48; a famine, 15:14; a questioning, John 3:25; a murmuring, Acts 6:1; a tribulation, 11:19 (RV); a stir in the city, 19:23; a dissension, 23:7; a great clamor, v. 9. See BECOME.

6. *anabainō* (ἀναβαίνω, 305), "to go up, to ascend," is once rendered "arise" in the RV, Luke 24:38, of reasonings in the heart; in Rev. 13:1, RV, "coming up," for KJV, "rise up," with reference to the beast; in 17:8, KJV, "ascend," for RV, "to come up"; in 19:3, RV, "goeth up," for KJV, "rose up. See CLIMB UP, GO.

7. *sunephistēmi* (συνεφίστημι, 4911), "to rise up together" (*sun*, together, *epi*, "up," *histēmi*, "to stand"), is used in Acts 16:22, of the "rising up" of a multitude against Paul and Silas.

8. *eiserchomai* (εἰσέρχομαι, 1525), lit., "to go in" (*eis*, "in," *erchomai*, "to go"), "to enter," is once rendered "arose," metaphorically, with reference to a reasoning among the disciples which of them should be the greatest, Luke 9:46. See GO.

9. *anatellō* (ἀνατέλλω, 393), "to arise," is used especially of things in the natural creation, e.g., "the rising" of the sun, moon and stars; metaphorically, of light, in Matt. 4:16, "did spring up"; of the sun, Matt. 5:45; 13:6 (RV); Mark 4:6; Jas. 1:11; in Mark 16:2 the RV has "when the sun was risen," keeping to the verb form, for the KJV, "at the rising of"; of a cloud, Luke 12:54; of the day-star, 2 Pet. 1:19; in Heb. 7:14 metaphorically, of the Incarnation of Christ: "Our Lord hath sprung out of Judah," more lit., "Our Lord hath arisen out of Judah," as of the rising of the light of the sun.

Notes: (1) A corresponding noun, *anatolē*, signifies "the east," i.e., the place of the "sunrising."

(2) In Acts 27:14, the verb *ballō*, "to beat" (intransitive), is translated "arose" in the KJV; RV, "beat."

ARK

kibōtos (κιβωτός, 2787), "a wooden box, a chest," is used of (a) Noah's vessel, Matt. 24:38; Luke 17:27; Heb. 11:7; 1 Pet. 3:20; (b) the "ark" of the covenant in the tabernacle, Heb. 9:4; (c) the "ark" seen in vision in the heavenly temple, Rev. 11:19.

ARM (physical)

1. *ankalē* (ἀγκάλη, 43), used in the plural, in Luke 2:28, originally denoted "the curve, or the inner angle, of the arm." The word is derived from a term signifying "to bend, to curve"; the Eng. "angle" is connected.

Note: Enankalizomai (*en*, "in," and a verb akin to No. 1), "to take into the arms, to embrace," is used in Mark 9:36 and 10:16, of the tenderness of Christ towards little children.

2. *brachiōn* (βραχίων, 1023), "the shorter part of the arm, from the shoulder to the elbow," is used metaphorically to denote strength, power, and always in the NT of the power of God, Luke 1:51; John 12:38; Acts 13:17; frequently so in the OT, especially in Deuteronomy, the Psalms and Isaiah; see, e.g., Deut. 4:34; 5:15; Ps. 44:3; 71:18, where "strength" is, lit., "arm"; 77:15; Isa. 26:11, where "hand" is, lit., "arm"; 30:30; 40:10-11, etc.

ART, ARTS

1. *technē* (τέχνη, 5078), "an art, handicraft, trade," is used in Acts 17:29, of the plastic art; in Acts 18:3, of a trade or craft (KJV, "occupation," RV, "trade"); in Rev. 18:22, "craft" (cf. *technitēs*, "a craftsman," Eng., "technical"). See OCCUPATION.

2. *periergos* (περίεργος, 4021), lit., "a work about" (*peri*, "about," *ergon*, "a work"), hence, "busy about trifles," is used, in the plural, of things superfluous, "curious (or magical) arts," Acts 19:19; in 1 Tim. 5:13, "busybodies."

For **ASCEND** see ARISE, No. 6

ASHAMED (to be), SHAME

A. Verbs.

1. *aischunō* (αἰσχύνω, 153), from *aischos*, "shame," always used in the passive voice, signifies (a) "to have a feeling of fear or shame which prevents a person from doing a thing," e.g., Luke 16:3; (b) "the feeling of shame arising from something that has been done," e.g., 2 Cor. 10:8; Phil. 1:20; 1 John 2:28, of the possibility of being "ashamed" before the Lord Jesus at His judgment seat in His Parousia with His saints; in 1 Pet. 4:16, of being ashamed of suffering as a Christian.

2. *epaischunomai* (ἐπαισχύνομαι, 1870), a strengthened form of No. 1 (*epi*, "upon," intensive), is used only in the sense (b) in the preceding paragraph. It is said of being "ashamed" of persons, Mark 8:38; Luke 9:26; the gospel, Rom. 1:16; former evil doing, Rom. 6:21; "the testimony of our Lord," 2 Tim. 1:8; suffering for the gospel, v. 12; rendering assistance and comfort to one who is suffering for the gospel's sake, v. 16. It is used in Heb., of Christ in calling those who are sanctified His brethren, 2:11, and of God in His not being "ashamed" to be called the God of believers, 11:16. In the Sept., in Job 34:19; Ps. 119:6; Isa. 1:29.

3. *kataischunō* (καταισχύνω, 2617), another strengthened form (*kata*, "down," intensive), is used (a) in the active voice, "to put to shame," e.g., Rom. 5:5; 1 Cor. 1:27 (KJV, "confound"); 11:4-5 ("dishonoreth"), and v. 22; (b) in the passive voice, Rom. 9:33; 10:11; 2 Cor. 7:14; 1 Pet. 2:6; 3:16. See CONFOUND, DISHONOR, SHAME.

4. *entrepō* (ἐντρέπω, 1788), "to put to shame," in the passive voice, to be ashamed, lit. means "to turn in" (*en*, "in," *trepō*, "to turn"), that is, to turn one upon himself and so produce a feeling of "shame," a wholesome "shame" which involves a change of conduct, 1 Cor. 4:14; 2 Thess. 3:14; Titus 2:8, the only places where it has this meaning. See also REGARD, REVERENCE.

B. Nouns.

1. *aischunē* (αἰσχύνη, 152), "shame," akin to A, No. 1, signifies (a) subjectively, the confusion of one who is "ashamed" of anything, a sense of "shame," Luke 14:9; those things which "shame" conceals, 2 Cor. 4:2; (b) objectively, ignominy, that which is visited on a person by the wicked, Heb. 12:2; that which should arise from guilt, Phil. 3:19; (c) concretely, a thing to be "ashamed" of, Rev. 3:18; Jude 13, where the word is in the plural, lit., "basenesses," "disgraces." See DISHONESTY.

2. *entropē* (ἐντροπή, 1791), akin to A, No. 4, lit., "a turning in upon oneself," producing a recoil from what is unseemly or vile, is used in 1 Cor. 6:5; 15:34. It is associated with *aischunē* in the Psalms, in the Sept., e.g., 35:26, where it follows *aischunē*, "let them be clothed with shame (*aischunē*) and confusion (*entropē*)"; 44:15, "all the day my shame is before me and the confusion of my face has covered me"; 69:19, "Thou knowest my reproach and my shame and my confusion"; so in 71:13. In 109:29 the words are in the opposite order.

Note: Aidōs, used in 1 Tim. 2:9, denotes "modesty, shamefastness" (the right spelling for the KJV, "shamefacedness"). In comparison with *aischunē, aidōs* is "the nobler word, and implies the nobler motive: in it is involved an innate moral repugnance to the doing of the dishonorable act, which moral repugnance scarcely or not at all exists in *aischunē*" (Trench, *Syn.* Sec. XIX). See SHAMEFASTNESS.

C. Adjectives.

1. *aischros* (αἰσχρός, 150), "base" (akin to No. 1), is used in 1 Cor. 11:6-14:35; Eph. 5:12. See FILTHY B, No. 1. Cf. *aischrotes*, "filthiness," Eph. 5:4.

2. *anepaischuntos* (ἀνεπαίσχυντος, 422), an intensive adjective (*a*, negative, *n* euphonic, *epi*, "upon," intensive, *aischunē*, "shame"), "not ashamed, having no cause for shame," is used in 2 Tim. 2:15.

ASHES

A. Noun.

spodos (σποδός, 4700), "ashes," is found three times, twice in association with sackcloth, Matt. 11:21 and Luke 10:13, as tokens of grief (cf. Esth. 4:1, 3; Isa. 58:5; 61:3; Jer. 6:26; Jonah 3:6); of the ashes resulting from animal sacrifices, Heb. 9:13; in the OT, metaphorically, of one who describes himself as dust and "ashes," Gen. 18:27, etc.

B. Verb.

tephroō (τεφρόω, 5077), "to turn to ashes," is found in 2 Pet. 2:6, with reference to the destruction of Sodom and Gomorrah.

Notes: (1) *Tephra*, frequently used of the "ashes" of a funeral pile, is not found in the NT.

(2) The Hebrew verb, rendered "accept" in Ps. 20:3, "accept thy burnt sacrifice," signifies "to turn to ashes" (i.e., by sending fire from heaven). See also Exod. 27:3, and Num. 4:13, "shall take away the ashes."

ASLEEP, SLEEP

A. Verbs.

1. *katheudō* (καθεύδω, 2518), "to go to sleep," is chiefly used of natural "sleep," and is found most frequently in the Gospels, especially Matthew and Luke. With reference to death it is found in the Lord's remark concerning Jairus' daughter, Matt. 9:24; Mark 5:39; Luke 8:52. In the epistles of Paul it is used as follows: (a) of natural "sleep," e.g., 1 Thess. 5:7; (b) of carnal indifference to spiritual things on the part of believers, Eph. 5:14; 1 Thess. 5:6, 10 (as in Mark 13:36), a condition of insensibility to divine things involving conformity to the world (cf. *hupnos* below).

2. *koimaomai* (κοιμάομαι, 2837) is used of natural "sleep," Matt. 28:13; Luke 22:45; John 11:12; Acts 12:6; of the death of the body, but only of such as are Christ's; yet never of Christ Himself, though He is "the firstfruits of them that have fallen asleep," 1 Cor. 15:20, of saints who departed before Christ came, Matt. 27:52; Acts 13:36; of Lazarus, while Christ was yet upon the earth, John 11:11; of believers since the Ascension, 1 Thess. 4:13-15, and Acts 7:60; 1 Cor. 7:39; 11:30; 15:6, 18, 51; 2 Pet. 3:4.

Note: "This metaphorical use of the word sleep is appropriate, because of the similarity in appearance between a sleeping body and a dead body; restfulness and peace normally characterize both. The object of the metaphor is to suggest that, as the sleeper does not cease to exist while his body sleeps, so the dead person continues to exist despite his absence from the region in which those who remain can communicate with him, and that, as sleep is known to be temporary, so the death of the body will be found to be ....

"That the body alone is in view in this metaphor is evident, (a) from the derivation of the word *koimaomai*, from *keimai*, to lie down (cf. *anastasis*, resurrection, from *ana*, 'up,' and *histēmi* to cause to stand); cf. Isa. 14:8, where for 'laid down,' the Sept. has 'fallen asleep'; (b) from the fact that in the NT the word resurrection is used of the body alone; (c) from Dan. 12:2, where the physically dead are described as 'them that sleep (Sept. *katheudō*, as at 1 Thess. 5:6) in the dust of the earth,' language inapplicable to the spiritual part of man; moreover, when the body returns whence it came, Gen. 3:19, the spirit returns to God who gave it, Eccl. 12:7.

"When the physical frame of the Christian (the earthly house of our tabernacle, 2 Cor. 5:1) is dissolved and returns to the dust, the spiritual part of his highly complex being, the seat of personality, departs to be with Christ, Phil. 1:23. And since that state in which the believer, absent from the body, is at home with the Lord, 2 Cor. 5:6-9, is described as 'very far better' than the present state of joy in communion with God and of happy activity in His service, everywhere reflected in Paul's writings, it is evident the word 'sleep,' where applied to the departed Christians, is not intended to convey the idea that the spirit is unconscious ....

"The early Christians adopted the word *koimētērion* (which was used by the Greeks of a rest-house for strangers) for the place of interment of the bodies of their departed; thence the English word 'cemetery,' 'the sleeping place,' is derived."

3. *exupnizō* (ἐξυπνίζω, 1852), "to awake" (*ek*, "out," *hupnos*, "sleep"), "to awake out of sleep," is used in John 11:11. In the Sept., Judg. 16:14, 20; 1 Kings 3:15; Job 14:12.

4. *aphupnoō* (ἀφυπνόω, 879), "to fall asleep" (*apo*, "away"), is used of natural "sleep," Luke 8:23, of the Lord's falling "asleep" in the boat on the lake of Galilee.

B. Adjective.

exupnos (ἔξυπνος, 1853), Acts 16:27, signifies "out of sleep."

C. Noun.

hupnos (ὕπνος, 5258) is never used of death. In five places in the NT it is used of physical "sleep"; in Rom. 13:11, metaphorically, of a slumbering state of soul, i.e., of spiritual conformity to the world, out of which believers are warned to awake.

ASP

aspis (ἀσπίς, 785), "a small and very venomous serpent," the bite of which is fatal, unless the part affected is at once cut away, in Rom. 3:13 is said, metaphorically, of the conversation of the ungodly.

ASS

1. *onos* (ὄνος, 3688) is the usual word. *Onarion*, the diminutive of *onos*, "a young ass, or ass's colt," is used in John 12:14, together with *onos*.

2. *hupozugion* (ὑποζύγιον, 5268), lit., "under a yoke" (*hupo*, "under," *zugos*, "a yoke"), is used as an alternative description of the same animal, in Matt. 21:5, where both words are found together, "Behold, thy king cometh unto thee, meek and riding upon an ass (*onos*), and upon a colt the foal of an ass (*hupozugion*)." It was upon the colt that the Lord sat, John 12:14. In 2 Pet. 2:16, it is used of Balaam's "ass."

ASSASSIN

sikarios (σικάριος, 4607) is a Latin word (*sicarius*, "from" *sica*, "a dagger") denoting "one who carries a dagger or short sword under his clothing, an assassin," Acts 21:38, RV. Here it is used as a proper name (see the RV) of the Sicarii, "assassins," the fanatical Jewish faction which arose in Judea after Felix had rid the country of the robbers referred to by Josephus (Ant., XX). They mingled with the crowds at festivals and stabbed their political opponents unobserved (KJV, "murderers").

ASSAULT

A. Verb.

ephistēmi (ἐφίστημι, 2186), lit., "to stand over" (*epi*, "over," *histēmi*, "to stand"), signifies "to assault"; said in Acts 17:5, of those who attacked the house of Jason. For its usual meanings see HAND (AT), PRESENT.

B. Noun.

hormē (ὁρμή, 3730), rendered "assault" in Acts 14:5, KJV; RV, "onset," corresponds to *hormaō*, to rush. See IMPULSE, ONSET.

For **ASSAY** see TRY, No. 2

ASSEMBLE

1. *sunagō* (συνάγω, 4863), "to assemble" (*sun*, "together," *ago*, "to bring"), is used of the "gathering together" of people or things; in Luke 12:17-18, "bestow," with reference to the act of "gathering" one's goods; so in Luke 15:13, suggesting that the Prodigal, having "gathered" all his goods together, sold them off; in John 6:12, of "gathering" up fragments; in John 18:2, "resorted," with reference to the "assembling" of Christ with His disciples in the garden of Gethsemane, there in the passive voice (unsuitable, however, in an English translation). In Acts 11:26, the RV has "were gathered together (with the church)," for KJV, "assembled themselves" (possibly "they were hospitably entertained by"). The verb is not found in the most authentic mss. in Rev. 13:10. See BESTOW, GATHER, LEAD.

Note: Episunagō, "to gather together," is found only in the synoptic Gospels; twice of the "gathering" together of people, Mark 1:33; Luke 12:1; twice of the desire of the Lord to "gather" together the inhabitants of Jerusalem, Matt. 23:37; Luke 13:34; twice of His future act in "gathering" together His elect through the instrumentality of the angels, Matt. 24:31; Mark 13:27. See GATHER.

2. *sunalizō* (συναλίζω, 4871), "to gather together, to assemble," with the suggestion of a crowded meeting (*sun*, "with," *halizō*, "to crowd, or mass:" the corresponding adjective is *halēs*, "thronged"), is used in Acts 1:4. The meaning "to eat with," suggested by some, as if the word were derived from *hals*, "salt," is not to be accepted.

3. *sunerchomai* (συνέρχομαι, 4905), "to come together" (*sun*, "together," *erchomai* "to come"), is once rendered "assemble," Mark 14:53, KJV. It is frequently used of "coming together," especially of the "gathering" of a local church, 1 Cor. 11:17-18, 20, 33-34; 14:23, 26; it is rendered "resorted" in Acts 16:13, KJV, where the RV adheres to the lit. rendering, "came together." See ACCOMPANY.

Notes: (1) In Acts 15:25, *ginomai*, "to become," is translated "having come to (one accord)," correcting the KJV, "being assembled with (one accord)."

(2) *Sunagōgē*, akin to A, No. 1, is, lit., "a place where people assemble." In Acts 13:43 the RV suitably has "synagogue," for the KJV "congregation," the building standing by metonymy for the people therein (cf. Matt. 10:17, etc.). In Jas. 2:2 (KJV, "assembly") the word is "synagogue" (RV). See SYNAGOGUE.

(3) *Episunagōgē*, akin to No. 1, *Note*, "an assembling together," is used in 2 Thess. 2:1, of the rapture of the saints into the air to meet the Lord, "our gathering together"; in Heb. 10:25, of the "gatherings" of believers on earth during the present period. See GATHERING.

ASSEMBLY

1. *ekklēsia* (ἐκκλησία, 1577), from *ek*, "out of," and *klēsis*, "a calling" (*kaleō*, "to call"), was used among the Greeks of a body of citizens "gathered" to discuss the affairs of state, Acts 19:39. In the Sept. it is used to designate the "gathering" of Israel, summoned for any definite purpose, or a "gathering" regarded as representative of the whole nation. In Acts 7:38 it

is used of Israel; in 19:32, 41, of a riotous mob. It has two applications to companies of Christians, (a) to the whole company of the redeemed throughout the present era, the company of which Christ said, "I will build My Church," Matt. 16:18, and which is further described as "the Church which is His Body," Eph. 1:22; 5:23, (b) in the singular number (e.g., Matt. 18:17, RV marg., "congregation"), to a company consisting of professed believers, e.g., Acts 20:28; 1 Cor. 1:2; Gal. 1:13; 1 Thess. 1:1; 2 Thess. 1:1; 1 Tim. 3:5, and in the plural, with reference to churches in a district.

There is an apparent exception in the RV of Acts 9:31, where, while the KJV has "churches," the singular seems to point to a district; but the reference is clearly to the church as it was in Jerusalem, from which it had just been scattered, 8:1. Again, in Rom. 16:23, that Gaius was the host of "the whole church," simply suggests that the "assembly" in Corinth had been accustomed to meet in his house, where also Paul was entertained.

2. *paneguris* (πανήγυρις, 3831), from *pan*, "all," and *agora*, "any kind of assembly," denoted, among the Greeks, an assembly of the people in contrast to the council of national leaders, or a "gathering" of the people in honor of a god, or for some public festival, such as the Olympic games. The word is used in Heb. 12:23, coupled with the word "church," as applied to all believers who form the body of Christ.

3. *plēthos* (πλῆθος, 4128), "a multitude, the whole number," is translated "assembly" in Acts 23:7, RV. See BUNDLE, COMPANY, MULTITUDE.

Note: For *sunagōgē*, see ASSEMBLE, *Note* (2).

For **ASSIST** see HELP, B, *Note*

ASSURANCE, ASSURE, ASSUREDLY

A. Nouns.

1. *pistis* (πίστις, 4102), "faith," has the secondary meaning of "an assurance or guarantee, e.g., Acts 17:31; by raising Christ from the dead, God has given "assurance" that the world will be judged by Him (the KJV margin, "offered faith" does not express the meaning). Cf. 1 Tim. 5:12, where "faith" means "pledge." See BELIEF, FAITH, FIDELITY.

2. *plērophoria* (πληροφορία, 4136), "a fullness, abundance," also means "full assurance, entire confidence"; lit., a "full-carrying" (*plēros*, "full," *pherō*, "to carry"). Some explain it as full fruitfulness (cf. RV, "fullness" in Heb. 6:11). In 1 Thess. 1:5 it describes the willingness and freedom of spirit enjoyed by those who brought the gospel to Thessalonica; in Col. 2:2, the freedom of mind and confidence resulting from an understanding in Christ; in Heb. 6:11 (KJV, "full assurance," RV, "fullness"), the engrossing effect of the expectation of the fulfillment of God's promises; in Heb. 10:22, the character of the faith by which we are to draw near to God. See FULLNESS.

3. *hupostasis* (ὑπόστασις, 5287), lit., "a standing under, support" (*hupo*, "under," *histēmi*, "to stand"), hence, an "assurance," is so rendered in Heb. 11:1, RV, for KJV, "substance." It here may signify a title-deed, as giving a guarantee, or reality. See CONFIDENCE, PERSON, SUBSTANCE.

Note: In Acts 16:10, for the KJV (of *sumbibazomai*), "assuredly gathering," see CONCLUDE.

B. Verbs.

1. *pistoō* (πιστόω, 4104), "to trust or give assurance to" (cf. A, No. 1), has a secondary meaning, in the passive voice, "to be assured of," 2 Tim. 3:14.

2. *plērophoreō* (πληροφορέω, 4135), akin to A, No. 2, "to bring in full measure, to fulfill," also signifies "to be fully assured," Rom. 4:21, RV, of Abrahams faith. In 14:5 it is said of the apprehension of the will of God. So in Col. 4:12 in the best mss. In these three places it is used subjectively, with reference to an effect upon the mind. For its other and objective use, referring to things external, see FULFILL; see also BELIEVE, KNOW, PERSUADE, PROOF. In the Sept., Eccl. 8:11.

3. *peithō* (πείθω, 3982), "to persuade," is rendered "assure" in 1 John 3:19 (marg., "persuade"), where the meaning is that of confidence toward God consequent upon loving in deed and in truth. See BELIEVE, CONFIDENCE, FRIEND, OBEY, PERSUADE, TRUST, YIELD.

C. Adverb.

asphalōs (ἀσφαλῶς, 806) means (a) "safely," Mark 14:44; Acts 16:23; (b) "assuredly," Acts 2:36; the knowledge there enjoined involves freedom from fear of contradiction, with an intimation of the impossibility of escape from the effects. See SAFELY.

For **ASTONISH and ASTONISHMENT** see AMAZE AND AMAZEMENT

For **ASTRAY** see ERR

For **ASUNDER** see PART

For **ATHIRST** see THIRST

ATONEMENT

katallagē (καταλλαγή, 2643), translated "atonement" in the KJV of Rom. 5:11, signifies, not "atonement," but "reconciliation," as in the RV. See also Rom. 11:15; 2 Cor. 5:18-19. So with the corresponding verb *katallassō*, see under RECONCILE. "Atonement" (the explanation of this English word as being "at-onement" is entirely fanciful) is frequently found in the OT. See, for instance, Leviticus, chapters 16 and 17. The corresponding NT words are *hilasmos*, "propitiation," 1 John

2:2; 4:10, and *hilastērion*, Rom. 3:25; Heb. 9:5, "mercy-seat," the covering of the ark of the covenant. These describe the means (in and through the person and work of the Lord Jesus Christ, in His death on the cross by the shedding of His blood in His vicarious sacrifice for sin) by which God shows mercy to sinners. See PROPITIATION.

ATTEND, ATTENDANCE, ATTENDANT

A. Verbs.

1. *prosechō* (προσέχω, 4337), "to take heed, give heed," is said of the priests who "gave attendance at the altar," Heb. 7:13. It suggests devotion of thought and effort to a thing. In 1 Tim. 4:13 (in the exhortation regarding the public reading of the Scriptures), the RV translates it "give heed," for the KJV, "give attendance." In Acts 16:14, "to give heed" (for KJV, "attended). See BEWARE, GIVE, No. 17, REGARD.

2. *proskartereō* (προσκαρτερέω, 4342), "to be steadfast," a strengthened form of *kartereō* (*pros*, "towards," intensive, *karteros*, "strong"), denotes to continue steadfastly in a thing and give unremitting care to it, e.g., Rom. 13:6, of rulers in the discharge of their functions. In the Sept., Num. 13:21.

B. Adjective.

euparedros (εὐπρόσεδρος, 2145), lit., "sitting well beside" (*eu*, "well," *para*, "beside," *hedra*, "a seat"), i.e., sitting constantly by, and so applying oneself diligently to, anything, is used in 1 Cor. 7:35, with *pros*, "upon," "that ye may attend upon." Some mss. have *euprosedron*.

C. Noun.

hupēretēs (ὑπηρέτης, 5257), lit., "an underrower"; hence, "a servant," is rendered "attendant" in Luke 4:20 and Acts 13:5, RV. See MINISTER, SERVANT.

For **ATTENTIVE**, in the KJV of Luke 19:48, see HANG, No. 2

For **AUDIENCE** see HEARING, A, No. 1, B, No. 1

AUSTERE

austēros (αὐστηρός, 840), akin to *auō*, "to dry up" (Eng., "austere"), primarily denotes "stringent to the taste," like new wine not matured by age, unripe fruit, etc., hence, "harsh, severe," Luke 19:21-22.

Note: Synonymous with *austēros*, but to be distinguished from it, is *sklēros* (from *skellō*, "to be dry"). It was applied to that which lacks moisture, and so is rough and disageeable to the touch, and hence came to denote "harsh, stern, hard." It is used by Matthew to describe the unprofitable servant's remark concerning his master, in the parable corresponding to that in Luke 19 (see *austēros*, above). *Austēros* is derived from a word having to do with the taste, *sklēros*, "with the touch." *Austēros* is not necessarily a term of reproach, whereas *sklēros* is always so, and indicates a harsh, even inhuman character. *Austēros* is "rather the exaggeration of a virtue pushed too far, than an absolute vice" (Trench, *Syn.* Sec. XIV). *Sklēros* is used of the character of a man, Matt. 25:24; of a saying, John 6:60; of the difficulty and pain of kicking against the ox-goads, Acts 9:5; 26:14; of rough winds, Jas. 3:4 and of harsh speeches, Jude 15. See FIERCE, HARD. Cf. *sklērotēs*, "hardness," *sklērunō*, "to harden," *sklērokardia*, "hardness of heart," and *sklērotrachēlos*, "stiff-necked."

AUTHOR

1. *aitios* (αἴτιος, 159), an adjective (cf. *aitia*, a cause), denotes "that which causes something." This and No. 2 are both translated "author" in Hebrews. *Aitios*, in Heb. 5:9, describes Christ as the "Author of eternal salvation unto all them that obey Him," signifying that Christ, exalted and glorified as our High Priest, on the ground of His finished work on earth, has become the personal mediating cause (RV, margin) of eternal salvation. It is difficult to find an adequate English equivalent to express the meaning here. Christ is not the merely formal cause of our salvation. He is the concrete and active cause of it. He has not merely caused or effected it, He is, as His name, "Jesus," implies, our salvation itself, Luke 2:30; 3:6.

2. *archēgos* (ἀρχηγός, 747), translated "Prince" in Acts 3:15 (marg., "Author") and 5:31, but "Author" in Heb. 2:10, RV, "Captain," RV marg., and KJV, and "Author" in 12:2, primarily signifies "one who takes a lead in, or provides the first occasion of, anything." In the Sept. it is used of the chief of a tribe or family, Num. 13:2 (RV, prince); of the "heads" of the children of Israel, v. 3; a captain of the whole people, 14:4; in Micah 1:13, of Lachish as the leader of the sin of the daughter of Sion: there, as in Heb. 2:10, the word suggests a combination of the meaning of leader with that of the source from whence a thing proceeds. That Christ is the Prince of life signifies, as Chrysostom says, that "the life He had was not from another; the Prince or Author of life must be He who has life from Himself." But the word does not necessarily combine the idea of the source or originating cause with that of leader. In Heb. 12:2 where Christ is called the "Author and Perfecter of faith," He is represented as the one who takes precedence in faith and is thus the perfect exemplar of it. The pronoun "our" does not correspond to anything in the original, and may well be omitted. Christ in the days of His flesh trod undeviatingly the path of faith, and as the Perfecter has brought it to a perfect end in His own person. Thus He is the leader of all others who tread that path. See PRINCE.

Note: In 1 Cor. 14:33, the KJV, "the author," represents no word in the original; RV "a God of."

AUTHORITY

A. Nouns.

1. *exousia* (ἐξουσία, 1849) denotes "authority" (from the impersonal verb *exesti*, "it is lawful"). From the meaning of "leave or permission," or liberty of doing as one pleases, it passed to that of "the ability or strength with which one is endued," then to that of the "power of authority," the right to exercise power, e.g., Matt. 9:6; 21:23; 2 Cor. 10:8; or "the power of rule or government," the power of one whose will and commands must be obeyed by others, e.g., Matt. 28:18; John 17:2; Jude 25; Rev. 12:10; 17:13; more specifically of apostolic "authority," 2 Cor. 10:8; 13:10; the "power" of judicial decision, John 19:10; of "managing domestic affairs," Mark 13:34. By metonymy, or name-change (the substitution of a suggestive word for the name of the thing meant), it stands for "that which is subject to authority or rule," Luke 4:6 (RV, "authority," for the KJV "power"); or, as with the English "authority," "one who possesses authority, a ruler, magistrate," Rom. 13:1-3; Luke 12:11; Titus 3:1; or "a spiritual potentate," e.g., Eph. 3:10; 6:12; Col. 1:16; 2:10, 15; 1 Pet. 3:22. The RV usually translates it "authority."

In 1 Cor. 11:10 it is used of the veil with which a woman is required to cover herself in an assembly or church, as a sign of the Lord's "authority" over the church. See LIBERTY, POWER, RIGHT, STRENGTH.

2. *epitagē* (ἐπιταγή, 2003), an injunction (from *epi*, "upon," *tassō*, "to order"), is once rendered "authority," Titus 2:15 (RV, marg. "commandment"). See COMMANDMENT.

Note: The corresponding verb is *epitassō*, "to command." See COMMAND.

3. *huperochē* (ὑπεροχή, 5247), primarily, "a projection, eminence," as a mountain peak, hence, metaphorically, "preeminence, superiority, excellency," is once rendered "authority," 1 Tim. 2:2, KJV (marg., "eminent place"), RV, "high place," of the position of magistrates; in 1 Cor. 2:1, "excellency" (of speech). Cf. *huperechō*, "to surpass." See EXCELLENCY.

4. *dunastēs* (δυνάστης, 1413), akin to *dunamis*, "power," (Eng., "dynasty,") signifies "a potentate, a high officer"; in Acts 8:27, of a high officer, it is rendered "of great authority"; in Luke 1:52, RV, "princes," (KJV, "the mighty"); in 1 Tim. 6:15 it is said of God ("Potentate"). See MIGHTY.

B. Verbs.

1. *exousiazō* (ἐξουσιάζω, 1850), akin to A, No. 1, signifies "to exercise power," Luke 22:25; 1 Cor. 6:12; 7:4 (twice). See POWER.

2. *katexousiazō* (κατεξουσιάζω, 2715), *kata*, "down," intensive, and No. 1, "to exercise authority upon," is used in Matt. 20:25, and Mark 10:42.

3. *authenteō* (αὐθεντέω, 831), from *autos*, "self," and a lost noun *hentēs*, probably signifying working (Eng., "authentic"), "to exercise authority on one's own account, to domineer over," is used in 1 Tim. 2:12, KJV, "to usurp authority," RV, "to have dominion." In the earlier usage of the word it signified one who with his own hand killed either others or himself. Later it came to denote one who acts on his own "authority"; hence, "to exercise authority, dominion." See DOMINION, *Note*.

AVENGE, AVENGER

A. Verb.

ekdikeō (ἐκδικέω, 1556), *ek*, "from," *dikē*, "justice," i.e., that which proceeds from justice, means (a) "to vindicate a person's right," (b) "to avenge a thing." With the meaning (a), it is used in the parable of the unjust judge, Luke 18:3, 5, of the "vindication" of the rights of the widow; with the meaning (b) it is used in Rev. 6:10 and 19:2, of the act of God in "avenging" the blood of the saints; in 2 Cor. 10:6, of the apostle's readiness to use his apostolic authority in punishing disobedience on the part of his readers; here the RV substitutes "avenge" for the KJV, "revenge"; in Rom. 12:19 of "avenging" oneself, against which the believer is warned.

Note: In Rev. 18:20, the KJV mistranslates *krinō* and *krima* "hath avenged you"; RV, "hath judged your judgment."

B. Nouns.

1. *ekdikos* (ἔκδικος, 1558), primarily, "without law," then, "one who exacts a penalty from a person, an avenger, a punisher," is used in Rom. 13:4 of a civil authority in the discharge of his function of executing wrath on the evildoer (KJV, wrongly, "revenger"); in 1 Thess. 4:6, of God as the avenger of the one who wrongs his brother, here particularly in the matter of adultery.

2. *ekdikēsis* (ἐκδίκησις, 1557), vengeance," is used with the verb *poieō*, "to make," i.e., to avenge, in Luke 18:7-8; Acts 7:24; twice it is used in statements that "vengeance" belongs to God, Rom. 12:19; Heb. 10:30. In 2 Thess. 1:8 it is said of the act of divine justice which will be meted out to those who know not God and obey not the gospel, when the Lord comes in flaming fire at His second advent. In the divine exercise of judgment there is no element of vindictiveness, nothing by way of taking revenge. In Luke 21:22, it is used of the "days of vengeance" upon the Jewish people; in 1 Pet. 2:14, of civil governors as those who are sent of God "for vengeance on evildoers" (KJV, "punishment"); in 2 Cor. 7:11, of the "self-avenging" of believers, in their godly sorrow for wrong doing, RV, "avenging," for KJV, revenge. See PUNISHMENT, VENGEANCE.

AWAKE

1. *egeirō* (ἐγείρω, 1453) is used, (a) in the active voice, of "arousing a person from sleep" in Matt. 8:25 of the act of the disciples in awaking the Lord; in Acts 12:7, of the awaking of Peter, RV, "awake him"; (b) in the passive voice, with a middle significance, of the virgins, in "arousing themselves" from their slumber, Matt. 25:7; in Rom. 13:11, and Eph. 5:14, metaphorically, "of awaking from a state of moral sloth. See ARISE.

2. *diegeirō* (διεγείρω, 1326), is used of "awaking from natural sleep," Matt. 1:24; Mark 4:38; of the act of the disciples in "awaking" the Lord, Luke 8:24 (cf. *egeirō*, in Matt. 8:25); metaphorically, "of arousing the mind," 2 Pet. 1:13; 3:1. See ARISE, STIR UP.

3. *eknēphō* (ἐκνήφω, 1594), primarily, "to return to one's sense from drunkenness, to become sober," is so used in the Sept., e.g., Gen. 9:24; metaphorically, in Joel 1:5; Hab. 2:7; lit., in 2:19, of the words of an idolater to an image; in the NT in 1 Cor. 15:34, "Awake up righteously and sin not" (RV), suggesting a return to soberness of mind from the stupor consequent upon the influence of evil doctrine.

4. *exupnizō* (ἐξυπνίζω, 1852), from *ek*, "out of," and *hupnos*, "sleep," "to rouse a person out of sleep," is used metaphorically, in John 11:11.

5. *diagrēgoreō* (διαγρηγορέω, 1235), *dia*, intensive, *grēgoreō*, "to watch," is used in Luke 9:32, RV, "were fully awake." KJV "were awake."

For **AWARE** see KNOW, A, No. 1, end of 1st par.

AWE

deos (δέος, 127), "awe," is so rendered in Heb. 12:28, RV; the previous word "reverence" represents the inferior reading *aidōs* (see SHAMEFASTNESS).

AXE

axinē (ἀξίνη, 513), "an axe," akin to *agnumi*, "to break," is found in Matt. 3:10, and Luke 3:9.

B

BABBLER, BABBLINGS

1. *spemologos* (σπερμολόγος, 4691), "a babbler," is used in Acts 17:18. Primarily an adjective, it came to be used as a noun signifying a crow, or some other bird, picking up seeds (*sperma*, "a seed," *legō*, "to collect"). Then it seems to have been used of a man accustomed to hang about the streets and markets, picking up scraps which fall from loads; hence a parasite, who lives at the expense of others, a hanger on.

Metaphorically it became used of a man who picks up scraps of information and retails them secondhand, a plagiarist, or of those who make a show, in unscientific style, of knowledge obtained from misunderstanding lectures. Prof. Ramsay points out that there does not seem to be any instance of the classical use of the word as a "babbler" or a mere talker. He finds in the word a piece of Athenian slang, applied to one who was outside any literary circle, an ignorant plagiarist. Other suggestions have been made, but without satisfactory evidence.

2. *kenophōnia* (κενοφωνία, 2757), "babbling" (from *kenos*, "empty," and *phonē*, "a sound"), signifies empty discussion, discussion on useless subjects, 1 Tim. 6:20 and 2 Tim. 2:16.

BABE

1. *brephos* (βρέφος, 1025) denotes (a) "an unborn child," as in Luke 1:41, 44; (b) "a newborn child, or an infant still older," Luke 2:12, 16; 18:15; Acts 7:19; 2 Tim. 3:15; 1 Pet. 2:2. See CHILD.

2. *nēpios* (νήπιος, 3516), lit., "without the power of speech," denotes "a little child," the literal meaning having been lost in the general use of the word. It is used (a) of "infants," Matt. 21:16; (b) metaphorically, of the unsophisticated in mind and trustful in disposition, Matt. 11:25 and Luke 10:21, where it stands in contrast to the wise; of those who are possessed merely of natural knowledge, Rom. 2:20; of those who are carnal, and have not grown, as they should have done, in spiritual understanding and power, the spiritually immature, 1 Cor. 3:1, those who are so to speak partakers of milk, and "without experience of the word of righteousness," Heb. 5:13; of the Jews, who, while the Law was in force, were in a state corresponding to that of childhood, or minority, just as the word "infant" is used of a minor, in English law, Gal. 4:3, "children"; of believers in an immature condition, impressionable and liable to be imposed upon instead of being in a state of spiritual maturity, Eph. 4:14, "children." "Immaturity" is always associated with this word. See CHILD, No. 7.

Note: The corresponding verb, *nēpiazō*, is found in 1 Cor. 14:20, where believers are exhorted to be as "babes" (RV) in malice, unable to think or speak maliciously.

For **BADE** see BID

BAD

1. *kakos* (κακός, 2556) indicates the lack in a person or thing of those qualities which should be possessed; it means "bad in character" (a) morally, by way of thinking, feeling or acting, e.g., Mark 7:21, "thoughts"; 1 Cor. 15:33, "company"; Col. 3:5, "desire"; 1 Tim. 6:10, "all kinds of evil"; 1 Pet. 3:9, "evil for evil"; (b) in the sense of what is injurious or baneful, e.g., the tongue as "a restless evil," Jas. 3:8; "evil beasts," Titus 1:12; "harm," Acts 16:28; once it is translated "bad," 2 Cor. 5:10. It is the opposite of *agathos*, "good." See EVIL, HARM, ILL, WICKED.

2. *ponēros* (πονηρός, 4190), connected with *ponos*, "labor," expresses especially the "active form of evil," and is practically the same in meaning as (b), under No. 1. It is used, e.g., of thoughts, Matt. 15:19 (cf. *kakos*, in Mark 7:21); of speech, Matt. 5:11 (cf. *kakos*, in 1 Pet. 3:10); of acts 2 Tim. 4:18. Where *kakos* and *ponēros* are put together, *kakos* is always put first and signifies "bad in character, base," *ponēros*, "bad in effect, malignant": see 1 Cor. 5:8, and Rev. 16:2. *Kakos* has a wider meaning, *ponēros* a stronger meaning. *Ponēros* alone is used of Satan and might well be translated "the malignant one," e.g., Matt. 5:37 and five times in 1 John (2:13-14; 3:12; 5:18-19, RV); of demons, e.g., Luke 7:21. Once it is translated bad, Matt. 22:10. See EVIL, GRIEVOUS, HARM, MALICIOUS, WICKED.

3. *sapros* (σαπρός, 4550), "corrupt, rotten" (akin to *sēpō*, "to rot"), primarily, of vegetable and animal substances, expresses what is of poor quality, unfit for use, putrid. It is said of a tree and its fruit, Matt. 7:17-18; 12:33; Luke 6:43; of certain fish, Matt. 13:48 (here translated "bad"); of defiling speech, Eph. 4:29. See CORRUPT.

BALANCE

zugos (ζυγός, 2218), "a yoke," also has the meaning of "a pair of scales," Rev. 6:5. So the Sept. of Lev. 19:36; Isa. 40:12 See YOKE.

BANDED

poieō sustrophēn (ποιέω, 4160, συστροφήν, 4963), Acts 23:12, of the Jews who "banded together" with the intention of killing Paul, consists of the verb *poieō*, "to make," and the noun *sustrophē*, primarily "a twisting up together, a binding together"; then, "a secret combination, a conspiracy." Accordingly it might be translated "made a conspiracy." The noun is used elsewhere in 19:40. See CONCOURSE.

BANK, BANKERS

1. *trapeza* (τράπεζα, 5132), primarily "a table," denotes (a) an eating-table, e.g., Matt. 15:27; (b) food, etc. placed on "a table," Acts 6:2; 16:34; (c) "a feast, a banquet," 1 Cor. 10:21; (d) "the table or stand" of a moneychanger, where he exchanged money for a fee, or dealt with loans and deposits, Matt. 21:12; Mark 11:15; Luke 19:23; John 2:15. See MEAT, TABLE.

2. *trapezitēs* (τραπεζίτης, 5133), a "moneychanger, broker, banker"; translated "bankers" in Matt. 25:27, RV (KJV, "exchangers").

For **BANQUETING** see CAROUSINGS

BAPTISM, BAPTIST, BAPTIZE

A. Nouns.

1. *baptisma* (βάπτισμα, 908), "baptism," consisting of the processes of immersion, submersion and emergence (from *baptō*, "to dip"), is used (a) of John's "baptism," (b) of Christian "baptism," see B. below; (c) of the overwhelming afflictions and judgments to which the Lord voluntarily submitted on the cross, e.g., Luke 12:50; (d) of the sufferings His followers would experience, not of a vicarious character, but in fellowship with the sufferings of their Master. Some mss. have the word in Matt. 20:22-23; it is used in Mark 10:38-39, with this meaning.

2. *baptismos* (βαπτισμός, 909), as distinct from *baptisma* (the ordinance), is used of the "ceremonial washing of articles," Mark 7:4, 8, in some texts; Heb. 9:10; once in a general sense, Heb. 6:2. See WASHING.

3. *baptistēs* (Βαπτιστής, 910), "a baptist," is used only of John the Baptist, and only in the Synoptists, 14 times.

B. Verb.

baptizō (βαπτίζω, 907), "to baptize," primarily a frequentative form of *baptō*, "to dip," was used among the Greeks to signify the dyeing of a garment, or the drawing of water by dipping a vessel into another, etc. Plutarchus uses it of the drawing of wine by dipping the cup into the bowl (*Alexis*, 67) and Plato, metaphorically, of being overwhelmed with questions (*Euthydemus*, 277 D).

It is used in the NT in Luke 11:38 of washing oneself (as in 2 Kings 5:14, "dipped himself," Sept.); see also Isa. 21:4, lit., "lawlessness overwhelms me." In the early chapters of the four Gospels and in Acts 1:5; 11:16; 19:4, it is used of the rite performed by John the Baptist who called upon the people to repent that they might receive remission of sins. Those who obeyed came "confessing their sins," thus acknowledging their unfitness to be in the Messiah's coming kingdom. Distinct from this is the "baptism" enjoined by Christ, Matt. 28:19, a "baptism" to be undergone by believers, thus witnessing to their identification with Him in death, burial and resurrection, e.g., Acts 19:5; Rom. 6:3-4; 1 Cor. 1:13-17; 12:13; Gal. 3:27; Col. 2:12. The phrase in Matt. 28:19, "baptizing them into the Name" (RV; cf. Acts 8:16, RV), would indicate that the "baptized" person was closely bound to, or became the property of, the one into whose name he was "baptized."

In Acts 22:16 it is used in the middle voice, in the command given to Saul of Tarsus, "arise and be baptized," the significance of the middle voice form being "get thyself baptized." The experience of those who were in the ark at the time of the Flood was a figure or type of the facts of spiritual death, burial, and resurrection, Christian "baptism" being an *antitupon*, "a corresponding type," a "like figure," 1 Pet. 3:21. Likewise the nation of Israel was figuratively baptized when made to pass through the Red Sea under the cloud, 1 Cor. 10:2. The verb is used metaphorically also in two distinct senses: firstly, of "baptism" by the Holy Spirit, which took place on the Day of Pentecost; secondly, of the calamity which would come upon the nation of the Jews, a "baptism" of the fire of divine judgment for rejection of the will and word of God, Matt. 3:11; Luke 3:16.

BARBARIAN, BARBAROUS

barbaros (βάρβαρος, 915) properly meant "one whose speech is rude, or harsh"; the word is onomatopoeic, indicating in the sound the uncouth character represented by the repeated syllable "bar-bar." Hence it signified one who speaks a strange or foreign language. See 1 Cor. 14:11. It then came to denote any foreigner ignorant of the Greek language and culture. After the Persian war it acquired the sense of rudeness and brutality. In Acts 28:2, 4, it is used unreproachfully of the inhabitants of Malta, who were of Phoenician origin. So in Rom. 1:14, where it stands in distinction from Greeks, and in implied contrast to both Greeks and Jews. Cf. the contrasts in Col. 3:11, where all such distinctions are shown to be null and void in Christ. "Berber" stood similarly in the language of the Egyptians for all non-Egyptian peoples.

BARE (Adjective)

gumnos (γυμνός, 1131), "naked," is once translated "bare," 1 Cor. 15:37, where, used of grain, the meaning is made clearer by translating the phrase by "a bare grain," RV. See NAKED.

BARREN

1. *steiros* (στεῖρος, 4723), from a root *ster-* meaning "hard, firm" (hence Eng., "sterile"), signifies "barren, not bearing children," and is used with the natural significance three times in the Gospel of Luke, 1:7, 36; 23:29; and with a spiritual significance in Gal. 4:27, in a quotation from Isa. 54:1. The circumstances of Sarah and Hagar, which Isaiah no doubt had in mind, are applied by the apostle to the contrast between the works of the Law and the promise by grace.

2. *argos* (ἀργός, 692), denoting "idle, barren, yielding no return, because of inactivity," is found in the best mss. in Jas. 2:20 (RV, "barren"); it is rendered "barren" in 2 Pet. 1:8, KJV, (RV, "idle"). In Matt. 12:36, the "idle word" means the word that is thoughtless or profitless. See IDLE; cf. *katargeō*, under ABOLISH.

BASE, BASER

1. *agenēs* (ἀγενής, 36), "of low birth" (*a*, negative, *genos*, "family, race"), hence denoted "that which is of no reputation, of no account," 1 Cor. 1:28, "the base things of the world," i.e., those which are of no account or fame in the world's esteem. That the neuter plural of the adjective bears reference to persons is clear from verse 26.

2. *tapeinos* (ταπεινός, 5011), primarily "that which is low, and does not rise far from the ground," as in the Sept. of Ezek. 17:24, hence, metaphorically, signifies "lowly, of no degree." So the RV in 2 Cor. 10:1. Cf. Luke 1:52 and Jas. 1:9, "of low degree." Cf. *tapeinophrosunē*, "lowliness of mind," and *tapeinoō*, "to humble." See HUMBLE, LOW, LOWLY.

3. *agoraios* (ἀγοραῖος, 60), translated in the KJV of Acts 17:5 "of the baser sort," RV, "of the rabble," signifies, lit., "relating to the market place"; hence, frequenting markets, and so sauntering about idly. It is also used of affairs usually transacted in the market-place, and hence of judicial assemblies, Acts 19:38, RV "courts" (KJV, "law"); the margin in both RV and KJV has "court days are kept." See COURT.

BASON

niptēr (νιπτήρ, 3537), the vessel into which the Lord poured water to wash the disciples' feet, was "a large ewer," John 13:5. The word is connected with the verb *nipto*, "to wash."

BASTARD

nothos (νόθος, 3541) denotes "an illegitimate child, one born out of lawful wedlock," Heb. 12:8.

BATTLE

polemos (πόλεμος, 4171), "a war," is incorrectly rendered "battle" in the KJV of 1 Cor. 14:8; Rev. 9:7, 9; 16:14; 20:8; RV, invariably, "war."

BEAM

dokos (δοκός, 1385), "a beam," is perhaps etymologically connected with the root *dek-*, seen in the word *dechomai*, "to receive," "beams" being received at their ends into walls or pieces of timber. The Lord used it metaphorically, in contrast to a mote, "of a great fault, or vice," Matt. 7:3-5; Luke 6:41-42.

BEAR (animal)

ark(t)os (ἄρκτος, 715), "a bear," occurs in Rev. 13:2.

BEAST

1. *zoon* (ζῶον, 2226) primarily denotes "a living being" (*zōē*, "life"). The Eng., "animal," is the equivalent, stressing the fact of life as the characteristic feature. In Heb. 13:11 the KJV and the RV translate it "beasts" ("animals" would be quite suitable). In 2 Pet. 2:12 and Jude 10, the KJV has "beasts," the RV "creatures." In the Apocalypse, where the word is found some 20 times, and always of those beings which stand before the throne of God, who give glory and honor and thanks to Him, 4:6, and act in perfect harmony with His counsels, 5:14; 6:1-7, e.g., the word "beasts" is most unsuitable; the RV, "living creatures," should always be used; it gives to *zēon* its appropriate significance. See CREATURE.

2. *thērion* (θηρίον, 2342), to be distinguished from *zōon*, almost invariably denotes "a wild beast." In Acts 28:4, "venomous beast" is used of the viper which fastened on Paul's hand. *Zēon* stresses the vital element, *thērion* the bestial. The idea of a "beast" of prey is not always present. Once, in Heb. 12:20, it is used of the animals in the camp of Israel, such, e.g., as were appointed for sacrifice: But in the Sept. *thērion* is never used of sacrificial animals; the word *ktēnos* (see below) is reserved for these.

Thērion, in the sense of wild "beast," is used in the Apocalypse for the two antichristian potentates who are destined to control the affairs of the nations with Satanic power in the closing period of the present era, 11:7; 13:1-18; 14:9, 11; 15:2; 16:2, 10, 13; 17:3-17; 19:19-20; 20:4, 10.

3. *ktēnos* (κτῆνος, 2934) primarily denotes "property" (the connected verb *ktaomai* means "to possess"); then, "property in flocks and herds." In Scripture it signifies, (a) a "beast" of burden, Luke 10:34; Acts 23:24, (b) "beasts" of any sort, apart from those signified by *thērion* (see above), 1 Cor. 15:39; Rev. 18:13, (c) animals for slaughter; this meaning is not found in the NT, but is very frequent in the Sept.

4. *tetrapous* (τετράπους, 5074), "a fourfooted beast" (*tetra*, "four," and *pous*, "a foot") is found in Acts 10:12; 11:6; Rom. 1:23.

5. *sphagion* (σφάγιον, 4968), from *sphazo*, "to slay," denotes "a victim slaughtered for sacrifice, a slain beast," Acts 7:42, in a quotation from Amos 5:25.

BEAT

1. *derō* (δέρω, 1194), from a root *der-*, "skin" (*derma*, "a skin," cf. Eng., "dermatology"), primarily "to flay," then "to beat, thrash or smite," is used of the treatment of the servants of the owner of the vineyard by the husbandmen, in the parable in Matt. 21:35; Mark 12:3, 5; Luke 20:10-11; of the treatment of Christ, Luke 22:63, RV, "beat," for KJV, "smote"; John 18:23; of the followers of Christ, in the synagogues, Mark 13:9; Acts 22:19; of the punishment of unfaithful servants, Luke 12:47-48; of the "beating" of apostles by the High Priest and the Council of the Sanhedrin, Acts 5:40; by magistrates, 16:37. The significance of flogging does not always attach to the word; it is used of the infliction of a single blow, John 18:23; 2 Cor. 11:20, and of "beating" the air, 1 Cor. 9:26. The usual meaning is that of "thrashing or cudgelling," and when used of a blow it indicates one of great violence.

2. *tuptō* (τύπτω, 5180), from a root *tup-*, meaning "a blow," (*tupos*, "a figure or print:" (Eng., "type") denotes "to smite, strike, or beat," usually not with the idea of giving a thrashing as with *derō*. It frequently signifies a "blow" of violence, and, when used in a continuous tense, indicates a series of "blows." In Matt. 27:30 the imperfect tense signifies that the soldiers kept on striking Christ on the head. So Mark 15:19. The most authentic mss. omit it in Luke 22:64. In that verse the word *paiō*, "to smite," is used of the treatment given to Christ (*derō* in the preceding verse). The imperfect tense of the verb is again used in Acts 18:17, of the beating given to Sosthenes. Cf. Acts 21:32, which has the present participle. It is used in the metaphorical sense of "wounding," in 1 Cor. 8:12. See WOUND.

3. *rhabdizō* (ῥαβδίζω, 4463), "to beat with a rod, or stick, to cudgel," is the verbal form of *rhabdos*, "a rod, or staff," Acts 16:22; 2 Cor. 11:25.

4. *ballō* (βάλλω, 906), "to throw or cast," is once rendered "beat," Acts 27:14 RV, of the tempestuous wind that "beat" down upon the ship. So the KJV margin.

5. *epiballō* (ἐπιβάλλω, 1911), No. 4, with *epi* "upon," "to cast upon, or lay hands upon," signifies to "beat" into, in Mark 4:37, of the action of the waves.

6. *proskoptō* (προσκόπτω, 4350), "to stumble, to strike against" (*pros*, "to or against," *koptō*, "to strike"), is once used of a storm "beating" upon a house, Matt. 7:27. See STUMBLE, and cf. *proskomma* and *proskopē*, "a stumbling-block, offense."

7. *prospiptō* (προσπίπτω, 4363), "to fall upon" (*pros*, "to," *piptō*, "to fall"), is translated "beat" in Matt. 7:25; elsewhere, "to fall down at or before."

prosrēgnumi (προσρήγνυμι, 4366), "to break upon," is translated "beat vehemently upon, or against" (*pros*, "upon," *rhēgnumi*, "to break"), in Luke 6:48-49, of the violent action of a flood (RV, "brake").

Note: In Luke 10:30, the phrase lit. rendered "inflicting blows," is translated "wounded" (KJV), RV, correctly, "beat."

BEAUTIFUL

1. *hōraios* (ὡραῖος, 5611) describes "that which is seasonable, produced at the right time," as of the prime of life, or the time when anything is at its loveliest and best (from *hora*, "a season," a period fixed by natural laws and revolutions, and so the best season of the year). It is used of the outward appearance of whited sepulchres in contrast to the corruption within Matt. 23:27; of the Jerusalem gate called "Beautiful," Acts 3:2, 10; of the feet of those that bring glad tidings, Rom. 10:15.

In the Sept. it is very frequent, and especially in Genesis and the Song of Solomon. In Genesis it is said of all the trees in the garden of Eden, 2:9, especially of the tree of the knowledge of good and evil, 3:6; of the countenances of Rebekah, 26:7, Rachel, 29:17 and Joseph, 39:6. It is used five times in the Song of Solomon, 1:16; 2:14; 4:3 and 6:3, 5.

2. *asteios* (ἀστεῖος, 791), connected with *astu*, "a city," was used primarily "of that which befitted the town, town-bred" (corresponding Eng. words are "polite," "polished," connected with *polis*, "a town"; cf. "urbane," from Lat., *urbs*, "a city"). Among Greek writers it is set in contrast to *agroikos*, "rustic," and *aischros*, "base," and was used, e.g., of clothing. It is found in the NT only of Moses, Acts 7:20, "(exceeding) fair," lit., "fair (to God)," and Heb. 11:23, "goodly" (KJV, "proper"). See GOODLY, *Note*.

Notes: (1) In the Sept. it is far less frequent than *hōraios*. It is said of Moses in Ex. 2:2; negatively, of Balaam's procedure in the sight of God, Num. 22:32; of Eglon in Jud. 3:17.

(2) *Asteios* belongs to the realm of art, *hōraios*, to that of nature. *Asteios* is used of that which is "beautiful" because it is elegant; *hōraios* describes that which is "beautiful" because it is, in its season, of natural excellence.

(3) *Kalos*, "good," describes that which is "beautiful" as being well proportioned in all its parts, or intrinsically excellent. See BETTER, GOOD, etc.

For **BECAME** see BECOME

BECKON

1. *neuō* (νεύω, 3506), lit., "to give a nod, to signify by a nod," is used in John 13:24, of Peter's beckoning to John to ask the Lord of whom He had been speaking; in Acts 24:10, of the intimation given by Felix to Paul to speak.

2. *dianeuō* (διανεύω, 1269), "to express one's meaning by a sign" (No. 1, with *dia*, "through," used intensively), is said of the act of Zacharias, Luke 1:22 (RV, "continued making signs," for KJV, "beckoned"). In Sept., Ps. 35:19, "wink."

3. *katane*u*ō* (κατανεύω, 2656), No. 1, with *kata*, "down," intensive, is used of the fishermen-partners in Luke 5:7, "beckoned."

4. *kataseiō* (κατασείω, 2678), lit., "to shake down" (*kata*, "down," *seiō*, "to shake"), of shaking the hand, of waving, expresses a little more vigorously the act of "beckoning," Acts 12:17; 13:16; 19:33; 21:40. *Neuō* and its compounds have primary reference to a movement of the head; *kataseiō*, to that of the hand.

BECOME (to be fitting) A. Verb.

prepō (πρέπω, 4241) means "to be conspicuous among a number, to be eminent, distinguished by a thing," hence, "to be becoming, seemly, fit." The adornment of good works "becometh women professing godliness," 1 Tim. 2:10. Those who minister the truth are to speak "the things which befit the sound doctrine," Titus 2:1. Christ, as a High Priest "became us," Heb. 7:26. In the impersonal sense, it signifies "it is fitting, it becometh," Matt. 3:15; 1 Cor. 11:13; Eph. 5:3; Heb. 2:10. See COMELINESS.

B. Adjective.

hieroprepēs (ἱεροπρεπής, 2412), from *hieros*, "sacred," with the adjectival form of *prepō*, denotes "suited to a sacred character, that which is befitting in persons, actions or things consecrated to God," Titus 2:3, RV, "reverent," KJV, "as becometh holiness," (marg., "holy women"). Trench (*Syn.* Sec. XCII) distinguishes this word from *kosmios*, "modest," and *semnos*, "grave, honorable.

Notes: (1) The KJV translates the adverb *axiōs*, "as becometh," in Rom. 16:2; Phil. 1:27 (RV corrects to "worthily" and "worthy").

(2) *Ginomai*, "to become," is mentioned under various other headings.

(3) For "become of no effect," Gal. 5:4, KJV, RV, "severed from," see ABOLISH.

BED

1. *klinē* (κλίνη, 2825), akin to *klinō*, "to lean" (Eng., "recline, incline" etc.), "a bed," e.g., Mark 7:30, also denotes a "couch" for reclining at meals, Mark 4:21, or a "couch" for carrying the sick, Matt. 9:2, 6. The metaphorical phrase "to cast into a bed," Rev. 2:22, signifies to afflict with disease (or possibly, to lay on a bier). In Mark 7:4 the KJV curiously translates the word "tables" (marg., "beds"), RV, marg. only, "couches."

2. *klinarion* (κλινάριον, 2825a), a diminutive of No. 1, "a small bed," is used in Acts 5:15. Some mss. have *klinōn*. See also No. 4.

3. *koitē* (κοίτη, 2845), primarily "a place for lying down" (connected with *keimai*, "to lie"), denotes a "bed," Luke 11:7; the marriage "bed," Heb. 13:4; in Rom. 13:13, it is used of sexual intercourse. By metonymy, the cause standing for the effect, it denotes conception, Rom. 9:10.

4. *krabbatos* (κράβ βατος, 2895), a Macedonian word (Lat. *grabatus*), is "a somewhat mean bed, pallet, or mattress for the poor," Mark 2:4, 9, 11-12; 6:55; John 5:8-11; Acts 5:15; 9:33. See also No. 2.

Note: The verb *strōnnuō* or *strōnnumi*, "to spread," signifies, in Acts 9:34, "to make a bed"; elsewhere it has its usual meaning.

BEG, BEGGAR, BEGGARLY

A. Verbs.

1. *epaiteō* (ἐπαιτέω, 1871), a strengthened form of *aiteo*, is used in Luke 16:3.

2. *prosaiteō* (προσαιτέω, 4319), lit., "to ask besides" (*pros*, "towards," used intensively, and *aiteo*), "to ask earnestly, to importune, continue asking," is said of the blind beggar in John 9:8. In Mark 10:46 and Luke 18:35 certain mss. have this verb; the most authentic have *prosaitēs*, "a beggar," a word used in John 9:8, as well as the verb (see the RV).

Note: "Begged" in Matt. 27:58 and Luke 23:52, RV, "asked for," translates the verb *aiteō*.

B. Adjective.

ptōchos (πτωχός, 4434), an adjective describing "one who crouches and cowers," is used as a noun, "a beggar" (from *ptōssō*, "to cower down or hide oneself for fear"), Luke 14:13, 21 ("poor"); 16:20, 22; as an adjective, "beggarly" in Gal. 4:9, i.e., poverty-stricken, powerless to enrich, metaphorically descriptive of the religion of the Jews.

While *prosaitēs* is descriptive of a "beggar," and stresses his "begging," *ptōchos* stresses his poverty-stricken condition. See POOR.

For **BEGAN** see BEGIN

BEGET, BEAR (of begetting), BORN

A. Verbs.

1. *gennaō* (γεννάω, 1080), "to beget," in the passive voice, "to be born," is chiefly used of men "begetting" children, Matt. 1:2-16; more rarely of women "begetting" children, Luke 1:13, 57, "brought forth" (for "delivered," in this v., see No. 4); 23:29; John 16:21, "is delivered of," and of the child, "is born" (for "is in travail" see No. 4). In Gal. 4:24, it is used allegorically, to contrast Jews under bondage to the Law, and spiritual Israel, KJV, "gendereth," RV, "bearing children," to contrast the natural birth of Ishmael and the supernatural birth of Isaac. In Matt. 1:20 it is used of conception, "that which is conceived in her." It is used of the act of God in the birth of Christ, Acts 13:33; Heb. 1:5; 5:5, quoted from Psalm

2:7, none of which indicate that Christ became the Son of God at His birth.

It is used metaphorically (a) in the writings of the apostle John, of the gracious act of God in conferring upon those who believe the nature and disposition of "children," imparting to them spiritual life, John 3:3, 5, 7; 1 John 2:29; 3:9; 4:7; 5:1, 4, 18; (b) of one who by means of preaching the gospel becomes the human instrument in the impartation of spiritual life, 1 Cor. 4:15; Philem. 10; (c) in 2 Pet. 2:12, with reference to the evil men whom the apostle is describing, the RV rightly has "born mere animals" (KJV, "natural brute beasts"); (d) in the sense of gendering strife, 2 Tim. 2:23. See A, No. 3, CONCEIVE, DELIVER.

2. *anagennaō* (ἀναγεννάω, 313), *ana*, "again, or from above," with No. 1, is found in 1 Pet. 1:3, 23.

Note: In John 3:3, 5, 7, the adverb *anōthen*, "anew, or from above," accompanies the simple verb *gennaō*. See ABOVE.

3. *apokueō* (ἀποκυέω, 616), "to give birth to, to bring forth" (from *kueō*, "to be pregnant"), is used metaphorically of spiritual birth by means of the Word of God, Jas. 1:18, and of death as the offspring of sin (v. 15; so in the best texts).

4. *tiktō* (τίκτω, 5088), "to bring forth," Luke 1:57; John 16:21; Heb. 11:11; Rev. 12:2, 4, or, "to be born," said of the Child, Matt. 2:2; Luke 2:11, is used metaphorically in Jas. 1:15, of lust as bringing forth sin. See *apokueō*, above, used in the same verse. See DELIVER, TRAVAIL (BE IN).

B. Nouns.

1. *genos* (γένος, 1085), "a generation, kind, stock," is used in the dative case, with the article, to signify "by race," in Acts 18:2 and 24, RV, for the KJV, "born." See COUNTRYMEN, DIVERSITY, GENERATION, KIND, NATION, OFFSPRING, STOCK.

2. *ektrōma* (ἔκτρωμα, 1626) denotes "an abortion, an untimely birth"; from *ektitrōskō*, "to miscarry." In 1 Cor. 15:8 the apostle likens himself to "one born out of due time"; i.e., in point of time, inferior to the rest of the apostles, as an immature birth comes short of a mature one.

C. Adjectives.

1. *gennētos* (γεννητός, 1084), "born" (related to *gennao*, verb No. 1), is used in Matt. 11:11 and Luke 7:28 in the phrase "born of women," a periphrasis for "men," and suggestive of frailty.

2. *artigennētos* (ἀρτιγέννητος, 738), "newborn" (*arti*, "newly, recently," and No. 1), is used in 1 Pet. 2:2.

Notes: (1) For *prōtotokos* see FIRSTBORN.

(2) For *monogenēs*, see ONLY BEGOTTEN.

For **BEGGAR** see BEG

For **BEGOTTEN** see BEGET

BEGUILE

1. *apataō* (ἀπατάω, 538), "to deceive," is rendered "beguiled" in the RV of 1 Tim. 2:14. See No. 2.

2. *exapataō* (ἐξαπατάω, 1818), a strengthened form of No. 1, is rendered "beguile," 2 Cor. 11:3; the more adequate rendering would be "as the serpent thoroughly beguiled Eve." So in 1 Tim. 2:14, in the best mss., this stronger form is used of Satan's deception of Eve, lit., "thoroughly beguiled"; the simpler verb, No. 1, is used of Adam. In each of these passages the strengthened form is used. So of the influence of sin, Rom. 7:11 (RV, "beguile"); of self-deception, 1 Cor. 3:18 (RV, "deceive"); of evil men who cause divisions, Rom. 16:18 (RV, "beguile"); of deceitful teachers, 2 Thess. 2:3 (RV, "beguile"). See DECEIVE. In the Sept., Exod. 8:29.

3. *paralogizomai* (παραλογίζομαι, 3884), lit. and primarily, "to reckon wrong," hence means "to reason falsely" (*para*, "from, amiss," *logizomai*, "to reason") or "to deceive by false reasoning"; translated "delude" in Col. 2:4, RV (KJV, "beguile") and Jas. 1:22 (KJV, "deceive"). See DECEIVE, DELUDE.

4. *deleazō* (δελεάζω, 1185) originally meant "to catch by a bait" (from *delear*, "a bait"); hence "to beguile, entice by blandishments": in Jas. 1:14, "entice"; in 2 Pet. 2:14, KJV, "beguile"; in v. 18, KJV, "allure"; RV, "entice" in both. See ENTICE.

Note: In Col. 2:18, the verb *katabrabeuō*, "to give judgment against, condemn," is translated "beguile ... of your reward," KJV; RV, "rob ... of your prize." The verb was used of an umpire's decision against a racer; hence the translations (or paraphrases) in the Eng. versions.

BEHAVE, BEHAVIOR

A. Verbs.

1. *anastrephō* (ἀναστρέφω, 390), "to turn back, return" (*ana*, "back," *strephō*, "to turn"), hence, "to move about in a place, to sojourn," and, in the middle and passive voices, "to conduct oneself," indicating one's manner of life and character, is accordingly rendered "behave" in 1 Tim. 3:15, lit., "how it is necessary to behave," not referring merely to Timothy himself, but to all the members of the local church (see the whole epistle); in Eph. 2:3, KJV, "we had our conversation," RV, "we lived"; in 2 Cor. 1:12 "behaved ourselves," for KJV "have had our conversation."

2. *ginomai* (γίνομαι, 1096), "to become," is rendered "behave" in 1 Thess. 2:10; lit., "we became among you" (cf. 1:5).

3. *atakteō* (ἀτακτέω, 812), lit., to be disorderly" (*a*, negative, and *taxis*, "order"), "to lead a disorderly life," is rendered "behave disorderly" in 2 Thess. 3:7. Cf. *ataktos*, "disorderly, unruly," and *ataktōs*, "disorderly."

4. *aschēmoneō* (ἀσχημονέω, 807), "to be unseemly" (*a*, negative, and *schēma*, "a form"), is used in 1 Cor. 7:36, "behave (himself) unseemly," i.e., so as to run the risk of bringing

the virgin daughter into danger or disgrace, and in 13:5, "doth (not) behave itself unseemly."

B. Nouns.

1. *anastrophē* (ἀναστροφή, 391), lit., "a turning back" (cf. No. 1, above), is translated "manner of life," "living," etc. in the RV, for KJV, "conversation," Gal. 1:13; Eph. 4:22; 1 Tim. 4:12; Heb. 13:7; Jas. 3:13; 1 Pet. 1:15, 18; 2:1 ("behavior"); 3:1, 2, 16 (ditto); 2 Pet. 2:7; 3:11. see LIFE.

2. *katastēma* (κατάστημα, 2688), akin to *kathistēmi* (see APPOINT, No. 2), denotes "a condition, or constitution of anything, or deportment," Titus 2:3, "demeanor," RV, for KJV, behavior.

C. Adjective.

kosmios (κόσμιος, 2887), "orderly, modest," is translated "orderly" in 1 Tim. 3:2, RV, for KJV, "of good behavior." Both have "modest" in 1 Tim. 2:9. Cf. *kosmeō*, "to adorn," *kosmos*, adornment."

BEHEAD

1. *apokephalizō* (ἀποκεφαλίζω, 607), *apo*, "from, off," *kephalē*, "a head," is found in Matt. 14:10; Mark 6:16, 27; Luke 9:9.

2. *pelekizō* (πελεκίζω, 3990) denotes "to cut with an axe" (from *pelekus*, "an axe"), Rev. 20:4.

BEHOLD, BEHELD

1. *horaō* (ὁράω, 3708), with its aorist form *eidon*, "to see" (in a few places the KJV uses the verb "to behold"), is said (a) of bodily vision, e.g., Mark 6:38; John 1:18, 46; (b) of mental perception, e.g., Rom. 15:21; Col. 2:18; (c) of taking heed, e.g., Matt. 8:4; 1 Thess. 5:15; (d) of experience, as of death, Luke 2:26; Heb. 11:5; life, John 3:36; corruption, Acts 2:27; (e) of caring for, Matt. 27:4; Acts 18:15 (here the form *opsomai* is used). See APPEAR, HEED, LOOK.

2. *blepō* (βλέπω, 991) is also used of (a) bodily and (b) mental vision, (a) "to perceive," e.g., Matt. 13:13; (b) "to take heed," e.g., Mark 13:23, 33; it indicates greater vividness than *horaō*, expressing a more intent, earnest contemplation; in Luke 6:41, of "beholding" the mote in a brother's eye; Luke 24:12, of "beholding" the linen clothes in the empty tomb; Acts 1:9, of the gaze of the disciples when the Lord ascended. The greater earnestness is sometimes brought out by the rendering "regardest," Matt. 22:16. See BEWARE, HEED, LIE, LOOK, REGARD, SIGHT.

3. *emblepō* (ἐμβλέπω, 1689), from *en*, "in" (intensive), and No. 2, (not to be rendered literally), expresses "earnest looking," e.g., in the Lord's command to "behold" the birds of the heaven, with the object of learning lessons of faith from them, Matt. 6:26. See also 19:26; Mark 8:25; 10:21, 27; 14:67; Luke 20:17; 22:61; John 1:36; of the Lord's looking upon Peter, John 1:42; Acts 1:11; 22:11. See LOOK.

4. *ide* and *idou* (ἴδε, 2396 and ἰδού, 2400) are imperative moods, active and middle voices, respectively, of *eidon*, "to see," calling attention to what may be seen or heard or mentally apprehended in any way. These are regularly rendered "behold." See especially the Gospels, Acts and the Apocalypse. See LO.

5. *epide* (ἔπιδε, 1896), a strengthened form of No. 4 (with *epi*, "upon," prefixed), is used in Acts 4:29 of the entreaty made to the Lord to "behold" the threatenings of persecutors.

6. *theōreō* (θεωρέω, 2334), from *theōros*, "a spectator," is used of one who looks at a thing with interest and for a purpose, usually indicating the careful observation of details; this marks the distinction from No. 2; see, e.g., Mark 15:47; Luke 10:18; 23:35; John 20:6 (RV, "beholdeth," for KJV, "seeth"); so in verses 12 and 14; "consider," in Heb. 7:4. It is used of experience, in the sense of partaking of, in John 8:51; 17:24. See LOOK. Cf. *theōria*, "sight," Luke 23:48, only.

7. *anatheōreō* (ἀναθεωρέω, 333), *ana*, "up" (intensive), and No. 6, "to view with interest, consider contemplatively," is translated "beheld," in Acts 17:23, RV, "observed"; "considering" in Heb. 13:7.

8. *theaomai* (θεάομαι, 2300), "to behold, view attentively, contemplate," had, in earlier Greek usage, the sense of a wondering regard. This idea was gradually lost. It signifies a more earnest contemplation than the ordinary verbs for "to see," "a careful and deliberate vision which interprets ... its object," and is more frequently rendered "behold" in the RV than the KJV. Both translate it by "behold" in Luke 23:55 (of the sepulchre); "we beheld," in John 1:14, of the glory of the Son of God; "beheld," RV, in John 1:32; Acts 1:11; 1 John 1:1 (more than merely seeing); 4:12, 14. See LOOK.

9. *epopteuō* (ἐποπτεύω, 2029), from *epi*, "upon," and a form of *horaō*, "to see," is used of "witnessing as a spectator, or overseer," 1 Pet. 2:12; 3:2.

Note: The corresponding noun *epoptēs*, "an eye-witness," found in 2 Pet. 1:16, was used by the Greeks of those who had attained to the highest grade of certain mysteries, and the word is perhaps purposely used here of those who were at the transfiguration of Christ. See EYEWITNESS.

10. *atenizō* (ἀτενίζω, 816) from *atenes*, "strained, intent," denotes "to gaze upon," "beholding earnestly," or "steadfastly" in Acts 14:9; 23:1. See LOOK.

11. *katanoeō* (κατανοέω, 2657), a strengthened form of *noeō*, "to perceive," (*kata*, intensive), denotes "the action of the mind in apprehending certain facts about a thing"; hence, "to consider"; "behold," Acts 7:31-32; Jas. 1:23-24.

12. *katoptrizō* (κατοπτρίζω, 2734), from *katoptron*, "a mirror" (*kata*, "down," *ōps*, "an eye or sight"), in the active

voice, signifies "to make to reflect, to mirror"; in the middle voice "to reflect as a mirror"; so the RV in 2 Cor. 3:18, for KJV, "beholding as in a glass." The whole context in the 3rd chapter and the first part of the 4th bears out the RV.

Note: For *epeidon* (from *ephoraō*), Acts 4:29, see LOOK, No. 9. For *prooraō*, Acts 2:25, RV, behold, see FORESEE.

BELIAL

belial (Βελίαλ or Βελίαρ, 955) is a word frequently used in the Old Testament, with various meanings, especially in the books of Samuel, where it is found nine times. See also Deut. 13:13; Jud. 19:22; 20:13; 1 Kings 21:10, 13; 2 Chron. 13:7. Its original meaning was either "worthlessness" or "hopeless ruin" (see the RV, margin). It also had the meanings of "extreme wickedness and destruction," the latter indicating the destiny of the former. In the period between the OT and the NT it came to be a proper name for Satan. There may be an indication of this in Nahum 1:15, where the word translated "the wicked one" is Belial. The oldest form of the word is "Beliar," possibly from a phrase signifying "Lord of the forest," or perhaps simply a corruption of the form "Belial," due to harsh Syriac pronunciation. In the NT, in 2 Cor. 6:15, it is set in contrast to Christ and represents a personification of the system of impure worship connected especially with the cult of Aphrodite.

BELIEF, BELIEVE, BELIEVERS

A. Verbs.

1. *pisteuō* (πιστεύω, 4100), "to believe," also "to be persuaded of," and hence, "to place confidence in, to trust," signifies, in this sense of the word, reliance upon, not mere credence. It is most frequent in the writings of the apostle John, especially the Gospel. He does not use the noun (see below). For the Lord's first use of the verb, see 1:50. Of the writers of the Gospels, Matthew uses the verb ten times, Mark ten, Luke nine, John ninety-nine. In Acts 5:14 the present participle of the verb is translated "believers. See INTRUST, TRUST.

2. *peithō* (πείθω, 3982), "to persuade," in the middle and passive voices signifies "to suffer oneself to be persuaded," e.g., Luke 16:31; Heb. 13:18; it is sometimes translated "believe" in the RV, but not in Acts 17:4, RV, "were persuaded," and 27:11, "gave (more) heed"; in Acts 28:24, "believed. See ASSURE, OBEY, PERSUADE, TRUST, YIELD.

Note: For *apisteō*, the negative of No. 1, and *apeitheō*, the negative of No. 2, see DISBELIEVE, DISOBEDIENT.

B. Noun.

pistis (πίστις, 4102), "faith," is translated "belief" in Rom. 10:17; 2 Thess. 2:13. Its chief significance is a conviction respecting God and His Word and the believer's relationship to Him. See ASSURANCE, FAITH, FIDELITY.

Note: In 1 Cor. 9:5 the word translated "believer" (RV), is *adelphē*, "a sister," so 7:15; Rom. 16:1; Jas. 2:15, used, in the spiritual sense, of one connected by the tie of the Christian faith.

C. Adjective.

pistos (πιστός, 4103), (a) in the active sense means "believing, trusting"; (b) in the passive sense, "trusty, faithful, trustworthy." It is translated "believer" in 2 Cor. 6:15; "them that believe" in 1 Tim. 4:12, RV (KJV, "believers "); in 1 Tim. 5:16, "if any woman that believeth," lit. "if any believing woman." So in 6:2, "believing masters." In 1 Pet. 1:21 the RV, following the most authentic mss., gives the noun form, "are believers in God" (KJV, "do believe in God"). In John 20:27 it is translated "believing." It is best understood with significance (a), above, e.g., in Gal. 3:9; Acts 16:1; 2 Cor. 6:15; Titus 1:6; it has significance (b), e.g., in 1 Thess. 5:24; 2 Thess. 3:3 (see *Notes on Thess.* p. 211, and *Gal.* p. 126, by Hogg and Vine). See FAITHFUL.

Notes: (1) The corresponding negative verb is *apisteō*, 2 Tim. 2:13, KJV, "believe not" RV, "are faithless," in contrast to the statement "He abideth faithful."

(2) The negative noun *apistia*, "unbelief," is used twice in Matthew (13:58); 17:20), three times in Mark (6:6; 9:24; 16:14), four times in Romans (3:3; 4:20; 11:20, 23); elsewhere in 1 Tim. 1:13 and Heb. 3:12, 19.

(3) The adjective *apistos* is translated "unbelievers" in 1 Cor. 6:6, and 2 Cor. 6:14; in v. 15, RV, "unbeliever" (KJV, "infidel"); so in 1 Tim. 5:8; "unbelieving" in 1 Cor. 7:12-15; 14:22- 24; 2 Cor. 4:4; Titus 1:15; Rev. 21:8; "that believe not" in 1 Cor. 10:27. In the Gospels it is translated "faithless" in Matt. 17:17; Mark 9:19; Luke 9:41; John 20:27, but in Luke 12:46, RV, "unfaithful," KJV, "unbelievers." Once it is translated "incredible," Acts 26:8. See FAITHLESS, INCREDIBLE, UNBELIEVER.

(4) *Plērophoreō*, in Luke 1:1 (KJV, "are most surely believed," lit., "have had full course"), the RV renders "have been fulfilled." See FULFILL, KNOW, PERSUADE, PROOF.

BELLY

1. *koilia* (κοιλία, 2836), from *koilos*, "hollow" (Lat., *coelum*, "heaven," is connected), denotes the entire physical cavity, but most frequently was used to denote "the womb." In John 7:38 it stands metaphorically for the innermost part of man, the soul, the heart. See WOMB.

2. *gastēr* (γαστήρ, 1064), (cf. Eng., "gastritis"), is used much as No. 1, but in Titus 1:12, by synecdoche (a figure of speech in which the part is put for the whole, or vice versa), it is used to denote "gluttons," RV, for KJV, "bellies." See WOMB.

BELOVED

A. Adjective.

agapētos (ἀγαπητός, 27), from *agapaō*, "to love," is used of Christ as loved by God, e.g., Matt. 3:17; of believers (ditto), e.g., Rom. 1:7; of believers, one of another, 1 Cor. 4:14; often, as a form of address, e.g., 1 Cor. 10:14. Whenever the KJV has "dearly beloved," the RV has "beloved"; so, "well beloved" in 3 John 1; in 1 John 2:7, KJV, "brethren" (*adelphos*), the RV has "beloved," according to the mss. which have *agapētos*. See DEAR.

B. Verb.

agapaō (ἀγαπάω, 25), in its perfect participle passive form, is translated "beloved" in Rom. 9:25; Eph. 1:6; Col. 3:12; 1 Thess. 1:4; 2 Thess. 2:13. In Jude 1 the best texts have this verb (RV); the KJV, "sanctified" follows those which have *hagiazō*. See LOVE.

Note: In Luke 9:35, the RV, translating from the most authentic mss., has "My chosen" (*eklegō*), for KJV, "beloved" (*agapētos*); so in Philem. 2, "sister" (*adelphē*).

BENEFIT, BENEFACTOR

1. *euergesia* (εὐεργεσία, 2108), lit., "good work" (*eu*, "well," *ergon*, "work"), is found in Acts 4:9, "good deed," and 1 Tim. 6:2, "benefit."

2. *euergetes* (εὐεργέτης, 2110), "a benefactor," expresses the agent, Luke 22:25.

Note: Cf. *euergeteō*, "to do good."

3. *charis* (χάρις, 5485), "grace," is once rendered "benefit," 2 Cor. 1:15; it stresses the character of the "benefit," as the effect of the gracious disposition of the benefactor. See FAVOR, GRACE, LIBERALITY, PLEASURE, THANK.

4. *agathon* (ἀγαθός, 18), the neuter of *agathos*, used as a noun in Philem. 14, is translated "benefit," KJV; RV, "goodness." See GOOD.

BENEVOLENCE

eunoia (εὔνοια, 2133), "good will" (*eu*, "well," *nous*, "the mind"), is rendered "benevolence" in 1 Cor. 7:3, KJV. The RV, following the texts which have *opheilēn* ("due"), has "her due," a more comprehensive expression; in Eph. 6:7, "good will."

BEREAVED, BEREFT

1. *aporphanizomai* (ἀπορφανίζω, 642), lit., "to be rendered an orphan" (*apo*, "from," with the thought of separation, and *orphanos*, "an orphan"), is used metaphorically in 1 Thess. 2:17 (KJV, "taken from"; RV, "bereaved"), in the sense of being "bereft" of the company of the saints through being compelled to leave them (cf. the similes in 7 and 11). The word has a wider meaning than that of being an orphan.

Note: The corresponding adjective, *orphanos*, is translated "desolate" in John 14:18 (KJV, "comfortless"); "fatherless" in Jas. 1:27; see DESOLATE, FATHERLESS.

2. *apostereō* (ἀποστερέω, 650), "to rob, defraud, deprive," is used in 1 Tim. 6:5, in the passive voice, of being deprived or "bereft" (of the truth), with reference to false teachers (KJV, destitute). See DEFRAUD, DESTITUTE, FRAUD.

BESIDE ONESELF (to be)

1. *existēmi* (ἐξίστημι, 1839), primarily and lit. means "to put out of position, displace": hence, (a) "to amaze," Luke 24:22 (for KJV, "make ... astonished"); Acts 8:9, 11 (KJV, "bewitched "); or "to be amazed, astounded," Matt. 12:23; Mark 6:51; (b) "to be out of one's mind, to be beside oneself," Mark 3:21; 2 Cor. 5:13, in the latter of which it is contrasted with *sōphroneō*, "to be of a sound mind, sober." See AMAZE.

2. *mainomai* (μαίνομαι, 3105), "to be mad, to rave," is said of one who so speaks that he appears to be out of his mind, Acts 26:24, translated "thou art beside thyself," KJV; RV, "thou art mad." In v. 25; John 10:20; Acts 12:15; 1 Cor. 14:23, both versions use the verb to be mad. See MAD.

Note: For *paraphroneō*, 2 Cor. 11:23, RV, see FOOL, B, No. 2.

BESTOW

1. *didōmi* (δίδωμι, 1325), "to give," is rendered "bestow" in 1 John 3:1, the implied idea being that of giving freely. The KJV has it in 2 Cor. 8:1; the RV adheres to the lit. rendering, "the grace of God which hath been given in the churches of Macedonia.

2. *sunagō* (συνάγω, 4863), "to bring together" (*sun*, "together," *agō*, "to bring"), is used in the sense of "bestowing," or stowing, by the rich man who laid up his goods for himself, Luke 12:17-18. See ASSEMBLE, GATHER, LEAD.

3. *kopiaō* (κοπιάω, 2872), (a) "to grow tired with toil," Matt. 11:28; John 4:6; Rev. 2:3, also means (b) "to bestow labor, work with toil," Rom. 16:6; Gal. 4:11; in John 4:38, KJV, "bestowed (no) labor," RV, "have (not) labored," and, in the same verse, KJV and RV, "labored." See LABOR, TOIL, WEARY.

4. *psōmizō* (ψωμίζω, 5595), primarily "to feed by putting little bits into the mouths of infants or animals," came to denote simply "to give out food, to feed," and is rendered by the phrase "bestow ... to feed" in 1 Cor. 13:3; "feed," Rom. 12:20; there the person to be fed is mentioned; in 1 Cor. 13:3 the material to be given is specified, and the rendering "bestow ... to feed" is necessary. See FEED.

5. *peritithēmi* (περιτίθημι, 4060), "to put around or on" (*peri*, "around," *tithēmi*, "to put"), is translated in 1 Cor. 12:23 (metaphorically) "bestow" (marg., "put on").

6. *charizomai* (χαρίζομαι, 5483), "to show favor, grant, bestow," is rendered "bestowed" in Luke 7:21, RV, for KJV, "gave." Here and in Gal. 3:18, the verb might be translated "graciously conferred. See DELIVER, FORGIVE, GIVE.

BETRAY, BETRAYER

A. Verb.

paradidōmi (παραδίδωμι, 3860), "to betray" (*para*, "up," *didōmi*, "to give"), lit., "to give over," is used either (a) in the sense of delivering a person or thing to be kept by another, to commend, e.g., Acts 28:16; (b) to deliver to prison or judgment, e.g., Matt. 4:12; 1 Tim. 1:20; (c) to deliver over treacherously by way of "betrayal," Matt. 17:22 (RV, "delivered"); 26:16; John 6:64 etc.; (d) to hand on, deliver, e.g., 1 Cor. 11:23; (e) to allow of something being done, said of the ripening of fruit, Mark 4:29, RV, "is ripe" (marg., "alloweth"). See DELIVER, GIVE, RECOMMEND.

B. Noun.

prodotēs (προδότης, 4273), "a betrayer" (akin to A), is translated "betrayers" in Acts 7:52; "traitor," "traitors," in Luke 6:16 and 2 Tim. 3:4. See TRAITOR.

BETROTH

mnēsteuō (μνηστεύω, 3423), in the active voice, signifies "to woo a woman and ask for her in marriage"; in the NT, only in the passive voice, "to be promised in marriage, to be betrothed," Matt. 1:18; Luke 1:27; 2:5, RV, "betrothed," (KJV, "espoused"). See ESPOUSED.

BETTER

1. *kreissōn* (κρείττων, 2909), from *kratos*, "strong" (which denotes power in activity and effect), serves as the comparative degree of *agathos*, "good" (good or fair, intrinsically). *Kreissōn* is especially characteristic of the Epistle to the Hebrews, where it is used 12 times; it indicates what is (a) advantageous or useful, 1 Cor. 7:9, 38; 11:17; Heb. 11:40; 12:24; 2 Pet. 2:21; Phil. 1:23, where it is coupled with *mallon*, "more," and *pollō*, "much, by far," "very far better" (RV); (b) excellent, Heb. 1:4; 6:9; 7:7, 19, 22; 8:6; 9:23; 10:34; 11:16, 35.

2. *kalon mallon* (καλόν, 2570 and μᾶλλον, 3123), the neuter of *kalos*, with *mallon*, "more," is used in Mark 9:42, "it were better (lit., 'much better') for him if a great millstone were hanged about his neck." In verses 43, 45, 47, *kalos* is used alone (RV, "good," for KJV, "better").

Note: In Luke 5:39 the most authentic texts have *chrēstos*, "good," instead of the comparative, *chrēstoteros*, "better."

BETTER (be)

1. *diapherō* (διαφέρω, 1308), used (a) transitively, means "to carry through" or "about" (*dia*, "through," *pherō*, "to carry"), Mark 11:16 ("carry ... through"); Acts 13:49; 27:27 ("driven to and fro"); (b) intransitively, (1) "to differ," Rom. 2:18; Gal. 2:6; Phil. 1:10; (2) "to excel, be better," e.g., Matt. 6:26; 10:31 ("of more value"); 12:12; Luke 12:7, 24; 1 Cor. 15:41; Gal. 4:1; some would put Rom. 2:18 and Phil. 1:10 here (see marg.). See EXCELLENT, PUBLISH.

2. *perisseuō* (περισσεύω, 4052), "to be over or above (a number), to be more than enough, to be pre-eminent, superior," Matt. 5:20, is translated "are we the better," in 1 Cor. 8:8 (cf. 15:58; Rom. 15:13; 2 Cor. 3:9; 8:7; Phil. 1:9; Col. 2:7; 1 Thess. 4:1, 10). See ABOUND.

3. *lusiteleō* (λυσιτελέω, 3081) signifies "to indemnify, pay expenses, pay taxes" (from *luō*, "to loose," *telos*, "toll, custom"); hence, "to be useful, advantageous, to be better" Luke 17:2.

4. *huperechō* (ὑπερέχω, 5242) lit. means "to hold or have above" (*huper*, "above," *echō*, "to hold"); hence, metaphorically, to be superior to, to be better than, Phil. 2:3; 1 Pet. 2:13, "supreme," in reference to kings; in Rom. 13:1, "higher"; Phil. 3:8, "excellency," more strictly "the surpassing thing, (namely, the knowledge of Christ)"; in 4:7 passeth. See EXCELLENCY, HIGHER, SUPREME.

Notes: (1) In Rom. 3:9 the RV rightly translates *proechō* (which there is used in the passive voice, not the middle) "are we in worse case than ...?," i.e., "are we surpassed?" "are we at a disadvantage?" The question is, are the Jews, so far from being better off than the Gentiles, in such a position that their very privileges bring them into a greater disadvantage or condemnation than the Gentiles? The KJV "are we better" does not convey the meaning.

(2) *Sumpherō*, in Matt. 18:6, KJV, is translated "it were better for him," RV, "profitable." See Matt. 5:29-30 etc. See EXPEDIENT, GOOD, D, *Note* (2).

BETTERED (to be)

ōpheleō (ὠφελέω, 5623) in the active voice signifies "to help, to succor, to be of service"; in the passive "to receive help, to derive profit or advantage"; in Mark 5:26, "was (nothing) bettered," of the woman who had an issue of blood.

BEWAIL

1. *klaiō* (κλαίω, 2799), "to wail," whether with tears or any external expression of grief, is regularly translated "weep" in the RV; once in the KJV it is rendered "bewail," Rev. 18:9. See WEEP.

Note: The associated noun is *klauthmos*, "weeping." Cf. *dakruō*, "to weep," John 11:35.

2. *koptō* (κόπτω, 2875), primarily, "to beat, smite"; then, "to cut off," Matt. 21:8; Mark 11:8, is used in the middle voice, of beating oneself, beating the breast, as a token of grief; hence, "to bewail," Matt. 11:17 (RV, "mourn," for KJV, "lament");

24:30, "mourn"; Rev. 1:7 (RV, "mourn"; KJV, "wail"); in Luke 8:52; 23:27 "bewail"; in Rev. 18:9, "wail" (for KJV, "lament"). See MOURN. Cf. *kopetos*, "lamentation," Acts 8:2.

3. *pentheō* (πενθέω, 3996) denotes "to lament, mourn," especially for the dead; in 2 Cor. 12:21, RV, "mourn" (KJV, "bewail"). See also Rev. 18:11, 15, 19. Cf. *penthos*, "mourning." See MOURN.

Notes: (1) *Thrēneō*, "to sing a dirge, to lament," is rendered "wail" in Matt. 11:17, RV; "mourned" in Luke 7:32; "to lament" in Luke 23:27 and John 16:20. *Threnos*, "lamentation," occurs in Matt. 2:18.

(2) *Odurmos* from *oduromai*, "to wail" (a verb not found in the NT), denotes "mourning," Matt. 2:18 and 2 Cor. 7:7.

(3) Cf. *lupeomai*, "to grieve"; see also Trench, *Syn.* Sec. LXV.

BEWARE

1. *blepō* (βλέπω, 991), "to see," is applied to mental vision, and is sometimes used by way of warning "to take heed" against an object, Mark 8:15; 12:38; Acts 13:40; Phil. 3:2 (three times); in Col. 2:8, RV, "take heed," marg., "see whether. See BEHOLD.

2. *prosechō* (προσέχω, 4337), lit., "to hold to" (*pros*, "to," *echō*, "to have, to hold"), hence, "to turn one's mind or attention to a thing by being on one's guard against it," is translated "beware" in Matt. 7:15; 10:17; 16:6, 11-12; Luke 12:1; 20:46. See ATTEND, HEED, REGARD.

3. *phulassō* (φυλάσσω, 5442), "to guard, watch, keep," is used, in the middle voice, of being "on one's guard against" (the middle v. stressing personal interest in the action), Luke 12:15, "beware of," RV, "keep yourselves from," as in Acts 21:25; in 2 Tim. 4:15, "be thou ware"; in 2 Pet. 3:17, "beware." See GUARD, KEEP, OBSERVE, SAVE.

BEWITCH

1. *baskainō* (βασκαίνω, 940), primarily, "to slander, to prate about anyone"; then "to bring evil on a person by feigned praise, or mislead by an evil eye, and so to charm, bewitch" (Eng., "fascinate" is connected), is used figuratively in Gal. 3:1, of leading into evil doctrine.

2. *existēmi* (ἐξίστημι, 1839) is rendered "bewitch" in Acts 8:9, 11, KJV, concerning Simon the sorcerer; it does not mean "to bewitch," as in the case of the preceding verb, but "to confuse, amaze" (RV). See AMAZE, B. No. 1.

BID FAREWELL

1. *apotassō* (ἀποτάσσω, 657) is used in the middle voice to signify "to bid adieu to a person." It primarily means "to set apart, separate" (*apo*, "from," *tassō*, "to set, arrange"); then, "to take leave of, to bid farewell to," Mark 6:46 (RV); Luke 9:61; "to give parting instructions to," Acts 18:18, 21; 2 Cor. 2:13; "to forsake, renounce," Luke 14:33. See FORSAKE, RENOUNCE, SEND, *Note* (2) at end.

2. *apaspazomai* (ἀπό, 575 and ἀσπάζομαι, 782), "to bid farewell" (*apo*, "from," *aspazomai*, "to greet"), is used in Acts 21:6, KJV, "had taken our leave of"; RV, "bade … farewell."

BIER

soros (σορός, 4673) originally denoted a receptacle for containing the bones of the dead, "a cinerary urn"; then "a coffin," Gen. 50:26; Job 21:32; then, "the funeral couch or bier" on which the Jews bore their dead to burial, Luke 7:14.

BILL

1. *biblion* (βιβλίον, 975), primarily "a small book, a scroll, or any sheet on which something has been written"; hence, in connection with *apostasion*, "divorce," signifies "a bill of divorcement," Matt. 19:7 (KJV, "writing"); Mark 10:4. See BOOK, SCROLL, WRITING.

2. *gramma* (γράμμα, 1121), from *graphō*, "to write" (Eng., "graph, graphic," etc.), in Luke 16:6, KJV, is translated "bill." It lit. signifies that which is drawn, a picture; hence, a written document; hence, a "bill," or bond, or note of hand, showing the amount of indebtedness. In the passage referred to the word is in the plural, indicating perhaps, but not necessarily, various "bills." The bonds mentioned in rabbinical writings, were formal, signed by witnesses and the Sanhedrin of three, or informal, when only the debtor signed. The latter were usually written on wax, and easily altered. See LEARNING, LETTER, SCRIPTURE, WRITING.

For **BILLOWS**, Luke 21:25, RV, see WAVE

BIND, BINDING (see also bound)

1. *deō* (δέω, 1210), "to bind," is used (a) literally, of any sort of "binding," e.g., Acts 22:5; 24:27, (b) figuratively, of the Word of God, as not being "bound," 2 Tim. 2:9, i.e., its ministry, course and efficacy were not hindered by the bonds and imprisonment suffered by the apostle. A woman who was bent together, had been "bound" by Satan through the work of a demon, Luke 13:16. Paul speaks of himself, in Acts 20:22, as being "bound in the spirit," i.e. compelled by his convictions, under the constraining power of the Spirit of God, to go to Jerusalem. A wife is said to be "bound" to her husband, Rom. 7:2; 1 Cor. 7:39; and the husband to the wife, 1 Cor. 7:27. The Lord's words to the apostle Peter in Matt. 16:19, as to "binding," and to all the disciples in 18:18, signify, in the former case, that the apostle, by his ministry of the Word of Life, would keep unbelievers outside the kingdom of God, and admit those who believed. So with regard to 18:18, including the exercise of disciplinary measures in the sphere of

the local church; the application of the rabbinical sense of forbidding is questionable. See BOND, TIE.

2. *perideō* (περιδέω, 4019), *peri*, "around," with No. 1, "to bind around," is used in John 11:44 of the napkin around the face of Lazarus. Cf. Job 12:18, Sept.

3. *hupodeō* (ὑποδέω, 5265), *hupo*, "under," with No. 1, "to bind underneath," is used of binding of sandals, Acts 12:8; rendered "shod" in Mark 6:9 and Eph. 6:15 See SHOD.

4. *katadeō* (καταδέω, 2611), *kata*, "down," with No. 1, "to bind or tie down, or bind up," is used in Luke 10:34 of the act of the good Samaritan.

5. *sundeō* (συνδέω, 4887), *sun*, "together," and No. 1, "to bind together," implying association, is used in Heb. 13:3 of those bound together in confinement.

6. *desmeuō* (δεσμεύω, 1195) or *desmeō* (δεσμέω, 1196) signifies "to put in fetters or any kind of bond," Luke 8:29; Acts 22:4, or "to bind a burden upon a person," Matt. 23:4. The verb is connected with No. 1.

Notes: (1) Cf. *desmos*, "a band, bond, fetter," e.g., Luke 13:16, and *desmios*, "bound," Acts 25:14, KJV (RV, "a prisoner"); in Heb. 13:3, "them that are in bonds." See BOND, PRISONER, STRING.

(2) *Sundesmos* (see No. 5, above), "that which binds together," is translated "bands," in Col. 2:19.

7. *proteinō* (προτείνω, 4385), lit., "to stretch forth" (*pro*, "forth," *teinō*, "to stretch"), is used in Acts 22:25, KJV, "they bound"; RV, "they had tied (him) up," in reference to the preparations made for scourging, probably, to stretch the body forward, to make it tense for severer punishment. See TIE.

BIRD (Fowl)

1. *orneon* (ὄρνεον, 3732) is probably connected with a word signifying "to perceive, to hear"; Rev. 18:2; 19:17, 21. Cf. *ornis*, a hen.

2. *peteinon* (πετεινόν, 4071) signifies "that which is able to fly, winged." It is connected with *ptenon* signifying "feathered, winged," which is used in 1 Cor. 15:39. Cf. *petomai* and *petaomai*, "to fly." In the Gospels the RV always translates it "birds," e.g., Matt. 6:26; but "fowls" in Acts 10:12; 11:6. The KJV unsuitably has "fowls," in the Gospels, except Matt. 8:20; 13:32; Luke 9:58.

BIRTH

1. *gennēsis* (γέννησις, 1083), "a birth, begetting, producing" (related to *gennaō*, "to beget"), is used in Matt. 1:18 and Luke 1:14. Some mss. have *genesis*, "lineage, birth" (from *ginomai*, "to become").

2. *genetē* (γενετή, 1079), "a being born, or the hour of birth" (related to *genea*, "race, generation"), is connected with *ginomai*, "to become, to be born," and is used in John 9:1.

Notes (1) For *genesis* and *gennēma* see FRUIT, GENERATION, NATURE.

(2) In Gal. 4:19, *ōdinō*, "to have birth pangs," is rendered "travail in birth," KJV; RV, "am in travail." See Rev. 12:2.

BIRTHDAY

genesia (γενέσια, 1077), a neuter plural (akin to *genesis*, "lineage," from *ginomai*), primarily denoted "the festivities of a birthday, a birthday feast," though among the Greeks it was also used of a festival in commemoration of a deceased friend. It is found in Matt. 14:6 and Mark 6:21. Some have regarded it as the day of the king's accession, but this meaning is not confirmed in Greek writings.

BIRTHRIGHT

prōtotokia (πρωτοτόκια, 4415), a birthright" (from *protos*, "first," *tiktō*, "to beget"), is found in Heb. 12:16, with reference to Esau (cf. *prōtotokos*, firstborn). The "birthright" involved preeminence and authority, Gen. 27:29; 49:3. Another right was that of the double portion, Deut. 21:17; 1 Chron. 5:1-2. Connected with the "birthright" was the progenitorship of the Messiah. Esau transferred his "birthright" to Jacob for a paltry mess of pottage, profanely despising this last spiritual privilege, Gen. 25 and 27. In the history of the nation God occasionally set aside the "birthright," to show that the objects of His choice depended not on the will of the flesh, but on His own authority. Thus Isaac was preferred to Ishmael, Jacob to Esau, Joseph to Reuben, David to his elder brethren, Solomon to Adonijah. See FIRSTBORN.

BISHOP (Overseer)

1. *episkopos* (ἐπίσκοπος, 1985), lit., an overseer" (*epi*, "over," *skopeō*, "to look or watch"), whence Eng. "bishop," which has precisely the same meaning, is found in Acts 20:28; Phil. 1:1; 1 Tim. 3:2; Titus 1:7; 1 Pet. 2:25. See OVERSEER.

Note: Presbuteros, "an elder," is another term for the same person as bishop or overseer. See Acts 20:17 with verse 28. The term "elder" indicates the mature spiritual experience and understanding of those so described; the term "bishop," or "overseer," indicates the character of the work undertaken. According to the divine will and appointment, as in the NT, there were to be "bishops" in every local church, Acts 14:23; 20:17; Phil. 1:1; Titus 1:5; Jas. 5:14. Where the singular is used, the passage is describing what a "bishop" should be, 1 Tim. 3:2; Titus 1:7. Christ Himself is spoken of as "the ... Bishop of our souls," 1 Pet. 2:25. See ELDER.

2. *episkopē* (ἐπισκοπή, 1984), besides its meaning, "visitation," e.g., 1 Pet. 2:12 (cf. the Sept. of Exod. 3:16; Isa. 10:3;

Jer. 10:15), is rendered "office," in Acts 1:20, RV (KJV, "bishoprick"); in 1 Tim. 3:1 "the office of a bishop," lit., "(if any one seeketh) overseership," there is no word representing office.

Note: The corresponding verb is *episkopeō*, which, in reference to the work of an overseer, is found in 1 Pet. 5:2, RV, "exercising the oversight," for KJV "taking the oversight." See OVERSIGHT.

BITTER, BITTERLY, BITTERNESS

A. Adjective.

pikros (πικρός, 4089), from a root *pik-*, meaning "to cut, to prick," hence, lit., "pointed, sharp, keen, pungent to the sense of taste, smell, etc.," is found in Jas. 3:11, 14. In v. 11 it has its natural sense, with reference to water; in v. 14 it is used metaphorically of jealousy, RV.

B. Verb.

pikrainō (πικραίνω, 4087), related to A, signifies, in the active voice, "to be bitter," Col. 3:19, or "to embitter, irritate, or to make bitter," Rev. 10:9; the passive voice, "to be made bitter," is used in Rev. 8:11; 10:10.

C. Noun.

pikria (πικρία, 4088) denotes "bitterness." It is used in Acts 8:23, metaphorically, of a condition of extreme wickedness, "gall of bitterness" or "bitter gall"; in Rom. 3:14, of evil speaking; in Eph. 4:31, of "bitter" hatred; in Heb. 12:15, in the same sense, metaphorically, of a root of "bitterness," producing "bitter" fruit.

D. Adverb.

pikrōs (πικρῶς, 4090), "bitterly," is used of the poignant grief of Peter's weeping for his denial of Christ, Matt. 26:75; Luke 22:62.

Note: In the Sept., *pikris* (not in the NT), "a bitter herb," is used in Exod. 12:8; Num. 9:11.

BLACK, BLACKNESS

A. Adjective.

melas (μέλας, 3189), "black," Matt. 5:36; Rev. 6:5, 12, is derived from a root *mal-*, meaning "to be dirty"; hence Latin, *malus*, bad.

B. Nouns.

1. *gnophos* (γνόφος, 1105), Heb. 12:18, "blackness, gloom," seems to have been associated with the idea of a tempest. It is related to *skotos*, "darkness," in that passage, and in the Sept. of Exod. 10:22; Deut. 4:11; Zeph. 1:15.

2. *zophos* (ζόφος, 2217), akin to No. 1, especially "the gloom of the regions of the lost," is used four times; 2 Pet. 2:4, "darkness" (RV); 2:17, RV, "blackness," for KJV, "mist"; Jude 6, "darkness"; v. 13, "blackness," suggesting a kind of emanation. See DARK, MIST.

For **BLADE** see GRASS

BLAME, BLAMELESS

A. Verb.

mōmaomai (μωμάομαι, 3469), "to find fault with, to blame, or calumniate," is used in 2 Cor. 6:3, of the ministry of the gospel; in 8:20, of the ministration of financial help.

Notes: (1) Cf. the synonymous verb, *memphomai*, "to find fault," Mark 7:2; Rom. 9:19; Heb. 8:8. See FAULT.

(2) In Gal. 2:11, *kataginōskō* is rightly rendered "stood condemned," RV, for KJV, "was to be blamed. See CONDEMN.

B. Adjectives.

1. *amōmos* (ἄμωμος, 299): See BLEMISH, B.

2. *amōmētos* (ἀμώμητος, 298), translated in Phil. 2:15 "without blemish" (KJV, "without rebuke"), is rendered "blameless" in 2 Pet. 3:14 (KJV and RV).

3. *amemptos* (ἄμεμπτος, 273), related to *memphomai* (A, *Note*), is translated "unblameable" in 1 Thess. 3:13; "blameless," in Luke 1:6; Phil. 2:15; 3:6; "faultless" in Heb. 8:7. See FAULTLESS, UNBLAMEABLE.

"If *amōmos* is the 'unblemished,' *amemptos* is the 'unblamed.' ... Christ was *amōmos* in that there was in Him no spot or blemish, and He could say, 'Which of you convinceth (convicteth) Me of sin?' but in strictness of speech He was not *amemptos* (unblamed), nor is this epithet ever given to Him in the NT, seeing that He endured the contradiction of sinners against Himself, who slandered His footsteps and laid to His charge 'things that He knew not' (i.e., of which He was guiltless)." Trench, *Syn.* Sec. CIII.

4. *anaitios* (ἀναίτιος, 338), "guiltless" (*a*, negative, *n*, euphonic, and *aitia*, "a charge"), is translated, "blameless" in the KJV of Matt. 12:5, "guiltless" in 12:7. The RV has "guiltless" in both places. In the Sept., in Deut. 19:10, 13, and 21:8-9. See GUILTLESS.

5. *anepilēptos* (ἀνεπίληπτος, 423), lit., "that cannot be laid hold of," hence, "not open to censure, irreproachable" (from *a*, negative, *n*, euphonic, and *epilambanō*, "to lay hold of"), is used in 1 Tim. 3:2; 5:7; 6:14 (in all three places the RV has "without reproach"; in the first two KJV, "blameless," in the last, "unrebukeable"; an alternative rendering would be "irreprehensible). See REPROACH, UNREBUKEABLE.

6. *anenklētos* (ἀνέγκλητος, 410) signifies "that which cannot be called to account" (from *a*, negative, *n*, euphonic, and *enkaleō*, "to call in"), i.e., with nothing laid to one's charge (as the result of public investigation), in 1 Cor. 1:8, RV, "unreproveable," KJV, "blameless"; in Col. 1:22, KJV and RV, "unreproveable"; in 1 Tim. 3:10 and Titus 1:6-7, KJV and RV, "blameless." It implies not merely acquittal, but the absence

of even a charge or accusation against a person. This is to be the case with elders.

C. Adverb.

amemptōs (ἀμέμπτως, 274), in 1 Thess. 2:10, "unblameably"; in 5:23, "without blame," KJV, "blameless," is said of believers at the judgment-seat of Christ in His Parousia (His presence after His coming), as the outcome of present witness and steadfastness. See B, No. 3, above.

BLASPHEME, BLASPHEMY, BLASPHEMER, BLASPHEMOUS

A. Noun.

blasphēmia (βλασφημία, 988), either from *blax*, "sluggish, stupid," or, probably, from *blaptō*, "to injure," and *phēmē*, "speech," (Eng. "blasphemy") is so translated thirteen times in the RV, but "railing" in Matt. 15:19; Mark 7:22; Eph. 4:31; Col. 3:8; 1 Tim. 6:4; Jude 9. The word "blasphemy" is practically confined to speech defamatory of the Divine Majesty. See *Note*, below. See EVIL SPEAKING, RAILING.

B. Verb.

blasphēmeō (βλασφημέω, 987), "to blaspheme, rail at or revile," is used (a) in a general way, of any contumelious speech, reviling, calumniating, railing at, etc., as of those who railed at Christ, e.g., Matt. 27:39; Mark 15:29; Luke 22:65 (RV, "reviling"); 23:39; (b) of those who speak contemptuously of God or of sacred things, e.g., Matt. 9:3; Mark 3:28; Rom. 2:24; 1 Tim. 1:20; 6:1; Rev. 13:6; 16:9, 11, 21; "hath spoken blasphemy," Matt. 26:65; "rail at," 2 Pet. 2:10; Jude 8, 10; "railing," 2 Pet. 2:12; "slanderously reported," Rom. 3:8; "be evil spoken of," Rom. 14:16; 1 Cor. 10:30; 2 Pet. 2:2; "speak evil of," Titus 3:2; 1 Pet. 4:4; "being defamed," 1 Cor. 4:13. The verb (in the present participial form) is translated "blasphemers" in Acts 19:37; in Mark 2:7, "blasphemeth," RV, for KJV, "speaketh blasphemies."

There is no noun in the original representing the English "blasphemer." This is expressed either by the verb, or by the adjective *blasphemos*. See DEFAME, RAIL, REPORT, REVILE.

C. Adjective.

blasphēmos (βλάσφημος, 989), "abusive, speaking evil," is translated "blasphemous," in Acts 6:11, 13; "a blasphemer," 1 Tim. 1:13; "railers," 2 Tim. 3:2, RV; "railing," 2 Pet. 2:11. See RAIL.

Note: As to Christ's teaching concerning "blasphemy" against the Holy Spirit, e.g., Matt. 12:32, that anyone, with the evidence of the Lord's power before His eyes, should declare it to be Satanic, exhibited a condition of heart beyond divine illumination and therefore hopeless. Divine forgiveness would be inconsistent with the moral nature of God. As to the Son of Man, in his state of humiliation, there might be misunderstanding, but not so with the Holy Spirit's power demonstrated.

BLAZE ABROAD

diaphēmizō (διαφημίζω, 1310), "to spread broad" (*dia*, "throughout," *phēmizō*, "to speak"), is so translated in the RV in Matt. 9:31; 28:15 (KJV, "commonly reported"); Mark 1:45 (KJV, "blaze abroad").

BLEMISH

A. Noun.

mōmos (μῶμος, 3470), akin to *mōmaomai* (see BLAME, A), signifies (a) "a blemish" (Sept. only); (b) "a shame, a moral disgrace," metaphorical of the licentious, 2 Pet. 2:13.

B. Adjective.

amōmos (ἄμωμος, 299), "without blemish"; is always so rendered in the RV, Eph. 1:4; 5:27; Phil. 2:15; Col. 1:22; Heb. 9:14; 1 Pet. 1:19; Jude 24; Rev. 14:5. This meaning is to be preferred to the various KJV renderings, "without blame," Eph. 1:4, "unblameable," Col. 1:22, "faultless," Jude 24, "without fault," Rev. 14:5. The most authentic mss. have *amōmos*, "without blemish," in Phil. 2:15, for *amometos*, "without rebuke." In the Sept., in reference to sacrifices, especially in Lev. and Num., the Psalms and Ezek., "of blamelessness in character and conduct." See BLAME, FAULT.

BLESS, BLESSED, BLESSEDNESS, BLESSING

A. Verbs.

1. *eulogeō* (εὐλογέω, 2127), lit., "to speak well of" (*eu*, "well," *logos*, "a word"), signifies, (a) "to praise, to celebrate with praises," of that which is addressed to God, acknowledging His goodness, with desire for His glory, Luke 1:64; 2:28; 24:51, 53; Jas. 3:9; (b) "to invoke blessings upon a person," e.g., Luke 6:28; Rom. 12:14. The present participle passive, "blessed, praised," is especially used of Christ in Matt. 21:9; 23:39, and the parallel passages; also in John 12:13; (c) "to consecrate a thing with solemn prayers, to ask God's blessing on a thing," e.g., Luke 9:16; 1 Cor. 10:16; (d) "to cause to prosper, to make happy, to bestow blessings on," said of God, e.g., in Acts 3:26; Gal. 3:9; Eph. 1:3. Cf. the synonym *aineō*, "to praise." See PRAISE.

2. *eneulogeō* (ἐνευλογέω, 1757), "to bless," is used in the passive voice, Acts 3:25, and Gal. 3:8. The prefix *en* apparently indicates the person on whom the blessing is conferred.

3. *makarizō* (μακαρίζω, 3106), from a root *mak-*, meaning "large, lengthy," found also in *makros*, "long," *mēkos*, "length," hence denotes "to pronounce happy, blessed," Luke 1:48 and Jas. 5:11. See HAPPY.

B. Adjectives.

1. *eulogētos* (εὐλογητός, 2128), akin to A, 1, means "blessed, praised"; it is applied only to God, Mark 14:61; Luke 1:68; Rom. 1:25; 9:5; 2 Cor. 1:3; 11:31; Eph. 1:3; 1 Pet. 1:3. In the Sept. it is also applied to man, e.g., in Gen. 24:31; 26:29; Deut. 7:14; Judg. 17:2; Ruth 2:20; 1 Sam. 15:13.

2. *makarios* (μακάριος, 3107), akin to A, No. 3, is used in the beatitudes in Matt. 5 and Luke 6, is especially frequent in the Gospel of Luke, and is found seven times in Revelation, 1:3; 14:13; 16:15; 19:9; 20:6; 22:7, 14. It is said of God twice, 1 Tim. 1:11; 6:15. In the beatitudes the Lord indicates not only the characters that are "blessed," but the nature of that which is the highest good.

C. Nouns.

1. *eulogia* (εὐλογία, 2129), akin to A, 1, lit., "good speaking, praise," is used of (a) God and Christ, Rev. 5:12-13; 7:12; (b) the invocation of blessings, benediction, Heb. 12:17; Jas. 3:10; (c) the giving of thanks, 1 Cor. 10:16; (d) a blessing, a benefit bestowed, Rom. 15:29; Gal. 3:14; Eph. 1:3; Heb. 6:7; of a monetary gift sent to needy believers, 2 Cor. 9:5-6; (e) in a bad sense, of fair speech, Rom. 16:18, RV, where it is joined with *chrēstologia*, "smooth speech," the latter relating to the substance, *eulogia* to the expression. See BOUNTY.

2. *makarismos* (Μακεδονία, 3109), akin to A, 3, "blessedness," indicates an ascription of blessing rather than a state; hence in Rom. 4:6, where the KJV renders it as a noun, "(describeth) the blessedness"; the RV rightly puts "(pronounceth) blessing." So v. 9. In Gal. 4:15 the KJV has "blessedness," RV, "gratulation." The Galatian believers had counted themselves happy when they heard and received the gospel. Had they lost that opinion? See GRATULATION.

Note: In Acts 13:34, *hosia*, lit., "holy things," is translated "mercies" (KJV), "blessings" (RV).

For **BLEW** see BLOW

BLIND, BLINDNESS

A. Verbs.

1. *tuphloō* (τυφλόω, 5186), "to blind" (from a root *tuph-*, "to burn, smoke"; cf. *tuphos*, "smoke"), is used metaphorically, of the dulling of the intellect, John 12:40; 2 Cor. 4:4; 1 John 2:11.

2. *pōroō* (πωρόω, 4456) signifies "to harden" (from *pōros*, "a thick skin, a hardening"); rendered "blinded," KJV, in Rom. 11:7 and 2 Cor. 3:14 (RV, "hardened"); cf. 4:4. See HARDEN.

B. Adjective.

tuphlos (τυφλός, 5185), "blind," is used both physically and metaphorically, chiefly in the Gospels; elsewhere four times; physically, Acts 13:11; metaphorically, Rom. 2:19; 2 Pet. 1:9; Rev. 3:17. The word is frequently used as a noun, signifying "a blind man."

C. Noun.

pōrōsis (πώρωσις, 4457), akin to A. No. 2, primarily means "a covering with a callus," a "hardening," Rom. 11:25 and Eph. 4:18, RV for KJV, "blindness"; Mark 3:5, RV, for KJV, "hardness." It is metaphorical of a dulled spiritual perception. See HARDNESS.

Note: In John 9:8, the most authentic mss. have *prosaitēs*, "a beggar," RV, instead of *tuphlos*, "blind."

BLOOD

A. Nouns.

1. *haima* (αἷμα, 129), (hence Eng., prefix *haem-*), besides its natural meaning, stands, (a) in conjunction with *sarx*, "flesh," "flesh and blood," Matt. 16:17; 1 Cor. 15:50; Gal. 1:16; the original has the opposite order, blood and flesh, in Eph. 6:12 and Heb. 2:14; this phrase signifies, by *synecdoche*, "man, human beings." It stresses the limitations of humanity; the two are essential elements in man's physical being; "the life of the flesh is in the blood," Lev. 17:11; (b) for human generation, John 1:13; (c) for "blood" shed by violence, e.g., Matt. 23:35; Rev. 17:6; (d) for the "blood" of sacrificial victims, e.g., Heb. 9:7; of the "blood" of Christ, which betokens His death by the shedding of His "blood" in expiatory sacrifice; to drink His "blood" is to appropriate the saving effects of His expiatory death, John 6:53. As "the life of the flesh is in the blood," Lev. 17:11, and was forfeited by sin, life eternal can be imparted only by the expiation made, in the giving up of the life by the sinless Savior.

2. *haimatekchusia* (αἱματεκχυσία, 130) denotes "shedding of blood," Heb. 9:22 (*haima*, "blood," *ekchunō*, "to pour out, shed").

B. Verb.

haimorrhoeō (αἱμοῤῥέω, 131), from *haima*, "blood," *rheō*, "to flow" (Eng., "hemorrhage"), signifies "to suffer from a flow of blood," Matt. 9:20.

Notes: (1) In Mark 5:25 and Luke 8:43, different constructions are used, the translations respectively being "having a flowing of blood" and "being in (i.e., with) a flowing of blood."

(2) In Acts 17:26 (RV, "of one"; KJV, "of one blood"), the most authentic mss. do not contain the noun *haima*, "blood." So with the phrase "through His blood," in Col. 1:14.

BLOT OUT

exaleiphō (ἐξαλείφω, 1813), from *ek*, "out," used intensively, and *aleiphō*, "to wipe," signifies "to wash, or to smear completely." Hence, metaphorically, in the sense of removal, "to wipe away, wipe off, obliterate"; Acts 3:19, of sins; Col. 2:14, of writing; Rev. 3:5, of a name in a book; Rev. 7:17; 21:4, of tears.

BLOW (Noun)

rhapisma (ῥάπισμα, 4475), (a) "a blow with a rod or staff," (b) "a blow with the hand, a slap or cuff," is found in three places; of the maltreatment of Christ by the officials or attendants of the high priest, Mark 14:65, RV, "received (according to the most authentic mss.) Him with blows of their hands," (KJV, "did strike Him with the palms of their hands"); that they received, or took, Him would indicate their rough handling of Him; John 18:22 and 19:3; in all three places the RV marg. gives the meaning (a), as to the use of a rod.

So with the corresponding verb *rhapizō*, in Matt. 26:67. The soldiers subsequently beat Him with a reed, 27:30, where *tuptō*, "to beat," is used; *rhapizō* occurs elsewhere in Matt. 5:39.

BLOW (Verb)

1. *pneō* (πνέω, 4154) signifies (a) "to blow," e.g., Matt. 7:25; John 3:8; in Acts 27:40 the present participle is used as a noun, lit., "to the blowing" (i.e., to the wind); (b) "to breathe." See BREATHE.

2. *hupopneō* (ὑποπνέω, 5285), *hupo*, "under" (indicating repression), and No. 1, denotes "to blow softly," Acts 27:13.

Note: In Acts 28:13, *epiginomai*, "to come on," is used of the springing up of a wind, KJV, "blew"; RV, "sprang up."

BOAST, BOASTER, BOASTFUL

A. Verbs.

1. *kauchaomai* (καυχάομαι, 2744), and its related words *katakauchaomai*, "to glory or boast" and the nouns *kauchēsis* and *kauchēma*, translated "boast," and "boasting," in the KJV, are always translated "glory," and "glorying" in the RV, e.g., 2 Cor. 10:15; 11:10, 17; Eph. 2:9. See GLORY.

2. *megalaucheō* (μεγαλαυχέω, 3166), from *megala*, "great things," and *aucheō*, "to lift up the neck," hence, "to boast," is found in some texts of Jas. 3:5. The most authentic mss. have the two words separated. It indicates any kind of haughty speech which stirs up strife or provokes others.

Note: In Acts 5:36, the verb *legō*, "to say," is rendered "boasting" in the KJV; "giving out" (RV).

B. Nouns.

1. *alazōn* (ἀλαζών, 213), "a boaster," Rom. 1:30 and 2 Tim. 3:2, KJV, "boasters," RV, "boastful," primarily signifies "a wanderer about the country" (from *alē*, "wandering"), "a vagabond," hence, "an impostor."

2. *alazoneia* (ἀλαζονεία, 212), the practice of an *alazōn*, denotes quackery; hence, "arrogant display, or boastings," Jas. 4:16, RV, "vauntings"; in 1 John 2:16, RV, "vainglory"; KJV, "pride." See PRIDE, VAUNT.

Note: In 2 Cor. 9:4, *hupostasis*, "a support, substance," means "confidence" (RV); KJV, "confident boasting."

BOAT

1. *ploiarion* (πλοιάριον, 4142), "a skiff or small boat," is a diminutive of *ploion* (No. 2), Mark 3:9; 4:36; John 6:22 (but No. 2 in the 2nd part of the verse), 23 (here some texts have No. 2), 24; 21:8.

2. *ploion* (πλοῖον, 4143), KJV, "ship," is preferably translated "boat" (RV) in the gospels, where it is of frequent use; it is found 18 times in Acts, where, as in Jas. 3:4; Rev. 8:9; 18:19, it signifies a ship.

3. *skaphē* (σκάφη, 4627) is, lit., "anything dug or scooped out" (from *skaptō*, "to dig"), "as a trough, a tub, and hence a light boat, or skiff, a boat belonging to a larger vessel," Acts 27:16, 30, 32.

BODY, BODILY

A. Nouns.

1. *sōma* (σῶμα, 4983) is "the body as a whole, the instrument of life," whether of man living, e.g., Matt. 6:22, or dead, Matt. 27:52; or in resurrection, 1 Cor. 15:44; or of beasts, Heb. 13:11; of grain, 1 Cor. 15:37-38; of the heavenly hosts, 1 Cor. 15:40. In Rev. 18:13 it is translated "slaves." In its figurative uses the essential idea is preserved.

Sometimes the word stands, by *synecdoche*, for "the complete man," Matt. 5:29; 6:22; Rom. 12:1; Jas. 3:6; Rev. 18:13. Sometimes the person is identified with his or her "body," Acts 9:37; 13:36, and this is so even of the Lord Jesus, John 19:40 with 42. The "body" is not the man, for he himself can exist apart from his "body," 2 Cor. 12:2-3. The "body" is an essential part of the man and therefore the redeemed are not perfected till the resurrection, Heb. 11:40; no man in his final state will be without his "body," John 5:28-29; Rev. 20:13.

The word is also used for physical nature, as distinct from *pneuma*, "the spiritual nature," e.g., 1 Cor. 5:3, and from *psuchē*, "the soul," e.g., 1 Thess. 5:23. "*Sōma*, 'body,' and *pneuma*, 'spirit,' may be separated; *pneuma* and *psuchē*, 'soul,' can only be distinguished" (Cremer).

It is also used metaphorically, of the mystic body of Christ, with reference to the whole church, e.g., Eph. 1:23; Col. 1:18, 22, 24; also of a local church, 1 Cor. 12:27.

2. *chrōs* (χρώς, 5559) signifies "the surface of a body," especially of the human body, Acts 19:12, with reference to the handkerchiefs carried from Paul's body to the sick.

3. *ptōma* (πτῶμα, 4430) denotes, lit., "a fall" (akin to *piptō*, "to fall"); hence, "that which is fallen, a corpse," Matt. 14:12; 24:28, "carcase"; Mark 6:29; 15:45, "corpse"; Rev. 11:8-9,

"dead bodies" (Gk., "carcase," but plural in the 2nd part of v. 9). See CARCASE, CORPSE.

B. Adjectives.

1. *sussōmos* (σύσσωμος, 4954), *sun*, "with," and A, No. 1., means "united in the same body," Eph. 3:6, of the church.

2. *sōmatikos* (σωματικός, 4984), "bodily," is used in Luke 3:22, of the Holy Spirit in taking a bodily shape; in 1 Tim. 4:8 of bodily exercise.

C. Adverb.

sōmatikōs (σωματικῶς, 4985), "bodily, corporeally," is used in Col. 2:9.

BOISTEROUS

Note: The KJV "boisterous" in Matt. 14:30 is a rendering of the word *ischuros*, "strong" (see margin); it is not in the most authentic mss.

BOLDNESS

parrhēsia (παῤῥησία, 3954), from *pas*, "all," *rhēsis*, "speech" (see A, No. 2), denotes (a), primarily, "freedom of speech, unreservedness of utterance," Acts 4:29, 31; 2 Cor. 3:12; 7:4; Philem. 8; or "to speak without ambiguity, plainly," John 10:24; or "without figures of speech," John 16:25; (b) "the absence of fear in speaking boldly; hence, confidence, cheerful courage, boldness, without any connection necessarily with speech"; the RV has "boldness" in the following; Acts 4:13; Eph. 3:12; 1 Tim. 3:13; Heb. 3:6; 4:16; 10:19, 35; 1 John 2:28; 3:21; 4:17; 5:14; (c) the deportment by which one becomes conspicuous, John 7:4; 11:54, acts openly, or secures publicity, Col. 2:15. See CONFIDENCE, OPENLY, PLAINNESS.

BOND

1. *desmos* (δεσμός, 1199), from *deō*, "to bind," is usually found in the plural, either masculine or neuter; (a) it stands thus for the actual "bonds" which bind a prisoner, as in Luke 8:29; Acts 16:26; 20:23 (the only three places where the neuter plural is used); 22:30; (b) the masculine plural stands frequently in a figurative sense for "a condition of imprisonment," Phil. 1:7, 13, i.e., "so that my captivity became manifest as appointed for the cause of Christ"; verses 14, 16; Col. 4:18; 2 Tim. 2:9; Philem. 10, 13; Heb. 10:34.

In Mark 7:35 "the bond (KJV, string)" stands metaphorically for "the infirmity which caused an impediment in his speech." So in Luke 13:16, of the infirmity of the woman who was bowed together. See STRING.

2. *desmios* (δέσμιος, 1198), "a binding," denotes "a prisoner," e.g., Acts 25:14, RV, for the KJV, "in bonds"; Heb. 13:3, "them that are in bonds." Paul speaks of himself as a prisoner of Christ, Eph. 3:1; 2 Tim. 1:8; Philem. 1, 9; "in the Lord," Eph. 4:1. See PRISONER.

3. *sundesmos* (σύνδεσμος, 4886), "that which binds together" (*sun*, "with," and No. 1), is said of "the bond of iniquity," Acts 8:23; "the bond of peace," Eph. 4:3; "the bond of perfectness," Col. 3:14 (figurative of the ligaments of the body); elsewhere; Col. 2:19, "bands," figuratively of the bands which unite the church, the body of Christ.

4. *halusis* (ἅλυσις, 254) denotes "a chain"; so the RV in Eph. 6:20, for KJV "bonds."

5. *gramma* (γράμμα, 1121), in Luke 16:6, RV, means "a bill or note of hand." See BILL, No. 2.

6. *cheirographon* (χειρόγραφον, 5498), "a handwriting," is rendered "bond" in Col. 2:14, RV.

BONDAGE

A. Noun.

douleia (δουλεία, 1397), akin to *deō*, "to bind," primarily "the condition of being a slave," came to denote any kind of bondage, as, e.g., of the condition of creation, Rom. 8:21; of that fallen condition of man himself which makes him dread God, v. 15, and fear death, Heb. 2:15; of the condition imposed by the Mosaic Law, Gal. 4:24. See SERVE.

B. Verbs.

1. *douleuō* (δουλεύω, 1398), "to serve as a slave, to be a slave, to be in bondage," is frequently used without any association of slavery, e.g., Acts 20:19; Rom. 6:6; 7:6; 12:11; Gal. 5:13. See SERVE.

2. *douloō* (δουλόω, 1402), different from No. 1, in being transitive instead of intransitive, signifies "to make a slave of, to bring into bondage," Acts 7:6; 1 Cor. 9:19, RV; in the passive voice, "to be brought under bondage," 2 Pet. 2:19; "to be held in bondage," Gal. 4:3 (lit., "were reduced to bondage"); Titus 2:3, "of being enslaved to wine"; Rom. 6:18, "of service to righteousness" (lit., "were made bondservants"). As with the purchased slave there were no limitations either in the kind or the time of service, so the life of the believer is to be lived in continuous obedience to God. See ENSLAVED, GIVE, SERVANT.

3. *doulagōgeō* (δουλαγωγέω, 1396), "to bring into bondage" (from A, above, and *agō*, "to bring"), is used in 1 Cor. 9:27, concerning the body, RV, "bondage," for KJV, "subjection."

4. *katadouloō* (καταδουλόω, 2615), "to bring into bondage," occurs in 2 Cor. 11:20; Gal. 2:4.

BONDMAN, BONDMAID

doulos (δοῦλος, 1401), from *deō*, "to bind," "a slave," originally the lowest term in the scale of servitude, came also to mean "one who gives himself up to the will of another," e.g., 1 Cor. 7:23; Rom. 6:17, 20, and became the most common and general word for "servant," as in Matt. 8:9, without any idea of bondage. In calling himself, however, a "bondslave of

Jesus Christ," e.g., Rom. 1:1, the apostle Paul intimates (1) that he had been formerly a "bondslave" of Satan, and (2) that, having been bought by Christ, he was now a willing slave, bound to his new Master. See SERVANT.

The feminine, *doulē*, signifies "a handmaid," Luke 1:38, 48; Acts 2:18.

paidiskē (παιδίσκη, 3814), "a young girl, maiden," also denoted "a young female slave, bondwoman, or handmaid." For the KJV, "bondmaid" or "bondwoman," in Ga. 4:22- 23, 30-31, the RV has "handmaid." See DAMSEL, MAID

For **BONDSERVANT** see SERVANT

BONE

osteon (ὀστέον, 3747), probably from a word signifying strength, or firmness, sometimes denotes "hard substances other than bones," e.g., the stone or kernel of fruit. In the NT it always denotes "bones," Matt. 23:27; Luke 24:39; John 19:36; Heb. 11:22.

Note: As to Eph. 5:30, RV, "We are members of His body" (in contrast to the KJV), "the words that follow in the common text are an unintelligent gloss, in which unsuccessful endeavor is made to give greater distinctness to the Apostle's statement" (Westcott).

BOOK

1. *biblos* (βίβλος, 976) (Eng. "Bible") was the inner part, or rather the cellular substance, of the stem of the papyrus (Eng. "paper"). It came to denote the paper made from this bark in Egypt, and then a written "book," roll, or volume. It is used in referring to "books" of Scripture, the "book," or scroll, of Matthew's Gospel, Matt. 1:1; the Pentateuch, as the "book" of Moses, Mark 12:26; Isaiah, as "the book of the words of Isaiah," Luke 3:4; the Psalms, Luke 20:42 and Acts 1:20; "the prophets," Acts 7:42; to "the Book of Life," Phil. 4:3; Rev. 3:5; 20:15. Once only it is used of secular writings, Acts 19:19.

2. *biblion* (βιβλίον, 975), a diminutive of No. 1, had in Hellenistic Greek almost lost its diminutive force and was ousting *biblos* in ordinary use; it denotes "a scroll or a small book." It is used in Luke 4:17, 20, of the "book" of Isaiah; in John 20:30, of the Gospel of John; in Gal. 3:10 and Heb. 10:7, of the whole of the OT; in Heb. 9:19, of the "book" of Exodus; in Rev. 1:11; 22:7, 9-10, 18 (twice), 19, of the Apocalypse; in John 21:25 and 2 Tim. 4:13, of "books" in general; in Rev. 13:8; 17:8; 20:12; 21:27, of the "Book" of Life (see *Note,* below); in Rev. 20:12, of other "books" to be opened in the Day of Judgment, containing, it would seem, the record of human deeds. In Rev. 5:1- 9 the "Book" represents the revelation of God's purposes and counsels concerning the world. So with the "little book" in Rev. 10:8. In 6:14 it is used of a scroll, the rolling up of which illustrates the removal of the heaven.

In Matt. 19:7 and Mark 10:4 the word is used of a bill of divorcement. See BILL.

Note: In Rev. 22:19, the most authentic mss. have *xulon*, "tree (of life)," instead of "*biblion*."

3. *biblaridion* (βιβλαρίδιον, 974), another diminutive of No. 1, is always rendered "little book," in Rev. 10:2, 9-10. Some texts have it also in verse 8, instead of *biblion* (but see beginning of No 2).

For **BORN** see BEGET

BOSOM

kolpos (κόλπος, 2859) signifies (a) "the front of the body between the arms"; hence, to recline in the "bosom" was said of one who so reclined at table that his head covered, as it were, the "bosom" of the one next to him, John 13:23. Hence, figuratively, it is used of a place of blessedness with another, as with Abraham in paradise, Luke 16:22-23 (plural in v. 23), from the custom of reclining at table in the "bosom," a place of honor; of the Lord's eternal and essential relation with the Father, in all its blessedness and affection as intimated in the phrase, "The Only-begotten Son, which is in the bosom of the Father" (John 1:18); (b) "of the bosom of a garment, the hollow formed by the upper forepart of a loose garment, bound by a girdle and used for carrying or keeping things"; thus figuratively of repaying one liberally, Luke 6:38; cf. Isa. 65:6; Jer. 39:18; (c) "of an inlet of the sea," because of its shape, like a bosom, Acts 27:39.

BOTTOM, BOTTOMLESS

abussos (ἄβυσσος, 12), "bottomless" (from *a*, intensive, and *bussos*, "a depth"; akin to *bathus*, "deep"; Eng., "bath"), is used as a noun denoting the abyss (KJV, "bottomless pit"). It describes an immeasurable depth, the underworld, the lower regions, the abyss of Sheol. In Rom. 10:7, quoted from Deut. 30:13, the abyss (the abode of the lost dead) is substituted for the sea (the change in the quotation is due to the facts of the death and resurrection of Christ); the KJV has "deep" here and in Luke 8:31; the reference is to the lower regions as the abode of demons, out of which they can be let loose, Rev. 11:7; 17:8, it is found seven times in the Apocalypse, 9:1-2, 11; 11:7; 17:8; 20:1, 3; in 9:1, 2 the RV has "the pit of the abyss." See DEEP.

For **BOUGHT** see BUY

BOUNTY, BOUNTIFULLY

1. *eulogia* (εὐλογία, 2129), "a blessing," has the meaning of "bounty" in 2 Cor. 9:5, of the offering sent by the church at Corinth to their needy brethren in Judea.

Note: In the next verse the adverb "bountifully" is a translation of the phrase *ep' eulogiais*, lit., "with blessings" (RV marg.), that is, that blessings may accrue. See BLESSING.

2. *haplotēs* (ἁπλότης, 572), from *haplous*, "simple, single," is translated "bountifulness" in 2 Cor. 9:11, KJV; RV, "liberality" (marg., "singleness"); cf. 8:2; 9:13; from sincerity of mind springs "liberality." The thought of sincerity is present in Rom. 12:8; 2 Cor. 11:3; Eph. 6:5; Col. 3:22. See LIBERAL, SIMPLICITY.

3. *charis* (χάρις, 5485), "grace," is rendered, "bounty" in 1 Cor. 16:3, RV, (KJV, "liberality"), by metonymy for a material gift. See BENEFIT, No. 3.

4. *hadrotēs* (ἁδρότης, 100), lit. "fatness" (from *hadros*, "thick, well-grown"), is used of a monetary gift, in 2 Cor. 8:20, KJV, "abundance," RV, "bounty."

BOW, BOWED (Verb)

1. *kamptō* (κάμπτω, 2578), "to bend," is used especially of bending the knees in religious veneration, Rom. 11:4; 14:11; Eph. 3:14; Phil. 2:10.

2. *sunkamptō* (συγκάμπτω, 4781) signifies "to bend completely together, to bend down by compulsory force," Rom. 11:10.

3. *sunkuptō* (συγκύπτω, 4794), "to bow together" (*sun*, "together with," *kuptō*, "to bow"), is said, in Luke 13:11, of the woman crippled with a physical infirmity.

4. *klinō* (κλίνω, 2827), "to incline, to bow down," is used of the women who in their fright "bowed" their faces to the earth at the Lord's empty tomb, Luke 24:5; of the act of the Lord on the cross immediately before giving up His Spirit. What is indicated in the statement "He bowed His head," is not the helpless dropping of the head after death, but the deliberate putting of His head into a position of rest, John 19:30. The verb is deeply significant here. The Lord reversed the natural order. The same verb is used in His statement in Matt. 8:20 and Luke 9:58, "the Son of Man hath not where to lay His head." It is used, too, of the decline of day, Luke 9:12; 24:29; of turning enemies to flight, Heb. 11:34.

5. *tithēmi* (τίθημι, 5087), "to put, or place," is said of the soldiers who mockingly bowed their knees to Christ, Mark 15:19. See APPOINT.

Note: For *gonupeteō*, "to bow the knee," Matt. 27:29, see KNEEL.

BOW (Noun)

toxon (τόξον, 5115), "a bow," is used in Rev. 6:2. Cf. Hab. 3:8-9. The instrument is frequently mentioned in the Sept., especially in the Psalms.

BOWELS

splanchnon (σπλάγχνον, 4698), always in the plural, properly denotes "the physical organs of the intestines," and is once used in this respect, Acts 1:18 (for the use by Greeks and Hebrews, see AFFECTION, No. 2). The RV substitutes the following for the word "bowels": "affections," 2 Cor. 6:12; "affection," 2 Cor. 7:15; "tender mercies," Phil. 1:8; 2:1; "a heart (of compassion)," Col. 3:12; "heart," Philem. 12, 20; "hearts," Philem. 7; "compassion," 1 John 3:17. The word is rendered "tender" in the KJV and RV of Luke 1:78, in connection with the word mercy. See AFFECTION, No. 2, COMPASSION, A, No. 2 and B, No 2.

BOWL

phialē (φιάλη, 5357) (Eng., "phial") denotes "a bowl"; so the RV, for KJV, "vial," in Rev. 5:8; 15:7; 16:1-4, 8, 10, 12, 17; 17:1; 21:9; the word is suggestive of rapidity in the emptying of the contents. While the seals (ch. 6) give a general view of the events of the last "week" or "hebdomad," in the vision given to Daniel, Dan. 9:23-27, the "trumpets" refer to the judgments which, in a more or less extended period, are destined to fall especially, though not only, upon apostate Christendom and apostate Jews. The emptying of the "bowls" betokens the final series of judgments in which this exercise of the wrath of God is "finished" (Rev. 15:1, RV). These are introduced by the 7th trumpet. See Rev. 11:15 and the successive order in v. 18, "the nations were wroth, and Thy wrath came ..."; see also 6:17; 14:19, 20; 19:11-12.

BOY

pais (παῖς, 3816) denotes "a boy" (in contrast to *paidion*, a diminutive of *pais*, and to *teknon*, "a child"). With reference to Christ, instead of the KJV "child," the RV suitably translates otherwise as follows: Luke 2:43, "the boy Jesus"; Acts 4:27, 30, "Thy Holy Servant, Jesus." So in the case of others, Matt. 17:18 and Luke 9:42 ("boy"). See CHILD, MAID, SERVANT, SON, YOUNG MAN.

For **BRAMBLE BUSH** see BUSH

BRANCH

1. *klados* (κλάδος, 2798), from *klaō*, "to break" (cf. *klasma*, "a broken piece"), properly a young tender shoot, "broken off" for grafting, is used for any kind of branch, Matt. 13:32; 21:8; 24:32; Mark 4:32; 13:28; Luke 13:19; the descendants of Israel, Rom. 11:16-19, 21.

2. *klēma* (κλῆμα, 2814), akin to *klaō*, "to break," denotes "a tender, flexible branch, especially the shoot of a vine, a vine sprout," John 15:2, 4-6.

3. *stoibas* or *stibas* (στοιβάς, 4746), from *steibō*, "to tread on," primarily denoted "a layer of leaves, reeds, twigs or straw,

serving for a bed"; then "a branch full of leaves, soft foliage," which might be used in making a bed, or for treading upon, Mark 11:8.

4. *baion* (βάϊον, 902), of Egyptian origin, frequent in the papyri writings, denotes "a branch of the palm tree," John 12:13.

Note: Matthew, Mark and John each use a different word for "branch" in narrating Christ's entry into Jerusalem.

BRANDED

kaustēriazō (καυστηριάζω, 2743), "to burn in with a branding iron" (cf. Eng., "caustic"), is found, in the best mss., in 1 Tim. 4:2, RV "branded." Others have *kautēriazō* (from *kautērion*, "a branding-iron," Eng., "cauterize"), to mark by "branding," an act not quite so severe as that indicated by the former. The reference is to apostates whose consciences are "branded" with the effects of their sin. See SEARED.

Note: In the RV of Gal. 6:17, "branded" does not represent a word in the original; it serves to bring out the force of the apostle's metaphor of bearing in his body the *stigmata*, the marks, of the Lord Jesus. The reference is not to the branding of slaves, soldiers and criminals, but rather to the religious devotee, who "branded" himself with the mark of the god whom he specially worshipped. So Paul describes the physical marks due to the lictor's rods at Philippi and to the stones at Lystra, marks which, while not self-inflicted, betokened his devotion to Christ and his rejoicing therein.

BREAD (Loaf)

1. *artos* (ἄρτος, 740), "bread" (perhaps derived from *arō*, "to fit together," or from a root *ar*-, "the earth"), signifies (a) "a small loaf or cake," composed of flour and water, and baked, in shape either oblong or round, and about as thick as the thumb; these were not cut, but broken and were consecrated to the Lord every Sabbath and called the "shewbread" (loaves of presentation), Matt. 12:4; when the "shewbread" was reinstituted by Nehemiah (Neh. 10:32) a poll-tax of 1/3 shekel was laid on the Jews, Matt. 17:24; (b) "the loaf at the Lord's Supper," e.g., Matt. 26:26 ("Jesus took a loaf," RV, marg.); the breaking of "bread" became the name for this institution, Acts 2:42; 20:7; 1 Cor. 10:16; 11:23; (c) "bread of any kind," Matt. 16:11; (d) metaphorically, "of Christ as the Bread of God, and of Life," John 6:33, 35; (e) "food in general," the necessities for the sustenance of life, Matt. 6:11; 2 Cor. 9:10, etc.

2. *azumos* (ἄζυμος, 106) denotes "unleavened bread," i.e., without any process of fermentation; hence, metaphorically, "of a holy, spiritual condition," 1 Cor. 5:7, and of "sincerity and truth" (v. 8). With the article it signifies the feast of unleavened bread, Matt. 26:17; Mark 14:1, 12; Luke 22:1, 7; Acts 12:3; 20:6.

BREAST

1. *stēthos* (στῆθος, 4738), connected with *histēmi*, "to stand," i.e., that which stands out, is used of mourners in smiting the "breast," Luke 18:13; 23:48; of John in reclining on the "breast" of Christ, John 13:25; 21:20; of the "breasts" of the angels in Rev. 15:6.

2. *mastos* (μαστός, 3149), used in the plural, "paps," Luke 11:27; 23:29; Rev. 1:13, KJV, is preferably rendered "breasts," in the RV.

BREASTPLATE

thōrax (θώραξ, 2382), primarily, "the breast," denotes "a breastplate or corselet," consisting of two parts and protecting the body on both sides, from the neck to the middle. It is used metaphorically of righteousness, Eph. 6:14; of faith and love, 1 Thess. 5:8, with perhaps a suggestion of the two parts, front and back, which formed the coat of mail (an alternative term for the word in the NT sense); elsewhere in Rev. 9:9, 17.

BREATH, BREATHE

A. Nouns.

1. *pnoē* (πνοή, 4157), akin to *pneō*, "to blow," lit., "a blowing," signifies (a) "breath, the breath of life," Acts 17:25; (b) "wind," Acts 2:2. See WIND.

2. *pneuma* (πνεῦμα, 4151), "spirit," also denotes "breath," Rev. 11:11 and 13:15, RV. In 2 Thess. 2:8, the KJV has "spirit" for RV, breath. See LIFE, SPIRIT, WIND.

B. Verbs.

1. *empneō* (ἐμπνέω, 1709), lit., "to breathe in, or on," is used in Acts 9:1, indicating that threatening and slaughter were, so to speak, the elements from which Saul drew and expelled his breath.

2. *emphusaō* (ἐμφυσάω, 1720), "to breathe upon," is used of the symbolic act of the Lord Jesus in breathing upon His apostles the communication of the Holy Spirit, John 20:22.

BRIDE, BRIDECHAMBER, BRIDEGROOM

numphē (νύμφη, 3565) (Eng. "nymph") "a bride, or young wife," John 3:29; Rev. 18:23; 21:2, 9; 22:17, is probably connected with the Latin *nubō*, "to veil"; the "bride" was often adorned with embroidery and jewels (see Rev. 21:2), and was led veiled from her home to the "bridegroom." Hence the secondary meaning of "daughter-in-law," Matt. 10:35; Luke 12:53. See DAUGHTER-IN-LAW. For the relationship between Christ and a local church, under this figure, see 2 Cor. 11:2; regarding the whole church, Eph. 5:23-32; Rev. 22:17.

numphios (νυμφίος, 3566), "a bridegroom," occurs fourteen times in the gospels, and in Rev. 18:23. "The friend of the bridegroom," John 3:29, is distinct from "the sons of the bridechamber" who were numerous. When John the Baptist speaks of "the friend of the Bridegroom," he uses language according to the customs of the Jews.

numphōn (νυμφών, 3567), signifies (a) "the room or dining hall in which the marriage ceremonies were held," Matt. 22:10; some mss. have *gamos*, "a wedding," here; (b) "the chamber containing the bridal bed," "the sons of the bridechamber" being the friends of the bridegroom, who had the charge of providing what was necessary for the nuptials, Matt. 9:15; Mark 2:19; Luke 5:34.

BRIGHT, BRIGHTNESS

A. Adjectives.

1. *phōteinos* (φωτεινός, 5460), "bright" (from *phōs*, "light"), is said of a cloud, Matt. 17:5; metaphorically of the body, Matt. 6:22, "full of light"; Luke 11:34, 36. See LIGHT.

2. *lampros* (λαμπρός, 2986), "shining, brilliant, bright," is used of the clothing of an angel, Acts 10:30 and Rev. 15:6; symbolically, of the clothing of the saints in glory, Rev. 19:8, RV, in the best texts (KJV, "white"); of Christ as the Morning Star, 22:16; of the water of life, 22:1, KJV, "clear." See CLEAR, GOODLY, GORGEOUS, WHITE.

Note: Cf. *lamprōs*, "sumptuously," Luke 16:19.

B. Nouns.

1. *lamprotēs* (λαμπρότης, 2987), "brightness," akin to A, No. 2, above is found in Acts 26:13.

2. *apaugasma* (ἀπαύγασμα, 541), "a shining forth" (*apo*, "from," *augē*, "brightness"), of a light coming from a luminous body, is said of Christ in Heb. 1:3, KJV, "brightness," RV, "effulgence," i.e., shining forth (a more probable meaning than reflected brightness).

Note: Epiphaneia, lit., "shining forth or upon," is rendered "brightness" in the KJV of 2 Thess. 2:8; RV, "manifestation." See APPEAR.

BRIMSTONE

1. *theion* (θεῖον, 2303) originally denoted "fire from heaven." It is connected with sulphur. Places touched by lightning were called *theia*, and, as lightning leaves a sulphurous smell, and sulphur was used in pagan purifications, it received the name of *theion* Luke 17:29; Rev. 9:17-18; 14:10; 19:20; 20:10; 21:8.

2. *theiōdēs* (θειώδης, 2306), akin to No. 1, signifies "brimstone-like, or consisting of brimstone," Rev. 9:17.

BROTHER, BRETHREN, BROTHERHOOD, BROTHERLY

adelphos (ἀδελφός, 80) denotes "a brother, or near kinsman"; in the plural, "a community based on identity of origin or life." It is used of:—

(1) male children of the same parents, Matt. 1:2; 14:3; (2) male descendants of the same parents, Acts 7:23, 26; Heb. 7:5; (3) male children of the same mother, Matt. 13:55; 1 Cor. 9:5; Gal. 1:19; (4) people of the same nationality, Acts 3:17, 22; Rom. 9:3. With "men" (*anēr*, "male"), prefixed, it is used in addresses only, Acts 2:29, 37, etc.; (5) any man, a neighbor, Luke 10:29; Matt. 5:22; 7:3; (6) persons united by a common interest, Matt. 5:47; (7) persons united by a common calling, Rev. 22:9; (8) mankind, Matt. 25:40; Heb. 2:17; (9) the disciples, and so, by implication, all believers, Matt. 28:10; John 20:17; (10) believers, apart from sex, Matt. 23:8; Acts 1:15; Rom. 1:13; 1 Thess. 1:4; Rev. 19:10 (the word "sisters" is used of believers, only in 1 Tim. 5:2); (11) believers, with *aner*, "male," prefixed, and with "or sister" added, 1 Cor. 7:14 (RV), 15; Jas. 2:15, male as distinct from female, Acts 1:16; 15:7, 13, but not 6:3. From *Notes on Thessolonians*, by Hogg and Vine, p. 32.

Notes: (1) Associated words are *adelphotēs*, primarily, "a brotherly relation," and so, the community possessed of this relation, "a brotherhood," 1 Pet. 2:17 (see 5:9, marg.).; *philadelphos*, (*phileō*, "to love," and *adelphos*), "fond of one's brethren," 1 Pet. 3:8; "loving as brethren," RV.; *philadelphia*, "brotherly love," Rom. 12:10; 1 Thess. 4:9; Heb. 13:1; "love of the brethren," 1 Pet. 1:22 and 2 Pet. 1:7, RV.; *pseudadelphos*, "false brethren," 2 Cor. 11:26; Gal. 2:4.

(2) In Luke 6:16 and Acts 1:13, the RV has "son," for KJV, "brother."

BRUTE

alogos (ἄλογος, 249), translated "brute" in the KJV of 2 Pet. 2:12 and Jude 10, signifies "without reason," RV, though, as J. Hastings points out, "brute beasts" is not at all unsuitable, as "brute" is from Latin *brutus*, which means "dull, irrational"; in Acts 25:27 it is rendered "unreasonable."

BUD

blastanō (βλαστάνω, 985), "to bud," is said of Aaron's rod, Heb. 9:14; "spring up," Matt. 13:26, and Mark 4:27; elsewhere, in Jas. 5:18.

BUILD, BUILDER, BUILDING

A. Verbs.

1. *oikodomeō* (οἰκοδομέω, 3618), lit., "to build a house" (*oikos*, "a house," *domeō*, "to build"), hence, to build anything, e.g., Matt. 7:24; Luke 4:29; 6:48, RV, "well builded" (last clause of verse); John 2:20; is frequently used figuratively, e.g., Acts 20:32 (some mss. have No. 3 here); Gal. 2:18; especially of edifying, Acts 9:31; Rom. 15:20; 1 Cor. 10:23; 14:4; 1 Thess. 5:11 (RV). In 1 Cor. 8:10 it is translated "emboldened" (marg., "builded up"). The participle with the article (equivalent to a noun) is rendered "builder," Matt. 21:42; Acts 4:11; 1 Pet. 2:7. See EDIFY, EMBOLDEN.

2. *anoikodomeō* (ἀνοικοδομέω, 456) signifies "to build again" (*ana*, "again"), Acts 15:16.

3. *epoikodomeō* (ἐποικοδομέω, 2026) signifies "to build upon" (*epi*, "upon"), 1 Cor. 3:10, 12, 14; Eph. 2:20; Jude 20; or up, Acts 20:32; Col. 2:7.

4. *sunoikodomeō* (συνοικοδομέω, 4925), "to build together" (*sun*, "with"), is used in Eph. 2:22, metaphorically, of the church, as a spiritual dwelling-place for God.

5. *kataskeuazō* (κατασκευάζω, 2680), "to prepare, establish, furnish," is rendered "builded" and "built" in Heb. 3:3-4. See ORDAIN, PREPARE.

B. Nouns.

1. *oikodomē* (οἰκοδομή, 3619), "a building, or edification" (see A, No. 1), is used (a) literally, e.g., Matt. 24:1; Mark 13:1-2; (b) figuratively, e.g., Rom. 14:19 (lit., "the things of building up"); 15:2 of a local church as a spiritual building, 1 Cor. 3:9, or the whole church, the body of Christ, Eph. 2:21. It expresses the strengthening effect of teaching, 1 Cor. 14:3, 5, 12, 26; 2 Cor. 10:8; 12:19; 13:10, or other ministry, Eph. 4:12, 16, 29 (the idea conveyed is progress resulting from patient effort). It is also used of the believer's resurrection body, 2 Cor. 5:1. See EDIFICATION, EDIFY.

2. *endōmēsis* (ἐνδώμησις, 1739), "a thing built, structure" (*en*, "in," *dōmaō*, "to build"), is used of the wall of the heavenly city, Rev. 21:18 (some suggest that the word means "a fabric"; others, "a roofing or coping"; these interpretations are questionable; the probable significance is "a building").

3. *ktisis* (κτίσις, 2937), "a creation," is so translated in the RV of Heb. 9:11 (KJV "building,). See CREATION, B, No. 1, CREATURE, ORDINANCE.

4. *technitēs* (τεχνίτης, 5079), "an artificer, one who does a thing by rules of art," is rendered "builder" in Heb. 11:10, marg., "architect," which gives the necessary contrast between this and the next noun in the verse.

BUNDLE

1. *desmē* (δεσμή, 1197), from *deō*, "to bind" (similarly, Eng. "bundle" is akin to "bind"), is used in Matt. 13:30.

2. *plēthos* (πλῆθος, 4128), "a great number" (akin to *pleō*, "to fill"), is the word for the "bundle of sticks" which Paul put on the fire, Acts 28:3. See COMPANY, MULTITUDE.

BURIAL, BURY, BURYING

A. Nouns.

1. *entaphiasmos* (ἐνταφιασμός, 1780), lit. "an entombing" (from *en*, "in," *taphos*, "a tomb"), "burying," occurs in Mark 14:8; John 12:7. Cf. B.1.

2. *taphē* (ταφή, 5027), "a burial" (cf. No. 1, and Eng., "epitaph"), is found in Matt. 27:7, with *eis*, "unto," lit. "with a view to a buriai (place) for strangers."

B. Verbs.

1. *entaphiazō* (ἐνταφιάζω, 1779), see A, No. 1, "to prepare a body for burial," is used of any provision for this purpose, Matt. 26:12; John 19:40.

2. *thaptō* (θάπτω, 2290) occurs in Matt. 8:21-22, and parallels in Luke; Matt. 14:12; Luke 16:22; Acts 2:29; 5:6, 9-10; of Christ's "burial," 1 Cor. 15:4.

3. *sunthaptō* (συνθάπτω, 4916), akin to A. 2, "to bury with, or together" (*sun*), is used in the metaphorical sense only, of the believer's identification with Christ in His "burial," as set forth in baptism, Rom. 6:4; Col. 2:12.

BURN, BURNING

A. Verbs.

1. *kaiō* (καίω, 2545), "to set fire to, to light"; in the passive voice, "to be lighted, to burn," Matt. 5:15; John 15:6; Heb. 12:18; Rev. 4:5; 8:8, 10; 19:20; 21:8; 1 Cor. 13:3, is used metaphorically of the heart, Luke 24:32; of spiritual light, Luke 12:35; John 5:35. See LIGHT.

2. *katakaiō* (κατακαίω, 2618), from *kata*, "down" (intensive), and No. 1, signifies "to burn up, burn utterly," as of chaff, Matt. 3:12; Luke 3:17; tares, Matt. 13:30, 40; the earth and its works, 2 Pet. 3:10; trees and grass, Rev. 8:7. This form should be noted in Acts 19:19; 1 Cor. 3:15; Heb. 13:11, Rev. 17:16. In each piace the full rendering "burn utterly" might be used, as in Rev. 18:8.

3. *ekkaiō* (ἐκκαίω, 1572), from *ek*, out (intensive), and No. 1, lit., "to burn out," in the passive voice, "to be kindled, burn up," is used of the lustful passions of men, Rom. 1:27.

4. *puroomai* (πυρόομαι, 4448), from *pur*, "fire, to glow with heat," is said of the feet of the Lord, in the vision in Rev. 1:15; it is translated "fiery" in Eph. 6:16 (of the darts of the evil one); used metaphorically of the emotions, in 1 Cor. 7:9; 2 Cor. 11:29; elsewhere literally, of the heavens, 2 Pet. 3:12; of gold, Rev. 3:18 (RV, "refined"). See FIERY, FIRE, TRY.

5. *empiprēmi* (ἐμπίπρημι, 1714), or *emprēthō*, "to burn up," occurs in Matt. 2:7.

B. Nouns.

1. *kausis* (καῦσις, 2740), akin to A, No. 1 (Eng., "caustic"), is found in Heb. 6:8, lit. "whose end is unto burning." Cf. BRANDED.

2. *kausōn* (καύσων, 2742) is rendered "burning heat" in Jas. 1:11, KJV (RV, "scorching). See HEAT.

3. *purōsis* (πύρωσις, 4451), akin to A. No. 4, is used literally in Rev. 18:9, 18; metaphorically in 1 Pet. 4:12, "fiery trial." See TRIAL.

BURNT (offering)

holokautōma (ὁλοκαύτωμα, 3646) denotes "a whole burnt offering" (*holos*, "whole," *kautos*, for *kaustos*, a verbal adjective from *kaiō*, "to burn"), i.e., "a victim," the whole of which is burned, as in Ex. 30:20; Lev. 5:12; 23:8, 25, 27. It is used in Mark 12:33, by the scribe who questioned the Lord as to the first commandment in the Law and in Heb. 10:6, 8, RV "whole burnt offerings." See OFFERING.

For **BURY** see BURIAL

BUSH

batos (βάτος, 942) denotes "a bramble bush," as in Luke 6:44. In Mark 12:26 and Luke 20:37 the phrase "in the place concerning the Bush" signifies in that part of the book of Exodus concerning it. See also Acts 7:30, 35.

C

CAGE

phulakē (φυλακή, 5438), from *phulassō*, "to guard," denotes (a) "a watching, keeping watch," Luke 2:8; (b) "persons keeping watch, a guard," Acts 12:10; (c) "a period during which watch is kept," e.g., Matt. 24:43; (d) "a prison, a hold." In Rev. 18:2, KJV, Babylon is described figuratively, first as a "hold" and then as a "cage" of every unclean and hateful bird (RV, "hold" in both clauses, marg., "prison"). The word is almost invariably translated prison. See HOLD, PRISON, WATCH.

CALF

moschos (μόσχος, 3448) primarily denotes "anything young," whether plants or the offspring of men or animals, the idea being that which is tender and delicate; hence "a calf, young bull, heifer," Luke 15:23, 27, 30; Heb. 9:12, 19; Rev. 4:7.

moschopoieō (μοσχοποιέω, 3447) signifies "to make a calf" (*moschos*, and *poieō*, "to make"), Acts 7:41.

CALL, CALLED, CALLING

A. Verbs.

1. *kaleō* (καλέω, 2564), derived from the root *kal-*, whence Eng. "call" and "clamor" (see B and C, below), is used (a) with a personal object, "to call anyone, invite, summon," e.g., Matt. 20:8; 25:14; it is used particularly of the divine call to partake of the blessings of redemption, e.g., Rom. 8:30; 1 Cor. 1:9; 1 Thess. 2:12; Heb. 9:15; cf. B and C, below; (b) of nomenclature or vocation, "to call by a name, to name"; in the passive voice, "to be called by a name, to bear a name." Thus it suggests either vocation or destination; the context determines which, e.g., Rom. 9:25-26; "surname," in Acts 15:37, KJV, is incorrect (RV, "was called"). See BID, NAME.

2. *eiskaleō* (εἰσκαλέω, 1528), lit., "to call in," hence, "to invite" (*eis*, "in," and No. 1), is found in Acts 10:23.

3. *epikaleō* (ἐπικαλέω, 1941), *epi*, "upon," and No. 1., denotes (a) "to surname"; (b) "to be called by a person's name"; hence it is used of being declared to be dedicated to a person, as to the Lord, Acts 15:17 (from Amos 9:12); Jas. 2:7; (c) "to call a person by a name by charging him with an offense," as the Pharisees charged Christ with doing His works by the help of Beelzebub, Matt. 10:25 (the most authentic reading has *epikaleō*, for *kaleō*); (d) "to call upon, invoke"; in the middle voice, "to call upon for oneself" (i.e., on one's behalf), Acts 7:59, or "to call upon a person as a witness," 2 Cor. 1:23, or to appeal to an authority, Acts 25:11, etc.; (e)"to call upon by way of adoration, making use of the Name of the Lord," Acts 2:21; Rom. 10:12-14; 2 Tim. 2:22. See SURNAME.

4. *metakaleō* (μετακαλέω, 3333), *meta*, implying "change," and No. 1, "to call from one place to another, to summon" (cf. the Sept. of Hos. 11:1), is used in the middle voice only, "to call for oneself, to send for, call hither," Acts 7:14; 10:32; 20:17; 24:25.

5. *proskaleō* (προσκαλέω, 4341), *pros*, "to," and No. 1, signifies (a) "to call to oneself, to bid to come"; it is used only in the middle voice, e.g., Matt. 10:1; Acts 5:40; Jas. 5:14; (b) "God's call to Gentiles through the gospel," Acts 2:39; (c) the divine call in entrusting men with the preaching of the gospel," Acts 13:2; 16:10.

6. *sunkaleō* (συγκαλέω, 4779) signifies "to call together," Mark 15:16; Luke 9:1; 15:6, 9; 23:13; Acts 5:21; 10:24; 28:17.

Notes: (1) *Enkaleō*, Acts 19:40, KJV, "called in question," signifies "to accuse," as always in the RV. See ACCUSE, IMPLEAD.

(2) *Parakaleō*, "to beseech, intreat," is rendered "have called for" in Acts 28:20, KJV; RV, "did intreat" (marg., "call for"). It is used only here with this meaning.

7. *aiteō* (αἰτέω, 154), "to ask," is translated "called for" in Acts 16:29 ("he called for lights").

8. *phōneō* (φωνέω, 5455), "to sound" (Eng.,"phone"), is used of the crowing of a cock, e.g., Matt. 26:34; John 13:38; of "calling" out with a clear or loud voice, to cry out, e.g. Mark 1:26 (some mss. have *krazō* here), Acts 16:28; of "calling" to come to oneself, e.g., Matt. 20:32; Luke 19:15; of "calling" forth, as of Christ's call to Lazarus to come forth from the tomb, John 12:17; of inviting, e.g., Luke 14:12; of "calling" by name, with the implication of the pleasure taken in the possession of those "called," e.g., John 10:3; 13:13. See CRY.

9. *legō* (λέγω, 3004), "to speak," is used of all kinds of oral communication, e.g. "to call to call by name," to surname, Matt. 1:16; 26:36; John 4:5; 11:54; 15:15; Rev. 2:2, RV, "call themselves," etc.

10. *epilegō* (ἐπιλέγω, 1951), *epi* "upon," and No. 9, signifies "to call in addition," i.e., by another name besides that already intimated John 5:2; for its other meaning in Acts 15:40, see CHOOSE.

11. *chrēmatizō* (χρηματίζω, 5537), occasionally means "to be called or named," Acts 11:26 (of the name "Christians") and Rom. 7:3, the only places where it has this meaning. Its

primary significance, "to have business dealings with," led to this. They "were (publicly) called" Christians, because this was their chief business. See ADMONISH, REVEAL, WARN.

12. *eipon* (εἶπον, 2046), "to say, speak," means "to call by a certain appellation," John 10:35. See BID, No. 3.

13. *krinō* (κρίνω, 2919), "to judge," is translated "to call in question," in Acts 23:6; 24:21.

Notes: (1) For *onoma*, "a name," translated "called," KJV, in Luke 24:13; Acts 10:1, *onomazō*, "to name," translated "called," KJV, 1 Cor. 5:11, and *eponomazō*, "to surname," translated "art called," Rom. 2:17, see NAME and SURNAME.

(2) *Legō*, "to say," is rendered "calleth" in 1 Cor. 12:3, KJV, which the RV corrects to "saith," what is meant is not calling Christ "Anathema," but making use of the phrase "Anathema Jesus," i.e., "Jesus is accursed."

(3) *Prosagoreuō*, Heb. 5:10, means "to be named." See NAME.

(4) *Metapempō*, rendered "call for," in Acts 10:5, KJV, and 11:13, signifies "to fetch," RV. See SEND, No. 9.

(5) *Sunathroizō*, "to assemble," is translated "he called together," in the KJV of Acts 19:25; RV, "he gathered together."

(6) *Lambanō*, "to take or receive," is found with the noun *hupomnēsis*, "remembrance," in 2 Tim. 1:5; RV, "having been reminded" (lit., "having received remembrance"), for KJV, "when I call to remembrance."

(7) In Acts 10:15 and 11:9, *koinoō*, "to make common" (RV) is translated "call common" in the KJV.

B. Noun.

klēsis (κλῆσις, 2821), "a calling" (akin to A, No. 1), is always used in the NT of that "calling" the origin, nature and destiny of which are heavenly (the idea of invitation being implied); it is used especially of God's invitation to man to accept the benefits of salvation, Rom. 11:29; 1 Cor. 1:26; 7:20 (said there of the condition in which the "calling" finds one); Eph. 1:18, "His calling"; Phil. 3:14, the "high calling"; 2 Thess. 1:11 and 2 Pet. 1:10, "your calling"; 2 Tim. 1:9, a "holy calling"; Heb. 3:1, a "heavenly calling"; Eph. 4:1, "the calling wherewith ye were called"; 4:4, "in one hope of your calling." See VOCATION.

C. Adjective.

klētos (κλητός, 2822), "called, invited," is used, (a) "of the call of the gospel," Matt. 20:16; 22:14, not there "an effectual call," as in the Epistles, Rom. 1:1, 6-7; 8:28; 1 Cor. 1:2, 24; Jude 1; Rev. 17:14; in Rom. 1:7 and 1 Cor. 1:2 the meaning is "saints by calling"; (b) of "an appointment to apostleship," Rom. 1:1; 1 Cor. 1:1.

CALM

galēnē (γαλήνη, 1055) primarily signifies "calmness, cheerfulness" (from a root *gal-*, from which *gelaō*, "to smile," is also derived, hence the "calm" of the sea, the smiling ocean being a favorite metaphor of the poets), Matt. 8:26; Mark 4:39; Luke 8:24.

CALVARY

kranion (κρανίον, 2898), *kara*, "a head" (Eng., "cranium"), a diminutive of *kranon*, denotes "a skull" (Latin *calvaria*), Matt. 27:33; Mark 15:22; Luke 23:33; John 19:17. The corresponding Aramaic word is *Golgotha* (Heb. *gulgōleth*, see Judg. 9:53; 2 Kings 9:35).

CAMEL

kamēlos (κάμηλος, 2574), from a Hebrew word signifying "a bearer, carrier," is used in proverbs to indicate (a) "something almost or altogether impossible," Matt. 19:24, and parallel passages, (b) "the acts of a person who is careful not to sin in trivial details, but pays no heed to more important matters," Matt. 23:24.

For **CANDLE and CANDLESTICK** see LAMP and LAMPSTAND

CARCASE

1. *kōlon* (κῶλον, 2966) primarily denotes "a member of a body," especially the external and prominent members, particularly the feet, and so, a dead body (see, e.g., the Sept., in Lev. 26:30; Num. 14:29, 32; Isa. 66:24, etc.). The word is used in Heb. 3:17, from Num. 14:29, 32.

2. *ptōma* (πτῶμα, 4430): see BODY, No. 3.

CARNAL, CARNALLY

1. *sarkikos* (σαρκικός, 4559), from *sarx*, "flesh," signifies (a) "having the nature of flesh," i.e., sensual, controlled by animal appetites, governed by human nature, instead of by the Spirit of God, 1 Cor. 3:3 (for v. 1, see below; same mss. have it in v. 4); having its seat in the animal nature, or excited by it, 1 Pet. 2:11, "fleshly"; or as the equivalent of "human," with the added idea of weakness, figuratively of the weapons of spiritual warfare, "of the flesh" (KJV, "carnal"), 2 Cor. 10:4; or with the idea of unspirituality, of human wisdom, "fleshly," 2 Cor. 1:12; (b) "pertaining to the flesh" (i.e., the body), Rom. 15:27; 1 Cor. 9:11.

2. *sarkinos* (σάρκινος, 4560), (a) "consisting of flesh," 2 Cor. 3:3, "tables that are hearts of flesh" (KJV, "fleshy tables of the heart"); (b) "pertaining to the natural, transient life of the body," Heb. 7:16, "a carnal commandment"; (c) given up to the flesh, i.e., with almost the same significance as *sarkikos*, above, Rom. 7:14, "I am carnal sold under sin"; 1 Cor. 3:1 (some texts have *sarkikos*, in both these places, and in those

in (a) and (b), but textual evidence is against it). It is difficult to discriminate between *sarkikos* and *sarkinos* in some passages. In regard to 1 Pet. 2:11, Trench (*Syn.* Sec. LXXI, LXXII) says that *sarkikos* describes the lusts which have their source in man's corrupt and fallen nature, and the man is *sarkikos* who allows to the flesh a place which does not belong to it of right; in 1 Cor. 3:1 *sarkinos* is an accusation far less grave than *sarkikos* would have been. The Corinthian saints were making no progress, but they were not anti-spiritual in respect of the particular point with which the apostle was there dealing. In vv. 3-4, they are charged with being *sarkikos* See FLESHLY, FLESHY.

CAROUSINGS

potos (πότος, 4224), lit., "a drinking," signifies not simply a banquet but "a drinking bout, a carousal," 1 Pet. 4:3 (RV, "carousings" KJV, "banquetings"). Synonymous is *kraipale*, "surfeiting," Luke 21:34.

CARPENTER

tektōn (τέκτων, 5045) denotes any craftsman, but especially a worker in wood, a carpenter, Matt. 13:55; Mark 6:3.

CARRYING AWAY

A. Noun.

metoikesia (μετοικεσία, 3350), "a change of abode, or a carrying away by force" (*meta*, implying "change," *oikia*, "a dwelling"), is used only of the carrying away to Babylon, Matt. 1:11-12, 17.

B. Verb.

metoikizō (μετοικίζω, 3351), akin to A, is used of the removal of Abraham into Canaan, Acts 7:4, and of the carrying into Babylon, 7:43.

CATTLE

1. *thremma* (θρέμμα, 2353), "whatever is fed or nourished" (from *trephō*, "to nourish, nurture, feed"), is found in John 4:12.

2. *ktēnos* (κτῆνος, 2934), "cattle as property": see BEAST, No. 3.

Note: The verb *poimainō*, "to act as a shepherd" (*poimēn*), "to keep sheep," is translated "keeping sheep" in Luke 17:7, RV, for KJV "feeding cattle."

CAVE

1. *opē* (ὀπή, 3692), perhaps from *ōps*, "sight," denotes "a hole, an opening," such as a fissure in a rock, Heb. 11:38. In Jas. 3:11, the RV has "opening," of the orifice of a fountain (KJV, "place").

2. *spēlaion* (σπήλαιον, 4693), "a grotto, cavern, den" (Lat., *spelunca*), "cave," John 11:38, is said of the grave of Lazarus; in the RV in Heb. 11:38 and Rev. 6:15 (KJV, "dens"); in the Lord's rebuke concerning the defilement of the Temple, Matt. 21:13; Mark 11:17; Luke 19:46, "den" is used.

For **CELESTIAL** see HEAVEN, HEAVENLY, B, No. 2

CELLAR

kruptē (κρυπτή, 2926) (Eng., "crypt"), "a covered way or vault" (akin to *kruptos*, "hidden, secret"), is used in Luke 11:33, of lighting a lamp and putting it "in a cellar," RV.

CENSER

1. *thumiatērion* (θυμιαστήριον, 2369), "a vessel for burning incense" (2 Chron. 26:19; Ezek. 8:11), is found in Heb. 9:4.

2. *libanōtos* (λιβανωτός, 3031) denotes "frankincense," the gum of the *libanos*, "the frankincense tree"; in a secondary sense, "a vessel in which to burn incense," Rev. 8:3, 5.

Note: No. 1 derives its significance from the act of burning (*thumia*); No. 2 from that which was burned in the vessel.

CHAFF

achuron (ἄχυρον, 892), "chaff, the stalk of the grain from which the kernels have been beaten out, or the straw broken up by a threshing machine," is found in Matt. 3:12 and Luke 3:17.

CHAMBER (Store-chamber)

1. *tameion* (ταμεῖον, 5009) denotes, firstly, "a store-chamber," then, "any private room, secret chamber," Matt. 6:6; RV, "inner chamber" (KJV, "closet"); 24:26, "inner (KJV, secret) chambers"; Luke 12:3, RV, ditto, for KJV, "closets"; it is used in Luke 12:24 ("store-chamber") of birds.

2. *huperōn* (ὑπερῷον, 5253), the neuter of *huperoos*, "above," denotes "an upper room, upper chamber" (*huper*, "above"), Acts 1:13; 9:37, 39; 20:8.

CHAMBERING

koitē (κοίτη, 2845), primarily a place in which to lie down, hence, "a bed, especially the marriage bed," denotes, in Rom. 13:13, "illicit intercourse." See BED, CONCEIVE.

CHANGER (Money-changer)

1. *kollubistēs* (κολλυβιστής, 2855), from *kollubos* (lit., "clipped"), "a small coin or rate of change" (*koloboō* signifies "to cut off, to clip, shorten," Matt. 24:22), denotes "a money-changer," lit., money-clipper, Matt. 21:12; Mark 11:15; John 2:15.

2. *kermatistēs* (κερματιστής, 2773), from *kermatizō* (not found in the NT), "to cut into small pieces, to make small change" (*kerma* signifies "a small coin," John 2:15; akin to *keirō*, "to cut short"). In the court of the Gentiles, in the temple precincts, were the seats of those who sold selected and approved animals for sacrifice, and other things. The

magnitude of this traffic had introduced the bankers' or brokers' business, John 2:14.

CHARIOT

1. *harma* (ἅρμα, 716), akin to *arariskō*, "to join," denotes "a war chariot with two wheels," Acts 8:28, 29, 38; Rev. 9:9.

2. *rhedē* (ῥέδη, 4480), "a wagon with four wheels," was chiefly used for traveling purposes, Rev. 18:13.

For **CHARITY** see LOVE

CHASTE

hagnos (ἁγνός, 53) signifies (a) "pure from every fault, immaculate," 2 Cor. 7:11 (KJV, "clear"); Phil. 4:8; 1 Tim. 5:22; Jas. 3:17; 1 John 3:3 (in all which the RV rendering is "pure"), and 1 Pet. 3:2, "chaste"; (b) "pure from carnality, modest," 2 Cor. 11:2, RV, "pure"; Titus 2:5, chaste. See CLEAR, HOLY, PURE.

Note: Cf. *hagios*, "holy, as being free from admixture of evil"; *hosios*, "holy, as being free from defilement"; *eilikrinēs*, "pure, as being tested," lit., "judged by the sunlight," *katharos*, "pure, as being cleansed."

CHASTEN, CHASTENING, CHASTISE, CHASTISEMENT

A. Verb.

paideuō (παιδεύω, 3811) primarily denotes "to train children," suggesting the broad idea of education (*pais*, "a child"), Acts 7:22; 22:3; see also Titus 2:12, "instructing" (RV), here of a training gracious and firm; grace, which brings salvation, employs means to give us full possession of it, hence, "to chastise," this being part of the training, whether (a) by correcting with words, reproving, and admonishing, 1 Tim. 1:20 (RV, "be taught"); 2 Tim. 2:25, or (b) by "chastening" by the infliction of evils and calamities, 1 Cor. 11:32; 2 Cor. 6:9; Heb. 12:6-7, 10; Rev. 3:19. The verb also has the meaning "to chastise with blows, to scourge," said of the command of a judge, Luke 23:16, 22. See CORRECTION, B, INSTRUCT, LEARN, TEACH, and cf. CHILD (Nos. 4 to 6).

B. Noun.

paideia (παιδεία, 3809) denotes "the training of a child, including instruction"; hence, "discipline, correction," "chastening," Eph. 6:4, RV (KJV, "nurture"), suggesting the Christian discipline that regulates character; so in Heb. 12:5, 7, 8 (in v. 8, KJV, "chastisement," the RV corrects to "chastening"); in 2 Tim. 3:16, "instruction. See INSTRUCTION, NURTURE.

CHEEK

siagōn (σιαγών, 4600) primarily denotes "the jaw, the jaw-bone"; hence "cheek," Matt. 5:39; Luke 6:29.

CHEER, CHEERFUL, CHEERFULLY, CHEERFULNESS

A. Verbs.

1. *euthumeō* (εὐθυμέω, 2114) signifies, in the active voice, "to put in good spirits, to make cheerful" (*eu*, "well," *thumos*, "mind or passion"); or, intransitively, "to be cheerful," Acts 27:22, 25; Jas. 5:13 (RV, "cheerful," for KJV, "merry"). See MERRY.

2. *tharseō* (θαρσέω, 2293), "to be of good courage, of good cheer" (*tharsos*, "courage, confidence"), is used only in the imperative mood, in the NT; "be of good cheer," Matt. 9:2, 22; 14:27; Mark 6:50; 10:49; Luke 8:48; John 16:33; Acts 23:11. See COMFORT, COURAGE.

B. Adjectives.

1. *euthumos* (εὔθυμος, 2115) means "of good cheer" (see A, No. 1), Acts 27:36.

2. *hilaros* (ἱλαρός, 2431), from *hileōs*, "propitious," signifies that readiness of mind, that joyousness, which is prompt to do anything; hence, "cheerful" (Eng., "hilarious"), 2 Cor. 9:7, "God loveth a cheerful (hilarious) giver."

Note: In the Sept. the verb *hilarunō* translates a Hebrew word meaning "to cause to shine," in Ps. 104:15.

C. Adverb.

euthumōs (εὐθύμως, 2115), cheerfully (see A, No. 1), is found in the most authentic mss. in Acts 24:10, instead of the comparative degree, *euthumoteron*.

D. Noun.

hilarotēs (ἱλαρότης, 2432), "cheerfulness" (akin to B, No. 2), is used in Rom. 12:8, in connection with showing mercy.

CHERISH

thalpō (θάλπω, 2282) primarily means "to heat, to soften by heat"; then, "to keep warm," as of birds covering their young with their feathers, Deut. 22:6, Sept.; metaphorically, "to cherish with tender love, to foster with tender care," in Eph. 5:29 of Christ and the church; in 1 Thess. 2:7 of the care of the saints at Thessalonica by the apostle and his associates, as of a nurse for her children.

CHERUBIM

cheroubim (χερουβίμ, 5502) are regarded by some as the ideal representatives of redeemed animate creation. In the tabernacle and Temple they were represented by the two golden figures of two-winged living creatures. They were all of one piece with the golden lid of the ark of the covenant in the Holy of Holies signifying that the prospect of redeemed and glorified creatures was bound up with the sacrifice of Christ.

This in itself would indicate that they represent redeemed human beings in union with Christ, a union seen, figuratively, proceeding out of the mercy seat. Their faces were towards this mercy seat, suggesting a consciousness of the means whereby union with Christ has been produced.

The first reference to the "cherubim" is in Gen. 3:24, which should read "... at the East of the Garden of Eden He caused to dwell in a tabernacle the cherubim, and the flaming sword which turned itself to keep the way of the Tree of Life." This was not simply to keep fallen human beings out; the presence of the "cherubim" suggests that redeemed men, restored to God on God's conditions, would have access to the Tree of Life. (See Rev. 22:14).

Certain other references in the OT give clear indication that angelic beings are upon occasion in view, e.g., Ps. 18:10; Ezek. 28:4. So with the vision of the cherubim in Ezek. 10:1-20; 11:22. In the NT the word is found in Heb. 9:5, where the reference is to the ark in the tabernacle, and the thought is suggested of those who minister to the manifestation of the glory of God.

We may perhaps conclude, therefore, that, inasmuch as in the past and in the present angelic beings have functioned and do function administratively in the service of God, and that redeemed man in the future is to act administratively in fellowship with Him, the "cherubim" in Scripture represent one or other of these two groups of created beings according to what is set forth in the various passages relating to them.

CHIEF, CHIEFEST, CHIEFLY

A. Adjective.

protōs (πρῶτος, 4413) denotes "the first," whether in time or place. It is translated "chief" in Mark 6:21, RV, of men of Galilee, in Acts 13:50, of men in a city; in 28:7, of the "chief" man in the island of Melita; in 17:4, of "chief" women in a city; in 28:17, of Jews; in 1 Tim. 1:15-16, of a sinner. In the following, where the KJV has "chief," or "chiefest," the RV renderings are different: Matt. 20:27 and Mark 10:44, "first"; Luke 19:47 and Acts 25:2, "principal men"; Acts 16:12, said of Philippi, "the first (city) of the district," RV, for incorrect KJV, "the chief city of that part of Macedonia." Amphipolis was the "chief" city of that part. *Protōs* here must mean the first in the direction in which the apostle came. See BEGINNING, FIRST, FORMER.

B. Nouns.

1. *kephalaion* (κεφάλαιον, 2774), akin to the adjective *kephalaios*, "belonging to the head," and *kephalē*, "the head," denotes the chief point or principal thing in a subject, Heb. 8:1, "the chief point is this" (KJV, "the sum"); elsewhere in Acts 22:28 (of principal, as to money), "(a great) sum." See SUM.

Certain compound nouns involving the significance of chief, are as follows:

2. *archiereus* (ἀρχιερεύς, 749), "a chief priest, high priest" (*archē*, "first," *hiereus*, "a priest"), is frequent in the gospels, Acts and Hebrews, but there only in the NT. It is used of Christ, e.g., in Heb. 2:17; 3:1; of "chief" priests, including ex-high-priests and members of their families, e.g., Matt. 2:4; Mark 8:31.

3. *archipoimēn* (ἀρχιποίμην, 750), "a chief shepherd" (*archē*, "chief," *poimēn*, "a shepherd"), is said of Christ only, 1 Pet. 5:4. Modern Greeks use it of tribal chiefs.

4. *architelōnēs* (ἀρχιτελώνης, 754) denotes "a chief tax-collector, or publican," Luke 19:2.

5. *akrogoniaios* (ἀκρογωνιαῖος, 204) denotes "a chief corner-stone" (from *akros*, "highest, extreme," *gōnia*, "a corner, angle"), Eph. 2:20 and 1 Pet. 2:6. In the Sept., Isa. 28:16.

6. *prōtokathedria* (πρωτοκαθεδρία, 4410), "a sitting in the first or chief seat" (*prōtos*, "first," *kathedra*, "a seat"), is found in Matt. 23:6; Mark 12:39; Luke 11:43; 20:46.

7. *prōtoklisia* (πρωτοκλισία, 4411), "the first reclining place, the chief place at table" (from *prōtos*, and *klisia*, "a company reclining at a meal"; cf. *klinō*, "to incline"), is found in Matt. 23:6; Mark 12:39 (as with No. 6); Luke 14:7-8; 20:46.

8. *chiliarchos* (χιλίαρχος, 5506) denotes "a chief captain."

9. *asiarchēs* (Ἀσιάρχης, 775), "an Asiarch," was one of certain officers elected by various cities in the province of Asia, whose function consisted in celebrating, partly at their own expense, the public games and festivals; in Acts 19:31, RV, the word is translated "chief officers of Asia" (KJV, "chief of Asia").

It seems probable, according to Prof. Ramsay, that they were "the high priests of the temples of the Imperial worship in various cities of Asia"; further, that "the Council of the Asiarchs sat at stated periods in the great cities alternately ... and were probably assembled at Ephesus for such a purpose when they sent advice to St. Paul to consult his safety." A festival would have brought great crowds to the city.

10. *archōn* (ἄρχων, 758), "a ruler," is rendered "chief" in the KJV of Luke 14:1 (RV, "ruler"); "chief rulers," in John 12:42, RV, "rulers (of the people)," i.e., of members of the Sanhedrin; "chief," in Luke 11:15 (RV, "prince"), in reference to Beelzebub, the prince of demons. See MAGISTRATE, PRINCE, RULER.

11. *archisunagōgos* (ἀρχισυνάγωγος, 752), "a ruler of a synagogue," translated "chief ruler of the synagogue," in Acts 18:8, 17, KJV, was the administrative officer supervising the worship.

C. Verb.

hēgeomai (ἡγέομαι, 2233), "to lead the way, to preside, rule, be the chief," is used of the ambition "to be chief" among the disciples of Christ, Luke 22:26; of Paul as the "chief" speaker in gospel testimony at Lystra, Acts 14:12; of Judas and Silas, as chief (or rather, "leading") men among the brethren at Jerusalem, Acts 15:22. See COUNT, ESTEEM, GOVERNOR, JUDGE.

D. Adverbs.

1. *huperlian* (χόρτος, 5528 and χόρτος, 3029), "chiefest" (*huper*, "over," *lian*, "exceedingly, pre-eminently, very much"), is used in 2 Cor. 11:5; 12:11, of Paul's place among the apostles.

2. *malista* (μάλιστα, 3122), the superlative of *mala*, "very, very much," is rendered "chiefly" in 2 Pet. 2:10 and in the KJV of Phil. 4:22 (RV, especially).

Note: In Rom. 3:2, RV, the adverb *prōton* is translated "first of all" (KJV, "chiefly").

CHILD, CHILDREN, CHILDBEARING, CHILDISH, CHILDLESS

1. *teknon* (τέκνον, 5043), "a child" (akin to *tiktō*, "to beget, bear"), is used in both the natural and the figurative senses. In contrast to *huios*, "son" (see below), it gives prominence to the fact of birth, whereas *huios* stresses the dignity and character of the relationship. Figuratively, *teknon* is used of "children" of (a) God, John 1:12; (b) light, Eph. 5:8; (c) obedience, 1 Pet. 1:14; (d) a promise, Rom. 9:8; Gal. 4:28; (e) the Devil, 1 John 3:10; (f) wrath, Eph. 2:3; (g) cursing, 2 Pet. 2:14; (h) spiritual relationship, 2 Tim. 2:1; Philem. 10. See DAUGHTER, SON.

2. *teknion* (τεκνίον, 5040), "a little child," a diminutive of No. 1, is used only figuratively in the NT, and always in the plural. It is found frequently in 1 John, see 2:1, 12, 28; 3:7, 18; 4:4; 5:21; elsewhere, once in John's Gospel, 13:33, once in Paul's epistles, Gal. 4:19. It is a term of affection by a teacher to his disciples under circumstances requiring a tender appeal, e.g., of Christ to the Twelve just before His death; the apostle John used it in warning believers against spiritual dangers; Paul, because of the deadly errors of Judaism assailing the Galatian churches. Cf. his use of *teknon* in Gal. 4:28.

3. *huios* (υἱός, 5207), "a son," is always so translated in the RV, except in the phrase "children of Israel," e.g., Matt. 27:9; and with reference to a foal, Matt. 21:5. The KJV does not discriminate between *teknon* and *huios*. In the First Epistle of John, the apostle reserves the word for the Son of God. See *teknia*, "little children" (above), and *tekna*, "children," in John 1:12; 11:52. See *paidion* (below). For the other use of *huios*, indicating the quality of that with which it is connected, see SON.

4. *pais* (παῖς, 3816) signifies (a) "a child in relation to descent," (b) "a boy or girl in relation to age," (c) "a servant, attendant, maid, in relation to condition." As an instance of (a) see Matt. 21:15, "children," and Acts 20:12 (RV, "lad"). In regard to (b) the RV has "boy" in Matt. 17:18 and Luke 9:42. In Luke 2:43 it is used of the Lord Jesus. In regard to (c), see Matt. 8:6, 8, 13, etc. As to (a) note Matt. 2:16, RV, male children. See MAID, SERVANT, SON, YOUNG MAN.

5. *paidion* (παιδίον, 3813), a diminutive of *pais*, signifies "a little or young child"; it is used of an infant just born, John 16:21, of a male child recently born, e.g., Matt. 2:8; Heb. 11:23; of a more advanced child, Mark 9:24; of a son, John 4:49; of a girl, Mark 5:39, 40, 41; in the plural, of "children," e.g., Matt. 14:21. It is used metaphorically of believers who are deficient in spiritual understanding, 1 Cor. 14:20, and in affectionate and familiar address by the Lord to His disciples, almost like the Eng., "lads," John 21:5; by the apostle John to the youngest believers in the family of God, 1 John 2:13, 18; there it is to be distinguished from *teknia*, which term he uses in addressing all his readers (vv. 1, 12, 28: see *teknia*, above). See DAMSEL.

Note: The adverb *paidiothen*, "from (or of) a child," is found in Mark 9:21.

6. *paidarion* (παιδάριον, 3808), another diminutive of *pais*, is used of "boys and girls," in Matt. 11:16 (the best texts have *paidiois* here), and a "lad," John 6:9; the tendency in colloquial Greek was to lose the diminutive character of the word.

7. *nēpios* (νήπιος, 3516), lit., "not-speaking" (from *ne*, a negative, and *epos*, a word is rendered "childish" in 1 Cor. 13:11 see BABE.

8. *monogenēs* (μονογενής, 3439), lit., "only-begotten," is translated "only child" in Luke 9:38. See ONLY BEGOTTEN.

9. *teknogonia* (τεκνογονία, 5042), *teknon* and a root *gen-*, whence *gennaō*, "to beget," denotes "bearing children," implying the duties of motherhood, 1 Tim. 2:15.

B. Verbs.

1. *nēpiazō* (νηπιάζω, 3515), "to be a babe," is used in 1 Cor. 14:20, "(in malice) be ye babes" (akin to No. 7, above).

2. *teknotropheō* (τεκνοτροφέω, 5044), "to rear young," *teknon*, and *trephō*, "to rear," signifies "to bring up children," 1 Tim. 5:10.

3. *teknogoneō* (τεκνογονέω, 5041), "to bear children" (*teknon*, and *gennaō*, "to beget"), see No. 9 above, is found in 1 Tim. 5:14.

C. Adjectives.

1. *enkuos* (ἔγκυος, 1471) denotes "great with child" (*en*, "in," and *kuō*, "to conceive"), Luke 2:5.

2.*philoteknos* (φιλότεκνος, 5388), from *phileō*, "to love," and *teknon*, signifies "loving one's children," Titus 2:4.

3. *ateknos* (ἄτεκνος, 815), from *a*, negative, and *teknon*, signifies "childless," Luke 20:28-30.

Notes: (1) For *brephos*, "a new born babe," always rendered "babe" or "babes" in the RV (KJV, "young children," Acts 7:19; "child," 2 Tim. 3:15), see under BABE.

(2) *Huiothesia*, "adoption of children," in the KJV of Eph. 1:5, is corrected to "adoption as sons" in the RV. See on ADOPTION.

CHOKE

1. *pnigō* (πνίγω, 4155) is used, in the passive voice, of "perishing by drowning," Mark 5:13; in the active, "to seize a person's throat, to throttle," Matt. 18:28.

2. *apopnigō* (ἀποπνίγω, 638), a strengthened form of No. 1 (*apo*, "from," intensive; cf. Eng., "to choke off"), is used metaphorically, of "thorns crowding out seed sown and preventing its growth," Matt. 13:7; Luke 8:7. It is Luke's word for "suffocation by drowning," Luke 8:33 (Cf. Mark 5:13, above).

3. *sumpnigō* (συμπνίγω, 4846) gives the suggestion of "choking together" (*sun*, "with"), i.e., by crowding, Matt. 13:22; Mark 4:7, 19; Luke 8:14. It is used in Luke 8:42, of the crowd that thronged the Lord, almost, so to speak, to suffocation.

CHOICE, CHOOSE, CHOSEN

A. Verbs.

1. *eklegō* (ἐκλέγοω, 1586), "to pick out, select," means, in the middle voice, "to choose for oneself," not necessarily implying the rejection of what is not chosen, but "choosing" with the subsidiary ideas of kindness or favor or love, Mark 13:20; Luke 6:13; 9:35 (RV); 10:42; 14:7; John 6:70; 13:18; 15:16, 19; Acts 1:2, 24; 6:5; 13:17; 15:22, 25; in 15:7 it is rendered "made choice"; 1 Cor. 1:27-28; Eph. 1:4; Jas. 2:5.

2. *epilegō* (ἐπιλέγω, 1951), in the middle voice, signifies "to choose," either in addition or in succession to another. It has this meaning in Acts 15:40, of Paul's choice of Silas. For its other meaning, "to call or name," John 5:2, see CALL.

3. *haireō* (αἱρεω, 138), "to take," is used in the middle voice only, in the sense of taking for oneself, choosing, 2 Thess. 2:13, of a "choice" made by God (as in Deut. 7:6-7; 26:18, Sept.); in Phil. 1:22 and Heb. 11:25, of human "choice." Its special significance is to select rather by the act of taking, than by showing preference or favor.

4. *hairetizō* (αἱρετίζω, 140), akin to the verbal adjective *hairetos*, "that which may be taken" (see No. 3), signifies "to take," with the implication that what is taken is eligible or suitable; hence, "to choose," by reason of this suitability, Matt. 12:18, of God's delight in Christ as His "chosen." It is frequent in the Sept., e.g., Gen. 30:20; Num. 14:8; Ps. 25:12; 119:30, 173; 132:13-14; Hos. 4:18; Hag. 2:23 ("he hath chosen the Canaanites"), Zech. 1:17; 2:12; Mal. 3:17.

5. *cheirotoneō* (χειροτονέω, 5500); see APPOINT, No. 11.

6. *procheirotoneō* (προχειροτονέω, 4401) signifies "to choose before," Acts 10:41, where it is used of a choice made before by God.

Notes: (1) For *procheirizō* see APPOINT, No. 12.

(2) *Stratologeō*, in 2 Tim. 2:4 (KJV, "chosen to be a soldier"), signifies to enroll as a soldier (RV).

B. Adjective.

eklektos (ἐκλεκτός, 1588), akin to A, No. 1, signifies "chosen out, select," e.g., Matt. 22:14; Luke 23:35; Rom. 16:13 (perhaps in the sense of "eminent"), Rev. 17:14. In 1 Pet. 2:4, 9, the RV translates it "elect." See ELECT.

C. Noun.

eklogē (ἐκλογή, 1589), akin to A, No. 1 and B, "a picking out, choosing" (Eng., "eclogue"), is translated "chosen" in Acts 9:15, lit., "he is a vessel of choice unto Me." In the six other places where this word is found it is translated "election." See ELECTION.

CHRIST

christos (Χριστός, 5547), "anointed," translates, in the Sept., the word "Messiah," a term applied to the priests who were anointed with the holy oil, particularly the high priest, e.g., Lev. 4:3, 5, 16. The prophets are called *hoi christoi Theou*, "the anointed of God," Ps. 105:15. A king of Israel was described upon occasion as *christos tou Kuriou*, "the anointed of the Lord," 1 Sam. 2:10, 35; 2 Sam. 1:14; Ps. 2:2; 18:50; Hab. 3:13; the term is used even of Cyrus, Isa. 45:1.

The title *ho Christos*, "the Christ," is not used of Christ in the Sept. version of the inspired books of the OT. In the NT the word is frequently used with the article, of the Lord Jesus, as an appellative rather than a title, e.g., Matt. 2:4; Acts 2:31; without the article, Luke 2:11; 23:2; John 1:41. Three times the title was expressly accepted by the Lord Himself, Matt. 16:17; Mark 14:61-62; John 4:26.

It is added as an appellative to the proper name "Jesus," e.g., John 17:3, the only time when the Lord so spoke of Himself; Acts 9:34; 1 Cor. 3:11; 1 John 5:6. It is distinctly a proper name in many passages, whether with the article, e.g., Matt. 1:17; 11:2; Rom. 7:4, 9:5; 15:19; 1 Cor. 1:6, or without the article, Mark 9:41; Rom. 6:4; 8:9, 17; 1 Cor. 1:12; Gal. 2:16. The single title Christos is sometimes used without the article to signify the One who by His Holy Spirit and power indwells believers and molds their character in conformity to His likeness, Rom. 8:10; Gal. 2:20; 4:19; Eph. 3:17. As to the use or absence of the article, the title with the article specifies the Lord Jesus as "the Christ"; the title without the article stresses His character and His relationship with believers. Again, speaking generally, when the title is the subject of a sentence it has the article; when it forms part of the predicate the article is absent. See also JESUS.

CHRISTS (FALSE)

pseudochristos (ψευδόχριστος, 5580) denotes "one who falsely lays claim to the name and office of the Messiah," Matt. 24:24; Mark 13:22. See *Note* under ANTICHRIST.

CHRISTIAN

christianos (Χριστιανός, 5546), "Christian," a word formed after the Roman style, signifying an adherent of Jesus, was first applied to such by the Gentiles and is found in Acts 11:26; 26:28; 1 Pet. 4:16.

Though the word rendered "were called" in Acts 11:26 (see under CALL) might be used of a name adopted by oneself or given by others, the "Christians" do not seem to have adopted it for themselves in the times of the apostles. In 1 Pet. 4:16, the apostle is speaking from the point of view of the persecutor, cf. "as a thief," "as a murderer." Nor is it likely that the appellation was given by Jews. As applied by Gentiles there was no doubt an implication of scorn, as in Agrippa's statement in Acts 26:28. Tacitus, writing near the end of the first century, says, "The vulgar call them Christians. The author or origin of this denomination, Christus, had, in the reign of Tiberius, been executed by the procurator, Pontius Pilate" (Annals xv. 44). From the second century onward the term was accepted by believers as a title of honor.

For **CHURCH** see ASSEMBLY and CONGREGATION

CIRCUMCISION, UNCIRCUMCISION, CIRCUMCISE

A. Nouns.

1. *peritomē* (περιτομή, 4061), lit., "a cutting round, circumcision" (the verb is *peritemnō*), was a rite enjoined by God upon Abraham and his male descendants and dependents, as a sign of the covenant made with him, Gen. 17; Acts 7:8; Rom. 4:11. Hence Israelites termed Gentiles "the uncircumcised," Judg. 15:18; 2 Sam. 1:20. So in the NT, but without the suggestion of contempt, e.g., Rom. 2:26; Eph. 2:11.

The rite had a moral significance, Ex. 6:12, 30, where it is metaphorically applied to the lips; so to the ear, Jer. 6:10, and the heart, Deut. 30:6; Jer. 4:4. Cf. Jer. 9:25-26. It refers to the state of "circumcision," in Rom. 2:25-28; 3:1; 4:10; 1 Cor. 7:19; Gal. 5:6; 6:15; Col. 3:11.

"In the economy of grace no account is taken of any ordinance performed on the flesh; the old racial distinction is ignored in the preaching of the gospel, and faith is the sole condition upon which the favor of God in salvation is to be obtained, Rom. 10:11-13; 1 Cor. 7:19. See also Rom. 4:9-12." From *Notes on Galatians,* by Hogg and Vine. p. 69.

Upon the preaching of the gospel to, and the conversion of, Gentiles, a sect of Jewish believers arose who argued that the gospel, without the fulfillment of "circumcision," would make void the Law and make salvation impossible, Acts 15:1. Hence this party was known as "the circumcision," Acts 10:45; 11:2; Gal. 2:12; Col. 4:11; Titus 1:10 (the term being used by metonymy, the abstract being put for the concrete, as with the application of the word to Jews generally, Rom. 3:30; 4:9, 12; 15:8; Gal. 2:7-9; Eph. 2:11). It is used metaphorically and spiritually of believers with reference to the act, Col. 2:11 and Rom. 2:29; to the condition, Phil. 3:3.

The apostle Paul's defense of the truth, and his contention against this propaganda, form the main subject of the Galatian epistle. Cf. *katatome*, "concision," Phil. 3:2. See CONCISION.

2. *akrobustia* (ἀκροβυστία, 203), "uncircumcision," is used (a) of the physical state, in contrast to the act of "circumcision," Acts 11:3 (lit., "having uncircumcision"); Rom. 2:25-26; 4:10-11 ("though they be in uncircumcision," RV), 12; 1 Cor. 7:18-19; Gal. 5:6; 6:15; Col. 3:11; (b) by metonymy, for Gentiles, e.g., Rom. 2:26-27; 3:30; 4:9; Gal. 2:7; Eph. 2:11; (d) in a metaphorical or transferred sense, of the moral condition in which the corrupt desires of the flesh still operate, Col. 2:13.

Note: In Rom. 4:11, the phrase "though they be in uncircumcision" translates the Greek phrase *di' akrobustias*, lit., "through uncircumcision"; here *dia* has the local sense of proceeding from and passing out.

B. Adjective.

aperitmētos (ἀπερίτμητος, 564), "uncircumcised" (*a*, negative, *peri*, "around," *temnō*, "to cut"), is used in Acts 7:51, metaphorically, of "heart and ears."

C. Verbs.

1. *peritemnō* (περιτέμνω, 4059), "to circumcise," is used (a) lit., e.g., Luke 1:59; 2:21; of receiving circumcision, Gal. 5:2-3; 6:13, RV; (b) metaphorically, of spiritual circumcision, Col. 2:11.

2. *epispaomai* (ἐπισπάομαι, 1986), lit., "to draw over, to become uncircumcised," as if to efface Judaism, appears in 1 Cor. 7:18.

CITIZEN, CITIZENSHIP

1. *politēs* (πολίτης, 4177), "a member of a city or state, or the inhabitant of a country or district," Luke 15:15, is used elsewhere in Luke 19:14; Acts 21:39, and, in the most authentic mss., in Heb. 8:11 (where some texts have *plēsion*, "a neighbor"). Apart from Heb. 8:11, the word occurs only in the writings of Luke (himself a Greek).

2. *sumpolitēs* (συμπολίτης, 4847), *sun*, "with," and No. 1, denotes "a fellow-citizen," i.e., possessing the same "citizenship," Eph. 2:19, used metaphorically in a spiritual sense.

3. *politeia* (πολιτεία, 4174) signifies (a) "the relation in which a citizen stands to the state, the condition of a citizen, citizenship," Acts 22:28, "with a great sum obtained I this citizenship" (KJV, "freedom"). While Paul's "citizenship" of Tarsus was not of advantagre outside that city, yet his Roman "citizenship" availed throughout the Roman Empire and, besides private rights, included (1) exemption from all degrading punishments; (2) a right of appeal to the emperor after a sentence; (3) a right to be sent to Rome for trial before the emperor if charged with a capital offense. Paul's father might have obtained "citizenship" (1) by manumission; (2) as a reward of merit; (3) by purchase; the contrast implied in Acts 22:28 is perhaps against the last mentioned; (b) "a civil polity, the condition of a state, a commonwealth," said of Israel, Eph. 2:12.

4. *politeuma* (πολίτευμα, 4175) signifies "the condition, or life, of a citizen, citizenship"; it is said of the heavenly status of believers, Phil. 3:20, "our citizenship (KJV, "conversation") is in Heaven." The RV marg. gives the alternative meaning, "commonwealth," i.e., community. See FREEDOM.

Note: Politeuō, Phil. 1:27, signifies "to be a *politēs*" (see No. 1), and is used in the middle voice, signifying, metaphorically, conduct characteristic of heavenly "citizenship," RV, "let your manner of life (KJV, "conversation") be worthy (marg., "behave as citizens worthily") of the gospel of Christ." In Acts 23:1 it is translated "I have lived." See LIVE.

CITY

polis (πόλις, 4172), primarily "a town enclosed with a wall" (perhaps from a root *plē-*, signifying "fullness," whence also the Latin *pleo*, "to fill," Eng., "polite, polish, politic, etc."), is used also of the heavenly Jerusalem, the abode and community of the redeemed, Heb. 11:10, 16; 12:22; 13:14. In the Apocalypse it signifies the visible capital of the heavenly kingdom, as destined to descend to earth in a coming age e.g., Rev. 3:12; 21:2, 14, 19. By metonymy the word stands for the inhabitants, as in the English use, e.g., Matt. 8:34; 12:25; 21:10; Mark 1:33; Acts 13:44.

Note: In Acts 16:13, the most authentic mss. have *pulē*, "gate," RV, "without the gate."

CLAY

pēlos (πηλός, 4081), "clay," especially such as was used by a mason or potter, is used of moist "clay," in John 9:6, 11, 14-15, in connection with Christ's healing the blind man; in Rom. 9:21, of potter's "clay," as to the potter's right over it as an illustration of the prerogatives of God in His dealings with men.

CLEAN, CLEANNESS, CLEANSE, CLEANSING

A. Adjective.

katharos (καθαρός, 2513), "free from impure admixture, without blemish, spotless," is used (a) physically, e.g., Matt. 23:26; 27:59; John 13:10 (where the Lord, speaking figuratively, teaches that one who has been entirely "cleansed," needs not radical renewal, but only to be "cleansed" from every sin into which he may fall); 15:3; Heb. 10:22; Rev. 15:6; 19:8, 14; 21:18, 21; (b) in a Levitical sense, Rom. 14:20; Titus 1:15, "pure"; (c) ethically, with the significance free from corrupt desire, from guilt, Matt. 5:8; John 13:10-11; Acts 20:26; 1 Tim. 1:5; 3:9; 2 Tim. 1:3; 2:22; Titus 1:15; Jas. 1:27; blameless, innocent (a rare meaning for this word), Acts 18:6; (d) in a combined Levitical and ethical sense ceremonially, Luke 11:41, "all things are clean unto you." See CLEAR, C, *Note* (2), PURE.

B. Verbs.

1. *katharizō* (καθαρίζω, 2511), akin to A, signifies (1) "to make clean, to cleanse" (a) from physical stains and dirt, as in the case of utensils, Matt. 23:25 (figuratively in verse 26); from disease, as of leprosy, Matt. 8:2; (b) in a moral sense, from the defilement of sin, Acts 15:9; 2 Cor. 7:1; Heb. 9:14; Jas. 4:8, "cleanse" from the guilt of sin, Eph. 5:26; 1 John 1:7; (2) "to pronounce clean in a Levitical sense," Mark 7:19, RV; Acts 10:15; 11:9; "to consecrate by cleansings," Heb. 9:22, 23; 10:2. See PURGE, PURIFY.

2. *diakatharizō* (διακαθαρίζω, 1245), "to cleanse thoroughly," is used in Matt. 3:12, RV.

Note: For *kathairō*, John 15:2, RV, see PURGE, No. 1. For *diakathairō*, Luke 3:17, RV, see PURGE, No. 3.

C. Nouns.

1. *katharismos* (καθαρισμός, 2512), akin to A, denotes "cleansing," (a) both the action and its results, in the Levitical sense, Mark 1:44; Luke 2:22, "purification"; 5:14, "cleansing"; John 2:6; 3:25, "purifying"; (b) in the moral sense, from sins, Heb. 1:3; 2 Pet. 1:9, RV, "cleansing. See PURGE, PURIFICATION, PURIFYING.

2. *katharotēs* (καθαρότης, 2514), akin to B, "cleanness, purity," is used in the Levitical sense in Heb. 9:13, RV, "cleanness." See PURIFY.

Note: In 2 Pet. 2:18, some inferior mss. have *ontōs*, "certainly" (KJV, "clean"), for *oligōs*, "scarcely" (RV, "just").

CLEAR, CLEARING, CLEARLY

A. Verb.

krustallizō (κρυσταλλίζω, 2929), "to shine like crystal, to be of crystalline brightness, or transparency," is found in Rev. 21:11, "clear as crystal." The verb may, however, have a transitive force, signifying "to crystallize or cause to become like crystal." In that case it would speak of Christ (since He is the

"Lightgiver," see the preceding part of the verse), as the One who causes the saints to shine in His own likeness.

B. Adjective.

lampros (λαμπρός, 2986) is said of crystal, Rev. 22:1, KJV, clear, RV, bright. See BRIGHT, GOODLY, GORGEOUS, WHITE.

Note: The corresponding adverb *lamprēs* signifies "sumptuously."

C. Adverb.

telaugōs (τηλαυγῶς, 5081), from *telē*, "afar," and *augē*, "radiance," signifies "conspicuously, or clearly," Mark 8:25, of the sight imparted by Christ to one who had been blind. Some mss. have *dēlaugōs*, "clearly" (*dēlos*, "clear").

Notes: (1) In 2 Cor. 7:11, KJV, *hagnos* is rendered "clear." See PURE. (2) In Rev. 21:18, *katharos*, ("pure," RV) is rendered "clear," in the KJV. SEE CLEAN. (3) *Apologia* (Eng., apology), "a defense against an accusation," signifies, in 2 Cor. 7:11, a clearing of oneself.

CLEAVE, CLAVE

1. *kollaō* (κολλάω, 2853), "to join fast together, to glue, cement," is primarily said of metals and other materials (from *kolla*, "glue"). In the NT it is used only in the passive voice, with reflexive force, in the sense of "cleaving unto," as of cleaving to one's wife, Matt. 19:5; some mss. have the intensive verb No. 2, here; 1 Cor. 6:16-17, "joined." In the corresponding passage in Mark 10:7, the most authentic mss. omit the sentence. In Luke 10:11 it is used of the "cleaving" of dust to the feet; in Acts 5:13; 8:29; 9:26; 10:28; 17:34, in the sense of becoming associated with a person so as to company with him, or be on his side, said, in the last passage, of those in Athens who believed: in Rom. 12:9, ethically, of "cleaving" to that which is good. See COMPANY.

2. *proskollaō* (προσκολλάω, 4347), in the passive voice, used reflexively, "to cleave unto," is found in Eph. 5:31 (KJV "joined to").

3. *prosmenō* (προσμένω, 4357), lit., "to abide with" (*pros*, "toward or with," and *menō*, "to abide"), is used of "cleaving" unto the Lord, Acts 11:23.

CLEMENCY

epieikeia (ἐπιείκεια, 1932), "mildness, gentleness, kindness" (what Matthew Arnold has called "sweet reasonableness"), is translated "clemency" in Acts 24:4; elsewhere, in 2 Cor. 10:1, of the gentleness of Christ. See GENTLENESS. Cf. *epieikēs* (see FORBEARANCE).

For **CLERK** see under TOWN CLERK

CLIMB UP

anabainō (ἀναβαίνω, 305), "to ascend," is used of climbing up, in Luke 19:4 and John 10:1. See ARISE.

CLOKE (Pretense)

1. *epikalumma* (ἐπικάλυμα, 1942) is "a covering, a means of hiding" (*epi*, "upon," *kaluptō*, "to cover"); hence, "a pretext, a cloke, for wickedness," 1 Pet. 2:16. In the Sept. it is used in Ex. 26:14; 39:21, "coverings"; 2 Sam. 17:19; Job 19:29, "deceit."

2. *prophasis* (πρόφασις, 4392), either from *pro*, "before," and *phainō*, "to cause to appear, shine," or, more probably, from *pro*, and *phēmi*, "to say," is rendered "cloke" (of covetousness) in 1 Thess. 2:5; "excuse" in John 15:22 (KJV "cloke"); "pretense" in Matt. 23:14; Mark 12:40; Luke 20:47 (KJV "show"); Phil. 1:18; "color" in Acts 27:30. It signifies the assuming of something so as to disguise one's real motives. See SHOW.

CLOKE (Garment). For the various words for garments see CLOTHING.

CLOSE (Verb)

1. *kammuō* (καμμύω, 2576), derived by syncope (i.e., shortening and assimilation of *t* to *m*) from *katamuō*, i.e., *kata*, "down," and *muō*, from a root *mu-*, pronounced by closing the lips, denotes "to close down"; hence, "to shut the eyes," Matt. 13:15 and Acts 28:27, in each place of the obstinacy of Jews in their opposition to the gospel.

2. *ptussō* (πτύσσω, 4428), "to fold, double up," is used of a scroll of parchment, Luke 4:20. Cf. *anaptussō*, "to open up," v. 17.

Notes: (1) For "close-sealed," Rev. 5:1, see SEAL.

(2) In Luke 9:36, *sigaō*, "to be silent," is translated "they kept it close," KJV (RV, "they held their peace").

For **CLOSET** see CHAMBER

CLOTH

rhakos (ῥάκος, 4470) denotes "a ragged garment, or a piece of cloth torn off, a rag"; hence, a piece of undressed "cloth," Matt. 9:16; Mark 2:21.

Note: For other words, *othonion, sindon*, See LINEN, Nos. 1 and 3.

CLOTHING, CLOTHS, CLOTHES, CLOKE, COAT

1. *phelonēs*, or *phailonēs* (φαιλόνης, 5341), probably by metathesis from *phainolēs* (Latin *paenula*), "a mantle," denotes a traveling "cloak" for protection against stormy weather, 2 Tim. 4:13. Some, however, regard it as a Cretan word for *chitōn*, "a tunic." It certainly was not an ecclesiastical vestment. The Syriac renders it a case for writings (some regard it as a book-cover), an explanation noted by Chrysostom, but improbable. It may have been "a light mantle like a cashmere dust-cloak, in which the books and parchments were wrapped" (Mackie in *Hastings' Dic. of the Bible*).

2. *himation* (ἱμάτιον, 2440), "an outer garment, a mantle, thrown over the *chitōn*" In the plural, "clothes" (the "cloke" and the tunic), e.g., Matt. 17:2; 26:65; 27:31, 35.

3. *chitōn* (χιτών, 5509) denotes "the inner vest or undergarment," and is to be distinguished, as such, from the *himation*. The distinction is made, for instance, in the Lord's command in Matt. 5:40: "If any man would go to law with thee, and take away thy coat (*chitōn*), (*himation*) also." The order is reversed in Luke 6:29, and the difference lies in this, that in Matt. 5:40 the Lord is referring to a legal process, so the claimant is supposed to claim the inner garment, the less costly. The defendant is to be willing to let him have the more valuable one too. In the passage in Luke an act of violence is in view, and there is no mention of going to law. So the outer garment is the first one which would be seized.

When the soldiers had crucified Jesus they took His garments (*himation*, in the plural), His outer garments, and the "coat," the *chitōn*, the inner garment, which was without seam, woven from the top throughout, John 19:23. The outer garments were easily divisible among the four soldiers, but they could not divide the *chitōn* without splitting it, so they cast lots for it.

Dorcas was accustomed to make coats (*chitōn*) and garments (*himation*), Acts 9:39, that is, the close fitting undergarments and the long, flowing outer robes.

A person was said to be "naked" (*gumnos*), whether he was without clothing, or had thrown off his outer garment, e.g., his *ependutēs*, (No. 6, below), and was clad in a light undergarment, as was the case with Peter, in John 21:7. The high priest, in rending his clothes after the reply the Lord gave him in answer to his challenge, rent his undergarments (*chitōn*), the more forcibly to express his assumed horror and indignation, Mark 14:63. In Jude 23, "the garment spotted by the flesh" is the *chitōn*, the metaphor of the undergarment being appropriate; for it would be that which was brought into touch with the pollution of the flesh.

4. *himatismos* (ἱματισμός, 2441), in form a collective word, denoting "vesture, garments," is used generally of "costly or stately raiment," the apparel of kings, of officials, etc. See Luke 7:25, where "gorgeously apparelled" is, lit., "in gorgeous vesture." See also Acts 20:33 and 1 Tim. 2:9, "costly raiment." This is the word used of the Lord's white and dazzling raiment on the Mount of Transfiguration, Luke 9:29. It is also used of His *chiton*, His undergarment (see note above), for which the soldiers cast lots, John 19:23-24, "vesture"; in Matt. 27:35 it is also translated vesture. See RAIMENT, VESTURE.

5. *enduma* (ἔνδυμα, 1742), akin to *enduō*, denotes "anything put on, a garment of any kind." It was used of the clothing of ancient prophets, in token of their contempt of earthly splendor, 1 Kings 19:13; 2 Kings 1:8, RV; Zech. 13:4. In the NT it is similarly used of John the Baptist's raiment, Matt. 3:4: of raiment in general, Matt. 6:25, 28; Luke 12:23; metaphorically, of sheep's clothing, Matt. 7:15; of a wedding garment, 22:11-12; of the raiment of the angel at the tomb of the Lord after His resurrection, 28:3. See GARMENT, RAIMENT.

6. *ependutēs* (ἐπενδύτης, 1903) denotes "an upper garment" (*epi*, "upon," *enduō*, "to clothe"). The word is found in John 21:7, where it apparently denotes a kind of linen frock, which fishermen wore when at their work. See No. 3.

7. *esthēs* (ἐσθής, 2066), "clothing," Acts 10:30.

8. *stolē* (στολή, 4749), (Eng., "stole"), denotes any "stately robe," a long garment reaching to the feet or with a train behind. It is used of the long clothing in which the scribes walked, making themselves conspicuous in the eyes of men, Mark 12:38; Luke 20:46; of the robe worn by the young man in the Lord's tomb, Mark 16:5; of the best or, rather, the chief robe, which was brought out for the returned prodigal, Luke 15:22; five times in the Apocalypse, as to glorified saints, 6:11; 7:9, 13-14; 22:14. In the Sept. it is used of the holy garments of the priests, e.g., Exod. 28:2; 29:21; 31:10.

Notes: (1) *Peribolaion*, from *periballō*, "to throw around," lit., "that which is thrown around," was a wrap or mantle. It is used in 1 Cor. 11:15, of the hair of a woman which is given to her as a veil; in Heb. 1:12, of the earth and the heavens, which the Lord will roll up "as a mantle," RV, for KJV, "vesture." The other word in that verse rendered "garment," RV, is *himation*.

(2) *Endusis*, is "a putting on (of apparel)," 1 Pet. 3:3. Cf. No. 5.

(3) *Esthēsis*.

(4) The *chlamus* was a short "cloak" or robe, worn over the *chitōn* (No. 3), by emperors, kings, magistrates, military officers, etc. It is used of the scarlet robe with which Christ was arrayed in mockery by the soldiers in Pilate's Judgment Hall, Matt. 27:28, 31.

What was known as purple was a somewhat indefinite color. There is nothing contradictory about its being described by Mark and John as "purple," though Matthew speaks of it as "scarlet." The soldiers put it on the Lord in mockery of His Kingship.

(5) The *podērēs* was another sort of outer garment, reaching to the feet (from *pous*, "the foot," and *arō*, "to fasten"). It was one of the garments of the high priests, a robe (Hebrew, *chetoneth*), mentioned after the ephod in Exod. 28:4, etc. It is used in Ezek. 9:2, where instead of "linen" the Sept. reads "a long robe"; and in Zech. 3:4, "clothe ye him with a long robe"; in the NT in Rev. 1:13, of the long garment in which the Lord is seen in vision amongst the seven golden lampstands. There, *podērēs* is described as "a garment down to the feet," indicative of His High Priestly character and acts.

CLOUD

1. *nephos* (νέφος, 3509) denotes "a cloudy, shapeless mass covering the heavens." Hence, metaphorically, of "a dense multitude, a throng," Heb. 12:1.

2. *nephelē* (νεφέλη, 3507), "a definitely shaped cloud, or masses of clouds possessing definite form," is used, besides the physical element, (a) of the "cloud" on the mount of transfiguration, Matt. 17:5; (b) of the "cloud" which covered Israel in the Red Sea, 1 Cor. 10:1-2; (c), of "clouds" seen in the Apocalyptic visions, Rev. 1:7; 10:1; 11:12; 14:14-16; (d) metaphorically in 2 Pet. 2:17, of the evil workers there mentioned; but RV, "and mists" (*homichlē*), according to the most authentic mss.

In 1 Thess. 4:17, the "clouds" referred to in connection with the rapture of the saints are probably the natural ones, as also in the case of those in connection with Christ's second advent to the earth. See Matt. 24:30; 26:64, and parallel passages. So at the Ascension, Acts 1:9.

COALS

1. *anthrax* (ἄνθραξ, 440), "a burning coal" (cf. Eng., "anthracite,") is used in the plural in Rom. 12:20, metaphorically in a proverbial expression, "thou shalt heap coals of fire on his head" (from Prov. 25:22), signifying retribution by kindness, i.e., that, by conferring a favor on your enemy, you recall the wrong he has done to you, so that he repents, with pain of heart.

2. *anthrakia* (ἀνθρακιά, 439), akin to No. 1, is "a heap of burning coals, or a charcoal fire," John 18:18; 21:9.

For **COAT** (*ependeutes*) see CLOTHING

COCK, COCK-CROWING

1. *alektōr* (ἀλέκτωρ, 220), "a cock," perhaps connected with a Hebrew phrase for the oncoming of the light, is found in the passages concerning Peter's denial of the Lord, Matt. 26:34, 74-75; Mark 14:30, 68, 72; Luke 22:34, 60-61; John 13:38; 18:27.

2. *alektorophōnia* (ἀλεκτοροφωνία, 219) denotes "cock-crowing" (*alektōr*, and *phonē*, "a sound"), Mark 13:35. There were two "cockcrowings," one after midnight, the other before dawn. In these watches the Jews followed the Roman method of dividing the night. The first "cock-crowing" was at the third watch of the night. That is the one mentioned in Mark 13:35. Mark mentions both; see 14:30. The latter, the second, is that referred to in the other Gospels and is mentioned especially as "the cock-crowing."

COLD

A. Noun.

psuchos (ψύχος, 5592), "coldness, cold," appears in John 18:18; Acts 28:2; 2 Cor. 11:27.

B. Adjective.

psuchros (ψυχρός, 5593), "cool, fresh, cold, chilly" (fuller in expression than *psuchos*), is used in the natural sense in Matt. 10:42, "cold water"; metaphorically in Rev. 3:15-16.

C. Verb.

psuchō (ψύχω, 5594), "to breathe, blow, cool by blowing," passive voice, "grow cool," is used metaphorically in Matt. 24:12, in the sense of waning zeal or love.

COMELINESS, COMELY

A. Noun.

euschēmosunē (εὐσχημοσύνη, 2157), "elegance of figure, gracefulness, comeliness" (*eu*, "well," *schēma*, "a form"), is found in this sense in 1 Cor. 12:23.

B. Adjective.

euschēmōn (εὐσχήμων, 2158), akin to A, "elegant in figure, well formed, graceful," is used in 1 Cor. 12:24, of parts of the body (see above); in 1 Cor. 7:35 RV, "(that which is) seemly," KJV, "comely"; "honourable," Mark 15:43; Acts 13:50; 17:12. See HONORABLE.

Note: In 1 Cor. 11:13, *prepō*, "to be becoming," is rendered in the KJV, "is it comely?" RV, "is it seemly?" See BECOME, SEEMLY.

COMFORT, COMFORTER, COMFORTLESS

A. Nouns.

1. *paraklēsis* (παράκλησις, 3874), means "a calling to one's side" (*para*, "beside," *kaleō*, "to call"); hence, either "an exhortation, or consolation, comfort," e.g., Luke 2:25 (here "looking for the consolation of Israel" is equivalent to waiting for the coming of the Messiah); 6:24; Acts 9:31; Rom. 15:4-5; 1 Cor. 14:3, "exhortation"; 2 Cor. 1:3, 4-7; 7:4, 7, 13; 2 Thess. 2:16; Philem. 7. In 2 Thess. 2:16 it combines encouragement with alleviation of grief. The RV changes "consolation" into "comfort," except in Luke 2:25; 6:24; Acts 15:31; in Heb. 6:18, "encouragement"; in Acts 4:36, "exhortation." RV (KJV, consolation"). See CONSOLATION, ENCOURAGEMENT, EXHORTATION, INTREATY.

2. *paramuthia* (παραμυθία, 3889), primarily "a speaking closely to anyone" (*para*, "near," *muthos*, "speech"), hence denotes "consolation, comfort," with a greater degree of tenderness than No. 1, 1 Cor. 14:3.

3. *paramuthion* (παραμύθιον, 3890) has the same meaning as No. 2, the difference being that *paramuthia* stresses the

process or progress of the act, *paramuthion* the instrument as used by the agent, Phil. 2:1.

4. *parēgoria* (παρηγορία, 3931), primarily "an addressing, address," hence denotes "a soothing, solace," Col. 4:11. A verbal form of the word signifies medicines which allay irritation (Eng., "paregoric").

5. *paraklētos* (παράκλητος, 3875), lit., "called to one's side," i.e., to one's aid, is primarily a verbal adjective, and suggests the capability or adaptability for giving aid. It was used in a court of justice to denote a legal assistant, counsel for the defense, an advocate; then, generally, one who pleads another's cause, an intercessor, advocate, as in 1 John 2:1, of the Lord Jesus. In the widest sense, it signifies a "succorer, comforter." Christ was this to His disciples, by the implication of His word "another (*allos*, "another of the same sort," not *heteros*, "different") Comforter," when speaking of the Holy Spirit, John 14:16. In 14:26; 15:26; 16:7 He calls Him "the Comforter." "Comforter" or "Consoler" corresponds to the name "*Menahem*," given by the Hebrews to the Messiah.

B. Verbs.

1. *parakaleō* (παρακαλέω, 3870) has the same variety of meanings as Noun, No. 1, above, e.g., Matt. 2:18; 1 Thess. 3:2, 7; 4:18. In 2 Cor. 13:11, it signifies "to be comforted" (so the RV).

2. *sumparakaleō* (συμπαρακαλέω, 4837), *sun*, "with," and No. 1, signifies "to comfort together," Rom. 1:12.

3. *paramutheomai* (παραμυθέομαι, 3888), akin to Noun No. 2, "to soothe, console, encourage," is translated, in John 11:31, "comforted," in v. 19, RV, "console." In 1 Thess. 2:11 and 5:14, RV, "encourage," as the sense there is that of stimulating to the earnest discharge of duties. See CONSOLE, ENCOURAGE.

4. *eupsucheō* (εὐψυχέω, 2174) signifies "to be of good comfort" (*eu*, "well," *psuchē*, "the soul"), Phil. 2:19.

Notes: (1) For the verb *tharseō*, "be of good comfort," see CHEER, No. 2. (2) *Orphanos* is rendered "comfortless" in John 14:18, KJV; RV, desolate. See DESOLATE, FATHERLESS.

COMING (Noun)

1. *eisodos* (εἴσοδος, 1529), "an entrance" (*eis*, "in," *hodos*, "a way"), "an entering in," is once translated "coming," Acts 13:24, of the coming of Christ into the nation of Israel. For its meaning "entrance" see 1 Thess. 1:9; 2:1; Heb. 10:19; 2 Pet. 1:11.

2. *eleusis* (ἔλευσις, 1660), "a coming" (from *erchomai*, "to come"), is found in Acts 7:52.

3. *parousia* (παρουσία, 3952), lit., "a presence," *para*, "with," and *ousia*, "being" (from *eimi*, "to be"), denotes both an "arrival" and a consequent "presence with." For instance, in a papyrus letter a lady speaks of the necessity of her parousia in a place in order to attend to matters relating to her property there. Paul speaks of his *parousia* in Philippi, Phil. 2:12 (in contrast to his *apousia*, "his absence"; see ABSENCE). Other words denote "the arrival" (see *eisodos* and *eleusis*, above). *Parousia* is used to describe the presence of Christ with His disciples on the Mount of Transfiguration, 2 Pet. 1:16. When used of the return of Christ, at the rapture of the church, it signifies, not merely His momentary "coming" for His saints, but His presence with them from that moment until His revelation and manifestation to the world. In some passages the word gives prominence to the beginning of that period, the course of the period being implied, 1 Cor. 15:23; 1 Thess. 4:15; 5:23; 2 Thess. 2:1; Jas. 5:7-8; 2 Pet. 3:4. In some, the course is prominent, Matt. 24:3, 37; 1 Thess. 3:13; 1 John 2:28; in others the conclusion of the period, Matt. 24:27; 2 Thess. 2:8.

The word is also used of the Lawless One, the Man of Sin, his access to power and his doings in the world during his *parousia*, 2 Thess. 2:9. In addition to Phil. 2:12 (above), it is used in the same way of the apostle, or his companions, in 1 Cor. 16:17; 2 Cor. 7:6-7; 10:10; Phil. 1:26; of the Day of God, 2 Pet. 3:12. See PRESENCE.

Note: The word *apokalupsis*, rendered "coming" in 1 Cor. 1:7, KJV, denotes a "revelation" (RV). For a fuller treatment of *Parousia*, see *Notes on Thessalonians,* by Hogg and Vine, pp. 87-88.

COMMAND (Verbs)

1. *diatassō* (διατάσσω, 1299) signifies "to set in order, appoint, command," Matt. 11:1; Luke 8:55; 17:9-10; Acts 18:2; 23:31; "gave order," 1 Cor. 16:1, RV. So in Acts 24:23, where it is in the middle voice. See APPOINT, No. 6.

2. *epō* (ἔπω, 2036) denotes "to speak" (connected with eipon, "to say"); hence, among various renderings, "to bid, command," Matt. 4:3; Mark 5:43; 8:7; Luke 4:3; 19:15. See BID.

Note: In 2 Cor. 4:6, the RV rightly has "said," followed by the quotation "Light shall shine out of darkness."

3. *entello* (ἐντέλλομαι, 1781) signifies "to enjoin upon, to charge with"; it is used in the Middle Voice in the sense of commanding, Matt. 19:7; 28:20; Mark 10:3; 13:34; John 8:5; 15:14, 17; Acts 13:47; Heb. 9:20; 11:22, "gave commandment."

4. *epitassō* (ἐπιτάσσω, 2004) signifies to appoint over, put in charge (*epi*, "over," *tassō*, "to appoint"); then, "to put upon one as a duty, to enjoin," Mark 1:27; 6:27, 39; 9:25; Luke 4:36; 8:25, 31; 14:22; Acts 23:2; Philem. 8.

5. *keleuo* (κελεύω, 2753), "to urge, incite, order," suggests a stronger injunction than No. 6, Matt. 14:9, 19; 15:35; 18:25; 27:58, 64; Luke 18:40; Acts 4:15 (frequently in Acts, not subsequently in the NT). See BID.

6. *parangellō* (παραγγέλλω, 3853), "to announce beside" (*para*, "beside," *angellō*, "to announce"), "to pass on an announcement," hence denotes "to give the word, order, give a charge, command," e.g., Mark 6:8; Luke 8:29; 9:21; Acts 5:28; 2 Thess. 3:4, 6, 10, 12.

7. *prostassō* (προστάσσω, 4367) denotes "to arrange or set in order towards" (*pros*, "towards," *tassō*, "to arrange"); hence "to prescribe, give command," Matt. 1:24; 8:4; Mark 1:44; Luke 5:14; Acts 10:33, 48. For Matt. 21:6 see *Note* (3) below. See BID.

Notes: (1) In Rev. 9:4, *rheō*, "to speak," is translated "said" in the RV (KJV, "commanded"). (2) in Heb. 12:20 *diastellomai*, "to charge, enjoin" (so in the RV), is rendered "commanded" in the KJV. (3) in Matt. 21:6, the RV, translating *suntassō*, as in the best mss., has "appointed," KJV, "commanded."

COMMANDMENT

1. *diatagma* (διάταγμα, 1297) signifies "that which is imposed by decree or law," Heb. 11:23. It stresses the concrete character of the "commandment" more than *epitagē* (No. 4). Cf. COMMAND, No. 1. For the verb in v. 22 see No. 3 under COMMAND.

2. *entolē* (ἐντολή, 1785), akin to No. 3, above, denotes, in general, "an injunction, charge, precept, commandment." It is the most frequent term, and is used of moral and religious precepts, e.g., Matt. 5:19; it is frequent in the Gospels, especially that of John, and in his Epistles. See also, e.g., Acts 17:15; Rom. 7:8-13; 13:9; 1 Cor. 7:19; Eph. 2:15; Col. 4:10. See PRECEPT.

3. *entalma* (ἔνταλμα, 1778), akin to No. 2, marks more especially "the thing commanded, a commission"; in Matt. 15:9; Mark 7:7; Col. 2:22, RV, "precepts," KJV, "commandments." See PRECEPT.

4. *epitagē* (ἐπιταγή, 2003), akin to No. 4, above, stresses "the authoritativeness of the command"; it is used in Rom. 16:26; 1 Cor. 7:6, 25; 2 Cor. 8:8; 1 Tim. 1:1; Tit. 1:3; 2:15.

Note: In Rev. 22:14 the RV, "wash their robes" (for KJV, "do His commandments") follows the most authentic mss.

COMMEND, COMMENDATION

A. Verbs.

1. *epaineō* (ἐπαινέω, 1867), "to praise," is an intensive form of *aineō*, Luke 16:8. It is elsewhere translated by the verb "to praise," in the RV, Rom. 15:11; 1 Cor. 11:2, 17, 22. See PRAISE.

2. *paradidōmi* (παραδίδωμι, 3860), lit., to give or deliver over" (*para*, "over" *didōmi*, "to give"), is said of "commending," or "committing," servants of God to Him (KJV, "recommend), Acts 14:26; 15:40. See BETRAY, DELIVER, GIVE, RECOMMEND.

3. *paratithēmi* (παρατίθημι, 3908), lit., "to put near" (*para*, "near"), in the Middle Voice, denotes "to place with someone, entrust, commit." In the sense of commending, it is said (a) of the Lord Jesus in "commending" His spirit into the Father's hands, Luke 23:46; (b) of "commending" disciples to God, Acts 14:23; (c) of "commending" elders to God, Acts 20:32. Cf. No.2.

4. *paristēmi* (παρίστημι, 3936), lit., "to place near, set before," (*para*, "near," *histēmi*, "to set"), is used of "self-commendation," 1 Cor. 8:8. See PRESENT, PROVE, PROVIDE, SHOW, YIELD.

5. *sunistēmi* (συνίστημι, 4921), or *sunistanō* (συνιστάω, 4921), lit., "to place together," denotes "to introduce one person to another, represent as worthy," e.g., Rom. 3:5; 5:8; 16:1; 2 Cor. 4:2; 6:4; 10:18; 12:11. In 2 Cor. 3:1; 5:12 and 10:12, the verb *sunistanō* is used. See CONSIST.

B. Adjective.

sustatikos (συστατικός, 4956), akin to A, No. 5, lit., "placing together," hence, "commendatory," is used of letters of "commendation," 2 Cor. 3:1, lit., "commendatory letters."

COMMON, COMMONLY

A. Adjective.

koinos (κοινός, 2839) denotes (a) "common, belonging to several" (Lat., *communis*), said of things had in common, Acts 2:44; 4:32; of faith, Titus 1:4; of salvation, Jude 3; it stands in contrast to *idios*, "one's own"; (b) "ordinary, belonging to the generality, as distinct from what is peculiar to the few," hence the application to religious practices of Gentiles in contrast with those of Jews; or of the ordinary people in contrast with those of the Pharisees; hence the meaning "unhallowed, profane," Levitically unclean (Lat., *profanus*), said of hands, Mark 7:2 (KJV, "defiled,") RV marg., "common"; of animals, ceremonially unclean, Acts 10:14; 11:8; of a man, 10:28; of meats, Rom. 14:14, "unclean"; of the blood of the covenant, as viewed by an apostate, Heb. 10:29, "unholy" (RV, marg., "common"); of everything unfit for the holy city, Rev. 21:27, RV, "unclean" (marg., "common"). Some mss. have the verb here. See DEFILE, UNCLEAN, UNHOLY.

B. Verb.

koinoō (κοινόω, 2840), "to make, or count, common," has this meaning in Acts 10:15; 11:9. See DEFILE, POLLUTE, UNCLEAN.

Notes: (1) *Polus*, used of number, signifies "many, numerous"; used of space, it signifies "wide, far reaching"; hence, with the article it is said of a multitude as being numerous; it is translated "common" (people) in Mark 12:37 (see the RV, marg.). It does not, however, mean the ordinary folk, but the many folk. See ABUNDANT, GREAT, LONG.

(2) *Ochlos* denotes "a crowd, a great multitude"; with the article it is translated "the common people," in John 12:9, 12 (RV, marg.). See COMPANY, CROWD, MULTITUDE, PEOPLE, PRESS.

(3) *Tunchanō*, "to happen," is used as an adjective in Acts 28:2, of the kindness shown by the people of Melita to the shipwrecked company; KJV, "(no) little"; RV, "(no) common"; the idea suggested by the verb is that which might happen anywhere or at all times; hence, "little, ordinary, or casual." See ENJOY.

(4) In Matt. 27:27, what the KJV describes as "the common hall," is the praetorium, RV, "palace," the official residence of the Governor of a Province (marg., "praetorium").

(5) In Acts 5:18, *dēmosios* (KJV, "common," with reference to the prison) signifies "public," belonging to the people, *demos*, (RV, "public").

(6) In 1 Cor. 5:1, *holōs*, "altogether" (KJV, "commonly") means "actually" (RV).

(7) In Matt. 28:15, *diaphēmizō*, "to spread abroad" (as in the RV), is rendered in the KJV, "is commonly reported.

For **COMMOTION** see CONFUSION, TUMULT

COMMUNE

1. *dialaleō* (διαλαλέω, 1255) signifies "to speak with anyone" (*dia*, "by turns," *laleo*, "to speak"), Luke 6:11; in 1:65, "to talk over, to noise abroad." The idea that *laleo* and its compounds bear no reference to the word spoken or the sentiment, is unfounded.

2. *homileō* (ὁμιλέω, 3656), from *homos*, "together," signifies "to be in company, to associate with any one"; hence, "to have intercourse with," Luke 24:14 (RV, "communed"; KJV, "talked"), 15; Acts 24:26; in 20:11, "talked with. See TALK.

3. *sullaleō* (συλλαλέω, 4814), "to talk together," is translated "communed" in Luke 22:4, of the conspiracy of Judas with the chief priests. See CONFER, TALK.

Note: Laleō and its compounds, and the noun *lalia*, "speech," have a more dignified meaning in the Hellenistic Greek than "to chatter," its frequent meaning in earlier times.

COMMUNICATE, COMMUNICATION

A. Verbs.

1. *koinoneō* (κοινωνέω, 2841) is used in two senses, (a) "to have a share in," Rom. 15:27; 1 Tim. 5:22; Heb. 2:14; 1 Pet. 4:13; 2 John 11; (b) "to give a share to, go shares with," Rom. 12:13, RV, "communicating," for KJV, "distributing"; Gal. 6:6, "communicate"; Phil. 4:15, KJV, "did communicate," RV, "had fellowship with." See FELLOWSHIP, PARTAKE.

2. *sunkoinōneō* (συγκοινωνέω, 4790), "to share together with" (*sun* "and" No. 1), is translated "communicated with" in Phil. 4:14; "have fellowship with," Eph. 5:11; "be ... partakers of," Rev. 18:4 (RV, "have fellowship"). The thought is that of sharing with others what one has, in order to meet their needs. See FELLOWSHIP, B, No. 2, PARTAKE, B, No. 2.

Note: Anatithēmi, "to set forth," is rendered "laid before" in Gal. 2:2, RV, for KJV, "communicated unto"; in Acts 25:14, RV, "laid before," for KJV, "declared."

B. Nouns.

1. *koinōnia* (κοινωνία, 2842), akin to A (which see), is translated in Heb. 13:16 "to communicate," lit., "be not forgetful of good deed and of fellowship"; "fellowship" (KJV, "communication") in Philem. 6, RV. See COMMUNION.

2. *logos* (λόγος, 3056), "a word, that which is spoken" (*legō*, "to speak"), is used in the plural with reference to a conversation; "communication," Luke 24:17. Elsewhere with this significance the RV renders it "speech," Matt. 5:37; Eph. 4:29.

Note: In Col. 3:8, where the KJV translates *aischrologia* by "filthy communication," the RV renders it "shameful speaking" (*aischros*, "base," *legō*, "to speak").

C. Adjective.

koinōnikos (κοινωνικός, 2843), akin to A, No. 1 and B, No. 1, means "apt, or ready, to communicate," 1 Tim. 6:18.

Note: Homilia, "a company, association, or intercourse with" (see COMMUNE, No. 2), is translated "company" in 1 Cor. 15:33, RV (KJV, "communications"); the word is in the plural, "evil companies," i.e., associations. See COMPANY, No. 6.

COMMUNION

A. Noun.

koinōnia (κοινωνία, 2842), "a having in common (*koinos*), partnership, fellowship" (see COMMUNICATE), denotes (a) the share which one has in anything, a participation, fellowship recognized and enjoyed; thus it is used of the common experiences and interests of Christian men, Acts 2:42; Gal. 2:9; of participation in the knowledge of the Son of God, 1 Cor. 1:9; of sharing in the realization of the effects of the blood (i.e., the death) of Christ and the body of Christ, as set forth by the emblems in the Lord's Supper, 1 Cor. 10:16; of participation in what is derived from the Holy Spirit, 2 Cor. 13:14 (RV, "communion"); Phil. 2:1; of participation in the sufferings of Christ, Phil. 3:10; of sharing in the resurrection life possessed in Christ, and so of fellowship with the Father and the Son, 1 John 1:3, 6-7; negatively, of the impossibility of "communion" between light and darkness, 2 Cor. 6:14; (b) fellowship manifested in acts, the practical effects of fellowship with God, wrought by the Holy Spirit in the lives of believers as the outcome of faith, Philem. 6, and finding expression in joint ministration to the needy, Rom. 15:26; 2 Cor. 8:4; 9:13;

Heb. 13:16, and in the furtherance of the Gospel by gifts, Phil. 1:5. See COMMUNICATION, CONTRIBUTION, FELLOWSHIP.

B. Adjective.

koinōnos (κοινωνός, 2844), "having in common," is rendered "have communion with (the altar),"—the altar standing by metonymy for that which is associated with it—in 1 Cor. 10:18, RV (for KJV, "are partakers of"), and in v. 20, for KJV, "have fellowship with (demons)." See COMPANION.

COMPACTED

1. *sunistēmi* (συνίστημι, 4921), and transitively *sunistaō*, "to stand together" (*sun*, "with," *histēmi*, "to stand"), is rendered "compacted," in 2 Pet. 3:5, of the earth as formerly arranged by God in relation to the waters. See COMMEND, CONSIST.

2. *sumbibazō* (συμβιβάζω, 4822), "to unite, to knit," is translated "compacted" in the KJV of Eph. 4:16 (RV, "knit together"), concerning the church as the body of Christ. See CONCLUDE, GATHER, INSTRUCT, PROVE.

COMPANION

1. *sunekdēmos* (συνέκδημος, 4898), "a fellow-traveler" (*sun*, "with," *ek*, "from," *dēmos*, "people"; i.e., "away from one's people"), is used in Acts 19:29, of Paul's companions in travel, in 2 Cor. 8:19, "travel with"; a closer rendering would be "(as) our fellow-traveler." See TRAVEL.

2. *koinōnos* (κοινωνός, 2844) is rendered "companions" in the KJV of Heb. 10:33 (RV "partakers"). So *sunkoinōnos* in Rev. 1:9, KJV, "companion"; RV, "partaker with you." See B, above, PARTAKER, PARTNER. Cf. COMMUNICATE.

3. *sunergos* (συνεργός, 4904), "a fellowworker" (*sun*, "with," *ergon*, "work"), is translated in Phil. 2:25 "companion in labor," KJV (RV, fellow-worker). See HELPER, LABORER.

COMPANY (Noun and Verb)

A. Nouns and Phrases.

1. *ochlos* (ὄχλος, 3793), "a throng of people, an irregular crowd," most usually "a disorganized throng"; in Acts 6:7, however, it is said of a company of the priests who believed; the word here indicates that they had not combined to bring this about. The RV usually translates this word "company" or "multitude." Cf. B, *Note* 3. See COMMON, CROWD, MULTITUDE, and Trench, *Syn.* Sec. XCVIII.

2. *sunodia* (συνοδία, 4923), lit., "a way or journey together" (*sun*, "with," *hodos*, "a way"), denotes, by metonymy, "a company of travelers"; in Luke 2:44, of the company from which Christ was missed by Joseph and Mary. (Eng., synod).

3. *sumposion* (συμπόσιον, 4849), lit. "denotes a drinking together (*sun*, "with," *pinō*, "to drink"), a drinking-party"; hence, by metonymy, "any table party or any company arranged as a party." In Mark 6:39 the noun is repeated, in the plural, by way of an adverbial and distributive phrase, *sumposia sumposia*, lit., "companies-companies" (i.e., by companies).

4. *klisia* (κλισία, 2828), akin to *klinō*, to recline," primarily means "a place for lying down in, and hence a reclining company," for the same purpose as No. 3. It is found in the plural in Luke 9:14, corresponding to Mark's word *sumposia* (No. 3, above), signifying "companies reclining at a meal."

5. *plēthos* (πλῆθος, 4128), lit., "a fullness," hence denotes "a multitude, a large or full company," Luke 23:1; "a multitude," v. 27 (KJV, "a great company). See BUNDLE, MULTITUDE.

6. *homilia* (ὁμιλία, 3657), "an association of people, those who are of the same company" (*homos*, "same"), is used in 1 Cor. 15:33, KJV, "(evil) communications"; RV, "(evil) company."

7. *homilos* (ὅμιλος, 3658), akin to No. 6, "a throng or crowd," is found, in some mss., in Rev. 18:17, "all the company in ships," KJV. *Homilos* denotes the concrete; *homilia* is chiefly an abstract noun.

8. *idios* (ἴδιος, 2398), "one's own," is used in the plural with the article in Acts 4:23, to signify "their own (company)."

Notes: (1) The preposition *ex* (i.e., *ek*), "of," with the first personal pronoun in the genitive plural (*hēmōn*, "us"); signifies "of our company," lit., "of us," in Luke 24:22; so *ex autōn*, in Acts 15:22, "men out of their company," lit., "men out of them." (2) The phrase in Acts 13:13, *hoi peri Paulon*, lit., "the (ones) about Paul," signifies "Paul and his company." (3) *Murias*, a noun connected with the adjective *murios* ("numberless, infinite"), signifies "a myriad" (whence the English word), and is used hyperbolically, of vast numbers, e.g., Heb. 12:22, KJV, "an innumerable company"; RV, "innumerable hosts." (Contrast *murioi*, 10,000, Matt. 18:24). (4) In Acts 21:8, the phrase translated "that were of Paul's company" is absent from the best texts.

B. Verbs.

1. *sunanamignumi* (συναναμίγνυμι, 4874), lit., "to mix up with" (*sun*, "with," *ana*, "up," *mignumi*, "to mix, mingle"), signifies "to have, or keep, company with," 1 Cor. 5:9, 11; 2 Thess. 3:14.

2. *sunerchomai* (συνέρχομαι, 4905), "to come, or go, with," is rendered "have companied" in Acts 1:21.

Notes: (1) *Aphorizō*, "to separate," is translated "separate (you) from (their) company," in Luke 6:22, the latter part being added in italics to supply the meaning of excommunication.

(2) *Kollaō*, "to join," is rendered "keep company," in Acts 10:28, KJV; RV, "join himself." See CLEAVE.

(3) *Ochlopoieō*, lit., "to make a crowd" (*ochlos*, "a crowd," *poieō*, "to make"), is translated "gathered a company," in Acts

17:5, KJV; the RV corrects this to "gathering a crowd." See CROWD.

COMPASSION, COMPASSIONATE

A. Verbs.

1. *oikteirō* (οἰκτείρω, 3627), "to have pity, a feeling of distress through the ills of others," is used of God's compassion, Rom. 9:15.

2. *splanchnizomai* (σπλαγχνίζομαι, 4697), "to be moved as to one's inwards (*splanchna*), to be moved with compassion, to yearn with compassion," is frequently recorded of Christ towards the multitude and towards individual sufferers, Matt. 9:36; 14:14; 15:32; 18:27; 20:34; Mark 1:41; 6:34; 8:2; 9:22 (of the appeal of a father for a demon-possessed son); Luke 7:13; 10:33; of the father in the parable of the Prodigal Son, 15:20. (Moulton and Milligan consider the verb to have been coined in the Jewish dispersion).

3. *sumpatheō* (συμπαθέω, 4834), "to suffer with another (*sun*, 'with,' *paschō*, 'to suffer'), to be affected similarly" (Eng., "sympathy"), to have "compassion" upon, Heb. 10:34, of "compassionating" those in prison, is translated "be touched with" in Heb. 4:15, of Christ as the High Priest. See TOUCH.

4. *eleeō* (ἐλεέω, 1653), "to have mercy (*eleos*, "mercy"), to show kindness, by beneficence, or assistance," is translated "have compassion" in Matt. 18:33 (KJV); Mark 5:19 and Jude 22. See MERCY.

5. *metriopatheō* (μετριοπαθέω, 3356) is rendered "have compassion," in Heb. 5:2, KJV.

B. Nouns.

1. *oiktirmos* (οἰκτιρμός, 3628), akin to A, No. 1, is used with *splanchna* (see below), "the viscera, the inward parts," as the seat of emotion, the "heart," Phil. 2:1; Col. 3:12, "a heart of compassion" (KJV, "bowels of mercies"). In Heb. 10:28 it is used with *chōris*, "without," (lit., "without compassions"). It is translated "mercies" in Rom. 12:1 and 2 Cor. 1:3. See MERCY.

2. *splanchnon* (σπλάγχνον, 4698), always used in the plural, is suitably rendered "compassion" in the RV of Col. 3:12 and 1 John 3:17; "compassions" in Phil. 2:1, Cf. A, No. 2. See BOWELS.

C. Adjective.

sumpathēs (συμπαθής, 4835) denotes suffering with, "compassionate," 1 Pet. 3:8, RV (KJV, "having compassion"). See A, No. 3.

COMPEL

1. *anankazō* (ἀναγκάζω, 315) denotes "to put constraint upon (from *anankē*, 'necessity'), to constrain, whether by threat, entreaty, force or persuasion"; Christ "constrained" the disciples to get into a boat, Matt. 14:22; Mark 6:45; the servants of the man who made a great supper were to constrain people to come in, Luke 14:23 (RV, "constrain"); Saul of Tarsus "strove" to make saints blaspheme, Acts 26:11, RV (KJV, "compelled"); Titus, though a Greek, was not "compelled" to be circumcised, Gal. 2:3, as Galatian converts were, 6:12, RV; Peter was "compelling" Gentiles to live as Jews, Gal. 2:14; Paul was "constrained" to appeal to Caesar, Acts 28:19, and was "compelled" by the church at Corinth to become foolish in speaking of himself, 2 Cor. 12:11. See CONSTRAIN.

2. *angareuō* (ἀγγαρεύω, 29), "to dispatch as an *angaros*" (a Persian courier kept at regular stages with power of impressing men into service), and hence, in general, "to impress into service," is used of "compelling" a person to go a mile, Matt. 5:41; of the impressing of Simon to bear Christ's cross, Matt. 27:32; Mark 15:21.

COMPLAINER, COMPLAINT

1. *mempsimoiros* (μεμψίμοιρος, 3202) denotes "one who complains," lit., "complaining of one's lot" (*memphomai*, "to blame," *moira*, "a fate, lot"); hence, "discontented, querulous, repining"; it is rendered "complainers" in Jude 16.

2. *momphē* (μομφή, 3437), denotes "blame" (akin to *memphomai* see No. 1), "an occasion of complaint," Col. 3:13 (KJV, "quarrel"). See QUARREL.

3. *aitiōma* (αἰτίωμα, 157), "a charge," is translated "complaints" in Acts 25:7, KJV.

For **COMPREHEND** see APPREHEND, John 1:5, KJV, and SUM UP

CONCEAL

parakaluptō (παρακαλύπτω, 3871), "to conceal thoroughly" (*para*, "beside," intensive, *kaluptō*, "to hide"), is found in Luke 9:45, of "concealing" from the disciples the fact of the delivering up of Christ.

CONCEITS

1. *en heautois* (ἐν ἑαυτοῖς, 1438), lit., "in yourselves," is used with *phronimos*, "wise," in Rom. 11:25, "(wise) in your own conceits (i.e., opinions)."

2. *par' heautois* (παρ' ἑαυτοῖς, 1438), (*para*, "with, in the estimation of"), in Rom. 12:16 has the same rendering as No. 1.

CONCEIVE

1. *gennaō* (γεννάω, 1080), "to conceive, beget": see BEGET, A, No. 1.

2. *sullambanō* (συλλαμβάνω, 4815), lit., "to take together" (*sun*, "with," *lambanō*, "to take or receive"), is used (a) of a woman, to "conceive," Luke 1:24, 31, 36; in the passive voice. Luke 2:21; (b) metaphorically, of the impulse of lust in the human heart, enticing to sin, Jas. 1:15.

3. *tithēmi* (τίθημι, 5087), to put, set, is used in Acts 5:4, of the sin of Ananias, in "conceiving" a lie in his heart.

Notes: (1) The phrase *echō*, "to have," with *koitē*, "a lying down, a bed," especially the marriage bed, denotes "to conceive," Rom. 9:10.

(2) The phrase *eis katabolēn*, lit., "for a casting down, or in," is used of conception in Heb. 11:11.

CONCISION

katatomē (κατατομή, 2699), lit., "a cutting off" (*kata*, "down," *temnō*, "to cut"), "a mutilation," is a term found in Phil. 3:2, there used by the apostle, by a paronomasia, contemptuously, for the Jewish circumcision with its Judaistic influence, in contrast to the true spiritual circumcision.

CONCLUDE

sumbibazō (συμβιβάζω, 4822), lit., "to make to come together," is translated "concluding" in Acts 16:10, RV, for the KJV, "assuredly gathering." See COMPACTED, INSTRUCT, PROVE.

Notes: (1) For *krinō*, "to judge, give judgment," rendered "concluded" in the KJV of Acts 21:25, RV, giving judgment, see JUDGMENT.

(2) For *logizomai*, "to reckon," translated "conclude" in Rom. 3:28, KJV, RV, "reckon," see RECKON.

(3) For *sunkleiō*, "to shut up with," translated "concluded" in Rom. 11:32; Gal. 3:22, KJV, RV, shut up, see SHUT.

CONCORD

sumphōnēsis (συμφώνησις, 4857), lit., "a sounding together" (*sun*, "with," *phonē*, "a sound"; Eng., "symphony"), is found in 2 Cor. 6:15, in the rhetorical question "what concord hath Christ with Belial?"

CONCOURSE

suntrophē (συστροφή, 4963), "a turning together" (*sun*, "with," *trepō*, "to turn"), signifies (a) that which is rolled together; hence (b) a dense mass of people, concourse, Acts 19:40. See BANDED.

For **CONCUPISCENCE** (KJV of Rom. 7:8; Col. 3:5; 1 Thess. 4:5) see COVET, DESIRE, LUST

CONDEMN, CONDEMNATION

A. Verbs.

1. *kataginōskō* (καταγινώσκω, 2607), "to know something against" (*kata*, "against," *ginōskō*, "to know by experience"), hence, "to think ill of, to condemn," is said, in Gal. 2:11, of Peter's conduct (RV, "stood condemned"), he being "self-condemned" as the result of an exercised and enlightened conscience, and "condemned" in the sight of others; so of "self-condemnation" due to an exercise of heart, 1 John 3:20-21. See BLAME.

2. *katadikazō* (καταδικάζω, 2613) signifies "to exercise right or law against anyone"; hence, "to pronounce judgment, to condemn" (*kata*, "down, or against," *dikē*, "justice"), Matt. 12:7, 37; Luke 6:37; Jas. 5:6.

3. *krinō* (κρίνω, 2919), "to distinguish, choose, give an opinion upon, judge," sometimes denotes "to condemn," e.g., Acts 13:27; Rom. 2:27; Jas. 5:9 (in the best mss.). Cf. No. 1, below. See CALL (No. 13), CONCLUDE, DECREE, ESTEEM, JUDGE, LAW (go to), ORDAIN, SUE.

4. *katakrinō* (κατακρίνω, 2632), a strengthened form of No. 3, signifies "to give judgment against, pass sentence upon"; hence, "to condemn," implying (a) the fact of a crime, e.g., Rom. 2:1; 14:23; 2 Pet. 2:6; some mss. have it in Jas. 5:9; (b) the imputation of a crime, as in the "condemnation" of Christ by the Jews, Matt. 20:18; Mark 14:64. It is used metaphorically of "condemning" by a good example, Matt. 12:41-42; Luke 11:31-32; Heb. 11:7.

In Rom. 8:3, God's "condemnation" of sin is set forth in that Christ, His own Son, sent by Him to partake of human nature (sin apart) and to become an offering for sin, died under the judgment due to our sin.

B. Nouns.

1. *krima* (κρίμα, 2917) denotes (a) "the sentence pronounced, a verdict, a condemnation, the decision resulting from an investigation," e.g., Mark 12:40; Luke 23:40; 1 Tim. 3:6; Jude 4; (b) "the process of judgment leading to a decision," 1 Pet. 4:17 ("judgment"), where *krisis* (see No. 3, below) might be expected. In Luke 24:20, "to be condemned" translates the phrase *eis krima*, "unto condemnation" (i.e., unto the pronouncement of the sentence of "condemnation"). For the rendering "judgment," see, e.g., Rom. 11:33; 1 Cor. 11:34; Gal. 5:10; Jas. 3:1. In these (a) the process leading to a decision and (b) the pronouncement of the decision, the verdict, are to be distinguished. In 1 Cor. 6:7 the word means a matter for judgment, a lawsuit. See JUDGMENT.

2. *katakrima* (κατάκριμα, 2631), cf. No. 4, above, is "the sentence pronounced, the condemnation" with a suggestion of the punishment following; it is found in Rom. 5:16, 18; 8:1.

3. *krisis* (κρίσις, 2920) (a) denotes "the process of investigation, the act of distinguishing and separating" (as distinct from *krima*, see No. 1 above); hence "a judging, a passing of judgment upon a person or thing"; it has a variety of meanings, such as judicial authority, John 5:22, 27; justice, Acts 8:33; Jas. 2:13; a tribunal, Matt. 5:21-22; a trial, John 5:24; 2 Pet. 2:4; a judgment, 2 Pet. 2:11; Jude 9; by metonymy, the standard of judgment, just dealing, Matt. 12:18, 20; 23:23; Luke 11:42; divine judgment executed, 2 Thess. 1:5; Rev. 16:7; (b)

sometimes it has the meaning "condemnation," and is virtually equivalent to *krima* (a); see Matt. 23:33; John 3:19; Jas. 5:12, *hupo krisin*, "under judgment." See ACCUSATION, A (Note), JUDGMENT.

Note: In John 9:39, "For judgment (*krima*) came I into this world," the meaning would appear to be, "for being judged" (as a touchstone for proving men's thoughts and characters), in contrast to 5:22, "hath given all judging (*krisis*) to the Son"; in Luke 24:20, "delivered Him up to be condemned to death," the latter phrase is, lit., "to a verdict (*krima*) of death" (which they themselves could not carry out); in Mark 12:40, "these shall receive greater condemnation" (*krima*), the phrase signifies a heavier verdict (against themselves).

4. *katakrisis* (κατάκρισις, 2633), a strengthened form of No. 3, denotes "a judgment against, condemnation," with the suggestion of the process leading to it, as of "the ministration of condemnation," 2 Cor. 3:9; in 7:3, "to condemn," more lit., "with a view to condemnation."

C. Adjectives.

1. *autokatakritos* (αὐτοκατάκριτος, 843), "self-condemned" (*auto*, "self," *katakrinō*, "to condemn"), i.e., on account of doing himself what he condemns in others, is used in Titus 3:11.

2. *akatagnōstos* (ἀκατάγνωστος, 176), akin to A, No. 1, with negative prefix, *a*, "not to be condemned," is said of sound speech, in Titus 2:8.

CONDUCT

A. Noun.

agōgē (ἀγωγή, 72), from *ago*, "to lead," properly denotes "a teaching"; then, figuratively, "a training, discipline," and so, the life led, a way or course of life, conduct, 2 Tim.3:10, RV, "conduct"; KJV, "manner of life." See LIFE.

B. Verbs.

1. *kathistēmi* (καθίστημι, 2525), lit., "to stand down or set down" (*kata*, "down," *histēmi*, "to stand"), has, among its various meanings, "the significance of bringing to a certain place, conducting," Acts 17:15 (so the Sept. in Josh. 6:23; 1 Sam. 5:3; 2 Chron. 28:15). See APPOINT.

2. *propempō* (προπέμπω, 4311) signifies "to set forward, conduct": see ACCOMPANY, No. 4.

CONFER, CONFERENCE

1. *prosanatithēmi* (προσανατίθημι, 4323), lit., "to put before" (*pros*, "towards," *ana*, "up," and *tithēmi*, "to put"), i.e., "to lay a matter before others so as to obtain counsel or instruction," is used of Paul's refraining from consulting human beings, Gal. 1:16 (translated "imparted" in 2:6; KJV, "added ... in conference"). Cf. the shorter form *anatithēmi*, in 2:2, "laid before," the less intensive word being used there simply to signify the imparting of information, rather than conferring with others to seek advice.

2. *sullaleō* (συλλαλέω, 4814), "to speak together with" (*sun*, "with," *laleō*, "to speak"), is translated "conferred" in Acts 25:12; elsewhere of talking with Matt. 17:3; Mark 9:4; Luke 4:36; 9:30; "communed" in Luke 22:4. See COMMUNE, TALK.

3. *sumballō* (συμβάλλω, 4820), lit., "to throw together" (*sun*, "with," *ballō*, "to throw"), is used of "conversation, to discourse or consult together, confer," Acts 4:15. See ENCOUNTER, HELP.

Note: For the KJV, "conference" in Gal. 2:6, see No. 1, above.

CONFESS, CONFESSION

A. Verbs.

1. *homologeō* (ὁμολογέω, 3670), lit., "to speak the same thing" (*homos*, "same," *legō*, "to speak"), "to assent, accord, agree with," denotes, (a) "to confess, declare, admit," John 1:20; e.g., Acts 24:14; Heb. 11:13; (b) "to confess by way of admitting oneself guilty of what one is accused of, the result of inward conviction," 1 John 1:9; (c) "to declare openly by way of speaking out freely, such confession being the effect of deep conviction of facts," Matt. 7:23; 10:32 (twice) and Luke 12:8 (see next par.); John 9:22; 12:42; Acts 23:8; Rom. 10:9-10 ("confession is made"); 1 Tim. 6:12 (RV); Titus 1:16; 1 John 2:23; 4:2, 15; 2 John 7 (in John's epistle it is the necessary antithesis to Gnostic doceticism); Rev. 3:5, in the best mss. (some have No. 2 here); (d) "to confess by way of celebrating with praise," Heb. 13:15; (e) "to promise," Matt. 14:7.

In Matt. 10:32 and Luke 12:8 the construction of this verb with *en*, "in," followed by the dative case of the personal pronoun, has a special significance, namely, to "confess" in a person's name, the nature of the "confession" being determined by the context, the suggestion being to make a public "confession." Thus the statement, "every one ... who shall confess Me (lit. "in Me," i.e., in My case) before men, him (lit., "in him," i.e., in his case) will I also confess before My Father ... ," conveys the thought of "confessing" allegiance to Christ as one's Master and Lord, and, on the other hand, of acknowledgment, on His part, of the faithful one as being His worshipper and servant, His loyal follower; this is appropriate to the original idea in *homologeō* of being identified in thought or language. See PROFFESS, PROMISE, THANK.

2. *exomologeō* (ἐξομολογέω, 1843), *ek*, "out," intensive, and No. 1, and accordingly stronger than No. 1, "to confess forth," i.e., "freely, openly," is used (a) "of a public acknowledgment or confession of sins," Matt. 3:6; Mark 1:5; Acts 19:18; Jas. 5:16; (b) "to profess or acknowledge openly," Matt.

11:25 (translated "thank," but indicating the fuller idea); Phil. 2:11 (some mss. have it in Rev. 3:5: see No. 1); (c) "to confess by way of celebrating, giving praise," Rom. 14:11; 15:9. In Luke 10:21, it is translated "I thank," the true meaning being "I gladly acknowledge." In Luke 22:6 it signifies to consent (RV), for KJV, "promised." See CONSENT, PROMISE, THANK.

B. Noun.

homologia (ὁμολογία, 3671), akin to A, No. 1, denotes "confession, by acknowledgment of the truth," 2 Cor. 9:13; 1 Tim. 6:12-13; Heb. 3:1; 4:14; 10:23 (KJV, incorrectly, "profession," except in 1 Tim. 6:13).

Note: For the adverb *homologoumenōs*, confessedly, see CONTROVERSY.

CONFIDENCE (Noun, or Verb with "have"), CONFIDENT (-LY)

A. Nouns.

1. *pepoithēsis* (πεποίθησις, 4006), akin to *peithō*, B, No. 1 below, denotes "persuasion, assurance, confidence," 2 Cor. 1:15; 3:4, KJV, "trust"; 8:22; 10:2; Eph. 3:12; Phil. 3:4. See TRUST.

2. *hupostasis* (ὑπόστασις, 5287), lit., "a standing under" (*hupo*, "under," *stasis*, "a standing"), "that which stands, or is set, under, a foundation, beginning"; hence, the quality of confidence which leads one to stand under, endure, or undertake anything, 2 Cor. 9:4; 11:17; Heb. 3:14. Twice in Heb. it signifies "substance," 1:3 (KJV, "Person") and 11:1. See SUBSTANCE.

3. *parrhēsia* (παῤῥησία, 3954), often rendered "confidence" in the KJV, is in all such instances rendered "boldness" in the RV, Acts 28:31; Heb. 3:6; 1 John 2:28; 3:21; 5:14. See BOLDNESS, OPENLY, PLAINNESS.

B. Verbs.

1. *peithō* (πείθω, 3982), "to persuade," or, intransitively, "to have confidence, to be confident" (cf. A, No. 1), has this meaning in the following, Rom. 2:19; 2 Cor. 2:3; Gal. 5:10; Phil. 1:6, 14 (RV, "being confident," for KJV, "waxing confident"), 25; 3:3-4; 2 Thess. 3:4; Philem. 21. See ASSURE, BELIEVE, OBEY, PERSUADE, TRUST, YIELD.

2. *tharreō* (θαῤῥέω, 2292), "to be of good courage," is so translated in the RV of 2 Cor. 5:6; 7:16 (KJV, "to have confidence, or be confident). See COURAGE.

Note: The adverb "confidently" is combined with the verb "affirm" to represent the verbs *diischurzomai*, Luke 22:59 and Acts 12:15, RV (KJV, "constantly affirmed"),, and *diabebaioomai*, 1 Tim. 1:7, KJV, "affirm," and Titus 3:8, KJV, "affirm constantly."

CONFIRM, CONFIRMATION

A. Verbs.

1. *bebaioō* (βεβαιόω, 950), "to make firm, establish, make secure" (the connected adjective *bebaios* signifies "stable, fast, firm"), is used of "confirming" a word, Mark 16:20; promises, Rom. 15:8; the testimony of Christ, 1 Cor. 1:6; the saints by the Lord Jesus Christ, 1 Cor. 1:8; the saints by God, 2 Cor. 1:21 ("stablisheth"); in faith, Col. 2:7; the salvation spoken through the Lord and "confirmed" by the apostles, Heb. 2:3; the heart by grace, Heb. 13:9 ("stablished").

2. *epistērizō* (ἐπιστηρίζω, 1991), "to make to lean upon, strengthen" (*epi*, "upon," *stērix*, "a prop, support"), is used of "confirming" souls Acts 14:22, brethren, 15:32; churches, 15:41; disciples, 18:23, in some mss. ("stablishing," RV, "strengthening," KJV); the most authentic mss. have *stērizō* in 18:23. See STRENGTHEN.

3. *kuroō* (κυρόω, 2964), "to make valid, ratify, impart authority or influence" (from *kuros*, "might," *kurios*, "mighty, a head, as supreme in authority"), is used of spiritual love, 2 Cor. 2:8; a human covenant, Gal. 3:15.. In the Sept., see Gen. 23:20, e.g.

4. *prokuroō* (προκυρόω, 4300), *pro*, "before," and No. 3, "to confirm or ratify before," is said of the divine confirmation of a promise given originally to Abraham, Gen. 12, and "confirmed" by the vision of the furnace and torch, Gen. 15, by the birth of Isaac, Gen. 21, and by the oath of God, Gen. 22, all before the giving of the Law, Gal. 3:17.

5. *mesiteuo* (μεσιτεύω, 3315), "to act as a mediator, to interpose," is rendered "confirmed," in the KJV of Heb. 6:17 (marg., and RV, "interposed").

B. Noun.

bebaiōsis (βεβαίωσις, 951), akin to A, No. 1, is used in two senses (a) "of firmness, establishment," said of the "confirmation" of the gospel, Phil. 1:7; (b) "of authoritative validity imparted," said of the settlement of a dispute by an oath to produce confidence, Heb. 6:16. The word is found frequently in the papyri of the settlement of a business transaction.

CONFLICT (Noun)

1. *agōn* (ἀγών, 73), from *agō*, "to lead," signifies (a) "a place of assembly," especially the place where the Greeks assembled for the Olympic and Pythian games; (b) "a contest of athletes," metaphorically, 1 Tim. 6:12; 2 Tim. 4:7, "fight"; Heb. 12:1, "race"; hence, (c) "the inward conflict of the soul"; inward "conflict" is often the result, or the accompaniment, of outward "conflict," Phil. 1:30; 1 Thess. 2:2, implying a contest against spiritual foes, as well as human adversaries; so Col. 2:1, "conflict," KJV; RV, "(how greatly) I strive," lit., "how

great a conflict I have." See CONTENTION, FIGHT, RACE. Cf. *agōnizomai* (Eng., "agonize"), 1 Cor. 9:25 etc.

2. *athlēsis* (ἄθλησις, 119) denotes "a combat, contest of athletes"; hence, "a struggle, 6ght," Heb. 10:32, with reference to affliction. See FIGHT. Cf. *athleō*, "to strive," 2 Tim. 2:5 (twice).

CONFORMED, CONFORMABLE

A. Verb.

summorphizō (συμμορφίζω, 4833), "to make of like form with another person or thing, to render like" (*sun*, "with," *morphē*, "a form"), is found in Phil. 3:10 (in the passive participle of the verb), "becoming conformed" (or "growing into conformity") to the death of Christ, indicating the practical apprehension of the death of the carnal self, and fulfilling his share of the sufferings following upon the sufferings of Christ. Some texts have the alternative verb *summorphoō*, which has practically the same meaning.

B. Adjectives.

1. *summorphos* (συμμορφός, 4832), akin to A, signifies "having the same form as another, conformed to"; (a) of the "conformity" of children of God "to the image of His Son," Rom. 8:29; (b), of their future physical "conformity" to His body of glory, Phil. 3:21. See FASHION.

2. *suschēmatizō* (συσχηματίζω, 4964), "to fashion or shape one thing like another," is translated "conformed" in Rom. 12:2, KJV; RV, "fashioned"; "fashioning" in 1 Pet. 1:14. This verb has more especial reference to that which is transitory, changeable, unstable; *summorphizō*, to that which is essential in character and thus complete or durable, not merely a form or outline. *Suschēmatizō* could not be used of inward transformation. See FASHION (*schēma*) and FORM (*morphē*).

CONFOUND, CONFUSE, CONFUSION

A. Nouns.

1. *akatastasia* (ἀκαταστασία, 181), "instability," (*a*, negative, *kata*, "down," *stasis*, "a standing"), denotes "a state of disorder, disturbance, confusion, tumult," 1 Cor. 14:33; Jas. 3:16, "revolution or anarchy"; translated "tumults" in Luke 21:9 (KJV, "commotions"); 2 Cor. 6:5; 12:20. See TUMULT.

2. *sunchusis* (σύγχυσις, 4799), "a pouring or mixing together" (*sun*, "with," *cheō*, "to pour"); hence "a disturbance, confusion, a tumultuous disorder, as of riotous persons," is found in Acts 19:29.

B. Verbs.

1. *suncheō* (συγχέω, 4797), or *sunchunno* or *sunchuno* (the verb form of A., No. 2), lit., "to pour together, commingle," hence (said of persons), means "to trouble or confuse, to stir up," Acts 19:32 (said of the mind); "to be in confusion," 21:31, RV (KJV, "was in an uproar"); 21:27, "stirred up"; Acts 2:6; 9:22, "confounded. See STIR, UPROAR.

2. *kataischunō* (καταισχύνω, 2617), "to put to shame," is translated "confound" in 1 Cor. 1:27, and 1 Pet. 2:6, KJV (RV, "put to shame"). See ASHAMED, DISHONOR, SHAME.

CONGREGATION

1. *ekklēsia* (ἐκκλησία, 1577) is translated "congregation" in Heb. 2:12, RV, instead of the usual rendering "church." See ASSEMBLY.

2. *sunagōgē* (συναγωγή, 4864) is translated "congregation" in Acts 13:43, KJV (RV, "synagogue). See SYNAGOGUE.

CONQUER, CONQUEROR

1. *nikaō* (νικάω, 3528), "to overcome" (its usual meaning), is translated "conquering" and "to conquer" in Rev. 6:2. See OVERCOME, PREVAIL, VICTORY.

2. *hupernikaō* (ὑπερνικάω, 5245), "to be more than conqueror" (*huper*, "over," and No. 1), "to gain a surpassing victory," is found in Rom. 8:37, lit., "we are hyper-conquerors," i.e., we are pre-eminently victorious.

CONSCIENCE

suneidēsis (συνείδησις, 4893), lit., "a knowing with" (*sun*, "with," *oida*, "to know"), i.e., "a co-knowledge (with oneself), the witness borne to one's conduct by conscience, that faculty by which we apprehend the will of God, as that which is designed to govern our lives"; hence (a) the sense of guiltiness before God; Heb. 10:2; (b) that process of thought which distinguishes what it considers morally good or bad, commending the good, condemning the bad, and so prompting to do the former, and avoid the latter; Rom. 2:15 (bearing witness with God's law); 9:1; 2 Cor. 1:12; acting in a certain way because "conscience" requires it, Rom. 13:5; so as not to cause scruples of "conscience" in another, 1 Cor. 10:28-29; not calling a thing in question unnecessarily, as if conscience demanded it, 1 Cor. 10:25, 27; "commending oneself to every man's conscience," 2 Cor. 4:2; cf. 5:11. There may be a "conscience" not strong enough to distinguish clearly between the lawful and the unlawful, 1 Cor. 8:7, 10, 12 (some regard consciousness as the meaning here). The phrase "conscience toward God," in 1 Pet. 2:19, signifies a "conscience" (or perhaps here, a consciousness) so controlled by the apprehension of God's presence, that the person realizes that griefs are to be borne in accordance with His will. Heb. 9:9 teaches that sacrifices under the Law could not so perfect a person that he could regard himself as free from guilt.

For various descriptions of "conscience" see Acts 23:1; 24:16; 1 Cor. 8:7; 1 Tim. 1:5, 19; 3:9; 4:2; 2 Tim. 1:3; Titus 1:15; Heb. 9:14; 10:22; 13:18; 1 Pet. 3:16, 2l.

CONSECRATE

Note: In Heb. 7:28 the verb *teleioō* is translated "perfected" in the RV, for KJV, "consecrated"; so in 9:18 and 10:20, *enkainizō*, RV, dedicated. See DEDICATE, PERFECT.

CONSENT

A. Verbs.

1. *exomologeō* (ἐξομολογέω, 1843), "to agree openly, to acknowledge outwardly, or fully" (*ex*, "for," *ek*, "out," intensive), is translated "consented" in the RV of Luke 22:6 (KJV, promised). See CONFESS, THANK.

2. *epineuō* (ἐπινεύω, 1962), lit. "signifies to nod to" (*epi*, "upon or to," *neuō*, "to nod"); hence, "to nod assent, to express approval, consent," Acts 18:20.

3. *proserchomai* (προσέρχομαι, 4334), "to come to," signifies "to consent," implying a coming to agreement with, in 1 Tim. 6:3.

4. *sunkatatithēmi* (συγκατατίθημι, 4784), lit., "to put or lay down together with" (*sun*, "with," *kata*, "down," *tithēmi*, "to put"), was used of depositing one's vote in an urn; hence, "to vote for, agree with, consent to." It is said negatively of Joseph of Arimathaea, who had not "consented" to the counsel and deed of the Jews, Luke 23:51 (middle voice).

5. *sumphēmi* (σύμφημι, 4852), lit., "to speak with" (*sun*, "with," *phemi*, "to speak"), hence, "to express agreement with," is used of "consenting" to the Law, agreeing that it is good, Rom. 7:16.

6. *suneudokeō* (συνευδοκέω, 4909), lit., "to think well with" (*sun*, "with," *eu*, "well," *dokeō*, "to think"), to take pleasure with others in anything, to approve of, to assent, is used in Luke 11:48, of "consenting" to the evil deeds of predecessors (KJV, "allow"); in Rom. 1:32, of "consenting" in doing evil; in Acts 8:1; 22:20, of "consenting" to the death of another. All these are cases of "consenting" to evil things. In 1 Cor. 7:12-13, it is used of an unbelieving wife's "consent" to dwell with her converted husband, and of an unbelieving husband's "consent" to dwell with a believing wife (KJV, "be pleased"; RV, "be content"). See ALLOW, CONTENT, PLEASE.

B. Phrases.

1. *apo mias*, lit., "from one," is found in Luke 14:18, some word like "consent" being implied; e.g., "with one consent."

2. *ek sumphōnou*, lit., "from (or by) agreement" (*sun*, "with," *phōnē*, "a sound"), i.e., "by consent," is found in 1 Cor. 7:5.

CONSIST

1. *eimi* (εἰμί, 1510), "to be," is rendered "consist" (lit., "is") in Luke 12:15.

2. *sunistēmi* (συνίστημι, 4921), *sun*, "with," *histēmi*, "to stand," denotes, in its intransitive sense, "to stand with or fall together, to be constituted, to be compact"; it is said of the universe as upheld by the Lord, Col. 1:17, lit., "by Him all things stand together," i.e., "consist" (the Latin *consisto*, "to stand together," is the exact equivalent of *sunistēmi*). See COMMEND.

CONSOLATION, CONSOLE

A. Nouns.

1. *paraklēsis* (παράκλησις, 3874) is translated "consolation," in both KJV and RV, in Luke 2:25; 6:24; Acts 15:31; in 1 Cor. 14:3, KJV, "exhortation," RV, "comfort"; in the following the KJV has "consolation," the RV, "comfort," Rom. 15:5; 2 Cor. 1:6-7; 7:7; Phil. 2:1; 2 Thess. 2:16; Philem. 7; in Acts 4:36, RV, "exhortation"; in Heb. 6:18, RV, "encouragement." See COMFORT.

2. *paramuthia* (παραμυθία, 3889), "a comfort, consolation": see COMFORT, A, No. 2.

3. *paramuthion* (παραμύθιον, 3890), "an encouragement, consolation," Phil. 2:1, RV, in the phrase "consolation of love." See COMFORT, A, No. 3.

B. Verb.

paramutheomai (παραμυθέομαι, 3888), "to speak soothingly to," is translated "console," John 11:19, RV; in v. 31 "were comforting"; in 1 Thess. 2:11 and 5:14, KJV, "comforted" and "comfort," RV, "encouraged" and "encourage."

CONSORT (with)

prosklēroō (προσκληρόω, 4345), lit., "to assign by lot" (*pros*, "to," *klēros*, "a lot"), "to allot," is found in Acts 17:4, "consorted with," imparting to the passive voice (the form of the verb there) a middle voice significance, i.e., "they joined themselves to," or "threw in their lot with." The passive voice significance can be retained by translating (in the stricter sense of the word), "they were allotted" (i.e., by God) to Paul and Silas, as followers or disciples.

CONSPIRACY

sunōmosia (συνωμοσία, 4945) denotes, lit., "a swearing together" (*sun*, "with," *omnumi*, "to swear"), a "being leagued by oath, and so a conspiracy," Acts 23:13.

CONSTRAIN, CONSTRAINT

A. Verbs.

1. *anankazō* (ἀναγκάζω, 315): see COMPEL, No. 1.

2. *parabiazomai* (παραβιάζομαι, 3849) primarily denotes "to employ force contrary to nature and right, to compel by using force" (*para*, "alongside," intensive, *biazō*, "to force"), and is used only of "constraining" by intreaty, as the two going to Emmaus did to Christ, Luke 24:29; as Lydia did to Paul and his companions, Acts 16:15.

3. *sunechō* (συνέχω, 4912), "to hold together, confine, secure, to hold fast" (*echō*, "to have or hold"), "to constrain," is said (a) of the effect of the word of the Lord upon Paul, Acts 18:5 (KJV, "was pressed in spirit," RV, "was constrained by the word"); of the effect of the love of Christ, 2 Cor. 5:14; (b) of being taken with a disease, Matt. 4:24; Luke 4:38; Acts 28:8; with fear, Luke 8:37; (c) of thronging or holding in a person, Luke 8:45; being straitened, Luke 12:50; being in a strait betwixt two, Phil. 1:23; keeping a city in on every side, Luke 19:43; keeping a tight hold on a person, as the men who seized the Lord Jesus did, after bringing Him into the High Priest's house, Luke 22:63; (d) of stopping the ears in refusal to listen, Acts 7:57. Luke uses the word nine times out of its twelve occurrences in the NT. See HOLD, KEEP, No. (1), PRESS, SICK (lie).

Note: The verb *echō*, "to have," with *ananke*, "a necessity," is translated "I was constrained," in Jude 3, RV (KJV, "it was needful").

B. Adverb.

anankastōs (ἀναγκαστῶς, 317), akin to A, No. 1, "by force, unwillingly, by constraint," is used in 1 Pet. 5:2.

CONSULT, CONSULTATION

A. Verbs.

1. *bouleuō* (βουλεύω, 1011), used in the middle voice, means (a) "to consult," Luke 14:31; (b) "to resolve," John 12:10, KJV, "consulted"; RV, took counsel." See COUNSEL.

2. *sumbouleuō* (συμβουλεύω, 4823), "to take counsel together," is translated "consulted together," in Matt. 26:4, KJV (RV, "took counsel.") See COUNSEL.

B. Noun.

sumboulion (συμβούλιον, 4824), a word of the Graeco-Roman period (akin to A, No. 2), "counsel, advice," is translated "consultation" in Mark 15:1 (with *poieō*, "to make"), "to hold a consultation"; elsewhere "counsel" in the RV, except in Acts 25:12, where, by metonymy, it means a "council." See COUNCIL.

CONSUME

1. *analiskō* (ἀναλίσκω, 355), "to use up, spend up, especially in a bad sense, to destroy," is said of the destruction of persons, (a) literally, Luke 9:54 and the RV marg. of 2 Thess. 2:8 (text, "shall slay"); (b) metaphorically, Gal. 5:15 "(that) ye be not consumed (one of another)."

2. *katanaliskō* (καταναλίσκω, 2654), "to consume utterly, wholly" (*kata*, intensive), is said, in Heb. 12:29, of God as "a consuming fire."

3. *aphanizō* (ἀφανίζω, 853), lit., "to cause to disappear, put out of sight," came to mean "to do away with" (*a*, negative, *phainō*, "to cause to appear"), said of the destructive work of moth and rust, Matt. 6:19-20 (RV, "consume," KJV, "corrupt"). See CORRUPT, DISFIGURE, PERISH, VANISH.

Note: Dapanaō, "to expend, be at an expense," is translated "consume" in the KJV of Jas. 4:3 (RV, "spend").

CONTAIN

1. *chōreō* (χωρέω, 5562) signifies (a), lit., "to give space, make room" (*chōra*, "a place"); hence, transitively, "to have space or room for a thing, to contain," said of the waterpots as "containing" a certain quantity, John 2:6; of a space large enough to hold a number of people, Mark 2:2; of the world as not possible of "containing" certain books, John 21:25; (b) "to go," Matt. 15:17; "to have place," John 8:37; "to come," 2 Pet. 3:9; (c) metaphorically, "of receiving with the mind," Matt. 19:11, 12; or "into the heart," 2 Cor. 7:2. See GO.

2. *periechō* (περιέχω, 4023), lit., "to have round" (*peri*, "around," *echō*, "to have"), means "to encompass, enclose, contain," as a writing contains details, 1 Pet. 2:6. Some mss. have it in Acts 23:25, lit., "having this form" (the most authentic have *echō*, "to have"). For the secondary meaning, "amazed" (KJV, "astonished"), Luke 5:9 (lit., "amazement encompassed," i.e., seized, him).

Notes: (1) The verb *allēgoreō* in Gal. 4:24, RV, is translated "contain an allegory" (KJV, "are an allegory"), i.e., they apply the facts of the narrative to illustrate principles. (2) In Eph. 2:15 "the law of commandments contained in ordinances" is, lit., "the law of commandments in ordinances." (3) In Rom. 2:14, the RV, translating literally, has "the things of the Law"; the KJV inserts the words "contained in." (4) In 1 Cor. 7:9, for the KJV, "if they cannot contain," see CONTINENCY.

CONTEND (-ING)

1. *athleō* (ἀθλέω, 118), "to engage in a contest" (cf. Eng., "athlete"), "to contend in public games," is used in 2 Tim. 2:5, RV, "contend in the games," for the KJV, "strive for the masteries." See STRIVE.

Note: In 1 Cor. 9:25, the verb *agōnizomai*, "to strive," is used in the same connection, RV, "striveth in the games." Cf. No. 3.

2. *diakrinō* (διακρίνω, 1252), lit., "to separate throughout or wholly" (*dia*, "asunder," *krinō*, "to judge," from a root *kri*, meaning "separation"), then, to distinguish, decide, signifies, in the middle voice, "to separate oneself from, or to contend with," as did the circumcisionists with Peter, Acts 11:2; as did Michael with Satan, Jude 9. See RV marg. of v. 22, where the thought may be that of differing in opinion. See DISCERN, DOUBT, JUDGE, PARTIAL, STAGGER, WAVER.

3. *epagonizomai* (ἐπαγωνίζομαι, 1864) signifies "to contend about a thing, as a combatant" (*epi*, "upon or about," intensive, *agōn*, "a contest"), "to contend earnestly," Jude 3. The

word "earnestly" is added to convey the intensive force of the preposition.

CONTENT (to be), CONTENTMENT

A. Verb.

1. *arkeō* (ἀρκέω, 714) primarily signifies "to be sufficient, to be possessed of sufficient strength, to be strong, to be enough for a thing"; hence, "to defend, ward off"; in the middle voice, "to be satisfied, contented with," Luke 3:14, with wages; 1 Tim. 6:8, with food and raiment; Heb. 13:5, with "such things as ye have"; negatively of Diotrephes, in 3 John 10, "not content therewith."

2. *suneudokeō* (συνευδοκέω, 4909), in 1 Cor. 7:12-13, RV, signifies "to be content": see CONSENT, No. 6.

B. Adjectives.

1. *autarkēs* (αὐτάρκης, 842), as found in the papyri writings, means "sufficient in oneself" (*autos*, "self," *arkeō*, "see" A), "self-sufficient, adequate, needing no assistance"; hence, "content," Phil. 4:11.

2. *hikanos* (ἱκανός, 2425), "sufficient," used with *poieō*, "to do," in Mark 15:15, is translated "to content (the multitude)," i.e., to do sufficient to satisfy them. See ABLE.

C. Noun.

autarkeia (αὐτάρκεια, 841), "contentment, satisfaction with what one has," is found in 1 Tim. 6:6.

CONTENTION, CONTENTIOUS

A. Nouns.

1. *eris* (ἔρις, 2054), "strife, quarrel, especially rivalry, contention, wrangling," as in the church in Corinth, 1 Cor. 1:11, is translated "contentions in Titus 3:9, KJV. See STRIFE, VARIANCE.

2. *paroxusmos* (παροξυσμός, 3948), (Eng., "paroxysm"), lit., "a sharpening," hence "a sharpening of the feeling, or action" (*para*, "beside," intensive, *oxus*, "sharp"), denotes an incitement, a sharp contention, Acts 15:39, the effect of irritation; elsewhere in Heb. 10:24, "provoke," unto love. See PROVOKE.

3. *philoneikia* (φιλονεικία, 5379), lit., "love of strife" (*phileō*, "to love," *neikos*, "strife"), signifies "eagerness to contend"; hence, a "contention," said of the disciples, Luke 22:24. Cf. B, 2.

B. Adjectives.

1. *amachos* (ἄμαχος, 269), lit., "not fighting" (*a*, negative, *machē*, "a fight, combat, quarrel"), primarily signifying "invincible," came to mean "not contentious," 1 Tim. 3:3, RV; Titus 3:2 (KJV, "not a brawler," "no brawlers").

2. *philoneikos* (φιλόνεικος, 5380), akin to A, No. 3, is used in 1 Cor. 11:16. In the Sept., Ezek. 3:7, "stubborn."

Notes: (1) *Eritheia*, "contention," KJV, in Phil. 1:17, is translated "faction," in the RV. The phrase *hoi ex eritheias*, Rom. 2:8, lit., "those of strife," is rendered "contentious," in the KJV; RV, factious. See FACTIOUS, STRIFE.

(2) For *agōn*, "a contest," "contention," 1 Thess. 2:2, KJV; conflict, RV, see CONFLICT.

CONTINENCY

enkrateuomai (ἐγκρατεύομαι, 1467), *en*, "in," *kratos*, "power, strength," lit., "to have power over oneself," is rendered "(if) they have (not) continency" (i.e., are lacking in self-control), in 1 Cor. 7:9, RV; KJV, "can (not) contain"; in 9:25, "is temperate." See TEMPERATE.

CONTINUAL, CONTINUALLY

A. Adverbial Phrases.

1. *eis telos* (εἰς τέλος, 5056), lit., "unto (the) end," signifies "continual," in Luke 18:5, of the importunate widow's applications to the unrighteous judge; see also Matt. 10:22; 24:13; Mark 13:13; John 13:1; 1 Thess. 2:16. Cf. *heōs telous*, lit., "until the end," 1 Cor. 1:8; 2 Cor. 1:13; *mechri telous*, ditto, Heb. 3:6, 14; *achri telous*, Heb. 6:11; Rev. 2:26.

2. *dia pantos* (διὰ παντός, 1275) is used of a "period throughout or during which anything is done"; it is said of the disciples' "continuance" in the Temple after the ascension of Christ, Luke 24:53; of the regular entrance of the priests into the first tabernacle, Heb. 9:6, RV (KJV "always"); of the constant sacrifice of praise enjoined upon believers, Heb. 13:15. See also Matt. 18:10; Mark 5:5; Acts 10:2; 24:16; Rom. 11:10; 2 Thess. 3:16, "at all times." (See ALWAYS, No. 3, and Note under No. 3 below).

3. *eis to diēnekes* (εἰς τὸ διηνεκές, 1336), lit., "unto the carried-through" (*dia*, "through," *enenka*, "to carry"), i.e., unto (the) unbroken "continuance," is used of the continuous priesthood of Christ, Heb. 7:3, and of the "continual" offering of sacrifices under the Law, Heb. 10:1. It is translated "for ever," in Heb. 10:12, of the everlasting session of Christ at the right hand of God; and in 10:14, of the everlasting effects of His sacrifice upon "them that are sanctified." See EVER.

Note: No. 2 indicates that a certain thing is done frequently throughout a period; No. 3 stresses the unbroken continuity of what is mentioned.

B. Adjective.

adialeiptos (ἀδιάλειπτος, 88), "continual, unceasing."

CONTRADICT, CONTRADICTION

A. Verb.

antilegō (ἀντίλεγω, 483), lit., "to speak against" (*anti*, "against," *legō*, "to speak"), is translated "contradict" in Acts 13:45. See ANSWER.

B. Noun.

antilogia (ἀντιλογία, 485), akin to A, is translated "contradiction" in the KJV of Heb. 7:7; 12:3, "dispute," and "gainsaying." See STRIFE.

CONTRIBUTION

koinōnia (κοινωνία, 2842) is twice rendered "contribution," Rom. 15:26, and 2 Cor. 9:13, RV, (KJV, "distribution). See COMMUNION.

CONTROVERSY (without)

homologoumenōs (ὁμολογουμένως, 3672), "confessedly, by common consent," akin to *homologeō*, "to confess" (*homos*, "same," *legō*, "to speak"), is rendered in 1 Tim. 3:16 "without controversy"; some translate it "confessedly." See CONFESS, A, No. 1, and B.

CONVERT, CONVERSION

A. Verbs.

1. *strephō* (στρέφω, 4762), "to turn," is translated "be converted" in Matt. 18:3, KJV.

2. *epistrephō* (ἐπιστρέφω, 1994), "to turn about, turn towards" (*epi*, "towards" and No. 1), is used transitively, and so rendered "convert" (of causing a person to turn) in Jas. 5:19-20. Elsewhere, where the KJV translates this verb, either in the middle voice and intransitive use, or the passive, the RV adheres to the middle voice significance, and translates by "turn again," Matt. 13:15; Mark 4:12; Luke 22:32; Acts 3:19; 28:27. See GO (again).

B. Noun.

epistrophē (ἐπιστροφή, 1995), akin to A, No. 2, "a turning about, or round, conversion," is found in Acts 15:3. The word implies "a turning from and a turning to"; corresponding to these are repentance and faith; cf. "turned to God from idols" (1 Thess. 1:9). Divine grace is the efficient cause, human agency the responding effect.

CONVEY

ekneuō (ἐκνεύω, 1593), primarily, "to bend to one side, to turn aside"; then "to take oneself away, withdraw," is found in John 5:13, of Christ's "conveying" Himself away from one place to another. Some have regarded the verb as having the same meaning as *ekneō*, "to escape," as from peril, "slip away secretly"; but the Lord did not leave the place where He had healed the paralytic in order to escape danger, but to avoid the applause of the throng.

CONVICT (*including the KJV, "convince"*)

1. *elenchō* (ἐλέγχω, 1651) signifies (a) "to convict, confute, refute," usually with the suggestion of putting the convicted person to shame; see Matt. 18:15, where more than telling the offender his fault is in view; it is used of "convicting" of sin, John 8:46; 16:8; gainsayers in regard to the faith, Titus 1:9; transgressors of the Law, Jas. 2:9; some texts have the verb in John 8:9; (b) "to reprove," 1 Cor. 14:24, RV (for KJV, "convince"), for the unbeliever is there viewed as being reproved for, or "convicted" of, his sinful state; so in Luke 3:19; it is used of reproving works, John 3:20; Eph. 5:11, 13; 1 Tim. 5:20; 2 Tim. 4:2; Titus 1:13; 2:15; all these speak of reproof by word of mouth. In Heb. 12:5 and Rev. 3:19, the word is used of reproving by action. See FAULT, REBUKE, REPROVE.

2. *exelenchō* (ἐξελέγχω, 1827), an intensive form of No. 1, "to convict thoroughly," is used of the Lord's future "conviction" of the ungodly, Jude 15.

COOL

katapsuchō (καταψύχω, 2711), Luke 16:24, denotes "to cool off, make cool" (*kata*, "down," *psuchō*, "to cool"). In the Sept., Gen. 18:4.

COPY

hupodeigma (ὑπόδειγμα, 5262), from *hupo*, "under," *deiknumi*, "to show," properly denotes "what is shown below or privately"; it is translated "example," Heb. 8:5, KJV (RV, "copy"). It signifies (a) a sign suggestive of anything, the delineation or representation of a thing, and so, a figure, "copy"; in Heb. 9:23 the RV has "copies," for the KJV, "patterns"; (b) an example for imitation, John 13:15; Jas. 5:10; for warning, Heb. 4:11; 2 Pet. 2:6 (KJV "ensample"). See EXAMPLE.

Note: Cf. *hupogrammos* (*hupo*, "under," *graphō*, "to write"), "an underwriting, a writing copy, an example," is used in 1 Pet. 2:21.

CORBAN

korban (κορβᾶν, 2878) signifies (a) "an offering," and was a Hebrew term for any sacrifice, whether by the shedding of blood or otherwise; (b) "a gift offered to God," Mark 7:11. Jews were much addicted to rash vows; a saying of the rabbis was, "It is hard for the parents, but the law is clear, vows must be kept." The Sept. translates the word by *dōron*, "a gift." See *korbanas*, under TREASURY, Matt. 27:6.

CORNER, CORNERSTONE

1. *gōnia* (γωνία, 1137), "an angle" (Eng., "coign"), signifies (a) "an external angle," as of the "corner" of a street, Matt. 6:5; or of a building, 21:42; Mark 12:10; Luke 20:17; Acts 4:11; 1 Pet. 2:7, "the corner stone or head-stone of the corner" (see below); or the four extreme limits of the earth, Rev. 7:1; 20:8; (b) "an internal corner," a secret place, Acts 26:26. See QUARTER.

2. *archē* (ἀρχή, 746), "a beginning" (its usual meaning), "first in time, order, or place," is used to denote the extremities or "corners" of a sheet, Acts 10:11; 11:5. See BEGINNING.

Note: For the adjective *akrogōniaios* (from *akros*, "extreme, highest," and No. 1), "a chief corner stone," see CHIEF. They were laid so as to give strength to the two walls with which they were connected. So Christ unites Jew and Gentile, Eph. 2:20; again, as one may carelessly stumble over the "corner stone," when turning the "corner," so Christ proved a stumbling stone to Jews, 1 Pet. 2:6.

CORPSE

ptōma (πτῶμα, 4430): see BODY, No. 3.

CORRECT, CORRECTION, CORRECTOR, CORRECTING

A. Nouns.

1. *diorthōma* (διόρθωμα, 1357a) signifies "a reform, amendment, correction," lit., "a making straight" (*dia*, "through," *orthoō*, "to make straight"). In Acts 24:2, lit., "reformations come about (or take place, lit., 'become')," the RV has "evils are corrected," KJV, "worthy deeds are done"; there is no word for "worthy" or for "deeds" in the original. Some texts have *katorthōma*, which has the same meaning. See *diorthōsis*, "reformation," Heb. 9:10.

2. *epanorthōsis* (ἐπανόρθωσις, 1882), lit., "a restoration to an upright or right state" (*epi*, "to," *ana*, "up, or again," and *orthoō*, see No. 1), hence, "correction," is used of the Scripture in 2 Tim. 3:16, referring to improvement of life and character.

3. *paideutēs* (παιδευτής, 3810) has two meanings, corresponding to the two meanings of the verb *paideuō* (see below) from which it is derived, (a) "a teacher, preceptor, corrector," Rom. 2:20 (KJV, "instructor"), (b) "a chastiser," Heb. 12:9, rendered "to chasten" (KJV, "which corrected"; lit., "chastisers"). See INSTRUCTOR.

B. Verb.

paideuō (παιδεύω, 3811), "to train up a child" (*pais*), is rendered "correcting in 2 Tim. 2:25, RV, KJV, "instructing." See CHASTEN.

CORRUPT, verb and adjective. CORRUPTION, CORRUPTIBLE, INCORRUPTION, INCORRUPTIBLE

A. Verbs.

1. *kapēleuō* (καπηλεύω, 2585) primarily signifies "to be a retailer, to peddle, to hucksterize" (from *kapelos*, "an innkeeper, a petty retailer, especially of wine, a huckster, peddler," in contrast to *emporos*, "a merchant"); hence, "to get base gain by dealing in anything," and so, more generally, "to do anything for sordid personal advantage." It is found in 2 Cor. 2:17, with reference to the ministry of the gospel. The significance can be best ascertained by comparison and contrast with the verb *doloō* in 4:2 (likewise there only in the NT), "to handle deceitfully." The meanings are not identical. While both involve the deceitful dealing of adulterating the word of truth, *kapēleuō* has the broader significance of doing so in order to make dishonest gain. Those to whom the apostle refers in 2:17 are such as make merchandise of souls through covetousness (cf. Titus 1:11; 2 Pet. 2:3, 14-15; Jude 11, 16; Ezek. 13:19); accordingly "hucksterizing" would be the most appropriate rendering in this passage, while "handling deceitfully" is the right meaning in 4:2. See Trench, *Syn.* Sec.LXII. In Isa. 1:22, the Sept. has "thy wine-merchants" (*kapēloi*, "hucksterizer").

2. *phtheirō* (φθείρω, 5351) signifies "to destroy by means of corrupting," and so "bringing into a worse state"; (a) with this significance it is used of the effect of evil company upon the manners of believers, and so of the effect of association with those who deny the truth and hold false doctrine, 1 Cor. 15:33 (this was a saying of the pagan poet Menander, which became a well known proverb); in 2 Cor. 7:2, of the effects of dishonorable dealing by bringing people to want (a charge made against the apostle); in 11:3, of the effects upon the minds (or thoughts) of believers by "corrupting" them "from the simplicity and the purity that is toward Christ"; in Eph. 4:22, intransitively, of the old nature in waxing "corrupt," "morally decaying, on the way to final ruin" (Moule), "after the lusts of deceit"; in Rev. 19:2, metaphorically, of the Babylonish harlot, in "corrupting" the inhabitants of the eanh by her false religion.

(b) With the significance of destroying, it is used of marring a local church by leading it away from that condition of holiness of life and purity of doctrine in which it should abide, 1 Cor. 3:17 (KJV, "defile"), and of God's retributive destruction of the offender who is guilty of this sin (id.); of the effects of the work of false and abominable teachers upon themselves, 2 Pet. 2:12 (some texts have *kataphtheirō*; KJV, "shall utterly perish"), and Jude 10 (KJV, "corrupt themselves." RV, marg., "are corrupted"). See DEFILE and DESTROY.

3. *diaphtheirō* (διαφθείρω, 1311), *dia*, "through," intensive, and No. 2, "to corrupt utterly, through and through," is said of men "corrupted in mind," whose wranglings result from the doctrines of false teachers, 1 Tim. 6:5 (the KJV wrongly renders it as an adjective, "corrupt"). It is translated "destroyeth" instead of "corrupteth," in the RV of Luke 12:33, of the work of a moth, in Rev. 8:9, of the effect of divine judgments hereafter upon navigation; in 11:18, of the divine retribution of destruction upon those who have destroyed the earth; in 2 Cor. 4:16 it is translated "is decaying," said of the human body. See DESTROY, PERISH.

4. *kataphtheirō* (καταφθείρω, 2704), *kata*, "down," intensive, and No. 2, is said of men who are reprobate concerning the faith, "corrupted in mind" (KJV, "corrupt"), 2 Tim. 3:8. For 2 Pet. 2:12, RV, "shall be destroyed," see No. 2.

5. *sēpō* (σήπω, 4595) signifies "to make corrupt, to destroy"; in the passive voice with middle sense, "to become corrupt or rotten, to perish," said of riches, Jas. 5:2, of the gold and silver of the luxurious rich who have ground down their laborers. The verb is derived from a root signifying "to rot off, drop to pieces."

6. *aphanizō* (ἀφανίζω, 853): see CONSUME, No. 3.

B. Nouns.

1. *phthora* (φθορά, 5356), connected with *phtheirō*, No. 2, above, signifies "a bringing or being brought into an inferior or worse condition, a destruction or corruption." It is used (a) physically, (1) of the condition of creation, as under bondage, Rom. 8:21; (2) of the effect of the withdrawal of life, and so of the condition of the human body in burial, 1 Cor. 15:42; (3) by metonymy, of anything which is liable to "corruption," 1 Cor. 15:50; (4) of the physical effects of merely gratifying the natural desires and ministering to one's own needs or lusts, Gal. 6:8, to the flesh in contrast to the Spirit, "corruption" being antithetic to "eternal life"; (5) of that which is naturally short-lived and transient, Col. 2:22, "perish"; (b) of the death and decay of beasts, 2 Pet. 2:12, RV, "destroyed" (first part of verse; lit., "unto ... destruction"); (c) ethically, with a moral significance, (1) of the effect of lusts, 2 Pet. 1:4; (2) of the effect upon themselves of the work of false and immoral teachers, 2 Pet. 2:12, RV, "destroying"; KJV, "corruption," and verse 19. See DESTROY, PERISH.

Note: There is nothing in any of these words suggesting or involving annihilation.

2. *diaphthora* (διαφθορά, 1312), an intensified form of No. 1, "utter or thorough corruption," referring in the NT to physical decomposition and decay, is used six times, five of which refer, negatively, to the body of God's "Holy One," after His death, which body, by reason of His absolute holiness, could not see "corruption," Acts 2:27, 31; 13:34-35, 37; once it is used of a human body, that of David, which, by contrast, saw "corruption," Acts 13:36.

3. *aphtharsia* (ἀφθαρσία, 861), "incorruption," *a*, negative, with A, No. 2, is used (a) of the resurrection body, 1 Cor. 15:42, 50, 53-54; (b) of a condition associated with glory and honor and life, including perhaps a moral significance, Rom. 2:7; 2 Tim. 1:10; this is wrongly translated "immortality" in the KJV; (c) of love to Christ, that which is sincere and undiminishing, Eph. 6:24 (translated "uncorruptness"). See IMMORTALITY, SINCERITY.

Note: For Titus 2:7 (where some texts have *aphtharsia*), see No. 4.

4. *aphthoria* (φθορά, 5356d), similar to No. 3, "uncorruptness, free from (moral) taint," is said of doctrine, Titus 2:7 (some texts have *adiaphthoria*, the negative form of No. 2, above).

C. Adjectives.

1. *phthartos* (φθαρτός, 5349), "corruptible," akin to A, No. 2, is used (a) of man as being mortal, liable to decay (in contrast to God), Rom. 1:23; (b) of man's body as death-doomed, 1 Cor. 15:53-54; (c) of a crown of reward at the Greek games, 1 Cor. 9:25; (d) of silver and gold, as specimens or "corruptible" things, 1 Pet. 1:18; (e) of natural seed, 1 Pet. 1:23.

2. *apthartos* (ἄφθαρτος, 862), "not liable to corruption or decay, incorruptible" (*a*, negative, and A, No. 2), is used of (a) God, Rom. 1:23; 1 Tim. 1:17 (KJV, "immortal"); (b) the raised dead, 1 Cor. 15:52; (c) rewards given to the saints hereafter, metaphorically described as a "crown," 1 Cor. 9:25; (d) the eternal inheritance of the saints, 1 Pet. 1:4; (e) the Word of God, as "incorruptible" seed, 1 Pet. 1:23; (f) a meek and quiet spirit, metaphorically spoken of as "incorruptible" apparel, 1 Pet. 3:4. See IMMORTAL.

3. *sapros* (σαπρός, 4550), "corrupt," akin to *sēpō*, A, No. S; see BAD, No. 3.

Note: (1) Trench, *Syn.* Sec. LXVIII, contrasts this with *amarantos*, and *amarantinos*, "unwithering, not fading away," 1 Pet. 1:4; 5:4. These are, however, distinct terms (see FADE) and are not strictly synonymous, though used in the same description of the heavenly inheritance.

COUNCIL, COUNCILLOR

1. *sumboulion* (συμβούλιον, 4824), "a uniting in counsel" (*sun*, "together," *boulē*, "counsel, advice"), denotes (a) "counsel" which is given, taken and acted upon, e.g., Matt. 12:14, RV, "took counsel," for KJV, "held a council"; 22:15; hence (b) "a council," an assembly of counsellors or persons in consultation, Acts 25:12, of the "council" with which Festus conferred concerning Paul. The governors and procurators of provinces had a board of advisers or assessors, with whom they took "counsel," before pronouncing judgment. See CONSULTATION.

2. *sunedrion* (συνέδριον, 4892), properly, "a settling together" (*sun*, "together," *hedra*, "a seat"), hence, (a) "any assembly or session of persons deliberating or adjusting," as in the Sept. of Ps. 26:4 (lit., "with a council of vanity"); Prov. 22:10; Jer. 15:17, etc.; in the NT, e.g., Matt. 10:17; Mark 13:9; John 11:47, in particular, it denoted (b) "the Sanhedrin," the Great Council at Jerusalem, consisting of 71 members, namely, prominent members of the families of the high priest, elders and scribes. The Jews trace the origin of this to Num.

11:16. The more important causes came up before this tribunal. The Roman rulers of Judea permitted the Sanhedrin to try such cases, and even to pronounce sentence of death, with the condition that such a sentence should be valid only if confirmed by the Roman procurator. In John 11:47, it is used of a meeting of the Sanhedrin; in Acts 4:15, of the place of meeting.

3. *bouleutēs* (βουλευτής, 1010): Joseph of Arimathaea is described as "a councillor of honorable estate," Mark 15:43, RV; cf. Luke 23:50 (not as KJV, "counsellor").

COUNSEL

For **COUNSELLOR** see above.

A. Nouns.

1. *boulē* (βουλή, 1012): see under ADVICE.

2. *sumboulos* (σύμβουλος, 4825), "a councillor with," occurs in Rom. 11:34.

B. Verbs.

1. *bouleuō* (βουλεύω, 1011), "to take counsel, to resolve," is used in the middle voice in the NT, "took counsel" in Acts 5:33, KJV (RV translates *boulomai*); both in 27:39; in Luke 14:31, RV "take counsel" (KJV, "consulteth"); in John 11:53, KJV and RV (so the best mss.); 12:10, RV, "took counsel," for KJV, "consulted"; in 2 Cor. 1:17 (twice), "purpose." See CONSULT, MINDED.

2. *sumbouleuō* (συμβουλεύω, 4823), in the active voice, "to advise, to counsel," John 18:14, "gave counsel"; in Rev. 3:18, "I counsel"; in the middle voice, "to take counsel, consult," Matt. 26:4, RV, "took counsel together," for KJV, "consulted"; Acts 9:23, "took counsel" (RV adds "together"); in some mss. John 11:53. See CONSULT.

COUNT

1. *echō* (ἔχω, 2192), "to have, to hold"; then, "to hold in the mind, to regard, to count," has this significance in Matt. 14:5, "they counted Him as a prophet"; Philem. 17, "If then thou countest me a partner"; Mark 11:32, KJV, (RV, "hold"); Acts 20:24, KJV. See ABLE.

2. *hēgeomai* (ἡγέομαι, 2233), primarily, "to lead the way"; hence, "to lead before the mind, account," is found with this meaning in Phil. 2:3, RV (KJV, "esteem"); 2:6, RV (KJV, "thought"); 2:25 (KJV, "supposed"); Phil. 3:7-8; 2 Thess. 3:15; 1 Tim. 1:12; 6:1; Heb. 10:29; Jas. 1:2; Heb. 11:11 (KJV, "judged"); 2 Pet. 2:13; 3:9.

3. *logizomai* (λογίζομαι, 3049), "to reckon," is rendered "count" in 2 Cor. 10:2, RV (KJV, "think"); "counted" in the KJV of Rom. 2:26; 4:3, 5; 9:8 (RV, "reckoned").

4. *psēphizō* (ψηφίζω, 5585), akin to *psēphos*, "a stone," used in voting, occurs in Luke 14:28; Rev. 13:18.

5. *sumpsēphizō* (συμψηφίζω, 4860), "to count up," occurs in Acts 19:19.

Note: In Jas. 5:11, *makarizō*, "to pronounce blessed," is rendered "count ... happy," KJV (RV, "call ..."). For "descent is counted" see GENEALOGY.

COUNTENANCE

1. *opsis* (ὄψις, 3799): only Rev. 1:16 has "countenance." See APPEARANCE.

2. *prosōpon* (πρόσωπον, 4383), is translated "countenance" in Luke 9:29; Acts 2:28, and in the KJV of 2 Cor. 3:7 (RV, "face"). See APPEARANCE.

3. *eidea* (εἰδέα, 2397), akin to *eidon*, "to see: see APPEARANCE.

Notes: (1) In Acts 13:24 *prosōpon* is translated "before" (lit., "before the presence of His coming").

(2) *Skuthrōpos*, "of a sad countenance" (*skuthros*, "gloomy, sad," *ōps*, "an eye"), is used in Matt. 6:16 and Luke 24:17, "sad."

(3) *Stugnazō*, "to be or become hateful, gloomy, in aspect," is translated "his countenance fell," Mark 10:22, RV (KJV, "he was sad"). It is used of the heaven or sky in Matt. 16:3, "lowring."

COUNTRYMEN

1. *genos* (γένος, 1085) properly denotes "an offspring"; then, "a family"; then, "a race, nation; otherwise, a kind or species"; it is translated "countrymen," in 2 Cor. 11:26, in Paul's reference to his fellow-nationals; so in Gal. 1:14, RV, for KJV, "nation. See BEGET.

2. *sumphuletēs* (συμφυλέτης, 4853), lit., "a fellow-tribesman" (*sun*, "with," *phulē*, "a tribe, race, nation, people"), hence, one who is of the same people, a fellow-countryman, is found in 1 Thess. 2:14.

COUPLED

Note: The word "coupled" is inserted in italics in 1 Pet. 3:2, the more adequately to express the original, which is, lit., "your chaste behavior in fear."

COURAGE

A. Noun.

tharsos (θάρσος, 2294), akin to *tharseo*, "to be of good cheer," is found in Acts 28:15.

B. Verb.

tharreō (θαῤῥέω, 2292) is translated by some form of the verb "to be of good courage," in the RV in five of the six places where it is used: 2 Cor. 5:6, "being of good courage" (KJV, "we are ... confident"); 5:8, "we are of good courage" (KJV, "we are confident"); 7:16, "I am of good courage" (KJV, "I have confidence"); 10:1, "I am of good courage" (KJV, "I am bold");

10:2, "show courage" (KJV, "be bold"); Heb. 13:6, "with good courage," lit., "being of good courage" (KJV, "boldly"). See CONFIDENCE.

Note: Tharreō is a later form of *tharseō*. Cf. *tolmaō*, "to be bold."

COURT

1. *agoraios* (ἀγοραῖος, 60) is an adjective, "signifying pertaining to the *agora*, any place of public meeting, and especially where trials were held," Acts 19:38; the RV translates the sentence "the courts are open"; a more literal rendering is "court days are kept." In Acts 17:5 it is translated in the RV, "rabble"; KJV, "baser sort," lit., "frequenters of the markets." See BASER.

2. *aulē* (αὐλή, 833), primarily, "an uncovered space around a house, enclosed by a wall, where the stables were," hence was used to describe (a) "the courtyard of a house"; in the OT it is used of the "courts" of the tabernacle and Temple; in this sense it is found in the NT in Rev. 11:2; (b) "the courts in the dwellings of well-to-do folk," which usually had two, one exterior, between the door and the street (called the *proaulion*, or "porch," Mark 14:68.), the other, interior, surrounded by the buildings of the dwellings, as in Matt. 26:69 (in contrast to the room where the judges were sitting); Mark 14:66; Luke 22:55; KJV, "hall"; RV "court" gives the proper significance, Matt. 26:3, 58; Mark 14:54; 15:16 (RV, "Praetorium"); Luke 11:21; John 18:15. It is here to be distinguished from the Praetorium, translated "palace." See HALL, PALACE.

3. *basileion* (βασίλειον, 933), an adjective meaning "royal," signifies, in the neuter plural, "a royal palace," translated "kings' courts" in Luke 7:25; in the singular, 1 Pet. 2:9, "royal." See ROYAL.

COURTEOUS, COURTEOUSLY

A. Adjective.

tapeinophrōn (ταπεινόφρων, 5391), "lowlyminded," is used in 1 Pet. 3:8, "be courteous," KJV (RV, "humble-minded").

B. Adverbs.

1. *philophronōs* (φιλοφρόνως, 5390), lit., "friendly," or, more fully, "with friendly thoughtfulness" (*philos*, "friend," *phrēn*, "the mind"), is found in Acts 28:7, of the hospitality showed by Publius to Paul and his fellow-shipwrecked travelers.

Note: Some mss. have the corresponding adjective *philophrōn*, "courteous," in 1 Pet. 3:8; the most authentic mss. have *tapeinophrōn*, "humble-minded."

2. *philanthrōpōs* (φιλανθρώπως, 5364) is translated "courteously" in Acts 27:3, KJV; RV, "kindly" (Eng., "philanthropically"). See KINDLY.

COVENANT (Noun and Verb)

A. Noun.

diathēkē (διαθήκη, 1242) primarily signifies "a disposition of property by will or otherwise." In its use in the Sept., it is the rendering of a Hebrew word meaning a "covenant" or agreement (from a verb signifying "to cut or divide," in allusion to a sacrificial custom in connection with "covenant-making," e.g., Gen. 15:10, "divided" Jer. 34:18-19). In contradistinction to the English word "covenant" (lit., "a coming together"), which signifies a mutual undertaking between two parties or more, each binding himself to fulfill obligations, it does not in itself contain the idea of joint obligation, it mostly signifies an obligation undertaken by a single person. For instance, in Gal. 3:17 it is used as an alternative to a "promise" (vv. 16-18). God enjoined upon Abraham the rite of circumcision, but His promise to Abraham, here called a "covenant," was not conditional upon the observance of circumcision, though a penalty attached to its nonobservance.

"The NT uses of the word may be analyzed as follows: (a) a promise or undertaking, human or divine, Gal. 3:15; (b) a promise or undertaking on the part of God, Luke 1:72; Acts 3:25; Rom. 9:4; 11:27; Gal. 3:17 Eph. 2:12; Heb. 7:22; 8:6, 8, 10; 10:16; (c) an agreement, a mutual undertaking, between God and Israel, see Deut. 29-30 (described as a 'commandment,' Heb. 7:18, cf. v. 22); Heb. 8:9; 9:20; (d) by metonymy, the token of the covenant, or promise, made to Abraham, Acts 7:8, (e) by metonymy, the record of the covenant, 2 Cor. 3:14; Heb. 9:4; cf. Rev. 11:19; (f) the basis, established by the death of Christ, on which the salvation of men is secured, Matt. 26:28; Mark 14:24; Luke 22:20; 1 Cor. 11:25; 2 Cor. 3:6; Heb. 10:29; 12:24; 13:20.

"This covenant is called the 'new,' Heb. 9:15, the 'second,' 8:7, the 'better,' 7:22. In Heb. 9:16-17, the translation is much disputed. There does not seem to be any sufficient reason for departing in these verses from the word used everywhere else. The English word 'Testament' is taken from the titles prefixed to the Latin Versions." See TESTAMENT.

B. Verb.

suntithēmi (συντίθημι, 4934), lit., "to put together," is used only in the middle voice in the NT, and, means "to determine, agree," John 9:22 and Acts 23:20; "to assent," Acts 24:9; "to covenant," Luke 22:5.

Note: In Matt. 26:15 the KJV translates *histēmi*, "to place (in the balances)," i.e., to weigh, "they covenanted with"; RV, "they weighed unto."

COVENANT-BREAKERS

asunthetos (ἀσύνθετος, 802), from *suntithēmi* (see above), with the negative prefix a hence signifies "not covenant-keeping," i.e., refusing to abide by "covenants" made, "covenant-breaking," faithless, Rom. 1:31.

In the Sept. it is found in Jer. 3:8-11. Cf. the corresponding verb *asuntithēmi*, in the Sept. of Ps. 73:15, "to deal treacherously" (RV), and the noun *asunthesua*, "transgression, or covenant-breaking," e.g., Ezra 9:2, 4; 10:6.

Note: Trench, *Syn.* Sec. LII, notes the distinction between *asunthetos* and *aspondos*, "implacable," the latter, in 2 Tim. 3:3 only, being derived from *spondē*, "a sacrificial libation," which accompanied treaty-making; hence, with the negative prefix *a*, "without a treaty or covenant," thus denoting a person who cannot be persuaded to enter into a "covenant." He points out that *asunthetos* presumes a state of peace interrupted by the unrighteous, *aspondos* a state of war, which the implacable refuse to terminate equitably. The words are clearly not synonymous.

COVET, COVETOUS, COVETOUSNESS

A. Verbs.

1. *epithumeō* (ἐπιθυμέω, 1937), "to fix the desire upon" (*epi*, "upon," used intensively, *thumos*, "passion"), whether things good or bad; hence, "to long for, lust after, covet," is used with the meaning "to covet evilly" in Acts 20:33, of "coveting money and apparel"; so in Rom. 7:7; 13:9. See DESIRE, FAIN, LUST.

2. *zēloō* (ζηλόω, 2206) is rendered "covet earnestly," in 1 Cor. 12:31, KJV; RV, "desire earnestly," as in 14:39 (KJV "covet"). See AFFECT, DESIRE, ENVY, JEALOUS, ZEALOUS.

3. *oregō* (ὀρέγω, 3713), "to stretch after," is rendered "covet after" in 1 Tim. 6:10, KJV; RV. "reaching after." See DESIRE.

B. Nouns.

1. *epithumētēs* (ἐπιθυμητής, 1938), "a luster after" (akin to A, No. 1), is translated in 1 Cor. 10:6, in verbal form, "should not lust after." See LUST.

2. *epithumia* (ἐπιθυμία, 1939) denotes "coveting," Rom. 7:7-8, RV; KJV, "lust" and "concupiscence"; the commandment here referred to convicted him of sinfulness in his desires for unlawful objects besides that of gain. See DESIRE, LUST.

3. *pleonexia* (πλεονεξία, 4124), "covetousness," lit., "a desire to have more" (*pleon*, "more," *echō*, "to have"), always in a bad sense, is used in a general way in Mark 7:22 (plural, lit., "covetings," i.e., various ways in which "covetousness" shows itself); Rom. 1:29; Eph. 5:3; 1 Thess. 2:5. Elsewhere it is used, (a) of material possessions, Luke 12:15; 2 Pet. 2:3; 2 Cor. 9:5 (RV, "extortion"), lit., "as (a matter of) extortion" i.e., a gift which betrays the giver's unwillingness to bestow what is due; (b) of sensuality, Eph. 4:19, "greediness"; Col. 3:5 (where it is called "idolatry"); 2 Pet. 2:14 (KJV, "covetous practices"). See EXTORTION.

Note: Cf. the corresponding verb *pleonekteō*, "to gain, take advantage of wrong." See DEFRAUD, WRONG.

C. Adjectives.

1. *pleonektēs* (πλεονέκτης, 4123), lit., "(eager) to have more" (see B, No. 3), i.e., to have what belongs to others; hence, "greedy of gain, covetous," 1 Cor. 5:10-11; 6:10; Eph. 5:5 ("covetous man").

2. *philarguros* (φιλάργυρος, 5366), lit., "money-loving," is rendered "covetous" in the KJV of Luke 16:14 and 2 Tim. 3:2; RV, "lovers of money," the wider and due significance.

3. *aphilarguros* (ἀφιλάργυρος, 866), No. 2, with negative prefix, is translated "without covetousness" in Heb. 13:5, KJV; RV, "free from the love of money." In 1 Tim. 3:3, the KJV has "not covetous," the RV, "no lover of money."

Note: Trench, *Syn.* Sec. XXIV, points out the main distinction between *pleonexia* and *philarguria* as being that between "covetousness" and avarice, the former having a much wider and deeper sense, being "the genus of which *philarguria* is the species." The "covetous" man is often cruel as well as grasping, while the avaricious man is simply miserly and stinting.

CRAFTINESS, CRAFTY

A. Noun.

panourgia (πανουργία, 3834), lit., "allworking," i.e., doing everything (*pan*, "all," *ergon*, "work"), hence, "unscrupulous conduct, craftiness," is always used in a bad sense in the NT, Luke 20:23; 1 Cor. 3:19; 2 Cor. 4:2; 11:3; Eph. 4:14, KJV, "cunning craftiness." See SUBTLETY. In the Sept. it is used in a good sense, Prov. 1:4; 8:5; indifferently in Num. 24:22 and Josh. 9:4.

B. Adjective.

panourgos (πανοῦργος, 3835), "cunning, crafty," is found in 2 Cor. 12:16, where the apostle is really quoting an accusation made against him by his detractors. In the Sept. it is used in a good sense in Prov. 13:1; 28:2.

C. Noun.

dolos (δόλος, 1388), primarily, "a bait," hence, "fraud, guile, deceit," is rendered "craft" in the KJV of Mark 14:1 (RV "subtilty"). See DECEIT, GUILE, SUBTLETY.

CRAVE

Note: The word "crave," found in the KJV of Mark 15:43, translates the verb *aiteō*, "to ask" (RV, "asked for").

CREATE, CREATION, CREATOR, CREATURE

A. Verb.

ktizō (κτίζω, 2936), used among the Greeks to mean the founding of a place, a city or colony, signifies, in Scripture, "to create," always of the act of God, whether (a) in the natural creation, Mark 13:19; Rom. 1:25 (where the title "The Creator" translates the article with the aorist participle of the verb); 1 Cor. 11:9; Eph. 3:9; Col. 1:16; 1 Tim. 4:3; Rev. 4:11; 10:6, or (b) in the spiritual creation, Eph. 2:10, 15; 4:24; Col. 3:10.

B. Nouns.

1. *ktisis* (κτίσις, 2937), primarily "the act of creating," or "the creative act in process," has this meaning in Rom. 1:20 and Gal. 6:15. Like the English word "creation," it also signifies the product of the "creative" act, the "creature," as in Mark 16:15, RV; Rom. 1:25; 8:19; Col. 1:15 etc.; in Heb. 9:11, KJV, "building." In Mark 16:15 and Col. 1:23 its significance has special reference to mankind in general. As to its use in Gal. 6:15 and 2 Cor. 5:17, in the former, apparently, "the reference is to the creative act of God, whereby a man is introduced into the blessing of salvation, in contrast to circumcision done by human hands, which the Judaizers claimed was necessary to that end. In 2 Cor. 5:17 the reference is to what the believer is in Christ; in consequence of the creative act he has become a new creature."

Ktisis is once used of human actions, 1 Pet. 2:13, "ordinance" (marg., "creation"). See BUILDING, ORDINANCE.

2. *ktisma* (κτίσμα, 2938) has the concrete sense, "the created thing, the creature, the product of the creative act," 1 Tim. 4:4; Jas. 1:18; Rev. 5:13; 8:9.

3. *ktistēs* (κτιστής, 2939), among the Greeks, the founder of a city, etc., denotes in Scripture "the Creator," 1 Pet. 4:19 (cf. Rom. 1:20, under B, No. 1, above).

Note: It is a significant confirmation of Rom. 1:20-21, that in all nonchristian Greek literature these words are never used by Greeks to convey the idea of a creator or of a creative act by any of their gods. The words are confined by them to the acts of human beings.

4. *zōon* (ζῷον, 2226), "a living creature": see BEAST.

For **CREDITOR** see LEND

CREEP, CREEPING, CREPT

A. Verbs.

1. *endunō* (ἐνδύνω, 1744), properly, "to envelop in" (*en*, "in," *dunō*, "to enter"), "to put on," as of a garment, has the secondary and intransitive significance of "creeping into, insinuating oneself into," and is found with this meaning in 2 Tim. 3:6. Cf. *enduō*, "to clothe."

2. *pareisdunō* (παρεισδύνω, 3921), "to enter in by the side" (*para*, "beside," *eis*, "in"), to insinuate oneself into, by stealth, to creep in stealthily, is used in Jude 4.

B. Noun.

herpeton (ἑρπετόν, 2062) signifies "a creeping thing" (*herpō*, "to creep"; Eng., "serpent," Jas. 3:7 (RV, "creeping things," for KJV, "serpents," which form only one of this genus); it is set in contrast to quadrupeds and birds, Acts 10:12; 11:6; Rom. 1:23. See SERPENT.

For **CRIPPLE** see HALT

CROOKED

skolios (σκολιός, 4646), "curved, crooked," was especially used (a) of a way, Luke 3:5, with spiritual import (see Prov. 28:18, Sept.); it is set in contrast to *orthos* and *euthus*, "straight"; (b) metaphorically, of what is morally "crooked," perverse, froward, of people belonging to a particular generation, Acts 2:40 (KJV, "untoward"); Phil. 2:15; of tyrannical or unjust masters, 1 Pet. 2:18, "froward"; in this sense it is set in contrast to *agathos*, "good."

CROSS, CRUCIFY

A. Noun.

stauros (σταυρός, 4716) denotes, primarily, "an upright pale or stake." On such malefactors were nailed for execution. Both the noun and the verb *stauroō*, "to fasten to a stake or pale," are originally to be distinguished from the ecclesiastical form of a two beamed "cross." The shape of the latter had its origin in ancient Chaldea, and was used as the symbol of the god Tammuz (being in the shape of the mystic Tau, the initial of his name) in that country and in adjacent lands, including Egypt. By the middle of the 3rd cent. A.D. the churches had either departed from, or had travestied, certain doctrines of the Christian faith. In order to increase the prestige of the apostate ecclesiastical system pagans were received into the churches apart from regeneration by faith, and were permitted largely to retain their pagan signs and symbols. Hence the Tau or T, in its most frequent form, with the cross-piece lowered, was adopted to stand for the "cross" of Christ.

As for the Chi, or X, which Constantine declared he had seen in a vision leading him to champion the Christian faith, that letter was the initial of the word "Christ" and had nothing to do with "the Cross" (for *xulon*, "a timber beam, a tree," as used for the *stauros*, see under TREE).

The method of execution was borrowed by the Greeks and Romans from the Phoenicians. The *stauros* denotes (a) "the cross, or stake itself," e.g., Matt. 27:32; (b) "the crucifixion suffered," e.g., 1 Cor. 1:17-18, where "the word of the cross," RV, stands for the gospel; Gal. 5:11, where crucifixion is metaphorically used of the renunciation of the world, that characterizes the true Christian life; 6:12, 14; Eph. 2:16; Phil. 3:18.

The judicial custom by which the condemned person carried his stake to the place of execution, was applied by the Lord to those sufferings by which His faithful followers were to express their fellowship with Him, e.g., Matt. 10:38.

B. Verbs.

1. *stauroō* (σταυρόω, 4717) signifies (a) "the act of crucifixion," e.g., Matt. 20:19; (b) metaphorically, "the putting off of the flesh with its passions and lusts," a condition fulfilled in the case of those who are "of Christ Jesus," Gal. 5:24, RV; so of the relationship between the believer and the world, 6:14.

2. *sustauroō* (συσταυρόω, 4957), "to crucify with" (*su*-, "for," *sun*, "with"), is used (a) of actual "crucifixion" in company with another, Matt. 27:44; Mark 15:32; John 19:32; (b) metaphorically, of spiritual identification with Christ in His death, Rom. 6:6, and Gal. 2:20.

3. *anastauroō* (ἀνασταυρόω, 388) (*ana*, again) is used in Heb. 6:6 of Hebrew apostates, who as merely nominal Christians, in turning back to Judaism, were thereby virtually guilty of "crucifying" Christ again.

4. *prospēgnumi* (προσπήγνυμι, 4362), "to fix or fasten to anything" (*pros*, "to," *pēgnumi*, "to fix"), is used of the "crucifixion" of Christ, Acts 2:23.

CROSS (Verb)

diaperaō (διαπεράω, 1276), "to pass over, to cross over" (*dia*, "through," *peraō*, "to pass": akin to this are *peran*, "across," *peras*, "a boundary," Latin, *porta*, "a gate," Eng., "portal, port," etc.), is translated by the verb "to cross" in the RV, but differently in the KJV; in Matt. 9:1; Mark 5:21; 6:53 (KJV, "passed"); Matt. 14:34 (KJV, "were gone "); Luke 16:26 (KJV, "neither can they pass"); Acts 21:2 (KJV, "sailing "). See GO. In the Sept., Deut. 30:13; Isa. 23:2.

For the verb **CROW (CREW)** see CALL, A, No. 8

CROWD

A. Noun.

ochlos (ὄχλος, 3793), "a confused throng," is usually translated "multitude."

The RV translates it "crowd" (KJV, "press" in some) in Matt. 9:23, 25; Mark 2:4; 3:9; 5:27, 30; Luke 8:19; 19:3; Acts 21:34-35; 24:12, 18. See COMPANY, MULTITUDE, PEOPLE.

B. Verb.

ochlopoieō (ὀχλοποιέω, 3792), "to make a crowd" (A, with *poieō*, "to make"), is translated "gathered a crowd" in Acts 17:5, RV (KJV, "company").

CROWN (Noun and Verb)

A. Nouns.

1. *stephanos* (στέφανος, 4735), primarily, "that which surrounds, as a wall or crowd" (from *stephō*, "to encircle"), denotes (a) "the victor's crown," the symbol of triumph in the games or some such contest; hence, by metonymy, a reward or prize; (b) "a token of public honor" for distinguished service, military prowess, etc., or of nuptial joy, or festal gladness, especially at the parousia of kings. It was woven as a garland of oak, ivy, parsley, myrtle, or olive, or in imitation of these in gold. In some passages the reference to the games is clear, 1 Cor. 9:25; 2 Tim. 4:8 ("crown of righteousness"); it may be so in 1 Pet. 5:4, where the fadeless character of "the crown of glory" is set in contrast to the garlands of earth. In other passages it stands as an emblem of life, joy, reward and glory, Phil. 4:1; 1 Thess. 2:19; Jas. 1:12 ("crown of life "); Rev. 2:10 (ditto); 3:11; 4:4, 10: of triumph, 6:2; 9:7; 12:1; 14:14.

It is used of "the crown of thorns" which the soldiers plaited and put on Christ's head, Matt. 27:29; Mark 15:17; John 19:2, 5. At first sight this might be taken as an alternative for *diadēma*, "a kingly crown" (see below), but considering the blasphemous character of that masquerade, and the materials used, obviously *diadēma* would be quite unfitting and the only alternative was *stephanos* (see Trench *Syn.* Sec. XXXII).

2. *diadēma* (διάδημα, 1238) is never used as *stephanos* is; it is always the symbol of kingly or imperial dignity, and is translated "diadem" instead of "crown" in the RV, of the claims of the Dragon, Rev. 12:3; 13:1; 19:12. See DIADEM.

B. Verb.

stephanoō (στεφανόω, 4737), "to crown," conforms in meaning to *stephanos;* it is used of the reward of victory in the games, in 2 Tim. 2:5; of the glory and honor bestowed by God upon man in regard to his position in creation, Heb. 2:7; of the glory and honor bestowed upon the Lord Jesus in His exaltation, v. 9.

For **CRUCIFY** see CROSS

CRY (Noun and Verb), CRYING

A. Nouns.

1. *kraugē* (κραυγή, 2906), an onomatopoeic word, is used in Matt. 25:6; Luke 1:42 (some mss. have *phōnē*); Acts 23:9, RV, "clamor"; Eph. 4:31, "clamor"; Heb. 5:7; Rev. 21:4, "crying." Some mss. have it in Rev. 14:18 (the most authentic have *phōnē*).

2. *boē* (βοή, 995), especially "a cry for help," an onomatopoeic word (cf. Eng., "boo"), connected with *boaō* (see B, No. 1), is found in Jas. 5:4.

B. Verbs.

1. *boaō* (βοάω, 994), akin to A, No. 2, signifies (a) "to raise a cry," whether of joy, Gal. 4:27, or vexation, Acts 8:7; (b) "to speak with a strong voice," Matt. 3:3; Mark 1:3; 15:34; Luke 3:4; 9:38 (some mss. have *anaboaō* here: see No. 2); John 1:23; Acts 17:6; 25:24 (some mss. have *epiboaō*, No. 3, here); (c) "to cry out for help," Luke 18:7, 38. For Acts 21:34, see No. 8.

2. *anaboaō* (ἀναβοάω, 310), *ana*, "up," intensive, and No. 1, "to lift up the voice, cry out," is said of Christ at the moment of His death, a testimony to His supernatural power in giving up His life, Matt. 27:46; in some mss. in Mark 15:8, of the shouting of a multitude; in some mss. in Luke 9:38, of the "crying" out of a man in a company (see No. 1).

3. *epiboaō* (ἐπιβοάω, 1916), *epi*, "upon," intensive, and No. 1, "to cry out, exclaim vehemently," is used in some mss. in Acts 25:24 (see No. 1.)

4. *krazō* (κράζω, 2896), akin to A, No. 1, "to cry out," an onomatopoeic word, used especially of the "cry" of the raven; then, of any inarticulate cries, from fear, pain etc.; of the "cry" of a Canaanitish woman, Matt. 15:22 (so the best mss., instead of *kraugazō*); of the shouts of the children in the Temple, Matt. 21:15; of the people who shouted for Christ to be crucified, 27:23; Mark 15:13-14; of the "cry" of Christ on the Cross at the close of His sufferings, Matt. 27:50; Mark 15:39 (see No. 2, above).

In John's gospel it is used three times, out of the six, of Christ's utterances, 7:28, 37; 12:44. In the Acts it is not used of "cries" of distress, but chiefly of the shouts of opponents; in the Apocalypse, chiefly of the utterances of heavenly beings concerning earthly matters; in Rom. 8:15 and Gal. 4:6, of the appeal of believers to God the Father; in Rom. 9:27, of a prophecy concerning Israel; in Jas. 5:4, metaphorically, of hire kept back by fraud.

Note: A recent translator renders this verb in Matt. 27:50 "uttered a scream," an utterly deplorable mistranslation and a misrepresentation of the nature of the Lord's "cry."

5. *anakrazō* (ἀνακράζω, 349), *ana*, "up," intensive, and No. 4, signifies "to cry out loudly," Mark 1:23; 6:49; Luke 4:33; 8:28; 23:18.

6. *kraugazō* (κραυγάζω, 2905), a stronger form of No. 4, "to make a clamor or outcry" (A, No. 1), is used in Matt. 12:19, in a prophecy from Isaiah of Christ; in Luke 4:41 (in the best mss., instead of *krazo*); John 11:43; 12:13 (in the best mss.); 18:40; 19:6, 12, 19:15; Acts 22:23.

7. *phōneō* (φωνέω, 5455), "to utter a loud sound or cry," whether of animals, e.g., Matt. 26:34; or persons, Luke 8:8; 16:24; this is the word which Luke uses to describe the "cry" of the Lord at the close of His sufferings on the cross, Luke 23:46 (see under *anaboaō* and *krazō*, above); also, e.g., Acts 16:28; Rev. 14:18. See CALL, A, No. 8.

8. *epiphōneō* (ἐπιφωνέω, 2019), No. 7, with *epi*, "upon," or "against," signifies "to shout," either against, Luke 23:21; Acts 21:34 (in the best mss., No. 1); 22:24, or in acclamation, Acts 12:22. See SHOUT.

Comparing the various verbs, *kaleō*, denotes "to call out for any purpose," *boaō*, "to cry out as an expression of feeling," *krazō*, to cry out loudly." *Kaleō* suggests intelligence, *boaō*, sensibilities, *krazō*, instincts.

CRYSTAL

A. Noun.

krustallos (κρύσταλλος, 2930), from *kruos*, "ice," and hence properly anything congealed and transparent, denotes "crystal," a kind of precious stone, Rev. 4:6; 22:1. Rock crystal is pure quartz; it crystallizes in hexagonal prisms, each with a pyramidical apex.

B. Verb.

krustallizō (κρυσταλλίζω, 2929), "to be of crystalline brightness and transparency, to shine like crystal," is found in Rev. 21:11, where it is said of Christ as the "Light-giver" (*phōster*) of the heavenly city (not *phōs*, "light," RV and KJV). Possibly there the verb has a transitive force, "to transform into crystal splendor," as of the effect of Christ upon His saints.

CUMBER

1. *katargeō* (καταργέω, 2673), lit., "to reduce to idleness or inactivity" (*kata*, "down," and *argos*, "idle"), is once rendered "cumber," Luke 13:7. See ABOLISH.

2. *perispaō* (περισπάω, 4049), lit., "to draw around" (*peri*), "draw away, distract," is used in the passive voice in the sense of being overoccupied about a thing, to be "cumbered," Luke 10:40.

CUP

potērion (ποτήριον, 4221), a diminutive of *potēr*, denotes, primarily, a "drinking vessel"; hence, "a cup" (a) literal, as, e.g., in Matt. 10:42. The "cup" of blessing, 1 Cor. 10:16, is so named from the third (the fourth according to Edersheim) "cup" in the Jewish Passover feast, over which thanks and praise were given to God. This connection is not to be rejected on the ground that the church at Corinth was unfamiliar with Jewish customs. That the contrary was the case, see 5:7; (b) figurative, of one's lot or experience, joyous or sorrowful (frequent in the Psalms; cf. Ps. 116:18, "cup of salvation"); in the NT it is used most frequently of the sufferings of Christ, Matt. 20:22-23; 26:39; Mark 10:38-39; 14:36; Luke 22:42; John 18:11; also of the evil deeds of Babylon, Rev. 17:4; 18:6; of divine punishments to be inflicted, Rev. 14:10; 16:19. Cf. Ps. 11:6; 75:8; Isa. 51:17; Jer. 25:15; Ezek. 23:32-34; Zech. 12:2.

CURE (Noun and Verb)

A. Noun.

iasis (ἴασις, 2392), "a healing, a cure" (akin to *iaomai*, "to heal," and *iatros*, "a physician"), is used in the plural in Luke 13:32; in Acts 4:22, "healing," in 4:30 with the preposition *eis* "unto," lit., "unto healing," translated "heal." See HEALING.

B. Verb.

therapeuō (θεραπεύω, 2323), (Eng., "therapeutics," etc.), denotes (a) primarily, "to serve" (cf. *therapeia* and *therapon*), Acts 17:25 (KJV, "worshiped"); then, (b) "to heal, restore to health, to cure"; it is usually translated "to heal," but "cure" in Matt. 17:16, 18; Luke 7:21; 9:1; John 5:10; Acts 28:9, RV. See HEAL, WORSHIP.

CURIOUS

Note: The adjective *periergos*, "busy about trifles," is used of magic arts in Acts 19:19 (lit., "things that are around work," and thus superfluous), i.e., the arts of those who pry into forbidden things, with the aid of evil spirits. See also 1 Tim. 5:13, where the meaning is "inquisitive," prying into other people's affairs.

CURSE, CURSING (Noun and Verb), CURSED, ACCURSED

A. Nouns.

1. *ara* (ἀρά, 685), in its most usual meaning, "a malediction, cursing" (its other meaning is "a prayer"), is used in Rom. 3:14 (often in the Sept.)

2. *katara* (κατάρα, 2671), *kata*, "down," intensive, and No. 1, denotes an "execration, imprecation, curse," uttered out of malevolence, Jas. 3:10; 2 Pet. 2:14; or pronounced by God in His righteous judgment, as upon a land doomed to barrenness, Heb. 6:8; upon those who seek for justification by obedience, in part or completely, to the Law, Gal. 3:10, 13; in this 13th verse it is used concretely of Christ, as having "become a curse" for us, i.e., by voluntarily undergoing on the cross the appointed penalty of the "curse." He thus was identified, on our behalf, with the doom of sin. Here, not the verb in the Sept. of Deut. 21:23 is used (see B, No. 3), but the concrete noun.

3. *anathema* (ἀνάθεμα, 331), transliterated from the Greek, is frequently used in the Sept., where it translates the Heb. *cherem*, "a thing devoted to God," whether (a) for His service, as the sacrifices, Lev. 27:28 (cf. *anathema*, a votive offering, gift), or (b) for its destruction, as an idol, Deut. 7:26, or a city, Josh. 6:17. Later it acquired the more general meaning of "the disfavor of Jehovah," e.g., Zech. 14:11. This is the meaning in the NT. It is used of (a) the sentence pronounced, Acts 23:14 (lit., "cursed themselves with a curse"; see *anathematizō* below); (b) of the object on which the "curse" is laid, "accursed"; in the following, the RV keeps to the word "anathema," Rom. 9:3; 1 Cor. 12:3; 16:22; Gal. 1:8-9, all of which the KJV renders by "accursed" except 1 Cor. 16:22, where it has "Anathema." In Gal. 1:8-9, the apostle declares in the strongest manner that the gospel he preached was the one and only way of salvation, and that to preach another was to nullify the death of Christ.

4. *katathema* (κατανάθεμα, 2652), or, as in some mss., the longer form *katanathema*, is stronger than No. 3 (*kata*, intensive), and denotes, by metonymy, "an accursed thing" (the object "cursed" being put for the "curse" pronounced), Rev. 22:3.

B. Verbs.

1. *anathematizō* (ἀναθεματίζω, 332), akin to No. 3, signifies "to declare anathema," i.e., "devoted to destruction, accursed, to curse," Mark 14:71, or "to bind by a curse," Acts 23:12, 14, 21.

2. *katanathematizō* (καταναθεματίζω, 2653), a strengthened form of No. 1, denotes "to utter curses against," Matt. 26:74; cf. Mark's word concerning the same occasion (No. 1).

3. *kataraomai* (καταράομαι, 2672), akin to A, No. 2, primarily signifies "to pray against, to wish evil against a person or thing"; hence "to curse," Matt. 25:41; Mark 11:21; Luke 6:28; Rom. 12:14; Jas. 3:9. Some mss. have it in Matt. 5:44.

4. *kakologeō* (κακολογέω, 2551), "to speak evil" (*kakos*, "evil," *legō*, "to speak"), is translated by the verb "to curse" in Matt. 15:4, and Mark 7:10, "to speak evil of father and mother," not necessarily "to curse," is what the Lord intended (RV). KJV and RV have the verb "to speak evil" in Mark 9:39 and Acts 19:9. See EVIL.

C. Adjectives.

1. *epikataratos* (ἐπικατάρατος, 1944), "cursed, accursed" (*epi* "upon," and A, No. 2), is used in Gal. 3:10, 13.

2. *eparatos* (ἐπάρατος, 1944), "accursed," is found, in the best mss., in John 7:49, RV, "accursed," instead of No. 1.

CUSTOM (Usage), ACCUSTOM (Verb)

A. Nouns.

1. *ethos* (ἔθος, 1485) denotes (a) "a custom, usage, prescribed by law," Acts 6:14; 15:1; 25:16; "a rite or ceremony," Luke 2:42; (b) a "custom, habit, manner," Luke 22:39; John 19:40; Heb. 10:25 (KJV, "manner").

2. *sunētheia* (συνήθεια, 4914), *sun*, "with," *ethos* (see No. 1), denotes (a) "an intercourse, intimacy," a meaning not found in the NT; (b) "a custom, customary usage," John 18:39; 1 Cor. 11:16; "or force of habit," 1 Cor. 8:7, RV, "being used to" (some mss. here have *suneidēsis*, "conscience"; whence KJV, "with conscience of").

B. Verbs.

1. *ethizō* (ἐθίζω, 1480), akin to A, No. 1, signifies "to accustom," or in the passive voice, "to be accustomed." In the participial form it is equivalent to a noun, "custom, Luke 2:27.

2. *ethō* (ἔθω, 1486), "to be accustomed," as in the case of No. 1, is used in the passive participle as a noun, signifying "a custom," Luke 4:16; Acts 17:2 (KJV, "manner"; RV, "custom"); in Matt. 17:15 and Mark 10:1, "was wont."

CUSTOM (Toll)

1. *telos* (τέλος, 5056) "an end, termination," whether of time or purpose, denotes, in its secondary significance, "what is paid for public ends, a toll, tax, custom," Matt. 17:25 (RV, "toll"); Rom. 13:7 (RV and KJV, "custom"). In Palestine the Herods of Galilee and Perea received the "custom"; in Judea it was paid to the procurator for the Roman government. See END, FINALLY, UTTERMOST.

2. *telōnion* (τελώνιον, 5058) denotes "a custom-house," for the collection of the taxes, Matt. 9:9; Mark 2:14; Luke 5:27 (RV, "place of toll").

CYMBAL

kumbalon (κύμβαλον, 2950), "a cymbal," was so called from its shape (akin to *kumbos*, "a hollow basin," *kumbē*, "a cup"), and was made of bronze, two being struck together, 1 Cor. 13:1.

D

DAINTY

liparos (λιπαρός, 3045) properly signifies "oily, or anointed with oil" (from *lipos*, "grease," connected with *aleiphō*, "to anoint"); it is said of things which pertain to delicate and sumptuous living; hence, "dainty," Rev. 18:14. In the Sept., Judg. 3:29; Neh. 9:35; Isa. 30:23.

For **DAMAGE** see LOSS

For **DAMNABLE, DAMNATION, and DAMNED** see CONDEMNATION, DESTRUCTION, JUDGE, JUDGMENT

DAMSEL

1. *korasion* (κοράσιον, 2877), a diminutive of *korē*, "a girl," denotes "a little girl" (properly a colloquial word, often used disparagingly, but not so in later writers); in the NT it is used only in familiar conversation, Matt. 9:24-25 (KJV, "maid"); 14:11; Mark 5:41-42; 6:22, 28.

2. *paidion* (παιδίον, 3813), a diminutive of *pais*, denotes "a young child (male or female)" in the KJV of Mark 5:39-41 (1st line); the RV corrects "damsel" to "child," so as to distinguish between the narrative of facts, and the homely address to the little girl herself, in which, and in the following sentence, *korasion* is used. (See No. 1). See CHILD.

3. *paidiskē* (παιδίσκη, 3814) denotes "a young girl, or a female slave"; "damsel," KJV, in John 18:17; Acts 12:13; 16:16; RV "maid" in each case. See BONDMAN, MAID, MAIDEN.

DANCE

orcheō (ὀρχέω, 3738), (cf. Eng., "orchestra"), probably originally signified "to lift up," as of the feet; hence, "to leap with regularity of motion." It is always used in the middle voice, Matt. 11:17; 14:6; Mark 6:22; Luke 7:32. The performance by the daughter of Herodias is the only clear instance of artistic dancing, a form introduced from Greek customs.

DANCING

choros (χορός, 5525), (Eng., "chorus"), primarily denoted "an enclosure for dancing"; hence, "a company of dancers and singers." The supposition that the word is connected with *orcheō* by metathesis (i.e., change of place, of the letters *ch* and *o*) seems to be without foundation. The word is used in Luke 15:25.

DANGER, DANGEROUS

A. Verb.

kinduneuō (κινδυνεύω, 2793) properly signifies "to run a risk, face danger," but is used in the NT in the sense of "being in danger, jeopardy," Acts 19:27, 40. It is translated "were in jeopardy" in Luke 8:23, and "stand we in jeopardy," 1 Cor. 15:30.

Note: Kindunos, akin to A, "peril, danger," is always rendered "peril," Rom. 8:35 and 2 Cor. 11:26 (eight times).

B. Adjectives.

1. *enochos* (ἔνοχος, 1777), lit., "held in, contained in" (*en*, "in," *echō*, "to have, hold"), hence, "bound under obligation to, liable to, subject to," is used in the sense of being in "danger" of the penal effect of a misdeed, i.e.. in a forensic sense, signifying the connection of a person with (a) his crime, "guilty of an eternal sin," Mark 3:29, RV; (b) the trial or tribunal, as a result of which sentence is passed, Matt. 5:21–22, "the judgment," "the council"; *enochos* here has the obsolete sense of control (J. Hastings); (c) the penalty itself, 5:22, "the hell of fire," and, with the translation "worthy" (KJV, "guilty"), of the punishment determined to be inflicted on Christ, Matt. 26:66 and Mark 14:64, "death"; (d) the person or thing against whom or which the offense is committed 1 Cor. 11:27, "guilty," the crime being against "the body and blood of the Lord"; Jas. 2:10, "guilty" of an offense against all the Law, because of a breach of one commandment.

Apart from the forensic sense, this adjective is used of the thing by which one is bound, "subject to" (bondage), in Heb. 2:15. See GUILTY, SUBJECT, WORTHY.

2. *episphalēs* (ἐπισφαλής, 2000), lit., "prone to fall" (*epi*, "upon," i.e., near upon, *sphallō*, "to fall"), hence, "insecure, dangerous," is used in Acts 27:9.

DARE, DARING, DURST

A. Verb.

tolmaō (τολμάω, 5111) signifies "to dare," (a) in the sense of not dreading or shunning through fear, Matt. 22:46; Mark 12:34; Mark 15:43, "boldly," lit., "having dared, went in"; Luke 20:40; John 21:12; Acts 5:13; 7:32; Rom. 15:18; 2 Cor. 10:2, RV, "show courage," (KJV, "be bold"); 10:12, RV, "are (not) bold," 11:21; Phil. 1:14, "are bold"; Jude 9; (b) in the sense of bearing, enduring, bringing oneself to do a thing, Rom. 5:7; 1 Cor. 6:1. Cf. *apotolmaō*, "to be very bold," Rom. 10:20.

B. Adjective.

tolmētēs (τολμητής, 5113), akin to A, "daring," is used in 2 Pet. 2:10, RV, "daring" (KJV "presumptuous"), "shameless and irreverent daring."

DARK, DARKEN, DARKLY, DARKNESS

A. Adjectives.

1. *skoteinos* (σκοτεινός, 4652), "full of darkness, or covered with darkness," is translated "dark" in Luke 11:36; "full of darkness," in Matt. 6:23 and Luke 11:34, where the physical condition is figurative of the moral. The group of *skot-* words is derived from a root *ska-*, meaning "to cover." The same root is to be found in *skēnē*, "a tent."

Note: Contrast *phōteinos*, "full of light," e.g., Matt. 6:22.

2. *auchmēros* (αὐχμηρός, 850), from *auchmos*, "drought produced by excessive heat," hence signifies "dry, murky, dark," 2 Pet. 1:19 (RV marg., "squalid"). No. 1 signifies "darkness" produced by covering; No. 2, "darkness" produced by being squalid or murky.

B. Nouns.

1. *skotia* (σκοτία, 4653) is used (a) of physical darkness, "dark," John 6:17, lit., "darkness had come on," and 20:1, lit., "darkness still being"; (b) of secrecy, in general, whether what is done therein is good or evil, Matt. 10:27; Luke 12:3; (c) of spiritual or moral "darkness," emblematic of sin, as a condition of moral or spiritual depravity, Matt. 4:16; John 1:5; 8:12; 12:35, 46; 1 John 1:5; 2:8-9, 11.

2. *skotos* (σκότος, 4655), an older form than No. 1, grammatically masculine, is found in some mss. in Heb. 12:18.

3. *skotos* (σκότος, 4655), a neuter noun frequent in the Sept., is used in the NT as the equivalent of No. 1; (a) of "physical darkness," Matt. 27:45; 2 Cor. 4:6; (b) of "intellectual darkness," Rom. 2:19 (cf. C, No. 1); (c) of "blindness," Acts 13:11; (d) by metonymy, of the "place of punishment," e.g., Matt. 8:12; 2 Pet. 2:17; Jude 13; (e) metaphorically, of "moral and spiritual darkness," e.g., Matt. 6:23; Luke 1:79; 11:35; John 3:19; Acts 26:18; 2 Cor. 6:14; Eph. 6:12; Col. 1:13; 1 Thess. 5:4-5; 1 Pet. 2:9; 1 John 1:6; (f) by metonymy, of "those who are in moral or spiritual darkness," Eph. 5:8; (g) of "evil works," Rom. 13:12; Eph. 5:11, (h) of the "evil powers that dominate the world," Luke 22:53; (i) "of secrecy" [as in No. 1, (b)]. While *skotos* is used more than twice as many times as *skotia* in the NT, the apostle John uses *skotos* only once, 1 John 1:6, but *skotia* 15 times out of the 18.

"With the exception of the significance of secrecy [No. 1, (b) and No. 3 (i)], darkness is always used in a bad sense. Moreover the different forms of darkness are so closely allied, being either cause and effect, or else concurrent effects of the same cause, that they cannot always be distinguished; 1 John 1:5; 2:8, e.g., are passages in which both spiritual and moral darkness are intended."

4. *zophos* (ζόφος, 2217) denotes "the gloom of the nether world," hence, "thick darkness darkness that may be felt"; it is rendered "darkness" in Heb. 12:18; 2 Pet. 2:4 and Jude 6; in 2 Pet. 2:17, RV, "blackness," KJV, "mists"; in Jude 13, RV and KJV, blackness. See BLACK, B, Nos. 1 and 2, MIST.

C. Verbs.

1. *skotizō* (σκοτίζω, 4654), "to deprive of light, to make dark," is used in the NT in the passive voice only, (a) of the heavenly bodies Matt. 24:29; Mark 13:24; Rev. 8:12; (b) metaphorically, of the mind, Rom. 1:21; 11:10; (some mss. have it in Luke 23:45).

2. *skotoō* (σκοτόω, 4656), "to darken," is used (a) of the heavenly bodies, Rev. 9:2; 16:10; (b) metaphorically, of the mind, Eph. 4:18.

Note: The phrase *en ainigmati*, lit., "in an enigma," is rendered "darkly" in 1 Cor. 13:12. *Ainigma* is akin to the verb *ainissomai* "to hint obscurely." The allusion is to Num. 12:8 (Sept.), "not in (*dia*, "by means of") dark speeches" (lit., "enigmas"); God's communications to Moses were not such as in the case of dreams, etc. After the same analogy, what we see and know now is seen "darkly" compared with the direct vision in the presence of God hereafter. The riddles of seeming obscurity in life will all be made clear.

DART

belos (βέλος, 956), akin to *ballō*, "to throw," denotes "a missile, an arrow, javelin, dart, etc.," Eph. 6:16 (see FIERY). Cf. *bolē*, "a stone's throw or cast," Luke 22:41,; *bolizō*, "to sound" (to fathom the depth of water), Acts 27:28.

Note: The noun *bolis*, "a dart," is found in some texts in Heb. 12:20 (see KJV).

DAUGHTER, DAUGHTER-IN-LAW

1. *thugatēr* (θυγάτηρ, 2364), "a daughter," (etymologically, Eng., "daughter" is connected), is used of (a) the natural relationship (frequent in the gospels); (b) spiritual relationship to God, 2 Cor. 6:18, in the sense of the practical realization of acceptance with, and the approval of, God (cf. Isa. 43:6), the only place in the NT where it applies to spiritual relationship; (c) the inhabitants of a city or region, Matt. 21:5; John 12:15 ("of Zion"); cf. Isa. 37:22; Zeph. 3:14 (Sept.); (d) the women who followed Christ to Calvary, Luke 23:28; (e) women of Aaron's posterity, Luke 1:5; (f) a female descendant of Abraham, Luke 13:16.

2. *thugatrion* (θυγάτριον, 2365), a diminutive of No. 1, denotes "a little daughter," Mark 5:23; 7:25.

3. *parthenos* (παρθένος, 3933), "a maiden, virgin," e.g., Matt. 1:23, signifies a virgin-daughter in 1 Cor. 7:36-38 (RV); in Rev. 14:4, it is used of chaste persons. See VIRGIN.

4. *numphē* (νύμφη, 3565), (Eng., "nymph"), denotes "a bride," John 3:29; also "a daughter-in-law, Matt. 10:35; Luke 12:53. See BRIDE.

Note: In 1 Pet. 3:6, *teknon*, "a child," is translated "daughters" (KJV), "children" (RV).

DAWN

A. Verbs.

1. *augazō* (αὐγάζω, 826), "to shine," is used metaphorically of the light of dawn, in 2 Cor. 4:4 (some texts have *kataugazō*). Cf. *augē*, "brightness or break of day," Acts 20:11. The word formerly meant "to see clearly," and it is possible that this meaning was continued in general usage.

2. *diaugazō* (διαυγάζω, 1306) signifies "to shine through" (*dia*, "through," *augē*, "brightness"); it describes the breaking of daylight upon the darkness of night, metaphorically in 2 Pet. 1:19, of the shining of spiritual light into the heart. A probable reference is to the day to be ushered in at the second coming of Christ: "until the Day gleam through the present darkness, and the Light-bringer dawn in your hearts."

Note: Cf. *diaugēs*, "translucent, transparent," Rev. 21:21 (some texts have *diaphanēs*, "transparent").

3. *epiphōskō* (ἐπιφώσκω, 2020), "to grow light" (*epi*, "upon," *phōs*, "light"), in the sense of shining upon, is used in Matt. 28:1; in Luke 23:54, "drew on" (of the Sabbath-day); RV, marg., "began to dawn."

B. Noun.

orthros (ὄρθρος, 3722), "daybreak," denotes "at early dawn," Luke 24:1 (RV), "early in the morning" (KJV), and John 8:2 (KJV and RV); in Acts 5:21, RV, "about daybreak," for KJV, "early in the morning."

Note: Cf. *orthrios*, "early," in some texts in Luke 24:22; *orthrinos*, a later form of *orthros*, in some mss. in Rev. 22:16; *orthrizō*, "to do anything early in the morning," in Luke 21:38.

DAY

A. Nouns.

1. *hēmera* (ἡμέρα, 2250), "a day," is used of (a) the period of natural light, Gen. 1:5; Prov. 4:18; Mark 4:35; (b) the same, but figuratively, for a period of opportunity for service, John 9:4; Rom. 13:13; (c) one period of alternate light and darkness, Gen. 1:5; Mark 1:13; (d) a period of undefined length marked by certain characteristics, such as "the day of small things," Zech. 4:10; of perplexity and distress, Isa. 17:11; Obad. 12-14; of prosperity and of adversity, Ecc. 7:14; of trial or testing, Ps. 95:8; of salvation, Isa. 49:8; 2 Cor. 6:2; cf. Luke 19:42; of evil, Eph. 6:13; of wrath and revelation of the judgments of God, Rom. 2:5; (e) an appointed time, Ecc. 8:6; Eph. 4:30; (f) a notable defeat in battle, etc., Isa. 9:4; Psa. 137:7; Ezek. 30:9; Hos. 1:11; (g) by metonymy = "when," "at the time when"; (1), of the past, Gen. 2:4; Num. 3:13; Deut. 4:10, (2), of the future, Gen. 2:17; Ruth 4:5; Matt. 24:50; Luke 1:20; (h) a judgment or doom, Job 18:20. (i) of a time of life, Luke 1:17-18 ("years").

As the "day" throws light upon things that have been in darkness, the word is often associated with the passing of judgment upon circumstances. In 1 Cor. 4:3, "man's day," KJV, "man's judgement," RV, denotes mere human judgment upon matters ("man's" translates the adjective *anthrōpinos*, "human"), a judgment exercised in the present period of human rebellion against "God"; probably therefore "the Lord's Day," Rev. 1:10, or "the Day of the Lord" (where an adjective, *kuriakos*, is similarly used), is the day of His manifested judgment on the world.

The phrases "the day of Christ," Phil. 1:10; 2:16; "the day of Jesus Christ," 1:6; "the day of the Lord Jesus," 1 Cor. 5:5; 2 Cor. 1:14; "the day of our Lord Jesus Christ," 1 Cor. 1:8, denote the time of the Parousia of Christ with His saints, subsequent to the Rapture, 1 Thess. 4:16-17. In 2 Pet. 1:19 this is spoken of simply as the day, (see DAY-STAR).

From these the phrase "the day of the Lord" is to be distinguished; in the OT it had reference to a time of the victorious interposition by God for the overthrow of the foes of Israel, e.g., Isa. 2:12; Amos 5:18; if Israel transgressed in the pride of their hearts, the Day of the Lord would be a time of darkness and judgment. For their foes, however, there would come "a great and terrible day of the Lord," Joel 2:31; Mal. 4:5. That period, still future, will see the complete overthrow of gentile power and the establishment of Messiah's kingdom, Isa. 13:9-11; 34:8; Dan. 2:34, 44; Obad. 15; cf. Isa. 61:2; John 8:56.

In the NT "the day of the Lord" is mentioned in 1 Thess. 5:2 and 2 Thess. 2:2, RV, where the apostle's warning is that the church at Thessalonica should not be deceived by thinking that "the Day of the Lord is now present." This period will not begin till the circumstances mentioned in verses 3 and 4 take place.

For the eventual development of the divine purposes in relation to the human race see 2 Pet. 3:12, "the Day of God."

2. *augē* (αὐγή, 827), "brightness, bright, shining, as of the sun"; hence, "the beginning of daylight," is translated "break of day" in Acts 20:11.

B. Adverb.

ennucha (ἔννυχα, 1773), the neuter plural of *ennuchos*, used adverbially, lit., "in night" (*en*, "in," *nux*, "night," with *lian*, "very"), signifies "very early, yet in the night," "a great while before day," Mark 1:35.

Notes: (1) In Mark 6:35, the clause "the day was far spent" is, lit., "a much hour (i.e., a late hour) having become," or, perhaps, "many an hour having become," i.e., many hours having passed. In the end of the V., RV, "day," for KJV, "time." (2) In Mark 2:26, KJV, "in the days of," there is no word for "days" in the original; RV (from best mss.), "when" in Acts 11:28, "in the days of" (3) In John 21:4, the adjective *prōios*, "at early morn," is translated "day" (RV, for KJV, "the morning"), see Matt. 27:1. (4) In 2 Thess. 2:3, "that day shall not come" (KJV) translates nothing in the original; it is inserted to supply the sense (see the RV); cf. Luke 7:11 (RV, "soon afterwards"); 1 Cor. 4:13 (RV, "even until now"). (5) For "day following" see MORROW.

For **DAYBREAK** (RV, in Acts 5:21) see DAWN, B

DAYSPRING

anatolē (ἀνατολή, 395), lit., "a rising up" (cf. *anatellō*, "to cause to rise"), is used of the rising of the sun and stars; it chiefly means the east, as in Matt. 2:1, etc.; rendered "dayspring" in Luke 1:78. Its other meaning, "a shoot," is found in the Sept. in Jer. 23:5; Zech. 6:12. See also the margin of Luke 1:78, "branch." See EAST.

DAY-STAR

phōsphoros (φωσφόρος, 5459), (Eng., "phosphorus," lit., "light-bearing" *phōs*, "light," *pherō*, "to bear"), is used of the morning star, as the light-bringer, 2 Pet. 1:19, where it indicates the arising of the light of Christ as the personal fulfillment, in the hearts of believers, of the prophetic Scriptures concerning His coming to receive them to Himself.

DAZZLING

1. *astraptō* (ἀστράπτω, 797), "to flash forth, lighten," is said of lightning, Luke 17:24, and of the apparel of the two men by the Lord's sepulchre, 24:4, KJV, "shining." See LIGHTEN, SHINE.

2. *exastraptō* (ἐξαστράπτω, 1823), a strengthened form of No. 1 (*ek*, out of), signifies "to flash like lightning, gleam, be radiant," in Luke 9:29 of the Lord's raiment at His transfiguration, RV, "dazzling"; KJV, "glistering." In the Sept., Ezek. 1:4, 7; Nahum 3:3.

DEACON

diakonos (διάκονος, 1249), (Eng., "deacon"), primarily denotes a "servant," whether as doing servile work, or as an attendant rendering free service, without particular reference to its character. The word is probably connected with the verb *diōkō*, "to hasten after, pursue" (perhaps originally said of a runner). "It occurs in the NT of domestic servants, John 2:5, 9; the civil ruler, Rom. 13:4; Christ, Rom. 15:8; Gal. 2:17; the followers of Christ in relation to their Lord, John 12:26; Eph. 6:21; Col. 1:7; 4:7; the followers of Christ in relation to one another, Matt. 20:26; 23:11, Mark 9:35; 10:43; the servants of Christ in the work of preaching and teaching, 1 Cor. 3:5; 2 Cor. 3:6; 6:4; 11:23; Eph. 3:7; Col. 1:23, 25; 1 Thess. 3:2; 1 Tim. 4:6; those who serve in the churches, Rom. 16:1 (used of a woman here only in NT); Phil. 1:1; 1 Tim. 3:8, 12; false apostles, servants of Satan, 2 Cor. 11:15. Once *diakonos* is used where, apparently, angels are intended, Matt. 22:13; in v. 3, where men are intended, *doulos* is used."

Diakonos is, generally speaking, to be distinguished from *doulos*, "a bondservant, slave"; *diakonos* views a servant in relationship to his work, *doulos* views him in relationship to his master. See, e.g., Matt. 22:2-14; those who bring in the guests (vv. 3-4, 6, 8, 10) are *douloi*, those who carry out the king's sentence (v. 13) are *diakonoi*.

Note: As to synonymous terms, *leitourgos* denotes "one who performs public duties"; *misthios* and *misthōtos*, "a hired servant"; *oiketēs*, "a household servant"; *hupēretēs*, "a subordinate official waiting on his superior" (originally an underrower in a war-galley); *therapōn*, "one whose service is that of freedom and dignity." See MINISTER, SERVANT.

The so-called "seven deacons" in Acts 6 are not there mentioned by that name, though the kind of service in which they were engaged was of the character of that committed to such.

DEAD

A. Noun and Adjective.

nekros (νεκρός, 3498) is used of (a) the death of the body, cf. Jas. 2:26, its most frequent sense: (b) the actual spiritual condition of unsaved men, Matt. 8:22; John 5:25; Eph. 2:1, 5; 5:14; Phil. 3:11; Col. 2:13; cf. Luke 15:24: (c) the ideal spiritual condition of believers in regard to sin, Rom. 6:11: (d) a church in declension, inasmuch as in that state it is inactive and barren, Rev. 3:1: (e) sin, which apart from law cannot produce a sense of guilt, Rom. 7:8: (f) the body of the believer in contrast to his spirit, Rom. 8:10: (g) the works of the Law, inasmuch as, however good in themselves, Rom. 7:13, they cannot produce life, Heb. 6:1; 9:14: (h) the faith that does not produce works, Jas. 2:17, 26; cf. v. 20.

B. Verbs.

1. *nekroō* (νεκρόω, 3499), "to put to death," is used in the active voice in the sense of destroying the strength of, depriving of power, with reference to the evil desires which work in the body, Col. 3:5. In the passive voice it is used of Abraham's body as being "as good as dead," Rom. 4:19 with Heb. 11:12.

2. *thanatoō* (θανατόω, 2289), "to put to death": see DEATH, C, No. 1.

DEADLY

1. *thanatēphoros* (θανατήφορος, 2287), lit., "death-bearing, deadly" (*thanatos*, "death," *pherō*, "to bear"), is used in Jas. 3:8. In the Sept., Num. 18:22; Job 33:23.

2. *thanasimos* (θανάσιμος, 2286), from *thanatos* (see No. 1), "belonging to death, or partaking of the nature of death," is used in Mark 16:18.

HALF DEAD

hēmithanēs (ἡμιθανής, 2253), from *hēmi*, "half," and *thneskō*, "to die," is used in Luke 10:30.

DEADNESS

nekrōsis (νέκρωσις, 3500), "a putting to death" (cf. DEAD, A and B), is rendered "dying" in 2 Cor. 4:10; "deadness" in Rom. 4:19, i.e., the state of being virtually "dead."

DEAF

kōphos (κωφός, 2974), akin to *koptō*, "to beat," and *kopiaō*, "to be tired" (from a root *kop-*, "to cut"), signifies "blunted, dull," as of a weapon; hence, "blunted in tongue, dumb," Matt. 9:32 etc.; "in hearing, deaf," Matt. 11:5; Mark 7:32, 37; 9:25; Luke 7:22. See DUMB.

DEAL

merizō (μερίζω, 3307) signifies "to divide into parts" (*meros*, "a portion, part"); hence, "to distribute, divide out, deal out to," translated "hath dealt" in Rom. 12:3. See DIVINE.

DEAR

1. *timios* (τίμιος, 5093), from *timē*, "honor, price," signifies (a), primarily, "accounted as of great price, precious, costly," 1 Cor. 3:12; Rev. 17:4; 18:12, 16; 21:19, and in the superlative degree, 18:12; 21:11; the comparative degree is found in 1 Pet. 1:7 (*polutimoteros*, in the most authentic mss., "much more precious"); (b) in the metaphorical sense, "held in honor, esteemed, very dear," Acts 5:34, "had in honor," RV (KJV, "had in reputation"); so in Heb. 13:4, RV, "let marriage be had in honor"; KJV, "is honorable"; Acts 20:24, "dear," negatively of Paul's estimate of his life; Jas. 5:7, "precious" (of fruit); 1 Pet. 1:19, "precious" (of the blood of Christ); 2 Pet. 1:4 (of God's promises). See HONORABLE, REPUTATION. Cf. *timiotēs*, preciousness, Rev. 18:19.

2. *entimos* (ἔντιμος, 1784), "held in honor" (*timē*, see above), "precious, dear," is found in Luke 7:2, of the centurion's servant; 14:8, "more honorable"; Phil. 2:29, "honor" (KJV, "reputation"), of devoted servants of Christ, in 1 Pet. 2:4, 6, "precious," of stones, metaphorically. See HONORABLE, REPUTATION.

3. *agapētos* (ἀγαπητός, 27), from *agapē*, "love," signifies "beloved"; it is rendered "very dear" in 1 Thess. 2:8 (KJV, "dear"), of the affection of Paul and his fellow workers for the saints at Thessalonica; in Eph. 5:1 and Col. 1:7, KJV, dear; RV, "beloved." See BELOVED.

Note: In Col. 1:13, *agapē* is translated "dear" in the KJV; the RV, adhering to the noun, has "the Son of His love."

For **DEARLY** see BELOVED

For **DEARTH** see FAMINE

DEATH, DEATH-STROKE (See also die)

A. Nouns

1. *thanatos* (θάνατος, 2288), "death," is used in Scripture of:

(a) the separation of the soul (the spiritual part of man) from the body (the material part), the latter ceasing to function and turning to dust, e.g., John 11:13; Heb. 2:15; 5:7; 7:23. In Heb. 9:15, the KJV, "by means of death" is inadequate; the RV, "a death having taken place" is in keeping with the subject. In Rev. 13:3, 12, the RV, "death-stroke" (KJV, "deadly wound") is, lit., "the stroke of death":

(b) the separation of man from God; Adam died on the day he disobeyed God, Gen. 2:17, and hence all mankind are born in the same spiritual condition, Rom. 5:12, 14, 17, 21, from which, however, those who believe in Christ are delivered, John 5:24; 1 John 3:14. "Death" is the opposite of life; it never denotes nonexistence. As spiritual life is "conscious existence in communion with God," so spiritual "death" is "conscious existence in separation from God."

"Death, in whichever of the above-mentioned senses it is used, is always, in Scripture, viewed as the penal consequence of sin, and since sinners alone are subject to death, Rom. 5:12, it was as the Bearer of sin that the Lord Jesus submitted thereto on the Cross, 1 Pet. 2:24. And while the physical death of the Lord Jesus was of the essence of His sacrifice, it was not the whole. The darkness symbolized, and His cry expressed, the fact that He was left alone in the Universe, He was 'forsaken;' cf. Matt. 27:45-46."

2. *anairesis* (ἀναίρεσις, 336), another word for "death," lit. signifies "a taking up or off" (*ana*, "up," *airō*, "to take"), as of the taking of a life, or "putting to death"; it is found in Acts 8:1, of the murder of Stephen. Some mss. have it in 22:20. See *anaireō*, under KILL. In the Sept., Num. 11:15; Judg. 15:17, "the lifting of the jawbone.

3. *teleutē* (τελευτή, 5054), "an end, limit" (cf. *telos*, see END), hence, "the end of life, death," is used of the "death" of Herod, Matt. 2:15.

B. Adjective.

epithanatios (ἐπιθανάτιος, 1935), "doomed to death" (*epi*, "upon," *thanatos*, A, No. 1), is said of the apostles, in 1 Cor. 4:9.

C. Verbs.

1. *thanatoō* (θανατόω, 2289), "to put to death" (akin to A, No. 1), in Matt. 10:21; Mark 13:12; Luke 21:16, is translated "shall ... cause (them) to be put to death," lit., "shall put (them) to death" (RV marg.). It is used of the death of Christ in Matt. 26:59; 27:1; Mark 14:55 and 1 Pet. 3:18. In Rom. 7:4 (passive voice) it is translated "ye ... were made dead," RV (for KJV, "are become"), with reference to the change from bondage to the Law to union with Christ; in 8:13, "mortify" (marg., "make to die"), of the act of the believer in regard to the deeds of the body; in 8:36, "are killed"; so in 2 Cor. 6:9. See KILL, MORTIFY.

2. *anaireō* (ἀναιρέω, 337), lit., "to take or lift up or away" (see A, No. 2), hence, "to put to death," is usually translated "to kill or slay"; in two places "put to death," Luke 23:32; Acts 26:10. It is used 17 times, with this meaning, in Acts. See KILL.

3. *apagō* (ἀπάγω, 520), lit., "to lead away" (*apo*, "away," *agō*, "to lead"), is used especially in a judicial sense, "to put to death," e.g., Acts 12:19. See LEAD.

4. *apokteinō* (ἀποκτείνω, 615), to kill, is so translated in the RV, for the KJV, "put to death," in Mark 14:1; Luke 18:33; in John 11:53; 12:10 and 18:31, RV, "put to death." See KILL.

Note: The phrase *eschatōs echō*, lit., "to have extremely," i.e., "to be in extremity," *in extremis*, "at the last (gasp), to be at the point of death," is used in Mark 5:23.

For the KJV **DEBATE** (Rom. 1:29 and 2 Cor. 12:20) see STRIFE

DEBTOR

1. *opheiletēs* (ὀφειλέτης, 3781), "one who owes anything to another," primarily in regard to money; in Matt. 18:24, "who owed" (lit., "one was brought, a debtor to him of ten thousand talents"). The slave could own property, and so become a "debtor" to his master, who might seize him for payment.

It is used metaphorically,

(a) of a person who is under an obligation, Rom. 1:14, of Paul, in the matter of preaching the gospel; in Rom. 8:12, of believers, to mortify the deeds of the body; in Rom. 15:27, of gentile believers, to assist afflicted Jewish believers; in Gal. 5:3, of those who would be justified by circumcision, to do the whole Law: (b) of those who have not yet made amends to those whom they have injured, Matt. 6:12, "our debtors"; of some whose disaster was liable to be regarded as a due punishment, Luke 13:4 (RV, "offenders"; KJV, "sinners"; marg, "debtors").

2. *chreōpheiletēs* (χρεωφειλέτης, 5533), lit., "a debt-ower" (*chreōs*, "a loan, a debt," and No. 1), is found in Luke 7:41, of the two "debtors" mentioned in the Lord's parable addressed to Simon the Pharisee, and in 16:5, of the "debtors" in the parable of the unrighteous steward. This parable indicates a system of credit in the matter of agriculture. In the Sept., Job 31:37, "having taken nothing from the debtor"; Prov. 29:13, "when the creditor and the debtor meet together." The word is more expressive than No. 1.

Note: In Matt. 23:16 *opheilō*, "to owe," is translated "he is a debtor." The RV marg., keeping the verbal form, has "bound by his oath" (KJV, marg., "bound"). In the 18th verse the KJV, "he is guilty," means that he is under obligation to make amends for his misdeeds.

DECAY

1. *palaioō* (παλαιόω, 3822), "to make old" (*palaios*), is translated in Heb. 8:13, firstly, "hath made ... old," secondly (passive voice), RV "is becoming old" (KJV, "decayeth"); "wax old," Luke 12:33 and Heb. 1:11. See OLD.

2. *diaphtheirō* (διαφθείρω, 1311), "to destroy utterly," as used in 2 Cor. 4:16 (here in the passive voice, lit., "is being destroyed"), is rendered "is decaying" (RV, for KJV, "perish"). See CORRUPT, DESTROY.

DECEASE

A. Noun.

exodos (ἔξοδος, 1841), (Eng., "exodus"), lit. signifies "a way out" (*ex*, "out," *hodos*, "a way"); hence, "a departure," especially from life, "a decease"; in Luke 9:31, of the Lord's death, "which He was about to accomplish"; in 2 Pet. 1:15, of Peter's death (marg., "departure" in each case); "departure" in Heb. 11:22, RV. See DEPARTURE.

B. Verb.

teleutaō (τελευτάω, 5053), lit., "to end," is used intransitively and translated "deceased" in Matt. 22:25. See DEATH, A, No. 3, DIE.

DECEIT, DECEITFUL, DECEITFULLY, DECEITFULNESS, DECEIVE, DECEIVABLENESS

A. Nouns.

1. *apatē* (ἀπάτη, 539), "deceit or deceitfulness" (akin to *apataō*, "to cheat, deceive, beguile"), that which gives a false impression, whether by appearance, statement or influence, is said of riches, Matt. 13:22; Mark 4:19; of sin, Heb. 3:13. The phrase in Eph. 4:22, "deceitful lusts," KJV, "lusts of deceit," RV, signifies lusts excited by "deceit," of which "deceit" is the source of strength, not lusts "deceitful" in themselves. In 2 Thess. 2:10, "all deceit of unrighteousness," RV, signifies all manner of unscrupulous words and deeds designed to "deceive" (see Rev. 13:13-15). In Col. 2:8, "vain deceit" suggests that "deceit" is void of anything profitable.

Note: In 2 Pet. 2:13, the most authentic texts have "revelling in their love-feasts," RV (*agapais*), for KJV, "deceivings" (*apatais*).

2. *dolos* (δόλος, 1388), primarily "a bait, snare"; hence, "craft, deceit, guile," is translated "deceit" in Mark 7:22; Rom. 1:29. See GUILE, SUBTLETY.

Notes: (1) *Planē,* rendered "deceit" in 1 Thess. 2:3, KJV, signifies wandering (cf. Eng., "planet"), hence, "error" (RV), i.e., a wandering from the right path; in Eph. 4:14, "wiles of error," KJV, "to deceive." See DELUDE, ERROR. (2) For *dolioō,* "to use deceit," see C, No. 4.

B. Adjective.

dolios (δόλιος, 1386), "deceitful," is used in 2 Cor. 11:13, of false apostles as "deceitful workers"; cf. A, No. 2 and *Note* (2).

C. Verbs.

1. *apataō* (ἀπατάω, 538), "to beguile, deceive" (see A, No. 1), is used (a) of those who "deceive" "with empty words," belittling the true character of the sins mentioned, Eph. 5:6; (b) of the fact that Adam was "not beguiled," 1 Tim. 2:14, RV (cf. what is said of Eve; see No. 2 below); (c) of the "self-deceit" of him who thinks himself religious, but bridles not his tongue, Jas. 1:26.

2. *exapataō* (ἐξαπατάω, 1818), *ek* (*ex*), intensive, and No. 1, signifies "to beguile thoroughly, to deceive wholly," 1 Tim. 2:14, RV. See BEGUILE.

3. *phrenapataō* (φρεναπατάω, 5422), lit., "to deceive in one's mind" (*phrēn,* "the mind," and No. 1), "to deceive by fancies" (Lightfoot), is used in Gal. 6:3, with reference to self-conceit, which is "self-deceit," a sin against common sense. Cf. Jas. 1:26 (above).

Note: Cf. *phrenapatēs,* No. 2, under DECEIVE.

4. *dolioō* (δολιόω, 1387), "to lure," as by a bait (see A, No. 2), is translated "have used deceit" in Rom. 3:13.

5. *doloō* (δολόω, 1389), a short form of No. 4, primarily signifies "to ensnare"; hence, "to corrupt," especially by mingling the truths of the Word of God with false doctrines or notions, and so handling it "deceitfully," 2 Cor. 4:2. Cf. *kapēleuō,* "to corrupt by way of hucksterizing," 2:17. For the difference between the words see CORRUPT, A, No. 1.

6. *planaō* (πλανάω, 4105), akin to *planē,* A, *Note* (1) (Eng., "planet"), in the passive form sometimes means "to go astray, wander," Matt. 18:12; 1 Pet. 2:25; Heb. 11:38; frequently active, "to deceive, by leading into error, to seduce," e.g., Matt. 24:4, 5, 11, 24; John 7:12, "leadeth astray," RV (cf. 1 John 3:7). In Rev. 12:9 the present participle is used with the definite article, as a title of the Devil, "the Deceiver," lit., "the deceiving one." Often it has the sense of "deceiving oneself," e.g., 1 Cor. 6:9; 15:33; Gal. 6:7; Jas. 1:16, "be not deceived," RV, "do not err," KJV. See ERR, LEAD (astray), SEDUCE, WANDER, WAY (be out of the).

7. *paralogizomai* (παραλογίζομαι, 3884); see BEGUILE, No. 3.

DECEIVER

1. *planos* (πλάνος, 4108) is, properly, an adjective, signifying "wandering, or leading astray, seducing," 1 Tim. 4:1, "seducing (spirits)," used as a noun, it denotes an impostor of the vagabond type, and so any kind of "deceiver" or corrupter, Matt. 27:63; 2 Cor. 6:8; 2 John 7 (twice), in the last of which the accompanying definite article necessitates the translation "the deceiver," RV. See SEDUCE.

2. *phrenapatēs* (φρεναπάτης, 5423), akin to C, No. 3, under DECEIVE, lit., "a mind-deceiver," is used in Titus 1:10.

Note: For "the deceiver," in Rev. 12:9, see DECEIVE, C, No. 6.

DECENTLY

euschēmonōs (εὐσχημόνως, 2156) denotes "gracefully, becomingly, in a seemly manner" (*eu,* "well," *schēma,* "a form, figure"); "honestly," in Rom. 13:13 (marg., "decently"), in contrast to the shamefulness of gentile social life; in 1 Thess. 4:12, the contrast is to idleness and its concomitant evils and the resulting bad testimony to unbelievers; in 1 Cor. 14:40, "decently," where the contrast is to disorder in oral testimony in the churches. See HONESTLY.

Note: Cf. *euschēmosunē,* "comeliness," 1 Cor. 12:23., and *euschēmōn,* "comely, honorable." See COMELINESS.

DECLARE, DECLARATION

A. Verbs.

1. *anangellō* (ἀναγγέλλω, 312) signifies "to announce, report, bring back tidings" (*ana,* "back," *angellō,* "to announce"). Possibly the *ana* carries the significance of upward, i.e., heavenly, as characteristic of the nature of the tidings. In the following, either the KJV or the RV translates the word by the verb "to declare"; in John 4:25, RV, "declare," KJV, "tell"; in 16:13-15, RV, "declare," KJV, "shew"; in Acts 15:4, RV, "rehearsed," KJV, "declared"; in 19:18, RV, "declaring," KJV, "shewed" (a reference, perhaps, to the destruction of their idols, in consequence of their new faith); in 20:20, RV, "declaring," KJV, "have shewed"; in 1 John 1:5, RV, "announce," KJV, "declare." See REHEARSE, REPORT.

2. *apangellō* (ἀπαγγέλλω, 518) signifies "to announce or report from a person or place" (*apo,* "from"); hence, "to declare, publish"; it is rendered "declare" in Luke 8:47; Heb. 2:12; 1 John 1:3. It is very frequent in the Gospels and Acts; elsewhere, other than the last two places mentioned, only in 1 Thess. 1:9 and 1 John 1:2.

3. *diangellō* (διαγγέλλω, 1229), lit., "to announce through," hence, "to declare fully, or far and wide" (*dia*, "through"), is translated "declaring" in Acts 21:26, RV (KJV, "to signify"); in Luke 9:60, RV, "publish abroad" (for KJV, "preach"), giving the verb its fuller significance; so in Rom. 9:17, for KJV, "declared." See PREACH, SIGNIFY.

4. *katangellō* (καταγγέλλω, 2605), lit., "to report down" (*kata*, intensive), is ordinarily translated "to preach"; "declare" in Acts 17:23, KJV (RV, "set forth"); in 1 Cor. 2:1, RV, "proclaiming," for KJV, "declaring." It is nowhere translated by "declare" in the RV. See PREACH, SHOW, TEACH.

5. *diēgeomai* (διηγέομαι, 1334), "to conduct a narration through to the end" (*dia*, "through," intensive, *hegēomai*, "to lead"), hence denotes "to recount, to relate in full," Mark 5:16; Luke 8:39; 9:10; Acts 8:33; 9:27; 12:17; in Mark 9:9 and Heb. 11:32, "tell." See SHOW.

6. *ekdiēgeomai* (ἐκδιηγέομαι, 1555), properly, "to narrate in full," came to denote, "to tell, declare"; it is used in Acts 13:41; 15:3.

7. *exēgeomai* (ἐξηγέομαι, 1834), lit., "to lead out," signifies "to make known, rehearse declare," Luke 24:35 (KJV, "told"; RV, "rehearsed"); Acts 10:8; 15:12, 14; 21:19. In John 1:18, in the sentence "He hath declared Him," the other meaning of the verb is in view, to unfold in teaching, "to declare" by making known.

8. *horizō* (ὁρίζω, 3724), "to mark off by boundaries," signifies "to determine," usually of time; in Rom. 1:4, Christ is said to have been "marked out" as the Son of God, by the fact of His resurrection; "declared" (RV, marg., "determined"). See DEFINE.

9. *dēloō* (δηλόω, 1213), "to make plain," is rendered "to declare" in 1 Cor. 1:11, KJV; 3:13; Col. 1:8. See SIGNIFY.

10. *phrazō* (φράζω, 5419), "to declare," occurs in Matt. 15:15 and (in some texts) in 13:36 (as KJV).

Note: For *gnorizō*, "to make known," rendered "to declare" in John 17:26; 1 Cor. 15:1 and Col. 4:7, see KNOW, A, No. 8. For *emphanizō*, "to declare plainly," Heb. 11:14, KJV, see MANIFEST, A, No. 2. For *phaneroō*, see MANIFEST, B, No. 1. For *anatithēmi*, Acts 25:14, KJV, see COMMUNICATE. For declare glad tidings" see TIDINGS.

B. Noun.

endeixis (ἔνδειξις, 1732), "a showing, pointing out" (*en*, "in," *deiknumi*, "to show"), is said of the "showing forth" of God's righteousness, in Rom. 3:25-26, KJV, "to declare"; RV, "to show," and "(for) the showing." In 2 Cor. 8:24, "proof"; Phil. 1:28, "an evident token." See SHOW, TOKEN.

Notes: (1) In Luke 1:1, *diēgēsis* is a "narrative" (RV), not a "declaration" (KJV).

(2) In 2 Cor. 8:19, "declaration" does not represent any word in the original.

DECREE (Noun and Verb)

dogma (δόγμα, 1378), transliterated in English, primarily denoted "an opinion or judgment" (from *dokeō*, "to be of opinion"), hence, an "opinion expressed with authority, a doctrine, ordinance, decree"; "decree," Luke 2:1; Acts 16:4; 17:7; in the sense of ordinances, Eph. 2:15; Col. 2:14. See ORDINANCE.

Note: Krinō, "to determine," is translated "hath decreed" in 1 Cor. 7:37, KJV; RV, "hath determined."

DEDICATE, DEDICATION

A. Verb.

enkainizō (ἐγκαινίζω, 1457) primarily means "to make new, to renew" (*en*, "in," *kainos*, "new"), as in the Sept. of 2 Chron. 15:8; then, to initiate or "dedicate," Heb. 9:18, with reference to the first covenant, as not "dedicated" without blood; in 10:20, of Christ's "dedication" of the new and living way (KJV, "consecrated"; RV, "dedicated"). See CONSECRATE. In the Sept. it has this meaning in Deut. 20:5; 2 Chron. 7:5; Isa. 16:11; 41:1; 45:16, "keep feast (to Me)."

B. Noun.

enkainia (ἐγκαίνια, 1456), akin to A, frequent in the Sept., in the sense of "dedication," became used particularly for the annual eight days' feast beginning on the 25th of Chisleu (mid. of Dec.), instituted by Judas Maccabaeus, 164, B.C., to commemorate the cleansing of the Temple from the pollutions of Antiochus Epiphanes; hence it was called the Feast of the Dedication, John 10:22. This feast could be celebrated anywhere. The lighting of lamps was a prominent feature; hence the description "Feast of Lights." Westcott suggests that John 9:5 refers to this.

DEED, DEEDS

1. *ergon* (ἔργον, 2041) denotes "a work" (Eng., "work" is etymologically akin), "deed, act." When used in the sense of a "deed or act," the idea of "working" is stressed, e.g., Rom. 15:18; it frequently occurs in an ethical sense of human actions, good or bad, e.g., Matt. 23:3; 26:10; John 3:20-21; Rom. 2:7, 15; 1 Thess. 1:3; 2 Thess. 1:11, etc.; sometimes in a less concrete sense, e.g., Titus 1:16; Jas. 1:25 (RV that worketh, lit., of work). See LABOR.

2. *praxis* (πρᾶξις, 4234) denotes "a doing, transaction, a deed the action of which is looked upon as incomplete and in progress" (cf. *prassō*, "to practice"); in Matt. 16:27, RV, "deeds," for KJV, "works"; in Luke 23:51, "deed"; in v. 41, the verb is used [see *Note* (2) below]; Acts 19:18; Rom. 8:13; Col.

3:9. In Rom. 12:4 it denotes an "action," business, or function, translated "office." See OFFICE.

Note: Contrast *pragma*, "that which has been done, an accomplished act," e.g., Jas. 3:16, RV, "deed," KJV, "work."

3. *poiēsis* (ποίησις, 4162), "a doing" (akin to *poieō*, "to do"), is translated "deed" in Jas. 1:25, KJV, (RV, "doing").

Note: Cf. *poiēma*, "a work done," Rom. 1:20; Eph. 2:10.

4. *euergesia* (εὐεργεσία, 2108): see BENEFIT, No. 1.

Notes: (1) *Katergazomai*, "to work out, bring about something, to perpetrate a deed," is used with the neuter demonstrative pronoun *touto* "this," in 1 Cor. 5:3, "hath (so) done this deed," KJV; RV, "hath (so) wrought this thing."

(2) *Prassō* (see No. 2), is used in Luke 23:41, with the neuter plural of the relative pronoun "of our deeds"; lit., "(the things) which we practiced."

(3) In 2 Cor. 12:12 the phrase "mighty deeds" (RV, "mighty works") translates *dunameis*, "powers" (marg.).

(4) In Acts 24:2, *diorthōma*, "a straightening," with *ginomai*, "to become," is translated in the KJV, "very worthy deeds are done," RV, "evils are corrected"; more lit., "reforms take place." For the variant reading *katorthōma*, see CORRECTION, No. 1.

DEEP (Noun and Adjective), DEEPNESS, DEEPLY, DEPTH

A. Nouns.

1. *bathos* (βάθος, 899) is used (a) naturally, in Matt. 13:5, "deepness"; Mark 4:5, KJV, "depth," RV, "deepness"; Luke 5:4, of "deep" water; Rom. 8:39 (contrasted with *hupsōma*, "height"); (b) metaphorically, in Rom. 11:33, of God's wisdom and knowledge; in 1 Cor. 2:10, of God's counsels; in Eph. 3:18, of the dimensions of the sphere of the activities of God's counsels, and of the love of Christ which occupies that sphere; in 2 Cor. 8:2, of "deep" poverty; some mss. have it in Rev. 2:24.

2. *buthos* (βυθός, 1037), "a depth," is used in the NT only in the natural sense, of the sea 2 Cor. 11:25.

Notes: (1) Cf. *buthizō*, "to sink" (intransitive), middle voice, Luke 5:7; (transitive) "to drown," 1 Tim. 6:9.

(2) *Abussos*, (Eng., "abyss"), is translated "the deep" in Luke 8:31 and Rom. 10:7, KJV. See BOTTOM.

B. Adjective and Adverb.

bathus (βαθύς, 901), akin to A, No. 1, "deep," is said in John 4:11, of a well; in Acts 20:9, of sleep; in Rev. 2:24 the plural is used, of the "deep things," the evil designs and workings, of Satan.

Notes: (1) In Luke 24:1, some mss. have *batheos*, the genitive case, with *orthros*, "dawn"; the most authentic mss. have *batheōs*, "deeply," i.e., very early.

(2) In Mark 8:12, "He sighed deeply" represents *anastenazō*, "to fetch a deep-drawn sigh" (*ana*, "up," *stenazō*, "to sigh or groan").

C. Verb.

bathunō (βαθύνω, 900), "to deepen, make deep," is used in Luke 6:48 (KJV, "digged deep"). The original has two separate verbs, *skaptō*, "to dig," and *bathunō;* the RV therefore has "digged and went deep."

DEFAME

dusphēmeō (δυσφημέω, 1426a), lit., "to speak injuriously" (from *dus-*, an inseparable prefix signifying "opposition, injury, etc.," and *phēmi*, "to speak"), is translated "defamed," 1 Cor. 4:13. Some mss. have *blasphēmeō*. See BLASPHEME.

DEFEND

amunō (ἀμύνω, 292), "to ward off," is used in the middle voice in Acts 7:24, of the assistance given by Moses to his fellow Israelite against an Egyptian (translated, "defended"). The middle voice indicates the special personal interest Moses had in the act.

DEFENSE

A. Noun.

apologia (ἀπολογία, 627), a speech made in defense. See ANSWER.

B. Verb.

apologeomai (ἀπολογέομαι, 626): see ANSWER, B, No. 4.

DEFILE, DEFILEMENT

A. Verbs.

1. *koinoō* (κοινόω, 2840) denotes (a) "to make common"; hence, in a ceremonial sense, "to render unholy, unclean, to defile," Matt. 15:11, 18, 20; Mark 7:15, 18, 20, 23; Acts 21:28 (RV, "defiled"; KJV, "polluted"); Heb. 9:13 (RV, "them that have been defiled," KJV, "the unclean"); (b) "to count unclean," Acts 10:15; 11:9. In Rev. 21:27, some mss. have this verb, "defileth"; the most authentic have the adjective, *koinos*, "unclean." See CALL, COMMON.

2. *miainō* (μιαίνω, 3392), primarily, "to stain, to tinge or dye with another color," as in the staining of a glass, hence, "to pollute, contaminate, soil, defile," is used (a) of "ceremonial defilement," John 18:28; so in the Sept., in Lev. 22:5, 8; Num. 19:13, 20 etc.; (b) of "moral defilement," Titus 1:15 (twice); Heb. 12:15; "of moral and physical defilement," Jude 8. See B, Nos. 1 and 2.

3. *molunō* (μολύνω, 3435) properly denotes "to besmear," as with mud or filth, "to befoul." It is used in the figurative sense, of a conscience "defiled" by sin, 1 Cor. 8:7; of believers who have kept themselves (their "garments") from

"defilement," Rev. 3:4, and of those who have not "soiled" themselves by adultery or fornication, Rev. 14:4.

Note: The difference between *miainō* and *molunō* is that the latter is not used in a ritual or ceremonial sense, as *miainō* is (Trench, *Syn.* Sec. XXXI).

4. *spiloō* (σπιλόω, 4695), "to make a stain or spot," and so "to defile," is used in Jas. 3:6 of the "defiling" effects of an evil use of the tongue; in Jude 23, "spotted," with reference to moral "defilement."

Note: (1) Cf. *spilos*, "a spot, a moral blemish," Eph. 5:27; 2 Pet. 2:13; *aspilos*, "without spot, spotless," 1 Tim. 6:14; Jas. 1:27; 1 Pet. 1:19; 2 Pet. 3:14; *spilas*, Jude 12, "hidden rocks," RV (KJV "spots," a late meaning, equivalent to spilos).

5. *phtheirō* (φθείρω, 5351): see CORRUPT, A, No. 2.

B. Nouns.

1. *miasma* (μίασμα, 3393), whence the Eng. word, denotes "defilement" (akin to A, No. 2), and is found in 2 Pet. 2:20, KJV, "pollutions," RV, "defilements," the vices of the ungodly which contaminate a person in his intercourse with the world.

2. *miasmos* (μιασμός, 3394), also akin to A, No. 2, primarily denotes "the act of defiling," the process, in contrast to the "defiling" thing (No. 1). It is found in 2 Pet. 2:10 (KJV, "uncleanness," RV, "defilement.").

3. *molusmos* (μολυσμός, 3436), akin to A, No. 3, denotes "defilement," in the sense of an action by which anything is "defiled," 2 Cor. 7:1. Cf. the synonymous word *spilos*, A, No. 4, *Note.*

C. Adjective.

koinos (κοινός, 2839), akin to A, No. 1, common, and, from the idea of coming into contact with everything, "defiled," is used in the ceremonial sense in Mark 7:2; in v. 5, RV, "defiled," for KJV, "unwashen" (the verb is used in 7:15). See COMMON, UNCLEAN.

DEFINE

horizō (ὁρίζω, 3724), (Eng., "horizon"), primarily means "to mark out the boundaries of a place" (as in the Sept. of Num. 34:6; Josh. 13:27); hence "to determine, appoint." In Heb. 4:7, where the reference is to the time of God's invitation to enter into His rest, in contrast to Israel's failure to do so, the word may mean either the appointing of the day (i.e., the period), or the "defining" of the day, i.e., marking its limits. So the RV (KJV, "limiteth"). See DECLARE, LIMIT, ORDAIN.

DEFRAUD

1. *apostereō* (ἀποστερέω, 650) signifies "to rob, despoil, defraud," Mark 10:19; 1 Cor. 6:8; 7:5 (of that which is due to the condition of natural relationship of husband and wife); in the middle voice, "to allow oneself to be defrauded," 1 Cor. 6:7; in the passive voice, "bereft," 1 Tim. 6:5, RV, with reference to the truth, with the suggestion of being retributively "robbed" of the truth, through the corrupt condition of the mind. Some mss. have this verb in Jas. 5:4 for *aphustereō*, "to keep back by fraud." See BEREAVED, DESTITUTE, FRAUD. In the Sept., Exod. 21:10; in some mss, Deut. 24:14.

2. *pleonekteō* (πλεονεκτέω, 4122), translated "defraud" in 1 Thess. 4:6, KJV (RV, "wrong"), the reference being to the latter part of the Tenth Commandment.

DEGREE

bathmos (βαθμός, 898) denotes "a step," primarily of a threshold or stair, and is akin to *bainō*, "to go"; figuratively, "a standing, a stage in a career, position, degree," 1 Tim. 3:13, of faithful deacons.

Note: Tapeinos, "low, humble," whether in condition or mind, is translated "of low degree" in Luke 1:52 and Jas. 1:9.

DELAY

A. Verbs.

1. *okneō* (ὀκνέω, 3635), akin to *oknos*, "a shrinking, to be loath or slow to do a thing, to hesitate, delay," is used in Acts 9:38. In the Sept. in Num. 22:16, "do not delay"; Judg. 18:9.

2. *chronizō* (χρονίζω, 5549), from *chronos*, "time," lit. means "to while away time," i.e., by way of lingering, tarrying, "delaying"; "delayeth," Matt. 24:48; Luke 12:45, "tarried" Matt. 25:5; "tarried so long," Luke 1:21; "will (not) tarry," Heb. 10:37.

B. Noun.

anabolē (ἀναβολή, 311) lit. signifies "that which is thrown up" (*ana*, "up," *ballō*, "to throw"); hence "a delay," Acts 25:17.

Note: In Rev. 10:6, *chronos* is translated "delay" in RV marg., and is to be taken as the true meaning.

DELICACIES

Note: For *strēnos*, rendered "delicacies" in Rev. 18:3, KJV, denoting "wantonness" (RV), i.e., arrogant luxury, see WANTON.

DELIGHT IN

sunēdomai (συνήδομαι, 4913), lit., "to rejoice with (anyone), to delight in (a thing) with (others)," signifies "to delight with oneself inwardly in a thing," in Rom. 7:22.

Note: Cf. *hēdonē*, "desire, pleasure."

DELIVER, DELIVERANCE, DELIVERER

A. Verbs.

1. *didōmi* (δίδωμι, 1325), "to give," is translated "delivered" in Luke 7:15; RV, "gave"; so 19:13. See GIVE.

2. *anadidōmi* (ἀναδίδωμι, 325), *ana*, "up," and No. 1, "to deliver over, give up," is used of "delivering" the letter mentioned in Acts 23:33.

Note: For the different verb in Acts 15:30, see No. 4.

3. *apodidōmi* (ἀποδίδωμι, 591), *apo*, "from," and No. 1, lit., "to give away," hence, "to give back or up," is used in Pilate's command for the Lord's body to be "given up," Matt. 27:58; in the sense of "giving back," of the Lord's act in giving a healed boy back to his father, Luke 9:42. See GIVE, PAY, PAYMENT, PERFORM, RESTORE, YIELD.

4. *epididōmi* (ἐπιδίδωμι, 1929), lit., "to give upon or in addition," as from oneself to another, hence, "to deliver over," is used of the "delivering" of the roll of Isaiah to Christ in the synagogue, Luke 4:17; of the "delivering" of the epistle from the elders at Jerusalem to the church at Antioch, Acts 15:30. See GIVE, OFFER.

5. *paradidōmi* (παραδίδωμι, 3860), "to deliver over," in Rom. 6:17, RV, "that form of teaching whereunto ye were delivered," the figure being that of a mold which gives its shape to what is cast in it (not as the KJV). In Rom. 8:32 it is used of God in "delivering" His Son to expiatory death; so 4:25; see Mark 9:31; of Christ in "delivering" Himself up, Gal. 2:20; Eph. 5:2, 25. See BETRAY, A. In Mark 1:14, RV, it is used of "delivering" John the Baptist to prison.

6. *apallassō* (ἀπαλλάσσω, 525), lit., "to change from" (*apo*, "from," *allassō*, "to change"), "to free from, release," is translated "might deliver" in Heb. 2:15; in Luke 12:58, it is used in a legal sense of being quit of a person, i.e., the opponent being appeased and withdrawing his suit.

7. *eleutheroō* (ἐλευθερόω, 1659), "to set free," is translated "deliver" in Rom. 8:21. In six other places it is translated "make free," John 8:32, 36; Rom. 6:18, 22; 8:2; Gal. 5:1, RV, "set free." See FREE.

8. *exaireō* (ἐξαιρέω, 1807), lit., "to take out," denotes, in the middle voice, "to take out for oneself," hence, "to deliver, to rescue," the person who does so having a special interest in the result of his act. Thus it is used, in Gal. 1:4, of the act of God in "delivering" believers "out of this present evil world," the middle voice indicating His pleasure in the issue of their "deliverance." It signifies to "deliver" by rescuing from danger, in Acts 12:11; 23:27; 26:17; from bondage, Acts 7:10, 34.

9. *katargeō* (καταργέω, 2673): see ABOLISH.

10. *rhuomai* (ῥύομαι, 4506), "to rescue from, to preserve from," and so, "to deliver," the word by which it is regularly translated, is largely synonymous with *sōzō*, "to save," though the idea of "rescue from" is predominant in *rhuomai* (see Matt. 27:43), that of "preservation from," in *sōzō*. In Rom. 11:26 the present participle is used with the article, as a noun, "the Deliverer." This is the construction in 1 Thess. 1:10, where Christ is similarly spoken of Here the KJV wrongly has "which delivered" (the tense is not past); RV, "which delivereth"; the translation might well be (as in Rom. 11:26), "our Deliverer," that is, from the retributive calamities with which God will visit men at the end of the present age. From that wrath believers are to be "delivered." The verb is used with *apo*, "away from," in Matt. 6:13; Luke 11:4 (in some mss.); so also in 11:4; Rom. 15:31; 2 Thess. 3:2; 2 Tim. 4:18; and with *ek*, "from, out of," in Luke 1:74; Rom. 7:24; 2 Cor. 1:10; Col. 1:13, from bondage; in 2 Pet. 2:9, from temptation, in 2 Tim. 3:11, from persecution; but *ek* is used of ills impending, in 2 Cor. 1:10; in 2 Tim. 4:17, *ek* indicates that the danger was more imminent than in v. 18, where *apo* is used. Accordingly the meaning "out of the midst of" cannot be pressed in 1 Thess. 1:10.

11. *charizomai* (χαρίζομαι, 5483), "to gratify, to do what is pleasing to anyone," is translated "deliver" in the KJV of Acts 25:11, 16; RV, "give up" (marg., "grant by favor," i.e., to give over to the Jews so as to gratify their wishes). See FORGIVE, GIVE.

Note: For *gennaō* and *tiktō*, "to bear, to be delivered" (said of women at childbirth), see BEGET.

B. Nouns.

1. *apolutrōsis* (ἀπολύτρωσις, 629) denotes "redemption" (*apo*, "from," *lutron*, "a price of release"). In Heb. 11:35 it is translated "deliverance"; usually the release is effected by the payment of a ransom, or the required price, the *lutron* (ransom). See REDEMPTION.

2. *aphesis* (ἄφεσις, 859) denotes "a release, from bondage, imprisonment, etc." (the corresponding verb is *aphiēmi*, "to send away, let go"); in Luke 4:18 it is used of "liberation" from captivity (KJV, "deliverance," RV, "release"). See FORGIVENESS, REMISSION.

3. *lutrōtēs* (λυτρωτής, 3086), "a redeemer, one who releases" (see No. 1), is translated "deliverer" in Acts 7:35 (RV marg., "redeemer").

Note: See also DELIVER, A, No. 10.

C. Verbal Adjective.

ekdotos (ἔκδοτος, 1560), lit., "given up" (*ek*, "out of," *didōmi*, "to give"), "delivered up" (to enemies, or to the power or will of someone), is used of Christ in Acts 2:23.

DELUDE, DELUSION

A. Verb.

paralogizomai (παραλογίζομαι, 3884): see BEGUILE.

B. Noun.

planē (πλάνη, 4106), lit., "a wandering," whereby those who are led astray roam hither and thither, is always used in the NT, of mental straying, wrong opinion, error in morals or religion. In 2 Thess. 2:11, KJV, it is translated delusion, RV, error. See DECEIT, ERROR.

DEMAND

Note: For DEMAND (Matt. 2:4 and Acts 21:33), see INQUIRE.

DEMON, DEMONIAC

A. Nouns.

1. *daimōn* (δαίμων, 1142), "a demon," signified, among pagan Greeks, an inferior deity, whether good or bad. In the NT it denotes "an evil spirit." It is used in Matt. 8:31, mistranslated "devils."

Some would derive the word from a root *da-*, meaning "to distribute." More probably it is from a similar root *da-*, meaning "to know," and hence means "a knowing one."

2. *daimonion* (δαιμόνιον, 1140), not a diminutive of *daimōn*, No. 1, but the neuter of the adjective *daimonios*, pertaining to a demon, is also mistranslated "devil," "devils." In Acts 17:18, it denotes an inferior pagan deity. "Demons" are the spiritual agents acting in all idolatry. The idol itself is nothing, but every idol has a "demon" associated with it who induces idolatry, with its worship and sacrifices, 1 Cor. 10:20-21; Rev. 9:20; cf. Deut. 32:17; Isa. 13:21; 34:14; 65:3, 11. They disseminate errors among men, and seek to seduce believers, 1 Tim. 4:1. As seducing spirits they deceive men into the supposition that through mediums (those who have "familiar spirits," Lev. 20:6, 27, e.g.) they can converse with deceased human beings. Hence the destructive deception of spiritism, forbidden in Scripture, Lev. 19:31; Deut. 18:11; Isa. 8:19. "Demons" tremble before God, Jas. 2:19; they recognized Christ as Lord and as their future Judge, Matt. 8:29; Luke 4:41. Christ cast them out of human beings by His own power. His disciples did so in His name, and by exercising faith, e.g., Matt. 17:20.

Acting under Satan (cf. Rev. 16:13-14), "demons" are permitted to afflict with bodily disease, Luke 13:16. Being unclean they tempt human beings with unclean thoughts, Matt. 10:1; Mark 5:2; 7:25; Luke 8:27-29; Rev. 16:13; 18:2, e.g. They differ in degrees of wickedness, Matt. 12:45. They will instigate the rulers of the nations at the end of this age to make war against God and His Christ, Rev. 16:14. See DEVIL.

B. Verb.

daimonizomai (δαιμονίζομαι, 1139) signifies "to be possessed of a demon, to act under the control of a demon." Those who were thus afflicted expressed the mind and consciousness of the "demon" or "demons" indwelling them, e.g., Luke 8:28. The verb is found chiefly in Matt. and Mark; Matt. 4:24; 8:16, 28, 33; 9:32; 12:22; 15:22; Mark 1:32; 5:15-16, 18; elsewhere in Luke 8:36 and John 10:21, "him that hath a devil (demon)."

C. Adjective.

daimoniōdes (δαιμονιώδης, 1141) signifies "proceeding from, or resembling, a demon, demoniacal"; see marg. of Jas. 3:15, RV (text, "devilish").

DEMONSTRATION

apodeixis (ἀπόδειξις, 585), lit., "a pointing out" (*apo*, "forth," *deiknumi*, "to show"), a "showing" or demonstrating by argument, is found in 1 Cor. 2:4, where the apostle speaks of a proof, a "showing" forth or display, by the operation of the Spirit of God in him, as affecting the hearts and lives of his hearers, in contrast to the attempted methods of proof by rhetorical arts and philosophic arguments.

DEN

spēlaion (σπήλαιον, 4693): see CAVE.

DEPOSE

kathaireō (καθαιρέω, 2507) lit. signifies "to take down" (*kata*, "down," *haireō*, "to take"), the technical term for "removing a body after crucifixion," e.g., Mark 15:36; hence, "to pull down, demolish"; in Acts 19:27, according to the most authentic mss., the translation is (as the RV) "that she (Diana) should even be deposed from her magnificence" (possibly, in the partitive sense of the genitive, "destroyed from, or diminished in, somewhat of her magnificence"). See DESTROY.

DEPTH

1. *bathos* (βάθος, 899): see DEEP.

2. *pelagos* (πέλαγος, 3989), "the sea," Acts 27:5, denotes also "the depth" (of the sea), Matt. 18:6. The word is most probably connected with a form of *plēssō*, "to strike," and *plēgē*, "a blow," suggestive of the tossing of the waves. Some would connect it with *plax*, "a level board," but this is improbable, and less applicable to the general usage of the word, which commonly denotes the sea in its restless character. See SEA.

DERIDE

Note: For *ekmuktērizō*, lit., "to turn up the nose at, to deride out and out," Luke 16:14; 23:35, see SCOFF.

2. *lego*, (λέγω, 3004) "to say," is rendered "describeth" in Rom. 4:6, KJV, "David describeth the blessedness ..."; this the RV corrects to, "David pronounceth blessing upon ..." This might be regarded as the meaning, if David is considered as the human agent acting for God as the real pronouncer of blessing. Otherwise the verb *lego* is to be taken in its ordinary sense of "telling or relating"; especially as the blessedness (*makarismos*) is not an act, but a state of felicity resulting from God's act of justification.

DESERT (Noun and Adjective)

A. Noun.

erēmia (ἐρημία, 2047), primarily "a solitude, an uninhabited place," in contrast to a town or village, is translated "deserts" in Heb. 11:38; "the wilderness" in Matt. 15:33, KJV, "a desert place," RV; so in Mark 8:4; "wilderness" in 2 Cor. 11:26. It does not always denote a barren region, void of vegetation; it is often used of a place uncultivated, but fit for pasturage. See WILDERNESS.

B. Adjective.

erēmos (ἔρημος, 2048), used as a noun, has the same meaning as *erēmia*, in Luke 5:16 and 8:29, RV, "deserts," for KJV, "wilderness"; in Matt. 24:26 and John 6:31, RV, "wilderness," for KJV, "desert." As an adjective, it denotes (a), with reference to persons, "deserted," desolate, deprived of the friends and kindred, e.g. of a woman deserted by a husband, Gal 4:21; (b) so of a city, as Jerusalem, Matt. 23:38; or uninhabited places, "desert," e.g., Matt. 14:13, 15; Acts 8:26; in Mark 1:35, RV, "desert," for KJV, solitary. See DESOLATE, WILDERNESS.

DESIRE (Noun and Verb), DESIROUS

A. Nouns.

1. *epithumia* (ἐπιθυμία, 1939), "a desire, craving, longing, mostly of evil desires," frequently translated "lust," is used in the following, of good "desires": of the Lord's "wish" concerning the last Passover, Luke 22:15, of Paul's "desire" to be with Christ, Phil. 1:23; of his "desire" to see the saints at Thessalonica again, 1 Thess. 2:17.

With regard to evil "desires," in Col. 3:5 the RV has "desire," for the KJV, "concupiscence"; in 1 Thess. 4:5, RV, "lust," for KJV, "concupiscence"; there the preceding word *pathos* is translated "passion," RV, for KJV, "lust" (see AFFECTION); also in Col. 3:5 *pathos* and *epithumia* are associated, RV, "passion," for KJV, "inordinate affection." *Epithumia* is combined with *pathēma*, in Gal. 5:24; for the KJV, "affections and lusts," the RV has "passions, and the lusts thereof." *Epithumia* is the more comprehensive term, including all manner of "lusts and desires"; *pathēma* denotes suffering; in the passage in Gal. (l.c.) the sufferings are those produced by yielding to the flesh; *pathos* points more to the evil state from which "lusts" spring. Cf *orexis*, "lust," Rom. 1:27. See LUST, and Trench, *Syn.* Sec. LXXXVII.

2. *eudokia* (εὐδοκία, 2107), lit., "good pleasure" (*eu*, "well," *dokeō*, "to seem"), implies a gracious purpose, a good object being in view, with the idea of a resolve, showing the willingness with which the resolve is made. It is often translated "good pleasure," e.g., Eph. 1:5, 9; Phil. 2:13; in Phil. 1:15, "good will"; in Rom. 10:1, "desire," (marg., "good pleasure"); in 2 Thess. 1:11, RV, "desire," KJV and RV, marg., "good pleasure."

It is used of God in Matt. 11:26 ("well pleasing," RV, for KJV, "seemed good"); Luke 2:14, RV, "men in whom He is well pleased," lit., "men of good pleasure" (the construction is objective); 10:21; Eph. 1:5, 9; Phil. 2:13. See PLEASURE, SEEM, WILL.

3. *epipothēsis* (ἐπιπόθησις, 1972), "an earnest desire, a longing for" (*epi*, "upon," intensive, *potheō*, "to desire"), is found in 2 Cor. 7:7, 11, KJV, "earnest desire," and "vehement desire"; RV, "longing" in both places. See LONGING.

4. *epipothia* (ἐπιποθία, 1974), with the same meaning as No. 3, is used in Rom. 15:23, RV, "longing," KJV, "great desire." Cf. *epipothētos*, Phil. 4:1, "longed for," and *epipotheō*, "to long for" [see B, Note (4)]. See LONGING.

5. *thelēma* (θέλημα, 2307) denotes "a will, that which is willed" (akin to B, No. 6). It is rendered "desires," in Eph. 2:3. See PLEASURE, WILL.

Note: In 1 Pet. 4:3, RV, *boulēma* is rendered "desire." See WILL.

B. Verbs.

1. *axioō* (ἀξιόω, 515), "to deem worthy," is translated "desire" in Acts 28:22, where a suitable rendering would be "We think it meet (or good) to hear of thee"; so in 15:38.

2. *epithumeō* (ἐπιθυμέω, 1937), "to desire earnestly" (as with A, No. 1), stresses the inward impulse rather than the object desired. It is translated "to desire" in Luke 16:21; 17:22; 22:15; 1 Tim. 3:1; Heb. 6:11; 1 Pet. 1:12; Rev. 9:6. See COVET.

3. *erōtaō* (ἐρωτάω, 2065), in Luke 7:36 is translated "desired"; in 14:32, RV, "asketh," for KJV, "desireth"; so in John 12:21; Acts 16:39; 18:20; 23:20; in v. 18 "asked," for KJV, "prayed."

4. *homeiromai* (ὁμείρομαι, 2442) or *himeiromai* (ἱμείρομαι, 2442), "to have a strong affection for, a yearning after," is found in 1 Thess. 2:8, "being affectionately desirous of you." It is probably derived from a root indicating remembrance.

5. *oregō* (ὀρέγω, 3713), "to reach or stretch out," is used only in the middle voice, signifying the mental effort of stretching oneself out for a thing, of longing after it, with stress upon the object desired (cf. No. 2); it is translated "desire" in Heb. 11:16; in 1 Tim. 3:1, RV, "seeketh," for KJV, "desireth"; in 1 Tim. 6:10, RV, "reached after," for KJV, "coveted after." In Heb. 11:16, a suitable rendering would be "reach after." See COVET. Cf. *orexis*, lust, Rom. 1:27.

6. *thelō* (θέλω, 2309), "to will, to wish," implying volition and purpose, frequently a determination, is most usually rendered "to will." It is translated "to desire" in the RV of the following: Matt. 9:13; 12:7; Mark 6:19; Luke 10:29; 14:28; 23:20;

Acts 24:27; 25:9; Gal. 4:17; 1 Tim. 5:11; Heb. 12:17; 13:18. See INTEND, LIST, LOVE, PLEASE, VOLUNTARY, WILL.

7. *boulomai* (βούλομαι, 1014), "to wish, to will deliberately," expresses more strongly than *thelō* (No. 6) the deliberate exercise of the will; it is translated "to desire" in the RV of the following: Acts 22:30; 23:28; 27:43; 28:18; 1 Tim. 2:8; 5:14; 6:9 and Jude 5. See INTEND, LIST, MINDED, WILLING.

8. *zēloō* (ζηλόω, 2206), "to have a zeal for, to be zealous towards," whether in a good or evil sense, the former in 1 Cor. 14:1, concerning spiritual gifts RV, "desire earnestly," KJV, "desire"; in an evil sense, in Jas. 4:2, RV, "covet," for KJV, "desire to have."

9. *aiteō* (αἰτέω, 154), "to ask," is rendered "to desire" in KJV, e.g., in Matt. 20:20; Luke 23:25 [RV, always "to ask (for)"].

10. *speudō* (σπεύδω, 4692) is translated "earnestly desiring" in 2 Pet. 3:12, RV. See HASTE.

Note: The following are translated by the verb "to desire" in the KJV.

(1) *Eperōtaō*, No. 3, with *epi*, intensive, "to ask, interrogate, inquire of, consult, or to demand of a person"; in Matt. 16:1, RV, "asked." (2) *Zēteō*, "to seek"; in Matt. 12:46–47, RV, "seeking"; in Luke 9:9, RV, "sought." See GO, *Note* (2), (a), INQUIRE. (3) *Epizēteō*, "to seek earnestly" (No. 2, with *epi*, intensive), in Acts 13:7, RV, "sought"; in Phil. 4:17, RV, "seek for" (twice). See INQUIRE. (4) *Epipotheō*, "to long after, to lust"; in 2 Cor. 5:2, RV, "longing"; in 1 Thess. 3:6 and 2 Tim. 1:4, RV, "longing"; in 1 Pet. 2:2, RV, "long for." See A, Hos. 3-4. See LONG, LUST. (5) *Exaiteomai*, intensive of No. 9, occurs in Luke 22:31. (6) For *parakaleō*, see EXHORT, INTREAT. (7) For desirous of vain glory," see VAINGLORY.

DESOLATE (Verb and Adjective), DESOLATION

A. Verbs.

1. *erēmoō* (ἐρημόω, 2049) signifies "to make desolate, lay waste." From the primary sense of "making quiet" comes that of "making lonely." It is used only in the passive voice in the NT; in Rev. 17:16, "shall make desolate" is, lit., "shall make her desolated"; in 18:17, 19, "is made desolate"; in Matt. 12:25 and Luke 11:17, "is brought to desolation." See NOUGHT (COME TO). Cf. DESERT.

2. *monoō* (μονόω, 3443), "to leave alone" (akin to *monos*, "alone"), is used in 1 Tim. 5:5, in the passive voice, but translated "desolate," lit., "was made desolate" or "left desolate."

B. Adjectives.

1. *erēmos* (ἔρημος, 2048) is translated "desolate" in the Lord's words against Jerusalem, Matt. 23:38; some mss. have it in Luke 13:35; in reference to the habitation of Judas, Acts 1:20, and to Sarah, from whom, being barren, her husband had turned, Gal. 4:27. See DESERT.

2. *orphanos* (ὀρφανός, 3737) (Eng., "orphan"; Lat., "*orbus*"), signifies "bereft of parents or of a father." In Jas. 1:27 it is translated "fatherless." It was also used in the general sense of being "friendless or desolate." In John 14:18 the Lord uses it of the relationship between Himself and His disciples, He having been their guide, teacher and protector; RV, "desolate," KJV, "comfortless." Some mss. have the word in Mark 12:40. See FATHERLESS.

C. Noun.

erēmōsis (ἐρήμωσις, 2050), akin to A, No. 1, denotes "desolation," (a) in the sense of "making desolate," e.g., in the phrase "the abomination of desolation," Matt. 24:15; Mark 13:14; the genitive is objective, "the abomination that makes desolate"; (b) with stress upon the effect of the process, Luke 21:20, with reference to the "desolation" of Jerusalem.

DESPAIR

1. *exaporeō* (ἐξαπορέω, 1820) is used in the NT in the passive voice, with middle sense, "to be utterly without a way" (*ek*, "out of," intensive, *a*, negative, *poros*, "a way through"; cf. *poreuō*, "to go through"; (Eng., "ferry" is connected); "to be quite at a loss, without resource, in despair." It is used in 2 Cor. 1:8, with reference to life; in 4:8, in the sentence "perplexed, yet not unto (KJV, 'in') despair," the word "perplexed" translates the verb *aporeō*, and the phrase "unto despair" translates the intensive form *exaporeō*, a play on the words. In the Sept., Ps. 88:15, where the translation is "having been lifted up, I was brought low and into despair.

2. *apelpizō* (ἀπελπίζω, 560), lit., "to hope away" (*apo*, "away from," *elpizō*, "to hope"). i.e., "to give up in despair, to despair," is use. in Luke 6:35, RV, "nothing despairing," i.e., without anxiety as to the result, or not "despairing" of the recompense from God; this is probably the true meaning; KJV, "hoping for nothing again." The marg., "of no man," is to be rejected.

DESPISE, DESPISER

A. Verbs.

1. *exoutheneō* (ἐξουθενέω, 1848), "to make of no account" (*ex*, "out," *oudeis*, "nobody," alternatively written, *outheis*), "to regard as nothing, to despise utterly, to treat with contempt." This is usually translated to "set at nought," Luke 18:9, RV, KJV, "despised." So in Rom. 14:3. Both have "set at nought" in Luke 23:11; Acts 4:11; Rom. 14:10. Both have "despise" in 1 Cor. 16:11; Gal. 4:14, and 1 Thess. 5:20; in 2 Cor. 10:10, RV, "of no account," for KJV, "contemptible"; in 1 Cor. 1:28, KJV and RV, "despised."

Note: In Mark 9:12 some mss. have this verb; the most authentic have the alternative spelling *exoudeneō*, "set at nought."

2. *kataphroneō* (καταφρονέω, 2706), lit., "to think down upon or against anyone" (*kata*, "down," *phrēn*, "the mind"), hence signifies "to think slightly of, to despise," Matt. 6:24; 18:10; Luke 16:13; Rom. 2:4; 1 Cor. 11:22; 1 Tim. 4:12; 6:2; Heb. 12:2; 2 Pet. 2:10.

3. *periphroneō* (περιφρονέω, 4065) lit. denotes "to think round a thing, to turn over in the mind"; hence, "to have thoughts beyond, to despise," Titus 2:15.

Notes: The following verbs, translated "to despise, etc." in the KJV, are given suitable meanings in the RV:

(1) *Atheteō*, lit., "to displace, to set aside," RV, "to reject," Luke 10:16; 1 Thess. 4:8; in 1 Tim. 5:12, "rejected," for KJV, "cast off"; in Heb. 10:28, "hath set at nought"; so Jude 8. See REJECT, VOID, No. 2. (2) *Atimazō*, "to dishonor" (*a*, negative, *timē*, "honor"); in Jas. 2:6, RV, "have dishonored." See DISHONOR, SHAME, C, No. 1, SHAMEFULLY. (3) *Oligōreō*, "to care little for, regard lightly" (*oligos*, "little"); in Heb. 12:5, RV, "regard lightly. See REGARD. (4) The phrase *logizomai eis ouden* signifies "to reckon as nothing"; in the passive voice, "to be counted as nothing"; in Acts 19:27, RV, "be made of no account."

B. Adjective.

atimos (ἄτιμος, 820), "without honor," see *Note* (2), above, is translated as a verb in 1 Cor. 4:10, KJV, "are despised"; RV, "have dishonor," lit., "(we are) without honor"; "without honor" in Matt. 13:57; Mark 6:4. The comparative degree *atimoteros*, "less honorable," is used in 1 Cor. 12:23.

Note: Aphilagathos, "not loving the good" (*a*, negative, *phileō*, "to love," *agathos*, "good"), is used in 2 Tim. 3:3, KJV, "despisers of those that are good," RV, "no lovers of good." See LOVER.

C. Noun.

kataphronētēs (καταφρονητής, 2707), lit., "one who thinks down against," hence, "a despiser" (see A, No. 2), is found in Acts 13:41. In the Sept., Hab. 1:5; 2:5 and Zeph. 3:4.

DESPITE, DESPITEFUL, DESPITEFULLY (use)

1. *enubrizō* (ἐνυβρίζω, 1796), "to treat insultingly, with contumely" (*en*, intensive, *hubrizō*, "to insult"; some connect it with *huper*, "above, over," Lat. *super*, which suggests the insulting disdain of one who considers himself superior), is translated "hath done despite" in Heb. 10:29.

Notes: (1) *Hubrizō*, "to insult, act with insolence," is translated "to use despitefully" in Acts 14:5, KJV; RV, "to entreat ... shamefully." See SHAMEFULLY, SPITEFULLY, REPROACH, B, No. 2.

(2) The noun *hubristēs*, "a violent man," is translated "despiteful" in Rom. 1:30, KJV; RV, "insolent"; in 1 Tim. 1:13, "injurious."

2. *epēreazō* (ἐπηρεάζω, 1908), for which see ACCUSE, B, No. 3, is found in some mss. in Matt. 5:44, and translated "despitefully use," KJV (the RV follows the mss. which omit the sentence). In the corresponding passage in Luke 6:28, the KJV and RV have "despitefully use"; in 1 Pet. 3:16, KJV, "falsely accuse," RV, "revile." See ACCUSE, REVILE.

DESTITUTE (be, etc.)

1. *apostereō* (ἀποστερέω, 650): see DEFRAUD.

2. *hustereō* (ὑστερέω, 5302), primarily, "to be behind, to be last," hence, "to lack, fail of, come short of," is translated "being destitute" in Heb. 11:37.

3. *leipō* (λείπω, 3007) signifies "to leave, forsake"; in the passive voice, "to be left, forsaken, destitute"; in Jas. 2:15, KJV, "destitute," RV, "be in lack." See LACK.

DESTROY, DESTROYER, DESTRUCTION, DESTRUCTIVE

A. Verbs.

1. *apollumi* (ἀπόλλυμι, 622), a strengthened form of *ollumi*, signifies "to destroy utterly"; in middle voice, "to perish." The idea is not extinction but ruin, loss, not of being, but of wellbeing. This is clear from its use, as, e.g., of the marring of wine skins, Luke 5:37; of lost sheep, i.e., lost to the shepherd, metaphorical of spiritual destitution, Luke 15:4, 6, etc.; the lost son, 15:24; of the perishing of food, John 6:27; of gold, 1 Pet. 1:7. So of persons, Matt. 2:13, "destroy"; 8:25, "perish"; 22:7; 27:20; of the loss of well-being in the case of the unsaved hereafter, Matt. 10:28; Luke 13:3, 5; John 3:16 (v. 15 in some mss.); 10:28; 17:12; Rom. 2:12; 1 Cor. 15:18; 2 Cor. 2:15, "are perishing"; 4:3; 2 Thess. 2:10; Jas. 4:12; 2 Pet. 3:9. Cf. B, II, No. 1. See DIE, LOSE, PERISH.

2. *katargeō* (καταργέω, 2673): see ABOLISH.

3. *kathaireō* (καθαιρέω, 2507), "to cast down, pull down by force, etc.," is translated "to destroy" in Acts 13:19. In Acts 19:27, KJV, "should be destroyed," the RV suitably has "should be deposed."

4. *luō* (λύω, 3089), "to loose, dissolve, sever, break, demolish," is translated "destroy," in 1 John 3:8, of the works of the Devil.

5. *kataluō* (καταλύω, 2647), *kata*, "down," intensive, and No. 4, "to destroy utterly, to overthrow completely," is rendered "destroy," in Matt. 5:17, twice, of the Law; Matt. 24:2; 26:61; 27:40; Mark 13:2; 14:58; 15:29; Luke 21:6, of the Temple; in Acts 6:14, of Jerusalem; in Gal. 2:18, of the Law as a means of justification; in Rom. 14:20 (KJV, "destroy," RV, "overthrow"), of the marring of a person's spiritual well-being (in v. 15 *apollumi*, No. 1, is used in the same sense); in Acts 5:38 and 39 (RV, "overthrow") of the failure of purposes; in 2 Cor.

5:1, of the death of the body ("dissolved). See DISSOLVE, NOUGHT (COME TO), OVERTHROW.

For its other meaning, "to lodge," see Luke 9:12 and 19:7.

6. *olothreuō* (ὀλοθρεύω, 3645), "to destroy," especially in the sense of slaying, is found in Heb. 11:28, where the RV translates the present participle with the article by the noun "destroyer." See B, below. The verb occurs frequently in the Sept., e.g., Ex. 12:23; Josh. 3:10; 7:25; Jer. 2:30; 5:6; 22:7.

7. *exolothreuō* (ἐξολοθρεύω, 1842), *ek*, "out of" (intensive), and No. 6, "to destroy utterly to slay wholly," is found in Acts 3:23, RV, "utterly destroyed," referring to the "destruction" of one who would refuse to hearken to the voice of God through Christ. This verb is far more abundantly used in the Sept. than No. 6; it occurs 35 times in Deut. 34 in Josh. 68 in the Psalms.

8. *phtheirō* (φθείρω, 5351): see CORRUPT, A, No. 2.

9. *diaphtheirō* (διαφθείρω, 1311); See CORRUPT, A, No. 3.

Note: Portheō, "to ruin by laying waste, to make havock of," is translated "destroyed" in Acts 9:21, of the attacks upon the church in Jerusalem by Saul of Tarsus; "wasted," in Gal. 1:13, with reference to the same; "destroyed" in Gal. 1:23, where "the faith" is put by metonymy (one thing being put for another associated with it), for those who held the faith. In each of these places the RV consistently translates by "made havock of." See HAVOC, WASTE.

B. Nouns.

(I) *(Personal: DESTROYER)*

olothreutēs (ὀλοθρευτής, 3644), akin to A, No. 6, "a destroyer," is found in 1 Cor. 10:10.

Note: For the construction in Heb. 11:28, "the destroyer," see A, No. 6. Cf. *apolluōn*, in Rev. 9:11, the present participle of *apollumi*, A, No. 1, used as a proper noun.

(II) *(Abstract: DESTRUCTION)*

1. *apōleia* (ἀπώλεια, 684), akin to A, No. 1, and likewise indicating "loss of well-being, not of being," is used (a) of things, signifying their waste, or ruin; of ointment, Matt. 26:8; Mark 14:4; of money, Acts 8:20 ("perish"); (b) of persons, signifying their spiritual and eternal perdition, Matt. 7:13; John 17:12; 2 Thess. 2:3, where "son of perdition" signifies the proper destiny of the person mentioned; metaphorically of men persistent in evil, Rom. 9:22, where "fitted" is in the middle voice, indicating that the vessels of wrath fitted themselves for "destruction," of the adversaries of the Lord's people, Phil. 1:28 ("perdition"); of professing Christians, really enemies of the cross of Christ, Phil. 3:19 (RV, "perdition"); of those who are subjects of foolish and hurtful lusts, 1 Tim. 6:9 (for the preceding word "destruction" see No. 3, below); of professing Hebrew adherents who shrink back into unbelief, Heb. 10:39; of false teachers, 2 Pet. 2:1, 3; of ungodly men, 3:7; of those who wrest the Scriptures, 3:16; of the Beast, the final head of the revived Roman Empire, Rev. 17:8, 11; (c) of impersonal subjects, as heresies, 2 Pet. 2:1, where "destructive heresies" (RV; KJV, "damnable") is, lit., "heresies of destruction" (marg., "sects of perdition"); in v. 2 the most authentic mss. have *aselgeiais*, "lascivious," instead of *apōleiais*. See PERDITION, PERNICIOUS, WASTE.

2. *kathairesis* (καθαίρεσις, 2506), akin to A, No. 3, "a taking down, a pulling down," is used three times in 2 Cor., "casting down" in the RV in each place; in 10:4 (KJV, "pulling down"); in 10:8 and 13:10 (KJV, "destruction").

3. *olethros* (ὄλεθρος, 3639), "ruin, destruction," akin to A, No. 6, always translated "destruction," is used in 1 Cor. 5:5, of the effect upon the physical condition of an erring believer for the purpose of his spiritual profit; in 1 Thess. 5:3 and 2 Thess. 1:9, of the effect of the divine judgments upon men at the ushering in of the Day of the Lord and the revelation of the Lord Jesus; in 1 Tim. 6:9, of the consequences of the indulgence of the flesh, referring to physical "ruin" and possibly that of the whole being, the following word *apōleia* (see No. 1) stressing the final, eternal and irrevocable character of the ruin.

4. *phthora* (φθορά, 5356), akin to A, No. 8, denotes "the destruction that comes with corruption." In 2 Pet. 2:12 it is used twice; for the KJV, "made to be taken and destroyed ... shall utterly perish (*phtheirō*) in their own corruption," the RV has "to be taken and destroyed (lit., 'unto capture and destruction,' *phthora*) ... shall in their destroying (*phthora*) surely be destroyed," taking the noun in the last clause in the sense of their act of "destroying" others. See CORRUPT, CORRUPTION.

5. *suntrimma* (σύντριμμα, 4938), "a breaking in pieces, shattering" (the corresponding verb is *suntribō*), hence, "ruin, destruction," is compounded of sun, "together," and *trimma*, "a rubbing or wearing away." The latter, and *tribō*, "to beat," are derived from a root, signifying "to rub, wear away"; hence Eng., "tribulation and trouble." It is used, metaphorically, of "destruction," in Rom. 3:16 (from Isa. 59:7), which, in a passage setting forth the sinful state of mankind in general, suggests the "wearing" process of the effects of cruelty. The word is frequent in the Sept., especially in Isaiah and Jeremiah.

DEVICE

1. *enthumēsis* (ἐνθύμησις, 1761), "a cogitation, an inward reasoning" (generally, evil surmising or supposition), is formed from *en*, "in," and *thumos*, "strong feeling, passion" (cf. *thumoō*, in the middle voice, "to be wroth, furious"); Eng., "fume" is akin; the root, *thu*, signifies "to rush, rage." The word is translated "device" in Acts 17:29, of man's production of images; elsewhere, "thoughts," Matt. 9:4; 12:25; Heb. 4:12,

where the accompanying word *ennoia* denotes inward intentions. See THOUGHT.

2. *noēma* (νόημα, 3540) denotes "thought, that which is thought out" (cf. *noeō*, "to understand"); hence, "a purpose, device"; translated "devices" in 2 Cor. 2:11; "minds" in 2 Cor. 3:14; 4:4; 11:3; in 2 Cor. 10:5, "thought"; in Phil. 4:7, KJV, "minds," RV, "thoughts." See MIND, THOUGHT.

DEVIL, DEVILISH

diabolos (διάβολος, 1228), "an accuser, a slanderer" (from *diaballō*, "to accuse, to malign"), is one of the names of Satan. From it the English word "Devil" is derived, and should be applied only to Satan, as a proper name. *Daimōn*, "a demon," is frequently, but wrongly, translated "devil"; it should always be translated "demon," as in the RV margin. There is one "Devil," there are many demons. Being the malignant enemy of God and man, he accuses man to God, Job 1:6-11; 2:1-5; Rev. 12:9, 10, and God to man, Gen. 3. He afflicts men with physical sufferings, Acts 10:38. Being himself sinful, 1 John 3:8, he instigated man to sin, Gen. 3, and tempts man to do evil, Eph. 4:27; 6:11, encouraging him thereto by deception, Eph. 2:2. Death having been brought into the world by sin, the "Devil" had the power of death, but Christ through His own death, has triumphed over him, and will bring him to nought, Heb. 2:14; his power over death is intimated in his struggle with Michael over the body of Moses, Jude 9. Judas, who gave himself over to the "Devil," was so identified with him, that the Lord described him as such, John 6:70 (see 13:2). As the "Devil" raised himself in pride against God and fell under condemnation, so believers are warned against similar sin, 1 Tim. 3:6; for them he lays snares, v. 7, seeking to devour them as a roaring lion, 1 Pet. 5:8; those who fall into his snare may be recovered therefrom unto the will of God, 2 Tim. 2:26, "having been taken captive by him (i.e., by the 'Devil')"; "by the Lord's servant" is an alternative, which some regard as confirmed by the use of *zōgreō* ("to catch alive") in Luke 5:10; but the general use is that of taking captive in the usual way. If believers resist he will flee from them, Jas. 4:7. His fury and malignity will be especially exercised at the end of the present age, Rev. 12:12. His doom is the lake of fire, Matt. 25:41; Rev. 20:10. The noun is applied to slanderers, false accusers, 1 Tim. 3:11; 2 Tim. 3:3; Titus 2:3.

Note: For devilish, Jas. 3:17, see DEMON, C.

DEVISED (cunningly)

sophizō (σοφίζω, 4679), from *sophos*, "wise" (connected etymologically with *sophēs*, "tasty"), in the active voice signifies "to make wise," 2 Tim. 3:15 (so in the Sept. of Ps. 19:7, e.g., "making babes wise"; in 119:98, "Thou hast made me wiser than mine enemies"). In the middle voice it means (a) "to become wise"; it is not used thus in the NT, but is so found in the Sept., e.g., in Eccles. 2:15, 19; 7:17; (b) "to play the sophist, to devise cleverly," it is used with this meaning in the passive voice in 2 Pet. 1:16, "cunningly devised fables." See WISE.

Note: Cf. *katasophizomai*, "to deal subtly." See DEAL WITH, *Note* (2).

DEVOTION

Note: For this word, in Acts 17:23, KJV, which translates *sebasma*, "devotions," marg., "gods that ye worship," RV, "objects of your worship," in 2 Thess. 2:4, "that is worshiped," see WORSHIP. Cf. Acts 14:15, where, in translating *mataia*, the KJV has "vanities," the abstract for the concrete (RV, "vain things").

DEVOUR

1. *esthiō* (ἐσθίω, 2068) is a strengthened form of an old verb *edo*, from the root *ed-*, whence Lat., *edo*, Eng., "eat." The form *ephagon*, used as the 2nd aorist tense of this verb, is from the root *phag-*, "to eat up." It is translated "devour" in Heb. 10:27; elsewhere, by the verb "to eat."

2. *katesthiō* and *kataphagō* (κατεσθίω and καταφάγω, 2719), *kata*, "down," intensive, and No. 1, signifies (a) "to consume by eating, to devour," said of birds, Matt. 13:4; Mark 4:4; Luke 8:5; of the Dragon, Rev. 12:4; of a prophet, "eating" up a book, suggestive of spiritually "eating" and digesting its contents, Rev. 10:9 (cf. Ezek. 2:8; 3:1-3; Jer. 15:16); (b) metaphorically, "to squander, to waste," Luke 15:30; "to consume" one's physical powers by emotion, John 2:17; "to devour" by forcible appropriation, as of widows' property, Matt. 23:14 (KJV only); Mark 12:40; "to demand maintenance," as false apostles did to the church at Corinth, 2 Cor. 11:20; "to exploit or prey on one another," Gal. 5:15, where "bite ... devour ... consume" form a climax, the first two describing a process, the last the act of swallowing down; to "destroy" by fire, Rev. 11:5; 20:9.

3. *katapinō* (καταπίνω, 2666), from *kato*, "down," intensive, *pinō*, "to drink," in 1 Pet. 5:8 is translated "devour," of Satan's activities against believers. The meaning "to swallow" is found in Matt. 23:24; 1 Cor. 15:54; 2 Cor. 2:7; 5:4; Heb. 11:29, RV (for KJV, "drowned"); Rev. 12:16. See SWALLOW.

DEVOUT

1. *eulabēs* (εὐλαβής, 2126), lit., "taking hold well" (*eu*, "well," *lambanō*, "to take hold"), primarily, "cautious," signifies in the NT, "careful as to the realization of the presence and claims of God, reverencing God, pious, devout," in Luke 2:25 it is said of Simeon, in Acts 2:5, of certain Jews; in 8:2, of those who bore Stephen's body to burial; of Ananias, 22:12 (see No. 2). "In that mingled fear and love which, combined, constitute the piety of man toward God, the Old Testament

placed its emphasis on the fear, the New places it on the love (though there was love in the fear of God's saints then, as there must be fear in their love now)," Trench, *Syn.*, Sec. XLVIII.

Note. Cf. the noun *eulabeia*, "reverence," and the verb *eulabeomai*, "to reverence."

2. *eusebēs* (εὐσεβής, 2152), from *eu*, "well," *sebomai*, "to reverence," the root *seb-* signifying "sacred awe," describes "reverence" exhibited especially in actions, reverence or awe well directed. Among the Greeks it was used, e.g., of practical piety towards parents. In the NT it is used of a pious attitude towards God, Acts 10:2, 7; (in some mss. in 22:12); "godly," in 2 Pet. 2:9. See GODLY. In the Sept., Prov. 12:12; Isa. 24:16; 26:7; 32:8; Mic. 7:2.

Notes: (1) While *eulabēs* especially suggests the piety which characterizes the inner being, the soul, in its attitude towards God, *eusebēs* directs us rather to the energy which, directed by holy awe of God, finds expression in devoted activity.

(2) Cf. *theosebeia*, and *theosebēs*, which, by their very formation (*theos*, "God," and *sebomai*, express "reverence" towards God. See Trench (Sec. XLVIII).

3. *sebomai* (σέβομαι, 4576), "to feel awe," whether before God or man, "to worship," is translated "devout," in Acts 13:43, RV (KJV, "religious"); 13:50; 17:4, 17. See WORSHIP.

DIADEM

diadēma (διάδημα, 1238) is derived from *diadeō*, "to bind round." It was the kingly ornament for the head, and especially the blue band marked with white, used to bind on the turban or tiara of Persian kings. It was adopted by Alexander the Great and his successors. Among the Greeks and Romans it was the distinctive badge of royalty. Diocletian was the first Roman emperor to wear it constantly. The word is found in Rev. 12:3; 13:1; 19:12, in which passages it symbolizes the rule respectively of the Dragon, the Beast, and Christ. In the Sept., Esth. 1:11; 2:17, in some mss. in 6:8 and 8:15; also in Isa. 62:3-4. For the distinction between this and *stephanos*, see CROWN.

DIE, DEAD (to be, become), DYING

1. *thnēskō* (θνήσκω, 2348), "to die" (in the perf. tense, "to be dead"), in the NT is always used of physical "death," except in 1 Tim. 5:6, where it is metaphorically used of the loss of spiritual life. The noun *thanatos*, and the verb *thanatoō* (below) are connected. The root of this group of words probably had the significance of the breathing out of the last breath. Cf words under DEATH.

2. *apothnēskō* (ἀποθνήσκω, 599), lit., "to die off or out," is used (a) of the separation of the soul from the body, i.e., the natural "death" of human beings, e.g., Matt. 9:24; Rom. 7:2; by reason of descent from Adam, 1 Cor. 15:22; or of violent "death," whether of men or animals; with regard to the latter it is once translated "perished," Matt. 8:32; of vegetation, Jude 12; of seeds, John 12:24; 1 Cor. 15:36; it is used of "death" as a punishment in Israel under the Law, in Heb. 10:28; (b) of the separation of man from God, all who are descended from Adam not only "die" physically, owing to sin, see (a) above, but are naturally in the state of separation from God, 2 Cor. 5:14. From this believers are freed both now and eternally, John 6:50; 11:26, through the "death" of Christ, Rom. 5:8, e.g.; unbelievers, who "die" physically as such, remain in eternal separation from God, John 8:24. Believers have spiritually "died" to the Law as a means of life, Gal. 2:19; Col. 2:20; to sin, Rom. 6:2, and in general to all spiritual association with the world and with that which pertained to their unregenerate state, Col. 3:3, because of their identification with the "death" of Christ, Rom. 6:8 (see No. 3, below). As life never means mere existence, so "death," the opposite of life, never means nonexistence. See PERISH.

3. *sunapothnēskō* (συναποθνήσκω, 4880), "to die with, to die together," is used of association in physical "death," Mark 14:31; in 2 Cor. 7:3, the apostle declares that his love to the saints makes separation impossible, whether in life or in "death." It is used once of association spiritually with Christ in His "death," 2 Tim. 2:11. See No. 2 (b).

4. *teleutaō* (τελευτάω, 5053), "to end" (from *telos*, "an end"), hence, "to end one's life," is used (a) of the "death" of the body, Matt. 2:19; 9:18; 15:4, where "die the death" means "surely die," RV, marg., lit., "let him end by death"; Mark 7:10; Matt. 22:25, "deceased"; Luke 7:2; John 11:39, some mss. have verb No. 1 here; Acts 2:29; 7:15; Heb. 11:22 (RV, "his end was nigh"); (b) of the gnawings of conscience in self reproach, under the symbol of a worm, Mark 9:48 (vv. 44 and 46, KJV). See DECEASE.

5. *koimaō* (κοιμάω, 2837), in the middle and passive voices, its only use in the NT, signifies "to fall asleep." It is connected etymologically with *keimai* "to lie down," the root *ki-* signifying "to lie." Hence it is used metaphorically of "death," Matt. 27:52, etc. It is translated "be dead" in 1 Cor. 7:39. See ASLEEP.

6. *apoginomai* (ἀπογίνομαι, 581), lit., "to be away from" (*apo*, "from," *ginomai*, "to be, become"; *apo* here signifies "separation"), is used in 1 Pet. 2:24 of the believer's attitude towards sin as the result of Christ's having borne our sins in His body on the tree; RV, "having died unto sins," the aorist or momentary tense, expressing an event in the past.

Note: Apollumi, "to destroy," is found in the middle voice in some mss. in John 18:14, and translated "die." The most authentic mss. have *apothnēskō* (No. 2, above).

DIGNITY, DIGNITIES

doxa (δόξα, 1391) primarily denotes "an opinion, estimation, repute"; in the NT, always "good opinion, praise, honor, glory, an appearance commanding respect, magnificence, excellence, manifestation of glory"; hence, of angelic powers, in respect of their state as commanding recognition, "dignities," 2 Pet. 2:10; Jude 8. See GLORY, HONOR, PRAISE, WORSHIP.

DILIGENCE, DILIGENT, DILIGENTLY

A. Nouns.

1. *ergasia* (ἐργασία, 2039), (a) lit., "a working" (akin to *ergon*, "work"), is indicative of a process, in contrast to the concrete, *ergon*, e.g., Eph. 4:19, lit., "unto a working" (RV marg., "to make a trade of"); contrast *ergon* in v. 12; (b) "business," Acts 19:25, RV (for KJV, "craft"); or gain got by "work," Acts 16:16, 19; 19:24; (c) endeavor, pains, "diligence," Luke 12:58.

2. *spoudē* (σπουδή, 4710), "earnestness, zeal," or sometimes "the haste accompanying this," Mark 6:25; Luke 1:39, is translated "diligence" in Rom. 12:8; in v. 11, KJV, "business" (RV, "diligence"); in 2 Cor. 8:7, KJV, "diligence," RV, "earnestness"; both have "diligence" in Heb. 6:11; 2 Pet. 1:5; Jude 3; in 2 Cor. 7:11, 12, RV, "earnest care," KJV, "carefulness," and "care."

B. Verbs.

1. *spoudazō* (σπουδάζω, 4704) has meanings corresponding to A, No. 2; it signifies "to hasten to do a thing, to exert oneself, endeavor, give diligence"; in Gal. 2:10, of remembering the poor, KJV, "was forward," RV, "was zealous"; in Eph. 4:3, of keeping the unity of the Spirit, KJV "endeavoring," RV, "giving diligence"; in 1 Thess. 2:17, of going to see friends, "endeavored"; in 2 Tim. 4:9; 4:21, "do thy diligence"; in the following the RV uses the verb "to give diligence": 2 Tim. 2:15, KJV, "study"; Titus 3:12, KJV, "be diligent"; Heb. 4:11, of keeping continuous Sabbath rest, KJV, "let us labor"; in 2 Pet. 1:10, of making our calling and election sure; in 2 Pet. 1:15, of enabling believers to call Scripture truth to remembrance, KJV, "endeavour"; in 2 Pet. 3:14, of being found in peace without fault and blameless, when the Lord comes, KJV, be diligent. See LABOR, STUDY, ZEALOUS.

2. *meletaō* (μελετάω, 3191), signifies "to care for, attend carefully" (from *melete*, "care"); in 1 Tim. 4:15, KJV, "meditate," RV, "be diligent in"; in Acts 4:25, "imagine" (marg., "meditate"), in Mark 13:11, the most authentic mss. have *promerimnaō*. See IMAGINE, MEDITATE.

C. Adjectives.

1. *spoudaios* (σπουδαῖος, 4705), akin to A, No. 2 and B, No. 1, primarily signifies "in haste"; hence, diligent, earnest, zealous, 2 Cor. 8:22, KJV, "diligent, RV, "earnest." See EARNEST. In the Sept., Ezek. 41:25, "stout (planks)."

2. *spoudaioteros* (σπουδαιότερος, 4707), the comparative degree of No. 1, 2 Cor. 8:22, KJV, "more diligent," RV, "more earnest," in v. 17 KJV, "more forward," RV, "very earnest." See EARNEST.

D. Adverbs.

1. *epimelōs* (ἐπιμελῶς, 1960), from *epi* intensive, and an adverbial form of the impersonal verb *melei*, "it is a care" (cf. B, No. 2), signifies "carefully, diligently," Luke 15:8.

2. *pugmē* (πυγμή, 4435), the dative case of *pugmē*, "a fist," lit. means "with the fist" (one hand being rubbed with the clenched fist of the other), a metaphorical expression for "thoroughly," in contrast to what is superficial; Mark 7:3, RV and KJV marg., "diligently" (KJV, text, "oft"). It also signified "boxing" (not in the NT); cf. *puktēs* and *pugmachos*, "a boxer" (Lat., *pugnus* and *pugno*; Eng., "pugilist"). In the Sept., Exod. 21:18; Isa. 58:4.

3. *spoudaiōs* (σπουδαίως, 4709), "speedily, earnestly, diligently" (cf. the corresponding noun, verb and adjective above), is translated "earnestly" in the RV of Luke 7:4 (KJV, "instantly"); "diligently" in Titus 3:13.

4. *spoudaioterōs* (σπουδαιοτέρως, 4708), the comparative degree of No. 3, "more diligently," is used in Phil. 2:28, RV, "the more diligently" (KJV, "the more carefully").

Notes: (1) Some mss. have the neuter of the comparative adjective *spoudaioteron* in 2 Tim. 1:17. The most authentic texts have the adverb No. 4.

(2) *Akribōs* (ἀκριβῶς, 199), means "accurately, exactly." The KJV translates it "diligently" in Matt. 2:8 and Acts 18:25; "perfectly" in 1 Thess. 5:2 (cf. Luke 1:3). See PERFECTLY.

DINE, DINNER

A. Verb.

aristaō (ἀριστάω, 709), primarily, "to breakfast" (see B), was later used also with the meaning "to dine," e.g., Luke 11:37; in John 21:12, 15, RV, "break your fast," and "had broken their fast," for KJV, "dine"; obviously there it was the first meal in the day. In the Sept., Gen. 43:25; 1 Sam. 14:24; 1 Chron. 13:7.

B. Noun.

ariston (ἄριστον, 712), primarily, "the first food," taken early in the morning before work; the meal in the Pharisee's house, in Luke 11:37, was a breakfast or early meal (see RV, marg.); the dinner was called *deipnon*. Later the breakfast was called *akratisma* (not in NT), and dinner, *ariston*, as in Matt. 22:4; Luke 11:38; 14:12.

2. *embaptō* (ἐμβάπτω, 1686), *en*, "in," and No. 1, "to dip into," is used of the act of Judas in "dipping" his hand with that of Christ in the dish, Matt. 26:23; Mark 14:20.

DIRECT

kateuthunō (κατευθύνω, 2720), "to make straight" (*kata*, "down," intensive, *euthus*, "straight," *euthunō*, "to straighten"), is translated "guide" in Luke 1:79, of the Lord's "guidance" of the feet of His people; "direct," in 1 Thess. 3:11, of His "directing" the way of His servants; in 2 Thess. 3:5, of His "directing" the hearts of His saints into the love of God. See GUIDE.

DISALLOW

apodokimazō (ἀποδοκιμάζω, 593), "to reject as the result of disapproval" (*apo*, "away from," *dokimazō*, "to approve"), is always translated "to reject," except in the KJV of 1 Pet. 2:4 and 7. See REJECT.

DISANNUL, DISANNULLING

DISBELIEVE

apisteō (ἀπιστέω, 569), "to be unbelieving" (*a*, negative, *pistis*, "faith"; cf. *apistos*, "unbelieving"), is translated "believed not," etc., in the KJV (except in 1 Pet. 2:7, "be disobedient"); "disbelieve" (or "disbelieved") in the RV, in Mark 16:11, 16; Luke 24:11, 41; Acts 28:24; "disbelieve" is the best rendering, implying that the unbeliever has had a full opportunity of believing and has rejected it; some mss. have *apeitheō*, "to be disobedient," in 1 Pet. 2:7; Rom. 3:3, RV, "were without faith"; 2 Tim. 2:13, RV, "are faithless." Cf. DISOBEDIENT, C. See BELIEVE.

DISCERN, DISCERNER, DISCERNMENT

A. Verbs.

1. *anakrinō* (ἀνακρίνω, 350), "to distinguish, or separate out so as to investigate (*krinō*) by looking throughout (*ana*, intensive) objects or particulars," hence signifies "to examine, scrutinize, question, to hold a preliminary judicial examination preceding the trial proper" (this first examination, implying more to follow, is often present in the nonlegal uses of the word), e.g. Luke 23:14; figuratively, in 1 Cor. 4:3; it is said of searching the Scriptures in Acts 17:11; of "discerning" or determining the excellence or defects of a person or thing, e.g., 1 Cor. 2:14, KJV, "discerned"; RV, "judged"; in 1 Cor. 10:27, "asking (no) question" (i.e., not raising the question as to whether the meat is the residue from an idolatrous sacrifice). Except in Luke 23:14, this word is found only in Acts and 1 Cor. See EXAMINE, JUDGE.

2. *diakrinō* (διακρίνω, 1252) signifies "to separate, discriminate"; then, "to learn by discriminating, to determine, decide." It is translated "discern" in Matt. 16:3, of discriminating between the varying conditions of the sky (see *dokimazō*, No. 3, below, in Luke 12:56), and in 1 Cor. 11:29, with reference to partaking of the bread and the cup of the Lord's Supper unworthily, by not "discerning" or discriminating what they represent; in v. 31, the RV has "discerned," for the KJV, "would judge," of trying oneself, "discerning" one's condition, and so judging any evil before the Lord; in 14:29, regarding oral testimony in a gathering of believers, it is used of "discerning" what is of the Holy Spirit, RV, "discern" (KJV, "judge"). See CONTEND, etc.

3. *dokimazō* (δοκιμάζω, 1381) signifies "to test, prove, scrutinize," so as "to decide." It is translated "discern" in the KJV of Luke 12:56; RV, "interpret" (marg., "prove").

B. Noun.

diakrisis (διάκρισις, 1253), cf. A, No. 2, "a distinguishing, a clear discrimination, discerning, judging," is translated "discernings" in 1 Cor. 12:10, of "discerning" spirits, judging by evidence whether they are evil or of God. In Heb. 5:14 the phrase consisting of pros, with this noun, lit., "towards a discerning," is translated "to discern," said of those who are capable of discriminating between good and evil. In Rom. 14:1 the word has its other sense of decision or judgment, and the phrase "doubtful disputations" is, lit., "judgments of reasonings" (marg., "not for decisions of doubts," i.e., not to act as a judge of the weak brother's scruples).

Note: For "discernment," Phil. 1:19, see JUDGMENT, *Note* (4).

C. Adjective.

kritikos (κριτικός, 2924) signifies "that which relates to judging (*krinō*, "to judge"), fit for, or skilled in, judging" (Eng., "critical"), found in Heb. 4:12, of the Word of God as "quick to discern the thoughts and intents of the heart," (lit., "critical of, etc."), i.e., discriminating and passing judgment on the thoughts and feelings.

DISCHARGED

katargeō (καταργέω, 2673) means "to reduce to inactivity." "Discharged" is the RV translation of the word in Rom. 7:2 and 6 (KJV, "is loosed," and "are delivered"). In v. 2 the meaning is that the death of a woman's first husband makes void her status as a wife in the eyes of the Law; she is therefore "discharged" from the prohibition against remarrying; the prohibition is rendered ineffective in her case. So, in v. 6, with the believer in relation to the Law, he has been made dead to the Law as a means of justification and life. It is not the Law that has died (KJV), but the believer (see the RV), who has been "discharged," through being put to death, as to the old nature, in identification with the death of Christ, that he might have life in Christ. See ABOLISH.

DISCIPLE

A. Nouns.

1. *mathētēs* (μαθητής, 3101), lit., "a learner" (from *manthanō*, "to learn," from a root *math-*, indicating thought

accompanied by endeavor), in contrast to *didaskalos*, "a teacher"; hence it denotes "one who follows one's teaching," as the "disciples" of John, Matt. 9:14; of the Pharisees, Matt. 22:16; of Moses, John 9:28; it is used of the "disciples" of Jesus (a) in a wide sense, of Jews who became His adherents, John 6:66; Luke 6:17, some being secretly so, John 19:38; (b) especially of the twelve apostles, Matt. 10:1; Luke 22:11, e.g.; (c) of all who manifest that they are His "disciples" by abiding in His Word, John 8:31, cf. 13:35; 15:8; (d) in the Acts, of those who believed upon Him and confessed Him, 6:1-2, 7; 14:20, 22, 28; 15:10; 19:1, etc.

A "disciple" was not only a pupil, but an adherent; hence they are spoken of as imitators of their teacher; cf. John 8:31; 15:8.

2. *mathētria* (μαθήτρια, 3102), "a female disciple," is said of Tabitha, Acts 9:36.

3. *summathētōs* (συμμαθητής, 4827) means "a fellow disciple" (*sun*, with, and No. 1), John 11:16.

Note: In Acts 1:15, the RV translates the mss. which have *adelphōn*, "brethren"; in 20:7, RV, "we," for KJV, "disciples."

B. Verb.

mathēteuō (μαθητεύω, 3100) is used in the active voice, intransitively, in some mss., in Matt. 27:57, in the sense of being the "disciple" of a person; here, however, the best mss. have the passive voice, lit., "had been made a disciple," as in Matt. 13:52, RV, "who hath been made a disciple." It is used in this transitive sense in the active voice in 28:19 and Acts 14:21.

DISCIPLINE

sōphronismōs (σωφρονισμός, 4995), from *sōphrōn*, lit., "saving the mind," from *saos*, "contracted to" *sōs*, "safe" (cf. *sōzō*, "to save"), *phrēn*, "the mind," primarily, "an admonishing or calling to soundness of mind, or to self-control," is used in 2 Tim. 1:7, KJV, "a sound mind"; RV, "discipline." Cf. *sōphroneō* ("to be of sound mind"), *sōphronizō* ("to admonish"), *sōphronōs* ("soberly"), and *sōphrōn*, "of sound mind. See MIND. Cf. CHASTISEMENT.

DISCOURAGE (-D)

athumeō (ἀθυμέω, 120), "to be disheartened, dispirited, discouraged" (*a*, negative, *thumos*, "spirit, courage," from the root *thu-*, found in *thuō*, "to rush," denoting "feeling, passion"; hence Eng., "fume"), is found in Col. 3:21.

DISCREET, DISCREETLY

A. Adjective.

sōphrōn (σώφρων, 4998), "of sound mind self-controlled" (for the derivation, see DISCIPLINE), is translated "soberminded," in its four occurrences in the RV, 1 Tim. 3:2 (KJV, "sober"); Titus 1:8 (KJV, "ditto"); 2:2 (KJV, "temperate"); 2:5 (KJV, "discreet"). See SOBER, TEMPERATE.

B. Adverb.

nounechōs (νουνεχῶς, 3562), lit., "mindpossessing" (*nous*, "mind, understanding," *echō*, "to have"), hence denotes "discreetly, sensibly prudently." Mark 12:34.

DISEASE, DISEASED (BE)

A. Nouns.

1. *astheneia* (ἀσθένεια, 769), lit., "lacking strength" (*a*, negative, *sthenos*, "strength"), "weakness, infirmity," is translated "diseases" in Matt. 8:17, RV, for KJV, "sicknesses," and in Acts 28:9. Its usual rendering is "infirmity" or "infirmities"; "sickness," in John 11:4. Cf. B, No. 1. See INFIRMITY, SICKNESS, WEAKNESS.

2. *malakia* (μαλακία, 3119) primarily denotes "softness" (cf. *malakos*, "soft," Matt. 11:8, etc.); hence, "debility, disease." It is found in Matthew only, 4:23; 9:35; 10:1. It is frequent in the Sept., e.g., Gen. 42:4; 44:29; Deut. 7:15; 28:61; Isa. 38:9; 53:3.

3. *nosos* (νόσος, 3554), akin to Lat. *nocere*, "to injure" (Eng., "nosology"), is the regular word for "disease, sickness," Matt. 4:23; 8:17; 9:35; 10:1, RV, "disease," KJV, "sickness"; in Matt. 4:24; Mark 1:34; Luke 4:40; 6:17; 9:1; Acts 19:12, KJV and RV render it "diseases." In Luke 7:21, KJV has "infirmities." The most authentic mss. omit the word in Mark 3:15. See SICKNESS.

4. *nosēma* (νόσημα, 3553), an alternative form of No. 3, is found in some mss. in John 5:4. Cf. *noseō*, "to dote about, have a diseased craving for," 1 Tim. 6:4.

B. Verbs.

1. *astheneō* (ἀσθενέω, 770), akin to A, No. 1, "to lack strength, to be weak, sick," is translated "were diseased" in John 6:2, KJV (RV, "were sick). See SICK, WEAK.

2. *echō kakos* (ἔχω κακῶς), lit., "to have badly," i.e., "to be ill or in an evil case," is used in Matt. 14:35 (KJV, "were diseased," RV, "were sick"); so in Mark 1:32; Luke 7:2. See SICK.

DISFIGURE

aphanizō (ἀφανίζω, 853) primarily means "to cause to disappear," hence (a) "to make unsightly, to disfigure," as of the face, Matt. 6:16; (b) "to cause to vanish away, consume," Matt. 6:19, 20; (c) in the passive voice, "to perish," Acts 13:41, or "to vanish away," Jas. 4:14. See CONSUME.

DISH

trublion (τρύβλιον, 5165) denotes "a bowl," somewhat deep, Matt. 26:23; Mark 14:20; among the Greeks it was a measure in medical prescriptions.

DISHONESTY

aischunē (αἰσχύνη, 152), "shame," so the RV in 2 Cor. 4:2 (for KJV, "dishonesty"), is elsewhere rendered "shame," Luke 14:9; Phil. 3:19; Heb. 12:2; Jude 13; Rev. 3:18. See SHAME.

DISHONOR

A. Noun.

atimia (ἀτιμία, 819), from *a*, negative, *timē*, "honor," denotes "dishonor, ignominy, disgrace," in Rom. 1:26, "vile passions" (RV), lit., 'passions of dishonor;' in Rom. 9:21, "dishonor," of vessels designed for meaner household purposes (in contrast to *timē*, "honor," as in 2 Tim. 2:20); in 1 Cor. 11:14, said of long hair, if worn by men, RV, "dishonor," for KJV, "shame," in contrast to *doxa*, glory, v. 15; so in 1 Cor. 15:43, of the "sowing" of the natural body, and in 2 Cor. 6:8, of the apostle Paul's ministry. In 2 Cor. 11:21 he uses it in selfdisparagement, KJV, "reproach," RV, "disparagement. See DISPARAGEMENT, REPROACH, SHAME, VILE.

B. Adjective.

atimos (ἄτιμος, 820), akin to A: see DESPISE, B.

C. Verbs.

1. *atimazō* (ἀτιμάζω, 818) akin to A, signifies "to dishonour, treat shamefully, insult," whether in word, John 8:49, or deed, Mark 12:4; Luke 20:11, RV "handled (him) shamefully," (RV "entreated ... shamefully"); Rom. 1:24; 2:23, "dishonorest;" Jas. 2:6, RV, "ye have dishonored (the poor)," (KJV, "despised"); in the passive voice, to suffer dishonor, Acts 5:41 (KJV, "suffer shame"). See DESPISE, A, *Note* (2).

Note: Atimaō is found in some mss. in Mark 12:4.

2. *kataischunō* (καταισχύνω, 2617): see ASHAMED, No. 3.

DISMISS (-ED)

apoluō (ἀπολύω, 630), lit., "to loose from" (*apo*, "from," *luō*, "to loose"), is translated "dismiss" in Acts 15:30, 33, RV (KJV, "let go") and 19:41. See DIVORCE, FORGIVE, GO, LIBERTY, LOOSE, RELEASE, SEND.

DISOBEDIENCE, DISOBEDIENT

A. Nouns.

1. *apeitheia* (ἀπείθεια, 543), lit., "the condition of being unpersuadable" (*a*, negative, *peithō*, "to persuade"), denotes "obstinacy, obstinate rejection of the will of God"; hence, "disobedience"; Eph. 2:2; 5:6; Col. 3:6, and in the RV of Rom. 11:30, 32 and Heb. 4:6, 11 (for KJV, "unbelief"), speaking of Israel, past and present. See UNBELIEF.

2. *parakoē* (παρακοή, 3876), primarily, "hearing amiss" (*para*, "aside," *akouō*, "to hear"), hence signifies "a refusal to hear"; hence, "an act of disobedience," Rom. 5:19; 2 Cor. 10:6; Heb. 2:2. It is broadly to be distinguished from No. 1, as an act from a condition, though *parakoē* itself is the effect, in transgression, of the condition of failing or refusing to hear. Carelessness in attitude is the precursor of actual "disobedience." In the OT "disobedience" is frequently described as "a refusing to hear," e.g., Jer. 11:10; 35:17; cf. Acts 7:57. See Trench, *Syn.* Sec. LXVI.

B. Adjective.

apeithēs (ἀπειθής, 545), akin to A, No. 1, signifies "unwilling to be persuaded, spurning belief, disobedient," Luke 1:17; Acts 26:19; Rom. 1:30; 2 Tim. 3:2; Titus 1:16; 3:3.

Note: In 1 Tim. 1:9 *anupotaktos*, "insubordinate, unsubjected" (*a*, negative, *n*, euphonic, *hupo*, "under," *tassō*, "to order"), is translated "disobedient" in the KJV; the RV has "unruly," as in Titus 1:6, 10; in Heb. 2:8, "not subject" (RV), "not put under" (KJV). See UNRULY.

C. Verb.

apeitheō (ἀπειθέω, 544), akin to A, No. 1, and B, "to refuse to be persuaded, to refuse belief, to be disobedient," is translated "disobedient," or by the verb "to be disobedient," in the RV of Acts 14:2 (KJV, "unbelieving"), and 19:9 (KJV, "believed not"); it is absent from the most authentic mss. in Acts 17:5; in John 3:36 "obeyeth not," RV (KJV, "believeth not"); in Rom. 2:8 "obey not"; in 10:21, "disobedient"; in 11:30, 31, "were disobedient" (KJV, "have not believed"); so in 15:31; Heb. 3:18; 11:31; in 1 Pet. 2:8, "disobedient"; so in 3:20; in 3:1 and 4:17, "obey not." In 2:7 the best mss. have *apisteō*, "to disbelieve." See OBEY, B, No. 4, UNBELIEVING.

DISPARAGEMENT

For this RV translation of *atimia* in 2 Cor. 11:21, see DISHONOR, A.

DISPENSATION

oikonomia (οἰκονομία, 3622) primarily signifies "the management of a household or of household affairs" (*oikos*, "a house," *nomos*, "a law"); then the management or administration of the property of others, and so "a stewardship," Luke 16:2-4; elsewhere only in the epistles of Paul, who applies it (a) to the responsibility entrusted to him of preaching the gospel, 1 Cor. 9:17 (RV, "stewardship," KJV, "dispensation"); (b) to the stewardship committed to him "to fulfill the Word of God," the fulfillment being the unfolding of the completion of the divinely arranged and imparted cycle of truths which are consummated in the truth relating to the church as the body of Christ, Col. 1:25 (RV and KJV, "dispensation"); so in Eph. 3:2, of the grace of God given him as a stewardship ("dispensation") in regard to the same "mystery"; (c) in Eph. 1:10 and 3:9, it is used of the arrangement or administration by God, by which in "the fullness of the times" (or seasons) God will sum up all things in the heavens and on earth in

Christ. In Eph. 3:9 some mss. have *koinōnia*, "fellowship," for *oikonomia*, "dispensation." In 1 Tim. 1:4 *oikonomia* may mean either a stewardship in the sense of (a) above, or a "dispensation" in the sense of (c). The reading *oikodomia*, "edifying," in some mss., is not to be accepted. See STEWARDSHIP.

Note: A "dispensation" is not a period or epoch (a common, but erroneous, use of the word), but a mode of dealing, an arrangement or administration of affairs. Cf. *oikonomos*, "a steward," and *oikonomeō*, "to be a steward."

DISPERSE, DISPERSION

A. Verbs.

1. *dialuō* (διαλύω, 1262), "to dissolve," is used in Acts 5:36 of the breaking up and dispersion of a company of men, RV, "dispersed," KJV, "scattered." See SCATTER.

2. *skorpizō* (σκορπίζω, 4650), "to scatter" (probably from a root, *skarp-*, signifying "to cut asunder," akin to *skorpios*, "a scorpion"), is used in Matt. 12:30; Luke 11:23; John 10:12; 16:32; in the RV of 2 Cor. 9:9, "scattered abroad" (KJV, "he hath dispersed abroad"), of one who liberally dispenses benefits. See SCATTER.

3. *diaskorpizō* (διασκορπίζω, 1287), *dia*, "through," and No. 2, signifies "to scatter abroad," in Matt. 26:31; Mark 14:27, metaphorically of sheep; in Luke 1:51, of the proud; in John 11:52, of the "scattering" of the children of God; in Acts 5:37, of the followers of Judas of Galilee (KJV, "were dispersed"); cf. No. 1, re v. 36; of "scattering" grain by winnowing Matt. 25:24, 26; in Luke 15:13 and 16:1, it signifies "to waste. See SCATTER, WASTE.

4. *diaspeirō* (διασπείρω, 1289), "to scatter abroad" (*dia*, "through," *speirō*, "to sow"), is used in Acts 8:1, 4; 11:19.

B. Noun.

diaspora (διασπορά, 1290), akin to A, No. 4, "a scattering, a dispersion," was used of the Jews who from time to time had been scattered among the Gentiles, John 7:35; later with reference to Jews, so "scattered," who had professed, or actually embraced, the Christian faith, "the Dispersion," Jas. 1:1, RV; especially of believers who were converts from Judaism and "scattered" throughout certain districts, "sojourners of the Dispersion," 1 Pet. 1:1, RV. In the Sept., of Israelites, "scattered" and exiled, e.g., Deut. 28:25; 30:4; Neh. 1:9.

DISPLEASED

1. *aganakteō* (ἀγανακτέω, 23), from *agan*, "much," and *achomai*, "to grieve," primarily meant "to feel a violent irritation, physically"; it was used, too, of the fermenting of wine hence, metaphorically, "to show signs of grief, to be displeased, to be grieved, vexed"; it is translated "sore displeased" in Matt. 21:15, KJV; "much displeased," in Mark 10:14, 41; the RV always renders it "to be moved with, or to have, indignation," as the KJV elsewhere, Matt. 20:24; 26:8; Mark 14:4; Luke 13:14. See INDIGNATION.

2. *prosochthizō* (προσοχθίζω, 4360), "to be wroth or displeased with" (*pros*, "toward," or "with," *ochtheō*, "to be sorely vexed"), is used in Heb. 3:10, 17 (KJV, "grieved"; RV, "displeased"). "Grieved" does not adequately express the righteous anger of God intimated in the passage. See GRIEVE.

3. *thumomacheō* (θυμομαχέω, 2371), lit., "to fight with great animosity" (*thumos*, "passion," *machomai*, "to fight"), hence, "to be very angry, to be highly displeased," is said of Herod's "displeasure" with the Tyrians and Sidonians, Acts 12:20.

DISPOSITION

diatagē (διαταγή, 1296), an ordinance, e.g., Rom. 13:2 (cf. *diatassō*, "to appoint, ordain"), is rendered "disposition" in Acts 7:53; RV, "as it (the law) was ordained by angels" (marg., "as the ordinance of angels"; lit., "unto ordinances of angels"). Angels are mentioned in connection with the giving of the Law of Moses in Deut. 33:2. In Gal. 3:19 and Heb. 2:2 the purpose of the reference to them is to show the superiority of the gospel to the Law. In Acts 7:53 Stephen mentions the angels to stress the majesty of the Law. See ORDAIN, ORDINANCE.

DISPUTATION

1. *zētēsis* (ζήτησις, 2214) denotes, firstly, "a seeking" (*zēteō*, "to seek"), then, "a debate, dispute, questioning," Acts 15:2, 7 (some texts have *suzētēsis*, "reasoning," in both verses), RV, "questioning," for KJV, "disputation" and "disputing."

2. *dialogismos* (διαλογισμός, 1261) is translated "disputations" in Rom. 14:1. See below.

DISREPUTE

apelegmos (ἀπελεγμός, 557), from *apo*, "from," and *elenchō*, "to refute," denotes "censure, repudiation" (of something shown to be worthless), hence, "contempt," "disrepute," Acts 19:27, RV, "(come into) disrepute," for KJV, "(to be) set at nought." It is akin to *apelenchō* "to convict, refute" (not in the NT), *elenchō*, "to convict," *elenxis*, "rebuke," and *elegmos*, "reproof." See NOUGHT.

For **DISSEMBLE** see DISSIMULATION

DISSENSION

stasis (στάσις, 4714), akin to *histēmi*, "to stand," denotes (a) "a standing, stability," Heb. 9:8, "(while as the first tabernacle) is yet standing"; (b) "an insurrection, uproar," Mark 15:7; Luke 23:19, 25; Acts 19:40; 24:5; (c) "a dissension, Acts 15:2; 23:7, 10. See INSURRECTION, SEDITION, UPROAR.

DISSIMULATION, DISSEMBLE

A. Noun.

hupokrisis (ὑπόκρισις, 5272), primarily, "a reply," came to mean "the acting of a stageplayer," because such answered one another in dialogue; hence the meaning "dissembling or pretense." It is translated "dissimulation" in Gal. 2:13 (see B). See HYPOCRISY.

B. Verb.

sunupokrinomai (συνυποκρίνομαι, 4942), *sun*, "with," *hupokrinomai*, akin to A, "to join in acting the hypocrite," in pretending to act from one motive, whereas another motive really inspires the act. So in Gal. 2:13, Peter with other believing Jews, in separating from believing Gentiles at Antioch, pretended that the motive was loyalty to the Law of Moses, whereas really it was fear of the Judaizers.

C. Adjective.

anupokritos (ἀνυπόκριτος, 505), from *a*, negative, *n*, euphonic, and an adjectival form corresponding to A, signifies "unfeigned"; it is said of love, 2 Cor. 6:6; 1 Pet. 1:22; Rom. 12:9, KJV, "without dissimulation," RV, "without hypocrisy"; of faith, 1 Tim. 1:5; 2 Tim. 1:5, "unfeigned"; of the wisdom that is from above, Jas. 3:17, "without hypocrisy." See HYPOCRISY.

DISSOLVE

1. *luō* (λύω, 3089), "to loose," is used of the future demolition of the elements or heavenly bodies, 2 Pet. 3:10-12; in v. 10, KJV, "shall melt," RV, "shall be dissolved"; in verses 11-12, KJV and RV, "dissolved."

2. *kataluō* (καταλύω, 2647): see DESTROY A, No. 5.

DISTRESS, DISTRESSED

A. Nouns.

1. *anankē* (ἀναγκή, 318) denotes (a) "a necessity," imposed whether by external circumstances, e.g., Luke 23:17, or inward pressure, e.g., 1 Cor. 9:16; (b) "straits, distress," Luke 21:23 (in v. 25 "distress" translates No. 3); 1 Cor. 7:26; 1 Thess. 3:7; the last two refer to the lack of material things. See NECESSITY.

2. *stenochōria* (στενοχωρία, 4730): see ANGUISH.

3. *sunochē* (συνόχη, 4928): see ANGUISH.

4. *thlipsis* (θλίψις, 2347): see AFFLICTION, B, No. 5.

B. Verbs.

1. *basanizō* (βασανίζω, 928), properly signifies "to test by rubbing on the touchstone" (*basanos*, "a touchstone"), then, "to question by applying torture"; hence "to vex, torment"; in the passive voice, "to be harassed, distressed"; it is said of men struggling in a boat against wind and waves, Matt. 14:24, RV, "distressed" (KJV, "tossed"); Mark 6:48, RV, "distressed" (KJV, toiling). See PAIN, TOIL, TORMENT, VEX.

2. *skullō* (σκύλλω, 4660) primarily signifies "to skin, to flay"; then "to rend, mangle"; hence, "to vex, trouble, annoy"; it is found in the most authentic mss. in Matt. 9:36, RV, "distressed" (of the multitudes who applied to the Lord for healing); KJV, "fainted," translating the alternative reading, *ekluō*, lit., "to loosen out." It is also used in Mark 5:35; Luke 7:6; 8:49. See TROUBLE.

3. *stenochōreō* (στενοχωρέω, 4729): see ANGUISH.

4. *kataponeō* (καταπονέω, 2669), primarily, "to tire down with toil, exhaust with labor" (*kata*, "down," *ponos*, "labor"), hence signifies "to afflict, oppress"; in the passive voice, "to be oppressed, much distressed"; it is translated "oppressed" in Acts 7:24, and "sore distressed" in 2 Pet. 2:7, RV, (KJV, "vexed"). See OPPRESS, VEX.

DIVERS

A. Adjectives.

1. *diaphoros* (διάφορος, 1313) is rendered divers in Heb. 9:10.

2. *poikilos* (ποικίλος, 4164) denotes "particolored, variegated" (*poikillo* means "to make gay": the root of the first syllable is *pik-*, found in Eng., "picture"), hence "divers," Matt. 4:24; Mark 1:34; Luke 4:40; 2 Tim. 3:6; Titus 3:3; Heb. 2:4 (RV, "manifold"), 13:9; Jas. 1:2 (RV, "manifold"); in 1 Pet. 1:6 and 4:10, "manifold," both KJV and RV.

Notes: (1) Cf. *polupoikilos*, Eph. 3:10, "manifold" (lit., "much varied").

(2) The pronoun *tines*, "some" (the plural of *tis*, "some-one"), is translated "divers" in the KJV of Mark 8:3 and Acts 19:9; RV, "some."

(3) In 1 Cor. 12:28, *genos*, in the plural, is rendered "divers kinds." See DIVERSITIES.

B. Adverb.

polutropōs (πολυτρόπως, 4187) means "in many ways" (*polus*, "much," *tropos*, "a manner, way"; Eng., "trope"), "in divers manners," Heb. 1:1.

Note: The phrase *kata topous*, lit., "throughout places" (*kata*, "down, or throughout," in a distributive sense, *topos*, "a place"), is translated "in divers places," in Matt. 24:7; Mark 13:8 and Luke 21:11.

DIVERSITY, DIVERSITIES

Note: Genos, "a kind, class, sort" (Eng., "genus"), is translated "diversities" in the KJV of 1 Cor. 12:28 (marg., "kinds"); RV, "divers kinds."

DIVINE

A. Adjective.

theios (θεῖος, 2304), "divine" (from *theos*, "God"), is used of the power of God, 2 Pet. 1:3, and of His nature, v. 4, in each place, as that which proceeds from Himself. In Acts 17:29 it is used as a noun with the definite article, to denote "the Godhead," the Deity (i.e., the one true God). This word, instead of *theos*, was purposely used by the apostle in speaking to Greeks on Mars Hill, as in accordance with Greek usage. Cf. DIVINITY. In the Sept., Exod. 31:3; 35:31; Job 27:3; 33:4; Prov. 2:17.

B. Noun.

latreia (λατρεία, 2999), akin to *latreuō*, "to serve," primarily, any service for hire denotes in Scripture the service of God according to the requirements of the Levitical Law, Rom. 9:4; Heb. 9:1, 6, "divine service." It is used in the more general sense of service to God, in John 16:2; Rom. 12:1. See SERVICE.

DIVINITY

theiotēs (θειότης, 2305), difinity, the RV rendering in Rom. 1:20 (KJV, "Godhead"), is derived from *theios* (see DIVINE, A), and is to be distinguished from *theotēs*, in Col. 2:9, "Godhead." In Rom. 1:20 the apostle "is declaring how much of God may be known from the revelation of Himself which He has made in nature, from those vestiges of Himself which men may everywhere trace in the world around them. Yet it is not the personal God whom any man may learn to know by these aids; He can be known only by the revelation of Himself in His Son; ... But in the second passage (Col. 2:9), Paul is declaring that in the Son there dwells all the fullness of absolute Godhead; they were no mere rays of Divine glory which gilded Him, lighting up His Person for a season and with a splendor not His own; but He was, and is, absolute and perfect God; and the apostle uses *theotēs* to express this essential and personal Godhead of the Son" (Trench, *Syn.* Sec. II). *Theotēs* indicates the "divine" essence of Godhood, the personality of God; *theiotēs*, the attributes of God, His "divine" nature and properties.

DIVISION

1. *diamerismos* (διαμερισμός, 1267), primarily, "a parting, distribution," denotes "a discussion, dissension, division or discord, breaking up as of family ties" (*dia*, "asunder," *meros*, "a part"), it is found in Luke 12:51, where it is contrasted with *eirēnē*, "peace." Cf. DIVIDE, A, No. 7.

2. *dichostasia* (διχοστασία, 1370), lit., "a standing apart" (*dichē*, "asunder, apart," *stasis*, "a standing," the root *di-* indicating "division," is found in many words in various languages), is used in Rom. 16:17, where believers are enjoined to mark those who cause "division" and to turn away from them; and in Gal. 5:20, RV (KJV, "seditions"), where "divisions" are spoken of as "works of the flesh." Some mss. have this noun in 1 Cor. 3:3.

3. *schisma* (σχίσμα, 4978), (Eng., "schism"), denotes "a cleft, a rent," Matt. 9:16; Mark 2:21, then, metaphorically, "a division dissension," John 7:43; 9:16; 10:19; 1 Cor. 1:10; 11:18; in 1 Cor. 12:25 it is translated "schism" (marg., "division"). The root is *skid-* seen in the corresponding verb *schizō*, "to cleave" (Lat. *scindo*). See SCHISM. Cf. *hairesis*, a sect.

DIVORCE, DIVORCEMENT

A. Verb.

apoluō (ἀπολύω, 630), "to let loose from, let go free" (*apo*, "from," *luō*, "to loose"), is translated "is divorced" in the KJV of Matt. 5:32 (RV, "is put away"); it is further used of "divorce" in Matt. 1:19; 19:3, 7-9; Mark 10:2, Mk 4:11; Luke 16:18. The Lord also used it of the case of a wife putting away her husband, Mark 10:12, a usage among Greeks and Romans, not among Jews. See DISMISS.

B. Noun.

apostasion (ἀποστάσιον, 647), primarily, "a defection," lit., "a standing off" (*apo*, "from," *stasis*, "a standing"; cf. *aphistēmi*, "to cause to withdraw"), denotes, in the NT, "a writing or bill of divorcement," Matt. 5:31; 19:7; Mark 10:4. In Sept., Deut. 24:3; Isa. 50:1; Jer. 3:8.

DOCTOR

1. *didaskalos* (διδάσκαλος, 1320), a teacher (from *didaskō*, "to teach"), cf. *didaskalia*, "teaching, doctrine, instruction," is translated "doctors," with reference to the teachers of the Jewish religion, Luke 2:46. Cf. *paideutēs*, "a teacher." See MASTER, TEACHER.

2. *nomodidaskalos* (νομοδιδάσκαλος, 3547), "a teacher of the Law" (*nomos*, "a law," and No. 1), with reference to the teachers of the Mosaic Law, is used in the same sense as No. 1, Luke 5:17; Acts 5:34; also of those who went about among Christians, professing to be instructors of the Law, 1 Tim. 1:7. See TEACHER. See under LAW.

DOCTRINE

1. *didachē* (διδαχή, 1322), akin to No. 1, under DOCTOR, denotes "teaching," either (a) that which is taught, e.g., Matt. 7:28, KJV, "doctrine," RV, "teaching"; Titus 1:9, RV; Rev. 2:14-15, 24, or (b) the act of teaching, instruction, e.g., Mark 4:2, KJV, "doctrine," RV, "teaching" the RV has "the doctrine" in Rom. 16:17. See NOTE (1) below.

2. *didaskalia* (διδασκαλία, 1319) denotes, as No. 1 (from which, however, it is to be distinguished), (a) "that which is taught, doctrine," Matt. 15:9; Mark 7:7; Eph. 4:14; Col. 2:22; 1 Tim. 1:10; 4:1, 6; 6:1, 3; 2 Tim. 4:3; Titus 1:9 ("doctrine," in last part of verse: see also No. 1); 2:1, 10; (b) "teaching, instruction," Rom. 12:7, "teaching"; 15:4, "learning," 1 Tim. 4:13, KJV, "doctrine," RV, "teaching"; v. 16, KJV, "the doctrine," RV,

(correctly) "thy teaching;" 5:17, KJV, "doctrine," RV "teaching"; 2 Tim. 3:10, 16 (ditto); Titus 2:7, "thy doctrine." Cf. No. 1, under DOCTOR. See LEARNING.

Notes: (I) Whereas *didachē* is used only twice in the Pastoral Epistles, 2 Tim. 4:2, and Titus 1:9, *didaskalia* occurs fifteen times. Both are used in the active and passive senses (i.e., the act of teaching and what is taught), the passive is predominant in *didachē*, the active in *didaskalia*, the former stresses the authority, the latter the act (Cremer). Apart from the apostle Paul, other writers make use of *didachē* only, save in Matt. 15:9 and Mark 7:7 (*didaskalia*).

(2) In Heb. 6:1, *logos*, "a word," is translated "doctrine," KJV; the RV margin gives the lit. rendering, "the word (of the beginning of Christ)," and, in the text, "the (first) principles (of Christ)."

DOG

1. *kuōn* (κύων, 2965) is used in two senses, (a) natural, Matt. 7:6; Luke 16:21; 2 Pet. 2:22; (b) metaphorical, Phil. 3:2; Rev. 22:15, of those whose moral impurity will exclude them from the New Jerusalem. The Jews used the term of Gentiles, under the idea of ceremonial impurity. Among the Greeks it was an epithet of impudence. Lat., *canis*, and Eng., "hound" are etymologically akin to it.

2. *kunarion* (κυνάριον, 2952), a diminutive of No. 1, "a little dog, a puppy," is used in Matt. 15:26-27; Mark 7:27, 28.

DOMINION (have ... over) A. Nouns.

1. *kratos* (κράτος, 2904), "force, strength, might," more especially "manifested power," is derived from a root *kra-*, "to perfect, to complete": "creator" is probably connected. It also signifies "dominion," and is so rendered frequently in doxologies, 1 Pet. 4:11; 5:11; Jude 25; Rev. 1:6; 5:13 (RV); in 1 Tim. 6:16, and Heb. 2:14 it is translated "power." See MIGHT, POWER, STRENGTH.

Note: Synonymous words are *bia*, "force," often oppressive, *dunamis*, "power," especially "inherent power"; *energeia*, "power" especially in exercise, operative power; *exousia*, primarily "liberty of action," then "authority" either delegated or arbitrary; *ischus*, "strength," especially physical, power as an endowment.

2. *kuriotēs* (κυριότης, 2963) denotes "lordship" (*kurios*, "a lord"), "power, dominion," whether angelic or human, Eph. 1:21; Col. 1:16; 2 Pet. 2:10 (RV, for KJV, "government"); Jude 8. In Eph. and Col. it indicates a grade in the angelic orders, in which it stands second.

B. Verbs.

1. *kurieuō* (κυριεύω, 2961), "to be lord over, rule over, have dominion over" (akin to A, No. 2), is used of (a) divine authority over men, Rom. 14:9, "might be Lord"; (b) human authority over men, Luke 22:25, "lordship," 1 Tim. 6:15, "lords" (RV, marg., "them that rule as lords"); (c) the permanent immunity of Christ from the "dominion" of death, Rom. 6:9; (d) the deliverance of the believer from the "dominion" of sin, Rom. 6:14; (e) the "dominion" of law over men, Rom. 7:1; (f) the "dominion" of a person over the faith of other believers, 2 Cor. 1:24 (RV, "lordship"). See LORD.

2. *katakurieuō* (κατακυριεύω, 2634), *kata*, "down" (intensive), and No. 1, "to exercise, or gain, dominion over, to lord it over," is used of (a) the "lordship" of gentile rulers, Matt. 20:25, KJV, "exercise dominion," RV, "lord it," Mark 10:42, KJV, "exercise lordship," RV, "lord it"; (b) the power of demons over men, Acts 19:16, KJV, "overcame," RV, "mastered"; (c) of the evil of elders in "lording" it over the saints under their spiritual care, 1 Pet. 5:3. See LORDSHIP, OVERCOME.

DOOMED

For RV in 1 Cor. 4:9, see APPOINT (*Note* at end), DEATH, B.

DOOR

thura (θύρα, 2374), "a door, gate" (Eng., "door" is connected), is used (a) literally, e.g., Matt. 6:6; 27:60; (b) metaphorically, of Christ, John 10:7, 9; of faith, by acceptance of the gospel, Acts 14:27; of "openings" for preaching and teaching the Word of God, 1 Cor. 16:9; 2 Cor. 2:12; Col. 4:3; Rev. 3:8; of "entrance" into the Kingdom of God, Matt. 25:10; Luke 13:24-25; of Christ's "entrance" into a repentant believer's heart, Rev. 3:20; of the nearness of Christ's second advent, Matt. 24:33; Mark 13:29; cf. Jas. 5:9; of "access" to behold visions relative to the purposes of God, Rev. 4:1.

DOTE

noseō (νοσέω, 3552) signifies "to be ill, to be ailing," whether in body or mind; hence, "to be taken with such a morbid interest in a thing as is tantamount to a disease, to dote," 1 Tim. 6:4 (marg., "sick"). The primary meaning of "dote" is to be foolish (cf. Jer. 50:36), the evident meaning of *noseō*, in this respect, is "to be unsound."

DOUBLE-MINDED

dipsuchos (δίψυχος, 1374) lit. means "twosouled" (*dis*, "twice," *psuchē*, "a soul"), hence, "double-minded," Jas. 1:8; 4:8.

DOUBLE-TONGUED

dilogos (δίλογος, 1351) primarily means "saying the same thing twice, or given to repetition" (*dis*, "twice," *logos*, "a word, or speech"); hence, "saying a thing to one person and giving a different view of it to another, double-tongued," 1 Tim. 3:8.

DOUBT (be in, make to), DOUBTFUL, DOUBTING

A. Verbs.

1. *aporeō* (ἀπορέω, 639), always used in the middle voice, lit. means "to be without a way" (*a*, negative, *poros*, "a way, transit"), "to be without resources, embarrassed, in doubt, perplexity, at a loss," as was Herod regarding John the Baptist, Mark 6:20 (RV, following the most authentic mss., "was much perplexed"); as the disciples were, regarding the Lord's betrayal, John 13:22, "doubting"; and regarding the absence of His body from the tomb, Luke 24:4, "were perplexed"; as was Festus, about the nature of the accusations brought against Paul, Acts 25:20, KJV "doubted," RV, "being perplexed"; as Paul was, in his experiences of trial 2 Cor. 4:8, "perplexed," and, as to the attitude of the believers of the churches in Galatia towards Judaistic errors, Gal. 4:20, KJV, "I stand in doubt," RV, "I am perplexed." Perplexity is the main idea. See PERPLEX. Cf. the noun *aporia*, "distress," Luke 21:25.

2. *diaporeō* (διαπορέω, 1280), *dia*, "asunder" (intensive), and No. 1, signifies "to be thoroughly perplexed," with a perplexity amounting to despair, Acts 2:12; 5:24 and 10:17, KJV, "were in doubt," "doubted," RV, "were (was) perplexed." See also Luke 9:7 (some mss. have it in Luke 24:4, where the most authentic have No. 1). See PERPLEX.

3. *diakrinō* (διακρίνω, 1252): see CONTEND; in Acts 11:12, KJV, "nothing doubting," RV, "making no distinction"; in Jude 22, RV, "who are in doubt" (KJV, "making a difference," RV, marg., "while they dispute"); in Jas. 1:6, KJV, "wavereth," RV, "doubteth." This verb suggests, not so much weakness of faith, as lack of it (contrast, Nos. 4 and 5).

4. *distazō* (διστάζω, 1365), "to stand in two ways" (*dis*, "double," *stasis*, "a standing"), implying "uncertainty which way to take," is used in Matt. 14:31 and 28:17; said of believers whose faith is small. Cf. No 5.

5. *meteōrizō* (μετεωρίζω, 3349), from *meteōros* (Eng., "meteor"), signifying "in mid air, raised on high," was primarily used of putting a ship out to sea, or of "raising" fortifications, or of the "rising" of the wind. In the Sept., it is used, e.g., in Micah 4:1, of the "exaltation" of the Lord's house; in Ezek. 10:16, of the "lifting" up of the wings of the cherubim; in Obad. 4, of the "mounting" up of the eagle; in the NT metaphorically, of "being anxious," through a "distracted" state of mind, of "wavering" between hope and fear, Luke 12:29, "neither be ye of doubtful mind" (KJV, marg., "live not in careful suspense"), addressed to those who have little faith. Cf. No. 4. The interpretation "do not exalt yourselves" is not in keeping with the context.

6. *psuchēn airō* (ψυχὴν αἴρω), lit., "to raise the breath, or to lift the soul," signifies "to hold in suspense," RV of John 10:24 (KJV, "make us to doubt"), suggestive of "an objective suspense due to lack of light" (Warfield), through a failure of their expectations, rather than, subjectively, through unbelief The meaning may thus be, "How long dost Thou raise our expectations without satisfying them?"

B. Noun.

dialogismos (διαλογισμός, 1261) expresses reasoning or questioning hesitation, 1 Tim. 2:8.

DOUBT (No), DOUBTLESS

pantōs (πάντως, 3843): *Notes:* (1) In 2 Cor. 12:1 the best texts have no word representing "doubtless." (2) In Luke 11:20, the particle *ara*, KJV, "no doubt," means "then" (RV). (3) In 1 Cor. 9:10 the conjunction *gar*, KJV, "no doubt," here means "assuredly," or "yea" (RV). (4) In Phil. 3:8, the opening phrase means "yea, verily," as RV. (5) In 1 Cor. 9:2, the RV, "at least," gives the right sense (not "doubtless").

DOVE, TURTLE-DOVE

1. *peristera* (περιστερά, 4058) denotes "a dove or pigeon," Matt. 3:16; 10:16 (indicating its proverbial harmlessness); 21:12; Mark 1:10; 11:15; Luke 2:24 (pigeons"); 3:22; John 1:32; 2:14, 16.

2. *trugōn* (τρυγών, 5167) denotes "a turtledove" (from *truzō*, "to murmur, to coo"), Luke 2:24.

DRAGON

drakōn (δράκων, 1404) denoted "a mythical monster, a dragon"; also a large serpent, so called because of its keen power of sight (from a root *derk-*, signifying "to see"). Twelve times in the Apocalypse it is used of the Devil 12:3-4, 7, 9, 13, 16-17; 13:2, 4, 11; 16:13; 20:2.

For **DRANK** see DRINK

DREAM (noun and verb), DREAMER

A. Nouns.

1. *onar* (ὄναρ, 3677) is "a vision in sleep," in distinction from a waking vision, Matt. 1:20; 2:12-13, 19, 22; 27:19.

2. *enupnion* (ἐνύπνιον, 1798), is, lit., "what appears in sleep" (*en*, "in," *hupnos*, "sleep"), an ordinary "dream," Acts 2:17. For synonymous nouns, see VISION.

B. Verb.

enupniazō (ἐνυπνιάζω, 1797), akin to A, No. 2, is used in Acts 2:17, in the passive voice in a phrase (according to the most authentic mss.) which means "shall be given up to dream by dreams," translated "shall dream dreams" metaphorically in Jude 8, of being given over to sensuous "dreamings," RV, KJV, "dreamers," and so defiling the flesh.

DRINK (-ETH, -ER, -ING), DRANK

A. Nouns.

1. *poma* (πόμα, 4188), akin to B, No. 1, denotes "the thing drunk" (from a root *po-*, found in the Eng., "potion"; it is connected with the root *pi-;* see B, No. 3), 1 Cor. 10:4; Heb. 9:10.

2. *posis* (πόσις, 4213), akin to B, No. 1, suggests "the act of drinking," John 6:55 (where it is practically equivalent to No. 1); Rom. 14:17, "drinking," RV; Col. 2:16.

3. *sikera* (σίκερα, 4608) is "a strong, intoxicating drink," made from any sweet ingredients, whether grain, vegetables, or the juice of fruits, or a decoction of honey; "strong drink," Luke 1:15. In the Sept., Lev. 10:9; Num. 6:3; 28:7; Deut. 14:26; 29:6; Isa. 5:11, 22; 24:9; 28:7; 29:9.

B. Verbs.

1. *pinō* (πίνω, 4095), "to drink," is used chiefly in the Gospels and in 1 Cor., whether literally (most frequently), or figuratively, (a) of "drinking" of the blood of Christ, in the sense of receiving eternal life, through His death, John 6:53-54, 56; (b) of "receiving" spiritually that which refreshes, strengthens and nourishes the soul, John 7:37; (c) of "deriving" spiritual life from Christ, John 4:14, as Israel did typically 1 Cor. 10:4; (d) of "sharing" in the sufferings of Christ humanly inflicted, Matt. 20:22-23; Mark 10:38-39; (e) of "participating" in the abominations imparted by the corrupt religious and commercial systems emanating from Babylon, Rev. 18:3; (f) of "receiving" divine judgment, through partaking unworthily of the Lord's Supper, 1 Cor. 11:29; (g) of "experiencing" the wrath of God, Rev. 14:10; 16:6; (h) of the earth's "receiving" the benefits of rain, Heb. 6:7.

2. *methuō* (μεθύω, 3184), from *methu*, "wine, to be drunk," is used in John 2:10 in the passive voice, and is translated in the RV, "have drunk freely"; KJV, "have well drunk." See DRUNK.

3. *potizō* (ποτίζω, 4222), "to give to drink, to make to drink," is used (a) in the material sense, in Matt. 10:42, 25:35, 37, 42 (here of "ministering" to those who beiong to Christ and thus doing so virtually to Him); 27:48; Mark 9:41; 15:36; Luke 13:15 ("to watering"); Rom. 12:20; 1 Cor. 3:7-8; (b) figuratively, with reference to "teaching" of an elementary character, 1 Cor. 3:2, "I fed (you with milk)"; of "spiritual watering by teaching" the Word of God, 3:6; of being "provided" and "satisfied" by the power and blessing of the Spirit of God, 1 Cor. 12:13; of the effect upon the nations of "partaking" of the abominable mixture, provided by Babylon, of paganism with details of the Christian faith Rev. 14:8. See FEED, WATER.

4. *sumpinō* (συμπίνω, 4844), "to drink together" (*sun*, "with," and B, No. 1), is found in Acts 10:41.

5. *hudropoteō* (ὑδροποτέω, 5202), "to drink water" (*hudōr*, "water," *poteō*, "to drink"), is found in 1 Tim. 5:23, RV, "be (no longer) a drinker of water."

DROP (Noun)

thrombos (θρόμβος, 2361), "a large, thick drop of clotted blood" (etymologically akin to *trepho*, "to curdle"), is used in Luke 22:44, in the plural, in the narrative of the Lord's agony in Gethsemane.

DROPSY

hudropikos (ὑδρωπικός, 5203), "dropsical, suffering from dropsy" (*hudrops*, "dropsy"), is found in Luke 14:2, the only instance recorded of the healing of this disease by the Lord.

DRUNK, (-EN, be), DRUNKARD, DRUNKENNESS

A. Verbs.

1. *methuō* (μεθύω, 3184) signifies "to be drunk with wine" (from *methu*, "mulled wine"; hence Eng., "mead, honey-wine"); originally it denoted simply "a pleasant drink." For John 2:10 see under DRINK. The verb is used of "being intoxicated" in Matt. 24:49; Acts 2:15; 1 Cor. 11:21; 1 Thess. 5:7*b*; metaphorically, of the effect upon men of partaking of the abominations of the Babylonish system, Rev. 17:2; of being in a state of mental "intoxication," through the shedding of men's blood profusely, v. 6.

2. *methuskō* (μεθύσκω, 3182) signifies "to make drunk, or to grow drunk" (an inceptive verb, marking the process or the state expressed in No. 1), "to become intoxicated," Luke 12:45; Eph. 5:18; 1 Thess. 5:7*a*.

B. Adjective.

methusos (μέθυσος, 3183), "drunken" (cf. No. 2), is used as noun, in the singular, in 1 Cor. 5:11, and in the plural, in 6:10, "drunkard," "drunkards."

C. Noun.

methē (μέθη, 3178), "strong drink" (akin to *methu*, "wine," see under A. 1, above), denotes "drunkenness, habitual intoxication," Luke 21:34; Rom. 13:13; Gal. 5:21.

DRY

A. Adjectives.

1. *xēros* (ξηρός, 3584) is used (a) naturally, of "dry" land, Heb. 11:29; or of land in general, Matt. 23:15, "land"; or of physical infirmity, "withered," Matt. 12:10; Mark 3:3; Luke 6:6, 8; John 5:3; (b) figuratively, in Luke 23:31, with reference to the spiritual "barrenness" of the Jews, in contrast to the character of the Lord. Cf. Ps. 1:3; Isa. 56:3; Ezek. 17:24; 20:47.

2. *anudros* (ἄνυδρος, 504), "waterless" (*a*, negative, *n*, euphonic, *hudōr*, "water"), is rendered "dry" in Matt. 12:43, KJV,

and Luke 11:24 (RV, "waterless"); "without water" in 2 Pet. 2:17 and Jude 12. See WATER.

B. Verb.

xērainō (ξηραίνω, 3583), akin to A. 1, "to dry, dry up, make dry, wither," is translated "dried" (of physical infirmity), in Mark 5:29; of a tree, in the KJV of Mark 11:20 (RV, "withered away"); of water, in Rev. 16:12. It is translated "ripe" (RV, "overripe") in Rev. 14:15, of a harvest (used figuratively of the gathered nations against Jerusalem at the end of this age); "pineth away," in Mark 9:18. See OVERRIPE, RIPE, WITHER.

DUE

A. Adjective.

idios (ἴδιος, 2398), "one's own," is applied to *kairos*, "a season," in Gal. 6:9, "in due season," i.e., in the season divinely appointed for the reaping. So in 1 Tim. 2:6, "the testimony to be borne in its own (KJV, 'due') times (seasons)"; 6:15, "in its own (*idios*) times (seasons)"; similarly in Titus 1:3.

B. Verbs.

1. *opheilō* (ὀφείλω, 3784) signifies "to owe, to be indebted," especially financially, Matt. 18:30, RV, "that which was due"; 18:34, "all that was due." See BOUND (TO BE).

2. *dei* (δεῖ, 1163), an impersonal verb signifying "it is necessary," is translated "was due" in Rom. 1:27, RV (KJV, "was meet").

C. Noun.

opheilē (ὀφειλή, 3782), akin to B, No. 1, is rendered "dues" in Rom. 13:7. In 1 Cor. 7:3, RV, it is translated "her due" (the KJV, "due benevolence" follows another reading).

Notes: (1) In the phrases "in due season" in Matt. 24:45; Luke 12:42; Rom. 5:6 (lit., "according to time"), and "in due time," 1 Pet. 5:6, there is no word representing "due" in the original, and the phrases are, lit., "in season," "in time."

(2) For the phrase "born out of due time," in 1 Cor. 15:8, see BEGET, B, No. 2.

DUMB

A. Adjectives.

1. *alolos* (ἄλαλος, 216), lit., "speechless" (*a*, negative, and *laleō*, "to speak"), is found in Mark 7:37; 9:17, 25. In the Sept., Ps. 38:13.

2. *aphōnos* (ἄφωνος, 880), lit., "voiceless, or soundless" (*a*, negative, and *phōnē*, "a sound"), has reference to voice, Acts 8:32; 1 Cor. 12:2; 2 Pet. 2:16, while *alalos* has reference to words. In 1 Cor. 14:10 it is used metaphorically of the significance of voices or sounds, "without signification." In the Sept. Isa. 53:7.

3. *kōphos* (κωφός, 2974) denotes "blunted or dulled"; see DEAF.

B. Verb.

siōpaō (σιωπάω, 4623), from *siōpē*, "silence, to be silent," is used of Zacharias' "dumbness," Luke 1:20. See PEACE (HOLD ONE'S).

DUNG

1. *skubalon* (σκύβαλον, 4657) denotes "refuse," whether (a) "excrement," that which is cast out from the body, or (b) "the leavings of a feast," that which is thrown away from the table. Some have derived it from *kusibalon* (with *metathesis* of k and s), "thrown to dogs"; others connect it with a root meaning "shred." Judaizers counted gentile Christians as dogs, while they themselves were seated at God's banquet. The apostle, reversing the image, counts the Judaistic ordinances as refuse upon which their advocates feed, Phil. 3:8.

2. *koprion* (κοπρία, 2874d), "manure," Luke 13:8, used in the plural with *ballō*, "to throw," is translated by the verb "to dung." Some mss. have the accusative case of the noun *kopria*, "a dunghill" See below.

DUNGHILL

kopria (κοπρία, 2874), "a dunghill," is found in Luke 14:35.

For **DURST** see DARE

DUST

A. Nouns.

1. *chous*, or *choos* (χοῦς or χόος, 5522), from *cheō*, "to pour," primarily, "earth dug out, an earth heap," then, "loose earth or dust," is used in Mark 6:11 and Rev. 18:19.

2. *koniortos* (κονιορτός, 2868), "raised or flying dust" (*konia*, "dust," *ornumi*, "to stir up"), is found in Matt. 10:14; Luke 9:5; 10:11; Acts 13:51; 22:23.

B. Verb.

likmaō (λικμάω, 3039), primarily, "to winnow" (from *likmos*, "a winnowing-fan"), hence, "to scatter" as chaff or dust, is used in Matt. 21:44 and Luke 20:18, RV, "scatter as dust," KJV, "grind to powder." There are indications in the papyri writings that the word came to denote "to ruin, to destroy."

DUTY

opheilō (ὀφείλω, 3784), "to owe, to be indebted," is translated "it was our duty," in Luke 17:10, lit., "we owe (ought) to do"; so in Rom. 15:27, KJV, "their duty is": RV, "they owe it." See BOUND.

For **DYING** see DEADNESS

E

EAGLE

aetos (ἀετός, 105), "an eagle" (also a vulture), is perhaps connected with *aēmi*, "to blow," as of the wind, on account of its windlike flight. In Matt. 24:28 and Luke 17:37 the vultures are probably intended. The meaning seems to be that, as these birds of prey gather where the carcass is, so the judgments of God will descend upon the corrupt state of humanity. The figure of the "eagle" is used in Ezek. 17 to represent the great powers of Egypt and Babylon, as being employed to punish corrupt and faithless Israel. Cf. Job 39:30; Prov. 30:17. The "eagle" is mentioned elsewhere in the NT in Rev. 4:7; 8:13 (RV); 12:14. There are eight species in Palestine.

EAR (of the body)

1. *ous* (οὖς, 3775), Latin *auris*, is used (a) of the physical organ, e.g., Luke 4:21; Acts 7:57; in Acts 11:22, in the plural with *akouō*, "to hear," lit., "was heard into the ears of someone," i.e., came to the knowledge of, similarly, in the singular, Matt. 10:27, in familiar private conversation; in Jas. 5:4 the phrase is used with *eiserchomai*, "to enter into"; in Luke 1:44, with *ginomai*, "to become, to come"; in Luke 12:3, with *lalein*, "to speak" and *pros*, "to," (b) metaphorically, of the faculty of perceiving with the mind, understanding and knowing, Matt. 13:16; frequently with *akouō*, "to hear," e.g., Matt. 11:15; 13:9, 43; Rev. 2 and 3, at the close of each of the messages to the churches, in Matt. 13:15 and Acts 28:27, with *bareōs*, "heavily," of being slow to understand and obey; with a negative in Mark 8:18; Rom. 11:8; in Luke 9:44 the lit. meaning is "put those words into your ears," i.e., take them into your mind and keep them there, in Acts 7:51 it is used with *aperitmētos*, "uncircumcised." As seeing is metaphorically associated with conviction, so hearing is with obedience (*hupakoē*, lit., "hearing under"; the Eng., "obedience" is etymologically "hearing over against," i.e., with response in the hearer).

2. *ōtion* (ὠτίον, 5621), a diminutive of No. 1, but without the diminutive force, it being a common tendency in everyday speech to apply a diminutive form to most parts of the body, is used in Matt. 26:51; Mark 14:47 (in some mss.); Luke 22:51; John 18:10 (in some mss.) and v. 26, all with reference to the "ear" of Malchus.

Note: The most authentic mss. have the alternative diminutive *otarion*, in Mark 14:47 and John 18:10.

3. *akoē* (ἀκοή, 189), "hearing," akin to *akouō*, "to hear," denotes (a) the sense of "hearing," e.g., 1 Cor. 12:17; 2 Pet. 2:8; (b) that which is "heard," a report, e.g., Matt. 4:24; (c) the physical organ, Mark 7:35, standing for the sense of "hearing"; so in Luke 7:1, RV, for KJV, "audience"; Acts 17:20; 2 Tim. 4:3-4 (in v. 3, lit., "being tickled as to the ears"); (d) a message or teaching, John 12:38; Rom. 10:16-17; Gal. 3:2, 5; 1 Thess. 2:13; Heb. 4:2, RV, "(the word) of hearing," for KJV, "(the word) preached." See FAME, HEARING, PREACH, REPORT, RUMOR.

Note: In Matt. 28:14, the verb *akouo* is used with the preposition *epi*, "upon or before" (or *hupo*, "by," in some mss.), lit., "if this come to a hearing before the governor."

EARNEST, EARNESTNESS, EARNESTLY

A. Noun.

spoudē (σπουδή, 4710), akin to *speudō*, "to hasten," denotes "haste," Mark 6:25; Luke 1:39; hence, "earnestness," 2 Cor. 8:7, RV, for KJV, "diligence," and v. 8, for KJV, "forwardness"; in 7:12, "earnest care," for KJV, "care"; in 8:16, earnest care. See DILIGENCE, HASTE.

B. Adjective.

spoudaios (σπουδαῖος, 4705), akin to A, denotes "active, diligent, earnest," 2 Cor. 8:22 RV, "earnest," for KJV, "diligent"; in the latter part of the verse the comparative degree, *spoudaioteros*, is used, RV, "more earnest," for KJV, "more diligent"; in v. 17, RV, in the superlative sense, "very earnest," for KJV, "more forward." See DILIGENT.

C. Adverbs.

1. *ektenōs* (ἐκτενῶς, 1619), "earnestly" (*ek*, "out," *teinō*, "to stretch"; Eng., "tension," etc.), is used in Acts 12:5, "earnestly," RV, for KJV, "without ceasing" (some mss. have the adjective *ektenēs*, "earnest"); in 1 Pet. 1:22, "fervently." The idea suggested is that of not relaxing in effort, or acting in a right spirit. See FERVENTLY.

2. *ektenesteron* (ἐκτενέστερον, 1617), the comparative degree of No. 1, used as an adverb in this neuter form, denotes "more earnestly, fervently," Luke 22:44.

3. *spoudaiōs* (σπουδαίως, 4709), akin to B, signifies "with haste," or "with zeal, earnestly," Luke 7:4, RV, "earnestly," for KJV, "instantly"; in 2 Tim. 1:17, RV, and Titus 3:13, "diligently"; in Phil. 2:28, the comparative *spoudaioterōs*, RV, "the more diligently," KJV, "the more carefully. See DILIGENTLY.

D. Adverbial Phrase.

en ekteneia (ἐν ἐκτενείᾳ), lit., "in earnestness," cf. C, No. 1, is translated "earnestly" in Acts 26:7, RV, for KJV, "instantly."

Notes: (1) In 1 Cor. 12:31; 14:1, 39, *zēloō*, "to be zealous about," is translated "desire earnestly." See DESIRE. (2) In 2 Pet. 3:12, *speudō* is translated "earnestly desiring," for KJV, "hasting unto." (3) In Jude 3, *epagōnizō*, "to contend earnestly," is so translated. (4) In Jas. 5:17 the dative case of the noun *proseuchē* is translated "earnestly" (KJV), in connection with the corresponding verb, lit., "he prayed with prayer" (RV, "fervently"), implying persevering continuance in prayer with fervor. Cf. e.g., Ps. 40:1, lit., "in waiting I waited." See FERVENT. (5) *Atenizō*, akin to C, No. 1, "to fix the eyes upon, gaze upon," is translated "earnestly looked" in Luke 22:56, KJV (RV, "looking steadfastly"); in Acts 3:12, KJV, "look ye earnestly," RV, "fasten ye your eyes on"; in Acts 23:1, KJV, "earnestly beholding," RV, "looking steadfastly on." (6) In Heb. 2:1, *prosechō*, "to give heed," is used with the adverb *perissoterōs*, "more abundantly," to signify "to give the more earnest heed"; lit., "to give heed more exceedingly." For the verb see ATTEND, GIVE, No. 16, HEED, REGARD.

EARTH

1. *gē* (γῆ, 1093) denotes (a) "earth as arable land," e.g., Matt. 13:5, 8, 23; in 1 Cor. 15:47 it is said of the "earthly" material of which "the first man" was made, suggestive of frailty; (b) "the earth as a whole, the world," in contrast, whether to the heavens, e.g., Matt. 5:18, 35, or to heaven, the abode of God, e.g., Matt. 6:19, where the context suggests the "earth" as a place characterized by mutability and weakness; in Col. 3:2 the same contrast is presented by the word "above"; in John 3:31 (RV, "of the earth," for KJV, "earthly") it describes one whose origin and nature are "earthly" and whose speech is characterized thereby, in contrast with Christ as the One from heaven; in Col. 3:5 the physical members are said to be "upon the earth," as a sphere where, as potential instruments of moral evils, they are, by metonymy, spoken of as the evils themselves; (c) "the inhabited earth," e.g., Luke 21:35; Acts 1:8; 8:33; 10:12; 11:6; 17:26; 22:22; Heb. 11:13; Rev. 13:8. In the following the phrase "on the earth" signifies "among men," Luke 12:49; 18:8; John 17:4, (d) "a country, territory," e.g. Luke 4:25; John 3:22; (e) "the ground," e.g., Matt. 10:29; Mark 4:26, RV, "(upon the) earth," for KJV, "(into the) ground"; (f) "land," e.g., Mark 4:1; John 21:8-9, 11. Cf. Eng. words beginning with *ge-*, e.g., "geodetic," "geodesy," "geology," "geometry," "geography." See GROUND, WORLD.

2. *oikoumenē* (οἰκουμένη, 3625), the present participle, passive voice, of *oikeō*, "to dwell, inhabit," denotes the "inhabited earth." It is translated "world" in every place where it has this significance, save in Luke 21:26, KJV, where it is translated "earth." See WORLD.

Note: For *epigeios*, translated "on earth" in Phil. 2:10, *ostrakinos*, "of earth," 2 Tim. 2:20, and *katachthonios*, "under the earth," Phil. 2:10, see EARTHEN.

EARTHEN, EARTHLY, EARTHY

1. *ostrakinos* (ὀστράκινος, 3749) signifies "made of earthenware or clay" (from *ostrakon*, "baked clay, potsherd, shell"; akin to *osteon*, "a bone"), 2 Tim. 2:20, "of earth"; 2 Cor. 4:7, "earthen."

2. *epigeios* (ἐπίγειος, 1919), "on earth" (*epi*, "on," *gē*, "the earth"), is rendered "earthly" in John 3:12; 2 Cor. 5:1; Phil. 3:19; Jas. 3:15; in Phil. 2:10, "on earth," RV; "terrestrial" in 1 Cor. 15:40 (twice). See TERRESTRIAL.

3. *choikos* (χοϊκός, 5517) denotes "earthy," made of earth, from *chous*, "soil, earth thrown down or heaped up," 1 Cor. 15:47-49.

4. *katachthonios* (καταχθόνιος, 2709), "under the earth, subterranean" (*kata*, "down," *chthōn*, "the ground," from a root signifying that which is deep), is used in Phil. 2:10.

EAST

anatolē (ἀνατολή, 395), primarily "a rising," as of the sun and stars, corresponds to *anatellō*, "to make to rise," or, intransitively, "to arise," which is also used of the sunlight, as well as of other objects in nature. In Luke 1:78 it is used metaphorically of Christ as "the Dayspring," the One through whom light came into the world, shining immediately into Israel, to dispel the darkness which was upon all nations. Cf. Mal. 4:2. Elsewhere it denotes the "east," as the quarter of the sun's rising, Matt. 2:1-2, 9; 8:11; 24:27; Luke 13:29; Rev. 7:2; 16:12; 21:13. The "east" in general stands for that side of things upon which the rising of the sun gives light. In the heavenly city itself, Rev. 21:13, the reference to the "east" gate points to the outgoing of the influence of the city "eastward." See DAYSPRING.

EASTER

pascha (πάσχα, 3957), mistranslated "Easter" in Acts 12:4, KJV, denotes the Passover (RV). The phrase "after the Passover" signifies after the whole festival was at an end. The term "Easter" is not of Christian origin. It is another form of *Astarte*, one of the titles of the Chaldean goddess, the queen of heaven. The festival of Pasch held by Christians in post-apostolic times was a continuation of the Jewish feast, but was not instituted by Christ, nor was it connected with Lent. From this Pasch the pagan festival of "Easter" was quite distinct and was introduced into the apostate Western religion, as part of the attempt to adapt pagan festivals to Christianity. See PASSOVER.

EDGE, EDGED

A. Noun.

stoma (στόμα, 4750), the mouth (cf. Eng., "stomach," from *stomachos*, 1 Tim. 5:23), has a secondary and figurative meaning in reference to the "edge of a sharp instrument, as of a sword," Luke 21:24; Heb. 11:34 (cf. the Sept., e.g., Gen. 34:26; Judg. 18:27). See FACE, MOUTH.

B. Adjective.

distomos (δίστομος, 1366), lit., "doublemouthed" (*dis*, "twice," and A.), "two-edged," is used of a sword with two edges, Heb. 4:12; Rev. 1:16; 212. In the Sept., Judg. 3:16; Psa. 149:6; Prov. 5:4.

EDIFICATION, EDIFY, EDIFYING

A. Noun.

oikodomē (οἰκοδομή, 3619) denotes (a) "the act of building" (*oikos*, "a home," and *demō*, "to build"); this is used only figuratively in the NT, in the sense of edification, the promotion of spiritual growth (lit., "the things of building up"), Rom. 14:19; 15:2; 1 Cor. 14:3, 5, 12, 26, e.g.; (b) "a building, edifice," whether material, Matt. 24:1, e.g., or figurative, of the future body of the believer, 2 Cor. 5:1, or of a local church, 1 Cor. 3:9, or the whole church, "the body of Christ, Eph. 2:21. See BUILDING.

B. Verb.

oikodomeō (οἰκοδομέω, 3618), lit., "to build a house" (see above), (a) usually signifies "to build," whether literally, or figuratively; the present participle, lit., "the (ones) building," is used as a noun, "the builders," in Matt. 21:42; Mark 12:10; Luke 20:17; Acts 4:11 (in some mss.; the most authentic have the noun *oikodomos;*) 1 Pet. 2:7; (b) is used metaphorically, in the sense of "edifying," promoting the spiritual growth and development of character of believers, by teaching or by example, suggesting such spintual progress as the result of patient labor. It is said (1) of the effect of this upon local churches, Acts 9:31; 1 Cor. 14:4; (2) of the individual action of believers towards each other, 1 Cor. 8:1; 10:23; 14:17; 1 Thess. 5:11; (3) of an individual in regard to himself, 1 Cor. 14:4. In 1 Cor. 8:10, where it is translated "emboldened," the apostle uses it with pathetic irony, of the action of a brother in "building up" his brother who had a weak conscience, causing him to compromise his scruples; "strengthened," or "confirmed," would be suitable renderings. See BUILD, EMBOLDEN.

EFFECT (of none)

1. *akuroō* (ἀκυρόω, 208) signifies "to render void, deprive of force and authority" (from *a*, negative, and *kuros*, "might, authority"; *kurios*, "a lord," is from the same root), the opposite to *kuroō*, "to confirm" (see CONFIRM). It is used of making "void" the Word of God, Matt. 15:6; Mark 7:13 (KJV, "making of none effect"), and of the promise of God to Abraham as not being deprived of authority by the Law 430 years after, Gal. 3:17, "disannul." *Kuroō* is used in v. 15. See VOID.

2. *katargeō* (καταργέω, 2673), "to reduce to inactivity, to render useless," is translated "to make of none effect," in Rom. 3:3, 31; 4:14; Gal. 3:17 (cf. *akuroō*, No. 1, in the same verse), and in the KJV of Gal. 5:4, RV, "ye are severed" (from Christ). For the meaning and use of the word see ABOLISH AND DESTROY.

3. *kenoō* (κενόω, 2758), "to make empty, to empty," is translated "should be made of none effect" in 1 Cor. 1:17, KJV (RV "made void"); it is used (a) of the Cross of Christ, there; (b) of Christ, in emptying Himself, Phil. 2:7; (c) of faith, Rom. 4:14; (d) of the apostle Paul's glorying in the gospel ministry, 1 Cor. 9:15; (e) of his glorying on behalf of the church at Corinth, 2 Cor. 9:3. See EMPTY, VAIN, VOID.

Note: In Rom. 9:6 the verb *ekpiptō*, lit., "to fall out of, as of a ship falling out of its course" (cf. the same word in Acts 27:17, "were driven"), is translated "hath taken none effect," KJV (RV, "hath come to nought"). See NOUGHT.

EFFEMINATE

malakos (μαλακός, 3120), "soft, soft to the touch" (Lat., *mollis*, Eng., "mollify," "emollient," etc.), is used (a) of raiment, Matt. 11:8 (twice); Luke 7:25; (b) metaphorically, in a bad sense, 1 Cor. 6:9, "effeminate," not simply of a male who practices forms of lewdness, but persons in general, who are guilty of addiction to sins of the flesh, voluptuous.

EFFULGENCE

apaugasma (ἀπαύγασμα, 541), "radiance, effulgence," is used of light shining from a luminous body (*apo*, "from," and *augē*, "brightness"). The word is found in Heb. 1:3, where it is used of the Son of God as "being the effulgence of His glory." The word "effulgence" exactly corresponds (in its Latin form) to *apaugasma*. The "glory" of God expresses all that He is in His nature and His actings and their manifestation. The Son, being one with the Father in Godhood, is in Himself, and ever was, the shining forth of the "glory," manifesting in Himself all that God is and does, all, for instance, that is involved in His being "the very image of His substance," and in His creative acts, His sustaining power, and in His making purification of sins, with all that pertains thereto and issues from it.

ELDER, ELDEST

A. Adjectives.

1. *presbuteros* (πρεσβύτερος, 4245), an adjective, the comparative degree of *presbus*, "an old man, an elder," is used

(a) of age, whether of the "elder" of two persons, Luke 15:25, or more, John 8:9, "the eldest," or of a person advanced in life, a senior, Acts 2:17; in Heb. 11:2, the "elders" are the forefathers in Israel so in Matt. 15:2; Mark 7:3, 5 the feminine of the adjective is used of "elder" women in the churches, 1 Tim. 5:2, not in respect of position but in seniority of age; (b) of rank or positions of responsibility, (1) among Gentiles, as in the Sept. of Gen. 50:7; Num. 22:7, (2) in the Jewish nation, firstly, those who were the heads or leaders of the tribes and families, as of the seventy who assisted Moses, Num. 11:16; Deut. 27:1, and those assembled by Solomon; secondly, members of the Sanhedrin, consisting of the chief priests, "elders" and scribes, learned in Jewish law, e.g., Matt. 16:21; 26:47; thirdly, those who managed public affairs in the various cities, Luke 7:3; (3) in the Christian churches those who, being raised up and qualified by the work of the Holy Spirit, were appointed to have the spiritual care of, and to exercise oversight over, the churches. To these the term "bishops," *episkopoi*, or "overseers," is applied (see Acts 20, v. 17 with v. 28, and Titus 1:5 and 7), the latter term indicating the nature of their work *presbuteroi* their maturity of spiritual experience. The divine arrangement seen throughout the NT was for a plurality of these to be appointed in each church, Acts 14:23; 20:17; Phil. 1:1; 1 Tim. 5:17; Titus 1:5. The duty of "elders" is described by the verb *episkopeō*. They were appointed according as they had given evidence of fulfilling the divine qualifications, Titus 1:6 to 9; cf. 1 Tim. 3:1-7 and 1 Pet. 5:2; (4) the twenty-four "elders" enthroned in heaven around the throne of God, Rev. 4:4, 10; 5:5-14; 7:11, 13; 11:16; 14:3; 19:4. The number twenty-four is representative of earthly conditions. The word "elder" is nowhere applied to angels. See OLD.

2. *sumpresbuteros* (συμπρεσβύτερος, 4850), "a fellow-elder" (*sun*, "with"), is used in 1 Pet. 5:1.

3. *meizōn* (μείζων, 3187), "greater," the comparative degree of *megas*, "great," is used of age, and translated "elder" in Rom. 9:12, with reference to Esau and Jacob. See GREATER, GREATEST.

B. Noun.

presbuterion (πρεσβυτέριον, 4244), "an assembly of aged men," denotes (a) the Council or Senate among the Jews, Luke 22:66; Acts 22:5; (b) the "elders" or bishops in a local church, 1 Tim. 4:14, "the presbytery." For their functions see A, No. 1, (3).

ELECT, ELECTED, ELECTION

A. Adjectives.

1. *eklektos* (ἐκλεκτός, 1588) lit. signifies "picked out, chosen" (*ek*, "from," *legō*, "to gather, pick out"), and is used of (a) Christ, the "chosen" of God, as the Messiah, Luke 23:35 (for the verb in 9:35 see Note below), and metaphorically as a "living Stone," "a chief corner Stone," 1 Pet. 2:4, 6; some mss. have it in John 1:34, instead of *huios*, "Son"; (b) angels, 1 Tim. 5:21, as "chosen" to be of especially high rank in administrative association with God, or as His messengers to human beings, doubtless in contrast to fallen angels (see 2 Pet. 2:4 and Jude 6); (c) believers (Jews or Gentiles), Matt. 24:22, 24, 31; Mark 13:20, 22, 27; Luke 18:7; Rom. 8:33; Col. 3:12; 2 Tim. 2:10; Titus 1:1; 1 Pet. 1:1; 2:9 (as a spiritual race); Matt. 20:16; 22:14 and Rev. 17:14, "chosen"; individual believers are so mentioned in Rom. 16:13; 2 John 1, 13.

Believers were "chosen" "before the foundation of the world" (cf. "before times eternal," 2 Tim. 1:9), in Christ, Eph. 1:4, to adoption, Eph. 1:5; good works, 2:10; conformity to Christ, Rom. 8:29; salvation from the delusions of the Antichrist and the doom of the deluded, 2 Thess. 2:13; eternal glory, Rom. 9:23.

The source of their "election" is God's grace, not human will, Eph. 1:4, 5; Rom. 9:11; 11:5. They are given by God the Father to Christ as the fruit of His death, all being foreknown and foreseen by God, John 17:6 and Rom. 8:29. While Christ's death was sufficient for all men, and is effective in the case of the "elect," yet men are treated as responsible, being capable of the will and power to choose. For the rendering "being chosen as firstfruits," an alternative reading in 2 Thess. 2:13, see FIRSTFRUITS. See CHOICE, B.

2. *suneklektos* (συνεκλεκτός, 4899) means "elect together with," 1 Pet. 5:13.

B. Noun.

eklogē (ἐκλογή, 1589) denotes "a picking out, selection" (Eng., "eclogue"), then, "that which is chosen"; in Acts 9:15, said of the "choice" of God of Saul of Tarsus, the phrase is, lit., "a vessel of choice." It is used four times in Romans; in 9:11, of Esau and Jacob, where the phrase "the purpose ... according to election" is virtually equivalent to "the electing purpose"; in 11:5, the "remnant according to the election of grace" refers to believing Jews, saved from among the unbelieving nation; so in v. 7; in v. 28, "the election" may mean either the "act of choosing" or the "chosen" ones; the context, speaking of the fathers, points to the former, the choice of the nation according to the covenant of promise. In 1 Thess. 1:4, "your election" refers not to the church collectively, but to the individuals constituting it; the apostle's assurance of their "election" gives the reason for his thanksgiving. Believers are to give "the more diligence to make their calling and election sure," by the exercise of the qualities and graces which make them fruitful in the knowledge of God, 2 Pet. 1:10. For the corresponding verb *eklegomai*, see CHOOSE.

ELOQUENT

logios (λόγιος, 3052), an adjective, from *logos*, "a word," primarily meant "learned, a man skilled in literature and the arts." In the KJV of Acts 18:24, it is translated "eloquent," said of Apollos; the RV is almost certainly right in translating it "learned." It was much more frequently used among the Greeks of one who was erudite than of one who was skilled in words. He had stores of "learning" and could use it convincingly.

EMBOLDEN

oikodomeō (οἰκοδομέω, 3618) is rendered "embolden" in 1 Cor. 8:10, in reference to blameworthy actions (see marg.), the delinquent being built up, so to speak, to do what is contrary to his conscience. See BUILD, EDIFICATION.

EMBRACE

1. *aspazomai* (ἀσπάζομαι, 782) lit. signifies "to draw to oneself"; hence, "to greet, salute, welcome," the ordinary meaning, e.g., in Rom. 16, where it is used 21 times. It also signifies "to bid farewell," e.g., Acts 20:1, RV, "took leave of" (KJV, "embraced"). A "salutation or farewell" was generally made by embracing and kissing (see Luke 10:4, which indicates the possibility of delay on the journey by frequent salutation). In Heb. 11:13 it is said of those who greeted the promises from afar, RV, "greeted," for KJV, "embraced." Cf. *aspasmos*, "a salutation. See GREET, SALUTE.

Note: In Acts 21:6 the most authentic texts have *apaspazomai* (*apo*, and No. 1), "to bid farewell."

2. *sumperilambanō* (συμπεριλαμβάνω, 4843), lit., "to take around with," (*sun*, "with" *peri* "around," *lambanō*, "to take"), "to embrace," is used in Acts 20:10, in connection with Paul's recovery of Eutychus. In the Sept., Ezra 5:3, "to enclose."

EMPEROR

sebastos (σεβαστός, 4575), "august, reverent," the masculine gender of an adjective (from *sebas*, "reverential awe"), became used as the title of the Roman emperor, Acts 25:21, 25, RV, for KJV, "Augustus"; then, taking its name from the emperor, it became a title of honor applied to certain legions or cohorts or battalions, marked for their valor, Acts 27:1. Cf. *sebazomai*, "to worship," Rom. 1:25; *sebasma*, "an object of worship," Acts 17:23; 2 Thess. 2:4.

EMPTY

A. Verbs.

1. *kenoō* (κενόω, 2758), "to empty," is so translated in Phil. 2:7, RV, for KJV, "made ... of no reputation." The clauses which follow the verb are exegetical of its meaning, especially the phrases "the form of a servant," and "the likeness of men." Christ did not "empty" Himself of Godhood. He did not cease to be what He essentially and eternally was. The KJV, while not an exact translation, goes far to express the act of the Lord (see GIFFORD on the Incarnation). For other occurrences of the word, see Rom. 4:14; 1 Cor. 1:17; 9:15; 2 Cor. 9:3. In the Sept., Jer. 14:2; 15:9.

2. *scholazō* (σχολάζω, 4980), from *scholē*, "leisure," that for which leisure is employed, such as "a lecture" (hence, "the place where lectures are given"; Eng., "school"), is used of persons, to have time for anything and so to be occupied in, 1 Cor. 7:5; of things, to be unoccupied, empty, Matt. 12:44 (some mss. have it in Luke 11:25). See GIVE (oneself to).

B. Adjective.

kenos (κενός, 2756) expresses the "hollowness" of anything, the "absence" of that which otherwise might be possessed. It is used (a) literally, Mark 12:3; Luke 1:53; 20:10-11; (b) metaphorically, of imaginations, Acts 4:25; of words which convey erroneous teachings, Eph. 5:6; of deceit, Col. 2:8; of a person whose professed faith is not accompanied by works, Jas. 2:20; negatively, concerning the grace of God, 1 Cor. 15:10; of refusal to receive it, 2 Cor. 6:1; of faith, 1 Cor. 15:14; of preaching (id.); and other forms of Christian activity and labor, 1 Cor. 15:58; Gal. 2:2; Phil. 2:16; 1 Thess. 2:1; 3:5. The synonymous word *mataios*, "vain," signifies "void" of result, it marks the aimlessness of anything. The vain (*kenos*) man in Jas. 2:20 is one who is "empty" of divinely imparted wisdom; in 1:26 the vain (mataios) religion is one that produces nothing profitable. *Kenos* stresses the absence of quality, *mataios*, the absence of useful aim or effect. Cf. the corresponding adverb *kenōs*, "in vain," in Jas. 4:5, the noun *kenodoxia*, "vainglory," Phil. 2:3, the adjective *kenodoxos*, "vainglorious," Gal. 5:26, and the noun *kenophōnia*, "vain," or "empty," babblings, 1 Tim. 6:20; 2 Tim. 2:16.

For **EMULATION**, KJV (Rom. 11:14; Gal. 5:20) see JEALOUSY

ENCOUNTER

sumballō (συμβάλλω, 4820), lit., "to throw together" (*sun*, "with," *ballō*, "to throw"), is used of "encountering" in war, Luke 14:31, RV, "to encounter ... (in war)," for KJV, "to make war against"; of meeting in order to discuss, in Acts 17:18, "encountered," of the philosophers in Athens and the apostle. See CONFER, HELP.

ENCOURAGE, ENCOURAGEMENT

A. Verbs.

1. *protrepō* (προτρέπω, 4389), "to urge forward, persuade," is used in Acts 18:27 in the middle voice, RV, "encouraged," indicating their particular interest in giving Apollos the

"encouragement" mentioned; the KJV, "exhorting," wrongly connects the verb.

2. *paramutheomai* (παραμυθέομαι, 3888), from *para*, "with," and *muthos*, "counsel, advice," is translated "encouraging" in 1 Thess. 2:11, RV, and "encourage" in 5:14, RV, there signifying to stimulate to the discharge of the ordinary duties of life. In John 11:19, 31, it means "to comfort." See COMFORT.

Cf. the nouns *paramuthia*, 1 Cor. 14:3, and *paramuthion*, Phil. 2:1, "comfort."

B. Noun.

paraklēsis (παράκλησις, 3874), "a calling to one's aid" (*para*, "by the side," *kaleō*, "to call"), then, "an exhortation, encouragement," is translated "encouragement" in Heb. 6:18, RV, for KJV, "consolation"; it is akin to *parakaleō*, "to beseech or exhort, encourage, comfort," and *paraklētos*, "a paraclete or advocate." See COMFORT, CONSOLATION, EXHORTATION, INTREATY.

END, ENDING

A. Nouns.

1. *telos* (τέλος, 5056) signifies (a) "the limit," either at which a person or thing ceases to be what he or it was up to that point, or at which previous activities were ceased, 2 Cor. 3:13; 1 Pet. 4:7; (b) "the final issue or result" of a state or process, e.g., Luke 1:33; in Rom. 10:4, Christ is described as "the end of the Law unto righteousness to everyone that believeth"; this is best explained by Gal. 3:23-26; cf. Jas. 5:11; the following more especially point to the issue or fate of a thing, Matt. 26:58; Rom. 6:21; 2 Cor. 11:15; Phil. 3:19; Heb. 6:8; 1 Pet. 1:9; (c) "a fulfillment," Luke 22:37, KJV, "(have) an end"; (d) "the utmost degree" of an act, as of the love of Christ towards His disciples, John 13:1; (e) "the aim or purpose" of a thing, 1 Tim. 1:5; (f) "the last" in a succession or series Rev. 1:8 (KJV, only, "ending"); 21:6; 22:13. See CONTINUAL, CUSTOM (TOLL), FINALLY, UTTERMOST.

Note: The following phrases contain *telos* (the word itself coming under one or other of the above): *eis telos*, "unto the end," e.g., Matt. 10:22; 24:13; Luke 18:5, "continual"; John 13:1 (see above); 2 Cor. 3:13, "on the end" (RV); *heos telous*, "unto the end," 1 Cor. 1:8; 2 Cor. 1:13; *achri telous*, "even to the end" (a stronger expression than the preceding); Heb. 6:11; Rev. 2:26 (where "even" might well have been added); *mechri telous*, with much the same meaning as *achri telous*, Heb. 3:6, 14. See other expressions in the *Notes* after C.

2. *sunteleia* (συντέλεια, 4930) signifies "a bringing to completion together" (*sun* "with," *teleō*, "to complete," akin to No. 1), marking the "completion" or consummation of the various parts of a scheme. In Matt. 13:39-40, 49; 24:3; 28:20, the rendering "the end of the world" (KJV and RV, text) is misleading; the RV marg., "the consummation of the age," is correct. The word does not denote a termination, but the heading up of events to the appointed climax. *Aiōn* is not the world, but a period or epoch or era in which events take place. In Heb. 9:26, the word translated "world" (KJV) is in the plural, and the phrase is "the consummation of the ages." It was at the heading up of all the various epochs appointed by divine counsels that Christ was manifested (i.e., in His Incarnation) "to put away sin by the sacrifice of Himself."

3. *peras* (πέρας, 4009), "a limit, boundary" (from *pera*, "beyond"), is used (a) of space, chiefly in the plural, Matt. 12:42, RV, "ends," for KJV, "uttermost parts"; so Luke 11:31 (KJV, "utmost"); Rom. 10:18 (KJV and RV, "ends"); (b) of the termination of something occurring in a period, Heb. 6:16, RV, "final," for KJV, "an end," said of strife. See UTTERMOST.

4. *ekbasis* (ἔκβασις, 1545) denotes "a way out" (*ek*, "out," *bainō*, "to go"), 1 Cor. 10:13, "way of escape"; or an issue, Heb. 13:7 (KJV, "end," RV, "issue").

B. Verbs.

1. *teleō* (τελέω, 5055), "to complete, finish, bring to an end," is translated "had made an end," in Matt. 11:1.

2. *sunteleō* (συντελέω, 4931), cf. A, No. 2, signifies (a) "to bring to an end, finish completely" (*sun*, "together," imparting a perfective significance to *teleō*), Matt. 7:28 (in some mss.); Luke 4:2, 13; Acts 21:27, RV, "completed"; (b) "to bring to fulfillment," Mark 13:4; Rom. 9:28; (c) "to effect, make," Heb. 8:8. See FULFILL.

3. *plēroō* (πληρόω, 4137), (a) "to fill," (b) "to fulfill, complete, end," is translated "had ended" in Luke 7:1; "were ended" (passive) in Acts 19:21.

Note: In John 13:2, the verb *ginomai*, there signifying "to be in progress," and used in the present participle, is translated "during supper" (RV). A less authentic reading, is *genomenou*, "being ended" (KJV).

C. Adjective.

eschatos (ἔσχατος, 2078), "last, utmost, extreme," is used as a noun (a) of time, rendered "end" in Heb. 1:2, RV, "at the "end" of these days," i.e., at the "end" of the period under the Law, for KJV, "in these last days"; so in 1 Pet. 1:20, "at the end of the times." In 2 Pet. 2:20, the plural, *ta eschata*, lit., "the last things," is rendered "the latter end," KJV, (RV, "the last state"); the same phrase is used in Matt. 12:45; Luke 11:26; (b) of place, Acts 13:47, KJV, "ends (of the earth)," RV, "uttermost part. See LAST, LOWEST, UTTERMOST.

Notes: (1) In Matt. 28:1, *opse*, "late (in the evening)," is rendered "in the end (of)," KJV, RV, "late (on)." (2) In 1 Pet. 1:13, *teleiōs*, "perfectly," RV, is rendered "to the end," in KJV (3) The phrase *eis touto*, lit., "unto this," signifies "to this end," John 18:37, RV (twice; KJV, "for this cause," in the second clause); so Mark 1:38; Acts 26:16; Rom. 14:9; 2 Cor. 2:9; 1 Tim. 4:10 (KJV, "therefore"); 1 Pet. 4:6; 1 John 3:8 (KJV, "for this purpose"). (4) *Eis*, "unto," followed by the article and the infinitive mood of a verb, signifies "to the end that ..." marking the aim of an action, Acts 7:19; Rom. 1:11; 4:16, 18; Eph. 1:12; 1 Thess. 3:13; 2 Thess. 1:5; 2:2, 6; 1 Pet. 3:7. In Luke 18:1, *pros*, "to," has the same construction and meaning. (5) The conjunction *hina*, "in order that," is sometimes rendered "to the end that," Eph. 3:17; 2 Thess. 3:14; Titus 3:8. (6) In Matt. 24:31, the prepositions *apo*, "from," and *heōs*, "unto," are used with the plural of *akros*, "highest, extreme," signifying "from one end ... to the other," lit., "from extremities ... to extremities."

ENDUE

enduō (ἐνδύω, 1746), in the middle voice, "to put on oneself, be clothed with," is used metaphorically of power, Luke 24:49, RV, clothed.

Note: In Jas. 3:13 the adjective *epistēmōn*, "knowing, skilled," is translated "endued with knowledge," KJV, RV, "understanding."

ENDURE, ENDURING

A. Verbs.

1. *menō* (μένω, 3306), "to abide," is rendered "to endure" in the KJV of John 6:27 and 1 Pet. 1:25 (RV, "abideth"); Heb. 10:34, KJV, "enduring (substance)," RV, "abiding."

2. *hupomenō* (ὑπομένω, 5278), a strengthened form of No. 1, denotes "to abide under, to bear up courageously" (under suffering), Matt. 10:22; 24:13; Mark 13:13; Rom. 12:12, translated "patient"; 1 Cor. 13:7; 2 Tim. 2:10, 12 (KJV, "suffer"); Heb. 10:32; 12:2-3, 7; Jas. 1:12; 5:11; 1 Pet. 2:20, "ye shall take it patiently." It has its other significance, "to tarry, wait for, await," in Luke 2:43; Acts 17:14 (in some mss., Rom. 8:24). Cf. B. See PATIENT, SUFFER. Cf. *makrothumeō*, to be longsuffering" (see No. 7).

3. *pherō* (φέρω, 5342), "to bear," is translated "endured" in Rom. 9:22 and Heb. 12:20.

4. *hupopherō* (ὑποφέρω, 5297), a strengthened form of No. 3, "to bear or carry," by being under, is said metaphorically of "enduring" temptation, 1 Cor. 10:13, KJV, "bear"; persecutions, 2 Tim. 3:11; griefs, 1 Pet. 2:19.

5. *anechō* (ἀνέχω, 430), "to hold up" (*ana*, "up," *echō*, "to hold or have"), always in the middle voice in the NT, is rendered "endure" in 2 Thess. 1:4, of persecutions and tribulations; in 2 Tim. 4:3, of sound doctrine.

6. *kartereō* (καρτερέω, 2594), "to be steadfast, patient," is used in Heb. 11:27, "endured," of Moses in relation to Egypt. In the Sept., Job 2:9; Isa. 42:14.

7. *makrothumeō* (μακροθυμέω, 3114), "to be long-tempered" (*makros*, "long," *thumos*, "mind"), is rendered "patiently endured" in Heb. 6:15, said of Abraham. See B, below. See LONGSUFFERING, PATIENCE, SUFFER.

Note: In 2 Tim. 2:9, *kakopatheō*, "to suffer evil" (*kakos*, "evil," *paschō*, "to suffer"), is translated "endure hardness," KJV; RV, "suffer hardship"; so in 4:5, KJV, "endure afflictions"; elsewhere in Jas. 5:13. In 2 Tim. 2:3 the most authentic mss. have *sunkakopatheō*, "to suffer hardship with," as in 1:8. See HARDSHIP, SUFFER.

B. Noun.

hupomonē (ὑπομονή, 5281), "patience," lit., "a remaining under" (akin to A, No. 2), is translated "patient enduring" in 2 Cor. 1:6, RV, for KJV, "enduring." Cf. *makrothumia*, "longsuffering" (akin to A, No. 7). See PATIENCE.

ENEMY

echthros (ἐχθρός, 2190), an adjective, primarily denoting "hated" or "hateful" (akin to *echthos*, "hate"; perhaps associated with *ekos*, "outside"), hence, in the active sense, denotes "hating, hostile"; it is used as a noun signifying an "enemy," adversary, and is said (a) of the Devil, Matt. 13:39; Luke 10:19; (b) of death, 1 Cor. 15:26; (c) of the professing believer who would be a friend of the world, thus making himself an enemy of God, Jas. 4:4; (d) of men who are opposed to Christ, Matt. 13:25, 28; 22:44; Mark 12:36; Luke 19:27; 20:43; Acts 2:35; Rom. 11:28; Phil. 3:18; Heb. 1:13; 10:13; or to His servants, Rev. 11:5, 12; to the nation of Israel, Luke 1:71, 74; 19:43; (e) of one who is opposed to righteousness, Acts 13:10; (f) of Israel in its alienation from God, Rom. 11:28; (g) of the unregenerate in their attitude toward God, Rom. 5:10; Col. 1:21; (h) of believers in their former state, 2 Thess. 3:15; (i) of foes, Matt. 5:43-44; 10:36; Luke 6:27, 35; Rom. 12:20; 1 Cor. 15:25; of the apostle Paul because he told converts "the truth," Gal. 4:16. See FOE. Cf. *echthra*, "enmity."

ENJOY

A. Verb.

tunchanō (τυγχάνω, 5177), used transitively, denotes "to hit upon, meet with"; then, "to reach, get, obtain"; it is translated "enjoy" (i.e., obtain to our satisfaction) in Acts 24:2. See COMMON, *Note* (3).

B. Noun.

apolausis (ἀπόλαυσις, 619), "enjoyment" (from *apolauō*, "to take hold of, enjoy a thing"), suggests the advantage or pleasure to be obtained from a thing (from a root, *lab-* seen in *lambanō*, "to obtain"); it is used with the preposition *eis*, in 1 Tim. 6:17, lit., "unto enjoyment," rendered "to enjoy"; with *echō*, "to have," in Heb. 11:25, lit., "to have pleasure (of sin)," translated "to enjoy the pleasures." See PLEASURE.

ENLARGE

1. *megalunō* (μεγαλύνω, 3170) denotes "to make great" (from *megas*, "great"), Matt. 23:5, "enlarge"; 2 Cor. 10:15, KJV, "enlarged," RV, "magnified"; elsewhere in the KJV it is rendered by the verb "to magnify," except in Luke 1:58, KJV, "had showed great (mercy)," RV, "had magnified (His mercy); see Luke 1:46; Acts 5:13; 10:46; 19:17; Phil. 1:20. See MAGNIFY.

2. *platunō* (πλατύνω, 4115), "to make broad," from *platus*, "broad," is translated "enlarged" in 2 Cor. 6:11, 13 (metaphorically), "make broad," Matt. 23:5 (literally). From the primary sense of freedom comes that of the joy that results from it. Cf. *platos*, "breadth," and *plateia*, "a street."

ENLIGHTEN

phōtizō (φωτίζω, 5461), from *phōs*, "light," (a), used intransitively, signifies "to give light, shine," Rev. 22:5; (b), used transitively, "to enlighten, illumine," is rendered "enlighten" in Eph. 1:18, metaphorically of spiritual "enlightenment"; so John 1:9, i.e., "lighting every man" (by reason of His coming); Eph. 3:9, "to make (all men) see" (RV marg., "to bring to light"); Heb. 6:4, "were enlightened"; 10:32, RV, "enlightened," KJV, "illuminated." See LIGHT. Cf. *phōtismos*, "light," and *phōteinos*, "full of light."

ENMITY

echthra (ἔχθρα, 2189), from the adjective *echthros* (see ENEMY) is rendered "enmity" in Luke 23:12; Rom. 8:7; Eph. 2:15-16; Jas. 4:4; "enmities," Gal. 5:20, RV, for KJV, "hatred." It is the opposite of *agapē*, "love."

For **ENQUIRE** see INQUIRE

ENRICH

ploutizō (πλουτίζω, 4148), "to make rich" (from *ploutos*, "wealth, riches"), is used metaphorically, of spiritual "riches," in 1 Cor. 1:5, "ye were enriched"; 2 Cor. 6:10, "making rich"; 2 Cor. 9:11, "being enriched." See RICH.

ENSAMPLE

1. *tupos* (τύπος, 5179) primarily denoted "a blow" (from a root *tup-*, seen also in *tuptō*, "to strike"), hence, (a) an impression, the mark of a "blow," John 20:25; (b) the "impress" of a seal, the stamp made by a die, a figure, image, Acts 7:43; (c) a "form" or mold, Rom. 6:17 (see RV); (d) the sense or substance of a letter, Acts 23:25; (e) "an ensample," pattern, Acts 7:44; Heb. 8:5, "pattern"; in an ethical sense, 1 Cor. 10:6; Phil. 3:17; 1 Thess. 1:7; 2 Thess. 3:9; 1 Tim. 4:12, RV, "ensample"; Titus 2:7, RV, "ensample," for KJV, "pattern"; 1 Pet. 5:3; in a doctrinal sense, a type, Rom. 5:14. See EXAMPLE, FASHION, FIGURE, FORM.

2. *hupotupōsis* (ὑποτύπωσις, 5296), "an outline, sketch," akin to *hupotupoō*, "to delineate," is used metaphorically to denote a "pattern," an "ensample," 1 Tim. 1:16, RV, "ensample," for KJV, "pattern"; 2 Tim. 1:13, RV, "pattern," for KJV, "form." See FORM.

3. *hupodeigma* (ὑπόδειγμα, 5262), lit., "that which is shown" (from *hupo*, "under," and *deiknumi*, "to show"), hence, (a) "a figure, copy," Heb. 8:5, RV, "copy," for KJV, "example"; 9:23; (b) "an example," whether for imitation, John 13:15; Jas. 5:10, or for warning, Heb. 4:11; 2 Pet. 2:6, RV, example. See EXAMPLE.

ENSLAVED

douloō (δουλόω, 1402), "to make a slave of," is rendered "enslaved" (to much wine) in Titus 2:3, RV, for KJV, given to. See BONDAGE.

ENSNARE

pagideuō (παγιδεύω, 3802), "to entrap, lay snares for" (from *pagis*, "anything which fixes or grips," hence, "a snare"), is used in Matt. 22:15, of the efforts of the Pharisees to "entrap" the Lord in His speech, KJV, "entangle." See ENTANGLE.

For **ENSUE** see PURSUE

ENTANGLE

1. *pagideuō*: see ENSNARE.

2. *emplekō* (ἐμπλέκω, 1707), "to weave in" (*en*, "in," *plekō*, "to weave"), hence, metaphorically, to be involved, entangled in, is used in the passive voice in 2 Tim. 2:4, "entangleth himself;" 2 Pet. 2:20, "are entangled." In the Sept., Prov. 28:18.

3. *enechō* (ἐνέχω, 1758), "to hold in," is said (a) of being "entangled" in a yoke of bondage, such as Judaism, Gal. 5:1. Some mss. have the word in 2 Thess. 1:4, the most authentic have *anechō*, "to endure"; (b) with the meaning to set oneself against, be urgent against, said of the plotting of Herodias against John the Baptist, Mark 6:19, RV, "set herself against," KJV, "had a quarrel against"; of the effort of the scribes and Pharisees to provoke the Lord to say something which would provide them with a ground of accusation against Him, Luke 11:53, RV, "to press upon," marg., "to set themselves vehemently against," KJV, "to urge."

ENTERTAIN

xenizō (ξενίζω, 3579) signifies (a) "to receive as a guest" (*xenos*, "a guest") rendered "entertained" in Acts 28:7, RV, for KJV, "lodged"; in Heb. 13:2, "have entertained"; (b) "to be astonished by the strangeness of a thing," Acts 17:20; 1 Pet. 4:4, 12. See STRANGE (think).

Note: In Heb. 13:2 (first part), *philoxenia*, lit., "love of strangers" (*phileō*, "to love," and *xenos*, "a stranger or guest"), is translated "to show love to," RV, for KJV, "entertain." See HOSPITALITY.

ENTICE, ENTICING

A. Verb.

deleazō (δελεάζω, 1185), primarily, "to lure by a bait" (from *delear*, "a bait"), is used metaphorically in Jas. 1:14, of the "enticement" of lust; in 2 Pet. 2:14, of seducers, RV, "enticing," for KJV, "beguiling"; in v. 18, RV, "entice (in)," for KJV, "allure (through)."

B. Adjective.

peithos (πειθός, 3981), "apt to persuade" (from *peithō*, "to persuade"), is used in 1 Cor. 2:4, KJV, "enticing," RV, "persuasive."

Note: In Col. 2:4, *pithanologia*, "persuasive speech" (from *pithanos*, "persuasive, plausible," akin to the above, and *logos*, "speech"), is rendered "enticing" in the KJV (RV, "persuasiveness of.") It signifies the employment of plausible arguments, in contrast to demonstration. Cf. *eulogia*, "fair speech," Rom. 16:18, i.e., "nice style."

ENTIRE

holoklēros (ὁλόκληρος, 3648), "complete, sound in every part" (*holos*, "whole," *klēros*, "a lot," i.e., with all that has fallen by lot), is used ethically in 1 Thess. 5:23, indicating that every grace present in Christ should be manifested in the believer; so Jas. 1:4. In the Sept. the word is used, e.g., of a "full" week, Lev. 23:15; of altar stones unhewn, Deut. 27:6 and Josh. 8:31; of a "full-grown" vine tree, useless for work, Ezek. 15:5; of the "sound" condition of a sheep, Zech. 11:16.

The corresponding noun *holoklēria* is used in Acts 3:16, "perfect soundness." The synonymous word *teleios*, used also in Jas. 1:4, "perfect," indicates the development of every grace into maturity.

The Heb. *shalom*, "peace," is derived from a root meaning "wholeness." See, e.g., Isa. 42:19, marg., "made perfect," for text, "at peace"; cf. 26:3. Cf. also Col. 1:28 with 2 Pet. 3:14.

For **ENTREAT, to request**, see INTREAT;
for ENTREATY see INTREATY

ENVY, ENVYING

A. Noun.

phthonos (φθόνος, 5355), "envy," is the feeling of displeasure produced by witnessing or hearing of the advantage or prosperity of others; this evil sense always attaches to this word, Matt. 27:18; Mark 15:10; Rom. 1:29; Gal. 5:21; Phil. 1:15; 1 Tim. 6:4; Titus 3:3; 1 Pet. 2:1; so in Jas. 4:5, where the question is rhetorical and strongly remonstrative, signifying that the Spirit (or spirit) which God made to dwell in us was certainly not so bestowed that we should be guilty of "envy."

Note: Zēlos, "zeal or jealousy," translated "envy" in the KJV, in Acts 13:45; Rom. 13:13; 1 Cor. 3:3; 2 Cor. 12:20; Jas. 3:14, 16, is to be distinguished from *phthonos*, and, apart from the meanings "zeal" and "indignation," is always translated "jealousy" in the RV. The distinction lies in this, that "envy" desires to deprive another of what he has, "jealousy" desires to have the same or the same sort of thing for itself See FERVENT, INDIGNATION, JEALOUSY, ZEAL.

B. Verbs.

1. *phthoneō* (φθονέω, 5354), "to envy" (akin to A.), is used in Gal. 5:26.

2. *zēloō* (ζηλόω, 2206) denotes "to be zealous, moved with jealousy," Acts 7:9 and 17:5, RV, "moved with jealousy" (KJV, "moved with envy"); both have "envieth" in 1 Cor. 13:4. See the *Note* under A. See AFFECT, COVET, DESIRE, JEALOUS, ZEALOUS.

EPHPHATHA

Note: Ephphatha is an Aramaic word signifying "to open," used in the imperative mood, "be opened," Mark 7:34; while the application in this case was to the ears, the tongue was remedially affected.

EPILEPTIC

selēniazomai (σεληνιάζομαι, 4583), lit., "to be moon struck" (from *selēnē*, "the moon"), is used in the passive voice with active significance, RV, "epileptic," for KJV, "lunatick," Matt. 4:24; 17:15; the corresponding English word is "lunatic." Epilepsy was supposed to be influenced by the moon.

EPISTLE

epistolē (ἐπιστολή, 1992), primarily "a message" (from *epistellō*, "to send to"), hence, "a letter, an epistle," is used in the singular, e.g., Acts 15:30; in the plural, e.g., Acts 9:2; 2 Cor. 10:10. "Epistle is a less common word for a letter. A letter affords a writer more freedom, both in subject and expression, than does a formal treatise. A letter is usually occasional, that is, it is written in consequence of some circumstance which requires to be dealt with promptly. The style of a letter depends largely on the occasion that calls it forth." "A broad line is to be drawn between the letter and the epistle. The one is essentially a spontaneous product dominated throughout by the image of the reader, his sympathies and interests, instinct also with the writer's own soul: it is virtually one half of an imaginary dialogue, the suppressed responses of the other party shaping the course of what is actually written .... the other has a general aim, addressing all and sundry whom it may concern: it is like a public speech and looks towards publication" (J. v. Bartlet, in *Hastings' Bib. Dic.*).

In 2 Pet. 3:16 the apostle includes the Epistles of Paul as part of the God-breathed Scriptures.

ERR

1. *planaō* (πλανάω, 4105), in the active voice, signifies "to cause to wander, lead astray, deceive" (*planē*, "a wandering"; cf. Eng., "planet"); in the passive voice, "to be led astray, to err." It is translated "err," in Matt. 22:29; Mark 12:24, 27; Heb. 3:10; Jas. 1:16 (KJV, "do not err," RV, "be not deceived"); 5:19. See DECEIVE, SEDUCE, WANDER, WAY, *Note* (4).

2. *apoplanaō* (ἀποπλανάω, 635), "to cause to wander away from, to lead astray from" (*apo*, "from," and No. 1), is used metaphorically of leading into error, Mark 13:22, KJV, "seduce," RV "lead astray"; 1 Tim. 6:10, in the passive voice, KJV, "have erred," RV, "have been led astray." See SEDUCE.

3. *astocheō* (ἀστοχέω, 795), "to miss the mark, fail" (*a*, negative, *stochos*, "a mark"), is used only in the Pastoral Epistles, 1 Tim. 1:6, "having swerved"; 6:21 and 2 Tim. 2:18, "have erred."

ERROR

1. *planē* (πλάνη, 4106), akin to *planaō* (see ERR, No. 1), "a wandering, a forsaking of the right path," see Jas. 5:20, whether in doctrine, 2 Pet. 3:17; 1 John 4:6, or in morals, Rom. 1:27; 2 Pet. 2:18; Jude 11, though, in Scripture, doctrine and morals are never divided by any sharp line. See also Matt. 27:64, where it is equivalent to 'fraud.'" "Errors" in doctrine are not infrequently the effect of relaxed morality, and vice versa.

In Eph. 4:14 the RV has "wiles of error," for KJV, "they lie in wait to deceive"; in 1 Thess. 2:3, RV, "error," for KJV, "deceit"; in 2 Thess. 2:11, RV, "a working of error," for KJV, "strong delusion." See DECEIT. Cf. *planētēs*, "a wandering," Jude 13, and the adjective *planos*, "leading astray, deceiving, a deceiver."

2. *agnoēma* (ἀγνόημα, 51), "a sin of ignorance" (cf. *agnoia*, "ignorance," and *agnoeō*, "to be ignorant"), is used in the plural in Heb. 9:7.

ESCAPE

A. Verbs.

1. *pheugō* (φεύγω, 5343), "to flee" (Lat., *fuga*, "flight," etc.; cf. Eng., "fugitive, subterfuge"), is rendered "escape" in Matt. 23:33; Heb. 11:34. See FLEE.

2. *apopheugō* (ἀποφεύγω, 668), "to flee away from" (*apo*, "from," and No. 1), is used in 2 Pet. 1:4; 2:18, 20.

3. *diapheugō* (διαφεύγω, 1309), lit., "to flee through," is used of the "escaping" of prisoners from a ship, Acts 27:42. For the word in v. 44, see No. 5.

4. *ekpheugō* (ἐκφεύγω, 1628), "to flee out of a place" (*ek*, "out of," and No. 1), is said of the "escape" of prisoners, Acts 16:27; of Sceva's sons, "fleeing" from the demoniac, 19:16; of Paul's escape from Damascus, 2 Cor. 11:33; elsewhere with reference to the judgments of God, Luke 21:36; Rom. 2:3; Heb. 2:3; 12:25; 1 Thess. 5:3. See FLEE.

5. *diasōzō* (διασώζω, 1295), in the active voice, "to bring safely through a danger" (*dia*, "through," intensive, *sōzō*, "to save"), to make completely whole, to heal, Luke 7:3; to bring "safe," Acts 23:24; "to save," 27:43; in the passive voice, Matt. 14:36, "were made whole"; 1 Pet. 3:20. It is also used in the passive voice, signifying "to escape," said of shipwrecked mariners, Acts 27:44; 28:1, 4. See HEAL, SAFE, SAVE.

Note: Exerchomai, "to come or go out of a place," is rendered, "He escaped," in John 10:39, KJV, an unsuitable translation, both in meaning and in regard to the circumstances of the Lord's departure from His would-be captors. The RV "went forth" is both accurate and appropriate to the dignity of the Lord's actions.

B. Noun.

ekbasis (ἔκβασις, 1545), "a way out" (*ek*, "out," *bainō*, "to go"), denotes (a) "an escape," 1 Cor. 10:13, used with the definite article and translated "the way of escape," as afforded by God in case of temptation; (b) "an issue or result," Heb. 13:7. See END. Cf. *ekbainō*, "to go out," Heb. 11:15 (some mss. have *exerchomai*).

ESCHEW

ekklinō (ἐκκλίνω, 1578), "to turn aside" (*ek*, "from," *klinō*, "to turn, bend"), is used metaphorically (a) of leaving the right path, Rom. 3:12, RV, "turned aside," for KJV, "gone out of the way"; (b) of turning away from divisionmakers, and errorists, 16:17, RV, "turn away from"; (c) of turning away from evil, 1 Pet. 3:11, RV, "turn away from," KJV, "eschew." In the Sept. the verb is frequently used of declining or swerving from God's ways, e.g., Job 23:11; Ps. 44:18; 119:51, 157.

ESPOUSED

1. *harmozō* (ἁρμόζω, 718), "to fit, join" (from *hamnos*, "a joint, joining"; the root *ar-*, signifying "to fit," is in evidence in various languages; cf. *arthron*, "a joint," *arithmos*, "a number," etc.), is used in the middle voice, of marrying or giving in marriage; in 2 Cor. 11:2 it is rendered "espoused," metaphorically of the relationship established between Christ and the local church, through the apostle's instrumentality. The thought may be that of "fitting" or "joining" to one husband, the middle voice expressing the apostle's interest or desire in doing so.

2. *mnēsteuō* (μνηστεύω, 3423), "to woo and win, to espouse or promise in marriage," is used in the passive voice in Matt. 1:18; Luke 1:27; 2:5, all with reference to the Virgin Mary, RV, "betrothed," for KJV, "espoused," in each case. See BETROTH.

ESTATE, STATE

1. *euschēmōn* (εὐσχήμων, 2158), signifying "elegant, graceful, comely" (*eu*, "well," *schēma*, "figure, fashion"), is used (a) in a moral sense, seemly, becoming, 1 Cor. 7:35; (b) in a physical sense, comely, 1 Cor. 12:24; (c) with reference to social degree, influential, a meaning developed in later Greek, and rendered of "honorable estate" in the RV of Mark 15:43; Acts 13:50; 17:12 (for KJV, "honorable"). See COMELINESS, HONORABLE.

2. *tapeinōsis* (ταπείνωσις, 5014) denotes "abasement, humiliation, low estate" (from *tapeinos*, "lowly"), Luke 1:48, "low estate"; Acts 8:33, "humiliation"; Phil. 3:21, RV, "of humiliation," for KJV, "vile"; Jas. 1:10, "is made low," lit., "in his low estate. See HUMILIATION, LOW, VILE.

3. *hupsos* (ὕψος, 5311), signifying "height," is rendered "(in his) high estate," Jas. 1:9, RV, for KJV, "in that he is exalted"; "on high," Luke 1:78; 24:49; Eph. 4:8; "height," Eph. 3:18; Rev. 21:16. See EXALT, HIGH.

Notes: (1) In Acts 22:5, *presbuterion*, "presbytery, a body of elders," is translated "estate of the elders," lit., "the presbytery," i.e., the Sanhedrin. (2) In Col. 4:7 the plural of the definite article with the preposition *kata*, and the singular personal pronoun with *panta*, "all," is rendered "all my state," KJV, RV, "all my affairs"; in v. 8 the preposition *peri*, with the personal pronoun, lit., "the things concerning us," is translated "our estate," i.e., "how we fare"; so in Phil. 2:19-20, "your state," i.e., "your condition." (3) In Mark 6:21 *prōtos*, lit., "first," is rendered "chief estates," KJV, RV, "the chief men," i.e., the men to whom belongs the dignity. (4) In Rom. 12:16 *tapeinos*, in the plural with the artide, lit., "the lowly," is translated "men of low estate," KJV, RV, "things that are lowly." (S) In Jude 6 *archē*, "principality," RV, KJV has "first estate," (6) For "last state" see LAST.

ESTEEM

1. *hēgeomai* (ἡγέομαι, 2233) signifies "to lead"; then, "to lead before the mind, to suppose, consider, esteem"; translated "esteem" in Phil. 2:3, KJV, RV, "counting"; in 1 Thess. 5:13, "esteem"; in Heb. 11:26, KJV, "esteeming," RV, "accounting."

2. *krinō* (κρίνω, 2919) signifies "to separate, choose"; then, "to approve, esteem"; translated "esteemeth" in Rom. 14:5 (twice), said of days; here the word "alike" (KJV) is rightly omitted in the RV, the meaning being that every day is especially regarded as sacred.

3. *logizomai* (λογίζομαι, 3049), "to reckon," is translated "esteemeth" in Rom. 14:14 (RV, "accounteth").

Notes: (1) In 1 Cor. 6:4, KJV, *exoutheneō*, "to set at nought," is rendered "are least esteemed"; the meaning is that judges in the world's tribunals have no place (are not of account) in the church. (2) In the KJV marg. of 1 Pet. 2:17, *timaō*, "to honor," is rendered "esteem." (3) For "highly esteemed," Luke 16:15, KJV, see EXALT, B.

ETERNAL

1. *aiōn* (αἰών, 165), "an age," is translated "eternal" in Eph. 3:11, lit., "(purpose) of the ages" (marg.), and 1 Tim. 1:17, lit. "(king) of the ages" (marg.). See AGE.

2. *aiōnios* (αἰώνιος, 166) "describes duration, either undefined but not endless, as in Rom. 16:25; 2 Tim. 1:9; Titus 1:2; or undefined because endless as in Rom. 16:26, and the other sixty-six places in the NT.

"The predominant meaning of *aiōnios*, that in which it is used everywhere in the NT, save the places noted above, may be seen in 2 Cor. 4:18, where it is set in contrast with *proskairos*, lit., 'for a season,' and in Philem. 15, where only in the NT it is used without a noun. Moreover it is used of persons and things which are in their nature endless, as, e.g., of God, Rom. 16:26; of His power, 1 Tim. 6:16, and of His glory, 1 Pet. 5:10; of the Holy Spirit, Heb. 9:14; of the redemption effected by Christ, Heb. 9:12, and of the consequent salvation of men, 5:9, as well as of His future rule, 2 Pet. 1:11, which is elsewhere declared to be without end, Luke 1:33; of the life received by those who believe in Christ, John 3:16, concerning whom He said, 'they shall never perish,' 10:28, and of the resurrection body, 2 Cor. 5:1, elsewhere said to be 'immortal,' 1 Cor. 15:53, in which that life will be finally realized, Matt. 25:46; Titus 1:2.

"*Aiōnios* is also used of the sin that 'hath never forgiveness,' Mark 3:29, and of the judgment of God, from which there is no appeal, Heb. 6:2, and of the fire, which is one of its instruments, Matt. 18:8; 25:41; Jude 7, and which is elsewhere said to be 'unquenchable,' Mark 9:43.

"The use of *aiōnios* here shows that the punishment referred to in 2 Thess. 1:9, is no temporary, but final, and, accordingly, the phraseology shows that its purpose is not remedial but retributive."

3. *aidios* (ἀΐδιος, 126); see EVERLASTING.

EUNUCH

A. Noun.

eunouchos (εὐνοῦχος, 2135) denotes (a) "an emasculated man, a eunuch," Matt. 19:12; (b) in the 3rd instance in that verse, "one naturally incapacitated for, or voluntarily abstaining from, wedlock"; (c) one such, in a position of high authority in a court, "a chamberlain," Acts 8:27-39.

B. Verb.

eunouchizō (εὐνουχίζω, 2134), "to make a eunuch" (from A), is used in Matt. 19:12, as under (b) in A; and in the passive voice, "were made eunuchs," probably an allusion by the

Lord to the fact that there were eunuchs in the courts of the Herods, as would be well known to His hearers.

EVANGELIST

euangelistēs (εὐαγγελιστής, 2099), lit., "a messenger of good" (*eu*, "well," *angelos*, "a messenger"), denotes a "preacher of the gospel," Acts 21:8; Eph. 4:11, which makes clear the distinctiveness of the function in the churches; 2 Tim. 4:5. Cf. *euangelizō*, "to proclaim glad tidings," and *euangelion*, "good news, gospel." Missionaries are "evangelists," as being essentially preachers of the gospel.

EVEN (Noun), EVENING, EVENTIDE

A. Nouns.

1. *hespera* (ἑσπέρα, 2073), properly, the feminine of the adjective *hesperos*, "of, or at, evening, western" (Lat., *vesper*, Eng., "vespers"), is used as a noun in Luke 24:29; Acts 4:3, "eventide"; 28:23. Some mss. have the word in 20:15, "in the evening (we touched)," instead of *hetera*, "next (day)."

2. *opsia* (ὀψία, 3798), the feminine of the adjective *opsios*, "late," used as a noun, denoting "evening," with *hora*, "understood" (see No. 1), is found seven times in Matthew, five in Mark, two in John, and in these places only in the NT (some mss. have it in Mark 11:11, see B). The word really signifies the "late evening," the latter of the two "evenings" as reckoned by the Jews, the first from 3 p.m. to sunset, the latter after sunset; this is the usual meaning. It is used, however, of both, e.g., Mark 1:32 (cf. *opsimos*, "latter," said of rain, Jas. 5:7).

B. Adverb.

opse (ὀψέ, 3796), "long after, late, late in the day, at evening" (in contrast to *proi*, "early," e.g., Matt. 20:1), is used practically as a noun in Mark 11:11, lit., "the hour being at eventide"; 11:19; 13:35; in Matt. 28:1 it is rendered "late on," RV, for KJV, "in the end of." Here, however, the meaning seems to be "after," a sense in which the word was used by late Greek writers. In the Sept., Gen. 24:11; Exod. 30:8; Jer. 2:23; Isa. 5:11.

Note: In Luke 12:38 some mss. have the adjective *hesperinos*, "of the evening" (see A, No. 1), lit., "in the evening watch."

EVER, FOREVER, EVERMORE

A. Adverbs.

1. *pantote* (πάντοτε, 3842), "at all times, always" (akin to *pas*, "all"), is translated "ever" in Luke 15:31; John 18:20; 1 Thess. 4:17; 5:15; 2 Tim. 3:7; Heb. 7:25; "evermore" in John 6:34; in 1 Thess. 5:16, RV, "alway," for KJV, "evermore." It there means "on all occasions," as, e.g., in 1 Thess. 1:2; 3:6; 5:15; 2 Thess. 1:3, 11; 2:13. See ALWAYS.

2. *aei* (ἀεί, 104), "ever," is used (a) of continuous time, signifying "unceasingly, perpetually," Acts 7:51; 2 Cor. 4:11; 6:10; Titus 1:12; Heb. 3:10; (b) of successive occurrences, signifying "on every occasion," 1 Pet. 3:15; 2 Pet. 1:12. Some texts have the word in Mark 15:8. See ALWAYS.

Note: The adjective *diēnekēs*, "unbroken, continuous," is used in a phrase with *eis*, "unto," and the article, signifying "perpetually, for ever," Heb. 7:3; 10:1, 12, 14.

B. Phrases.

The following phrases are formed in connection with *aiōn*, "an age": they are idiomatic expressions betokening undefined periods and are not to be translated literally: (a) *eis aiōna*, lit., "unto an age," Jude 13, "for ever"; (b) *eis ton aiōna*, lit., "unto the age," "for ever" (or, with a negative, "never"), Matt. 21:19; Mark 3:29; 11:14; Luke 1:55; John 4:14; 6:51, 58; 8:35 (twice), 51-52; 10:28; 11:26; 12:34; 13:8; 14:16; 1 Cor. 8:13; 2 Cor. 9:9; Heb. 5:6; 6:20; 7:17, 21, 24, 28; 1 Pet. 1:25; 1 John 2:17; 2 John 2; (c) *eis tous aiōnas*, lit., "unto the ages," "for ever," Matt. 6:13 (KJV only); Luke 1:33; Rom. 1:25; 9:5; 11:36; 16:27 (some mss. have the next phrase here); 2 Cor. 11:31; Heb. 13:8; (d) *eis tous aiōnas tōn aiōnōn*, lit. "unto the ages of the ages," "for ever and ever," or "for evermore," Gal. 1:5; Phil. 4:20; 1 Tim. 1:17; 2 Tim. 4:18; Heb. 13:21; 1 Pet. 4:11; 5:11 [(c) in some mss.]; Rev. 1:6 [(c) in some mss.]; 1:18, "for evermore"; 4:9-10; 5:13; 7:12; 10:6; 11:15; 15:7; 19:3; 20:10; 22:5; (e) *eis aiōnas aiōnōn*, lit., "unto ages of ages," "for ever and ever," Rev. 14:11; (f) *eis ton aiōna tou aiōnos*, lit., "unto the age of the age," "for ever and ever," Heb. 1:8; (g) *tou aiōnos tōn aiōnōn*, lit., "of the age of the ages," "for ever and ever," Eph. 3:21; (h) *eis pantas tous aiōnas*, lit., "unto all the ages," Jude 25 ("for evermore," RV; "ever," KJV); (i) *eis hēmeran aiōnos*, lit., "unto a day of an age," "for ever," 2 Pet. 3:18.

EVERLASTING

1. *aiōnios* (αἰώνιος, 166): see ETERNAL.

2. *aidios* (ἀΐδιος, 126) denotes "everlasting" (from *aei*, "ever"), Rom. 1:20, RV, "everlasting," for KJV, "eternal"; Jude 6, KJV and RV "everlasting." *Aiōnios*, should always be translated "eternal" and *aidios*, "everlasting." "While *aiōnios* ... negatives the end either of a space of time or of unmeasured time, and is used chiefly where something future is spoken of, *aidios* excludes interruption and lays stress upon permanence and unchangeableness" (Cremer).

EVIL, EVIL-DOER

A. Adjectives.

1. *kakos* (κακός, 2556) stands for "whatever is evil in character, base," in distinction (wherever the distinction is observable) from *ponēros* (see No. 2), which indicates "what is evil in influence and effect, malignant." *Kakos* is the wider term and often covers the meaning of *ponēros*. *Kakos* is antithetic to *kalos*, "fair, advisable, good in character," and to *agathos*, "beneficial, useful, good in act"; hence it denotes what

is useless, incapable, bad; *poneros* is essentially antithetic to *chrēstos*, "kind, gracious, serviceable"; hence it denotes what is destructive, injurious, evil. As evidence that *ponēros* and *kakos* have much in common, though still not interchangeable, each is used of thoughts, cf. Matt. 15:19 with Mark 7:21; of speech, Matt. 5:11 with 1 Pet. 3:10; of actions, 2 Tim. 4:18 with 1 Thess. 5:15; of man, Matt. 18:32 with 24:48.

The use of *kakos* may be broadly divided as follows: (a) of what is morally or ethically "evil," whether of persons, e.g., Matt. 21:41; 24:48; Phil. 3:2; Rev. 2:2, or qualities, emotions, passions, deeds, e.g., Mark 7:21; John 18:23, 30; Rom. 1:30; 3:8; 7:19, 21; 13:4; 14:20; 16:19; 1 Cor. 13:5; 2 Cor. 13:7; 1 Thess. 5:15; 1 Tim. 6:10; 2 Tim. 4:14; 1 Pet. 3:9, 12; (b) of what is injurious, destructive, baneful, pernicious, e.g., Luke 16:25; Acts 16:28; 28:5; Titus 1:12; Jas. 3:8; Rev. 16:2, where *kakos* and *ponēros* come in that order, "noisome and grievous." See B, No. 3. For compounds of *kakos*, see below.

2. *ponēros* (πονηρός, 4190), akin to *ponos*, "labor, toil," denotes "evil that causes labor, pain, sorrow, malignant evil" (see No. 1); it is used (a) with the meaning bad, worthless, in the physical sense, Matt. 7:17-18; in the moral or ethical sense, "evil," wicked; of persons, e.g., Matt. 7:11; Luke 6:45; Acts 17:5; 2 Thess. 3:2; 2 Tim. 3:13; of "evil" spirits, e.g., Matt. 12:45; Luke 7:21; Acts 19:12-13, 15-16; of a generation, Matt. 12:39, 45; 16:4; Luke 11:29; of things, e.g., Matt. 5:11; 6:23; 20:15; Mark 7:22; Luke 11:34; John 3:19; 7:7; Acts 18:14; Gal. 1:4; Col. 1:21; 1 Tim. 6:4; 2 Tim. 4:18; Heb. 3:12; 10:22; Jas. 2:4; 4:16; 1 John 3:12; 2 John 11; 3 John 10; (b) with the meaning toilsome, painful, Eph. 5:16; 6:13; Rev. 16:2. Cf. *ponēria*, "iniquity, wickedness." For its use as a noun see B, No. 2.

3. *phaulos* (φαῦλος, 5337) primarily denotes "slight, trivial, blown about by every wind"; then, "mean, common, bad," in the sense of being worthless, paltry or contemptible, belonging to a low order of things; in John 5:29, those who have practiced "evil" things, RV, "ill" (*phaula*), are set in contrast to those who have done good things (*agatha*); the same contrast is presented in Rom. 9:11 and 2 Cor. 5:10, in each of which the most authentic mss. have *phaulos* for *kakos*; he who practices "evil" things (RV, "ill") hates the light, John 3:20; jealousy and strife are accompanied by "every vile deed," Jas. 3:16. It is used as a noun in Titus 2:8 (see B, No. 4). See BAD, ILL, VILE.

B. Nouns.

1. *kakia* (κακία, 2549), primarily, "badness" in quality (akin to A, No. 1), denotes (a) "wickedness, depravity, malignity," e.g., Acts 8:22, "wickedness"; Rom. 1:29, "maliciousness"; in Jas. 1:21, KJV, "naughtiness"; (b) "the evil of trouble, affliction," Matt. 6:34, only, and here alone translated "evil." See MALICE, MALICIOUSNESS, WICKEDNESS.

2. *ponēros* (πονηρός, 4190), the adjective (A, No. 2), is used as a noun, (a) of Satan as the "evil" one, Matt. 5:37; 6:13; 13:19, 38; Luke 11:4 (in some texts); John 17:15; Eph. 6:16; 2 Thess. 3:3; 1 John 2:13-14; 3:12; 5:18-19; (b) of human beings, Matt. 5:45; (probably v. 39); 13:49; 22:10; Luke 6:35; 1 Cor. 5:13; (c) neuter, "evil (things)," Matt. 9:4; 12:35; Mark 7:23; Luke 3:19; "that which is evil," Luke 6:45; Rom. 12:9; Acts 28:21, "harm."

3. *kakon* (κακός, 2556), the neuter of A, No. 1, is used with the article, as a noun, e.g., Acts 23:9; Rom. 7:21; Heb. 5:14; in the plural, "evil things," e.g., 1 Cor. 10:6; 1 Tim. 6:10, "all kinds of evil," RV.

4. *phaulon* (φαῦλον, 5337), the neuter of A, No. 3, is used as a noun in Titus 2:8.

5. *kakopoios* (κακοποιός, 2555), properly the masculine gender of the adjective, denotes an "evil-doer" (*kakon*, "evil," *poieō*, "to do"), 1 Pet. 2:12, 14; 4:15; in some mss. in 3:16 and John 18:30 (so the KJV). For a synonymous word see *Note* (1). Cf. the verb below. In the Sept., Prov. 12:4; 24:19. See MALEFACTOR.

Notes: (1) *Kakourgos*, "an evil-worker" (*kakon*, "evil," *ergon*, "a work"), is translated "evil-doer" in 2 Tim. 2:9, KJV (RV, "malefactor"). Cf. Luke 23:32-33, 39.

(2) *Adikēma*, "an injustice" (*a*, negative, *dikaios*, "just"), is translated "evil-doing," in Acts 24:20, KJV, RV, "wrong-doing." See INIQUITY, WRONG.

C. Verbs.

1. *kakoō* (κακόω, 2559), "to ill-treat" (akin to A, No. 1), is rendered "to entreat evil" in Acts 7:6, 19; "made (them) evil affected," 14:2. See AFFECT, AFFLICT, HARM, HURT, VEX.

2. *kakopoieō* (κακοποιέω, 2554) signifies "to do evil" (cf. B, No. 5), Mark 3:4 (RV, "to do harm"); so, Luke 6:9; in 3 John 11, "doeth evil"; in 1 Pet. 3:17, "evil doing." See HARM.

Note: Cf. *kakologeō*, "to speak evil" (see CURSE); *kakopatheō*, "to endure evil" (see ENDURE, SUFFER); *kakopatheia*, "suffering affliction" (see SUFFER); *kakoucheo*, "to suffer adversity" (see SUFFER).

D. Adverb.

kakōs (κακῶς, 2560), "badly, evilly," akin to A, No. 1, is used in the physical sense, "to be sick," e.g., Matt. 4:24; Mark 1:32, 34; Luke 5:31 (see DISEASE). In Matt. 21:41 this adverb is used with the adjective, "He will miserably destroy those miserable men," more lit., "He will evilly destroy those men (evil as they are)," with stress on the adjective; (b) in the moral sense, "to speak evilly," John 18:23; Acts 23:5; to ask evilly, Jas. 4:3. See AMISS, GRIEVOUSLY, SICK.

EVIL SPEAKING

1. *blasphēmia* (βλασφημία, 988) is translated "evil speaking" in Eph. 4:31, KJV (RV, railing). See BLASPHEMY.

2. *katalalia* (καταλαλία, 2636), "evil speaking, 1 Pet. 2:1.

EXACT (Verb)

1. *prassō* (πράσσω, 4238), "to do, to practice," also has the meaning of "transacting," or "managing in the matter of payment, to exact, to get money from a person," Luke 3:13 (RV, "extort"). Cf. the English idiom "to do a person in." This verb is rendered "required," in 19:23.

2. *sukophanteō* (συκοφαντέω, 4811), "to accuse falsely," Luke 3:14, has its other meaning, "to exact wrongfully," in 19:8. See ACCUSE.

EXACT, EXACTLY

akribesteron (ἀκριβέστερον, 197), the comparative degree of *akribos*, "accurately, carefully," is used in Acts 18:26, KJV, "more perfectly," RV, "more carefully"; 23:15, KJV, "more perfectly," RV, "more exactly"; so v. 20; 24:22, KJV, "more perfect," RV, "more exact" (lit., "knowing more exactly"). See PERFECTLY.

Cf. *akribeia*, "precision, exactness," Acts 22:3, and *akriboō*, "to learn carefully, to enquire with exactness," Matt. 2:7, 16.

EXALT, EXALTED

A. Verbs.

1. *hupsoō* (ὑψόω, 5312), "to lift up" (akin to *hupsos*, "height"), is used (a) literally of the "lifting" up of Christ in His crucifixion, John 3:14; 8:28; 12:32, 34; illustratively, of the serpent of brass, John 3:14; (b) figuratively, of spiritual privileges bestowed on a city, Matt. 11:23; Luke 10:15; of "raising" to dignity and happiness, Luke 1:52; Acts 13:17; of haughty self-exaltation, and, contrastingly, of being "raised" to honor, as a result of self-humbling, Matt. 23:12; Luke 14:11; 18:14; of spiritual "uplifting" and revival, Jas. 4:10; 1 Pet. 5:6; of bringing into the blessings of salvation through the gospel, 2 Cor. 11:7; (c) with a combination of the literal and metaphorical, of the "exaltation" of Christ by God the Father, Acts 2:33; 5:31.

2. *huperupsoō* (ὑπερυψόω, 5251), "to exalt highly" (*huper*, "over," and No. 1), is used of Christ, as in No. 1, (c), in Phil. 2:9.

3. *epairō* (ἐπαίρω, 1869), "to lift up" (*epi*, "up," *airō*, "to raise"), is said (a) literally, of a sail, Acts 27:40; hands, Luke 24:50; 1 Tim. 2:8; heads, Luke 21:28; eyes, Matt. 17:8, etc.; (b) metaphorically, of "exalting" oneself, being "lifted up" with pride, 2 Cor. 10:5; 11:20.

4. *huperairō* (ὑπεραίρω, 5229), "to raise over" (*huper*, "above," and *airō*, see No. 3), is used in the middle voice, of "exalting" oneself exceedingly, 2 Cor. 12:7; 2 Thess. 2:4.

B. Adjective.

hupsēlos (ὑψηλός, 5308), "high, lofty," is used metaphorically in Luke 16:15, as a noun with the article, RV, "that which is exalted," KJV, "that which is highly esteemed." See ESTEEM, HIGH.

Note: For Jas. 1:9, RV, "in his high estate," see ESTATE, No. 3.

EXAMINATION, EXAMINE

A. Noun.

anakrisis (ἀνάκρισις, 351), from *ana*, "up or through," and *krinō*, "to distinguish," was a legal term among the Greeks, denoting the preliminary investigation for gathering evidence for the information of the judges, Acts 25:26.

B. Verbs.

1. *anakrinō* (ἀνακρίνω, 350), "to examine, investigate," is used (a) of searching or enquiry, Acts 17:11; 1 Cor. 9:3; 10:25, 27; (b) of reaching a result of the enquiry, judging, 1 Cor. 2:14-15; 4:3-4; 14:24; (c) forensically, of examining by torture, Luke 23:14; Acts 4:9; 12:19; 24:8; 28:18. See DISCERN, JUDGE, SEARCH.

2. *anetazō* (ἀνετάζω, 426), "to examine judicially" (*ana*, "up," *etazō*, "to test"), is used in Acts 22:24, 29. Cf. the synonymous verb *exetazō*, "to search" or "enquire carefully," Matt. 2:8; 10:11; John 21:12.

3. *dokimazō* (δοκιμάζω, 1381), "to prove, test, approve," is rendered "examine" in 1 Cor. 11:28, KJV (RV, prove).

4. *peirazō* (πειράζω, 3985), "to tempt, try," is rendered "examine" in 2 Cor. 13:5, KJV (RV, try). See GO, PROVE, TEMPT, TRY.

EXAMPLE

A. Nouns.

1. *deigma* (δεῖγμα, 1164), primarily "a thing shown, a specimen" (akin to *deiknumi*, "to show"), denotes an "example" given as a warning, Jude 7.

Note: The corresponding word in 2 Pet. 2:6 is No. 2.

2. *hupodeigma* (ὑπόδειγμα, 5262): see ENSAMPLE, No. 3.

3. *tupos* (τύπος, 5179): see ENSAMPLE, No. 1.

4. *hupogrammos* (ὑπογραμμός, 5261), lit., "an underwriting" (from *hupographō*, "to write under, to trace letters" for copying by scholars); hence, "a writing-copy, an example," 1 Pet. 2:21, said of what Christ left for believers, by His sufferings (not expiatory, but exemplary), that they might "follow His steps."

B. Verbs.

1. *deigmatizō* (δειγματίζω, 1165), "to make a show of, to expose" (akin to A, No. 1), is translated "to make a public example," in Matt. 1:19 (some mss. have the strengthened form

paradeigmatizō here; "put ... to an open shame," Heb. 6:6,); in Col. 2:15, "made a show of."

2. *hupodeiknumi* (ὑποδείκνυμι, 5263), primarily, "to show secretly" (*hupo*, "under," *deiknumi*, "to show"), "to show by tracing out" (akin to A, No. 2); hence, "to teach, to show by example," Acts 20:35, RV, "I gave you an example," for KJV, "I showed you." Elsewhere, "to warn," Matt. 3:7; Luke 3:7; 12:5, RV, for KJV, "forewarn"; "to show," Luke 6:47; Acts 9:16. See FOREWARN, SHOW, WARN.

EXCEED, EXCEEDING, EXCEEDINGLY

A. Verbs.

1. *huperballō* (ὑπερβάλλω, 5235), "to throw over or beyond" (*huper*, "over," *ballō*, "to throw"), is translated "exceeding" in 2 Cor. 9:14; Eph. 1:19; 2:7; "excelleth" (RV, "surpasseth") in 2 Cor. 3:10; "passeth" in Eph. 3:19 ("surpasseth" might be the meaning here). See EXCEL, SURPASS. Cf. *huperbolē*, under EXCEL, B, No. 1.

2. *perisseuō* (περισσεύω, 4052), "to be over and above, over a certain number or measure, to abound, exceed," is translated "exceed" in Matt. 5:20; 2 Cor. 3:9. See ABUNDANCE, B, No. 1.

B. Adverbs and Adverbial Phrases.

1. *lian* (λίαν, 3029), "very, exceedingly," is translated "exceeding" in Matt. 2:16 (for v. 10, see No. 2); 4:8; 8:28; Mark 9:3; Luke 23:8.

2. *sphodra* (σφόδρα, 4970), properly the neuter plural of *sphodros*, "excessive, violent" (from a root indicating restlessness), signifies "very, very much, exceedingly," Matt. 2:10; 17:6, "sore"; 17:23; 18:31, RV, "exceeding," for KJV, "very"; 19:25; 26:22; 27:54, RV, "exceedingly" for KJV, "greatly"; Mark 16:4, "very"; Luke 18:23 (ditto); Acts 6:7, RV, "exceedingly," for KJV, greatly; Rev. 16:21.

3. *sphodrōs* (σφοδρῶς, 4971), "exceedingly" (see No. 2), is used in Acts 27:18.

4. *perissōs* (περισσῶς, 4057) is used in Matt. 27:23, RV, "exceedingly," for KJV, "the more"; Mark 10:26, RV, "exceedingly," for KJV, "out of measure"; in Acts 26:11, "exceedingly." In Mark 15:14, the most authentic mss. have this word (RV, "exceedingly") for No. 5 (KJV, "the more exceedingly").

5. *perissoterōs* (περισσοτέρως, 4056), the comparative degree of No. 4, "abundantly, exceedingly" (akin to A, No. 2), Gal. 1:14, "more exceedingly"; 1 Thess. 2:17, RV, "the more exceedingly," for KJV, "the more abundantly; see ABUNDANCE, D, No. 2.

6. *huperekperissou* (ὑπερεκπερισσοῦ), (ὑπερ, 5228, and εκ, 1537, and περισσός, 4053) denotes "superabundantly" (*huper*, "over," *ek*, "from," *perissos*, "abundant"); in 1 Thess. 3:10, "exceedingly"; Eph. 3:20, "exceeding abundantly." Another form, *huperekperissōs* (*huper*, "and," *ek* and No. 4), is used in 1 Thess. 5:13 (in the best mss.), "exceeding highly." Cf. the verb *huperperisseuō*, "to abound more exceedingly," Rom. 5:21; in 2 Cor. 7:4, "I overflow (with joy)," RV, for KJV, "I am exceeding (joyful)." See ABUNDANT, D, No. 2.

Notes: (1) In Acts 7:20, the phrase "exceeding fair" (*asteios*) is, lit., "fair to God" (see marg.). (2) In Matt. 26:7, *barutimos* (*barus*, "weighty," *timē* "value"), is rendered "exceeding precious," RV, for KJV, "very precious." (3) In Mark 4:41, "they feared exceedingly" is, lit., "they feared a great fear." See FEAR. (4) For other combinations of the adverb, see GLAD, GREAT, JOYFUL, SORROWFUL, SORRY.

EXCEL, EXCELLENCY, EXCELLENT

A. Verbs.

1. *huperballō* (ὑπερβάλλω, 5235), lit., "to throw over: see EXCEED, No. 1.

2. *perisseuō* (περισσεύω, 4052), "to be over and above," is rendered "abound in 1 Cor. 14:12, RV, for KJV, excel. See ABUNDANCE, B, No. 1, and EXCEED, A, No. 2.

3. *huperechō* (ὑπερέχω, 5242), lit., "to have over" (*huper*, "over," *echō*, "to have"), is translated "excellency" in Phil. 3:8, "the surpassingness" (Moule); the phrase could be translated "the surpassing thing, which consists in the knowledge of Christ Jesus," and this is the probable meaning. This verb is used three times in Philippians, here and in 2:3; 4:7. See also Rom. 13:1; 1 Pet. 2:13. See BETTER, No. 4.

4. *diapherō* (διαφέρω, 1308), "to differ," is used in the neuter plural of the present participle with the article, in Phil. 1:10, "the things that are excellent" (marg., "the things that differ"), lit., "the excellent things."

B. Nouns.

1. *huperbolē* (ὑπερβολή, 5236), lit., "a throwing beyond," hence, "a surpassing, an excellence," is translated "excellency" in 2 Cor. 4:7, KJV; RV, "exceeding greatness." It always betokens preeminence. It is used with *kata*, "according to," in the phrase *kath' huperbolēn*, signifying "beyond measure, exceedingly," Rom. 7:13, "exceeding sinful"; in 2 Cor. 1:8, RV, "exceedingly," for KJV, "out of measure"; in Gal. 1:13, "beyond measure"; in 1 Cor. 12:31, "more excellent." In 2 Cor. 4:17, there is an expanded phrase *kath' huperbolēn eis huperbolēn*, lit., "according to a surpassing unto a surpassing," RV, "more and more exceedingly," which corrects the KJV, "a far more exceeding"; the phrase refers to "worketh," showing the surpassing degree of its operation, and not to the noun "weight" (nor does it qualify, "eternal"). In 2 Cor. 12:7, the RV has "exceeding greatness," the KJV, "abundance." See ABUNDANCE.

2. *huperochē* (ὑπεροχή, 5247), akin to A, No. 3, strictly speaking, "the act of overhanging" (*huper*, and *echō*, "to

hold") or "the thing which overhangs," hence, "superiority, preeminence," is translated "excellency (of speech)" in 1 Cor. 2:1; elsewhere, in 1 Tim. 2:2, RV, "high place," for KJV, "authority."

Note: In 1 Pet. 2:9 RV renders *aretē* (virtue) "excellencies."

C. Adjectives.

1. *megaloprepēs* (μεγαλοπρεπής, 3169) signifies "magnificent, majestic, that which is becoming to a great man" (from *megas*, "great," and *prepo*, "to be fitting or becoming"), in 2 Pet. 1:17, "excellent."

2. *diaphorōteros* (διαφορώτερος, 1313), comparative degree of *diaphoros*, "excellent," akin to A, No. 4, is used twice, in Heb. 1:4, "more excellent (name)," and 8:6, "more excellent (ministry)." For the positive degree see Rom. 12:6; Heb. 9:10.

3. *pleiōn* (πλείων, 4119), "more, greater," the comparative degree of *polus*, "much," is translated "more excellent" in Heb. 11:4, of Abel's sacrifice; *pleion* is used sometimes of that which is superior by reason of inward worth, cf. 3:3, "more (honor)"; in Matt. 6:25, of the life in comparison with meat.

4. *kratistos* (κράτιστος, 2903), "mightiest, noblest, best," the superlative degree of *kratus*, "strong" (cf. *kratos*, "strength"), is used as a title of honor and respect, "most excellent," Luke 1:3 (Theophilus was quite possibly a man of high rank); Acts 23:26; 24:3 and 26:25, RV, for KJV, "most noble."

Note: The phrase *kath' huperbolēn* (for which see B, No. 1) is translated "more excellent" in 1 Cor. 12:31.

EXCESS

1. *akrasia* (ἀκρασία, 192) lit. denotes "want of strength" (*a*, negative, *kratos*, "strength"), hence, "want of self-control, incontinence," Matt. 23:25, "excess"; 1 Cor. 7:5, "incontinency." Cf. *akratēs*, "powerless, incontinent," 2 Tim. 3:3, RV, "without self-control."

2. *anachusis* (ἀνάχυσις, 401), lit., "a pouring out, overflowing" (akin to *anacheō*, "to pour out"), is used metaphorically in 1 Pet. 4:4, "excess," said of the riotous conduct described in v. 3.

Notes: (1) *Asōtia* denotes "prodigality, profligacy, riot" (from *a*, negative, and *sōzō*, "to save"); it is translated "riot" in Eph. 5:18, RV, for KJV, "excess"; in Titus 1:6 and 1 Pet. 4:4, "riot" in KJV and RV. See RIOT. Cf. the adverb *asōtōs*, "wastefully," "in riotous living," Luke 15:13. A synonymous noun is *aselgeia*, "lasciviousness, outrageous conduct, wanton violence."

(2) In 1 Pet. 4:3, *oinophlugia*, "drunkenness, debauchery" (*oinos*, "wine," *phluō*, "to bubble up, overflow"), is rendered "excess of wine," KJV (RV, "winebibbings").

EXCLUDE

ekkleiō (ἐκκλείω, 1576), "to shut out" (*ek*, "from," *kleiō*, "to shut"), is said of glorying in works as a means of justification, Rom. 3:27; of Gentiles, who by Judaism would be "excluded" from salvation and Christian fellowship, Gal. 4:17.

EXCUSE

A. Noun.

prophasis (πρόφασις, 4392), "a pretense, pretext" (from *pro*, "before," and *phēmi*, "to say"), is translated "excuse" in John 15:22, RV, for KJV, "cloke"; "cloke in 1 Thess. 2:5. KJV and RV. See SHOW (Noun).

B. Adjective (negative).

anapologētos (ἀναπολόγητος, 379), "without excuse, inexcusable" (*a*, negative, *n*, euphonic, and *apologeomai*, see C, No. 1, below), is used, Rom. 1:20, "without excuse," of those who reject the revelation of God in creation; 2:1, RV, for KJV, "inexcusable," of the Jew who judges the Gentile.

C. Verbs.

1. *apologeomai* (ἀπολογέομαι, 626), lit., "to speak oneself off," hence "to plead for oneself," and so, in general, (a) "to defend," as before a tribunal; in Rom. 2:15, RV, "excusing them," means one "excusing" others (not themselves); the preceding phrase "one with another" signifies one person with another, not one thought with another; it may be paraphrased, "their thoughts with one another, condemning or else excusing one another"; conscience provides a moral standard by which men judge one another; (b) "to excuse" oneself, 2 Cor. 12:19; cf. B. See ANSWER.

2. *paraiteomai* (παραιτέομαι, 3868) is used in the sense of "begging off, asking to be excused or making an excuse," in Luke 14:18 (twice) and v. 19. In the first part of v. 18 the verb is used in the middle voice, "to make excuse" (acting in imagined self-interest); in the latter part and in v. 19 it is in the passive voice, "have me excused."

EXECUTE

1. *poieō* (ποιέω, 4160), "to do, to make," is thrice rendered "execute," of the Lord's authority and acts in "executing" judgment, (a) of His authority as the One to whom judgment is committed, John 5:27; (b) of the judgment which He will mete out to all transgressors at His second advent, Jude 15; (c) of the carrying out of His Word (not "work," as in the KJV) in the earth, especially regarding the nation of Israel, the mass being rejected, the remnant saved, Rom. 9:28. That He will "execute His Word finishing and cutting it short," is expressive of the summary and decisive character of His action.

2. *hierateuō* (ἱερατεύω, 2407), "to be a priest, to officiate as such," is translated "executed the priest's office," in Luke 1:8. It occurs frequently in the Sept., and in inscriptions. Cf.

hierateuma, "priesthood," 1 Pet. 2:5, 9,, *hierateia*, "a priest's office," Luke 1:9; Heb. 7:5, *hiereus*, "a priest," and *hieros*, "sacred."

For **EXECUTIONER,** Mark 6:27, see GUARD, A, No. 2

EXERCISE

A. Verbs.

1. *gumnazō* (γυμνάζω, 1128) primarily signifies "to exercise naked" (from *gumnos*, "naked"); then, generally, "to exercise, to train the body or mind" (Eng., "gymnastic"), 1 Tim. 4:7, with a view to godliness; Heb. 5:14, of the senses, so as to discern good and evil; 12:11, of the effect of chastening, the spiritual "exercise producing the fruit of righteousness"; 2 Pet. 2:14, of certain evil teachers with hearts "exercised in covetousness," RV.

2. *askeō* (ἀσκέω, 778) signifies "to form by art, to adorn, to work up raw material with skill"; hence, in general, "to take pains, endeavor, exercise by training or discipline," with a view to a conscience void of offense, Acts 24:16.

3. *poieō* (ποιέω, 4160), "to do," is translated "exerciseth" in Rev. 13:12, said of the authority of the second "Beast." Cf. EXECUTE.

Notes: The following verbs contain in translation the word "exercise" but belong to other headings: *exousiazō*, "to exercise authority over," Luke 22:25 (*exousia*, "authority"); in the first part of this verse, the verb *kurieuō*, "to be lord," is translated "exercise lordship," KJV (RV, "have lordship"); *katexousiazō*, a strengthened form of the preceding (*kata*, "down," intensive), Matt. 20:25; Mark 10:42, "exercise authority" (in the first part of these verses the synonymous verb *katakurieuō*, is rendered "lord it," RV, for KJV, "exercise dominion," and "exercise lordship," respectively); *episkopeō*, "to look over or upon" (*epi*, "over," *skopeō*, "to look"), "to care for," 1 Pet. 5:2 (absent in some mss.), RV, "exercising the oversight," for KJV "taking, etc."

B. Noun.

gumnasia (γυμνασία, 1129) primarily denotes "gymnastic exercise" (akin to A, No. 1), 1 Tim. 4:8, where the immediate reference is probably not to mere physical training for games but to discipline of the body such as that to which the apostle refers in 1 Cor. 9:27, though there may be an allusion to the practices of asceticism.

EXHORT, EXHORTATION

A. Verbs.

1. *parakaleō* (παρακαλέω, 3870), primarily, "to call to a person" (*para*, "to the side," *kaleō*, "to call"), denotes (a) "to call on, entreat"; (b) to admonish, exhort, to urge one to pursue some course of conduct (always prospective, looking to the future, in contrast to the meaning to comfort, which is retrospective, having to do with trial experienced), translated "exhort" in the RV of Phil. 4:2; 1 Thess. 4:10; Heb. 13:19, 22, for KJV, "beseech"; in 1 Tim. 5:1, for KJV, "intreat"; in 1 Thess. 5:11, for KJV, "comfort"; "exhorted" in 2 Cor. 8:6 and 12:18, for KJV, "desired"; in 1 Tim. 1:3, for KJV, "besought."

2. *paraineō* (παραινέω, 3867), primarily, "to speak of near" (*para*, "near," and *aineō*, "to tell of, speak of," then, "to recommend"), hence, "to advise, exhort, warn," is used in Acts 27:9, "admonished," and v. 22, "I exhort." See ADMONISH.

3. *protrepō* (προτρέπω, 4389), lit., "to turn forward, propel" (*pro*, "before," *trepō*, "to turn"); hence, "to impel morally, to urge forward, encourage," is used in Acts 18:27, RV, "encouraged him" (Apollos), with reference to his going into Achaia; KJV, "exhorting the disciples"; while the encouragement was given to Apollos, a letter was written to the disciples in Achaia to receive him.

B. Noun.

paraklēsis (παράκλησις, 3874), akin to A, No. 1, primarily "a calling to one's side," and so "to one's aid," hence denotes (a) an appeal, "entreaty," 2 Cor. 8:4; (b) encouragement, "exhortation," e.g., Rom. 12:8; in Acts 4:36, RV, "exhortation," for KJV, "consolation"; (c) "consolation and comfort," e.g., Rom. 15:4. See COMFORT. Cf. *paraklētos*, "an advocate, comforter."

EXIST

huparchō (ὑπάρχω, 5225), primarily, "to make a beginning" (*hupo*, "under," *archē*, "a beginning"), denotes "to be, to be in existence," involving an "existence" or condition both previous to the circumstances mentioned and continuing after it. This is important in Phil. 2:6, concerning the deity of Christ. The phrase "being (existing) in the form (*morphē*, the essential and specific form and character) of God," carries with it the two facts of the antecedent Godhood of Christ, previous to His incarnation, and the continuance of His Godhood at and after the event of His Birth (see Gifford, on the Incarnation, pp. 11, sqq.). It is translated "exist" in 1 Cor. 11:18, RV, for KJV, "there be." Cf. Luke 16:14; 23:50; Acts 2:30; 3:2; 17:24; 22:3 etc. See GOODS, LIVE, POSSESS, SUBSTANCE.

EXORCIST

exorkistēs (ἐξορκιστής, 1845) denotes (a) "one who administers an oath"; (b) "an exorcist" (akin to *exorkizō*, "to adjure," from *orkos*, "an oath"), "one who employs a formula of conjuration for the expulsion of demons," Acts 19:13. The practice of "exorcism" was carried on by strolling Jews, who used their power in the recitation of particular names.

EXPECT, EXPECTATION

A. Verbs.

1. *ekdechomai* (ἐκδέχομαι, 1551), lit. and primarily, "to take or receive from" (*ek*, "from," *dechomai*, "to receive"), hence denotes "to await, expect," the only sense of the word in the NT; it suggests a reaching out in readiness to receive something; "expecting," Heb. 10:13; "expect," 1 Cor. 16:11, RV (KJV, "look for"); to wait for, John 5:3 (KJV only); Acts 17:16; 1 Cor. 11:33, RV (KJV, "tarry for"); Jas. 5:7; to wait, 1 Pet. 3:20 in some mss.; "looked for," Heb. 11:10. Cf. B, No. 1. See LOOK.

2. *prosdokaō* (προσδοκάω, 4328), "to watch toward, to look for, expect" (*pros*, "toward," *dokeō*, "to think": *dokaō* "does not exist"), is translated "expecting" in Matt. 24:50 and Luke 12:46, RV (KJV, "looketh for"); Luke 3:15, "were in expectation"; Acts 3:5,"expecting" (KJV and RV); 28:6 (twice), "expected that," RV (KJV, "looked when") and "when they were long in expectation" (KJV, "after they had looked a great while"). See LOOK.

B. Nouns.

1. *apokaradokia* (ἀποκαραδοκία, 603), primarily "a watching with outstretched head" (*apo*, "from," *kara*, "the head," and *dokeō*, "to look, to watch"), signifies "strained expectancy, eager longing," the stretching forth of the head indicating an "expectation" of something from a certain place, Rom. 8:19 and Phil. 1:20. The prefix *apo* suggests "abstraction and absorption" (Lightfoot), i.e., abstraction from anything else that might engage the attention, and absorption in the object expected "till the fulfillment is realized" (Alford). The intensive character of the noun, in comparison with No. 2 (below), is clear from the contexts; in Rom. 8:19 it is said figuratively of the creation as waiting for the revealing of the sons of God ("waiting" translates the verb *apekdechomai*, a strengthened form of A, No. 1). In Phil. 1:20 the apostle states it as his "earnest expectation" and hope, that, instead of being put to shame, Christ shall be magnified in his body, "whether by life, or by death," suggesting absorption in the person of Christ, abstraction from aught that hinders.

2. *prosdokia* (προσδοκία, 4329), "a watching for, expectation" (akin to A, No. 2, which see), is used in the NT only of the "expectation" of evil, Luke 21:26, RV, "expectation," KJV, "looking for," regarding impending calamities; Acts 12:11, "the expectation" of the execution of Peter.

3. *ekdochē* (ἐκδοχή, 1561), primarily "a receiving from," hence, "expectation" (akin to A, No. 1), is used in Heb. 10:27 (RV, "expectation"; KJV, "looking for"), of judgment.

EXPEDIENT

sumpherō (συμφέρω, 4851) signifies (a), transitively, lit., "to bring together," (*sun*, "with," *pherō*, "to bring"), Acts 19:19; (b) intransitively, "to be an advantage, profitable, expedient" (not merely 'convenient'); it is used mostly impersonally, "it is (it was) expedient"; so in Matt. 19:10, RV (negatively), KJV, "it is (not) good"; John 11:50; 16:7; 18:14; 1 Cor. 6:12; 10:23; 2 Cor. 8:10; 12:1; "it is profitable," Matt. 5:29-30; 18:6, RV; "was profitable," Acts 20:20; "to profit withal," 1 Cor. 12:7; in Heb. 12:10, used in the neuter of the present participle with the article as a noun, "for (our) profit." Cf. the adjective *sumphoros* (or *sumpheron*), "profitable," used with the article as a noun, 1 Cor. 7:35; 10:33.

EXPERIENCE (without), EXPERIMENT

1. *apeiros* (ἄπειρος, 552), "without experience" (*a*, negative, *peira*, "a trial, experiment") is used in Heb. 5:13, RV, "without experience," KJV, "unskillful," with reference to "the word of righteousness." In the Sept., Num. 14:23, of youths; Jer. 2:6, of a land, "untried"; Zech. 11:15, of a shepherd.

2. *dokimē* (δοκιμή, 1382) means (a) "the process of proving"; it is rendered "experiment" in 2 Cor. 9:13, KJV, RV, "the proving (of you)"; in 8:2, KJV, "trial," RV, "proof"; (b) "the effect of proving, approval, approvedness," RV, "probation," Rom. 5:4 (twice), for KJV, "experience"; KJV and RV, "proof" in 2 Cor. 2:9; 13:3 and Phil. 2:22. See EXPERIENCE, PROOF. Cf. *dokimos*, "approved," *dokimazō*, "to prove, approve."

EXPERT

gnōstēs (γνώστης, 1109), "one who knows" (akin to *ginosko*, "to know"), denotes "an expert, a connoisseur," Acts 26:3. Cf. *gnostos*, "known."

EXPLAIN

diasapheō (διασαφέω, 1285), "to make clear, explain fully" (*dia* "through," intensive, and *saphēs*, "clear"), is translated "explain" in Matt. 13:36 RV (KJV, "declare") translates *phrazō*; in 18:31, "told," of the account of the unforgiving debtor's doings given by his fellowservants. The preferable rendering would be "they made clear" or "they explained," suggesting a detailed explanation of the circumstances.

EXTORT, EXTORTION, EXTORTIONER

A. Verb.

prassō (πράσσω, 4238), "to practice," has the special meaning "extort" in Luke 3:13, RV (KJV, "exact"). In Luke 19:23 it is translated "required"; it may be that the master, in addressing the slothful servant, uses the word "extort" or "exact" (as in 3:13), in accordance with the character attributed to him by the servant.

B. Nouns.

1. *harpagē* (ἁρπαγή, 724) denotes "pillage, plundering, robbery, extortion" (akin to *harpazō*, "to seize, carry off by force," and *harpagmos*, "a thing seized, or the act of seizing";

from the root *arp*, seen in Eng., "rapacious"; an associated noun, with the same spelling, denoted a rake, or hook for drawing up a bucket); it is translated "extortion" in Matt. 23:25; Luke 11:39, RV, KJV, "ravening"; Heb. 10:34, "spoiling. See RAVENING. Cf. c. below.

2. *pleonexia* (πλεονεξία, 4124), "covetousness, desire for advantage," is rendered "extortion" in 2 Cor. 9:5, RV (KJV and RV marg., "covetousness"). See COVET.

C. Adjective.

harpax (ἅρπαξ, 727), "rapacious" (akin to No. 1), is translated as a noun, "extortioners," in Luke 18:11; 1 Cor. 5:10-11; 6:10; in Matt. 7:15 "ravening" (of wolves). In the Sept., Gen. 49:27.

EYE

1. *ophthalmos* (ὀφθαλμός, 3788), akin to *opsis*, "sight," probably from a root signifying "penetration, sharpness" (Curtius, Gk. Etym.) (cf. Eng., "ophthalmia," etc.). is used (a) of the physical organ, e.g., Matt. 5:38; of restoring sight, e.g., Matt. 20:33; of God's power of vision, Heb. 4:13; 1 Pet. 3:12; of Christ in vision, Rev. 1:14; 2:18; 19:12; of the Holy Spirit in the unity of Godhood with Christ, Rev. 5:6; (b) metaphorically, of ethical qualities, evil, Matt. 6:23; Mark 7:22 (by metonymy, for envy); singleness of motive, Matt. 6:22; Luke 11:34; as the instrument of evil desire, "the principal avenue of temptation," 1 John 2:16; of adultery, 2 Pet. 2:14; (c) metaphorically, of mental vision, Matt. 13:15; John 12:40; Rom. 11:8; Gal. 3:1, where the metaphor of the "evil eye" is altered to a different sense from that of bewitching (the posting up or placarding of an "eye" was used as a charm, to prevent mischief); by gospel-preaching Christ had been, so to speak, placarded before their "eyes"; the question may be paraphrased, "What evil teachers have been malignly fascinating you?"; Eph. 1:18, of the "eyes of the heart," as a means of knowledge.

2. *omma* (ὄμμα, 3659), "sight," is used in the plural in Matt. 20:34 (No. 1 is used in v. 33); Mark 8:23 (No. 1 is used in v. 25). The word is more poetical in usage than No. 1, and the writers may have changed the word with a view to distinguishing the simple desire of the blind man from the tender act of the Lord Himself.

3. *trumalia* (τρυμαλιά, 5168) is used of the "eye" of a needle, Mark 10:25 (from *trumē*, "a hole," *truō*, "to wear away"). Cf. *trēma*, "a hole, perforation," Matt. 19:24 (some texts have *trupēma*, "a hole," from *trupaō*, "to bore a hole") and Luke 18:25, as in the most authentic mss. (some texts have *trumalia* here).

EYE (withone)

monophthalmos (μονόφθαλμος, 3442), "oneeyed, deprived of one eye" (*monos*, "only," and No. 1, above), is used in the Lord's warning in Matt. 18:9; Mark 9:47.

EYE-SERVICE

ophthalmodoulia (ὀφθαλμοδουλεία, 3787) denotes "service performed only under the master's eye" (*ophthalmos*, "an eye," *doulos*, "a slave"), diligently performed when he is looking, but neglected in his absence, Eph. 6:6 and Col. 3:22.

EYEWITNESS

1. *autoptēs* (αὐτόπτης, 845) signifies "seeing with one's own eyes" (*autos*, "self," and a form, *optanō*, "to see"), Luke 1:2.

2. *epoptēs* (ἐπόπτης, 2030), primarily "an overseer" (*epi*, "over"), then, a "spectator, an eyewitness" of anything, is used in 2 Pet. 1:16 of those who were present at the transfiguration of Christ. Among the Greeks the word was used of those who had attained to the third grade, the highest, of the Eleusinian mysteries, a religious cult at Eleusis, with its worship, rites, festival and pilgrimages; this brotherhood was open to all Greeks. In the Sept., Esth. 5:1, where it is used of God as the Overseer and Preserver of all things. Cf. *epopteuō*, "to behold," 1 Pet. 2:12 and 3:2.

F

FABLE

muthos (μῦθος, 3454) primarily signifies "speech, conversation." The first syllable comes from a root *mu-*, signifying "to close, keep secret, be dumb"; whence, *muō*, "to close" (eyes, mouth) and *mustērion*, "a secret, a mystery"; hence, "a story, narrative, fable, fiction" (Eng., "myth"). The word is used of gnostic errors and of Jewish and profane fables and genealogies, in 1 Tim. 1:4; 4:7; 2 Tim. 4:4; Titus 1:14; of fiction, in 2 Pet. 1:16.

Muthos is to be contrasted with *alētheia*, "truth," and with *logos*, "a story, a narrative purporting to set forth facts," e.g., Matt. 28:15, a "saying" (i.e., an account, story, in which actually there is a falsification of facts); Luke 5:15, RV, "report."

FACE

1. *prosōpon* (πρόσωπον, 4383) denotes "the countenance," lit., "the part towards the eyes" (from *pros*, "towards," *ōps*, "the eye"), and is used (a) of the "face," Matt. 6:16-17; 2 Cor. 3:7, 2nd part (KJV, "countenance"); in 2 Cor. 10:7, in the RV, "things that are before your face" (KJV, "outward appearance"), the phrase is figurative of superficial judgment; (b) of the look i.e., the "face," which by its various movements affords an index of inward thoughts and feelings. e g., Luke 9:51, 53; 1 Pet. 3:12; (c) the presence of a person, the "face" being the noblest part, e.g., Acts 3:13, RV, "before the face of," KJV, "in the presence of"; 5:41, "presence"; 2 Cor. 2:10, "person"; 1 Thess. 2:17 (first part), "presence"; 2 Thess. 1:9, RV, "face," KJV, "presence"; Rev. 12:14, "face"; (d) the person himself, e.g., Gal. 1:22; 1 Thess. 2:17 (second part); (e) the appearance one presents by his wealth or poverty, his position or state, Matt. 22:16; Mark 12:14; Gal. 2:6; Jude 16; (f) the outward appearance of inanimate things, Matt. 16:3; Luke 12:56; 21:35; Acts 17:26.

"To spit in a person's face" was an expression of the utmost scorn and aversion, e.g., Matt. 26:67 (cf. 27:30; Mark 10:34; Luke 18:32). See APPEARANCE.

2. *opsis* (ὄψις, 3799) is primarily "the act of seeing"; then, (a) "the face"; of the body of Lazarus, John 11:44; of the "countenance" of Christ in a vision, Rev. 1:16; (b) the "outward appearance" of a person or thing, John 7:24. See APPEARANCE.

Note: The phrase "face to face" translates two phrases in Greek: (1) *kata prosōpon* (*kata*, "over against," and No. 1), Acts 25:16; (2) *stoma pros stoma*, lit., "mouth to mouth" (*stoma*, "a mouth"), 2 John 12; 3 John 14. See MOUTH. (3) For *antophthalmō*, Acts 27:15, RV has "to face."

FACTION, FACTIOUS

erithia (or *—eia*) (ἐριθεία, 2052) denotes "ambition, self-seeking, rivalry," self-will being an underlying idea in the word; hence it denotes "party-making." It is derived, not from *eris*, "strife," but from *erithos*, "a hireling"; hence the meaning of "seeking to win followers," "factions," so rendered in the RV of 2 Cor. 12:20, KJV, "strifes"; not improbably the meaning here is rivalries, or base ambitions (all the other words in the list express abstract ideas rather than factions); Gal. 5:20 (ditto); Phil. 1:17 (RV; KJV, v. 16, "contention"); 2:3 (KJV, "strife"); Jas. 3:14, 16 (ditto); in Rom. 2:8 it is translated as an adjective, "factious" (KJV, "contentious"). The order "strife, jealousy, wrath, faction," is the same in 2 Cor. 12:20 and Gal. 5:20. "Faction" is the fruit of jealousy. Cf. the synonymous adjective *hairetikos*, Titus 3:10, causing division (marg., "factious"), not necessarily "heretical," in the sense of holding false doctrine.

FADE (away)

A. Verb.

marainō (μαραίνω, 3133) was used (a) to signify "to quench a fire," and in the passive voice, of the "dying out of a fire"; hence (b) in various relations, in the active voice, "to quench, waste, wear out"; in the passive, "to waste away," Jas. 1:11, of the "fading" away of a rich man, as illustrated by the flower of the field. In the Sept., Job 15:30; 24:24.

B. Adjectives (negative).

1. *amarantos* (ἀμάραντος, 263), "unfading" (*a*, negative, and A, above), whence the "amaranth," an unfading flower, a symbol of perpetuity (see *Paradise Lost*, iii. 353), is used in 1 Pet. 1:4 of the believer's inheritance, "that fadeth not away." It is found in various writings in the language of the *Koinē*, e.g., on a gladiator's tomb; and as a proper name (Moulton and Milligan, Vocab.).

2. *amarantinos* (ἀμαράντινος, 262) primarily signifies "composed of amaranth" (see No. 1); hence, "unfading," 1 Pet. 5:4, of the crown of glory promised to faithful elders. Cf. *rhodinos*, "made of roses" (*rhodon*, "a rose").

FAIN

1. *boulomai* (βούλομαι, 1014), "to will deliberately, wish, desire, be minded," implying the deliberate exercise of

volition (contrast No. 3), is translated "would fain" in Philem. 13 (in the best mss.).

2. *epithumeō* (ἐπιθυμέω, 1937), "to set one's heart upon, desire," is translated "would fain" in Luke 15:16, of the Prodigal Son. See DESIRE.

3. *thelō* (θέλω, 2309), "to wish, to design to do anything," expresses the impulse of the will rather than the intention (see No. 1); the RV translates it "would fain" in Luke 13:31, of Herod's desire to kill Christ, KJV, "will (kill)"; in 1 Thess. 2:18, of the desire of the missionaries to return to the church in Thessalonica.

Note: In Acts 26:28, in Agrippa's statement to Paul, the RV rendering is "with but little persuasion thou wouldest fain make me a Christian." The lit. rendering is "with (or in) little (labor or time) thou art persuading me so as to make (me) a Christian." There is no verb for "wouldest" in the original, but it brings out the sense.

FAINT

1. *ekluō* (ἐκλύω, 1590) denotes (a) "to loose, release" (*ek*, "out," *luō*, "to loose"); (b) "to unloose," as a bow-string, "to relax," and so, "to enfeeble," and is used in the passive voice with the significance "to be faint, grow weary," (1) of the body, Matt. 15:32; (some mss. have it in 9:36); Mark 8:3; (2) of the soul, Gal. 6:9 (last clause), in discharging responsibilities in obedience to the Lord; in Heb. 12:3, of becoming weary in the strife against sin; in v. 5, under the chastening hand of God. It expresses the opposite of *anazōnnumi*, "to gird up," 1 Pet. 1:13.

2. *enkakeō* or *ekkakeō* (ἐκκακέω, 1573), "to lack courage, lose heart, be fainthearted" (*en*, "in," *kakos*, "base"), is said of prayer, Luke 18:1; of gospel ministry, 2 Cor. 4:1, 16; of the effect of tribulation, Eph. 3:13; as to well doing, 2 Thess. 3:13, "be not weary" (KJV marg., "fain not"). Some mss. have this word in Gal. 6:9 (No. 1).

3. *kamnō* (κάμνω, 2577) primarily signified "to work"; then, as the effect of continued labor, "to be weary"; it is used in Heb. 12:3, of becoming "weary" (see also No. 1), RV, "wax not weary"; in Jas. 5:15, of sickness; some mss. have it in Rev. 2:3, KJV, "hast (not) fainted," RV, "grown weary." See SICK, WEARY.

FAINTHEARTED

oligopsuchos (ὀλιγόψυχος, 3642), lit., "small-souled" (*oligos*, "small," *psuchē*, "the soul"), denotes "despondent"; then, "fainthearted," 1 Thess. 5:14, RV, for the incorrect KJV, "feeble-minded." In the Sept., similarly, in a good sense, Isa. 57:15, "who giveth endurance to the fainthearted," for RV, "to revive the spirit of the humble"; in a bad sense, Prov. 18:14, "who can endure a fainthearted man?"

FAITH

pistis (πίστις, 4102), primarily, "firm persuasion," a conviction based upon hearing (akin to *peithō*, "to persuade"), is used in the NT always of "faith in God or Christ, or things spiritual."

The word is used of (a) trust, e.g., Rom. 3:25 [see *Note* (4) below]; 1 Cor. 2:5; 15:14, 17; 2 Cor. 1:24; Gal. 3:23 [see *Note* (5) below]; Phil. 1:25; 2:17; 1 Thess. 3:2; 2 Thess. 1:3; 3:2; (b) trust-worthiness, e.g., Matt. 23:23; Rom. 3:3, RV, "the faithfulness of God"; Gal. 5:22 (RV, "faithfulness"); Titus 2:10, "fidelity"; (c) by metonymy, what is believed, the contents of belief, the "faith," Acts 6:7; 14:22; Gal. 1:23; 3:25 [contrast 3:23, under (a)]; 6:10; Phil. 1:27; 1 Thess. 3:10; Jude 3, 20 (and perhaps 2 Thess. 3:2); (d) a ground for "faith," an assurance, Acts 17:31 (not as in KJV, marg., "offered faith"); (e) a pledge of fidelity, plighted "faith," 1 Tim. 5:12.

The main elements in "faith" in its relation to the invisible God, as distinct from "faith" in man, are especially brought out in the use of this noun and the corresponding verb, *pisteuō*; they are (1) a firm conviction, producing a full acknowledgement of God's revelation or truth, e.g., 2 Thess. 2:11-12; (2) a personal surrender to Him, John 1:12; (3) a conduct inspired by such surrender, 2 Cor. 5:7. Prominence is given to one or other of these elements according to the context. All this stands in contrast to belief in its purely natural exercise, which consists of an opinion held in good "faith" without necessary reference to its proof. The object of Abraham's "faith" was not God's promise (that was the occasion of its exercise); his "faith" rested on God Himself, Rom. 4:17, 20-21. See ASSURANCE, BELIEF, FAITHFULNESS, FIDELITY.

Notes: (1) In Heb. 10:23, *elpis*, "hope," is mistranslated "faith" in the KJV (RV, "hope"). (2) In Acts 6:8 the most authentic mss. have *charis*, "grace," RV, for *pistis*, "faith." (3) In Rom. 3:3, RV, *apistia*, is rendered "want of faith," for KJV, "unbelief" (so translated elsewhere). See UNBELIEF. The verb *apisteō* in that verse is rendered "were without faith," RV, for KJV, "did not believe." (4) In Rom. 3:25, the KJV wrongly links "faith" with "in His blood," as if "faith" is reposed in the blood (i.e., the death) of Christ; the *en* is instrumental; "faith" rests in the living Person; hence the RV rightly puts a comma after "through faith," and renders the next phrase "by His blood," which is to be connected with "a propitiation." Christ became a propitiation through His blood (i.e., His death in expiatory sacrifice for sin). (5) In Gal. 3:23, though the article stands before "faith" in the original, "faith" is here to be taken as under (a) above, and as in v. 22, and not as under (c), "the faith"; the article is simply that of renewed mention. (6) For the difference between the teaching of Paul and that of James, on "faith" and works, see *Notes on Galatians,* by Hogg and Vine, pp. 117-119.

FAITH (of little)

oligopistos (ὀλιγόπιστος, 3640), lit., "little of faith" (*oligos*, "little," *pistis*, "faith"), is used only by the Lord, and as a tender rebuke, for anxiety, Matt. 6:30 and Luke 12:28; for fear, Matt. 8:26; 14:31; 16:8.

FAITHFUL, FAITHFULLY, FAITHLESS

1. *pistos* (πιστός, 4103), a verbal adjective, akin to *peithō* (see FAITH), is used in two senses, (a) passive, "faithful, to be trusted, reliable," said of God, e.g., 1 Cor. 1:9; 10:13; 2 Cor. 1:18 (KJV, "true"); 2 Tim. 2:13; Heb. 10:23; 11:11; 1 Pet. 4:19; 1 John 1:9; of Christ, e.g., 2 Thess. 3:3; Heb. 2:17; 3:2; Rev. 1:5; 3:14; 19:11; of the words of God, e.g., Acts 13:34, "sure"; 1 Tim. 1:15; 3:1 (KJV, "true"); 4:9; 2 Tim. 2:11; Titus 1:9; 3:8; Rev. 21:5; 22:6; of servants of the Lord, Matt. 24:45; 25:21, 23; Acts 16:15; 1 Cor. 4:2, 17; 7:25; Eph. 6:21; Col. 1:7; 4:7, 9; 1 Tim. 1:12; 3:11; 2 Tim. 2:2; Heb. 3:5; 1 Pet. 5:12; 3 John 5; Rev. 2:13; 17:14; of believers, Eph. 1:1; Col. 1:2; (b) active, signifying "believing, trusting, relying," e.g., Acts 16:1 (feminine); 2 Cor. 6:15; Gal. 3:9 seems best taken in this respect, as the context lays stress upon Abraham's "faith" in God, rather than upon his "faithfulness." In John 20:27 the context requires the active sense, as the Lord is reproaching Thomas for his want of "faith." See No. 2.

With regard to believers, they are spoken of sometimes in the active sense, sometimes in the passive, i.e., sometimes as believers, sometimes as "faithful." See Lightfoot on Galatians, p. 155.

Note: In 3 John 5 the RV has "thou doest a faithful work," for KJV, "thou doest faithfully." The lit. rendering is "thou doest (*poieō*) a faithful thing, whatsoever thou workest (*ergazō*)." That would not do as a translation. To do a "faithful" work is to do what is worthy of a "faithful" man. The KJV gives a meaning but is not exact as a translation. Westcott suggests "thou makest sure (*piston*) whatsoever thou workest" (i.e., it will not lose its reward). The change between *poieō*, "to do," and *ergazō*, "to work," must be maintained. Cf. Matt. 26:10 (*ergazō* and *ergon*).

2. *apistos* (ἄπιστος, 571) is used with meanings somewhat parallel to No. 1; (a) "untrustworthy" (*a*, negative, and No. 1), not worthy of confidence or belief, is said of things "incredible," Acts 26:8 (b) "unbelieving, distrustful," used as a noun, "unbeliever," Luke 12:46; 1 Tim. 5:8 (RV, for KJV, "infidel"); in Titus 1:15 and Rev. 21:8, "unbelieving"; "faithless" in Matt. 17:17; Mark 9:19; Luke 9:41; John 20:27. The word is most frequent in 1 and 2 Corinthians. See BELIEVE, INCREDIBLE, UNBELIEVER, UNFAITHFUL. (In the Sept., Prov. 17:6; 28:25; Isa. 17:10.).

FAITHFULNESS

Note: This is not found in the KJV. The RV corrects the KJV "faith" to "faithfulness" in Rom. 3:3; Gal. 5:22. See FAITH.

FALSE, FALSEHOOD, FALSELY

A. Adjectives.

1. *pseudēs* (ψευδής, 5571), is used of "false witnesses," Acts 6:13; "false apostles," Rev. 2:2, RV, "false," KJV, "liars"; Rev. 21:8, "liars."

Note: For compound words with this adjective, see APOSTLE, CHRIST, PROPHET, WITNESS.

2. *pseudōnumos* (ψευδώνυμος, 5581), "under a false name" (No. 1, and *onoma*, "a name"; Eng., "pseudonym"), is said of the knowledge professed by the propagandists of various heretical cults, 1 Tim. 6:20.

B. Noun.

pseudos (ψεῦδος, 5579), "a falsehood" (akin to A, No. 1), is so translated in Eph. 4:25, RV (KJV, "lying"); in 2 Thess. 2:9, "lying wonders" is lit. "wonders of falsehood," i.e., wonders calculated to deceive; it is elsewhere rendered "lie," John 8:44; Rom. 1:25; 2 Thess. 2:11; 1 John 2:21, 27; Rev. 14:5, RV; 21:27; 22:15. See GUILE, LIE.

C. Verb.

pseudō (ψεύδω, 5574), "to deceive by lies," is used in the middle voice, translated "to say ... falsely," in Matt. 5:11; it is elsewhere rendered "to lie," Acts 5:3-4; Rom. 9:1; 2 Cor. 11:31; Gal. 1:20; Col. 3:9; 1 Tim. 2:7. See LIE.

FAME

A. Noun.

phēmē (φήμη, 5345) originally denoted "a divine voice, an oracle"; hence, "a saying or report" (akin to *phēmi*, "to say," from a root meaning "to shine, to be clear"; hence, Lat., *fama*, Eng., "fame"), is rendered "fame" in Matt. 9:26 and Luke 4:14.

Notes: (1) In Luke 5:15, RV, *logos*, "a word, report, account," is translated "report," for KJV, "fame." See REPORT. (2) *Akoē*, "a hearing," is translated "report" in the RV of Matt. 4:24; 14:1; Mark 1:28, for KJV, "fame." See EAR, No. 3. HEARING. (3) *Ēchos*, "a noise, report, sound," is translated "rumor," in the RV of Luke 4:37, for KJV, "fame"; "sound" in Acts 2:2; Heb. 12:19. See RUMOR, SOUND.

B. Verb.

diaphēmizo (διαφημίζω, 1310) signifies "to spread abroad a matter," Matt. 28:15, RV; Mark 1:45, RV (from *dia*, "throughout," and *phēmi*, "to say"); hence, "to spread abroad one's fame," Matt. 9:31. All the passages under this heading relate to the testimony concerning Christ in the days of His flesh.

FAMILY

1. *oikos* (οἶκος, 3624) signifies (a) "a dwelling, a house" (akin to *oikeo*, to dwell); (b) "a household, family," translated "family" in 1 Tim. 5:4, RV, for KJV, "at home." See HOME, HOUSE, TEMPLE.

2. *patria* (πατριά, 3965), primarily "an ancestry, lineage," signifies in the NT "a family or tribe" (in the Sept. it is used of related people, in a sense wider than No. 1, but narrower than *phulē*, "a tribe," e.g., Exod. 12:3; Num. 32:28); it is used of the "family" of David, Luke 2:4, RV, for KJV, "lineage"; in the wider sense of "nationalities, races," Acts 3:25, RV, "families," for KJV, "kindreds"; in Eph. 3:15, RV, "every family," for KJV, "the whole family," the reference being to all those who are spiritually related to God the Father, He being the Author of their spiritual relationship to Him as His children, they being united to one another in "family" fellowship (*patria* is akin to *patēr*, "a father"); Luther's translation, "all who bear the name of children," is advocated by Cremer, p. 474. The phrase, however, is lit., "every family."

FAMINE

limos (λιμός, 3042) is translated "hunger" in Luke 15:17; 2 Cor. 11:27; elsewhere it signifies "a famine," and is so translated in each place in the RV; the KJV has the word "dearth" in Acts 7:11 and 11:28, and "hunger" in Rev. 6:8; the RV "famine" is preferable there; see Matt. 24:7; Mark 13:8; Luke 4:25; 15:14; 21:11; Rom. 8:35; Rev. 18:8.

FARE, FAREWELL

1. *euphrainō* (εὐφραίνω, 2165), in the active voice, signifies "to cheer, gladden," 2 Cor. 2:2; in the passive, "to rejoice, make merry"; translated "faring sumptuously" in Luke 16:19, especially of food (RV, marg., "living in mirth and splendor"). See GLAD, MERRY, REJOICE.

2. *rhōnnumi* (ῥώννυμι, 4517), "to strengthen, to be strong," is used in the imperative mood as a formula at the end of letters, signifying "Farewell," Acts 15:29; some mss. have it in 23:30 (the RV omits it, as do most Versions).

3. *echō* (ἔχω, 2192), "to have," is used idiomatically in Acts 15:36, RV, "(how) they fare," KJV, "how they do."

4. *chairō* (χαίρω, 5463), "to joy, rejoice, be glad," is used in the imperative mood in salutations, (a) on meeting, "Hail," e.g., Matt. 26:49; or with *legō*, "to say, to give a greeting," 2 John 11; in letters, "greeting," e.g., Acts 15:23; (b) at parting, the underlying thought being joy, 2 Cor. 13:11 (RV, marg., "rejoice"); (c) on other occasions, see the RV marg. in Phil. 3:1; 4:4. See GLAD, GREETING, No. 2, HAIL, JOY, JOYFUL.

Note: As "farewell" is inadequate to express *chairō*, which always conveys the thought of joy or cheer, (b) properly comes under (c).

5. *apotassō* (ἀποτάσσω, 657) primarily denotes "to set apart"; then, in the middle voice, (a) "to take leave of, bid farewell to," Mark 6:46, "had taken leave of"; cf. Acts 18:18, 21; 2 Cor. 2:13 (in these three verses, the verb may signify to give final instructions to); Luke 9:61, "to bid farewell"; (b) "to forsake," Luke 14:33. In the papyri, besides saying goodbye, the stronger meaning is found of getting rid of a person (Moulton and Milligan). See FORSAKE, RENOUNCE, SEND (away).

FASHION

A. Nouns.

1. *eidos* (εἶδος, 1491), "that which is seen, an appearance," is translated "fashion" in Luke 9:29, of the Lord's countenance at the Transfiguration. See APPEARANCE, and *Note* under IMAGE, No. 1.

2. *prosōpon* (πρόσωπον, 4383), "the face, countenance," is translated "fashion" in Jas. 1:11, of the flower of grass. See COUNTENANCE. Cf. v. 24, "what manner of man," which translates *hopoios*, "of what sort."

3. *schēma* (σχῆμα, 4976), "a figure, fashion" (akin to *echō*, "to have"), is translated "fashion" in 1 Cor. 7:31, of the world, signifying that which comprises the manner of life, actions, etc. of humanity in general; in Phil. 2:8 it is used of the Lord in His being found "in fashion" as a man, and signifies what He was in the eyes of men, "the entire outwardly perceptible mode and shape of His existence, just as the preceding words *morphē*, "form," and *homoiōma*, "likeness," describe what He was in Himself as Man" (Gifford on the Incarnation, p. 44). "Men saw in Christ a human form, bearing, language, action, mode of life ... in general the state and relations of a human being, so that in the entire mode of His appearance He made Himself known and was recognized as a man" (Meyer).

4. *tupos* (τύπος, 5179), "a type, figure, example," is translated "fashion" in the KJV of Acts 7:44, RV, "figure," said of the tabernacle. See ENSAMPLE.

B. Adverb.

houtōs (οὕτως, 3779), "thus, so, in this way," is rendered "on this fashion" in Mark 2:12. See EVEN, No. 5, WHAT.

C. Verbs.

1. *metaschēmatizō* (μετασχηματίζω, 3345), "to change in fashion or appearance" (*meta*, "after," here implying change, *schēma*, see A, No. 3), is rendered "shall fashion anew" in Phil. 3:21, RV; KJV, "shall change," of the bodies of believers as changed or raised at the Lord's return; in 2 Cor. 11:13, 14, 15, the RV uses the verb "to fashion oneself," for KJV, to transform, of Satan and his human ministers, false apostles; in 1 Cor. 4:6 it is used by way of a rhetorical device, with the significance of transferring by a figure. See TRANSFORM.

2. *suschēmatizō* (συσχηματίζω, 4964), "to give the same figure or appearance as, to conform to" (*sun*, "with," *schēma*, cf. No. 1), used in the passive voice, signifies "to fashion oneself, to be fashioned," Rom. 12:2, RV, "be not fashioned according to," for KJV, "be not conformed to"; 1 Pet. 1:14, "(not) fashioning yourselves." See CONFORMED.

Note: In Rom. 12:2 being outwardly "conformed" to the things of this age is contrasted with being "transformed" (or transfigured) inwardly by the renewal of the thoughts through the Holy Spirit's power. A similar distinction holds good in Phil. 3:21; the Lord will "fashion anew," or change outwardly, the body of our humiliation, and "conform" it in its nature (*summorphos*) to the body of His glory.

D. Adjective.

summorphos (συμμορφός, 4832), "having like form with" (*sun*, "with," *morphē*, "form"), is used in Rom. 8:29 and Phil. 3:21 (KJV, "fashioned," RV, "conformed").

FAST, FASTING

A. Nouns.

1. *nēsteia* (νηστεία, 3521), "a fasting, fast" (from *nē*, a negative prefix, and *esthiō*, "to eat"), is used (a) of voluntary abstinence from food, Luke 2:37; Acts 14:23 (some mss. have it in Matt. 17:21 and Mark 9:29); "fasting" had become a common practice among Jews, and was continued among Christians; in Acts 27:9, "the Fast" refers to the Day of Atonement, Lev. 16:29; that time of the year would be one of dangerous sailing; (b) of involuntary abstinence (perhaps voluntary is included), consequent upon trying circumstances, 2 Cor. 6:5; 11:27.

2. *nēstis* (νῆστις, 3523), "not eating" (see No. 1), "fasting," is used of lack of food, Matt. 15:32; Mark 8:3.

Note: Asitia, Acts 27:21, means "without food" (not through lack of supplies), i.e., abstinence from food. See ABSTINENCE, and cf. C, below.

B. Verb.

nesteuō (νηστεύω, 3522), "to fast, to abstain from eating" (akin to A, Nos. 1 and 2), is used of voluntary "fasting," Matt. 4:2; 6:16, 17, 18; 9:14, 15; Mark 2:18, 19, 20; Luke 5:33, 34, 35; 18:12; Acts 13:2, 3. Some of these passages show that teachers to whom scholars or disciples were attached gave them special instructions as to "fasting." Christ taught the need of purity and simplicity of motive.

The answers of Christ to the questions of the disciples of John and of the Pharisees reveal His whole purpose and method. No doubt He and His followers observed such a fast as that on the Day of Atonement, but He imposed no frequent "fasts" in addition. What He taught was suitable to the change of character and purpose which He designed for His disciples. His claim to be the Bridegroom, Matt. 9:15, and the reference there to the absence of "fasting," virtually involved a claim to be the Messiah (cf. Zech. 8:19). Some mss. have the verb in Acts 10:30.

C. Adjective.

asitos (ἄσιτος, 777), "without food" (*a*, negative, *sitos*, "corn, food"), is used in Acts 27:33, "fasting." Cf. *asitia, Note* under A, No. 2.

FATHER

A. Noun.

patēr (πατήρ, 3962), from a root signifying "a nourisher, protector, upholder" (Lat., *pater*, Eng., "father," are akin), is used (a) of the nearest ancestor, e.g., Matt. 2:22; (b) of a more remote ancestor, the progenitor of the people, a "forefather," e.g., Matt. 3:9; 23:30; 1 Cor. 10:1; the patriarchs, 2 Pet. 3:4; (c) one advanced in the knowledge of Christ, 1 John 2:13; (d) metaphorically, of the originator of a family or company of persons animated by the same spirit as himself, as of Abraham, Rom. 4:11, 12, 16, 17, 18, or of Satan, John 8:38, 41, 44; (e) of one who , as a preacher of the gospel and a teacher, stands in a "father's" place, caring for his spiritual children, 1 Cor. 4:15 (not the same as a mere title of honor, which the Lord prohibited, Matt. 23:9); (f) of the members of the Sanhedrin, as of those who exercised religious authority over others, Acts 7:2; 22:1; (g) of God in relation to those who have been born anew (John 1:12, 13), and so are believers, Eph. 2:18; 4:6 (cf. 2 Cor. 6:18), and imitators of their "Father," Matt. 5:45, 48; 6:1, 4, 6, 8, 9, etc. Christ never associated Himself with them by using the personal pronoun "our"; He always used the singular, "My Father," His relationship being unoriginated and essential, whereas theirs is by grace and regeneration, e.g., Matt. 11:27; 25:34; John 20:17; Rev. 2:27; 3:5, 21; so the apostles spoke of God as the "Father" of the Lord Jesus Christ, e.g., Rom. 15:6; 2 Cor. 1:3; 11:31; Eph. 1:3; Heb. 1:5; 1 Pet. 1:3; Rev. 1:6; (h) of God, as the "Father" of lights, i.e., the Source or Giver of whatsoever provides illumination, physical and spiritual, Jas. 1:17; of mercies, 2 Cor. 1:3; of glory, Eph. 1:17; (i) of God, as Creator, Heb. 12:9 (cf. Zech. 12:1).

Note: Whereas the everlasting power and divinity of God are manifest in creation, His "Fatherhood" in spiritual relationship through faith is the subject of NT revelation, and waited for the presence on earth of the Son, Matt. 11:27; John 17:25. The spiritual relationship is not universal, John 8:42, 44 (cf. John 8:12 and Gal. 3:26).

B. Adjectives.

1. *patrōos* (πατρῷος, 3971) signifies "of one's fathers," or "received from one's fathers" (akin to A), Acts 22:3; 24:14; 28:17. In the Sept., Prov. 27:10.

2. *patrikos* (πατρικός, 3967), "from one's fathers, or ancestors," is said of that which is handed down from one's "forefathers," Gal. 1:14.

3. *apatōr* (ἀπάτωρ, 540), "without father" (*a*, negative, and *patēr*), signifies, in Heb. 7:3, with no recorded genealogy.

4. *patroparadotos* (πατροπαράδοτος, 3970), "handed down from one's fathers" (*patēr*, and *paradidomi*, "to hand down"), is used in 1 Pet. 1:18.

FATHER-IN-LAW

pentheros (πενθερός, 3995), "a wife's father" (from a root signifying "a bond, union"), is found in John 18:13.

FATHERLESS

orphanos (ὀρφανός, 3737), properly, "an orphan," is rendered "fatherless" in Jas. 1:27; "desolate" in John 14:18, for KJV, "comfortless. See COMFORTLESS.

FAULT, FAULTLESS

A. Noun.

aition (αἴτιον, 158), properly the neuter of *aitios*, causative of, responsible for, is used as a noun, "a crime, a legal ground for punishment," translated "fault" in Luke 23:4, 14; in v. 22, cause. See AUTHOR.

Notes: (1) For *aitia*, rendered "fault" in John 18:38; 19:4, 6, KJV (like *aition*, denoting "a ground for punishment"), see ACCUSATION. (2) For *paraptōma*, "a false step, a trespass," translated "fault" in Gal. 6:1, KJV, and "faults" in Jas. 5:16, KJV, see SIN, A, No. 2, *Note* (1), TRESPASS.

B. Adjective.

amemptos (ἄμεμπτος, 273), "without blame," is rendered "faultless," in Heb. 8:7. See BLAMELESS.

Note: For *amōmos*, "without blemish," rendered "faultless," i,e., without any shortcoming, in Jude 24, and "without fault" in Rev. 14:5, KJV, see BLEMISH.

C. Verbs.

1. *memphomai* (μέμφομαι, 3201), "to blame," is translated "to find fault" in Rom. 9:19 and Heb. 8:8. Some mss. have the verb in Mark 7:2. See BLAME.

2. *elenchō* (ἐλέγχω, 1651), "to convict, reprove, rebuke," is translated "shew (him) his fault" in Matt. 18:15. See CONVICT.

Note: In 1 Pet. 2:20, KJV, the verb *hamartanō*, "to sin" (strictly, to miss the mark) is rendered "for your faults." The RV corrects to "when ye sin (and are buffeted for it)."

FAVOR, FAVORED

A. Noun.

charis (χάρις, 5485) denotes (a) objectively, "grace in a person, graciousness," (b) subjectively, (1) "grace on the part of a giver, favor, kindness," (2) "a sense of favor received, thanks." It is rendered "favor" in Luke 1:30; 2:52; Acts 2:47; 7:10, 46; 24:27 and 25:9, RV (for KJV, "pleasure"); 25:3; see more fully under GRACE.

B. Verb.

charitoō (χαριτόω, 5487), akin to A, to endow with *charis*, primarily signified "to make graceful or gracious," and came to denote, in Hellenistic Greek, "to cause to find favor," Luke 1:28, "highly favored" (marg., "endued with grace"); in Eph. 1:6, it is translated "made ... accepted," KJV, "freely bestowed," RV (lit., "graced"); it does not here mean to endue with grace. Grace implies more than favor; grace is a free gift, favor may be deserved or gained.

FEAR, FEARFUL, FEARFULNESS

A. Nouns.

1. *phobos* (φόβος, 5401) first had the meaning of "flight," that which is caused by being scared; then, "that which may cause flight," (a) "fear, dread, terror," always with this significance in the four Gospels; also e.g., in Acts 2:43; 19:17; 1 Cor. 2:3; 1 Tim. 5:20 (lit., "may have fear"); Heb. 2:15; 1 John 4:18; Rev. 11:11; 18:10, 15; by metonymy, that which causes "fear," Rom. 13:3; 1 Pet. 3:14, RV, "(their) fear," KJV "(their) terror," an adaptation of the Sept. of Isa. 8:12, "fear not their fear"; hence some take it to mean, as there, "what they fear," but in view of Matt. 10:28, e.g., it seems best to understand it as that which is caused by the intimidation of adversaries; (b) "reverential fear," (1) of God, as a controlling motive of the life, in matters spiritual and moral, not a mere "fear" of His power and righteous retribution, but a wholesome dread of displeasing Him, a "fear" which banishes the terror that shrinks from His presence, Rom. 8:15, and which influences the disposition and attitude of one whose circumstances are guided by trust in God, through the indwelling Spirit of God, Acts 9:31; Rom. 3:18; 2 Cor. 7:1; Eph. 5:21 (RV, "the fear of Christ"); Phil. 2:12; 1 Pet. 1:17 (a comprehensive phrase: the reverential "fear" of God will inspire a constant carefulness in dealing with others in His "fear"); 3:2, 15; the association of "fear and trembling," as, e.g., in Phil. 2:12, has in the Sept. a much sterner import, e.g., Gen. 9:2; Exod. 15:16; Deut. 2:25; 11:25; Ps. 55:5; Isa. 19:16; (2) of superiors, e.g., Rom. 13:7; 1 Pet. 2:18. See TERROR.

2. *deilia* (δειλία, 1167), "fearfulness" (from *deos*, "fright"), is rightly rendered "fearfulness" in 2 Tim. 1:7, RV (for KJV, "fear"). That spirit is not given us of God. The word denotes "cowardice and timidity" and is never used in a good sense, as No. 1 is. Cf. *deilos*, B, No. 2, below, and *deiliaō*, to be fearful (KJV, "afraid"), John 14:27.

3. *eulabeia* (εὐλάβεια, 2124) signifies, firstly, "caution"; then, "reverence, godly fear," Heb. 5:7; 12:28, in best mss.,

"reverence"; in general, "apprehension, but especially holy fear," "that mingled fear and love which, combined, constitute the piety of man toward God; the OT places its emphasis on the fear, the NT ... on the love, though there was love in the fear of God's saints then, as there must be fear in their love now" (Trench, *Syn.* Sec. XLVIII). In the Sept., Josh. 22:24; Prov. 28:14.

Note: In Luke 21:11, *phobētron* (akin to No. 1) denotes a terror, RV, "terrors," for KJV, "fearful sights," i.e., objects or instruments of terror.

B. Adjectives.

1. *phoberos* (φοβερός, 5398), "fearful" (akin to A, No. 1), is used only in the active sense in the NT, i.e., causing "fear," terrible, Heb. 10:27, 31; 12:21, RV, "fearful," for KJV, "terrible."

2. *deilos* (δειλός, 1169), "cowardly" (see A, No. 2), "timid," is used in Matt. 8:26; Mark 4:40; Rev. 21:8 (here "the fearful" are first in the list of the transgressors).

3. *ekphobos* (ἔκφοβος, 1630), signifies "frightened outright" (*ek*, "out," intensive, and A, No. 1), Heb. 12:21 (with *eimi*, "I am"), "I exceedingly fear" (see No. 4); Mark 9:6, "sore afraid."

4. *entromos* (ἔντρομος, 1790), "trembling with fear" (*en*, "in," intensive, and *tremō*, "to tremble, quake"; Eng., "tremor," etc.), is used with *ginomai*, "to become," in Acts 7:32, "trembled"; 16:29, RV, "trembling for fear"; with *eimi*, "to be," in Heb. 12:21, "quake" (some mss. have *ektromos* here). See QUAKE, TREMBLE. The distinction between No. 3 and No. 4, as in Heb. 12:21, would seem to be that *ekphobos* stresses the intensity of the "fear," *entromos* the inward effect, "I inwardly tremble (or quake)."

C. Adverb.

aphōbos (ἀφωνος, 880) denotes "without fear" (*a*, negative, and A, No. 1), and is said of serving the Lord, Luke 1:74; of being among the Lord's people as His servant, 1 Cor. 16:10; of ministering the Word of God, Phil. 1:14; of the evil of false spiritual shepherds, Jude 12. In the Sept., Prov. 1:33.

D. Verbs.

1. *phobeō* (φοβέω, 5399), in earlier Greek, "to put to flight" (see A, No. 1), in the NT is always in the passive voice, with the meanings either (a) "to fear, be afraid," its most frequent use, e.g., Acts 23:10, according to the best mss. (see No. 2); or (b) "to show reverential fear" [see A, No. 1, (b)], (1) of men, Mark 6:20; Eph. 5:33, RV, "fear," for KJV, "reverence"; (2) of God, e.g., Acts 10:2, 22; 13:16, 26; Col. 3:22 (RV, "the Lord"); 1 Pet. 2:17; Rev. 14:7; 15:4; 19:5; (a) and (b) are combined in Luke 12:4, 5, where Christ warns His followers not to be afraid of men, but to "fear" God. See MARVEL, B, No. 1, *Note.*

2. *eulbeomai* (εὐλαβέομαι, 2125), "to be cautious, to beware" (see A, No. 3), signifies to act with the reverence produced by holy "fear," Heb. 11:7, "moved with godly fear."

Notes: (1) In Acts 23:10 some mss. have this verb with the meaning (a) under No. 1.

(2) In Luke 3:14, *diaseiō*, "to shake violently, to intimidate, to extort by violence, blackmail," is rendered "put no man in fear" in KJV marg. See VIOLENCE.

FEAST

A. Nouns.

1. *heortē* (ἑορτή, 1859), "a feast or festival," is used (a) especially of those of the Jews, and particularly of the Passover; the word is found mostly in John's gospel (seventeen times); apart from the Gospels it is used in this way only in Acts 18:21; (b) in a more general way, in Col. 2:16, KJV, "holy day," RV, "a feast day."

2. *deipnon* (δεῖπνον, 1173) denotes (a) "the chief meal of the day," dinner or supper, taken at or towards evening; in the plural "feasts," Matt. 23:6; Mark 6:21; 12:39; Luke 20:46; otherwise translated "supper," Luke 14:12, 16, 17, 24; John 12:2; 13:2, 4; 21:20; 1 Cor. 11:21 (of a social meal); (b) "the Lord's Supper," 1 Cor. 11:20; (c) "the supper or feast" which will celebrate the marriage of Christ with His spiritual Bride, at the inauguration of His Kingdom, Rev. 19:9; (d) figuratively, of that to which the birds of prey will be summoned after the overthrow of the enemies of the Lord at the termination of the war of Armageddon, 19:17 (cf. Ezek. 39:4, 17-20). See SUPPER.

3. *dochē* (δοχή, 1403), "a reception feast, a banquet" (from *dechomai*, "to receive"), Luke 5:29; 14:13 (not the same as No 2; see v. 12).

4. *gamos* (γάμος, 1062), "a wedding," especially a wedding "feast" (akin to *gameō*, "to marry"); it is used in the plural in the following passages (the RV rightly has "marriage feast" for the KJV, "marriage," or "wedding"), Matt. 22:2, 3, 4, 9 (in verses 11, 12, it is used in the singular, in connection with the wedding garment); 25:10; Luke 12:36; 14:8; in the following it signifies a wedding itself, John 2:1, 2; Heb. 13:4; and figuratively in Rev. 19:7, of the marriage of the Lamb; in v. 9 it is used in connection with the supper, the wedding supper (or what in English is termed "breakfast"), not the wedding itself, as in v. 7.

5. *agapē* (ἀγάπη, 26), "love," is used in the plural in Jude 12, signifying "love feasts," RV (KJV, "feasts of charity"); in the corresponding passage, 2 Pet. 2:13, the most authentic mss. have the word *apate*, in the plural, "deceivings."

Notes: (1) In 1 Cor. 10:27 the verb *kaleō*, "to call," in the sense of inviting to one's house, is translated "biddeth you (to a feast)"; in the most authentic texts there is no separate phrase representing "to a feast," as in some mss., *eis deipnon* (No. 2). (2) In Mark 14:2 and John 2:23 the KJV translates *heortē* (see No. 1) by "feast day" (RV, "feast"). (3) For the "Feast of the Dedication," John 10:22, see DEDICATION.

B. Verbs.

1. *heortizō* (ἑορτάζω, 1858), "to keep festival" (akin to A, No. 1) is translated "let us keep the feast," in 1 Cor. 5:8. This is not the Lord's Supper, nor the Passover, but has reference to the continuous life of the believer as a festival or holy-day (see KJV, margin), in freedom from "the leaven of malice and wickedness, but with the unleavened bread of sincerity and truth."

2. *suneuōcheō* (συνευωχέω, 4910), "to entertain sumptuously with," is used in the passive voice, denoting "to feast sumptuously with" (*sun*, "together," and *euōchia*, "good cheer"), "to revel with," translated "feast with" in 2 Pet. 2:13 and Jude 12.

FEEBLE

asthenēs (ἀσθενής, 772), "without strength" (*a*, negative, and *sthenos*, "strength"), is translated "feeble" in 1 Cor. 12:22, of members of the body. See SICK, STRENGTH, B, *Note* (5), WEAK.

Notes: (1) In Heb. 12:12 *paraluō*, "to weaken, enfeeble," in the passive voice, "to be enfeebled," as by a paralytic stroke, is translated "feeble" in the KJV (RV, "palsied"). (2) For "feeble-minded" in 1 Thess. 5:14, KJV, see FAINTHEARTED.

FEED, FED

1. *boskō* (βόσκω, 1006), "to feed," is primarily used of a herdsman (from *boō*, "to nourish," the special function being to provide food; the root is *bo*, found in *botēr*, "a herdsman or herd," and *botanē*, "fodder, pasture"), its uses are (a) literal, Matt. 8:30; in v. 33, the RV corrects the KJV, "they that kept," to "they that fed," as in Mark. 5:14 (KJV and RV) and Luke 8:34; in Mark 5:11 and Luke 8:32, "feeding"; Luke 15:15; (b) metaphorical, of spiritual ministry, John 21:15, 17 (see *Note* on No. 2). See KEEP.

2. *poimainō* (ποιμαίνω, 4165), "to act as a shepherd" (from *poimēn*, "a shepherd"), is used (a) literally, Luke 17:7, RV, "keeping sheep," for KJV, "feeding cattle"; 1 Cor. 9:7, (b) metaphorically, "to tend, to shepherd"; said of Christ Matt. 2:6, RV, "shall be Shepherd of" (for KJV, "shall rule"); of those who act as spiritual shepherds under Him, John 21:16, RV, "tend" (for KJV "feed"), so 1 Pet. 5:2; Acts 20:28, "to feed" ("to tend" would have been a consistent rendering; a shepherd does not only "feed" his flock); of base shepherds, Jude 12. See RULE.

Note: In John 21:15, 16, 17, the Lord, addressing Peter, first uses No. 1, *boskō* (v. 15) then No. 2, *poimainō* (v. 16), and then returns to *boskō* (v. 17). These are not simply interchangeable (nor are other variations in His remarks); a study of the above notes will show this. Nor, again, is there a progression of ideas. The lesson to be learnt, as Trench points out (*Syn.* Sec. XXV), is that, in the spiritual care of God's children, the "feeding" of the flock from the Word of God is the constant and regular necessity; it is to have the foremost place. The tending (which includes this) consists of other acts, of discipline, authority, restoration, material assistance of individuals, but they are incidental in comparison with the "feeding."

3. *trephō* (τρέφω, 5142) signifies (a) "to make to grow, bring up, rear," Luke 4:16, "brought up"; (b) "to nourish, feed," Matt. 6:26; 25:37; Luke 12:24; Acts 12:20; Rev. 12:6, 14; of a mother, "to give suck," Luke 23:29 (some mss. here have *thēlazō*, "to suckle"); "to fatten," as of fattening animals, Jas. 5:5, "ye have nourished (your hearts)."

4. *chortazō* (χορτάζω, 5526), "to feed, to fatten," is used (a) primarily of animals, Rev. 19:21; (b) of persons, to fill or satisfy with food. It is usually translated by the verb "to fill," but is once rendered "to be fed," in Luke 16:21, of Lazarus, in his desire for the crumbs (he could be well supplied with them) that fell from the rich man's table, a fact which throws light upon the utter waste that went on at the table of the latter. The crumbs that fell would provide no small meal. See SATISFY.

5. *psōmizō* (ψωμίζω, 5595) primarily denotes "to feed with morsels," as nurses do child dren; then, "to dole out or supply with food," Rom. 12:20; 1 Cor. 13:3. Cf. *psōmion*, "a fragment, morsel," John 13:26, 27, 30 ("sop").

6. *potizō* (ποτίζω, 4222), to give to drink, is translated "I fed (you with milk)" in 1 Cor. 3:2. See DRINK, WATER.

FEEL, FEELING, FELT

1. *ginōskō* (γινώσκω, 1097), "to know, perceive," is translated "she felt (in her body)," of the woman with the issue of blood, Mark 5:29, i.e., she became aware of the fact. See KNOW.

2. *phroneō* (φρονέω, 5426), "to think, to be minded," is translated "I felt" in the RV of 1 Cor. 13:11 (for KJV, I understood).

3. *psēlaphaō* (ψηλαφάω, 5584), "to feel or grope about" (from *psaō*, "to touch"), expressing the motion of the hands over a surface, so as to "feel" it, is used (a) metaphorically, of seeking aher God, Acts 17:27; (b) literally, of physical handling or touching, Luke 24:39 with 1 John 1:1; Heb. 12:18. See TOUCH.

4. *sumpatheō* (συμπαθέω, 4834), "to have a fellow-feeling for or with," is rendered "touched with the feeling of" in Heb. 4:15; "have compassion" in 10:34. See COMPASSION.

5. *apalgeō* (ἀπαλγέω, 524) signifies "to cease to feel pain for" (*apo*, "from," *algeō*, "to feel pain"; cf. Eng., "neuralgia"); hence, to be callous, "past feeling," insensible to honor and shame, Eph. 4:19.

Note: In Acts 28:5 *paschō*, "to suffer," is rendered "felt (no harm)," RV, "took," lit., "suffered no ill (effect)."

FEIGN, FEIGNED

A. Verb.

hupokrinomai (ὑποκρίνομαι, 5271) primarily denotes "to answer"; then, "to answer on the stage, play a part," and so, metaphorically, "to feign, pretend," Luke 20:20. Cf. *hupokritēs*, "a hypocrite," and *hupokrisis*, "hypocrisy."

B. Adjective.

plastos (πλαστός, 4112) primarily denotes "formed, molded" (from *plassō*, to mold; Eng., "plastic"); then, metaphorically, "made up, fabricated, feigned," 2 Pet. 2:3. Cf. *plasma*, "that which is molded," Rom. 9:20.

FELLOW

1. *anēr* (ἀνήρ, 435) denotes "a man," in relation to his sex or age; in Acts 17:5 (plural) it is rendered "fellows," as more appropriate to the accompanying description of them. See HUSBAND, SIR.

2. *hetairos* (ἑταῖρος, 2083), "a companion, comrade," is translated "fellows" in Matt. 11:16 [where, however, the most authentic mss. have *heterois*, "(the) others"]. The word is used only by Matthew and is translated "friend" in 20:13; 22:12; 26:50. See FRIEND.

3. *metochos* (μέτοχος, 3353), properly an adjective, signifying "sharing in, partaking of," is translated "partners" in Luke 5:7; "partakers" in Heb. 3:1, 14; 6:4; 12:8; "fellows" in Heb. 1:9, of those who share in a heavenly calling, or have held, or will hold, a regal position in relation to the earthly, messianic kingdom. (Cf *summetochos*, "fellow-partakers," in Eph. 3:6, RV). See PARTAKER, PARTNER.

Notes: (1) In Acts 24:5 *loimos*, "a plague, a pest," is rendered "a pestilent fellow." This is a sample of the strongest use of the epithet "fellow." (2) *Toioutos*, an adjective, "such a one," is often used as a noun, e.g., Acts 22:22, where it is translated "such a fellow." (3) *Houtos*, "this," is translated "this fellow" in the KJV of Luke 23:2 (RV, "this man"). So in John 9:29. Both versions have "this man," e.g., in Mark 2:7; John 6:52, in the same contemptuous sense. (4) For the word in combination with various nouns see CITIZEN, DISCIPLE, ELDER, HEIR, HELPER, LABORER, MEMBER, PARTNER, PRISONER, SERVANT.

FELLOWSHIP

A. Nouns.

1. *koinōnia* (κοινωνία, 2842), (a) "communion, fellowship, sharing in common" (from *koinos*, "common"), is translated "communion" in 1 Cor. 10:16; Philem. 6, RV, "fellowship," for KJV, "communication"; it is most frequently translated "fellowship"; (b) "that which is the outcome of fellowship, a contribution," e.g., Rom. 15:26; 2 Cor. 8:4. See COMMUNION, CONTRIBUTION, etc.

Note: In Eph. 3:9, some mss. have *koinōnia*, instead of *oikonomia*, "dispensation," RV.

2. *metochē* (μετοχή, 3352), "partnership" (akin to No. 3, under FELLOW), is translated "fellowship" in 2 Cor. 6:4. In the Sept., Ps. 122:3, "Jerusalem is built as a city whose fellowship is complete." The word seems to have a more restricted sense than *koinōnia*. Cf. the verb form in Heb. 2:14.

3. *koinōnos* (κοινωνός, 2844) denotes "a partaker" or "partner" (akin to No. 1); in 1 Cor. 10:20 it is used with *ginomai*, "to become," "that ye should have communion with," RV (KJV, fellowship with). See COMPANION, PARTAKER, PARTNER.

B. Verbs.

1. *koinōneō* (κοινωνέω, 2841), "to have fellowship," is so translated in Phil. 4:15, RV, for KJV, "did communicate." See COMMUNICATE.

2. *sunkoinōneō* (συγκοινωνέω, 4790), "to have fellowship with or in" (*sun*, "with," and No. 1), is used in Eph. 5:11; Phil. 4:14, RV, "ye had fellowship," for KJV, "ye did communicate"; Rev. 18:4, RV, "have (no) fellowship with," for KJV, "be (not) partakers of" See COMMUNICATE, PARTAKER.

For **FELT** see FEEL

FEMALE

thēlus (θῆλυς, 2338), an adjective (from *thēlē*, "a breast"), is used in the form *thēlu* (grammatically neuter) as a noun, "female," in Matt. 19:4; Mark 10:6; Gal. 3:28; in the feminine form *thēleia*, in Rom. 1:26, "women"; v. 27 "woman." See WOMAN.

FERVENT, FERVENTLY

A. Adjective.

ektenēs (ἐκτενής, 1618) denotes "strained, stretched" (*ek*, "out," *teino*, "to stretch"); hence, metaphorically, "fervent," 1 Pet. 4:8. Some mss. have it in Acts 12:5, for the adverb (see B). Cf. *ekteneia* (with *en*), "intently, strenuously," in Acts 26:7, KJV, "instantly," RV, "earnestly." Cf. EARNEST.

B. Adverb.

ektenōs (ἐκτενῶς, 1619), "fervently" (akin to A), is said of love, in 1 Pet. 1:22; of prayer, in some mss., Acts 12:5 (see under A); for the comparative degree in Luke 22:44, see EARNESTLY.

C. Verb.

zeō (ζέω, 2204), "to be hot, to boil" (Eng. "zeal" is akin), is metaphorically used of "fervency" of spirit, Acts 18:25; Rom. 12:11.

Notes: (1) In Col. 4:12, the verb *agōnizomai*, "to strive," is translated "laboring fervently," KJV (RV, "striving"). (2) In 2 Cor. 7:7, the noun *zēlos*, "zeal" (akin to C.), is translated "fervent mind," KJV (RV, "zeal"). (3) In Jas. 5:17, "he prayed fervently" (KJV, "earnestly") translates the noun *proseuchē*, followed by the corresponding verb, lit., "he prayed with prayer." In v. 16 *deēsis*, "supplication," is so translated in the RV, for the KJV, "effectual fervent prayer." There is nothing in the original corresponding to the word "effectual." The phrase, including the verb *energeomai*, "to work in," is, lit., "the inworking supplication," suggesting a supplication consistent with inward conformity to the mind of God. (4) For "fervent heat" see HEAT, B.

FEVER (to be sick of) A. Noun.

puretos (πυρετός, 4446), "feverish heat" (from *pur*, "fire"), hence, "a fever," occurs in Matt. 8:15; Mark 1:31; John 4:52; Acts 28:8; in Luke 4:38, with *megas*, "great, a high fever"; v. 39. Luke, as a physician, uses the medical distinction by which the ancients classified fevers into great and little. In the Sept., Deut. 28:22.

B. Verb.

puressō (πυρέσσω, 4445) signifies "to be ill of a fever" (akin to A), Matt. 8:14; Mark 1:30.

FIDELITY

pistis (πίστις, 4102), "faith, faithfulness," is translated "fidelity" in Titus 2:10. See FAITH (b).

FIERCE, FIERCENESS

A. Adjectives.

1. *anēmeros* (ἀνήμερος, 434) signifies "not tame, savage" (from *a* negative, and *hemeros*, "gentle"), 2 Tim. 3:3. Epictetus describes those who forget God as their creator, as resembling lions, "wild, savage and fierce" (*anemeroi*) (Moulton and Milligan, Greek Test Vocab.).

2. *chalepos* (χαλεπός, 5467) "hard," (a) "hard to do or deal with, difficult, fierce," is said of the Gadarene demoniacs, Matt. 8:28; (b) "hard to bear, painful, grievous," said of the last times, 2 Tim. 3:1, RV, "grievous," for KJV, "perilous." See GRIEVOUS.

Notes: (1) In Jas. 3:4, *sklēros*, "hard, rough, violent," is said of winds, RV, "rough," for KJV, "fierce." (2) In Luke 23:5, the verb *epischuō*, "to make or grow stronger" (from *epi*, "over," intensive, and *ischus*, "strength"), is used metaphorically, "they were the more urgent," RV, for KJV, "the more fierce."

B. Nouns.

1. *thumos* (θυμός, 2372), "hot anger, wrath," is rendered "fierceness" in Rev. 16:19; 19:15, of the wrath of God. See ANGER (A, *Notes*), INDIGNATION, WRATH.

2. *zeēos* (ζῆλος, 2205), "zeal, jealousy," is rendered "fierceness" in Heb. 10:27, RV (of fire).

FIERY

puroō (πυρόω, 4448), "to set on fire, burn up" (from *pur*, "fire"), always used in the passive voice in the NT, is translated "fiery" in Eph. 6:16, metaphorically of the darts of the evil one; "fire-tipped" would perhaps bring out the verbal force of the word. The most ancient mss. have the article repeated, lit., "the darts of the evil one, the fiery (darts)," marking them as particularly destructive. Some mss. omit the repeated article. In ancient times, darts were often covered with burning material. See BURN, FIRE, TRY, *Note* (1).

Notes: (1) For Heb. 10:27, RV, see FIRE (cf. FIERCE, B, No. 2). (2) For *purōsis*, "a fiery trial," 1 Pet. 4:12, (lit., "a burning," as in Rev. 18:9, 18), "a refining, or trial by fire," see TRIAL.

FIG

1. *sukon* (σῦκον, 4810) denotes "the ripe fruit of a *sukē*, a fig-tree" (see below; cf. No. 2), Matt. 7:16; Mark 11:13; Luke 6:44; Jas. 3:12.

2. *olunthos* (ὄλυνθος, 3653) denotes "an unripe fig," which grows in winter and usually falls off in the spring, Rev. 6:13. In the Sept. Song of Sol., 2:13.

FIG TREE

sukē or *sukea* (συκῆ, 4808), "a fig tree," is found in Matt. 21:19, 20, 21; 24:32; Mark 11:13, 20, 21; 13:28; Luke 13:6, 7; 21:29; John 1:48, 50, Jas. 3:12; Rev. 6:13 (see *sukon*, above).

Note: A "fig tree" with leaves must have young fruits already, or it will be barren for the season. The first figs ripen in late May or early June. The tree in Mark 11:13 should have had fruit, unripe indeed, but existing. In some lands "fig trees" bear the early fruit under the leaves and the later fruit above the leaves. In that case the leaves were a sign that there should have been fruit, unseen from a distance, underneath the leaves. The condemnation of this fig tree lay in the absence of any sign of fruit.

FIGHT

A. Nouns.

1. *agōn* (ἀγών, 73), akin to *ago*, "to lead," primarily "a gathering," then, "a place of assembly," and hence, "a contest,

conflict," is translated "fight" in 1 Tim. 6:12; 2 Tim. 4:7. See CONFLICT.

2. *athlēsis* (ἄθλησις, 119) is translated fight in Heb. 10:32, KJV. See CONFLICT.

Note: In Heb. 11:34, *polemos*, "war," is translated "fight," KJV (RV, "war"); it is misrendered "battle" in the KJV of 1 Cor. 14:8; Rev. 9:7, 9; 16:14; 20:8.

B. Verbs.

1. *agōnizomai* (ἀγωνίζομαι, 75), from A, No. 1, denotes (a) "to contend" in the public games, 1 Cor. 9:25 ("striveth in the games," RV); (b) "to fight, engage in conflict," John 18:36; (c) metaphorically, "to contend" perseveringly against opposition and temptation, 1 Tim. 6:12; 2 Tim. 4:7 (cf. A, No. 1; in regard to the meaning there, the evidence of *Koinē* inscriptions is against the idea of games-contests); to strive as in a contest for a prize, straining every nerve to attain to the object Luke 13:24; to put forth every effort, involving toil, Col. 1:29; 1 Tim. 4:10 (some mss. have *oneidizomai* here, "to suffer reproach"); to wrestle earnestly in prayer, Col. 4:12 (cf. *sunagōnizomai*, Rom. 15:30). See LABOR, STRIVE.

2. *pukteuō* (πυκτέω, 4438), "to box" (from *puktēs*, "a pugilist"), one of the events in the Olympic games, is translated "fight" in 1 Cor. 9:26.

3. *machomai* (μάχομαι, 3164), "to fight," is so rendered in Jas. 4:2 (cf. "fightings," v. 1, see below), and translated "strive" in 2 Tim. 2:24; "strove" in John 6:52; Acts 7:26. See STRIVE.

4. *thēriomacheō* (θηριομαχέω, 2341) signifies "to fight with wild beasts" (*thērion*, "a beast," and No. 3), 1 Cor. 15:32. Some think that the apostle was condemned to fight with wild beasts; if so, he would scarcely have omitted it from 2 Cor. 11:23-end. Moreover, he would have lost his status as a Roman citizen. Probably he uses the word figuratively of contending with ferocious men. Ignatius so uses it in his Ep. to the Romans.

Notes: (1) In Rev. 2:16 and 12:7, KJV, *polemeō*, "to war," is translated "to fight," RV, "will make war," "*going forth* to war," and "warred." (2) In Acts 23:9 some mss. have the verb *theomacheō*, "to fight against God." Cf. the corresponding adjective, below, under FIGHTING.

FIGHTING

A. Noun.

machē (μάχη, 3163), "a fight, strife" (akin to B, No. 3, under FIGHT), is always used in the plural in the NT, and translated "fightings" in 2 Cor. 7:5; Jas. 4:1; and Titus 3:9, RV (for KJV, "strivings"); "strifes in 2 Tim. 2:23. See STRIFE.

B. Adjective.

theomachos (θεόμαχος, 2314), "fighting against God" (theos, "God," and A, occurs in Acts 5:39 (KJV, "to fight"), lit., "God-fighters."

FIGURE

1. *tupos* (τύπος, 5179), "a type, figure, pattern," is translated "figures" (i.e., representations of gods) in Acts 7:43; in the RV of v. 44 (for KJV, "fashion") and in Rom. 5:14, of Adam as a "figure of Christ." See ENSAMPLE.

2. *antitupos* (ἀντίτυπον, 499), an adjective, used as a noun, denotes, lit., "a striking back"; metaphorically, "resisting, adverse"; then, in a passive sense, "struck back"; in the NT metaphorically, "corresponding to," (a) a copy of an archetype (*anti*, "corresponding to, and No. 1), i.e., the event or person or circumstance corresponding to the type, Heb. 9:24, RV, "like in pattern" (KJV, "the figure of"), of the tabernacle, which, with its structure and appurtenances, was a pattern of that "holy place," "Heaven itself," "the true," into which Christ entered, "to appear before the face of God for us." The earthly tabernacle anticipatively represented what is now made good in Christ; it was a "figure" or "parable" (9:9), "for the time now present," RV, i.e., pointing to the present time, not "then present," KJV (see below); (b) "a corresponding type," 1 Pet. 3:21, said of baptism; the circumstances of the flood, the ark and its occupants, formed a type, and baptism forms "a corresponding type" (not an antitype), each setting forth the spiritual realities of the death, burial, and resurrection of believers in their identification with Christ. It is not a case of type and antitype, but of two types, that in Genesis, the type, and baptism, the corresponding type.

3. *parabolē* (παραβολή, 3850), "a casting or placing side by side" (*para*, "beside," *ballō*, "to throw") with a view to comparison or resemblance, a parable, is translated "figure" in the KJV of Heb. 9:9 (RV, "a parable for the time now present") and 11:19, where the return of Isaac was (parabolically, in the lit. sense of the term) figurative of resurrection (RV, "parable"). See No. 2 (a). See PARABLE.

Notes: (1) The synonymous noun *hupotupōsis*, "an example, pattern," 1 Tim. 1:16; 2 Tim. 1:13, denotes simply a delineation or outline. (2) For *metaschēmaizō*, rendered "I have in a figure transferred" in 1 Cor. 4:6, where the fact stated is designed to change its application, i.e., from Paul and Apollos to circumstances in Corinth, see FASHION.

FILTH

1. *perikatharma* (περικάθαρμα, 4027) denotes "offscouring, refuse" (lit., "cleanings," i.e., that which is thrown away in cleansing; from *perikathairō*, "to purify all around," i.e., completely, as in the Sept. of Deut. 18:10; Josh. 5:4.) It is

once used in the Sept. (Prov. 21:18) as the price of expiation; among the Greeks the term was applied to victims sacrificed to make expiation; they also used it of criminals kept at the public expense, to be thrown into the sea, or otherwise killed, at the outbreak of a pestilence, etc. It is used in 1 Cor. 4:13 much in this sense (not of sacrificial victims), "the filth of the world" representing "the most abject and despicabie men" (Grimm-Thayer), the scum or rubbish of humanity.

2. *rhupos* (ῥύπος, 4509) denotes "dirt, filth," 1 Pet. 3:2l. Cf. *rhuparia*, "filthiness" (see A, No. 2, below); *rhuparos*, "vile," Jas. 2:2; Rev. 22:11, in the best mss. (see B, No. 3, below); *rhupoō*, "to make filthy," Rev. 22:11; *rhupainō* (see D below).

FILTHINESS, FILTHY (to make) A. Nouns.

1. *aischrotēs* (αἰσχρότης, 151), "baseness" (from *aischos*, "shame, disgrace"), is used in Eph, 5:4, of obscenity, all that is contrary to purity.

2. *rhuparia* (ῥυπαρία, 4507) denotes "dirt, filth" (cf. No. 2, under FILTH), and is used metaphorically of moral "defilement" in Jas. 1:21.

3. *molusmos* (μολυσμός, 3436), "a soiling, defilement," is used in 2 Cor. 7:1. See DEFILE.

4. *aselgeia* (ἀσέλγεια, 766), "wantonness, licentiousness, lasciviousness," is translated "filthy (conversation)," in 2 Pet. 2:7, KJV; RV, lascivious (life). See LASCIVIOUSNESS, WANTONNESS.

Notes: (1) Broadly speaking, *aischrotēs* signifies "whatever is disgraceful"; *rhuparia*, "that which is characterized by moral impurity," *molumos*, "that which is defiling by soiling the clean"; *aselgeia*, "that which is an insolent disregard of decency." (2) In Col. 3:8 *aischrologia*, which denotes any kind of "base utterance," the utterance of an uncontrolled tongue, is rendered "filthy communication" in the KJV; but this is only part of what is included in the more comprehensive RV rendering, "shameful speaking." In the papyri writings the word is used of "abuse." In general it seems to have been associated more frequently with "foul" or "filthy," rather than abusive, "speaking" (Moulton and Milligan).

B. Adjectives.

1. *aischros* (αἰσχρός, 150), "base, shameful" (akin to A, No. 1), is used of "base gain," "filthy (lucre)," Titus 1:11, and translated "shame" in 1 Cor. 11:6, with reference to a woman with shorn hair; in 14:35, of oral utterances of women in a church gathering (RV, "shameful"); in Eph. 5:12, of mentioning the base and bestial practices of those who live lascivious lives. See SHAME.

2. *aischrokerdēs* (αἰσχροκερδής, 146), "greedy of base gain" (No. 1, and *kerdos*, "gain"), is used in 1 Tim. 3:8 and Titus 1:7, "greedy of filthy lucre"; some mss. have it also in 1 Tim. 3:3.

3. *rhuparos* (ῥυπαρός, 4508), akin to A, No. 2 (see also FILTH, No. 2), "dirty," is said of shabby clothing, Jas. 2:2: metaphorically, of moral "defilement," Rev. 22:11 (in the best mss.).

Note: For *akathartos* see UNCLEAN, No. 1.

C. Adverb.

aischrokerdōs (αἰσχροκερδῶς, 147), "eagerness for base gain" (akin to B, No. 2), is used in 1 Pet. 5:2, "for filthy lucre."

D. Verb.

rhupainō (ῥυπαίνω, 4510v), "to make filthy, defile" (from A, No. 2), is used in the passive voice, in an ethical sense, in Rev. 22:11 (cf. B, No. 3, in the same verse), "let him be made filthy," RV. The tense (the aorist) marks the decisiveness of that which is decreed. Some texts have *rhupareuomai*, here, with the same meaning; some have *rhupoō*, in the middle voice, "to make oneself filthy.

FINAL, FINALLY

A. Nouns.

1. *peras* (πέρας, 4009), "a limit, end," is translated "final" in Heb. 6:16, RV, "an oath is final for confirmation" (the KJV connects the clauses differently). See END.

2. *telos* (τέλος, 5056), "an end," most frequently of the termination of something, is used with the article adverbially, meaning "finally" or "as to the end," i.e., as to the last detail, 1 Pet. 3:8. See END.

B. Adverb.

loipon (λοιπόν, 3063) is the neuter of the adjective *loipos*, remaining (which is used in its different genders as a noun, "the rest"), and is used either with the article or without, to signify "finally," lit., "for the rest." The apostle Paul uses it frequently in the concluding portion of his epistles, introducing practical exhortations, not necessarily implying that the letter is drawing to a close, but marking a transition in the subject-matter, as in Phil. 3:1, where the actual conclusion is for the time postponed and the farewell injunctions are resumed in 4:8. See also 1 Thess. 4:1 (KJV, "furthermore"); 2 Thess. 3:1.

For **FINE** see GOODLY, *Note,* LINEN

FIRE

A. Nouns.

1. *pur* (πῦρ, 4442), (akin to which are No. 2, *pura*, and *puretos*, "a fever," Eng., "fire," etc.) is used (besides its ordinary natural significance):

(a) of the holiness of God, which consumes all that is inconsistent therewith, Heb. 10:27; 12:29; cf. Rev. 1:14; 2:18; 10:1; 15:2; 19:12; similarly of the holy angels as His ministers

Heb. 1:7 in Rev. 3:18 it is symbolic of that which tries the faith of saints, producing what will glorify the Lord:

(b) of the divine judgment, testing the deeds of believers, at the judgment seat of Christ 1 Cor. 3:13 and 15:

(c) of the fire of divine judgment upon the rejectors of Christ, Matt. 3:11 (where a distinction is to be made between the baptism of the Holy Spirit at Pentecost and the "fire" of divine retribution; Acts 2:3 could not refer to baptism): Luke 3:16:

(d) of the judgments of God at the close of the present age previous to the establishment of the kingdom of Christ in the world, 2 Thess. 1:8; Rev. 18:8:

(e) of the "fire" of Hell, to be endured by the ungodly hereafter, Matt. 5:22; 13:42, 50; 18:8, 9; 25:41; Mark 9:43, 48; Luke 3:17:

(f) of human hostility both to the Jews and to Christ's followers, Luke 12:49:

(g) as illustrative of retributive judgment upon the luxurious and tyrannical rich, Jas. 5:3:

(h) of the future overthrow of the Babylonish religious system at the hands of the Beast and the nations under him, Rev. 17:16:

(i) of turning the heart of an enemy to repentance by repaying his unkindness by kindness, Rom. 12:20:

(j) of the tongue, as governed by a "fiery" disposition and as exercising a destructive influence over others, Jas. 3:6:

(k) as symbolic of the danger of destruction, Jude 23.

Note: See also under FLAME.

2. *pura* (πυρά, 4443), from No. 1, denotes "a heap of fuel" collected to be set on fire (hence Eng., "pyre"), Acts 28:2, 3.

Note: In Mark 14:54, the italicized phrase "of the fire" is added in the Eng. versions to indicate the light as coming from the "fire."

B. Adjective.

purinos (πύρινος, 4447), "fiery" (akin to A, No. 1), is translated "of fire" in Rev. 9:17. In the Sept., Ezek. 28:14, 16.

C. Verbs.

1. *puroō* (πυρόω, 4448) is translated "being on fire" (middle voice) in 2 Pet. 3:12. See FIERY.

2. *phlogizō* (φλογίζω, 5394), "to set on fire, burn up," is used figuratively, in both active and passive voices, in Jas. 3:6, of the tongue, firstly of its disastrous effects upon the whole round of the circumstances of life; secondly, of satanic agency in using the tongue for this purpose.

FIRST

A. Adjective.

prōtos (πρῶτος, 4413), the superlative degree of *pro*, "before," is used (I) "of time or place," (a) as a noun, e.g., Luke 14:18; Rev. 1:17; opposite to "the last," in the neuter plural, Matt. 12:45; Luke 11:26; 2 Pet. 2:20; in the neuter singular, opposite to "the second," Heb. 10:9; in 1 Cor. 15:3, *en protois*, lit., "in the first (things, or matters)" denotes "first of all"; (b) as an adjective, e.g., Mark 16:9, used with "day" understood, lit., "the first (day) of (i.e., after) the Sabbath," in which phrase the "of" is objective, not including the Sabbath, but following it (cf. B, No. 3); in John 20:4, 8; Rom. 10:19, e.g., equivalent to an English adverb; in John 1:15, lit., "first of me," i.e., "before me" (of superiority); (II) "of rank or dignity," see CHIEF. Cf. B, Nos. 3 and 4.

B. Adverbs.

1. *proteron* (πρότερον, 4386), the comparative degree of *pro* (see No. 1), "former, before," denotes "first" in Heb. 7:27; in 4:6, RV, "before" (KJV, "first"), speaking of Israel as having heard God's good tidings previously to the ministry of the Gospel; in Gal. 4:13, "I preached ... unto you the first time" means on the former of his two previous visits.

2. *anōthen* (ἄνωθεν, 509), "from above," is rendered "from the first" in Luke 1:3, RV, it may mean "from their beginning, or source."

3. *prōtōs* (πρώτως, 4413), "firstly," is used in Acts 11:26, "first" (some mss. have No. 4 here).

4. *prōton* (πρῶτον, 4412), the neuter of the adjective *prōtos*, is used as an adverb, signifying "first, firstly," e.g., of time, Matt. 8:21; of order, Rom. 3:2 (KJV, "chiefly"); in John 7:51, RV, "except it first hear from himself" (the KJV "before it hear him," follows the mss. which have No. 1).

C. Numeral.

mia (μία, 3391), a grammatically feminine form of *heis*, "one," is translated "first" in certain occurrences of the phrase "on the first day of the week," e.g., Luke 24:1; 1 Cor. 16:2; cf. A, and see DAY; also in Titus 3:10, of a "first" admonition to a heretical man.

D. Noun.

archē (ἀρχή, 746), "a beginning," is translated "first" in Heb. 5:12, "of the first (principles of the oracles of God)," lit. "(the principles) of the beginning (of the oracles of God)"; in 6:1 "the first (principles) of Christ," lit., "(the account) of the beginning of Christ," i.e., the elementary teaching concerning Christ. In Acts 26:4, where the word is preceded by *apo*, "from," the KJV has "at the first," the RV, "from the beginning."

Notes: (1) In Jude 6 *archē* has the meaning "principality," as in the RV and the KJV margin.

(2) In 2 Cor. 8:12 *prokeimai*, "to be present," lit., "to lie beforehand" (*pro*, "before," *keimai*, "to lie"), RV renders "(if the readiness) is there," for KJV, "if there be first (a willing mind)."

FIRST-BEGOTTEN, FIRSTBORN

prōtotokos (πρωτοτόκος, 4416), "firstborn" (from *prōtos*, "first," and *tiktō*, "to beget"), is used of Christ as born of the Virgin Mary, Luke 2:7; further, in His relationship to the Father, expressing His priority to, and preeminence over, creation, not in the sense of being the "first" to be born. It is used occasionally of superiority of position in the OT, see Exod. 4:22; Deut. 21:16, 17, the prohibition being against the evil of assigning the privileged position of the "firstborn" to one born subsequently to the "first" child.

The five passages in the NT relating to Christ may be set forth chronologically thus: (a) Col. 1:15, where His eternal relationship with the Father is in view, and the clause means both that He was the "Firstborn" before all creation and that He Himself produced creation (the genitive case being objective, as v. 16 makes clear); (b) Col. 1:18 and Rev. 1:5, in reference to His resurrection; (c) Rom. 8:29, His position in relationship to the church; (d) Heb. 1:6, RV, His second advent (the RV "when He again bringeth in," puts "again" in the right place, the contrast to His first advent, at His birth, being implied); cf. Ps. 89:27. The word is used in the plural, in Heb. 11:28, of the firstborn sons in the families of the Egyptians, and in 12:23, of the members of the Church.

Note: With (a) cf. John 1:30, "He was before me," lit., "He was first (*prōtos*) of me," i.e., "in regard to me," expressing all that is involved in His preexistence and priority.

FIRSTFRUIT(S)

aparchē (ἀπαρχή, 536) denotes, primarily, "an offering of firstfruits" (akin to *aparchomai*, "to make a beginning"; in sacrifices, "to offer firstfruits"). "Though the English word is plural in each of its occurrences save Rom. 11:16, the Greek word is always singular. Two Hebrew words are thus translated, one meaning the "chief" or "principal part," e.g., Num. 18:12; Prov. 3:9; the other, "the earliest ripe of the crop or of the tree," e.g., Exod. 23:16; Neh. 10:35; they are found together, e.g., in Exod. 23:19, "the first of the firstfruits."

"The term is applied in things spiritual, (a) to the presence of the Holy Spirit with the believer as the firstfruits of the full harvest of the Cross, Rom. 8:23; (b) to Christ Himself in resurrection in relation to all believers who have fallen asleep, 1 Cor. 15:20, 23; (c) to the earliest believers in a country in relation to those of their countrymen subsequently converted, Rom. 16:5; 1 Cor. 16:15; (d) to the believers of this age in relation to the whole of the redeemed, 2 Thess. 2:13 (see *Note* below) and Jas. 1:18. Cf. Rev. 14:4.

Notes: (1) In Jas. 1:15 the qualifying phrase, "a kind of," may suggest a cerain falling short, on the part of those mentioned, of what they might be. (2) In 2 Thess. 2:13, instead of *ap' archēs*, "from the beginning," there is an alternative reading, well supported, viz., *aparchēn*, "(God chose you) as firstfruits."

FISH

1. *ichthus* (ἰχθύς, 2486) denotes "a fish," Matt. 7:10; Mark 6:38, etc.; apart from the Gospels, only in 1 Cor. 15:39.

2. *ichthudion* (ἰχθύδιον, 2485) is a diminutive of No. 1, "a little fish," Matt. 15:34; Mark 8:7.

3. *opsarion* (ὀψάριον, 3795) is a diminutive of *opson*, "cooked meat," or "a relish, a dainty dish, especially of fish"; it denotes "a little fish," John 6:9, 11; 21:9, 10, 13.

FISH (Verb), FISHER, FISHERMAN

A. Noun.

halieus (ἁλιεύς, 231), "a fisherman, fisher" (from *hals*, "the sea"), occurs in Matt. 4:18, 19; Mark 1:16, 17; Luke 5:2.

B. Verb

halieuō (ἁλιεύω, 232), "to fish" (akin to A.), occurs in John 2:3. In the Sept., Jer. 16:16.

A. Adjectives.

1. *euthetos* (εὔθετος, 2111), "ready for use, fit, well adapted," lit., "well placed" (*eu*, "well," *tithemi*, "to place"), is used (a) of persons, Luke 9:62, negatively, of one who is not fit for the kingdom of God; (b) of things, Luke 14:35, of salt that has lost its savor; rendered "meet" in Heb. 6:7, of herbs.

2. *arestos* (ἀρεστός, 701), "pleasing" (akin to *aresko*, "to please"), is translated "(it is not) fit," RV (KJV, "reason"), in Acts 6:2. See PLEASE, REASON.

B. Verbs.

1. *aneko* (ἀνήκω, 433), properly, "to have come up to" (*ana*, "up," and *heko*, "to arrive"), is translated "is fitting," in Col. 3:18, RV.

2. *katheko* (καθήκω, 2520), "to come or reach down to" (*kata*, "down"), hence, "to befit, be proper," is translated "is (not fit)" in Acts 22:22; in Rom. 1:28, RV, "fitting" (KJV, "convenient").

3. *katartizo* (καταρτίζω, 2675), "to make fit, to equip, prepare" (*kata*, "down," *artos*, "a joint"), is rendered "fitted" in Rom. 9:22, of vessels of wrath; here the middle voice signifies that those referred to "fitted" themselves for destruction (as illustrated in the case of Pharaoh, the self-hardening of whose heart is accurately presented in the RV in the first part of the series of incidents in the Exodus narrative, which records Pharaoh's doings; only after repeated and persistent obstinacy on his part is it recorded that God hardened his heart.) See FRAME, PERFECT, PREPARE, RESTORE.

4. *sunarmologeo* (συναρμολογέω, 4883), "to fit or frame together" (*sun*, "with," *harmos*, "a joint, in building," and *lego*, "to choose"), is used metaphorically of the various parts of the

church as a building, Eph. 2:21, "fitly framed together"; also of the members of the church as the body of Christ, 4:16, RV, "fitly framed ... together."

FLAME, FLAMING

phlox (φλόξ, 5395), akin to Lat. *fulgeo*, "to shine," is used apart from *pur*, "fire," in Luke 16:24; with *pur*, it signifies "a fiery flame," lit., "a flame of fire," Acts 7:30; 2 Thess. 1:8, where the fire is to be understood as the instrument of divine judgment; Heb. 1:7, where the meaning probably is that God makes His angels as active and powerful as a "flame" of fire; in Rev. 1:14; 2:18; 19:12, of the eyes of the Lord Jesus as emblematic of penetrating judgment, searching out evil.

FLATTERY (-ING)

kolakia (or *-eia*) (κολακεία, 2850), akin to *kolakeuō*, "to flatter," is used in 1 Thess. 2:5 of "words of flattery" (RV), adopted as "a cloke of coveousness," i.e., words which "flattery" uses, not simply as an effort to give pleasure, but with motives of self-interest.

FLEE, FLED

1. *pheugō* (φεύγω, 5343), "to flee from or away" (Lat., *fugio;* Eng., "fugitive," etc.), besides its literal significance, is used metaphorically, (a) transitively, of "fleeing" fornication, 1 Cor. 6:18; idolatry, 10:14; evil doctrine, questionings, disputes of words, envy, strife, railings, evil surmisings, wranglings, and the love of money, 1 Tim. 6:11; youthful lusts, 2 Tim. 2:22; (b) intransitively, of the "flight" of physical matter, Rev. 16:20; 20:11; of death, 9:6. See ESCAPE.

2. *ekpheugō* (ἐκφεύγω, 1628), "to flee away, escape" (*ek*, "from," and No. 1), is translated "fled" in Acts 16:27 (KJV only); 19:16. In Heb. 12:25 the best mss. have this verb instead of No. 1. See ESCAPE.

3. *katapheugō* (καταφεύγω, 2703), "to flee for refuge" (*kata*, used intensively, and No. 1), is used (a) literally in Acts 14:6; (b) metaphorically in Heb. 6:18, of "fleeing" for refuge to lay hold upon hope.

Note: For *apopheugō* and *diapheugō*, see ESCAPE.

FLESH

1. *sarx* (σάρξ, 4561) has a wider range of meaning in the NT than in the OT. Its uses in the NT may be analyzed as follows:

"(a) "the substance of the body," whether of beasts or of men, 1 Cor. 15:39; (b) "the human body," 2 Cor. 10:3a; Gal. 2:20; Phil. 1:22; (c) by synecdoche, of "mankind," in the totality of all that is essential to manhood, i.e., spirit, soul, and body, Matt. 24:22; John 1:13; Rom. 3:20; (d) by synecdoche, of "the holy humanity" of the Lord Jesus, in the totality of all that is essential to manhood, i.e., spirit, soul, and body John 1:14; 1 Tim. 3:16; 1 John 4:2; 2 John 7, in Heb. 5:7, "the days of His flesh," i.e., His past life on earth in distinction from His present life in resurrection; (e) by synecdoche, for "the complete person," John 6:51-57; 2 Cor. 7:5; Jas. 5:3; (f) "the weaker element in human nature," Matt. 26:41; Rom. 6:19; 8:3a; (g) "the unregenerate state of men," Rom. 7:5; 8:8, 9; (h) "the seat of sin in man" (but this is not the same thing as in the body), 2 Pet. 2:18; 1 John 2:16; (i) "the lower and temporary element in the Christian," Gal. 3:3; 6:8, and in religious ordinances, Heb. 9:10; (j) "the natural attainments of men," 1 Cor. 1:26; 2 Cor. 10:2, 3b; (k) "circumstances," 1 Cor. 7:28; the externals of life, 2 Cor. 7:1; Eph. 6:5; Heb. 9:13; (l) by metonymy, "the outward and seeming," as contrasted with the spirit, the inward and real, John 6:63; 2 Cor. 5:16; (m) "natural relationship, consanguine," 1 Cor. 10:18; Gal. 4:23, or marital, Matt. 19:5."

In Matt. 26:41; Rom. 8:4, 13; 1 Cor. 5:5; Gal. 6:8 (not the Holy Spirit, here), "flesh" is contrasted with spirit, in Rom. 2:28, 29, with heart and spirit; in Rom. 7:25, with the mind; cf. Col. 2:1, 5. It is coupled with the mind in Eph. 2:3, and with the spirit in 2 Cor. 7:1.

Note: In Col. 2:18 the noun *sarx* is used in the phrase "(by his) fleshly mind," lit., "by the mind of his flesh" [see (h) above], whereas the mind ought to be dominated by the Spirit.

2. *kreas* (κρέας, 2907) denotes "flesh" in the sense of meat. It is used in the plural in Rom. 14:21; 1 Cor. 8:13.

FLESHLY, FLESHY

1. *sarkikos* (σαρκικός, 4559), akin to No. 1, under FLESH, signifies (a) associated with or pertaining to, "the flesh, carnal," Rom. 15:27; 1 Cor. 9:11; (b) of "the nature of the flesh, sensual," translated "fleshly" in 2 Cor. 1:12, of wisdom, in 1 Pet. 2:11, of lusts; in 2 Cor. 10:4, negatively, of the weapons of the Christian's warfare, RV, "of the flesh" (KJV, "carnal"). See CARNAL.

2. *sarkinos* (σάρκινος, 4560) denotes "of the flesh, fleshly" (the termination *-inos* signifying the substance or material of a thing); in 2 Cor. 3:3, RV, "(tables that are hearts) of flesh," KJV, fleshly (tables), etc. See CARNAL.

Note: The adjectives "fleshly," "carnal" are contrasted with spiritual qualities in Rom. 7:14; 1 Cor. 3:1, 3, 4; 2 Cor. 1:12; Col. 2:18 (lit., "mind of flesh"). Speaking broadly, the carnal denotes the sinful element in man's nature, by reason of descent from Adam; the spiritual is that which comes by the regenerating operation of the Holy Spirit.

FLIGHT

A. Noun.

phugē (φυγή, 5437), akin to *pheugō* (see FLEE), is found in Matt. 24:20. Some inferior mss. have it in Mark 13:18.

B. Verb.

klinō (κλίνω, 2827), "to make to bend," is translated "turned to flight" in Heb. 11:34. See BOW.

FLOCK

1. *poimnē* (ποίμνη, 4167), akin to *poimēn*, "a shepherd," denotes "a flock" (properly, of sheep), Matt. 26:31; Luke 2:8; 1 Cor. 9:7; metaphorically, of Christ's followers, John 10:16, RV, for the erroneous KJV, "fold." What characterizes Christ's sheep is listening to His voice, and the "flock" must be one as He is one.

2. *poimnion* (ποίμνιον, 4168), possibly a diminutive of No. 1, is used in the NT only metaphorically, of a group of Christ's disciples, Luke 12:32; of local churches cared for by elders, Acts 20:28, 29; 1 Pet. 5:2, 3.

FLOOD

A. Nouns.

1. *kataklusmos* (κατακλυσμός, 2627), "a deluge" (Eng., "cataclysm"), akin to *katakluzō*, "to inundate," 2 Pet. 3:6, is used of the "flood" in Noah's time, Matt. 24:38, 39; Luke 17:27; 2 Pet. 2:5.

2. *plēmmura* (πλημμύρα, 4132), akin to *plēthō* and *pimplēmi*, "to fill, a flood of sea or river," the latter in Luke 6:4. In the Sept., Job 40:18 (v. 23 in the EV).

3. *potamos* (ποταμός, 4215), "a river, stream, torrent," is translated "flood" in Matt. 7:25, 27; in Rev. 12:15, 16, KJV, flood, RV, "river. See RIVER, WATER

B. Adjective.

potamophorētos (ποταμοφόρητος, 4216) signifies "carried away by a stream or river" (A, No. 3, and *pherō*, "to carry"), Rev. 12:15, RV, "carried away by the stream" (KJV, "of the flood").

FLOWER

A. Noun.

anthos (ἄνθος, 438), "a blossom, flower" (used in certain names of flowers), occurs in Jas. 1:10, 11; 1 Pet. 1:24 (twice).

B. Adjective.

huperakmos (ὑπέρακμος, 5230), "past the bloom of youth" (from *huper*, "beyond," and *akmē*, "the highest point of anything," the full bloom of a flower: Eng., "acme"), is used in 1 Cor. 7:36, "past the flower of her age"; Lightfoot prefers the rendering "of full age."

FLUTE-PLAYERS

aulētēs (αὐλητής, 834), "a flute-player" (from *auleō*, "to play the flute"), occurs in Matt. 9:23 (KJV, "minstrel"), and Rev. 18:22 (KJV "pipers"). In the papyri writings of the time the word is chiefly associated with religious matters (Moulton and Milligan, *Vocab.*). Cf. MINSTREL.

FOAL

huios (υἱός, 5207), "a son," primarily signifying the relation of offspring to parent, is used of the "foal" of an ass in Matt. 21:5. See SON.

FOE

echthros (ἐχθρός, 2190), an adjective signifying "hated, hateful, or hostile," is used also as a noun denoting "an enemy," translated "foes" in Matt. 10:36 and the KJV of Acts 2:35. See ENEMY.

For **FOLK** see SICK, B, No. 2

FOLLY

anoia (ἄνοια, 454) lit. signifies "without understanding" (*a*, negative, *nous*, "mind"); hence, "folly," or, rather, "senselessness," 2 Tim. 3:9; in Luke 6:11 it denotes violent or mad rage, "madness." See MADNESS. Cf. *anoētos*, "foolish."

Note: For *aphrosunē*, rendered "folly" in 2 Cor. 11:1, KJV, see FOOLISHNESS (RV).

FOOD

1. *trophē* (τροφή, 5160) denotes "nourishment, food" (akin to *trephō*, "to rear, nourish, feed"); it is used literally, in the Gospels, Acts and Jas. 2:15; metaphorically, in Heb. 5:12, 14, RV, "(solid) food," KJV, "(strong) meat," i.e., deeper subjects of the faith than that of elementary instruction. The word is always rendered "food" in the RV, where the KJV has "meat"; e.g., Matt. 3:4; 6:25; 10:10; 24:45; Luke 12:23; John 4:8; Acts 2:46, "did take their food," RV (KJV, "did eat their meat"); 9:19, "took food"; 27:33, 34, 36. The KJV also has "food" in Acts 14:17 and Jas. 2:15.

2. *diatrophē* (διατροφή, 1305), "sustenance, food," a strengthened form of No. 1 (*dia*, "through," suggesting a sufficient supply), is used in 1 Tim. 6:8.

3. *brōsis* (βρῶσις, 1035), "eating, the act of eating" (akin to *bibroskō*, "to eat") is translated "food" in 2 Cor. 9:10. See MEAT.

4. *sitometrion* (σιτόμετρον, 4620), a measured "portion of food" (*sitos*, "corn," *metreō*, "to measure"), is used in Luke 12:42, RV.

5. *brōma* (βρῶμα, 1033), akin to No. 3, frequently translated "meat," and always so in the KJV except in Matt. 14:15, "victuals," is rendered "food" in the RV in Matt. 14:15; Luke 3:11; 9:13.

Note: For *asitia*, "without food," see ABSTINENCE.

FOOL, FOOLISH, FOOLISHLY, FOOLISHNESS

A. Adjectives.

1. *aphrōn* (ἄφρων, 878) signifies "without reason" (*a*, negative, *phrēn*, "the mind"), "want of mental sanity and sobriety, a reckless and inconsiderate habit of mind" (Hort), or "the lack of commonsense perception of the reality of things natural and spiritual ... or the imprudent ordering of one's life in regard to salvation" (G. Vos, in *Hastings' Bible Dic.*); it is mostly translated "foolish" or "foolish ones" in the RV; Luke 11:40; 12:20; Rom. 2:20; 1 Cor. 15:36; 2 Cor. 11:16 (twice), 19 (contrasted with *phronimos*, "prudent"); 12:6, 11; Eph. 5:17; 1 Pet. 2:15.

2. *anoētos* (ἀνόητος, 453) signifies "not understanding" (*a*, negative, *noeō*, "to perceive, understand"), not applying *nous*, "the mind," Luke 24:25; in Rom. 1:14 and Gal. 3:1, 3 it signifies "senseless," an unworthy lack of understanding; sometimes it carries a moral reproach (in contrast with *sōphrōn*, "sober-minded, selfcontrolled") and describes one who does not govern his lusts, Titus 3:3; in 1 Tim. 6:9 it is associated with evil desires, lusts. See UNWISE.

3. *mōros* (μωρός, 3474) primarily denotes "dull, sluggish" (from a root *muh*, "to be silly"); hence, "stupid, foolish"; it is used (a) of persons, Matt. 5:22, "Thou fool"; here the word means morally worthless, a scoundrel, a more serious reproach than "Raca"; the latter scorns a man's mind and calls him stupid; *mōros* scorns his heart and character; hence the Lord's more severe condemnation; in 7:26, "a foolish man"; 23:17, 19, "fools"; 25:2, 3, 8, "foolish"; in 1 Cor. 3:18, "a fool"; the apostle Paul uses it of himself and his fellow-workers, in 4:10, "fools" (i.e., in the eyes of opponents); (b) of things, 2 Tim. 2:23, "foolish and ignorant questionings"; so Titus 3:9; in 1 Cor. 1:25, "the foolishness of God," not *mōria*, "foolishness" as a personal quality (see C, No. 1), but adjectivally, that which is considered by the ignorant as a "foolish" policy or mode of dealing, lit., "the foolish (thing)"; so in v. 27, "the foolish (things) of the world."

4. *asunetos* (ἀσύνετος, 801) denotes "without discernment," or "understanding" (*a*, negative, *suniēmi*, "to understand"); hence "senseless," as in the RV of Rom. 1:21 (KJV, "foolish"), of the heart; in 10:19, KJV, "foolish," RV, "void of understanding." See UNDERSTANDING.

Note: For "fools," Eph. 5:15, see UNWISE, No. 3.

B. Verbs.

1. *mōrainō* (μωραίνω, 3471) is used (a) in the causal sense, "to make foolish," 1 Cor. 1:20; (b) in the passive sense, "to become foolish," Rom. 1:22; in Matt. 5:13 and Luke 14:34 it is said of salt that has lost its flavor, becoming tasteless.

2. *paraphroneō* (παραφρονέω, 3912), "to be beside oneself" (from *para*, "contrary to," and *phrēn*, "the mind"), "to be deranged," 2 Cor. 11:23, RV, "as one beside himself," for KJV, "as a fool."

C. Nouns.

1. *mōria* (μωρία, 3472) denotes "foolishness" (akin to A, No. 3 and B, No. 1), and is used in 1 Cor. 1:18, 21, 23; 2:14; 3:19.

2. *aphrosunē* (ἀφροσύνη, 877), "senselessness," is translated "foolishness" in Mark 7:22; 2 Cor. 11:1, 17, 21, "foolishness," RV (KJV "folly" and "foolishly"). See FOLLY.

Note: Mōrologia denotes "foolish talking," Eph. 5:4. See TALKING.

FOOT, FEET

A. Nouns.

1. *pous* (πούς, 4228), besides its literal meaning, is used, by metonymy, of "a person in motion," Luke 1:79; Acts 5:9; Rom. 3:15; 10:15; Heb. 12:13. It is used in phrases expressing subjection, 1 Cor. 15:27, RV; of the humility and receptivity of discipleship, Luke 10:39; Acts 22:3; of obeisance and worship, e.g., Matt. 28:9; of scornful rejection, Matt. 10:14; Acts 13:51. Washing the "feet" of another betokened the humility of the service and the comfort of the guest, and was a feature of hospitality, Luke 7:38; John 13:5; 1 Tim. 5:10 (here figuratively).

Note: In Acts 7:5 *bēma*, "a step," is used with podos, the genitive case of *pous*, lit., "the step of a foot," i.e., "a foot breadth," what the "foot" can stand on, "(not so much as) to set his foot on."

2. *basis* (βάσις, 939), lit., "a step" (akin to *bainō*, "to go"), hence denotes that with which one steps, "a foot," and is used in the plural in Acts 3:7.

B. Adjectives.

1. *podērēs* (ποδήρης, 4158) signifies "reaching to the feet," from *pous*, and *arō*, "to fit" (akin to A, No. 1), and is said of a garment, Rev. 1:13. In the Sept. it is used of the high priest's garment, e.g., Ex. 28:4. 2. *pezos* (πεζός, 3978), an adjective, "on foot," is used in one of its forms as an adverb in Matt. 14:3, and Mark 6:33, in each place signifying "by land," in contrast to by sea. Cf. *pezeuō*, "to go on foot," Acts 20:3, RV, "to go by land" (marg., "on foot"). *Notes:* (1) In Acts 20:18, the RV "set foot in" expresses more literally the verb *epibainō* (lit. "to go upon") than the KJV "came into." So again in 21:4 (some mss. have *anabainō* here). (2) In Luke 8:5, *katapateō*, "to tread down" (*kata*, "down," *pateō*, "to tread, trample"), is translated "was trodden under foot," RV (KJV "was trodden down").

FOOTSTOOL

hupopodion (ὑποπόδιον, 5286), from *hupo*, "under," and *pous*, "a foot," is used (a) literally in Jas. 2:3, (b) metaphorically, of the earth as God's "footstool," Matt. 5:35; of the foes of the Lord, Matt. 22:44 (in some mss.); Mark 12:36, "underneath" (in some mss.), Luke 20:43; Acts 2:35; 7:49; Heb. 1:13; 10:13. The RV, adhering to the literal rendering, translates the phrase "the footstool of My (Thy, His) feet," for the KJV, "My (etc.) footstool," but in Matt. 22:44, "(till I put Thine enemies) underneath thy feet."

For **FORBADE** see FORBID

FORBEAR, FORBEARANCE

A. Verbs.

1. *anechō* (ἀνέχω, 430), "to hold up" (*ana*, "up," *echō*, "to have or hold"), is used in the middle voice in the NT, signifying "to bear with, endure"; it is rendered "forbearing (one another)" in Eph. 4:2 and Col. 3:13. Cf. B, No. 1, below.

2. *aniēmi* (ἀνίημι, 447), lit., "to send up or back" (*ana*, "up," *hiēmi*, "to send"), hence, "to relax, loosen," or, metaphorically, "to desist from," is translated "forbearing" (threatening) in Eph. 6:9 ("giving up your threatening," T. K. Abbott). See LOOSE.

3. *pheidomai* (φείδομαι, 5339), "to spare" (its usual meaning), "to refrain from doing something," is rendered "I forbear" in 2 Cor. 12:6.

4. *stegō* (στέγω, 4722) properly denotes "to protect by covering"; then, "to conceal"; then, by covering, "to bear up under"; it is translated "forbear" in 1 Thess. 3:1, 5.

Note: In 1 Cor. 9:6, the verb *ergazomai*, "to work," is used in the present infinitive, with a negative, and translated "to forbear working" (lit., "not working").

B. Noun.

anochē (ἀνοχή, 463), "a holding back" (akin to A, No. 1), denotes "forbearance." a delay of punishment, Rom. 2:4; 3:25, in both places of God's "forbearance" with men, in the latter passage His "forbearance" is the ground, not of His forgiveness, but of His pretermission of sins, His withholding punishment. In 2:4 it represents a suspense of wrath which must eventually be exercised unless the sinner accepts God's conditions; in 3:25 it is connected with the passing over of sins in times past, previous to the atoning work of Christ.

Note: Cf. the noun *epieikeia*, Acts 24:4 "clemency"; 2 Cor. 10:1, "gentleness." Synonymous with this are *makrothumia*, "longsuffering," and *hupomonē*, "patience" (see Col. 1:11). *Anochē* and *makrothumia* are used together in Rom. 2:4. See also Eph. 4:2 (where A, No. 1, is used in this combination). Trench (*Syn.*) and Abbott-Smith (Lex.) state that *huponomē* expresses patience with regard to adverse things, *makrothumia* patience with regard to antagonistic persons. It must be observed, however that in Heb. 6:15 the verb *makrothumeō* is used of Abraham's patience under the pressure of trying circumstances (cf. also Jas. 5:7, 8). *Makrothumia* and *hupomonē* are often found together, e.g., 2 Cor. 6:4 and 6; 2 Tim. 3:10. "Longsuffering is that quality of self-restraint in the face of provocation which does not hastily retaliate or promptly punish; it is the opposite of anger and is associated with mercy, and is used of God, Exod. 34:6, Sept.; Rom. 2:4; 1 Pet. 3:20. Patience is the quality that does not surrender to circumstances or succumb under trial; it is the opposite of despondency and is associated with hope, in 1 Thess. 1:3; it is not used of God."

C. Adjectives.

1. *anexikakos* (ἀνεξίκακος, 420) denotes "patiently forbearing evil," lit., "patient of wrong," (from *anechō*, A, No. 1 and *kakos*, "evil"), "enduring"; it is rendered "forbearing" in 2 Tim. 2:24.

2. *epieikēs* (ἐπιεικής, 1933), an adjective (from *epi*, used intensively, and *eikos*, "reasonable"), is used as a noun with the article in Phil. 4:5, and translated "forbearance" in the RV; KJV, "moderation," RV, marg., "gentleness," "sweet reasonableness" (Matthew Arnold). See GENTLE.

FORBID, FORBADE

A. Verb.

kōluō (κωλύω, 2967), "to hinder, restrain, withhold, forbid" (akin to *kolos*, "docked, lopped, clipped"), is most usually translated "to forbid," often an inferior rendering to that of hindering or restraining, e.g., 1 Thess. 2:16; Luke 23:2; 2 Pet. 2:16, where the RV has "stayed"; in Acts 10:47 "forbid." In Luke 6:29, the RV has "withhold not (thy coat also)." See HINDER, KEEP, *Note* (7), SUFFER, A, *Note* (3), WITHHOLD, WITHSTAND, No. 1.

Notes: (1) The strengthened form *diakōluō* (*dia*, "through," used intensively) is used in Matt. 3:14, where, for the KJV, "forbad" the RV has "would have hindered him" ["forbad" is unsuitable with reference to the natural and persistent (*dia*) effort to prevent Christ from being baptized.]

(2) The phrase *mē genoito*, lit., "let it not be" (*mē*, negative, and *ginomai*, "to become"), is idiomatically translated "God forbid" in Luke 20:16; Rom. 3:4, 6, 31; 6:2, 15; 7:7, 13; 9:14; 11:1, 11; 1 Cor. 6:15; Gal. 2:17; 3:21, and in the KJV of 6:14; here the RV has "far be it from me (to glory)," which the American RV uses in the OT. In Paul's Epistles it is almost entirely used to express the apostle's repudiation of an inference which he apprehends may be drawn from his argument.

B. Adverb.

akōlutōs (ἀκωλύτως, 209), "without hindrance" (*a*, negative, and A, No. 1, is translated "none forbidding him," in Acts 28:31. From the 2nd century A.D. onwards the word is found constantly in legal documents (Moulton and Milligan,

Vocab., who draw attention to the triumphant note on which the word brings the Acts to a close).

FORCE

A. Adjective.

bebaios (βέβαιος, 949), "firm, secure," is translated "of force" (present usage would translate it "in force") in Heb. 9:17, of a testament, or covenant, in relation to a death.

B. Verb.

1. *harpazō* (ἁρπάζω, 726), "to snatch away, carry off by force," is used in the next sentence in Matt. 11:12, to that referred to under No. 1, "men of violence (KJV 'the violent') take it by force," the meaning being, as determined by the preceding clause, that those who are possessed of eagerness and zeal, instead of yielding to the opposition of religious foes, such as the scribes and Pharisees, press their way into the kingdom, so as to possess themselves of it. It is elsewhere similarly rendered in John 6:15, of those who attempted to seize the Lord, and in Acts 23:10, of the chief captain's command to the soldiers to rescue Paul. Cf. *diarpazō*, "to plunder," e.g., Matt. 12:29, and *sunarpazō*, "to seize and carry away," e.g., Acts 6:12, and *harpax*, "rapacious, ravening," e.g., Matt. 7:15.

Notes: (1) *Biazō*, "to force" (from *bia*, "force"), is used in the passive voice in Matt. 11:12, of the kingdom of heaven as 'suffering violence;' so in Luke 16:16, "entereth violently into it," here in the middle voice, expressive of the special interest which the doer of the act has in what he is doing. This meaning is abundantly confirmed by the similar use in the papyri. Moulton and Milligan (*Vocab.*) remark that Luke's statement can be naturally rendered "everyone is entering it violently." See VIOLENCE.

(2) In Matt. 11:12, the corresponding noun, *biastēs*, "violence," is rendered "men of violence," RV (see No. 2). See VIOLENCE.

FOREFATHER

1. *progonos* (πρόγονος, 4269), an adjective, primarily denoting "born before" (*pro*, "before," and *ginomai*, "to become"), is used as a noun in the plural, 2 Tim. 1:3, "forefathers" (in 1 Tim. 5:4, "parents"). See PARENTS.

2. *propatōr* (προπάτωρ, πρό, 4253 and πατήρ, 3962), "a forefather" (*pro*, "before," *patēr*, "a father"), is used of Abraham in Rom. 4:1.

FOREHEAD

metōpon (μέτωπον, 3359), from *meta*, "with," and *ops*, "an eye," occurs only in the Apocalypse, 7:3; 9:4; 13:16; 14:1, 9; 17:5; 20:4; 22:4.

FOREIGN, FOREIGNER

exō (ἔξω, 1854), an adverb, signifying "outside, without," is used in Acts 26:11, RV, "foreign," for KJV "strange," of cities beyond the limits of Palestine, lit., "unto (the) cities without," including Damascus. See STRANGE.

Note: In Eph. 2:19, *paroikos*, lit., "dwelling near" (*para*, "near," *oikos*, a "dwelling"), denotes "an alien, a sojourner," in contrast to fellow-citizens, RV, "sojourners" (KJV, "foreigners"); in 1 Pet. 2:11, KJV, "strangers"; see also Acts 7:6, 29. See SOJOURNER, STRANGER. Cf. *allotrios*, e.g., Acts 7:6; Heb. 11:9, 34; *allophulos*, Acts 10:28; *xenos*, Matt. 25:35, 38, 43; 27:7; Acts 17:21, etc.

FOREKNOW, FOREKNOWLEDGE

A. Verb.

proginōskō (προγινώσκω, 4267), "to know before" (*pro*, "before," *ginōskō*, "to know"), is used (a) of divine knowledge, concerning (1) Christ, 1 Pet. 1:20, RV, "foreknown" (KJV, "foreordained"); (2) Israel as God's earthly people, Rom. 11:2; (3) believers, Rom. 8:29; "the foreknowledge" of God is the basis of His foreordaining counsels; (b) of human knowledge, (1) of persons, Acts 26:5; (2) of facts, 2 Pet. 3:17.

B. Noun.

prognōsis (πρόγνωσις, 4268), "a foreknowledge" (akin to A.), is used only of divine "foreknowledge," Acts 2:23; 1 Pet. 1:2. "Foreknowledge" is one aspect of omniscience; it is implied in God's warnings, promises and predictions. See Acts 15:18. God's "foreknowledge" involves His electing grace, but this does not preclude human will. He "foreknows" the exercise of faith which brings salvation. The apostle Paul stresses especially the actual purposes of God rather than the ground of the purposes, see, e.g., Gal. 1:16; Eph. 1:5, 11. The divine counsels will ever be unthwartable. Cf. FORESHEW.

For **FOREORDAIN** see FOREKNOW, A

FORERUNNER

prodromos (πρόδρομος, 4274), an adjective signifying "running forward, going in advance," is used as a noun, of "those who were sent before to take observations," acting as scouts, especially in military matters; or of "one sent before a king" to see that the way was prepared, Isa. 40:3; (cf. Luke 9:52; and, of John the Baptist, Matt. 11:10, etc). In the NT it is said of Christ in Heb. 6:20, as going in advance of His followers who are to be where He is, when He comes to receive them to Himself. In the Sept., Num. 13:21, "forerunners (of the grape)"; Isa. 28:4, "an early (fig)."

FORESEE, FORESEEN

1. *prooraō* (προοράω, 4308), with the aorist form *proeidon* (used to supply tenses lacking in *prooraō*), "to see before" (*pro*,

"before," *horaō*, "to see"), is used with reference (a) to the past, of seeing a person before, Acts 21:29; (b) to the future, in the sense of "foreseeing" a person or thing, Acts 2:25, with reference to Christ and the Father, RV, "beheld" (here the middle voice is used).

2. *proeidon* (προεῖδον, 4275), an aorist tense form without a present, "to foresee," is used of David, as foreseeing Christ, in Acts 2:31, RV, "foreseeing" (KJV, "seeing before"); in Gal. 3:8 it is said of the Scripture, personified, personal activity being attributed to it by reason of its divine source (cf. v. 22). "What saith the Scripture?" was a common formula among the Rabbis. In the Sept., Gen. 37:18; Ps. 16:8 (*proorao*); 139:3.

3. *problepō* (προβλέπω, 4265), from *pro*, "before," and *blepō*, "to see, perceive," is translated "having provided" in Heb. 11:40 (middle voice), marg., "foreseen," which is the lit. meaning pf the verb, as with Eng. "provide." In the Sept., Ps. 37:13.

FORESHEW

prokatangellō (προκαταγγέλλω, 4293), "to announce beforehand" (*pro*, "before," *katangellō*, "to proclaim"), is translated "foreshewed" in Acts 3:18, RV (KJV, "before had shewed"); in 7:52, KJV and RV, "shewed before."

FORETELL

prolegō (προλέγω, 4302), with the aorist form *proeipon*, and a perfect form *proeirēka* (from *proereō*), signifies (1) "to declare openly" or "plainly," or "to say" or "tell beforehand" (*pro*, "before," *legō*, "to say"), translated in 2 Cor. 13:2 (in the first sentence), RV, "I have said beforehand," KJV, "I told ... before," in the next sentence, KJV, "I foretell," RV, "I do say beforehand" (marg., "plainly"); not prophecy is here in view, but a warning given before and repeated (see under FOREWARN); (2) "to speak before, of prophecy," as "foretelling" the future, Mark 13:23, KJV, "have foretold," RV, "have told ... beforehand"; Acts 1:16 (of the prophecy concerning Judas); Rom. 9:29; 2 Pet. 3:2; Jude 17; some inferior mss. have it in Heb. 10:15. See FOREWARN.

Note: In Acts 3:24 some mss. have *prokatangellō* (see FORESHEW); the most authentic have *katangellō*, RV, "told."

FOREWARN

prolegō (προλέγω, 4302), with verbal forms as mentioned above, is translated "I forewarn" and "I did forewarn," in the RV of Gal. 5:21, KJV, "I tell (you) before" and "I have told (you) in time past"; here, however, as in 2 Cor. 13:2 and 1 Thess. 3:4 (see below), the RV marg., "plainly" is to be preferred to "beforehand" or "before" (see under FORETELL); the meaning in Gal. 5:21 is not so much that Paul prophesied the result of the practice of the evils mentioned but that he had told them before of the consequence and was now repeating his warning, as leaving no possible room for doubt or misunderstanding; in 1 Thess. 3:4, the subject told before was the affliction consequent upon the preaching of the Gospel; in 1 Thess. 4:6, "we forewarned," the warning was as to the consequences of whatsoever violates chastity.

Note: In Luke 12:5 the verb *hupodeiknumi*, "to shew, teach, make known," is translated "will warn" in the RV (KJV, "forewarn"). See EXAMPLE (B, No. 2), WARN.

FORFEIT

zēmioō (ζημιόω, 2210), in the active voice signifies "to damage"; in the passive, "to suffer loss, forfeit," Matt. 16:26 and Mark 8:36, of the "life," RV; KJV, and RV marg., "soul"; in each place the RV has "forfeit," for uv, "lose"; Luke 9:25,"his own self" (RV, "forfeit," KJV, "be cast away"; here the preceding word "lose" translates *apollumi*, "to destroy"). What is in view here is the act of "forfeiting" what is of the greatest value, not the casting away by divine judgment, though that is involved, but losing or penalizing one's own self, with spiritual and eternal loss. The word is also used in 1 Cor. 3:15; 2 Cor. 7:9; Phil. 3:8. See LOSE, LOSS (suffer).

FORGET, FORGETFUL

A. Verbs.

1. *lanthanō* (λανθάνω, 2990), "to escape notice," is translated "they (wilfully) forget" in 2 Pet. 3:5, RV, lit., "this escapes them (i.e., their notice, wilfully on their part)," KJV, "they willingly are ignorant of"; in v. 8, RV, "forget not," lit., "let not this one thing escape you" (your notice), KJV, "be not ignorant of" See HIDE, IGNORANT.

2. *epilanthanomai* (ἐπιλανθάνομαι, 1950), "to forget, or neglect" (*epi*, "upon," used intensively, and No. 1), is said (a) negatively of God, indicating His remembrance of sparrows, Luke 12:6, and of the work and labor of love of His saints, Heb. 6:10; (b) of the disciples regarding taking bread, Matt. 16:5: Mark 8:14; (c) of Paul regarding "the things which are behind," Phil. 3:13; (d) of believers, as to showing love to strangers, Heb. 13:2, RV, and as to doing good and communicating, v. 16; (e) of a person who after looking at himself in a mirror, forgets what kind of person he is, Jas. 1:24.

3. *eklanthanomai* (ἐκλανθάνομαι, 1585), "to forget utterly" (*ek*, "out," intensive), is used in the middle voice in Heb. 12:5, of "forgetting" an exhortation.

B. Nouns.

1. *lēthē* (λήθη, 3024), "forgetfulness" (from *lēthō*, "to forget," an old form of *lanthanō*, see A, No. 1; cf. Eng. "lethal," "lethargy," and the mythical river "Lethe," which was supposed to cause forgetfulness of the past to those who drank of it), is used with *lambanō*, "to take," in 2 Pet. 1:9, "having forgotten,"

lit., "having taken forgetfulness" (cf. 2 Tim. 1:5, lit., "having taken reminder"), a periphrastic expression for a single verb.

2. *epilēsmonē* (ἐπιλησμονή, 1953), "forgetfulness" (akin to A, No. 2), is used in Jas. 1:25, "a forgetful hearer," RV, "a hearer that forgetteth," lit., "a hearer of forgetfulness," i.e., a hearer characterized by "forgetfulness."

FORGIVE, FORGAVE, FORGIVENESS

A. Verbs.

1. *aphiēmi* (ἀφίημι, 863), primarily, "to send forth, send away" (*apo*, "from," *hiēmi*, "to send"), denotes, besides its other meanings, "to remit or forgive" (a) debts, Matt. 6:12; 18:27, 32, these being completely cancelled; (b) sins, e.g., Matt. 9:2, 5, 6; 12:31, 32; Acts 8:22 ("the thought of thine heart"); Rom. 4:7; Jas. 5:15; 1 John 1:9; 2:12. In this latter respect the verb, like its corresponding noun (below), firstly signifies the remission of the punishment due to sinful conduct, the deliverance of the sinner from the penalty divinely, and therefore righteously, imposed; secondly, it involves the complete removal of the cause of offense; such remission is based upon the vicarious and propitiatory sacrifice of Christ. In the OT atoning sacrifice and "forgiveness" are often associated, e.g., Lev. 4:20, 26. The verb is used in the NT with reference to trespasses (*paraptōma*), e.g., Matt. 6:14, 15; sins (*hamartia*), e.g., Luke 5:20; debts (see above) (*opheilēma*), Matt. 6:12; (*opheilē*), 18:32; (*daneion*), 18:27; the thought (*dianoia*) of the heart, Acts 8:22. Cf. *kalupōo*, "to cover," 1 Pet. 4:8; Jas. 5:20; and *epikaluptō*, "to cover over," Rom. 4:7, representing the Hebrew words for "atonement."

Human "forgiveness" is to be strictly analogous to divine "forgiveness," e.g., Matt. 6:12. If certain conditions are fulfilled, there is no limitation to Christ's law of "forgiveness," Matt. 18:21, 22. The conditions are repentance and confession, Matt. 18:15-17; Luke 17:3.

As to limits to the possibility of divine "forgiveness," see Matt. 12:32, 2nd part (see BLASPHEMY) and 1 John 5:16 (see DEATH). See FORSAKE, REMIT, SEND, *Note*, (1), SUFFER, YIELD.

2. *charizomai* (χαρίζομαι, 5483), "to bestow a favor unconditionally," is used of the act of "forgiveness," whether divine, Eph. 4:32; Col. 2:13; 3:13; or human, Luke 7:42, 43 (debt); 2 Cor. 2:7, 10; 12:13; Eph. 4:32 (1st mention). Paul uses this word frequently, but No. 1 only, in Rom. 4:7, in this sense of the word. See DELIVER.

Note: Apoluō, "to let loose from" (*apo*, "from," *luō*, "to loose"), "to release," is translated "forgive," "ye shall be forgiven," Luke 6:37, KJV (RV, "release," "ye shall be released"), the reference being to setting a person free as a quasi-judicial act. The verb does not mean "to forgive." See DISMISS, RELEASE.

B. Noun.

aphesis (ἄφεσις, 859) denotes "a dismissal, release" (akin to A, No. 1); it is used of the remission of sins, and translated "forgiveness" in Mark 3:29; Eph. 1:7; Col. 1:14, and in the KJV of Acts 5:31; 13:38; 26:18, in each of which the RV has "remission." Eleven times it is followed by "of sins," and once by "of trespasses." It is never used of the remission of sins in the Sept., but is especially connected with the Year of Jubilee (Lev. 25:10, etc.). Cf. the RV of Luke 4:18, "release" (KJV, "liberty"). For the significance in connection with remission of sins and the propitiatory sacrifice of Christ, see A, No. 1. See DELIVERANCE, LIBERTY, RELEASE, REMISSION. Cf. the different word *paresis*, "a passing over, a remission," of sins committed under the old covenant, Rom. 3:25. The RV should be used here. This passing over, or by, was neither forgetting nor "forgiving"; it was rather a suspension of the just penalty; cf. Acts 17:30, "the times of ignorance God overlooked," RV; see also, e.g., Ps. 78:38.

FORM (Noun)

1. *morphē* (μορφή, 3444) denotes "the special or characteristic form or feature" of a person or thing; it is used with particular significance in the NT, only of Christ, in Phil. 2:6, 7, in the phrases "being in the form of God," and "taking the form of a servant." An excellent definition of the word is that of Gifford: "*morphē* is therefore properly the nature or essence, not in the abstract, but as actually subsisting in the individual, and retained as long as the individual itself exists .... Thus in the passage before us *morphē Theou* is the Divine nature actually and inseparably subsisting in the Person of Christ .... For the interprehtion of 'the form of God' it is sufficient to say that (1) it includes the whole nature and essence of Deity, and is inseparable from them, since they could have no actual existence without it; and (2) that it does not include in itself anything 'accidental' or separable, such as particular modes of manifestation, or conditions of glory and majesty, which may at one time be attached to the 'form,' at another separated from it ....

"The true meaning of *morphē* in the expression 'form of God' is confirmed by its recurrence in the corresponding phrase, 'form of a servant.' It is universally admitted that the two phrases are directly antithetical, and that 'form' must therefore have the same sense in both."

The definition above mentioned applies to its use in Mark 16:12, as to the particular ways in which the Lord manifested Himself.

Note: For the synonymous word *schēma*, see FASHION. For the verb *morphoō*, see FORMED, No. 1, below.

2. *morphōsis* (μόρφωσις, 3446), "a form or outline," denotes, in the NT, "an image or impress, an outward semblance,"

Rom. 2:20, of knowledge of the truth; 2 Tim. 3:5, of godliness. It is thus to be distinguished from *morphē* (No. 1); it is used in almost the same sense as *schēma*, "fashion" (which see), but is not so purely the outward "form" as *schēma* is.

3. *tupos* (τύπος, 5179), "the representation or pattern" of anything (for which see ENSAMPLE), is rendered "form" in Rom. 6:17, "that form (or mold) of teaching whereunto ye were delivered," RV. The metaphor is that of a cast or frame into which molten material is poured so as to take its shape. The Gospel is the mould; those who are obedient to its teachings become conformed to Christ, whom it presents. In Acts 23:25, it is used of a letter, RV, "form" (KJV, "manner"), with reference to the nature of the contents.

4. *eidos* (εἶδος, 1491), lit., "that which is seen" (*eidon*, "to see"), "an appearance or external form," is rendered "form" in the RV of Luke 3:22, of the Holy Spirit's appearance at the baptism of Christ; in John 5:37, in the Lord's testimony concerning the Father; in Luke 9:29 it is said of Christ Himself; it is translated "sight" in 2 Cor. 5:7, the Christian being guided by what he knows to be true, though unseen; in 1 Thess. 5:22 Christians are exhorted to abstain from "every form of evil," RV (the KJV, "appearance" is inadequate), i.e., from every kind of evil. See FASHION, SHAPE, SIGHT.

5. *hupotupōsis* (ὑποτύπωσις, 5296), "an outline, sketch" (akin to *hupotupoō*, "to delineate," *hupo*, "under," and No. 3), is used metaphorically to denote "a pattern, example," "form," in 2 Tim. 1:13, "of sound words" (RV, "pattern"); in 1 Tim. 1:16, "pattern" and "ensample." See ENSAMPLE.

FORMED

A. Verbs.

1. *morphoō* (μορφόω, 3445), like the noun (A, No. 1), refers, not to the external and transient, but to the inward and real; it is used in Gal. 4:19, expressing the necessity of a change in character and conduct to correspond with inward spiritual condition, so that there may be moral conformity to Christ.

Cf. *metamorphoō*, "to transform, transfigure," *summorphizō* and *suschematizō*, "to conform to."

2. *plassō* (πλάσσω, 4111), "to mold, to shape," was used of the artist who wrought in clay or wax (Eng., "plastic," "plasticity"), and occurs in Rom. 9:20; 1 Tim. 2:13.

B. Noun.

plasma (πλάσμα, 4110) denotes "anything molded or shaped into a form" (akin to A, No. 2), Rom. 9:20, "the thing formed." Cf. the adjective *plastos*, "made up, fabricated, feigned," 2 Pet. 2:3.

FORMER

1. *prōtos* (πρῶτος, 4413), "first," is translated "former" in Acts 1:1, of Luke's first treatise; in Rev. 21:4, RV, "first" (KJV, "former"). See FIRST.

2. *proteros* (πρότερος, 4387), "before, former," is translated "former" in Eph. 4:22; Heb. 10:32; 1 Pet. 1:14.

FORNICATION, FORNICATOR

A. Nouns.

1. *porneia* (πορνεία, 4202) is used (a) of "illicit sexual intercourse," in John 8:41; Acts 15:20, 29; 21:25; 1 Cor. 5:1; 6:13, 18; 2 Cor. 12:21; Gal. 5:19; Eph. 5:3; Col. 3:5; 1 Thess. 4:3; Rev. 2:21; 9:21; in the plural in 1 Cor. 7:2; in Matt. 5:32 and 19:9 it stands for, or includes, adultery; it is distinguished from it in 15:19 and Mark 7:21; (b) metaphorically, of "the association of pagan idolatry with doctrines of, and professed adherence to, the Christian faith," Rev. 14:8; 17:2, 4; 18:3; 19:2; some suggest this as the sense in 2:21.

2. *pornos* (πόρνος, 4205) denotes "a man who indulges in fornication, a fornicator," 1 Cor. 5:9, 10, 11; 6:9; Eph. 5:5, RV; 1 Tim. 1:10, RV; Heb. 12:16; 13:4, RV; Rev. 21:8 and 22:15, RV (KJV, "whoremonger").

B. Verbs.

1. *porneuō* (πορνεύω, 4203) "to commit fornication," is used (a) literally, Mark 10:19; 1 Cor. 6:18; 10:8; Rev. 2:14, 20, see (a) and (b) above; (b) metaphorically, Rev. 17:2; 18:3, 9.

2. *ekporneuō* (ἐκπορνεύω, 1608), a strengthened form of No. 1 (*ek*, used intensively), "to give oneself up to fornication," implying excessive indulgence, Jude 7.

FORSAKE

A. Verbs.

1. *kataleipō* (καταλείπω, 2641), a strengthened form of *leipō*, "to leave," signifies (a) "to leave, to leave behind," e.g., Matt. 4:13; (b) "to leave remaining, reserve," e.g., Luke 10:40; (c) "to forsake," in the sense of abandoning, translated "to forsake" in the RV of Luke 5:28 and Acts 6:2; in Heb. 11:27 and 2 Pet. 2:15, KJV and RV. In this sense it is translated "to leave," in Mark 10:7; 14:52; Luke 15:4; Eph. 5:31.

2. *enkataleipō* (ἐγκαταλείπω, 1459), from *en*, "in," and No. 1, denotes (a) "to leave behind, among, leave surviving," Rom. 9:29; (b) "to forsake, abandon, leave in straits, or helpless," said by, or of, Christ, Matt. 27:46; Mark 15:34; Acts 2:27, 31 (No. 1 in some mss.); of men, 2 Cor. 4:9; 2 Tim. 4:10, 16; by God, Heb. 13:5; of things, by Christians (negatively), Heb. 10:25.

3. *aphiēmi* (ἀφίημι, 863) sometimes has the significance of "forsaking," Mark 1:18; 14:50 (RV, "left"); so Luke 5:11. See FORGIVE.

4. *apotassō* (ἀποτάσσω, 657), primarily, "to set apart" (*apo*, off, "from," *tasso*, "to arrange"), is used in the middle voice, meaning (a) "to take leave of," e.g., Mark 6:46, (b) "to renounce, forsake," Luke 14:33, KJV, "forsaketh," RV, "renounceth" ("all that he hath"). See BID FAREWELL, RENOUNCE, SEND, *Note* (2) at end.

B. Noun.

apostasia (ἀποστασία, 646), "an apostasy, defection, revolt," always in NT of religious defection, is translated "to forsake" in Acts 2:2 lit., "(thou teachest) apostasy (from Moses)"; in 2 Thess. 2:3, "falling away."

FORSWEAR

epiorkeō (ἐπιορκέω, 1964) signifies "to swear falsely, to undo one's swearing, forswear oneself" (*epi*, "against," *orkos*, "an oath"), Matt. 5:33. Cf. *epiorkos*, "a perjured person, a perjurer," 1 Tim. 1:10, "false swearers."

FORTY

tessarakonta (τεσσαράκοντα, 5062) is used in circumstances in Scripture which indicate the number as suggesting probation, separation or judgment, e.g., Matt. 4:2; Acts 1:3; Heb. 3:9, 17.

Note: Tessarakontaetēs, "forty years" (*etos*, "a year"), is found in Acts 7:23; 13:18.

FOSTER-BROTHER

suntrophos (σύντροφος, 4939) primarily denotes "one nourished or brought up with another" (*sun*, "with," *trephō*, "to rear"); it is rendered "foster-brother" in Acts 13:1, RV. It has, however, been found in Hellenistic usage as a court term, signifying an intimate friend of a king (Deissmann), and this would seem to be the meaning regarding Manaen and Herod the Tetrarch.

FOUL

akathartos (ἀκάθαρτος, 169) denotes "unclean, impure" (*a*, negative, and *kathairō*, "to purify"), (a) ceremonially, e g., Acts 10:14, 28; (b) morally, always, in the Gospels, of unclean spirits; it is translated "foul" in the KJV of Mark 9:25 and Rev. 18:2, but always "unclean" in the RV. Since the word primarily had a ceremonial significance, the moral significance is less prominent as applied to a spirit, than when *ponēros*, "wicked," is so applied. Cf. *akatharsia*, "uncleanness." See UNCLEAN.

Note: In Rev. 17:4 the best mss. have this word in the plural, RV. "the unclean things" (*akathartēs*, "filthiness," in some mss.).

FOUNDATION (to lay), FOUNDED

A. Nouns.

1. *themelios*, or *themelion* (θεμέλιος, 2310, or θεμέλιον, 2310a) is properly an adjective denoting "belonging to a foundation" (connected with *tithēmi*, "to place"). It is used (1) as a noun, with *lithos*, "a stone," understood, in Luke 6:48, 49; 14:29; Heb. 11:10; Rev. 21:14, 19; (2) as a neuter noun in Acts 16:26, and metaphorically, (a) of "the ministry of the gospel and the doctrines of the faith," Rom. 15:20; 1 Cor. 3:10, 11, 12; Eph. 2:20, where the "of" is not subjective (i.e., consisting of the apostles and prophets), but objective, (i.e., laid by the apostles, etc.); so in 2 Tim. 2:19, where "the foundation of God" is "the foundation laid by God,"—not the Church (which is not a "foundation"), but Christ Himself, upon whom the saints are built; Heb. 6:1; (b) "of good works, 1 Tim. 6:19.

2. *katabolē* (καταβολή, 2602), lit., "a casting down," is used (a) of "conceiving seed," Heb. 11:11; (b) of "a foundation," as that which is laid down, or in the sense of founding; metaphorically, of "the foundation of the world"; in this respect two phrases are used, (1) "from the foundation of the world," Matt. 25:34 (in the most authentic mss. in 13:35 there is no phrase representing "of the world"); Luke 11:50; Heb. 4:3; 9:26; Rev. 13:8; 17:8; (2) "before the foundation of the world," John 17:24; Eph. 1:4; 1 Pet. 1:20. The latter phrase looks back to the past eternity.

B. Verb.

themelioō (θεμελιόω, 2311), "to lay a foundation, to found" (akin to A, No. 1), is used (a) literally, Matt. 7:25; Luke 6:48; Heb. 1:10; (b) metaphorically, Eph. 3:17, "grounded (in love)"; Col. 1:23 (ditto, "in the faith"); 1 Pet. 5:10, KJV, "settle." See GROUND.

FOUNTAIN

pēgē (πηγή, 4077), "a spring or fountain," is used of (a) "an artificial well," fed by a spring, John 4:6; (b) metaphorically (in contrast to such a well), "the indwelling Spirit of God," 4:14; (c) "springs," metaphorically in 2 Pet. 2:17, RV, for KJV, "wells"; (d) "natural fountains or springs," Jas. 3:11, 12; Rev. 8:10; 14:7; 16:4; (e) metaphorically, "eternal life and the future blessings accruing from it," Rev. 7:17; 21:6; (f) "a flow of blood," Mark 5:29.

For **FOWL** see BIRD

FRAME (Verb)

1. *katartizō* (καταρτίζω, 2675), "to fit, to render complete," is translated "have been framed" in Heb. 11:3, of the worlds or ages. See FIT.

2. *sunarmologeō* (συναρμολογέω, 4883), "to fit or frame together" (*sun*, "with," *harmos*, "a joint," *legō*, "to choose"), is used metaphorically of the church as a spiritual temple, the parts being "fitly framed together," Eph. 2:21; as a body, 4:16, RV, "fitly framed," (for KJV, "fitly joined").

FRANKINCENSE

libanos (λίβανος, 3030), from a Semitic verb signifying "to be white," is a vegetable resin, bitter and glittering, obtained by incisions in the bark of the *arbor thuris*, "the incense tree," and especially imported through Arabia; it was used for fumigation at sacrifices, Exod. 30:7, etc., or for perfume, Song of Sol., 3:6. The Indian variety is called *looban*. It was among the offerings brought by the wise men, Matt. 2:11. In Rev. 18:13 it is listed among the commodities of Babylon. The "incense" of Rev. 8:3 should be "frankincense." Cf. INCENSE.

FRANKLY

Note: In Luke 7:42, the verb *charizomai*, "to forgive" (as a matter of grace), is rendered "frankly forgave," so as to bring out the force of the grace in the action. Older versions had "forgave," and to this the RV returns.

FRAUD

aphustereō (ἀφυστερέω, ἀπό, 575 and ὑστερέω, 5302), "to keep back, deprive" (*apo*, "from," *hustereō*, "to be lacking"), is used in Jas. 5:4, "is kept back by fraud" (some mss. have *apostereō*, "to defraud"). The word is found in a papyrus writing of A.D. 42, of a bath insufficiently warmed (Moulton and Milligan, *Vocab.*). The Law required the prompt payment of the laborer, Deut. 24:15.

FREE, FREEDOM, FREELY, FREEMAN, FREEDMAN, FREEWOMAN

A. Adjective.

eleutheros (ἐλεύθερος, 1658), primarily of "freedom to go wherever one likes," is used (a) of "freedom from restraint and obligation" in general, Matt. 17:26; Rom. 7:3; 1 Cor. 7:39, RV, "free," of the second marriage of a woman; 9:1, 19; 1 Pet. 2:16; from the Law, Gal. 4:26; from sin, John 8:36; with regard to righteousness, Rom. 6:20 (i.e., righteousness laid no sort of bond upon them, they had no relation to it); (b) in a civil sense, "free" from bondage or slavery, John 8:33; 1 Cor. 7:21, 22, 2nd part (for v. 22, 1st part, see C, No. 2); 12:13; Gal. 3:28; Eph. 6:8; Rev. 13:16; 19:18; as a noun, "freeman," Col. 3:11, RV; Rev. 6:15; "f reewoman," Gal. 4:22, 23, 30, and v. 31. RV.

Notes: (1) In Matt. 15:6 and Mark 7:11, the words "he shall be free," KJV, have nothing to represent them in the Greek. (2) In Heb. 13:5, RV, "be ye free from the love of money," is an abbreviated rendering of the adjective *aphilarguros* ("not loving money") with the noun *tropos*, "turn (of mind)"; hence the marg., "let your turn of mind be free, etc.," for KJV, "let your conversation be without covetousness."

B. Verb.

eleutheroō (ἐλευθερόω, 1659), "to make free" (akin to A), is used of deliverance from (a) sin, John 8:32, 36; Rom. 6:18, 22; (b) the Law, Rom. 8:2; Gal. 5:1 (see, however under C); (c) the bondage of corruption, Rom. 8:21. See DELIVER.

Note: In Rom. 6:7, the verb *dikaioō*, translated "is freed," signifies "to justify," as in the RV, "is justified," i.e., in the legal sense; death annuls all obligations. The death penalty which Christ endured holds good for the believer, through his identification with Christ in His death; having been crucified as to his unregenerate nature, and justified from sin, he walks in newness of life in Christ.

C. Nouns.

1. *eleutheria* (ἐλευθερία, 1657), "liberty" (akin to A and B), is rendered "freedom" in Gal. 5:1, "with freedom did Christ set us free." The combination of the noun with the verb stresses the completeness of the act, the aorist (or point) tense indicating both its momentary and comprehensive character; it was done once for all. The RV margin "for freedom" gives perhaps the preferable meaning, i.e., "not to bring us into another form of bondage did Christ liberate us from that in which we were born, but in order to make us free from bondage."

The word is twice rendered "freedom" in the RV of Gal. 5:13 (KJV, "liberty"). The phraseology is that of manumission from slavery, which among the Greeks was effected by a legal fiction, according to which the manumitted slave was purchased by a god; as the slave could not provide the money, the master paid it into the temple treasury in the presence of the slave, a document being drawn up containing the words "for freedom." No one could enslave him again, as he was the property of the god. Hence the word *apeleutheros*, No. 2. The word is also translated "freedom" in 1 Pet. 2:16, RV. In 2 Cor. 3:17 the word denotes "freedom" of access to the presence of God. See LIBERTY.

2. *apeleutheros* (ἀπελεύθερος, 558), "a freed man" (*apo*, "from," and A), is used in 1 Cor. 7:22, "the Lord's freedman." See the illustration above under No. 1. Here the fuller word brings out the spiritual emancipation in contrast to the natural "freedman."

Note: (1) In Acts 22:28, the word *politeia*, rendered "freedom" (KJV), denotes citizenship, as in the RV (see CITIZENSHIP); in the next sentence the Greek is, lit., "But I was even born"; the necessary word to be supplied is "Roman," from the previous verse; hence the RV, "But I am a Roman born." (2) For "free gift" (*charisma*), Rom. 5:15, 16; 6:23, see GIFT.

D. Adverb.

dōrean (δωρεάν, 1432), from *dōrea*, "a gift" is used as an adverb in the sense "freely," in Matt. 10:8; Rom. 3:24; 2 Cor. 11:7 (RV, "for nought"); Rev. 21:6; 22:17. Here the prominent thought is the grace of the Giver.

Notes: (1) In Acts 26:26 *parrhēsiazomai*, "to be bold in speech," is translated, "to speak freely." (2) In Acts 2:29 the noun *parrhēsia* with the preposition *meta*, "with," is rendered "freely," lit., "with free-spokenness." (3) For *charizomai*, "to give freely," Rom. 8:32; 1 Cor. 2:12, see GIVE. (4) In 2 Thess. 3:1, KJV, the verb *trechō*, "to run," is rendered "may have free course"; this the RV corrects to "may run." (5) For "have drunk freely," John 2:10, RV, see DRINK, B, No. 2.

For **FREQUENT**, 2 Cor. 11:23, see ABUNDANT, D

FRIEND (make one's)

A. Nouns.

1. *philos* (φίλος, 5384), primarily an adjective, denoting "loved, dear, or friendly," became used as a noun, (a) masculine, Matt. 11:19; fourteen times in Luke (once feminine, 15:9); six in John; three in Acts; two in James, 2:23, "the friend of God"; 4:4, "a friend of the world"; 3 John 14 (twice); (b) feminine, Luke 15:9, "her friends."

2. *hetairos* (ἑταῖρος, 2083), "a comrade, companion, partner," is used as a term of kindly address in Matt. 20:13; 22:12; 26:50. This, as expressing comradeship, is to be distinguished from No. 1, which is a term of endearment. Some mss. have the word in Matt. 11:16; the best have *heterois*, others, KJV and RV, "fellows." See FELLOW.

Notes: (1) The phrase *hoi para autou*, in Mark 3:21, "his friends," lit. means "the (ones) beside Him," i.e., those belonging to him. (2) In Mark 5:19, "thy friends" represents the phrase *hoitsoi*, lit., "the (ones) to thee," i.e., "thine own."

B. Verb.

peithō (πείθω, 3982), "to persuade, influence," is rendered "having made ... their friend" in Acts 12:20, of the folks of Tyre and Sidon in winning the good will of Blastus, Herod's chamberlain, possibly with bribes. See ASSURE, B, No. 3.

FRIENDSHIP

philia (φιλία, 5373), akin to *philos*, "a friend" (see above), is rendered in Jas. 4:4, "the friendship (of the world)." It involves "the idea of loving as well as being loved" (Mayor); cf. the verb in John 15:19.

For **FROWARD** see CROOKED

FRUIT (bear), FRUITFUL, UNFRUITFUL

A. Nouns.

1. *karpos* (καρπός, 2590), "fruit," is used (I) of the fruit of trees, fields, the earth, that which is produced by the inherent energy of a living organism, e.g., Matt. 7:17; Jas. 5:7, 18; plural, e.g., in Luke 12:17 [for the next verse, see *Note* (1) below] and 2 Tim. 2:6; of the human body, Luke 1:42; Acts 2:30; (II), metaphorically, (a) of works or deeds, "fruit" being the visible expression of power working inwardly and invisibly, the character of the "fruit" being evidence of the character of the power producing it, Matt. 7:16. As the visible expressions of hidden lusts are the works of the flesh, so the invisible power of the Holy Spirit in those who are brought into living union with Christ (John 15:2-8, 16) produces "the fruit of the Spirit," Gal. 5:22, the singular form suggesting the unity of the character of the Lord as reproduced in them, namely, "love, joy, peace, longsuffering, kindness, goodness, faithfulness, meekness, temperance," all in contrast with the confused and often mutually antagonistic "works of the flesh." So in Phil. 1:11, marg., "fruit of righteousness." In Heb. 12:11, "the fruit of righteousness" is described as "peaceable fruit," the outward effect of divine chastening; "the fruit of righteousness is sown in peace," Jas. 3:18, i.e., the seed contains the fruit; those who make peace, produce a harvest of righteousness; in Eph. 5:9, "the fruit of the light" (RV, and see context) is seen in "goodness and righteousness and truth," as the expression of the union of the Christian with God (Father, Son and Holy Spirit); for God is good, Mark 10:18, the Son is "the righteous One," Acts 7:52, the Spirit is "the Spirit of truth," John 16:13; (b) of advantage, profit, consisting (1) of converts as the result of evangelistic ministry, John 4:36; Rom. 1:13; Phil. 1:22; (2) of sanctification, through deliverance from a life of sin and through service to God, Rom. 6:22, in contrast to (3) the absence of anything regarded as advantageous as the result of former sins, v. 21; (4) of the reward for ministration to servants of God, Phil. 4:17; (5) of the effect of making confession to God's Name by the sacrifice of praise, Heb. 13:15.

2. *genēma* (γένημα, 1096d), from *ginomai*, "to come into being," denotes "fruit" (a) as the produce of the earth, e.g., the vine; in the following the best mss. have this noun, Matt. 26:29; Mark 14:25; Luke 22:18; [12:18 in some mss., see *Note* (1)]; (b) metaphorically, as "the fruits of ... righteousness" (i.e., of material ministrations to the needy), 2 Cor. 9:10.

Notes: (1) In Luke 12:18 some mss. have *gennēmata*, a mistake for *genēmata*; the best have *sitos*, "corn." (2) *Genēma* is to be distinguished from *gennēma*, "offspring" (from *gennaō*, "to beget"), Matt. 3:7; 12:34; 23:33; Luke 3:7.

3. *opōra* (ὀπώρα, 3703) primarily denotes "late summer or early autumn," i.e., late July, all August and early September.

Since that is the time of "fruit-bearing," the word was used, by metonymy, for the "fruits" themselves, Rev. 18:14.

Note: Cf. *phthinoporinos*, "autumnal," in Jude 12, "autumn trees," bearing no "fruit" when "fruit" should be expected.

B. Adjectives.

1. *karpophoros* (καρποφόρος, 2593) denotes "fruitful" (A, No. 1, and *pherō*, "to bear"), Acts 14:17. Cf. C, below.

2. *akarpos* (ἄκαρπος, 175), "unfruitful" (*a*, negative, and A, No. 1), is used figuratively (a) of "the word of the Kingdom," rendered "unfruitful" in the case of those influenced by the cares of the world and the deceitfulness of riches, Matt. 13:22; Mark 4:19; (b) of the understanding of one praying with a "tongue," which effected no profit to the church without an interpretation of it, 1 Cor. 14:14; (c) of the works of darkness, Eph. 5:11; (d) of believers who fail "to maintain good works," indicating the earning of one's living so as to do good works to others, Titus 3:14; of the effects of failing to supply in one's faith the qualities of virtue, knowledge, temperance, patience, godliness, love of the brethren, and love, 2 Pet. 1:8. In Jude 12 it is rendered "without fruit," of ungodly men, who oppose the gospel while pretending to uphold it, depicted as "autumn trees" (see *Note* under A, No. 3). In the Sept., Jer. 2:6.

C. Verb.

karpophoreō (καρποφορέω, 2592), "to bear or bring forth fruit" (see B, No. 1), is used (a) in the natural sense, of the "fruit of the earth," Mark 4:28; (b) metaphorically, of conduct, or that which takes effect in conduct, Matt. 13:23; Mark 4:20; Luke 8:15; Rom. 7:4, 5 (the latter, of evil "fruit," borne "unto death," of activities resulting from a state of alienation from God); Col. 1:6 in the middle voice; Col. 1:10.

Note: For "bring forth fruit to perfection," Luke 8:14, see PERFECTION, B.

For **FRUSTRATE**, Gal. 2:21, see VOID

FULFILL, FULFILLING, FULFILLMENT

A. Verbs.

1. *plēroō* (πληρόω, 4137) signifies (1) "to fill"; (2) "to fulfill, complete," (a) of time, e.g., Mark 1:15; Luke 21:24; John 7:8 (KJV, "full come"); Acts 7:23, RV, "he was wellnigh forty years old" (KJV, "was full" etc.), lit., "the time of forty years was fulfilled to him"; v. 30, KJV, "were expired"; 9:23; 24:27 (KJV, "after two years"; RV, "when two years were fulfilled"); (b) of number, Rev. 6:11; (c) of good pleasure, 2 Thess. 1:11; (d) of joy, Phil. 2:2; in the passive voice, "to be fulfilled," John 3:29 and 17:13; in the following the verb is rendered "fulfilled" in the RV, for the KJV, "full," John 15:11; 16:24; 1 John 1:4; 2 John 12; (e) of obedience, 2 Cor. 10:6; (f) of works, Rev. 3:2; (g) of the future Passover, Luke 22:16; (h) of sayings, prophecies, etc., e.g., Matt. 1:22 (twelve times in Matt., two in Mark, four in Luke, eight in John, two in Acts); Jas. 2:23; in Col. 1:25 the word signifies to preach "fully," to complete the ministry of the Gospel appointed.

2. *anaplēroō* (ἀναπληρόω, 378), "to fill up fill completely" (*ana*, "up, up to," and No. 1), is used (a) of Isaiah's prophecy of Israel's rejection of God, fulfilled in the rejection of His Son, Matt. 13:14; (b) of the status of a person in a church, RV, "filleth the place," for KJV, "occupieth the room," 1 Cor. 14:16; (c) of an adequate supply of service, 1 Cor. 16:17, "supplied"; Phil. 2:30, "to supply"; (d) of sins, 1 Thess. 2:16; (e) of the law of Christ; Gal. 6:2.

3. *teleō* (τελέω, 5055), "to end" (akin to *telos*, "an end"), signifies, among its various meanings, "to give effect to," and is translated "fulfill," of the Law, intentionally, Jas. 2:8, or unconsciously, Rom. 2:27; of the prophetic Scriptures concerning the death of Christ, Acts 13:29; prohibitively, of the lust of the flesh, Gal. 5:16.

Notes: (1) In regard to this word in Rev. 15:1 and 8, the RV, "finished," corrects the KJV, "filled up," and "fulfilled," as the judgments there indicated finish the whole series of those consisting of the wrath of God; so in 20:3, of the thousand years of the Millennium (cf. vv. 5, 7). (2) In 17:17, the RV has "should be accomplished," for KJV, "shall be fulfilled." (3) In Luke 22:37 the KJV has "be accomplished" (RV, "be fulfilled").

4. *sunteleō* (συντελέω, 4931), "to complete," is translated "fulfilled" in the KJV of Mark 13:4 (RV, "accomplished). See COMPLETE.

5. *teleioō* (τελειόω, 5048), "to bring to an end, fulfill," is rendered "to fulfill," of days. Luke 2:43; of the Scripture, John 19:28.

6. *plērophoreō* (πληροφορέω, 4135), "to bring in full measure," from *plēroō* (see No. 1), and *phoreō*, "to bring"; hence, "to fulfill," of circumstances relating to Christ, Luke 1:1, RV, "have been fulfilled" (KJV "are most surely believed"); of evangelical ministry, 2 Tim. 4:5, "fulfill" (KJV, "make full proof"); so in v. 17, RV, "fully proclaimed" (KJV, "fully known"). See ASSURE, PERSUADE.

7. *ekplēroō* (ἐκπληρόω, 1603), a strengthened form of No. 1, occurs in Acts 13:33.

Notes: (1) *Poieō*, "to do," is so rendered in the RV, for KJV "fulfill," in Acts 13:22; Eph. 2:3; Rev. 17:17 [for the end of this verse see *Note* (2) under *teleō*, above]. (2) *Ginomai*, "to become, to take place," is rendered "fulfilled" in the KJV of Matt. 5:18; 24:34; Luke 21:32, RV, "accomplished," in each place.

B. Nouns.

1. *plērōma* (πλήρωμα, 4138) stands for the result of the action expressed in *plēroō*, "to fill." It is used to signify (a) "that which has been completed, the complement, fullness,"

e.g., John 1:16; Eph. 1:23; some suggest that the "fullness" here points to the body as the filled receptacle of the power of Christ (words terminating in *-ma* are frequently concrete in character; cf. *dikaiōma* in Rom. 5:18, act of righteousness); in Mark 8:20 the rendering "basketfuls" (RV) represents the plural of this word, lit., "the fulnesses of (how many baskets)"; (b) "that which fills up," Matt. 9:16; Mark 2:21; (C) "a filling up, fulfillment," Rom. 13:10, of the fulfilling of the Law. See FULLNESS (below).

2. *teleiōsis* (τελώνιον, 5058), a fulfillment, is so rendered in Luke 1:45, RV (KJV, "performance"). See PERFECTION.

FULL

A. Adjectives.

1. *plērēs* (πλήρης, 4134) denotes "full," (a) in the sense of "being filled," materially, Matt. 14:20; 15:37; Mark 8:19 (said of baskets "full" of bread crumbs); of leprosy, Luke 5:12; spiritually, of the Holy Spirit, Luke 4:1; Acts 6:3; 7:55; 11:24; grace and truth, John 1:14; faith, Acts 6:5; grace and power, 6:8; of the effects of spiritual life and qualities, seen in good works, Acts 9:36; in an evil sense, of guile and villany, Acts 13:10; wrath, 19:28; (b) in the sense of "being complete," "full corn in the ear," Mark 4:28; of a reward hereafter, 2 John 8.

2. *mestos* (μεστός, 3324) probably akin to a root signifying "to measure," hence conveys the sense of "having full measure," (a) of material things, a vessel, John 19:29; a net, 21:11; (b) metaphorically, of thoughts and feelings, exercised (1) in evil things, hypocrisy, Matt. 23:28; envy, murder, strife, deceit, malignity, Rom. 1:29; the utterances of the tongue, Jas. 3:8; adultery, 2 Pet. 2:14; (2) in virtues, goodness, Rom. 15:14; mercy, etc, Jas. 3:17.

B. Verb.

gemō (γέμω, 1073), "to be full, to be heavily laden with," was primarily used of a ship; it is chiefly used in the NT of evil contents, such as extortion and excess, Matt. 23:25; dead men's bones, v. 27; extortion and wickedness, Luke 11:39; cursing, Rom. 3:14; blasphemy, Rev. 17:3; abominations, v. 4; of divine judgments 15:7; 21:9; (RV, "laden," KJV, "full"); of good things, 4:6, 8; 5:8.

Notes: (1) *Gemizō* is always rendered "to fill" in RV (2) For "fullgrown," Heb. 5:14, RV, see AGE, No. 2.

FULLER

gnapheus (γναφεύς, 1102), akin to *knaptō*, "to card wool," denotes "a clothcarder, or dresser" (*gnaphos*, "the prickly teasel-cloth"; hence, "a carding comb"); it is used of the raiment of the Lord in Mark 9:3.

For **FULLY** see ASSURED, NOW, PERSUADE, PREACH, RIPE

FULLNESS

plērōma (πλήρωμα, 4138) denotes "fullness," that of which a thing is "full"; it is thus used of the grace and truth manifested in Christ, John 1:16; of all His virtues and excellencies, Eph. 4:13; "the blessing of Christ," Rom. 15:29, RV (not as KJV); the conversion and restoration of Israel, Rom. 11:12; the completion of the number of Gentiles who receive blessing through the gospel, v. 25; the complete products of the earth, 1 Cor. 10:26; the end of an appointed period, Gal. 4:4; Eph. 1:10; God, in the completeness of His Being, Eph. 3:19; Col. 1:19; 2:9; the church as the complement of Christ, Eph. 1:23. In Mark 6:43, "basketfuls," RV, is, lit., "fullnesses of baskets." For Mark 8:20 see FULFILL, B.

Note: For *plērophoria*, "fullness," Heb. 6:11, RV, see ASSURANCE.

FURNACE

kaminos (κάμινος, 2575), "an oven, furnace, kiln" (whence Lat. *caminus*, Eng., chimney), used for smelting, or for burning earthenware, occurs in Matt. 13:42, 50; Rev. 1:15; 9:2.

FURTHERANCE

Notes: (1) In Phil. 1:12, 25, KJV, *prokopē*, "a striking forward" (*pro*, "forward," *koptō*, "to cut"), is translated "furtherance"; "progress" in RV, as in 1 Tim. 4:15. Originally the word was used of a pioneer cutting his way through brushwood. (2) In Phil. 1:5 the RV "(for your fellowship) in furtherance of the gospel," and in 2:22, "in furtherance of the Gospel," are, lit., "unto the Gospel."

G

GALL

cholē (χολή, 5521), a word probably connected with *chloē*, "yellow," denotes "gall," (a) literal, Matt. 27:34 (cf. Ps. 69:21); some regard the word here as referring to myrrh, on account of Mark 15:23; (b) metaphorical, Acts 8:23, where "gall of bitterness" stands for extreme wickedness, productive of evil fruit. In the OT it is used (a) of a plant characterized by bitterness (probably wormwood), Deut. 29:18; Hos. 10:4; Amos 6:12; (b) as the translation of the word *mererah*, "bitterness," Job. 13:26, e.g.; (c) as the translation of *rôsh*, "venom"; in Deut. 32:32 "(grapes) of gall." In Job 20:25, the gall bladder is referred to (the receptacle of bile). The ancients supposed that the poison of serpents lay in the gall (see Job 20:14).

For **GAMES** see CONTEND

GARDEN

kēpos (κῆπος, 2779), "a garden," occurs in Luke 13:19, in one of the Lord's parables; in John 18:1, 26, of the garden of Gethsemane; in 19:41, of the garden near the place of the Lord's crucifixion.

GARDENER

kēpouros (κηπουρός, 2780), lit., "a gardenkeeper" (from *kēpos*, see above, and *ouros*, "a watcher"), occurs in John 20:15.

GARMENT

Note: For *himation*, the usual word for "garment," see CLOTHING, where see also *esthēsis* (translated "garments" in the KJV of Luke 24:4, RV, "apparel"), *enduma, chitōn*, and *stolē* (RV, "robe" in Mark 16:5). The fact of the wedding garment, *enduma* in Matt. 22, vv. 11, 12, indicates that persons of high rank showed their magnificence by providing the guests with festal garments.

For **GARRISON** see GUARD, B, No. 3

GATE

1. *pulē* (πύλη, 4439) is used (a) literally, for a larger sort of "gate," in the wall either of a city or palace or temple, Luke 7:12, of Nain (burying places were outside the "gates" of cities); Acts 3:10; 9:24; 12:10; Heb. 13:12; (b) metaphorically, of the "gates" at the entrances of the ways leading to life and to destruction, Matt. 7:13, 14; some mss. have *pulē*, for *thura*, "a door," in Luke 13:24 (see the RV); of the "gates" of Hades, Matt. 16:18, than which nothing was regarded as stronger. The importance and strength of "gates" made them viewed as synonymous with power. By metonymy, the "gates" stood for those who held government and administered justice there.

2. *pulōn* (πυλών, 4440), akin to No. 1, primarily signifies "a porch or vestibule," e.g., Matt. 26:71; Luke 16:20; Acts 10:17; 12:13, 14; then, the "gateway" or "gate tower" of a walled town, Acts 14:13; Rev. 21:12, 13, 15, 21, 25; 22:14.

Notes: (1) In Acts 3:2 *thura* denotes, not a "gate," but a "door," RV. See DOOR. (2) *Probatikos*, signifying "of, or belonging to, sheep," denotes a sheep "gate" in John 5:2, RV, and KJV marg. (3) The conjectural emendation which suggests the idea of "floods" for "gates" in Matt. 16:18 is not sufficiently substantiated to be accepted.

GATHER, GATHERING

A. Verbs.

1. *sunagō* (συνάγω, 4863), "to gather or bring together," is said of (a) persons, e.g., Matt. 2:4; (b) things, e.g., Matt. 13:30; in Luke 15:13 the idea is that of "gathering" his goods together for sale, i.e., "having sold off all." See ASSEMBLE, BESTOW.

2. *episunagō* (ἐπισυνάγω, 1996), "to gather together," suggesting stress upon the place at which the "gathering" is made (*epi*, "to"), is said of a hen and her chickens, Matt. 23:37; and so of the Lord's would-be protecting care of the people of Jerusalem, *id*, and Luke 13:34; of the "gathering" together of the elect, Matt. 24:31; Mark 13:27; of the "gathering" together of a crowd, Mark 1:33; Luke 12:1.

3. *sullegō* (συλλέγω, 4816), "to collect, gather up or out" (*sun*, "with" *legō*, "to pick out"), is said of "gathering" grapes and figs, Matt. 7:16; Luke 6:44 (cf. No. 5); tares, Matt. 13:28, 29, 30, 40; good fish, 13:48; "all things that cause stumbling, and them that do iniquity," 13:41.

4. *sustrephō* (συστρέφω, 4962) signifies (a) "to twist together or roll into a mass" (*sun*, "together," *strephō*, "to turn"), said of the bundle of sticks "gathered" by Paul, Acts 28:3; (b) "to assemble or gather together" (possibly, to journey about together), of persons, Matt. 17:22 (in the best mss.), RV, marg.

5. *trugaō* (τρυγάω, 5166) signifies "to gather in," of harvest, vintage, ripe fruits (*trugē* denotes "fruit," etc., gathered in autumn), Luke 6:44, of grapes (last part of v.; for the previous clause, as to figs, see No. 3); metaphorically, of the clusters of "the vine of the earth," Rev. 14:18; of that from which they are "gathered," v. 19.

6. *athroizō* (ἀθροίζω, 4867) denotes "to assemble, gather together," Luke 24:33 (according to the best mss.); the word is akin to *athroos*, "assembled in crowds" (not found in the NT).

7. *sunathroizō* (συναθροίζω, 4867), *sun*, "together," and No. 6, signifies (a) "to gather together," Acts 19:25, RV (KJV, "called together"); in the passive voice, 12:12.

8. *epathroizō* (ἐπαθροίζω, 1865), "to assemble besides" (*epi*), said of multitudes, Luke 11:29, is rendered "were gathering together" (middle voice), RV (KJV, "were gathered thick together").

Notes: (1) In Eph. 1:10, KJV, the verb *anakephalaioō*, "to sum up, head up," is rendered "might gather together in one" (RV, "sum up"). (2) In Luke 8:4, KJV (*suneimi*, "to come together") as "were gathered together" (see RV). (4) For "assuredly gathering," see CONCLUDE.

B. Noun.

episunagogē (ἐπισυναγωγή, 1997), "a gathering together," is used in 2 Thess. 2:1, of the "rapture" of the saints; for Heb. 10:25, see ASSEMBLE.

For **GAY** see GOODLY, A, *Note*.

For **GAZE** see BEHOLD, No. 3.

GAZINGSTOCK

theatrizō (θεατρίζω, 2301) signifies "to make a spectacle" (from *theatron*, "a theater, spectacle, show"); it is used in the passive voice in Heb. 10:33, "being made a gazingstock."

For **GENDER** see BEGET, No. 1

GENEALOGY

A. Noun.

genealogia (γενεαλογία, 1076) is used in 1 Tim. 1:4 and Titus 3:9, with reference to such "genealogies" as are found in Philo, Josephus and the book of Jubilees, by which Jews traced their descent from the patriarchs and their families, and perhaps also to Gnostic "genealogies" and orders of aeons and spirits. Amongst the Greeks, as well as other nations, mythological stories gathered round the birth and "genealogy" of their heroes. Probably Jewish "genealogical" tales crept into Christian communities. Hence the warnings to Timothy and Titus.

B. Verb.

genealogeō (γενεαλογέω, 1075), "to reckon or trace a genealogy" (from *genea*, "a race," and *legō*, "to choose, pick out"), is used, in the passive voice, of Melchizedek in Heb. 7:6, RV, "whose genealogy (KJV, 'descent') is not counted."

C. Adjective (*negative*).

agenealogētos (ἀγενεαλόγητος, 35), denoting "without recorded pedigree" (*a*, negative, and an adjectival form from B), is rendered "without genealogy" in Heb. 7:3. The narrative in Gen. 14 is so framed in facts and omissions as to foreshadow the person of Christ.

For **GENERAL (Assembly)** see ASSEMBLY, No. 2

GENERATION

1. *genea* (γενεά, 1074): see AGE, No. 2.

2. *genesis* (γένεσις, 1078) denotes "an origin, a lineage, or birth," translated "generation" in Matt. 1:1. See NATURAL, NATURE.

Notes: (1) For *gennēma*, translated "generation" in the KJV of Matt. 3:7; 12:34; 23:33; Luke 3:7, see OFFSPRING. (2) For *genos*, translated "generation" in 1 Pet. 2:9, KJV, see KIND.

GENTILES

A. Nouns.

1. *ethnos* (ἔθνος, 1484), whence Eng., "heathen," denotes, firstly, "a multitude or company"; then, "a multitude of people of the same nature or genus, a nation, people"; it is used in the singular, of the Jews, e.g., Luke 7:5; 23:2; John 11:48, 50-52; in the plural, of nations (Heb., *goiim*) other than Israel, e.g., Matt. 4:15; Rom. 3:29; 11:11; 15:10; Gal. 2:8; occasionally it is used of gentile converts in distinction from Jews, e.g., Rom. 11:13; 16:4; Gal. 2:12, 14; Eph. 3:1.

2. *hellēn* (Ἕλλην, 1672) originally denoted the early descendants of Thessalian Hellas; then, Greeks as opposed to barbarians, Rom. 1:14. It became applied to such Gentiles as spoke the Greek language, e.g., Gal. 2:3; 3:28. Since that was the common medium of intercourse in the Roman Empire, Greek and Gentile became more or less interchangeable terms. For this term the RV always adheres to the word "Greeks," e.g., John 7:35; Rom. 2:9, 10; 3:9; 1 Cor. 10:32, where the local church is distinguished from Jews and Gentiles; 12:13.

B. Adjective.

ethnikos (ἐθνικός, 1482) is used as noun, and translated "Gentiles" in the RV of Matt. 5:47; 6:7; "the Gentile" in 18:17 (KJV, "an heathen man"); "the Gentiles" in 3 John 7, KJV and RV.

C. Adverb.

ethnikōs (ἐθνικῶς, 1483), "in Gentile fashion, in the manner of Gentiles," is used in Gal. 2:14, "as do the Gentiles," RV.

Notes: (1) For the synonymous word *laos*, "a people," see PEOPLE. (2) When, under the new order of things introduced by the gospel the mystery of the church was made known, the word *ethnos* was often used in contrast to the local church, 1 Cor. 5:1; 10:20; 12:2; 1 Thess. 4:5; 1 Pet. 2:12.

GENTLE, GENTLENESS, GENTLY

A. Adjectives.

1. *epieikēs* (ἐπιεικής, 1933), from *epi*, "unto," and *eikos*, "likely," denotes "seemly, fitting"; hence, "equitable, fair, moderate, forbearing, not insisting on the letter of the law"; it expresses that considerateness that looks "humanely and reasonably at the facts of a case"; it is rendered "gentle" in 1 Tim. 3:3, RV (KJV, "patient"), in contrast to contentiousness; in Titus 3:2, "gentle," in association with meekness, in Jas. 3:17, as a quality of the wisdom from above, in 1 Pet. 2:18, in association with the good; for the RV rendering "forbearance" in Phil. 4:5, RV, see FORBEARANCE. Cf. B. See PATIENT. In the Sept., Esth. 8:13; Ps. 86:5.

2. *ēpios* (ἤπιος, 2261), "mild, gentle," was frequently used by Greek writers as characterizing a nurse with trying children or a teacher with refractory scholars, or of parents toward their children. In 1 Thess. 2:7, the apostle uses it of the conduct of himself and his fellow missionaries towards the converts at Thessalonica (cf. 2 Cor. 11:13, 20); in 2 Tim. 2:24, of the conduct requisite for a servant of the Lord.

B. Noun.

epieikeia (ἐπιείκεια, 1932), or *epieikia*, denotes "fairness, moderation, gentleness," "sweet reasonableness" (Matthew Arnold); it is said of Christ, 2 Cor. 10:1, where it is coupled with *prautēs*, "meekness"; for its meaning in Acts 24:4, see CLEMENCY.. Trench (*Syn.* Sec. XLVIII) considers that the ideas of equity and justice which are essential to the meaning, do not adequately express it in English. In contrast with *prautēs* ("meekness"), which is more especially a temperament or habit of mind, *epieikeia* expresses an active dealing with others.

Note: For *chrēstotēs*, "kindness, goodness of heart," rendered "gentleness" in Gal. 5:22, KJV, see KINDNESS. The corresponding adjective *chrēstos* is translated "good," "kind," "easy," "gracious."

For **GHOST** see SPIRIT

GHOST (give up the)

1. *ekpneō* (ἐκπνέω, 1606), lit., "to breathe out" (*ek*, "out," *pneō*, "to breathe"), "to expire," is used in the NT, without an object, "soul" or "life" being understood, Mark 15:37, 39, and Luke 23:46, of the death of Christ. In Matt. 27:50 and John 19:30, where different verbs are used, the act is expressed in a way which stresses it as of His own volition: in the former, "Jesus ... yielded up His spirit (*pneuma*); in the latter, "He gave up His spirit."

2. *ekpsuchō* (ἐκψύχω, 1634), "to expire," lit., "to breathe out the soul (or life), to give up the ghost" (*ek*, "out," *psuchē*, "the soul"), is used in Acts 5:5, 10; 12:23.

GIFT, GIVING

1. *dōron* (δῶρον, 1435), akin to *didōmi*, "to give," is used (a) of "gifts" presented as an expression of honor, Matt. 2:11; (b) of "gifts" for the support of the temple and the needs of the poor, Matt. 15:5; Mark 7:11; Luke 21:1, 4; (c) of "gifts" offered to God, Matt. 5:23, 24; 8:4; 23:18, 19; Heb. 5:1; 8:3, 4; 9:9; 11:4; (d) of salvation by grace as the "gift" of God, Eph. 2:8; (e) of "presents" for mutual celebration of an occasion, Rev. 11:10. See OFFERING.

2. *dōrea* (δωρεά, 1431) denotes "a free gift," stressing its gratuitous character; it is always used in the NT of a spiritual or supernatural gift, John 4:10; Acts 8:20; 11:17; Rom. 5:15; 2 Cor. 9:15; Eph. 3:7; Heb. 6:4; in Eph. 4:7, "according to the measure of the gift of Christ," the "gift" is that given by Christ; in Acts 2:28, "the gift of the Holy Ghost," the clause is epexegetical, the "gift" being the Holy Ghost Himself; cf. 10:45; 11:17, and the phrase, "the gift of righteousness," Rom. 5:17.

Note: For *dōrean*, a form of this noun, used adverbially, see FREELY.

3. *doma* (δόμα, 1390) lends greater stress to the concrete character of the "gift," than to its beneficent nature, Matt. 7:11; Luke 11:13; Eph. 4:8; Phil. 4:17.

4. *dosis* (δόσις, 1394) denotes, properly, "the act of giving," Phil. 4:15, euphemistically referring to "gifts" as a matter of debt and credit accounts; then, objectively, "a gift," Jas. 1:17 (1st mention).

5. *charisma* (χάρισμα, 5486), "a gift of grace, a gift involving grace" (*charis*) on the part of God as the donor, is used (a) of His free bestowments upon sinners, Rom. 5:15, 16; 6:23; 11:29; (b) of His endowments upon believers by the operation of the Holy Spirit in the churches, Rom. 12:6; 1 Cor. 1:7; 12:4, 9, 28, 30, 31; 1 Tim. 4:14; 2 Tim. 1:6; 1 Pet. 4:10; (c) of that which is imparted through human instruction, Rom. 1:11; (d) of the natural "gift" of continence, consequent upon the grace of God as Creator, 1 Cor. 7:7; (e) of gracious deliverances granted in answer to the prayers of fellow believers, 2 Cor. 1:11.

Note: In the KJV of 2 Cor. 8:4 *charis*, "grace," is translated "gift." The RV, "in regard of this grace," adheres to the true meaning, as in v. 6.

6. *merismos* (μερισμός, 3311), "a dividing" (from *meros*, "a part"), is translated "gifts" in Heb. 2:4, "gifts of the Holy Ghost" (marg., "distributions"); in 4:12, "dividing."

Note: In the KJV of Luke 21:5 *anathēma*, "a votive offering," is translated "gifts" (RV, "offerings").

GIRD, GIRDED, GIRT (about, up)

1. *zōnnumi* (ζώννυμι, 2224), or *zōnnuō*, "to gird" in the middle voice, "to gird oneself," is used of the long garments worn in the east, John 21:18; Acts 12:8 (*perizōnnumi* in some mss.).

2. *anazōnnumi* (ἀναζώννυμι, 328), "to gird up" (*ana*, "up," and No. 1), is used metaphorically of the loins of the mind, 1 Pet. 1:13; cf. Luke 12:35 (see No. 4). The figure is taken from the circumstances of the Israelites as they ate the Passover in readiness for their journey, Exod. 12:11; the Christian is to have his mental powers alert in expectation of Christ's coming. The verb is in the middle voice, indicating the special interest the believer is to take in so doing.

3. *diazonnumi* (διαζώννυμι, 1241), "to gird round," i.e., firmly (*dia*, "throughout," used intensively), is used of the Lord's act in "girding" Himself with a towel, John 13:4, 5, and of Peter's girding himself with his coat, 21:7.

4. *perizonnumi* (περιζώννυμι, 4024), "to gird around or about," is used (a) literally, of "girding" oneself for service, Luke 12:37; 17:8; for rapidity of movement, Acts 12:8; (b) figuratively, of the condition for service on the part of the followers of Christ, Luke 12:35; Eph. 6:14; (c) emblematically, of Christ's priesthood, Rev. 1:13, indicative of majesty of attitude and action, the middle voice suggesting the particular interest taken by Christ in "girding" Himself thus; so of the action of the angels mentioned in 15:6.

GIRDLE

zōnē (ζώνη, 2223), Eng., "zone," denotes "a belt or girdle," Matt. 3:4; Mark 1:6; Acts 21:11; Rev. 1:13; 15:6; it was often hollow, and hence served as a purse, Matt. 10:9; Mark 6:8.

GIVER

dotēs (δότης, 1395), akin to *didōmi*, "to give," is used in 2 Cor. 9:7 of him who gives cheerfully (hilariously) and is thereby loved of God.

GLAD (be, make), GLADLY

A. Verbs.

1. *chairō* (χαίρω, 5463) is the usual word for "rejoicing, being glad"; it is rendered by the verb "to be glad" in Mark 14:11; Luke 15:32; 22:5; 23:8; John 8:56; 11:15; 20:20; Acts 11:23; 13:48; in the following the RV has "to rejoice" for KJV, "to be glad," Rom. 16:19; 1 Cor. 16:17; 2 Cor. 13:9; 1 Pet. 4:13; Rev. 19:7. See FAREWELL, No. 4, GREETING, HAIL, JOY, REJOICE.

2. *agalliaō* (ἀγαλλιάω, 21), "to exult, rejoice greatly," is chiefly used in the middle voice (active in Luke 1:47; some mss. have the passive in John 5:35, "to be made glad"). In the OT, it is found abundantly in the Psalms, from 2:11 onward to 149:2, 5 (Sept.). It conveys the idea of jubilant exultation, spiritual "gladness," Matt. 5:12, "be exceeding glad," the Lord's command to His disciples; Luke 1:47, in Mary's song; 10:21, of Christ's exultation ("rejoiced"); cf Acts 2:26, "(My tongue) was glad," KJV (RV, "rejoiced"); John 8:56, of Abraham; Acts 16:34, RV, "rejoiced greatly" (of the Philippian jailor); 1 Pet. 1:6, 8; 4:13 ("with exceeding joy"), of believers in general; in Rev. 19:7, RV, "be exceeding glad" (KJV, "rejoice"). See REJOICE.

3. *euphrainō* (εὐφραίνω, 2165), "to cheer, gladden," is rendered "maketh ... glad" in 2 Cor. 2:2. See FARE, MERRY, REJOICE.

B. Adverbs.

1. *hēdeōs* (ἡδέως, 2234), "gladly" (from *hēdus*, "sweet"), is used in Mark 6:20; 12:37; 2 Cor. 11:19.

2. *hēdista* (ἥδιστα, 2236), the superlative degree of No. 1, "most gladly, most delightedly, with great relish," is rendered "most gladly" in 2 Cor. 12:9, and in v. 15 (RV; KJV, "very gladly").

3. *asmenōs* (ἀσμένως, 780), "with delight, delightedly, gladly," is found in Acts 21:17. It is absent from the best texts in 2:41 (see the RV).

GLADNESS

1. *chara* (χαρά, 5479), "joy, delight" (akin to A, No. 1 above), is rendered "gladness" in the KJV of Mark 4:16; Acts 12:14 and Phil. 2:29 (RV "joy," as elsewhere in both versions). See JOY.

2. *agalliasis* (ἀγαλλίασις, 20), "exultation, exuberant joy" (akin to A, No. 2), is translated "gladness" in Luke 1:14; Acts 2:6; Heb. 1:9; "joy" in Luke 1:44; "exceeding joy" in Jude 24. It indicates a more exultant "joy" than No. 1. In the Sept. this word is found chiefly in the Psalms, where it denotes "joy" in God's redemptive work, e.g., 30:5; 42:4; 45:7, 15. See JOY.

3. *euphrosunē* (εὐφροσύνη, 2167), "good cheer, joy, mirth, gladness of heart" (akin to A, No. 3), from *eu*, "well," and *phrēn*, "the mind," is rendered "gladness" in Acts 2:28, RV (KJV, "joy") and 14:17. See JOY.

GLASS, GLASSY

A. Nouns.

1. *hualos* (ὕαλος, 5194) primarily denoted anything transparent, e.g., a transparent stone or gem, hence, "a lens of crystal, a glass," Rev. 21:18, 21.

2. *esoptron* (ἔσοπτρον, 2072), "a mirror," is rendered "glass" in the KJV of 1 Cor. 13:12 and Jas. 1:23. See MIRROR.

Note: For the corresponding verb *katoptrizō* in 2 Cor. 3:18 (middle voice), see BEHOLD, No. 12.

B. Adjective.

hualinos (ὑάλινος, 5193) signifies "glassy, made of glass" (akin to A, No. 1), Rev. 4:6; 15:2 (twice), RV, "glassy."

For **GLISTERING** see DAZZLING and SHINE, No. 4

GLORIFY

1. *doxazō* (δοξάζω, 1392) primarily denotes "to suppose" (from *doxa*, "an opinion"); in the NT (a) "to magnify, extol, praise" (see *doxa* below), especially of "glorifying"; God, i.e., ascribing honor to Him, acknowledging Him as to His being, attributes and acts, i.e., His glory (see GLORY), e.g., Matt. 5:16; 9:8; 15:31; Rom. 15:6, 9; Gal. 1:24; 1 Pet. 4:16; the Word of the Lord, Acts 13:48; the Name of the Lord, Rev. 15:4; also of "glorifying" oneself, John 8:54; Rev. 18:7; (b) "to do honor to, to make glorious," e.g., Rom. 8:30; 2 Cor. 3:10; 1 Pet. 1:8, "full of glory," passive voice (lit., "glorified"); said of Christ, e.g., John 7:39; 8:54, RV, "glorifieth," for KJV, "honor" and "honoreth" (which would translate *timaō*, "to honor"); of the Father, e.g., John 13:31, 32; 21:19; 1 Pet. 4:11; of "glorifying" one's ministry, Rom. 11:13, RV, "glorify" (KJV, "magnify"); of a member of the body, 1 Cor. 12:26, "be honored" (RV marg., "be glorified").

"As the glory of God is the revelation and manifestation of all that He has and is ..., it is said of a Self-revelation in which God manifests all the goodness that is His, John 12:28. So far as it is Christ through whom this is made manifest, He is said to glorify the Father, John 17:1, 4; or the Father is glorified in Him, 13:31; 14:13; and Christ's meaning is analogous when He says to His disciples, 'Herein is My Father glorified, that ye bear much fruit; and so shall ye be My disciples,' John 15:8. When *doxazō* is predicated of Christ ..., it means simply that His innate glory is brought to light, is made manifest; cf. 11:4. So 7:39; 12:16, 23; 13:31; 17:1, 5. It is an act of God the Father in Him .... As the revelation of the Holy Spirit is connected with the glorification of Christ, Christ says regarding Him, 'He shall glorify Me,' 16:14" (Cremer).

2. *endoxazō* (ἐνδοξάζω, 1740), No. 1 prefixed by *en*, "in," signifies, in the passive voice, "to be glorified," i.e., to exhibit one's glory; it is said of God, regarding His saints in the future, 2 Thess. 1:10, and of the name of the Lord Jesus as "glorified" in them in the present, v. 12.

3. *sundoxazō* (συνδοξάζω, 4888), "to glorify together" (*sun*, "with"), is used in Rom. 8:17.

GLORY, GLORIOUS

A. Nouns.

1. *doxa* (δόξα, 1391), "glory" (from *dokeō*, "to seem"), primarily signifies an opinion, estimate, and hence, the honor resulting from a good opinion. It is used (I) (a) of the nature and acts of God in self-manifestation, i.e., what He essentially is and does, as exhibited in whatever way he reveals Himself in these respects, and particularly in the person of Christ, in whom essentially His "glory" has ever shone forth and ever will do, John 17:5, 24; Heb. 1:3; it was exhibited in the character and acts of Christ in the days of His flesh, John 1:14; John 2:11; at Cana both His grace and His power were manifested, and these constituted His "glory," so also in the resurrection of Lazarus 11:4, 40; the "glory" of God was exhibited in the resurrection of Christ, Rom. 6:4, and in His ascension and exaltation, 1 Pet. 1:21, likewise on the Mount of Transfiguration, 2 Pet. 1:17. In Rom. 1:23 His "everlasting power and Divinity" are spoken of as His "glory," i.e., His attributes and power as revealed through creation; in Rom. 3:23 the word denotes the manifested perfection of His character, especially His righteousness, of which all men fall short; in Col. 1:11 "the might of His glory" signifies the might which is characteristic of His "glory"; in Eph. 1:6, 12, 14, "the praise of the glory of His grace" and "the praise of His glory" signify the due acknowledgement of the exhibition of His attributes and ways; in Eph. 1:17, "the Father of glory" describes Him as the source from whom all divine splendor and perfection proceed in their manifestation, and to whom they belong; (b) of the character and ways of God as exhibited through Christ to and through believers, 2 Cor. 3:18 and 4:6; (c) of the state of blessedness into which believers are to enter hereafter through being brought into the likeness of Christ, e.g., Rom. 8:18, 21; Phil. 3:21 (RV, "the body of His glory"); 1 Pet. 5:1, 10; Rev. 21:11; (d) brightness or splendor, (1) supernatural, emanating from God (as in the *shekinah* "glory," in the pillar of cloud and in the Holy of Holies, e.g., Exod. 16:10; 25:22), Luke 2:9; Acts 22:11; Rom. 9:4; 2 Cor. 3:7; Jas. 2:1; in Titus 2:13 it is used of Christ's return, "the appearing of the glory of our great God and Savior Jesus Christ" (RV); cf. Phil. 3:21, above; (2) natural, as of the heavenly bodies, 1 Cor. 15:40, 41; (II) of good reputation, praise, honor, Luke 14:10 (RV, "glory," for KJV, "worship"); John 5:41 (RV, "glory," for KJV, "honor"); 7:18; 8:50; 12:43 (RV, "glory," for KJV, "praise"); 2 Cor. 6:8 (RV, "glory," for KJV "honor"); Phil. 3:19; Heb. 3:3; in 1 Cor. 11:7, of man as representing the authority of God, and of woman as rendering conspicuous the authority of man; in 1 Thess. 2:6, "glory" probably stands, by metonymy, for material gifts, an honorarium, since in human estimation "glory" is usually expressed in things material.

The word is used in ascriptions of praise to God, e.g.. Luke 17:18; John 9:24, RV, "glory" (KJV, "praise"); Acts 12:23; as in doxologies (lit., "glory-words"), e.g., Luke 2:14; Rom. 11:36; 16:27; Gal. 1:5; Rev. 1:6. See DIGNITY, HONOR, PRAISE, WORSHIP.

2. *kleos* (κλέος, 2811), "good report, fame, renown," is used in 1 Pet. 2:20. The word is derived from a root signifying "hearing"; hence, the meaning "reputation."

Note: In 2 Cor. 3:11 the phrase *dia doxes*, "through (i.e.. by means of) glory," is rendered "with glory" in the RV (KJV, "glorious"); in the same verse *en doxe*, "in glory" (RV), i.e., "accompanied by glory," is rendered "glorious" in the KJV. The first is said of the ministration of the Law, the second of that of the gospel.

B. Adjective.

endoxos (ἔνδοξος, 1741) signifies (a) "held in honor" (*en*, "in," *doxa*, "honor"), "of high repute," 1 Cor. 4:10, RV "have glory" (KJV, "are honorable"); (b) "splendid, glorious," said of apparel, Luke 7:25, "gorgeously"; of the works of Christ, 13:17; of the church, Eph. 5:27. See GORGEOUSLY, HONORABLE.

GLORY (to boast), GLORYING

A. Verbs.

1. *kauchaomai* (καυχάομαι, 2744), "to boast or glory," is always translated in the RV by the verb "to glory," where the KJV uses the verb "to boast" (see, e.g., Rom. 2:17, 23; 2 Cor. 7:14; 9:2; 10:8, 13, 15, 16); it is used (a) of "vainglorying," e.g., 1 Cor. 1:29; 3:21; 4:7; 2 Cor. 5:12; 11:12, 18; Eph. 2:9; (b) of "valid glorying," e.g., Rom. 5:2, "rejoice"; 5:3, 11 (RV, "rejoice"); 1 Cor. 1:31; 2 Cor. 9:2; 10:8, 12:9; Gal. 6:14; Phil. 3:3 and Jas. 1:9, RV, "glory" (KJV, "rejoice"). See BOAST, JOY, REJOICE.

2. *katakauchaomai* (κατακαυχάομαι, 2620), a strengthened form of No. 1 (*kata*, intensive), signifies "to boast against, exult over," Rom. 11:18, RV, "glory" (KJV, "boast"); Jas. 2:13, RV, "glorieth" (KJV, "rejoiceth"); 3:14, "glory (not)." See BOAST, REJOICE.

3. *enkauchaomai* (ἐνκαυχάομαι), *en*, "in," and No. 1, "to glory in," is found, in the most authentic mss., in 2 Thess. 1:4.

Note: Cf. *perpereuomai*, "to vaunt oneself, to be *perperos*, vainglorious," 1 Cor. 13:4.

B. Nouns.

1. *kauchēma* (καύχημα, 2745), akin to A, No. 1, denotes "that in which one glories, a matter or ground of glorying," Rom. 4:2 and Phil. 2:16, RV, "whereof to glory" (for Rom. 3:27, see No. 2); in the following the meaning is likewise "a ground of glorying": 1 Cor. 5:6; 9:15, "glorying," 16, "to glory of"; 2 Cor. 1:14 RV; 9:3, RV; Gal. 6:4, RV (KJV, "rejoicing"); Phil. 1:26 (ditto); Heb. 3:6 (ditto). In 2 Cor. 5:12 and 9:3 the word denotes the boast itself, yet as distinct from the act (see No. 2).

2. *kauchēsis* (καύχησις, 2746) denotes "the act of boasting," Rom. 3:27; 15:17, RV, "(my) glorying" (KJV, "whereof I may glory"); 1 Cor. 15:31, RV, "glorying"; 2 Cor. 1:12 (ditto); 7:4, 14 (KJV, "boasting"); 8:24; 11:10, and 17 (ditto); 1 Thess. 2:19 (KJV, "rejoicing"); Jas. 4:16 (ditto). The distinction between this and No. 1 is to be observed in 2 Cor. 8:24, speaking of the apostle's act of "glorying" in the liberality of the Corinthians, while in 9:3 he exhorts them not to rob him of the ground of his "glorying" (No. 1). Some take the word in 2 Cor. 1:12 (see above) as identical with No. 1, a boast, but there seems to be no reason for regarding it as different from its usual sense, No. 2.

Note: Cf. *alazoneia* (or *-ia*), "vainglory, ostentatious (or arrogant) display," Jas. 4:16 and 1 John 2:16, and *alazōn*, "a boaster," Rom. 1:30 and 2 Tim. 3:2.

GOAD

kentron (κέντρον, 2759), from *kenteō*, "to prick," denotes (a) "a sting," Rev. 9:10; metaphorically, of sin as the "sting" of death, 1 Cor. 15:55, 56; (b) "a goad," Acts 26:14, RV, "goad" (marg., "goads"), for KJV, "pricks" (in some mss. also in 9:5), said of the promptings and misgivings which Saul of Tarsus had resisted before conversion.

GOAL

skopos (σκοπός, 4649), primarily, "a watcher" (from *skopeo*, "to look at"; Eng., "scope"), denotes "a mark on which to fix the eye," and is used metaphorically of an aim or object in Phil. 3:14, RV, "goal" (KJV, "mark"). See MARK.

GOAT

1. *eriphos* (ἔριφος, 2056) denotes "a kid or goat," Matt. 25:32 (RV, marg., "kids"); Luke 15:29, "a kid"; some mss. have No. 2 here, indicating a sneer on the part of the elder son, that his father had never given him even a tiny kid.

2. *eriphion* (ἐρίφιον, 2055), a diminutive of No. 1, is used in Matt. 25:33. In v. 32 *eriphos* is purely figurative; in v. 33, where the application is made, though metaphorically, the change to the diminutive is suggestive of the contempt which those so described bring upon themselves by their refusal to assist the needy.

3. *tragos* (τράγος, 5131) denotes "a he-goat," Heb. 9:12, 13, 19; 10:4, the male prefiguring the strength by which Christ laid down His own life in expiatory sacrifice.

GOD

theos (θεός, 2316), (I) in the polytheism of the Greeks, denoted "a god or deity," e.g., Acts 14:11; 19:26; 28:6; 1 Cor. 8:5; Gal. 4:8.

(II) (a) Hence the word was appropriated by Jews and retained by Christians to denote "the one true God." In the Sept. *theos* translates (with few exceptions) the Hebrew words *Elohim* and *Jehovah*, the former indicating His power and preeminence, the latter His unoriginated, immutable, eternal and self-sustained existence.

In the NT, these and all the other divine attributes are predicated of Him. To Him are ascribed, e.g., His unity, or monism, e.g., Mark 12:29; 1 Tim. 2:5; self-existence, John 5:26; immutability, Jas. 1:17; eternity, Rom. 1:20; universality, Matt. 10:29; Acts 17:26-28; almighty power Matt. 19:26; infinite knowledge, Acts 2:23; 15:18; Rom. 11:33, creative power, Rom. 11:36; 1 Cor. 8:6; Eph. 3:9; Rev. 4:11; 10:6; absolute holiness, 1 Pet. 1:15; 1 John 1:5; righteousness, John 17:25; faithfulness, 1 Cor. 1:9; 10:13; 1 Thess. 5:24; 2 Thess. 3:3; 1 John 1:9; love, 1 John 4:8, 16; mercy, Rom. 9:15, 18; truthfulness, Titus 1:2; Heb. 6:18. See GOOD, No. 1 (b).

(b) The divine attributes are likewise indicated or definitely predicated of Christ, e.g., Matt. 20:18-19; John 1:1-3; 1:18, RV, marg.; 5:22-29; 8:58; 14:6; 17:22-24; 20:28; Rom. 1:4; 9:5; Phil. 3:21; Col. 1:15; 2:3; Titus 2:13, RV; Heb. 1:3; 13:8; 1 John 5:20; Rev. 22:12, 13.

(c) Also of the Holy Spirit, e.g., Matt. 28:19; Luke 1:35; John 14:16; 15:26; 16:7-14; Rom. 8:9, 26; 1 Cor. 12:11; 2 Cor. 13:14.

(d) *Theos* is used (1) with the definite article, (2) without (i.e., as an anarthrous noun). "The English may or may not have need of the article in translation. But that point cuts no figure in the Greek idiom. Thus in Acts 27:23 ('the God whose I am,' RV) the article points out the special God whose Paul is, and is to be preserved in English. In the very next verse (*ho theos*) we in English do not need the article" (A. T. Robertson, *Gram. of Greek, NT*, p. 758).

As to this latter it is usual to employ the article with a proper name, when mentioned a second time. There are, of course, exceptions to this, as when the absence of the article serves to lay stress upon, or give precision to, the character or nature of what is expressed in the noun. A notable instance of this is in John 1:1, "and the Word was God"; here a double stress is on *theos*, by the absence of the article and by the emphatic position. To translate it literally, "a god was the Word," is entirely misleading. Moreover, that "the Word" is the subject of the sentence, exemplifies the rule that the subject is to be determined by its having the article when the predicate is anarthrous (without the article). In Rom. 7:22, in the phrase "the law of God," both nouns have the article; in v. 25, neither has the article. This is in accordance with a general rule that if two nouns are united by the genitive case (the "of" case), either both have the article, or both are without. Here, in the first instance, both nouns, "God" and "the law" are definite, whereas in v. 25 the word "God" is not simply titular; the absence of the article stresses His character as lawgiver.

Where two or more epithets are applied to the same person or thing, one article usually serves for both (the exceptions being when a second article lays stress upon different aspects of the same person or subject, e.g., Rev. 1:17). In Titus 2:13 the RV correctly has "our great God and Savior Jesus Christ." Moulton (*Prol.*, p. 84) shows, from papyri writings of the early Christian era, that among Greek-speaking Christians this was "a current formula" as applied to Christ. So in 2 Pet. 1:1 (cf. 1:11; 3:18).

In the following titles God is described by certain of His attributes; the God of glory, Acts 7:2; of peace, Rom. 15:33; 16:20; Phil. 4:9; 1 Thess. 5:23; Heb. 13:20; of love and peace, 2 Cor. 13:11; of patience and comfort, Rom. 15:5; of all comfort, 2 Cor. 1:3; of hope, Rom. 15:13; of all grace, 1 Pet. 5:10. These describe Him, not as in distinction from other persons, but as the source of all these blessings; hence the employment of the definite article. In such phrases as "the God of a person," e.g., Matt. 22:32, the expression marks the relationship in which the person stands to God and God to him.

(e) In the following the nominative case is used for the vocative, and always with the article; Mark 15:34; Luke 18:11, 13; John 20:28; (Acts 4:24 in some mss.); Heb. 1:8; 10:7.

(f) The phrase "the things of God" (translated literally or otherwise) stands for (1) His interests, Matt. 16:23; Mark 8:33; (2) His counsels, 1 Cor. 2:11; (3) things which are due to Him, Matt. 22:21; Mark 12:17; Luke 20:25. The phrase "things pertaining to God," Rom. 15:17; Heb. 2:17; 5:1, describes, in the Heb. passages, the sacrificial service of the priest; in the Rom. passage the gospel ministry as an offering to God.

(III) The word is used of divinely appointed judges in Israel, as representing God in His authority, John 10:34, quoted from Ps. 82:6, which indicates that God Himself sits in judgment on those whom He has appointed. The application of the term to the Devil, 2 Cor. 4:4, and the belly, Phil. 3:19, virtually places these instances under (I).

For **GOD-SPEED** see GREETING

GOD (without)

atheos (ἄθεος, 112), cf. Eng., "atheist," primarily signifies "godless" (*a*, negative), i.e., destitute of God; in Eph. 2:12 the phrase indicates, not only that the Gentiles were void of any true recognition of God, and hence became morally "godless" (Rom. 1:19-32) but that being given up by God, they were excluded from communion with God and from the privileges granted to Israel (see the context and cf. Gal. 4:8). As to pagan ideas, the popular cry against the early Christians was "away with the atheists" (see the account of the martyrdom of Polycarp, in Eusebius, *Eccles. Hist.* iv. 15, 19).

GODDESS

thea (θεά, 2299) is found in Acts 19:27 (in some mss. in vv. 35, 37).

For **GODHEAD** see DIVINE, DIVINITY

GODLINESS, GODLY

A. Nouns.

1. *eusebeia* (εὐσέβεια, 2150), from *eu*, "well," and *sebomai*, "to be devout," denotes that piety which, characterized by a

Godward attitude, does that which is well-pleasing to Him. This and the corresponding verb and adverb (see below) are frequent in the Pastoral Epistles, but do not occur in previous epistles of Paul. The apostle Peter has the noun four times in his 2nd Epistle, 1:3, 6, 7; 3:11. Elsewhere it occurs in Acts 3:12; 1 Tim. 2:2; 3:16; 4:7, 8; 6:3, 5, 6, 11; 2 Tim. 3:5; Titus 1:1. In 1 Tim. 6:3 "the doctrine which is according to godliness" signifies that which is consistent with "godliness," in contrast to false teachings; in Titus 1:1, "the truth which is according to godliness" is that which is productive of "godliness"; in 1 Tim. 3:16, "the mystery of godliness" is "godliness" as embodied in, and communicated through, the truths of the faith concerning Christ; in 2 Pet. 3:11, the word is in the plural, signifying acts of "godliness."

2. *theosebeia* (θεοσέβεια, 2317) denotes "the fear or reverence of God," from *theos*, "god," and *sebomai* (see No. 1), 1 Tim. 2:10. Cf. the adjective *theosebēs*, "God-fearing," John 9:31. In the Sept., Gen. 20:11 and Job 28:28.

Note: For *eulabeia*, "godly fear," Heb. 5:7; 12:28 see FEAR, A, No. 3; for *eulabeomai*, "to reverence," Heb. 11:7 ("for His godly fear") see FEAR, D, No. 2; for the verb *eusebeō*, "to show piety," 1 Tim. 5:4; "to worship," Acts 17:23, see PIETY and WORSHIP.

B. Adjective.

eusebēs (εὐσεβής, 2152), akin to A, No. 1, denotes "pious, devout, godly," indicating reverence manifested in actions; it is rendered "godly" in 2 Pet. 2:9. See DEVOUT.

C. Adverb.

eusebōs (εὐσεβῶς, 2153) denotes "piously, godly"; it is used with the verb "to live" (of manner of life) in 2 Tim. 3:12; Titus 2:12.

Notes: (1) In the following the word "godly" translates the genitive case of the noun *theos*, lit., "of God," 2 Cor. 1:12, KJV, "godly (sincerity)," RV, "(sincerity) of God"; 2 Cor. 11:2, "a godly jealousy," lit., "a jealousy of God" (RV, marg.); 1 Tim. 1:4, RV, "a dispensation of God" (*oikonomia*, in the best mss.), KJV, "godly edifying" (*oikodomē* lit., "an edifying of, i.e., by, God"). (2) In 2 Cor. 7:10, "godly (sorrow)," and in vv. 9 and 11, "after a godly sort," are in all three place, lit., "according to God." (3) In 3 John 6, where the KJV translates the adverb *axios*, with the noun *theos*, "after a godly sort," the RV rightly substitutes "worthily of God."

GODWARD

Note: This translates the phrase *pros ton theon*, lit., "toward God," in 2 Cor. 3:4, and 1 Thess. 1:8.

GOOD, GOODLY, GOODNESS

A. Adjectives.

1. *agathos* (ἀγαθός, 18) describes that which, being "good" in its character or constitution, is beneficial in its effect; it is used (a) of things physical, e.g., a tree, Matt. 7:17; ground, Luke 8:8; (b) in a moral sense, frequently of persons and things. God is essentially, absolutely and consummately "good," Matt. 19:17; Mark 10:18; Luke 18:19. To certain persons the word is appiied in Matt. 20:15; 25:21, 23; Luke 19:17; 23:50; John 7:12; Acts 11:24; Titus 2:5; in a general application, Matt. 5:45; 12:35; Luke 6:45; Rom. 5:7; 1 Pet. 2:18.

The neuter of the adjective with the definite article signifies that which is "good," lit., "the good," as being morally honorable, pleasing to God, and therefore beneficial. Christians are to prove it, Rom. 12:2; to cleave to it, 12:9; to do it, 13:3; Gal. 6:10; 1 Pet. 3:11 (here, and here only, the article is absent); John 5:29 (here, the neuter plural is used, "the good things"); to work it, Rom. 2:10; Eph. 4:28; 6:8; to follow after it, 1 Thess. 5:15; to be zealous of it, 1 Pet. 3:13; to imitate it, 3 John 11; to overcome evil with it, Rom. 12:21. Governmental authorities are ministers of "good," i.e., that which is salutary, suited to the course of human affairs, Rom. 13:4. In Philem. 14, "thy goodness," RV (lit., "thy good"), means "thy benefit." As to Matt. 19:17, "why askest thou Me concerning that which is good?" the RV follows the most ancient mss.

The neuter plural is also used of material "goods," riches, etc., Luke 1:53; 12:18, 19; 16:25; Gal. 6:6 (of temporal supplies); in Rom. 10:15; Heb. 9:11; 10:1, the "good" things are the benefits provided through the sacrifice of Christ, in regard both to those conferred through the gospel and to those of the coming messianic kingdom. See further under No. 2. See BENEFIT, GOODS.

2. *kalos* (καλός, 2570) denotes that which is intrinsically "good," and so, "goodly, fair, beautiful," as (a) of that which is well adapted to its circumstances or ends, e.g., fruit, Matt. 3:10; a tree, 12:33; ground, 13:8, 23; fish, 13:48; the Law, Rom. 7:16; 1 Tim. 1:8; every creature of God, 1 Tim. 4:4; a faithful minister of Christ and the doctrine he teaches, 4:6; (b) of that which is ethically good, right, noble, honorable e.g., Gal. 4:18; 1 Tim. 5:10, 25; 6:18; Titus 2:7, 14; 3:8, 14. The word does not occur in the Apocalypse, nor indeed after 1 Peter.

Christians are to "take thought for things honorable" (*kalos*), 2 Cor. 8:21, RV; to do that which is honorable, 13:7; not to be weary in well doing, Gal. 6:9; to hold fast "that which is good," 1 Thess. 5:21; to be zealous of good works, Titus 2:14; to maintain them, 3:8; to provoke to them, Heb. 10:24; to bear testimony by them, 1 Pet. 2:12.

Kalos and *agathos* occur together in Luke 8:15, an "honest" (*kalos*) heart, i.e., the attitude of which is right towards

God; a "good" (*agathos*) heart, i.e., one that, instead of working ill to a neighbor, acts beneficially towards him. In Rom. 7:18, "in me ... dwelleth no good thing" (*agathos*) signifies that in him is nothing capable of doing "good," and hence he lacks the power "to do that which is good" (*kalos*). In 1 Thess. 5:15, "follow after that which is good" (*agathos*), the "good" is that which is beneficial; in v. 21, "hold fast that which is good (*kalos*)," the "good" describes the intrinsic value of the teaching. See BETTER, HONEST, WORTHY.

3. *chrestos* (χρηστός, 5543), said of things, "that which is pleasant," said of persons, "kindly, gracious," is rendered "good" in 1 Cor. 15:33, "goodness" in Rom. 2:4.

Note: Lampros denotes "gay, bright," "goodly" in Jas. 2:2, KJV, (RV, "fine"); in 2:3, KJV, "gay"; in Rev. 18:14 (RV, "sumptuous"). See GORGEOUS, SUMPTUOUS. For *asteios*, "goodly," Heb. 11:23, RV, see BEAUTIFUL.

B. Nouns.

1. *chrēstotēs* (χρηστότης, 5544), akin to A, No. 3, denotes "goodness" (a) in the sense of what is upright, righteous, Rom. 3:12 (translated "good"); (b) in the sense of kindness of heart or act, said of God, Rom. 2:4; 11:22 (thrice); Eph. 2:7 ("kindness"); Titus 3:4 ("kindness"); said of believers and rendered "kindness," 2 Cor. 6:6; Col. 3:12; Gal. 5:22 (RV; KJV, "gentleness"). It signifies "not merely goodness as a quality, rather it is goodness in action, goodness expressing itself in deeds; yet not goodness expressing itself in indignation against sin, for it is contrasted with severity in Rom. 11:22, but in grace and tenderness and compassion." See GENTLENESS, KINDNESS.

2. *agathōsunē* (ἀγαθωσύνη, 19), "goodness," signifies that moral quality which is described by the adjective *agathos* (see A, No. 1). It is used, in the NT, of regenerate persons, Rom. 15:14; Gal. 5:22; Eph. 5:9; 2 Thess. 1:11; in the last, the phrase "every desire of goodness" (RV; the addition of "His" in the KJV is an interpolation; there is no pronoun in the original) may be either subjective, i.e., desire characterized by "goodness," "good" desire, or objective, i.e., desire after "goodness," to be and do good.

Trench, following Jerome, distinguishes between *chrēstotēs* and *agathōsunē* in that the former describes the kindlier aspects of "goodness," the latter includes also the sterner qualities by which doing "good" to others is not necessarily by gentle means. He illustrates the latter by the act of Christ in cleansing the temple, Matt. 21:12, 13, and in denouncing the scribes and Pharisees, 23:13-29; but *chrēstotēs* by His dealings with the penitent woman, Luke 7:37-50. Lightfoot regards *chrēstotēs* as a kindly disposition towards others; *agathōsunē* as a kindly activity on their behalf.

J. A. Robertson (on Eph. 5:9) remarks that *agathōsunē* is "the kindlier, as *dikaiosunē* (righteousness) the sterner, element in the ideal character."

3. *eupoiia* (εὐποιΐα, 2140), "beneficence, doing good" (*eu*, "well," *poieō*, "to do"), is translated as a verb in Heb. 13:16, "to do good."

C. Adverbs.

1. *kalōs* (καλῶς, 2573), "well, finely," is used in some mss. in Matt. 5:44, with *poieō*, "to do," and translated "do good." In Jas. 2:3 it is rendered "in a good place" (KJV marg., "well" or "seemly"). See WELL.

2. *eu* (εὖ, 2095), "well," used with *poieō*, is translated "do ... good" in Mark 14:7. See WELL.

D. Verbs (to do, or be, good).

1. *agathopoieō* (ἀγαθοποιέω, 15), from A, No. 1, and *poieō*, "to do," is used (a) in a general way, "to do well," 1 Pet. 2:15, 20; 3:6, 17; 3 John 11; (b) with pointed reference "to the benefit of another," Luke 6:9, 33, 35; in Mark 3:4 the parts of the word are separated in some mss. Some mss. have it in Acts 14:17, for No. 2. Cf. the noun *agathopoiia*, "well-doing," 1 Pet. 4:19, and the adjective *agathopoios*, "doing well," 1 Pet. 2:14.

2. *agathourgeō* (ἀγαθοεργέω, 14), for *agathoergeō*, "to do good" (from A, No. 1, and *ergon*, "a work"), is used in Acts 14:17 (in the best mss.; see No. 1), where it is said of God's beneficence towards man, and 1 Tim. 6:18, where it is enjoined upon the rich.

3. *euergeteō* (εὐεργετέω, 2109), "to bestow a benefit, to do good" (*eu*, "well," and a verbal form akin to *ergon*), is used in Acts 10:38.

Notes: (1) The verb *ischuō*, "to be strong" (*ischus*, "strength"), "to have efficacy, force or value," is said of salt in Matt. 5:13, negatively, "it is good for nothing." (2) In Matt. 19:10, KJV, *sumpherō*, "to be profitable, expedient" (*sun*, "together," *pherō*, "to bring"); is rendered with a negative "it is not good" (RV, "it is not expedient"). (3) In Mark 14:7, the two words *eu*, "well," and *poieō*, "to do," are in some mss. treated as one verb *eupoieo*, "to do good."

GOODMAN

oikodespotēs (οἰκοδεσπότης, 3617) denotes "the master of a house" (*oikos*, "a house," *despotēs*, "a master"), "a householder." It occurs only in the Synoptists, and there 12 times. It is rendered "goodman" in Luke 22:11, where "of the house" is put separately; in Matt. 20:11, where the KJV has "the goodman of the house" for the one word, the RV renders it by "householder," as in v. 1; in 24:43, "master"; so in Luke 12:39; in Mark 14:14, both have "the goodman of the house. See MASTER.

GOODS

1. For the neuter plural of *agathos*, used as a noun, "goods," see Luke 12:18, 19, where alone this word is so rendered.

2. *huparxis* (ὕπαρξις, 5223), primarily, "subsistence," then, "substance, property, goods" (akin to *huparchō*, "to exist, be, belong to"), is translated "goods" in Acts 2:45; "possession." RV (KJV, "substance") in Heb. 10:34.

3. *bios* (βίος, 979), which denotes (a) "life, lifetime," (b) "livelihood, living, means of living," is translated "goods" in 1 John 3:17, RV (KJV, "good). See LIFE, No. 2.

4. *skeuos* (σκεῦος, 4632), "a vessel," denotes "goods" in Matt. 12:29; Mark 3:27; Luke 17:31, RV (KJV, stuff). See VESSEL.

Notes: (1) The neuter plural of the present participle of *huparchō*, is used as a noun denoting "goods," in Matt. 24:47, KJV "his goods," RV, "that he hath"; "goods" in Matt. 25:14; Luke 11:21; 16:1; 19:8; 1 Cor. 13:3; in Heb. 10:34 (1st part). (2) In Luke 6:30 "thy goods" translates the neuter plural of the possessive pronoun with the article, lit., "thy things," or possessions. (3) In Rev. 3:17, the KJV "I am ... increased with goods" translates the perfect tense of the verb *plouteō*, "to be rich"; RV, "I have gotten riches." (4) See SUBSTANCE.

GORGEOUS, GORGEOUSLY

lampros (λαμπρός, 2986), "bright, splendid," is rendered "gorgeous" in Luke 23:11 of the apparel in which Herod and his soldiers arrayed Christ. See BRIGHT.

Note: For the KJV, "gorgeously apparelled" in Luke 7:25, see GLORIOUS, B.

GOSPEL (Noun and Verb: to preach)

A. Noun.

euangelion (εὐαγγέλιον, 2098) originally denoted a reward for good tidings; later, the idea of reward dropped, and the word stood for "the good news" itself. The Eng. word "gospel," i.e. "good message," is the equivalent of *euangelion* (Eng., "evangel"). In the NT it denotes the "good tidings" of the kingdom of God and of salvation through Christ, to be received by faith, on the basis of His expiatory death, His burial, resurrection, and ascension, e.g., Acts 15:7; 20:24; 1 Pet. 4:17. Apart from those references and those in the gospels of Matthew and Mark, and Rev. 14:6, the noun is confined to Paul's epistles. The apostle uses it of two associated yet distinct things, (a) of the basic facts of the death, burial and resurrection of Christ, e.g., 1 Cor. 15:1-3; (b) of the interpretation of these facts, e.g., Rom. 2:16; Gal. 1:7, 11; 2:2; in (a) the "gospel" is viewed historically, in (b) doctrinally, with reference to the interpretation of the facts, as is sometimes indicated by the context.

The following phrases describe the subjects or nature or purport of the message; it is the "gospel" of God, Mark 1:14; Rom. 1:1; 15:16; 2 Cor. 11:7; 1 Thess. 2:2, 9; 1 Pet. 4:17; God, concerning His Son, Rom. 1:1-3; His Son, Rom. 1:9; Jesus Christ, the Son of God, Mark 1:1; our Lord Jesus, 2 Thess. 1:8; Christ, Rom. 15:19, etc.; the glory of Christ, 2 Cor. 4:4; the grace of God, Acts 20:24; the glory of the blessed God, 1 Tim. 1:11; your salvation, Eph. 1:13; peace, Eph. 6:15. Cf. also "the gospel of the Kingdom," Matt. 4:23; 9:35; 24:14; "an eternal gospel," Rev. 14:6.

In Gal. 2:14, "the truth of the gospel" denotes, not the true "gospel," but the true teaching of it, in contrast to perversions of it.

The following expressions are used in connection with the "gospel": (a) with regard to its testimony; (1) *kērussō*, "to preach it as a herald, e.g., Matt. 4:23; Gal. 2:2 (see PREACH); (2) *laleō*, "to speak," 1 Thess. 2:2; (3) *diamarturomai*, "to testify (thoroughly)," Acts 20:24; (4) *euangelizō*, "to preach," e.g., 1 Cor. 15:1; 2 Cor. 11:7; Gal. 1:11 (see B, No. 1 below); (5) *katangellō*, "to proclaim," 1 Cor. 9:14; (6) *douleuō eis*, "to serve unto" ("in furtherance of"), Phil. 2:22; (7) *sunathleō en*, "to labor with in," Phil. 4:3; (8) *hierourgeō*, "to minister," Rom. 15:16; (8) *plēroō*, "to preach fully," Rom. 15:19; (10) *sunkakopatheō*, "to suffer hardship with," 2 Tim. 1:8; (b) with regard to its reception ol otherwise: (1) *dechomai*, "to receive," 2 Cor. 11:4; *hupakouō*, "to hearken to, or obey," Rom. 10:16; 2 Thess. 1:8; *pisteuō en*, "to believe in," Mark 1:15; *metastrephō*, "to pervert," Gal. 1:7.

Note: In connection with (a), the apostle's statement in 1 Cor. 9:23 is noticeable, "I do all things for the Gospel's sake, that I may be a joint partaker thereof," RV, for the incorrect KJV, "that I might be partaker thereof with you."

B. Verbs.

1. *euangelizō* (εὐαγγελίζω, 2097), "to bring or announce glad tidings" (Eng., "evangelize"), is used (a) in the active voice in Rev. 10:7 ("declared") and 14:6 ("to proclaim," RV, KJV, "to preach"); (b) in the passive voice, of matters to be proclaimed as "glad tidings," Luke 16:16; Gal. 1:11; 1 Pet. 1:25; of persons to whom the proclamation is made, Matt. 11:5; Luke 7:22; Heb. 4:2, 6; 1 Pet. 4:6; (c) in the middle voice, especially of the message of salvation, with a personal object, either of the person preached, e.g., Acts 5:42; 11:20; Gal. 1:16, or, with a preposition, of the persons evangelized, e.g., Acts 13:32, "declare glad tidings"; Rom. 1:15; Gal. 1:8; with an impersonal object, e.g., "the word," Acts 8:4; "good tidings," 8:12; "the word of the Lord," 15:35; "the gospel," 1 Cor. 15:1; 2 Cor. 11:7; "the faith," Gal. 1:23; "peace," Eph. 2:17; "the unsearchable riches of Christ, 3:8. See PREACH, TIDINGS.

2. *proeuangelizomai* (προευαγγελίζομαι, 4283), "to announce glad tidings beforehand," is used in Gal. 3:8.

Note: For other verbs see above.

GOVERNMENT

kubernēsis (κυβέρνησις, 2941), from *kubernaō*, "to guide" (whence Eng., "govern"), denotes (a) "steering, pilotage"; (b) metaphorically, "governments or governings," said of those who act as guides in a local church, 1 Cor. 12:28. Cf. *kubernētēs*, "a pilot," Acts 27:11; Rev. 18:17.

Note: For *kuriotēs*, "lordship, dominion," rendered "government" in 2 Pet. 2:10, KJV, see DOMINION.

GOVERNOR

A. Nouns.

1. *hēgemōn* (ἡγεμών, 2232) is a term used (a) for "rulers" generally, Mark 13:9; 1 Pet. 2:14; translated "princes" (i.e., leaders) in Matt. 2:6; (b) for the Roman procurators, referring, in the gospels to Pontius Pilate, e.g., Matt. 27:2; Luke 20:20 (so designated by Tacitus, *Annals,* xv. 44); to Felix, Acts 23:26. Technically the procurator was a financial official under a proconsul or propretor, for collecting the imperial revenues, but entrusted also with magisterial powers for decisions of questions relative to the revenues. In certain provinces, of which Judea was one (the procurator of which was dependent on the legate of Syria), he was the general administrator and supreme judge, with sole power of life and death. Such a governor was a person of high social standing. Felix, however, was an ex-slave, a freedman, and his appointment to Judea could not but be regarded by the Jews as an insult to the nation. The headquarters of the governor of Judea was Caesarea, which was made a garrison town. See PRINCE, RULER.

2. *ethnarchēs* (ἐθνάρχης, 1481), "an ethnarch," lit. "a ruler of a nation" (*ethnos*, "a people," *archē*, "rule"), is translated "governor" in 2 Cor. 11:32; it describes normally the ruler of a nation possessed of separate laws and customs among those of a different race. Eventually it denoted a ruler of a province, superior to a tetrarch, but inferior to a king (e.g., Aretas).

3. *oikonomos* (οἰκονόμος, 3623), lit., "one who rules a house" (*oikos*, "a house," *nomos*, "a law"), Gal. 4:2, denotes a superior servant responsible for the family housekeeping, the direction of other servants, and the care of the children under age. See STEWARD.

4. *architriklinos* (ἀρχιτρίκλινος, 755), from *archē*, "rule," and *triklinos*, "a room with three couches," denotes "the ruler of a feast," John 2:8, RV (KJV, "the governor of the feast"), a man appointed to see that the table and couches were duly placed and the courses arranged, and to taste the food and wine.

B. Verbs.

1. *hēgeomai* (ἡγέομαι, 2233), akin to A, No. 1, is used in the present participle to denote "a governor," lit., "(one) governing," Matt. 2:6; Acts 7:10.

2. *hēgemoneuō* (ἡγεμονεύω, 2230), to be a *hēgemōn*, "to lead the way," came to signify to be "a governor of a province"; it is used of Quirinius, governor of Syria, Luke 2:2, RV, of Pontius Pilate, governor of Judea, 3:1. In the first clause of this verse the noun *hēgemonia*, "a rule or sovereignty," is translated "reign"; Eng., "hegemony."

Note. In Jas. 3:4, the verb *euthunō*, "to make or guide straight," is used in the present participle, as a noun, denoting the "steersman" (RV) or pilot of a vessel, KJV, "governor."

GRACE

1. *charis* (χάρις, 5485) has various uses, (a) objective, that which bestows or occasions pleasure, delight, or causes favorable regard; it is applied, e.g., to beauty, or gracefulness of person, Luke 2:40; act, 2 Cor. 8:6, or speech, Luke 4:22, RV, "words of grace" (KJV, "gracious words"); Col. 4:6; (b) subjective, (1) on the part of the bestower, the friendly disposition from which the kindly act proceeds, graciousness, loving-kindness, goodwill generally, e.g., Acts 7:10; especially with reference to the divine favor or "grace," e.g., Acts 14:26; in this respect there is stress on its freeness and universality, its spontaneous character, as in the case of God's redemptive mercy, and the pleasure or joy He designs for the recipient; thus it is set in contrast with debt, Rom. 4:4, 16, with works, 11:6, and with law, John 1:17; see also, e.g., Rom. 6:14, 15; Gal. 5:4; (2) on the part of the receiver, a sense of the favor bestowed, a feeling of gratitude, e.g., Rom. 6:17 ("thanks"); in this respect it sometimes signifies "to be thankful," e.g., Luke 17:9 ("doth he thank the servant?" lit., "hath he thanks to"); 1 Tim. 1:12; (c) in another objective sense, the effect of "grace," the spiritual state of those who have experienced its exercise, whether (1) a state of "grace," e.g., Rom. 5:2; 1 Pet. 5:12; 2 Pet. 3:18, or (2) a proof thereof in practical effects, deeds of "grace," e.g., 1 Cor. 16:3, RV, "bounty" (KJV, "liberality"); 2 Cor. 8:6, 19 (in 2 Cor. 9:8 it means the sum of earthly blessings); the power and equipment for ministry, e.g., Rom. 1:5; 12:6; 15:15; 1 Cor. 3:10; Gal. 2:9; Eph. 3:2, 7.

To be in favor with is to find "grace" with, e.g., Acts 2:47; hence it appears in this sense at the beginning and the end of several epistles, where the writer desires "grace" from God for the readers, e.g., Rom. 1:7; 1 Cor. 1:3; in this respect it is connected with the imperative mood of the word *chairō*, "to rejoice," a mode of greeting among Greeks, e.g., Acts 15:23; Jas. 1:1 (marg.); 2 John 10, 11, RV, "greeting" (KJV, "God speed").

The fact that "grace" is received both from God the Father, 2 Cor. 1:12, and from Christ, Gal. 1:6; Rom. 5:15

(where both are mentioned), is a testimony to the deity of Christ. See also 2 Thess. 1:12, where the phrase "according to the grace of our God and the Lord Jesus Christ" is to be taken with each of the preceding clauses, "in you," "and ye in Him."

In Jas. 4:6, "But He giveth more grace" (Greek, "a greater grace," RV, marg.), the statement is to be taken in connection with the preceding verse, which contains two remonstrating, rhetorical questions, "Think ye that the Scripture speaketh in vain?" and "Doth the Spirit (the Holy Spirit) which He made to dwell in us long unto envying?" (see the RV). The implied answer to each is "it cannot be so." Accordingly, if those who are acting so flagrantly, as if it were so, will listen to the Scripture instead of letting it speak in vain, and will act so that the Holy Spirit may have His way within, God will give even "a greater grace," namely, all that follows from humbleness and from turning away from the world. See BENEFIT, BOUNTY, LIBERALITY, THANK.

Note: The corresponding verb *charitoō*, "to endue with divine favor or grace," is used in Luke 1:28, "highly favored" (marg., "endued with grace") and Eph. 1:6, KJV, "hath made ... accepted"; RV, "freely bestowed" (marg., "endued.").

2. *euprepeia* (εὐπρέπεια, 2143), "comeliness, goodly appearance," is said of the outward appearance of the flower of the grass, Jas. 1:11.

GRACIOUS

chrēstos (χρηστός, 5543) is rendered "gracious" in 1 Pet. 2:3, as an attribute of the Lord. See GOOD, KIND.

Note: Euphēmos, "fair-sounding" (*eu*, "well," *phēmē*, "a saying, or report"), "of good report," Phil. 4:8, is rendered "gracious" in the RV marg.

GRAIN

kokkos (κόκκος, 2848) denotes "a grain," Matt. 13:31; 17:20; Mark 4:31; Luke 13:19; 17:6; John 12:24 (KJV, "corn"); 1 Cor. 15:37 (where the RV has "a ... grain," to distinguish it from "grain" in general).

GRAPE

staphulē (σταφυλή, 4718) denotes "a bunch of grapes, or a grape," Matt. 7:16; Luke 6:44; Rev. 14:18. It is to be distinguished from *omphax*, "an unripe grape" (not in NT), e.g., in the Sept. of Job 15:33, and from *botrus*, "a cluster," used together with *staphulē* in Rev. 14:18.

GRASS

chortos (χόρτος, 5528) primarily denoted "a feeding enclosure" (whence Latin *hortus*, "a garden"; Eng.. "yard," and "garden"); then, "food," especially grass for feeding cattle; it is translated "grass" in Matt. 6:30; 14:19; Mark 6:39 (where "the green grass" is the first evidence of early spring); Luke 12:28; John 6:10; Jas. 1:10, 11; 1 Pet. 1:24; Rev. 8:7; 9:4; "blade" in Matt. 13:26; Mark 4:28; "hay" in 1 Cor. 3:12, used figuratively. In Palestine or Syria there are 90 genera and 243 species of grass.

GRATULATION

makarismos (μακαρισμός, 3108) denotes "a declaration of blessedness, a felicitation"; it is translated "gratulation" in Gal. 4:15, RV (KJV, "blessedness"); the Galatian converts had counted themselves happy when they heard and received the gospel from Paul; he asks them rhetorically what had become of that spirit which had animated them; the word is rendered blessing in Rom. 4:6, 9. See BLESSING, C, No. 2.

GRAVE (Noun)

1. *mnēmeion* (μνημεῖον, 3419) primarily denotes "a memorial" (akin to *mnaomai*, "to remember"), then, "a monument" (the significance of the word rendered "tombs," KJV, "sepulchres," in Luke 11:47), anything done to preserve the memory of things and persons; it usually denotes a tomb, and is translated either "tomb" or "sepulchre" or "grave." Apart from the Gospels, it is found only in Acts 13:29. Among the Hebrews it was generally a cavern, closed by a door or stone, often decorated. Cf. Matt. 23:29. See TOMB.

2. *mnēma* (μνῆμα, 3418), akin to No. 1, like which it signified "a memorial" or "record of a thing or a dead person," then "a sepulchral monument," and hence "a tomb"; it is rendered "graves" in the KJV of Rev. 11:9 (RV, "a tomb"); "tomb" or "tombs," Mark 5:3, 5 (some mss. have No. 1, as in 15:46, KJV, "sepulchre") and 16:2 (KJV, "sepulchre"); Luke 8:27; Acts 2:29 and 7:16 (KJV, "sepulchre"). See TOMB.

Note: In 1 Cor. 15:55, where some texts have "Hades," KJV, "grave," the most authentic have *thanatos*, "death."

GRAVE (Adjective)

semnos (σαβαχθανί, 4518) first denoted "reverend, august, venerable" (akin to *sebomai*, "to reverence"); then, "serious, grave," whether of persons, 1 Tim. 3:8, 11 (deacons and their wives); Titus 2:2 (aged men); or things, Phil. 4:8, RV, "honorable" (marg., "reverend"), KJV, "honest." Trench (*Syn.* Sec. XCII) points out that "grave" and "gravity" fail to cover the full meaning of their original; "the word we want is one in which the sense of gravity and dignity is combined." Cremer describes it as denoting what inspires reverence and awe, and says that *semnos* and *hosios*, "holy, consecrated," are only secondary designations of the conception of holiness. "The word points to seriousness of purpose and to self-respect in conduct" (Moule). Cf. *semnotēs*, "gravity" (see below).

GRAVE-CLOTHES

keiria (κειρία, 2750) denotes, firstly, "a band" either for a bed girth, or bed sheets themselves (Sept. of Prov. 7:16.); then, "the swathings wrapped round a corpse"; it is used in the plural in John 11:44.

GRAVEN

charagma (χάραγμα, 5480), from *charassō*, "to engrave" (akin to *charaktēr*, "an impress," RV, marg., of Heb. 1:3), denotes (a) "a mark" or "stamp," e.g., Rev. 13:16, 17; 14:9, 11; 16:2; 19:20; 20:4; 15:2 in some mss.; (b) "a thing graven," Acts 17:29.

GRAVITY

semnotēs (σεμνότης, 4587) denotes "venerableness, dignity"; it is a necessary characteristic of the life and conduct of Christians, 1 Tim. 2:2, RV, "gravity" (KJV, "honesty"), a qualification of a bishop or overseer in a church, in regard to his children, 1 Tim. 3:4; a necessary characteristic of the teaching imparted by a servant of God, Titus 2:7. Cf. the adjective *semnos*, under GRAVE.

GREATNESS

1. *megethos* (μέγεθος, 3174), akin to *megas* (see GREAT, No. 1), is said of the power of God, in Eph. 1:19.

2. *huperbolē* (ὑπερβολή, 5236) denotes "exceeding greatness," 2 Cor. 4:7; 12:7. see EXCEL, B, No. 1.

For **GREEDINESS** see COVETOUSNESS, B, No. 3

GREEN

1. *chlōros* (χλωρός, 5515), akin to *chloē*, "tender foliage" (cf. the name "Chloe," 1 Cor. 1:11, and Eng., "chlorine"), denotes (a) "pale green," the color of young grass, Mark 6:39; Rev. 8:7; 9:4, "green thing"; hence, (b) "pale," Rev. 6:8, the color of the horse whose rider's name is Death.

2. *hugros* (ὑγρός, 5200) denotes "wet, moist" (the opposite of *xēros*, "dry"); said of wood, sappy, "green," Luke 23:31, i.e., if they thus by the fire of their wrath treated Christ, the guiltless, holy, the fruitful, what would be the fate of the perpetrators, who were like the dry wood, exposed to the fire of divine wrath.

GREET, GREETING

A. Verbs.

1. *aspazomai* (ἀσπάζομαι, 782) signifies "to greet welcome," or "salute." In the KJV it is chiefly rendered by either of the verbs "to greet" or "to salute." "There is little doubt that the revisers have done wisely in giving 'salute' ... in the passages where KJV has 'greet.' For the cursory reader is sure to imagine a difference of Greek and of meaning when he finds, e.g., in Phil. 4:21, 'Salute every saint in Christ Jesus. The brethren which are with me greet you,' or in 3 John 14, 'Our friends salute thee. Greet the friends by name'" (Hastings, *Bible Dic.*). In Acts 25:13 the meaning virtually is "to pay his respects to."

In two passages the renderings vary otherwise; in Acts 20:1, of bidding farewell, KJV, "embraced them," RV, "took leave of them," or, as Ramsay translates it, "bade them farewell"; in Heb. 11:13, of welcoming promises, KJV, "embraced," RV, "greeted."

The verb is used as a technical term for conveying "greetings" at the close of a letter, often by an amanuensis, e.g., Rom. 16:22, the only instance of the use of the first person in this respect in the NT; see also 1 Cor. 16:19, 20; 2 Cor. 13:13; Phil. 4:22; Col. 4:10-15; 1 Thess. 5:26; 2 Tim. 4:21; Titus 3:15; Philem. 23; Heb. 13:24; 1 Pet. 5:13, 14; 2 John 13. This special use is largely illustrated in the papyri, one example of this showing how keenly the absence of the greeting was felt. The papyri also illustrate the use of the addition "by name," when several persons are included in the greeting, as in 3 John 14 (Moulton and Milligan, *Vocab*). See EMBRACE, SALUTE.

2. *chairō* (χαίρω, 5463), "to rejoice," is thrice used as a formula of salutation in Acts 15:23, KJV, "send greeting," RV, "greeting"; so 23:26; Jas. 1:1. In 2 John 10, 11, the RV substitutes the phrase (to give) "greeting," for the KJV (to bid) "God speed." See FAREWELL, GLAD, HAIL, JOY, REJOICE.

B. Noun.

aspamos (ἀσπασμός, 783), a salutation, is always so rendered in the RV; KJV, "greetings" in Matt. 23:7; Luke 11:43; 20:46, it is used (a) orally in those instances and in Mark 12:38; Luke 1:29, 41, 44; (b) in written salutations, 1 Cor. 16:21 (cf. A, No. 1, in v. 20); Col. 4:18; 2 Thess. 3:17.

GRIEF, GRIEVE

A. Noun.

lupē (λύπη, 3077) signifies "pain," of body or mind; it is used in the plural in 1 Pet. 2:19 only, RV, "griefs" (KJV, "grief"); here, however, it stands, by metonymy, for "things that cause sorrow, grievances"; hence Tyndale's rendering, "grief," for Wycliffe's "sorews"; everywhere else it is rendered "sorrow," except in Heb. 12:11, where it is translated "grievous" (lit., "of grief"). See HEAVINESS, SORROW.

B. Verbs.

1. *lupeō* (λυπέω, 3076), akin to A, denotes (a), in the active voice, "to cause pain, or grief, to distress, grieve," e.g., 2 Cor. 2:2 (twice, active and passive voices); v. 5 (twice), RV, "hath caused sorrow" (KJV, "have caused grief," and "grieved"); 7:8, "made (you) sorry"; Eph. 4:30, of grieving the Holy Spirit of God (as indwelling the believer); (b) in the passive voice, "to be grieved, to be made sorry, to be sorry, sorrowful," e.g., Matt. 14:9, RV, "(the king) was grieved" (KJV,

"was sorry"); Mark 10:22, RV, "(went away) sorrowful" (KJV, "grieved"); John 21:17, "(Peter) was grieved," Rom. 14:15, "(if... thy brother) is grieved"; 2 Cor. 2:4, "(not that) ye should be made sorry," RV, KJV, "ye should be grieved." See HEAVINESS, SORROW, SORROWFUL, SORRY.

2. *sunlupeō* (συλλυπέω, 4818), or *sullupeō*, is used in the passive voice in Mark 3:5, "to be grieved" or afflicted together with a person, said of Christ's "grief" at the hardness of heart of those who criticized His healing on the Sabbath day; it here seems to suggest the sympathetic nature of His grief because of their self-injury. Some suggest that the *sun* indicates the mingling of "grief" with His anger.

3. *stenazō* (στενάζω, 4727), "to groan" (of an inward, unexpressed feeling of sorrow), is translated "with grief" in Heb. 13:17 (marg. "groaning"). It is rendered "sighed" in Mark 7:34; "groan," in Rom. 8:23; 2 Cor. 5:2, 4; "murmur," in Jas. 5:9, RV (KJV, "grudge"). See MURMUR.

Notes: (1) *Diaponeō*, "to work out with labor," in the passive voice, "to be sore troubled," is rendered "being grieved" in Acts 4:2 and 16:18, KJV (RV, "sore troubled"). See TROUBLE. In some mss., Mark 14:4. (2) *Prosochthizō*, "to be angry with," is rendered "was grieved" in Heb. 3:10, 17, KJV (RV, "was displeased"). See DISPLEASED.

GRIEVOUS, GRIEVOUSLY

A. Adjectives.

1. *barus* (βαρύς, 926) denotes "heavy, burdensome"; it is always used metaphorically in the NT, and is translated "heavy" in Matt. 23:4, of Pharisaical ordinances; in the comparative degree "weightier," 23:23, of details of the law of God; "grievous," metaphorically of wolves, in Acts 20:29; of charges, 25:7; negatively of God's commandments, 1 John 5:3 (causing a burden on him who fulfills them); in 2 Cor. 10:10, "weighty," of Paul's letters. See HEAVY.

2. *ponēros* (πονηρός, 4190), "painful, bad," is translated "grievous" in Rev. 16:2, of a sore inflicted retributively. See BAD.

3. *dusbastaktos* (δυσβάστακτος, 1419), "hard to be borne" (from *dus*, an inseparable prefix, like Eng. "mis-," and "un-," indicating "difficulty, injuriousness, opposition," etc., and *bastazō*, "to bear"), is used in Luke 11:46 and, in some mss., in Matt. 23:4, "grievous to be borne"; in the latter the RV marg. has "many ancient authorities omit."

4. *chalepos* (χαλεπός, 5467), "hard," signifies (a) "hard to deal with," Matt. 8:28 (see FIERCE); (b) "hard to bear, grievous," 2 Tim. 3:1, RV, "grievous" (KJV, "perilous"), said of a characteristic of the last days of this age. See FIERCE.

Notes: (1) For the noun *lupē*, "grievous," in Heb. 12:11, see GRIEF. (2) In Phil. 3:1, the adjective *oknēros*, "shrinking," or "causing shrinking," hence, "tedious" (akin to *okneō*, "to shrink"), is rendered "irksome" in the RV (KJV, "grievous"); the apostle intimates that, not finding his message tedious, he has no hesitation in giving it. In Matt. 25:26 and Rom. 12:11, "slothful."

B. Adverbs.

1. *deinōs* (δεινῶς, 1171), akin to *deos*, "fear," signifies (a) "terribly," Matt. 8:6, "grievously (tormented)"; (b) "vehemently," Luke 11:53.

2. *kakōs* (κακῶς, 2560), "badly, ill," is translated "grievously (vexed)," in Matt. 15:22. See AMISS, EVIL, MISERABLY.

Notes: (1) In Mark 9:20 and Luke 9:42, the RV renders the verb *susparassō* "tare (him) grievously," the adverb bringing out the intensive force of the prefix *su-* (i.e., *sun*); the meaning may be "threw violently to the ground." (2) In Matt. 17:15, the idiomatic phrase, consisting of No. 2 (above) with *echō*, "to have," (lit., "hath badly"), is rendered "suffereth grievously," RV (KJV, "is ... sore vexed").

GROUND, GROUNDED

A. Nouns.

1. *gē* (γῆ, 1093), "the earth, land," etc., often denotes "the ground," e.g., Matt. 10:29; Mark 8:6. See EARTH.

2. *edaphos* (ἔδαφος, 1475), "a bottom, base," is used of the "ground" in Acts 22:7, suggestive of that which is level and hard. Cf. B, No. 1, below.

3. *chōra* (χώρα, 5561), "land, country," is used of property, "ground," in Luke 12:16, "the ground (of a certain rich man)."

4. *chōrion* (χωρίον, 5564), a diminutive of No. 3, "a piece of land, a place, estate," is translated "parcel of ground" in John 4:5.

5. *hedraiōma* (ἑδραίωμα, 1477), "a support, bulwark, stay" (from *hedraios*, "steadfast, firm"; from *hedra*, "a seat"), is translated "ground" in 1 Tim. 3:15 (said of a local church); the RV marg., "stay" is preferable.

Notes: (1) In Mark 4:16 the RV rightly has "rocky places" (*petrōdēs*) for KJV, "stony ground." (2) In Acts 27:29, for the KJV, "rocks" the RV has "rocky ground," lit., "rough places," i.e., a rocky shore. (3) In Luke 14:18, *agros*, "a field," is translated "a piece of ground," KJV, RV, a field.

B. Verbs.

1. *edaphizō* (ἐδαφίζω, 1474), akin to A, No. 2.

2. *themelioō* (θεμελιόω, 2311) signifies "to lay the foundation of, to found" (akin to *themelios*, "a foundation"; from *tithēmi*, "to put"), and is rendered "grounded" in Eph. 3:17, said of the condition of believers with reference to the love of Christ; in Col. 1:23, of their continuance in the faith. See FOUND.

C. Adverb.

chamai (χαμαί, 5476) (akin to Lat., *humi*, "on the ground," and *homo*, "man"), signifies "on the ground," John 9:6, of the act of Christ in spitting on the "ground" before anointing the eyes of a blind man; in 18:6, "to the ground," of the fall of the rabble that had come to seize Christ in Gethsemane.

For **GRUDGE** (Jas. 5:9), see GRIEVE, B, No. 3, MURMUR

GRUDGINGLY

Note: In 2 Cor. 9:7, the phrase *ek lupēs*, lit., "out of sorrow" (*ek*, "out of," or "from," *lupē*, "sorrow, grief"), is translated "grudgingly" (RV marg., "of sorrow"); the "grudging" regret is set in contrast to cheerfulness enjoined in giving, as is the reluctance expressed in "of necessity."

GUARD (Noun and Verb)

A. Nouns.

1. *koustōdia* (κουστωδία, 2892); "a guard," (Latin, *custodia*, Eng., "custodian"), is used of the soldiers who "guarded" Christ's sepulchre, Matt. 27:65, 66 and 28:11, and is translated "(ye have) a guard," "the guard (being with them)," and "(some of) the guard," RV, KJV, "... a watch," "(setting a) watch," and "... the watch." This was the Temple guard, stationed under a Roman officer in the tower of Antonia, and having charge of the high priestly vestments. Hence the significance of Pilate's words "Ye have a guard." See WATCH.

2. *spekoulatōr* (σπεκουλάτωρ, 4688), Latin, *speculator*, primarily denotes "a lookout officer," or "scout," but, under the emperors, "a member of the bodyguard"; these were employed as messengers, watchers and executioners; ten such officers were attached to each legion; such a guard was employed by Herod Antipas, Mark 6:27, RV, "a soldier of his guard" (KJV, "executioner").

3. *phulax* (φύλαξ, 5441), "a guard, keeper" (akin to *phulassō*, "to guard, keep"), is translated "keepers" in Acts 5:23; in 12:6, 19, RV, "guards" (KJV, "keepers"). See KEEPER.

Notes: (1) In Acts 28:16, some mss. have the sentence containing the word *stratopedarchēs*, "a captain of the guard." (2) In Phil. 1:13, the noun *praitōrion*, the "praetorian guard," is so rendered in the RV (KJV, "palace").

B. Verbs.

1. *phulassō* (φυλάσσω, 5442), "to guard, watch, keep" (akin to A, No. 3), is rendered by the verb "to guard" in the RV (KJV, "to keep") of Luke 11:21; John 17:12; Acts 12:4; 28:16; 2 Thess. 3:3; 1 Tim. 6:20; 2 Tim. 1:12, 14; 1 John 5:21; Jude 24. In Luke 8:29, "was kept under guard, RV (KJV, kept). See BEWARE, KEEP, OBSERVE, PRESERVE, SAVE, WATCH.

2. *diaphulassō* (διαφυλάσσω, 1314), a strengthened form of No. 1 (*dia*, "through," used intensively), "to guard carefully, defend," is found in Luke 4:10 (from the Sept. of Ps. 91:11), RV, "to guard" (KJV, "to keep").

3. *phroureō* (φρουρέω, 5432), a military term, "to keep by guarding, to keep under guard," as with a garrison (*phrouros*, "a guard, or garrison"), is used, (a) of blocking up every way of escape, as in a siege; (b) of providing protection against the enemy, as a garrison does; see 2 Cor. 11:32, "guarded." KJV, "kept," i.e., kept the city, "with a garrison." It is used of the security of the Christian until the end, 1 Pet. 1:5, RV, "are guarded," and of the sense of that security that is his when he puts all his matters into the hand of God, Phil. 4:7, RV, "shall guard." In these passages the idea is not merely that of protection, but of inward garrisoning as by the Holy Spirit; in Gal. 3:23 ("were kept in ward"), it means rather a benevolent custody and watchful guardianship in view of worldwide idolatry (cf. Isa. 5:2). See KEEP.

GUARDIAN

epitropos (ἐπίτροπος, 2012), lit., "one to whose care something is committed" (*epi*, "upon," *trepō*, "to turn" or "direct"), is rendered "guardians" in Gal. 4:2, RV, KJV, "tutors" (in Matt. 20:8 and Luke 8:3, "steward").

"The corresponding verb, *epitrepō*, is translated "permit, give leave, suffer"; see 1 Cor. 14:34; 16:7; 1 Tim. 2:12, e.g., ... An allied noun, *epitropē*, is translated "commission" in Acts 26:12 () and refers to delegated authority over persons. This usage of cognate words suggests that the *epitropos* was a superior servant responsible for the persons composing the household, whether children or slaves."

GUIDE (Noun and Verb)

A. Noun.

hodēgos (ὁδηγός, 3595), "a leader on the way" (*hodos*, "a way," *hēgeomai*, "to lead"), "a guide," is used (a) literally, in Acts 1:16; (b) figuratively, Matt. 15:14, RV, "guides" (KJV, "leaders"); Matt. 23:16, 24, "guides"; Rom. 2:19, "a guide." Cf. B, No. 1.

B. Verbs.

1. *hodēgeō* (ὁδηγέω, 3594), "to lead the way" (akin to A), is used (a) literally, RV, "guide" (KJV, "lead"), of "guiding" the blind, in Matt. 15:14; Luke 6:39; of "guiding" unto foun tains of waters of life, Rev. 7:17; (b) figuratively, in John 16:13, of "guidance" into the truth by the Holy Spirit; in Acts 8:31, of the interpretation of Scripture. See LEAD.

2. *kateuthunō* (κατευθύνω, 2720), "to make straight," is said of "guiding" the feet into the way of peace, Luke 1:79. See DIRECT.

Notes: (1) 1 Tim. 5:14, the RV rightly translates the verb *oikodespoteō* by "rule the household" (KJV, "guide the house"), the meaning being that of the management and direction of household affairs. See RULE. (2) *Hēgeomai,* "to lead," in Heb. 13:7, 24, is rendered "that had the rule over" and "that have, etc.," more lit., "them that were (are) your leaders," or "guides."

GUILE

dolos (δόλος, 1388), "a bait, snare, deceit," is rendered "guile" in John 1:47, negatively of Nathanael; Acts 13:10, RV, KJV, "subtlety" (of Bar-Jesus); 2 Cor. 12:16, in a charge made against Paul by his detractors, of catching the Corinthian converts by "guile" (the apostle is apparently quoting the language of his critics); 1 Thess. 2:3, negatively, of the teaching of the apostle and his fellow missionaries; 1 Pet. 2:1, of that from which Christians are to be free; 2:22, of the guileless speech of Christ (cf. GUILELESS, No. 2); 3:10, of the necessity that the speech of Christians should be guileless. See also Matt. 26:4; Mark 7:22; 14:1. See DECEIT, SUBTLETY.

Note: In Rev. 14:5, some mss. have *dolos;* the most authentic have *pseudos,* a "lie."

GUILELESS (WITHOUT GUILE)

1. *adolos* (ἄδολος, 97), "without guile" (*a,* negative, and *dolos,* see GUILE), "pure, unadulterated," is used metaphorically of the teaching of the Word of God, 1 Pet. 2:2, RV. It is used in the papyri writings of seed, corn, wheat, oil, wine, etc.

2. *akakos* (ἄκακος, 172), lit., "without evil" (*a,* negative, *kakos,* "evil"), signifies "simple, guileless," Rom. 16:18, "simple," of believers (perhaps = unsuspecting, or, rather, innocent, free from admixture of evil); in Heb. 7:26, RV, "guileless" (KJV, "harmless"), the character of Christ (more lit., "free from evil"). Cf. Sept., Job 2:3; 8:20; Prov. 1:4; 14:15. See HARMLESS.

GUILTLESS

anaitios (ἀναίτιος, 338), "innocent, guiltless" (*a,* negative, *n,* euphonic, *aitia,* "a charge of crime"), is translated "blameless" in Matt. 12:5, KJV, "guiltless" in v. 7; RV, "guiltless" in each place. See BLAMELESS.

GUILTY (Adjective)

enochos (ἔνοχος, 1777), lit., "held in, bound by, liable to a charge or action at law": see DANGER.

Notes: (1) In Rom. 3:19, KJV, *hupodikos,* "brought to trial," lit., 'under judgment' (*hupo,* "under," *dikē,* "justice"), is incorrectly rendered "guilty"; RV, "under the judgement of." See JUDGMENT. (2) In Matt. 23:18, *opheilō,* to owe, to be indebted, to fail in duty, be a delinquent," is misrendered "guilty" in the KJV; RV, "a debtor."

GUSH OUT

ekchunō (ἐκχύνω, 1632), or *ekchunnō* (ἐκχύννω, 1632), a Hellenistic form of *ekcheō,* "to pour forth," is translated "gushed out" in Acts 1:18, of the bowels of Judas Iscariot.

H

For **HA** (Mark 15:29, RV) see AH

HABITATION

1. *oikētērion* (οἰκητήριον, 3613), "a habitation" (from *oikētēr*, "an inhabitant," and *oikos*, "a dwelling"), is used in Jude 6, of the heavenly region appointed by God as the dwelling place of angels; in 2 Cor. 5:2, RV, "habitation," KJV, "house," figuratively of the spiritual bodies of believers when raised or changed at the return of the Lord. See HOUSE.

2. *katoikētērion* (κατοικητήριον, 2732), (*kata*, "down," used intensively, and No. 1), implying more permanency than No. 1, is used in Eph. 2:22 of the church as the dwelling place of the Holy Spirit; in Rev. 18:2 of Babylon, figuratively, as the dwelling place of demons.

3. *katoikia* (κατοικία, 2733), "a settlement, colony, dwelling" (*kata*, and *oikos*, see above), is used in Acts 17:26, of the localities divinely appointed as the dwelling places of the nations.

4. *epaulis* (ἔπαυλις, 1886), "a farm, a dwelling" (*epi*, "upon," *aulis*, "a place in which to pass the night, a country house, cottage or cabin, a fold"), is used in Acts 1:20 of the habitation of Judas.

5. *skēnē* (σκηνή, 4633), akin to *skēnoō*, "to dwell in a tent or tabernacle," is rendered "habitations" in Luke 16:9, KJV (RV, "tabernacles") of the eternal dwelling places of the redeemed. See TABERNACLE.

6. *skēnōma* (σκήνωμα, 4638), "a booth," or "tent pitched" (akin to No. 5), is used of the Temple as God's dwelling, as that which David desired to build, Acts 7:46 (RV, "habitation," KJV, "tabernacle"); metaphorically of the body as a temporary tabernacle, 2 Pet. 1:13, 14. See TABERNACLE.

HADES

hadēs (ᾅδης, 86), "the region of departed spirits of the lost" (but including the blessed dead in periods preceding the ascension of Christ). It has been thought by some that the word etymologically meant "the unseen" (from *a*, negative, and *eidō*, "to see"), but this derivation is questionable; a more probable derivation is from *hadō*, signifying "all-receiving." It corresponds to "Sheol" in the OT. In the KJV of the OT and NT; it has been unhappily rendered "hell," e.g., Ps. 16:10; or "the grave," e.g., Gen. 37:35; or "the pit," Num. 16:30, 33; in the NT the revisers have always used the rendering "hades"; in the OT, they have not been uniform in the translation, e.g. in Isa. 14:15 "hell" (marg., "Sheol"); usually they have "Sheol" in the text and "the grave" in the margin. It never denotes the grave, nor is it the permanent region of the lost; in point of time it is, for such, intermediate between decease and the doom of Gehenna. For the condition, see Luke 16:23-31.

The word is used four times in the Gospels, and always by the Lord, Matt. 11:23; 16:18; Luke 10:15; 16:23; it is used with reference to the soul of Christ, Acts 2:27, 31; Christ declares that He has the keys of it, Rev. 1:18; in Rev. 6:8 it is personified, with the signification of the temporary destiny of the doomed; it is to give up those who are therein, 20:13, and is to be cast into the lake of fire, v. 14.

Note: In 1 Cor. 15:55 the most authentic mss. have *thanatos*, "death," in the 2nd part of the verse, instead of "hades," which the KJV wrongly renders "grave" ("hell," in the marg.).

HAIL (Verb)

chairō (χαίρω, 5463), "to rejoice," is used in the imperative mood, (a) as a salutation, only in the Gospels; in this respect it is rendered simply "hail," in mockery of Christ, Matt. 26:49; 27:29; Mark 15:18; John 19:3; (b) as a greeting, by the angel Gabriel to Mary, Luke 1:28, and, in the plural, by the Lord to the disciples after His resurrection, Matt. 28:9.

HALL

1. *aulē* (αὐλή, 833), "a court," most frequently the place where a governor dispensed justice, is rendered "hall" in Mark 15:16 and Luke 22:55, KJV (RV, "court"). See COURT, PALACE.

2. *praitōrion* (πραιτώριον, 4232) is translated "common hall" in Matt. 27:27, KJV (RV, "palace"); "Praetorium" in Mark 15:16; "hall of judgment" or "judgment hall" in John 18:28, 33; 19:9; Acts 23:35 (RV, "palace," in each place); "praetorian guard," Phil. 1:13 (KJV, "palace"). See PALACE.

HALLELUJAH

hallēlouia (ἀλληλουϊά, 239) signifies "Praise ye Jah." It occurs as a short doxology in the Psalms, usually at the beginning, e.g., 111, 112, or the end, e.g., 104, 105, or both, e.g., 106, 135 (where it is also used in v. 3), 146-150. In the NT it is found in Rev. 19:1, 3, 4, 6, as the keynote in the song of the great multitude in heaven. "Alleluia," without the initial "H," is a misspelling.

HALLOW

hagiazō (ἁγιάζω, 37), "to make holy" (from *hagios*, "holy"), signifies to set apart for God, to sanctify, to make a person or thing the opposite of *koinos*, "common"; it is translated "Hallowed," with reference to the name of God the Father in the Lord's Prayer, Matt. 6:9; Luke 11:2. See SANCTIFY.

HAND

cheir (χείρ, 5495), "the hand" (cf. Eng., "chiropody"), is used, besides its ordinary significance, (a) in the idiomatic phrases, "by the hand of," "at the hand of," etc., to signify "by the agency of," Acts 5:12; 7:35; 17:25; 14:3; Gal. 3:19 (cf. Lev. 26:46); Rev. 19:2; (b) metaphorically, for the power of God, e.g., Luke 1:66; 23:46; John 10:28, 29; Acts 11:21; 13:11; Heb. 1:10; 2:7; 10:31; (c) by metonymy, for power, e.g., Matt. 17:22; Luke 24:7; John 10:39; Acts 12:11.

AT HAND

A. Adverb.

engus (ἐγγύς, 1451), "near, nigh," frequently rendered "at hand," is used (a) of place, e.g., of the Lord's sepulchre, John 19:42, "nigh at hand"; (b) of time, e.g., Matt. 26:18; Luke 21:30, 31, RV, "nigh," KJV, "nigh at hand"; in Phil. 4:5, "the Lord is at hand," it is possible to regard the meaning as that either of (a) or (b); the following reasons may point to (b): (1) the subject of the preceding context has been the return of Christ, 3:20, 21; (2) the phrase is a translation of the Aramaic "Maranatha," 1 Cor. 16:22, a Christian watchword, and the use of the title "the Lord" is appropriate; (3) the similar use of the adverb in Rev. 1:3 and 22:10; (4) the similar use of the corresponding verb (see B) in Rom. 13:12; Heb. 10:25, "drawing nigh," RV; Jas. 5:8; cf. 1 Pet. 4:7.

B. Verb.

engizō (ἐγγίζω, 1448): See APPROACH, A.

Notes: (1) In 2 Thess. 2:2, KJV, the verb *enistēmi*, "to be present" (*en*, "in," *histēmi*, "to cause to stand"), is wrongly translated "is at hand"; the RV correctly renders it, "is (now) present"; the apostle is counteracting the error of the supposition that "the Day of the Lord" (RV), a period of divine and retributive judgments upon the world, had already begun.

(2) In 2 Tim. 4:6, KJV, the verb *ephistēmi*, "to stand by, to come to or upon" (*epi*, "upon," *histēmi*, "to make to stand"), is rendered "is at hand," of the apostle's departure from this life; the RV "is come" represent the vivid force of the statement, expressing suddenness or imminence.

HAND (lead by the)

A. Adjective.

cheiragōgos (χειραγωγός, 5497), lit., "a hand-leader" (*cheir*, "the hand," *agō*, "to lead"), is used as a noun (plural) in Acts 13:11, "some to lead him by the hand."

B. Verb.

cheiragōgeō (χειραγωγέω, 5496), "to lead by the hand," is used in Acts 9:8; 22:11.

HANDED DOWN

patroparadotos (πατροπαράδοτος, 3970), an adjective, denoting "handed down from one's fathers," is used in 1 Pet. 1:18, RV, for KJV, "*received* by tradition from your fathers" (from *patēr*, "a father," and *paradidōmi*, "to hand down").

HAND (with one's own)

autocheir (αὐτόχειρ, 849), a noun (*autos*, "self," *cheir*, "the hand"), is used in the plural in Acts 27:19, "with their own hands."

HAND (take in)

epicheireō (ἐπιχειρέω, 2021), "to put the hand to" (*epi*, "to," *cheir*, "the hand"), is rendered "have taken in hand" in Luke 1:1.

For **LAY HANDS ON** (*krateō* in Matt. 18:28; 21:46; *piazō* in John 8:20), see HOLD and APPREHEND

HANDS (made by, not made with)

1. *cheiropoiētos* (χειροποίητος, 5499), "made by hand," of human handiwork (*cheir*, and *poieō*, "to make"), is said of the temple in Jerusalem, Mark 14:58; temples in general, Acts 7:48 (RV, "houses"); 17:24; negatively, of the heavenly and spiritual tabernacle, Heb. 9:11; of the holy place in the earthly tabernacle, v. 24; of circumcision, Eph. 2:11. In the Sept., of idols, Lev. 26:1, 30; Isa. 2:18; 10:11; 16:12; 19:1; 21:9; 31:7; 46:6.

2. *acheiropoiētos* (ἀχειροποίητος, 886), "not made by hands" (*a*, negative, and No. 1), is said of an earthly temple, Mark 14:58; of the resurrection body of believers, metaphorically as a house, 2 Cor. 5:1; metaphorically, of spiritual circumcision, Col. 2:11. This word is not found in the Sept.

For **HANDMAID and HANDMAIDEN** see under BONDMAN

For **HANDWRITING** see BOND

HANG

1. *kremannumi* (κρεμάννυμι, 2910) is used (a) transitively in Acts 5:30; 10:39; in the passive voice, in Matt. 18:6, of a millstone about a neck, and in Luke 23:39, of the malefactors; (b) intransitively, in the middle voice, in Matt. 22:40, of the dependence of "the Law and the prophets" (i.e., that which they enjoin) upon the one great principle of love to God and one's neighbor (as a door "hangs" on a hinge, or as articles "hang" on a nail); in Acts 28:4, of the serpent "hanging" from Paul's hand; in Gal. 3:13 the word is used in a quotation from the Sept. of Deut. 21:23.

2. *ekkremannumi* (ἐκκρεμάννυμι, 1582), "to hang from, or upon" (*ek*, and No. 1), is used in the middle voice (*ekkremamai*) metaphorically in Luke 19:48, RV, "(the people all) "hung" upon (Him, listening)," KJV, "were very attentive." In the Sept, Gen. 44:30.

3. *pariēmi* (παρίημι, 3935) signifies (a) "to disregard, leave alone, leave undone," Luke 11:42 (some mss. have *aphiēmi*, here); (b) "to relax, loosen," and, in the passive voice, "to be relaxed, exhausted," said of hands that "hang" down in weakness, Heb. 12:12.

4. *perikeimai* (περίκειμαι, 4029) signifies "to lie round" (*peri*, "around," *keimai*, "to lie"); then, "to be hanged round," said of "a great millstone" (lit., "a millstone turned by an ass"), Mark 9:42, RV, and marg., to be "hung" round the neck of him who causes one of Christ's "little ones" to stumble; in Luke 17:2, "a millstone." See BOUND (TO BE).

5. *apanchō* (ἀπάγχω, 519) signifies "to strangle"; in the middle voice, to "hang" oneself, Matt. 27:5. In the Sept. it is said of Ahithophel (2 Sam. 17:23).

HAPPY, HAPPIER

A. Adjective.

makarios (μακάριος, 3107), "blessed, happy," is rendered "happy" in the RV, in two places only, as in the KJV, Acts 26:2 and Rom. 14:22 (where "blessed" would have done); also the comparative "happier" in 1 Cor. 7:40. Elsewhere the RV uses "blessed" for KJV "happy," e.g., John 13:17; 1 Pet. 3:14; 4:14. See BLESS.

B. Verb.

makarizō (μακαρίζω, 3106), "to call blessed," Luke 1:48, is rendered "we count ... happy" in Jas. 5:11. See BLESS.

HARD, HARDEN, HARDENING, HARDNESS

A. Adjectives.

1. *sklēros* (σκληρός, 4642), from *skello*, "to dry," signifies "trying, exacting": see AUSTERE.

2. *duskolos* (δύσκολος, 1422) primarily means "hard to satisfy with food" (*dus*, a prefix like Eng., *un-* or *mis-*, indicating "difficulty, opposition, injuriousness," etc., the opposite of, *eu*, "well," and *kolon*, "food"); hence, "difficult," Mark 10:24, of the "difficulty," for those who trust in riches, to enter into the Kingdom of God.

B. Nouns.

1. *sklērotēs* (σκληρότης, 4643), akin to A, No. 1, is rendered "hardness" in Rom. 2:5.

2. *pōrōsis* (πώρωσις, 4457) denotes "a hardening," a covering with a *poros*, a kind of stone, indicating "a process" (from *pōroō*, C, No. 1), and is used metaphorically of dulled spiritual perception, Mark 3:5, RV, "at the hardening of their hearts"; Rom. 11:25, RV, "a hardening" (KJV, "blindness"), said of the state of Israel; Eph. 4:8, RV, "hardening," of the heart of Gentiles. See BLIND.

Note: See also under HARDSHIP and HEART (HARDNESS OF).

C. Verbs.

1. *pōroō* (πωρόω, 4456), "to make hard, callous, to petrify" (akin to B, No. 2), is used metaphorically, of the heart, Mark 6:52; 8:17; John 12:40; of the mind (or thoughts), 2 Cor. 3:14, of those in Israel who refused the revealed will and ways of God in the gospel, as also in Rom. 11:7, RV, "hardened" (KJV, "blinded"), in both places. See BLIND.

2. *sklērunō* (σκληρύνω, 4645), "to make dry or hard" (akin to A, No. 1 and B, No. 1), is used in Acts 19:9; in Rom. 9:18, illustrated by the case of Pharaoh, who first persistently "hardened" his heart (see the RV marg. of Ex. 7:13, 22; 8:19; text of v. 32 and 9:7), all producing the retributive "hardening" by God, after His much long-suffering, 9:12, etc.; in Heb. 3:8, 13, 15; 4:7, warnings against the "hardening" of the heart.

HARDSHIP (to suffer)

1. *kakopatheō* (κακοπαθέω, 2553), "to suffer evil," is translated "suffer hardship" in three places in the RV, 2 Tim. 2:3 (in some mss.; see No. 2), KJV, "endure hardness"; 2:9, KJV, "suffer trouble"; 4:5, KJV, "endure affliction"; in Jas. 5:13, RV, "suffering" (KJV, "afflicted"). See AFFLICT, ENDURE, SUFFER. In the Sept., Jonah 4:10.

2. *sunkakopatheō* (συγκακοπαθέω, 4777), "to suffer hardship with," is so rendered in 2 Tim. 1:8, RV, KJV, "be thou partaker of the afflictions" (of the gospel), and, in the best mss., in 2:3, "suffer hardship with me." See AFFLICTION, No. 3, *Note*.

HARLOT

pornē (πόρνη, 4204), "a prostitute, harlot" (from *pernēmi*, "to sell"), is used (a) literally, in Matt. 21:31, 32, of those who were the objects of the mercy shown by Christ; in Luke 15:30, of the life of the Prodigal; in 1 Cor. 6:15, 16, in a warning to the Corinthian church against the prevailing licentiousness which had made Corinth a byword; in Heb. 11:31 and Jas. 2:25, of Rahab; (b) metaphorically, of mystic Babylon, Rev. 17:1, 5 (KJV, "harlots"), 15, 16; 19:2, RV, for KJV, "whore."

HARM

A. Nouns.

1. *kakos* (κακός, 2556), "evil," is rendered "harm" in Acts 16:28; 28:5. See EVIL.

2. *ponēros* (πονηρός, 4190), "evil," generally of a more malignant sort than No. 1, is translated "harm" in Acts 28:21. See EVIL.

3. *atopos* (ἄτοπος, 824): see AMISS.

4. *hubris* (ὕβρις, 5196) primarily denotes "wantonness, insolence": then, "an act of wanton violence, an outrage, injury," 2 Cor. 12:10, RV, "injuries," KJV, "reproaches" (more than reproach is conveyed by the term); metaphorically of a loss by sea, Acts 27:10, RV, "injury," KJV, "hurt," and v. 21, RV, "injury," KJV, harm. See HURT, INJURY, REPROACH.

B. Verb.

1. *kakoō* (κακόω, 2559), "to do evil to a person" (akin to A, No. 1), is rendered "harm" in 1 Pet. 3:13, and in the RV of Acts 18:10 (KJV, "hurt"). See AFFECT, EVIL.

2. *kakopoieō* (κακοποιέω, 2554), "to do harm" (A, No. 1, and *poieō*, "to do"), is so rendered in the RV of Mark 3:4 and Luke 6:9 (KJV, "to do evil"), with reference to the moral character of what is done; in 1 Pet. 3:17, "evil doing"; 3 John 11, "doeth evil."

HARMLESS

1. *akeraios* (ἀκέραιος, 185), lit., "unmixed, with absence of foreign mixture" (from *a*, negative, and *kerannumi*, "to mix"), "pure," is used metaphorically in the NT of what is guileless, sincere, Matt. 10:16, "harmless" (marg., "simple"), i.e., with the simplicity of a single eye, discerning what is evil, and choosing only what glorifies God; Rom. 16:19, "simple (unto that which is evil)," KJV marg., "harmless"; Phil. 2:15, "harmless," KJV marg., "sincere." The Greeks used it of wine unmixed with water, of unalloyed metal; in the papyri writings it is used of a loan the interest of which is guaranteed (Moulton and Milligan, *Vocab.*). Trench compares it and synonymous words as follows: "as the *akakos* (see No. 2, below) has no harmfulness in him, and the *adolos* no guile, so the *akeraios* no foreign mixture, and the *haplous* no folds" (*Syn.* Sec. LVI). *Haplous* is said of the single eye, Matt. 6:22; Luke 11:34.

2. *akakos* (ἄκακος, 172), the negative of *kakos* (see HARM, A, No. 1), "void of evil," is rendered "harmless" in Heb. 7:26 (RV, "guileless"), of the character of Christ as a High Priest; in Rom. 16:18, RV, "innocent," KJV, "simple."

HASTE, WITH HASTE, HASTILY

A. Noun.

spoudē (σπουδή, 4710) denotes (a) "haste, speed," accompanied by "with," Mark 6:25; Luke 1:39; (b) "zeal, diligence, earnestness": see DILIGENCE.

B. Verb.

speudō (σπεύδω, 4692) denotes (a) intransitively, "to hasten," Luke 2:16, "with haste," lit., "(they came) hastening"; Luke 19:5, 6; Acts 20:16; 22:18; (b) transitively, "to desire earnestly," 2 Pet. 3:12, RV, "earnestly desiring" (marg., "hastening"), KJV, "hasting" (the day of God), i.e., in our practical fellowship with God as those who are appointed by Him as instruments through prayer and service for the accomplishment of His purposes, purposes which will be unthwartably fulfilled both in time and manner of accomplishment. In this way the earnest desire will find its fulfillment.

C. Adverb.

tacheōs (ταχέως, 5030), "quickly," is used in a warning to lay hands "hastily" on no man (with a suggestion of rashness), 1 Tim. 5:22, RV (KJV, "suddenly"); in John 11:31, RV, "(she rose up) quickly" (KJV, hastily).

HATE, HATEFUL, HATER, HATRED

A. Verb.

miseō (μισέω, 3404), "to hate," is used especially (a) of malicious and unjustifiable feelings towards others, whether towards the innocent or by mutual animosity, e.g., Matt. 10:22; 24:10; Luke 6:22, 27; 19:14; John 3:20, of "hating" the light (metaphorically); 7:7; 15:18, 19, 23-25; Titus 3:3; 1 John 2:9, 11; 3:13, 15; 4:20; Rev. 18:2, where "hateful" translates the perfect participle passive voice of the verb, lit., "hated," or "having been hated"; (b) of a right feeling of aversion from what is evil; said of wrongdoing, Rom. 7:15; iniquity, Heb. 1:9; "the garment (figurative) spotted by the flesh," Jude 23; "the works of the Nicolaitans," Rev. 2:6 (and v. 15, in some mss.; see the KJV); (c) of relative preference for one thing over another, by way of expressing either aversion from, or disregard for, the claims of one person or thing relatively to those of another, Matt. 6:24, and Luke 16:13, as to the impossibility of serving two masters; Luke 14:26, as to the claims of parents relatively to those of Christ; John 12:25, of disregard for one's life relatively to the claims of Christ; Eph. 5:29, negatively, of one's flesh, i.e. of one's own, and therefore a man's wife as one with him.

Note: In 1 John 3:15, he who "hates" his brother is called a murderer; for the sin lies in the inward disposition, of which the act is only the outward expression.

B. Adjective.

stugētos (στυγνητός, 4767), "hateful" (from *stugeō*, "to hate," not found in the NT), is used in Titus 3:3.

C. Nouns.

1. *echthra* (ἔχθρα, 2189), "hatred": see ENMITY.

2. *theostugēs* (θεοστυγής, 2319), from *theos*, "God," and *stugeō* (see B), is used in Rom. 1:30, KJV, and RV, marg., "haters of God," RV, "hateful to God"; the former rendering is appropriate to what is expressed by the next words, "insolent," "haughty," but the RV text seems to give the true meaning.

Lightfoot quotes from the Epistle of Clement of Rome, in confirmation of this, "those who practice these things are hateful to God."

HAUGHTY

huperēphanos (ὑπερήφανος, 5244), "showing oneself above others" (*huper*, "over," *phainomai*, "to appear"), though often denoting preeminent, is always used in the NT in the evil sense of "arrogant, disdainful, haughty"; it is rendered "haughty" in Rom. 1:30 and 2 Tim. 3:2, RV, KJV, "proud," but "proud" in both versions in Luke 1:51; Jas. 4:6, and 1 Pet. 5:5; in the last two it is set in opposition to *tapeinos*, "humble, lowly." Cf. the noun *huperēphania*, Mark 7:22, "pride."

HAVOC

1. *portheō* (πορθέω, 4199), "to destroy, ravage, lay waste," is used of the persecution inflicted by Saul of Tarsus on the church in Jerusalem, Acts 9:21, and Gal. 1:23, RV, "made havoc," for KJV, "destroyed"; Gal. 1:13, ditto, for KJV, "wasted." See DESTROY, *Note*.

2. *lumainomai* (λυμαίνομαι, 3075), "to maltreat, outrage" (*lumē*, "an outrage"), is translated "made havock" in Acts 8:3, KJV (RV, "laid waste.")

For **HAY** see GRASS

HEAD

kephalē (κεφαλή, 2776), besides its natural significance, is used (a) figuratively in Rom. 12:20, of heaping coals of fire on a "head" (see COALS); in Acts 18:6, "Your blood be upon your own heads," i.e., "your blood-guiltiness rest upon your own persons," a mode of expression frequent in the OT, and perhaps here directly connected with Ezek. 3:18, 20; 33:6, 8; see also Lev. 20:16; 2 Sam. 1:16; 1 Kings 2:37; (b) metaphorically, of the authority or direction of God in relation to Christ, of Christ in relation to believing men, of the husband in relation to the wife, 1 Cor. 11:3; of Christ in relation to the Church, Eph. 1:22; 4:15; 5:23; Col. 1:18; 2:19; of Christ in relation to principalities and powers, Col. 2:10. As to 1 Cor. 11:10, taken in connection with the context, the word "authority" probably stands, by metonymy, for a sign of authority (RV), the angels being witnesses of the preeminent relationship as established by God in the creation of man as just mentioned, with the spiritual significance regarding the position of Christ in relation to the Church; cf. Eph. 3:10; it is used of Christ as the foundation of the spiritual building set forth by the Temple, with its "corner stone," Matt. 21:42; symbolically also of the imperial rulers of the Roman power, as seen in the apocalyptic visions, Rev. 13:1, 3; 17:3, 7, 9.

HEAD (to wound in the)

kephalioō (κεφαλιόω, 2775), or *kephalaioō* (κεφαλαιόω, 2775), from *kephalion*, a diminutive of *kephalē*, usually meant "to sum up, to bring under heads"; in Mark 12:4 it is used for "wounding on the head," the only place where it has this meaning.

HEADLONG (to cast, to fall)

1. *katakrēmnizō* (κατακρημνίζω, 2630) signifies "to throw over a precipice" (*kata*, "down," *krēmnos*, "a steep bank," etc.), said of the purpose of the people of Nazareth to destroy Christ, Luke 4:29.

2. *prēnēs* (πρηνής, 4248), an adjective denoting "headlong, prone," is used with the verb *ginomai*, "to become," in Acts 1:18, of the death of Judas, "falling headlong"; various suggestions have been made as to the actual details; some ascribe to the word the meaning "swelling up."

HEADSTRONG (RV), HEADY (KJV)

propetēs (προπετής, 4312) lit. means "falling forwards" (from *pro*, "forwards," and *piptō*, "to fall"); it is used metaphorically to signify "precipitate, rash, reckless," and is said (a) of persons, 2 Tim. 3:4; "headstrong" is the appropriate rendering; (b) of things, Acts 19:36, RV, "(nothing) rash" (KJV, "rashly").

HEAL, HEALING

A. Verbs.

1. *therapeuō* (θεραπεύω, 2323) primarily signifies "to serve as a *therapōn*, an attendant"; then, "to care for the sick, to treat, cure, heal" (Eng., "therapeutics"). It is chiefly used in Matthew and Luke, once in John (5:10), and, after the Acts, only Rev. 13:3 and 12. See CURE.

2. *iaomai* (ἰάομαι, 2390), "to heal," is used (a) of physical treatment 22 times; in Matt. 5:28, KJV, "made whole," RV, "healed"; so in Acts 9:34; (b) figuratively, of spiritual "healing," Matt. 13:15; John 12:40; Acts 28:27; Heb. 12:13; 1 Pet. 2:24; possibly, Jas. 5:16 includes both (a) and (b); some mss. have the word, with sense (b), in Luke 4:18. Apart from this last, Luke, the physician, uses the word fifteen times. See WHOLE.

3. *sōzō* (σώζω, 4982), "to save," is translated by the verb "to heal" in the KJV of Mark 5:23 and Luke 8:36 (RV, "to make whole"; so KJV frequently); the idea is that of saving from disease and its effects. See SAVE.

4. *diasōzō* (διασώζω, 1295), "to save thoroughly" (*dia*, "through," and No. 3), is translated "heal" in Luke 7:3, KJV (RV, "save"). See ESCAPE.

B. Nouns.

1. *therapeia* (θεραπεία, 2322), akin to A, No. 1, primarily denotes "care, attention," Luke 12:42; then, "medical service,

healing" (Eng., "therapy"), Luke 9:11; Rev. 22:2, of the effects of the leaves of the tree of life, perhaps here with the meaning "health."

2. *iama* (ἴαμα, 2386), akin to A, No. 2, formerly signified "a means of healing"; in the NT, "a healing" (the result of the act), used in the plural, in 1 Cor. 12:9, 28, 30, RV, "healings"; of divinely imparted gifts in the churches in apostolic times.

3. *iasis* (ἴασις, 2392), akin to A, No. 2, stresses the process as reaching completion, Luke 13:32, "cures," of the acts of Christ in the days of His flesh; Acts 4:22, 30, "to heal," lit. 'unto healing.'

HEALTH (to be in)

hugianiō (ὑγιαίνω, 5198) denotes "to be healthy, sound, in good health" (Eng., "hygiene"), rendered "mayest be in health," in 3 John 2; rendered "safe and sound" in Luke 15:27. See SAFE, D, No. 2, SOUND, WHOLE, B, No. 1.

Note: In Acts 27:34, *sōtēria*, "salvation, safety," is translated "health" in the KJV; the RV, gives the right meaning, "safety."

HEAR, HEARING

A. Verbs.

1. *akouō* (ἀκούω, 191), the usual word denoting "to hear," is used (a) intransitively, e.g., Matt. 11:15; Mark 4:23; (b) transitively when the object is expressed, sometimes in the accusative case, sometimes in the genitive. Thus in Acts 9:7, "hearing the voice," the noun "voice" is in the partitive genitive case [i.e., hearing (something) of], whereas in 22:9, "they heard not the voice," the construction is with the accusative. This removes the idea of any contradiction. The former indicates a "hearing" of the sound, the latter indicates the meaning or message of the voice (this they did not hear). "The former denotes the sensational perception, the latter (the accusative case) the thing perceived" (Cremer). In John 5:25, 28, the genitive case is used, indicating a "sensational perception" that the Lord's voice is sounding; in 3:8, of "hearing" the wind, the accusative is used, stressing "the thing perceived."

That God "hears" prayer signifies that He answers prayer, e.g., John 9:31; 1 John 5:14, 15. Sometimes the verb is used with *para* ("from beside"), e.g., John 1:40, "one of the two which heard John speak," lit., "heard from beside John," suggesting that he stood beside him; in John 8:26, 40, indicating the intimate fellowship of the Son with the Father; the same construction is used in Acts 10:22 and 2 Tim. 2:2, in the latter case, of the intimacy between Paul and Timothy. See HEARKEN.

2. *eisakouō* (εἰσακούω, 1522), "to listen to" (*eis*, to, and No. 1), has two meanings, (a) "to hear and to obey," 1 Cor. 14:21, "they will not hear"; (b) "to hear so as to answer," of God's answer to prayer, Matt. 6:7; Luke 1:13; Acts 10:31; Heb. 5:7.

3. *diakouō* (διακούω, 1251), "to hear through, hear fully" (*dia*, "through," and No. 1), is used technically, of "hearing" judicially, in Acts 23:35, of Felix in regard to the charges against Paul. In the Sept., Deut. 1:16; Job 9:33.

4. *epakouō* (ἐπακούω, 1873), "to listen to, hear with favor, at or upon an occasion" (*epi*, "upon," and No. 1), is used in 2 Cor. 6:2 (RV, "hearken").

5. *epakroaomai* (ἐπακροάομαι, 1874), "to listen attentively to" (*epi*, used intensively, and a verb akin to No. 1), is used in Acts 16:25, "(the prisoners) were listening to (them)," RV, expressive of rapt attention.

6. *proakouō* (προακούω, 4257) signifies "to hear before" (*pro*), Col. 1:5, where Lightfoot suggests that the preposition contrasts what they heard before, the true gospel, with the false gospel of their recent teachers.

7. *parakouō* (παρακούω, 3878) primarily signifies "to overhear, hear amiss or imperfectly" (*para*, "beside, amiss," and No. 1); then (in the NT) "to hear without taking heed, to neglect to hear," Matt. 18:17 (twice); in Mark 5:36 the best mss. have this verb, which the RV renders "not heeding" (marg., "overhearing"); some mss. have No. 1, KJV, "hearing." It seems obvious that the Lord paid no attention to those from the ruler's house and their message that his daughter was dead. Cf. the noun *parakoē*, "disobedience."

B. Nouns.

1. *akoē* (ἀκοή, 189), akin to A, No. 1, denotes (a) "the sense of hearing," 1 Cor. 12:17; 2 Pet. 2:8; a combination of verb and noun is used in phrases which have been termed Hebraic as they express somewhat literally an OT phraseology, e.g., "By hearing ye shall hear," Matt. 13:14; Acts 28:26, RV, a mode of expression conveying emphasis; (b) "the organ of hearing," Mark 7:35, "ears"; Luke 7:1, RV, "ears," for KJV, "audience"; Acts 17:20; 2 Tim. 4:3, 4; Heb. 5:11, "dull of hearing," lit., "dull as to ears"; (c) "a thing heard, a message or teaching," John 12:38, "report"; Rom. 10:16; 1 Thess. 2:13, "the word of the message," lit. "the word of hearing" (KJV, "which ye heard"); Heb. 4:2, "the word of hearing," RV, for KJV, "the word preached"; in a somewhat similar sense, "a rumor, report," Matt. 4:24; 14:1; Mark 1:28, KJV, "fame," RV, "report"; Matt. 24:6; Mark 13:7, "rumors (of wars)"; (d) "the receiving of a message," Rom. 10:17, something more than the mere sense of "hearing" [see (a)]; so with the phrase "the hearing of faith," Gal. 3:2, 5, which it seems better to understand so than under (c). See EAR, FAME, PREACH, REPORT, RUMOR.

HEARER

akroatēs (ἀκροατής, 202), from *akroaomai*, "to listen," is used in Rom. 2:13, "of a law"; Jas. 1:22, 23, "of the word"; v. 25, "a (forgetful) hearer."

Note: In Eph. 4:29 and 2 Tim. 2:14, the verb *akouō*, "to hear," is rendered "hearers" in the KJV (RV, "them that hear").

HEARKEN

1. *akouō* (ἀκούω, 191), "to hear," is rendered "hearken" in the KJV and RV, in Mark 4:3; Acts 4:19; 7:2; 15:13; Jas. 2:5; in the RV only, in Acts 3:22, 23; 13:16 (KJV, "give audience"); 15:12, "hearkened" (KJV "gave audience"). See HEAR, No. 1.

Note: In Acts 12:13, *hupakouō*, lit., "to hearken," with the idea of stillness, or attention (*hupo*, "under," *akouō*, "to hear"), signifies "to answer a knock at a door," RV, "to answer" (KJV, "to hearken"). See OBEY.

2. *epakouō* (ἐπακούω, 1873), denotes "to hearken to," 2 Cor. 6:2, RV (see HEAR, A, No. 4).

3. *enōtizomai* (ἐνωτίζομαι, 1801), "to give ear to, to hearken" (from *en*, "in," and *ous*, "an ear"), is used in Acts 2:14, in Peter's address to the men of Israel.

4. *peitharcheō* (πειθαρχέω, 3980), "to obey one in authority, be obedient" (*peithomai*, "to be persuaded," *archē*, "rule"), is translated "to hearken unto" in Acts 27:21, in Paul's reminder to the shipwrecked mariners that they should have given heed to his counsel. See OBEY.

HEART, HEARTILY

kardia (καρδία, 2588), "the heart" (Eng., "cardiac," etc.), the chief organ of physical life ("for the life of the flesh is in the blood," Lev. 17:11), occupies the most important place in the human system. By an easy transition the word came to stand for man's entire mental and moral activity, both the rational and the emotional elements. In other words, the heart is used figuratively for the hidden springs of the personal life. "The Bible describes human depravity as in the 'heart,' because sin is a principle which has its seat in the center of man's inward life, and then 'defiles' the whole circuit of his action, Matt. 15:19, 20. On the other hand, Scripture regards the heart as the sphere of Divine influence, Rom. 2:15; Acts 15:9 .... The heart, as lying deep within, contains 'the hidden man,' 1 Pet. 3:4, the real man. It represents the true character but conceals it" (J. Laidlaw, in *Hastings' Bible Dic.*).

As to its usage in the NT it denotes (a) the seat of physical life, Acts 14:17; Jas. 5:5; (b) the seat of moral nature and spiritual life, the seat of grief, John 14:1; Rom. 9:2; 2 Cor. 2:4; joy, John 16:22; Eph. 5:19; the desires, Matt. 5:28; 2 Pet. 2:14; the affections, Luke 24:32; Acts 21:13; the perceptions, John 12:40; Eph. 4:18; the thoughts, Matt. 9:4; Heb. 4:12; the understanding, Matt. 13:15; Rom. 1:21; the reasoning powers, Mark 2:6; Luke 24:38; the imagination, Luke 1:51; conscience, Acts 2:37; 1 John 3:20; the intentions, Heb. 4:12, cf. 1 Pet. 4:1; purpose, Acts 11:23; 2 Cor. 9:7; the will, Rom. 6:17; Col. 3:15; faith, Mark 11:23; Rom. 10:10; Heb. 3:12.

The heart, in its moral significance in the OT, includes the emotions, the reason and the will.

2. *psuchē* (ψυχή, 5590), the soul, or life, is rendered "heart" in Eph. 6:6 (marg., "soul"), "doing the will of God from the heart." In Col. 3:23, a form of the word *psuchē* preceded by *ek*, from, lit., "from (the) soul," is rendered "heartily."

Notes: (1) The RV, "heart" is substituted for KJV, "bowels," in Col. 3:12; Philem. 7, 12, 20. (2) In 2 Cor. 3:3, the RV has "tables that are hearts of flesh," for KJV, "fleshy tables of the heart." (3) In Eph. 1:18, the best mss. have *kardia*, "(the eyes of your) heart"; some have *dianoia*, "understanding" (KJV). (4) In Heb. 8:10 and 10:16, the KJV has "in their hearts" and "into their hearts"; RV, "on their heart." (5) In Luke 21:26, where there is no word for "hearts" in the original, the RV has "men fainting (for fear)." (6) In 2 Cor. 7:2, the verb *chōreō*, to make room for, "receive" (KJV), is translated, or rather, interpreted, "open your hearts," RV, marg., "make room for (us)."

HEART (hardness of)

sklērokardia (σκληροκαρδία, 4641), "hardness of heart" (*sklēros*, "hard," and *kardia*), is used in Matt. 19:8; Mark 10:5; 16:14. In the Sept., Deut. 10:16; Jer. 4:4.

HEART (knowing the)

kardiognōstēs (καρδιογνώστης, 2589), "a knower of hearts" (*kardia* and *ginōskō*, "to know"), is used in Acts 1:24; 15:8.

HEAT

A. Nouns.

1. *kausōn* (καύσων, 2742) denotes "a burning heat" (from *kaiō*, "to burn"; cf. Eng., "caustic," "cauterize"), Matt. 20:12; Luke 12:55 (KJV, "heat"), RV, in each place, "scorching heat" (marg. "hot wind"); in Jas. 1:11, "a burning heat," KJV, RV, "the scorching wind" like the sirocco. Cf. Amos 4:9, where the Sept. has *purōsis*, "burning" (*pur*, "fire"). See BURNING.

2. *kauma* (καῦμα, 2738), "heat" (akin to No. 1), signifies "the result of burning," or "the heat produced," Rev. 7:16; 16:9; cf. *kaumatizō*, "to scorch," *kausis*, "burning," *kautēriazomai*, "to brand, sear."

3. *thermē* (θέρμη, 2329) denotes "warmth, heat," Acts 28:3 (Eng., "thermal," etc.).

B. Verb.

kausoō (καυσόω, 2741) was used as a medical term, of "a fever"; in the NT, "to burn with great heat" (akin to A, No. 1), said of the future destruction of the natural elements, 2 Pet. 3:10, 12, "with fervent heat," passive voice, lit.. "being burned."

For **HEATHEN** see GENTILES

HEAVEN, HEAVENLY (-IES)

A. Nouns.

1. *ouranos* (οὐρανός, 3772), probably akin to *ornumi*, "to lift, to heave," is used in the NT (a) of "the aerial heavens," e.g., Matt. 6:26; 8:20; Acts 10:12; 11:6 (RV, "heaven," in each place, KJV, "air"); Jas. 5:18; (b) "the sidereal," e.g., Matt. 24:29, 35; Mark 13:25, 31; Heb. 11:12, RV, "heaven," KJV, "sky"; Rev. 6:14; 20:11; they, (a) and (b), were created by the Son of God, Heb. 1:10, as also by God the Father, Rev. 10:6; (c) "the eternal dwelling place of God," Matt. 5:16; 12 :50; Rev. 3:12; 11:13; 16:11; 20:9. From thence the Son of God descended to become incarnate, John 3:13, 31; 6:38, 42. In His ascension Christ "passed through the heavens," Heb. 4:14, RV; He "ascended far above all the heavens," Eph. 4:10, and was "made higher than the heavens," Heb. 7:26; He "sat down on the right hand of the throne of the Majesty in the heavens," Heb. 8:1; He is "on the right hand of God," having gone into heaven, 1 Pet. 3:22. Since His ascension it is the scene of His present life and activity, e.g., Rom. 8:34; Heb. 9:24. From thence the Holy Spirit descended at Pentecost, 1 Pet. 1:12. It is the abode of the angels, e.g., Matt. 18:10; 22:30; cf. Rev. 3:5. Thither Paul was "caught up," whether in the body or out of the body, he knew not, 2 Cor. 12:2. It is to be the eternal dwelling place of the saints in resurrection glory, 2 Cor. 5:1. From thence Christ will descend to the air to receive His saints at the Rapture, 1 Thess. 4:16; Phil. 3:20, 21, and will subsequently come with His saints and with His holy angels at His second advent, Matt. 24:30; 2 Thess. 1:7. In the present life "heaven" is the region of the spiritual citizenship of believers, Phil. 3:20. The present "heavens," with the earth, are to pass away, 2 Pet. 3:10, "being on fire," v. 12 (see v. 7); Rev. 20:11, and new "heavens" and earth are to be created, 2 Pet. 3:13; Rev. 21:1, with Isa. 65:17, e.g.

In Luke 15:18, 21, "heaven" is used, by metonymy, for God. See AIR.

Notes: (1) For the phrase in Luke 11:13, see *Note* on B, No. 2. (2) In Luke 11:2, the KJV, "as in heaven," translates a phrase found in some mss.

2. *mesouranēma* (μεσουράνημα, 3321) denotes "mid-heaven," or the midst of the heavens (*mesos*, "middle," and No. 1), Rev. 8:13; 14:6; 19:17.

B. Adjectives.

1. *ouranios* (οὐράνιος, 3770), signifying "of heaven, heavenly," corresponding to A, No. 1, is used (a) as an appellation of God the Father, Matt. 6:14, 26, 32, "your heavenly Father"; 15:13, "My heavenly Father"; (b) as descriptive of the holy angels, Luke 2:13; (c) of the vision seen by Paul, Acts 26:19.

2. *epouranios* (ἐπουράνιος, 2032), "heavenly," what pertains to, or is in, heaven (*epi*, in the sense of "pertaining to," not here, "above"), has meanings corresponding to some of the meanings of *ouranos*, A, No. 1. It is used (a) of God the Father, Matt. 18:35; (b) of the place where Christ "sitteth at the right hand of God" (i.e., in a position of divine authority), Eph. 1:20; and of the present position of believers in relationship to Christ, Eph 2:6; where they possess "every spiritual blessing," 1:3; (c) of Christ as "the Second Man," and all those who are related to Him spiritually, 1 Cor. 15:48; (d) of those whose sphere of activity or existence is above, or in contrast to that of earth, of "principalities and powers," Eph. 3:10; of "spiritual hosts of wickedness," 6:12, RV, "in heavenly places," for KJV, "in high places"; (e) of the Holy Spirit, Heb. 6:4; (f) of "heavenly things," as the subjects of the teaching of Christ, John 3:12, and as consisting of the spiritual and "heavenly" sanctuary and "true tabernacle" and all that appertains thereto in relation to Christ and His sacrifice as antitypical of the earthly tabernacle and sacrifices under the Law, Heb. 8:5; 9:23; (g) of the "calling" of believers, Heb. 3:1; (h) of heaven as the abode of the saints, "a better country" than that of earth, Heb. 11:16, and of the spiritual Jerusalem, 12:22; (i) of the kingdom of Christ in its future manifestation, 2 Tim. 4:18; (j) of all beings and things, animate and inanimate, that are "above the earth," Phil. 2:10; (k) of the resurrection and glorified bodies of believers, 1 Cor. 15:49; (l) of the "heavenly orbs," 1 Cor. 15:40 ("celestial," twice, and so rendered here only).

Note: In connection with (a), the word "heavenly," used of God the Father in Luke 11:13, represents the phrase *ex ouranou*, "from heaven."

C. Adverb.

ouranothen (οὐρανόθεν, 3771), formed from A, No. 1, and denoting "from heaven," is used of (a) the aerial heaven, Acts 14:17; (b) heaven, as the uncreated sphere of God's abode, 26:13.

HEAVY, HEAVINESS

A. Nouns.

1. *lupē* (λύπη, 3077), "grief, sorrow," is rendered "heaviness" in the KJV of Rom. 9:2; 2 Cor. 2:1 (RV, "sorrow," in both places). See GRIEF, SORROW.

2. *katēpheia* (κατήφεια, 2726) probably denotes a downcast look, expressive of sorrow; hence, "dejection, heaviness"; it is used in Jas. 4:9.

B. Verbs.

1. *adēmoneō* (ἀδημονέω, 85), "to be troubled, much distressed," is used of the Lord's sorrow in Gethsemane, Matt. 26:37; Mark 14:33, KJV, "to be very heavy," RV, "to be sore troubled"; of Epaphroditus, because the saints at Philippi had received news of his sickness, Phil. 2:26, KJV, "was full of heaviness," RV, "was sore troubled. See TROUBLE, B, No 12.

2. *lupeō* (λυπέω, 3076), "to distress, grieve" (akin to A, No. 1), is rendered "are in heaviness" in 1 Pet. 1:6, KJV (RV, "have been put to grief"); here, as frequently, it is in the passive voice. See GRIEF, SORROWFUL.

3. *bareō* (βαρέω, 916), always in the passive voice in the NT, is rendered "were heavy" in Matt. 26:43; Mark 14:40; Luke 9:32.

C. Adjective.

barus (βαρύς, 926), "heavy" (akin to B, No. 3), is so rendered in Matt. 23:4. See GRIEVOUS.

HEED (to give, to take)

1. *blepō* (βλέπω, 991), "to look," see, usually implying more especially an intent, earnest contemplation, is rendered "take heed" in Matt. 24:4; Mark 4:24; 13:5, 9, 23, 33; Luke 8:18; 21:8; 1 Cor. 3:10; 8:9; 10:12; Gal. 5:15; Col. 2:8 (KJV, "beware"); 4:17; Heb. 3:12. See BEHOLD, BEWARE, LIE, LOOK, REGARD.

2. *horaō* (ὁράω, 3708), "to see," usually expressing the sense of vision, is rendered "take heed" in Matt. 16:6; 18:10, KJV (RV, "see"); Mark 8:15; Luke 12:15; Acts 22:26 (KJV only). See BEHOLD.

3. *prosechō* (προσέχω, 4337), lit., "to hold to," signifies "to turn to, turn one's attention to"; hence, "to give heed"; it is rendered "take heed" in Matt. 6:1; Luke 17:3; 21:34; Acts 5:35; 20:28; 2 Pet. 1:19; to give heed to, in Acts 8:6, 10; in v. 11 (KJV, "had regard to"); 16:14 (KJV, "attended unto"); 1 Tim. 1:4; 4:1, 13 (KJV, "give attendance to"); Titus 1:14; Heb. 2:1, lit., "to give heed more earnestly." See ATTEND, BEWARE, GIVE, REGARD.

4. *epechō* (ἐπέχω, 1907), lit., "to hold upon," then, "to direct towards, to give attention to," is rendered "gave heed," in Acts 3:5; "take heed," in 1 Tim. 4:16. See HOLD (FORTH), MARK.

Notes: (1) In Luke 11:35, KJV, *skopeō*, "to look," is translated "take heed (that)," RV, "look (whether)." (2) Nos. 2 and 3 are used together in Matt. 16:6; Nos. 2 and 1, in that order, in Mark 8:15; but in Luke 12:15 the RV rightly follows No. 2 by "keep yourselves from" (*phulassō*, "to guard"). (3) For the RV of Mark 5:36, "not heeding," see under HEAR, No. 7. (4) In Rom. 11:21 the KJV adds "take heed," because of a variant reading which introduces the clause by a conjunctive phrase signifying "lest."

HEIR

A. Noun.

1. *klēronomos* (κληρονόμος, 2818) lit. denotes "one who obtains a lot or portion (*klēros*, "a lot," *nemomai*, "to possess"), especially of an inheritance. The NT usage may be analyzed as under: "(a) the person to whom property is to pass on the death of the owner, Matt. 21:38; Mark 12:7; Luke 20:14; Gal. 4:1; (b) one to whom something has been assigned by God, on possession of which, however, he has not yet entered, as Abraham, Rom. 4:13, 14; Heb. 6:17; Christ, Heb. 1:2; the poor saints, Jas. 2:5; (c) believers, inasmuch as they share in the new order of things to be ushered in at the return of Christ, Rom. 8:17; Gal. 3:29; 4:7; Titus 3:7; (d) one who receives something other than by merit, as Noah, Heb. 11:7."

In the Sept., Judg. 18:7; 2 Sam. 14:7; Jer. 8:10; Mic. 1:15.

2. *sunklēronomos* (συγκληρονόμος, 4789), "a joint-heir, co-inheritor" (*sun*, "with," and No. 1), "is used of Isaac and Jacob as participants with Abraham in the promises of God, Heb. 11:9; of husband and wife who are also united in Christ, 1 Pet. 3:7; of Gentiles who believe, as participants in the gospel with Jews who believe, Eph. 3:6; and of all believers as prospective participants with Christ in His glory, as recompense for their participation in His sufferings, Rom. 8:17."

B. Verb.

klēronomeō (κληρονομέω, 2816), "to be an heir to, to inherit" (see A, No. 1), is rendered "shall (not) inherit with" in Gal. 4:30, RV, KJV, "shall (not) be heir with"; in Heb. 1:14, RV, "shall inherit," KJV, "shall be heirs of." See INHERIT. Cf. *klēroomai*, "to be taken as an inheritance," *klēronomia*, "an inheritance," *klēros*, "a lot, an inheritance."

HELL

1. *geenna* (γέεννα, 1067) represents the Hebrew Ge-Hinnom (the valley of Tophet) and a corresponding Aramaic word; it is found twelve times in the NT, eleven of which are in the Synoptists, in every instance as uttered by the Lord Himself. He who says to his brother, Thou fool (see under FOOL), will be in danger of "the hell of fire," Matt. 5:22; it is better to pluck out (a metaphorical description of irrevocable law) an eye that causes its possessor to stumble, than that his "whole body be cast into hell," v. 29; similarly with the hand, v. 30; in Matt. 18:8, 9, the admonitions are repeated, with an additional mention of the foot; here, too, the warning concerns the person himself (for which obviously the "body" stands in chapt. 5); in v. 8, "the eternal fire" is mentioned as the doom, the character of the region standing for the region itself, the two being combined in the phrase "the hell of fire," v. 9. To the passage in Matt. 18, that in Mark 9:43-47, is parallel; here to the word "hell" are applied the

extended descriptions "the unquenchable fire" and "where their worm dieth not and the fire is not quenched."

That God, "after He hath killed, hath power to cast into hell," is assigned as a reason why He should be feared with the fear that keeps from evil doing, Luke 12:5; the parallel passage to this in Matt. 10:28 declares, not the casting in, but the doom which follows, namely, the destruction (not the loss of being, but of wellbeing) of "both soul and body."

In Matt. 23 the Lord denounces the scribes and Pharisees, who in proselytizing a person "make him two-fold more a son of hell" than themselves (v. 15), the phrase here being expressive of moral characteristics, and declares the impossibility of their escaping "the judgment of hell," v. 33. In Jas. 3:6 "hell" is described as the source of the evil done by misuse of the tongue; here the word stands for the powers of darkness, whose characteristics and destiny are those of "hell."

For terms descriptive of "hell," see e.g., Matt. 13:42; 25:46; Phil. 3:19; 2 Thess. 1:9; Heb. 10:39; 2 Pet. 2:17; Jude 13; Rev. 2:11; 19:20; 20:6, 10, 14; 21:8.

Notes: (1) For the rendering "hell" as a translation of hades, corresponding to Sheol, wrongly rendered "the grave" and "hell," see HADES. (2) The verb *tartaroō*, translated "cast down to hell" in 2 Pet. 2:4, signifies to consign to Tartarus, which is neither Sheol nor hades nor hell, but the place where those angels whose special sin is referred to in that passage are confined "to be reserved unto judgment"; the region is described as "pits of darkness." RV

HELPER, FELLOW-HELPER

1. *boēthos* (βοηθός, 998), an adjective, akin to A, No. 2, and B, No. 4, under HELP, signifying "helping," is used as a noun in Heb. 13:6, of God as the helper of His saints.

2. *sunergos* (συνεργός, 4904), an adjective, akin to B, No. 7, under HELP, "a fellow worker," is translated "helper" in the KJV of Rom. 16:3, 9, RV, "fellow worker"; in 2 Cor. 1:24, KJV and RV, "helpers"; in 2 Cor. 8:23, KJV, "fellow helper," RV, "fellow worker"; so the plural in 3 John 8: See COMPANION, LABORER, etc.

HERD

agelē (ἀγέλη, 34), from *agō*, "to lead," is used, in the NT, only of swine, Matt. 8:30, 31, 32; Mark 5:11, 13; Luke 8:32, 33.

HEREAFTER

Notes: (1) This adverb translates the phrase *meta tauta*, lit., "after these things," John 13:7; Rev. 1:19, and frequently in the Apocalypse, see 4:1 (twice); 7:9; 9:12; 15:5; 18:1; 19:1; 20:3, (2) In John 14:30, *ouk eti* is rendered "no more" in the RV (KJV, "Hereafter … not"). (3) In 1 Tim. 1:16, "hereafter" translates the verb *mellō*, "to be about to."

HERESY

hairesis (αἵρεσις, 139) denotes (a) "a choosing, choice" (from *haireomai*, "to choose"); then, "that which is chosen," and hence, "an opinion," especially a self-willed opinion, which is substituted for submission to the power of truth, and leads to division and the formation of sects, Gal. 5:20 (marg., "parties"); such erroneous opinions are frequently the outcome of personal preference or the prospect of advantage; see 2 Pet. 2:1, where "destructive" (RV) signifies leading to ruin; some assign even this to (b); in the papyri the prevalent meaning is "choice" (Moulton and Milligan, *Vocab.*); (b) "a sect"; this secondary meaning, resulting from (a), is the dominating significance in the NT, Acts 5:17; 15:5; 24:5, 14; 26:5; 28:22; "heresies" in 1 Cor. 11:19 (see marg.). See SECT.

HERETICAL

hairetikos (αἱρετικός, 141), akin to the above, primarily denotes "capable of choosing" (*haireomai*); hence, "causing division by a party spirit, factious," Titus 3:10, RV, "heretical."

For **HERETOFORE** see SIN, C, No. 2

HERITAGE

klēroō (κληρόω, 2820), primarily, "to cast lots" or "to choose by lot," then, "to assign a portion," is used in the passive voice in Eph. 1:11, "we were made a heritage," RV (KJV, "we have obtained an inheritance"). The RV is in agreement with such OT passages as Deut. 4:20, "a people of inheritance"; 9:29; 32:9; Ps. 16:6. The meaning "were chosen by lot," as in the Vulgate, and in 1 Sam. 14:41, indicating the freedom of election without human will (so Chrysostom and Augustine), is not suited to this passage.

HIDE, HID, HIDDEN

A. Verbs.

1. *kruptō* (κρύπτω, 2928), "to cover, conceal, keep secret" (Eng., "crypt," "cryptic," etc.), is used (a) in its physical significance, e.g., Matt. 5:14; 13:44; 25:18 (some mss. have No. 2); (b) metaphorically, e.g., Matt. 11:25 (some mss. have No. 2 here); 13:35, RV, "(things) hidden"; KJV, "(things) which have been kept secret"; Luke 18:34; 19:42; John 19:38, "secretly." See SECRET.

2. *apokruptō* (ἀποκρύπτω, 613), "to conceal from, to keep secret" (*apo*, "from," and No. 1), is used metaphorically, in Luke 10:21, of truths "hidden" from the wise and prudent and revealed to babes; 1 Cor. 2:7, of God's wisdom; Eph. 3:9, of the mystery of the unsearchable riches of Christ, revealed through the gospel Col. 1:26, of the mystery associated with the preceding.

3. *enkruptō* (ἐγκρύπτω, 1470), "to hide in anything" (*en*, "in," and No. 1), is used in Matt. 13:33, of leaven "hidden" in meal.

4. *perikruptō* (περικρύπτω, 4032) signifies "to hide by placing something around, to conceal entirely, to keep hidden" (*peri*, "around," used intensively, and No. 1), Luke 1:24.

5. *kaluptō* (καλύπτω, 2572) signifies "to cover, conceal," so that no trace of it can be seen (hence somewhat distinct from No. 1): it is not translated "to hide" in the RV; in 2 Cor. 4:3 it is rendered "veiled," suitably continuing the subject of 3:13-18; in Jas. 5:20, "shall hide," KJV (RV, "shall cover").

6. *parakaluptō* (παρακαλύπτω, 3871), lit., "to cover with a veil," KJV, "hid," in Luke 9:45, "it was veiled from them"; see CONCEAL.

7. *lanthanō* (λανθάνω, 2990), "to escape notice, to be hidden from," is rendered "(could not) be hid" in Mark 7:24, of Christ; "was (not) hid," Luke 8:47, of the woman with the issue of blood; "is hidden," Acts 26:26, of the facts concerning Christ; the sentence might be rendered "none of these things has escaped the king's notice." See FORGET.

B. Adjectives.

1. *kruptos* (κρυπτός, 2927), akin to A, No. 1, "hidden, secret," is translated "hid" in Matt. 10:26; Mark 4:22; Luke 8:17, RV, for KJV, "secret"; 12:2 (last part); in 1 Cor. 4:5, "hidden (things of darkness)"; 2 Cor. 4:2, "hidden (things of shame)"; 1 Pet. 3:4, "hidden (man of the heart)." See SECRET.

2. *apokruphos* (ἀπόκρυφος, 614), "hidden away from" (corresponding to A, No. 2; cf Eng., "apocryphal"), is translated, "made (KJV, kept) secret," in Mark 4:22; in Luke 8:17, RV, "secret," for KJV, "hid"; in Col. 2:3, RV, "hidden," KJV, "hid." See SECRET.

HIGH (from on, most), HIGHLY

A. Adjectives.

1. *hupsēlos* (ὑψηλός, 5308), "high, lofty," is used (a) naturally, of mountains, Matt. 4:8; 17:1; Mark 9:2; Rev. 21:10; of a wall, Rev. 21:12; (b) figuratively, of the arm of God, Acts 13:17; of heaven, "on high," plural, lit., "in high (places)," Heb. 1:3; (c) metaphorically, Luke 16:15, RV, "exalted" (KJV, "highly esteemed"); Rom. 11:20, in the best texts, "high-minded" [lit., "mind (not) high things"]; 12:16.

2. *hupsistos* (ὕψιστος, 5310), "most high," is a superlative degree, the positive not being in use; it is used of God in Luke 1:32, 35, 76; 6:35, in each of which the RV has "the most High," for KJV, "the highest," KJV and RV in Mark 5:7; Luke 8:28; Acts 7:48; 16:17; Heb. 7:1. See HIGHEST (below).

3. *megas* (μέγας, 3173), "great," is translated "high" in John 19:31, of the Sabbath day at the Passover season; here the meaning is virtually equivalent to "holy." See GREAT.

Note: In Heb. 10:21, the RV rightly has "a great (priest)," KJV, "high." For "high places," Eph. 6:12, KJV, see HEAVENLY, B, No. 2.

B. Nouns.

1. *hupsos* (ὕψος, 5311), "height," is used with *ex* (*ek*) "from," in the phrase "on high," Luke 1:78; 24:49; with *eis*, "in" or "into," Eph. 4:8. See ESTATE.

2. *hupsōma* (ὕψωμα, 5313), "high thing," 2 Cor. 10:5; in Rom. 8:39, "height."

C. Adverb.

anō (ἄνω, 507), "above, upward," is used in Phil. 3:14, of the "high calling of God in Christ Jesus," the prize of which is set before believers as their goal, lit., "calling upward" (RV, marg.), a preferable rendering to "heavenly calling." See ABOVE.

HIGHER

A. Adverb.

1. *anōteron* (ἀνώτερος, 511), the neuter of *anōteros*, "higher," the comparative of *ano* (see C, under HIGH), is used as an adverb of place in Luke 14:10; for the meaning "above," in Heb. 10:8, see ABOVE.

B. Verb.

huperechō (ὑπερέχω, 5242), lit., "to hold over anything," as being superior, is used metaphorically in Rom. 13:1, of rulers, as the "higher" powers; cf. 1 Pet. 2:13, "supreme." See BETTER, EXCELLENCY, SUPREME.

HIGHEST

hupsistos (ὕψιστος, 5310) is used in the plural in the phrase "in the highest," i.e., in the "highest" regions, the abode of God, Matt. 21:9; Mark 11:10; Luke omits the article, Luke 2:14; 19:38; for its use as a title of God, see HIGH, A, No. 2.

For **HIGHLY** see DISPLEASED, EXALT, EXCEEDING, FAVOR

HIGH-MINDED

1. *tuphoō* (τυφόω, 5187) properly means "to wrap in smoke" (from *tuphos*, "smoke"; metaphorically, for "conceit"); it is used in the passive voice, metaphorically in 1 Tim. 3:6, "puffed up," RV (KJV, "lifted up with pride"); so 6:4, KJV, "proud," and 2 Tim. 3:4, KJV, "highminded." See PROUD, PUFF (UP). Cf. *tuphomai*, "to smoke," Matt. 12:20, and *tuphōnikos*, "tempestuous" (with *anemos*, "wind," understood), Acts 27:14.

2. *hupsēlophroneō* (ὑψηλοφρονέω, 5309), "to be high-minded," is used in 1 Tim. 6:17.

HINDER, HINDRANCE

A. Verbs.

1. *enkoptō* (ἐγκόπτω, 1465), lit., "to cut into" (*en*, "in," *koptō*, "to cut"), was used of "impeding" persons by breaking up the road, or by placing an obstacle sharply in the path; hence, metaphorically, of "detaining" a person unnecessarily, Acts 24:4, of "hindrances" in the way of reaching others, Rom. 15:22; or returning to them, 1 Thess. 2:18; of "hindering" progress in the Christian life, Gal. 5:7 (*anakoptō* in some mss.), where the significance virtually is "who broke up the road along which you were travelling so well?"; of "hindrances" to the prayers of husband and wife, through low standards of marital conduct, 1 Pet. 3:7 (*ekkoptō*, "to cut out, repulse," in some mss.).

2. *kōluō* (κωλύω, 2967), "to hinder, forbid, restrain," is translated "to hinder" in Luke 11:52; Acts 8:36; Rom. 1:13, RV (KJV, "was let"); Heb. 7:23, RV (KJV, "were not suffered"). See FORBID.

3. *diakōluō* (διακωλύω, 1254), a strengthened form of No. 2, "to hinder thoroughly," is used in Matt. 3:14, of John the Baptist's endeavor to "hinder" Christ from being baptized, KJV, "forbad," RV, "would have hindered," lit., "was hindering."

B. Noun.

enkopē (ἐγκοπή, 1464), "a hindrance," lit., "a cutting in," akin to A, No. 1, with corresponding significance, is used in 1 Cor. 9:12, with *didōmi*, "to give," RV, "(that) we may cause (no) hindrance," KJV, "(lest) we should hinder."

For **HINDER** (part) see STERN

HOLINESS, HOLY, HOLILY

A. Nouns.

1. *hagiasmos* (ἁγιασμός, 38), translated "holiness" in the KJV of Rom. 6:19, 22; 1 Thess. 4:7; 1 Tim. 2:15; Heb. 12:14, is always rendered "sanctification" in the RV. It signifies (a) separation to God, 1 Cor. 1:30; 2 Thess. 2:13; 1 Pet. 1:2; (b) the resultant state, the conduct befitting those so separated, 1 Thess. 4:3, 4, 7, and the four other places mentioned above. "Sanctification" is thus the state predetermined by God for believers, into which in grace He calls them, and in which they begin their Christian course and so pursue it. Hence they are called "saints" (*hagioi*). See SANCTIFICATION.

Note: The corresponding verb *hagiazō* denotes "to set apart to God." See HALLOW, SANCTIFY.

2. *hagiōsunē* (ἁγιωσύνη, 42) denotes the manifestation of the quality of "holiness" in personal conduct; (a) it is used in Rom. 1:4, of the absolute "holiness" of Christ in the days of His flesh, which distinguished Him from all merely human beings; this (which is indicated in the phrase "the spirit of holiness") and (in vindication of it) His resurrection from the dead, marked Him out as (He was "declared to be") the Son of God; (b) believers are to be "perfecting holiness in the fear of God," 2 Cor. 7:1, i.e., bringing "holiness" to its predestined end, whereby (c) they may be found "unblameable in holiness" in the Parousia of Christ, 1 Thess. 3:13.

"In each place character is in view, perfect in the case of the Lord Jesus, growing toward perfection in the case of the Christian. Here the exercise of love is declared to be the means God uses to develop likeness to Christ in His children. The sentence may be paraphrased thus:— The Lord enable you more and more to spend your lives in the interests of others, in order that He may so establish you in Christian character now, that you may be vindicated from every charge that might possibly be brought against you at the Judgment-seat of Christ;' cf. 1 John 4:16, 17."

3. *hagiotēs* (ἁγιότης, 41), "sanctity," the abstract quality of "holiness," is used (a) of God, Heb. 12:10; (b) of the manifestation of it in the conduct of the apostle Paul and his fellowlaborers, 2 Cor. 1:12 (in the best mss., for *haplotēs*).

4. *hosiotēs* (ὁσιότης, 3742) is to be distinguished from No. 3, as denoting that quality of "holiness" which is manifested in those who have regard equally to grace and truth; it involves a right relation to God; it is used in Luke 1:75 and Eph. 4:24, and in each place is associated with righteousness.

Notes: (1) In Acts 3:12, the KJV translates *eusebeia*, by "holiness," RV, "godliness," as everywhere, the true meaning of the word. See GODLINESS. (2) In Titus 2:3, KJV, *hieroprepēs*, which denotes "suited to a sacred character, reverent," is rendered "as becometh holiness," RV, "reverent." See REVERENT.

B. Adjectives.

1. *hagios* (ἅγιος, 40), akin to A, Nos. 1 and 2, which are from the same root as *hagnos* (found in *hazō*, "to venerate"), fundamentally signifies "separated" (among the Greeks, dedicated to the gods), and hence, in Scripture in its moral and spiritual significance, separated from sin and therefore consecrated to God, sacred.

(a) It is predicated of God (as the absolutely "Holy" One, in His purity, majesty and glory): of the Father, e.g., Luke 1:49; John 17:11; 1 Pet. 1:15, 16; Rev. 4:8; 6:10; of the Son, e.g., Luke 1:35; Acts 3:14; 4:27, 30; 1 John 2:20; of the Spirit, e.g., Matt. 1:18 and frequently in all the Gospels, Acts, Romans, 1 and 2 Cor., Eph., 1 Thess.; also in 2 Tim. 1:14; Titus 3:5; 1 Pet. 1:12; 2 Pet. 1:21; Jude 20.

(b) It is used of men and things (see below) in so far as they are devoted to God. Indeed the quality, as attributed to God, is often presented in a way which involves divine demands upon the conduct of believers. These are called *hagioi*, "saints," i.e., "sanctified" or "holy" ones.

This sainthood is not an attainment, it is a state into which God in grace calls men; yet believers are called to sanctify themselves (consistently with their calling, 2 Tim. 1:9), cleansing themselves from all defilement, forsaking sin, living a "holy" manner of life, 1 Pet. 1:15; 2 Pet. 3:11, and experiencing fellowship with God in His holiness. The saints are thus figuratively spoken of as "a holy temple," 1 Cor. 3:17 (a local church); Eph. 2:21 (the whole Church), cp. 5:27; "a holy priesthood," 1 Pet. 2:5; "a holy nation," 2:9.

"It is evident that *hagios* and its kindred words ... express something more and higher than *hieros*, sacred, outwardly associated with God; ... something more than *semnos*, worthy, honorable; something more than *hagnos*, pure, free from defilement. *Hagios* is ... more comprehensive .... It is characteristically godlikeness" (G. B. Stevens, in Hastings' *Bib. Dic.*).

The adjective is also used of the outer part of the tabernacle, Heb. 9:2 (RV, "the holy place"); of the inner sanctuary, 9:3, RV, "the Holy of Holies"; 9:4, "a holy place," RV; v. 25 (plural), of the presence of God in heaven, where there are not two compartments as in the tabernacle, all being "the holy place"; 9:8, 12 (neuter plural); 10:19, "the holy place," RV (KJV, "the holiest," neut. plural), see SANCTUARY; of the city of Jerusalem. Rev. 11:2; its temple, Acts 6:13; of the faith. Jude 20; of the greetings of saints, 1 Cor. 16:20; of angels, e.g., Mark 8:38; of apostles and prophets, Eph. 3:5; of the future heavenly Jerusalem, Rev. 21:2, 10; 22:19.

2. *hosios* (ὅσιος, 3741), akin to A, No. 4, signifies "religiously right, holy," as opposed to what is unrighteous or polluted. It is commonly associated with righteousness (see A, No. 4). It is used "of God, Rev. 15:4; 16:5; and of the body of the Lord Jesus, Acts 2:27; 13:35, citations from Ps. 16:10, Sept.; Heb. 7:26; and of certain promises made to David, which could be fulfilled only in the resurrection of the Lord Jesus, Acts 13:34. In 1 Tim. 2:8 and Titus 1:8, it is used of the character of Christians .... In the Sept., *hosios* frequently represents the Hebrew word *chasid*, which varies in meaning between 'holy' and 'gracious,' or 'merciful;' cf. Ps. 16:10 with 145:17."

Notes: (1) For Acts 13:34, see the RV and the KJV marg.; the RV in Rev. 16:5, "Thou Holy One," translates the most authentic mss. (KJV "and shalt be"). (2) For *hieros* (see No. 1), subserving a sacred purpose, translated "holy" in 2 Tim. 3:15, KJV (of the Scriptures), see SACRED.

C. Adverb.

hosios (ὁσίως, 3743), akin to A, No. 4, and B, No. 2, "holily," i.e., pure from evil conduct, and observant of God's will, is used in 1 Thess. 2:10, of the conduct of the apostle and his fellow missionaries.

D. Verb.

hagiazō (ἁγιάζω, 37), "to hallow, sanctify," in the passive voice, "to be made holy, be sanctified," is translated "let him be made holy" in Rev. 22:11, the aorist or point tense expressing the definiteness and completeness of the divine act; elsewhere it is rendered by the verb "to sanctify." See HALLOW, SANCTIFY.

For **HOLY GHOST** see under SPIRIT and HOLY, B, No. 1 (a)

HOLYDAY

heortē (ἑορτή, 1859) denotes "a feast, festival"; it is translated "a holy day" in the KJV of Col. 2:16; RV, "a feast day." See FEAST.

HOME, AT HOME (to be; workers)

A. Noun and Phrases.

1. *oikos* (οἶκος, 3624), "a house, dwelling," is used (a) with the preposition *eis*, "unto," with the meaning "to home," lit., "to a house," in Mark 8:3, RV, "to (their) home," KJV, "to (their own) houses"; so 8:26, "to (his) home"; Luke 15:6, "home," lit., "into the house"; (b) with the preposition *en*, "in," 1 Cor. 11:34, "(let him eat) at home"; 14:35, "(let them ask ...) at home"; (c) with the preposition *kata*, "down," Acts 2:46, "(breaking bread) at home," RV (KJV, "from house to house"); so in 5:42 (KJV, "in every house").

Notes: (1) In Mark 3:19, the KJV and RV marg., have "home," for the text "to a house"; the latter seems the more probable. See HOUSE. (2) In 1 Tim. 5:4, the phrase *ton idion oikon*, is rendered "at home," of the necessity that children should show piety there; RV, "towards their own family," the house being put by metonymy for the family.

2. The neuter plural of *idios*, "one's own," with the article, preceded by *eis*, "unto," lit., "unto one's own (things)," is translated "home" in Acts 21:6; in John 19:27, "unto his own home" ("home" being italicized).

Note: In John 16:32, this phrase is rendered "to his own" (of the predicted scattering of the disciples), KJV marg., "his own home"; cf. John 1:11, "His own things," RV, marg. (i.e., "His possessions").

For *oikia* in Matt. 8:6, KJV, "at home," see HOUSE.

3. In Luke 24:12 the reflexive pronoun *hauton* (in some mss. *heauton*), preceded by *pros*, to, is rendered "to his home," RV (lit., "to himself"), of the departure of Peter from the Lord's tomb; in John 20:10, the same construction is used, in the plural, of Peter and John on the same occasion, and rendered "unto their own home."

B. Adjective.

oikourgos (οἰκουρός, 3626), "working at home" (*oikos*, and a root of *ergon*, "work"), is used in Titus 2:5, "workers at home," RV, in the injunction given to elder women regarding the training of the young women. Some mss. have *oikouros*, "watching" or "keeping the home" (*oikos*, and *ouros*, "a keeper"), KJV, "keepers at home."

C. Verb.

endēmeō (ἐνδημέω, 1736), lit., "to be among one's people" (*en*, "in," *dēmos*, "people"; *endēmos*, "one who is in his own place or land"), is used metaphorically of the life on earth of believers, 2 Cor. 5:6, "at home (in the body)"; in v. 8 of the life in Heaven of the spirits of believers, after their decease, "at home (with the Lord)," RV (KJV, "present"); in v. 9, "at home" (KJV, "present") refers again to the life on earth. In each verse the verb is contrasted with *ekdēmeō*, "to be away from home, to be absent"; in v. 6, "we are absent," i.e., away from "home" (from the Lord); in v. 8, "to be absent" (i.e., away from the "home" of the body); so in v. 9, "absent." The implication in being "at home with the Lord" after death is a testimony against the doctrine of the unconsciousness of the spirit, when freed from the natural body.

HONEST, HONESTLY, HONESTY

A. Adjectives.

1. *kalos* (καλός, 2570), "good, admirable, becoming," has also the ethical meaning of what is "fair, right, honorable, of such conduct as deserves esteem"; it is translated "honest" [cf. Latin *honestus* (from *honos*, "honor")], which has the same double meaning as "honest" in the KJV, namely, regarded with honor, honorable, and bringing honor, becoming; in Luke 8:15 (KJV, and RV), "an honest and good (*agathos*) heart"; Rom. 12:17; 2 Cor. 8:21 and 13:7, RV, "honorable" (KJV, "honest"), of things which are regarded with esteem; in 1 Pet. 2:12, of behavior, RV, "seemly," KJV, "honest" (i.e., becoming). See GOOD.

Note: In Titus 3:14, the RV and KJV margins give what is probably the accurate meaning, "(to profess) honest occupations" (KJV, "trades"); in the texts "(to maintain) good works."

2. *semnos* (σεμνός, 4586), "august, venerable," is rendered "honest" in Phil. 4:8, KJV (marg., "venerable"), RV, "honorable" (marg., "reverent"). Matthew Arnold suggests "nobly serious." See GRAVE.

Note: In Acts 6:3, "men of honest (RV, 'good') report" translates the passive voice of *martureō*, lit., "having had witness borne."

B. Adverbs.

1. *kalōs* (καλῶς, 2573), corresponding to A, No. 1, is used in Heb. 13:18, "honestly," i.e., honorably. See WELL.

2. *euschēmonōs* (εὐσχημόνως, 2156), "becomingly, decently," is rendered "honestly" in Rom. 13:13, where it is set in contrast with the confusion of gentile social life, and in 1 Thess. 4:12, of the manner of life of believers as a witness to "them that are without"; in 1 Cor. 14:40, "decently," in contrast with confusion in the churches. See DECENTLY.

C. Noun.

semnotēs (σεμνότης, 4587) denotes "gravity, dignified seriousness"; it is rendered "honesty" in the KJV of 1 Tim. 2:2, RV, "gravity." See GRAVITY.

HONOR (Noun and Verb)

A. Nouns.

1. *timē* (τιμή, 5092), primarily "a valuing," hence, objectively, (a) "a price paid or received," e.g., Matt. 27:6, 9; Acts 4:34; 5:2, 3; 7:16, RV, "price" (KJV, "sum"); 19:19; 1 Cor. 6:20; 7:23; (b) of "the preciousness of Christ" unto believers, 1 Pet. 2:7, RV, i.e., the honor and inestimable value of Christ as appropriated by believers, who are joined, as living stones, to Him the cornerstone; (c) in the sense of value, of human ordinances, valueless against the indulgence of the fiesh, or, perhaps of no value in attempts at asceticism, Col. 2:23 (see extended note under INDULGENCE, No. 2); (d) "honor, esteem," (1) used in ascriptions of worship to God, 1 Tim. 1:17; 6:16; Rev. 4:9, 11; 5:13; 7:12; to Christ, 5:12, 13; (2) bestowed upon Christ by the Father, Heb. 2:9; 2 Pet. 1:17; (3) bestowed upon man, Heb. 2:7; (4) bestowed upon Aaronic priests, Heb. 5:4; (5) to be the reward hereafter of "the proof of faith" on the part of tried saints, 1 Pet. 1:7, RV; (6) used of the believer who as a vessel is "meet for the Master's use," 2 Tim. 2:21; (7) to be the reward of patience in well-doing, Rom. 2:7, and of working good (a perfect life to which man cannot attain, so as to be justified before God thereby), 2:10; (8) to be given to all to whom it is due, Rom. 13:7 (see 1 Pet. 2:17, under B, No. 1); (9) as an advantage to be given by believers one to another instead of claiming it for self, Rom. 12:10; (10) to be given to elders that rule well ("double honor"), 1 Tim. 5:17 (here the meaning may be an honorarium); (11) to be given by servants to their master, 1 Tim. 6:1; (12) to be given to wives by husbands, 1 Pet. 3:7; (13) said of the husband's use of the wife, in contrast to the exercise of the passion of lust, 1 Thess. 4:4 (some regard the "vessel" here as the believer's body); (14) of that bestowed upon; parts of the body, 1 Cor. 12:23, 24; (15) of that which belongs to the builder of a house in contrast to the house itself, Heb. 3:3; (16) of that which is not enjoyed by a prophet in his own country, John 4:44; (17) of that bestowed by the inhabitants of Melita upon Paul and his fellow-passengers, in gratitude for his benefits of healing, Acts 28:10; (18) of the festive honor to be possessed

by nations, and brought into the Holy City, the heavenly Jerusalem, Rev. 21:26 (in some mss., v. 24); (19) of honor bestowed upon things inanimate, a potters' vessel, Rom. 9:21; 2 Tim. 2:20. See SUM, VALUE.

Note: For *entimos*, "in honor," see HONORABLE, No. 2.

2. *doxa* (δόξα, 1391), "glory," is translated "honor" in the KJV of John 5:41, 44 (twice); 8:54; 2 Cor. 6:8, and Rev. 19:7; the RV keeps to the word "glory," as the KJV everywhere else. See GLORY.

B. Verbs.

1. *timaō* (τιμάω, 5091), "to honor" (akin to A, No. 1), is used of (a) valuing Christ at a price, Matt. 27:9, cf. A, No. 1, (a); (b) "honoring" a person: (1) the "honor" done by Christ to the Father, John 8:49; (2) "honor" bestowed by the Father upon him who serves Christ, John 12:26; (3) the duty of all to "honor" the Son equally with the Father, 5:23; (4) the duty of children to "honor" their parents, Matt. 15:4; 19:19; Mark 7:10; 10:19; Luke 18:20; Eph. 6:2; (5) the duty of Christians to "honor" the king, and all men, 1 Pet. 2:17; (6) the respect and material assistance to be given to widows "that are widows indeed," 1 Tim. 5:3; (7) the "honor" done to Paul and his companions by the inhabitants of Melita, Acts 28:10; (8) mere lip profession of "honor" to God, Matt. 15:8: Mark 7:6.

2. *doxazō* (δοξάζω, 1392), "to glorify" (from *doxa*, A, No. 2), is rendered "honor" and "honoreth" in the KJV of John 8:54; in 1 Cor. 12:26, however, in reference to the members of the body, both KJV and RV have "honored" (RV marg., "glorified"). Everywhere else it is translated by some form of the verb "to glorify," "have glory," or "be made glorious," except in Rom. 11:13, "magnify," KJV. See GLORIFY.

HONORABLE, WITHOUT HONOR

1. *endoxos* (ἔνδοξος, 1741) denotes (a) "held in honor" (*en*, "in," *doxa*, "honor"; cf. HONOR, A, No. 2), "of high repute," 1 Cor. 4:10, KJV "(are) honorable," RV, "(have) glory," in contrast to *atimos*, "without honor" (see No. 6 below). See GLORIOUS, GORGEOUSLY.

2. *entimos* (ἔντιμος, 1784), lit., "in honor" (*en*, "in," *timē*, "honor": see HONOR, A, No. 1), is used of the centurion's servant in Luke 7:2. "dear" (RV marg., "precious ... or honorable"): of self-sacrificing servants of the Lord, said of Epaphroditus, Phil. 2:29, RV "(hold such) in honor" (KJV, "in reputation"; marg., "honor such"); of Christ, as a precious stone, 1 Pet. 2:4, 6 (RV marg., "honorable"). Cf. *timios* in 1:7, 19; see No. 4.

The comparative degree, *entimoteros*, is used (in the best mss.) of degrees of honor attached to persons invited to a feast, a marriage feast, Luke 14:8, "a more honorable man."

3. *euschēmōn* (εὐσχήμων, 2158) signifies "elegant, comely, of honorable position," KJV, "honorable," RV, "of honorable estate," Mark 15:43; Acts 13:50; 17:12; for other renderings in 1 Cor. 7:35 and 12:24 see COMELINESS, B.

4. *timios* (τίμιος, 5093), "precious, valuable, honorable" (akin to *time*, "honor"; see No. 2), is used of marriage in Heb. 13:4, KJV, as a statement, "(marriage) is honorable (in all)," RV, as an exhortation, "let (marriage) be had in honor (among all)." See DEAR, REPUTATION.

5. *kalos* (καλός, 2570), "good, fair," is translated "honorable" in Rom. 12:17; 2 Cor. 8:21; 13:7, RV (KJV, "honest"). See GOOD, HONEST.

6. *atimos* (ἄτιμος, 820), without honor (*a*, negative, or privative, *time*, "honor"), "despised," is translated "without honor" in Matt. 13:57; Mark 6:4; "dishonor" in 1 Cor. 4:10, RV (KJV, "despised"). See DESPISE.

The comparative degree *atimoteros* is used in the best mss. in 1 Cor. 12:23, "less honorable."

Note: For *semnos*, honorable, Phil. 4:8, RV, see GRAVE.

HOPE (Noun and Verb), HOPE (for)

A. Noun.

elpis (ἐλπίς, 1680), in the NT, "favorable and confident expectation" (contrast the Sept. in Isa. 28:19, "an evil hope"). It has to do with the unseen and the future, Rom. 8:24, 25. "Hope" describes (a) the happy anticipation of good (the most frequent significance), e.g., Titus 1:2; 1 Pet. 1:21; (b) the ground upon which "hope" is based, Acts 16:19; Col. 1:27, "Christ in you the hope of glory"; (c) the object upon which the "hope" is fixed, e.g., 1 Tim. 1:1.

Various phrases are used with the word "hope," in Paul's epistles and speeches: (1) Acts 23:6, "the hope and resurrection of the dead"; this has been regarded as a hendiadys (one by means of two), i.e., the "hope" of the resurrection; but the *kai*, "and," is epexegetic, defining the "hope," namely, the resurrection; (2) Acts 26:6, 7, "the hope of the promise (i.e., the fulfillment of the promise) made unto the fathers"; (3) Gal. 5:5, "the hope of righteousness"; i.e., the believer's complete conformity to God's will, at the coming of Christ; (4) Col. 1:23, "the hope of the Gospel," i.e., the "hope" of the fulfillment of all the promises presented in the gospel; cf. 1:5; (5) Rom. 5:2, "(the) hope of the glory of God," i.e., as in Titus 2:13, "the blessed hope and appearing of the glory of our great God and Savior Jesus Christ"; cf. Col. 1:27; (6) 1 Thess. 5:8, "the hope of salvation," i.e., of the rapture of believers, to take place at the opening of the Parousia of Christ; (7) Eph. 1:18, "the hope of His (God's) calling," i.e., the prospect before those who respond to His call in the gospel; (8) Eph. 4:4, "the hope of your calling," the same as (7), but regarded from the point of view of the called; (9) Titus 1:2, and 3:7, "the hope of eternal life," i.e., the full manifestation and realization of that life which is already the believer's possession; (10)

Acts 28:20, "the hope of Israel," i.e., the expectation of the coming of the Messiah. See *Notes on Galatians* by Hogg and Vine, pp. 248, 249.

In Eph. 1:18; 2:12 and 4:4, the "hope" is objective. The objective and subjective use of the word need to be distinguished, in Rom. 15:4, e.g., the use is subjective.

In the NT three adjectives are descriptive of "hope": "good," 2 Thess. 2:16; "blessed," Titus 2:13; "living," 1 Pet. 1:3. To these may be added Heb. 7:19, "a better hope," i.e., additional to the commandment, which became disannulled (v. 18), a hope centered in a new priesthood.

In Rom. 15:13 God is spoken of as "the God of hope," i.e., He is the author, not the subject, of it. "Hope" is a factor in salvation, Rom. 8:24; it finds its expression in endurance under trial, which is the effect of waiting for the coming of Christ, 1 Thess. 1:3; it is "an anchor of the soul," staying it amidst the storms of this life, Heb. 6:18, 19; it is a purifying power, "every one that hath this hope set on Him (Christ) purifieth himself, even as He is pure," 1 John 3:3, RV (the apostle John's one mention of "hope").

The phrase "fullness of hope," Heb. 6:11, RV, expresses the completeness of its activity in the soul; cf. "fullness of faith," 10:22, and "of understanding," Col. 2:2 (RV, marg.).

B. Verbs.

1. *elpizō* (ἐλπίζω, 1679), "to hope," is not infrequently translated in the KJV, by the verb "to trust"; the RV adheres to some form of the verb "to hope," e.g., John 5:45, "Moses, on whom ye have set your hope"; 2 Cor. 1:10, "on whom we have set our hope"; so in 1 Tim. 4:10; 5:5; 6:17; see also, e.g., Matt. 12:21; Luke 24:21; Rom. 15:12, 24.

The verb is followed by three prepositions: (1) *eis*, rendered "on" in John 5:45 (as above); the meaning is really "in" as in 1 Pet. 3:5, "who hoped in God"; the "hope" is thus said to be directed to, and to center in, a person; (2) *epi*, "on," Rom. 15:12, "On Him shall the Gentiles hope," RV; so 1 Tim. 4:10; 5:5 (in the best mss.); 6:17, RV; this expresses the ground upon which "hope" rests; (3) *en*, "in," 1 Cor. 15:19, "we have hoped in Christ," RV, more lit., "we are (men) that have hoped in Christ," the preposition expresses that Christ is not simply the ground upon whom, but the sphere and element in whom, the "hope" is placed. The form of the verb (the perfect participle with the verb to be, lit., "are having hoped") stresses the character of those who "hope," more than the action; "hope" characterizes them, showing what sort of persons they are. See TRUST.

2. *proelpizō* (προελπίζω, 4276), "to hope before" (*pro*, "before," and No. 1), is found in Eph. 1:12.

3. *apelpizō* (ἀπελπίζω, 560), lit., "to hope from" (*apo*, and No, 1): see DESPAIR.

HORN

keras (κέρας, 2768), "a horn," is used in the plural, as the symbol of strength, (a) in the apocalyptic visions; (1) on the head of the Lamb as symbolic of Christ, Rev. 5:6; (2) on the heads of beasts as symbolic of national potentates, Rev. 12:3; 13:1, 11; 17:3, 7, 12, 16 (cf. Dan. 7:8; 8:9; Zech. 1:18, etc.); (3) at the corners of the golden altar, Rev. 9:13 (cf. Exod. 30:2; the horns were of one piece with the altar, as in the case of the brazen altar, 27:2, and were emblematic of the efficacy of the ministry connected with it); (b) metaphorically, in the singular, "a horn of salvation," Luke 1:69 (a frequent metaphor in the OT, e.g., Ps. 18:2; cf. 1 Sam. 2:10; Lam. 2:3).

HOSANNA

hōsanna (ὡσαννά, 5614), in the Hebrew, means "save, we pray." The word seems to have become an utterance of praise rather than of prayer, though originally, probably, a cry for help. The people's cry at the Lord's triumphal entry into Jerusalem (Matt. 21:9, 15; Mark 11:9, 10; John 12:13) was taken from Ps. 118, which was recited at the Feast of Tabernacles (see FEAST) in the great Hallel (Psalms 113 to 118) in responses with the priest, accompanied by the waving of palm and willow branches. "The last day of the feast" was called "the great Hosanna"; the boughs also were called "hosannas."

HOSPITALITY

A. Noun.

philoxenia (φιλονεξία, 5381), "love of strangers" (*philos*, "loving," *xenos*, "a stranger"), is used in Rom. 12:13; Heb. 13:2, lit. "(be not forgetful of) hospitality. See ENTERTAIN, *Note.*

B. Adjective.

philoxenos (φιλόξενος, 5382), "hospitable," occurs in 1 Tim. 3:2; Titus 1:8; 1 Pet. 4:9.

Note: For *xenodocheō*, 1 Tim. 5:10, see STRANGER, B.

HOST (of angels, etc.)

stratia (στρατία, 4756), "an army," is used of angels, Luke 2:13; of stars, Acts 7:42; some mss. have it instead of *strateia*, in 2 Cor. 10:4 ("warfare"). Cf. *strateuma*, "an army."

HOT

zestos (ζεστός, 2200), "boiling hot" (from *zeō*, "to boil, be hot, fervent"; cf. Eng., "zest"), is used, metaphorically, in Rev. 3:15, 16.

HOUR

hōra (ὥρα, 5610), whence Lat., *hora*, Eng., "hour," primarily denoted any time or period, expecially a season. In the NT it is used to denote (a) "a part of the day," especially a twelfth part of day or night, an "hour," e.g., Matt. 8:13; Acts

10:3, 9; 23:23; Rev. 9:15; in 1 Cor. 15:30, "every hour" stands for "all the time"; in some passages it expresses duration, e.g., Matt. 20:12; 26:40; Luke 22:59; inexactly, in such phrases as "for a season," John 5:35; 2 Cor. 7:8; "for an hour," Gal. 2:5; "for a short season," 1 Thess. 2:17, RV (KJV, "for a short time," lit., "for the time of an hour"); (b) "a period more or less extended," e.g., 1 John 2:18, "it is the last hour," RV; (C) "a definite point of time," e.g., Matt. 26:45, "the hour is at hand"; Luke 1:10; 10:21; 14:17, lit., "at the hour of supper"; Acts 16:18; 22:13; Rev. 3:3; 11:13; 14:7; a point of time when an appointed action is to begin, Rev. 14:15; in Rom. 13:11, "it is high time," lit., "it is already an hour," indicating that a point of time has come later than would have been the case had responsibility been realized. In 1 Cor. 4:11, it indicates a point of time previous to which certain circumstances have existed.

Notes: (1) In 1 Cor. 8:7, KJV, "unto this hour," the phrase in the original is simply, "until now," as RV (2) In Rev. 8:1, *hēmiōron*, "half an hour" (*hēmi*, "half," and *hōra*), is used with *hōs*, "about," of a period of silence in Heaven after the opening of the 7th seal, a period corresponding to the time customarily spent in silent worship in the Temple during the burning of incense.

HOUSE

A. Nouns.

1. *oikos* (οἶκος, 3624) denotes (a) "a house, a dwelling," e.g., Matt. 9:6, 7; 11:8; it is used of the Tabernacle, as the House of God, Matt. 12:4, and the Temple similarly, e.g., Matt. 21:13; Luke 11:51, KJV, "temple," RV, "sanctuary"; John 2:16, 17; called by the Lord "your house" in Matt. 23:38 and Luke 13:35 (some take this as the city of Jerusalem); metaphorically of Israel as God's house, Heb. 3:2, 5, where "his house" is not Moses', but God's; of believers, similarly, v. 6, where Christ is spoken of as "over God's House" (the word "own" is rightly omitted in the RV); Heb. 10:21; 1 Pet. 2:5; 4:17; of the body, Matt. 12:44; Luke 11:24; (b) by metonymy, of the members of a household or family, e.g., Luke 10:5; Acts 7:10; 11:14; 1 Tim. 3:4, 5, 12; 2 Tim. 1:16; 4:19, RV (KJV, "household"); Titus 1:11 (plural); of a local church, 1 Tim. 3:15; of the descendants of Jacob (Israel) and David, e.g., Matt. 10:6; Luke 1:27, 33; Acts 2:36; 7:42. See HOME, A, No. 1. *Note* (1).

2. *oikia* (οἰκία, 3614), is akin to No. 1, and used much in the same way; in Attic law *oikos* denoted the whole estate, *oikia* stood for the dwelling only; this distinction was largely lost in later Greek. In the NT it denotes (a) "a house, a dwelling," e.g., Matt. 2:11; 5:15; 7:24-27; 2 Tim. 2:20; 2 John 10; it is not used of the Tabernacle or the Temple, as in the case of No. 1; (b) metaphorically, the heavenly abode, spoken of by the Lord as "My Father's house," John 14:2, the eternal dwelling place of believers; the body as the dwelling place of the soul, 2 Cor. 5:1; similarly the resurrection body of believers (*id.*); property, e.g., Mark 12:40; by metonymy, the inhabitants of a house, a household, e.g., Matt. 12:25; John 4:53; 1 Cor. 16:15.

B. Adverb.

panoikei (πανοικί, 3832) denotes "with all the house," Acts 16:34, i.e., "the household."

Notes: (1) In 2 Cor. 5:2, *oikētērion*, "a habitation" (see RV) is translated "house" in the KJV, of the resurrection body (cf. *oikia* in the preceding verse; see above). (2) In 1 Tim. 5:13, "from house to house" is, lit., "the houses." (3) For "in every house," Acts 5:42 (cf. 2:46), see HOME.

For **HOW GREAT** see GREAT, Nos. 4, 5, 6

HUMBLE (Adjective and Verb)

A. Adjectives.

1. *tapeinos* (ταπεινός, 5011) primarily signifies "low-lying." It is used always in a good sense in the NT, metaphorically, to denote (a) "of low degree, brought low," Luke 1:52; Rom. 12:16, KJV, "(men) of low estate," RV, "(things that are) lowly" (i.e., of low degree); 2 Cor. 7:6, KJV, "cast down," RV, "lowly"; the preceding context shows that this occurrence belongs to (a); Jas. 1:9, "of low degree"; (b) humble in spirit, Matt. 11:29; 2 Cor. 10:1, RV, "lowly," KJV "base"; Jas. 4:6; 1 Pet. 5:5. See BASE, DEGREE (*Note*), LOWLY.

2. *tapeinophrōn* (ταπεινόφρων), "humbleminded" (*phrēn*, "the mind"), 1 Pet. 3:8; see COURTEOUS.

B. Verb.

tapeinoō (ταπεινόω, 5013), akin to A, signifies "to make low," (a) literally, "of mountains and hills," Luke 3:5 (passive voice); (b) metaphorically, in the active voice, Matt. 18:4; 23:12 (2nd part); Luke 14:11 (2nd part); 18:14 (2nd part); 2 Cor. 11:7 ("abasing"); 12:21; Phil. 2:8; in the passive voice, Matt. 23:12 (1st part), RV, "shall be humbled," KJV, "shall be abased"; Luke 14:11 (ditto); 18:14 (ditto); Phil. 4:12, "to be abased"; in the passive, with middle voice sense, Jas. 4:10, "humble yourselves"; 1 Pet. 5:6 (ditto). See ABASE, LOW (to bring).

HUMBLENESS OF MIND, HUMILITY

tapeinophrosunē (ταπεινοφροσύνη, 5012), "lowliness of mind" (*tapeinos*, see A, above, under HUMBLE, and *phrēn*, "the mind"), is rendered "humility of mind" in Acts 20:19, KJV (RV, "lowliness of mind"); in Eph. 4:2, "lowliness"; in Phil. 2:3, "lowliness of mind"; in Col. 2:18, 23, of a false "humility"; in Col. 3:12, KJV, "humbleness of mind," RV, "humility"; 1 Pet. 5:5, "humility." See LOWLINESS.

HUMILIATION

tapeinōsis (ταπείνωσις, 5014), akin to *tapeinos* (see above), is rendered "low estate" in Luke 1:48; "humiliation," Acts 8:33; Phil. 3:21, RV "(the body of our) humiliation," KJV, "(our) vile (body)"; Jas. 1:10, where "in that he is made low," is, lit., "in his humiliation." See ESTATE, LOW.

HURT (Noun and Verb), HURTFUL

A. Noun.

hubris (ὕβρις, 5196) is rendered "hurt" in Acts 27:10, KJV only. See HARM.

B. Verbs.

1. *adikeō* (ἀδικέω, 91) signifies, intransitively, "to do wrong, do hurt, act unjustly" (*a*, negative, and *dikē*, "justice"), transitively, "to wrong, hurt or injure a person." It is translated "to hurt" in the following: (a), intransitively, Rev. 9:19; (b) transitively, Luke 10:19; Rev. 2:11 (passive); 6:6; 7:2, 3; 9:4, 10; 11:5. See INJURY, OFFENDER, UNJUST, UNRIGHTEOUSNESS, WRONG, WRONG-DOER.

2. *blaptō* (βλάπτω, 984) signifies "to injure, mar, do damage to," Mark 16:18, "shall (in no wise) hurt (them)"; Luke 4:35, "having done (him no) hurt," RV. *Adikeō* stresses the unrighteousness of the act, *blaptō* stresses the injury done.

3. *kakoō* (κακόω, 2559), "to do evil to anyone": see HARM.

C. Adjective.

blaberos (βλαβερός, 983), akin to B, No. 2, signifies "hurtful," 1 Tim. 6:9, said of lusts. In the Sept., Prov. 10:26.

HUSBAND

A. Noun.

anēr (ἀνήρ, 435) denotes, in general, "a man, an adult male" (in contrast to *anthropos*, which generically denotes "a human being, male or female"); it is used of man in various relations, the context deciding the meaning; it signifies "a husband," e.g., Matt. 1:16, 19; Mark 10:12; Luke 2:36; 16:18; John 4:16, 17, 18; Rom. 7:23.

B. Adjectives

1. *philandros* (φίλανδρος, 5362), primarily, "loving man," signifies "loving a husband," Titus 2:4, in instruction to young wives to love their husbands, lit., "(to be) lovers of their husbands." The word occurs frequently in epitaphs.

2. *hupandros* (ὕπανδρος, 5220), lit., "under (i.e. subject to) a man," married, and therefore, according to Roman law under the legal authority of the husband, occurs in Rom. 7:2, "that hath a husband."

HYMN (Noun and Verb)

A. Noun.

humnos (ὕμνος, 5215) denotes "a song of praise addressed to God" (Eng., "hymn"), Eph. 5:19; Col. 3:16, in each of which the punctuation should probably be changed; in the former "speaking to one another" goes with the end of v. 18, and should be followed by a semicolon; similarly in Col. 3:16, the first part of the verse should end with the words "admonishing one another," where a semicolon should be placed.

Note: The *psalmos* denoted that which had a musical accompaniment; the *ōdē* (Eng., "ode") was the generic term for a song; hence the accompanying adjective "spiritual."

B. Verb.

humneō (ὑμνέω, 5214), akin to A, is used (a) transitively, Matt. 26:30; Mark 14:26, where the "hymn" was that part of the Hallel consisting of Psalms 113-118; (b) intransitively, where the verb itself is rendered "to sing praises" or "praise," Acts 16:25; Heb. 2:12. The Psalms are called, in general, "hymns," by Philo; Josephus calls them "songs and hymns."

HYPOCRISY

hupokrisis (ὑπόκρισις, 5272) primarily denotes "a reply, an answer" (akin to *hupokrinomai*, "to answer"); then, "play-acting," as the actors spoke in dialogue; hence, "pretence, hypocrisy"; it is translated "hypocrisy" in Matt. 23:28; Mark 12:15; Luke 12:1; 1 Tim. 4:2; the plural in 1 Pet. 2:1. For Gal. 2:13 and *anupokritos*, "without hypocrisy," in Jas. 3:17, see DISSIMULATION.

HYPOCRITE

hupokritēs (ὑποκριτής, 5273), corresponding to the above, primarily denotes "one who answers"; then, "a stage-actor"; it was a custom for Greek and Roman actors to speak in large masks with mechanical devices for augmenting the force of the voice; hence the word became used metaphorically of "a dissembler, a hypocrite." It is found only in the Synoptists, and always used by the Lord, fifteen times in Matthew; elsewhere, Mark 7:6; Luke 6:42; 11:44 (in some mss.); 12:56; 13:15.

I

For **IDLE TALES** (Luke 24:11, RV, "idle talk") see TALK

IDOL

eidōlon (εἴδωλον, 1497), primarily "a phantom or likeness" (from *eidos*, "an appearance," lit., "that which is seen"), or "an idea, fancy," denotes in the NT (a) "an idol," an image to represent a false god, Acts 7:41; 1 Cor. 12:2; Rev. 9:20; (b) "the false god" worshipped in an image, Acts 15:20; Rom. 2:22; 1 Cor. 8:4, 7; 10:19; 2 Cor. 6:16; 1 Thess. 1:9; 1 John 5:21.

"The corresponding Heb. word denotes 'vanity,' Jer. 14:22; 18:15; 'thing of nought,' Lev. 19:4, marg., cf. Eph. 4:17. Hence what represented a deity to the Gentiles, was to Paul a 'vain thing,' Acts 14:15; 'nothing in the world,' 1 Cor. 8:4; 10:19. Jeremiah calls the idol a 'scarecrow' ('pillar in a garden,' 10:5, marg.), and Isaiah, 44:9-20, etc., and Habakkuk, 2:18, 19 and the Psalmist, 115:4-8, etc., are all equally scathing. It is important to notice, however, that in each case the people of God are addressed. When he speaks to idolaters, Paul, knowing that no man is won by ridicule, adopts a different line, Acts 14:15-18; 17:16, 21-31."

IDOLS (full of)

kateidōlos (κατείδωλος, 2712), an adjective denoting "full of idols" (*kata*, "throughout," and *eidōlon*), is said of Athens in Acts 17:16, RV, and KJV, marg. (KJV, "wholly given to idolatry").

IDOLS (offered to, sacrificed to)

1. *eidōlothutos* (εἰδωλόθυτον, 1494) is an adjective signifying "sacrificed to idols" (*eidōlon*, as above, and *thuō*, "to sacrifice"), Acts 15:29; 21:25; 1 Cor. 8:1, 4, 7, 10; 10:19 (in all these the RV substitutes "sacrificed" for the KJV); Rev. 2:14, 20 (in these the RV and KJV both have "sacrificed"). Some inferior mss. have this adjective in 1 Cor. 10:28; see No. 2. The flesh of the victims, after sacrifice, was eaten or sold.

2. *nierothutos*, "offered in sacrifice" (*hieros*, "sacred," and *thuō*, "to sacrifice"), is found in the best mss. in 1 Cor. 10:28 (see No. 1).

IDOL'S TEMPLE

eidōlion (or *eidōleion*) (ειδώλιον, εἰδωλεῖον, 1493), an "idol's temple," is mentioned in 1 Cor. 8:10; feasting in the temple usually followed the sacrifice.

IDOLATER

eidōlolatrēs (εἰδωλολάτρης, 1496), an "idolater" (from *eidōlon*, and *latris*, "a hireling"), is found in 1 Cor. 5:10, 11; 6:9; 10:7; the warning is to believers against turning away from God to idolatry, whether "openly or secretly, consciously or unconsciously" (Cremer); Eph. 5:5; Rev. 21:8; 22:15.

IDOLATRY

eidōlolatria (or *-eia*) (εἰδωλολατρεία, 1495), whence Eng., "idolatry," (from *eidōlon*, and *latreia*, "service"), is found in 1 Cor. 10:14; Gal. 5:20; Col. 3:5; and, in the plural, in 1 Pet. 4:3.

Heathen sacrifices were sacrificed to demons, 1 Cor. 10:19; there was a dire reality in the cup and table of demons and in the involved communion with demons. In Rom. 1:22-25, "idolatry," the sin of the mind against God (Eph. 2:3), and immorality, sins of the flesh, are associated, and are traced to lack of the acknowledgment of God and of gratitude to Him. An "idolater" is a slave to the depraved ideas his idols represent, Gal. 4:8, 9; and thereby, to divers lusts, Titus 3:3 (see *Notes on Thess.* by Hogg and Vine, p. 44).

For **IDOLATRY** (wholly given to) see IDOLS (FULL OF)

IF: See † p. 1.

IGNORANCE, IGNORANT, IGNORANTLY

A. Nouns.

1. *agnoia* (ἄγνοια, 52), lit., "want of knowledge or perception" (akin to *agnoeō*, "to be ignorant"), denotes "ignorance" on the part of the Jews regarding Christ, Acts 3:17; of Gentiles in regard to God, 17:30; Eph. 4:18 (here including the idea of willful blindness: see Rom. 1:28, not the "ignorance" which mitigates guilt); 1 Pet. 1:14, of the former unregenerate condition of those who became believers (RV, "in *the time of* your ignorance").

2. *agnōsia* (ἀγνωσία, 56) denotes "ignorance" as directly opposed to *gnōsis*, which signifies "knowledge" as a result of observation and experience (*a*, negative, *ginōskō*, "to know"; cf. Eng., "agnostic"); 1 Cor. 15:34 ("no knowledge"); 1 Pet. 2:15. In both these passages reprehensible "ignorance" is suggested. See KNOWLEDGE.

3. *agnoēma* (ἀγνόημα, 51), "a sin of ignorance," occurs in Heb. 9:7, "errors" (RV marg., "ignorances"). For the corresponding verb in Heb. 5:2 see B, No. 1. What is especially in view in these passages is unwitting error. For Israel a sacrifice

was appointed, greater in proportion to the culpability of the guilty, greater, for instance, for a priest or ruler than for a private person. Sins of "ignorance," being sins, must be expiated. A believer guilty of a sin of "ignorance" needs the efficacy of the expiatory sacrifice of Christ, and finds "grace to help." Yet, as the conscience of the believer receives enlightenment, what formerly may have been done in "ignorance" becomes a sin against the light and demands a special confession, to receive forgiveness, 1 John 1:8, 9.

4. *idiōtēs* (ἰδιώτης, 2399), primarily "a private person" in contrast to a state official, hence, "a person without professional knowledge, unskilled, uneducated, unlearned," is translated "unlearned" in 1 Cor. 14:16, 23, 24, of those who have no knowledge of the facts relating to the testimony borne in and by a local church; "rude" in 2 Cor. 11:6, of the apostle's mode of speech in the estimation of the Corinthians; "ignorant men," in Acts 4:13, of the speech of the apostle Peter and John in the estimation of the rulers, elders and scribes in Jerusalem.

While *agrammatoi* ("unlearned") may refer to their being unacquainted with rabbinical learning, *idiōtai* would signify "laymen," in contrast with the religious officials. See UNLEARNED.

B. Verbs.

1. *agnoeō* (ἀγνοέω, 50), signifies (a) "to be ignorant, not to know," either intransitively, 1 Cor. 14:38 (in the 2nd occurrence in this verse, the RV text translates the active voice, the margin the passive); 1 Tim. 1:13, lit., "being ignorant (I did it)"; Heb. 5:2, "ignorant"; or transitively, 2 Pet. 2:12, KJV, "understand not," RV, "are ignorant (of)"; Acts 13:27, "knew (Him) not"; 17:23, RV, "(what ye worship) in ignorance," for KJV, "(whom ye) ignorantly (worship)," lit., "(what) not knowing (ye worship"; also rendered by the verb "to be ignorant that," or "to be ignorant of," Rom. 1:13; 10:3; 11:25; 1 Cor. 10:1; 12:1; 2 Cor. 1:8; 2:11; 1 Thess. 4:13; to know not, Rom. 2:4; 6:3; 7:1; to be unknown (passive voice), 2 Cor. 6:9; Gal. 1:22; (b) "not to understand," Mark 9:32; Luke 9:45. See KNOW.

2. *lanthanō* (λανθάνω, 2990); for 2 Pet. 3:5, 8, KJV, see FORGET.

Note: For adjectives see UNLEARNED.

ILL

kakos (κακός, 2556), "bad," is used in the neuter as a noun in Rom. 13:10, and translated "ill." See BAD.

Note: For *phaulos*, John 5:29, RV, see EVIL, A, No. 3.

For **ILLUMINATED** (Heb. 10:32) see ENLIGHTEN

IMAGE

1. *eikōn* (εἰκών, 1504) denotes "an image"; the word involves the two ideas of representation and manifestation. "The idea of perfection does not lie in the word itself, but must be sought from the context" (Lightfoot); the following instances clearly show any distinction between the imperfect and the perfect likeness.

The word is used (1) of an "image" or a coin (not a mere likeness), Matt. 22:20; Mark 12:16; Luke 20:24; so of a statue or similar representation (more than a resemblance), Rom. 1:23; Rev. 13:14, 15 (thrice); 14:9, 11; 15:2; 16:2; 19:20; 20:4; of the descendants of Adam as bearing his image, 1 Cor. 15:49, each a representation derived from the prototype; (2) of subjects relative to things spiritual, Heb. 10:1, negatively of the Law as having "a shadow of the good things to come, not the very image of the things," i.e., not the essential and substantial form of them; the contrast has been likened to the difference between a statue and the shadow cast by it; (3) of the relations between God the Father, Christ, and man, (a) of man as he was created as being a visible representation of God, 1 Cor. 11:7, a being corresponding to the original; the condition of man as a fallen creature has not entirely effaced the "image"; he is still suitable to bear responsibility, he still has Godlike qualities, such as love of goodness and beauty, none of which are found in a mere animal; in the Fall man ceased to be a perfect vehicle for the representation of God; God's grace in Christ will yet accomplish more than what Adam lost; (b) of regenerate persons, in being moral representations of what God is, Col. 3:10; cf. Eph. 4:24; (c) of believers, in their glorified state, not merely as resembling Christ but representing Him, Rom. 8:29; 1 Cor. 15:49; here the perfection is the work of divine grace; believers are yet to represent, not something like Him, but what He is in Himself, both in His spiritual body and in His moral character; (d) of Christ in relation to God, 2 Cor. 4:4, "the image of God," i.e., essentially and absolutely the perfect expression and representation of the Archetype, God the Father; in Col. 1:15, "the image of the invisible God" gives the additional thought suggested by the word "invisible," that Christ is the visible representation and manifestation of God to created beings; the likeness expressed in this manifestation is involved in the essential relations in the Godhead, and is therefore unique and perfect; "he that hath seen Me hath seen the Father," John 14:9. "The epithet 'invisible' ... must not be confined to the apprehension of the bodily senses, but will include the cognizance of the inward eye also" (Lightfoot).

As to synonymous words, *homoiōma*, "likeness," stresses the resemblance to an archetype, though the resemblance may not be derived, whereas *eikōn* is a "derived likeness" (see LIKENESS); *eidos*, "a shape, form," is an appearance, "not necessarily based on reality" (see FORM); *skia*, is "a shadowed resemblance" (see SHADOW); *morphē* is "the form, as indicative of the inner being" (Abbott-Smith); see FORM. For *charaktēr*, see No. 2.

2. *charaktēr* (χαρακτήρ, 5481) denotes, firstly, "a tool for graving" (from *charassō*, "to cut into, to engross"; cf. Eng., "character," "characteristic"); then, "a stamp" or "impress," as on a coin or a seal, in which case the seal or die which makes an impression bears the "image" produced by it, and, *vice versa*, all the features of the "image" correspond respectively with those of the instrument producing it. In the NT it is used metaphorically in Heb. 1:3, of the Son of God as "the very image (marg., 'the impress') of His substance." RV. The phrase expresses the fact that the Son "is both personally distinct from, and yet literally equal to, Him of whose essence He is the adequate imprint" (Liddon). The Son of God is not merely his "image" (His *charaktēr*), He is the "image" or impress of His substance, or essence. It is the fact of complete similarity which this word stresses in comparison with those mentioned at the end of No. 1. In the Sept., Lev. 13:28, "the mark (of the inflammation)."

"In John 1:1-3, Col. 1:15-17, and Heb. 1:2, 3, the special function of creating and upholding the universe is ascribed to Christ under His titles of Word, Image, and Son, respectively. The kind of Creatorship so predicated of Him is not that of a mere instrument or artificer in the formation of the world, but that of One 'by whom, in whom, and for whom' all things are made, and through whom they subsist. This implies the assertion of His true and absolute Godhood" (Laidlaw, in *Hastings' Bib. Dic.*).

Note: The similar word *charagma*, "a mark" (see GRAVEN and MARK), has the narrower meaning of "the thing impressed," without denoting the special characteristic of that which produces it, e.g., Rev. 13:16, 17. In Acts 17:29 the meaning is not "graven (*charagma*) by art," but "an engraved work of art."

IMAGINATION

1. *logismos* (λογισμός, 3053), "a reasoning, a thought" (akin to *logizomai*, "to count, reckon"), is translated "thoughts" in Rom. 2:15, suggestive of evil intent, not of mere reasonings; "imaginations" in 2 Cor. 10:5 (RV, marg., "reasonings," in each place). The word suggests the contemplation of actions as a result of the verdict of conscience. See THOUGHT.

2. *dialogismos* (διαλογισμός, 1261), *dia*, and No. 1, is rendered "imaginations" in Rom. 1:21, carrying with it the idea of evil purposes, RV, "reasonings"; it is most frequently translated thoughts.

3. *dianoia* (διάνοια, 1271), strictly, "a thinking over," denotes "the faculty of thinking"; then, "of knowing"; hence, "the understanding," and in general, "the mind," and so, "the faculty of moral reflection"; it is rendered "imagination" in Luke 1:51, "the imagination of their heart" signifying their thoughts and ideas. See MIND, UNDERSTANDING.

IMAGINE

meletaō (μελετάω, 3191) signifies "to care for" (*melete*, "care"); then, "to attend to," "be diligent in," 1 Tim. 4:15, RV, i.e., to practice as the result of devising or planning; thirdly, "to ponder," "imagine," Acts 4:25, RV, marg., "meditate." Some inferior mss. have it in Mark 13:11. See DILIGENT, MEDITATE.

IMITATE, IMITATOR

A. Verb.

mimeomai (μιμέομαι, 3401), "a mimic, an actor" (Eng., "mime," etc.), is always translated "to imitate" in the RV, for KJV, "to follow," (a) of imitating the conduct of missionaries, 2 Thess. 3:7, 9; the faith of spiritual guides, Heb. 13:7; (b) that which is good, 3 John 11. The verb is always used in exhortations, and always in the continuous tense, suggesting a constant habit or practice.

B. Nouns.

1. *mimētēs* (μιμητής, 3402), akin to A, "an imitator," so the RV for KJV, "follower," is always used in a good sense in the NT. In 1 Cor. 4:16; 11:1; Eph. 5:1; Heb. 6:12, it is used in exhortations, accompanied by the verb *ginomai*, "to be, become," and in the continuous tense (see A) except in Heb. 6:12, where the aorist or momentary tense indicates a decisive act with permanent results; in 1 Thess. 1:6; 2:14, the accompanying verb is in the aorist tense, referring to the definite act of conversion in the past. These instances, coupled with the continuous tenses referred to, teach that what we became at conversion we must diligently continue to be thereafter.

2. *summimētēs* (συμμιμητής, 4831) denotes "a fellow imitator" (*sun*, "with," and No. 1), Phil. 3:17, RV, "imitators together" (KJV, "followers together").

IMMEDIATELY

parachrēma (παραχρῆμα, 3916), lit., "with the matter (or business) itself" (*para*, "with," *chrēma*, "a business," or "event"), and so, "immediately," Matt. 21:19 (KJV, "presently"), 20; Luke 1:64; 4:39; 5:25; 8:44, 47, 55; 13:13; 18:43; 19:11; 22:60; Acts 3:7; 5:10; 12:23; 13:11; 16:26, 33; it is thus used by Luke only, save for the two instances in Matthew. It is also rendered "presently," "soon," "straightway."

IMMORTAL, IMMORTALITY

athanasia (ἀθανασία, 110), lit., "deathlessness" (*a*, negative, *thanatos*, "death"), is rendered "immortality" in 1 Cor. 15:53, 54, of the glorified body of the believer; 1 Tim. 6:16, of the nature of God. Moulton and Milligan (*Vocab.*) show that in early times the word had the wide connotation of freedom from death; they also quote Ramsay (*Luke the Physician*, p.

273), with reference to the use of the word in sepulchral epitaphs. In a papyrus writing of the sixth century, "a petitioner says that he will send up 'unceasing (*athanatous*)' hymns to the Lord Christ for the life of the man with whom he is pleading." In the NT, however, *athanasia* expresses more than deathlessness, it suggests the quality of the life enjoyed, as is clear from 2 Cor. 5:4; for the believer what is mortal is to be "swallowed up of life."

Note: The adjective *aphthartos*, translated "immortal" in 1 Tim. 1:17, KJV, does not bear that significance, it means "incorruptible." So with the noun *aphtharsia*, "incorruption," translated "immortality," in the KJV of Rom. 2:7 and 2 Tim. 1:10. See CORRUPT, B, No. 3, and C, No. 2.

IMMUTABLE, IMMUTABILITY

ametathetos (ἀμετάθετος, 276), an adjective signifying "immutable" (*a*, negative, *metatithēmi*, "to change"), Heb. 6:18, where the "two immutable things" are the promise and the oath. In v. 17 the word is used in the neuter with the article, as a noun, denoting "the immutability," with reference to God's counsel. Examples from the papyri show that the word was used as a technical term in connection with wills, "The connotation adds considerably to the force of Heb. 6:17 (and foll.)" (Moulton and Milligan).

IMPENITENT

ametanoētos (ἀμετανόητος, 279), lit., "without change of mind" (*a*, negative, *metanoeō*, "to change one's mind," *meta*, signifying "change," *nous*, "the mind"), is used in Rom. 2:5, "impenitent" (or "unrepentant"). Moulton and Milligan show from the papyri writings that the word is also used "in a passive sense, 'not affected by change of mind,' like *ametamelētos* in Rom. 11:29," "without repentance."

IMPLACABLE

aspondos (ἄσπονδος, 786) lit. denotes "without a libation" (*a*, negative, *spondē*, "a libation"), i.e., "without a truce," as a libation accompanied the making of treaties and compacts; then, "one who cannot be persuaded to enter into a covenant," "implacable," 2 Tim. 3:3 (KJV, "truce-breakers"). Some mss. have this word in Rom. 1:31.

Note: Trench (*Syn.* Sec. LII) contrasts *aspondos* with *asunthetos*; see *Note* under COVENANT-BREAKERS. *Aspondos* may signify "untrue to one's promise," *asunthetos* "not abiding by one's covenant, treacherous."

For **IMPLEAD** see ACCUSE, B, No. 2

IMPLANTED

emphutos (ἔμφυτος, 1721), "implanted," or "rooted" (from *emphuō*, "to implant"), is used in Jas. 1:21, RV, "implanted," for KJV, "engrafted," of the Word of God, as the "rooted word," i.e., a word whose property it is to root itself like a seed in the heart. "The KJV seems to identify it with *emphuteuton*, which however would be out of place here, since the word is sown, not grafted, in the heart" (Mayor).

IMPOSTORS

goēs (γόης, 1114) primarily denotes "a wailer" (*goaō*, "to wail"); hence, from the howl in which spells were chanted, "a wizard, sorcerer, enchanter," and hence, "a juggler, cheat, impostor," rendered "impostors" in 2 Tim. 3:13, RV (KJV, "seducers"); possibly the false teachers referred to practiced magical arts; cf. v. 8.

IMPULSE

hormē (ὁρμή, 3730) denotes (a) "an impulse" or "violent motion," as of the steersman of a vessel, Jas. 3:4, RV, "impulse" (KJV omits); (b) "an assault, onset," Acts 14:5. See ASSAULT.

IMPUTE

1. *logizomai* (λογίζομαι, 3049), "to reckon, take into account," or, metaphorically, "to put down to a person's account," is never rendered in the RV by the verb "to impute." In the following, where the KJV has that rendering, the RV uses the verb "to reckon," which is far more suitable, Rom. 4:6, 8, 11, 22, 23, 24; 2 Cor. 5:19; Jas. 2:23. See especially, in the above respect, RECKON.

2. *ellogaō*, or *-eō* (ἐλλογάω, -έω, 1677) (the *-aō* termination is the one found in the *Koinē*, the language covering the NT period), denotes "to charge to one's account, to lay to one's charge," and is translated "imputed" in Rom. 5:13, of sin as not being "imputed when there is no law." This principle is there applied to the fact that between Adam's transgression and the giving of the Law at Sinai, sin, though it was in the world, did not partake of the character of transgression; for there was no law. The law of conscience existed, but that is not in view in the passage, which deals with the fact of external commandments given by God. In Philem. 18 the verb is rendered "put (that) to (mine) account."

INCENSE (burn)

A. Noun.

thumiama (θυμίαμα, 2368) denotes "fragrant stuff for burning, incense" (from *thuō*, "to offer in sacrifice"), Luke 1:10, 11; in the plural, Rev. 5:8 and 18:13, RV (KJV, "odors"); 8:3, 4, signifying "frankincense" here. In connection with the tabernacle, the "incense" was to be prepared from stacte, onycha, and galbanum, with pure frankincense, an equal weight of each; imitation for private use was forbidden, Exod. 30:34-38. Cf. *thumiatērion*, "a censer," Heb. 9:4, and *libanos*, "frankincense," Rev. 18:13; see FRANKINCENSE.

B. Verb.

thumiaō (θυμιάω, 2370), "to burn incense" (see A), is found in Luke 1:9.

INCONTINENCY, INCONTINENT

A. Noun.

akrasia (ἀκρασία, 192) denotes "want of power" (*a*, negative, *kratos*, "power"); hence, "want of self-control, incontinency," 1 Cor. 7:5: in Matt. 23:25, "excess." See EXCESS.

B. Adjective.

akratēs (ἀκράτης, 193) denotes "powerless, impotent"; in a moral sense, unrestrained, "without self-control," 2 Tim. 3:3, RV (KJV, "incontinent"). See SELF-CONTROL.

For **INCORRUPTIBLE and INCORRUPTION,** see under CORRUPT

INCREDIBLE

apistos (ἄπιστος, 571) is once rendered "incredible," Acts 26:8, of the doctrine of resurrection; elsewhere it is used of persons, with the meaning "unbelieving." See BELIEF, C, *Note* (3).

INDEBTED (to be)

opheilō (ὀφείλω, 3784), "to owe, to be a debtor," is translated "is indebted" in Luke 11:4. Luke does not draw a parallel between our forgiving and God's; he speaks of God's forgiving sins, of our forgiving "debts," moral debts, probably not excluding material debts. Matthew speaks of our sins as *opheilēmata*, "debts," and uses parallel terms. Ellicott and others suggest that Luke used a term more adapted to the minds of gentile readers. The inspired language provides us with both, as intended by the Lord.

INDIGNATION

A. Noun.

aganaktēsis (ἀγανάκτησις, 24) is rendered "indignation" in 2 Cor. 7:11. See ANGER, A, *Note* (3).

Notes: (1) *Orgē*, "wrath," is translated "indignation" in Rev. 14:10, KJV; RV, "anger." See ANGER, A, No. 1. (2) For *thumos*, see ANGER, A, *Notes* (1) and (2). (3) In Acts 5:17, the KJV translates *zēlos* by "indignation" (RV "jealousy"); in Heb. 10:27, KJV, "indignation" (RV, "fierceness"; marg., "jealousy"). See JEALOUSY.

B. Verb.

aganakteō (ἀγανακτέω, 23), "to be indignant, to be moved with indignation" (from *agan*, "much," *achomai*, "to grieve"), is translated "were moved with indignation" of the ten disciples against James and John, Matt. 20:24; in Mark 10:41, RV (KJV, "they began to be much displeased"); in Matt. 21:15, of the chief priests and scribes, against Christ and the children, RV, "they were moved with indignation" (KJV, "they were sore displeased"); in 26:8, of the disciples against the woman who anointed Christ's feet, "they had indignation"; so Mark 14:4; in Mark 10:14, of Christ, against the disciples, for rebuking the children, "He was moved with indignation," RV (KJV, "he was much displeased"); in Luke 13:14, of the ruler of the synagogue against Christ for healing on the Sabbath, "being moved with indignation," RV, KJV, "(answered) with indignation." See ANGER, B, *Note* (3).

INDULGENCE

1. *anesis* (ἄνεσις, 425), "a loosening, relaxation of strain" (akin to *aniemi*, "to relax, loosen"), is translated "indulgence" in Acts 24:23, RV (KJV, "liberty"), in the command of Felix to the centurion, to moderate restrictions upon Paul. The papyri and inscriptions illustrate the use of the word as denoting relief (Moulton and Milligan, *Vocab.*) In the NT it always carries the thought of relief from tribulation or persecution; so 2 Thess. 1:7, "rest"; in 2 Cor. 2:13 and 7:5 it is rendered "relief," RV (KJV, "rest"); in 8:13, "eased." Josephus speaks of the rest or relief (*anesis*) from plowing and tillage, given to the land in the Year of Jubilee. See LIBERTY, RELIEF, REST.

2. *plēsmonē* (πλησμονή, 4140), "a filling up, satiety" (akin to *pimplēmi*, "to fill"), is translated "indulgence (of the flesh)" in Col. 2:23, RV (KJV, "satisfying"). Lightfoot translates the passage "yet not really of any value to remedy indulgence of the flesh." A possible meaning is, "of no value in attempts at asceticism." Some regard it as indicating that the ascetic treatment of the body is not of any honor to the satisfaction of the flesh (the reasonable demands of the body): this interpretation is unlikely. The following paraphrase well presents the contrast between the asceticism which "practically treats the body as an enemy, and the Pauline view which treats it as a potential instrument of a righteous life": ordinances, "which in fact have a specious look of wisdom (where there is no true wisdom), by the employment of self-chosen acts of religion and humility (and) by treating the body with brutality instead of treating it with due respect, with a view to meeting and providing against over-indulgence of the flesh" (Parry, in the *Camb. Greek Test.*).

For **INEXCUSABLE** see EXCUSE

For **INFALLIBLE** see PROOF

For **INFANT** see BABE

INFERIOR

hēttaomai (ἡττάομαι, 2274), or *hessoomai* (ἑσσόομαι, 2274), "to be less or inferior," is used in the passive voice, and translated "ye were made inferior," in 2 Cor. 12:13, RV, for KJV, "ye were inferior," i.e., were treated with less consideration than other churches, through his independence in not receiving gifts from them. In 2 Pet. 2:19, 20 it signifies to be overcome, in the sense of being subdued and enslaved. See OVERCOME. Cf. *hēssōn*, "less," 2 Cor. 12:15; in 1 Cor. 11:17, "worse"; *hēttēma*, "a loss, a spiritual defect," Rom. 11:12; 1 Cor. 6:7. Also *elattoō*, "to decrease, make lower," John 3:30; Heb. 2:7, 9.

For **INFIDEL** (RV , **UNBELIEVER**) see BELIEF, C, *Note* (3)

INFIRMITY

1. *ostheneia* (ἀσθένεια, 769), lit., "want of strength" (*a*, negative, *sthenos*, "strength"), "weakness," indicating inability to produce results, is most frequently translated "infirmity," or "infirmities"; in Rom. 8:26, the RV has "infirmity" (KJV, "infirmities"); in 2 Cor. 12:5, 9, 10, "weaknesses" and in 11:30, "weakness" (KJV, "infirmities"); in Luke 13:11 the phrase "a spirit of infirmity" attributes her curvature directly to satanic agency. The connected phraseology is indicative of trained medical knowledge on the part of the writer.

2. *asthenēma* (ἀσθένημα, 771), akin to No. 1, is found in the plural in Rom. 15:1, "infirmities," i.e., those scruples which arise through weakness of faith. The strong must support the infirmities of the weak (*adunatos*) by submitting to self-restraint.

Note: In Luke 7:21, KJV, *nosos*, "a disease," is translated "infirmities" (RV, "diseases").

INFLICTED

Note: This is inserted in 2 Cor. 2:6 to complete the sentence; there is no corresponding word in the original, which lit. reads "this punishment, the (one) by the majority."

INFORM

1. *emphanizō* (ἐμφανίζω, 1718), "to manifest, exhibit," in the middle and passive voices, "to appear, also signifies to declare, make known," and is translated "informed" in Acts 24:1; 25:2, 15. For all the occurrences of the word see APPEAR, A, No. 5.

2. *katēcheō* (κατηχέω, 2727) primarily denotes "to resound" (*kata*, "down," *echos* "a sound"); then, "to sound down the ears, to teach by word of mouth, instruct, inform" (Eng., "catechize, catechumen"); it is rendered, in the passive voice, by the verb "to inform," in Acts 21:21, 24. Here it is used of the large numbers of Jewish believers at Jerusalem whose zeal for the Law had been stirred by information of accusations made against the Apostle Paul, as to certain anti-Mosaic teaching he was supposed to have given the Jews. See INSTRUCT, TEACH.

INHERIT, INHERITANCE

A. Verbs.

1. *klēronomeō* (κληρονομέω, 2816) strictly means "to receive by lot" (*klseros*, "a lot," *nemomai*, "to possess"); then, in a more general sense, "to possess oneself of, to receive as one's own, to obtain." The following list shows how in the NT the idea of inheriting broadens out to include all spiritual good provided through and in Christ, and particularly all that is contained in the hope grounded on the promises of God.

The verb is used of the following objects:

"(a) birthright, that into the possession of which one enters in virtue of sonship, not because of a price paid or of a task accomplished, Gal. 4:30; Heb. 1:4; 12:17:

(b) that which is received as a gift, in contrast with that which is received as the reward of law-keeping, Heb. 1:14; 6:12 ("through," i.e., "through experiences that called for the exercise of faith and patience,' but not 'on the ground of the exercise of faith and patience.'):

(c) that which is received on condition of obedience to certain precepts, 1 Pet. 3:9, and of faithfulness to God amidst opposition, Rev. 21:7:

(d) the reward of that condition of soul which forbears retaliation and self-vindication, and expresses itself in gentleness of behavior .... Matt. 5:5. The phrase "inherit the earth," or "land," occur several times in OT. See especially Ps. 37:11, 22:

(e) the reward (in the coming age, Mark 10:30) of the acknowledgment of the paramountcy of the claims of Christ, Matt. 19:29. In the three accounts given of this incident, see Mark 10:17-31; Luke 18:18-30, the words of the question put to the Lord are, in Matthew, "that I may have," in Mark and Luke, "that I may inherit." In the report of the Lord's word to Peter in reply to his subsequent question, Matthew has "inherit eternal life," while Mark and Luke have "receive eternal life." It seems to follow that the meaning of the word "inherit" is here ruled by the words "receive" and "have," with which it is interchanged in each of the three Gospels, i.e., the less common word "inherit" is to be regarded as equivalent to the more common words "receive" and "have." Cf. Luke 10:25:

(f) the reward of those who have shown kindness to the "brethren" of the Lord in their distress, Matt. 25:34:

(g) the kingdom of God, which the morally corrupt cannot "inherit," 1 Cor. 6:9, 10, the "inheritance" of which is likewise impossible to the present physical constitution of man, 1 Cor. 15:50:

(h) incorruption, impossible of "inheritance" by corruption, 1 Cor. 15:50."

See HEIR.

Note: In regard to (e), the word clearly signifies entrance into eternal life without any previous title; it will not bear the implication that a child of God may be divested of his "inheritance" by the loss of his right of succession.

2. *klēroō* (κληρόω, 2820) is used in the passive voice in Eph. 1:11, KJV, "we have obtained an inheritance"; RV, "we were made a heritage." See HERITAGE.

B. Nouns.

1. *klēronomia* (κληρονομία, 2817), "a lot" (see A), properly "an inherited property, an inheritance." "It is always rendered inheritance in NT, but only in a few cases in the Gospels has it the meaning ordinarily attached to that word in English, i.e., that into possession of which the heir enters only on the death of an ancestor. The NT usage may be set out as follows: (a) that property in real estate which in ordinary course passes from father to son on the death of the former, Matt. 21:38; Mark 12:7; Luke 12:13; 20:14; (b) a portion of an estate made the substance of a gift, Acts 7:5; Gal. 3:18, which also is to be included under (c); (c) the prospective condition and possessions of the believer in the new order of things to be ushered in at the return of Christ, Acts 20:32; Eph. 1:14; 5:5; Col. 3:24; Heb. 9:15; 1 Pet. 1:4; (d) what the believer will be to God in that age, Eph. 1:18."

Note: In Gal. 3:18, "if the inheritance is of the Law," the word "inheritance" stands for "the title to the inheritance."

2. *klēros* (κλῆρος, 2819), (whence Eng., "clergy"), denotes (a) "a lot," given or cast (the latter as a means of obtaining divine direction), Matt. 27:35; Mark 15:24; Luke 23:24; John 19:24; Acts 1:26; (b) "a person's share" in anything, Acts 1:17, RV, "portion" (KJV, "part"); 8:21, "lot"; (c) "a charge" (lit., "charges") "allotted," to elders, 1 Pet. 5:3, RV [KJV, "(God's) heritage"]; the figure is from portions of lands allotted to be cultivated; (d) "an inheritance," as in No. 1 (c); Acts 26:18; Col. 1:12. See LOT(S), PART.

INIQUITY

1. *anomia* (ἀνομία, 458), lit., "lawlessness" (*a*, negative, *nomos*, "law"), is used in a way which indicates the meaning as being lawlessness or wickedness. Its usual rendering in the NT is "iniquity," which lit. means unrighteousness. It occurs very frequently in the Sept., especially in the Psalms, where it is found about 70 times. It is used (a) of iniquity in general, Matt. 7:23; 13:41; 23:28; 24:12; Rom. 6:19 (twice); 2 Cor. 6:14, RV, "iniquity" (KJV, "unrighteousness"); 2 Thess. 2:3, in some mss.; the KJV and RV follow those which have *hamartia*, "(man of) sin"; 2:7, RV, "lawlessness" (KJV, "iniquity"); Titus 2:14; Heb. 1:9; 1 John 3:4 (twice), RV, "(doeth) ... lawlessness" and "lawlessness" (KJV, "transgresseth the law" and "transgression of the law"); (b) in the plural, of acts or manifestations of lawlessness, Rom. 4:7; Heb. 10:17 (some inferior mss. have it in 8:12, for the word *hamartia*). See LAWLESSNESS, TRANSGRESSION, UNRIGHTEOUSNESS.

Note: In the phrase "man of sin," 2 Thess. 2:3, the word suggests the idea of contempt of Divine law, since the Antichrist will deny the existence of God.

2. *adikia* (ἀδικία, 93) denotes "unrighteousness," lit., "unrightness" (*a*, negative, *dikē*, "right"), a condition of not being right, whether with God, according to the standard of His holiness and righteousness, or with man, according to the standard of what man knows to be right by his conscience. In Luke 16:8 and 18:6, the phrases lit. are, "the steward of unrighteousness" and "the judge of injustice," the subjective genitive describing their character; in 18:6 the meaning is "injustice" and so perhaps in Rom. 9:14. The word is usually translated "unrighteousness," but is rendered "iniquity" in Luke 13:27; Acts 1:18; 8:23; 1 Cor. 13:6, KJV (RV, "unrighteousness"); so in 2 Tim. 2:19; Jas. 3:6.

3. *adikēma* (ἀδίκημα, 92) denotes "a wrong, injury, misdeed" (akin to No. 2; from *adikeō*, "to do wrong"), the concrete act, in contrast to the general meaning of No. 2, and translated "a matter of wrong," in Acts 18:14; "wrongdoing," 24:20 (KJV, "evil-doing"); "iniquities," Rev. 18:5. See EVIL, WRONG.

4. *ponēria* (πονηρία, 4189), akin to *poneō*, "to toil" (cf. *ponēros*, "bad, worthless"; see BAD), denotes "wickedness," and is so translated in Matt. 22:18; Mark 7:22 (plural); Luke 11:39; Rom. 1:29; 1 Cor. 5:8; Eph. 6:12; in Acts 3:26, "iniquities." See WICKEDNESS. Cf. *kakia*, "evil."

5. *paranomia* (παρανομία, 3892), "lawbreaking" (*para*, "against," *nomos*, "law"), denotes "transgression," so rendered in 2 Pet. 2:16, for KJV, "iniquity."

INJURE, INJURIOUS, INJURY

A. Verb.

adikeō (ἀδικέω, 91), akin to Nos. 2 and 3, under INIQUITY, is usually translated either "to hurt," or by some form of the verb "to do wrong." In the KJV of Gal. 4:12, it is rendered "ye have (not) injured me," which the RV corrects, both in tense and meaning, to "ye did (me no) wrong." See HURT.

B. Adjective.

hubristēs (ὑβριστής, 5197), "a violent, insolent man" (akin to C), is translated "insolent" in Rom. 1:30, RV, for KJV, "despiteful"; in 1 Tim. 1:13, "injurious." See DESPITEFUL, INSOLENT.

C. Noun.

hubris (ὕβρις, 5196): see HARM, A, No. 4.

INNOCENT

1. *athōos* (ἄθωος, 121) primarily denotes "unpunished" (*a*, negative, *thoe*, "a penalty"); then, "innocent," Matt. 27:4,

"innocent blood," i.e., the blood of an "innocent" person, the word "blood" being used both by synecdoche (a part standing for the whole), and by metonymy (one thing standing for another), i.e., for death by execution (some mss. have *dikaion*, "righteous"); v. 24, where Pilate speaks of himself as "innocent."

2. *akakos* (ἄκακος, 172), lit., "not bad" (*a*, negative, *kakos*, "bad"), denotes "guileless, innocent," Rom. 16:18, RV, "innocent" (KJV, "simple"); "harmless" in Heb. 7:26. See HARMLESS.

For **INORDINATE** see AFFECTION, No. 1

INQUIRE, INQUIRY (make)

A. Verbs.

1. *punthanomai* (πυνθάνομαι, 4441), "to inquire," is translated "inquired" in Matt. 2:4, and Acts 21:33, RV (KJV, "demanded"); in Luke 15:26; 18:36 and Acts 4:7 (KJV, "asked"); "inquired" (KJV, "inquired") in John 4:52; "inquire" (KJV, "inquire") in Acts 23:20; in Acts 23:34 it denotes "to learn by inquiry," KJV, and RV, "when (he) understood"; elsewhere it is rendered by the verb "to ask," Acts 10:18, 29; 23:19.

2. *zēteō* (ζητέω, 2212), "to seek," is rendered "inquire" in John 16:19; "inquire ... for" in Acts 9:11. See ABOUT, B, *Note*, DESIRE, GO, *Note* (2), *a*.

3. *dierōtaō* (διερωτάω, 1331), "to find by inquiry, to inquire through to the end" (*dia*, intensive, *erōtaō*, "to ask") is used in Acts 10:17.

4. *exetazō* (ἐξετάζω, 1833), "to examine, seek out, inquire thoroughly," is translated "inquire" in Matt. 10:11, KJV (RV, "search out"); in John 21:12, "durst inquire," RV [KJV, "(durst) ask"]; in Matt. 2:8, RV, "search out" (KJV, "search"). See SEARCH.

Notes: (1) *Epizēteō*, "to seek after or for" (*epi*, "after," *zēteō*, "to seek"), is rendered "inquire" in Acts 19:39, KJV (RV, "seek"). (2) *Sunzēteō*, "to search" or "examine together," is rendered "to inquire" in Luke 22:23, KJV (RV, "to question"). (3) *Ekzēteō*, "to seek out, search after," is rendered "have inquired" in 1 Pet. 1:10, KJV (RV, "sought"). (4) *Diaginōskō*, "to ascertain exactly," or "to determine," is rendered "inquire" in Acts 23:15, KJV (RV, "judge"). (5) *Akriboō*, "to learn by diligent or exact inquiry," is rendered "inquired diligently" and "had diligently inquired" respectively, in Matt. 2:7, 16, KJV (RV, "learned carefully," and "had carefully learned"). (6) In 2 Cor. 8:23, the words "any inquire" are inserted to complete the meaning, lit., "whether about Titus."

B. Noun.

zētēsis (ζήτησις, 2214) primarily denotes "a search"; then, "an inquiry, a questioning, debate"; it forms part of a phrase translated by the verb "to inquire," in Acts 25:20, RV, "how to inquire," lit. "(being perplexed as to) the inquiry."

INSCRIPTION

epigraphō (ἐπιγράφω, 1924), "to write upon, inscribe" (*epi*, "upon," *graphō*, "to write"), is usually rendered by the verb "to write upon, over, or in," Mark 15:26; Heb. 8:10; 10:16; Rev. 21:12; it is translated by a noun phrase in Acts 17:23, "(with this) inscription," lit., "(on which) had been inscribed." Cf. the noun *epigraphē*, "a superscription."

INSOLENT

hubristēs (ὑβριστής, 5197), "violent, injurious, insolent," is rendered "insolent" in Rom. 1:30, RV (KJV, "despiteful"). See DESPITEFUL, INJURIOUS.

INSPIRATION OF GOD, INSPIRED OF GOD

theopneustos (θεόπνευστος, 2315), "inspired by God" (*Theos*, "God," *pneō*, "to breathe"), is used in 2 Tim. 3:16, of the Scriptures as distinct from non-inspired writings. Wycliffe, Tyndale, Coverdale and the Great Bible have the rendering "inspired of God."

INSTRUCT, INSTRUCTION, INSTRUCTOR

A. Verbs.

1. *katēcheō* (κατηχέω, 2727), "to teach orally, inform, instruct," is translated by the verb "to instruct" in Luke 1:4; Acts 18:25 (RV marg., "taught by word of mouth"); Rom. 2:18; 1 Cor. 14:19, RV (KJV, "teach"). See INFORM, TEACH.

2. *paideuō* (παιδεύω, 3811), "to train children, teach," is rendered "was instructed," in Acts 7:22, RV (KJV, "learned"); "instructing" in 2 Tim. 2:25, KJV (RV, "correcting"); Titus 2:12, RV, "instructing" (KJV, "teaching"). The verb is used of the family discipline, as in Heb. 12:6, 7, 10; cf. 1 Cor. 11:32; 2 Cor. 6:9; Rev. 3:19. In 1 Tim. 1:20 (passive voice) it is translated "might be taught," RV (KJV, "may learn"), but, "however the passage is to be understood, it is clear that not the impartation of knowledge but severe discipline is intended. In Luke 23:16, 22, Pilate, since he had declared the Lord guiltless of the charge brought against Him, and hence could not punish Him, weakly offered, as a concession to the Jews, to 'chastise, *paideuō*, Him, and let Him go.'"

This sense of *paideuō* is confirmed by Heb. 12:6, where it is joined (in a quotation from the Sept. of Prov. 3:12) with "to lash or scourge." Cf. the scene in the *Pilgrim's Progress* where a shining one with a whip of small cords "chastised sore" the pilgrims foolishly caught in the net of the flatterer and said to them, "As many as I love I rebuke and chasten" (*paideuō*). See CORRECT, TEACH.

3. *mathēteuō* (μαθητεύω, 3100), used transitively, "to make a disciple," is translated "which is instructed" in Matt. 13:52, KJV (RV, "who hath been made a disciple"). See DISCIPLE.

4. *mueō* (μυέω, 3453), "to initiate into the mysteries," is used in the passive voice, in Phil. 4:12, KJV, "I am instructed," RV, "have I learned the secret." See LEARN.

5. *probibazō* (προβιβάζω, 4264), "to lead forward, lead on" (the causal of *probainō*, "to go forward"; *pro*, "forward," *bibazō*, "to lift up"), is used in the passive voice In Matt. 14:8, and translated, KJV, "being before instructed," RV, "being put forward." Some mss. have it in Acts 19:33, instead of No. 6.

6. *sumbibazō* (συμβιβάζω, 4822), "to join, knit, unite" (*sun*, "with"), then, "to compare," and so, "to prove," hence, "to teach, instruct," is so rendered in 1 Cor. 2:16; it is found in the best mss. in Acts 19:33 (RV marg., "instructed"). See COMPACTED, CONCLUDE, PROVE.

B. Nouns.

(INSTRUCTION)

paideia (παιδεία, 3809), "training, instruction," is translated "instruction" in 2 Tim. 3:16. See CHASTEN.

(INSTRUCTOR)

1. *paidagōgos* (παιδαγωγός, 3807), "a guide," or "guardian" or "trainer of boys," lit., "a child-leader" (*pais*, "a boy, or child," *agō*, "to lead"), "a tutor," is translated "instructors" in 1 Cor. 4:15, KJV (RV, "tutors"); here the thought is that of pastors rather than teachers; in Gal. 3:24, 25, KJV, "schoolmaster" (RV, "tutor,"), but here the idea of instruction is absent. "In this and allied words the idea is that of training, discipline, not of impartation of knowledge. The *paidagōgos* was not the instructor of the child; he exercised a general supervision over him and was responsible for his moral and physical well-being. Thus understood, *paidagōgos* is appropriately used with 'kept in ward' and 'shut up,' whereas to understand it as equivalent to 'teacher' introduce, an idea entirely foreign to the passage, and throws the Apostle's argument into confusion." Cf. *epitropos*, "a steward, guardian, tutor."

2. *paideutēs* (παιδευτής, 3810), akin to A, No. 2, denotes (a) "an instructor, a teacher," Rom. 2:20, KJV, "an instructor" (RV, "a corrector"); (b) "one who disciplines, corrects, chastens," Heb. 12:9, RV, "to chasten" [KJV, "which corrected" (lit., "correctors")]. In (a) the discipline of the school is in view; in (b) that of the family. See CORRECTOR.. Cf. *epitropos*, "a steward, guardian, tutor."

INSURRECTION

A. Nouns.

1. *stasis* (στάσις, 4714), akin to *histēmi*, "to make to stand," denotes (a) primarily, "a standing or place," Heb. 9:8; (b) "an insurrection, sedition," translated "insurrection" in Mark 15:7; "insurrections" in Acts 24:5, RV (KJV, "sedition"); in Luke 23:19, 25 (KJV "sedition"), "riot," Acts 19:40, RV (KJV, "uproar"); (c) "a dissension," Acts 15:2; in Acts 23:7, 10, "dissension." See DISSENSION.

2. *stasiastēs* (συστασιαστής, 4955v) denotes "a rebel, revolutionist, one who stirs up sedition" (from *stasiazō*, "to stir up sedition"), Mark 15:7, "had made insurrection." Some mss. have *sustasiastēs*, a fellow-rioter, a fellow-mover of sedition, KJV, "had made insurrection with (him)."

B. Verb.

katephistēmi (κατεφίστημι, 2721) signifies "to rise up against" (lit., "to cause to stand forth against," *kata*, "against," *epi*, "forth," *histēmi*, "to cause to stand"), Acts 18:12, KJV, "made insurrection" (RV, "rose up against").

INTEND

1. *boulomai* (βούλομαι, 1014), "to will, wish, desire, purpose" (expressing a fixed resolve, the deliberate exercise of volition), is translated "intend" in Acts 5:28, and "intending" in 12:4. See DESIRE.

2. *thelō* (θέλω, 2309), "to will, be willing, desire" (less strong, and more frequent than No. 1), is translated "intending" in Luke 14:28, KJV (RV, "desiring"). See DESIRE.

3. *mellō* (μέλλω, 3195), "to be about to do a thing," indicating simply the formation of a design, is translated "intend" in Acts 5:35, KJV (RV, "are about"); "intending," in Acts 20:7, RV (KJV, "ready"); 20:13 (1st part); in the 2nd part of the v., RV, "intending" (KJV, "minding").

INTENT

1. *ennoia* (ἔννοια, 1771), primarily "a thinking, idea, consideration," denotes "purpose, intention, design" (*en*, in, *nous*, mind); it is rendered "intents" in Heb. 4:12; "mind," in 1 Pet. 4:1 (RV, marg., "thought"). See MIND. Cf. *Enthumesis*, "thought" (see DEVICE).

2. *logos* (λόγος, 3056), "a word, account, etc.," sometimes denotes "a reason, cause; intent," e.g., Matt. 5:32, "cause"; it is rendered "intent" in Acts 10:29.

Notes: (1) The phrase *eis touto*, lit., "unto this," i.e., "for this purpose," is rendered "for this (KJV, 'that') intent" in Acts 9:21, RV (2) The phrase *eis to*, "unto the," followed by a verb in the infinitive mood, is translated "to the intent" in 1 Cor. 10:6. (3) The phrase *pros ti*, lit., "in reference to what," is rendered "for what intent" in John 13:28. (4) In John 11:15 the conjunction *hina*, "to the end that," is translated "to the intent," and in Eph. 3:10, "to the intent that."

INTERCESSIONS

A. Noun.

enteuxis (ἔντευξις, 1783) primarily denotes "a lighting upon, meeting with" (akin to B); then, "a conversation"; hence, "a petition," a meaning frequent in the papyri; it is a technical term for approaching a king, and so for approaching God in "intercession"; it is rendered "prayer" in 1 Tim. 4:5; in the plural in 2:1 (i.e., seeking the presence and hearing of God on behalf of others). For the synonymous words, *proseuchē, deēsis*, see PRAYER.

B. Verbs.

1. *entunchanō* (ἐντυγχάνω, 1793), primarily "to fall in with, meet with in order to converse"; then, "to make petition," especially "to make intercession, plead with a person," either for or against others; (a) against, Acts 25:24, "made suit to (me)," RV [KJV, "have dealt with (me)"], i.e., against Paul; in Rom. 11:2, of Elijah in "pleading" with God, RV (KJV, "maketh intercession to"), against Israel; (b) for, in Rom. 8:27, of the intercessory work of the Holy Spirit for the saints; v. 34, of the similar intercessory work of Christ; so Heb. 7:25. See DEAL WITH, PLEAD.

2. *huperentunchanō* (ὑπερεντυγχάνω, 5241), "to make a petition" or "intercede on behalf of another" (*huper*, "on behalf of," and No. 1), is used in Rom. 8:26 of the work of the Holy Spirit in making "intercession" (see No. 1, v. 27).

INTERPRET, INTERPRETATION, INTERPRETER

A. Verbs.

1. *hermēneuō* (ἑρμηνεύω, 2059), (cf. *Hermēs*, the Greek name of the pagan god Mercury, who was regarded as the messenger of the gods), denotes "to explain, interpret" (Eng., "hermeneutics"), and is used of explaining the meaning of words in a different language, John 1:38 (in some mss.), see No. 3; 9:7 ("Siloam," interpreted as "sent"); Heb. 7:2 (Melchizedec, "by interpretation," lit., "being interpreted," King of righteousness).

2. *diermēneuō* (διερμηνεύω, 1329), a strengthened form of No. 1 (*dia*, "through," used intensively), signifies "to interpret fully, to explain." In Luke 24:27, it is used of Christ in interpreting to the two on the way to Emmaus "in all the Scriptures the things concerning Himself," RV, "interpreted" (KJV, "expounded"); in Acts 9:36, it is rendered "is by interpretation," lit., "being interpreted" (of Tabitha, as meaning Dorcas); in 1 Cor. 12:30 and 14:5, 13, 27, it is used with reference to the temporary gift of tongues in the churches; this gift was inferior in character to that of prophesying unless he who spoke in a "tongue" interpreted his words, 14:5; he was, indeed, to pray that he might interpret, v. 13; only two, or at the most three, were to use the gift in a gathering, and that "in turn" (RV); one was to interpret; in the absence of an interpreter, the gift was not to be exercised, v. 27.

3. *methermēneuō* (μεθερμηνεύω, 3177), "to change or translate from one language to another (*meto*, implying change, and No. 1), to interpret," is always used in the passive voice in the NT, "being interpreted," of interpreting the names, Immanuel, Matt. 1:23; Golgotha, Mark 15:22; Barnabas, Acts 4:36; in Acts 13:8, of Elymas, the verb is rendered "is ... by interpretation," lit., "is interpreted"; it is used of interpreting or translating sentences in Mark 5:41; 15:34; in the best mss., John 1:38 (Rabbi, interpreted as "Master"); v. 41 (Messiah, interpreted as "Christ"); see No. 1.

B. Nouns.

(INTERPRETATION)

1. *hermēneia* (or *-ia*) (ἑρμηνεία, 2058), akin to A, No. 1, is used in 1 Cor. 12:10; 14:26 (see A, No. 2).

2. *epilusis* (ἐπίλυσις, 1955), from *epiluō*, "to loose, solve, explain," denotes "a solution, explanation," lit., "a release" (*epi*, "up," *luō*, "to loose"), 2 Pet. 1:20, "(of private) interpretation"; i.e., the writers of Scripture did not put their own construction upon the "Godbreathed" words they wrote.

(INTERPRETER)

diermēneutēs (διερμηνευτής, 1328), lit., "a thorough interpreter" (cf. A, No. 2), is used in 1 Cor. 14:28 (some mss. have *hermēneutēs*).

INTERROGATION

eperōtēma (ἐπερώτημα, 1906), primarily a question or inquiry, denotes "a demand or appeal"; it is found in 1 Pet. 3:21, RV, "interrogation" (KJV, "answer"). See ANSWER, *Note.* Some take the word to indicate that baptism affords a good conscience, an appeal against the accuser.

INTREAT, INTREATY

A. Verbs.

1. *erōtaō* (ἐρωτάω, 2065), "to ask, beseech," is rendered "intreat," e.g., in Phil. 4:3, KJV (RV, "beseech").

2. *parakaleō* (παρακαλέω, 3870), "to beseech, comfort, exhort," is rendered by the verb "to intreat" in Luke 8:31, RV, "intreated" (KJV, "besought"); 15:28; Acts 9:38, RV, "intreating" (KJV, "desiring"); 28:20, RV (KJV, "called for"); 1 Cor. 4:13; 2 Cor. 9:5, RV (KJV, "exhort"); 10:1, RV (KJV, "beseech"); 1 Tim. 5:1, KJV (RV, "exhort").

3. *paraiteomai* (παραιτέομαι, 3868), "to ask to be excused, to beg," etc., is rendered "intreated" in Heb. 12:19.

B. Adjective.

eupeithēs (εὐπειθής, 2138), "ready to obey" (*eu*, "well," *peithomai*, "to obey, to be persuaded"), "compliant," is translated "easy to be intreated" in Jas. 3:17, said of the wisdom that is from above.

C. Noun.

paraklēsis (παράκλησις, 3874), "an appeal, a comfort, exhortation," etc., is translated "intreaty" in 2 Cor. 8:4.

INTRUST

pisteuō (πιστεύω, 4100), "to believe," also means "to entrust," and in the active voice is translated "to commit," in Luke 16:11; John 2:24; in the passive voice, "to be intrusted with," Rom. 3:2, RV, "they were intrusted with" (KJV, "unto them were committed"), of Israel and the oracles of God; 1 Cor. 9:17, RV, "I have ... intrusted to me" (KJV, "is committed unto me"), of Paul and the stewardship of the gospel; so Gal. 2:7; Titus 1:3; in 1 Thess. 2:4, where he associates with himself his fellow missionaries, RV, "to be intrusted with" (KJV, "to be put in trust with"). See BELIEVE.

INVENTORS

epheuretēs (ἐφευρέτης, 2182), "an inventor, contriver" (akin to *epheuriskō*, "to find out"; *epi*, "on," used intensively, *heurisko*, "to find"), occurs in the plural in Rom. 1:30.

INVISIBLE

aoratos (ἀόρατος, 517), lit., "unseen" (*a*, negative, *horaō*, "to see"), is translated "invisible" in Rom. 1:20, of the power and divinity of God; of God Himself, Col. 1:15; 1 Tim. 1:17; Heb. 11:27; of things unseen, Col. 1:16. In the Sept., Gen. 1:2; Isa. 45:3, "unseen (treasures)."

IVORY

elephantinos (ἐλεφάντινος, 1661), an adjective from *elephas* (whence Eng., elephant), signifies "of ivory," Rev. 18:12.

J

For **JANGLING** (1 Tim. 1:6, KJV) see TALKING (vain)

JEALOUS, JEALOUSY

A. Noun.

zēlos (ζῆλος, 2205), "zeal, jealousy," is rendered "jealousy" in the RV (KJV, "envying") in Rom. 13:13; 1 Cor. 3:3; Jas. 3:14, 16; in 2 Cor. 12:20 (KJV, "envyings"); in Gal. 5:20, RV "jealousies" (KJV, "emulations"); in Acts 5:17 (KJV, "indignation"); in 13:45 (KJV, "envy"); in 2 Cor. 11:2 it is used in the phrase "with a godly jealousy," lit., "with a jealousy of God" (RV, marg.). See ENVY.

B. Verbs.

1. *zēloō* (ζηλόω, 2206), akin to A, "to be jealous, to burn with jealousy" (otherwise, to seek or desire eagerly), is rendered "moved with jealousy," in Acts 7:9 and 17:5, RV (KJV, "moved with envy"); in 1 Cor. 13:4, "envieth (not)," KJV and RV; in Jas. 4:2, RV marg., "are jealous" (text "covet;" KJV, "desire to have"). See AFFECT, *Note,* DESIRE.

2. *parazēloō* (παραζηλόω, 3863), "to provoke to jealousy" (*para*, "beside," used intensively, and No. 1), is found in Rom. 10:19 and 11:11, of God's dealings with Israel through his merciful dealings with Gentiles; in 11:14, RV, "I may provoke to jealousy" (KJV, "... emulation"), of the apostle's evangelical ministry to Gentiles with a view to stirring his fellow nationals to a sense of their need and responsibilities regarding the gospel; in 1 Cor. 10:22, of the provocation of God on the part of believers who compromise their divine relationship by partaking of the table of demons; in Gal. 5:20, of the works of the flesh.

For **JEOPARDY** see DANGER

JESUS

iēsous (Ἰησοῦς, 2424) is a transliteration of the Heb. "Joshua," meaning "Jehovah is salvation," i.e., "is the Savior," "a common name among the Jews, e.g., Ex. 17:9; Luke 3:29 (RV); Col. 4:11. It was given to the Son of God in Incarnation as His personal name, in obedience to the command of an angel to Joseph, the husband of His Mother, Mary, shortly before He was born, Matt. 1:21. By it He is spoken of throughout the Gospel narratives generally, but not without exception, as in Mark 16:19, 20; Luke 7:13, and a dozen other places in that Gospel, and a few in John.

" 'Jesus Christ' occurs only in Matt. 1:1, 18; 16:21, marg.; Mark 1:1; John 1:17; 17:3. In Acts the name 'Jesus' is found frequently. 'Lord Jesus' is the normal usage, as in Acts 8:16; 19:5, 17; see also the reports of the words of Stephen, 7:59, of Ananias, 9:17, and of Paul, 16:31; though both Peter, 10:36, and Paul, 16:18, also used 'Jesus Christ.'

"In the Epistles of James, Peter, John and Jude, the personal name is not once found alone, but in Rev. eight times (RV), 1:9; 12:17; 14:12; 17:6; 19:10 (twice); 20:4; 22:16.

"In the Epistles of Paul 'Jesus' appears alone just thirteen times, and in the Hebrews eight times; in the latter the title 'Lord' is added once only, at 13:20. In the Epistles of James, Peter, John, and Jude, men who had companied with the Lord in the days of His flesh, 'Jesus Christ' is the invariable order (in the RV) of the Name and Title, for this was the order of their experience; as 'Jesus' they knew Him first, that He was Messiah they learnt finally in His resurrection. But Paul came to know Him first in the glory of heaven, Acts 9:1-6, and his experience being thus the reverse of theirs, the reverse order, 'Christ Jesus,' is of frequent occurrence in his letters, but, with the exception of Acts 24:24, does not occur elsewhere in the RV.

"In Paul's letters the order is always in harmony with the context. Thus 'Christ Jesus' describes the Exalted One who emptied Himself, Phil. 2:5, and testifies to His pre-existence; 'Jesus Christ' describes the despised and rejected One Who was afterwards glorified, Phil. 2:11, and testifies to His resurrection. 'Christ Jesus' suggests His grace, 'Jesus Christ' suggests His glory." From *Notes on Thessalonians,* by Hogg and Vine, pp. 16, 29.

JEW(-S) (live as do the), JEWESS, JEWISH, JEWRY, JEWS' RELIGION

A. Adjectives.

1. *ioudaios* (Ἰουδαῖος, 2453), is used (a) adjectivally, with the lit. meaning, "Jewish," sometimes with the addition of *anēr*, "a man," Acts 10:28; 22:3; in 21:39 with *anthrōpos*, in some mss. (a man in the generic sense); the best mss. omit the phrase here; in 13:6, lit., "a Jewish false-prophet"; in John 3:22, with the word *chōra*, "land" or "country," signifying "Judean," lit., "Judean country"; used by metonymy for the people of the country; (b) as a noun, "a Jew, Jews," e.g., Matt. 2:2; Mark 7:3. The name "Jew" is primarily tribal (from Judah). It is first found in 2 Kings 16:6, as distinct from Israel, of the northern kingdom. After the Captivity it was chiefly used to distinguish the race from Gentiles, e.g., John 2:6; Acts 14:1; Gal.

2:15, where it denotes Christians of "Jewish" race; it distinguishes Jews from Samaritans, in John 4:9; from proselytes, in Acts 2:10. The word is most frequent in John's gospel and the Acts; in the former "it especially denotes the typical representatives of Jewish thought contrasted with believers in Christ ... or with other Jews of less pronounced opinions, e.g., John 3:25; 5:10; 7:13; 9:22" (Lukyn Williams, in *Hastings' Bib. Dic.*); such representatives were found, generally, in opposition to Christ; in the Acts they are chiefly those who opposed the apostles and the gospel. In Rom. 2:28, 29 the word is used of ideal "Jews," i.e., "Jews" in spiritual reality, believers, whether "Jews" or Gentiles by natural birth. The feminine, "Jewess," is found in Acts 16:1; 24:24.

It also denotes Judea, e.g., Matt. 2:1; Luke 1:5; John 4:3, the word "country" being understood [cf. (a) above]. In Luke 23:5 and John 7:1, where the KJV has "Jewry," the RV translates it as usual, "Judea."

2. *ioudaikos* (Ἰουδαϊκός, 2451) denotes "Jewish," Titus 1:14.

B. Noun.

ioudaismos (Ἰουδαϊσμός, 2454), "Judaism," denotes "the Jews' religion," Gal. 1:13, 14, and stands, not for their religious beliefs, but for their religious practices, not as instituted by God, but as developed and extended from these by the traditions of the Pharisees and scribes. In the Apocrypha it denotes comprehensively "the Government, laws, institutions and religion of the Jews."

C. Verb.

ioudaizō (Ἰουδαΐζω, 2450), lit., "to Judaize," i.e., to conform to "Jewish" religious practices and manners, is translated "to live as do the Jews," in Gal. 2:14.

D. Adverb.

ioudaikōs (Ἰουδαϊκῶς, 2452), "in Jewish fashion." is translated "as do the Jews," in Gal. 2:14.

For **JOINT-HEIR** see HEIR

JOY (Noun and Verb), JOYFULNESS, JOYFULLY, JOYOUS

A. Nouns.

1. *chara* (χαρά, 5479), "joy, delight" (akin to *chairō*, "to rejoice"), is found frequently in Matthew and Luke, and especially in John, once in Mark (4:16, RV, "joy," KJV, "gladness"); it is absent from 1 Cor. (though the verb is used three times), but is frequent in 2 Cor., where the noun is used five times (for 7:4, RV, see *Note* below), and the verb eight times, suggestive of the apostle's relief in comparison with the circumstances of the I st Epistle; in Col. 1:11, KJV, "joyfulness," RV, "joy." The word is sometimes used, by metonymy, of the occasion or cause of "joy," Luke 2:10 (lit., "I announce to you a great joy"); in 2 Cor. 1:15, in some mss., for *charis*, "benefit"; Phil. 4:1, where the readers are called the apostle's "joy"; so 1 Thess. 2:19, 20; Heb. 12:2, of the object of Christ's "joy"; Jas. 1:2, where it is connected with falling into trials; perhaps also in Matt. 25:21, 23, where some regard it as signifying, concretely, the circumstances attending cooperation in the authority of the Lord. See also the *Note* following No. 3.

Note: In Heb. 12:11, "joyous" represents the phrase *meta*, "with," followed by *chara*, lit., "with joy." So in 10:34, "joyfully"; in 2 Cor. 7:4 the noun is used with the middle voice of *huperperisseuō*, "to abound more exceedingly," and translated "(I overflow) with joy," RV (KJV, "I am exceeding joyful").

2. *agalliasis* (ἀγαλλίασις, 20), "exultation, exuberant joy." Cf. B, No. 3, below. See GLADNESS.

3. *euphrosunē* (εὐφροσύνη, 2167) is rendered "joy" in the KJV of Acts 2:28, RV, "gladness," as in 14:17. See GLADNESS.

Note: "Joy" is associated with life, e.g. 1 Thess. 3:8, 9. Experiences of sorrow prepare for, and enlarge, the capacity for "joy," e.g., John 16:20; Rom. 5:3, 4; 2 Cor. 7:4; 8:2; Heb. 10:34; Jas. 1:2. Persecution for Christ's sake enhances "joy," e.g., Matt. 5:11, 12; Acts 5:41. Other sources of "joy" are faith, Rom. 15:13; Phil. 1:25; hope, Rom. 5:2 (*kauchaomai*, see B, No. 2); 12:12 (*chairo*, see B, No. 1); the "joy" of others, 12:15, which is distinctive of Christian sympathy. Cf. 1 Thess. 3:9. In the OT and the NT God Himself is the ground and object of the believer's "joy," e.g., Ps. 35:9; 43:4; Isa. 61:10; Luke 1:47; Rom. 5:11; Phil. 3:1; 4:4.

B. Verbs.

1. *chairō* (χαίρω, 5463), "to rejoice, be glad," is translated "joyfully" in Luke 19:6, lit., "rejoicing"; "we joyed," 2 Cor. 7:13; "I joy," Phil. 2:17; "do ye joy," 2:18; "joying," Col. 2:5; "we joy," 1 Thess. 3:9. It is contrasted with weeping and sorrow, e.g., in John 16:20, 22; Rom. 12:15; 1 Cor. 7:30 (cf. Ps. 30:5). See FAREWELL, GLAD, GREETING, HAIL, REJOICE.

2. *kauchaomai* (καυχάομαι, 2744), "to boast, glory, exult," is rendered "we joy," in Rom. 5:11, KJV (RV, "we rejoice"). It would have been an advantage to translate this word distinctively by the verbs "to glory" or "to exult."

3. *agalliaō* (ἀγαλλιάω, 21), "to exult, rejoice greatly," is translated "with exceeding joy" in 1 Pet. 4:13 (middle voice), lit., "(ye rejoice, *chairō*) exulting." Cf. A, No. 2. See GLAD, REJOICE.

4. *oninēmi* (ὀνίνημι, 3685), "to benefit, profit," in the middle voice, "to have profit, derive benefit," is translated "let me have joy" in Philem. 20 (RV marg., "help"); the apostle is doubtless continuing his credit and debit metaphors and using the verb in the sense of "profit."

JUDGE (Noun and Verb)

A. Nouns.

1. *kritēs* (κριτής, 2923), "a judge" (from *krinō*, see B, No. 1), is used (a) of God, Heb. 12:23, where the order in the original is "to a Judge who is God of all"; this is really the significance; it suggests that He who is the Judge of His people is at the same time their God; that is the order in 10:30; the word is also used of God in Jas. 4:12, RV; (b) of Christ, Acts 10:42; 2 Tim. 4:8; Jas. 5:9; (c) of a ruler in Israel in the times of the Judges, Acts 13:20; (d) of a Roman procurator, Acts 24:10; (e) of those whose conduct provides a standard of "judging," Matt. 12:27; Luke 11:19; (f) in the forensic sense, of one who tries and decides a case, Matt. 5:25 (twice); Luke 12:14 (some mss. have No. 2 here); 12:58 (twice); 18:2; 18:6 (lit., "the judge of unnghteousness," expressing subjectively his character); Acts 18:15; (g) of one who passes, or arrogates to himself, judgment on anything, Jas. 2:4 (see the RV); 4:11.

2. *dikastēs* (δικαστής, 1348) denotes "a judge" (from *dikē*, "right, a judicial hearing, justice"; akin to *dikazō*, "to judge"), Acts 7:27, 35; some mss. have it in Luke 12:14 (see No. 1); while *dikastēs* is a forensic term, *krites* "gives prominence to the mental process" (Thayer). At Athens the *dikastēs* acted as a juryman, the *kritēs* being the presiding "judge."

B. Verbs.

1. *krinō* (κρίνω, 2919) primarily denotes "to separate, select, choose"; hence, "to determine," and so "to judge, pronounce judgment." "The uses of this verb in the NT may be analyzed as follows: (a) to assume the office of a judge, Matt. 7:1; John 3:17; (b) to undergo process of trial, John 3:18; 16:11; 18:31; Jas. 2:12; (c) to give sentence, Acts 15:19; 16:4; 21:25; (d) to condemn, John 12:48; Acts 13:27; Rom. 2:27; (e) to execute judgment upon, 2 Thess. 2:12; Acts 7:7; (f) to be involved in a lawsuit, whether as plaintiff, Matt. 5:40; 1 Cor. 6:1; or as defendant, Acts 23:6; (g) to administer affairs, to govern, Matt. 19:28; cf. Judg. 3:10; (h) to form an opinion, Luke 7:43; John 7:24; Acts 4:19; Rom. 14:5; (i) to make a resolve, Acts 3:13; 20:16 1 Cor. 2:2." From *Notes on Thessalonians* by Hogg and Vine, p. 267.

See CALL, No. 13, CONCLUDE, CONDEMN, DECREE, ESTEEM, LAW (go to), ORDAIN, SENTENCE.

Note: In Acts 21:25, the RV has "giving judgement" (KJV, "concluded"); see JUDGMENT, *Note* (5).

2. *anakrinō* (ἀνακρίνω, 350), "to examine, investigate, question" (*ana*, "up," and No. 1), is rendered "judged" in 1 Cor. 2:14, RV (KJV, "are ... discerned;" RV marg., "examined"), said of the things of the Spirit of God; in v. 15, "judgeth" (RV marg., "examineth"), said of the exercise of a discerning "judgment" of all things as to their true value, by one who is spiritual; in the same verse, "is judged (of no man)," RV marg., "examined," i.e., the merely natural mind cannot estimate the motives of the spiritual; in 4:3, "I should be judged," i.e., as to examining and passing sentence on the fulfillment or nonfulfillment of the apostle's stewardship; so in the same verse, "I judge (not mine own self)," and in v. 4 "(he that) judgeth (me is the Lord)"; in 14:24, "he is judged (of all)," i.e., the light of the heart-searching testimony of the assembly probes the conscience of the unregenerate, sifting him judicially. See DISCERN, A, No. 1.

3. *diakrinō* (διακρίνω, 1252) denotes "to separate throughout" (*dia*, and No. 1), "discriminate, discern," and hence "to decide, to judge" (also "to contend, to hesitate, to doubt"); it is rendered "to judge" in 1 Cor. 6:5, in the sense of arbitrating; in 11:31 (1st part), the RV has "(if we) discerned (ourselves)," KJV "(if we would) judge" (*krinō*, No. 1, is used in the 2nd part); so in 14:29, RV, "discern" (KJV, "judge"). See DISCERN, A. No. 2.

Notes: (1) In 1 Cor. 6:2 (last clause) "to judge" represents the noun *kritērion*, which denotes "a tribunal, a law court," and the meaning thus is "are ye unworthy of sitting upon tribunals of least importance?" (see RV marg.), i.e., to "judge" matters of smallest importance. Some would render it "cases," but there is no clear instance elsewhere of this meaning. See JUDGMENT SEAT. (2) In Heb. 11:11, the verb *hēgeomai*, "to consider, think, account," is rendered "she judged (Him faithful)," KJV (RV, "she counted"). See COUNT, No. 2.

JUDGMENT

1. *krisis* (κρίσις, 2920) primarily denotes "a separating," then, "a decision, judgment," most frequently in a forensic sense, and especially of divine "judgment." For the variety of its meanings, with references, see CONDEMNATION, B, No. 3.

Notes: (1) The Holy Spirit, the Lord said, would convict the world of (*peri*, "in respect of"), i.e., of the actuality of, God's "judgment," John 16:8, 11. Cf. 2 Thess. 1:5. (2) In Rom. 2:5 the word *dikaiokrisia*, "righteous judgment," combines the adjective *dikaios*, "righteous," with *krisis*, the two words which are used separately in 2 Thess. 1:5.

2. *krima* (κρίμα, 2917) denotes the result of the action signified by the verb *krinō*, "to judge"; for its general significance see CONDEMNATION, B, No. 1: it is used (a) of a decision passed on the faults of others, Matt. 7:2; (b) of "judgment" by man upon Christ, Luke 24:20; (c) of God's "judgment" upon men, e.g., Rom. 2:2, 3; 3:8; 5:16; 11:33; 13:2; 1 Cor. 11:29; Gal. 5:10; Heb. 6:2; Jas. 3:1; through Christ, e.g., John 9:39; (d) of the right of "judgment," Rev. 20:4; (e) of a lawsuit, 1 Cor. 6:7.

3. *hēmera* (ἡμέρα, 2250), "a day," is translated "judgment" in 1 Cor. 4:3, where "man's judgment" (lit., "man's day," marg.) is used of the present period in which man's mere

"judgment" is exercised, a period of human rebellion against God. The adjective *anthrōpinos*, "human, belonging to man" (*anthrōpos*), is doubtless set in contrast here to *kuriakos*, "belonging to the Lord" (*kurios*, "a lord"), which is used in the phrase "the Day of the Lord," in Rev. 1:10, "The Lord's Day," a period of divine judgments. See DAY.

4. *gnōmē* (γνώμη, 1106), primarily "a means of knowing" (akin to *ginōskō*, "to know"), came to denote "a mind, understanding"; hence (a) "a purpose," Acts 20:3, lit., "(it was his) purpose"; (b) "a royal purpose, a decree," Rev. 17:17, RV, "mind" (KJV, "will"); (c) "judgment, opinion," 1 Cor. 1:10, "(in the same) judgment"; Rev. 17:13, "mind"; (d) "counsel, advice," 1 Cor. 7:25, "(I give my) judgment;" 7:40, "(after my) judgment"; Philem. 14, mind. See MIND, WILL.

Notes: (1) In 1 Cor. 6:4, KJV, *kritērion*, "a tribunal," is rendered "judgments" (RV, "to judge," marg., "tribunals"). See JUDGE, B, No. 3, Note (1). (2) In Rom. 1:32, KJV, *dikaioma*, "an ordinance, righteous act," is translated "judgment" (RV "ordinance"); in Rev. 15:4, "judgments" (RV, "righteous acts"). (3) In Acts 25:15, KJV, *katadikē*, "a sentence, condemnation," is translated "judgment" (RV, "sentence"). Some mss. have *dikē*. See SENTENCE. (4) In Phil. 1:9, KJV, *aisthēsis*, "perception, discernment," is translated "judgment" (RV, "discernment"). (5) In Acts 21:25, in the record of the decree from the apostles and elders at Jerusalem to the churches of the Gentiles, the verb *krinō* (see JUDGE, B, No. 1), is translated "giving judgment," RV (KJV, "concluded").

B. Adjective.

hupodikos (ὑπόδικος, 5267), "brought to trial, answerable to" (*hupo*, "under," *dikē*, "justice"), Rom. 3:19, is translated "under the judgment," RV (KJV, "guilty").

For **HALL OF JUDGMENT, JUDGMENT HALL**, see HALL.

JUDGMENT SEAT

1. *bēma* (βῆμα, 968), primarily, "a step, a pace" (akin to *bainō*, "to go"), as in Acts 7:5, translated "to set (his foot) on," lit., "footroom," was used to denote a raised place or platform, reached by steps, originally that at Athens in the Pnyx Hill, where was the place of assembly; from the platform orations were made. The word became used for a tribune, two of which were provided in the law courts of Greece, one for the accuser and one for the defendant; it was applied to the tribunal of a Roman magistrate or ruler, Matt. 27:19; John 19:13; Acts 12:21, translated "throne"; 18:12, 16, 17; 25:6, 10, 17.

In two passages the word is used of the divine tribunal before which all believers are hereafter to stand. In Rom. 14:10 it is called "The judgement seat of God," RV (KJV, "of Christ"), according to the most authentic mss. The same tribunal is called "the judgment seat of Christ," 2 Cor. 5:10, to whom the Father has given all judgment, John 5:22, 27. At this *bēma* believers are to be made manifest, that each may "receive the things done in (or through) the body," according to what he has done, "whether it be good or bad." There they will receive rewards for their faithfulness to the Lord. For all that has been contrary in their lives to His will they will suffer loss, 1 Cor. 3:15. This judgment seat is to be distinguished from the premillennial, earthly throne of Christ, Matt. 25:31, and the postmillennial "Great White Throne," Rev. 20:11, at which only "the dead" will appear. The judgment seat of Christ will be a tribunal held "in His Parousia," i.e., His presence with His saints after His return to receive them to Himself.

2. *kritērion* (κριτήριον, 2922) primarily "a means of judging" (akin to *krinō*, "to judge": Eng., "criterion"), then, a tribunal, law court, or "lawsuit," 1 Cor. 6:2 (last clause), for which see JUDGE, B, No. 3, Note (1); 6:4, for which see JUDGMENT, Note (1) at end; Jas. 2:6.

JUST, JUSTLY

A. Adjectives.

1. *dikaios* (δίκαιος, 1342) was first used of persons observant of *dikē*, "custom, rule, right," especially in the fulfillment of duties towards gods and men, and of things that were in accordance with right. The Eng. word "righteous" was formerly spelt "rightwise," i.e., (in a) straight way. In the NT it denotes "righteous," a state of being right, or right conduct, judged whether by the divine standard, or according to human standards, of what is right. Said of God, it designates the perfect agreement between His nature and His acts (in which He is the standard for all men). See RIGHTEOUSNESS. It is used (1) in the broad sense, of persons: (a) of God, e.g., John 17:25; Rom. 3:26; 1 John 1:9; 2:29; 3:7; (b) of Christ, e.g., Acts 3:14; 7:52; 22:14; 2 Tim. 4:8; 1 Pet. 3:18; 1 John 2:1; (c) of men, Matt. 1:19; Luke 1:6; Rom. 1:17; 2:13; 5:7. (2) of things; blood (metaphorical), Matt. 23:35; Christ's judgment, John 5:30; any circumstance, fact or deed, Matt. 20:4 (v. 7, in some mss.); Luke 12:57; Acts 4:19; Eph. 6:1; Phil. 1:7; 4:8; Col. 4:1; 2 Thess. 1:6; "the commandment" (the Law), Rom. 7:12; works, 1 John 3:12, the ways of God, Rev. 15:3. See RIGHTEOUS.

2. *endikos* (ἔνδικος, 1738), "just, righteous" (*en*, "in," *dikē*, "right"), is said of the condemnation of those who say "Let us do evil, that good may come," Rom. 3:8; of the recompense of reward of transgressions under the Law, Heb. 2:2.

Note: As to the distinction between No. 1 and No. 2, "*dikaios* characterizes the subject so far as he or it is (so to speak) one with *dikē*, right; *endikos*, so far as he occupies a due relation to *dikē*; ... in Rom. 3:8 *endikos* presupposes that which has been decided righteously, which leads to the just sentence" (Cremer).

B. Adverb.

dikaiōs (δικαίως, 1346), "justly, righteously, in accordance with what is right," is said (a) of God's judgment, 1 Pet. 2:23; (b) of men, Luke 23:41, "justly;" 1 Cor. 15:34, RV, "righteously" (KJV, "to righteousness"); 1 Thess. 2:10, RV, "righteously;" Titus 2:12.

JUSTICE

dikē (δίκη, 1349), primarily "custom, usage," came to denote "what is right"; then, "a judicial hearing"; hence, "the execution of a sentence," "punishment," 2 Thess. 1:9, RV; Jude 7, "punishment," RV (KJV, "vengeance"). In Acts 28:4 (KJV, "vengeance") it is personified and denotes the goddess Justice or Nemesis (Lat., *Justitia*), who the Melita folk supposed was about to inflict the punishment of death upon Paul by means of the viper. See PUNISHMENT, VENGEANCE.

JUSTIFICATION, JUSTIFIER, JUSTIFY

A. Nouns.

1. *dikaiōsis* (δικαίωσις, 1347) denotes "the act of pronouncing righteous, justification, acquittal"; its precise meaning is determined by that of the verb *dikaioō*, "to justify" (see B); it is used twice in the Ep. to the Romans, and there alone in the NT, signifying the establishment of a person as just by acquittal from guilt. In Rom. 4:25 the phrase "for our justification," is, lit., "because of our justification" (parallel to the preceding clause "for our trespasses," i.e., because of trespasses committed), and means, not with a view to our "justification," but because all that was necessary on God's part for our "justification" had been effected in the death of Christ. On this account He was raised from the dead. The propitiation being perfect and complete, His resurrection was the confirmatory counterpart. In 5:18, "justification of life" means "justification which results in life" (cf. v. 21). That God "justifies" the believing sinner on the ground of Christ's death, involves His free gift of life. On the distinction between *dikaiosis* and *dikaiōma*, see below. In the Sept., Lev. 24:22.

2. *dikaiōma* (δικαίωμα, 1345) has three distinct meanings, and seems best described comprehensively as "a concrete expression of righteousness"; it is a declaration that a person or thing is righteous, and hence, broadly speaking, it represents the expression and effect of *dikaiōsis* (No. 1). It signifies (a) "an ordinance," Luke 1:6; Rom. 1:32, RV, "ordinance," i.e., what God has declared to be right, referring to His decree of retribution (KJV, "judgment"); Rom. 2:26, RV, "ordinances of the Law" (i.e., righteous requirements enjoined by the Law); so 8:4, "ordinance of the Law," i.e., collectively, the precepts of the Law, all that it demands as right; in Heb. 9:1, 10, ordinances connected with the tabernacle ritual; (b) "a sentence of acquittal," by which God acquits men of their guilt, on the conditions (1) of His grace in Christ, through His expiatory sacrifice, (2) the acceptance of Christ by faith, Rom. 5:16; (c) "a righteous act," Rom. 5:18, "(through one) act of righteousness," RV, not the act of "justification," nor the righteous character of Christ (as suggested by the KJV: *dikaiōma* does not signify character, as does *dikaiōsunē*, righteousness), but the death of Christ, as an act accomplished consistently with God's character and counsels; this is clear as being in antithesis to the "one trespass" in the preceding statement. Some take the word here as meaning a decree of righteousness, as in v. 16; the death of Christ could indeed be regarded as fulfilling such a decree, but as the apostle's argument proceeds, the word, as is frequently the case, passes from one shade of meaning to another, and here stands not for a decree, but an act; so in Rev. 15:4, RV, "righteous acts" (KJV, "judgments"), and 19:8, "righteous acts (of the saints)" (KJV, "righteousness").

Note: For *dikaiōsune*, always translated "righteousness," see RIGHTEOUSNESS.

B. Verb.

dikaioō (δικαιόω, 1344) primarily "to deem to be right," signifies, in the NT, (a) "to show to be right or righteous"; in the passive voice, to be justified, Matt. 11:19; Luke 7:35; Rom. 3:4; 1 Tim. 3:16; (b) "to declare to be righteous, to pronounce righteous," (1) by man, concerning God, Luke 7:29 (see Rom. 3:4, above); concerning himself, Luke 10:29; 16:15; (2) by God concerning men, who are declared to be righteous before Him on certain conditions laid down by Him.

Ideally the complete fulfillment of the law of God would provide a basis of "justification" in His sight, Rom. 2:13. But no such case has occurred in mere human experience, and therefore no one can be "justified" on this ground, Rom. 3:9-20; Gal. 2:16; 3:10, 11; 5:4. From this negative presentation in Rom. 3, the apostle proceeds to show that, consistently with God's own righteous character, and with a view to its manifestation, He is, through Christ, as "a propitiation ... by (*en*, "instrumental") His blood," 3:25, RV, "the Justifier of him that hath faith in Jesus" (v. 26), "justification" being the legal and formal acquittal from guilt by God as Judge, the pronouncement of the sinner as righteous, who believes on the Lord Jesus Christ. In v. 24, "being justified" is in the present continuous tense, indicating the constant process of "justification" in the succession of those who believe and are "justified." In 5:1, "being justified" is in the aorist, or point, tense, indicating the definite time at which each person, upon the exercise of faith, was justified. In 8:1, "justification" is presented as "no condemnation." That "justification" is in view here is confirmed by the preceding chapters and by verse 34. In 3:26, the word rendered "Justifier" is the present participle of the verb, lit., "justifying"; similarly in 8:33 (where the artide is used), "God that justifieth," is, more lit., "God is the (One) justifying," with stress upon the word "God."

"Justification" is primarily and gratuitously by faith, subsequently and evidentially by works. In regard to "justification" by works, the so-called contradiction between James and the apostle Paul is only apparent. There is harmony in the different views of the subject. Paul has in mind Abraham's attitude toward God, his acceptance of God's word. This was a matter known only to God. The Romans epistle is occupied with the effect of this Godward attitude, not upon Abraham's character or actions, but upon the contrast between faith and the lack of it, namely, unbelief, cf. Rom. 11:20. James (2:21-26) is occupied with the contrast between faith that is real and faith that is false, a faith barren and dead, which is not faith at all.

Again, the two writers have before them different epochs in Abraham's life—Paul, the event recorded in Gen. 15, James, that in Gen. 22. Contrast the words "believed" in Gen. 15:6 and "obeyed" in 22:18.

Further, the two writers use the words "faith" and "works" in somewhat different senses. With Paul, faith is acceptance of God's word; with James, it is acceptance of the truth of certain statements about God, (v. 19), which may fail to affect one's conduct. Faith, as dealt with by Paul, results in acceptance with God., i.e., "justification," and is bound to manifest itself. If not, as James says "Can that faith save him?" (v. 14). With Paul, works are dead works, with James they are life works. The works of which Paul speaks could be quite independent of faith: those referred to by James can be wrought only where faith is real, and they will attest its reality. So with righteousness, or "justification": Paul is occupied with a right relationship with God, James, with right conduct. Paul testifies that the ungodly can be "justified" by faith, James that only the right-doer is "justified." See also under RIGHTEOUS, RIGHTEOUSNESS.

K

KEY

kleis (κλείς, 2807), "a key," is used metaphorically (a) of "the keys of the kingdom of heaven," which the Lord committed to Peter, Matt. 16:19, by which he would open the door of faith, as he did to Jews at Pentecost, and to Gentiles in the person of Cornelius, acting as one commissioned by Christ, through the power of the Holy Spirit; he had precedence over his fellow disciples, not in authority, but in the matter of time, on the ground of his confession of Christ (v. 16); equal authority was committed to them (18:18); (b) of "the key of knowledge," Luke 11:52, i.e., knowledge of the revealed will of God, by which men entered into the life that pleases God; this the religious leaders of the Jews had presumptuously "taken away," so that they neither entered in themselves, nor permitted their hearers to do so; (c) of "the keys of death and of Hades," Rev. 1:18, RV (see HADES), indicative of the authority of the Lord over the bodies and souls of men; (d) of "the key of David," Rev. 3:7, a reference to Isa. 22:22, speaking of the deposition of Shebna and the investiture of Eliakim, in terms evidently messianic, the metaphor being that of the right of entrance upon administrative authority; the mention of David is symbolic of complete sovereignty; (e) of "the key of the pit of the abyss," Rev. 9:1; here the symbolism is that of competent authority; the pit represents a shaft or deep entrance into the region, from whence issued smoke, symbolic of blinding delusion; (f) of "the key of the abyss," Rev. 20:1; this is to be distinguished from (e): the symbolism is that of the complete supremacy of God over the region of the lost, in which, by angelic agency, Satan is destined to be confined for a thousand years.

For **KID** see GOAT

KILL

1. *apokteinō* (ἀποκτείνω, 615), "to kill," is used (a) physically, e.g., Matt. 10:28; 14:5, "put ... to death," similarly rendered in John 18:31; often of Christ's death; in Rev. 2:13, RV "was killed" (KJV, "was slain"); 9:15, RV, "kill" (KJV, "slay"); 11:13, RV, "were killed" (KJV, "were slain"); so in 19:21; (b) metaphorically, Rom. 7:11, of the power of sin, which is personified, as "finding occasion, through the commandment," and inflicting deception and spiritual death, i.e., separation from God, realized through the presentation of the commandment to conscience, breaking in upon the fancied state of freedom; the argument shows the power of the Law, not to deliver from sin, but to enhance its sinfulness; in 2 Cor. 3:6, "the letter killeth," signifies not the literal meaning of Scripture as contrasted with the spiritual, but the power of the Law to bring home the knowledge of guilt and its punishment; in Eph. 2:16 "having slain the enmity" describes the work of Christ through His death in annulling the enmity, "the Law" (v. 15), between Jew and Gentile, reconciling regenerate Jew and Gentile to God in spiritual unity "in one body." See DEATH, C, No. 4.

2. *anaireō* (ἀναιρέω, 337) denotes (a) "to take up" (*ana*, "up," *haireō*, "to take"), said of Pharaoh's daughter, in "taking up" Moses, Acts 7:21; (b) "to take away" in the sense of removing, Heb. 10:9, of the legal appointment of sacrifices, to bring in the will of God in the sacrificial offering of the death of Christ; (c) "to kill," used physically only (not metaphorically as in No. 1), e.g., Luke 22:2; in 2 Thess. 2:8, instead of the future tense of this verb, some texts (followed by RV marg.) read the future of *analiskō*, "to consume." See DEATH, C, No. 2.

3. *thuō* (θύω, 2380) primarily denotes "to offer firstfruits to a god"; then (a) "to sacrifice by slaying a victim," Acts 14:13, 18, to do sacrifice; 1 Cor. 10:20, to sacrifice; 1 Cor. 5:7, "hath been sacrificed," of the death of Christ as our Passover; (b) "to slay, kill," Matt. 22:4; Mark 14:12; Luke 15:23, 27, 30; 22:7; John 10:10; Acts 10:13; 11:7.

4. *phoneuō* (φονεύω, 5407), "to murder," akin to *phoneus*, "a murderer," is always rendered by the verb "to kill" (except in Matt. 19:18, KJV, "do ... murder," and in Matt. 23:35, KJV and RV, "ye slew"); Matt. 5:21 (twice); 23:31; Mark 10:19; Luke 18:20; Rom. 13:9; Jas. 2:11 (twice); 4:2; 5:6.

5. *thanatoō* (θανατόω, 2289), "to put to death" (from *thanatos*, "death"), is translated "are killed" in Rom. 8:36; "killed" in 2 Cor. 6:9. See DEATH, C, No. 1.

6. *diacheirizō* (διαχειρίζω, 1315), primarily, "to have in hand, manage" (*cheir*, "the hand"), is used in the middle voice, in the sense of "laying hands on" with a view to "kill," or of actually "killing," Acts 5:30, "ye slew"; 26:21, "to kill."

7. *sphazō*, or *sphattō* (σφάζω or σφάττω, 4969), "to slay, to slaughter," especially victims for sacrifice, is most frequently translated by the verb "to slay"; so the RV in Rev. 6:4 (KJV, "should kill"), in 13:3, RV, "smitten unto death" (KJV, "wounded"). See WOUND. Cf. *katasphazō*, "to kill off," Luke 19:27; *sphagē*, "slaughter," e.g., Acts 8:32, and *sphagion*, "a victim for slaughter," Acts 7:42.

KIND (Adjective), KIND (be), KINDLY, KINDNESS

A. Adjectives.

1. *chrēstos* (χρηστός, 5543), "serviceable, good, pleasant" (of things), "good, gracious, kind" (of persons), is translated "kind" in Luke 6:35, of God; in Eph. 4:32, enjoined upon believers. See BETTER, GOOD, GOODNESS, GRACIOUS.

2. *agathos* (ἀγαθός, 18), "good," is translated "kind" in Titus 2:5, RV. See GOOD.

B. Verb.

chrēsteuomai (χρηστευομαι, 5541), akin to A, No. 1, "to be kind," is said of love, 1 Cor. 13:4.

C. Nouns.

1. *chrēstotēs* (χρηστότης, 5544), akin to A, No. 1, and B, used of "goodness of heart, kindness," is translated "kindness" in 2 Cor. 6:6; Gal. 5:22, RV (KJV, "gentleness"); Eph. 2:7; Col. 3:12; Titus 3:4. See GOODNESS.

2. *philanthrōpia* (φιλανθρωπία, 5363), from *philos*, "loving," *anthrōpos*, "man" (Eng., "philanthropy"), denotes "kindness," and is so translated in Acts 28:2, of that which was shown by the inhabitants of Melita to the shipwrecked voyagers; in Titus 3:4, of the "kindness" of God, translated "(His) love toward man." See LOVE.

D. Adverb.

philanthrōpōs (φιλανθρώπως, 5364), akin to C, No. 2, "humanely, kindly," is translated "kindly" in Acts 27:3 (KJV, "courteously"). See COURTEOUSLY.

KINDLE

1. *haptō* (ἅπτω, 681), properly, "to fasten to," is used in Acts 28:2 (in the most authentic mss., some mss. have No. 3), of "kindling a fire." See No. 2.

Note: Haptō is used of "lighting a lamp," in Luke 8:16; 11:33; 15:8. For the middle voice see TOUCH.

2. *periaptō* (περί, 4012 and περί, 681), properly, "to tie about, attach" (*peri*, "around," and No. 1), is used of "lighting" a fire in the midst of a court in Luke 22:55 (some mss. have No. 1).

3. *anaptō* (ἀνάπτω, 381), "to light up" (*ana*, "up," and No. 1), is used (a) literally, in Jas. 3:5, "kindleth"; (b) metaphorically, in the passive voice, in Luke 12:49, of the "kindling" of the fire of hostility; see FIRE, A (f). For Acts 28:2, see No. 1, above.

KING

A. Noun.

basileus (βασιλεύς, 935), "a king" (cf. Eng., "Basil"), e.g., Matt. 1:6, is used of the Roman emperor in 1 Pet. 2:13, 17 (a command of general application); this reference to the emperor is illustrated frequently in the *koinē* (see Preface to this volume); of Herod the Tetrarch (used by courtesy), Matt. 14:9; of Christ, as the "King" of the Jews, e.g., Matt, 2:2; 27:11, 29, 37; as the "King" of Israel, Mark 15:32; John 1:49; 12:13; as "King of kings," Rev. 17:14; 19:16; as "the King" in judging nations and men at the establishment of the millennial kingdom, Matt. 25:34, 40; of God, "the great King," Matt. 5:35; "the King eternal, incorruptible, invisible," 1 Tim. 1:17; "King of kings," 1 Tim. 6:15, see *Note* (2) below; "King of the ages," Rev. 15:3, RV (KJV, "saints"). Christ's "kingship" was predicted in the OT, e.g., Ps. 2:6, and in the NT, e.g., Luke 1:32, 33; He came as such e.g., Matt. 2:2; John 18:37; was rejected and died as such, Luke 19:14; Matt. 27:37; is now a "King" Priest, after the order of Melchizedek, Heb. 5:6; 7:1, 17; and will reign for ever and ever, Rev. 11:15.

Notes: (1) In Rev. 1:6 and 5:10, the most authentic mss. have the word *basileia*, "kingdom," instead of the plural of *basileus*, KJV, "kings;" RV, "a kingdom (to be priests)," and "a kingdom (and priests)." The kingdom was conditionally offered by God to Israel, that they should be to Him "a kingdom of priests," Exod. 19:6, the entire nation fulfilling priestly worship and service. Their failure to fulfill His covenant resulted in the selection of the Aaronic priesthood. The bringing in of the new and better covenant of grace has constituted all believers a spiritual kingdom, a holy and royal priesthood, 1 Pet. 2:5, 9. (2) In 1 Tim. 6:15, the word "kings" translates the present participle of the verb *basileuō*, "to be king, to have kingship," lit., "of (those) who are kings." See REIGN, (3). Deissmann has shown that the title "king of kings" was "in very early eastern history a decoration of great monarchs and also a divine title" (*Light from the Ancient East*, pp. 367ff.). Moulton and Milligan illustrate the use of the title among the Persians, from documents discovered in Media.

B. Adjectives.

1. *basileios* (βασίλειος, 934), denoting "royal," as in 1 Pet. 2:9, is used in the plural, of the courts or palaces of kings, Luke 7:25, "kings' courts"; a possible meaning is "among royal courtiers or persons."

2. *basilikos* (βασιλικός, 937), "royal, belonging to a king," is used in Acts 12:20 with "country" understood, "their country was fed from the king's," lit., "the royal (country)." See ROYAL.

KINGDOM

basileia (βασιλεία, 932) is primarily an abstract noun, denoting "sovereignty, royal power, dominion," e.g., Rev. 17:18, translated "(which) reigneth," lit., "hath a kingdom" (RV marg.); then, by metonymy, a concrete noun, denoting the territory or people over whom a king rules, e.g., Matt. 4:8; Mark 3:24. It is used especially of the "kingdom" of God and of Christ.

"The Kingdom of God is (a) the sphere of God's rule, Ps. 22:28; 145:13; Dan. 4:25; Luke 1:52; Rom. 13:1, 2. Since, however, this earth is the scene of universal rebellion against God, e.g., Luke 4:5, 6; 1 John 5:19; Rev. 11:15-18, the "kingdom" of God is (b) the sphere in which, at any given time, His rule is acknowledged. God has not relinquished His sovereignty in the face of rebellion, demoniac and human, but has declared His purpose to establish it, Dan. 2:44; 7:14; 1 Cor. 15:24, 25. Meantime, seeking willing obedience, He gave His law to a nation and appointed kings to administer His "kingdom" over it, 1 Chron. 28:5. Israel, however, though declaring still a nominal allegiance shared in the common rebellion, Isa. 1:2-4, and, after they had rejected the Son of God, John 1:11 (cf. Matt. 21:33-43), were "cast away," Rom. 11:15, 20, 25. Henceforth God calls upon men everywhere, without distinction of race or nationality, to submit voluntarily to His rule. Thus the "kingdom" is said to be "in mystery" now, Mark 4:11, that is, it does not come within the range of the natural powers of observation, Luke 17:20, but is spiritually discerned, John 3:3 (cf. 1 Cor. 2:14). When, hereafter, God asserts His rule universally, then the "kingdom" will be in glory, that is, it will be manifest to all; cf. Matt. 25:31-34; Phil. 2:9-11; 2 Tim. 4:1, 18.

"Thus, speaking generally, references to the Kingdom fall into two classes, the first, in which it is viewed as present and involving suffering for those who enter it, 2 Thess. 1:5; the second, in which it is viewed as future and is associated with reward, Matt. 25:34, and glory, 13:43. See also Acts 14:22.

"The fundamental principle of the Kingdom is declared in the words of the Lord spoken in the midst of a company of Pharisees, "the Kingdom of God is in the midst of you," Luke 17:21, marg., that is, where the King is, there is the Kingdom. Thus at the present time and so far as this earth is concerned, where the King is and where His rule is acknowledged, is, first, in the heart of the individual believer, Acts 4:19; Eph. 3:17; 1 Pet. 3:15; and then in the churches of God, 1 Cor. 12:3, 5, 11; 14:37; cf. Col. 1:27, where for "in" read "among."

"Now, the King and His rule being refused, those who enter the Kingdom of God are brought into conflict with all who disown its allegiance, as well as with the desire for ease, and the dislike of suffering and unpopularity, natural to all. On the other hand, subjects of the Kingdom are the objects of the care of God, Matt. 6:33, and of the rejected King, Heb. 13:5.

"Entrance into the Kingdom of God is by the new birth, Matt. 18:3; John 3:5, for nothing that a man may be by nature, or can attain to by any form of self-culture, avails in the spiritual realm. And as the new nature, received in the new birth, is made evident by obedience, it is further said that only such as do the will of God shall enter into His Kingdom, Matt. 7:21, where, however, the context shows that the reference is to the future, as in 2 Pet. 1:10, 11. Cf. also 1 Cor. 6:9, 10; Gal. 5:21; Eph. 5:5.

"The expression 'Kingdom of God' occurs four times in Matthew, 'Kingdom of the Heavens' usually taking its place. The latter (cf. Dan. 4:26) does not occur elsewhere in NT, but see 2 Tim. 4:18, "His heavenly Kingdom." ... This Kingdom is identical with the Kingdom of the Father (cf. Matt. 26:29 with Mark 14:25), and with the Kingdom of the Son (cf. Luke 22:30). Thus there is but one Kingdom, variously described: of the Son of Man, Matt. 13:41; of Jesus, Rev. 1:9; of Christ Jesus, 2 Tim. 4:1; "of Christ and God," Eph. 5:5; "of our Lord, and of His Christ," Rev. 11:15; "of our God, and the authority of His Christ," 12:10; "of the Son of His love," Col. 1:13.

"Concerning the future, the Lord taught His disciples to pray, "Thy Kingdom come," Matt. 6:10, where the verb is in the point tense, precluding the notion of gradual progress and development, and implying a sudden catastrophe as declared in 2 Thess. 2:8.

"Concerning the present, that a man is of the Kingdom of God is not shown in the punctilious observance of ordinances, which are external and material, but in the deeper matters of the heart, which are spiritual and essential, viz., "righteousness, and peace, and joy in the Holy Spirit," Rom. 14:17." From *Notes on Thessalonians* by Hogg and Vine, pp. 68-70.

"With regard to the expressions "the Kingdom of God" and the "Kingdom of the Heavens," while they are ohen used interchangeably, it does not follow that in every case they mean exactly the same and are quite identical.

"The Apostle Paul often speaks of the Kingdom of God, not dispensationally but morally, e.g., in Rom. 14:17; 1 Cor. 4:20, but never so of the Kingdom of Heaven. 'God' is not the equivalent of 'the heavens.' He is everywhere and above all dispensations, whereas 'the heavens' are distinguished from the earth, until the Kingdom comes in judgment and power and glory (Rev. 11:15, RV) when rule in heaven and on earth will be one.

"While, then, the sphere of the Kingdom of God and the Kingdom of Heaven are at times identical, yet the one term cannot be used indiscriminately for the other. In the 'Kingdom of Heaven' (32 times in Matt.), heaven is in antithesis to earth, and the phrase is limited to the Kingdom in its earthly aspect for the time being, and is used only dispensationally and in connection with Israel. In the 'Kingdom of God', in its broader aspect, God is in antithesis to 'man' or 'the world,' and the term signifies the entire sphere of God's rule and action in relation to the world. It has a moral and spiritual force and is a general term for the Kingdom at any time. The Kingdom of Heaven is always the Kingdom of God, but the Kingdom of God is not limited to the Kingdom of Heaven, until in their final form, they become identical, e.g., Rev. 11:15, RV; John 3:5; Rev. 12:10." (*An Extract*).

KISS (Noun and Verb)

A. Noun.

philēma (φίλημα, 5370), "a kiss" (akin to B), Luke 7:45; 22:48, was a token of Christian brotherhood, whether by way of welcome or farewell, "a holy kiss," Rom. 16:16; 1 Cor. 16:20; 2 Cor. 13:12; 1 Thess. 5:26, "holy" (*hagios*), as free from anything inconsistent with their calling as saints (*hagioi*); "a kiss of love," 1 Pet. 5:14. There was to be an absence of formality and hypocrisy, a freedom from prejudice arising from social distinctions, from discrimination against the poor, from partiality towards the well-to-do. In the churches masters and servants would thus salute one another without any attitude of condescension on the one part or disrespect on the other. The "kiss" took place thus between persons of the same sex. In the "Apostolic Constitutions," a writing compiled in the 4th century, A.D., there is a reference to the custom whereby men sat on one side of the room where a meeting was held and women on the other side of the room (as is frequently the case still in parts of Europe and Asia), and the men are bidden to salute the men, and the women the women, with "the kiss of the Lord."

B. Verbs.

1. *phileō* (φιλέω, 5368), "to love," signifies "to kiss," in Matt. 26:48; Mark 14:44; Luke 22:47.

2. *kataphileō* (καταφιλέω, 2705) denotes "to kiss fervently" (*kata*, intensive, and No. 1); the stronger force of this verb has been called in question, but the change from *phileō* to *kataphileō* in Matt. 26:49 and Mark 14:45 can scarcely be without significance, and the act of the traitor was almost certainly more demonstrative than the simple kiss of salutation. So with the kiss of genuine devotion, Luke 7:38, 45; 15:20; Acts 20:37, in each of which this verb is used.

KNEEL

1. *gonupeteō* (γονυπετέω, 1120) denotes "to bow the knees, kneel," from *gonu* (see above) and *piptō*, "to fall prostrate," the act of one imploring aid, Matt. 17:14; Mark 1:40; of one expressing reverence and honor, Mark 10:17; in mockery, Matt. 27:29.

2. A phrase consisting of *tithēmi*, "to put," with *gonata*, the plural of *gonu*, "the knee" (see above), signifies "to kneel," and is always used of an attitude of prayer, Luke 22:41 (lit., "placing the knees"); Acts 7:60; 9:40; 20:36; 21:5.

KNOW, KNOWN, KNOWLEDGE, UNKNOWN

A. Verbs.

1. *ginōskō* (γινώσκω, 1097) signifies "to be taking in knowledge, to come to know, recognize, understand," or "to understand completely," e.g., Mark 13:28, 29; John 13:12; 15:18; 21:17; 2 Cor. 8:9; Heb. 10:34; 1 John 2:5; 4:2, 6 (twice), 7, 13; 5:2, 20; in its past tenses it frequently means "to know in the sense of realizing," the aorist or point tense usually indicating definiteness, Matt. 13:11; Mark 7:24; John 7:26; in 10:38 "that ye may know (aorist tense) and understand, (present tense)"; 19:4; Acts 1:7; 17:19; Rom. 1:21; 1 Cor. 2:11 (2nd part), 14; 2 Cor. 2:4; Eph. 3:19; 6:22; Phil. 2:19; 3:10; 1 Thess. 3:5; 2 Tim. 2:19; Jas. 2:20; 1 John 2:13 (twice), 14; 3:6; 4:8; 2 John 1; Rev. 2:24; 3:3, 9. In the passive voice, it often signifies "to become known," e.g., Matt. 10:26; Phil. 4:5. In the sense of complete and absolute understanding on God's part, it is used, e.g., in Luke 16:15; John 10:15 (of the Son as well as the Father); 1 Cor. 3:20. In Luke 12:46, KJV, it is rendered "he is ... aware."

In the NT *ginōskō* frequently indicates a relation between the person "knowing" and the object known; in this respect, what is "known" is of value or importance to the one who knows, and hence the establishment of the relationship, e.g., especially of God's "knowledge," 1 Cor. 8:3, "if any man love God, the same is known of Him"; Gal. 4:9, "to be known of God"; here the "knowing" suggests approval and bears the meaning "to be approved"; so in 2 Tim. 2:19; cf. John 10:14, 27; Gen. 18:19; Nah. 1:7; the relationship implied may involve remedial chastisement, Amos 3:2. The same idea of appreciation as well as "knowledge" underlies several statements concerning the "knowledge" of God and His truth on the part of believers, e.g., John 8:32; 14:20, 31; 17:3; Gal. 4:9 (1st part); 1 John 2:3-13, 14; 4:6, 8, 16; 5:20; such "knowledge" is obtained, not by mere intellectual activity, but by operation of the Holy Spirit consequent upon acceptance of Christ. Nor is such "knowledge" marked by finality; see e.g., 2 Pet. 3:18; Hos. 6:3, RV.

The verb is also used to convey the thought of connection or union, as between man and woman, Matt. 1:25; Luke 1:34.

2. *oida* (οἶδα, Perf. of εἴδω, 1492), from the same root as *eidon*, "to see," is a perfect tense with a present meaning, signifying, primarily, "to have seen or perceived"; hence, "to know, to have knowledge of," whether absolutely, as in divine knowledge, e.g., Matt. 6:8, 32; John 6:6, 64; 8:14; 11:42; 13:11; 18:4; 2 Cor. 11:31; 2 Pet. 2:9; Rev. 2:2, 9, 13, 19; 3:1, 8, 15; or in the case of human "knowledge," to know from observation, e.g., 1 Thess. 1:4, 5; 2:1; 2 Thess. 3:7.

The differences between *ginōskō* (No. 1) and *oida* demand consideration: (a) *ginōskō*, frequently suggests inception or progress in "knowledge," while *oida* suggests fullness of "knowledge," e.g., John 8:55, "ye have not known Him" (*ginōskō*), i.e., begun to "know," "but I know Him" (*oida*), i.e., "know Him perfectly"; 13:7, "What I do thou knowest not now," i.e. Peter did not yet perceive (*oida*) its significance, "but thou shalt understand," i.e., "get to know (*ginōskō*), hereafter"; 14:7, "If ye had known Me" (*ginōskō*), i.e., "had definitely come to know Me," "ye would have known My Father also" (*oida*), i.e., "would have had perception of": "from henceforth ye know Him" (*ginōskō*), i.e., having unconsciously been coming to the Father, as the One who was in Him, they would now consciously be in the constant and progressive experience of "knowing" Him; in Mark 4:13, "Know ye not (*oida*) this parable? and how shall ye know (*ginōskō*) all the parables?" (RV), i.e., "Do ye not understand this parable? How shall ye come to perceive all . . ." the intimation being that the first parable is a leading and testing one; (b) while *ginōskō* frequently implies an active relation between the one who "knows" and the person or thing "known" (see No. 1, above), *oida* expresses the fact that the object has simply come within the scope of the "knower's" perception; thus in Matt. 7:23 "I never knew you" (*ginōskō*) suggests "I have never been in approving connection with you," whereas in 25:12, "I know you not" (*oida*) suggests "you stand in no relation to Me."

3. *epiginōskō* (ἐπιγινώσκω, 1921) denotes (a) "to observe, fully perceive, notice attentively, discern, recognize" (*epi*, "upon," and No. 1); it suggests generally a directive, a more special, recognition of the object "known" than does No. 1; it also may suggest advanced "knowledge" or special appreciation; thus, in Rom. 1:32, "knowing the ordinance of God" (*epiginōskō*) means "knowing full well," whereas in verse 21 "knowing God" (*ginōskō*) simply suggests that they could not avoid the perception. Sometimes *epiginōskō* implies a special participation in the object "known," and gives greater weight to what is stated; thus in John 8:32, "ye shall know the truth," *ginosko* is used, whereas in 1 Tim. 4:3, "them that believe and know the truth," *epiginōskō* lays stress on participation in the truth. Cf. the stronger statement in Col. 1:6 (*epiginōskō*) with that in 2 Cor. 8:9 (*ginōskō*), and the two verbs in 1 Cor. 13:12, "now I know in part (*ginōskō*); but then shall I know (*piginōskō*) even as also I have been known (*epiginōskō*)," "a knowledge" which perfectly unites the subject with the object; (b) "to discover, ascertain, determine," e.g., Luke 7:37; 23:7; Acts 9:30; 19:34; 22:29; 28:1; in 24:11 the best mss. have this verb instead of No. 1; hence the RV, "take knowledge." J. Armitage Robinson (on Ephesians) points out that *epignōsis* is "knowledge directed towards a particular object, perceiving, discerning," whereas *gnōsis* is knowledge in the abstract. See ACKNOWLEDGE.

4. *proginōskō* (προγινώσκω, 4267), "to know beforehand," is used (a) of the divine "foreknowledge" concerning believers, Rom. 8:29; Israel, 11:2; Christ as the Lamb of God, 1 Pet. 1:20, RV, "foreknown" (KJV, "foreordained"); (b) of human previous "knowledge," of a person, Acts 26:5, RV, "having knowledge of" (KJV, "which knew"); of facts, 2 Pet. 3:17. See FOREKNOW.

5. *epistamai* (ἐπίσταμαι, 1987), "to know, know of, understand" (probably an old middle voice form of *ephistemi*, "to set over"), is used in Mark 14:68, "understand," which follows *oida* "I (neither) know"; most frequently in the Acts, 10:28; 15:7; 18:25; 19:15, 25; 20:18; 22:19; 24:10; 26:26; elsewhere, 1 Tim. 6:4; Heb. 11:8; Jas. 4:14; Jude 10.

6. *sunoida* (συνοδία, 4923), *sun*, "with," and No. 2, a perfect tense with a present meaning, denotes (a) "to share the knowledge of, be privy to," Acts 5:2; (b) "to be conscious of," especially of guilty consciousness, 1 Cor. 4:4, "I know nothing against (KJV, by) myself." The verb is connected with *suneidon*, found in Acts 12:12; 14:6 (in the best texts).

7. *agnoeō* (ἀγνοέω, 50), "not to know, to be ignorant": see IGNORANT.

8. *gnōrizō* (γνωρίζω, 1107) signifies (a) "to come to know, discover, know," Phil. 1:22, "I wot (not)," i.e., "I know not," "I have not come to know" (the RV, marg. renders it, as under (b), "I do not make known"); (b) "to make known," whether (I) communicating things before "unknown," Luke 2:15, 17; in the latter some mss. have the verb *diagnorizō* (hence the KJV, "made known abroad)"; John 15:15, "I have made known"; 17:26; Acts 2:28; 7:13 (1st part), see *Note* (3) below; Rom. 9:22, 23; 16:26 (passive voice); 2 Cor. 8:1, "we make known (to you)," RV, KJV, "we do (you) to wit"; Eph. 1:9; 3:3, 5, 10 (all three in the passive voice); 6:19, 21; Col. 1:27; 4:7, 9, "shall make known" (KJV, "shall declare"); 2 Pet. 1:16; or (II), reasserting things already "known," 1 Cor. 12:3, "I give (you) to understand" (the apostle reaffirms what they knew); 15:1, of the gospel; Gal. 1:11 (he reminds them of what they well knew, the ground of his claim to apostleship); Phil. 4:6 (passive voice), of requests to God. See DECLARE (*Note*), WIT, WOT.

Notes: (1) In 2 Tim. 3:10, KJV, *parakoloutheō*, "to follow closely, follow as a standard of conduct," is translated "hast fully known" (RV, "didst follow"). (2) In 2 Tim. 4:17, KJV, *plērophoreō*, "to fulfill, accomplish," is translated "might be fully known" (RV, "might be fully proclaimed"). See FULFILL. (3) In Acts 7:13, some mss. have the verb *anagnorizō*, "to make oneself known," "was made known," instead of No. 8 (which see). (4) In Acts 7:13 (2nd part) the KJV, "was made known" translates the phrase *phaneros ginomai*, "to become manifest" (RV, "became manifest"). See MANIFEST. (5) For *diagnōrizō*, "to make known," in Luke 2:17, see No. 8.

B. Adjectives.

1. *gnōstos* (γνωστός, 1110), a later form of *gnōtos* (from No. 1), most frequently denotes "known"; it is used ten times in the Acts, always with that meaning (save in 4:16, where it means "notable"); twice in the Gospel of John, 18:15, 16; in Luke 2:44 and 23:49 it denotes "acquaintance"; elsewhere only in Rom. 1:19, "(that which) may be known (of God)," lit., "the knowable of God," referring to the physical universe, in the creation of which God has made Himself "knowable," that is, by the exercise of man's natural faculties, without such supernatural revelations as those given to Israel. See ACQUAINTANCE.

2. *phaneros* (φανερός, 5318), "visible, manifest," is translated "known" in Matt. 12:16 and Mark 3:12. See APPEAR, MANIFEST, OPENLY.

3. *epistēmōn* (ἐπιστήμων, 1990), akin to A, No. 5, "knowing, skilled," is used in Jas. 3:13, KJV, "endued with knowledge" (RV "understanding").

4. *agnōstos* (ἄγνωστος, 57), the negative of No. 1, "unknown," is found in Acts 17:23.

C. Nouns.

1. *gnōsis* (γνῶσις, 1108), primarily "a seeking to know, an enquiry, investigation" (akin to A, No. 1), denotes, in the NT, "knowledge," especially of spiritual truth; it is used (a) absolutely, in Luke 11:52; Rom. 2:20; 15:14; 1 Cor. 1:5; 8:1 (twice), 7, 10, 11; 13:2, 8; 14:6; 2 Cor. 6:6; 8:7; 11:6; Eph. 3:19; Col. 2:3; 1 Pet. 3:7; 2 Pet. 1:5, 6; (b) with an object: in respect of (1) God, 2 Cor. 2:14; 10:5; (2) the glory of God, 2 Cor. 4:6; (3) Christ Jesus, Phil. 3:8; 2 Pet. 3:18; (4) salvation, Luke 1:77; (c) subjectively, of God's "knowledge," Rom. 11:33; the word of "knowledge," 1 Cor. 12:8; "knowledge" falsely so called, 1 Tim. 6:20.

2. *epignōsis* (ἐπίγνωσις, 1922), akin to A, No. 3, denotes "exact or full knowledge, discernment, recognition," and is a strengthened form of No. 1, expressing a fuller or a full "knowledge," a greater participation by the "knower" in the object "known," thus more powerfully influencing him. It is not found in the Gospels and Acts. Paul uses it 15 times (16 if Heb. 10:26 is included) out of the 20 occurrences; Peter 4 times, all in his 2nd Epistle. Contrast Rom. 1:28 (*epignōsis*) with the simple verb in v. 21. "In all the four Epistles of the first Roman captivity it is an element in the Apostle's opening prayer for his correspondents' well-being, Phil. 1:9; Eph. 1:17; Col. 1:9; Philem. 6" (Lightfoot).

It is used with reference to God in Rom. 1:28; 10:2; Eph. 1:17; Col. 1:10; 2 Pet. 1:3; God and Christ, 2 Pet. 1:2; Christ, Eph. 4:13; 2 Pet. 1:8; 2:20; the will of the Lord, Col. 1:9; every good thing, Philem. 6, RV (KJV, "acknowledging"); the truth, 1 Tim. 2:4; 2 Tim. 2:25, RV; 3:7; Titus 1:1, RV; the mystery of God. Col. 2:2, RV, "(that they) may know" (KJV, "to the acknowledgment of"), lit., "into a full knowledge." It is used without the mention of an object in Phil. 1:9; Col. 3:10, RV, "(renewed) unto knowledge." See ACKNOWLEDGE.

3. *agnōsia* (ἀγνωσία, 56), the negative of No. 1, "ignorance," is rendered "no knowledge" in 1 Cor. 15:34, RV (KJV, "not the knowledge"); in 1 Pet. 2:15, ignorance. See IGNORANCE.

Note: In Eph. 3:4, KJV, *sunesis*, "understanding," is translated "knowledge"; RV, "understanding." For *kardiognōstēs* see p. 297.

L

LABOR (Noun and Verb)

A. Nouns.

1. *kopos* (κόπος, 2873) primarily denotes "a striking, beating" (akin to *koptō*, "to strike, cut"), then, "toil resulting in weariness, laborious toil, trouble"; it is translated "labor" or "labors" in John 4:38; 1 Cor. 3:8; 15:58; 2 Cor. 6:5; 10:15; 11:23, 27, RV, "labor" (KJV, "weariness"); 1 Thess. 1:3; 2:9; 3:5; 2 Thess. 3:8; (in some mss., Heb. 6:10); Rev. 2:2 (RV "toil"); 14:13. In the following the noun is used as the object of the verb *parechō*, "to afford, give, cause," the phrase being rendered "to trouble," lit., "to cause toil or trouble," to embarrass a person by giving occasion for anxiety, as some disciples did to the woman with the ointment, perturbing her spirit by their criticisms, Matt. 26:10; Mark 14:6; or by distracting attention or disturbing a person's rest, as the importunate friend did, Luke 11:7; 18:5; in Gal. 6:17, "let no man trouble me," the apostle refuses, in the form of a peremptory prohibition, to allow himself to be distracted further by the Judaizers, through their proclamation of a false gospel and by their malicious attacks upon himself.

2. *ponos* (πόνος, 4192) denotes (a) "labors, toil," Col. 4:13, in the best mss. (some have *zēlos*, "zeal," KJV); (b) "the consequence of toil," viz., distress, suffering, pain, Rev. 16:10, 11; 21:4. See PAIN.

Notes: (1) In Phil. 1:22, KJV, *ergon*, "work," is translated "labor" (RV, "work"); work refers to what is done, and may be easy and pleasant; *kopos* suggests the doing, and the pains taken therein. (2) A synonymous word is *mochthos*, "toil, hardship, distress," 2 Cor. 11:27; 1 Thess. 2:9; 2 Thess. 3:8.

B. Verbs.

1. *kopiaō* (κοπιάω, 2872), akin to A, No. 1, has the two different meanings (a) "growing weary," (b) "toiling"; it is sometimes translated "to bestow labor" (see under BESTOW, No. 3). It is translated by the verb "to labor" in Matt. 11:28; John 4:38 (2nd part); Acts 20:35; Rom. 16:12 (twice); 1 Cor. 15:10; 16:16; Eph. 4:28; Phil. 2:16; Col. 1:29; 1 Thess. 5:12; 1 Tim. 4:10; 5:17; 2 Tim. 2:6; Rev. 2:3; 1 Cor. 4:12, RV, "toil" (KJV, "labor"). See TOIL.

2. *cheimazō* (χειμάζω, 5492), from *cheima*, "winter cold," primarily, "to expose to winter cold," signifies "to drive with a storm"; in the passive voice, "to be driven with storm, to be tempest-tossed," Acts 27:18, RV, "as (we) labored with the storm" (KJV, "being... tossed with a tempest").

3. *sunathleō* (συναθλέω, 4866), "to contend along with a person" (*sun*, "with," *athleō*, "to contend"), is said in Phil. 4:3 of two women who "labored with" the apostle in the gospel; in 1:27, RV, "striving (for)," marg., "with," KJV, "striving together (for)." See STRIVE.

Notes: (1) In John 6:27 and 1 Thess. 2:9, KJV, *ergazomai*, "to work," is translated respectively "labor" and "laboring" (RV, "working"). It is used of manual work here and in 4:11 and Eph. 4:28; of work for Christ in general, in 1 Cor. 16:10. (2) In Heb. 4:11, KJV, *spoudazō*, "to be diligent," is translated "let us labor" (RV, "let us give diligence"). (3) In Col. 4:12, KJV, *agōnizomai*, "to strive, wrestle," is translated "laboring fervently" (RV, and KJV, marg., "striving"). (4) In 2 Cor. 5:9, KJV, *philotimeomai*, "to seek after honor," and hence, "to be ambitious," is translated "we labor," marg., "endeavor" (RV, "we make it our aim," marg., "are ambitious"); cf. Rom. 15:20; 1 Thess. 4:11, RV, marg.

LABORER, FELLOW LABORER

ergatēs (ἐργάτης, 2040), akin to *ergazomai*, "to work," and *ergon*, "work," denotes (a) "a field laborer, a husbandman," Matt. 9:37, 38; 20:1, 2, 8; Luke 10:2 (twice); Jas. 5:4; (b) "a workman, laborer," in a general sense, Matt. 10:10; Luke 10:7; Acts 19:25; 1 Tim. 5:18; it is used (c) of false apostles and evil teachers, 2 Cor. 11:13; Phil. 3:2, (d) of a servant of Christ, 2 Tim. 2:15; (e) of evildoers, Luke 13:27.

Note: In the KJV of Philem. 1 and 24, *sunergos*, "a fellow worker," is translated "fellow laborer," RV, "fellow worker"; in Phil. 4:3, the plural, RV, "fellow workers;" in Phil. 2:25, KJV, "companion in labor," RV, "fellow worker"; in 1 Cor. 3:9, KJV, "laborers together (with God)," RV, "God's fellow workers," i.e., fellow workers belonging to and serving God; in 3 John 8, KJV, "fellow helpers" (to the truth), RV, "fellow workers (with the truth)," i.e., acting together with the truth as an operating power; in 1 Thess. 3:2, some ancient authorities have the clause "fellow worker (with God)," RV, marg.; it is absent from the most authentic mss. See HELPER.

LACK, LACKING

A. Noun.

husterēma (ὑστέρημα, 5303) denotes (a) "that which is lacking, deficiency, shortcoming" (akin to *hustereō*, "to be behind, in want"), 1 Cor. 16:17; Phil. 2:30; Col. 1:24, RV, "that which is lacking" [KJV, "that which is behind" (of the afflictions of Christ)], where the reference is not to the vicarious sufferings of Christ but to those which He endured previously, and those which must be endured by His faithful servants; 1 Thess. 3:10, where "that which is lacking" means that which Paul had not been able to impart to them, owing to the interruption of his spiritual instruction among them; (b) "need, want, poverty," Luke 21:4, RV, "want" (KJV, "penury"); 2 Cor. 8:14 (twice) "want;" 9:12, "wants" (KJV, "want"); 11:9, RV, "(the measure of my) want" [KJV, "that which was lacking (to me)"]. See PENURY.

Note: In 1 Thess. 4:12, KJV, *chreia*, "need," is translated "lack" (RV, "need").

B. Adjective.

endeēs (ἐνδεής, 1729), from *endeō*, "to lack," signifies "needy, in want," translated "that lacked" in Acts 4:34.

C. Verbs.

1. *hustereō* (ὑστερέω, 5302), akin to A, "to come or be behind," is used in the sense of "lacking" certain things, Matt. 19:20; Mark 10:21 ("one thing"; cf. No. 3 in Luke 18:22); Luke 22:35; in the sense of being inferior, 1 Cor. 12:24 (middle voice). Elsewhere it is translated in various ways; see DESTITUTE.

2. *elattoneō* (ἐλαττονέω, 1641), "to be less" (from *elattōn*, "less"), is translated "had no lack," 2 Cor. 8:15 (quoted from the Sept. of Exod. 16:18), the circumstance of the gathering of the manna being applied to the equalizing nature of cause and effect in the matter of supplying the wants of the needy.

3. *leipō* (λείπω, 3007), "to leave," denotes (a) transitively, in the passive voice, "to be left behind, to lack," Jas. 1:4, "ye may be lacking in (nothing)," RV (KJV, "wanting"); v. 5, "lacketh" (KJV, "lack"); 2:15, RV, "be ... in lack" (KJV, "be ... destitute"); (b) intransitively, active voice, Luke 18:22, "(one thing thou) lackest," is, lit., "(one thing) is lacking (to thee)"; Titus 1:5, "(the things) that were wanting"; 3:13, "(that nothing) be wanting." See DESTITUTE.

Note: In 2 Pet. 1:9, "he that lacketh" translates a phrase the lit. rendering of which is "(he to whom these things) are not present" (*pareimi*, "to be present").

For **LAD**, in John 6:9, see CHILD, A, No. 6

LADING

phortion (φορτίον, 5413), "a burden, load" (a diminutive of *phortos*, "a load," from *pherō*, "to bear"), is used of the cargo of a ship, Acts 27:10, "lading," (some mss. have *phortos*).

LADY

kuria (Κυρία, 2959) is the person addressed in 2 John 1 and 5. Not improbably it is a proper name (Eng., "Cyria"), in spite of the fact that the full form of address in v. 1 is not quite in accord, in the original, with those in v. 13 and in 3 John 1. The suggestion that the church is addressed is most unlikely. Possibly the person is one who had a special relation with the local church.

LAMA

lama (λαμά, 2982) is the Hebrew word for "Why?" (the variant *lema* is the Aramaic form), Matt. 27:46; Mark 15:34.

LAMB

1. *arēn* (ἀρήν, 704), a noun the nominative case of which is found only in early times occurs in Luke 10:3. In normal usage it was replaced by *arnion* (No. 2), of which it is the equivalent.

2. *arnion* (ἀρνίον, 721) is a diminutive in form, but the diminutive force is not to be pressed (see *Note* under No. 3). The general tendency in the vernacular was to use nouns in *-ion* freely, apart from their diminutive significance. It is used only by the apostle John, (a) in the plural, in the Lord's command to Peter, John 21:15, with symbolic reference to young converts; (b) elsewhere, in the singular, in the Apocalypse, some 28 times, of Christ as the "Lamb" of God, the symbolism having reference to His character and His vicarious Sacrifice, as the basis both of redemption and of divine vengeance. He is seen in the position of sovereign glory and honor, e.g., 7:17, which He shares equally with the Father, 22:1, 3, the center of angelic beings and of the redeemed and the object of their veneration, e.g. 5:6, 8, 12, 13; 15:3, the Leader and Shepherd of His saints, e.g., 7:17; 14:4, the Head of his spiritual bride, e.g., 21:9, the luminary of the heavenly and eternal city, 21:23, the One to whom all judgment is committed, e.g., 6:1, 16; 13:8, the Conqueror of the foes of God and His people, 17:14; the song that celebrates the triumph of those who "gain the victory over the Beast," is the song of Moses ... and the song of the Lamb 15:3. His sacrifice, the efficacy of which avails for those who accept the salvation thereby provided, forms the ground of the execution of divine wrath for the rejector, and the defier of God, 14:10; (c) in the description of the second "Beast," Rev. 13:11, seen in the vision "like a lamb," suggestive of his acting in the capacity of a false messiah, a travesty of the true. For the use in the Sept. see *Note* under No. 3.

3. *amnos* (ἀμνός, 286), "a lamb," is used figuratively of Christ, in John 1:29, 36, with the article, pointing Him out as the expected One, the One to be well known as the personal fulfillment and embodiment of all that had been indicated in the OT, the One by whose sacrifice deliverance from divine judgment was to be obtained; in Acts 8:32 (from the Sept. of Is. 53:7) and 1 Pet. 1:19, the absence of the article stresses the nature and character of His sacrifice as set forth in the symbolism. The reference in each case is to the lamb of God's

providing, Gen. 22:8, and the Paschal lamb of God's appointment for sacrifice in Israel, e.g., Ex. 12:5, 14, 27 (cf. 1 Cor. 5:7).

Note: The contrast between *arnion* and *amnos* does not lie in the diminutive character of the former as compared with the latter. As has been pointed out under No. 2, *arnion* lost its diminutive force. The contrast lies in the manner in which Christ is presented in the two respects. The use of *amnos* points directly to the fact, the nature and character of His sacrifice; *arnion* (only in the Apocalypse) presents Him, on the ground, indeed, of His sacrifice, but in His acquired majesty, dignity, honor, authority and power.

In the Sept. *arnion* is used in Ps. 114:4, 6, in Jer. 11:19, with the adjective *akakos*, "innocent"; in Jer. 27:45, "lambs." There is nothing in these passages to suggest a contrast between a "lamb" in the general sense of the term and the diminutive; the contrast is between "lambs" and sheep. Elsewhere in the Sept. *amnos* is in general used some 100 times in connection with "lambs" for sacrifice.

For **LAME** see HALT

For **LAMENT and LAMENTATION** see BEWAIL

LAMP

1. *lampas* (λαμπάς, 2985) denotes "a torch" (akin to *lampō*, "to shine"), frequently fed, like a "lamp," with oil from a little vessel used for the purpose (the *angeion* of Matt. 25:4); they held little oil and would frequently need replenishing. Rutherford (*The New Phrynichus*) points out that it became used as the equivalent of *luchnos* (No. 2), as in the parable of the ten virgins, Matt. 25:1, 3, 4, 7, 8; John 18:3, "torches"; Acts 20:8, "lights"; Rev. 4:5; 8:10 (RV, "torch," KJV, "lamp"). See *Note* below. Cf. *phanos*, "a torch," John 18:3 (translated "lanterns").

2. *luchnos* (λύχνος, 3088) frequently mistranslated "candle," is a portable "lamp" usually set on a stand (see LAMPSTAND); the word is used literally, Matt. 5:15; Mark 4:21; Luke 8:16; 11:33, 36; 15:8; Rev. 18:23; 22:5; (b) metaphorically, of Christ as the Lamb, Rev. 21:23, RV, "lamp" (KJV, "light"); of John the Baptist, John 5:35, RV, "the lamp" (KJV, "a ... light"); of the eye, Matt. 6:22, and Luke 11:34, RV, "lamp"; of spiritual readiness, Luke 12:35, RV, "lamps"; of "the word of prophecy," 2 Pet. 1:19, RV, "lamp." See LIGHT.

"In rendering *luchnos* and *lampas* our translators have scarcely made the most of the words at their command. Had they rendered *lampas* by 'torch' not once only (John 18:3), but always, this would have left 'lamp,' now wrongly appropriated by lampas, disengaged. Altogether dismissing 'candle,' they might then have rendered *luchnos* by 'lamp' wherever it occurs. At present there are so many occasions where 'candle' would manifestly be inappropriate, and where, therefore, they are obliged to fall back on 'light,' that the distinction between *phōs* and *luchnos* nearly, if not quite, disappears in our Version. The advantages of such a re-distribution of the words would be many. In the first place, it would be more accurate. *Luchnos* is not a 'candle' ('*candela,*' from '*candeo,*' the white wax light, and then any kind of taper), but a hand-lamp, fed with oil. Neither is *lampas* a 'lamp,' but a 'torch'" (Trench *Syn.*, Sec. XLVI).

Note: There is no mention of a candle in the original either in the OT or in the NT. The figure of that which feeds upon its own substance to provide its light would be utterly inappropriate. A lamp is supplied by oil, which in its symbolism is figurative of the Holy Spirit.

LAMPSTAND

luchnia (λυχνία, 3087) is mistranslated "candlestick" in every occurrence in the KJV and in certain places in the RV; the RV has "stand" in Matt. 5:15; Mark 4:21; Luke 8:16; 11:33; "candlestick" in Heb. 9:2; Rev. 1:12, 13, 20 (twice); 2:1, 5; 11:4; the RV marg., gives "lampstands" in the passages in Rev., but not in Heb. 9:2.

LANGUAGE

dialektos (διάλεκτος, 1258), primarily "a conversation, discourse" (akin to *dialegomai*, "to discourse or discuss"), came to denote "the language or dialect of a country or district," in the KJV and RV of Acts 2:6 it is translated "language"; in the following the RV retains "language," for KJV, "tongue," Acts 1:19; 2:8; 21:40; 22:2; 26:14. See TONGUE. In the Sept., Esth. 9:26.

LANTERN

phanos (φανός, 5322) denotes either "a torch" or "a lantern" (from *phainō*, "to cause to shine, to give light"), John 18:3, where it is distinguished from *lampas* (see LAMP, No. 1); it was "a link or torch consisting of strips of resinous wood tied together" (Rutherford). "Torch" would seem to be the meaning.

LASCIVIOUS, LASCIVIOUSNESS

aselgeia (ἀσέλγεια, 766) denotes "excess, licentiousness, absence of restraint, indecency, wantonness"; "lasciviousness" in Mark 7:22, one of the evils that proceed from the heart; in 2 Cor. 12:21, one of the evils of which some in the church at Corinth had been guilty; in Gal. 5:19, classed among the works of the flesh; in Eph. 4:19, among the sins of the unregenerate who are "past feeling"; so in 1 Pet. 4:3; in Jude 4, of that into which the grace of God had been turned by ungodly men; it is translated "wantonness" in Rom. 13:13, one of the sins against which believers are warned; in 2 Pet. 2:2, according to the best mss., "lascivious (doings)," RV (the KJV "pernicious ways" follows those texts which have *apōleiais*); in v. 7, RV, "lascivious (life)," KJV, "filthy (conversation)," of the people of Sodom and Gomorrah; in 2:18, RV, "lasciviousness" (KJV, "wantonness"), practiced by the same persons as mentioned in Jude. The prominent idea is shameless conduct. Some have derived the word from *a*, negative, and *selgē*, "a city in Pisidia." Others, with similar improbability, trace it to *a*, negative, and *selgō*, or *thelgō*, "to charm." See WANTONNESS.

LAST

A. Adjective.

eschatos (ἔσχατος, 2078), "last, utmost, extreme," is used (a) of place, e.g., Luke 14:9, 10, "lowest;" Acts 1:8 and 13:47, "uttermost part;" (b) of rank, e.g., Mark 9:35; (c) of time, relating either to persons or things, e.g., Matt. 5:26, "the last (farthing)," RV (KJV, "uttermost"); Matt. 20:8, 12, 14; Mark 12:6, 22; 1 Cor. 4:9, of apostles as "last" in the program of a spectacular display; 1 Cor. 15:45, "the last Adam"; Rev. 2:19; of the "last" state of persons, Matt. 12:45, neuter plural, lit., "the last (things)"; so Luke 11:26; 2 Pet. 2:20, RV, "the last state" (KJV, "the latter end"); of Christ as the Eternal One, Rev. 1:17 (in some mss. v. 11); 2:8; 22:13; in eschatological phrases as follows: (a) "the last day," a comprehensive term including both the time of the resurrection of the redeemed, John 6:39, 40, 44, 54 and 11:24, and the ulterior time of the judgment of the unregenerate, at the Great White Throne, John 12:48; (b) "the last days," Acts 2:17, a period relative to the supernatural manifestation of the Holy Spirit at Pentecost and the resumption of the divine interpositions in the affairs of the world at the end of the present age, before "the great and notable Day of the Lord," which will usher in the messianic kingdom; (c) in 2 Tim. 3:1, "the last days" refers to the close of the present age of world conditions; (d) in Jas. 5:3, the phrase "in the last days" (RV) refers both to the period preceding the Roman overthrow of the city and the land in A.D. 70, and to the closing part of the age in consummating acts of gentile persecution including "the time of Jacob's trouble" (cf. verses 7, 8); (e) in 1 Pet. 1:5, "the last time" refers to the time of the Lord's second advent; (f) in 1 John 2:18,"the last hour" (RV) and, in Jude 18, "the last time" signify the present age previous to the Second Advent.

Notes: (1) In Heb. 1:2, RV, "at the end of these days" (KJV, "in these last days"), the reference is to the close of the period of the testimony of the prophets under the Law, terminating with the presence of Christ and His redemptive sacrifice and its effects, the perfect tense "hath spoken" indicating the continued effects of the message embodied in the risen Christ; so in 1 Pet. 1:20, RV, "at the end of the times" (KJV, "in these last times").

B. Adverb.

husteron (ὕστερον, 5305), the neuter of the adjective *husteros*, is used as an adverb signifying "afterwards, later."

Note: In Phil. 4:10 the particle *pote*, "sometime," used after *ēdē*, "now, already," to signify "now at length," is so rendered in the RV, KJV, "(now) at the last."

For **LAUD** (Rom. 15:11, KJV) see PRAISE, B, No. 1

LAUGH, LAUGH TO SCORN

1. *gelaō* (γελάω, 1070), "to laugh," is found in Luke 6:21, 25. This signifies loud laughter in contrast to demonstrative weeping.

2. *katagelaō* (καταγελάω, 2606) denotes "to laugh scornfully at," more emphatic than No. 1 (*kata*, "down," used intensively, and No. 1), and signifies derisive laughter, Matt. 9:24; Mark 5:40; Luke 8:53. Cf. *ekmuktērizō*, "to deride."

Note: The laughter of incredulity, as in Gen. 17:17 and 18:12, is not mentioned in the NT.

LAUGHTER

gelōs (γέλως, 1071) denotes "laughter," Jas. 4:9. This corresponds to the kind of "laughter" mentioned above (see LAUGH, No. 1).

LAW

A. Nouns.

1. *nomos* (νόμος, 3551), akin to *nemō*, "to divide out, distribute," primarily meant "that which is assigned"; hence, "usage, custom," and then, "law, law as prescribed by custom, or by statute"; the word *ēthos*, "custom," was retained for unwritten "law," while *nomos* became the established name for "law" as decreed by a state and set up as the standard for the administration of justice.

In the NT it is used (a) of "law" in general, e.g., Rom. 2:12, 13, "a law" (RV), expressing a general principle relating to "law"; v. 14, last part; 3:27, "By what manner of law?" i.e., "by what sort of principle (has the glorying been excluded)?"; 4:15 (last part); 5:13, referring to the period between Adam's trespass and the giving of the Law; 7:1 (1st part, RV marg., "law"); against those graces which constitute the fruit of the Spirit "there is no law," Gal. 5:23; "the ostensible aim of the law is to restrain the evil tendencies natural to man in his fallen estate, yet in experience law finds itself not merely ineffective, it actually provokes those tendencies to greater activity. The intention of the gift of the Spirit is to constrain the believer to a life in which the natural tendencies shall have no place, and to produce in him their direct contraries. Law, therefore, has nothing to say against the fruit of the Spirit; hence the believer is not only not under law, ver. 18, the law finds no scope in his life, inasmuch as, and in so far as, he is led by the Spirit;"

(b) of a force or influence impelling to action, Rom. 7:21, 23 (1st part), "a different law," RV;

(c) of the Mosaic Law, the "law" of Sinai, (1) with the definite article, e.g., Matt. 5:18; John 1:17; Rom. 2:15, 18, 20, 26, 27; 3:19; 4:15; 7:4, 7, 14, 16, 22; 8:3, 4, 7; Gal. 3:10, 12, 19, 21, 24; 5:3; Eph. 2:15; Phil. 3:6; 1 Tim. 1:8; Heb. 7:19; Jas. 2:9; (2) without the article, thus stressing the Mosaic Law in its quality as "law," e.g., Rom. 2:14 (1st part); 5:20; 7:9, where the stress in the quality lies in this, that "the commandment which was unto (i.e., which he thought would be a means of) life," he found to be "unto (i.e., to have the effect of revealing his actual state of) death"; 10:4; 1 Cor. 9:20; Gal. 2:16, 19, 21; 3:2, 5, 10 (1st part), 11, 18, 23; 4:4, 5, 21 (1st part); 5:4, 18; 6:13; Phil. 3:5, 9; Heb. 7:16; 9:19; Jas. 2:11; 4:11; (in regard to the statement in Gal. 2:16, that "a man is not justified by the works of the Law," the absence of the article before *nomos* indicates the assertion of a principle, "by obedience to law," but evidently the Mosaic Law is in view. Here the apostle is maintaining that submission to circumcision entails the obligation to do the whole "Law." Circumcision belongs to the ceremonial part of the "Law," but, while the Mosaic Law is actually divisible into the ceremonial and the moral, no such distinction is made or even assumed in Scripture. The statement maintains the freedom of the believer from the "law" of Moses in its totality as a means of justification);

(d) by metonymy, of the books which contain the "law," (1) of the Pentateuch, e.g., Matt. 5:17; 12:5; Luke 16:16; 24:44; John 1:45; Rom. 3:21; Gal. 3:10; (2) of the Psalms, John 10:34; 15:25; of the Psalms, Isaiah, Ezekiel and Daniel, 12:34, the Psalms and Isaiah, Rom. 3:19 (with vv. 10-18); Isaiah, 1 Cor. 14:21; from all this it may be inferred that "the law" in the most comprehensive sense was an alternative title to "The Scriptures."

The following phrases specify "laws" of various kinds; (a) "the law of Christ," Gal. 6:2, i.e., either given by Him (as in the Sermon on the Mount and in John 13:14, 15; 15:4), or the "law" or principle by which Christ Himself lived (Matt. 20:28; John 13:1); these are not actual alternatives, for the "law" imposed by Christ was always that by which He Himself lived in the "days of His flesh." He confirmed the "Law" as being of divine authority (cf. Matt. 5:18); yet He presented a higher standard of life than perfunctory obedience to the current legal rendering of the "Law," a standard which, without annulling the "Law," He embodied in His own character and life (see, e.g., Matt. 5:21-48; this breach with legalism is especially seen in regard to the ritual or ceremonial part of the "Law" in its wide scope); He showed Himself superior to all human interpretations of it; (b) "a law of faith," Rom. 3:27, i.e., a principle which demands only faith on man's part; (c) "the law of my mind," Rom. 7:23, that principle which governs the new nature in virtue of the new birth; (d) "the law of sin," Rom. 7:23, the principle by which sin exerts its influence and power despite the desire to do what is right; "of sin and death," 8:2, death being the effect; (e) "the law of liberty," Jas. 1:25; 2:12, a term comprehensive of all the Scriptures, not a "law" of compulsion enforced from without, but meeting with ready obedience through the desire and delight of the renewed being who is subject to it; into it he looks, and in its teaching he delights; he is "under law (*ennomos*, "in law," implying union and subjection) to Christ," 1 Cor. 9:21; cf, e.g., Ps. 119:32, 45, 97; 2 Cor. 3:17; (f) "the royal law," Jas. 2:8, i.e., the "law" of love, royal in the majesty of its power, the "law" upon which all others hang, Matt. 22:34-40; Rom. 13:8; Gal. 5:14; (g) "the law of the Spirit of life," Rom. 8:2, i.e., the animating principle by which the Holy Spirit acts as the imparter of life (cf. John 6:63); (h) "a law of righteousness," Rom. 9:31, i.e., a general principle presenting righteousness as the object and outcome of keeping a "law," particularly the "Law" of Moses (cf. Gal. 3:21); (i) "the law of a carnal commandment," Heb. 7:16, i.e., the "law" respecting the Aaronic priesthood, which appointed men conditioned by the circumstances and limitations of the flesh. In the Epistle to the Hebrews the "Law" is treated of especially in regard to the contrast between the Priesthood of Christ and that established under the "law" of Moses, and in regard to access to God and to worship. In these respects the "Law" "made nothing perfect," 7:19. There was "a disannulling of a foregoing commandment ... and a bringing in of a better hope." This is established under the "new Covenant," a covenant instituted on the basis of "better promises," 8:6.

Notes: (1) In Gal. 5:3, the statement that to receive circumcision constitutes a man a debtor to do "the whole Law," views the "Law" as made up of separate commands, each essential to the whole, and predicates the unity of the "Law"; in v. 14, the statement that "the whole law" is fulfilled in the one commandment concerning love, views the separate commandments as combined to make a complete "law." (2) In Rom. 8:3, "what the law could not do," is lit., "the inability (*adunaton*, the neuter of the adjective *adunatos*, 'unable,' used as a noun) of the Law"; this may mean either "the weakness of the Law" or "that which was impossible for the Law"; the latter is preferable; the significance is the same in effect; the "Law" could neither give freedom from condemnation nor impart life. (3) For the difference between the teaching of Paul and that of James in regard to the "Law," see under JUSTIFICATION. (4) For Acts 19:38, KJV, "the law is open" (RV, "courts," etc.) see COURT, No. 1. (5) For *nomodidaskaloi*, "doctors of the law," Luke 5:17, singular in Acts 5:34, "teachers of the law," 1 Tim. 1:7, see DOCTOR.

2. *nomothesia* (νομοθεσία, 3548) denotes "legislation, lawgiving" (No. 1, and *tithēmi*, "to place, to put"), Rom. 9:4, "(the) giving of the law." cf. B, No 1.

B. Verbs.

1. *nomotheteō* (νομοθετέω, 3549), (a) used intransitively, signifies "to make laws" (cf. A, No. 2, above); in the passive voice, "to be furnished with laws," Heb. 7:11, "received the law," lit., "was furnished with (the) law"; (b) used transitively, it signifies "to ordain by law, to enact"; in the passive voice, Heb. 8:6.

2. *krinō* (κρίνω, 2919), "to esteem, judge," etc., signifies "to go to law," and is so used in the middle voice in Matt. 5:40, RV, "go to law" (KJV, "sue ... at the law"); 1 Cor. 6:1, 6. See ESTEEM.

Note: In 1 Cor. 6:7, the KJV, "go to law," is a rendering of the phrase *echō krimata,* "to have lawsuits," as in the RV.

3. *paranomeō* (παρανομέω, 3891), "to transgress law" (*para,* "contrary to," and *nomos*), is used in the present participle in Acts 23:3, and translated "contrary to the law," lit., "transgressing the law."

C. Adjectives.

1. *nomikos* (νομικός, 3544) denotes "relating to law"; in Titus 3:9 it is translated "about the law," describing "fightings" (KJV, "strivings"); see LAWYER.

2. *ennomos* (ἔννομος, 1772), (a) "lawful, legal," lit., "in law" (*en,* "in," and *nomos*), or strictly, "what is within the range of law," is translated "lawful" in Acts 19:39, KJV (RV, "regular"), of the legal tribunals in Ephesus; (b) "under law" (RV), in relation to Christ, 1 Cor. 9:21, where it is contrasted with *anomos* (see No. 3 below); the word as used by the apostle suggests not merely the condition of being under "law," but the intimacy of a relation established in the loyalty of a will devoted to his Master. See LAWFUL.

3. *anomos* (ἄνομος, 459) signifies "without law" (*a,* negative) and has this meaning in 1 Cor. 9:21 (four times). See LAWLESS, TRANSGRESSOR, UNLAWFUL, WICKED.

D. Adverb.

anomōs (ἀνόμως, 460), "without law" (the adverbial form of C, No. 3), is used in Rom. 2:12 (twice), where "(have sinned) without law" means in the absence of some specifically revealed "law," like the "law" of Sinai; "(shall perish) without law" predicates that the absence of such a "law" will not prevent their doom; the "law" of conscience is not in view here. The succeeding phrase "under law" is lit., "in law," not the same as the adjective *ennomos* (C, No. 2), but two distinct words.

LAWFUL, LAWFULLY

A. Verb.

exesti (ἔξεστι, 1832), an impersonal verb, signifying "it is permitted, it is lawful" (or interrogatively, "is it lawful?"), occurs most frequently in the synoptic Gospels and the Acts; elsewhere in John 5:10; 18:31; 1 Cor. 6:12; 10:23; 2 Cor. 12:4; in Acts 2:29, it is rendered "let me (speak)," lit., "it being permitted"; in the KJV of 8:37, "thou mayest," lit., "it is permitted;" 16:21; in 21:37, "may I," lit., "is it permitted?"

Note: For *ennomos,* see C, No. 2, (under LAW).

B. Adverb.

nomimōs (νομίμως, 3545), "lawfully," is used in 1 Tim. 1:8, "the Law is good, if a man use it lawfully," i.e., agreeably to its design; the meaning here is that, while no one can be justified or obtain eternal life through its instrumentality, the believer is to have it in his heart and to fulfill its requirements; walking "not after the flesh but after the spirit," Rom. 8:4, he will "use it lawfully." In 2 Tim. 2:5 it is used of contending in the games and adhering to the rules.

LAWGIVER

nomothetēs (νομοθέτης, 3550), "a lawgiver" (see LAW, A, No. 2, and B, No. 1), occurs in Jas. 4:12, of God, as the sole "Lawgiver"; therefore, to criticize the Law is to presume to take His place, with the presumption of enacting a better law.

LAWLESS, LAWLESSNESS

A. Adjective.

anomos (ἄνομος, 459), "without law," also denotes "lawless," and is so rendered in the RV of Acts 2:23, "lawless (men)," marg., "(men) without the law," KJV, "wicked (hands);" 2 Thess. 2:8, "the lawless one" (KJV, "that wicked"), of the man of sin (2Th 2:4]; in 2 Pet. 2:8, of deeds (KJV, "unlawful"), where the thought is not simply that of doing what is unlawful, but of flagrant defiance of the known will of God. See LAW, C, No. 3.

B. Noun.

anomia (ἀνομία, 458), "lawlessness," akin to A, is most frequently translated "iniquity;" in 2 Thess. 2:7, RV, "lawlessness" (KJV, "iniquity"); "the mystery of lawlessness" is not recognized by the world, for it does not consist merely in confusion and disorder (see A); the display of "lawlessness" by the "lawless" one (v. 8) will be the effect of the attempt by the powers of darkness to overthrow the divine government. In 1 John 3:4, the RV adheres to the real meaning of the word, "every one that doeth sin (a practice, not the committal of an act) doeth also lawlessness: and sin is lawlessness." This definition of sin sets forth its essential character as the rejection of the law, or will, of God and the substitution of the will of self. See INIQUITY and synonymous words.

LAWYER

nomikos (νομικός, 3544), an adjective, "learned in the law" (see Titus 3:9, under LAW, C, No. 1), is used as a noun, "a lawyer," Matt. 22:35; Luke 7:30; 10:25; 11:45, 46, 52 (v. 53 in some mss.); 14:3; Titus 3:13, where Zenas is so named. As there is no evidence that he was one skilled in Roman jurisprudence, the term may be regarded in the usual NT sense as applying to one skilled in the Mosaic Law.

The usual name for a scribe is *grammateus*, a man of letters; for a doctor of the law, *nomodidaskalos* (see DOCTOR), "A comparison of Luke 5:17 with v. 21 and Mark 2:6 and Matt. 9:3 shows that the three terms were used synonymously, and did not denote three distinct classes. The scribes were originally simply men of letters, students of Scripture, and the name first given to them contains in itself no reference to the law; in course of time, however, they devoted themselves mainly, though by no means exclusively, to the study of the law. They became jurists rather than theologians, and received names which of themselves called attention to that fact. Some would doubtless devote themselves more to one branch of activity than to another; but a 'lawyer' might also be a 'doctor,' and the case of Gamaliel shows that a 'doctor' might also be a member of the Sanhedrin, Acts 5:34" (Eaton, in *Hastings' Bib. Dic.*).

For **LAY WAIT** see LIE IN WAIT

LAYING ON

epithesis (ἐπίθεσις, 1936), "a laying on" (*epi*, "on," *tithēmi*, "to put"), is used in the NT (a) of the "laying" on of hands by the apostles accompanied by the impartation of the Holy Spirit in outward demonstration, in the cases of those in Samaria who had believed, Acts 8:18; such supernatural manifestations were signs especially intended to give witness to Jews as to the facts of Christ and the faith, they were thus temporary; there is no record of their continuance after the time and circumstances narrated in Acts 19 (in v. 6 of which the corresponding verb *epitithēmi* is used; see below), nor was the gift delegated by the apostles to others; (b) of the similar act by the elders of a church on occasions when a member of a church was set apart for a particular work, having given evidence of qualifications necessary for it, as in the case of Timothy, 1 Tim. 4:14; of the impartation of a spiritual gift through the laying on of the hands of the apostle Paul, 2 Tim. 1:6, RV, "laying" (KJV, "putting"); cf. the verb *epitithēmi* in Acts 6:6, on the appointment of the seven, and in the case of Barnabas and Saul, 13:3, also in 19:6, (c) in Heb. 6:2, the doctrine of the "laying" on of hands refers to the act enjoined upon an Israelite in connection, e.g., with the peace offerings, Lev. 3:2, 8, 13; 4:29, 33; upon the priests in connection with the sin offering, 4:4; 16:21; upon the elders, 4:15; upon a ruler, 4:24.

The principle underlying the act was that of identification on the part of him who did it with the animal or person upon whom the hands were laid. In the Sept., 2 Chron. 25:27; Ezek. 23:11.

LEAD, LED

1. *agō* (ἄγω, 71), "to bear, bring, carry, lead," is translated by the verb "to lead," e.g., in Mark 13:11; Luke 4:1; 4:9, RV; 4:29; 22:54; 23:1, KJV only; 23:32; John 18:28 (present tense, RV), Acts 8:32; metaphorically in Rom. 2:4, of the goodness of God; 8:14 and Gal. 5:18, of the Spirit of God; 1 Cor. 12:2, of the powers of darkness instigating to idolatry; 2 Tim. 3:6, of divers lusts (in some mss., *aichmalōteuō*). In Luke 24:21 *agō* is used of the passing (or spending) of a day, and translated "it is (now the third day)"; here the verb is probably to be taken impersonally, according to idiomatic usage, in the sense "there is passing the third day." See KEEP, *Note* (2).

2. *anagō* (ἀνάγω, 321), "to lead up" (*ana*, "up"), is used of Christ in being "led" up by the Spirit into the wilderness, Matt. 4:1; Luke 4:5 (KJV, "taking up"); by the elders of the people into their council, Luke 22:66, "led away."

3. *apagō* (ἀπάγω, 520), "to lead away" (*apo*, "away"), is used of a way "leading" to destruction, Matt. 7:13, to life, v. 14; of those who "led" Christ away from Gethsemane, Mark 14:44; in some mss., John 18:13, to Annas (the best mss. have No. 1 here); to Caiaphas, Matt. 26:57; Mark 14:53; to Pilate, Matt. 27:2; to the Praetorium, Mark 15:16; to crucifixion, Matt. 27:31; Luke 23:26; in some mss. John 19:16; of "leading" an animal away to watering, Luke 13:15; of being "led" away to idolatry, 1 Cor. 12:2, RV, "led away" (KJV, "carried away"). Some mss. have it in Acts 24:7 (KJV, "took away"). It is translated "bring" in 23:17. In 12:19 it signifies "to put to death." See DEATH, C, No. 3.

4. *periagō* (περιάγω, 4013), used transitively, denotes "to lead about," 1 Cor. 9:5. For the intransitive use, see GO, No. 9.

5. *pherō* (φέρω, 5342), "to bear, carry," is used metaphorically of a gate, as "leading" to a city, Acts 12:10.

6. *hodegeō* (ὁδηγέω, 3594), "to lead the way": see GUIDE, B, No. 1.

7. *eisagō* (εἰσάγω, 1521), "to bring into," is translated "to be led into" in Acts 21:37, KJV (RV, "to be brought into").

8. *sunapagō* (συναπάγω, 4879), always in the passive voice, "to be carried or led away with," is translated "being led away with" in 2 Pet. 3:17, KJV (RV, "being carried away with").

9. *exagō* (ἐξάγω, 1806), "to lead out," is rendered by the verb "to lead, out or forth," in Mark 15:20 (in some mss. in

8:23, the best have *ekpherō*, "to bring out)"; Luke 24:50; John 10:3; Acts 7:36, 40 (KJV "brought"), and 13:17, RV; Acts 21:38; Heb. 8:9.

10. *anapherō* (ἀναφέρω, 399), "to carry or lead up," is translated "leadeth ... up" in the KJV of Mark 9:2 (RV "bringeth ... up").

11. *eispherō* (εἰσφέρω, 1533), "to bring in, or into," is translated "lead (us not) into," in Matt. 6:13 and Luke 11:4 (RV, "bring ... into"), of temptation.

12. *planaō* (πλανάω, 4105), "to lead astray" (akin to *planē*, "a wandering"), is translated "lead ... astray," metaphorically, in Matt. 24:4, 5, 11 and Mark 13:5, 6 (KJV, "deceive").

13. *apoplanaō* (ἀποπλανάω, 635), "to cause to go astray" (*apo*, "away from," and No. 12), is used metaphorically of "leading into error," Mark 13:22, RV, "lead astray" (KJV, "seduce"); passive voice in 1 Tim. 6:10 (KJV, "erred").

Notes: (1) In Rev. 13:10, some mss. have *sunagō*, "to bring together," translated "leadeth (into captivity)," KJV and RV marg. (RV text, "is for"). (2) For the verb *diagō*, "to lead a life," 1 Tim. 2:2, see LIVE, No. 7. (3) For *thriambeuō*, to "lead in triumph," 2 Cor. 2:14, RV, see TRIUMPH. (4) See also HAND (lead by the).

For **LEADERS** (Matt. 15:14) see GUIDE

LEAP

1. *hallomai* (ἅλλομαι, 242), "to leap" (akin to *halma*, "a leap"), is used (a) metaphorically, of the "springing" up of water, John 4:14; (b) literally, of the "leaping" of healed cripples, Acts 3:8 (2nd part); 14:10.

2. *skirtaō* (σκιρτάω, 4640), "to leap," is found in Luke 1:41, 44 and 6:23, there translated "leap for joy"; in 1:44 the words "for joy" are expressed separately.

3. *exallomai* (ἐξάλλομαι, 1814), "to leap up" (lit., "out," *ek*, and No. 1), is said in Acts 3:8 (1st part) of the cripple healed by Peter (cf. No. 1, above).

4. *ephallomai* (ἐφάλλομαι, 2177), "to leap upon" (*epi*, "upon," and No. 1), is said of the demoniac in Acts 19:16.

LEARN, LEARNED (be)

1. *manthanō* (μανθάνω, 3129) denotes (a) "to learn" (akin to *mathētēs*, "a disciple"), "to increase one's knowledge," or "be increased in knowledge," frequently "to learn by inquiry, or observation," e.g., Matt. 9:13; 11:29; 24:32; Mark 13:28; John 7:15; Rom. 16:17; 1 Cor. 4:6; 14:35; Phil. 4:9; 2 Tim. 3:14; Rev. 14:3; said of "learning" Christ, Eph. 4:20, not simply the doctrine of Christ, but Christ Himself, a process not merely of getting to know the person but of so applying the knowledge as to walk differently from the rest of the Gentiles; (b) "to ascertain," Acts 23:27, RV, "learned" (KJV, "understood"); Gal. 3:2, "This only would I learn from you," perhaps with a tinge of irony in the enquiry, the answer to which would settle the question of the validity of the new Judaistic gospel they were receiving; (c) "to learn by use and practice, to acquire the habit of, be accustomed to," e.g., Phil. 4:11; 1 Tim. 5:4, 13; Titus 3:14; Heb. 5:8.

2. *ginoskō* (γινώσκω, 1097), "to know by observation and experience," is translated "to learn," in the RV of Mark 15:45; John 12:9. See ALLOW

3. *akriboō* (ἀκριβόω, 198), "to learn carefully," is so translated in Matt. 2:7, 16, RV (KJV, "diligently enquired").

4. *mueō* (μυέω, 3453), "to initiate into mysteries," is translated "I have learned the secret" (passive voice, perfect tense) in Phil. 4:12, RV (KJV, "I am instructed"). See INSTRUCT.

Note: Paideuō, "to teach, instruct, train," is translated "instructed" in Acts 7:22, RV (KJV, "learned"); in 1 Tim. 1:20, "(that) they might be taught," KJV, "(that) they may learn."

LEARNING (Noun)

1. *gramma* (γράμμα, 1121), "a letter," is used in the plural in Acts 26:24, with the meaning "learning": "(thy much) learning (doth turn thee to madness)," RV, possibly an allusion to the Jewish Scriptures, to which the apostle had been appealing; in John 7:15, "(How knoweth this Man) letters" (KJV marg., "learning"), the succeeding phrase "not having learned" is illustrated in the papyri, where it indicates inability to write. See BILL.

2. *didaskalia* (διδασκαλία, 1319), "teaching, instruction" (akin to *didaskō*, "to teach"), is translated "learning" in Rom. 15:4. See DOCTRINE.

LEAST

1. *elachistos* (ἐλάχιστος, 1646), "least," is a superlative degree formed from the word *elachus*, "little," the place of which was taken by *mikros* (the comparative degree being *elassōn*, "less"); it is used of (a) size, Jas. 3:4; (b) amount; of the management of affairs, Luke 16:10 (twice), 19:17, "very little"; (c) importance, 1 Cor. 6:2, "smallest (matters)"; (d) authority: of commandments, Matt. 5:19; (e) estimation, as to persons, Matt. 5:19 (2nd part); 25:40, 45; 1 Cor. 15:9; as to a town, Matt. 2:6; as to activities or operations, Luke 12:26; 1 Cor. 4:3, "a very small thing."

2. *elachistoteros* (ἐλαχιστότερος, 1647), a comparative degree formed from No. 1, is used in Eph. 3:8, "less than the least."

3. *mikros* (μικρός, 3398), "small, little," is translated "the least" in Acts 8:10 and Heb. 8:11, with reference to rank or influence.

4. *mikroteros* (μικρός, 3398), the comparative of No. 3, is used of (a) size, Matt. 13:32, KJV, "the least," RV, "less;" Mark 4:31 [cf. No. 1 (a)]; (b) estimation, Matt. 11:11 and Luke 7:28,

KJV, "least," RV, "but little," marg., "lesser" (in the kingdom of heaven), those in the kingdom itself being less than John the Baptist [cf. No. 1 (e)]; Luke 9:48.

Notes: (1) In 1 Cor. 6:4, KJV, *exoutheneō*, in the passive voice, "to be of no account," is translated "is least esteemed" (RV, "are of no account"). (2) In Luke 19:42, the adverbial phrase *kai ge*, "at least," is found in some mss.; the RV follows those in which it is absent. (3) In 1 Cor. 9:2, KJV, the phrase *alla ge* is rendered "doubtless;" RV, "at least." (4) In Acts 5:15, the phrase *k'an* (for *kai ean*, "even if") denotes "at the least."

LEAVEN (Noun and Verb)

A. Noun.

zumē (ζύμη, 2219), "leaven, sour dough, in a high state of fermentation," was used in general in making bread. It required time to fulfill the process. Hence, when food was required at short notice, unleavened cakes were used, e.g., Gen. 18:6; 19:3; Exod. 12:8. The Israelites were forbidden to use "leaven" for seven days at the time of Passover, that they might be reminded that the Lord brought them out of Egypt "in haste," Deut. 16:3, with Exod. 12:11; the unleavened bread, insipid in taste, reminding them, too, of their afflictions, and of the need of self-judgment, is called "the bread of affliction." "Leaven" was forbidden in all offerings to the Lord by fire, Lev. 2:11; 6:17. Being bred of corruption and spreading through the mass of that in which it is mixed, and therefore symbolizing the pervasive character of evil, "leaven" was utterly inconsistent in offerings which typified the propitiatory sacrifice of Christ.

In the OT "leaven" is not used in a metaphorical sense. In the NT it is used (a) metaphorically (1) of corrupt doctrine, Matt. 13:33 and Luke 13:21, of error as mixed with the truth (there is no valid reason for regarding the symbol here differently from its application elsewhere in the NT); Matt. 16:6, 11; Mark 8:15 (1st part); Luke 12:1; that the kingdom of heaven is likened to "leaven," does not mean that the kingdom is "leaven." The same statement, as made in other parables, shows that it is the whole parable which constitutes the similitude of the kingdom; the history of Christendom confirms the fact that the pure meal of the doctrine of Christ has been adulterated with error; (2) of corrupt practices, Mark 8:15 (2nd part), the reference to the Herodians being especially applied to their irreligion; 1 Cor. 5:7, 8; (b) literally in Matt. 16:12, and in the general statements in 1 Cor. 5:6 and Gal. 5:9, where the implied applications are to corrupt practice and corrupt doctrine respectively.

B. Verb.

zumoō (ζυμόω, 2220) signifies "to leaven, to act as leaven," passive voice in Matt. 13:33 and Luke 13:21; active voice in 1 Cor. 5:6 and Gal. 5:9.

For **LED** see LEAD

LEGION

legiōn (λεγεών, 3003), otherwise spelled *legeōn*, "a legion," occurs in Matt. 26:53, of angels; in Mark 5:9, 15, and Luke 8:30, of demons. Among the Romans a "legion" was primarily a chosen (*lego*, "to choose") body of soldiers divided into ten cohorts, and numbering from 4,200 to 6,000 men (Gk. *speira*). In the time of our Lord it formed a complete army of infantry and cavalry, of upwards of 5,000 men. The "legions" were not brought into Judea till the outbreak of the Jewish war (A.D. 66), as they were previously employed in the frontier provinces of the Empire. Accordingly in its NT use the word has its other and more general significance "of a large number."

LEPER

lepros (λεπρός, 3015), an adjective, primarily used of "psoriasis," characterized by an eruption of rough scaly patches; later, "leprous," but chiefly used as a noun, "a leper," Matt. 8:2; 10:8; 11:5; Mark 1:40; Luke 4:27; 7:22; 17:12; especially of Simon. mentioned in Matt. 26:6; Mark 14:3.

LEPROSY

lepra (λέπρα, 3014), akin to *lepros* (above), is mentioned in Matt. 8:3; Mark 1:42; Luke 5:12, 13. In the removal of other maladies the verb "to heal" (*iaomai*) is used, but in the removal of "leprosy," the verb "to cleanse" (*katharizō*), save in the statement concerning the Samaritan, Luke 17:15, "when he saw that he was healed." Matt. 10:8 and Luke 4:27 indicate that the disease was common in the nation. Only twelve cases are recorded in the NT, but these are especially selected. For the Lord's commands to the leper mentioned in Matthew 8 and to the ten in Luke 17, see Lev. 14:2-32.

For **LET** (KJV in Rom. 1:13 and 2 Thess. 2:7) see HINDER

LETTER

1. *gramma* (γράμμα, 1121) primarily denotes "that which is traced or drawn, a picture"; then, "that which is written," (a) "a character, letter of the alphabet," 2 Cor. 3:7; "written," lit., "(in) letters," Gal. 6:11; here the reference is not to the length of the epistle (Paul never uses *gramma*, either in the singular or the plural of his epistles; of these he uses *epistolē*, No. 2), but to the size of the characters written by his own hand (probably from this verse to the end, as the use of the past tense, "I have written," is, according to Greek idiom,

the equivalent of our "I am writing"). Moreover, the word for "letters" is here in the dative case, *grammasin*, "with (how large) letters"; (b) "a writing, a written document, a bond" (KJV, "bill") Luke 16:6, 7; (c) "a letter, by way of correspondence," Acts 28:21; (d) the Scriptures of the OT, 2 Tim. 3:15; (e) "learning," John 7:15, "letters"; Acts 26:24, "(much) learning" (lit., "many letters"); in the papyri an illiterate person is often spoken of as one who does not know "letters," "which never means anything else than inability to write" (Moulton and Milligan); (f) "the letter," the written commandments of the Word of God, in contrast to the inward operation of the Holy Spirit under the New Covenant, Rom. 2:27, 29; 7:6; 2 Cor. 3:6; (g) "the books of Moses," John 5:47.

2. *epistolē* (ἐπιστολή, 1992): see EPISTLE.

For **LEWD and LEWDNESS** see VILE

LIAR

A. Nouns.

pseustēs (ψεύστης, 5583), "a liar," occurs in John 8:44, 55; Rom. 3:4; 1 Tim. 1:10; Titus 1:12; 1 John 1:10; 2:4, 22; 4:20; 5:10.

B. Adjective.

pseudēs (ψευδής, 5571), "lying, false" (Eng. "pseudo-"), rendered "false" in Acts 6:13 and in the RV of Rev. 2:2 (KJV, "liars"), is used as a noun, "liars," in Rev. 21:8; See FALSE.

Note: Many compound nouns are formed by the prefix *pseudo-*: see, e.g., APOSTLES, CHRISTS, PROPHET, TEACHERS, WITNESS.

LIBERAL, LIBERALITY, LIBERALLY

A. Noun.

1. *haplotēs* (ἁπλότης, 572) denotes (a) "simplicity, sincerity, unaffectedness" (from *haplous*, "single, simple," in contrast to *diplous*, "double"), Rom. 12:8, "simplicity"; 2 Cor. 11:3 (in some mss. in 1:12); Eph. 6:5 and Col. 3:22, "singleness"; (b) "simplicity as manifested in generous giving," "liberality," 2 Cor. 8:2; 9:11 (KJV, "bountifulness," RV marg., "singleness"); 9:13 (KJV, "liberal"). See BOUNTY, No. 2.

2. *charis* (χάρις, 5485) is rendered "liberality" in 1 Cor. 16:3, KJV. See BOUNTY, No. 3.

B. Adverb.

haplōs (ἁπλῶς, 574), "liberally, with singleness of heart," is used in Jas. 1:5 of God as the gracious and "liberal" Giver. The word may be taken either (a) in a logical sense, signifying unconditionally, simply, or (b) in a moral sense, generously; for the double meaning compare A, No. 3. On this passage Hort writes as follows: "Later writers comprehend under the one word the whole magnanimous and honorable type of character in which singleness of mind is the central feature."

LIBERTY

A. Nouns.

1. *anesis* (ἄνεσις, 425), "a loosening, relaxation," is translated "liberty" in Acts 24:23, KJV. See INDULGENCE.

2. *aphesis* (ἄφεσις, 859), "dismissal, release, forgiveness," is rendered "liberty" in the KJV of Luke 4:18, RV, "release." See FORGIVENESS.

3. *eleutheria* (ἐλευθερία, 1657): see FREEDOM.

4. *exousia* (ἐξουσία, 1849), "authority, right," is rendered "liberty" in 1 Cor. 8:9 (marg., "power"), "this liberty of yours," or "this right which you assert."

B. Adjective.

eleutheros (ἐλεύθερος, 1658) is rendered "at liberty" in 1 Cor. 7:39, KJV (RV "free"). See FREE.

C. Verbs.

1. *apoluō* (ἀπολύω, 630) is translated "to set at liberty" in Acts 26:32 and Heb. 13:23. See DISMISS.

2. *apostellō* (ἀποστέλλω, 649), "to send away," is translated "to set at liberty" in Luke 4:18. See SEND.

Note: In Acts 27:3, KJV, *epitrepō* is rendered "gave ... liberty" (RV "gave ... leave").

LIE (falsehood: Noun and Verb) A. Nouns.

1. *pseudos* (ψεῦδος, 5579), "a falsehood, lie" (see also under LIAR), is translated "lie" in John 8:44 (lit., "the lie"); Rom. 1:25, where it stands by metonymy for an idol, as, e.g., in Isa. 44:20; Jer. 10:14; 13:25; Amos 2:4 (plural); 2 Thess. 2:11, with special reference to the lie of v. 4, that man is God (cf. Gen. 3:5); 1 John 2:21, 27; Rev. 21:27; 22:15; in Eph. 4:25, KJV "lying," RV, "falsehood," the practice; in Rev. 14:5, RV, "lie." (some mss. have *dolos*, "guile," KJV); 2 Thess. 2:9, where "lying wonders" is, lit., "wonders of falsehood," i.e., wonders calculated to deceive (cf. Rev. 13:13-15), the purpose being to deceive people into the acknowledgement of the spurious claim to deity on the part of the Man of Sin.

Note: In Rom. 1:25 the "lie" or idol is the outcome of pagan religion; in 1 John 2:21, 22 the "lie" is the denial that Jesus is the Christ; in 2 Thess. 2:11 the "lie" is the claim of the Man of Sin.

2. *pseusma* (ψεῦσμα, 5582), "a falsehood," or "an acted lie," Rom. 3:7, where "my lie" is not idolatry, but either the universal false attitude of man toward God or that with which his detractors charged the apostle; the former seems to be the meaning.

B. Adjectives.

1. *pseudologos* (ψευδολόγος, 5573) denotes "speaking falsely" (*pseudēs*, "false," *logos*, "a word") in 1 Tim. 4:2, where the adjective is translated "that speak lies," RV (KJV, "speaking

lies") and is applied to "demons," the actual utterances being by their human agents.

2. *apseudēs* (ἀψευδής, 893) denotes "free from falsehood" (*a*, negative, *pseudēs*, "false"), truthful, Titus 1:2, of God, "who cannot lie."

C. Verb.

pseudō (ψεύδω, 5574), "to deceive by lies" (always in the middle voice in the NT), is used (a) absolutely, in Matt. 5:11, "falsely," lit., "lying" (v, marg.); Rom. 9:1; 2 Cor. 11:31; Gal. 1:20; Col. 3:9 (where the verb is followed by the preposition *eis*, "to"); 1 Tim. 2:7; Heb. 6:18; Jas. 3:14 (where it is followed by the preposition *kata*, "against"); 1 John 1:6; Rev. 3:9; (b) transitively, with a direct object (without a preposition following), Acts 5:3 (with the accusative case) "to lie to (the Holy Ghost)," RV marg., "deceive"; v. 4 (with the dative case) "thou hast (not) lied (unto men, but unto God)."

LIFE, LIVING, LIFETIME, LIFE-GIVING

A. Nouns.

1. *zōē* (ζωή, 2222) (Eng., "zoo," "zoology") is used in the NT "of life as a principle, life in the absolute sense, life as God has it, that which the Father has in Himself, and which He gave to the Incarnate Son to have in Himself, John 5:26, and which the Son manifested in the world, 1 John 1:2. From this life man has become alienated in consequence of the Fall, Eph. 4:18, and of this life men become partakers through faith in the Lord Jesus Christ, John 3:15, who becomes its Author to all such as trust in Him, Acts 3:15, and who is therefore said to be 'the life' of the believer, Col. 3:4, for the life that He gives He maintains, John 6:35, 63. Eternal life is the present actual possession of the believer because of his relationship with Christ, John 5:24; 1 John 3:14, and that it will one day extend its domain to the sphere of the body is assured by the Resurrection of Christ, 2 Cor. 5:4; 2 Tim. 1:10. This life is not merely a principle of power and mobility, however, for it has moral associations which are inseparable from it, as of holiness and righteousness. Death and sin, life and holiness, are frequently contrasted in the Scriptures.

"*Zōē* is also used of that which is the common possession of all animals and men by nature, Acts 17:25; 1 John 5:16, and of the present sojourn of man upon the earth with reference to its duration, Luke 16:25; 1 Cor. 15:19; 1 Tim. 4:8; 1 Pet. 3:10. 'This life' is a term equivalent to 'the gospel,' 'the faith,' 'Christianity,' Acts 5:20."

Death came through sin, Rom. 5:12, which is rebellion against God. Sin thus involved the forfeiting of the "life." "The life of the flesh is in the blood," Lev. 17:11. Therefore the impartation of "life" to the sinner must be by a death caused by the shedding of that element which is the life of the flesh. "It is the blood that maketh atonement by reason of the life" (*id.* RV). The separation from God caused by the forfeiting of the "life" could be removed only by a sacrifice in which the victim and the offerer became identified. This which was appointed in the typical offerings in Israel received its full accomplishment in the voluntary sacrifice of Christ. The shedding of the blood in the language of Scripture involves the taking or the giving of the "life." Since Christ had no sins of his own to die for, His death was voluntary and vicarious, John 10:15 with Isa. 53:5, 10, 12; 2 Cor. 5:21. In His sacrifice He endured the divine judgment due to man's sin. By this means the believer becomes identified with Him in His deathless "life," through His resurrection, and enjoys conscious and eternal fellowship with God.

2. *bios* (βίος, 979) (cf. Eng. words beginning with *bio*), is used in three respects (a) of "the period or duration of life," e.g., in the KJV of 1 Pet. 4:3, "the time past of our life" (the RV follows the mss. which omit "of our life"); Luke 8:14; 2 Tim. 2:4; (b) of "the manner of life, life in regard to its moral conduct," 1 Tim. 2:2; 1 John 2:16; (c) of "the means of life, livelihood, maintenance, living," Mark 12:44; Luke 8:43; 15:12, 30; 21:4; 1 John 3:17, "goods," RV (KJV, "good"). See GOODS.

Note: "While *zōē* is 'life' intensive ... *bios* is 'life' extensive .... In *bios*, used as manner of 'life,' there is an ethical sense often inhering which, in classical Greek at least, *zōē* does not possess." In Scripture *zōē* is "the nobler word, expressing as it continually does, all of highest and best which the saints possess in God" (Trench, *Syn.* Sec. XXVII).

3. *psuchē* (ψυχή, 5590), besides its meanings, "heart, mind, soul," denotes "life" in two chief respects, (a) "breath of life, the natural life," e.g., Matt. 2:20; 6:25; Mark 10:45; Luke 12:22; Acts 20:10; Rev. 8:9; 12:11 (cf. Lev. 17:11; Esth. 8:11); (b) "the seat of personality," e.g., Luke 9:24, explained in v. 25 as "own self" See list under SOUL. See also HEART, MIND.

Notes: (1) "Speaking generally, *psuchō*, is the individual life, the living being, whereas *zōē*, is the life of that being, cf. Ps. 66:9, 'God ... which holdeth our soul (*psuchē*) in life (*zōē*),' and John 10:10, 'I came that they may have life (*zōē*),' with v. 11, 'The Good Shepherd layeth down His life (*psuchē*) for the sheep.'" (2) In Rev. 13:15, KJV, *pneuma*, "breath," is translated "life" (RV, "breath"). (3) In 2 Cor. 1:8, "we despaired even of life," the verb *zaō*, "to live," is used in the infinitive mood, as a noun, and translated "life" (lit., "living"). In Heb. 2:15 the infinitive mood of the same verb is translated "lifetime."

4. *biōsis* (βίωσις, 981), from *bioō*, "to spend one's life, to live," denotes "a manner of life," Acts 26:4.

5. *agōgē* (ἀγωγή, 72), "a manner of life," 2 Tim. 3:10; see CONDUCT.

6. *anastrophē* (ἀναστροφή, 391), "behavior, conduct," is translated "manner of life" (KJV "conversation") in the RV of

Gal. 1:13; 1 Tim. 4:12; 1 Pet. 1:18; 3:16; "living," in 1 Pet. 1:15. See BEHAVIOR.

B. Adjectives.

1. *biōtikos* (βιωτικός, 982), "pertaining to life" (*bios*), is translated "of this life," in Luke 21:34, with reference to cares; in 1 Cor. 6:3 "(things) that pertain to this life," and v. 4, "(things) pertaining to this life," i.e., matters of this world, concerning which Christians at Corinth were engaged in public lawsuits one with another; such matters were to be regarded as relatively unimportant in view of the great tribunals to come under the jurisdiction of saints hereafter. Moulton and Milligan (*Vocab.*) illustrate the word from phrases in the papyri, e.g., "business (documents)"; "business concerning my livelihood"; "(stories) of ordinary life."

2. *apsuchos* (ἄψυχος, 895) denotes "lifeless inanimate" (*a*, negative, and *psuchē*, see A, No. 3), "without life," 1 Cor. 14:7.

C. Verb.

zōopoieō (ζωοποιέω, 2227), "to make alive, cause to live, quicken" (from *zōē*, "life," and *poieō*, "to make"), is used as follows:

"(a) of God as the bestower of every kind of life in the universe, 1 Tim. 6:13 (*zōogoneō*, to preserve alive, is the alternative reading adopted by most editors; see LIVE, No. 6), and, particularly, of resurrection life, John 5:21; Rom. 4:17; (b) of Christ, who also is the bestower of resurrection life, John 5:21 (2nd part); 1 Cor. 15:45; cf. v. 22; (c) of the resurrection of Christ in "the body of His glory," 1 Pet. 3:18; (d) of the power of reproduction inherent in seed, which presents a certain analogy with resurrection, 1 Cor. 15:36; (e) of the 'changing,' or 'fashioning anew,' of the bodies of the living, which corresponds with, and takes place at the same time as, the resurrection of the dead in Christ, Rom. 8:11; (f) of the impartation of spiritual life, and the communication of spiritual sustenance generally, John 6:63; 2 Cor. 3:6; Gal. 3:2. See QUICKEN, and cf. *sunzōopoieō*, "to quicken together with," Eph. 2:5 and Col. 2:13.

Notes: (1) For the verb *diagō*, "to lead a life," see LIVE, No. 7. (2) For *politeuō*, in Phil. 1:27, RV, "let your manner of life be," see LIVE, No. 8.

LIGHT, Noun, and Verb (bring to, give), LIGHTEN

A. Nouns.

1. *phōs* (φῶς, 5457), akin to *phaō*, "to give light" (from roots *pha-* and *phan-*, expressing "light as seen by the eye," and, metaphorically, as "reaching the mind," whence *phainō*, "to make to appear," *phaneros*, "evident," etc.); cf. Eng., "phosphorus" (lit., "light-bearing"). "Primarily light is a luminous emanation, probably of force, from certain bodies, which enables the eye to discern form and color. Light requires an organ adapted for its reception (Matt. 6:22). Where the eye is absent, or where it has become impaired from any cause, light is useless. Man, naturally, is incapable of receiving spiritual light inasmuch as he lacks the capacity for spiritual things, 1 Cor. 2:14. Hence believers are called 'sons of light,' Luke 16:8, not merely because they have received a revelation from God, but because in the New Birth they have received the spiritual capacity for it.

"Apart from natural phenomena, light is used in Scripture of (a) the glory of God's dwellingplace, 1 Tim. 6:16; (b) the nature of God, 1 John 1:5; (c) the impartiality of God, Jas. 1:17; (d) the favor of God, Ps. 4:6; of the King, Prov. 16:15; of an influential man, Job 29:24; (e) God, as the illuminator of His people, Isa. 60:19, 20; (f) the Lord Jesus as the illuminator of men, John 1:4, 5, 9; 3:19; 8:12; 9:5; 12:35, 36, 46; Acts 13:47; (g) the illuminating power of the Scriptures, Ps. 119:105; and of the judgments and commandments of God, Isa. 51:4; Prov. 6:23, cf. Ps. 43:3; (h) the guidance of God Job 29:3; Ps. 112:4; Isa. 58:10; and, ironically, of the guidance of man, Rom. 2:19; (i) salvation, 1 Pet. 2:9; (j) righteousness, Rom. 13:12; 2 Cor. 11:14, 15; 1 John 2:9, 10; (k) witness for God, Matt. 5:14, 16; John 5:35; (l) prosperity and general well-being, Esth. 8:16; Job 18:18; Isa. 58:8-10."

2. *phōstēr* (φωστήρ, 5458) denotes "a luminary, light," or "light-giver"; it is used figuratively of believers, as shining in the spiritual darkness of the world, Phil. 2:15; in Rev. 21:11 it is used of Christ as the "Light" reflected in and shining through the heavenly city (cf. v. 23). In the Sept., Gen. 1:14, 16.

3. *phōtismos* (φωτισμός, 5462), "an illumination, light," is used metaphorically in 2 Cor. 4:4, of the "light" of the gospel, and in v. 6, of the knowledge of the glory of God. In the Sept., Job 3:9; Ps. 27:1; 44:3; 78:14; 90:8; 139:11.

4. *phengos* (φέγγος, 5338), "brightness, luster," is used of the "light" of the moon, Matt. 24:29; Mark 13:24; of a lamp, Luke 11:33 (some mss. have *phōs*, here).

5. *luchnos* (λύχνος, 3088), "a hand-lamp": see LAMP.

6. *lampas* (λαμπάς, 2985), "a torch": see LAMP.

B. Verbs.

1. *phōtizō* (φωτίζω, 5461), used (a) intransitively, signifies "to shine, give light," Rev. 22:5; (b) transitively, (1) "to illumine, to light, enlighten, to be lightened," Luke 11:36; Rev. 21:23; in the passive voice, Rev. 18:1; metaphorically, of spiritual enlightenment, John 1:9; Eph. 1:18; 3:9, "to make ... see;" Heb. 6:4; 10:32, "ye were enlightened," RV (KJV, "... illuminated"); (2) "to bring to light," 1 Cor. 4:5 (of God's act in the future); 2 Tim. 1:10 (of God's act in the past). See ENLIGHTEN.

2. *epiphauskō* (ἐπιφαύσκω, 2017), or possibly *epiphauō*, "to shine forth," is rendered "shall give ... light," in Eph. 5:14, KJV (RV, "shall shine upon"), of the glory of Christ,

illumining the believer who fulfills the conditions, so that being guided by His "light" he reflects His character. See SHINE. Cf. *epiphōskō*, "to dawn" (really a variant form of *epiphauskō*).

3. *lampō* (λάμπω, 2989), "to give the light of a torch," is rendered "giveth light" in Matt. 5:15, KJV (RV, "shineth). See SHINE.

4. *epiphainō* (ἐπιφαίνω, 2014), transitively, "to show forth" (*epi*, "upon," *phainō*, "to cause to shine"), is used intransitively and metaphorically in Luke 1:79, and rendered "to give light," KJV (RV, "to shine upon"). See APPEAR, SHINE.

5. *haptō* (ἅπτω, 681), "to kindle a fire" and so give "light."

6. *kaiō* (καίω, 2545), "to burn," is translated "do (men) light" in Matt. 5:15. See BURN.

7. *astraptō* (ἀστράπτω, 797), "to flash forth lighten as lightning" (akin to *astrapē*, "lightning"), occurs in Luke 17:24; 24:4 (KJV "shining"; RV, "dazzling"). See DAZZLING.

Note: In Luke 2:32, KJV, the noun *apokalupsis*, "an unveiling, revelation," preceded by *eis*, "unto, with a view to," is rendered "to lighten" (RV, "for revelation"; marg., "(the) unveiling"). See REVELATION.

C. Adjective.

phōteinos (φωτεινός, 5460), from *phos* (A No. 1), "bright," is rendered "full of light" in Matt. 6:22; Luke 11:34, 36 (twice), figuratively, of the single-mindedness of the eye, which acts as the lamp of the body; in Matt. 17:5, "bright," of a cloud. See BRIGHT.

LIGHT (to light upon)

Notes: (1) In Matt. 3:16, KJV, *erchomai*, "to come," is translated "lighting"; RV, "coming." (2) In Rev. 7:16. KJV, *piptō*, "to fall," is translated "shall ... light" (RV, "shall ... strike").

LIGHT, LIGHTEN (as to weight)

A. Adjective.

elaphros (ἐλαφρός, 1645), "light in weight, easy to bear," is used of the burden imparted by Christ, Matt. 11:30; of affliction, 2 Cor. 4:17.

B. Verb.

kouphizo (κουφίζω, 2893), "to make light, lighten" (the adjective *kouphos*, not in NT, denotes "slight, light, empty"), is used of "lightening" the ship, in Acts 27:38.

C. Noun.

elaphria (ἐλαφρία, 1644), "lightness," 2 Cor. 1:17, KJV.

LIGHT OF (make), LIGHTLY

ameleō (ἀμελέω, 272) denotes "to be careless, not to care" (*a*, negative, and *melei*, an impersonal verb, signifying "it is a care"), Matt. 22:5, "they made light of (it)," lit. "making light of (it)," aorist participle, indicating the definiteness of their decision. See NEGLECT, NEGLIGENT, REGARD.

Note: In Mark 9:39, KJV, the adverb *tachu*, "quickly," is translated "lightly" (RV, "quickly").

LIGHTNING

astrapē (ἀστραπή, 796) denotes (a) "lightning" (akin to LIGHT, B, No. 7), Matt. 24:27; 28:3; Luke 10:18; 17:24; in the plural, Rev. 4:5; 8:5; 11:19; 16:18; (b) "bright shining," or "shining brightness," Luke 11:36. See SHINING.

LIKE, LIKE (as to, unto), (be) LIKE, (make) LIKE, LIKE (things), LIKEN

A. Adjectives.

1. *homoios* (ὅμοιος, 3664), "like, resembling, such as, the same as," is used (a) of appearance or form John 9:9; Rev. 1:13, 15; 2:18; 4:3 (twice), 6, 7; 9:7 (twice), 10, 19; 11:1; 13:2, 11; 14:14; (b) of ability, condition, nature, Matt. 22:39; Acts 17:29; Gal. 5:21, "such like," lit., "and the (things) similar to these"; 1 John 3:2; Rev. 13:4; 18:18; 21:11, 18; (c) of comparison in parables, Matt. 13:31, 33, 44, 45, 47; 20:1; Luke 13:18, 19, 21; (d) of action, thought, etc. Matt. 11:16; 13:52; Luke 6:47, 48, 49; 7:31, 32; 12:36; John 8:55; Jude 7.

2. *isos* (ἴσος, 2470), "equal" (the same in size, quality, etc.), is translated "like," of the gift of the Spirit, Acts 11:17. .

3. *paromoios* (παρόμοιος, 3946), "much like" (*para*, "beside," and No. 1), is used in Mark 7:13, in the neuter plural, "(many such) like things."

B. Verbs.

1. *homoioō* (ὁμοιόω, 3666), "to make like" (akin to A, No. 1), is used (a) especially in the parables, with the significance of comparing, "likening," or, in the passive voice, "being likened," Matt. 7:24, 26; 11:16; 13:24; 18:23; 22:2 (RV, "likened"); 25:1; Mark 4:30; Luke 7:31; 13:18, RV, "liken" (KJV, "resemble"); v. 20; in several of these instances the point of resemblance is not a specific detail, but the whole circumstances of the parable; (b) of making "like," or, in the passive voice, of being made or becoming "like," Matt. 6:8; Acts 14:11, "in the likeness of (men)," lit., "being made like" (aorist participle, passive); Rom. 9:29; Heb. 2:17, of Christ in being "made like" unto His brethren, i.e., in partaking of human nature, apart from sin (cf. v. 14).

2. *eoika* (ἔοικα, 1503v), a perfect tense with a present meaning (from an obsolete present, *eikō*), denotes "to be like, to resemble," Jas. 1:6, 23. In the Sept., Job 6:3, 25.

3. *paromoiazō* (παρομοιάζω, 3945), "to be like" (from *para*, "by," and a verbal form from *homoios*, A, No. 1), is used in Matt. 23:27 (perhaps with intensive force), in the Lord's comparison of the scribes and Pharisees to whitened sepulchres.

4. *aphomoioō* (ἀφομοιόω, 871), "to make like" (*apo*, "from," and No. 1), is used in Heb. 7:3, of Melchizedek as "made like"

the Son of God, i.e., in the facts related and withheld in the Genesis record.

Note: For the KJV of Rom. 1:23, "made like," see LIKENESS, No. 1.

C. Adverbs.

1. *hōs* (ὡς, 5613), used as a relative adverb of manner, means "as, like as," etc. and is translated "like," e.g., in Matt. 6:29; Mark 4:31; Luke 12:27; in Acts 3:22 and 7:37 (see RV, marg.); in 8:32 (2nd part), RV, "as" (KJV, "like"); Rev. 2:18, RV (the rendering should have been "as" here); 18:21, RV, "as it were" (KJV, "like"); 21:11, 2nd part (ditto).

2. *hōsper* (ὥσπερ, 5618), "just as," is rendered "like as" in Rom. 6:4.

Notes: (1) In Heb. 4:15, the phrase *kath'homoiotēta* (*kata*, "according to," *homoiotēs*, "a likeness," i.e., "after the similitude"), is rendered "like as," in the statement that Christ has been tempted in all points "like as we are, yet without sin"; this may mean either "according to the likeness of our temptations," or "in accordance with His likeness to us." (2) In the following the most authentic mss. have *hōs*, "as," for *hōsei*, "like," in the KJV; Mark 1:10; Luke 3:22; John 1:32; Rev. 1:14. (3) In John 7:46, KJV, the combination of the adverb *houtōs*, thus, with *hōs*, "as," is translated "like," RV "(never man) so (spake)." (4) In 1 Thess. 2:14, KJV, *ta auta*, "the same (things)," is translated "like (things)," RV, "the same (things)."

LIKEMINDED

1. *isopsuchos* (ἰσόψυχος, 2473), lit., "of equal soul" (*isos*, "equal," *psuchē*, "the soul"), is rendered "likeminded" in Phil. 2:20. In the Sept., Ps. 55:13.

2. *homophrōn* (ὁμόφρων, 3675), (*homos*, "the same," *phrēn*, "the mind"), occurs in 1 Pet. 3:8, RV, "likeminded" (KJV, "of one mind").

Note: In Rom. 15:5; Phil. 2:2, *phroneō to auto*, "to think the same thing," is translated, KJV, "be likeminded" (RV, "be of the same, mind").

LIKENESS, LIKENESS OF (in the)

1. *homoiōma* (ὁμοίωμα, 3667) denotes "that which is made like something, a resemblance," (a) in the concrete sense, Rev. 9:7, "shapes" (RV, marg., "likenesses"); (b) in the abstract sense, Rom. 1:23, RV, "(for) the likeness (of an image)"; the KJV translates it as a verb, "(into an image) made like to"; the association here of the two words *homoiōma* and *eikōn* (see IMAGE) serves to enhance the contrast between the idol and "the glory of the incorruptible God," and is expressive of contempt; in 5:14, "(the) likeness of Adam's transgression" (KJV, "similitude"); in 6:5, "(the) likeness (of His death); in 8:3, "(the) likeness (of sinful flesh); in Phil. 2:7, "the likeness of men." "The expression 'likeness of men' does not of itself imply, still less does it exclude or diminish, the reality of the nature which Christ assumed. That ... is declared in the words 'form of a servant.' 'Paul justly says *in the likeness of men*, because, in fact, Christ, although certainly perfect Man (Rom. 5:15; 1 Cor. 15:21; 1 Tim. 2:5), was, by reason of the Divine nature present in Him, not simply and merely man ... but the Incarnate Son of God'" (Gifford, quoting Meyer). See SHAPE. Cf. LIKE, B, (b).

2. *homoiōsis* (ὁμοίωσις, 3669), "a making like," is translated "likeness" in Jas. 3:9, RV (KJV, "similitude").

3. *homoiotēs* (ὁμοιότης, 3665) is translated "likeness" in Heb. 7:15, RV (KJV, "similitude").

4. *antitupon* (ἀντίτυπον, 499) is rendered "after a true likeness," in 1 Pet. 3:21, RV (marg., "in the antitype"). See FIGURE, No. 2.

For **LIMIT**, in Heb. 4:7, KJV, see DEFINE

For **LINE** see PROVINCE, No. 2

For **LINEAGE** in Luke 2:4, KJV, see FAMILY

LINEN, LINEN CLOTH, FINE LINEN

1. *sindōn* (σινδών, 4616) was "a fine linen cloth, an article of domestic manufacture" (Prov. 31:24) used (a) as a garment or wrap, the "linen cloth" of Mark 14:51, 52; (b) as shrouds or winding sheets, Matt. 27:59; Mark 15:46, RV, "linen cloth," for KJV, "linen"; Luke 23:53 (ditto). In the Sept., Judg. 14:2, "(thirty) sheets"; Prov. 31:24 (see above). The Mishna (the great collection of legal decisions by the ancient Rabbis) records that the material was sometimes used for curtains.

2. *linon* (λίνον, 3043) denotes (a) "flax," Matt. 12:20; (b) "linen," in Rev. 15:6, KJV; the best texts have *lithos*, "stone," RV.

3. *othonion* (ὀθόνιον, 3608), "a piece of fine linen," is used in the plural, of the strips of cloth with which the body of the Lord was bound, after being wrapped in the *sindōn*, Luke 24:12; John 19:40; 20:5, 6, 7. In the Sept., Judg. 14:13, "changes of raiment"; Hos. 2:5, 9. The word is a diminutive of *othonē*, "a sheet."

4. *bussos* (βύσσος, 1040), "fine linen," made from a special species of flax, a word of Aramean origin, used especially for the Syrian *byssus* (Arab. *bûs* is still used for native "linen"). Cf. Heb. *bûs*, in all OT passages quoted here, except Ezek. 27:7; Syriac *bûsâ* In Luke 16:9. It is the material mentioned in 1 Chron. 4:21, wrought by the house of Ashbea; 15:27, *bussinos*, No. 5 (David's robe); 2 Chron. 3:14, *bussos* (the veil of the Temple); 5:12, *bussinos* (the clothing of the Levite singers); Esth. 1:6 (the cords of the hangings in the king's garden); 8:15 (Mordecai's dress); Ezek. 27:7 (*bussos*, in Syrian trade with Tyre). In the NT, Luke 16:19, the clothing of the "rich man."

5. *bussinos* (βύσσινος, 1039), an adjective formed from No. 4, denoting "made of fine linen." This is used of the clothing of the mystic Babylon, Rev. 18:12; 16, and of the suitable attire of the Lamb's wife, 19:8, 14, figuratively describing "the righteous acts of the saints." The presumption of Babylon is conspicuous in that she arrays herself in that which alone befits the bride of Christ. For examples of the use in the Sept. see No. 4.

LIST (Verb)

1. *thelō* (θέλω, 2309), "to will, wish," is translated by the verb "to list" in Matt. 17:12; Mark 9:13; John 3:8. See DESIRE, B, No. 6.

2. *boulomai* (βούλομαι, 1014), "to will, be minded," is translated "listeth" in Jas. 3:4 (RV, "willeth"). See DESIRE, B, No. 7.

For **(NO) LITTLE** see COMMON, B, *Note* (3)

LIVE

1. *zaō* (ζάω, 2198), "to live, be alive," is used in the NT of "(a) God, Matt. 16:16; John 6:57; Rom. 14:11; (b) the Son in Incarnation, John 6:57; (c) the Son in Resurrection, John 14:19; Acts 1:3; Rom. 6:10; 2 Cor. 13:4; Heb. 7:8; (d) spiritual life, John 6:57; Rom. 1:17; 8:13b; Gal. 2:19, 20; Heb. 12:9; (e) the present state of departed saints, Luke 20:38; 1 Pet. 4:6; (f) the hope of resurrection, 1 Pet. 1:3; (g) the resurrection of believers, 1 Thess. 5:10; John 5:25; Rev. 20:4, and of unbelievers, v. 5, cf. v. 13; (h) the way of access to God through the Lord Jesus Christ, Heb. 10:20; (i) the manifestation of divine power in support of divine authority, 2 Cor. 13:4b; cf. 12:10, and 1 Cor. 5:5; (j) bread, figurative of the Lord Jesus, John 6:51; (k) a stone, figurative of the Lord Jesus, 1 Pet. 2:4; (l) water, figurative of the Holy Spirit, John 4:10; 7:38; (m) a sacrifice, figurative of the believer, Rom. 12:1; (n) stones, figurative of the believer, 1 Pet. 2:5; (o) the oracles, *logion*, Acts 7:38, and word, *logos*, Heb. 4:12; 1 Pet. 1:23, of God; (p) the physical life of men, 1 Thess. 4:15; Matt. 27:63; Acts 25:24; Rom. 14:9; Phil. 1:21 (in the infinitive mood used as a noun with the article, 'living'), 22; 1 Pet. 4:5; (q) the maintenance of physical life, Matt. 4:4; 1 Cor. 9:14; (r) the duration of physical life, Heb. 2:15; (s) the enjoyment of physical life, 1 Thess. 3:8; (t) the recovery of physical life from the power of disease, Mark 5:23; John 4:50; (u) the recovery of physical life from the power of death, Matt. 9:18; Acts 9:41; Rev. 20:5; (v) the course, conduct, and character of men, (1) good, Acts 26:5; 2 Tim. 3:12; Titus 2:12; (2) evil, Luke 15:13; Rom. 6:2; 8:13a; 2 Cor. 5:15b; Col. 3:7; (3) undefined, Rom. 7:9; 14:7; Gal. 2:14; (w) restoration after alienation, Luke 15:32.

Note: In 1 Thess. 5:10, to live means to experience that change, 1 Cor. 15:51, which is to be the portion of all in Christ who will be alive upon the earth at the Parousia of the Lord Jesus, cf. John 11:25, and which corresponds to the resurrection of those who had previously died in Christ, 1 Cor. 15:52-54.

2. *sunzaō* (συζάω, 4800), "to live together with" (*sun*, "with," and *zaō*, "to live"), may be included with *zao* in the above analysis as follows: (g) Rom. 6:8; 2 Tim. 2:11; (s), 2 Cor. 7:3.

3. *anazaō* (ἀναζάω, 326) *ana*, "again," and *zao*, denotes "to live again," "to revive," Luke 15:24; cf. (w) in list above, and Rom. 7:9, to manifest activity again.

Note: Zaō is translated "quick" (i.e., "living") in Acts 10:42; 2 Tim. 4:1; 1 Pet. 4:5; in Heb. 4:12, KJV (RV, "living").

4. *bioō* (βιόω, 980), "to spend life, to pass one's life," is used in 1 Pet. 4:2.

5. *anastrephō* (ἀναστρέφω, 390), used metaphorically, in the middle voice, "to conduct oneself, behave, live," is translated "to live," in Heb. 13:18 ("honestly"); in 2 Pet. 2:18 ("in error"). See BEHAVE, etc.

6. *zōogoneō* (ζωογονέω, 2225) denotes "to preserve alive" (from *zōos*, "alive," and *ginomai*, "to come to be, become, be made"); in Luke 17:33, "shall preserve (it)," i.e., his life, RV marg., "save (it) alive"; cf. the parallels *sōzō*, "to save," in Matt. 16:25, and *phulasō*, "to keep," in John 12:25; in Acts 7:19, "live," negatively of the efforts of Pharaoh to destroy the babes in Israel; in 1 Tim. 6:13, according to the best mss. (some have *zōopoieō*, "to cause to live"), "quickeneth" (RV, marg., "preserveth ... alive," the preferable rendering). See PRESERVE, QUICKEN.

7. *diagō* (διάγω, 1236) is used of time in the sense of passing a life, 1 Tim. 2:2, "(that) we may lead (a tranquil and quiet, RV) life"; Tit. 3:3, "living (in malice and envy)."

8. *politeuō* (πολιτεύω, 4176), "to be a citizen (*politēs*), to live as a citizen," is used metaphorically of conduct as in accordance with the characteristics of the heavenly community; in Acts 23:1, "I have lived"; in Phil. 1:27, "let your manner of life (KJV, conversation) be." See CITIZENSHIP, No. 4, *Note*.

9. *huparchō* (ὑπάρχω, 5225), "to be in existence, to be," is translated "live (delicately)" in Luke 7:25.

Note: In 1 Cor. 9:13, KJV, *esthiō*, "to eat," is translated "live of." In Tim. 5:6 the KJV renders *spatalaō* "liveth in pleasure."

LIVE LONG

makrochronios (μακροχρόνιος, 3118), an adjective denoting "of long duration, longlived" (*makros*, "long," *chronos*, "time"), is used in Eph. 6:3, "(that thou mayest) live long," lit., "(that thou mayest be) long-lived." In the Sept., Ex. 20:12; Deut. 4:40; 5:16; 17:20.

LIVELY

Note: This is the KJV translation of the present participle of the verb; *zao*, "to live," in three passages, in each of which the RV has "living," Acts 7:38; 1 Pet. 1:3; 2:5.

For **LIVING** see BEHAVIOR, B, No. 1, LIFE, Nos. 2, 6, and LIVE, No. 3, *Note*

For **LIVING CREATURES** see BEAST

LO!

1. *ide* (ἴδε, 2396), an aorist or point tense, marking a definite point of time, of the imperative mood of *eidon*, "to see" (taken as part of *horaō*, "to see"), is used as an interjection, addressed either to one or many persons, e.g., Matt. 25:20, 22, 25; John 1:29, 36, 47; Gal. 5:2, the only occurrence outside Matthew, Mark and John. See BEHOLD.

2. *idou* (ἰδού, 2400) a similar tense of No. 1, but in the middle voice, e.g., Matt. 1:20, 23; very frequent in the Synoptists and Acts and the Apocalypse.

For **LOAF** see BREAD

LOCUST

akris (ἀκρίς, 200) occurs in Matt. 3:4 and Mark 1:6, of the animals themselves, as forming part of the diet of John the Baptist; they are used as food; the Arabs stew them with butter, after removing the head, legs and wings. In Rev. 9:3, 7, they appear as monsters representing satanic agencies, let loose by divine judgments inflicted upon men for five months, the time of the natural life of the "locust." For the character of the judgment see the whole passage.

LOINS

osphus (ὀσφύς, 3751) is used (a) in the natural sense in Matt. 3:4; Mark 1:6; (b) as "the seat of generative power," Heb. 7:5, 10; metaphorically in Acts 2:30; (c) metaphorically, (1) of girding the "loins" in readiness for active service for the Lord, Luke 12:35; (2) the same, with truth, Eph. 6:14, i.e., bracing up oneself so as to maintain perfect sincerity and reality as the counteractive in Christian character against hypocrisy and falsehood; (3) of girding the "loins" of the mind, 1 Pet. 1:13, RV, "girding," suggestive of the alertness necessary for sobriety and for setting one's hope perfectly on "the grace to be brought ... at the revelation of Jesus Christ" (the present participle, "girding," is introductory to the rest of the verse).

LONG (Verb), LONG (after, for), LONGING

A. Verb.

epipotheō (ἐπιποθέω, 1971), "to long for greatly" (a strengthened form of *potheō*, "to long for," not found in the NT), is translated "I long," in Rom. 1:11; in 2 Cor. 5:2, RV, "longing" (KJV, "earnestly desiring"); in 1 Thess. 3:6 and 2 Tim. 1:4, RV, "longing" (KJV, "desiring greatly"); to long after, in 2 Cor. 9:14; Phil. 1:8; 2:26; to long for, in 1 Pet. 2:2, RV (KJV, "desire"); Jas. 4:5, RV, "long." See DESIRE.

B. Adjective.

epipothētos (ἐπιπόθητος, 1973), akin to A, and an intensive form of *pothetos*, "desired, greatly desired," "longed for," is used in Phil. 4:1.

C. Nouns.

1. *epipothia* (ἐπιποθία, 1974), "a longing" (akin to A and B), is found in Rom. 15:23, RV "longing" (KJV, "great desire"). See DESIRE.

2. *epipothēsis* (ἐπιπόθησις, 1972), "a longing" (perhaps stressing the process more than No. 1), is found in 2 Cor. 7:7, RV, "longing" (KJV, "earnest desire"); 7:11, RV, "longing" (KJV, "vehement desire").

LONGSUFFERING (Noun and Verb)

A. Noun.

makrothumia (μακροθυμία, 3115), "forbearance, patience, longsuffering" (*makros*, "long," *thumos*, "temper"), is usually rendered "longsuffering," Rom. 2:4; 9:22; 2 Cor. 6:6; Gal. 5:22; Eph. 4:2; Col. 1:11; 3:12; 1 Tim. 1:16; 2 Tim. 3:10; 4:2; 1 Pet. 3:20; 2 Pet. 3:15; "patience" in Heb. 6:12 and Jas. 5:10. See PATIENCE, and *Note* under FORBEAR.

B. Verb.

makrothumeō (μακροθυμέω, 3114), akin to A, "to be patient, longsuffering, to bear with," lit., "to be long-tempered," is rendered by the verb "to be longsuffering" in Luke 18:7, RV (KJV, "bear long"); in 1 Thess. 5:14, RV (KJV, "be patient"); so in Jas. 5:7, 8; in 2 Pet. 3:9, KJV and RV, "is longsuffering." See ENDURE, PATIENT, SUFFER.

Note: "Longsuffering is that quality of selfrestraint in the face of provocation which does not hastily retaliate or promptly punish; it is the opposite of anger, and is associated with mercy, and is used of God, Ex. 34:6 (Sept.); Rom. 2:4; 1 Pet. 3:20. Patience is the quality that does not surrender to circumstances or succumb under trial; it is the opposite of despondency and is associated with hope, 1 Thess. 1:3; it is not used of God."

LOOK

A. Verbs.

1. *blepō* (βλέπω, 991), primarily, "to have sight, to see," then, "observe, discern, perceive," frequently implying special contemplation (cf. No. 4), is rendered by the verb "to look" in Luke 9:62, "looking (back)"; John 13:22 "(the disciples) looked (one on another)"; Acts 1:9, RV, "were looking" (KJV, "beheld"); 3:4, "look (on us)"; 27:12, RV, looking," KJV, "that

lieth (towards)," of the haven Phenix; Eph. 5:15, RV, "look (therefore carefully how ye walk)," KJV, "see (that ye walk circumspectly)"; Rev. 11:9 and 18:9, RV, "look upon" (KJV, "shall see"). See BEHOLD.

2. *anablepō* (ἀναβλέπω, 308), denotes (a) "to look up" (*ana*, "up," and No. 1), e.g., Matt. 14:19; Mark 8:24 (in some mss. v. 25); (b) "to recover sight," e.g., Matt. 11:5; 20:34, RV, "received their sight"; John 9:11. See SIGHT. Cf. *anablepsis*, "recovering of sight," Luke 4:18.

3. *periblepō* (περιβλέπω, 4017), "to look about, or round about, on" (*peri*, "around," and No. 1), is used in the middle voice, Mark 3:5, 34, 5:32; 9:8; 10:23; 11:11; Luke 6:10.

4. *apoblepō* (ἀποβλέπω, 578) signifies "to look away from" (*apo*) all else at one object; hence, "to look steadfastly," Heb. 11:26, RV, "he looked" (KJV, "he had respect"). Cf. No. 8.

5. *emblepō* (ἐμβλέπω, 1689), to look at (*en*, in, and No. 1), is translated "to look upon" in Mark 10:27; 14:67; Luke 22:61; John 1:36. This verb implies a close, penetrating "look," as distinguished from Nos. 6 and 9. See BEHOLD, No. 3.

6. *epiblepō* (ἐπιβλέπω, 1914), "to look upon" (*epi*, "upon"), is used in the NT of favorable regard, Luke 1:48, RV, "he hath looked upon" (KJV, "hath regarded"), of the low estate of the Virgin Mary; in 9:38, in a request to the Lord to "look" upon an afflicted son; in Jas. 2:3, RV, "ye have regard" (KJV, "... respect"), of having a partial regard for the well-to-do. See REGARD, RESPECT.

7. *eidon* (εἶδον, 3708), used as the aorist tense of *horaō*, "to see," in various senses, is translated "to look," in the KJV of John 7:52, RV, "see;" Rev. 4:1 (RV, "I saw"); so in 6:8; 14:1, 14 (as in KJV of v. 6), and 15:5. See BEHOLD, HEED, No. 2.

8. *aphoraō* (ἀφοράω, 872), "to look away from one thing so as to see another" (*apo*, "from," and No. 7), "to concentrate the gaze upon," occurs in Phil. 2:23, "I shall see;" Heb. 12:2, "looking."

9. *epeidon* (ἐπεῖδον, 1896) denotes "to look upon" (*epi*, "upon"), (a) favorably, Luke 1:25 (b) unfavorably, in Acts 4:29.

10. *parakuptō* (παρακύπτω, 3879), lit. and primarily, "to stoop sideways" *para*, "aside," *kuptō*, "to bend forward"), denotes "to stoop to look into," Luke 24:12, "stooping and looking in" (KJV, "stooping down"), John 20:5, 11; metaphorically in Jas. 1:25, of "looking" into the perfect law of liberty; in 1 Pet. 1:12 of things which the angels desire "to look into.

11. *anakuptō* (ἀνακύπτω, 352), "to lift oneself up" (*ana*, "up"), is translated "look up" in Luke 21:28, of being elated in joyous expectation (followed by *epairō*, "to lift up").

12. *skopeō* (σκοπέω, 4648), "to look at, consider" (Eng., "scope"), implying mental consideration, is rendered "while we look ... at" in 2 Cor. 4:18; "looking to" (KJV, "on") in Phil. 2:4. See HEED, MARK.

13. *episkopeō* (ἐπισκοπέω, 1983), lit., "to look upon" (*epi*, and No. 12), is rendered "looking carefully" in Heb. 12:15, RV (KJV, "looking diligently"), *epi* being probably intensive here; in 1 Pet. 5:2, "to exercise the oversight, to visit, care for." See OVERSIGHT.

14. *episkeptomai* (ἐπισκέπτομαι, 1980), a later form of No. 13, "to visit," has the meaning of "seeking out," and is rendered "look ye out" in Acts 6:3. See VISIT.

15. *atenizō* (ἀτενίζω, 816), "to look fixedly, gaze," is translated "looking steadfastly" in Luke 22:56, RV (KJV, "... earnestly"); in Acts 1:10, "looking steadfastly;" in 3:12, KJV, "look ... earnestly" (RV, "fasten ye your eyes," as in 3:4 and 11:6); so in the RV of 6:15; 10:4; 13:9; 14:9; in 7:55, "looked up steadfastly," in 23:1, "looking steadfastly on" (KJV, "earnestly beholding"); in 2 Cor, 3:7, RV, "look steadfastly" (KJV, "steadfastly behold"); in 3:13, RV, ditto (KJV, "steadfastly look"). In Luke 4:20, "were fastened" (*ophthalmoi*, "eyes," being used separately). See BEHOLD, No. 10.

16. *theaomai* (θεάομαι, 2300), "to behold" (of careful contemplation), is translated "look" in John 4:35, of "looking" on the fields; in 1 John 1:1, KJV (RV, "we beheld"), of the apostles' personal experiences of Christ in the days of His flesh, and the facts of His Godhood and Manhood. See BEHOLD, No. 8.

17. *theōreō* (θεωρέω, 2334), "to look at, gaze at, behold," is translated "looking on" in Mark 15:40, KJV (RV, "beholding"). See BEHOLD, No. 6.

B. Noun.

horasis (ὅρασις, 3706), akin to A, No. 7, denotes (a) a vision (so the associated noun *horama*, e.g., Acts 7:31; *horasis* signifies especially the act of seeing, *horama* that which is seen), Acts 2:17; Rev. 9:17; (b) an appearance, Rev. 4:3, translated "to look upon" (twice in the RV; In the second instance the KJV has "in sight").

LOOK (for), LOOKING (after, for)

A. Verbs.

1. *prosdokaō* (προσδοκάω, 4328), "to await, expect" (*pros*, "to" or "towards," *dokeō*, "to think, be of opinion"), is translated "to look for," e.g., in Matt. 11:3; 2 Pet. 3:12, 13, 14; the RV renders it by the verb "to expect, to be in expectation," in some instances, as does the KJV in Luke 3:15; Acts 3:5, See EXPECT.

2. *prosdechomai* (προσδέχομαι, 4327), "to receive favorably," also means "to expect," and is rendered "to look for," e.g., in Luke 2:38; 23:51; Acts 24:15, RV (KJV, "allow"); Titus 2:13; Jude 21. See ALLOW, No. 4.

3. *ekdechomai* (ἐκδέχομαι, 1551), primarily "to receive from another," hence, "to expect, to await," is translated "he

looked for" in Heb. 11:10; in 1 Cor. 16:11, KJV, "I look for" (RV, "I expect"). See EXPECT, No. 1.

Notes: (1) In Phil. 3:20 and Heb. 9:28, KJV, *apekdechomai* (the verb in the preceding No. extended by *apo*, "from"), "to await" or "expect eagerly," is translated "look for" (RV, "wait for"; so KJV everywhere else). (2) In Acts 28:6, KJV, *prosdokaō*, "to expect," is translated "they looked" (RV, "they expected"), and "they had looked" (RV, "they were long in expectation").

B. Nouns.

1. *prosdokia* (προσδοκία, 4329); akin to A, No. 1, is translated "a looking after" in Luke 21:26, KJV ("expectation," as in Acts 12:11, KJV and RV).

2. *ekdochē* (ἐκδοχή, 1561), akin to A, No. 3, is translated "looking for" in Heb. 10:27, KJV.

LOOK (to)

1. *blepō* (βλέπω, 991), "to look" (see LOOK, No. 1), has the meaning of "taking heed, looking to oneself," in 2 John 8. See HEED.

2. *horaō* (ὁράω, 3708), "to see" (see LOOK, No. 7), has the meaning of "seeing to" or "caring for a thing" in Matt. 27:4, "see (thou to it);" in Acts 18:15, "look to it (yourselves)"; the future (sing. *opsei*, plural, *opsesthe*), is used for the tense which is wanting in *horaō*, and stands for the imperative.

LOOSE

A. Verbs.

1. *luō* (λύω, 3089) denotes (a) "to loose, unbind, release," (1) of things, e.g., in Acts 7:33, RV, "loose (the shoes)," KJV, "put off"; Mark 1:7; (2) of animals, e.g., Matt. 21:2; (3) of persons, e.g., John 11:44; Acts 22:30; (4) of Satan, Rev. 20:3, 7, and angels, Rev. 9:14, 15; (5) metaphorically, of one diseased, Luke 13:16; of the marriage tie, 1 Cor. 7:27; of release from sins, Rev. 1:5 (in the most authentic mss.); (b) "to loosen, break up, dismiss, dissolve, destroy"; in this sense it is translated "to loose" in Acts 2:24, of the pains of death; in Rev. 5:2, of the seals of a roll. See DESTROY, DISSOLVE, UNLOOSE.

2. *apoluō* (ἀπολύω, 630), *apo*, "from," and No. 1, denotes (a) "to set free, release," translated "loosed" in Luke 13:12, of deliverance from an infirmity; in Matt. 18:27, KJV, "loosed" (RV, "released"), of a debtor; (b) "to let go, dismiss," e.g., Matt. 14:15, 22. See DISMISS, DIVORCE, FORGIVE, LIBERTY, RELEASE, SEND (away).

3. *aniēmi* (ἀνίημι, 447), "to send back" (*ana*, "back," *hiēmi*, "to send"), "to leave, forbear," is translated "to loose," in Acts 16:26, of the "loosening" of bonds; 27:40, rudder bands. Elsewhere, Eph. 6:9; Heb. 13:5. See FORBEAR.

Notes: (1) In Acts 27:13, KJV, *airō*, "to lift," is translated "loosing (thence)" (RV, "they weighed anchor"). (2) For *katargeō*, translated "she is loosed" in Rom. 7:2, KJV (RV "discharged"), see ABOLISH.

B. Noun.

lusis (λύσις, 3080), "a loosening" (akin to A, No. 1), 1 Cor. 7:27, of divorce, is translated "to be loosed," lit., "loosing." In the second part of the verse the verb *luo* is used. In the Sept., Eccl. 8:1, with the meaning "interpretation."

LORD, LORDSHIP

A. Nouns.

1. *kurios* (κύριος, 2962), properly an adjective, signifying "having power" (*kuros*) or "authority," is used as a noun, variously translated in the NT, " 'Lord,' 'master,' 'Master,' 'owner,' 'Sir,' a title of wide significance, occurring in each book of the NT save Titus and the Epistles of John. It is used (a) of an owner, as in Luke 19:33, cf. Matt. 20:8; Acts 16:16; Gal. 4:1; or of one who has the disposal of anything, as the Sabbath, Matt. 12:8; (b) of a master, i.e., one to whom service is due on any ground, Matt. 6:24; 24:50; Eph. 6:5; (c) of an Emperor or King, Acts 25:26; Rev. 17:14; (d) of idols, ironically, 1 Cor. 8:5, cf. Isa. 26:13; (e) as a title of respect addressed to a father, Matt. 21:30, a husband, 1 Pet. 3:6, a master, Matt. 13:27; Luke 13:8, a ruler, Matt. 27:63, an angel, Acts 10:4; Rev. 7:14; (f) as a title of courtesy addressed to a stranger, John 12:21; 20:15; Acts 16:30; from the outset of His ministry this was a common form of address to the Lord Jesus, alike by the people, Matt. 8:2; John 4:11, and by His disciples, Matt. 8:25; Luke 5:8; John 6:68; (g) *kurios* is the Sept. and NT representative of Heb. Jehovah ('LORD' in Eng. versions), see Matt. 4:7; Jas. 5:11, e.g., of *adon*, Lord, Matt. 22:44, and of *Adonay*, Lord, 1:22; it also occurs for *Elohim*, God, 1 Pet. 1:25.

"Thus the usage of the word in the NT follows two main lines: one, *a-f*, customary and general, the other, *g*, peculiar to the Jews, and drawn from the Greek translation of the OT.

"Christ Himself assumed the title, Matt. 7:21, 22; 9:38; 22:41-45; Mark 5:19 (cf. Ps. 66:16; the parallel passage, Luke 8:39, has 'God'); Luke 19:31; John 13:13, apparently intending it in the higher senses of its current use, and at the same time suggesting its OT associations.

"His purpose did not become clear to the disciples until after His resurrection, and the revelation of His Deity consequent thereon. Thomas, when he realized the significance of the presence of a mortal wound in the body of a living man, immediately joined with it the absolute title of Deity, saying, 'My Lord and my God,' John 20:28. Thereafter, except in Acts 10:4 and Rev. 7:14, there is no record that *kurios* was ever again used by believers in addressing any save God and the Lord Jesus; cf Acts 2:47 with 4:29, 30.

"How soon and how completely the lower meaning had been superseded is seen in Peter's declaration in his first sermon after the resurrection, 'God hath made Him—Lord,' Acts 2:36, and that in the house of Cornelius, 'He is Lord of all,' 10:36, cf. Deut. 10:14; Matt. 11:25; Acts 17:24. In his writings the implications of his early teaching are confirmed and developed. Thus Ps. 34:8, 'O taste and see that Jehovah is good,' is applied to the Lord Jesus, 1 Pet. 2:3, and 'Jehovah of Hosts, Him shall ye sanctify,' Isa. 8:13, becomes 'sanctify in your hearts Christ as Lord,' 3:15.

"So also James who uses *kurios* alike of God, 1:7 (cf. v. 5); 3:9; 4:15; 5:4, 10, 11, and of the Lord Jesus, 1:1 (where the possibility that *kai* is intended epexegetically, i.e. = even, cf. 1 Thess. 3:11, should not be overlooked); 2:1 (lit., 'our Lord Jesus Christ of glory,' cf. Ps. 24:7; 29:3; Acts 7:2; 1 Cor. 2:8); 5:7, 8, while the language of 4:10; 5:15, is equally applicable to either.

"Jude, v. 4, speaks of 'our only—Lord, Jesus Christ,' and immediately, v. 5, uses 'Lord' of God (see the remarkable marg. here), as he does later, vv. 9, 14.

"Paul ordinarily uses *kurios* of the Lord Jesus, 1 Cor. 1:3, e.g., but also on occasion, of God, in quotations from the OT, 1 Cor. 3:20, e.g., and in his own words, 1 Cor. 3:5, cf. v. 10. It is equally appropriate to either in 1 Cor. 7:25; 2 Cor. 3:16; 8:21; 1 Thess. 4:6, and if 1 Cor. 11:32 is to be interpreted by 10:21, 22, the Lord Jesus is intended, but if by Heb. 12:5-9, then *kurios* here also = God. 1 Tim. 6:15, 16 is probably to be understood of the Lord Jesus, cf. Rev. 17:14.

"Though John does not use 'Lord' in his Epistles, and though, like the other Evangelists, he ordinarily uses the personal Name in his narrative, yet he occasionally speaks of Him as 'the Lord,' John 4:1; 6:23; 11:2; 20:20; 21:12.

"The full significance of this association of Jesus with God under the one appellation, 'Lord,' is seen when it is remembered that these men belonged to the only monotheistic race in the world. To associate with the Creator one known to be a creature, however exalted, though possible to Pagan philosophers, was quite impossible to a Jew.

"It is not recorded that in the days of His flesh any of His disciples either addressed the Lord, or spoke of Him, by His personal Name. Where Paul has occasion to refer to the facts of the gospel history he speaks of what the Lord Jesus said, Acts 20:35, and did, 1 Cor. 11:23, and suffered, 1 Thess. 2:15; 5:9, 10. It is our Lord Jesus who is coming, 1 Thess. 2:19, etc. In prayer also the title is given, 3:11; Eph. 1:3; the sinner is invited to believe on the Lord Jesus, Acts 16:31; 20:21, and the saint to look to the Lord Jesus for deliverance, Rom. 7:24, 25, and in the few exceptional cases in which the personal Name stands alone a reason is always discernible in the immediate context.

"The title 'Lord,' as given to the Savior, in its full significance rests upon the resurrection, Acts 2:36; Rom. 10:9; 14:9, and is realized only in the Holy Spirit, 1 Cor. 12:3."

2. *despotēs* (δεσπότης, 1203), "a master, lord, one who possesses supreme authority," is used in personal address to God in Luke 2:29; Acts 4:24; Rev. 6:10; with reference to Christ, 2 Pet. 2:1; Jude 4; elsewhere it is translated "master," "masters," 1 Tim. 6:1, 2; 2 Tim. 2:21 (of Christ); Titus 2:9; 1 Pet. 2:18. See MASTER.

Note: For *rabboni*, rendered "Lord" in the KJV of Mark 10:51, see RABBONI.

3. *megistan* (μεγιστάν, 3175), akin to *megistos*, "greatest," the superlative degree of *megas*, "great," denotes "chief men, nobles," it is rendered "lords" in Mark 6:21, of nobles in Herod's entourage; "princes" in Rev. 6:15 and 18:23, RV (KJV, "great men").

B. Verbs.

1. *kurieuō* (κυριεύω, 2961) denotes "to be lord of, to exercise lordship over," Luke 22:25; Rom. 6:9, 14; 7:1; 14:9; 2 Cor. 1:24; 1 Tim. 6:15; see DOMINION, B, No. 1.

2. *katakurieuō* (κατακυριεύω, 2634), a strengthened form of No. 1, is rendered "lording it" in 1 Pet. 5:3, RV: see DOMINION, B, No. 2.

C. Adjective.

kuriakos (κυριακός, 2960), from *kurios* (A, No. 1), signifies "pertaining to a lord or master"; "lordly" is not a legitimate rendering for its use in the NT, where it is used only of Christ; in 1 Cor. 11:20, of the Lord's Supper, or the Supper of the Lord (see FEAST); in Rev. 1:10, of the Day of the Lord (see DAY, No. 1).

LOSE, (suffer) LOSS, LOST

1. *apollumi* (ἀπόλλυμι, 622) signifies (I) In the active voice, (a) "to destroy, destroy utterly, kill," e.g., Matt. 10:28; Mark 1:24; 9:22; (b) "to lose utterly," e.g., Matt. 10:42, of "losing" a reward; Luke 15:4 (1st part), of "losing" a sheep; Luke 9:25, of "losing" oneself (of the "loss" of well-being hereafter); metaphorically, John 6:39, of failing to save; 18:9, of Christ's not "losing" His own; (II), in the middle voice (a) "to perish," of things, e.g., John 6:12 "(that nothing) be lost"; of persons, e.g., Matt. 8:25, "we perish;" of the "loss" of eternal life, usually (always in the RV) translated to perish, John 3:16; 17:12, KJV, "is lost," RV, "perished"; 2 Cor. 4:3, "are perishing," KJV, "are lost" (see PERISH); (b) "to be lost," e.g., Luke 15:4 (2nd part), "which is lost"; metaphorically, from the relation between shepherd and flock, of spiritual destitution and alienation from God, Matt. 10:6, "(the) lost (sheep)" of the house of Israel; Luke 19:10 (the perfect tense translated "lost" is here intransitive). See DESTROY.

2. *zēmioō* (ζημιόω, 2210), "to damage" (akin to *zēmia*, "damage," e.g., Acts 27:10, 21), is used in the NT, in the passive voice, signifying "to suffer loss, forfeit, lose," Matt. 16:26; Mark 8:36, of losing one's soul or life; Luke 9:25, RV, "forfeit (his own self)," KJV, "be cast away" (for the preceding verb see No. 1); 1 Cor. 3:15, "he shall suffer loss," i.e., at the Judgment-Seat of Christ (see v. 13 with 2 Cor. 5:10); 2 Cor. 7:9, "(that) ye might suffer loss," RV (KJV, "might receive damage"); though the apostle did regret the necessity of making them sorry by his letter, he rejoiced that they were made sorry after a godly sort, and that they thus suffered no spiritual loss, which they would have done had their sorrow been otherwise than after a godly manner; in Phil. 3:8, "I suffered the loss (of all things)," RV, i.e., of all things which he formerly counted gain (especially those in verses 5 and 6, to which the article before "all things" points). See FORFEIT.

LOSS

1. *zēmia* (ζημία, 2209), akin to No. 2, above, is used in Acts 27:10, RV, "loss" (KJV, "damage"); v. 21, KJV and RV, "loss," of ship and cargo; in Phil. 3:7, 8 of the apostle's estimate of the things which he formerly valued, and of all things on account of "the excellency of the knowledge of Christ Jesus."

2. *apobolē* (ἀποβολή, 580), lit., "casting away" (*apo*, "away," *ballō*, "to cast"), is translated "loss" in Acts 27:22; in Rom. 11:15, "casting away," of the temporary exclusion of the nation of Israel from its position of divine favor involving the reconciling of the world (i.e., the provision made through the gospel, which brings the world within the scope of reconciliation).

3. *hēttēma* (ἥττημα, 2275) denotes "a defect, loss," Rom. 11:12, RV, "loss," KJV, "diminishing" (for the meaning of which in regard to Israel see No. 2); 1 Cor. 6:7, RV, "defect" (KJV, "fault").

Note: For "suffer loss" see LOSE, No. 2.

LOT, LOTS

A. Noun.

klēros (κλῆρος, 2819) denotes (a) an object used in casting or drawing lots, which consisted of bits, or small tablets, of wood or stone (the probable derivation is from *klaō*, "to break"); these were sometimes inscribed with the names of persons, and were put into a receptacle or a garment ("a lap," Prov. 16:33), from which they were cast, after being shaken together; he whose "lot" first fell out was the one chosen. The method was employed in a variety of circumstances, e.g., of dividing or assigning property, Matt. 27:35; Mark 15:24; Luke 23:34; John 19:24 (cf., e.g., Num. 26:55); of appointing to office, Acts 1:26 (cf, e.g., 1 Sam. 10:20); for other occurrences in the OT, see, e.g., Josh. 7:14 (the earliest instance in Scripture), Lev.16:7-10; Esth. 3:7; 9:24; (b) "what is obtained by lot, an allotted portion," e.g., of the ministry allotted to the apostles, Acts 1:17, RV, "portion," marg., "lot" (KJV, "part"); in some mss. v. 25, KJV, "part" (the RV follows those which have *topos*, "place"); Acts 8:21; it is also used like *klēronomia*, "an inheritance," in Acts 26:18, of what God has in grace assigned to the sanctified; so Col. 1:12; in 1 Pet. 5:3 it is used of those the spiritual care of, and charge over, whom is assigned to elders, RV, "the charge allotted to you" (plural, lit., "the charges"), KJV, "(God's) heritage." From *klēros* the word "clergy" is derived (a transposition in the application of the term).

B. Verb.

lanchanō (λαγχάνω, 2975) denotes (a) "to draw lots," John 19:24; (b) "to obtain by lot, to obtain," Luke 1:9, "his lot was," lit., "he received by lot," i.e., by divine appointment; Acts 1:17, of the portion "allotted" by the Lord to His apostles in their ministry (cf. A, above); 2 Pet. 1:1, "that have obtained (a like precious faith)," i.e., by its being "allotted" to them, not by acquiring it for themselves, but by divine grace (an act independent of human control, as in the casting of "lots").

LOUD

megas (μέγας, 3173), "great," is used, besides other meanings, of intensity, as, e.g., of the force of a voice, e.g., Matt. 27:46, 50; in the following the RV has "great" for the KJV, "loud," Rev. 5:2, 12; 6:10; 7:2, 10; 8:13; 10:3; 12:10; 14:7, 9, 15, 18. See GREAT.

LOVE (Noun and Verb)

A. Verbs.

1. *agapaō* (ἀγαπάω, 25) and the corresponding noun *agapē* (B, No. 1 below) present "the characteristic word of Christianity, and since the Spirit of revelation has used it to express ideas previously unknown, inquiry into its use, whether in Greek literature or in the Septuagint, throws but little light upon its distinctive meaning in the NT. Cf, however, Lev. 19:18; Deut. 6:5.

"*Agapē* and *agapaō* are used in the NT (a) to describe the attitude of God toward His Son, John 17:26; the human race, generally, John 3:16; Rom. 5:8, and to such as believe on the Lord Jesus Christ particularly John 14:21; (b) to convey His wiil to His children concerning their attitude one toward another, John 13:34, and toward all men, 1 Thess. 3:12; 1 Cor. 16:14; 2 Pet. 1:7; (c) to express the essential nature of God, 1 John 4:8.

"Love can be known only from the actions it prompts. God's love is seen in the gift of His Son, 1 John 4:9, 10. But obviously this is not the love of complacency, or affection, that is, it was not drawn out by any excellency in its objects, Rom. 5:8. It was an exercise of the divine will in deliberate choice, made without assignable cause save that which lies in the nature of God Himself, Cf. Deut. 7:7, 8.

"Love had its perfect expression among men in the Lord Jesus Christ, 2 Cor. 5:14; Eph. 2:4; 3:19; 5:2; Christian love is the fruit of His Spirit in the Christian, Gal. 5:22.

"Christian love has God for its primary object, and expresses itself first of all in implicit obedience to His commandments, John 14:15, 21, 23; 15:10; 1 John 2:5; 5:3; 2 John 6. Self-will, that is, self-pleasing, is the negation of love to God.

"Christian love, whether exercised toward the brethren, or toward men generally, is not an impulse from the feelings, it does not always run with the natural inclinations, nor does it spend itself only upon those for whom some affinity is discovered. Love seeks the welfare of all, Rom. 15:2, and works no ill to any, 13:8-10; love seeks opportunity to do good to 'all men, and especially toward them that are of the household of the faith,' Gal. 6:10. See further 1 Cor. 13 and Col. 3:12-14."

In respect of *agapaō* as used of God, it expresses the deep and constant "love" and interest of a perfect Being towards entirely unworthy objects, producing and fostering a reverential "love" in them towards the Giver, and a practical "love" towards those who are partakers of the same, and a desire to help others to seek the Giver. See BELOVED.

2. *phileō* (φιλέω, 5368) is to be distinguished from *agapaō* in this, that *phileō* more nearly represents "tender affection." The two words are used for the "love" of the Father for the Son, John 3:35 (No. 1), and 5:20 (No. 2); for the believer, 14:21 (No. 1) and 16:27 (No. 2); both, of Christ's "love" for a certain disciple, 13:23 (No. 1), and 20:2 (No. 2). Yet the distinction between the two verbs remains, and they are never used indiscriminately in the same passage; if each is used with reference to the same objects, as just mentioned, each word retains its distinctive and essential character.

Phileō is never used in a command to men to "love" God; it is, however, used as a warning in 1 Cor. 16:22; *agapaō* is used instead, e.g., Matt. 22:37; Luke 10:27; Rom. 8:28; 1 Cor. 8:3; 1 Pet. 1:8; 1 John 4:21. The distinction between the two verbs finds a conspicuous instance in the narrative of John 21:15-17. The context itself indicates that *agapaō* in the first two questions suggests the "love" that values and esteems (cf. Rev. 12:11). It is an unselfish "love," ready to serve. The use of *phileō* in Peter's answers and the Lord's third question, conveys the thought of cherishing the Object above all else, of manifesting an affection characterized by constancy, from the motive of the highest veneration. See also Trench, *Syn.*, Sec. XII.

Again, to "love" (*phileō*) life, from an undue desire to preserve it, forgetful of the real object of living, meets with the Lord's reproof, John 12:25. On the contrary, to "love" life (*agapaō*) as used in 1 Pet. 3:10, is to consult the true interests of living. Here the word *phileō* would be quite inappropriate.

Note: In Mark 12:38, KJV, *thelō*, "to wish," is translated "love" (RV, "desire").

B. Nouns.

1. *agapē* (ἀγάπη, 26), the significance of which has been pointed out in connection with A, No. 1, is always rendered "love" in the RV where the KJV has "charity," a rendering nowhere used in the RV; in Rom. 14:15, where the KJV has "charitably," the RV, adhering to the translation of the noun, has "in love."

Note: In the two statements in 1 John 4:8 and 16, "God is love," both are used to enjoin the exercise of "love" on the part of believers. While the former introduces a declaration of the mode in which God's love has been manifested (vv. 9, 10), the second introduces a statement of the identification of believers with God in character, and the issue at the Judgment Seat hereafter (v. 17), an identification represented ideally in the sentence "as He is, so are we in this world."

2. *philanthrōpia* (φιλανθρωπία, 5363) denotes, lit., "love for man" (*phileō* and *anthrōpos*, "man"); hence, "kindness," Acts 28:2, in Titus 3:4, "(His) love toward man." Cf. the adverb *philanthrōpōs*, "humanely, kindly," Acts 27:3.

Note: For *philarguria*, "love of money," 1 Tim. 6:10, see MONEY (love of). For *philadelphia*, see BROTHER, *Note* (1).

LOVE FEASTS

agapē (ἀγάπη, 26) is used in the plural in Jude 12, and in some mss. in 2 Pet. 2:13; RV marg., "many ancient authorities read 'deceivings,'" (*apatais*); so the KJV. These love feasts arose from the common meals of the early churches (cf. 1 Cor. 11:21). They may have had this origin in the private meals of Jewish households, with the addition of the observance of the Lord's Supper. There were, however, similar common meals among the pagan religious brotherhoods. The evil dealt with at Corinth (l.c.) became enhanced by the presence of immoral persons, who degraded the feasts into wanton banquets, as mentioned in 2 Pet. and Jude. In later times the *agapē* became detached from the Lord's Supper.

LOVELY

prosphilēs (προσφιλής, 4375), "pleasing, agreeable, lovely" (*pros*, "toward," *phileō*, "to love"), occurs in Phil. 4:8. In the Sept., Esth. 5:1 (3rd sentence).

LOVER

This is combined with other words, forming compound adjectives as follows:

1. *philotheos* (φιλόθεος, 5377), "a lover of God," 2 Tim. 3:4.

2. *philoxenos* (φιλόξενος, 5382), "loving strangers" (*xenia*, "hospitality"), translated "a lover of hospitality" in Titus 1:8, KJV (RV, "given to h."); elsewhere, in 1 Tim. 3:2; 1 Pet. 4:9. See HOSPITALITY.

3. *philagathos* (φιλάγαθος, 5358), "loving that which is good" (*agathos*), Titus 1:8, "a lover of good," RV.

Note: The negative *aphilagathos* is found in 2 Tim. 3:3, "no lovers of good."

4. *philarguros* (φιλάργυρος, 5366), "loving money" (*arguros*, "silver"), translated "lovers of money" in Luke 16:14; 2 Tim. 3:2, RV (KJV, "covetous"). See COVETOUS.

5. *philautos* (φίλαυτος, 5367), "loving oneself," 2 Tim. 3:2, RV.

6. *philēdonos* (φιλήδονος, 5369), "loving pleasure" (*hēdonē*, "pleasure"), 2 Tim. 3:4, "lovers of pleasure."

Note: For "loving warmly," Rom. 12:10, see AFFECTION, B, No. 2. For *aphilarguros*, "no lover of money," 1 Tim. 3:3, RV, and Heb. 13:5, RV, see COVETOUS.

LOW (to bring, to make), LOW (estate, degree)

A. Verb.

tapeinoō (ταπεινόω, 5013), "to bring low, to humble," is translated "shall be brought low" in Luke 3:5. See HUMBLE.

B. Adjective.

tapeinos (ταπεινός, 5011) denotes "of low degree or estate," Rom. 12:16, "things that are lowly," RV (KJV, "men of low estate"). See BASE, DEGREE, ESTATE, HUMBLE, LOWLY.

C. Noun.

tapeinōsis (ταπείνωσις, 5014), "abasement, humiliation, low estate," is translated "low estate" in Luke 1:48; in Jas. 1:10, "that he is made low," lit., "in his abasement." See HUMILIATION.

LOWER (Adjective, and Verb, to make), LOWEST

A. Adjectives.

1. *katōteros* (κατώτερος, 2737), the comparative degree of *kato*, "beneath," is used in Eph. 4:9, of Christ's descent into "the lower parts of the earth"; two of the various interpretations of this phrase are (1) that the earth is in view in contrast to heaven, (2) that the region is that of hades, the Sheol of the OT. Inasmuch as the passage is describing the effects not merely of the Incarnation but of the death and resurrection of Christ, the second interpretation is to be accepted; cf., e.g., Ps. 16:10; 63:9; where the Sept. has the superlative; 139:15; Acts 2:31. Moreover, as Westcott says, it is most unlikely that the phrase would be used to describe the earth. The word *merē* (plural of *meros*), "parts," would have no force in such a meaning.

2. *eschatos* (ἔσχατος, 2078), "last, utmost, lowest," is rendered "lowest" in Luke 14:9, 10, of the "lowest" place at a meal. See LAST.

B. Verb.

elattoō (ἐλαττόω, 1642) denotes "to make less" (*elattōn*, "less"), and is used in the active voice in Heb. 2:7, "Thou madest (Him) ... lower," and in the passive in v. 9, "was made ... lower," and John 3:30, "(I must) decrease," (lit., "be made less").

LOWLINESS, LOWLY

A. Noun.

tapeinophrosunē (ταπεινοφροσύνη, 5012), "lowliness of mind, humbleness," is translated "lowliness" or "lowliness of mind" in Acts 20:19, RV; Eph. 4:2; Phil. 2:3. See HUMBLENESS OF MIND.

B. Adjective.

tapeinos (ταπεινός, 5011), "low, lowly": see HUMBLE and LOW, B.

For **LUNATIC** see EPILEPTIC

LUST (Noun and Verb)

A. Nouns.

1. *epithumia* (ἐπιθυμία, 1939) denotes "strong desire" of any kind, the various kinds being frequently specified by some adjective (see below). The word is used of a good desire in Luke 22:15; Phil. 1:23, and 1 Thess. 2:17 only. Everywhere else it has a bad sense. In Rom. 6:12 the injunction against letting sin reign in our mortal body to obey the "lust" thereof, refers to those evil desires which are ready to express themselves in bodily activity. They are equally the "lusts" of the flesh, Rom. 13:14; Gal. 5:16, 24; Eph. 2:3; 2 Pet. 2:18; 1 John 2:16, a phrase which describes the emotions of the soul, the natural tendency towards things evil. Such "lusts" are not necessarily base and immoral, they may be refined in character, but are evil if inconsistent with the will of God.

Other descriptions besides those already mentioned are:—"of the mind," Eph. 2:3; "evil (desire)," Col. 3:5; "the passion of," 1 Thess. 4:5, RV; "foolish and hurtful," 1 Tim. 6:9; "youthful," 2 Tim. 2:22; "divers," 2 Tim. 3:6 and Titus 3:3; "their own," 2 Tim. 4:3; 2 Pet. 3:3; Jude 16; "worldly," Titus 2:12; "his own," Jas. 1:14; "your former," 1 Pet. 1:14, RV; "fleshly," 2:11; "of men," 4:2; "of defilement," 2 Pet. 2:10; "of the eyes," 1 John 2:16; of the world ("thereof"), v. 17; "their own ungodly," Jude 18. In Rev. 18:14 "(the fruits) which thy soul lusted after" is, lit., "of thy soul's lust." See DESIRE, A, No. 1 (where associated words are noted).

2. *orexis* (ὄρεξις, 3715), lit., "a reaching" or "stretching after" (akin to *oregomai*, "to stretch oneself out, reach after"),

a general term for every kind of desire, is used in Rom. 1:27, "lust."

3. *hēdonē* (ἡδονή, 2237), "pleasure," is translated "lusts," in the KJV of Jas. 4:1, 3 (RV, "pleasures"). See PLEASURE.

Note: In 1 Thess. 4:5, KJV, *pathos*, "passion" (RV, "passion"), is translated "lust," which is the better rendering of the next word *epithumia*, rendered "concupiscence." *Pathos* is described by Trench as "the diseased condition out of which *epithumia* springs." In 1 Cor. 12:6: *epithumētēs*, a luster after, is rendered "to lust."

B. Verb.

epithumeō (ἐπιθυμέω, 1937), akin to A, No. 1, has the same twofold meaning as the noun, namely (a) "to desire," used of the Holy Spirit against the flesh, Gal. 5:17 (see below); of the Lord Jesus, Luke 22:15, "I have desired;" of the holy angels, 1 Pet. 1:12; of good men, for good things, Matt. 13:17; 1 Tim. 3:1; Heb. 6:11; of men, for things without moral quality, Luke 15:16; 16:21; 17:22; Rev. 9:6; (b) of "evil desires," in respect of which it is translated "to lust" in Matt. 5:28; 1 Cor. 10:6; Gal. 5:17 (1st part; see below); Jas. 4:2; to covet, Acts 20:23; Rom. 7:7; 13:9. See COVET, DESIRE, B, No. 2.

Notes: (1) In Gal. 5:17, in the statement, "the flesh lusteth against the Spirit, and the Spirit against the flesh," the Holy Spirit is intended, as in the preceding verse. To walk by the Spirit involves the opposition here referred to. The verb "lusteth" is not repeated in the second part of the statement, but must in some way be supplied. Since in modern English the word "lust" is used exclusively in a bad sense, it is unsuitable as a translation of *epithumeō*, where the word is used in a good sense. As the rendering "desire" is used of the Lord Jesus (as mentioned above), it may be best so understood here in respect of the Holy Spirit.

(2) In James 4:5 the RV translates correctly in giving two questions, each of a rhetorical character, asked by way of remonstrance. The first draws attention to the fact that it is impossible for the Scripture to speak in vain; the second to the impossibility that the Holy Spirit, whom God has caused to dwell in the believer, should "long (unto envying)," *epipotheō* (KJV, "lust"). Here again, not the human spirit is in view, but the Spirit of God; cf. 1 Cor. 6:19. See LONG.

For **LYING (falsehood)** See LIE, and for LYING (in wait) See LIE IN WAIT

M

MAD, MADNESS

A. Verbs.

1. *mainomai* (μαίνομαι, 3105), "to rage, be mad," is translated by the verb "to be mad" in John 10:20; Acts 12:15; 26:24, 25; 1 Cor. 14:23; see BESIDE ONESELF, No. 2.

2. *emmainomai* (ἐμμαίνομαι, 1693), an intensive form of No. 1, prefixed by *en*, "in," implying "fierce rage, to be furious against"; it is rendered "being exceedingly mad" in Acts 26:11 (cf. 9:1).

B. Nouns.

1. *mania* (μανία, 3130), akin to A, and transliterated into English, denotes "frenzy, madness," Acts 26:24 "(thy much learning doth turn thee to) madness," RV; KJV, "(doth make thee) mad."

2. *anoia* (ἄνοια, 454), lit., "without understanding" (*a*, negative, *nous*, "mind, understanding"), denotes "folly," 2 Tim. 3:9, and this finding its expression in violent rage, Luke 6:11. See FOLLY.

3. *paraphronia* (παραφρονία, 3913), "madness" (from *para*, "contrary to," and *phrēn*, "the mind"), is used in 2 Pet. 2:16. Cf. *paraphroneō*, 2 Cor. 11:23, "I speak like one distraught."

MAGISTRATE

1. *stratēgos* (στρατηγός, 4755), besides its application to "the captain of the Temple," denotes "a magistrate or governor," Acts 16:20, 22, 35, 36, 38. These were, in Latin terminology, the *duumviri* or *praetores*, so called in towns which were Roman colonies. They were attended by lictors or "sergeants," who executed their orders. In the circumstances of Acts 16 they exceeded their powers, in giving orders for Roman citizens to be scourged; hence they became suppliants.

2. *archōn* (ἄρχων, 758), "a ruler," denotes, in Luke 12:58, "a local authority, a magistrate," acting in the capacity of one who received complaints, and possessing higher authority than the judge, to whom the "magistrate" remits the case. See CHIEF, PRINCE, RULER.

Notes: (1) In Luke 12:11, KJV, *archē*, "a beginning, rule, principality," is translated "magistrates"; the word, however, denotes "rulers" in general: hence the RV, "rulers." (2) For the KJV of Titus 3:1, "to obey magistrates," see OBEY, B, No. 3.

MAGNIFICENCE

megaleiotēs (μεγαλειότης, 3168) denotes "splendor, magnificence" (from *megaleios*, "magnificent," mighty," Acts 2:11, *megas*, "great"), translated "magnificence" in Acts 19:27, of the splendor of the goddess Diana. In Luke 9:43, RV (KJV, "mighty power"); in 2 Pet. 1:16, "majesty." In the papyri writings it is frequent as a ceremonial title.

MAGNIFY

megalunō (μεγαλύνω, 3170), "to make great" (*megas*), is translated "to magnify" in Luke 1:46; in v. 58, RV, "had magnified (His mercy)," KJV, "had shewed great (mercy)"; Acts 5:13; 10:46; 19:17; 2 Cor. 10:15, RV (KJV, "we shall be enlarged"), i.e., by their faith in its practical effect he will be so assisted as to enlarge the scope of his gospel ministry and carry its message to regions beyond them; in Phil. 1:20, of the "magnifying" of Christ by him in his body, i.e., in all his activities and ways. In Matt. 23:5, it signifies "to enlarge." See ENLARGE.

Note: In Rom. 11:13, KJV, the verb *doxazō*, "to glorify," is translated "I magnify (my office)," RV, "I glorify (my ministry)." See GLORIFY.

MAID, MAIDEN, MAIDSERVANT

1. *pais* (παῖς, 3816), "a child," denotes "a maid" or "maiden" in Luke 8:51 and 54, RV, "maiden in both places." See CHILD, SERVANT, SON, YOUNG MAN.

2. *paidiskē* (παιδίσκη, 3814), a diminutive of No. 1, is translated "maid," "maids," in the KJV and RV in Mark 14:66, 69; Luke 22:56, in the RV (KJV, "damsel"), in Matt. 26:69; John 18:17; Acts 12:13; 16:16; in Luke 12:45, "maidservants" (KJV "maidens"); in Gal. 4:22, 23, 30, 31, RV, "handmaid" (KJV, "bondmaid" or "bondwoman"). See BONDMAID, DAMSEL.

3. *korasion* (κοράσιον, 2877), a colloquial familiar term, is translated "maid" in Matt. 9:24, 25, KJV (RV, "damsel"). See DAMSEL, No. 1.

MAJESTY

1. *megaleiotēs* (μεγαλειότης, 3168): see MAGNIFICENCE.

2. *megalōsunē* (μεγαλωσύνη, 3172), from *megas*, "great," denotes "greatness, majesty"; it is used of God the Father, signifying His greatness and dignity, in Heb. 1:3, "the Majesty (on high)," and 8:1, "the Majesty (in the Heavens)"; and in an ascription of praise acknowledging the attributes of God in Jude 25.

MAKER

dēmiourgos (δημιουργός, 1217), lit., "one who works for the people" (from *dēmos*, "people," *ergon*, "work"; an ancient inscription speaks of the magistrates of Tarsus as *dēmiourgoi:*

the word was formerly used thus regarding several towns in Greece; it is also found used of an artist), came to denote, in general usage, a builder or "maker," and is used of God as the "Maker" of the heavenly city, Heb. 11:10. In that passage the first word of the two, *technitēs*, denotes "an architect, designer," the second, *dēmiourgos*, is the actual Framer, the city is the archetype of the earthly one which God chose for His earthly people. Cf. *ktistēs*, "creator."

MALE

arsēn (ἄρσην, 730), or *arrēn* (ἄῤῥην, 730) is translated "men" in Rom. 1:27 (three times); "man child" in Rev. 12:5 (v. 13 in some mss.); "male" in Matt. 19:4; Mark 10:6; Luke 2:23; Gal. 3:28, "(there can be no) male (and female)," RV, i.e. sex distinction does not obtain in Christ; sex is no barrier either to salvation or the development of Christian graces.

MALEFACTOR

1. *kakourgos* (κακοῦργος, 2557), an adjective, lit., "evil-working" (*kakos*, "evil," *ergon*, "work"), is used as a noun, translated "malefactor(-s)" in Luke 23:32, 33, 39, and in the RV in 2 Tim. 2:9 (KJV, "evil doer"). See EVIL, B, *Note* (1). In the Sept., Prov. 21:15.

2. *kakopoios* (κακοποιός, 2555), an adjective, lit., "doing evil," is used in 1 Pet. 2:12, 14; 3:16 (in some mss.); 4:15. See EVIL, B, No. 5.

MALICE, MALICIOUSNESS, MALICIOUS

kakia (κακία, 2549), "badness in quality" (the opposite of *aretē*, "excellence"), "the vicious character generally" (Lightfoot), is translated "malice" in 1 Cor. 5:8; 14:20; Eph. 4:31; Col. 3:8; Titus 3:3; 1 Pet. 2:1, KJV (RV, "wickedness"; marg., "malice"); "maliciousness" in Rom. 1:29; in 1 Pet. 2:16, KJV (RV, "wickedness"; marg., "malice"). Elsewhere, Matt. 6:34; Acts 8:22; Jas. 1:21 (RV marg., "malice"). See EVIL, B, No. 1.

Note: In 2 John 10, KJV, *ponēros*, "evil, wicked" (see EVIL, A. No. 2) is translated "malicious" (RV, "wicked").

MALIGNITY

kakoētheia (κακοήθεια, 2550), lit., "bad manner or character" (*kakos*, "bad," *ēthos*, "manner"), hence, "an evil disposition" that tends to put the worst construction on everything, "malice, malevolence, craftiness," occurs in Rom. 1:29, as the accompaniment of *dolos*, "guile."

MAMMON

mamonas (μαμμωνᾶς, 3126), a common Aramaic word for "riches," akin to a Hebrew word signifying "to be firm, steadfast" (whence "Amen"), hence, "that which is to be trusted"; Gesenius regards it as derived from a Heb. word signifying "treasure" (Gen. 43:23); it is personified in Matt. 6:24; Luke 16:9, 11, 13.

For **MAN CHILD** see MALE

MANGER

phatnē (φάτνη, 5336), "a manger," Luke 2:7, 12, 16, also denotes "a stall," 13:15. So in the Sept., the word denoted not only a "manger" but, by metonymy, the stall or crib (Prov. 14:4) containing the "manger."

MANIFEST (Adjective and Verb)

A. Adjectives.

1. *emphanēs* (ἐμφανής, 1717), manifest (akin to *emphainō*, "to show in, to exhibit"; *en*, "in," *phainō*, "to cause to shine"), is used (a) literally in Acts 10:40, RV "(gave Him to be made) manifest"; (b) metaphorically in Rom. 10:20, "(I was made) manifest." See OPENLY. Cf. B, No. 2.

2. *phaneros* (φανερός, 5318), "open to sight, visible, manifest" (the root *phan-*, signifying "shining," exists also in No. 1), is translated "manifest" in Luke 8:17; Acts 4:16; 7:13, RV (KJV, "known"); Rom. 1:19; 1 Cor. 3:13; 11:19; 14:25; Gal. 5:19; Phil. 1:13; 1 Tim. 4:15 (KJV "appear"); 1 John 3:10. See APPEAR, B, *Note* (2), KNOW, B, No. 2, OPENLY.

3. *aphanēs* (ἀφανής, 852) denotes "unseen, hidden," Heb. 4:13, "not manifest" (*a*, negative and *phainō*). In the Sept., Neh. 4:8; Job 24:20.

Notes: (1) In 1 Cor. 15:27, KJV *dēlos*, "evident," is translated "manifest" (RV, "evident"). (2) So with *ekdēlos*, 2 Tim. 3:9, an intensive form of *dēlos*, signifying "quite evident." (3) In 1 Tim. 5:25, KJV, *prodēlos*, "evident beforehand, clearly evident," is translated "manifest beforehand" (RV, "evident"). (4) For "manifest token," see TOKEN.

B. Verbs.

1. *phaneroō* (φανερόω, 5319), "to make visible, clear, manifest," known (akin to A, No. 2), is used especially in the writings of the apostles John and Paul), occurring 9 times in the Gospel, 9 times in 1 John, 2 in Rev.; in the Pauline Epistles (including Heb.) 24 times; in the other Gospels, only in Mark, 3 times; elsewhere in 1 Pet. 1:20; 5:4.

The true meaning is "to uncover, lay bare reveal." The following are variations in the rendering, which should be noted: Mark 16:12, 14 (RV, "was manifested," KJV, "appeared"); John 21:1 (RV, "manifested," KJV, "shewed"; cf. v. 14); Rom. 1:19 (RV, "manifested," KJV, "hath shewed"); 2 Cor. 3:3 (RV, "being made manifest," KJV, "are manifestly declared"); 2 Cor. 5:10; 7:12 and Rev. 3:18 (RV, "be made manifest," KJV, "appear"); 2 Cor. 11:6 (RV, "we have made it manifest," KJV, "we have been throughly made manifest"); Col. 1:26 (RV "hath it been manifested," KJV, "is made manifest");

3:4 (RV, "be manifested," KJV, "appear"; so 1 Pet. 5:4); 1 Tim. 3:16 (RV, "was manifested," KJV, "was manifest"); 2 Tim. 1:10 (RV, "hath ... been manifested," KJV, "is ... made manifest"; cf. Rom. 16:26, 2 Cor. 4:10, 11; 1 Pet. 1:20); Heb. 9:26 (RV, "hath He been manifested," KJV, "hath He appeared"); 1 John 2:28; 3:2 (RV, "is ... made manifest," KJV, "doth appear"). See APPEAR, A, No. 4.

2. *emphanizō* (ἐμφανίζω, 1718), akin to A, No. 1, is translated "to manifest, make manifest," in John 14:21, 22; Heb. 11:14, RV; see APPEAR, A, No. 5.

Note: For the adverb *phanerōs*, "manifestly," see OPENLY.

MANIFESTATION

phanerōsis (φανέρωσις, 5321), "a manifestation" (akin to *phaneros* and *phaneroō*; see MANIFEST), occurs in 1 Cor. 12:7 and 2 Cor. 4:2.

Note: In Rom. 8:19, KJV, *apokalupsis*, "an uncovering, laying bare, revealing, revelation," is translated "manifestation" (RV, "revealing"). See REVELATION.

MANNA

manna (μάννα, 3131), the supernaturally provided food for Israel during their wilderness journey (for details see Exod. 16 and Num. 11). The Hebrew equivalent is given in Exod. 16:15, RV marg., "*man hu.*" The translations are, RV, "what is it?"; KJV and RV marg., "it is manna." It is described in Ps. 78:24, 25 as "the corn of heaven" and "the bread of the mighty," RV text and KJV marg. ("angels' food," KJV text), and in 1 Cor. 10:3, as "spiritual meat." The vessel a pointed to contain it as a perpetual memorial, was of gold, Heb. 9:4, with Exod. 16:33. The Lord speaks of it as being typical of Himself, the true Bread from Heaven, imparting eternal life and sustenance to those who by faith partake spiritually of Him, John 6:31-35. The "hidden manna" is promised as one of the rewards of the overcomer, Rev. 2:17; it is thus suggestive of the moral excellence of Christ in His life on earth, hid from the eyes of men, by whom He was "despised and rejected"; the path of the overcomer is a reflex of His life. None of the natural substances called "manna" is to be identified with that which God provided for Israel.

MANSLAYERS

androphonos (ἀνδροφόνος, 409), from *anēr*, "a man," and *phoneus*, "a murderer," occurs in the plural in 1 Tim. 5:9.

MARAN-ATHA

maran-atha (μαρὰν ἀθά, 3134), an expression used in 1 Cor. 16:22, is the Greek spelling for two Aramaic words, formerly supposed by some to be an imprecatory utterance or "a curse reinforced by a prayer," an idea contrary to the intimations conveyed by its use in early Christian documents, e.g., "The Teaching of the Apostles," a document of the beginning of the 2nd cent., and in the "Apostolic Constitutions" (vii. 26), where it is used as follows: "Gather us all together into Thy Kingdom which Thou hast prepared. Maranatha, Hosanna to the Son of David; blessed is He that cometh, etc."

The first part, ending in 'n,' signifies "Lord"; as to the second part, the Fathers regarded it as a past tense, "has come." Modern expositors take it as equivalent to a present, "cometh," or future, "will come." Certain Aramaic scholars regard the last part as consisting of *tha*, and regard the phrase as an ejaculation, "Our Lord, come," or "O Lord, come." The character of the context, however, indicates that the apostle is making a statement rather than expressing a desire or uttering a prayer.

As to the reason why it was used, most probably it was a current ejaculation among early Christians, as embodying the consummation of their desires.

"At first the title *Marana* or *Maran*, used in speaking to and of Christ was no more than the respectful designation of the Teacher on the part of the disciples." After His resurrection they used the title of or to Him as applied to God, "but it must here be remembered that the Aramaic-speaking Jews did not, save exceptionally, designate God as 'Lord'; so that in the 'Hebraist' section of the Jewish Christians the expression 'our Lord' (*Marana*) was used in reference to Christ only" (Dalman, *The Words of Jesus*).

MARK (Noun)

1. *charagma* (χάραγμα, 5480) denotes "a stamp, impress," translated "mark" in Rev. 13:16, 17, etc. See GRAVEN.

2. *stigma* (στίγμα, 4742) denotes "a tattooed mark" or "a mark burnt in, a brand" (akin to *stizo*, "to prick"), translated "marks" in Gal. 6:17. "It is probable that the apostle refers to the physical sufferings he had endured since he began to proclaim Jesus as Messiah and Lord [e.g., at Lystra and Philippi]. It is probable, too, that this reference to his scars was intended to set off the insistence of the Judaizers upon a body-mark which cost them nothing. Over against the circumcision they demanded as a proof of obedience to the law he set the indelible tokens, sustained in his own body, of his loyalty to the Lord Jesus. As to the origin of the figure, it was indeed customary for a master to brand his slaves, but this language does not suggest that the apostle had been branded by His Master. Soldiers and criminals also were branded on occasion; but to neither of these is the case of Paul as here described analogous. The religious devotee branded himself with the peculiar mark of the god whose cult he affected; so was Paul branded with the marks of his devotion to the Lord Jesus. It is true such markings were forbidden by the law, Lev. 19:28, but then Paul had not inflicted these on himself

"The marks of Jesus cannot be taken to be the marks which the Lord bears in His body in consequence of the Crucifixion; they were different in character."

3. *skopos* (σκοπός, 4649), primarily "a watcher, watchman" (as in the Sept., e.g., Ezek. 3:17), then, "a mark on which to fix the eye" (akin to *skopeo*, "to look at"), is used metaphorically in Phil. 3:14, of "an aim or object," RV, "goal." See GOAL.

MARK (Verb)

1. *epechō* (ἐπέχω, 1907), lit., "to hold upon" (*epi*, "upon," *echō*, "to hold"), signifies (like *parechō*) "to hold out," Phil. 2:16, of the word of life; then, "to hold one's mind towards, to observe," translated "marked" in Luke 14:7, of the Lord's observance of those who chose the chief seats. See HEED, HOLD.

2. *skopeō* (σκοπέω, 4648), "to look at, behold, watch, contemplate," (akin to *skopos*, "a mark," see Noun above), is used metaphorically of "looking to," and translated "mark" in Rom. 16:17, of a warning against those who cause divisions, and in Phil. 3:17, of observing those who walked after the example of the apostle and his fellow workers, so as to follow their ways. See HEED, *Note* (1), LOOK.

MARKET, MARKETPLACE

agora (ἀγορά, 58), primarily "an assembly," or, in general, "an open space in a town" (akin to *ageirō*, "to bring together"), became applied, according to papyri evidences, to a variety of things, e.g., "a judicial assembly," "a market," or even "supplies, provisions" (Moulton and Milligan, *Vocab.*). In the NT it denotes "a place of assembly, a public place or forum, a marketplace." A variety of circumstances, connected with it as a public gathering place, is mentioned, e.g., business dealings such as the hiring of laborers, Matt. 20:3; the buying and selling of goods, Mark 7:4 (involving risk of pollution); the games of children, Matt. 11:16; Luke 7:32; exchange of greetings, Matt. 23:7; Mark 12:38; Luke 11:43; 20:46; the holding of trials, Acts 16:19; public discussions, Acts 17:17. Mark 6:56 records the bringing of the sick there. The word always carries with it the idea of publicity, in contrast to private circumstances.

The RV always translates it "marketplace" or in the plural. The KJV sometimes changes the rendering to "markets" and translates it "streets" in Mark 6:56.

MARRIAGE (give in), MARRY

A. Noun.

gamos (γάμος, 1062), "a marriage, wedding," or "wedding feast," is used to denote (a) the ceremony and its proceedings, including the "marriage feast," John 2:1, 2; of the "marriage ceremony" only, figuratively, Rev. 19:7, as distinct from the "marriage feast" (v. 9); (b) "the marriage feast," RV in Matt. 22:2-4, 9; in v. 8, 10, "wedding;" in 25:10, RV "marriage feast;" so Luke 12:36; 14:8; in Matt. 22:11, 12, the "wedding garment" is, lit., "a garment of a wedding." In Rev. 19, where, under the figure of a "marriage," the union of Christ, as the Lamb of God, with His heavenly bride is so described, the marriage itself takes place in heaven during the Parousia, v. 7 (the aorist or point tense indicating an accomplished fact; the bride is called "His wife"); the "marriage feast" or supper is to take place on earth, after the Second Advent, v. 9. That Christ is spoken of as the Lamb points to His atoning sacrifice as the ground upon which the spiritual union takes place. The background of the phraseology lies in the OT description of the relation of God to Israel, e.g., Isa. 54:4,ff.; Ezek. 16:7,ff.; Hos. 2:19; (c) "marriage" in general, including the "married" state, which is to be "had in honor," Heb. 13:4, RV.

Note: Among the Jews the "marriage supper" took place in the husband's house and was the great social event in the family life. Large hospitality, and resentment at the refusal of an invitation, are indicated in Matt. 22:1-14. The "marriage" in Cana exhibits the way in which a "marriage feast" was conducted in humbler homes. Special honor attached to the male friends of the bridegroom, "the sons of the bridechamber," Matt. 9:15, RV (see BRIDECHAMBER). At the close the parents conducted the bride to the nuptial chamber (cf. Judg. 15:1)

B. Verbs.

1. *gameō* (γαμέω, 1060), "to marry" (akin to A), is used (a) of "the man," Matt. 5:32; 19:9, 10; 22:25 (RV; KJV, "married a wife"); v. 30; 24:38; Mark 6:17; 10:11; 12:25; Luke 14:20; 16:18; 17:27, RV, "married" (KJV, "married wives"); 20:34, 35; 1 Cor. 7:28 (1st part); v. 33; (b) of "the woman," in the active voice, Mark 10:12; 1 Cor. 7:28 (last part); ver. 34; 1 Tim. 5:11, 14; in the passive voice, 1 Cor. 7:39; (c) of "both sexes," 1 Cor. 7:9, 10, 36; 1 Tim. 4:3.

2. *gamizō* (γαμίζω, 1061), "to give in marriage," is used in the passive voice in Matt. 22:30 (2nd clause), some mss. have No. 5 here; Mark 12:25 (No. 3 in some mss.); Luke 17:27 (No. 5 in some mss.); 20:35 (last word), passive (Nos. 3 and 4 in some mss.); in the active voice Matt. 24:38 (Nos. 3 and 5 in some mss.); further, of giving a daughter in "marriage," 1 Cor. 7:38 (twice), RV (No. 5 in some mss.), which, on the whole, may be taken as the meaning. In this part of the Epistle, the apostle was answering a number of questions on matters about which the church at Corinth had written to him, and in this particular matter the formal transition from "marriage" in general to the subject of giving a daughter in "marriage," is simple. Eastern customs naturally would involve the inclusion of the latter in the inquiry and the reply.

3. *gamiskō* (γαμίσκω, 1061), an alternative for No. 2, Luke 20:34 (some mss. have No. 4); in some mss. in Mark 12:25; Luke 20:35.

4. *ekgamiskō* (ἐκγαμίσκω, 1548), "to give out in marriage" (*ek*, "out," and No. 3): see Nos. 2 and 3.

5. *ekgamizō* (ἐκγαμίζω, 1547), an alternative for No. 4: see Nos. 2 and 3.

6. *epigambreuō* (ἐπιγαμβρεύω, 1918), "to take to wife after" (*epi*, "upon," *gambros*, "a connection by marriage"), signifies "to marry" (of a deceased husband's next of kin, Matt. 22:24). Cf. Gen. 38:8.

Note: In Rom. 7:3 (twice) and v. 4, KJV, *ginomai*, "to become" (here, "to become another man's"), is translated "be married" (RV, "be joined").

MARROW

muelos (μυελός, 3452), "marrow," occurs in Heb. 4:12, where, by a natural metaphor, the phraseology changes from the material to the spiritual.

For **MARTYR** see WITNESS

MARVEL (Noun and Verb), MARVELLOUS

A. Noun.

thauma (θαῦμα, 2295), "a wonder" (akin to *theaomai*, "to gaze in wonder"), is found in the most authentic mss. in 2 Cor. 11:14 (some mss. have the adjective *thaumastos:* see C, below), "(no) marvel"; in Rev. 17:6, RV, "wonder" (KJV, "admiration"), said of John's astonishment at the vision of the woman described as Babylon the Great. In the Sept., Job 17:8; 18:20; in some mss., 20:8 and 21:5. Cf. *teras*, "a wonder"; *semeion*, "a sign"; *thambos*, "wonder"; *ekstasis*, "amazement."

B. Verbs.

1. *thaumazō* (θαυμάζω, 2296) signifies "to wonder at, marvel" (akin to A); the following are RV differences from the KJV: Luke 2:33, "were marveling" for "marveled"; Luke 8:25 and 11:14, "marveled" for "wondered"; 9:43, "were marveling" for "wondered"; 2 Thess. 1:10, "marveled at" for "admired" (of the person of Christ at the time of the shining forth of His Parousia, at the Second Advent). See WONDER.

Note: In Matt. 9:8, KJV translates this verb; RV, *phobeō*, "were afraid."

2. *ekthaumazō* (ἐκ, 1537) and (ἐκ, 2296), a strengthened form of No. 1 (*ek*, intensive), is found in the best mss. in Mark 12:17, RV, "wondered greatly" (some mss. have No. 1).

C. Adjective.

thaumastos (θαυμαστός, 2298), "marvellous" (akin to A and B), is said (a) of the Lord's doing in making the rejected Stone the Head of the corner, Matt. 21:42; Mark 12:11; (b) of the erstwhile blind man's astonishment that the Pharisees knew not from whence Christ had come, and yet He had given him sight, John 9:30, RV, "the marvel," KJV, "a marvellous thing"; (c) of the spiritual light into which believers are brought, 1 Pet. 2:9; (d) of the vision of the seven angels having the seven last plagues, Rev. 15:1; (e) of the works of God, 15:3.

MASTER (Noun and Verb)

A. Nouns.

1. *didaskalos* (διδάσκαλος, 1320), "a teacher" (from *didaskō*, "to teach"), is frequently rendered "Master" in the four Gospels, as a title of address to Christ, e.g., Matt. 8:19; Mark 4:38 (there are more instances in Luke than in the other Gospels); John 1:38, where it interprets "Rabbi"; 20:16, where it interprets "Rabboni." It is used by Christ of Himself in Matt. 23:8 (see No. 6) and John 13:13-14; by others concerning Him, Matt. 17:24; 26:18; Mark 5:35; 14:14; Luke 8:49; 22:11; John 11:28. In John 3:10, the Lord uses it in addressing Nicodemus, RV, "the teacher" (KJV, "a master"), where the article does not specify a particular "teacher," but designates the member of a class; for the class see Luke 2:46, "the doctors" (RV, marg., "teachers"). It is used of the relation of a disciple to his "master," in Matt. 10:24, 25; Luke 6:40. It is not translated "masters" in the rest of the NT, save in the KJV of Jas. 3:1 "(be not many) masters," where obviously the RV "teachers" is the meaning. See TEACHER.

2. *kurios* (κύριος, 2962), "a lord, one who exercises power," is translated "masters" in Matt. 6:24; 15:27; Mark 13:35; Luke 16:13; Acts 16:16, 19; Rom. 14:4, KJV (RV, "lord"); Eph. 6:5, 9 (twice), the 2nd time of Christ; so in Col. 3:22; 4:1. See LORD.

3. *despotēs* (δεσπότης, 1203), one who has "absolute ownership and uncontrolled power," is translated "masters" in 1 Tim. 6:1, 2; Titus 2:9; 1 Pet. 2:18; of Christ, 2 Tim. 2:21; 2 Pet. 2:1, RV (for KJV, Lord); in Jude 4, RV, it is applied to Christ "(our only) Master (and Lord, Jesus Christ)," KJV "(the only) Lord (God)"; in Rev. 6:10, RV, in an address to God, "O Master" (KJV, "O Lord"). It is rendered "Lord" in Luke 2:29 and Acts 4:24. See LORD.

Note: For "master of the house," see GOODMAN.

4. *rabbei* (ῥαββί, 4461) was an Aramaic word signifying "my master," a title of respectful address to Jewish teachers.

"The Aramaic word *rabbei*, transliterated into Greek, is explicitly recognized as the common form of address to Christ, Matt. 26:25 (cf., however, v. 22, *kurios*); 26:49; Mark 9:5, but Matt. 17:4, *kurios*" (Dalman, *The Words of Jesus*).

In the following the RV has "Rabbi" for KJV "Master"; Matt. 26:25, 49; Mark 9:5; 11:21; 14:45; John 4:31; 9:2; 11:8. In other passages the KJV has "Rabbi," Matt 23:7-8; John 1:38, 49; 3:2, 26; 6:25.

Note: The form *Rabbounei* (*Rabboni*), in Mark 10:51, is retained in the RV (for KJV, "Lord"); in John 20:16, in both KJV and RV. This title is said to be Galilean; hence it would be natural in the lips of a woman of Magdala. It does not differ materially from "Rabbi."

5. *epistatēs* (ἐπιστάτης, 1988) denotes "a chief, a commander, overseer master." It is used by the disciples in addressing the Lord, in recognition of His authority rather than His instruction (Nos. 1 and 6); it occurs only in Luke 5:5; 8:24, 45; 9:33, 49; 17:13. In the Sept., 2 Kings 25:19; 2 Chron. 31:12; Jer. 36:26; 52:25.

Note: "The form *epistata* ... alongside of the commoner *didaskale* is ... a Greek synonym for the latter, and both are to be traced back to the Aramaic *rabbei.*" Christ forbade His disciples to allow themselves to be called *rabbi*, "on the ground that He alone was their Master, Matt. 23:8. In reference to Himself the designation was expressive of the real relation between them. The form of address 'Good Master' He, however, refused to allow, Mark 10:17, 18 ... in the mouth of the speaker it was mere insolent flattery ... the Lord was unwilling that anyone should thoughtlessly deal with such an epithet; and here, as always, the honor due to the Father was the first consideration with Him .... The primitive community never ventured to call Jesus 'Our Teacher' after He had been exalted to the Throne of God. The title *rabbi*, expressing the relation of the disciple to the teacher, vanished from use; and there remained only the designation *maran*, the servant's appropriate acknowledgement of his Lord" (Dalman).

6. *kathēgētēs* (καθηγητής, 2519), properly "a guide" (akin to *kathēgeomai*, "to go before, guide"; *kata*, "down," *hēgeomai*, "to guide"), denotes "a master, a teacher," Matt. 23:10 (twice); some mss. have it in v. 8, where the most authentic have No. 1.

7. *kubernētēs* (κυβερνήτης, 2942), "the pilot or steersman of a ship," or, metaphorically, "a guide or governor" (akin to *kubernaō*, "to guide": Eng., "govern" is connected; cf. *kubernēsis*, "a steering, pilotage," 1 Cor. 12:28, "governments"), is translated "master" in Acts 27:11; "shipmaster" in Rev. 18:17. In the Sept., Prov. 23:34; Ezek. 27:8, 27-28.

B. Verb.

katakurieuō (κατακυριεύω, 2634), "to exercise lordship" (*kata*, "down upon," *kurios*, "a lord"), is translated "mastered" in Acts 19:16, RV, of the action of the evil spirit on the sons of Sceva (KJV, "overcame"). In translating the word *amphoterōn* by its primary meaning, "both," the RV describes the incident as referring to two only. It has been shown, however, that in the period of the *Koinē* (see Foreword) *amphoteroi*, "both," was no longer restricted to two persons. Ramsay ascribes the abruptness of the word here to the vivid narrative of an eye witness. See DOMINION, LORD, LORDSHIP.

MEAL

aleuron (ἄλευρον, 224), "meal" (akin to *aleuō*, "to grind," and therefore, lit., "what is ground"), occurs in Matt. 13:33; Luke 13:21.

MEANING

dunamis (δύναμις, 1411),"power, force," is used of the significance or force of what is spoken, 1 Cor. 14:11. See MIGHT, POWER.

MEAT

1. *brōma* (βρῶμα, 1033), "food" (akin to *bibrōskō*, "to eat," John 6:13), solid food in contrast to milk, is translated "food" in Matt. 14:15, RV (KJV, "victuals"); "meats," Mark 7:19; 1 Cor. 6:13 (twice); 1 Tim. 4:3; Heb. 9:10; 13:9; "meat," John 4:34; Rom. 14:15 (twice), 20; 1 Cor. 3:2; 8:8, 13; 10:3; "food," RV, for KJV, "meat," Luke 3:11; 9:13.

2. *brōsis* (βρῶσις, 1035), akin to No. 1, denotes (a) "the act of eating," 1 Cor. 8:4; (b) "food," translated "meat" in John 4:32 (for v. 34, see No. 1); 6:27 (twice, the second time metaphorically, of spiritual food); 6:55, RV, marg., "(true) meat"; Rom. 14:17, KJV, "meat," RV, "eating"; Col. 2:16; in Heb. 12:16, RV, "mess of meat," KJV, "morsel of meat"; in 2 Cor. 9:10, "food"; in Matt. 6:19, 20, "rust."

3. *brōsimos* (βρώσιμος, 1034), "eatable," Luke 24:41, KJV, "any meat" (RV, "anything to eat").

4. *trophē* (τροφή, 5160), "nourishment, food," is translated "meat" in the KJV (RV "food") except in two instances. See FOOD, No. 1.

5. *phagō* (φάγω, 5315), "to eat," is used as a noun, in the infinitive mood, and translated "meat" in Matt. 25:35, 42 (lit., "to eat"); in Luke 8:55 the RV translates it literally, "to eat" (KJV, "meat").

6. *trapeza* (τράπεζα, 5132), "a table" (Eng., "trapeze"), is used, by metonymy, of "the food on the table," in Acts 16:34 (RV, marg., "a table") and translated "meat"; cf. "table" in Rom. 11:9; 1 Cor. 10:21. See TABLE.

Notes: (1) In Luke 12:42, *sitometrion* denotes "a measured portion of food" (*sitos*, "food," metrios, "within measure"). (2) In Matt. 15:37 and Mark 8:8, the KJV translates the plural of *klasma*, "a broken piece" (from *klaō*, "to break"), "broken meat" (RV, "broken pieces"). (3) In John 12:2, RV, *anakeimai*, "to recline at table," is translated "sat at meat" (KJV, "sat at the table"); in Mark 6:26, RV, according to the best mss., "sat at meat," some have *sunanakeimai* (KJV, "sat with him"); in Mark 6:22, RV, *sunanakeimai*, "to recline at table together," is translated "that sat at meat with him." (4) In Acts 15:29, KJV, the neuter plural of *eidōlothutos*, "sacrificed to idols," is translated "meats offered to idols" (RV, "things ...," as elsewhere in the KJV). See IDOLS (OFFERED TO).

MEDIATOR

mesitēs (μεσίτης, 3316), lit., "a go-between" (from *mesos*, "middle," and *eimi*, "to go"), is used in two ways in the NT, (a) "one who mediates" between two parties with a view to producing peace, as in 1 Tim. 2:5, though more than mere "mediatorship" is in view, for the salvation of men necessitated that the Mediator should Himself possess the nature and attributes of Him towards whom He acts, and should likewise participate in the nature of those for whom He acts (sin apart); only by being possessed both of deity and humanity could He comprehend the claims of the one and the needs of the other; further, the claims and the needs could be met only by One who, Himself being proved sinless, would offer Himself an expiatory sacrifice on behalf of men; (b) "one who acts as a guarantee" so as to secure something which otherwise would not be obtained. Thus in Heb. 8:6; 9:15; 12:24 Christ is the Surety of "the better covenant," "the new covenant," guaranteeing its terms for His people.

In Gal. 3:19 Moses is spoken of as a "mediator," and the statement is made that "a mediator is not a mediator of one," v. 20, that is, of one party. Here the contrast is between the promise given to Abraham and the giving of the Law. The Law was a covenant enacted between God and the Jewish people, requiring fulfillment by both parties. But with the promise to Abraham, all the obligations were assumed by God, which is implied in the statement, "but God is one." In the Sept., Job 9:33, daysman.

MEDITATE

1. *meletaō* (μελετάω, 3191), primarily, "to care for" (akin to *meletē*, "care"; cf. *melei*, "it is a care"), denotes (a) "to attend to, practice," 1 Tim. 4:15, RV, "be diligent in" (KJV, "meditate upon"); to practice is the prevalent sense of the word, and the context is not against this significance in the RV rendering; some mss. have it in Mark 13:11; (b) "to ponder, imagine," Acts 4:25. See IMAGINE.

2. *promeletaō* (προμελετάω, 4304), "to premeditate," is used in Luke 21:14. *Note:* In the corresponding passage in Mark 13:11, the most authentic mss. have the verb *promerimnaō*, "to be anxious beforehand" (RV); see No. 1.

MEEK, MEEKNESS

A. Adjective.

praus or *praos* (πραΰς or πρᾷος, 4239) denotes "gentle, mild, meek"; for its significance see the corresponding noun, below, B. Christ uses it of His own disposition, Matt. 11:29; He gives it in the third of His Beatitudes, 5:5; it is said of Him as the King Messiah, 21:5, from Zech. 9:9; it is an adornment of the Christian profession, 1 Pet. 3:4. Cf. *ēpios*, "gentle, of a soothing disposition," 1 Thess. 2:7; 2 Tim. 2:24.

B. Nouns.

1. *prautēs*, or *praotēs*, an earlier form, (πραΰτης, 4240) denotes "meekness." In its use in Scripture, in which it has a fuller, deeper significance than in nonscriptural Greek writings, it consists not in a person's "outward behavior only; nor yet in his relations to his fellow-men; as little in his mere natural disposition. Rather it is an inwrought grace of the soul; and the exercises of it are first and chiefly towards God. It is that temper of spirit in which we accept His dealings with us as good, and therefore without disputing or resisting; it is closely linked with the word *tapeinophrosunē* [humility], and follows directly upon it, Eph. 4:2; Col. 3:12; cf. the adjectives in the Sept. of Zeph. 3:12, "meek and lowly"; ... it is only the humble heart which is also the meek, and which, as such, does not fight against God and more or less struggle and contend with Him. This meekness, however, being first of all a meekness before God, is also such in the face of men, even of evil men, out of a sense that these, with the insults and injuries which they may inflict, are permitted and employed by Him for the chastening and purifying of His elect" (Trench, *Syn.* Sec. XLII). In Gal. 5:23 it is associated with *enkrateia*, "self-control."

The meaning of *prautēs* "is not readily expressed in English, for the terms meekness, mildness, commonly used, suggest weakness and pusillanimity to a greater or less extent, whereas *prautēs* does nothing of the kind. Nevertheless, it is difficult to find a rendering less open to objection than 'meekness'; 'gentleness' has been suggested, but as *prautēs* describes a condition of mind and heart, and as 'gentleness' is appropriate rather to actions, this word is no better than that used in both English Versions. It must be clearly understood, therefore, that the meekness manifested by the Lord and commended to the believer is the fruit of power. The common assumption is that when a man is meek it is because he cannot help himself; but the Lord was 'meek' because he had the infinite resources of God at His command. Described negatively, meekness is the opposite to self-assertiveness and self-interest; it is equanimity of spirit that is neither elated nor cast down, simply because it is not occupied with self at all.

"In 2 Cor. 10:1 the apostle appeals to the 'meekness ... of Christ.' Christians are charged to show 'all meekness toward all men,' Titus 3:2, for meekness becomes 'God's elect,' Col. 3:12. To this virtue the 'man of God' is urged; he is to 'follow after meekness' for his own sake, 1 Tim. 6:11 (the best texts have No. 2 here however), and in his service, and more especially in his dealings with the 'ignorant and erring,' he is to exhibit 'a spirit of meekness,' 1 Cor. 4:21, and Gal. 6:1; even 'they that oppose themselves' are to be corrected in meekness, 2 Tim. 2:25. James exhorts his 'beloved brethren' to 'receive with meekness the implanted word,' 1:21. Peter enjoins 'meekness' in setting forth the grounds of the Christian hope, 3:15."

2. *praupathia*, "a meek disposition, meekness" (*praus*, "meek," *paschō*, "to suffer"), is found in the best texts in 1 Tim. 6:11.

MELODY (Verb)

psallō (ψάλλω, 5567), primarily "to twitch, twang," then, "to play a stringed instrument with the fingers," and hence, in the Sept., "to sing with a harp, sing psalms," denotes, in the NT, "to sing a hymn, sing praise"; in Eph. 5:19, "making melody" (for the preceding word *adō*, see SING). Elsewhere it is rendered "sing," Rom. 15:9; 1 Cor. 14:15; in Jas. 5:13, RV, "let him sing praise" (KJV, "let him sing psalms"). See SING.

MEMBER

melos (μέλος, 3196), "a limb of the body," is used (a) literally, Matt. 5:29-30; Rom. 6:13 (twice), 19 (twice); 7:5, 23 (twice); 12:4 (twice); 1 Cor. 12:12 (twice), 14, 18-20, 22, 25-26 (twice); Jas. 3:5, 6; 4:1; in Col. 3:5, "mortify therefore your members which are upon the earth"; since our bodies and their "members" belong to the earth, and are the instruments of sin, they are referred to as such (cf. Matt. 5:29-30; Rom. 7:5, 23, mentioned above); the putting to death is not physical, but ethical; as the physical "members" have distinct individualities, so those evils, of which the physical "members" are agents, are by analogy regarded as examples of the way in which the "members" work if not put to death; this is not precisely the same as "the old man," v. 9, i.e., the old nature, though there is a connection; (b) metaphorically, "of believers as members of Christ," 1 Cor. 6:15 (1st part); of one another, Rom. 12:5 (as with the natural illustration, so with the spiritual analogy, there is not only vital unity, and harmony in operation, but diversity, all being essential to effectivity; the unity is not due to external organization but to common and vital union in Christ); there is stress in v. 5 upon "many" and "in Christ" and "members;" 1 Cor. 12:27 (of the "members" of a local church as a body); Eph. 4:25 (of the "members" of the whole Church as the mystical body of Christ); in 1 Cor. 6:15 (2nd part), of one who practices fornication.

MEMORIAL

mnēmosunon (μνημόσυνον, 3422) denotes "a memorial," that which keeps alive the memory of someone or something (from *mnēmōn*, "mindful"), Matt. 26:13; Mark 14:9; Acts 10:4.

For **MEMORY (keep in)** see KEEP, *Note* (8)

MEN-PLEASERS

anthrōpareskos (ἀνθρωπάρεσκος, 441), an adjective signifying "studying to please men" (*anthrōpos*, "man," *areskō*, "to please"), designates, "not simply one who is pleasing to men ..., but one who endeavors to please men and not God" (Cremer). It is used in Eph. 6:6 and Col. 3:22. In the Sept., Ps. 53:5.

MEN-STEALERS

andrapodistēs (ἀνδραποδιστής, 405), "a slave dealer, kidnapper," from *andrapodon*, "a slave captured in war," a word found in the plural in the papyri, e.g., in a catalogue of property and in combination with *tetrapoda*, "four-footed things" (*andrapodon, anēr*, "a man," *pous*, "a foot"); *andrapodon* "was never an ordinary word for slave; it was too brutally obvious a reminder of the principle which made quadruped and human chattels differ only in the number of their legs" (Moulton and Milligan, *Vocab.*). The verb *andrapodizō* supplied the noun "with the like odious meaning," which appears in 1 Tim. 1:10.

MENTION (Noun and Verb)

A. Noun.

mneia (μνεία, 3417), "remembrance, mention" (akin to *mimnēskō*, "to remind, remember"), is always used in connection with prayer, and translated "mention" in Rom. 1:9; Eph. 1:16; 1 Thess. 1:2; Philem. 4, in each of which it is preceded by the verb to make; "remembrance" in Phil. 1:3; 1 Thess. 3:6; 2 Tim. 1:3. Some mss. have it in Rom. 12:13, instead of *chreiais*, necessities. See REMEMBRANCE. Cf. *mnēmē*, "memory, remembrance," 2 Pet. 1:15.

B. Verb.

mnēmoneuō (μνημονεύω, 3421), which most usually means "to call to mind, remember," signifies "to make mention of," in Heb. 11:22. See REMEMBER.

MERCIFUL (Adjective, and Verb, to be), MERCY (Noun, and Verb, to have, etc.)

A. Nouns.

1. *eleos* (ἔλεος, 1656) "is the outward manifestation of pity; it assumes need on the part of him who receives it, and resources adequate to meet the need on the part of him who shows it. It is used (a) of God, who is rich in mercy, Eph. 2:4, and who has provided salvation for all men, Titus 3:5, for Jews, Luke 1:72, and Gentiles, Rom. 15:9. He is merciful to those who fear him, Luke 1:50, for they also are compassed with infirmity, and He alone can succor them. Hence they are to pray boldly for mercy, Heb. 4:16, and if for themselves, it is seemly that they should ask for mercy for one another, Gal. 6:16; 1 Tim. 1:2. When God brings His salvation to its issue at the Coming of Christ, His people will obtain His mercy, 2 Tim. 1:16; Jude 21; (b) of men; for since God is

merciful to them, He would have them show mercy to one another, Matt. 9:13; 12:7; 23:23; Luke 10:37; Jas. 2:13.

"Wherever the words mercy and peace are found together they occur in that order, except in Gal. 6:16. Mercy is the act of God, peace is the resulting experience in the heart of man. Grace describes God's attitude toward the lawbreaker and the rebel; mercy is His attitude toward those who are in distress."

"In the order of the manifestation of God's purposes of salvation grace must go before mercy ... only the forgiven may be blessed .... From this it follows that in each of the apostolic salutations where these words occur, grace precedes mercy, 1 Tim. 1:2; 2 Tim. 1:2; Titus 1:4 (in some mss.); 2 John 3" (Trench, *Syn.* Sec. XLVII).

2. *oiktirmos* (οἰκτιρμός, 3628), "pity, compassion for the ills of others," is used (a) of God, Who is "the Father of mercies," 2 Cor. 1:3; His "mercies" are the ground upon which believers are to present their bodies a living sacrifice, holy, acceptable to God, as their reasonable service, Rom. 12:1; under the Law he who set it at nought died without compassion, Heb. 10:28; (b) of men; believers are to feel and exhibit compassions one toward another, Phil. 2:1, RV "compassions," and Col. 3:12, RV "(a heart) of compassion"; in these two places the word is preceded by No. 3, rendered "tender mercies" in the former, and "a heart" in the latter, RV.

3. *splanchnon* (σπλάγχνον, 4698), "affections, the heart," always in the plural in the NT, has reference to "feelings of kindness, goodwill, pity," Phil. 2:1, RV, "tender mercies;" see AFFECTION, No. 2, and BOWELS.

Note: In Acts. 13:34 the phrase, lit., "the holy things, the faithful things (of David)" is translated, "the holy and sure blessings," RV; the KJV, following the mss. in which the words "holy and" are absent, has "the sure mercies," but notices the full phrase in the margin.

B. Verbs.

1. *eleeō* (ἐλεέω, 1653), akin to A, No. 1, signifies, in general, "to feel sympathy with the misery of another," and especially sympathy manifested in act, (a) in the active voice, "to have pity or mercy on, to show mercy" to, e.g., Matt. 9:27; 15:22; 17:15; 18:33; 20:30, 31 (three times in Mark, four in Luke); Rom. 9:15, 16, 18; 11:32; 12:8; Phil. 2:27; Jude 22, 23; (b) in the passive voice, "to have pity or mercy shown one, to obtain mercy," Matt. 5:7; Rom. 11:30, 31; 1 Cor. 7:25; 2 Cor. 4:1; 1 Tim. 1:13, 16; 1 Pet. 2:10.

2. *oikteirō* (οἰκτείρω, 3627), akin to A, No. 2, "to have pity on" (from *oiktos*, "pity": *oi*, an exclamation, = oh!), occurs in Rom. 9:15 (twice), where it follows No. 1 (twice); the point established there and in Exod. 33:19, from the Sept. of which it is quoted, is that the "mercy" and compassion shown by God are determined by nothing external to His attributes. Speaking generally *oikteirō* is a stronger term than *eleeō*.

3. *hilaskomai* (ἱλάσκομαι, 2433) in profane Greek meant "to conciliate, appease, propitiate, cause the gods to be reconciled"; their goodwill was not regarded as their natural condition, but as something to be earned. The heathen believed their gods to be naturally alienated in feeling from man. In the NT the word never means to conciliate God; it signifies (a) "to be propitious, merciful," Luke 18:13, in the prayer of the publican; (b) "to expiate, make propitiation for," Heb. 2:17, "make propitiation."

That God is not of Himself already alienated from man, see John 3:16. His attitude toward the sinner does not need to be changed by his efforts. With regard to his sin, an expiation is necessary, consistently with God's holiness and for His righteousness' sake, and that expiation His grace and love have provided in the atoning sacrifice of His Son; man, himself a sinner, justly exposed to God's wrath (John 3:36), could never find an expiation. As Lightfoot says, "when the NT writers speak at length on the subject of Divine wrath, the hostility is represented, not as on the part of God, but of men." Through that which God has accomplished in Christ, by His death, man, on becoming regenerate, escapes the merited wrath of God. The making of this expiation [(b) above], with its effect in the mercy of God (a) is what is expressed in *hilaskomai*. The Sept. uses the compound verb *exilaskomai*, e.g., Gen. 32:20; Exod. 30:10, 15, 16; 32:30, and frequently in Lev. and Num. See PROPITIATION.

C. Adjectives.

1. *eleēmōn* (ἐλεήμων, 1655), "merciful," akin to A, No. 1, not simply possessed of pity but actively compassionate, is used of Christ as a High Priest, Heb. 2:17, and of those who are like God, Matt. 5:7 (cf. Luke 6:35, 36, where the RV, "sons" is to be read, as representing characteristics resembling those of their Father).

2. *oiktirmōn* (οἰκτίρμων, 3629) "pitiful, compassionate for the ills of others," a stronger term than No. 1 (akin to A, No. 2), is used twice in Luke 6:36, "merciful" (of the character of God, to be expressed in His people); Jas. 5:11, RV, "merciful," KJV, "of tender mercy."

3. *hileōs* (ἵλεως, 2436), "propitious, merciful" (akin to B, No. 3), was used in profane Greek just as in the case of the verb (which see). There is nothing of this in the use of the word in Scripture. The quality expressed by it there essentially appertains to God, though man is undeserving of it. It is used only of God, Heb. 8:12; in Matt. 16:22, "Be it far from Thee" (Peter's word to Christ) may have the meaning given in the RV marg., "(God) have mercy on Thee," lit.,

"propitious to Thee" (KJV marg., "Pity Thyself") Cf. the Sept., 2 Sam. 20:20; 23:17.

4. *aneleos* or *anileōs* (ἀνέλεος or ἀνίλεως, 448), "unmerciful, merciless" (*a*, negative, *n*, euphonic, and A, No. 2, or C, No. 3), occurs in Jas. 2:13, said of judgment on him who shows no mercy.

MERCY SEAT

hilastērion (ἱλαστήριον, 2435), "the lid or cover of the ark of the covenant," signifies the Propitiatory, so called on account of the expiation made once a year on the great Day of Atonement, Heb. 9:5. For the formation see Exod. 25:17-21. The Heb. word is *kapporeth*, "the cover," a meaning connected with the covering or removal of sin (Ps. 32:1) by means of expiatory sacrifice. This mercy seat, together with the ark, is spoken of as the footstool of God, 1 Chron. 28:2; cf. Ps. 99:5; 132:7. The Lord promised to be present upon it and to commune with Moses "from above the mercy seat, from between the two cherubim," Exod. 25:22 (see CHERUBIM). In the Sept. the word *epithēma*, which itself means "a cover," is added to *hilastērion; epithēma* was simply a translation of *kapporeth;* accordingly, *hilastērion*, not having this meaning, and being essentially connected with propitiation, was added. Eventually *hilasterion* stood for both. In 1 Chron. 28:11 the Holy of Holies is called "the House of the Kapporeth" (see RV, marg.).

Through His voluntary expiatory sacrifice in the shedding of His blood, under divine judgment upon sin, and through His resurrection, Christ has become the Mercy Seat for His people. See Rom. 3:25, and see PROPITIATION, B, No. 1.

MERRY (to be, to make)

1. *euphrainō* (εὐφραίνω, 2165), in the active voice, "to cheer, make glad," 2 Cor. 2:2, is used everywhere else in the passive voice, signifying, "to be happy, rejoice, make merry," and translated "to be merry" in Luke 12:19; 15:23, 24, 29, 32; in 16:19, "fared (sumptuously)"; in Rev. 11:10, make merry. See FARE, GLAD, REJOICE.

2. *euthumeō* (εὐθυμέω, 2114), from *eu*, "well," and *thumos*, "the soul," as the principle of feeling, especially strong feeling, signifies "to make cheerful"; it is used intransitively in the NT, "to be of good cheer," Acts 27:22, 25; in Jas. 5:13, RV, "is (any) cheerful?" (KJV, "... merry?"). See CHEER.

MESSAGE

1. *angelia* (ἀγγελία, 31), akin to *angellō*, "to bring a message, proclaim," denotes a "message, proclamation, news," 1 John 1:5 [some mss. have *epangelia*. see *Note* (1)]; 1 John 3:11, where the word is more precisely defined (by being followed by the conjunction "that," expressing the purpose that we should love one another) as being virtually equivalent to an order.

Notes: (1) *Epangelia* (*epi*, "upon," and No. 1), "a promise," is found in some mss. in 1 John 1:5, "message" (see No. 1). See PROMISE. (2) In Luke 19:14, KJV, *presbeia*, is translated "a message"; RV, "an ambassage," as in 14:32. See AMBASSAGE.

2. *akoē* (ἀκοή, 189), "hearing," also denotes "the thing heard, a message"; in 1 Thess. 2:13, it is associated with *logos*, "a word," lit., "the word of hearing" (RV marg.), RV, "the word of the message," KJV, "the word ... which ye heard"; so in Heb. 4:2, RV, "the word of hearing" (KJV, "the word preached). See HEARING.

3. *kērugma* (κήρυγμα, 2782), "that which is proclaimed by a herald, a proclamation, preaching," is translated "the message" in Titus 1:3, RV (KJV, preaching). See PREACHING.

MESSENGER

1. *angelos* (ἄγγελος, 32), "a messenger, an angel, one sent," is translated "messenger," of John the Baptist, Matt. 11:10; Mark 1:2; Luke 7:27; in the plural, of John's "messengers," 7:24; of those whom Christ sent before Him when on His journey to Jerusalem, 9:52; of Paul's "thorn in the flesh," "a messenger of Satan," 2 Cor. 12:7; of the spies as received by Rahab, Jas. 2:25. See ANGEL.

2. *apostolos* (ἀπόστολος, 652), "an apostle," is translated "messengers" in 2 Cor. 8:23 regarding Titus and "the other brethren," whom Paul describes to the church at Corinth as "messengers of the churches," in respect of offerings from those in Macedonia for the needy in Judea; in Phil. 2:25, of Epaphroditus as the "messenger" of the church at Philippi to the apostle in ministering to his need; RV marg. in each case, "apostle." See APOSTLE.

MIDDAY

Note: In Acts 26:13, "at midday" translates the adjective *mesos*, "middle," and the noun *hēmera*, "a day," in a combined adverbial phrase.

MIDNIGHT

mesonuktion (μεσονύκτιον, 3317), an adjective denoting "at, or of, midnight," is used as a noun in Mark 13:35; Luke 11:5; Acts 16:25; 20:7.

Note: In Matt. 25:6 "at midnight" translates the adjective *mesos*, and noun *nux*, "night," in the combined adverbial phrase. In Acts 27:27 "about midnight" translates an adverbial phrase consisting of *kata*, "towards," followed by *mesos*, "middle" and *nux*, "night," with the article, lit., "towards (the) middle of the night."

MIGHT (Noun), MIGHTY, MIGHTILY, MIGHTIER

A. Nouns.

1. *dunamis* (δύναμις, 1411), "power," (a) used relatively, denotes "inherent ability, capability, ability to perform anything," e.g., Matt. 25:15, "ability"; Acts 3:12, "power"; 2 Thess. 1:7, RV, "(angels) of His power" (KJV, "mighty"); Heb. 11:11, RV, "power" (KJV, "strength"); see ABILITY; (b) used absolutely, denotes (1) "power to work, to carry something into effect," e.g., Luke 24:49; (2) "power in action," e.g., Rom. 1:16; 1 Cor. 1:18; it is translated "might" in the KJV of Eph. 1:21 (RV, "power"); so 3:16; Col. 1:11 (1st clause); 2 Pet. 2:11; in Rom. 15:19, KJV, this noun is rendered "mighty"; RV, "(in the) power of signs." The RV consistently avoids the rendering "might" for *dunamis;* the usual rendering is "power." Under this heading comes the rendering "mighty works," e.g., Matt. 7:22, RV (KJV, "wonderful works"); 11:20-23; singular number in Mark 6:5; in Matt. 14:2 and Mark 6:14 the RV has "powers"; in 2 Cor. 12:12, RV, "mighty works" (KJV, "mighty deeds"). See MIRACLE, especially POWER.

Note: Dunamis, "power," is to be distinguished from *exousia*, "the right to exercise power." See DOMINION, *Note*.

2. *ischus* (ἰσχύς, 2479) denotes "might, strength, power," (a) inherent and in action as used of God, Eph. 1:19, RV, "(the strength, *kratos*, of His) might," KJV, "(His mighty) power," i.e., power (over external things) exercised by strength; Eph. 6:10, "of His might"; 2 Thess. 1:9, RV, "(from the glory) of His might" (KJV "power"); Rev. 5:12, RV, "might" (KJV, "strength"); 7:12, "might"; (b) as an endowment, said (1) of angels, 2 Pet. 2:11; here the order is No. 2 and No. 1, RV, "might and power," which better expresses the distinction than the KJV, "power and might"; in some mss. in Rev. 18:2 it is said of the voice of an angel [see E, (c)]; the most authentic mss. have the adjective *ischuros*, "mighty"; (2) of men, Mark 12:30, 33; Luke 10:27 (RV and KJV, "strength," in all three verses); 1 Pet. 4:11, RV, "strength" (KJV, "ability": this belongs rather to No. 1). Either "strength" or "might" expresses the true significance of *ischus*. See ABILITY, POWER, STRENGTH.

Notes: (1) In Luke 9:43, KJV, *megaleiotēs*, "greatness, majesty," is translated "mighty power" (RV, "majesty"). (2) Cf. *kratos* (see POWER).

B. Adjectives.

1. *dunatos* (δυνατός, 1415), "powerful, mighty" (akin to A, No. 1), is used, with that significance, (1) of God, Luke 1:49, "mighty"; Rom. 9:22, "power" (here the neuter of the adjective is used with the article, as a noun, equivalent to *dunamis*); frequently with the meaning "able" (see ABLE, C, No. 1); (2) of Christ, regarded as a prophet, Luke 24:19 ("in deed and word"); (3) of men: Moses, Acts 7:22 ("in his words and works"); Apollos, 18:24, "in the Scriptures"; of those possessed of natural power, 1 Cor. 1:26; of those possessed of spiritual power, 2 Cor. 10:4. For the shades of meaning in the translation "strong," see Rom. 15:1; 2 Cor. 12:10; 13:9. For Rev. 6:15, see No. 2, below; see STRONG.

2. *ischuros* (ἰσχυρός, 2478), "strong, mighty" (akin to A, No. 2, and with corresponding adjectival significance), is usually translated "strong"; "mighty" in Luke 15:14 (of a famine); Rev. 19:6 (of thunders); 19:18 (of men): in the following, where the KJV has "mighty," the RV substitutes "strong," 1 Cor. 1:27; Rev. 6:15 (KJV, "mighty men"); 18:10, 21; Heb. 11:34, RV, "(waxed) mighty" (KJV, "valiant"). See BOISTEROUS, POWERFUL, STRONG (where the word is analyzed).

3. *ischuroteros* (ἰσχυρότερος, 2478), "stronger, mightier," the comparative degree of No. 2, is translated "mightier" in Matt. 3:11; Mark 1:7; Luke 3:16; "stronger" in Luke 11:22; 1 Cor. 1:25; 10:22. See STRONG.

4. *biaios* (βίαιος, 972), "violent" (from *bia*, "force, violence, strength," found in Acts 5:26; 21:35; 24:7; 27:41), occurs in Acts 2:2, of wind.

5. *krataios* (κραταιός, 2900), "strong, mighty" (akin to *kratos*, "strength," relative and manifested power: see MIGHTILY, below), is found in 1 Pet. 5:6, of the "mighty" hand of God.

6. *megaleios* (μεγαλεῖος, 3167) is rendered "mighty" in Acts 2:11, RV See WONDERFUL, *Note* (2).

Notes: (1) In Luke 1:52, KJV, *dunastēs*, "a potentate, prince," is translated "mighty" (RV, "princes"). (2) In Rev. 6:13, KJV, *megas*, "great," is translated "mighty" (RV, "great"), of a wind. (3) In Rev. 16:18, KJV, *tēlikoutos*, "so great" (when said of things), is translated "so mighty" (RV, "so great"), of an earthquake.

C. Verb.

dunateō (δυνατέω, 1414), "to be powerful" (akin to A, No. 1 and B, No. 1), is found in the most authentic mss. in Rom. 14:4 (some have *dunatos*, B, No. 1), RV "(the Lord) hath power," KJV, "(God) is able"; similarly, as regard mss., in 2 Cor. 9:8, where the RV and KJV have "(God) is able"; in 2 Cor. 13:3, KJV, "is mighty," RV, "is powerful" (according to the general significance of *dunamis*).

Note: In Gal. 2:8, KJV, *energeō*, "to work, work in" (*en*, "in," *ergon*, "work"), is first translated "wrought effectually," then "was mighty in" (RV, "wrought for," in both places; the probable meaning is "in me").

D. Adverb.

eutonōs (εὐτόνως, 2159), "vigorously, vehemently" (*eu*, "well," *teinō*, "to stretch"), is translated "mightily" in Acts 18:28, KJV, of the power of Apollos in "confuting" the Jews (RV, "powerfully"); in Luke 23:10 it is rendered "vehemently." See POWERFUL. In the Sept., Josh. 6:7, "(let them sound) loudly."

E. Phrases.

The following phrases signify "mightily:" (a) *en dunamei,* Col. 1:29, of the inward power of God's working, lit., "in power," as RV marg. (*en,* "in," and A, No. 1); (b) *kata kratos,* Acts 19:20, of the increase of the word of the Lord in a place, lit, "according to might"; (c) in Rev. 18:2 some mss. have *en ischui,* lit., "in strength" (*en,* "in," and A, No. 2), of the voice of an angel.

MILK

gala (γάλα, 1051) is used (a) literally, 1 Cor. 9:7; (b) metaphorically, of rudimentary spiritual teaching, 1 Cor. 3:2; Heb. 5:12, 13; 1 Pet. 2:2; here the meaning largely depends upon the significance of the word *logikos,* which the KJV renders "of the word," RV "spiritual." While *logos* denotes "a word," the adjective *logikos* is never used with the meaning assigned to it in the KJV, nor does the context in 1:23 compel this meaning. While it is true that the Word of God, like "milk," nourishes the soul, and this is involved in the exhortation, the only other occurrence in the NT is Rom. 12:1, where it is translated "reasonable," i.e., rational, intelligent (service), in contrast to the offering of an irrational animal; so here the nourishment may be understood as of that spiritually rational nature which, acting through the regenerate mind, develops spiritual growth. God's Word is not given so that it is impossible to understand it, or that it requires a special class of men to interpret it; its character is such that the Holy Spirit who gave it can unfold its truths even to the young convert. Cf. 1 John 2:27.

MILLSTONE

A. Noun.

mulos (μύλος, 3458) denotes "a handmill," consisting of two circular stones, one above the other, the lower being fixed. From the center of the lower a wooden pin passes through a hole in the upper, into which the grain is thrown, escaping as flour between the stones and falling on a prepared material below them. The handle is inserted into the upper stone near the circumference. Small stones could be turned by one woman (millgrinding was a work deemed fit only for women and slaves; cf. Judg. 16:21); larger ones were turned by two (cf. Matt. 24:41) or more.

Still larger ones were turned by an ass (*onikos*), Matt. 18:6, RV, "a great millstone" (marg., "a millstone turned by an ass"), indicating the immediate and overwhelming drowning of one who causes one young believer to stumble; Mark 9:42 (where some mss. have *lithos mulikos,* "a stone of a mill," as in Luke 17:2); Rev. 18:22 (some mss. have it in v. 21, see below).

B. Adjectives.

1. *mulikos* (μυλικός, 3457), "of a mill," occurs in Luke 17:2 (see above).

2. *mulinos* (3458(v)), "made of millstone," is used with *lithos,* "a stone"; and with the adjective *megas,* "great," in the best mss. in Rev. 18:21 (some have the word *mulos;* see A).

MIND (Noun and Verb)

A. Nouns.

1. *nous* (νοῦς, 3563), "mind," denotes, speaking generally, the seat of reflective consciousness, comprising the faculties of perception and understanding, and those of feeling, judging and determining.

Its use in the NT may be analyzed as follows: it denotes (a) the faculty of knowing, the seat of the understanding, Luke 24:45; Rom. 1:28; 14:5; 1 Cor. 14:15, 19; Eph. 4:17; Phil. 4:7; Col. 2:18; 1 Tim. 6:5; 2 Tim. 3:8; Titus 1:15; Rev. 13:18; 17:9; (b) counsels, purpose, Rom. 11:34 (of the "mind" of God); 12:2; 1 Cor. 1:10; 2:16, twice (1) of the thoughts and counsels of God, (2) of Christ, a testimony to His Godhood; Eph. 4:23; (c) the new nature, which belongs to the believer by reason of the new birth, Rom. 7:23, 25, where it is contrasted with "the flesh," the principle of evil which dominates fallen man. Under (b) may come 2 Thess. 2:2, where it stands for the determination to be steadfast amidst afflictions, through the confident expectation of the day of rest and recompense mentioned in the first chapter.

2. *dianoia* (διάνοια, 1271), lit. "a thinking through, or over, a meditation, reflecting," signifies (a) like No. 1, "the faculty of knowing, understanding, or moral reflection," (1) with an evil significance, a consciousness characterized by a perverted moral impulse, Eph. 2:3 (plural); 4:18; (2) with a good significance, the faculty renewed by the Holy Spirit, Matt. 22:37; Mark 12:30; Luke 10:27; Heb. 8:10; 10:16; 1 Pet. 1:13; 1 John 5:20; (b) "sentiment, disposition" (not as a function but as a product); (1) in an evil sense, Luke 1:51, "imagination"; Col. 1:21; (2) in a good sense, 2 Pet. 3:1.

3. *ennoia* (ἔννοια, 1771), "an idea, notion. intent," is rendered "mind" in 1 Pet. 4:1; see INTENT.

4. *noēma* (νόημα, 3540), "thought, design," is rendered "minds" in 2 Cor. 3:14; 4:4; 11:3; Phil. 4:7; see DEVICE, No. 2.

5. *gnōmē* (γνώμη, 1106), "a purpose, judgment, opinion," is translated "mind" in Philem. 14 and Rev. 17:13. See JUDGMENT, No. 4.

6. *phronēma* (φρόνημα, 5427) denotes "what one has in the mind, the thought" (the content of the process expressed in *phroneō,* "to have in mind, to think"); or "an object of thought"; in Rom. 8:6 (KJV, "to be carnally minded" and "to be spiritually minded"), the RV, adhering to the use of the noun, renders by "the mind of the flesh," in vv. 6 and 7, and

"the mind of the spirit," in v. 6. In v. 27 the word is used of the "mind" of the Holy Spirit.

Notes: (1) This word is to be distinguished from *phronēsis*, which denotes "an understanding, leading to right action, prudence," Luke 1:17; Eph. 1:8. (2) In three places, Acts 14:2; Phil. 1:27; Heb. 12:3, the KJV translates *psuchē*, "the soul," by "mind" (RV, "soul").

B. Verbs.

1. *phroneō* (φρονέω, 5426) signifies (a) "to think, to be minded in a certain way"; (b) "to think of, be mindful of." It implies moral interest or reflection, not mere unreasoning opinion. Under (a) it is rendered by the verb "to mind" in the following: Rom. 8:5, "(they that are after the flesh) do mind (the things of the flesh)"; 12:16, "be of (the same) mind," lit., "minding the same," and "set (not) your mind on," RV, KJV, "mind (not)"; 15:5, "to be of (the same) mind," RV, (KJV, "to be like-minded"); so the RV in 2 Cor. 13:11, KJV, "be of (one) mind"; Gal. 5:10, "ye will be (none otherwise) minded"; Phil. 1:7, RV, "to be (thus) minded," KJV, "to think (this)"; 2:2, RV, "be of (the same) mind," KJV, "be likeminded," and "being ... of (one) mind," lit., "minding (the one thing)"; 2:5, RV, "have (this) mind," KJV, "let (this) mind be," lit., "mind this"; 3:15, "let us ... be (thus) minded," and "(if) ... ye are (otherwise) minded" (some mss. have the verb in v. 16); 3:19, "(who) mind (earthly things)"; 4:2, "be of (the same) mind"; Col. 3:2, RV and KJV marg., "set your mind," lit., "mind (the things above)," KJV, "set your affection." See REGARD.

2. *anamimnēskō* (ἀναμιμνήσκω, 363), "to remind, call to remembrance" (*ana*, "up," *mimnēskō*, "to remind"), is translated "called to mind," in Mark 14:72 (passive voice). See REMEMBRANCE.

Note: The lengthened form *epanamimnēskō* is used in Rom. 15:15, KJV, "putting (you) in mind"; RV, "putting (you) again (*epi*) in remembrance."

3. *hupomimnēskō* (ὑπομιμνήσκω, 5279), "to cause one to remember, put one in mind" (*hupo*, "under"), is translated "put (them) in mind" in Titus 3:1. See REMEMBER, REMEMBRANCE.

4. *hupotithēmi* (ὑποτίθημι, 5294), lit., "to place under" (*hupo*, "under," *tithēmi*, "to place"), "to lay down" (of risking the life, Rom. 16:4), also denotes "to suggest, put into one's mind," 1 Tim. 4:6, RV, "put ... in mind" (KJV, "put ... in remembrance").

5. *sōphroneō* (σωφρονέω, 4993) signifies (a) "to be of sound mind," or "in one's right mind, sober-minded" (*sozo*, "to save," *phrēn*, "the mind"), Mark 5:15 and Luke 8:35, "in his right mind"; 2 Cor. 5:13, RV, "we are of sober mind" (KJV, "we be sober"); (b) "to be temperate, self-controlled," Titus 2:6, "to be sober-minded"; 1 Pet. 4:7, RV, "be ye ... of sound mind" (KJV, "be ye sober"). See also Rom. 12:3. See SOBER.

Note: In Acts 20:13, KJV, *mellō*, "to be about to, to intend," is translated "minding" (RV, "intending"). See INTEND.

C. Adjective.

homophrōn (ὁμόφρων, 3675), "agreeing, of one mind" (*homos*, "same," *phrēn*, "the mind"), is used in 1 Pet. 3:8.

Notes: (1) For the noun *sōphronismos*, in 2 Tim. 1:7, see DISCIPLINE. (2) In Rom. 15:6, KJV, the adverb *homothumadon*, "of one accord," is translated "with one mind" (RV, "of one accord"). See ACCORD. (3) See also DOUBTFUL, FERVENT, HUMBLENESS, HUMILITY, LOWLINESS, READINESS, WILLING.

MINDED

1. *phroneō* (φρονέω, 5426): see MIND, B, No. 1.

2. *boulomai* (βούλομαι, 1014), "to wish, will, desire, purpose" (akin to *boulē*, "counsel, purpose"), is translated "was minded" in Matt. 1:19; Acts 15:37, RV (KJV, "determined"); 18:27, RV (KJV, "was disposed"); 19:30, RV (KJV, "would have"); 5:33, RV, "were minded" (KJV, "took counsel"); 18:15, RV, "I am (not) minded (to be)," KJV, "I will (be no)"; Heb. 6:17, "being minded," RV (KJV, "willing"), said of God. See COUNSEL.

3. *bouleuō* (βουλεύω, 1011), "to take counsel," is translated "to be minded" in Acts 27:39; 2 Cor. 1:17, middle voice in each case. See COUNSEL, B, No. 1.

Note: For the noun *phronēma* in Rom. 8:6, see MIND, A, No. 6.

MINDFUL OF (to be)

1. *mimnēskō* (μιμνήσκω, 3403), the tenses of which are from the older verb *mnaomai*, signifies "to remind"; but in the middle voice, "to remember, to be mindful of," in the sense of caring for, e.g., Heb. 2:6, "Thou art mindful"; in 13:3, "remember"; in 2 Tim. 1:4, RV, "remembering" (KJV, "being mindful of"); so in 2 Pet. 3:2. See REMEMBER.

2. *mnēmoneuō* (μνημονεύω, 3421), "to call to mind, remember," is rendered "they had been mindful" in Heb. 11:15. See MENTION, B, REMEMBER.

MINISTER (Noun and Verb)

A. Nouns.

1. *diakonos* (διάκονος, 1249), "a servant, attendant, minister, deacon," is translated "minister" in Mark 10:43; Rom. 13:4 (twice); 15:8; 1 Cor. 3:5; 2 Cor. 3:6; 6:4; 11:15 (twice); Gal. 2:17; Eph. 6:21; Col. 1:7, 23, 25; 4:7; 1 Thess. 3:2; 1 Tim. 4:6. See DEACON.

2. *leitourgos* (λειτουργός, 3011) denoted among the Greeks, firstly, "one who discharged a public office at his own

expense," then, in general, "a public servant, minister." In the NT it is used (a) of Christ, as a "Minister of the sanctuary" (in the Heavens), Heb. 8:2; (b) of angels, Heb. 1:7 (Ps. 104:4); (c) of the apostle Paul, in his evangelical ministry, fulfilling it as a serving priest, Rom. 15:16; that he used it figuratively and not in an ecclesiastical sense, is obvious from the context; (d) of Epaphroditus, as ministering to Paul's needs on behalf of the church at Philippi, Phil. 2:25; here, representative service is in view; (e) of earthly rulers, who though they do not all act consciously as servants of God, yet discharge functions which are the ordinance of God, Rom. 13:6.

3. *hupēretēs* (ὑπηρέτης, 5257), properly "an under rower" (*hupo*, "under," *eretēs*, "a rower"), as distinguished from *nautēs*, "a seaman" (a meaning which lapsed from the word), hence came to denote "any subordinate acting under another's direction"; in Luke 4:20, RV, "attendant," KJV, "minister" it signifies the attendant at the synagogue service; in Acts 13:5, it is said of John Mark, RV, "attendant," KJV, "minister;" in Acts 26:16, "a minister," it is said of Paul as a servant of Christ in the gospel; so in 1 Cor. 4:1, where the apostle associates others with himself, as Apollos and Cephas, as "ministers of Christ." See ATTEND, C.

Note: Other synonymous nouns are *doulos*, "a bondservant"; *oiketēs*, "a household servant"; *misthios*, "a hired servant"; *misthōtos* (ditto); *pais*, "a boy, a household servant." For all these see SERVANT. Speaking broadly, *diakonos* views a servant in relation to his work; doulos, in relation to his master; *hupēretēs*, in relation to his superior; *leitourgos*, in relation to public service.

B. Verbs.

1. *diakoneō* (διακονέω, 1247), akin to A, No. 1, signifies "to be a servant, attendant, to serve, wait upon, minister." In the following it is translated "to minister," except where "to serve" is mentioned: it is used (a) with a general significance, e.g., Matt. 4:11; 20:28; Mark 1:13; 10:45; John 12:26 ("serve," twice); Acts 19:22; Philem. 13; (b) of waiting at table, "ministering" to the guests, Matt. 8:15; Luke 4:39; 8:3; 12:37; 17:8, "serve"; 22:26, "serve," v. 27, "serveth," twice; the 2nd instance, concerning the Lord, may come under (a); so of women preparing food, etc., Mark 1:31; Luke 10:40, "serve"; John 12:2, "served"; (c) of relieving one's necessities, supplying the necessaries of life, Matt. 25:44; 27:55; Mark 15:41; Acts 6:2, "serve"; Rom. 15:25; Heb. 6:10; more definitely in connection with such service in a local church, 1 Tim. 3:10, 13 [there is nothing in the original representing the word "office"; RV, "let them serve as deacons," "they that have served (well) as deacons"]; (d) of attending, in a more general way, to anything that may serve another's interests, as of the work of an amanuensis, 2 Cor. 3:3 (metaphorical): of the conveyance of material gifts for assisting the needy, 2 Cor. 8:19, 20, RV, "is ministered" (KJV, "is administered"); of a variety of forms of service, 2 Tim. 1:18; of the testimony of the OT prophets, 1 Pet. 1:12; of the ministry of believers one to another in various ways, 1 Pet. 4:10, 11 (not here of discharging ecclesiastical functions).

Note: In Heb. 1:14, KJV (2nd part), the phrase *eis diakonian* is translated "to minister," RV, "to do service," lit., "for service"; for the noun "ministering" in the 1st part, see MINISTERING, B.

2. *leitourgeō* (λειτουργέω, 3008), (akin to A, No. 2), in classical Greek, signified at Athens "to supply public offices at one's own cost, to render public service to the State"; hence, generally, "to do service," said, e.g., of service to the gods. In the NT (see *Note* below) it is used (a) of the prophets and teachers in the church at Antioch, who "ministered to the Lord," Acts 13:2; (b) of the duty of churches of the Gentiles to "minister" in "carnal things" to the poor Jewish saints at Jerusalem, in view of the fact that the former had "been made partakers" of the "spiritual things" of the latter, Rom. 15:27; (c) of the official service of priests and Levites under the Law, Heb. 10:11 (in the Sept., e.g., Exod. 29:30; Num. 16:9).

Note: The synonymous verb *latreuō* (properly, "to serve for hire"), which is used in the Sept. of the service of both priests and people (e.g., Exod. 4:3; Deut. 10:12, and in the NT, e.g., Heb. 8:5), and, in the NT, of Christians in general, e.g., Rev. 22:3, is to be distinguished from *leitourgeō*, which has to do with the fulfillment of an office, the discharge of a function, something of a representative character (Eng., "liturgy").

3. *hupēreteō* (ὑπηρετέω, 5256), "to do the service of a *hupēretēs*" (see A, No. 3), properly, "to serve as a rower on a ship," is used (a) of David, as serving the counsel of God in his own generation, Acts 13:36, RV, expressive of the lowly character of his service for God; (b) of Paul's toil in working with his hands, and his readiness to avoid any pose of ecclesiastical superiority, Acts 20:34; (c) of the service permitted to Paul's friends to render to him, 24:23.

4. *hierourgeō* (ἱερουργέω, 2418), "to minister in priestly service" (akin to *hierourgos*, "a sacrificing priest," a word not found in the Sept. or NT: from *hieros*, "sacred," and *ergon*, "work"), is used by Paul metaphorically of his ministry of the Gospel, Rom. 15:16; the offering connected with his priestly ministry is "the offering up of the Gentiles," i.e., the presentation by gentile converts of themselves to God. The apostle uses words proper to the priestly and Levitical ritual, to explain metaphorically his own priestly service. Cf. *prosphora*, "offering up," and *leitourgos*, in the same verse.

5. *parechō* (παρέχω, 3930), "to furnish, provide, supply," is translated "minister" in 1 Tim. 1:4, of the effect of "fables and endless genealogies."

6. *ergazomai* (ἐργάζομαι, 2038), "to work, work out, perform," is translated "minister" in 1 Cor. 9:13; the verb is frequently used of business, or employment, and here the phrase means "those employed in sacred things" or "those who are assiduous in priestly functions."

Notes: (1) The verb *chorēgeō*, rendered "minister" in the KJV of 2 Cor. 9:10, and the strengthened form *epichorēgeō*, rendered by the same verb in the KJV of 2 Cor. 9:10; Gal. 3:5; Col. 2:19; 2 Pet. 1:11, in v. 5, "add," are always translated "to supply" in the RV. Both verbs suggest an abundant supply, and are used of material or of spiritual provision. (2) In Eph. 4:29, KJV, *didōmi*, "to give," is translated "minister" (RV, "give").

MINISTERING, MINISTRATION, MINISTRY

A. Nouns.

1. *diakonua* (διακονία, 1248), "the office and work of a *diakonos*" (see MINISTER, A, No. 1), "service, ministry," is used (a) of domestic duties, Luke 10:40; (b) of religious and spiritual "ministration," (1) of apostolic "ministry," e.g., Acts 1:17, 25; 6:4; 12:25; 21:19; Rom. 11:13, RV (KJV, "office"); (2) of the service of believers, e.g., Acts 6:1; Rom. 12:7; 1 Cor. 12:5, RV, "ministrations" (KJV, "administrations"); 1 Cor. 16:15; 2 Cor. 8:4; 9:1, 12, RV, "ministration"; v. 13; Eph. 4:12, RV, "ministering" (KJV, "the ministry," not in the sense of an ecclesiastical function); 2 Tim. 4:11, RV, "(for) ministering"; collectively of a local church, Acts 11:29, "relief" (RV marg. "for ministry"); Rev. 2:19, RV, "ministry" (KJV, "service"); of Paul's service on behalf of poor saints, Rom. 15:31; (3) of the "ministry" of the Holy Spirit in the gospel, 2 Cor. 3:8; (4) of the "ministry" of angels, Heb. 1:14, RV, "to do service" (KJV, "to minister"); (5) of the work of the gospel, in general, e.g., 2 Cor. 3:9, "of righteousness;" 5:18, "of reconciliation"; (6) of the general "ministry" of a servant of the Lord in preaching and teaching, Acts 20:24; 2 Cor. 4:1; 6:3; 11:8; 1 Tim. 1:12, RV, "(to His) service"; 2 Tim. 4:5; undefined in Col. 4:17; (7) of the Law, as a "ministration" of death, 2 Cor. 3:7; of condemnation, 3:9.

2. *leitourgia* (λειτουργία, 3009), akin to *leitourgos* (see MINISTER, A, No. 2.), to which the meanings of *leitourgia* correspond, is used in the NT of "sacred ministrations," (a) priestly, Luke 1:23; Heb. 8:6; 9:21; (b) figuratively, of the practical faith of the members of the church at Philippi regarded as priestly sacrifice, upon which the apostle's lifeblood might be poured out as a libation, Phil. 2:17; (c) of the "ministration" of believers one to another, regarded as priestly service, 2 Cor. 9:12; Phil. 2:30. See SERVICE.

B. Adjective.

leitourgikos (λειτουργικός, 3010), "of or pertaining to service, ministering," is used in Heb. 1:14, of angels as "ministering spirits" (for the word "do service" in the next clause, see A, No. 1). In the Sept., Exod. 31:10; 39:13; Num. 4:12, 26; 7:5; 2 Chron. 24:14.

MINSTREL

mousikos (μουσικός, 3451) is found in Rev. 18:22, RV, "minstrels" (KJV, "musicians"); inasmuch as other instrumentalists are mentioned, some word like "minstrels" is necessary to make the distinction, hence the RV; Bengel and others translate it "singers." Primarily the word denoted "devoted to the Muses" (the nine goddesses who presided over the principal departments of letters), and was used of anyone devoted to or skilled in arts and sciences, or "learned."

MIRACLE

1. *dunamis* (δύναμις, 1411), "power, inherent ability," is used of works of a supernatural origin and character, such as could not be produced by natural agents and means. It is translated "miracles" in the RV and KJV in Acts 8:13 (where variant readings give the words in different order); 19:11; 1 Cor. 12:10, 28, 29; Gal. 3:5; KJV only, in Acts 2:22 (RV, "mighty works"); Heb. 2:4 (RV, "powers"). In Gal. 3:5, the word may be taken in its widest sense, to include "miracles" both physical and moral. See MIGHT, A, No. 1, POWER.

2. *sēmeion* (σημεῖον, 4592), "a sign, mark, token" (akin to *sēmainō*, "to give a sign"; *sēma*, "a sign"), is used of "miracles" and wonders as signs of divine authority; it is translated "miracles" in the RV and KJV of Luke 23:8; Acts 4:16, 22; most usually it is given its more appropriate meaning "sign," "signs," e.g., Matt. 12:38, 39, and in every occurrence in the Synoptists, excep Luke 23:8; in the following passages in John's Gospel the RV substitutes "sign" or "signs" for the KJV "miracle or miracles"; 2:11, 23; 3:2; 4:54; 6:2, 14, 26; 7:31; 9:16; 10:41; 11:47; 12:18, 37; the KJV also has "signs" elsewhere in this Gospel; in Acts, RV, "signs," KJV, "miracles," in 6:8; 8:6; 15:12; elsewhere only in Rev. 13:14; 16:14; 19:20. See SIGN, TOKEN, WONDER.

MIRROR

esoptron (ἔσοπτρον, 2072), rendered "glass" in the KJV, is used of any surface sufficiently smooth and regular to reflect rays of light uniformly, and thus produce images of objects which actually in front of it appear to the eye as if they were behind it. "Mirrors" in Biblical times were, it seems, metallic; hence the RV adopts the more general term "mirror"; in 1 Cor. 13:12, spiritual knowledge in this life is represented metaphorically as an image dimly perceived in a "mirror"; in Jas. 1:23, the "law of liberty" is figuratively compared to a "mirror"; the hearer who obeys not is like a person who, having looked into the "mirror," forgets the reflected image after turning away; he who obeys is like one who gazes into the "mirror" and retains in his soul the image of what he should be.

Note: For the verb *katoptrizō*, "to reflect as a mirror" (some regard it as meaning "beholding in a mirror"), in 2 Cor. 3:18, see BEHOLD, No. 12.

MISERABLE, MISERABLY, MISERY

A. Adjectives.

1. *eleeinos* (ἐλεεινός, 1652), "pitiable, miserable" (from *eleos*, "mercy, pity"; see MERCY), is used in Rev. 3:17, in the Lord's description of the church at Laodicea; here the idea is probably that of a combination of "misery" and pitiableness.

2. *kakos* (κακός, 2556), "bad, evil," is translated "miserable" in Matt. 21:41, RV (KJV, "wicked"). See BAD.

B. Adverb.

kakōs (κακῶς, 2560), "badly, ill," is translated "miserably" in Matt. 21:41 (see A, No. 2). Adhering to the meaning "evil," and giving the designed stress, the sentence may be rendered, "evil (as they are) he will evilly destroy them."

C. Noun.

talaipōria (ταλαιπωρία, 5004), "hardship, suffering, distress" (akin to *talaiporōs*, "wretched," Rom. 7:24; Rev. 3:17, and to *talaipōreō*, in the middle voice, "to afflict oneself," in Jas. 4:9, "be afflicted"), is used as an abstract noun, "misery," in Rom. 3:16; as a concrete noun, "miseries," in Jas. 5:1.

MIST

1. *achlus* (ἀχλύς, 887), "a mist," especially a dimness of the eyes, is used in Acts 13:11. "In the single place of its NT use it attests the accuracy in the selection of words, and not least of medical words, which 'the beloved physician' so often displays. For him it expresses the mist of darkness ... which fell on the sorcerer Elymas, being the outward and visible sign of the inward spiritual darkness which would be his portion for a while in punishment for his resistance to the truth" (Trench, *Syn.*, Sec. C).

2. *homichlē* (ὁμίχλη), "a mist" (not so thick as *nephos* and *nephelē*, "a cloud"), occurs in 2 Pet. 2:17 (1st part), RV, "mists"; some mss. have *nephelai*, "clouds" (KJV)."

3. *zophos* (ζόφος, 2217) is rendered "mist" in the KJV of 2 Pet. 2:17 (2nd part), RV, "blackness"; "murkiness" would be a suitable rendering. For this and other synonymous terms see BLACK, DARK.

MOCK, MOCKER, MOCKING

A. Verbs.

1. *empaizō* (ἐμπαίζω, 1702), a compound of *paizō*, "to play like a child" (*pais*), "to sport, jest," prefixed by *en*, "in" or "at," is used only in the Synoptists, and, in every instance, of the "mockery" of Christ, except in Matt. 2:16 (there in the sense of deluding, or deceiving, of Herod by the wise men) and in Luke 14:29, of ridicule cast upon the one who after laying a foundation of a tower is unable to finish it. The word is used (a) prophetically by the Lord, of His impending sufferings, Matt. 20:19; Mark 10:34; Luke 18:32; (b) of the actual insults inflicted upon Him by the men who had taken Him from Gethsemane, Luke 22:63; by Herod and his soldiers, Luke 23:11; by the soldiers of the governor, Matt. 27:29, 31; Mark 15:20; Luke 23:36; by the chief priests, Matt. 27:41; Mark 15:31.

2. *muktērizō* (μυκτηρίζω, 3456), from *muktēr*, "the nose," hence, "to turn up the nose at, sneer at, treat with contempt," is used in the passive voice in Gal. 6:7, where the statement "God is not mocked" does not mean that men do not mock Him (see Prov. 1:30, where the Sept. has the same verb); the apostle vividly contrasts the essential difference between God and man. It is impossible to impose upon Him who discerns the thoughts and intents of the heart.

Note: Ekmuktērizō, a strengthened form of the above, "to scoff at," is used in Luke 16:14 and 23:35 (RV, "scoffed at"; KJV, "derided"). See DERIDE, SCOFF.

3. *chleuazō* (χλευάζω, 5512), "to jest, mock, jeer at" (from *chleuē*, "a jest"), is said of the ridicule of some of the Athenian philosophers at the apostle's testimony concerning the resurrection of the dead, Acts 17:32.

4. *diachleuazō*, an intensive form of No. 3, "to scoff at," whether by gesture or word, is said of those who jeered at the testimony given on the Day of Pentecost, Acts 2:13 (some mss. have No. 3).

B. Nouns.

1. *empaiktēs* (ἐμπαίκτης, 1703), "a mocker" (akin to A, No. 1), is used in 2 Pet. 3:3, RV, "mockers." (KJV, "scoffers"); Jude 18, RV and KJV, "mockers." In the Sept., Isa. 3:4.

2. *empaigmos* (ἐμπαιγμός, 1701), the act of the *empaiktēs*, "a mocking," is used in Heb. 11:36, "mockings." In the Sept., Ps. 38:7; Ezek. 22:4.

3. *empaigmonē* (ἐμπαιγμονή, 1701), an abstract noun, "mockery," is used in 2 Pet. 3:3 (some mss. omit it, as in KJV): (see also No. 1, above).

For **MODERATION**, Phil. 4:5, KJV, see FORBEARANCE, C, No. 2

MODEST

kosmios (κόσμιος, 2887), "orderly, wellarranged, decent, modest" (akin to *kosmos*, in its primary sense as "harmonious arrangement adornment"; cf. *kosmikos*, of the world, which is related to *kosmos* in its secondary sense as the world), is used in 1 Tim. 2:9 of the apparel with which Christian women are to adorn themselves; in 3:2 (RV, "orderly;" KJV, "of good behavior"), of one of the qualifications essential for a bishop or overseer. "The well-ordering is not of dress and demeanor only, but of the inner life, uttering indeed and expressing itself in the outward conversation" (Trench, *Syn.*, Sec. XCII). In the Sept., Eccl. 12:9.

MOISTURE

ikmas (ἰκμάς, 2429), "moisture" (probably from an Indo-European root *sik-* indicating "wet"), is used in Luke 8:6. In the Sept., Job 26:14; Jer. 17:8.

MONEY

1. *argurion* (ἀργύριον, 694), properly, "a piece of silver," denotes (a) "silver," e.g., Acts 3:6; (b) a "silver coin," often in the plural, "pieces of silver," e.g., Matt. 26:15; so 28:12, where the meaning is "many, (*hikanos*) pieces of silver"; (c) "money"; it has this meaning in Matt. 25:18, 27; 28:15; Mark 14:11; Luke 9:3; 19:15, 23; 22:5; Acts 8:20 (here the RV has "silver").

Note: In Acts 7:16, for the KJV, "(a sum of) money," the RV has "(a price in) silver." See SILVER.

2. *chrēma* (χρῆμα, 5536), lit., "a thing that one uses" (akin to *chraomai* "to use"), hence, (a) "wealth, riches," Mark 10:23, 24; Luke 18:24; (b) "money," Acts 4:37, singular number, "a sum of money"; plural in 8:18, 20; 24:26. See RICHES.

3. *chalkos* (χαλκός, 5475), "copper," is used, by metonymy, of "copper coin," translated "money," in Mark 6:8; 12:41.

4. *kerma* (κέρμα, 2772), primarily "a slice" (akin to *keirō*, "to cut short"), hence, "a small coin, change," is used in the plural in John 2:15, "the changers' money," probably considerable heaps of small Coins.

5. *nomisma* (νόμισμα, 3546), primarily "that which is established by custom" (*nomos*, "a custom, law"), hence, "the current coin of a state, currency," is found in Matt. 22:19, "(tribute) money." In the Sept., Neh. 7:71.

Note: In Matt. 17:27, KJV, *statēr* ("a coin," estimated at a little over three shillings, equivalent to four *drachmae*, the temple-tax for two persons), is translated "piece of money" (RV, "shekel").

For **MONEY-CHANGER, CHANGER OF MONEY** see CHANGER

MONEY (love of)

philarguria (φιλαργυρία, 5365), from *phileō*, "to love," and *arguros*, "silver," occurs in 1 Tim. 6:10 (cf. *philarguros*, "covetous, avaricious"). Trench contrasts this with *pleonexia*, "covetousness." See under COVET, COVETOUSNESS.

MOON

1. *selēnē* (σελήνη, 4582), from *selas*, "brightness" (the Heb. words are *yarēach*, "wandering," and *lebānāh*, "white"), occurs in Matt. 24:29; Mark 13:24; Luke 21:25; Acts 2:20; 1 Cor. 15:41; Rev. 6:12; 8:12; 12:1; 21:23. In Rev. 12:1, "the moon under her feet" is suggestive of derived authority, just as her being clothed with the sun is suggestive of supreme authority, everything in the symbolism of the passage centers in Israel. In 6:12 the similar symbolism of the sun and "moon" is suggestive of the supreme authority over the world, and of derived authority, at the time of the execution of divine judgments upon nations at the close of the present age.

2. *neomēnia* (νεομηνία, 3561), or *noumēnia* (νουμηνία, 3561), denoting "a new moon" (*neos*, "new," *mēn*, "a month"), is used in Col. 2:16, of a Jewish festival. Judaistic tradition added special features in the liturgy of the synagogue in connection with the observance of the first day of the month, the new "moon" time.

In the OT the RV has "new moon" for KJV, "month" in Num. 29:6; 1 Sam. 20:27; Hos. 5:7. For the connection with feast days see Lev. 23:24; Num. 10:10; 29:1; Ps. 81:3.

MORNING (in the, early in the)

A. Adjectives.

1. *prōios* (πρωΐα, 4405), "early, at early morn" (from *pro*, "before"), is used as a noun in the feminine form *prōia*, "morning" in Matt. 27:1 and John 21:4 (in some mss. in Matt. 21:18 and John 18:28, for B, No. 1, which see). Its adjectival force is retained by regarding it as qualifying the noun *hōra*, "an hour," i.e., "at an early hour."

2. *prōinos* (πρωϊνός, 4407), a later form of No. 1, qualifies *astēr*, "star," in Rev. 2:28 and 22:16 (where some mss. have No. 3). That Christ will give to the overcomer "the morning star" indicates a special interest for such in Himself, as He thus describes Himself in the later passage. For Israel He will appear as "the sun of righteousness"; as the "morning" Star which precedes He will appear for the rapture of the church.

3. *orthrinos* or *orthrios* (ὄρθριος, 3721), "pertaining to dawn or morning," in some mss. in Rev. 22:16 (see No. 2); see DAWN, B, *Note*.

B. Adverb.

prōi (πρωΐ, 4404), "early," is translated "in the morning" in Matt. 16:3; 20:1 (with *hama*, "early"); 21:18; Mark 1:35; 11:20; 13:35; 15:1; "early" in Mark 16:2 (with *lian*, "very"; KJV, "early in the morning"); 16:9; Matt. 21:18 and John 18:28 (in the best texts for A, No. 1); 20:1; Acts 28:23 (with *apo*, "from").

C. Noun.

orthros (ὄρθρος, 3722) denotes "daybreak, dawn," Luke 24:1; John 8:2; Acts 5:21; see DAWN, B.

D. Verb.

orthrizō (ὀρθρίζω, 3719), "to do anything early in the morning," is translated "came early in the morning," in Luke 21:38.

MORROW

1. *aurion* (αὔριον, 839), an adverb denoting "tomorrow," is used (a) with this meaning in Matt. 6:30; Luke 12:28; 13:32, 33; Acts 23:15 (in some mss.), 20; 25:22; 1 Cor. 15:32; Jas. 4:13, (b) with the word *hēmera*, "day," understood (occurring thus in the papyri), translated as a noun, "(the) morrow," Matt. 6:34 (twice); Luke 10:35; Acts 4:3 (KJV, "next day"); 4:5; Jas. 4:14.

2. *epaurion* (ἐπαύριον, 1887), epi, "upon," and No. 1, is used as in (b) above; the RV always translates it "on (the) morrow"; in the following the KJV has "(the) next day," Matt. 27:62; John 1:29, 35 ("the next day after"); 12:12; Acts 14:20; 21:8; 25:6; "(the) day following," John 1:43; 6:22; "the morrow after," Acts 10:24.

Note: In Acts 25:17, KJV, the adverb *hexēs*, "next, successively, in order," is translated "on (the) morrow."

For **MORSEL** see MEAT, No. 2

MORTAL, MORTALITY

thnētos (θνητός, 2349), "subject or liable to death, mortal" (akin to *thnēskō*, "to die"), occurs in Rom. 6:12, of the body, where it is called "mortal," not simply because it is liable to death, but because it is the organ in and through which death carries on its death-producing activities; in 8:11, the stress is on the liability to death, and the quickening is not reinvigoration but the impartation of life at the time of the Rapture, as in 1 Cor. 15:53, 54 and 2 Cor. 5:4 (RV, "what is mortal"; KJV, "mortality"); in 2 Cor. 4:11, it is applied to the flesh, which stands, not simply for the body, but the body as that which consists of the element of decay, and is thereby death-doomed. Christ's followers are in this life delivered unto death, that His life may be manifested in that which naturally is the seat of decay and death. That which is subject to suffering is that in which the power of Him who suffered here is most manifested.

MORTIFY

1. *thanatoō* (θανατόω, 2289), "to put to death" (from *thanatos*, "death," akin to *thnētos*, "mortal," see above), is translated "mortify" in Rom. 8:13 (Amer. RV, "put to death"); in 7:4, "ye were made dead" (passive voice), betokens the act of God on the believer, through the death of Christ; here in 8:13 it is the act of the believer himself, as being responsible to answer to God's act, and to put to death "the deeds of the body. See DEATH, C, No. 1.

2. *nekroō* (νεκρόω, 3499), "to make dead" (from *nekros*, see DEAD, A), is used figuratively in Col. 3:5 and translated "mortify" (Amer. RV, "put to death"). See DEAD, B, No. 1.

MOTE

karphos (κάρφος, 2595), "a small, dry stalk, a twig, a bit of dried stick" (from *karpho*, "to dry up"), or "a tiny straw or bit of wool," such as might fly into the eye, is used metaphorically of a minor fault, Matt. 7:3, 4, 5; Luke 6:41, 42 (twice), in contrast with *dokos*, "a beam supporting the roof of a building" (see BEAM). In the Sept., Gen. 8:11.

MOTHER

1. *mētēr* (μήτηρ, 3384) is used (a) of the natural relationship, e.g., Matt. 1:18; 2 Tim. 1:5; (b) figuratively, (1) of "one who takes the place of a mother," Matt. 12:49, 50; Mark 3:34, 35; John 19:27; Rom. 16:13; 1 Tim. 5:2; (2) of "the heavenly and spiritual Jerusalem," Gal. 4:26, which is "free" (not bound by law imposed externally, as under the Law of Moses), "which is our mother" (RV), i.e., of Christians, the metropolis, mother-city, used allegorically, just as the capital of a country is "the seat of its government, the center of its activities, and the place where the national characteristics are most fully expressed"; (3) symbolically, of "Babylon," Rev. 17:5, as the source from which has proceeded the religious harlotry of mingling pagan rites and doctrines with the Christian faith.

Note: In Mark 16:1 the article, followed by the genitive case of the name "James," the word "mother" being omitted, is an idiomatic mode of expressing the phrase "the mother of James."

2. *mētrolōas* (μητρολῴας, 3389), or *mētralōas* (μητραλῴας, 3389) denotes "a matricide" (No. 1, and *aloiaō*, to smite); 1 Tim. 1:9, "murderers of mothers"; it probably has, however, the broader meaning of "smiters" (RV, marg.), as in instances elsewhere than the NT.

3. *amētōr* (ἀμήτωρ, 282), "without a mother" (*a*, negative, and No. 1), is used in Heb. 7:3, of the Genesis record of Melchizedek, certain details concerning him being purposely omitted, in order to conform the description to facts about Christ as the Son of God. The word has been found in this sense in the writings of Euripides the dramatist and Herodotus the historian. See also under FATHER.

For **MOTION**, Rom. 7:5, KJV, see PASSION

MOUNT, MOUNTAIN

oros (ὄρος, 3735) is used (a) without specification, e.g., Luke 3:5 (distinct from *bounos*, "a hill"); John 4:20; (b) of "the

Mount of Transfiguration," Matt. 17:1, 9; Mark 9:2, 9; Luke 9:28, 37 (KJV, "hill"); 2 Pet. 1:18; (c) of "Zion," Heb. 12:22; Rev. 14:1; (d) of "Sinai," Acts 7:30, 38; Gal. 4:24, 25; Heb. 8:5; 12:20; (e) of "the Mount of Olives," Matt. 21:1; 24:3; Mark 11:1; 13:3; Luke 19:29, 37; 22:39; John 8:1; Acts 1:12; (f) of "the hill districts as distinct from the lowlands," especially of the hills above the Sea of Galilee, e.g., Matt. 5:1; 8:1; 18:12; Mark 5:5; (g) of "the mountains on the east of Jordan" and "those in the land of Ammon" and "the region of Petra," etc., Matt. 24:16; Mark 13:14; Luke 21:21; (h) proverbially, "of overcoming difficulties, or accomplishing great things," 1 Cor. 13:2; cf. Matt. 17:20; 21:21; Mark 11:23; (i) symbolically, of "a series of the imperial potentates of the Roman dominion, past and future," Rev. 17:9.

MOURN, MOURNING

A. Verbs.

1. *koptō* (κόπτω, 2875), to cut or beat, used in the middle voice of "beating the breast or head in mourning" (cf. Luke 23:27), is translated "shall mourn" in Matt. 24:30. See BEWAIL, No. 2, WAIL.

2. *pentheō* (πενθέω, 3996), "to mourn for, lament," is used (a) of mourning in general, Matt. 5:4; 9:15; Luke 6:25; (b) of sorrow for the death of a loved one, Mark 16:10; (c) of "mourning" for the overthrow of Babylon and the Babylonish system, Rev. 18:11, 15, RV, "mourning" (KJV, "wailing"); v. 19 (ditto); (d) of sorrow for sin or for condoning it, Jas. 4:9; 1 Cor. 5:2; (e) of grief for those in a local church who show no repentance for evil committed, 2 Cor. 12:21, RV, "mourn" (KJV, "bewail"). See BEWAIL, No. 3.

3. *thrēneō* (θρηνέω, 2354), "to lament, wail" (akin to *thrēnos*, "a lamentation, a dirge"), is used (a) in a general sense, of the disciples during the absence of the Lord, John 16:20, "lament"; (b) of those who sorrowed for the sufferings and the impending crucifixion of the Lord, Luke 23:27, "lamented"; the preceding word is *koptō* (No. 1); (c) of "mourning" as for the dead, Matt. 11:17, RV, "wailed" (KJV, "have mourned"); Luke 7:32 (ditto). See BEWAIL, *Note* (1).

Notes: (1) Trench points out that *pentheō* is often joined with *klaiō*, "to weep," 2 Sam. 19:1; Mark 16:10; Jas. 4:9; Rev. 18:15, indicating that *pentheō* is used especially of external manifestation of grief (as with *koptō* and *thrēneō*), in contrast to *lupeomai* which may be used of inward grief (*Syn.* Sec. XLV); though in Classical Greek *pentheō* was used of grief without violent manifestations (Grimm-Thayer). (2) Among the well-to-do it was common to hire professional mourners (men and women), who accompanied the dead body to the grave with formal music and the singing of dirges. At the death of Jairus' daughter male flute players were present, Matt. 9:23 (see, however, Jer. 9:17).

B. Nouns.

1. *odurmos* (ὀδυρμός, 3602), "lamentation, mourning," is translated "mourning" in Matt. 2:18 and 2 Cor. 7:7: see BEWAIL, *Note* (2).

2. *penthos* (πένθος, 3997), akin to A, No. 2, "mourning," is used in Jas. 4:9; Rev. 18:7 (twice), RV, "mourning" (KJV, "sorrow"); v. 8, "mourning"; 21:4, RV, "mourning" (KJV, "sorrow"). See SORROW.

MOUTH

A. Noun.

stoma (στόμα, 4750), akin to *stomachos* (which originally meant "a throat, gullet"), is used (a) of "the mouth" of man, e.g., Matt. 15:11; of animals, e.g., Matt. 17:27; 2 Tim. 4:17 (figurative); Heb. 11:33; Jas. 3:3; Rev. 13:2 (2nd occurrence); (b) figuratively of "inanimate things," of the "edge" of a sword, Luke 21:24; Heb. 11:34; of the earth, Rev. 12:16; (c) figuratively, of the "mouth," as the organ of speech, (1) of Christ's words, e.g., Matt. 13:35; Luke 11:54; Acts 8:32; 22:14; 1 Pet. 2:22; (2) of human, e.g., Matt. 18:16; 21:16; Luke 1:64; Rev. 14:5; as emanating from the heart, Matt. 12:34; Rom. 10:8, 9; of prophetic ministry through the Holy Spirit, Luke 1:70; Acts 1:16; 3:18; 4:25; of the destructive policy of two world potentates at the end of this age, Rev. 13:2, 5, 6; 16:13 (twice); of shameful speaking, Eph. 4:29 and Col. 3:8; (3) of the Devil speaking as a dragon or serpent, Rev. 12:15, 16; 16:13; (d) figuratively, in the phrase "face to face" (lit., "mouth to mouth"), 2 John 12; 3 John 14; (e) metaphorically, of "the utterances of the Lord, in judgment," 2 Thess. 2:8; Rev. 1:16; 2:16; 19:15, 21; of His judgment upon a local church for its lukewarmness, Rev. 3:16; (f) by metonymy, for "speech," Matt. 18:16; Luke 19:22; 21:15; 2 Cor. 13:1.

Note: In Acts 15:27, *logos*, "a word," is translated "word of mouth," RV (KJV, "mouth," marg., "word").

B. Verb.

epistomizō (ἐπιστομίζω, 1993), "to bridle" (*epi*, "upon," and A), is used metaphorically of "stopping the mouth, putting to silence," Titus 1:11. Cf. *phrassō*, "to stop, close," said of stopping the "mouths" of men, in Rom. 3:19.

MULTIPLY

1. *plēthunō* (πληθύνω, 4129), used (a) transitively, denotes "to cause to increase, to multiply," 2 Cor. 9:10; Heb. 6:14 (twice); in the passive voice, "to be multiplied," Matt. 24:12, RV, "(iniquity) shall be multiplied" (KJV, "shall abound"); Acts 6:7; 7:17; 9:31; 12:24; 1 Pet. 1:2; 2 Pet. 1:2; Jude 2; (b) intransitively it denotes "to be multiplying," Acts 6:1, RV, "was multiplying" (KJV, "was multiplied"). See ABUNDANCE, B, No. 5.

2. *pleonazdo* (πλεονάζω, 4121), used intransitively, "to abound," is translated "being multiplied" in the RV of 2 Cor. 4:15 (KJV, "abundant"); the active voice, aorist tense, here would be more accurately rendered "having superabounded" or "superabounding" or "multiplying." See ABUNDANCE, B, No. 3.

MULTITUDE

1. *ochlos* (ὄχλος, 3793) is used frequently in the four Gospels and the Acts; elsewhere only in Rev. 7:9; 17:15; 19:1, 6; it denotes (a) "a crowd or multitude of persons, a throng," e.g., Matt. 14:14, 15; 15:33; often in the plural, e.g., Matt. 4:25; 5:1; with *polus*, "much" or "great," it signifies "a great multitude," e.g., Matt. 20:29, or "the common people," Mark 12:37, perhaps preferably "the mass of the people." Field supports the meaning in the text, but either rendering is suitable. The mass of the people was attracted to Him (for the statement "heard Him gladly" cf. what is said in Mark 6:20 of Herod Antipas concerning John the Baptist); in John 12:9, "the common people," RV, stands in contrast with their leaders (v. 10); Acts 24:12, RV, "crowd"; (b) "the populace, an unorganized multitude," in contrast to *dēmos*, "the people as a body politic," e.g., Matt. 14:5; 21:26; John 7:12 (2nd part); (c) in a more general sense, "a multitude or company," e.g., Luke 6:17, RV, "a (great) multitude (of His disciples)," KJV, "the company"; Acts 1:15, "a multitude (of persons)," RV, KJV, "the number (of names)"; Acts 24:18, RV, "crowd" (KJV, "multitude"). See COMPANY, No. 1.

2. *plēthos* (πλῆθος, 4128), lit., "a fullness," hence, "a large company, a multitude," is used (a) of things: of fish, Luke 5:6; John 21:6; of sticks ("bundle"), Acts 28:3; of stars and of sand, Heb. 11:12; of sins, Jas. 5:20; 1 Pet. 4:8; (b) of persons, (1) a "multitude": of people, e.g., Mark 3:7, 8; Luke 6:17; John 5:3; Acts 14:1; of angels, Luke 2:13; (2) with the article, the whole number, the "multitude," the populace, e.g., Luke 1:10; 8:37; Acts 5:16; 19:9; 23:7; a particular company, e.g., of disciples, Luke 19:37; Acts 4:32; 6:2, 5; 15:30; of elders, priests, and scribes, 23:7; of the apostles and the elders of the Church in Jerusalem, Acts 15:12. See ASSEMBLY, No. 3, BUNDLE, No. 2, COMPANY, No. 5.

Note: In Luke 12:1. KJV, the phrase, lit., "the myriads of the multitude" is translated "an innumerable multitude of people" (where "people" translates No. 1, above), RV, "the many thousands of the multitude" (where "multitude" translates No. 1).

MURDER

phonos (φόνος, 5408) is used (a) of a special act, Mark 15:7; Luke 23:19, 25; (b) in the plural, of "murders" in general, Matt. 15:19; Mark 7:21 (Gal. 5:21, in some inferior mss.); Rev. 9:21; in the singular, Rom. 1:29; (c) in the sense of "slaughter," Heb. 11:37, "they were slain with the sword," lit., "(they died by) slaughter (of the sword)"; in Acts 9:1, "slaughter." See SLAUGHTER.

Note: In Matt. 19:18, KJV, *phoneuō*, "to kill" (akin to *phoneus*, see below), is translated "thou shalt do (no) murder" (RV, "thou shalt (not) kill"). See KILL.

MURDERER

1. *phoneus* (φονεύς, 5406), akin to *phoneuō* and *phonos* (see above), is used (a) in a general sense, in the singular, 1 Pet. 4:15; in the plural, Rev. 21:8; 22:15; (b) of those guilty of particular acts, Matt. 22:7; Acts 3:14, lit. "a man (*anēr*), a murderer"; 7:52; 28:4.

2. *anthrōpoktonos* (ἀνθρωποκτόνος, 443), an adjective, lit., "manslaying," used as a noun, "a manslayer, murderer" (*anthrōpos*, "a man," *kteinō*, "to slay"), is used of Satan, John 8:44; of one who hates his brother, and who, being a "murderer," has not eternal life, 1 John 3:15 (twice).

3. *patrolōas* (or *patral-*) (πατραλῴας, 3964) "a murderer of one's father," occurs in 1 Tim. 1:9.

Note: For *sikarios*, in the plural, "murderers," in Acts 21:38, see ASSASSIN. See MOTHER, No. 2.

MURMUR, MURMURING

A. Verbs.

1. *gonguzō* (γογγύζω, 1111), "to mutter, murmur, grumble, say anything in a low tone" (Eng., "gong"), an onomatopoeic word, representing the significance by the sound of the word, as in the word "murmur" itself, is used of the laborers in the parable of the householder, Matt. 20:11; of the scribes and Pharisees, against Christ, Luke 5:30; of the Jews, John 6:41, 43, of the disciples, 6:61; of the people, 7:32 (of debating secretly); of the Israelites, 1 Cor. 10:10 (twice), where it is also used in a warning to believers. In the papyri it is used of the "murmuring" of a gang of workmen, also in a remark interposed, while the Emperor (late 2nd cent. A.D.) was interviewing a rebel, that the Romans were then "murmuring" (Moulton and Milligan, *Vocab.*).

2. *diagonguzō* (διαγογγύζω, 1234), lit., "to murmur through" (*dia*, i.e., "through a whole crowd," or "among themselves"), is always used of indignant complaining, Luke 15:2; 19:7.

3. *embrimaomai* (ἐμβριμάομαι, 1690) is rendered "murmured against" in Mark 14:5; it expresses indignant displeasure.

Note: For *stenazō*, Jas. 5:9, RV, "murmur," see GRIEVE, No. 3.

B. Noun.

gongusmos (γογγυσμός, 1112), "a murmuring, muttering" (akin to A, No. 1), is used (a) in the sense of secret debate among people, John 7:12 (as with the verb in v. 32); (b) of displeasure or complaining (more privately than in public), said of Grecian Jewish converts against Hebrews, Acts 6:1; in general admonitions, Phil. 2:14; 1 Pet. 4:9, RV, "murmuring" (KJV "grudging").

MURMURER

gongustēs (γογγυστής, 1113), "a murmurer" (akin to A, No. 1, and B, above), "one who complains," is used in Jude 16, especially perhaps of utterances against God (see v. 15).

For **MUSING** (*dialogizomai*, in Luke 3:15, KJV) see REASON (Verb)

MUSIC

sumphōnia (συμφωνία, 4858), lit., "a sounding together" (Eng., "symphony"), occurs in Luke 15:25. In the Sept., Dan. 3:5, 7, 10, 15, for Aramaic *sumpōnyâ* (not in v. 7), itself a loan word from the Greek; translated "dulcimer" (RV, marg., "bagpipe").

For **MUSICIAN,** Rev. 18:22, KJV, see MINSTREL

MYRRH

A. Noun.

smurna (σμύρνα, 4666), whence the name "Smyrna," a word of Semitic origin, Heb., *mōr*, from a root meaning "bitter," is a gum resin from a shrubby tree, which grows in Yemen and neighboring regions of Africa; the fruit is smooth and somewhat larger than a pea. The color of myrrh varies from pale reddish-yellow to reddish-brown or red. The taste is bitter, and the substance astringent, acting as an antiseptic and a stimulant. It was used as a perfume, Ps. 45:8, where the language is symbolic of the graces of the Messiah; Prov. 7:17; Song of Sol. 1:13; 5:5; it was one of the ingredients of the "holy anointing oil" for the priests, Ex. 30:23 (RV, "flowing myrrh"); it was used also for the purification of women, Esth. 2:12; for embalming, John 19:39; as an anodyne see B), it was one of the gifts of the Magi, Matt. 2:11.

B. Verb.

smurnizō (σμυρνίζω, 4669) is used transitively in the NT, with the meaning "to mingle or drug with myrrh," Mark 15:23; the mixture was doubtless offered to deaden the pain (Matthew's word "gall" suggests that "myrrh" was not the only ingredient). Christ refused to partake of any such means of alleviation; He would retain all His mental power for the complete fulfillment of the Father's will.

MYSTERY

mustērion (μυστήριον, 3466), primarily that which is known to the *mustēs*, "the initiated" (from *mueō*, "to initiate into the mysteries"; cf. Phil. 4:12, *mueomai*, "I have learned the secret," RV). In the NT it denotes, not the mysterious (as with the Eng. word), but that which, being outside the range of unassisted natural apprehension, can be made known only by divine revelation, and is made known in a manner and at a time appointed by God, and to those only who are illumined by His Spirit. In the ordinary sense a "mystery" implies knowledge withheld; its Scriptural significance is truth revealed. Hence the terms especially associated with the subject are "made known," "manifested," "revealed," "preached," "understand," "dispensation." The definition given above may be best illustrated by the following passage: "the mystery which hath been hid from all ages and generations: but now hath it been manifested to His saints" (Col. 1:26, RV). "It is used of:

"(a) spiritual truth generally, as revealed in the gospel, 1 Cor. 13:2; 14:2 [cf. 1 Tim. 3:9]. Among the ancient Greeks 'the mysteries' were religious rites and ceremonies practiced by secret societies into which any one who so desired might be received. Those who were initiated into these 'mysteries' became possessors of certain knowledge, which was not imparted to the uninitiated, and were called 'the perfected,' cf. 1 Cor. 2:6-16 where the Apostle has these 'mysteries' in mind and presents the gospel in contrast thereto; here 'the perfected' are, of course the believers, who alone can perceive the things revealed; (b) Christ, who is God Himself revealed under the conditions of human life, Col. 2:2; 4:3, and submitting even to death, 1 Cor. 2:1 [in some mss., for *marturion*, testimony], 7, but raised from among the dead, 1 Tim. 3:16, that the will of God to coordinate the universe in Him, and subject it to Him, might in due time be accomplished, Eph. 1:9 (cf. Rev. 10:7), as is declared in the gospel Rom. 16:25; Eph. 6:19; (c) the Church, which is Christ's Body, i.e., the union of redeemed men with God in Christ, Eph. 5:32 [cf. Col. 1:27]; (d) the rapture into the presence of Christ of those members of the Church which is His Body who shall be alive on the earth at His Parousia, 1 Cor. 15:51; (e) the operation of those hidden forces that either retard or accelerate the Kingdom of Heaven (i.e., of God), Matt. 13:11; Mark 4:11; (f) the cause of the present condition of Israel, Rom. 11:25; (g) the spirit of disobedience to God, 2 Thess. 2:7; Rev. 17:5, 7, cf. Eph. 2:2."

To these may be added (h) the seven local churches, and their angels, seen in symbolism, Rev. 1:20; (i) the ways of God in grace, Eph. 3:9. The word is used in a comprehensive way in 1 Cor. 4:1.

N

NAIL (Noun and Verb)

A. Noun.

hēlos (ἧλος, 2247) occurs in the remarks of Thomas regarding the print of the nails used in Christ's crucifixion, John 20:25.

B. Verb.

prosēloō (προσηλόω, 4338), "to nail to" (*pros*, "to," and a verbal form of A), is used in Col. 2:14, in which the figure of a bond (ordinances of the Law) is first described as cancelled, and then removed; the idea in the verb itself is not that of the cancellation, to which the taking out of the way was subsequent, but of nailing up the removed thing in triumph to the cross. The death of Christ not only rendered the Law useless as a means of salvation, but gave public demonstration that it was so.

NAKED (Adjective and Verb), NAKEDNESS

A. Adjective.

gumnos (γυμνός, 1131) signifies (a) "unclothed," Mark 14:52; in v. 51 it is used as a noun ("*his*" and "*body*" being italicized); (b) "scantily or poorly clad," Matt. 25:36, 38, 43, 44; Acts 19:16 (with torn garments); Jas. 2:15; (c) "clad in the undergarment only" (the outer being laid aside), John 21:7 (see CLOTHING); (d) metaphorically, (1) of "a bare seed," 1 Cor. 15:37; (2) of "the soul without the body," 2 Cor. 5:3; (3) of "things exposed to the allseeing eye of God," Heb. 4:13; (4) of "the carnal condition of a local church," Rev. 3:17; (5) of "the similar state of an individual," 16:15; (6) of "the desolation of religious Babylon," 17:16.

B. Verb.

gumnēteōo (γυμνητεύω, 1130), "to be naked or scantily clad" (akin to A), is used in 1 Cor. 4:11. In the *Koinē* writings (see Preface to Vol. 1) it is used of being light-armed.

C. Noun.

gumnotēs (γυμνότης, 1132), "nakedness" (akin to A), is used (a) of "want of sufficient clothing," Rom. 8:35; 2 Cor. 11:27; (b) metaphorically, of "the nakedness of the body," said of the condition of a local church, Rev. 3:18.

NAME

A. Noun.

onoma (ὄνομα, 3686) is used (I) in general of the "name" by which a person or thing is called, e.g., Mark 3:16, 17, "(He) surnamed," lit., "(He added) the name"; 14:32, lit., "(of which) the name (was)"; Luke 1:63; John 18:10, sometimes translated "named," e.g., Luke 8:5, "named (Zacharias)," lit., "by name"; in the same verse, "named (Elizabeth)," lit., "the name of her," an elliptical phrase, with "was" understood; Acts 8:9, RV, "by name," 10:1; the "name" is put for the reality in Rev. 3:1; in Phil. 2:9, the "Name" represents "the title and dignity" of the Lord, as in Eph. 1:21 and Heb. 1:4;

(II) for all that a "name" implies, of authority, character, rank, majesty, power, excellence, etc., of everything that the "name" covers: (a) of the "Name" of God as expressing His attributes, etc., e.g., Matt. 6:9; Luke 1:49; John 12:28; 17:6, 26; Rom. 15:9; 1 Tim. 6:1; Heb. 13:15; Rev. 13:6; (b) of the "Name" of Christ, e.g., Matt. 10:22; 19:29; John 1:12; 2:23; 3:18; Acts 26:9; Rom. 1:5; Jas. 2:7; 1 John 3:23; 3 John 7; Rev. 2:13; 3:8; also the phrases rendered "in the name"; these may be analyzed as follows: (1) representing the authority of Christ, e.g., Matt. 18:5 (with *epi*, "on the ground of My authority"); so Matt. 24:5 (falsely) and parallel passages; as substantiated by the Father, John 14:26; 16:23 (last clause), RV; (2) in the power of (with *en*, "in"), e.g., Mark 16:17; Luke 10:17; Acts 3:6; 4:10; 16:18; Jas. 5:14; (3) in acknowledgement or confession of, e.g., Acts 4:12; 8:16; 9:27, 28; (4) in recognition of the authority of (sometimes combined with the thought of relying or resting on), Matt. 18:20; cf. 28:19; Acts 8:16; 9:2 (*eis*, "into"); John 14:13; 15:16; Eph. 5:20; Col. 3:17; (5) owing to the fact that one is called by Christ's "Name" or is identified with Him, e.g. 1 Pet. 4:14 (with *en*, "in"); with *heneken*, "for the sake of," e.g., Matt. 19:29; with *dia*, "on account of," Matt. 10:22; 24:9; Mark 13:13; Luke 21:17; John 15:21; 1 John 2:12; Rev. 2:3 (for 1 Pet. 4:16, see *Note* below);

(III) as standing, by metonymy, for "persons," Acts 1:15; Rev. 3:4; 11:13 (RV, "persons").

Note: In Mark 9:41, the use of the phrase *en* with the dative case of *onoma* (as in the best mss.) suggests the idea of "by reason of" or "on the ground of" (i.e., "because ye are My disciples"); 1 Pet. 4:16, RV, "in this Name" (KJV, "on this behalf"), may be taken in the same way.

B. Verbs.

1. *onomazō* (ὀνομάζω, 3687) denotes (a) "to name," "mention," or "address by name," Acts 19:13, RV, "to name" (KJV, "to call"); in the passive voice, Rom. 15:20; Eph. 1:21; 5:3; to make mention of the "Name" of the Lord in praise and worship, 2 Tim. 2:19; (b) "to name, call, give a name to," Luke 6:13, 14;

passive voice, 1 Cor. 5:11, RV, "is named" (KJV, "is called"); Eph. 3:15 (some mss. have the verb in this sense in Mark 3:14 and 1 Cor. 5:1). See CALL, *Note* (1).

2. *eponomazō* (ἐπονομάζω, 2028), "to call by a name, surname" (*epi*, "on," and No. 1), is used in Rom. 2:17, passive voice, RV, "bearest the name of" (KJV, "art called"). See CALL, *Note* (1).

3. *prosagoreuō* (προσαγορεύω, 4316) primarily denotes "to address, greet, salute"; hence, "to call by name," Heb. 5:10, RV, "named (of God a High Priest)" (KJV, "called"), expressing the formal ascription of the title to Him whose it is; "called" does not adequately express the significance. Some suggest the meaning "addressed," but this is doubtful. The reference is to Ps. 110:4, a prophecy confirmed at the Ascension. In the Sept., Deut. 23:6.

4. *kaleō* (καλέω, 2564), "to call," is translated "named" in Acts 7:58, RV (KJV, "whose name was"). See CALL, No. 1 (b).

Notes: (1) In Luke 19:2, KJV, *kaleō*, "to call" (with the dative case of *onoma*, "by name"), is translated "named" (RV, "called by name"); in Luke 2:21, KJV, the verb alone is rendered "named" (RV, "called"). (2) In Matt. 9:9 and Mark 15:7, KJV, the verb *legō*, "to speak, to call by name," is rendered "named" (RV, "called"). See CALL, No. 9.

NARRATIVE

diēgēsis (διήγησις, 1335), translated "a declaration" in the KJV of Luke 1:1, denotes a "narrative," RV (akin to *diēgeomai*, "to set out in detail, recount, describe"). See DECLARE, B, Note (1). In the Sept., Judg. 7:15; Hab. 2:6.

NARROW

A. Adjective.

stenos (στενός, 4728), from a root *sten-*, seen in *stenazō*, "to groan," *stenagmos*, "groaning" (Eng., "stenography," lit., "narrow writing"), is used figuratively in Matt. 7:13, 14, of the gate which provides the entrance to eternal life, "narrow" because it runs counter to natural inclinations, and "the way" is similarly characterized; so in Luke 13:24 (where the more intensive word *agōnizomai*, "strive," is used); RV, "narrow" (KJV, "strait") in each place. Cf. *stenochōreō*, "to be straitened," and *stenochōria*, "narrowness, anguish, distress."

B. Verb.

thlibō (θλίβω, 2346), "to press," is translated "narrow" in Matt. 7:14, KJV, lit., "narrowed" (RV, "straitened"; the verb is in the perfect participle, passive voice), i.e., hemmed in, like a mountain gorge; the way is rendered "narrow" by the divine conditions, which make it impossible for any to enter who think the entrance depends upon self-merit, or who still incline towards sin, or desire to continue in evil. See AFFLICT, No. 4.

NATION

1. *ethnos* (ἔθνος, 1484), originally "a multitude," denotes (a) "a nation" or "people," e.g., Matt. 24:7; Acts 10:35; the Jewish people, e.g., Luke 7:5; 23:2; John 11:48, 50-52; Acts 10:22; 24:2, 10, 17; in Matt. 21:43, the reference is to Israel in its restored condition, (b) in the plural "the nations" as distinct from Israel. See GENTILES.

2. *genos* (γένος, 1085), "a race": see KIND (Noun).

3. *allophulos* (ἀλλόφυλος, 246), "foreign, of another race" (*allos*, "another," *phulon*, "a tribe"), is used in Acts 10:28, "one of another nation."

Note: For Phil. 2:15, *genea* (KJV, "nation," RV, "generation"), see AGE.

NATURAL, NATURALLY

A. Adjectives.

1. *phusikos* (φυσικός, 5446) originally signifying "produced by nature, inborn," from *phusis*, "nature" (see below), cf. Eng., "physical," "physics," etc., denotes (a) "according to nature," Rom. 1:26, 27; (b) "governed by mere natural instincts," 2 Pet. 2:12, RV, "(born) mere animals," KJV and RV marg., "natural (brute beasts)."

2. *psuchikos* (ψυχικός, 5591), "belonging to the *psuchē*, soul" (as the lower part of the immaterial in man), "natural, physical," describes the man in Adam and what pertains to him (set in contrast to *pneumatikos* "spiritual"), 1 Cor. 2:14; 15:44 (twice), 46 (in the latter used as a noun); Jas. 3:15, "sensual" (RV marg., "natural" or "animal"), here relating perhaps more especially to the mind, a wisdom in accordance with, or springing from, the corrupt desires and affections; so in Jude 19.

B. Noun.

genesis (γένεσις, 1078), "birth," is used in Jas. 1:23, of the "natural face," lit., "the face of his birth," "what God made him to be" (Hort). See GENERATION, NATURE, No. 2.

Note: In Rom. 11:21, 24 the preposition *kata*, "according to," with the noun *phusis*, "nature," is translated "natural," of branches, metaphorically describing members of the nation of Israel.

C. Adverb.

phusikōs (φυσικῶς, 5447), "naturally, by nature" (akin to A, No. 1), is used in Jude 10.

Note: In Phil. 2:20, KJV, *gnēsiōs*, "sincerely, honorably, truly" (from the adjective *gnēsios*, "true, sincere, genuine"; see, e.g., Phil. 4:3), is translated "naturally" (RV, "truly," marg., "genuinely").

NATURE

1. *phusis* (φύσις, 5449), from *phuō*, "to bring forth, produce," signifies (a) "the nature" (i.e., the natural powers or

constitution) of a person or thing, Eph. 2:3; Jas. 3:7 ("kind"); 2 Pet. 1:4; (b) "origin, birth," Rom. 2:27, one who by birth is a Gentile, uncircumcised, in contrast to one who, though circumcised, has become spiritually uncircumcised by his iniquity; Gal. 2:15; (c) "the regular law or order of nature," Rom. 1:26, against "nature" (*para*, "against"); 2:14, adverbially, "by nature" (for 11:21, 24, see NATURAL, Note); 1 Cor. 11:14; Gal. 4:8, "by nature (are no gods)," here "nature" is the emphatic word, and the phrase includes demons, men regarded as deified, and idols; these are gods only in name (the negative, *mē*, denies not simply that they were gods, but the possibility that they could be).

2. *genesis* (γένεσις, 1078) is used in the phrase in Jas. 3:6, "the wheel of nature," RV (marg., "birth"). Some regard this as the course of birth or of creation, or the course of man's "nature" according to its original divine purpose; Mayor (on the Ep. of James) regards *trochos* here as a wheel, "which, catching fire from the glowing axle, is compared to the widespreading mischief done by the tongue," and shows that "the fully developed meaning" of genesis denotes "the incessant change of life ... the sphere of this earthly life, meaning all that is contained in our life." The significance, then, would appear to be the whole round of human life and activity. Moulton and Milligan illustrate it in this sense from the papyri. See NATURAL, B.

For **NAUGHTINESS**, Jas. 1:21, KJV, see WICKEDNESS

NECESSITY (-TIES)

1. *ananke* (ἀναγκή, 318) signifies (a) "a necessity," what must needs be, translated "necessity" (in some mss. in Luke 23:17) in 1 Cor. 7:37; 9:16; 2 Cor. 9:7 (with *ek* "out of"); Philem. 14 (with *kata*, "according to"); Heb. 7:12; 9:16; (b) "distress, pain," translated "necessities" in 2 Cor. 6:4; 12:10. See DISTRESS, No. 1, and the synonymous words there (also CONSTRAIN, *Note*).

2. *chreia* (χρεία, 5532), "a need," and almost always so translated, is used in the plural in Acts 20:34, "necessities"; Rom. 12:13, RV (KJV, "necessity"); in Phil. 4:16, KJV, "necessity," RV, "need."

NEGLECT, NEGLIGENT

1. *ameleō* (ἀμελέω, 272) denotes (a) "to be careless, not to care" (*a*, negative, *melei*, "it is a care"; from *melō*, "to care, to be a care"), Matt. 22:5, "made light of"; (b) "to be careless of, neglect," 1 Tim. 4:14; Heb. 2:3; 8:9, "I regarded (them) not." See LIGHT OF (make), REGARD. (In the Sept., Jer. 4:17; 38:32.)

2. *paratheōreō* (παραθεωρέω, 3865), primarily, "to examine side by side, compare" (*para*, "beside," *theōreō*, "to look at"), hence, "to overlook, to neglect," is used in Acts 6:1, of the "neglect" of widows in the daily ministration in Jerusalem.

Note: In 2 Pet. 1:12, some mss. have No. 1, hence the KJV, "I will not be negligent;" the RV follows those which have the future tense of *mellō*, "to be ready." For "neglect to hear" see HEAR, No. 7.

For **NEGLECTING** (Col. 2:23) see SEVERITY

NEIGHBOR

1. *geitōn* (γείτων, 1069), lit., "one living in the same land," denotes "a neighbor," always plural in the NT, Luke 14:12; 15:6, 9; John 9:5.

2. *perioikos* (περίοικος, 4040), an adjective, lit., "dwelling around" (*peri*, "around," *oikos*, "a dwelling"), is used as a noun in Luke 1:58, "neighbors."

3. *plēsion* (πλησίον, 4139), the neuter of the adjective *plēsios* (from *pelas*, "near"), is used as an adverb accompanied by the article, lit., "the (one) near"; hence, one's "neighbor"; see refs. below.

This and Nos. 1 and 2 have a wider range of meaning than that of the Eng. word "neighbor." There were no farmhouses scattered over the agricultural areas of Palestine; the populations, gathered in villages, went to and fro to their toil. Hence domestic life was touched at every point by a wide circle of neighborhood. The terms for neighbor were therefore of a very comprehensive scope. This may be seen from the chief characteristics of the privileges and duties of neighborhood as set forth in Scripture, (a) its helpfulness, e.g., Prov. 27:10; Luke 10:36; (b) its intimacy, e.g., Luke 15:6, 9 (see No. 1); Heb. 8:11; (c) its sincerity and sanctity, e.g., Ex. 22:7, 10; Prov. 3:29; 14:21; Rom. 13:10; 15:2; Eph. 4:25; Jas. 4:12. The NT quotes and expands the command in Lev. 19:18, "to love one's neighbor as oneself"; see, e.g., Matt. 5:43; 19:19; 22:39; Mark 12:31, 33; Luke 10:27; Gal. 5:14; Jas. 2:8. See also Acts 7:27.

Note: In Rom. 13:8, for *heteron*, "another," RV has "his neighbor."

NEIGHBORHOOD

Note: This, in Acts 28:7, RV, translates a phrase consisting of the dative plural of the article followed by *peri*, "around," governed by the preposition *en*, "in," "in the neighborhood of (that place)," KJV, "in the (same quarters)," lit., "in the (parts) around (that place)."

NET

1. *amphibleētron* (ἀμφίβληστρον, 293), lit., "something thrown around" (*amphi*, "around," *ballō*, "to throw"), denotes "a casting net," a somewhat small "net," cast over the shoulder, spreading out in a circle and made to sink by weights, Matt.

4:18 (in some mss. in Mark 1:16: the best have the verb *amphiballo* alone).

2. *diktuon* (δίκτυον, 1350), a general term for a "net" (from an old verb *dikō*, "to cast": akin to *diskos*, "a quoit"), occurs in Matt. 4:20-21; Mark 1:18-19; Luke 5:2, 4-6; John 21:6, 8, 11 (twice). In the Sept. it was used for a "net" for catching birds, Prov. 1:17, in other ways, e.g., figuratively of a snare, Job 18:8; Prov. 29:5.

3. *sagēnē* (σαγήνη, 4522) denotes "a dragnet, a seine"; two modes were employed with this, either by its being let down into the water and drawn together in a narrowing circle, and then into the boat, or as a semicircle drawn to the shore, Matt. 13:47, where Nos. 1 and 2 would not have suited so well. The Greek historian Herodotus uses the corresponding verb *sagēneuō* of a device by which the Persians are said to have cleared a conquered island of its inhabitants.

NEW

1. *kainos* (καινός, 2537) denotes "new," of that which is unaccustomed or unused, not "new" in time, recent, but "new" as to form or quality, of different nature from what is contrasted as old. " 'The new tongues,' kainos, of Mark 16:17 are the 'other tongues,' heteros, of Acts 2:4. These languages, however, were 'new' and 'different,' not in the sense that they had never been heard before, or that they were new to the hearers, for it is plain from v. 8 that this is not the case; they were new languages to the speakers, different from those in which they were accustomed to speak.

"The new things that the Gospel brings for present obedience and realization are: a new covenant, Matt. 26:28 in some texts; a new commandment, John 13:34; a new creative act, Gal. 6:15; a new creation, 2 Cor. 5:17; a new man, i.e., a new character of manhood, spiritual and moral, after the pattern of Christ, Eph. 4:24; a new man, i.e., 'the Church which is His (Christ's) body,' Eph. 2:15.

"The new things that are to be received and enjoyed hereafter are: a new name, the believer's, Rev. 2:17; a new name, the Lord's, Rev. 3:12; a new song, Rev. 5:9; a new Heaven and a new Earth, Rev. 21:1; the new Jerusalem, Rev. 3:12; 21:2; 'And He that sitteth on the Throne said, Behold, I make all things new,' Rev. 21:5."

Kainos is translated "fresh" in the RV of Matt. 9:17; Mark 2:22 (in the best texts) and Luke 5:38, of wineskins. Cf. *kainotēs*, "newness" (below).

2. *neos* (νέος, 3501) signifies "new" in respect of time, that which is recent; it is used of the young, and so translated, especially the comparative degree "younger"; accordingly what is *neos* may be a reproduction of the old in quality or character. *Neos* and *kainos* are sometimes used of the same thing, but there is a difference, as already indicated. Thus the "new man" in Eph. 2:15 (*kainos*) is "new" in differing in character; so in 4:24 (see No. 1); but the "new man" in Col. 3:10 (*neos*) stresses the fact of the believer's "new" experience, recently begun, and still proceeding. "The old man in him ... dates as far back as Adam; a new man has been born, who therefore is fitly so called" [i.e., *neos*], Trench, *Syn.* Sec. LX. The "New" Covenant in Heb. 12:24 is "new" (*neos*) compared with the Mosaic, nearly fifteen hundred years before; it is "new" (*kainos*) compared with the Mosaic, which is old in character, ineffective, 8:8, 13; 9:15.

The "new" wine of Matt. 9:17; Mark 2:22; Luke 5:37-39, is *neos*, as being of recent production; the "new" wine of the kingdom, Matt. 26:29; Mark 14:25, is *kainos*, since it will be of a different character from that of this world. The rendering "new" (*neos*) is elsewhere used metaphorically in 1 Cor. 5:7, "a new lump." See YOUNG, YOUNGER.

3. *prosphatos* (πρόσφατος, 4372), originally signifying "freshly slain," acquired the general sense of "new," as applied to flowers, oil, misfortune, etc. It is used in Heb. 10:20 of the "living way" which Christ "dedicated for us ... through the veil ... His flesh" (which stands for His expiatory death by the offering of His body, v. 10). In the Sept., Num. 6:3; Deut. 32:17; Ps. 81:9; Eccl. 1:9. Cf. the adverb *prosphatōs*, "lately, recently," Acts 18:2.

Note: In Matt. 9:16 and Mark 2:21, KJV, *agnaphos* is translated "new" (RV, "undressed"). Moulton and Milligan give an instance in the papyri of its use in respect of a "new white shirt.

For **NEWBORN,** 1 Pet. 2:2, see BEGET, C, No. 2

NEWNESS

kainotēs (καινότης, 2538), akin to *kainos*, is used in the phrases (a) "newness of life," Rom. 6:4, i.e., life of a new quality; the believer, being a new creation (2 Cor. 5:17), is to behave himself consistently with this in contrast to his former manner of life; (b) "newness of the spirit," RV, Rom. 7:6, said of the believer's manner of serving the Lord. While the phrase stands for the new life of the quickened spirit of the believer, it is impossible to dissociate this (in an objective sense) from the operation of the Holy Spirit, by whose power the service is rendered.

NIGHT (by, in the)

nux (νύξ, 3571) is used (1) literally, (a) of "the alternating natural period to that of the day," e.g., Matt. 4:2; 12:40; 2 Tim. 1:3; Rev. 4:8; (b) of "the period of the absence of light," the time in which something takes place, e.g., Matt. 2:14 (27:64), in some mss.); Luke 2:8; John 3:2 (7:50, in some mss.); Acts 5:19; 9:25; (c) of "point of time," e.g., Matt. 14:27 (in some mss.), 30; Luke 12:20; Acts 27:23; (d) of "duration of time," e.g., Luke 2:37; 5:5; Acts 20:31; 26:7 (note the difference in the phrase in Mark 4:27); (II) metaphorically, (a) of "the period of man's alienation from God," Rom. 13:12; 1 Thess. 5:5, lit., "not of night," where "of" means 'belonging to;' cf. "of the Way," Acts 9:2; "of shrinking back" and "of faith," Heb. 10:39, marg.; (b) of "death," as the time when work ceases, John 9:4.

NIGHT AND A DAY (A)

nuchthēmeros (νυχθήμερον, 3574), an adjective denoting "lasting a night and a day" (from *nux*, "night," and *hēmera*, "a day"), is used in 2 Cor. 11:25, in the neuter gender, as a noun, the object of the verb *poieō*, to do, lit., 'I have done a night-and-a-day.'

NOBLE

1. *eugenēs* (εὐγένης, 2104), an adjective, lit., "well born" (*eu*, "well," and *genos*, "a family, race"), (a) signifies "noble," 1 Cor. 1:26; (b) is used with *anthrōpos*, "a man," i.e., "a nobleman," in Luke 19:12. In the Sept., Job 1:3.

2. *eugenesteros* (εὐγενέστερος, , 2104), the comparative degree of No. 1, occurs in Acts 17:11, "more noble," i.e., "more nobleminded."

3. *kratistos* (κράτιστος, 2903) is translated "most noble" in the KJV of Acts 24:3 and 26:25 (RV, most excellent), See EXCELLENT.

NOON

mesēmbria (μεσημβρία, 3314), lit., "middleday" (*mesos*, "middle," and *hēmera*, "a day"), signifies (a) "noon," Acts 22:6; (b) "the south," Acts 8:26.

NOTABLE, OF NOTE

1. *gnōstos* (γνωστός, 1110), an adjective, signifying "known" (from *ginōskō*, "to know"), is used (a) as an adjective, most usually translated "known," whether of facts, e.g., Acts 1:19; 2:14; 4:10; or persons, John 18:15-16; it denotes "notable" in Acts 4:16, of a miracle; (b) as a noun, "acquaintance," Luke 2:44 and 23:49. See ACQUAINTANCE, KNOWN.

2. *episēmos* (ἐπίσημος, 1978), primarily meant "bearing a mark," e.g., of money "stamped, coined," (from *epi*, "upon," and *sēma*, "a mark, a sign"; cf. *sēmainō*, "to give a sign, signify, indicate," and *sēmeioō*, "to note"; see below); it is used in the NT, metaphorically, (a) in a good sense, Rom. 16:7, "of note, illustrious," said of Andronicus and Junias; (b) in a bad sense, Matt. 27:16, "notable," of the prisoner Barabbas. In the Sept., Gen. 30:42; Esth. 5:4; 8:13, toward the end of the verse, "a distinct (day)."

3. *epiphanēs* (ἐπιφανής, 2016), "illustrious, renowned, notable" (akin to *epiphainō*, "to show forth, appear"; Eng., "epiphany"), is translated "notable" in Acts 2:20, of the great Day of the Lord. The appropriateness of this word (compared with Nos. 1 and 2) to that future occasion is obvious.

NOTE (Verb)

sēmeioō (σημειόω, 4593), from *sēmeion*, "a sign, token," signifies "to mark, to note," in the middle voice, "to note for oneself," and is so used in 2 Thess. 3:14, in an injunction to take cautionary note of one who refuses obedience to the apostle's word by the Epistle. In the Sept. Ps. 5:6.

NOURISH, NOURISHMENT

1. *trephō* (τρέφω, 5142), "to rear, feed, nourish," is translated by the verb "to nourish" in Jas. 5:5 (of luxurious living); Rev. 12:14 (of God's care for Israel against its enemies); so v. 6, RV (KJV, feed); in Acts 12:20, RV, "was fed" (KJV, "was nourished"). See FEED.

2. *anatrephō* (ἀνατρέφω, 397), "to nurse, bring up" (*ana*, "up," and No. 1), is translated "nourished" in Acts 7:20 (KJV, "nourished up"); in 21, "nourished," KJV and RV.

3. *ektrephō* (ἐκτρέφω, 1625), *ek*, "from, out of," and No. 1, primarily used of children, "to nurture, rear," is translated "nurture" of the care of one's own flesh, Eph. 5:29, and in Eph. 6:4, RV (KJV, "bring ... up").

4. *entrephō* (ἐντρέφω, 1789), "to train up, nurture," is used metaphorically, in the passive voice, in 1 Tim. 4:6, of being "nourished" in the faith.

NOVICE

neophutos (νεόφυτος, 3504), an adjective, lit., "newly-planted" (from *neos*, "new," and *phuō*, "to bring forth, produce"), denotes "a new convert, neophyte, novice," 1 Tim. 3:6, of one who by inexperience is unfitted to act as a bishop or overseer in a church. In the Sept., Job 14:9; Ps. 128:3; 144:12; Isa. 5:7.

NOW

1. *nun* (νῦν, 3568) is used (a) of time, the immediate present, whether in contrast to the past, e.g., John 4:18; Acts 7:52, or to the future, e.g., John 12:27; Rom. 11:31; sometimes with the article, singular or plural, e.g., Acts 4:29; 5:38; (b) of logical sequence, often partaking also of the character of (a), "now therefore, now however," as it is, e.g., Luke 11:39; John 8:40; 9:41; 15:22, 24; 1 Cor. 5:11, RV marg., "as it is."

Note: Under (a) comes the phrase in 2 Cor. 8:14, with *kairos*, "a time," all governed by *en*, "in," or "at," KJV, "now at this time" (RV, "at this present time").

2. *nuni* (νυνί, 3570), a strengthened form of No. 1, is used (a) of time, e.g., Acts 22:1 (in the best mss.); 24:13; Rom. 6:22; 15:23, 25; (b) with logical import, e.g., Rom. 7:17; 1 Cor. 13:13, which some regard as temporal (a); but if this is the significance, "the clause" means, 'but faith, hope, love, are our

abiding possession now in this present life.' The objection to this rendering is that the whole course of thought has been to contrast the things which last only for the present time with the things which survive. And the main contrast so far has been between love and the special [then] present activity of prophecy, tongues, knowledge. There is something of disappointment, and even of bathos, in putting as a climax to these contrasts the statement that in this present state faith, hope, love abide; that is no more than can be said of [the then existing] prophecies, tongues and knowledge. If there is to be a true climax the 'abiding' must cover the future as well as the present state. And that involves as a consequence that *nuni* must be taken in its logical meaning, i.e., 'as things are,' 'taking all into account' ... This logical sense of *nuni* ... is enforced by the dominant note of the whole passage" (R. St. John Parry, in the *Camb. Greek Test.*).

It is certain that love will continue eternally; and hope will not cease at the Parousia of Christ, for hope will ever look forward to the accomplishment of God's eternal purposes, a hope characterized by absolute assurance; and where hope is in exercise faith is its concomitant. Faith will not be lost in sight.

3. *ēdē* (ἤδη, 2235) denotes "already, now already," "the subjective present, with a suggested reference to some other time, or to some expectation" (Thayer), e.g., Matt. 3:10; 14:24; Luke 11:7; John 6:17; Rom. 1:10; 4:19; 13:11; Phil. 4:10.

4. *arti* (ἄρτι, 737), expressing "coincidence," and denoting "strictly present time," signifies "just now, this moment," in contrast (a) to the past, e.g., Matt. 11:12; John 2:10; 9:19, 25; 13:33; Gal. 1:9-10; (b) to the future, e.g., John 13:37; 16:12, 31; 1 Cor. 13:12 (cf. No. 2 in v. 13); 2 Thess. 2:7; 1 Pet. 1:6, 8; (c) sometimes without necessary reference to either, e.g., Matt. 3:15; 9:18; 26:53; Gal. 4:20; Rev. 12:10.

5. *aparti* (ἀπάρτι, 534), sometimes written separately, *ap'arti*, i.e., *apo*, "from," and No. 4, denotes "from now, henceforth," John 13:19; 14:7; Rev. 14:13.

6. *loipon* (λοιπόν, 3063), the neuter of *loipos*, "the rest, from now," is used adverbially with the article and translated "now" in Mark 14:41.

NURSE

trophos (τροφός, 5162), translated "nurse" in 1 Thess. 2:7, there denotes a "nursing" mother, as is clear from the statement "cherisheth her own children"; this is also confirmed by the word *epios*, "gentle" (in the same verse), which was commonly used of the kindness of parents towards children. Cf. *trephō*, "to bring up" (see NOURISH).

For **NURTURE** (Eph. 6:4) see CHASTENING

O

OATH

1. *horkos* (ὅρκος, 3727) is primarily equivalent to *herkos*, "a fence, an enclosure, that which restrains a person"; hence, "an oath." The Lord's command in Matt. 5:33 was a condemnation of the minute and arbitrary restrictions imposed by the scribes and Pharisees in the matter of adjurations, by which God's Name was profaned. The injunction is repeated in Jas. 5:12. The language of the apostle Paul, e.g., in Gal. 1:20 and 1 Thess. 5:27 was not inconsistent with Christ's prohibition, read in the light of its context. Contrast the "oaths" mentioned in Matt. 14:7, 9; 26:72; Mark 6:26.

Heb. 6:16 refers to the confirmation of a compact among men, guaranteeing the discharge of liabilities; in their disputes "the oath is final for confirmation." This is referred to in order to illustrate the greater subject of God's "oath" to Abraham, confirming His promise; cf. Luke 1:73; Acts 2:30. Cf. the verbs *horkizō*, and *exorkizō*, under ADJURE.

2. *horkōmosia* (ὁρκωμοσία, 3728) denotes "an affirmation on oath" (from No. 1 and *omnumi*, "to swear"). This is used in Heb. 7:20-21 (twice), 28, of the establishment of the Priesthood of Christ, the Son of God, appointed a Priest after the order of Melchizedek, and "perfected for evermore." In the Sept., Ezek. 17:18, 19.

Note: For *anathematizō* in Acts 23:21, KJV, "have bound (themselves) with an oath," see CURSE.

OBEDIENCE, OBEDIENT, OBEY

A. Nouns.

1. *hupakoē* (ὑπακοή, 5218), "obedience" (*hupo*, "under," *akouō*, "to hear"), is used (a) in general, Rom. 6:16 (1st part), RV, "(unto) obedience," KJV, "(to) obey"; here "obedience" is not personified, as in the next part of the verse, "servants ... of obedience" [see (c)], but is simply shown to be the effect of the presentation mentioned; (b) of the fulfillment of apostolic counsels, 2 Cor. 7:15; 10:6; Philem. 21; (c) of the fulfillment of God's claims or commands, Rom. 1:5 and 16:26, "obedience of faith," which grammatically might be objective, to the faith (marg.), or subjective, as in the text. Since faith is one of the main subjects of the Epistle, and is the initial act of obedience in the new life, as well as an essential characteristic thereof, the text rendering is to be preferred; Rom. 6:16 (2nd part); 15:18, RV "(for) the obedience," KJV, "(to make) obedient"; 16:19; 1 Pet. 1:2, 14, RV, "(children of) obedience," i.e., characterized by "obedience," KJV, "obedient (children)"; v. 22, RV, "obedience (to the truth)," KJV, "obeying (the truth)"; (d) of "obedience" to Christ (objective), 2 Cor. 10:5; (e) of Christ's "obedience," Rom. 5:19 (referring to His death; cf. Phil. 2:8); Heb. 5:8, which refers to His delighted experience in constant "obedience" to the Father's will (not to be understood in the sense that He learned to obey).

2. *hupotagē* (ὑποταγή, 5292), subjection (*hupo*, "under," *tassō*, "to order"), is translated "obedience" in 2 Cor. 9:13, RV (KJV, "subjection"). See SUBJECTION.

B. Verbs.

1. *hupakouō* (ὑπακούω, 5219), "to listen, attend" (as in Acts 12:13), and so, "to submit, to obey," is used of "obedience" (a) to God, Heb. 5:9; 11:8; (b) to Christ, by natural elements, Matt. 8:27; Mark 1:27; 4:41; Luke 8:25; (c) to disciples of Christ, Luke 17:6; (d) to the faith, Acts 6:7; the gospel, Rom. 10:16; 2 Thess. 1:8; Christian doctrine, Rom. 6:17 (as to a form or mold of teaching); (e) to apostolic injunctions, Phil. 2:12; 2 Thess. 3:14; (f) to Abraham by Sarah, 1 Pet. 3:6; (g) to parents by children, Eph. 6:1; Col. 3:20; (h) to masters by servants, Eph. 6:5; Col. 3:22; (i) to sin, Rom. 6:12; (j) in general, Rom. 6:16.

2. *peithō* (πείθω, 3982), "to persuade, to win over," in the passive and middle voices, "to be persuaded, to listen to, to obey," is so used with this meaning, in the middle voice, e.g., in Acts 5:36-37 (in v. 40, passive voice, "they agreed"); Rom. 2:8; Gal. 5:7; Heb. 13:17; Jas. 3:3. The "obedience" suggested is not by submission to authority, but resulting from persuasion.

"*Peithō* and *pisteuō*, 'to trust,' are closely related etymologically; the difference in meaning is that the former implies the obedience that is produced by the latter, cf. Heb. 3:18-19, where the disobedience of the Israelites is said to be the evidence of their unbelief Faith is of the heart, invisible to men; obedience is of the conduct and may be observed. When a man obeys God he gives the only possible evidence that in his heart he believes God. Of course it is persuasion of the truth that results in faith (we believe because we are persuaded that the thing is true, a thing does not become true because it is believed), but *peithō*, in NT suggests an actual and outward result of the inward persuasion and consequent faith." See ASSURANCE, B, No. 3.

3. *peitharcheō* (πειθαρχέω, 3980), "to obey one in authority" (No. 2, and *archē*, "rule"), is translated "obey" in

Acts 5:29, 32; "to be obedient," Titus 3:1, RV (KJV, "to obey magistrates"); in Acts 27:21, "hearkened." See HEARKEN.

4. *apeitheō* (ἀπειθέω, 544), "to disobey, be disobedient" (*a*, negative, and No. 2), is translated "obey not" in Rom. 2:8; 1 Pet. 3:1; 4:17. See DISOBEDIENT.

Note: In 1 Cor. 14:34, KJV, *hupotassō*, "to be in subjection" (RV), is translated "to be under obedience"; so Titus 2:5, RV, "being in subjection" (KJV, "obedient"); and v. 9, RV (KJV, "to be obedient"). See SUBJECTION.

C. Adjective.

hupēkoos (ὑπήκοος, 5255), "obedient" (akin to A, No. 1), "giving ear, subject," occurs in Acts 7:39, RV, "(would not be) obedient," KJV, "(would not) obey"; 2 Cor. 2:9; Phil. 2:8, where the RV "*even*" is useful as making clear that the "obedience" was not to death but to the Father.

OBSERVATION, OBSERVE

A. Noun.

paratērēsis (παρατήρησις, 3907), "attentive watching" (akin to *paratēreō*, "to observe"), is used in Luke 17:20, of the manner in which the kingdom of God (i.e., the operation of the spiritual kingdom in the hearts of men) does not come, "in such a manner that it can be watched with the eyes" (Grimm-Thayer), or, as KJV marg., "with outward show."

B. Verbs.

1. *anatheōreō* (ἀναθεωρέω, 333), "to observe carefully, consider well" (*ana*, "up," intensive, and *theōreō*, "to behold"), is used in Acts 17:23, RV, "observed" (of Paul's notice of the objects of Athenian worship), and Heb. 13:7, "considering." See BEHOLD.

2. *tēreō* (τηρέω, 5083): see KEEP, No. 1.

3. *suntēreō* (συντηρέω, 4933): see KEEP, No. 3.

4. *paratēreō* (παρατηρέω, 3906), "to watch closely, observe narrowly" (*para*, used intensively, and No. 2), is translated "ye observe" in Gal. 4:10, where the middle voice suggests that their religious observance of days, etc. was not from disinterested motives, but with a view to their own advantage. See WATCH. Cf. *phroneō* ("to think"), "regardeth" in Rom. 14:6, where the subject is connected with the above, though the motive differs.

5. *phulassō* (φυλάσσω, 5442): see KEEP, No. 4.

6. *poieō* (ποιέω, 4160), "to do," is translated "to observe" in Acts 16:21.

OCCUPATION

Note: The phrase "of like occupation" in Acts 19:25 translates the phrase *peri* ("about") *ta* ("the") *toiauta* ("such things"), i.e., lit., "(occupied) about such things."

OFFENCE (OFFENSE)

A. Nouns.

1. *skandalon* (σκάνδαλον, 4625) originally was "the name of the part of a trap to which the bait is attached, hence, the trap or snare itself, as in Rom. 11:9, RV, 'stumblingblock,' quoted from Psa. 69:22, and in Rev. 2:14, for Balaam's device was rather a trap for Israel than a stumblingblock to them, and in Matt. 16:23, for in Peter's words the Lord perceived a snare laid for Him by Satan.

"In NT *skandalon* is always used metaphorically, and ordinarily of anything that arouses prejudice, or becomes a hindrance to others, or causes them to fall by the way. Sometimes the hindrance is in itself good, and those stumbled by it are the wicked."

Thus it is used (a) of Christ in Rom. 9:33, "(a rock) of offense"; so 1 Pet. 2:8; 1 Cor. 1:23 (KJV and RV, "stumblingblock"), and of His cross, Gal. 5:11 (RV, ditto); of the "table" provided by God for Israel, Rom. 11:9 (see above); (b) of that which is evil, e.g., Matt. 13:41, RV, "things that cause stumbling" (KJV, "things that offend"), lit., "all stumblingblocks"; 18:7, RV, "occasions of stumbling" and "occasion"; Luke 17:1 (ditto); Rom. 14:13, RV, "an occasion of falling" (KJV, "an occasion to fall"), said of such a use of Christian liberty as proves a hindrance to another; 16:17, RV, "occasions of stumbling," said of the teaching of things contrary to sound doctrine; 1 John 2:10, "occasion of stumbling," of the absence of this in the case of one who loves his brother and thereby abides in the light. Love, then, is the best safeguard against the woes pronounced by the Lord upon those who cause others to stumble. Cf. the Sept. in Hos. 4:17, "Ephraim partaking with idols hath laid stumblingblocks in his own path."

2. *proskomma* (πρόσκομμα, 4348), "an obstacle against which one may dash his foot" (akin to *proskoptō*, "to stumble" or "cause to stumble"; *pros*, "to or against," *koptō*, "to strike"), is translated "offense" in Rom. 14:20, in v. 13, "a stumblingblock," of the spiritual hindrance to another by a selfish use of liberty (cf. No. 1 in the same verse); so in 1 Cor. 8:9. It is used of Christ, in Rom. 9:32-33, RV, "(a stone) of stumbling," and 1 Pet. 2:8, where the KJV also has this rendering. Cf. the Sept. in Ex. 23:33, "these (the gods of the Canaanites) will be an offense (stumblingblock) unto thee."

3. *proskopē* (προσκοπή, 4349), like No. 2, and formed from the same combination, occurs in 2 Cor. 6:3, RV, "occasion of stumbling" (KJV, "offense"), something which leads others into error or sin. Cf. the Sept. in Prov. 16:18, "a haughty spirit (becomes) a stumblingblock" (i.e., to oneself).

Notes: (1) In the KJV of Rom. 4:25; 5:15 (twice), 16-18, 20, *paraptōma*, "a trespass," is translated "offense." See TRES-

PASS. (2) In 2 Cor. 11:7, KJV, *hamartia*, a sin, is translated "an offense." See SIN.

B. Adjective.

aproskopos (ἀπρόσκοπος, 677), akin to A, No. 3, with *a*, negative, prefixed, is used (a) in the active sense, "not causing to stumble," in 1 Cor. 10:32, metaphorically of "refraining from doing anything to lead astray" either Jews or Greeks or the church of God (i.e., the local church), RV, "no occasion of stumbling" (KJV, "none offense"); (b) in the passive sense, "blameless, without stumbling," Acts 24:16, "(a conscience) void of offense;" Phil. 1:10, "void of (KJV, without) offense." The adjective is found occasionally in the papyri writings.

OFFEND

skandalizō (σκανδαλίζω, 4624), from *skandalon* (OFFENSE, No. 1), signifies "to put a snare or stumblingblock in the way," always metaphorically in the NT, in the same ways as the noun, which see. It is used 14 times in Matthew, 8 in Mark, twice in Luke, twice in John; elsewhere in 1 Cor. 8:13 (twice) and 2 Cor. 11:29. It is absent in the most authentic mss. in Rom. 14:21. The RV renders it by the verb "to stumble," or "cause to stumble," in every place save the following, where it uses the verb "to offend," Matt. 13:57; 15:12; 26:31, 33; Mark 6:3; 14:27, 29.

Notes: (1) In Jas. 2:10; 3:2 (twice), KJV, *ptaiō*, "to stumble," is translated "offend;" see STUMBLE. (2) In Acts 25:8, KJV, *hamartanō*, to sin," is translated "have I offended;" see SIN.

OFFENDER

opheiletēs (ὀφειλέτης, 3781), "a debtor," is translated "offenders" in Luke 13:4, RV (RV and KJV marg., "debtors;" KJV, "sinners"). See DEBTOR.

Note: In Acts 25:11, KJV, *adikeō*, "to do wrong," is translated "be an offender" (RV, "am a wrong-doer").

OFFER, OFFERING

A. Verbs.

1. *prospherō* (προσφέρω, 4374), primarily, "to bring to" (*pros*, "to," *pherō*, "to bring"), also denotes "to offer," (a) of the sacrifice of Christ Himself, Heb. 8:3; of Christ in virtue of his High Priesthood (RV, "this *high priest*"; KJV, "this man"); 9:14, 25 (negative), 28; 10:12; (b) of offerings under, or according to, the Law, e.g., Matt. 8:4; Mark 1:44; Acts 7:42; 21:26; Heb. 5:1, 3; 8:3; 9:7, 9; 10:1-2, 8, 11; (c) of "offerings" previous to the Law, Heb. 11:4, 17 (of Isaac by Abraham); (d) of gifts "offered" to Christ, Matt. 2:11, RV, "offered" (KJV, "presented unto"); (e) of prayers "offered" by Christ, Heb. 5:7; (f) of the vinegar "offered" to Him in mockery by the soldiers at the cross, Luke 23:36; (g) of the slaughter of disciples by persecutors, who think they are "offering" service to God, John 16:2, RV (KJV, "doeth"); (h) of money "offered" by Simon the sorcerer, Acts 8:18. See DEAL WITH, No. 2.

2. *anapherō* (ἀναφέρω, 399), primarily, "to lead" or "carry up" (*ana*), also denotes "to offer," (a) of Christ's sacrifice, Heb. 7:27; (b) of sacrifices under the Law, Heb. 7:27; (c) of such previous to the Law, Jas. 2:21 (of Isaac by Abraham); (d) of praise, Heb. 13:15; (e) of spiritual sacrifices in general, 1 Pet. 2:5.

3. *didōmi* (δίδωμι, 1325), to give, is translated "to offer" in Luke 2:24; in Rev. 8:3, KJV, "offer" (RV, "add;" marg., "give"). See GIVE.

4. *parechō* (παρέχω, 3930), "to furnish, offer, present, supply," is used in Luke 6:29, of "offering" the other cheek to be smitten after receiving a similar insult; for the KJV marg., in Acts 17:31, see ASSURANCE, A, No. 1.

5. *spendō* (σπένδω, 4689), "to pour out as a drink offering, make a libation," is used figuratively in the passive voice in Phil. 2:17, "offered" (RV marg., "poured out as a drink offering"; KJV marg., "poured forth"). In 2 Tim. 4:6, "I am already being offered," RV (marg., "poured out as a drink-offering"), the apostle is referring to his approaching death, upon the sacrifice of his ministry. This use of the word is exemplified in the papyri writings.

Notes: (1) In Luke 11:12, KJV *epididōmi*, "to give" (*epi*, "over," in the sense of "instead of," and No. 3), is translated "will he offer" (RV, and KJV marg., "will he give"). (2) In Acts 7:41, KJV, *anagō*, "to lead up" or "bring up," is rendered "offered" (RV, "brought"). (3) In Acts 15:29; 21:25 and 1 Cor. 8:1, 4, 10; 10:19, KJV, *eidōlothutos*, "sacrificed to idols," is translated "offered to idols" (*thuō* denotes "to sacrifice"). See SACRIFICE.

B. Nouns.

1. *prosphora* (προσφορά, 4376), lit., "a bringing to" (akin to A, No. 1), hence an "offering," in the NT a sacrificial "offering," (a) of Christ's sacrifice, Eph. 5:2; Heb. 10:10 (of His body); 10:14; negatively, of there being no repetition, 10:18; (b) of "offerings" under, or according to, the Law, Acts 21:26; Heb. 10:5, 8; (c) of gifts in kind conveyed to needy Jews, Acts 24:17; (d) of the presentation of believers themselves (saved from among the Gentiles) to God, Rom. 15:16.

2. *holokautōma* (ὁλοκαύτωμα, 3646), "a burnt offering": see BURNT.

3. *anathēma* (ἀνάθημα, 334) denotes "a gift set up in a temple, a votive offering" (*ana*, "up," *tithēmi*, "to place"), Luke 21:5, RV "offerings" (KJV, "gifts") Cf. *anathēma* (see CURSE).

Notes: (1) In Luke 21:4, KJV, the plural of *dōron*, "a gift," is translated "offerings" (RV, "gifts"). (2) In Rom. 8:3 and Heb. 13:11, the RV, "as an offering" is added to complete the sacrificial meaning of *peri*.

OFFICE

A. Nouns.

1. *praxis* (πρᾶξις, 4234), "a doing, deed" (akin to *prassō*, "to do or practice"), also denotes "an acting" or "function," translated "office" in Rom. 12:4. See DEED.

2. *hieroteia* (ἱερατεία, 2405), or *hieratia*, denotes "a priests's office," Luke 1:9; Heb. 7:5, RV, "priest's office" (KJV "office of the priesthood").

B. Verb.

hierateuō (ἱερατεύω, 2407), "to officiate as a priest" (akin to A, No. 2), is translated "he executed the priest's office" in Luke 1:8. The word is frequent in inscriptions.

Notes: (1) In Rom. 11:13, KJV, *diakonia*, "a ministry," is translated "office" (RV, "ministry"). (2) In Acts 1:20, RV, *episkopē*, "an overseership," is translated "office" (marg., "overseership"; KJV, "bishopric"). (3) In 1 Tim. 3:1, the word "office," in the phrase "the office of a bishop," has nothing to represent it in the original; the RV marg. gives "overseer" for "bishop," and the phrase lit. is "overseership"; so in vv. 10, 13, where the KJV has "use (and 'used') the office of a deacon," the RV rightly omits "office," and translates the verb *diakoneō*, "to serve," "let them serve as deacons" and "(they that) have served (well) as deacons."

OFFSPRING

1. *gennēma* (γέννημα, 1081), akin to *gennaō*, "to beget," denotes "the offspring of men and animals," Matt. 3:7; 12:34; 23:33; Luke 3:7, RV, "offspring" (KJV, "generation"). See FRUIT.

2. *genos* (γένος, 1085), "a race, family" (akin to *ginomai*, "to become"), denotes "an offspring," Acts 17:28, 29; Rev. 22:16. See GENERATION, KIND.

OIL

elaion (ἔλαιον, 1637), "olive oil," is mentioned over 200 times in the Bible. Different kinds were known in Palestine. The "pure," RV (KJV, beaten), mentioned in Exod. 27:20; 29:40; Lev. 24:2; Num. 28:5 (now known as virgin oil), extracted by pressure, without heat, is called "golden" in Zech. 4:12. There were also inferior kinds. In the NT the uses mentioned were (a) for lamps, in which the "oil" is a symbol of the Holy Spirit, Matt. 25:3-4, 8; (b) as a medicinal agent, for healing, Luke 10:34; (c) for anointing at feasts, Luke 7:46; (d) on festive occasions, Heb. 1:9, where the reference is probably to the consecration of kings; (e) as an accompaniment of miraculous power, Mark 6:13, or of the prayer of faith, Jas. 5:14. For its general use in commerce, see Luke 16:6; Rev. 6:6; 18:13.

OINTMENT

muron (μύρον, 3464), a word derived by the ancients from *murō*, "to flow," or from *murra*, "myrrh-oil" (it is probably of foreign origin; see MYRRH). The "ointment" is mentioned in the NT in connection with the anointing of the Lord on the occasions recorded in Matt. 26:7, 9, 12; Mark 14:3-4; Luke 7:37-38, 46; John 11:2; 12:3 (twice), 5. The alabaster cruse mentioned in the passages in Matthew, Mark and Luke was the best of its kind, and the spikenard was one of the costliest of perfumes. "Ointments" were used in preparing a body for burial, Luke 23:56 ("ointments"). Of the act of the woman mentioned in Matt. 26:6-13, the Lord said, "she did it to prepare Me for burial"; her devotion led her to antedate the customary ritual after death, by showing both her affection and her understanding of what was impending. For the use of the various kinds of "ointments" as articles of commerce, see Rev. 18:13.

OLD

A. Adjectives.

1. *archaios* (ἀρχαῖος, 744), "original, ancient" (from *archē*, "a beginning": Eng., "archaic," "archaeology," etc.), is used (a) of persons belonging to a former age,"(to) them of old time," Matt. 5:21, 33, RV; in some mss. v. 27; the RV rendering is right; not ancient teachers are in view; what was said to them of old time was "to be both recognized in its significance and estimated in its temporary limitations, Christ intending His words to be regarded not as an abrogation, but a deepening and fulfilling" (Cremer); of prophets, Luke 9:8, 19; (b) of time long gone by, Acts 15:21; (c) of days gone by in a person's experience, Acts 15:7, "a good while ago," lit., "from old (days)," i.e., from the first days onward in the sense of originality, not age; (d) of Mnason, "an early disciple," Acts 21:16, RV, not referring to age, but to his being one of the first who had accepted the gospel from the beginning of its proclamation; (e) of things which are "old" in relation to the new, earlier things in contrast to things present, 2 Cor. 5:17, i.e., of what characterized and conditioned the time previous to conversion in a believer's experience, RV, "they are become new," i.e., they have taken on a new complexion and are viewed in an entirely different way; (f) of the world (i.e., the inhabitants of the world) just previous to the Flood, 2 Pet. 2:5; (g) of the Devil, as "that old serpent," Rev. 12:9; 20:2, "old," not in age, but as characterized for a long period by the evils indicated.

Note: For the difference between this and No. 2, see below.

2. *palaios* (παλαιός, 3820), akin to C, No. 1 (Eng., "paleontology," etc.), "of what is of long duration, old in years," etc., a garment, wine (in contrast to *neos*), Matt. 9:16:17; Mark 2:21-22 (twice); Luke 5:36-37, 39 (twice); of the treasures of divine truth, Matt. 13:52 (compared with *kainos*); of what belongs to the past, e.g., the believer's former self before his conversion, his "old man," "old" because it has been superseded

by that which is new, Rom. 6:6; Eph. 4:22 (in contrast to *kainos*); Col. 3:9 (in contrast to *neos*); of the covenant in connection with the Law, 2 Cor. 3:14; of leaven, metaphorical of moral evil, 1 Cor. 5:7, 8 (in contrast to *neos*); of that which was given long ago and remains in force, an "old" commandment, 1 John 2:7 (twice), that which was familiar and well known in contrast to that which is fresh (*kainos*).

Note: Palaios denotes "old," "without the reference to beginning and origin contained in *archaios*" (Abbott-Smith), a distinction observed in the papyri (Moulton and Milligan). While sometimes any difference seems almost indistinguishable, yet "it is evident that wherever an emphasis is desired to be laid on the reaching back to a beginning, whatever that beginning may be, *archaios* will be preferred (e.g., of Satan, Rev. 12:9; 20:2, see No. 1). That which ... is old in the sense of more or less worn out ... is always *palaios*" (Trench).

3. *presbuteros* (πρεσβύτερος, 4245), "older, elder," is used in the plural, as a noun, in Acts 2:17, "old men." See ELDER.

B. Nouns.

1. *gerōn* (γέρων, 1088) denotes "an old man" (from the same root comes Eng., "gray"), John 3:4.

2. *presbutēs* (πρεσβύτης, 4246), "an old man," Luke 1:18, is translated "aged" in Titus 2:2; Philem. 9 (for this, however, see the RV marg.) See AGED.

3. *gēras* (γῆρας, 1094), "old age," occurs in Luke 1:36.

Note: Augustine (quoted by Trench, Sec. CVII, 2) speaks of the distinction observed among Greeks, that *presbutēs* conveys the suggestion of gravity.

C. Adverbs.

1. *palai* (πάλαι, 3819) denotes "long ago, of old," Heb. 1:1, RV, "of old time" (KJV, "in time past"); in Jude 4, "of old"; it is used as an adjective in 2 Pet. 1:9, "(his) old (sins)," lit., "his sins of old."

2. *ekpalai* (ἔκπαλαι, 1597), "from of old, for a long time" (*ek*, "from," and No. 1), occurs in 2 Pet. 2:3, RV, "from of old" (KJV, "of a long time"); 3:5. See LONG, B, *Note* (2).

Note: In 1 Pet. 3:5, KJV, the particle *pote*, "once, formerly, ever, sometime," is translated "in the old time" (RV, "aforetime"); in 2 Pet. 1:21, "in old time" (RV, "ever"), KJV marg., "at any time."

D. Verbs.

1. *palaioō* (παλαιόω, 3822), akin to A, No. 2, denotes, in the active voice, "to make or declare old," Heb. 8:13 (1st part); in the passive voice, "to become old," of things worn out by time and use, Luke 12:33; Heb. 1:11, "shall wax old," lit., "shall be made old," i.e., worn out; in 8:13 (2nd part), RV, "is becoming old" (KJV "decayeth"); here and in the 1st part of the verse, the verb may have the meaning "to abrogate"; for the next verb in the verse, see No. 2.

2. *gēraskō* (γηράσκω, 1095), from *gēras*, "old age" (akin to B, No. 1), "to grow old," is translated "thou shalt be old," in John 21:18; "waxeth aged," Heb. 8:13, RV (KJV, "waxeth old").

Notes: (1) In John 8:57, *echō*, "to have," is used with "fifty years" as the object, signifying, "Thou art (not yet fifty years) old," lit., "Thou hast not yet fifty years." (2) In Mark 5:42, RV, the verb *eimi*, "to be," with the phrase "of twelve years" is translated "was ... old" (KJV, "was *of the age* of").

OLDNESS

palaiotēs (παλαιότης, 3821), from *palaios* (see A, No. 2, above), occurs in Rom. 7:6, of "the letter," i.e., "the law," with its rules of conduct, mere outward conformity to which has yielded place in the believer's service to a response to the inward operation of the Holy Spirit. The word is contrasted with *kainotēs*, "newness."

OLIVES (OLIVE BERRIES), OLIVE TREE

1. *elaia* (ἐλαία, 1636) denotes (a) "an olive tree," Rom. 11:17, 24; Rev. 11:4 (plural); the Mount of Olives was so called from the numerous olive trees there, and indicates the importance attached to such; the Mount is mentioned in the NT in connection only with the Lord's life on earth, Matt. 21:1; 24:3; 26:30; Mark 11:1; 13:3; 14:26; Luke 19:37; 22:39; John 8:1; (b) "an olive," Jas. 3:12, RV (KJV, "olive berries").

2. *elaiōn* (ἐλαιών, 1638), "an olive grove" or "olive garden," the ending *-ōn*, as in this class of noun, here indicates "a place set with trees of the kind designated by the primitive" (Thayer); hence it is applied to the Mount of Olives, Luke 19:29; 21:37; Acts 1:12 ("Olivet"): in the first two of these and in Mark 11:1, some mss. have the form of the noun as in No. 1.

3. *kallielaios* (καλλιέλαιος, 2565), "the garden olive" (from *kallos*, "beauty," and No. 1), occurs in Rom. 11:24, "a good olive tree."

4. *agrielaios* (ἀγριέλαιος, 65), an adjective (from *agrios*, "growing in the fields, wild," and No. 1), denoting "of the wild olive," is used as a noun in Rom. 11:17, 24, "a wild olive tree" (RV, in the latter Verse).

For **OMNIPOTENT** (Rev. 19:6) see ALMIGHTY

ONLY BEGOTTEN

monogenēs (μονογενής, 3439) is used five times, all in the writings of the apostle John, of Christ as the Son of God; it is translated "only begotten" in Heb. 11:17 of the relationship of Isaac to Abraham.

With reference to Christ, the phrase "the only begotten from the Father," John 1:14, RV (see also the marg.), indicates that as the Son of God He was the sole representative of the Being and character of the One who sent Him. In the original the definite article is omitted both before "only begotten" and before "Father," and its absence in each case serves to lay stress upon the characteristics referred to in the terms used. The apostle's object is to demonstrate what sort of glory it was that he and his fellow apostles had seen. That he is not merely making a comparison with earthly relationships is indicated by *para*, "from." The glory was that of a unique relationship and the word "begotten" does not imply a beginning of His Sonship. It suggests relationship indeed, but must be distinguished from generation as applied to man.

We can only rightly understand the term "the only begotten" when used of the Son, in the sense of unoriginated relationship. "The begetting is not an event of time, however remote, but a fact irrespective of time. The Christ did not *become*, but necessarily and eternally *is* the Son. He, a Person, possesses every attribute of pure Godhood. This necessitates eternity, absolute being; in this respect He is not 'after' the Father" (Moule). The expression also suggests the thought of the deepest affection, as in the case of the OT word *yachid*, variously rendered, "only one," Gen. 22:2, 12; "only son," Jer. 6:26; Amos 8:10; Zech. 12:10; "only beloved," Prov. 4:3, and "darling," Ps. 22:20; 35:17.

In John 1:18 the clause "the only begotten son, which is in the bosom of the Father," expresses both His eternal union with the Father in the Godhead and the ineffable intimacy and love between them, the Son sharing all the Father's counsels and enjoying all His affections. Another reading is *monogenēs Theos*, "God only-begotten." In John 3:16 the statement, "God so loved the world that He gave His only begotten son," must not be taken to mean that Christ became the only begotten son by incarnation. The value and the greatness of the gift lay in the Sonship of Him who was given. His Sonship was not the effect of His being given. In John 3:18 the phrase "the name of the only begotten son of God" lays stress upon the full revelation of God's character and will, His love and grace, as conveyed in the name of One who, being in a unique relationship to Him, was provided by Him as the object of faith. In 1 John 4:9 the statement "God hath sent His only begotten son into the world" does not mean that God sent out into the world one who at His birth in Bethlehem had become His Son. Cf. the parallel statement, "God sent forth the Spirit of His Son," Gal. 4:6, RV, which could not mean that God sent forth One who became His Spirit when He sent Him.

For **ONSET,** Acts 14:5, RV, see ASSAULT and IMPULSE

For **ONWARD,** 2 John 9, RV, see GO, No. 10

OPENLY

1. *parrhēsia* (παῤῥησία, 3954), "freedom of speech, boldness," is used adverbially in the dative case and translated "openly" in Mark 8:32, of a saying of Christ; in John 7:13, of a public statement; in 11:54, of Christ's public appearance; in 7:26 and 18:20, of His public testimony; preceded by the preposition *en*, "in," John 7:4, lit., "in boldness" (cf. v. 10, RV, "publicly).

2. *phanerōs* (φανερῶς, 5318), manifestly, openly.

Notes: (1) In Gal. 3:1, "openly set forth" translates the verb *prographō*, lit., "to write before," as of the OT, Rom. 15:4 (cf. Jude 4), and of a previous letter, Eph. 3:3. In Gal. 3:1, however, "it is probably used in another sense, unexampled in the Scriptures but not uncommon in the language of the day, = 'proclaimed,' 'placarded,' as a magistrate proclaimed the fact that an execution had been carried out, placarding his proclamation in a public place. The Apostle carries on his metaphor of the 'evil eye;' as a preventive of such mischief it was common to post up charms on the walls of houses, a glance at which was supposed to counteract any evil influence to which a person may have been subjected. 'Notwithstanding,' he says, in effect, 'that the fact that Christ had been crucified was placarded before your very eyes in our preaching, you have allowed yourselves to be ... fascinated by the enemies of the Cross of Christ, when you had only to look at Him to escape their malignant influence;' cf. the interesting and instructive parallel in Num. 21:9." (2) In some mss. in Matt. 6:4, 6, 18, the phrase *en tō phanerō*, lit., "in the manifest," is found (KJV, "openly"); see the RV (3) For *emphanēs*, rendered "openly" in Acts 10:40, KJV, see MANIFEST. (4) In Acts 16:37, KJV, the dative case of the adjective *dēmosios*, "belonging to the people" (*dēmos*, "a people"), "public" (so RV), used adverbially, is translated "openly"; in 18:28 and 20:20, "publicly." For the adjective itself, "public," see Acts 5:18.

For **OPERATION** see WORKING

OPPOSE

1. *antikeimai* (ἀντίκειμαι, 480): see ADVERSARY, B.

2. *antitassō* (ἀντιτάσσω, 498) is used in the middle voice in the sense of setting oneself against (*anti*, "against," *tassō*, "to order, set"), "opposing oneself to," Acts 18:6; elsewhere rendered by the verb "to resist," Rom. 13:2; Jas. 4:6; 5:6; 1 Pet. 5:5.

3. *antidiatithemi* (ἀντιδιατίθεμαι, 475) signifies "to place oneself in opposition, oppose" (*anti*, "against," *dia*, "through," intensive, *tithēmi*, "to place"), 2 Tim. 2:25. The KJV and RV translate this as a middle voice, "them (KJV, 'those') that oppose themselves." Field (*Notes on the Trans. of the NT*) points out that in the only other known instance of the verb it is passive. The sense is practically the same if it is rendered "those who are opposed."

OPPOSITIONS

antithesis (ἀντίθεσις, 477), "a contrary position" (*anti*, "against," *tithēmi*, "to place"; Eng., "antithesis"), occurs in 1 Tim. 6:20.

OPPRESS

1. *katadunasteuō* (καταδυναστεύω, 2616), "to exercise power over" (*kata*, "down," *dunastēs*, "a potentate": *dunamai* "to have power"), "to oppress," is used, in the passive voice, in Acts 10:38; in the active, in Jas. 2:6.

2. *kataponeō* (καταπονέω, 2669): see DISTRESS, B, No. 4.

ORACLE

logion (λόγιον, 3051), a diminutive of *logos*, "a word, narrative, statement," denotes "a divine response or utterance, an oracle"; it is used of (a) the contents of the Mosaic Law, Acts 7:38; (b) all the written utterances of God through OT writers, Rom. 3:2; (c) the substance of Christian doctrine, Heb. 5:12; (d) the utterances of God through Christian teachers, 1 Pet. 4:11.

Note: Divine "oracles" were given by means of the breastplate of the high priest, in connection with the service of the tabernacle, and the Sept. uses the associated word *logeion* in Exod. 28:15, to describe the breastplate.

ORATION

dēmēgoreō (δημηγορέω, 1215), from *dēmos*, "the people" and *agoreuō*, "to speak in the public assembly, to deliver an oration," occurs in Acts 12:21.

ORATOR

rhētōr (ῥήτωρ, 4489), from an obsolete present tense, *rheo*, "to say" (cf. Eng., "rhetoric"), denotes "a public speaker, an orator," Acts 24:1, of Tertullus. Such a person, distinct from the professional lawyer, was hired, as a professional speaker, to make a skillful presentation of a case in court. His training was not legal but rhetorical.

ORDAIN

1. *tithēmi* (τίθημι, 5087), to put: see APPOINT, No. 3.

2. *kathistēmi* (καθίστημι, 2525), from *kata*, "down," or "over against," and *histēmi*, "to cause to stand, to set," is translated "to ordain" in the KJV of Titus 1:5; Heb. 5:1; 8:3. See APPOINT, No. 2.

3. *tassō* (τάσσω, 5021) is translated "to ordain," in Acts 13:48 and Rom. 13:1. See APPOINT, No. 5.

4. *diatassō* (διατάσσω, 1299) is translated "to ordain" in 1 Cor. 7:17; 9:14; Gal. 3:19, the last in the sense of "administered." Cf. *diatagē*, under DISPOSITION. See APPOINT, No. 6.

5. *horizō* (ὁρίζω, 3724) is twice used of Christ as divinely "ordained" to be the Judge of men, Acts 10:42; 17:31.

6. *krinō* (κρίνω, 2919), "to divide, separate, decide, judge," is translated "ordained" in Acts 16:4, of the decrees by the apostles and elders in Jerusalem. See JUDGE.

Notes: (1) In 1 Cor. 2:7, KJV, *proorizō*, "to foreordain" (see RV) is translated "ordained." (2) In Mark 3:14, KJV, *poieō*, "to make," is translated "ordained" (RV, "appointed"). (3) In Heb. 9:6, KJV, *kataskeuazō*, "to prepare" (so RV), is translated "were ... ordained. See PREPARE. (4) In Acts 14:23, KJV, *cheirotoneō*, "to appoint" (RV), is translated "they had ordained." See APPOINT, No. 11. (5) In Eph. 2:10, KJV, *proetoimazō*, "to prepare before," is translated "hath before ordained" (RV, "afore prepared"); see PREPARE. (6) In Jude 4, KJV, *prographō*, lit., "to write before," is translated "were before ... ordained" (RV, "were ... set forth"). (7) In Acts 1:22, KJV, *ginomai* "to become," is translated "be ordained" (RV, "become"). (8) In Rom. 7:10, KJV, "*ordained*" represents no word in the original (see RV).

ORDINANCE

A. Nouns.

1. *dikaiōma* (δικαίωμα, 1345): see JUSTIFICATION, No. 2.

2. *diatagē* (διαταγή, 1296) is translated "ordinances," in Rom. 13:2. See DISPOSITION.

3. *dogma* (δόγμα, 1378) is translated "ordinances" in Eph. 2:15 and Col. 2:14. See DECREE.

4. *ktisis* (κτίσις, 2937), "a creation, creature," is translated "ordinance" in 1 Pet. 2:13. See CREATE, B, No. 1. *NOTE:* In 1 Cor. 11:2, KJV, *paradosis*, "a tradition" (marg., and RV, "traditions"), is translated "ordinances." See TRADITION.

B. Verb.

dogmatizō (δογματίζω, 1379), akin to A, No. 3, "to decree," signifies, in the middle voice, "to subject oneself to an ordinance," Col. 2:20. In the Sept., Esth. 3:9; in some texts, Dan. 2:13, 15.

OVERCOME

1. *nikaō* (νικάω, 3528), is used (a) of God, Rom. 3:4 (a law term), RV, "mightest prevail"; (b) of Christ, John 16:33; Rev. 3:21; 5:5; 17:14; (c) of His followers, Rom. 12:21 (2nd part); 1 John 2:13-14; 4:4; 5:4-5; Rev. 2:7, 11, 17, 26; 3:5, 12, 21; 12:11; 15:2; 21:7; (d) of faith, 1 John 5:4; (e) of evil (passive voice), Rom. 12:21; (f) of predicted human potentates, Rev. 6:2; 11:7; 13:7.

2. *hēttaomai* (ἡττάομαι, 2274), "to be made inferior, be enslaved," is rendered "is (are) overcome," in 2 Pet. 2:19-20. See INFERIOR.

3. *katakurieuō* (κατακυριεύω, 2634) is translated "overcome" in Acts 19:16; see MASTER, B.

OVERFLOW, OVERFLOWING

A. Verbs.

1. *huperperisseuō* (ὑπερπερισσεύω, 5248), "to abound more exceedingly," Rom. 5:20, is med in the middle voice in 2 Cor. 7:4, RV, "I overflow (with joy)," KJV, "I am exceeding (joyful)." See ABUNDANCE, B, No. 2.

2. *katakluzō* (κατακλύζω, 2626), "to inundate, deluge" (*kata*, "down," *kluzō*, "to wash" or "dash over," said, e.g., of the sea), is used in the passive voice in 2 Pet. 3:6, of the Flood.

B. Noun.

perisseia (περισσεία, 4050) is translated "overflowing" in Jas. 1:21, RV. See ABUNDANCE, A, No. 2.

OVERRIPE

xērainō (ξηραίνω, 3583) denotes "to dry up, wither," translated in Rev. 14:15, "overripe," RV (KJV, "ripe"), said figuratively of the harvest of the earth, symbolizing the condition of the world, political, especially connected with Israel (Joel 3:9, 14), and religious, comprehensive of the whole scene of Christendom (Matt. 13:38). See DRY.

For **OVERSEER** see BISHOP

OVERSHADOW

1. *episkiazō* (ἐπισκιάζω, 1982), "to throw a shadow upon" (*epi*, "over," *skia*, "a shadow"), "to overshadow," is used (a) of the bright cloud at the Transfiguration, Matt. 17:5; Mark 9:7; Luke 9:34; (b) metaphorically of the power of "the Most High" upon the Virgin Mary, Luke 1:35; (c) of the apostle Peter's shadow upon the sick, Acts 5:15.

2. *kataskiazō* (κατασκιάζω, 2683), lit., "to shadow down," is used of the "overshadowing" (RV) of the cherubim of glory above the mercy seat, Heb. 9:5 (KJV, "shadowing").

OVERSIGHT (exercise, take)

episkopeō (ἐπισκοπέω, 1983), lit., "to look upon" (*epi*, "upon," *skopeō*, "to look at, contemplate"), is found in 1 Pet. 5:2 (some ancient authorities omit it), "exercising the oversight," RV (KJV, "taking ..."); "exercising" is the right rendering; the word does not imply the entrance upon such responsibility, but the fulfillment of it. It is not a matter of assuming a position, but of the discharge of the duties. The word is found elsewhere in Heb. 12:15, "looking carefully," RV. See LOOK. Cf. *episkopē* in 1 Tim. 3:1 (see BISHOP, No. 2).

OVERTAKE

1. *katalambanō* (καταλαμβάνω, 2638), "to lay hold of," has the significance of "overtaking," metaphorically, in John 12:35 (RV, "overtake," KJV, "come upon") and 1 Thess. 5:4. See APPREHEND, No. 1.

2. *prolambanō* (προλαμβάνω, 4301), "to anticipate" (*pro*, "before," *lambanō*, "to take"), is used of the act of Mary, in Mark 14:8; of forestalling the less favored at a social meal, 1 Cor. 11:21; of being "overtaken" in any trespass, Gal. 6:1, where the meaning is not that of detecting a person in the act, but of his being caught by the trespass, through his being off his guard (see 5:21 and contrast the premeditated practice of evil in 5:26). The modern Greek version is "even if a man, through lack of circumspection, should fall into any sin."

OVERTHROW (Noun and Verb)

A. Noun.

katastrophē (καταστροφή, 2692), lit., "a turning down" (*kata*, "down," *strophē*, "a turning"; Eng., "catastrophe"), is used (a) literally, 2 Pet. 2:6, (b) metaphorically, 2 Tim. 2:14 "subverting," i.e., the "overthrowing" of faith. Cf. *kathairesis*, "a pulling down," 2 Cor. 10:4, 8; 13:10.

B. Verbs.

1. *katastrephō* (καταστρέφω, 2690), akin to A, lit. and primarily, "to turn down" or "turn over," as, e.g., the soil, denotes to "overturn, overthrow," Matt. 21:12; Mark 11:15; in Acts 15:16, passive voice, "ruins," lit., "the overthrown (things) of it" (some mss. have *kataskaptō*, "to dig down"). See RUIN.

2. *anastrephō* (ἀναστρέφω, 390) is found in some mss. in John 2:15 (see No. 3).

3. *anatrepō* (ἀνατρέπω, 396), lit., "to turn up or over" (*ana*, "up," *trepō*, "to turn"), "to upset," is used (a) literally, in the most authentic mss., in John 2:15 (see No. 2); (b) metaphorically, in 2 Tim. 2:18, "overthrow (the faith of some);" in Titus 1:11, RV, "overthrow (whole homes)," KJV, "subvert ...," i.e., households. Moulton and Milligan (*Vocab.*) give an apt illustration from a 2nd cent. papyrus, of the complete upsetting of a family by the riotous conduct of a member.

4. *kataluō* (καταλύω, 2647), lit., "to loosen down," signifies "to overthrow" in Acts 5:38, RV, "it will be overthrown" (KJV, "it will come to nought"); Rom. 14:20, RV, "overthrow" (KJV, "destroy"). See DESTROY.

5. *katastrōnnumi* (καταστρώννυμι, 2693), primarily, "to strew" or "spread over" (*kata*, "down," *strōnnumi*, or *strōnnuō*, "to spread"), then, "to overthrow," has this meaning in 1 Cor. 10:5, "they were overthrown." In the Sept., Num. 14:16; Job 12:23.

OWE

A. Verbs.

1. *opheilō* (ὀφείλω, 3784), "to owe, to be a debtor" (in the passive voice, "to be owed, to be due"), is translated by the verb "to owe" in Matt. 18:28 (twice); Luke 7:41; 16:5, 7; Rom. 13:8; in 15:27, RV, "they (gentile converts) owe it" (KJV, "it is their duty"); Philem. 18. See DUE, DUTY, GUILTY, INDEBTED.

2. *prosopheilō* (προσοφείλω, 4359), "to owe besides" (*pros,* "in addition," and No. 1), is used in Philem. 19, "thou owest (to me even thine own self) besides," i.e., "thou owest me already as much as Onesimus' debt, and in addition even thyself" (not "thou owest me much more").

B. Noun.

opheiletēs (ὀφειλέτης, 3781), "a debtor" (akin to A, No. 1), is translated "which owed" in Matt. 18:24, lit., "a debtor (of ten thousand talents)." See DEBTOR.

OWNER

1. *kurios* (κύριος, 2962), "one having power" (*kuros*) or "authority, a lord, master," signifies "an owner" in Luke 19:33. See LORD, MASTER, SIR.

2. *nauklēros* (ναύκληρος, 3490), "a ship owner" (*naus,* "a ship," *klēros,* "a lot"), "a shipmaster," occurs in Acts 27:11, "(the) owner of the ship."

P

PAIN (Noun and Verb)

A. Nouns.

1. *ponos* (πόνος, 4192) is translated "pain" in Rev. 16:10; 21:4; "pains" in 16:11. See LABOR.

2. *ōdin* (ὠδίν, 5604), "a birth pang, travail pain," is rendered "travail," metaphorically, in Matt. 24:8 and Mark 13:8, RV (KJV, "sorrows"); by way of comparison, in 1 Thess. 5:3; translated "pains (of death)," Acts 2:24 (RV, "pangs"). See SORROW, TRAVAIL. Cf. *ōdinō*, "to travail in birth."

B. Verb.

bosanizō (βασανίζω, 928) primarily signifies "to rub on the touchstone, to put to the test" (from *basanos*, "a touchstone," a dark stone used in testing metals); hence, "to examine by torture," and, in general, "to distress"; in Rev. 12:2, "in pain," RV (KJV, "pained"), in connection with parturition. See TORMENT. (In the Sept., 1 Sam. 5:3.).

Note: For Rom. 8:22, "travaileth in pain together," see TRAVAIL.

For **PAINFULNESS** (2 Cor. 11:27, KJV) see TRAVAIL

PALACE

1. *aulē* (αὐλή, 833), "a court, dwelling, palace": see COURT.

2. *praitōrion* (πραιτώριον, 4232) signified originally "a general's (praetor's) tent." Then it was applied to "the council of army officers"; then to "the official residence of the governor of a province"; finally, to "the imperial bodyguard." In the KJV the word appears only once, Mark 15:16, "the hall, called Praetorium" (RV, "within the court which is the Praetorium," marg., "palace"); in the Greek of the NT it also occurs in Matt. 27:27, KJV, "the common hall," marg., "the governor's house"; RV, "palace," see marg.; John 18:28 (twice), KJV, "the hall of judgment"; and "judgment hall," marg., "Pilate's house," RV, "palace"; 18:33 and 19:9, KJV, "judgment hall," RV, "palace," see marg.; so in Acts 23:35; in Phil. 1:13, KJV, "in all the palace," marg., "Caesar's court," RV, "throughout the whole praetorian guard," marg., "in the whole Praetorium."

"In the Gospels the term denotes the official residence in Jerusalem of the Roman governor, and the various translations of it in our versions arose from a desire either to indicate the special purpose for which that residence was used on the occasion in question, or to explain what particular building was intended. But whatever building the governor occupied was the Praetorium. It is most probable that in Jerusalem he resided in the well-known palace of Herod .... Pilate's residence has been identified with the castle of Antonia, which was occupied by the regular garrison. The probability is that it was the same as Herod's palace. Herod's palace in Caesarea was used as the Praetorium there, and the expression in Acts 23:35, marg., 'Herod's praetorium,' is abbreviated from 'the praetorium of Herod's palace.'" (*Hastings Bib. Dic.*).

In Phil. 1:13, marg., "the whole Praetorium" has been variously explained. It has been spoken of as "the palace," in connection with 4:22, where allusion is made to believers who belong to Caesar's household. Others have understood it of the barracks of the "praetorian" guard, but Lightfoot shows that this use of the word cannot be established, neither can it be regarded as referring to the barracks of the "palace" guard. The phrase "and to all the rest" in 1:13 indicates that persons are meant. Mommsen, followed by Ramsay (*St. Paul the Traveller*, p. 357) regards it as improbable that the apostle was committed to the "praetorian" guard and holds the view that Julius the centurion, who brought Paul to Rome, belonged to a corps drafted from legions in the provinces, whose duty it was to supervise the corn supply and perform police service, and that Julius probably delivered his prisoners to the commander of his corps. Eventually Paul's case came before the praetorian council, which is the "praetorium" alluded to by the apostle, and the phrase "to all the rest" refers to the audience of the trial.

Note: Some scholars, believing that this epistle was written during an Ephesian imprisonment, take the "Praetorium" here to be the residence in Ephesus of the proconsul of the province of Asia, and "Caesar's household" to be the local imperial civil service (Deissmann etc.).

PALM (of the hand)

Note: For *rhapisma*, "a blow," with *didōmi*, "to give," translated "did strike (and, struck) ... with the palm of his hand" (KJV, in Mark 14:65; John 18:22), see BLOW.

PALM (palm tree)

phoinix (φοῖνιξ, 5404) denotes "the date palm"; it is used of "palm" trees in John 12:13, from which branches were taken; of the branches themselves in Rev. 7:9. The "palm" gave its name to Phoenicia and to Phoenix in Crete, Acts 27:12, RV. Jericho was the city of "palm trees," Deut. 34:3; Judg. 1:16; 3:13; 2 Chron. 28:15. They were plentiful there in the time of Christ.

PALSY (sick of)

A. Adjective.

paralutikos (παραλυτικός, 3885), "paralytic, sick of the palsy," is found in Matt. 4:24 (RV, "palsied"); 8:6; 9:2 (twice), 6; Mark 2:3, 4, 5, 9, 10; in some mss. Luke 5:24 (see B).

B. Verb

paraluō (παραλύω, 3886), lit., "to loose from the side," hence, "to set free," is used in the passive voice of "being enfeebled by a paralytic stroke, palsied," Luke 5:18, RV, "palsied" (KJV, "taken with a palsy"); 5:24 (ditto), in the best mss.; Acts 8:7 (ditto); 9:33, RV, "he was palsied" (KJV, "was sick of the palsy"); Heb. 12:12, RV, "palsied (knees)," KJV, "feeble." See FEEBLE.

For **PANGS,** Acts 2:24, RV, see PAIN

For **PAPS** see BREAST

PARABLE

1. *parabolē* (παραβολή, 3850) lit. denotes "a placing beside" (akin to *paraballō*, "to throw" or "lay beside, to compare"). It signifies "a placing of one thing beside another" with a view to comparison (some consider that the thought of comparison is not necessarily contained in the word). In the NT it is found outside the gospels, only in Heb. 9:9 and 11:19. It is generally used of a somewhat lengthy utterance or narrative drawn from nature or human circumstances, the object of which is to set forth a spiritual lesson, e.g., those in Matt. 13 and Synoptic parallels; sometimes it is used of a short saying or proverb, e.g., Matt. 15:15; Mark 3:23; 7:17; Luke 4:23; 5:36; 6:39. It is the lesson that is of value; the hearer must catch the analogy if he is to be instructed (this is true also of a proverb). Such a narrative or saying, dealing with earthly things with a spiritual meaning, is distinct from a fable, which attributes to things what does not belong to them in nature.

Christ's "parables" most frequently convey truths connected with the subject of the kingdom of God. His withholding the meaning from His hearers as He did from the multitudes, Matt. 13:34, was a divine judgment upon the unworthy.

Two dangers are to be avoided in seeking to interpret the "parables" in Scripture, that of ignoring the important features, and that of trying to make all the details mean something.

2. *paroimia* (παροιμία, 3942) denotes "a wayside saying" (from *paroimos*, "by the way"), "a byword," "maxim," or "problem," 2 Pet. 2:22. The word is sometimes spoken of as a "parable," John 10:6, i.e., a figurative discourse (RV marg., "proverb"); see also 16:25, 29, where the word is rendered "proverbs" (marg. "parables") and "proverb."

PARADISE

paradeisos (παράδεισος, 3857) is an Oriental word, first used by the historian Xenophon, denoting "the parks of Persian kings and nobles." It is of Persian origin (Old Pers. *pairidaeza*, akin to Gk. *peri*, "around," and *teichos*, "a wall") whence it passed into Greek. See the Sept., e.g., in Neh. 2:8; Eccl. 2:5; Song of Sol. 4:13. The Sept. translators used it of the garden of Eden, Gen. 2:8, and in other respects, e.g., Num. 24:6; Isa. 1:30; Jer. 29:5; Ezek. 31:8-9.

In Luke 23:43, the promise of the Lord to the repentant robber was fulfilled the same day; Christ, at His death, having committed His spirit to the Father, went in spirit immediately into Heaven itself, the dwelling place of God (the Lord's mention of the place as "paradise" must have been a great comfort to the malefactor; to the oriental mind it expressed the sum total of blessedness). Thither the apostle Paul was caught up, 2 Cor. 12:4, spoken of as "the third heaven" (v. 3 does not introduce a different vision), beyond the heavens of the natural creation (see Heb. 4:14, RV, with reference to the Ascension). The same region is mentioned in Rev. 2:7, where the "tree of life," the figurative antitype of that in Eden, held out to the overcomer, is spoken of as being in "the Paradise of God" (RV), marg., "garden," as in Gen. 2:8.

For **PARCEL** see GROUND, No. 4

PARENTS

1. *goneus* (γονεύς, 1118), "a begetter, a father" (akin to *ginomai*, "to come into being, become"), is used in the plural in the NT, Matt. 10:21; Mark 13:12; six times in Luke (in Luke 2:43, RV, "His parents," KJV, "Joseph and His mother"); six in John; elsewhere, Rom. 1:30; 2 Cor. 12:14 (twice); Eph. 6:1; Col. 3:20; 2 Tim. 3:2.

2. *progonos* (πρόγονος, 4269), an adjective signifying "born before" (*pro*, before, and *ginomai*, see No. 1), is used as a noun, in the plural, (a) of ancestors, "forefathers," 2 Tim. 1:3; (b) of living "parents," 1 Tim. 5:4. See FOREFATHER.

3. *patēr* (πατήρ, 3962), "a father," is used in Heb. 11:23, in the plural, of both father and mother, the "parents" of Moses. See FATHER.

PART (Verb, to separate)

1. *diamerizō* (διαμερίζω, 1266), "to part among, to distribute," is translated by the verb "to part" (a) in the middle voice, with reference to the Lord's garments, Matt. 27:35, 1st part (in some mss., 2nd part); Mark 15:24; Luke 23:34; John 19:24; (b) in the active voice, of "the proceeds of the sale of possessions and goods," Acts 2:45; (c) in the passive voice in Acts 2:3, of the "parting asunder" (RV) of tongues like fire (KJV, "cloven").

2. *diistēmi* (διΐστημι, 1339), "to set apart, separate" (*dia*, "apart," *histēmi*, "to cause to stand"), is used in the active voice in Luke 24:51, RV, "He parted (from them)," KJV, "was parted." See GO.

3. *apospaō* (ἀποσπάω, 645), "to draw off" or "tear away," is used in the passive voice in Luke 22:41, RV, "He was parted" (KJV, "was withdrawn"), lit. "He was torn away," indicating the reluctance with which Christ parted from the loving sympathy of the disciples. Moulton and Milligan suggest that the ordinary use of the verb does not encourage this stronger meaning, but since the simpler meaning is not found in the NT, except in Acts 21:1, and since the idea of withdrawal is expressed in Matt. by *anachōreō*, Luke may have used *apospaō* here in the stronger sense.

4. *chōrizō* (χωρίζω, 5563), in Philem. 15, RV, "parted."

5. *apochōrizō* (ἀποχωρίζω, 673), "to part from," Acts 15:39, RV.

PARTAKE, PARTAKER

A. Nouns.

1. *koinōnos* (κοινωνός, 2844), an adjective, signifying "having in common" (*koinos*, "common"), is used as a noun, denoting "a companion, partner, partaker," translated "partakers" in Matt. 23:30; 1 Cor. 10:18, KJV (see COMMUNION, B); 2 Cor. 1:7; Heb. 10:33, RV (see COMPANION, No. 2); 2 Pet. 1:4; "partaker" in 1 Pet. 5:1. See PARTNER.

2. *sunkoinōnos* (συγκοινωνός, 4791) denotes "partaking jointly with" (*sun*, and No. 1), Rom. 11:17, RV, "(didst become) partaker with them" (KJV, "partakest"); 1 Cor. 9:23, RV, "a joint partaker," i.e., with the gospel, as cooperating in its activity; the KJV misplaces the "with" by attaching it to the superfluous italicized pronoun "*you*"; Phil. 1:7, "partakers with (me of grace)," RV, and KJV marg.; not as KJV text, "partakers (of my grace)"; Rev. 1:9, "partaker with (you in the tribulation, etc.)," KJV, "companion." See COMPANION.

3. *metochos* (μέτοχος, 3353): see FELLOW, No. 3, PARTNER.

4. *summetochos* (συμμέτοχος, 4830), "partaking together with" (*sun*, "with," and No. 3), is used as a noun, a joint partaker, Eph. 3:6, RV, "fellow partakers" (KJV, "partakers"); in 5:7, RV and KJV, "partakers."

Notes: (1) For *antilambanō*, "to partake of," rendered "partakers" in 1 Tim. 6:2, KJV, see B, No. 4. (2) For the phrase "to be partakers," Col. 1:12, see PART, A, No. 2.

B. Verbs.

1. *koinōneō* (κοινωνέω, 2841), "to have a share of, to share with, take part in" (akin to A, No. 1), is translated "to be partaker of" in 1 Tim. 5:22; Heb. 2:14 (1st part), KJV, "are partakers of," RV, "are sharers in" (for the 2nd part see No. 3); 1 Pet. 4:13; 2 John 11, RV, "partaketh in" (KJV, "is partaker of"); in the passive voice in Rom. 15:27. See COMMUNICATE.

2. *sunkoinōneō* (συγκοινωνέω, 4790): see FELLOWSHIP, B, No. 2.

3. *metechō* (μετέχω, 3348), "to partake of, share in" (*meta*, "with," *echō*, "to have"), akin to A, No. 3, is translated "of partaking" in 1 Cor. 9:10, RV (KJV, "be partaker of"); "partake of" in 9:12, RV (KJV, "be partakers of"); so in 10:17, 21: in v. 30 "partake"; in Heb. 2:14, the KJV "took part of" is awkward; Christ "partook of" flesh and blood, RV; cf. No. 1 in this verse; in Heb. 5:13, metaphorically, of receiving elementary spiritual teaching, RV, "partaketh of (milk)," KJV, "useth"; in Heb. 7:13, it is said of Christ (the antitype of Melchizedek) as "belonging to" (so RV) or "partaking of" (RV marg.) another tribe than that of Levi (KJV, "pertaineth to"). See PARTNER, *Note*.

4. *antilambanō* (ἀντιλαμβάνω, 482), "to take hold of, to lay hold of" something before one, has the meaning "to partake of" in 1 Tim. 6:2, RV, "partake of," marg., "lay hold of," KJV, "are ... partakers of" (*anti*, "in return for," *lambanō*, "to take or receive"); the benefit mentioned as "partaken" of by the masters would seem to be the improved quality of the service rendered; the benefit of redemption is not in view here. See HELP.

5. *metalambanō* (μεταλαμβάνω, 3335), "to have, or get, a share of," is translated "to be partaker (or partakers) of" in 2 Tim. 2:6 and Heb. 12:10. See HAVE.

6. *summerizō* (συμμερίζω, 4829), primarily, "to distribute in shares" (*sun*, "with," *meros*, "a part"), in the middle voice, "to have a share in," is used in 1 Cor. 9:13, KJV, "are partakers with (the altar)," RV, "have their portion with," i.e., they feed with others on that which, having been sacrificed, has been placed upon an altar; so the believer feeds upon Christ (who is the altar in Heb. 13:10).

PARTIAL, PARTIALITY

A. Verb.

diakrinō (διακρίνω, 1252), "to separate, distinguish, discern, judge, decide" (*dia*, "asunder," *krinō*, "to judge"), also came to mean "to be divided in one's mind, to hesitate, doubt," and had this significance in Hellenistic Greek (though not so found in the Sept.). " 'This meaning seems to have had its beginning in near proximity to Christianity.' It arises very naturally out of the general sense of making distinctions" (Moulton and Milligan).

B. Noun.

prosklisis (πρόσκλισις, 4346) denotes "inclination" (*pros*, "towards," *klinō*, "to lean"); it is used with *kata* in 1 Tim. 5:21, lit., "according to partiality."

C. Adjective.

adiakritos (ἀδιάκριτος, 87) primarily signifies "not to be parted" (*a*, negative, and an adjectival form akin to A), hence, "without uncertainty," or "indecision," Jas. 3:17, KJV, "without partiality" (marg. "wrangling"), RV, "without variance" (marg., "Or, doubtfulness Or, partiality"). See VARIANCE. In the Sept., Prov. 25:1.

PARTITION

phragmos (φραγμός, 5418), primarily "a fencing" in (akin to *phrassō*, "to fence in, stop, close"), is used metaphorically in Eph. 2:14, of "the middle wall of partition"; "the partition" is epexegetic of "the middle wall," namely, the "partition" between Jew and Gentile. J. A. Robinson suggests that Paul had in mind the barrier between the outer and inner courts of the Temple, notices fixed to which warned Gentiles not to proceed further on pain of death (see Josephus, *Antiq.* xv. 11. 5; *B. J.* v. 5. 2; vi. 2. 4; cf. Acts 21:29). See HEDGE.

PARTNER

1. *koinōnos* (κοινωνός, 2844), an adjective, signifying "having in common" (*koinos*), is used as a noun, "partners" in Luke 5:10, "partner" in 2 Cor. 8:23; Philem. 17 (in spiritual life and business). See COMMUNION, B, COMPANION, No. 2, PARTAKER.

2. *metochos* (μέτοχος, 3353), an adjective, signifying "having with, sharing," is used as a noun, "partners" in Luke 5:7. See FELLOW, PARTAKER.

Note: Koinōnos stresses the fact of having something in common, *metochos*, "the fact of sharing"; the latter is less thorough in effect than the former.

PASSING OVER

paresis (πάρεσις, 3929), primarily "a letting go, dismissal" (akin to *pariēmi*, "to let alone, loosen"), denotes "a passing by" or "praetermission (of sin)," "a suspension of judgment," or "withholding of punishment," Rom. 3:25, RV, "passing over" (KJV, "remission"), with reference to sins committed previously to the propitiatory sacrifice of Christ, the "passing by" not being a matter of divine disregard but of forbearance.

PASSION

A. Nouns.

1. *pathēma* (πάθημα, 3804), "a suffering" or "a passive emotion," is translated "passions" in Rom. 7:5, RV, "(sinful) passions," KJV, "motions," and Gal. 5:24, RV; see AFFECTION, A, No. 3, AFFLICT, B, No. 3.

2. *pathos* (πάθος, 3806): see AFFECTION, A, No. 1.

B. Verb.

paschō (πάσχω, 3958), "to suffer," is used as a noun, in the aorist infinitive with the article, and translated "passion" in Acts 1:3, of the suffering of Christ at Calvary. See SUFFER.

C. Adjective.

homoiopathēs (ὁμοιοπαθής, 3663), "of like feelings or affections" (*homoios*, "like," and A, No. 2; Eng., "homeopathy"), is rendered "of like passions" in Acts 14:15 (RV marg., "nature"); in Jas. 5:17, RV, ditto (KJV, "subject to like passions").

PASSOVER

pascha (πάσχα, 3957), the Greek spelling o the Aramaic word for the Passover, from the Hebrew *pāsach*, "to pass over, to spare," a feast instituted by God in commemoration of the deliverance of Israel from Egypt, and anticipatory of the expiatory sacrifice of Christ. The word signifies (I) "the Passover Feast," e.g., Matt. 26:2; John 2:13, 23; 6:4; 11:55; 12:1; 13:1; 18:39; 19:14; Acts 12:4; Heb. 11:28; (II), by metonymy, (a) "the Paschal Supper," Matt. 26:18, 19; Mark 14:16; Luke 22:8, 13; (b) "the Paschal lamb," e.g., Mark 14:12 (cf. Exod. 12:21); Luke 22:7; (c) "Christ Himself," 1 Cor. 5:7.

PAST

A. Verbs.

1. *ginomai* (γίνομαι, 1096), "to become, come to pass," is translated "was past" in Luke 9:36, KJV, and RV marg. (RV, "came"), of the voice of God the Father at the Transfiguration; "is past," 2 Tim. 2:18.

2. *diaginomai* (διαγίνομαι, 1230), *dia*, "through," a stronger form than No. 1, used of time, denotes "to intervene, elapse, pass," Mark 16:1, "was past"; Acts 25:13, RV, "were passed"; 27:9, "was spent."

3. *proginomai* (προγίνομαι, 4266), "to happen before" (*pro*, before, and No. 1), is used in Rom. 3:25, KJV, "that are past" (RV, "done aforetime"), of sins committed in times previous to the atoning sacrifice of Christ (see PASSING OVER).

B. Particle.

pote (ποτέ, 4218), "once, formerly, sometime," is translated "in time (or times) past," in Rom. 11:30; Gal. 1:13, 23, KJV (RV, "once"); Eph. 2:2, 11 (RV, "aforetime"); v. 3 (RV, "once"); Philem. 11 (RV, "aforetime"); 1 Pet. 2:10.

PASTOR

poimēn (ποιμήν, 4166), "a shepherd, one who tends herds or flocks" (not merely one who feeds them), is used metaphorically of Christian "pastors," Eph. 4:11. "Pastors" guide as well as feed the flock, cf. Acts 20:28, which with v. 17, indicates that this was the service committed to elders (overseers or bishops); so also in 1 Pet. 5:1, 2, "tend the flock

... exercising the oversight," RV; this involves tender care and vigilant superintendence. See SHEPHERD.

PASTURE

nomē (νομή, 3542) denotes (a) "pasture, pasturage," figuratively in John 10:9; (b) "grazing, feeding," figuratively in 2 Tim. 2:17, of the doctrines of false teachers, lit., "their word will have feeding as a gangrene."

PATH

1. *tribos* (τρίβος, 5147), "a beaten track" (akin to *tribō*, "to rub, wear down"), "a path," is used in Matt. 3:3; Mark 1:3; Luke 3:4.

2. *trochia* (τροχιά, 5163), "the track of a wheel" (*trochos*, "a wheel"; *trechō*, "to run") hence, "a track, path," is used figuratively in Heb. 12:13. In the Sept., Prov. 2:15; 4:11, 26, 27; 5:6, 21; in some texts, Ezek. 27:19.

PATIENCE, PATIENT, PATIENTLY

A. Nouns.

1. *hupomonē* (ὑπομονή, 5281), lit., "an abiding under" (*hupo*, "under," *menō*, "to abide"), is almost invariably rendered "patience." "Patience, which grows only in trial, Jas. 1:3 may be passive, i.e., = "endurance," as, (a) in trials, generally, Luke 21:19 (which is to be understood by Matt. 24:13), cf. Rom. 12:12; Jas. 1:12; (b) in trials incident to service in the gospel, 2 Cor. 6:4; 12:12; 2 Tim. 3:10; (c) under chastisement, which is trial viewed as coming from the hand of God our Father, Heb. 12:7; (d) under undeserved affliction, 1 Pet. 2:20; or active, i.e. = "persistence, perseverance," as (e) in well doing, Rom. 2:7 (KJV, "patient continuance"); (f) in fruit bearing, Luke 8:15; (g) in running the appointed race, Heb. 12:1.

"Patience perfects Christian character, Jas. 1:4, and fellowship in the patience of Christ is therefore the condition upon which believers are to be admitted to reign with Him, 2 Tim. 2:12; Rev. 1:9. For this patience believers are 'strengthened with all power,' Col. 1:11, 'through His Spirit in the inward man,' Eph. 3:16.

"In 2 Thess. 3:5, the phrase 'the patience of Christ,' RV, is possible of three interpretations, (a) the patient waiting for Christ, so KJV paraphrases the words, (b) that they might be patient in their sufferings as Christ was in His, see Heb. 12:2, (c) that since Christ is 'expecting till His enemies be made the footstool of His feet,' Heb. 10:13, so they might be patient also in their hopes of His triumph and their deliverance. While a too rigid exegesis is to be avoided it may, perhaps, be permissible to paraphrase: 'the Lord teach and enable you to love as God loves, and to be patient as Christ is patient.'"

In Rev. 3:10, "the word of My patience" is the word which tells of Christ's patience, and its effects in producing "patience" on the part of those who are His (see above on 2 Thess. 3:5).

2. *makrothumia* (μακροθυμία, 3115), "longsuffering" (see B, No. 2), is rendered "patience" in Heb. 6:12; Jas. 5:10; see LONGSUFFERING.

B. Verbs.

1. *hupomenō* (ὑπομένω, 5278), akin to A, No. 1, (a) used intransitively, means "to tarry behind, still abide," Luke 2:43; Acts 17:14; (b) transitively, "to wait for," Rom. 8:24 (in some mss.), "to bear patiently, endure," translated "patient" (present participle) in Rom. 12:12; "ye take it patiently," 1 Pet. 2:20 (twice). See also under A, No. 1.

2. *makrothumeō* (μακροθυμέω, 3114), akin to A, No. 2, "to be long-tempered," is translated "to have patience," or "to be patient," in Matt. 18:26, 29; 1 Thess. 5:14, KJV (RV, "be longsuffering"); Jas. 5:7 (1st part, "be patient"; 2nd part, RV, "being patient," KJV, "hath long patience"); in Heb. 6:15, RV, "having (KJV, after he had) patiently endured." See LONGSUFFERING.

C. Adjectives.

Notes: (1) For *epieikēs*, translated "patient" in 1 Tim. 3:3, KJV, see GENTLE. (2) For *anexikakos*, translated "patient" in 2 Tim. 2:24, KJV, see FORBEAR.

D. Adverb.

makrothumōs (μακροθυμώς, 3116), akin to A, No. 2, and B, No. 2, denotes "patiently," Acts 26:3.

PATRIARCH

patriarchēs (πατριάρχης, 3966), from *patria*, "a family," and *archō*, "to rule," is found in Acts 2:29; 7:8, 9; Heb. 7:4. In the Sept., 1 Chron. 24:31; 27:22; 2 Chron. 19:8; 23:20; 26:12.

PAY (Verb), PAYMENT

1. *apodidōmi* (ἀποδίδωμι, 591), "to give back, to render what is due, to pay," used of various obligations in this respect, is translated "to pay, to make payment," in Matt. 5:26; 18:25 (twice), 26, 28, 29, 30, 34; 20:8, RV (KJV, "give"). See DELIVER.

2. *teleō* (τελέω, 5055), "to bring to an end, complete, fulfill," has the meaning "to pay" in Matt. 17:24 and Rom. 13:6.

Notes: (1) In Matt. 23:23, KJV, *apodekatoō*, "to tithe," is translated "ye pay tithe" (RV, "ye tithe"). (2) In Heb. 7:9, *dekatoō* (passive voice), "to pay tithe," is translated "hath paid tithes," RV (perfect tense). See TITHE.

PEACE, PEACEABLE, PEACEABLY

A. Noun.

eirēnē (εἰρήνη, 1515) "occurs in each of the books of the NT, save 1 John and save in Acts 7:26 ['(at) one again'] it is translated "peace" in the RV. It describes (a) harmonious relationships between men, Matt. 10:34; Rom. 14:19; (b) between nations, Luke 14:32; Acts 12:20; Rev. 6:4; (c) friendliness, Acts 15:33; 1 Cor. 16:11; Heb. 11:31; (d) freedom from molestation, Luke 11:21; 19:42; Acts 9:31 (RV, 'peace,' KJV, 'rest'); 16:36; (e) order, in the State, Acts 24:2 (RV, 'peace,' KJV, 'quietness'); in the churches, 1 Cor. 14:33; (f) the harmonized relationships between God and man, accomplished through the gospel, Acts 10:36; Eph. 2:17; (g) the sense of rest and contentment consequent thereon, Matt. 10:13; Mark 5:34; Luke 1:79; 2:29; John 14:27; Rom. 1:7; 3:17; 8:6; in certain passages this idea is not distinguishable from the last, Rom. 5:1."

"The God of peace" is a title used in Rom. 15:33; 16:20; Phil. 4:9; 1 Thess. 5:23; Heb. 13:20; cf. 1 Cor. 14:33; 2 Cor. 13:11. The corresponding Heb. word *shalom* primarily signifies "wholeness": see its use in Josh. 8:31, "unhewn"; Ruth 2:12, "full"; Neh. 6:15, "finished"; Isa. 42:19, marg., "made perfect." Hence there is a close connection between the title in 1 Thess. 5:23 and the word *holoklēros*, "entire," in that verse. In the Sept. *shalom* is often rendered by *sōtēria*, "salvation, e.g., Gen. 26:31; 41:16; hence the "peace-offering" is called the "salvation offering." Cf. Luke 7:50; 8:48. In 2 Thess. 3:16, the title "the Lord of peace" is best understood as referring to the Lord Jesus. In Acts 7:26, "would have set them at one" is, lit., "was reconciling them (conative imperfect tense, expressing an earnest effort) into peace."

B. Verbs.

1. *eirēneuō* (εἰρηνεύω, 1514), primarily, "to bring to peace, reconcile," denotes in the NT, "to keep peace or to be at peace": in Mark 9:50, RV, the Lord bids the disciples "be at peace" with one another, gently rebuking their ambitious desires; in Rom. 12:18 (RV, "be at peace," KJV, "live peaceably") the limitation "if it be possible, as much as in you lieth," seems due to the phrase "with all men," but is not intended to excuse any evasion of the obligation imposed by the command; in 2 Cor. 13:11 it is rendered "live in peace," a general exhortation to believers; in 1 Thess. 5:13, "be at peace (among yourselves)."

2. *eirēnopoieō* (εἰρηνοποιέω, 1517), "to make peace" (*eirēnē*, and *poieō*, "to make"), is used in Col. 1:20. In the Sept., Prov. 10:10.

C. Adjective.

eirēnikos (εἰρηνικός, 1516), akin to A, denotes "peaceful." It is used (a) of the fruit of righteousness, Heb. 12:11, "peaceable" (or "peaceful") because it is produced in communion with God the Father, through His chastening; (b) of "the wisdom that is from above," Jas. 3:17.

Note: In 1 Tim. 2:2, KJV, *hēsuchios*, "quiet," is translated "peaceable" (RV, "quiet").

PEACE (hold one's)

1. *sigaō* (σιγάω, 4601) signifies (a), used intransitively, "to be silent" (from *sigē*, "silence"), translated "to hold one's peace," in Luke 9:36; 18:39; 20:26; Acts 12:17; 15:13 (in v. 12, "kept silence"; similarly rendered in 1 Cor. 14:28, 30, KJV, "hold his peace," 34); (b) used transitively, "to keep secret"; in the passive voice, "to be kept secret," Rom. 16:25, RV, "hath been kept in silence." See SECRET, SILENCE.

2. *siōpaō* (σιωπάω, 4623), "to be silent or still, to keep silence" (from *siōpē*, "silence"), is translated "to hold one's peace," in Matt. 20:31; 26:63; Mark 3:4; 9:34; 10:48; 14:61; Luke 19:40; Acts 18:9; in the Lord's command to the sea, in Mark 4:39, it is translated "peace" (for the next word "be still" see No. 4); in Luke 1:20, RV, "thou shalt be silent" (KJV, "dumb"). See DUMB, B.

3. *hēsuchazō* (ἡσυχάζω, 2270) signifies "to be still"; it is used of holding one's "peace," being silent, Luke 14:4; Acts 11:18; 21:14, "we ceased. See QUIET.

4. *phimoō* (φιμόω, 5392), "to muzzle," is used metaphorically in the passive voice, in Mark 1:25 and Luke 4:35, "hold thy peace"; in Mark 4:39, "be still."

PEACEMAKER

eirēnopoios (εἰρηνοποιός, 1518), an adjective signifying peace making (*eirēnē*, and *poieō*, "to make"), is used in Matt. 5:9, "peacemakers." Cf. PEACE, B, No. 2.

For **PECULIAR** see POSSESSION, B, No. 3, and C

PENTECOST

pentēkostos (πεντηκοστός, 4005), an adjective denoting "fiftieth," is used as a noun, with "day" understood, i.e., the "fiftieth" day after the Passover, counting from the second day of the Feast, Acts 2:1; 20:16; 1 Cor. 16:8. For the divine instructions to Israel see Exod. 23:16; 34:22; Lev. 23:15-21; Num. 28:26-31; Deut. 16:9-11.

For **PENURY** (Luke 21:4, KJV, RV, "want") see LACK

PEOPLE

1. *laos* (λαός, 2992) is used of (a) "the people at large," especially of people assembled, e.g., Matt. 27:25; Luke 1:21; 3:15; Acts 4:27; (b) "a people of the same race and language," e.g., Rev. 5:9; in the plural, e.g., Luke 2:31; Rom. 15:11; Rev. 7:9; 11:9; especially of Israel, e.g., Matt. 2:6; 4:23; John 11:50; Acts 4:8; Heb. 2:17; in distinction from their rulers and priests, e.g., Matt. 26:5; Luke 20:19; Heb. 5:3; in distinction from Gentiles, e.g., Acts 26:17, 23; Rom. 15:10; (c) of Christians as the people of God, e.g., Acts 15:14; Titus 2:14; Heb. 4:9; 1 Pet. 2:9.

2. *ochlos* (ὄχλος, 3793), "a crowd, throng": see CROWD, MULTITUDE.

3. *dēmos* (δῆμος, 1218), "the common people, the people generally" (Eng., "demagogue," "democracy," etc.), especially the mass of the "people" assembled in a public place, Acts 12:22; 17:5; 19:30, 33.

4. *ethnos* (ἔθνος, 1484) denotes (a) "a nation," e.g., Matt. 24:7; Acts 10:35; "the Jewish people," e.g., Luke 7:5; Acts 10:22; 28:19; (b) in the plural, "the rest of mankind" in distinction from Israel or the Jews, e.g., Matt. 4:15; Acts 28:28; (c) "the people of a city," Acts 8:9; (d) gentile Christians, e.g., Rom. 10:19; 11:13; 15:27; Gal. 2:14. See GENTILES, NATION.

5. *anthrōpos* (ἄνθρωπος, 444), "man," without distinction of sex (cf. *aner*, "a male"), is translated "people" in John 6:10, RV (KJV, "men").

For **PERDITION** see DESTRUCTION, No. 1

PERFECT (Adjective and Verb), PERFECTLY

A. Adjectives.

1. *teleios* (τέλειος, 5046) signifies "having reached its end" (*telos*), "finished, complete perfect." It is used (I) of persons, (a) primarily of physical development, then, with ethical import, "fully grown, mature," 1 Cor. 2:6; 14:20 ("men"; marg., "of full age"); Eph. 4:13; Phil. 3:15; Col. 1:28; 4:12; in Heb. 5:14, RV, "full-grown" (marg., "perfect"), KJV, "of full age" (marg., "perfect"); (b) "complete," conveying the idea of goodness without necessary reference to maturity or what is expressed under (a) Matt. 5:48; 19:21; Jas. 1:4 (2nd part); 3:2. It is used thus of God in Matt. 5:48; (II), of "things, complete, perfect," Rom. 12:2; 1 Cor. 13:10 (referring to the complete revelation of God's will and ways, whether in the completed Scriptures or in the hereafter); Jas. 1:4 (of the work of patience); v. 25; 1 John 4:18.

2. *teleioteros* (τελειότερος), the comparative degree of No. 1, is used in Heb. 9:11, of the very presence of God.

3. *artios* (ἄρτιος, 739) is translated "perfect" in 2 Tim. 3:17: see COMPLETE, B.

B. Verbs.

1. *teleioō* (τελειόω, 5048), "to bring to an end by completing or perfecting," is used (I) of "accomplishing" (see FULFILL); (II), of "bringing to completeness," (a) of persons: of Christ's assured completion of His earthly course, in the accomplishment of the Father's will, the successive stages culminating in His death, Luke 13:32; Heb. 2:10, to make Him "perfect," legally and officially, for all that He would be to His people on the ground of His sacrifice; cf. 5:9; 7:28, RV, "perfected" (KJV, "consecrated"); of His saints, John 17:23, RV, "perfected" (KJV, "made perfect"); Phil. 3:12; Heb. 10:14; 11:40 (of resurrection glory); 12:23 (of the departed saints); 1 John 4:18, of former priests (negatively), Heb. 9:9; similarly of Israelites under the Aaronic priesthood, 10:1; (b) of things, Heb. 7:19 (of the ineffectiveness of the Law); Jas. 2:22 (of faith made "perfect" by works); 1 John 2:5, of the love of God operating through him who keeps His word; 4:12, of the love of God in the case of those who love one another; 4:17, of the love of God as "made perfect with" (RV) those who abide in God, giving them to be possessed of the very character of God, by reason of which "as He is, even so are they in this world."

2. *epiteleō* (ἐπιτελέω, 2005), "to bring through to the end" (*epi*, intensive, in the sense of "fully," and *teleō*, "to complete"), is used in the middle voice in Gal. 3:3, "are ye (now) perfected," continuous present tense, indicating a process, lit., "are ye now perfecting yourselves"; in 2 Cor. 7:1, "perfecting (holiness)"; in Phil. 1:6, RV, "will perfect (it)," KJV, "will perform."

3. *katartizō* (καταρτίζω, 2675), "to render fit, complete" (*artios*), "is used of mending nets, Matt. 4:21; Mark 1:19, and is translated 'restore' in Gal. 6:1. It does not necessarily imply, however, that that to which it is applied has been damaged, though it may do so, as in these passages; it signifies, rather, right ordering and arrangement, Heb. 11:3, 'framed;' it points out the path of progress, as in Matt. 21:16; Luke 6:40; cf. 2 Cor. 13:9; Eph. 4:12, where corresponding nouns occur. It indicates the close relationship between character and destiny, Rom. 9:22, 'fitted.' It expresses the pastor's desire for the flock, in prayer, Heb. 13:21, and in exhortation, 1 Cor. 1:10, RV, 'perfected' (KJV, 'perfectly joined'); 2 Cor. 13:11, as well as his conviction of God's purpose for them, 1 Pet. 5:10. It is used of the Incarnation of the Word in Heb. 10:5, 'prepare,' quoted from Ps. 40:6 (Sept.), where it is apparently intended to describe the unique creative act involved in the Virgin Birth, Luke 1:35. In 1 Thess. 3:10 it means to supply what is necessary, as the succeeding words show." See FIT, B, No. 3.

Note: Cf. *exartizō*, rendered "furnished completely," in 2 Tim. 3:17, RV.

C. Adverbs.

1. *akribōs* (ἀκριβῶς, 199), accurately, is translated "perfectly" in 1 Thess. 5:2, where it suggests that Paul and his companions were careful ministers of the Word. See Note (2) below.

2. *akribesteron* (ἀκριβέστερον, 197), the comparative degree of No. 1, Acts 18:26; 23:15: see EXACTLY.

3. *teleiōs* (τελείως, 5049), "perfectly," is so translated in 1 Pet. 1:13, RV (KJV, "to the end"), of setting one's hope on coming grace. See END.

Notes: (1) In Rev. 3:2, KJV, *plēroō*, "to fulfill," is translated "perfect" (RV, "fulfilled"). (2) For the adverb *akribōs* in Acts 24:22, KJV, see EXACT.

PERFECTION, PERFECTING (noun), PERFECTNESS

A. Nouns.

1. *katartisis* (κατάρτισις, 2676), "a making fit," is used figuratively in an ethical sense in 2 Cor. 13:9, RV, "perfecting" (KJV, "perfection"), implying a process leading to consummation (akin to *katartizō*, see PERFECT, B, No. 3).

2. *katartismos* (καταρτισμός, 2677) denotes, in much the same way as No. 1, "a fitting or preparing fully," Eph. 4:12.

3. *teleiōsis* (τελείωσις, 5050) denotes "a fulfillment, completion, perfection, an end accomplished as the effect of a process," Heb. 7:11; in Luke 1:45, RV, "fulfillment" (KJV, "performance").

4. *teleiotēs* (τελειότης, 5047) denotes much the same as No. 3, but stressing perhaps the actual accomplishment of the end in view, Col. 3:14, "perfectness"; Heb. 6:1, "perfection." In the Sept., Judg. 9:16, 19; Prov. 11:3; Jer. 2:2.

B. Verb.

telesphoreō (τελεσφορέω, 5052), "to bring to a completion" or "an end in view" (*telos*, "an end," *pherō*, "to bear"), is said of plants, Luke 8:14.

PERFORM, PERFORMANCE

1. *teleō* (τελέω, 5055), "to finish," is translated "performed" in Luke 2:39, KJV.

2. *apoteleō* (ἀποτελέω, 658), "to bring to an end, accomplish," is translated "I perform" in Luke 13:32, RV (KJV, "I do"); some mss. have No. 3; in Jas. 1:15, it is used of sin, "full-grown" RV (KJV, "finished").

3. *epiteleō* (ἐπιτελέω, 2005), Rom. 15:28, KJV, "performed" (RV, "accomplished"); 2 Cor. 8:11, KJV, "perform" (RV, "complete"); Phil. 1:6, KJV, "perform" (RV, "perfect").

4. *poieō* (ποιέω, 4160), "to do," is translated "to perform" in Rom. 4:21; in Luke 1:72, KJV (RV, "to show").

5. *apodidōmi* (ἀποδίδωμι, 591), "to give back, or in full," is translated "thou ... shalt perform" in Matt. 5:33. See DELIVER. No. 3.

Notes: (1) In Rom. 7:18, KJV, *katergazomai*, "to work," is translated "to perform" (RV, "to do"; marg., "work"). (2) In Luke 1:20, KJV, *ginomai* "to come to pass" (RV), is translated "shall be performed." (3) For "performance" in Luke 1:45, see FULFILLMENT.

For **PERIL**, see DANGER, *Note:* PERILOUS see GRIEVOUS

PERISH

1. *apollumi* (ἀπόλλυμι, 622), "to destroy," signifies, in the middle voice, "to perish," and is thus used (a) of things, e.g., Matt. 5:29, 30; Luke 5:37; Acts 27:34, RV, "perish" (in some texts *piptō*, "to fall," as KJV); Heb. 1:11; 2 Pet. 3:6; Rev. 18:14 (2nd part), RV, "perished" (in some texts *aperchomai*, "to depart," as KJV); (b) of persons, e.g., Matt. 8:25; John 3:15), 16; 10:28; 17:12, RV, "perished" (KJV, "is lost"); Rom. 2:12; 1 Cor. 1:18, lit., "the perishing," where the perfective force of the verb implies the completion of the process of destruction (Moulton, *Proleg.*, p. 114); 8:11; 15:18; 2 Pet. 3:9; Jude 11. For the meaning of the word see DESTROY, No. 1.

2. *sunapollumi* (συναπόλλυμι, 4881), in the middle voice, denotes "to perish together" (*sun*, "with," and No. 1), Heb. 11:31.

3. *apothnēskō* (ἀποθνήσκω, 599), "to die"; in Matt. 8:32 "perished." See DIE, No. 2.

4. *aphanizō* (ἀφανίζω, 853), "to make unseen" (*a*, negative, *phainō*, "to cause to appear"), in the passive voice, is translated "perish" in Acts 13:41 (RV, marg., "vanish away"). See DISFIGURE.

5. *diaphtheirō* (διαφθείρω, 1311), "to corrupt," is rendered "perish" in 2 Cor. 4:16, KJV (RV, "is decaying"). See CORRUPT, No. 3, DECAY.

Notes: (I) In Acts 8:20, "(thy money) perish" is a translation of a phrase, lit, "be unto destruction," *apōleia*, see DESTRUCTION, B, (II), No. 1. (2) In Col. 2:22, "to perish" is a translation of the phrase *eis pthoran*, lit., "unto corruption"; see CORRUPT, B, No. 1. (3) For "shall utterly perish," in 2 Pet. 2:12, KJV, see CORRUPT, B, No. 1 (b).

For **PERJURED PERSON** see FORSWEAR

PERMISSION

sungnōmē (συγγνώμη, 4774), lit., "a joint opinion, mind or understanding" (*sun*, "with," *gnōmē*, "an opinion"), "a fellow feeling," hence, "a concession, allowance," is translated "permission," in contrast to "commandment," in 1 Cor. 7:6.

PERMIT

epitrepō (ἐπιτρέπω, 2010), lit., "to turn to" (*epi*, "to," *trepō*, "to turn"), "to entrust," signifies "to permit," Acts 26:1; 1 Cor. 14:34; 1 Cor. 16:7; 1 Tim. 2:12, RV "permit" (KJV,"suffer"); Heb. 6:3.

For **PERNICIOUS,** 2 Pet. 2:2, KJV, see LASCIVIOUS

PERPLEX, PERPLEXITY

A. Verbs

1. *aporeō* (ἀπορέω, 639) is rendered "perplexed" in 2 Cor. 4:8, and in the most authentic mss. in Luke 24:4; see DOUBT, A, No. 1.

2. *diaporeō* (διαπορέω, 1280), "was much perplexed" in Luke 9:7; see DOUBT, A, No. 2.

B. Noun.

aporia (ἀπορία, 640), akin to A, No. 1, is translated "perplexity" in Luke 21:25 (lit., "at a loss for a way," *a*, negative, *poros*, "a way, resource"), of the distress of nations, finding no solution to their embarrassments; papyri illustrations are in the sense of being at one's wit's end, at a loss how to proceed, without resources.

PERSECUTE, PERSECUTION

A. Verbs.

1. *diōkō* (διώκω, 1377) has the meanings (a) "to put to flight, drive away," (b) "to pursue," whence the meaning "to persecute," Matt. 5:10-12, 44; 10:23; 23:34; Luke 11:49 (No. 2 in some mss.); 21:12; John 5:16; 15:20 (twice); Acts 7:52; 9:4, 5, and similar passages; Rom. 12:14; 1 Cor. 4:12; 15:9; 2 Cor. 4:9, KJV (RV, "pursued"); Gal. 1:13, 23; 4:29; Gal. 5:11, RV, "am ... persecuted" (KJV, "suffer persecution"); so 6:12; Phil. 3:6; 2 Tim. 3:12, "shall suffer persecution"; Rev. 12:13. See PURSUE.

2. *ekdiōkō* (ἐκδιώκω, 1559), *ek*, "out," and No. 1, is used in 1 Thess. 2:15, KJV, "persecuted" (RV, "drove out"). See also No. 1.

B. Noun.

diōgmos (διωγμός, 1375), akin to A, No. 1 occurs in Matt. 13:21; Mark 4:17; 10:30; Acts 8:1; 13:50; Rom. 8:35; 2 Cor. 12:10; 2 Thess. 1:4; 2 Tim. 3:11, twice (for v. 12, see A, No. 1. In the Sept., Prov. 11:19; Lam. 3:19.

Note: In Acts 11:19, KJV, *thlipsis*, "tribulation" (RV), is translated "persecution."

PERSECUTOR

diōktēs (διώκτης, 1376), akin to *diōkō* (see above), occurs in 1 Tim. 1:13.

PERSON

1. *prosōpon* (πρόσωπον, 4383), for the meaning of which see APPEARANCE, No. 2, is translated "person" or "persons" in Matt. 22:16; Mark 12:14; Luke 20:21; 2 Cor. 1:11; 2 Cor. 2:10; Gal. 2:6; Jude 16, lit., "(admiring, or showing respect of, RV) persons."

2. *anthrōpos* (ἄνθρωπος, 444), a generic name for man, is translated "persons" in Rev. 11:13, RV (KJV, "men").

Notes: (1) In Heb. 1:3, KJV, *hupostasis*, "substance," is translated "person"; see SUBSTANCE. (2) In Matt. 27:24, RV, *toutou*, "of this ... (man)," is translated "of this ... person" (KJV). (3) In Philem. 12, the pronoun *autos*, "he," placed in a position of strong emphasis, is translated "in his own person," RV, stressing the fact that in spite of the apostle's inclination to retain Onesimus, he has sent him, as being, so to speak, "his very heart," instead of adopting some other method. (4) In 1 Cor. 5:13, KJV, the adjective *ponēros*, "wicked," used as a noun, is translated "wicked person" (RV, "... man"). (5) In 2 Pet. 2:5, KJV, *ogdoos*, "eighth," is translated "the (lit., 'an') eighth *person*" (RV, "with seven others"). (b) Various adjectives are used with the word "persons," e.g., "devout, perjured, profane."

PERSONS (respect of)

A. Nouns.

1. *prosōpolēmptēs* (προσωπολήπτης, 4381) denotes "a respecter of persons" (*prosopōn*, "a face" or "person," *lambanō*, "to lay hold of"), Acts 10:34.

2. *prosopolēmpsia* (in inferior texts without the letter m) (προσωποληψία, 4382) denotes "respect of persons, partiality" (akin to No. 1), the fault of one who, when responsible to give judgment, has respect to the position, rank, popularity, or circumstances of men, instead of their intrinsic conditions, preferring the rich and powerful to those who are not so, Rom. 2:11; Eph. 6:9; Col. 3:25; Jas. 2:1.

B. Verb.

prosōpolēmpteō (προσωποληπτέω, 4380), "to have respect of persons" (see above), occurs in Jas. 2:9.

C. Adverb.

aprosōpolēmptōs (ἀπροσωπολήπτως, 678), "without respect of persons, impartially" (*a*, negative), occurs in 1 Pet. 1:17.

PERSUADE

1. *peithō* (πείθω, 3982) in the active voice, signifies "to apply persuasion, to prevail upon or win over, to persuade," bringing about a change of mind by the influence of reason or moral considerations, e.g., in Matt. 27:20; 28:14; Acts 13:43; 19:8; in the passive voice, "to be persuaded, believe" (see BELIEVE, No. 2, and OBEY), e.g., Luke 16:31; 20:6; Acts 17:4, RV (KJV, "believed"); 21:14; 26:26; Rom. 8:38; 14:14; 15:14; 2 Tim. 1:5, 12; Heb. 6:9; 11:13, in some mss.; 13:18, RV (KJV, "trust"). See ASSURANCE, B, No. 3.

Note: For Acts 26:28, KJV, "thou persuadest," see FAIN, *Note*.

2. *anapeithō* (ἀναπείθω, 374), "to persuade, induce," in an evil sense (*ana*, "back," and No. 1), is used in Acts 18:13. In the Sept., Jer. 29:8.

Note: For *plērophoreō*, rendered "being fully persuaded," in Rom. 4:21 and 14:5, KJV, see ASSURANCE, B, No. 2.

PERSUASIVE, PERSUASIVENESS

A. Adjective.

peithos (πειθός, 3981), an adjective (akin to *peithō*), not found elsewhere, is translated "persuasive" in 1 Cor. 2:4, RV (KJV, "enticing"); see ENTICE, B.

B. Noun.

pithanologia (πιθανολογία, 4086), "persuasiveness of speech," is used in Col. 2:4, RV. See ENTICE, B, *Note*.

PERSUASION

peismonē (πεισμονή, 3988), akin to *peithō*, is used in Gal. 5:8, where the meaning is "this influence that has won you over, or that seems likely to do so"; the use of *peithō*, in the sense of "to obey," in v. 7, suggests a play upon words here.

PERVERSE, PERVERT

1. *apostrephō* (ἀποστρέφω, 654), "to turn away" (*apo*, "from," *strephō*, "to turn"), is used metaphorically in the sense of "perverting" in Luke 23:14 (cf. No. 2 in Lu 23:2).

2. *diastrephō* (διαστρέφω, 1294), "to distort, twist" (*dia*, "through," and *strephō*), is translated "to pervert" in Luke 23:2 (cf. No. 1 in v. 14); Acts 13:10 [in v. 8, "to turn aside" (KJV, "away")]; in the perfect participle, passive voice, it is translated "perverse," lit., "turned aside, corrupted," in Matt. 17:17; Luke 9:41; Acts 20:30; Phil. 2:15.

3. *metastrephō* (μεταστρέφω, 3344), "to transform into something of an opposite character" (*meta*, signifying "a change," and *strephō*,) as the Judaizers sought to "pervert the gospel of Christ," Gal. 1:7; cf. "the sun shall be turned into darkness," Acts 2:20; laughter into mourning and joy to heaviness, Jas. 4:9.

4. *ekstrephō* (ἐκστρέφω, 1612), "to turn inside out" (*ek*, "out"), "to change entirely," is used metaphorically in Titus 3:11, RV, "is perverted" (KJV, "is subverted").

PESTILENCE, PESTILENT FELLOW

loimos (λοιμός, 3061), "a pestilence, any deadly infectious malady," is used in the plural in Luke 21:11 (in some mss., Matt. 24:7); in Acts 24:5, metaphorically, "a pestilent fellow." See FELLOW.

PETITION

aitēma (αἴτημα, 155), from *aiteō*, "to ask" is rendered "petitions" in 1 John 5:15. Cf. *deēsis* (see PRAYER).

PHARISEES

pharisaios (Φαρισαῖος, 5330), from an Aramaic word *peras* (found in Dan. 5:28), signifying "to separate," owing to a different manner of life from that of the general public. The "Pharisees" and Sadducees appear as distinct parties in the latter half of the 2nd cent. B.C., though they represent tendencies traceable much earlier in Jewish history, tendencies which became pronounced after the return from Babylon (537), B.C.). The immediate progenitors of the two parties were, respectively, the Hasidaeans and the Hellenizers; the latter, the antecedents of the Sadducees, aimed at removing Judaism from its narrowness and sharing in the advantages of Greek life and culture. The Hasidaeans, a transcription of the Hebrew *chasidim*, i.e., "pious ones," were a society of men zealous for religion, who acted under the guidance of the scribes, in opposition to the godless Hellenizing party; they scrupled to oppose the legitimate high priest even when he was on the Greek side. Thus the Hellenizers were a political sect, while the Hasidaeans, whose fundamental principle was complete separation from non-Jewish elements, were the strictly legal party among the Jews, and were ultimately the more popular and influential party. In their zeal for the Law they almost deified it and their attitude became merely external, formal, and mechanical. They laid stress, not upon the righteousness of an action, but upon its formal correctness. Consequently their opposition to Christ was inevitable; His manner of life and teaching was essentially a condemnation of theirs; hence His denunciation of them, e.g., Matt. 6:2, 5, 16; 15:7 and chapter 23.

While the Jews continued to be divided into these two parties, the spread of the testimony of the gospel must have produced what in the public eye seemed to be a new sect, and in the extensive development which took place at Antioch, Acts 11:19-26, the name "Christians" seems to have become a popular term applied to the disciples as a sect, the primary cause, however, being their witness to Christ (see CALL, A, No. 11). The opposition of both "Pharisees" and Sadducees (still mutually antagonistic, Acts 23:6-10) against the new "sect" continued unabated during apostolic times.

PHILOSOPHER

philosophos (φιλόσοφος, 5386), lit., "loving wisdom" (*philos*, "loving," *sophia*, "wisdom"), occurs in Acts 17:18.

PHILOSOPHY

philosophia (φιλοσοφία, 5385) denotes "the love and pursuit of wisdom," hence, "philosophy," the investigation of truth and nature; in Col. 2:8, the so-called "philosophy" of false teachers. "Though essentially Greek as a name and as an idea, it had found its way into Jewish circles ... Josephus speaks of the three Jewish sects as three 'philosophies' ... It is worth observing that this word, which to the Greeks denoted the highest effort of the intellect, occurs here alone in Paul's writings ... the Gospel had deposed the term as inadequate to the higher standard whether of knowledge or of practice, which it had introduced (Lightfoot).

PHYLACTERY

phulaktērion (φυλακτήριον, 5440), primarily "an outpost," or "fortification" (*phulax*, "a guard"), then, "any kind of safeguard," became used especially to denote "an amulet." In the NT it denotes a prayer fillet, "a phylactery," a small strip of parchment, with portions of the Law written on it; it was fastened by a leather strap either to the forehead or to the left arm over against the heart, to remind the wearer of the duty of keeping the commandments of God in the head and in the heart; cf. Ex. 13:16; Deut. 6:8; 11:18. It was supposed to have potency as a charm against evils and demons. The Pharisees broadened their "phylacteries" to render conspicuous their superior eagerness to be mindful of God's Law, Matt. 23:5.

PHYSICIAN

iatros (ἰατρός, 2395), akin to *iaomai*, "to heal," "a physician," occurs in Matt. 9:12; Mark 2:17; 5:26; Luke 4:23; 5:31 (in some mss., 8:43); Col. 4:14.

PIERCE

1. *diikneomai* (διϊκνέομαι, 1338), "to go through, penetrate" (*dia*, "through," *ikneomai*, "to go"), is used of the power of the Word of God, in Heb. 4:12, "piercing." In the Sept., Ex. 26:28.

2. *dierchomai* (διέρχομαι, 1330), "to go through," is translated "shall pierce through" in Luke 2:35.

3. *ekkenteō* (ἐκκεντέω, 1574), primarily, "to prick out" (*ek*, "out," *kenteō*, "to prick"), signifies "to pierce," John 19:37; Rev. 1:7.

4. *nussō* (νύσσω, 3572), "to pierce" or "pierce through," often of inflicting severe or deadly wounds, is used of the piercing of the side of Christ, John 19:34 (in some mss., Matt. 27:49).

5. *peripeirō* (περιπείρω, 4044), "to put on a spit," hence, "to pierce," is used metaphorically in 1 Tim. 6:10, of torturing one's soul with many sorrows, "have pierced (themselves) through."

PIETY (to shew)

eusebeō (εὐσεβέω, 2151), "to reverence, to show piety" towards any to whom dutiful regard is due (akin to *eusebēs*, "pious, godly, devout"), is used in 1 Tim. 5:4 of the obligation on the part of children and grandchildren (RV) to express in a practical way their dutifulness "towards their own family"; in Acts 17:23 of worshiping God. See WORSHIP.

For **PIGEON** see DOVE, No. 1

PILGRIM

parepidēmos (παρεπίδημος, 3927), an adjective signifying "sojourning in a strange place, away from one's own people" (*para*, "from," expressing a contrary condition, and *epidēmeō*, "to sojourn"; *dēmos*, "a people"), is used of OT saints, Heb. 11:13, "pilgrims" (coupled with *xenos*, "a foreigner"); of Christians, 1 Pet. 1:1, "sojourners (of the Dispersion)," RV; 2:11, "pilgrims" (coupled with *paroikos*, "an alien, sojourner"); the word is thus used metaphorically of those to whom Heaven is their own country, and who are sojourners on earth.

For **PIPERS,** Rev. 18:22, KJV, see FLUTE-PLAYERS

PITIFUL, PITY

1. *polusplanchnos* (πολύσπλαγχνος, 4184) denotes "very pitiful" or "full of pity" (*polus*, "much," *splanchnon*, "the heart"; in the plural, "the affections"), occurs in Jas. 5:11, RV, "full of pity."

2. *eusplanchnos* (εὔσπλαγχνος, 2155), "compassionate, tenderhearted," lit., "of good heartedness" (*eu*, "well," and *splanchnon*), is translated "pitiful" in 1 Pet. 3:8, KJV, RV, "tenderhearted," as in Eph. 4:32.

PIT

1. *phrear* (φρέαρ, 5421), "a well, dug for water" (distinct from *pēgē*, "a fountain"), denotes "a pit" in Rev. 9:1, 2, RV, "the pit (of the abyss)," "the pit," i.e., the shaft leading down to the abyss, KJV, "(bottomless) pit"; in Luke 14:5, RV, well (KJV, "pit"); in John 4:11, 12, "well." See WELL.

2. *bothunos* (βόθυνος, 999) is rendered "pit" in Matt. 12:11.

3. *abussos* (ἄβυσσος, 12): see BOTTOM.

4. *hupolēnion* (ὑπολήνιον, 5276) denotes "a vessel or trough beneath a winepress," to receive the juice, Mark 12:1, RV, "a pit for the winepress" (KJV, "a place for ... the wine-fat").

PLAGUE

1. *mastix* (μάστιξ, 3148), "a whip, scourge," Acts 22:24, "by scourging"; Heb. 11:36, "scourgings," is used metaphorically of "disease" or "suffering," Mark 3:10; 5:29, 34; Luke 7:21. See SCOURGING.

2. *plēgē* (πληγή, 4127), "a stripe, wound" (akin to *plēssō*, "to smite"), is used metaphorically of a calamity, "a plague," Rev. 9:20; 11:6; 15:1, 6, 8; 16:9, 21 (twice); 18:4, 8; 21:9; 22:18. See STRIPE, WOUND.

PLANT (Noun, Verb, Adjective)

A. Noun.

phuteia (φυτεία, 5451), firstly, "a planting," then "that which is planted, a plant" (from *phuō*, "to bring forth, spring up, grow," *phuton*, "a plant"), occurs in Matt. 15:13. In the Sept. 2 Kings 19:29; Ezek. 17:7; Mic. 1:6.

B. Verb.

phuteuō (φυτεύω, 5452), "to plant," is used (a) literally, Matt. 21:33; Mark 12:1; Luke 13:6; 17:6, 28; 20:9; 1 Cor. 9:7; (b) metaphorically Matt. 15:13; 1 Cor. 3:6, 7, 8.

C. Adjective.

sumphutos (σύμφυτος, 4854), firstly, "congenital, innate" (from *sumphuō*, "to make to grow together"), then, "planted" or "grown along with, united with," Rom. 6:5, KJV, "planted together," RV, "united with *Him*," indicating the union of the believer with Christ in experiencing spiritually "the likeness of His death." Cf. *emphutos*, Jas. 1:21, RV, "implanted" (marg., "inborn").

PLEAD

entunchanō (ἐντυγχάνω, 1793), "to make petition," is used of the "pleading" of Elijah against Israel, Rom. 11:2, RV, "pleadeth with" (KJV, "maketh intercession to"). See DEAL WITH.

PLEASE, PLEASING (Noun), WELL-PLEASING, PLEASURE

A. Verbs.

1. *areskō* (ἀρέσκω, 700) signifies (a) "to be pleasing to, be acceptable to," Matt. 14:6; Mark 6:22; Acts 6:5; Rom. 8:8; 15:2; 1 Cor. 7:32-34; Gal. 1:10; 1 Thess. 2:15; 4:1 (where the preceding *kai*, "and," is epexegetical, "even," explaining the "walking," i.e., Christian manner of life as "pleasing" God; in Gen. 5:22, where the Hebrew has "Enoch walked with God," the Sept. has "Enoch pleased God"; cf. Mic. 6:8; Heb. 11:5); 2 Tim. 2:4; (b) "to endeavor to please," and so, "to render service," doing so evilly in one's own interests, Rom. 15:1, which Christ did not, v. 3; or unselfishly, 1 Cor. 10:33; 1 Thess. 2:4. This sense of the word is illustrated by Moulton and Milligan (*Vocab.*) from numerous inscriptions, especially describing "those who have proved themselves of use to the commonwealth."

2. *euaresteō* (εὐαρεστέω, 2100) signifies "to be well-pleasing" (*eu*, "well," and a form akin to No. 1); in the active voice, Heb. 11:5, RV, "he had been "well-pleasing" (unto God)," KJV, "he pleased"; so v. 6; in the passive voice Heb. 13:16.

3. *eudokeō* (εὐδοκέω, 2106) signifies (a) "to be well pleased, to think it good" [*eu*, "well," and *dokeō*, see *Note* (1) below], not merely an understanding of what is right and good as in *dokeō*, but stressing the willingness and freedom of an intention or resolve regarding what is good, e.g., Luke 12:32, "it is (your Father's) good pleasure"; so Rom. 15:26, 27, RV; 1 Cor. 1:21; Gal. 1:15; Col. 1:19; 1 Thess. 2:8, RV, "we were well pleased" (KJV, "we were willing"); this meaning is frequently found in the papyri in legal documents; (b) "to be well pleased with," or "take pleasure in," e.g., Matt. 3:17; 12:18; 17:5; 1 Cor. 10:5; 2 Cor. 12:10; 2 Thess. 2:12; Heb. 10:6, 8, 38; 2 Pet. 1:17.

4. *thelō* (θέλω, 2309), "to will, wish, desire," is translated "it pleased (Him)" in 1 Cor. 12:18; 15:38, RV. See DESIRE, B, No. 6.

5. *spatalaō* (σπαταλάω, 4684), "to live riotously," is translated "giveth herself to pleasure" in 1 Tim. 5:6, RV (KJV, "liveth in pleasure"); "taken your pleasure" in Jas. 5:5, KJV, "been wanton."

Notes: (1) In Acts 15:22, KJV, *dokeō*, "to seem good to" (RV), is translated "it pleased" (in some mss., v. 34); in Heb. 12:10, KJV, "(after their own) pleasure," RV, "(as) seemed good (to them)." (2) For *suneudokeō*, rendered "have pleasure in" in Rom. 1:32, KJV, see CONSENT, No. 6.

B. Adjectives.

1. *arestos* (ἀρεστός, 701) denotes "pleasing, agreeable," John 8:29, RV, "(the things that are) pleasing," KJV, "(those things that) please," KJV and RV in 1 John 3:22; in Acts 6:2, "fit" (RV marg., "pleasing"); 12:3, "it pleased," lit., "it was pleasing." See FIT.

2. *euarestos* (εὐάρεστος, 2101), *eu*, "well," and No. 1, is translated "well-pleasing" in the RV except in Rom. 12:1, 2 (see marg., however).

C. Noun.

areskeia (or *-ia*) (ἀρέσκεια, 699), a "pleasing," a giving pleasure, Col. 1:10, of the purpose Godward of a walk worthy of the Lord (cf. 1 Thess. 4:1). It was used frequently in a bad sense in classical writers. Moulton and Milligan illustrate from the papyri its use in a favorable sense, and Deissmann (*Bible Studies*) from an inscription. In the Sept, Prov. 31:30.

PLEASURE

A. Nouns.

1. *hēdonē* (ἡδονή, 2237), "pleasure," is used of the gratification of the natural desire or sinful desires (akin to *hēdormai*, "to be glad," and *hēdeōs*, "gladly"), Luke 8:14; Titus 3:3; Jas. 4:1, 3, RV, "pleasures" (KJV, "lusts"); in the singular, 2 Pet. 2:13. See LUST.

2. *eudokia* (εὐδοκία, 2107), "good pleasure" (akin to *eudokeō*, PLEASE, No. 3), Eph. 1:5, 9; Phil. 2:13; 2 Thess. 1:11. See DESIRE, A, No. 2.

3. *apolausis* (ἀπόλαυσις, 619), "enjoyment," is used with *echō*, "to have," and rendered "enjoy the pleasures" (lit., "pleasure") in Heb. 11:25. See ENJOY.

Notes: (1) In Rev. 4:11, KJV, *thelēma*, "a will," is translated "(for Thy) pleasure," RV, "(because of Thy) will." (2) For *charis*, translated "pleasure" in the KJV of Acts 24:27 and 25:9, see FAVOR, A.

B. Adjective.

philēdonos (φιλήδονος, 5369), "loving pleasure" (*philos*, "loving," and A, No. 1), occurs in 2 Tim. 3:4, RV, "lovers of pleasure" (KJV, "... pleasures"). See LOVER.

Note: In 1 Tim. 5:6 the RV renders *spatalaō* "giveth herself to pleasure."

POET

poiētēs (ποιητής, 4163), primarily "a maker," later "a doer" (*poieo* "to make, to do"), was used, in classical Greek, of "an author," especially a "poet"; so Acts 17:28.

POISON

ios (ἰός, 2447) denotes "something active" as (a) "rust," as acting on metals, affecting their nature, Jas. 5:3; (b) "poison," as of asps, acting destructively on living tissues, figuratively of the evil use of the lips as the organs of speech, Rom. 3:13; so of the tongue, Jas. 3:8.

For **POLLUTE** see DEFILE, A, No. 1

POLLUTION

alisgema (ἀλίσγεμα, 234), akin to a late verb *alisgeō*, "to pollute," denotes "a pollution, contamination," Acts 15:20, "pollutions of idols," i.e., all the contaminating associations connected with idolatry including meats from sacrifices offered to idols.

Note: For *miasma*, KJV, "pollutions," in 2 Pet. 2:20. see DEFILE, B, No. 1.

POMP

phantasia (φαντασία, 5325), as a philosophic term, denoted "an imagination"; then, "an appearance," like *phantasma*, "an apparition"; later, "a show, display, pomp" (Eng., "phantasy"), Acts 25:23. In the Sept., Hab. 2:18; 3:10; Zech. 10:1.

POOL

kolumbēthra (κολυμβήθρα, 2861) denotes "a swimming pool" (akin to *kolumbaō*, "to swim," Acts 27:43), John 5:2 (v. 4 in some mss.), 7; 9:7 (v. 11 in some mss.).

POOR

A. Adjectives.

1. *ptōchos* (πτωχός, 4434), for which see BEG, B, has the broad sense of "poor," (a) literally, e.g., Matt. 11:5; 26:9, 11; Luke 21:3 (with stress on the word, "a conspicuously poor widow"); John 12:5, 6, 8; 13:29; Jas. 2:2, 3, 6; the "poor" are constantly the subjects of injunctions to assist them, Matt. 19:21; Mark 10:21; Luke 14:13, 21; 18:22; Rom. 15:26; Gal. 2:10; (b) metaphorically, Matt. 5:3; Luke 6:20; Rev. 3:17.

2. *penichros* (πενιχρός, 3998), akin to B, "needy, poor," is used of the widow in Luke 21:2 (cf. No. 1, of the same woman, in v. 3); it is used frequently in the papyri. In the Sept., Ex. 22:25; Prov. 28:15; 29:7.

B. Noun.

penēs (πένης, 3993), "a laborer" (akin to *penomai*, "to work for one's daily bread"), is translated "poor" in 2 Cor. 9:9.

C. Verb.

ptōcheuō (πτωχεύω, 4433), "to be poor as a beggar" (akin to A, No. 1), "to be destitute," is said of Christ in 2 Cor. 8:9.

POSSESS, POSSESSION

A. Verbs.

1. *katechō* (κατέχω, 2722), "to hold fast, hold back," signifies "to possess," in 1 Cor. 7:30 and 2 Cor. 6:10. See HOLD.

2. *ktaomai* (κτάομαι, 2932), "to procure for oneself, acquire, obtain," hence, "to possess" (akin to B, No. 1), has this meaning in Luke 18:12 and 1 Thess. 4:4; in Luke 21:19, RV, "ye shall win" (KJV, "possess ye"), where the probable meaning is "ye shall gain the mastery over your souls," i.e., instead of giving way to adverse circumstances.

3. *huparchō* (ὑπάρχω, 5225), "to be in existence," and, in a secondary sense, "to belong to," is used with this meaning in the neuter plural of the present participle with the article signifying one's "possessions," "the things which he possesseth," Luke 12:15; Acts 4:32; in Heb. 10:34, RV, "possessions" (KJV, "goods"); cf. B, No. 4. See GOODS.

4. *daimonizomai* (δαιμονίζομαι, 1139), "to be possessed of a demon or demons": see DEMON, B.

Note: In Acts 8:7 and 16:16, KJV, *echō*, "have," is translated "to be possessed of," in the sense of No. 4, above, RV, "had" and "having."

B. Nouns.

1. *ktēma* (κτῆμα, 2933), akin to A, No. 2, denotes "a possession, property," Matt. 19:22; Mark 10:22; Acts 2:45; 5:1.

2. *kataschesis* (κατάσχεσις, 2697), primarily "a holding back" (akin to A, No. 1), then, "a holding fast," denotes "a possession," Acts 7:5, or "taking possession," v. 45, with the article, lit., "in the (i.e., their) taking possession."

3. *peripoiēsis* (περιποίησις, 4047), "an obtaining, an acquisition," is translated "(God's own) possession" in Eph. 1:14, RV, which may mean "acquisition," KJV, "purchased possession," 1 Pet. 2:9, RV, "*God's* own possession," KJV, "a peculiar (people)."

4. *huparxis* (ὕπαρξις, 5223), primarily "subsistence" (akin to A, No. 3), later denoted "substance, property, possession" in Heb. 10:34, RV (KJV, substance). See GOODS, SUBSTANCE.

Note: In Acts 28:7, KJV, *chōria*, "lands" (RV), is translated "possessions."

C. Adjective.

periousios (περιούσιος, 4041), "of one's own possession, one's own," qualifies the noun *laos*, "people," in Titus 2:14, KJV, "peculiar," see RV. In the Sept., Ex. 19:5; 23:22; Deut. 7:6; 14:2; 26:18.

POSSESSOR

ktētōr (κτήτωρ, 2935), "a possessor, an owner" (akin to *ktaomai*, see POSSESS, No. 2), occurs in Acts 4:34.

POVERTY

ptōcheia (πτωχεία, 4432), "destitution" (akin to *ptōcheuō*, see POOR), is used of the "poverty" which Christ voluntarily experienced on our behalf, 2 Cor. 8:9; of the destitute condition of saints in Judea, v. 2; of the condition of the church in Smyrna, Rev. 2:9, where the word is used in a general sense. Cf. synonymous words under POOR.

POWER (Noun, and Verb, to have, bring under)

A. Nouns.

1. *dunamis* (δύναμις, 1411), for the different meanings of which see ABILITY, MIGHT, is sometimes used, by metonymy, of persons and things, e.g., (a) of God, Matt. 26:64; Mark 14:62; (b) of angels, e.g., perhaps in Eph. 1:21, RV, "power," KJV, "might" (cf. Rom. 8:38; 1 Pet. 3:22); (c) of that which manifests God's "power": Christ, 1 Cor. 1:24; the gospel, Rom. 1:16; (d) of mighty works (RV, marg., "power" or "powers"), e.g., Mark 6:5, "mighty work"; so 9:39, RV (KJV, "miracle"); Acts 2:22 (ditto); 8:13, "miracles"; 2 Cor. 12:12, RV, "mighty works" (KJV, "mighty deeds").

Note: For different meanings of synonymous terms, see *Note* under DOMINION, A, No. 1.

2. *exousia* (ἐξουσία, 1849) denotes "freedom of action, right to act"; used of God, it is absolute, unrestricted, e.g., Luke 12:5 (RV marg., "authority"); in Acts 1:7 "right of disposal" is what is indicated; used of men, authority is delegated. Angelic beings are called "powers" in Eph. 3:10 (cf. 1:21); 6:12; Col. 1:16; 2:15 (cf. 2:10). See also PRINCIPALITY.

3. *ischus* (ἰσχύς, 2479), "ability force, strength," is nowhere translated "power" in the RV (KJV in 2 Thess. 1:9). See ABILITY, No. 2.

4. *kratos* (κράτος, 2904) is translated "power" in the RV and KJV in 1 Tim. 6:16; Heb. 2:14; in Eph. 1:19 (last part); 6:10, KJV, "power" (RV, "strength"): see DOMINION, A, No. 1, STRENGTH, A, No. 3.

5. *dunaton* (δυνατός, 1415), the neuter of the adjective *dunatos*, "powerful" (akin to No. 1), is used as a noun with the article in Rom. 9:22, "(to make His) power (known)." See ABLE.

6. *archē* (ἀρχή, 746), "a beginning, rule," is translated "power" in Luke 20:20, KJV (RV, "rule"). See BEGINNING, B.

B. Verb.

exousiazō (ἐξουσιάζω, 1850), "to exercise authority" (akin to A, No. 2), is used (a) in the active voice, Luke 22:25, RV, "have authority" (KJV, "exercise authority"), of the "power" of rulers; 1 Cor. 7:4 (twice), of marital relations and conditions; (b) in the passive voice, 1 Cor. 6:12, to be brought under the "power" of a thing; here, this verb and the preceding one connected with it, *exesti*, present a *paronomasia*, which Lightfoot brings out as follows: "All are within my power; but I will not put myself under the power of any one of all things."

Notes: (1) In Rev. 13:14, 15, KJV, *didōmi*, "to give," is translated "(he) had power"; RV, "it was given (him)" and "it was given *unto him*"; the KJV misses the force of the permissive will of God in the actings of the Beast. (2) In Rom. 16:25, KJV, *dunamai*, "to be able," is translated "that is of power" (RV, "that is able"). See ABLE. (3) The subject of power in Scripture may be viewed under the following heads: (a) its original source, in the Persons in the Godhead; (b) its exercise by God in creation, its preservation and its government; (c) special manifestations of divine "power," past, present and future; (d) "power" existent in created beings, other than man, and in inanimate nature; (e) committed to man, and misused by him; (f) committed to those who, on becoming believers, were "empowered" by the Spirit of God, are indwelt by Him, and will exercise it hereafter for God's glory.

POWERFUL, POWERFULLY

A. Adjectives.

1. *energēs* (ἐνεργής, 1756): see ACTIVE.

2. *ischuros* (ἰσχυρός, 2478), "strong, mighty," akin to *ischus* (see POWER, A, No. 3), is translated "powerful" in 2 Cor. 10:10, KJV (RV, "strong"). See STRONG.

B. Adverb.

eutonōs (εὐτόνως, 2159) signifies "vigorously, vehemently" (*eu*, "well," *teinō*, "to stretch"), Luke 23:10, "vehemently," of the accusation of the chief priests and scribes against Christ; Acts 18:28, RV, "powerfully" (KJV, "mightily"), of Apollos in confuting Jews. In the Sept., Josh. 6:8.

Note: For "is powerful," 2 Cor. 13:3, RV, see MIGHTY, C.

For **PRACTICES** see COVETOUS, B, No. 3

PRAISE

A. Nouns.

1. *ainos* (αἶνος, 136), primarily "a tale, narration," came to denote "praise"; in the NT only of praise to God, Matt. 21:16; Luke 18:43.

2. *epainos* (ἔπαινος, 1868), a strengthened form of No. 1 (*epi* upon), denotes "approbation, commendation, praise"; it is used (a) of those on account of, and by reason of, whom as God's heritage, "praise" is to be ascribed to God, in respect of His glory (the exhibition of His character and operations), Eph. 1:12 in v. 14, of the whole company, the church, viewed as "*God's* own possession" (RV); in v. 6, with particular reference to the glory of His grace towards them; in Phil. 1:11,

as the result of "the fruits of righteousness" manifested in them through the power of Christ; (b) of "praise" bestowed by God, upon the Jew spiritually (Judah = "praise"), Rom. 2:29; bestowed upon believers hereafter at the judgment seat of Christ, 1 Cor. 4:5 (where the definite article indicates that the "praise" will be exactly in accordance with each person's actions); as the issue of present trials, "at the revelation of Jesus Christ," 1 Pet. 1:7; (c) of whatsoever is "praiseworthy," Phil. 4:8; (d) of the approbation by churches of those who labor faithfully in the ministry of the gospel, 2 Cor. 8:18; (e) of the approbation of well-doers by human rulers, Rom. 13:3; 1 Pet. 2:14.

3. *ainesis* (αἴνεσις, 133), "praise" (akin to No. 1), is found in Heb. 13:15, where it is metaphorically represented as a sacrificial offering.

Notes: (1) In 1 Pet. 2:9, KJV, *aretē*, "virtue, excellence," is translated "praises" (RV, "excellencies"). (2) In the following the KJV translates *doxa*, "glory," by "praise" (RV, "glory"); John 9:24, where "give glory to God" signifies "confess thy sins" (cf. Josh. 7:19, indicating the genuine confession of facts in one's life which gives glory to God); 12:43 (twice); 1 Pet. 4:11.

B. Verbs

1. *aineō* (αἰνέω, 134), "to speak in praise of, to praise" (akin to A, No. 1), is always used of "praise" to God, (a) by angels, Luke 2:13; (b) by men, Luke 2:?; 19:37; 24:53; Acts 2:20, 47; 3:8, 9; Rom. 15:11 (No. 2 In some texts); Rev. 19:5.

2. *epaineō* (ἐπαινέω, 1867), akin to A, No. 2, is rendered "praise," 1 Cor. 11:2, 17, 22: see COMMEND, No. 1.

3. *humneō* (ὑμνέω, 5214) denotes (a) transitively, "to sing, to laud, sing to the praise of" (Eng., "hymn"), Acts 16:25, KJV, "sang praises" (RV, "singing hymns"); Heb. 2:12, RV, "will I sing (Thy) praise," KJV, "will I sing praise (unto Thee)," lit., "I will hymn Thee"; (b) intransitively, "to sing," Matt. 26:30; Mark 14:26, in both places of the singing of the paschal hymns (Ps. 113-118, and 136), called by Jews the Great Hallel.

4. *psallō* (ψάλλω, 5567), primarily, "to twitch" or "twang" (as a bowstring, etc.), then, "to play" (a stringed instrument with the fingers), in the Sept., to sing psalms, denotes, in the NT, to sing a hymn, sing "praise"; in Jas. 5:13, RV, "sing praise" (KJV, "sing psalms"). See MELODY, SING.

5. *exomologeō* (ἐξομολογέω, 1843) in Rom. 15:9, RV, "will I give praise" (KJV, and RV marg., "I will confess"): see CONFESS, A, No. 2 (c).

Note: In Luke 1:64, KJV, *eulogeō*, "to bless," is translated "praised" (RV, "blessing").

PRATE

phluareo (φλυαρέω, 5396) signifies "to talk nonsense" (from *phluo*, "to babble"; cf. the adjective *phluaros*, "babbling, garrulous, tattlers," 1 Tim. 5:13), "to raise false accusations," 3 John 10.

PRAY, PRAYER

A. Verbs.

1. *euchomai* (εὔχομαι, 2172), "to pray (to God)," is used with this meaning in 2 Cor. 13:7; v. 9, RV, "pray" (KJV, "wish"); Jas. 5:16; 3 John 2, RV, "pray" (KJV, wish). Even when the RV and KJV translate by "I would," Acts 26:29, or "wished for," Acts 27:29 (RV, marg., "prayed"), or "could wish," Rom. 9:3 (RV, marg., "could pray"), the indication is that "prayer" is involved.

2. *proseuchomai* (προσεύχομαι, 4336), "to pray," is always used of "prayer" to God, and is the most frequent word in this respect, especially in the Synoptists and Acts, once in Romans, 8:26; in Ephesians, 6:18; in Philippians, 1:9; in 1 Timothy, 2:8; in Hebrews, 13:18; in Jude, v. 20.

3. *erōtaō* (ἐρωτάω, 2065), "to ask," is translated by the verb to pray in Luke 14:18, 19; 16:27; John 4:31; 14:16; 16:26; 17:9, 15, 20; in Acts 23:18, RV, "asked" (KJV "prayed"); in 1 John 5:16, RV, "should make request" (KJV "shall pray").

4. *deomai* (δέομαι, 1189), "to desire," in 2 Cor. 5:20; 8:4, RV, "beseech" (KJV, "pray").

Notes: (1) *Parakale*, "to call to one's aid," is rendered by the verb "to pray" in the KJV in the following: Matt. 26:53 (RV, "beseech"); so Mark 5:17, 18; Acts 16:9; in 24:4, RV, "intreat"; in 27:34, RV, "beseech." (2) In 1 Thess. 5:23 and 2 Tim. 4:16, there is no word in the original for "I pray," see the RV.

B. Nouns.

1. *euchē* (εὐχή, 2171), akin to A, No. 1, denotes "a prayer," Jas. 5:15; "a vow," Acts 18:18 and 21:23. See VOW.

2. *proseuchē* (προσευχή, 4335), akin to A, No. 2, denotes (a) "prayer" (to God), the most frequent term, e.g., Matt. 21:22; Luke 6:12, where the phrase is not to be taken literally as if it meant, "the prayer of God" (subjective genitive), but objectively, "prayer to God." In Jas. 5:17, "He prayed fervently," RV, is, lit., "he prayed with prayer" (a Hebraistic form); in the following the word is used with No. 3: Eph. 6:18; Phil. 4:6; 1 Tim. 2:1; 5:5; (b) "a place of prayer," Acts 16:13, 16, a place outside the city wall, RV.

3. *deēsis* (δέησις, 1162), primarily "a wanting, a need" (akin to A, No. 4), then, "an asking, entreaty, supplication," in the NT is always addressed to God and always rendered "supplication" or "supplications" in the RV; in the KJV "prayer," or "prayers," in Luke 1:13; 2:37; 5:33; Rom. 10:1; 2 Cor. 1:11; 9:14; Phil. 1:4 (in the 2nd part, "request"); 1:19; 2 Tim. 1:3; Heb. 5:7; Jas. 5:16; 1 Pet. 3:12.

4. *enteuxis* (ἔντευξις, 1783) is translated "prayer" in 1 Tim. 4:5.

Notes: (1) *Proseuchē* is used of "prayer" in general; *deēsis* stresses the sense of need; it is used sometimes of request from man to man.

(2) In the papyri *enteuxis* is the regular word for a petition to a superior. For the synonymous word *aitēma* see PETITION; for *hiketēria*, Heb. 5:7, see SUPPLICATION.

(3) "Prayer is properly addressed to God the Father Matt. 6:6; John 16:23; Eph. 1:17; 3:14, and the Son, Acts 7:59; 2 Cor. 12:8; but in no instance in the NT is prayer addressed to the Holy Spirit distinctively, for whereas the Father is in Heaven, Matt. 6:9, and the Son is at His right hand, Rom. 8:34, the Holy Spirit is in and with the believers, John 14:16, 17.

"Prayer is to be offered in the Name of the Lord Jesus, John 14:13, that is, the prayer must accord with His character, and must be presented in the same spirit of dependence and submission that marked Him, Matt. 11:26; Luke 22:42.

"The Holy Spirit, being the sole interpreter of the needs of the human heart, makes His intercession therein; and inasmuch as prayer is impossible to man apart from His help, Rom. 8:26, believers are exhorted to pray at all seasons in the Spirit, Eph. 6:18; cf. Jude 20, and Jas. 5:16, the last clause of which should probably be read 'the inwrought [i.e., by the Holy Spirit] supplication of righteous man availeth much' (or 'greatly prevails' *ischuō*, as in Acts 19:16, 20).

"None the less on this account is the understanding to be engaged in prayer, 1 Cor. 14:15, and the will, Col. 4:12; Acts 12:5 (where 'earnestly' is, lit., 'stretched out') and so in Luke 22:44.

"Faith is essential to prayer, Matt. 21:22; Mark 11:24; Jas. 1:5-8, for faith is the recognition of, and the committal of ourselves and our matters to, the faithfulness of God.

"Where the Jews were numerous, as at Thessalonica, they had usually a Synagogue, Acts 17:1; where they were few, as at Philippi, they had merely a *proseuchē*, or 'place of prayer,' of much smaller dimensions, and commonly built by a river for the sake of the water necessary to the preliminary ablutions prescribed by Rabbinic tradition, Acts 16:13, 16."

PREACH, PREACHING

A. Verbs.

1. *euangelizō* (εὐαγγελίζω, 2097) is almost always used of "the good news" concerning the Son of God as proclaimed in the gospel [exceptions are e.g., Luke 1:19; 1 Thess. 3:6, in which the phrase "to bring (or show) good (or glad) tidings" does not refer to the gospel]; Gal. 1:8 (2nd part). With reference to the gospel the phrase "to bring, or declare, good, or glad, tidings" is used in Acts 13:32; Rom. 10:15; Heb. 4:2.

In Luke 4:18 the RV "to preach good tidings" gives the correct quotation from Isaiah, rather than the KJV "to preach the Gospel." In the Sept. the verb is used of any message intended to cheer the hearers, e.g. 1 Sam. 31:9; 2 Sam. 1:20. See GOSPEL, B, No. 1.

2. *kērussō* (κηρύσσω, 2784) signities (a) "to be a herald," or, in general, "to proclaim," e.g., Matt. 3:1; Mark 1:45, "publish"; in Luke 4:18, RV, "to proclaim," KJV, "to preach"; so verse 19; Luke 12:3; Acts 10:37; Rom. 2:21; Rev. 5:2. In 1 Pet. 3:19 the probable reference is, not to glad tidings (which there is no real evidence that Noah preached, nor is there evidence that the spirits of antediluvian people are actually "in prison"), but to the act of Christ after His resurrection in proclaiming His victory to fallen angelic spirits; (b) "to preach the gospel as a herald," e.g., Matt. 24:14; Mark 13:10, RV, "be preached" (KJV, "be published"); 14:9; 16:15, 20; Luke 8:1; 9:2; 24:47; Acts 8:5; 19:13; 28:31; Rom. 10:14, present participle, lit., "(one) preaching," "a preacher"; 10:15 (1st part); 1 Cor. 1:23; 15:11, 12; 2 Cor. 1:19; 4:5; 11:4; Gal. 2:2; Phil. 1:15; Col. 1:23; 1 Thess. 2:9; 1 Tim. 3:16; (c) "to preach the word," 2 Tim. 4:2 (of the ministry of the Scriptures, with special reference to the gospel). See PROCLAIM, PUBLISH.

3. *proeuangelizomai* (προευαγγελίζομαι, 4283): see GOSPEL, B, No. 2.

4. *prokērussō* (προκηρύσσω, 4296), lit., "to proclaim as a herald" (*pro*, before, and No. 2), is used in Acts 13:24, "had first preached." Some mss. have the verb in Acts 3:20; for the best see APPOINT, No. 12.

5. *parrhēsiazomai* (παῤῥησιάζομαι, 3955), "to be bold in speech," is translated "to preach boldly" in Acts 9:27 (2nd part); in v. 29, RV (KJV, "he spake boldly").

Notes: (1) For *diangellō*, translated "preach" in Luke 9:60, see DECLARE, A, No. 3. (2) *Katangellō*, "to proclaim," is always so translated in the RV; the KJV renders it by "to preach" in Acts 4:2; 13:5, 38; 15:36; 17:3, 13; 1 Cor. 9:14; Col. 1:28. (3) *Laleō*, "to speak," is translated "preached," Mark 2:2, KJV, "preached" (RV, "spake"); in Acts 8:25, 1st part, KJV (RV, "spoken"); so in 13:42 and 14:25; "preaching" in Acts 11:19, KJV, but what is indicated here is not a formal "preaching" by the believers scattered from Jerusalem, but a general testimony to all with whom they came into contact; in 16:6, RV, "to speak" (KJV, "to preach"). (4) For KJV, "preached" in Heb. 4:2 (2nd part), see HEARING. (5) In Rom. 15:19 *plēroō*, "to fulfill" (RV, marg.), is rendered "I have fully preached."

B. Nouns.

kērugma (κήρυγμα, 2782), "a proclamation by a herald" (akin to A, No. 2), denotes "a message, a preaching" (the substance of what is "preached" as distinct from the act of "preaching"), Matt. 12:41; Luke 11:32; Rom. 16:25; 1 Cor. 1:21; 2:4; 15:14; in 2 Tim. 4:17 and Titus 1:3, RV, "message," marg., "proclamation," KJV, "preaching." See MESSAGE. In the Sept., 2 Chron. 30:5; Prov. 9:3; Jonah 3:2.

Note: In 1 Cor. 1:18, KJV, *logos*, "a word," is translated "preaching," RV, "the word (of the Cross)," i.e., not the act of "preaching," but the substance of the testimony, all that God has made known concerning the subject. For Heb. 4:2, KJV, see HEAR, B, No. 1.

PREACHER

kērux (κῆρυξ, 2783), "a herald" (akin to A, No. 2 and B, above), is used (a) of the "preacher" of the gospel, 1 Tim. 2:7; 2 Tim. 1:11; (b) of Noah, as a "preacher" of righteousness, 2 Pet. 2:5.

Notes: (1) For "a preacher," in Rom. 10:14, where the verb *kerusso* is used, see PREACH, A, No. 2. (2) *Kērux* indicates the "preacher" as giving a proclamation; *euangelistēs* points to his message as glad tidings; *apostolos* suggests his relationship to Him by whom he is sent.

PRECEPT

1. *entolē* (ἐντολή, 1785), "a commandment," is translated "precept" in Mark 10:5 (RV, "commandment"); so Heb. 9:19. See COMMANDMENT, No. 2.

2. *entalma* (ἔνταλμα, 1778) is always translated "precepts" in the RV; see COMMANDMENT, No. 3.

PREDESTINATE

proorizō (προορίζω, 4309) is to be distinguished from *proginōskō*, "to foreknow"; the latter has special reference to the persons foreknown by God; *proorizō* has special reference to that to which the subjects of His foreknowledge are "predestinated." See FOREKNOW, A and B.

PREEMINENCE (to have the)

1. *prōteuō* (πρωτεύω, 4409), "to be first" (*protos*), "to be preeminent," is used of Christ in relation to the Church, Col. 1:18.

2. *philoprōteuō* (φιλοπρωτεύω, 5383), lit., "to love to be preeminent" (*philos*, "loving"), "to strive to be first," is said of Diotrephes, 3 John 9.

PREJUDICE

prokrima (πρόκριμα, 4299) denotes "prejudging" (akin to *prokrinō*, "to judge beforehand"), 1 Tim. 5:21, RV, "prejudice" (marg., "preference"), preferring one person, another being put aside, by unfavorable judgment due to partiality.

PREMEDITATE

Note: This is the KJV rendering of *meletaō*, "to care for," which occurs in some mss. in Mark 13:11, "(neither) do ye premeditate." It is absent from the best mss. See IMAGINE.

PREPARATION, PREPARE, PREPARED

A. Nouns.

1. *hetoimasia* (ἑτοιμασία, 2091) denotes (a) "readiness," (b) "preparation"; it is found in Eph. 6:15, of having the feet shod with the "preparation" of the gospel of peace; it also has the meaning of firm footing (foundation), as in the Sept. of Ps. 89:14 (RV, "foundation"); if that is the meaning in Eph. 6:15, the gospel itself is to be the firm footing of the believer, his walk being worthy of it and therefore a testimony in regard to it.

2. *paraskeuē* (παρασκευή, 3904) denotes "preparation, equipment." The day on which Christ died is called "the Preparation" in Mark 15:42 and John 19:31; in John 19:42 "the Jews' Preparation," RV; in 19:14 it is described as "the Preparation of the Passover"; in Luke 23:54, RV, "the day of the Preparation (and the Sabbath drew on)." The same day is in view in Matt. 27:62, where the events recorded took place on "the day after the Preparation" (RV). The reference would be to the 6th day of the week. The title arose from the need of preparing food etc. for the Sabbath. Apparently it was first applied only to the afternoon of the 6th day; later, to the whole day. In regard to the phraseology in John 19:14, many hold this to indicate the "preparation" for the paschal feast. It probably means "the Preparation day," and thus falls in line with the Synoptic Gospels. In modern Greek and ecclesiastical Latin, *Parascevē* = Friday.

B. Verbs.

1. *hetoimazō* (ἑτοιμάζω, 2090), "to prepare, make ready," is used (I) absolutely, e.g., Mark 14:15; Luke 9:52; (II), with an object, e.g., (a) of those things which are ordained (1) by God, such as future positions of authority, Matt. 20:23; the coming Kingdom, 25:34; salvation personified in Christ, Luke 2:31; future blessings, 1 Cor. 2:9; a city, Heb. 11:16; a place of refuge for the Jewish remnant, Rev. 12:6; Divine judgments on the world, Rev. 8:6; 9:7, 15; 16:12; eternal fire, for the Devil and his angels, Matt. 25:41; (2) by Christ: a place in Heaven for His followers, John 14:2, 3; (b) of human "preparation" for the Lord, e.g., Matt. 3:3; 26:17, 19; Luke 1:17 ("make ready"), 76; 3:4, KJV (RV, "make ye ready"); 9:52 ("to make ready"); 23:56; Rev. 19:7; 21:2; in 2 Tim. 2:21, of "preparation" of oneself for "every good work"; (c) of human "preparations" for human objects, e.g., Luke 12:20, RV, "thou hast prepared" (KJV, "provided"); Acts 23:23; Philem. 22.

2. *katartizō* (καταρτίζω, 2675), "to furnish completely, prepare," is translated "didst Thou prepare" in Heb. 10:5 (KJV, "hast Thou prepared"), of the body of the Lord Jesus. See FIT, B, No. 3.

3. *kataskeuazō* (κατασκευάζω, 2680), "to prepare, make ready" (*kata*, used intensively, *skeuē*, "equipment"), is so

translated in Matt. 11:10; Mark 1:2; Luke 1:17; 7:27; Heb. 9:2, RV (KJV, "made"); 9:6, RV (KJV, "were ... ordained"); 11:7; 1 Pet. 3:20. See BUILD, No. 5.

4. *paraskeuazō* (παρασκευάζω, 3903), "to prepare, make ready" (*para*, "beside"), is used of making ready a meal, Acts 10:10: in the middle voice, of "preparing" oneself for war, 1 Cor. 14:8, RV; in the passive voice, of "preparing" an offering for the needy, 2 Cor. 9:2, "hath been prepared," RV (KJV, "was ready"); v. 3, "ye may be prepared," RV (KJV, "ye may be ready").

5. *proetoimazō* (προετοιμάζω, 4282), "to prepare beforehand" (*pro*, "before," and No. 1), is used of good works which God "afore prepared," for fulfillment by believers, Eph. 2:10, RV (KJV, "hath before ordained," marg., "prepared"); of "vessels of mercy," as "afore prepared" by God "unto glory," Rom. 9:23. See ORDAIN.

Notes: (1) Etymologically, the difference between *hetoimazō* and *paraskeuazō*, is that the former is connected with what is real (*etumos*) or ready, the latter with *skeuos*, an article ready to hand, an implement, vessel. (2) In Mark 14:15, KJV, *hetoimos*, "ready," is translated "prepared" (RV, "ready"). It is absent in some mss.

For **PRESBYTERY** see ELDER, A and B

PRESENCE

A. Nouns.

1. *prosōpon* (πρόσωπον, 4383): see FACE, No. 1 (also APPEARANCE, No. 2).

2. *parousi* (παρουσία, 3952): see COMING (Noun), No. 3.

B. Adverbs and Prepositions.

1. *enōpion* (ἐνώπιον, 1799) is translated "in the presence of" in Luke 1:19; 13:26; 14:10; 15:10; John 20:30; Rev. 14:10 (twice); in 1 Cor. 1:29 KJV, "in His presence" (RV, "before God").

2. *katenōpion* (κατενώπιον, 2714), *kata*, "down," and No. 2, "in the very presence of," is translated "before the presence of" in Jude 24.

3. *apenanti* (ἀπέναντι, 561), "over against, opposite to," is translated "in the presence of" in Acts 3:16.

PRESENT (to be)

A. Verbs.

1. *pareimi* (πάρειμι, 3918) signifies (a) "to be by, at hand or present," of persons, e.g., Luke 13:1; Acts 10:33; 24:19; 1 Cor. 5:3; 2 Cor. 10:2, 11; Gal. 4:18, 20; of things, John 7:6, of a particular season in the Lord's life on earth, "is (not yet) come," or "is not yet at hand"; Heb. 12:11, of chastening "(for the) present" (the neuter of the present participle, used as a noun); in 13:5 "such things as ye have" is, lit., "the things that are present"; 2 Pet. 1:12, of the truth "(which) is with (you)" (not as KJV, "the present truth," as if of special doctrines applicable to a particular time); in v. 9 "he that lacketh" is lit., "to whom are not present"; (b) "to have arrived or come," Matt. 26:50, "thou art come," RV; John 11:28; Acts 10:21; Col. 1:6.

2. *enistēmi* (ἐνίστημι, 1764), "to set in," or, in the middle voice and perfect tense of the active voice, "to stand in, be present," is used of the present in contrast with the past, Heb. 9:9, where the RV correctly has "(for the time) *now* present" (for the incorrect KJV, "then present"); in contrast to the future, Rom. 8:38; 1 Cor. 3:22; Gal. 1:4, "present"; 1 Cor. 7:26, where "the present distress" is set in contrast to both the past and the future; 2 Thess. 2:2, where the RV, "is *now* present" gives the correct meaning (KJV, incorrectly, "is at hand"); the saints at Thessalonica, owing to their heavy afflictions were possessed of the idea that "the day of the Lord," RV (not as KJV, "the day of Christ"), had begun; this mistake the apostle corrects; 2 Tim. 3:1, "shall come."

3. *ephistēmi* (ἐφίστημι, 2186), "to set over, stand over," is translated "present" in Acts 28:2. See ASSAULT, A.

4. *paraginomai* (παραγίνομαι, 3854), "to be beside" (*para*, "by," *ginomai*, "to become"), is translated "were present" in Acts 21:18.

5. *parakeimai* (παράκειμαι, 3873), "to lie beside" (*para*, and *keimai*, "to lie"), "to be near," is translated "is present" in Rom. 7:18, 21.

6. *sumpareimi* (συμπάρειμι, 4840), "to be present with" (sun, with, and No. 1), is used in Acts 25:24.

B. Adverbs.

1. *arti* (ἄρτι, 737), "just, just now, this moment," is rendered "(this) present (hour)" in 1 Cor. 4:11; in 1 Cor. 15:6, RV, "now" (KJV, "this present"). See NOW.

2. *nun* (νῦν, 3568), "now," is translated "present," with reference to this age or period ("world"), in Rom. 8:18; 11:5; 2 Tim. 4:10; Titus 2:12. See NOW.

Notes: (1) *Endēmeō*, "to be at home," is so rendered in 2 Cor. 5:6 (KJV and RV); in vv. 8, 9, RV, "at home" (KJV, "present"). See HOME. (2) In John 14:25, KJV, *menō*, "to abide," is translated "being present" (RV, "abiding"). (3) In Luke 5:17 the RV has "with Him," for KJV, italicized, "*present.*"

PRESENT (Verb)

1. *paristēmi* (παρίστημι, 3936) denotes, when used transitively, "to place beside" (*para*, "by," *histēmi*, "to set"), "to present," e.g., Luke 2:22; Acts 1:3, "He shewed (Himself)"; 9:41; 23:33; Rom. 6:13 (2nd part), RV, "present," KJV "yield"; so 6:19 (twice); 12:1; 2 Cor. 4:14; 11:2; Eph. 5:27; Col. 1:22, 28; 2 Tim. 2:15, RV (KJV, "shew").

2. *paristanō* (παριστάνω, 3936), a late present form of No. 1, is used in Rom. 6:13 (1st part) and v. 16, RV, "present" (KJV, "yield").

Notes: (1) In Jude 24, KJV, *histēmi*, "to cause to stand, to set," is translated "to present" (RV, "to set"). (2) In Matt. 2:11, KJV, *prospherō*, "to offer," is translated "presented" (RV, "offered").

For **PRESENTLY** see IMMEDIATELY, No. 1

PRESERVE

1. *tēreō* (τηρέω, 5083) is translated "to preserve" in 1 Thess. 5:23, where the verb is in the singular number, as the threefold subject, "spirit and soul and body," is regarded as the unit, constituting the person. The aorist or "point" tense regards the continuous "preservation" of the believer as a single, complete act, without reference to the time occupied in its accomplishment; in Jude 1, KJV (RV, "kept"). See KEEP, No. 1.

2. *suntēreō* (συντηρέω, 4933): see KEEP, No. 3.

3. *zōogoneō* (ζωογονέω, 2225), "to preserve alive": see LIVE, No. 6.

4. *phulassō* (φυλάσσω, 5442), "to guard, protect, preserve," is translated "preserved" in 2 Pet. 2:5, RV (KJV, "saved"). See GUARD.

Note: In 2 Tim. 4:18, KJV, *sōzō*, "to save," is translated "will preserve" (RV, "will save").

For **PRESS** (Noun) see CROWD, A

For **PRESUMPTUOUS** see DARING, B

PREVAIL

1. *ischuō* (ἰσχύω, 2480), "to be strong, powerful," is translated "to prevail" in Acts 19:16, 20; Rev. 12:8. See ABLE, B, No. 4.

2. *katischuō* (κατισχύω, 2729), "to be strong against" (*kata*, "against," and No. 1), is used in Matt. 16:18, negatively of the gates of hades; in Luke 21:36 (in the most authentic mss., some have *kataxioō*, "to count worthy"; see KJV), of "prevailing" to escape judgments at the close of this age; in Luke 23:23, of the voices of the chief priests, rulers and people against Pilate regarding the crucifixion of Christ.

3. *ōpheleō* (ὠφελέω, 5623), "to benefit, do good, profit," is translated "prevailed" in Matt. 27:24, RV (KJV, "could prevail"), of the conclusion formed by Pilate concerning the determination of the chief priests, elders and people. The meaning of the verb with the negative is better expressed by the phrase "he would do no good"; so in John 12:19, "ye prevail (nothing)," lit., "ye are doing no good."

4. *nikaō* (νικάω, 3528), "to conquer, prevail," is used as a law term in Rom. 3:4, "(that) Thou ... mightest prevail [KJV, 'overcome'] (when Thou comest into judgment)"; that the righteousness of the judge's verdict compels an acknowledgement on the part of the accused, is inevitable where God is the judge. God's promises to Israel provided no guarantee that an unrepentant Jew would escape doom. In Rev. 5:5, KJV, "hath prevailed" (RV, "hath overcome"). See CONQUER, No. 1.

For **PRICK** (Noun) see GOAD

PRIDE

A. Nouns.

1. *alazonia* (or *—eia*) (ἀλαζονεία, 212) is translated "pride" in 1 John 2:16, KJV. See BOAST, B, No. 2, VAINGLORY.

2. *huperēphania* (ὑπερηφανία, 5243), "pride," Mark 7:22: see HAUGHTY.

B. Verb.

tuphoō (τυφόω, 5187), "lifted up with pride," 1 Tim. 3:6, KJV (RV, "puffed up"). See HIGH-MINDED.

PRIEST

1. *hiereus* (ἱερεύς, 2409), "one who offers sacrifice and has the charge of things pertaining thereto," is used (a) of a "priest" of the pagan god Zeus, Acts 14:13; (b) of Jewish "priests," e.g., Matt. 8:4; 12:4, 5; Luke 1:5, where allusion is made to the 24 courses of "priests" appointed for service in the Temple (cf. 1 Chron. 24:4ff.); John 1:19; Heb. 8:4; (c) of believers, Rev. 1:6; 5:10; 20:6. Israel was primarily designed as a nation to be a kingdom of "priests," offering service to God, e.g., Ex. 19:6, the Israelites having renounced their obligations, Ex. 20:19, the Aaronic priesthood was selected for the purpose, till Christ came to fulfil His ministry in offering up Himself; since then the Jewish priesthood has been abrogated, to be resumed nationally, on behalf of Gentiles, in the millennial kingdom, Is. 61:6; 66:21. Meanwhile all believers, from Jews and Gentiles, are constituted "a kingdom of priests," Rev. 1:6 (see above), "a holy priesthood," 1 Pet. 2:5, and "royal," v. 9. The NT knows nothing of a sacerdotal class in contrast to the laity; all believers are commanded to offer the sacrifices mentioned in Rom. 12:1; Phil. 2:17; 4:18; Heb. 13:15, 16; 1 Pet. 2:5; (d) of Christ, Heb. 5:6; 7:11, 15, 17, 21; 8:4 (negatively); (e) of Melchizedek, as the foreshadower of Christ, Heb. 7:1, 3.

2. *archiereus* (ἀρχιερεύς, 749) designates (a) "the high priests" of the Levitical order, frequently called "chief priests" in the NT, and including "ex-high priests" and members of "high priestly" families, e.g., Matt. 2:4; 16:21; 20:18; 21:15; in the singular, a "high priest," e.g., Abiathar, Mark 2:26; Annas and Caiaphas, Luke 3:2, where the RV rightly has "in the high priesthood of A. and C." (cf. Acts 4:6). As to the combination of the two in this respect, Annas was the "high priest"

from A.D. 7-14, and, by the time referred to, had been deposed for some years; his son-in-law, Caiaphas, the fourth "high priest" since his deposition, was appointed about A.D. 24. That Annas was still called the "high priest" is explained by the facts (1) that by the Mosaic law the high priesthood was held for life, Num. 35:25; his deposition was the capricious act of the Roman procurator, but he would still be regarded legally and religiously as "high priest" by the Jews; (2) that he probably still held the office of deputy-president of the Sanhedrin (cf. 2 Kings 25:18); (3) that he was a man whose age, wealth and family connections gave him a preponderant influence, by which he held the real sacerdotal power; indeed at this time the high priesthood was in the hands of a clique of some half dozen families; the language of the writers of the gospels is in accordance with this, in attributing the high priesthood rather to a caste than a person; (4) the "high priests" were at that period mere puppets of Roman authorities who deposed them at will, with the result that the title was used more loosely than in former days.

The divine institution of the priesthood culminated in the "high priest," it being his duty to represent the whole people, e.g., Lev. 4:15, 16; ch. 16. The characteristics of the Aaronic "high priests" are enumerated in Heb. 5:1-4; 8:3; 9:7, 25; in some mss., 10:11 (RV, marg.); 13:11.

(b) Christ is set forth in this respect in the Ep. to the Hebrews, where He is spoken of as "a high priest," 4:15; 5:5, 10; 6:20; 7:26; 8:1, 3 (RV); 9:11; "a great high priest," 4:14; "a great priest," 10:21; "a merciful and faithful high priest," 2:17; "the Apostle and high priest of our confession," 3:1, RV; "a high priest after the order of Melchizedek," 5:10. One of the great objects of this Epistle is to set forth the superiority of Christ's High Priesthood as being of an order different from and higher than the Aaronic, in that He is the Son of God (see especially 7:28), with a priesthood of the Melchizedek order. Seven outstanding features of His priesthood are stressed, (1) its character, 5:6, 10; (2) His commission, 5:4, 5; (3) His preparation, 2:17; 10:5; (4) His sacrifice, 8:3; 9:12, 14, 27, 28; 10:4-12; (5) His sanctuary, 4:14; 8:2; 9:11, 12, 24; 10:12, 19; (6) His ministry, 2:18; 4:15; 7:25; 8:6; 9:15, 24; (7) its effects, 2:15; 4:16; 6:19, 20; 7:16, 25; 9:14, 28; 10:14-17, 22, 39; 12:1; 13:13-17.

Note: In Acts 4:6 the adjective *hieratikos*, "high priestly," is translated "of the high priest."

PRIESTHOOD, PRIEST'S OFFICE

A. Nouns.

1. *hierateuma* (ἱεράτευμα, 2406) denotes "a priesthood" (akin to *hierateuo*, see below), "a body of priests," consisting of all believers, the whole church (not a special order from among them), called "a holy priesthood," 1 Pet. 2:5; "a royal priesthood," v. 9; the former term is associated with offering spiritual sacrifices, the latter with the royal dignity of showing forth the Lord's excellencies (RV). In the Sept., Exod. 19:6; 23:22.

2. *hierōsunē* (ἱερωσύνη, 2420), "a priesthood," signifies the office, quality, rank and ministry of "a priest," Heb. 7:11, 12, 24, where the contrasts between the Levitical "priesthood" and that of Christ are set forth. In the Sept., 1 Chron. 29:22.

3. *hierateia* (ἱερατεία, 2405), "a priesthood," denotes the priest's office, Luke 1:9; Heb. 7:5, RV, "priest's office."

B. Verb.

hierateuō (ἱερατεύω, 2407) signifies "to officiate as a priest," Luke 1:8, "he executed the priest's office."

PRINCE

1. *archēgos* (ἀρχηγός, 747), primarily an adjective signifying "originating, beginning," is used as a noun, denoting "a founder, author, prince or leader," Acts 3:15, "Prince" (marg., "Author"); 5:31; see AUTHOR, No. 2.

2. *archōn* (ἄρχων, 758), the present participle of the verb *archo*, "to rule"; denotes "a ruler, a prince." It is used as follows ("p" denoting "prince," or "princes"; "r," "ruler" or "rulers"): (a) of Christ, as "the Ruler (KJV, Prince) of the kings of the earth," Rev. 1:5; (b) of rulers of nations, Matt. 20:25, RV, "r," KJV, "p"; Acts 4:26, "r"; 7:27, "r"; 7:35, "r" (twice); (c) of judges and magistrates, Acts 16:19, "r"; Rom. 13:3, "r"; (d) of members of the Sanhedrin, Luke 14:1, RV, "r" (KJV, "chief"); 23:13, 35, "r"; so 24:20, John 3:1; 7:26, 48; 12:42, RV, "r" (KJV, "chief r."); "r" in Acts 3:17; 4:5, 8; 13:27; 14:5; (e) of rulers of synagogues, Matt. 9:18, 23, "r"; so Luke 8:41; 18:18; (f) of the Devil, as "prince" of this world, John 12:31; 14:30; 16:11; of the power of the air, Eph. 2:2, "the air" being that sphere in which the inhabitants of the world live and which, through the rebellious and godless condition of humanity, constitutes the seat of his authority; (g) of Beelzebub, the "prince" of the demons, Matt. 9:24; 12:24; Mark 3:22; Luke 11:15. See CHIEF, B, No. 10.

3. *hegemōn* (ἡγεμών, 2232), "a leader, ruler," is translated "princes" (i.e., leaders) in Matt. 2:6: see GOVERNOR, A, No. 1.

Note: For *megistan*, Rev. 6:15; 18:23, RV, "princes," see LORD, No. 3.

PRINCIPALITY

archē (ἀρχή, 746), "beginning, government, rule," is used of supramundane beings who exercise rule, called "principalities"; (a) of holy angels, Eph. 3:10, the church in its formation being to them the great expression of "the manifold (or "much-varied") wisdom of God"; Col. 1:16; (b) of evil angels, Rom. 8:38; Col. 2:15, some would put this under (a); (a) and (b) are indicated in Col. 2:10. In Eph. 1:21, the RV renders it "rule" (KJV, "principality") and in Titus 3:1, "rulers"

(KJV, "principalities"). In Jude 6, RV, it signifies, not the first estate of fallen angels (as KJV), but their authoritative power, "their own" indicating that which had been assigned to them by God, which they left, aspiring to prohibited conditions. See BEGIN, B.

PRINCIPLES

1. *archē* (ἀρχή, 746), "beginning," is used in Heb. 6:1, in its relative significance, of the beginning of the thing spoken of; here "the first principles of Christ," lit., "the account (or word) of the beginning of Christ," denotes the teaching relating to the elementary facts concerning Christ. See BEGIN, B.

2. *stoicheion* (στοιχεῖον, 4747) is translated "principles" in Heb. 5:12.

PRISON, PRISON-HOUSE

1. *desmōtērion* (δεσμωτήριον, 1201), "a place of bonds" (from *desmos*, "a bond," *deō*, "to bind"), "a prison," occurs in Matt. 11:2, in Acts 5:21, 23 and 16:26, RV, "prison house" (KJV, "prison").

2. *phulakē* (φυλακή, 5438), for the various meanings of which see CAGE, denotes a "prison," e.g., Matt. 14:10; Mark 6:17; Acts 5:19; 2 Cor. 11:23; in 2 Cor. 6:5 and Heb. 11:36 it stands for the condition of imprisonment; in Rev. 2:10; 18:2, "hold" (twice, RV, marg., "prison"; in the 2nd case, KJV, "cage"); 20:7.

3. *tērēsis* (τήρησις, 5084), "a watching, keeping," then "a place of keeping" is translated "prison" in Acts 5:18 KJV (RV "ward").

Note: In Matt. 4:12, KJV, *paradidomi*, "to betray, deliver up," is translated "was cast into prison" (RV, "was delivered up"); see BETRAY. In Mark 1:14, KJV, "was put in prison," RV, as in Matt. 4:12.

PRISONER

1. *desmios* (δέσμιος, 1198), an adjective, primarily denotes "binding, bound," then, as a noun, "the person bound, a captive, prisoner" (akin to *deō*, "to bind"), Matt. 27:15, 16; Mark 15:6; Acts 16:25, 27; 23:18; 25:14, RV (KJV, "in bonds"), 27; 28:16, 17; Eph. 3:1; 4:1; 2 Tim. 1:8; Philem. 1, 9; in Heb. 10:34 and 13:3, "in bonds." See BOND, No. 2.

Note: The prison at Jerusalem (Acts 5) was controlled by the priests and probably attached to the high priest's palace, or the Temple. Paul was imprisoned at Jerusalem in the fort Antonia, Acts 23:10; at Caesarea, in Herod's Praetorium, 23:35; probably his final imprisonment in Rome was in the Tullianum dungeon.

2. *desmōtēs* (δεσμώτης, 1202), akin to No. 1, occurs in Acts 27:1, 42.

3. *sunaichmalōtos* (συναιχμάλωτος, 4869), "a fellow prisoner," primarily "one of fellow captives in war" (from *aichmē*, "a spear," and *haliskomai*, "to be taken"), is used by Paul of Andronicus and Junias, Rom. 16:7 of Epaphras, Philem. 23; of Aristarchus, Col. 4:10, on which Lightfoot remarks that probably his relations with the apostle in Rome excited suspicion and led to a temporary confinement, or that he voluntarily shared his captivity by living with him.

PRIVILY

lathra (λάθρα, 2977), "secretly, covertly" (from a root *lath-* indicating "unnoticed, unknown," seen in *lanthano*, "to escape notice," *lēthē*, "forgetfulness"), is translated "privily" in Matt. 1:19; 2:7; Acts 16:37; "secretly" in John 11:28 (in some mss., Mark 5:33). See SECRETLY.

Note: In Gal. 2:4, *pareisaktos*, an adjective (akin to *pareisagō*, lit., "to bring in beside," i.e., "secretly," from *para*, "by the side," *eis*, "into," *agō*, "to bring"), is used, "privily brought in," RV (KJV, "unawares, etc."), i.e., as spies or traitors. Strabo, a Greek historian contemporary with Paul, uses the word of enemies introduced secretly into a city by traitors within. In the same verse the verb *pareiserchomai* is translated "came in privily," of the same Judaizers, brought in by the circumcision party to fulfill the design of establishing the ceremonial law, and thus to accomplish the overthrow of the faith; cf. in Jude 4 the verb *pareisduō* (or *-dunō*), "to slip in secretly, steal in," RV, "crept in privily" (KJV, "... unawares"). See CREEP, No. 2.

For **PROBATION,** RV in Rom. 5:4, see EXPERIENCE, No. 2

PROCLAIM

1. *kērussō* (κηρύσσω, 2784) is translated "to proclaim" in the RV, for KJV, "to preach," in Matt. 10:27; Luke 4:19; Acts 8:5; 9:20. See PREACH, No. 2.

2. *katangellō* (καταγγέλλω, 2605), "to declare, proclaim," is translated "to proclaim" in the RV, for KJV, to "show," in Acts 16:17; 26:23; 1 Cor. 11:26, where the verb makes clear that the partaking of the elements at the Lord's Supper is a "proclamation" (an evangel) of the Lord's death; in Rom. 1:8, for KJV, "spoken of"; in 1 Cor. 2:1, for KJV, "declaring." See also PREACH, *Note* (2), and DECLARE, A, No. 4.

3. *plērophoreō* (πληροφορέω, 4135), "to bring in full measure" (*plērēs*, "full," *pherō*, "to bring"), hence, "to fulfill, accomplish," is translated "might be fully proclaimed," in 2 Tim. 4:17, RV, with *kērugma*, marg., "proclamation" (KJV "... known"). See ASSURE, B, No. 2, BELIEVE, C, *Note* (4), FULFILL, No. 6, KNOW, *Note* (2), PERSUADE, No. 2, *Note*, PROOF.

PROFANE (Adjective and Verb)

A. Adjective.

bebēlos (βέβηλος, 952), primarily, "permitted to be trodden, accessible" (from *bainō*, "to go," whence *bēlos*, "a threshold"), hence, "unhallowed, profane" (opposite to *hieros*, "sacred"), is used of (a) persons, 1 Tim. 1:9; Heb. 12:16; (b) things, 1 Tim. 4:7; 6:20; 2 Tim. 2:16. "The natural antagonism between the profane and the holy or divine grew into a moral antagonism .... Accordingly *bebēlos* is that which lacks all relationship or affinity to God" (Cremer, who compares *koinos*, "common," in the sense of ritual uncleanness).

B. Verb.

bebēloō (βεβηλόω, 953), primarily, "to cross the threshold" (akin to A, which see), hence, "to profane, pollute," occurs in Matt. 12:5 and Acts 24:6 (the latter as in 21:28, 29: cf. DEFILE, A, No. 1, PARTITION).

PROFESS, PROFESSION

A. Verbs.

1. *epangellō* (ἐπαγγέλλω, 1861), "to announce, proclaim, profess," is rendered "to profess" in 1 Tim. 2:10, of godliness, and 6:21, of "the knowledge ... falsely so called." See PROMISE.

2. *homologeō* (ὁμολογέω, 3670) is translated "to profess" in Matt. 7:23 and Titus 1:16; in 1 Tim. 6:12, KJV (RV, "confess"). See CONFESS.

3. *phaskō* (φάσκω, 5335), "to affirm, assert."

B. Noun.

homologia (ὁμολογία, 3671), akin to A, No. 2, "confession," is translated "profession" and "professed" in the KJV only. See CONFESS.

PROMISE (Noun and Verb)

A. Noun.

1. *epangelia* (ἐπαγγελία, 1860), primarily a law term, denoting "a summons" (*epi*, "upon," *angellō*, "to proclaim, announce"), also meant "an undertaking to do or give something, a promise." Except in Acts 23:21 it is used only of the "promises" of God. It frequently stands for the thing "promised," and so signifies a gift graciously bestowed, not a pledge secured by negotiation; thus, in Gal. 3:14, "the promise of the Spirit" denotes "the promised Spirit": cf. Luke 24:49; Acts 2:33 and Eph. 1:13; so in Heb. 9:15, "the promise of the eternal inheritance" is "the promised eternal inheritance." On the other hand, in Acts 1:4, "the promise of the Father," is the "promise" made by the Father.

In Gal. 3:16, the plural "promises" is used because the one "promise" to Abraham was variously repeated (Gen. 12:1-3; 13:14-17; 15:18; 17:1-14; 22:15-18), and because it contained the germ of all subsequent "promises"; cf. Rom. 9:4; Heb. 6:12; 7:6; 8:6; 11:17; Gal. 3 is occupied with showing that the "promise" was conditional upon faith and not upon the fulfillment of the Law. The Law was later than, and inferior to, the "promise," and did not annul it, v. 21; cf. 4:23, 28. Again, in Eph. 2:12, "the covenants of the promise" does not indicate different covenants, but a covenant often renewed, all centering in Christ as the "promised" Messiah-Redeemer, and comprising the blessings to be bestowed through Him.

In 2 Cor. 1:20 the plural is used of every "promise" made by God: cf. Heb. 11:33; in 7:6, of special "promises" mentioned. For other applications of the word, see, e.g., Eph. 6:2; 1 Tim. 4:8; 2 Tim. 1:1; Heb. 4:1; 2 Pet. 3:4, 9; in 1 John 1:5 some mss. have this word, instead of *angelia*, "message."

The occurrences of the word in relation to Christ and what centers in Him, may be arranged under the headings (1) the contents of the "promise," e.g., Acts 26:6; Rom. 4:20; 1 John 2:25; (2) the heirs, e.g., Rom. 9:8; 15:8; Gal. 3:29; Heb. 11:9; (3) the conditions, e.g., Rom. 4:13, 14; Gal. 3:14-22; Heb. 10:36.

2. *epangelma* (ἐπάγγελμα, 1862) denotes "a promise made," 2 Pet. 1:4; 3:13.

B. Verbs.

1. *epangellō* (ἐπαγγέλλω, 1861), "to announce, proclaim," has in the NT the two meanings "to profess" and "to promise," each used in the middle voice; "to promise" (a) of "promises" of God, Acts 7:5; Rom. 4:21; in Gal. 3:19, passive voice; Titus 1:2; Heb. 6:13; 10:23; 11:11; 12:26; Jas. 1:12; 2:5; 1 John 2:25; (b) made by men, Mark 14:11; 2 Pet. 2:19. See PROFESS.

2. *proepangellō* (προεπαγγέλλω, 4279), in the middle voice, "to promise before" *pro*, and No. 1), occurs in Rom. 1:2; 2 Cor. 9:5. See AFOREPROMISED.

3. *homologeō* (ὁμολογέω, 3670), "to agree, confess," signifies "to promise" in Matt. 14:7. See CONFESS.

Note: For *exomologeō* in Luke 22:6, see CONSENT, No. 1.

PROOF

1. *dokimē* (δοκιμή, 1382): see EXPERIENCE, No. 2.

2. *dokimion* (δοκίμιον, 1383), "a test, a proof," is rendered "proof" in Jas. 1:3, RV (KJV, "trying"); it is regarded by some as equivalent to *dokimeion*, "a crucible, a test"; it is the neuter form of the adjective *dokimios*, used as a noun, which has been taken to denote the means by which a man is tested and "proved" (Mayor), in the same sense as *dokime* (No. 1) in 2 Cor. 8:2; the same phrase is used in 1 Pet. 1:7, RV, "the proof (of your faith)," KJV, "the trial"; where the meaning probably is "that which is approved [i.e., as genuine] in your faith"; this interpretation, which was suggested by Hort, and may hold good for Jas. 1:3, has been confirmed from the papyri by Deissmann (*Bible Studies*, p. 259ff.). Moulton and Milligan (*Vocab.*) give additional instances.

3. *endeixis* (ἔνδειξις, 1732): see DECLARE, B. Cf. the synonymous word *endeigma*, "a token," 2 Thess. 1:5, which refers rather to the thing "proved," while *endeixis* points to the act of "proving."

4. *tekmērion* (τεκμήριον, 5039), "a sure sign, a positive proof" (from *tekmar*, "a mark, sign"), occurs in Acts 1:3, RV, "proofs" (KJV, "infallible proofs"; a "proof" does not require to be described as infallible, the adjective is superfluous).

Note: For the KJV in 2 Tim. 4:5, "make full proof," RV, "fulfill" (*plerophoreo*), see FULFILL.

PROPHECY, PROPHESY, PROPHESYING

A. Noun.

propheteia (προφητεία, 4394) signifies "the speaking forth of the mind and counsel of God" (*pro*, "forth," *phēmi*, "to speak": see PROPHET); in the NT it is used (a) of the gift, e.g., Rom. 12:6; 1 Cor. 12:10; 13:2; (b) either of the exercise of the gift or of that which is "prophesied," e.g., Matt. 13:14; 1 Cor. 13:8; 14:6, 22 and 1 Thess. 5:20, "prophesying (s)"; 1 Tim. 1:18; 4:14; 2 Pet. 1:20, 21; Rev. 1:3; 11:6; 19:10; 22:7, 10, 18, 19.

"Though much of OT prophecy was purely predictive, see Micah 5:2, e.g., and cf. John 11:51, prophecy is not necessarily, nor even primarily, fore-telling. It is the declaration of that which cannot be known by natural means, Matt. 26:68, it is the forth-telling of the will of God, whether with reference to the past, the present, or the future, see Gen. 20:7; Deut. 18:18; Rev. 10:11; 11:3 ....

"In such passages as 1 Cor. 12:28; Eph. 2:20, the 'prophets' are placed after the 'Apostles,' since not the prophets of Israel are intended, but the 'gifts' of the ascended Lord, Eph. 4:8, 11; cf. Acts 13:1; ... ; the purpose of their ministry was to edify, to comfort, and to encourage the believers, 1 Cor. 14:3, while its effect upon unbelievers was to show that the secrets of a man's heart are known to God, to convict of sin, and to constrain to worship, vv. 24, 25.

"With the completion of the canon of Scripture prophecy apparently passed away, 1 Cor. 13:8, 9. In his measure the teacher has taken the place of the prophet, cf. the significant change in 2 Pet. 2:1. The difference is that, whereas the message of the prophet was a direct revelation of the mind of God for the occasion, the message of the teacher is gathered from the completed revelation contained in the Scriptures."

B. Adjective.

prophētikos (προφητικός, 4397), "of or relating to prophecy," or "proceeding from a prophet, prophetic," is used of the OT Scriptures, Rom. 16:26, "of the prophets," lit., "(by) prophetic (Scriptures)"; 2 Pet. 1:19, "the word of prophecy (*made more sure*)," i.e., confirmed by the person and work of Christ (KJV, "a more sure, etc."), lit., "the prophetic word."

C. Verb.

prophēteuo (προφητεύω, 4395), "to be a prophet, to prophesy," is used (a) with the primary meaning of telling forth the divine counsels, e.g., Matt. 7:22; 26:68; 1 Cor. 11:4, 5; 13:9; 14:1, 3-5, 24, 31, 39; Rev. 11:3; (b) of foretelling the future, e.g., Matt. 15:7; John 11:51; 1 Pet. 1:10; Jude 14.

PROPHET

1. *prophētēs* (προφήτης, 4396), "one who speaks forth or openly" (see PROPHECY, A), "a proclaimer of a divine message," denoted among the Greeks an interpreter of the oracles of the gods.

In the Sept. it is the translation of the word *rôeh*, "a seer"; 1 Sam. 9:9, indicating that the "prophet" was one who had immediate intercourse with God. It also translates the word *nābhî*, meaning "either one in whom the message from God springs forth" or "one to whom anything is secretly communicated." Hence, in general, "the prophet" was one upon whom the Spirit of God rested, Num. 11:17-29, one, to whom and through whom God speaks, Num. 12:2; Amos 3:7, 8. In the case of the OT prophets their messages were very largely the proclamation of the divine purposes of salvation and glory to be accomplished in the future; the "prophesying" of the NT "prophets" was both a preaching of the divine counsels of grace already accomplished and the foretelling of the purposes of God in the future.

In the NT the word is used (a) of "the OT prophets," e.g., Matt. 5:12; Mark 6:15; Luke 4:27; John 8:52; Rom. 11:3; (b) of "prophets in general," e.g., Matt. 10:41; 21:46; Mark 6:4; (c) of "John the Baptist," Matt. 21:26; Luke 1:76; (d) of "prophets in the churches," e.g., Acts 13:1; 15:32; 21:10; 1 Cor. 12:28, 29; 14:29, 32, 37; Eph. 2:20; 3:5; 4:11; (e) of "Christ, as the aforepromised Prophet," e.g., John 1:21; 6:14; 7:40; Acts 3:22; 7:37, or, without the article, and, without reference to the Old Testament, Mark 6:15; Luke 7:16; in Luke 24:19 it is used with *aner*, "a man"; John 4:19; 9:17; (f) of "two witnesses" yet to be raised up for special purposes, Rev. 11:10, 18; (g) of "the Cretan poet Epimenides," Titus 1:12; (h) by metonymy, of "the writings of prophets," e.g., Luke 24:27; Acts 8:28.

2. *pseudoprophētēs* (ψευδοπροφήτης, 5578), "a false prophet," is used of such (a) in OT times, Luke 6:26; 2 Pet. 2:1; (b) in the present period since Pentecost, Matt. 7:15; 24:11, 24; Mark 13:22; Acts 13:6; 1 John 4:1; (c) with reference to a false "prophet" destined to arise as the supporter of the "Beast" at the close of this age, Rev. 16:13; 19:20; 20:10 (himself described as "another beast," 13:11).

PROPHETESS

prophētis (προφῆτις, 4398), the feminine of *prophetes* (see above), is used of Anna, Luke 2:36; of the self-assumed title of "the woman Jezebel" in Rev. 2:20.

PROPITIATION

A. Verb.

hilaskomai (ἱλάσκομαι, 2433) was used amongst the Greeks with the significance "to make the gods propitious, to appease, propitiate," inasmuch as their good will was not conceived as their natural attitude, but something to be earned first. This use of the word is foreign to the Greek Bible, with respect to God whether in the Sept. or in the NT. It is never used of any act whereby man brings God into a favorable attitude or gracious disposition. It is God who is "propitiated" by the vindication of His holy and righteous character, whereby through the provision He has made in the vicarious and expiatory sacrifice of Christ, He has so dealt with sin that He can show mercy to the believing sinner in the removal of his guilt and the remission of his sins.

Thus in Luke 18:13 it signifies "to be propitious" or "merciful to" (with the person as the object of the verb), and in Heb. 2:17 "to expiate, to make propitiation for" (the object of the verb being sins); here the RV, "to make propitiation" is an important correction of the KJV "to make reconciliation." Through the "propitiatory" sacrifice of Christ, he who believes upon Him is by God's own act delivered from justly deserved wrath, and comes under the covenant of grace. Never is God said to be reconciled, a fact itself indicative that the enmity exists on man's part alone, and that it is man who needs to be reconciled to God, and not God to man. God is always the same and, since He is Himself immutable, His relative attitude does change towards those who change. He can act differently towards those who come to Him by faith, and solely on the ground of the "propitiatory" sacrifice of Christ, not because He has changed, but because He ever acts according to His unchanging righteousness.

The expiatory work of the Cross is therefore the means whereby the barrier which sin interposes between God and man is broken down. By the giving up of His sinless life sacrificially, Christ annuls the power of sin to separate between God and the believer.

In the OT the Hebrew verb *kaphar* is connected with *kopher*, "a covering" (see MERCY SEAT), and is used in connection with the burnt offering, e.g., Lev. 1:4; 14:20; 16:24, the guilt offering, e.g., Lev. 5:16, 18, the sin offering, e.g., Lev. 4:20, 26, 31, 35, the sin offering and burnt offering together, e.g., Lev. 5:10; 9:7, the meal offering and peace offering, e.g., Ezek. 45:15, 17, as well as in other respects. It is used of the ram offered at the consecration of the high priest, Ex. 29:33, and of the blood which God gave upon the altar to make "propitiation" for the souls of the people, and that because "the life of the flesh is in the blood," Lev. 17:11, and "it is the blood that maketh atonement by reason of the life" (RV). Man has forfeited his life on account of sin and God has provided the one and only way whereby eternal life could be bestowed, namely, by the voluntary laying down of His life by His Son, under divine retribution. Of this the former sacrifices appointed by God were foreshadowings.

B. Nouns.

1. *hilasterion* (ἱλαστήριον, 2435), akin to A, is regarded as the neuter of an adjective signifying "propitiatory." In the Sept. it is used adjectivally in connection with *epithēma*, "a cover," in Exod. 25:17 and 37:6, of the lid of the ark (see MERCY SEAT), but it is used as a noun (without *epithēma*), of locality, in Exod. 25:18, 19, 20, 21, 22; 31:7; 35:12; 37:7, 8, 9; Lev. 16:2, 13, 14, 15; Num. 7:89, and this is its use in Heb. 9:5.

Elsewhere in the NT it occurs in Rom. 3:25, where it is used of Christ Himself; the RV text and punctuation in this verse are important: "whom God set forth *to be* a propitiation, through faith, by His blood." The phrase "by His blood" is to be taken in immediate connection with "propitiation." Christ, through His expiatory death, is the personal means by whom God shows the mercy of His justifying grace to the sinner who believes. His "blood" stands for the voluntary giving up of His life, by the shedding of His blood in expiatory sacrifice under divine judgment righteously due to us as sinners, faith being the sole condition on man's part.

Note: "By metonymy, 'blood' is sometimes put for 'death,' inasmuch as, blood being essential to life, Lev. 17:11, when the blood is shed life is given up, that is, death takes place. The fundamental principle on which God deals with sinners is expressed in the words 'apart from shedding of blood,' i.e., unless a death takes place, 'there is no remission' of sins, Heb. 9:22.

"But whereas the essential of the type lay in the fact that blood was shed, the essential of the antitype lies in this, that the blood shed was that of Christ. Hence, in connection with Jewish sacrifices, 'the blood' is mentioned without reference to the victim from which it flowed, but in connection with the great antitypical sacrifice of the NT the words 'the blood' never stand alone; the One Who shed the blood is invariably specified, for it is the Person that gives value to the work; the saving efficacy of the Death depends entirely upon the fact that He Who died was the Son of God."

2. *hilasmos* (ἱλασμός, 2434), akin to *hileōs* ("merciful, propitious"), signifies "an expiation, a means whereby sin is covered and remitted." It is used in the NT of Christ Himself as "the propitiation," in 1 John 2:2 and 4:10, signifying that

He Himself, through the expiatory sacrifice of His death, is the personal means by whom God shows mercy to the sinner who believes on Christ as the One thus provided. In the former passage He is described as "the propitiation for our sins; and not for ours only, but also for the whole world." The italicized addition in the KJV, "*the sins of*," gives a wrong interpretation. What is indicated is that provision is made for the whole world, so that no one is, by divine predetermination, excluded from the scope of God's mercy; the efficacy of the "propitiation," however, is made actual for those who believe. In 4:10, the fact that God "sent His Son to be the propitiation for our sins," is shown to be the great expression of God's love toward man, and the reason why Christians should love one another. In the Sept., Lev. 25:9; Num. 5:8; 1 Chron. 28:20; Ps. 130:4; Ezek. 44:27; Amos 8:14.

PROSELYTE

prosēlutos (προσήλυτος, 4339), akin to *proserchomai*, "to come to," primarily signifies "one who has arrived, a stranger"; in the NT it is used of converts to Judaism, or foreign converts to the Jewish religion, Matt. 23:15; Acts 2:10; 6:5; 13:43. There seems to be no connection necessarily with Palestine, for in Acts 2:10 and 13:43 it is used of those who lived abroad. Cf. the Sept., e.g., in Exod. 22:21; 23:9; Deut. 10:19, of the "stranger" living among the children of Israel.

PROSPER

euodoō (εὐοδόω, 2137), "to help on one's way" (*eu*, "well," *hodos*, "a way or journey"), is used in the passive voice signifying "to have a prosperous journey," Rom. 1:10; metaphorically, "to prosper, be prospered," 1 Cor. 16:2, RV, "(as) he may prosper," KJV, "(as God) hath prospered (him)," lit., "in whatever he may be prospered," i.e., in material things; the continuous tense suggests the successive circumstances of varying prosperity as week follows week; in 3 John 2, of the "prosperity" of physical and spiritual health.

PROUD

huperēphanos (ὑπερήφανος, 5244) signifies "showing oneself above others, preeminent" (*huper*, "above," *phainomai*, "to appear, be manifest"); it is always used in Scripture in the bad sense of "arrogant, disdainful, proud," Luke 1:51; Rom. 1:30; 2 Tim. 3:2; Jas. 4:6; 1 Pet. 5:5.

Note: For the KJV renderings of the verb *tuphoo*, in 1 Tim. 3:6; 6:4; 2 Tim. 3:4, see HIGHMINDED.

PROVE

A. Verbs.

1. *dokimazō* (δοκιμάζω, 1381), "to test, prove," with the expectation of approving, is translated "to prove" in Luke 14:19; Rom. 12:2; 1 Cor. 3:13, RV (KJV, "shall try"); 11:28, RV (KJV, "examine"); 2 Cor. 8:8, 22; 13:5; Gal. 6:4; Eph. 5:10; 1 Thess. 2:4 (2nd part), RV (KJV, "trieth"); 5:21; 1 Tim. 3:10; in some mss., Heb. 3:9 (the most authentic have the noun *dokimasia*, "a proving"); 1 Pet. 1:7, RV (KJV, "tried"); 1 John 4:1, RV (KJV, "try").

2. *apodeiknumi* (ἀποδείκνυμι, 584), "to show forth," signifies "to prove" in Acts 25:7.

3. *paristēmi* (παρίστημι, 3936), "to present," signifies "to prove" in Acts 24:13. See COMMEND, No. 4.

4. *peirazō* (πειράζω, 3985), "to try," either in the sense of attempting, e.g., Acts 16:7, or of testing, is rendered "to prove" in John 6:6. See EXAMINE, TEMPT.

5. *sumbibazō* (συμβιβάζω, 4822), "to join together," signifies "to prove" in Acts 9:22. See COMPACTED, No. 2.

6. *sunistēmi* (συνίστημι, 4921) or *sunistanō* (συνιστάω, 4921), "to commend, to prove," is translated "I prove (myself a transgressor)" in Gal. 2:18 (KJV, "I make"). See COMMEND.

B. Noun.

peirasmos (πειρασμός, 3986), (a) "a trying, testing," (b) "a temptation," is used in sense (a) in 1 Pet. 4:12, with the preposition *pros*, "towards" or "with a view to," RV, "to prove" (KJV, "to try"), lit., "for a testing." See TEMPTATION.

Notes: (1) In Luke 10:36, RV, *ginomai*, "to become, come to be," is translated "proved (neighbor)," KJV, "was ..."; so in Heb. 2:2. (2) In Rom. 3:9, KJV, *proaitiaomai*, "to accuse beforehand," is translated "we have before proved" (marg., "charged").

For **PROVERB** see PARABLE, No. 2

PROVIDE, PROVIDENCE, PROVISION

A. Verbs.

1. *hetoimazō* (ἑτοιμάζω, 2090), "to prepare," is translated "hast provided" in Luke 12:20, KJV. See PREPARE.

2. *ktaomai* (κτάομαι, 2932), "to get, to gain," is rendered "provide" in Matt. 10:9. See POSSESS.

3. *paristēmi* (παρίστημι, 3936), "to present," signifies "to provide" in Acts 23:24. See COMMEND, PROVE, No. 3.

4. *problepō* (προβλέπω, 4265), "to foresee," is translated "having provided" in Heb. 11:40. See FORESEE.

5. *pronoeō* (προνοέω, 4306), "to take thought for, provide," is translated "provide ... for" in 1 Tim. 5:8; in Rom. 12:17 and 2 Cor. 8:21, RV, to take thought for (KJV, "to provide").

Note: In Luke 12:33, KJV, *poieō*, "to make" (RV), is translated "provide."

B. Noun.

pronoia (πρόνοια, 4307), "forethought" (*pro*, "before," *noeō*, "to think"), is translated "providence" in Acts 24:2; "provision" in Rom. 13:14.

PROVINCE

1. *eparcheia*, or *-ia* (ἐπαρχία, 1885) was a technical term for the administrative divisions of the Roman Empire. The original meaning was the district within which a magistrate, whether consul or pretor, exercised supreme authority. The word *provincia* acquired its later meaning when Sardinia and Sicily were added to the Roman territories, 227 B.C. On the establishment of the empire the proconsular power over all "provinces" was vested in the emperor. Two "provinces," Asia and Africa, were consular, i.e., held by ex-consuls; the rest were praetorian. Certain small "provinces," e.g. Judea and Cappadocia, were governed by procurators. They were usually districts recently added to the empire and not thoroughly Romanized. Judea was so governed in the intervals between the rule of native kings; ultimately it was incorporated in the "province" of Syria. The "province" mentioned in Acts 23:34 and 25:1 was assigned to the jurisdiction of an *eparchos*, "a prefect or governor" (cf. GOVERNOR). In the Sept., Esth. 4:11.

2. *kanōn* (κανών, 2583) originally denoted "a straight rod," used as a ruler or measuring instrument, or, in rare instances, "the beam of a balance," the secondary notion being either (a) of keeping anything straight, as of a rod used in weaving, or (b) of testing straightness, as a carpenter's rule; hence its metaphorical use to express what serves "to measure or determine" anything. By a common transition in the meaning of words, "that which measures," was used for "what was measured"; thus a certain space at Olympia was called a *kanon*. So in music, a canon is a composition in which a given melody is the model for the formation of all the parts. In general the word thus came to serve for anything regulating the actions of men, as a standard or principle. In Gal. 6:16, those who "walk by this rule (*kanōn*)" are those who make what is stated in vv. 14 and 15 their guiding line in the matter of salvation through faith in Christ alone, apart from works, whether following the principle themselves or teaching it to others. In 2 Cor. 10:13, 15, 16, it is translated "province," RV (KJV, "rule" and "line of things"; marg., "line"; RV marg., "limit" or "measuring rod.") Here it signifies the limits of the responsibility in gospel service as measured and appointed by God.

For **PROVING** (*elenchos*) see REPROOF, A

PROVOCATION, PROVOKE

A. Nouns.

1. *parapikrasmos* (παραπικρασμός, 3894), from *para*, "amiss" or "from," used intensively, and *pikrainō*, "to make bitter" (*pikros*, "sharp, bitter"), "provocation," occurs in Heb. 3:8, 15. In the Sept., Ps. 95:8.

2. *paroxusmos* (παροξυσμός, 3948) denotes "a stimulation" (Eng., "paroxysm"), (cf. B, No. 2): in Heb. 10:24, "to provoke," lit., "unto a stimulation (of love)." See CONTENTION, No. 2.

B. Verbs.

1. *parapikrainō* (παραπικραίνω, 3893), "to embitter, provoke" (akin to A, No. 1), occurs in Heb. 3:16.

2. *paroxunō* (παροξύνω, 3947), primarily, "to sharpen" (akin to A, No. 2), is used metaphorically, signifying "to rouse to anger, to provoke," in the passive voice, in Acts 17:16, RV, "was provoked" (KJV, "was stirred"); in 1 Cor. 13:5, RV, "is not provoked" (the word "easily" in KJV, represents no word in the original). See STIR.

3. *erethizō* (ἐρεθίζω, 2042), "to excite, stir up, provoke," is used (a) in a good sense in 2 Cor. 9:2, KJV, "hath provoked," RV, "hath stirred up;" (b) in an evil sense in Col. 3:21, "provoke." See STIR.

4. *parorgizō* (παροργίζω, 3949), "to provoke to wrath": see ANGER, B, No. 2.

5. *parazeloō* (παραζηλόω, 3863), "to provoke to jealousy": see JEALOUSY.

6. *apostomatizō* (ἀποστοματίζω, 653) in classical Greek meant "to speak from memory, to dictate to a pupil" (*apo*, "from," *stoma*, "a mouth"); in later Greek, "to catechize"; in Luke 11:53, "to provoke (Him) to speak."

7. *prokaleō* (προκαλέω, 4292), "to call forth," as to a contest, hence "to stir up what is evil in another," occurs in the middle voice in Gal. 5:26.

PRUDENCE, PRUDENT

A. Nouns.

1. *phronēsis* (φρόνησις, 5428), akin to *phroneō*, "to have understanding" (*phrēn*, "the mind"), denotes "practical wisdom, prudence in the management of affairs." It is translated "wisdom" in Luke 1:17; "prudence" in Eph. 1:8. See WISDOM.

2. *sunesis* (σύνεσις, 4907), "understanding," is rendered "prudence" in 1 Cor. 1:19, RV (KJV, "understanding"); it suggests quickness of apprehension, the penetrating consideration which precedes action. Cf. B, in the same verse. See KNOWLEDGE, UNDERSTANDING.

B. Adjective.

sunetos (συνετός, 4908) signifies "intelligent, sagacious, understanding" (akin to *suniemi*, "to perceive"), translated "prudent" in Matt. 11:25, KJV (RV, "understanding"); Luke 10:21 (ditto); Acts 13:7, RV, "(a man) of understanding"; in 1 Cor. 1:19, "prudent," RV and KJV. Cf. *asunetos*, "without understanding."

PSALM

psalmos (ψαλμός, 5568) primarily denoted "a striking or twitching with the fingers (on musical strings)"; then, "a sacred song, sung to musical accompaniment, a psalm." It is used (a) of the OT book of "Psalms," Luke 20:42; 24:44; Acts 1:20; (b) of a particular "psalm," Acts 13:33 (cf. v. 35); (c) of "psalms" in general, 1 Cor. 14:26; Eph. 5:19; Col. 3:16.

Note: For *psallō*, rendered "let him sing psalms" in Jas. 5:13, see MELODY, SING.

PUBLISH

1. *kērussō* (κηρύσσω, 2784), "to be a herald, to proclaim, preach," is translated "to publish" in Mark 1:45; 5:20; 7:36; 13:10, KJV (RV, "preached"); Luke 8:39. See PREACH, PROCLAIM.

2. *diapherō* (διαφέρω, 1308), "to bear through," is translated "was published" in Acts 13:49, KJV (RV, "was spread abroad"). See BETTER (be), No. 1.

3. *ginomai* (γίνομαι, 1096), "to become, come to be," is translated "was published" in Acts 10:37, lit., "came to be."

4. *diangellō* (διαγγέλλω, 1229), "to publish abroad," is so translated in Luke 9:60, RV (KJV, "preach"), and Rom. 9:17. See DECLARE, A, No. 3.

PUFF (up)

1. *phusioō* (φυσιόω, 5448), "to puff up, blow up, inflate" (from *phusa*, "bellows"), is used metaphorically in the NT, in the sense of being "puffed" up with pride, 1 Cor. 4:6, 18, 19; 5:2; 8:1; 13:4; Col. 2:18.

2. *tuphoō* (τυφόω, 5187) is always rendered "to puff up" in the RV. See HIGH-MINDED, PROUD.

PUNISH

1. *kolazō* (κολάζω, 2849) primarily denotes "to curtail, prune, dock" (from *kolos*, "docked"); then, "to check, restrain, punish"; it is used in the middle voice in Acts 4:21; passive voice in 2 Pet. 2:9, KJV, "to be punished" (RV, "under punishment," lit., "being punished"), a futurative present tense.

2. *timōreō* (τιμωρέω, 5097), primarily, "to help," then, "to avenge" (from *timē*, "value, honor," and *ouros*, "a guardian"), i.e., "to help" by redressing injuries, is used in the active voice in Acts 26:11, RV, "punishing" (KJV, "I punished"); passive voice in 22:5, lit., "(that) they may be punished." Cf. No. 5, below.

Note: For 2 Thess. 1:9, "shall suffer punishment," RV, see JUSTICE. See SUFFER, *Note* (10).

PUNISHMENT

1. *ekdikēsis* (ἐκδίκησις, 1557): for 1 Pet. 2:14, KJV, "punishment" (RV, "vengeance"), see AVENGE, B, No. 2.

2. *epitimia* (ἐπιτιμία, 2009) in the NT denotes "penalty, punishment," 2 Cor. 2:6. Originally it signified the enjoyment of the rights and privileges of citizenship; then it became used of the estimate (*timē*) fixed by a judge on the infringement of such rights, and hence, in general, a "penalty."

3. *kolasis* (κόλασις, 2851), akin to *kolazō* (PUNISH, No. 1), "punishment," is used in Matt. 25:46, "(eternal) punishment," and 1 John 4:18, "(fear hath) punishment," RV (KJV, "torment"), which there describes a process, not merely an effect; this kind of fear is expelled by perfect love; where God's love is being perfected in us, it gives no room for the fear of meeting with His reprobation; the "punishment" referred to is the immediate consequence of the sense of sin, not a holy awe but a slavish fear, the negation of the enjoyment of love.

4. *dikē* (δίκη, 1349), "justice," or "the execution of a sentence," is translated "punishment" in Jude 7, RV (KJV, "vengeance"). See JUSTICE.

5. *timōria* (τιμωρία, 5098), primarily "help" (see PUNISH, No. 2), denotes "vengeance, punishment," Heb. 10:29.

Note: The distinction, sometimes suggested, between No. 3 as being disciplinary, with special reference to the sufferer, and No. 5, as being penal, with reference to the satisfaction of him who inflicts it, cannot be maintained in the *Koinē* Greek of NT times.

PURE, PURENESS, PURITY

A. Adjectives.

1. *hagnos* (ἁγνός, 53), "pure from defilement, not contaminated" (from the same root as *hagios*, "holy"), is rendered "pure" in Phil. 4:8; 1 Tim. 5:22; Jas. 3:17; 1 John 3:3; see CHASTE.

2. *katharos* (καθαρός, 2513), "pure," as being cleansed, e.g., Matt. 5:8; 1 Tim. 1:5; 3:9; 2 Tim. 1:3; 2:22; Titus 1:15; Heb. 10:22; Jas. 1:27; 1 Pet. 1:22; Rev. 15:6; 21:18; 22:1 (in some mss.). See CHASTE, Note, CLEAN, A.

Note: In 1 Pet. 1:22 the KJV, "with a pure heart," follows those mss. which have this adjective (RV, "from the heart").

3. *eilikrinēs* (εἰλικρινής, 1506) signifies "unalloyed, pure"; (a) it was used of unmixed substances; (b) in the NT it is used of moral and ethical "purity," Phil. 1:10, "sincere"; so the RV in 2 Pet. 3:1 (KJV, "pure"). Some regard the etymological meaning as "tested by the sunlight" (Cremer). See CHASTE, Note, SINCERE.

Note: Wine mixed with water may be *hagnos*, "not being contaminated"; it is not *katharos*, when there is the admixture of any element even though the latter is "pure" in itself.

B. Nouns.

1. *hagnotes* (ἁγνότης, 54), the state of being *hagnos* (A, No. 1), occurs in 2 Cor. 6:6, "pureness"; 11:3, in the best mss., "(and the) purity," RV.

2. *hagneia* (ἁγνεία, 47), synonymous with No. 1, "purity," occurs in 1 Tim. 4:12; 5:2, where it denotes the chastity which excludes all impurity of spirit, manner, or act.

PURGE

1. *kathairō* (καθαίρω, 2508), akin to *katharos* (see PURE, A, No. 2), "to cleanse," is used of pruning, John 15:2, KJV, "purgeth" (RV, "cleanseth"). In the Sept., 2 Sam. 4:6; Isa. 28:27; Jer. 38:28.

2. *ekkathairō* (ἐκκαθαίρω, 1571), "to cleanse out, cleanse thoroughly," is said of "purging" out leaven, 1 Cor. 5:7; in 2 Tim. 2:21, of "purging" oneself from those who utter "profane babblings," vv. 16-18.

3. *diakathairō* (διακαθαίρω) (διά, 1223 and καθαίρω, 2508), "to cleanse thoroughly," is translated "will throughly purge" in Luke 3:17, KJV (RV, "thoroughly to cleanse"; less authentic mss. have No. 5).

4. *kathakizō* (καθαρίζω, 2511), "to cleanse, make clean," is translated "purging (all meats)," in Mark 7:19, KJV, RV, "making (all meats) clean"; Heb. 9:14, KJV, "purge" (RV, "cleanse"); so 9:22 (for v. 23, see PURIFY) and 10:2. See CLEAN, B, No. 1.

5. *diakatharizō* (διακαθαρίζω, 1245), "to cleanse thoroughly," is translated "will throughly purge" in Matt. 3:12, KJV. See CLEAN, B, No. 2. Cf. the synonymous verb No. 3.

Notes: (1) For Heb. 1:3, KJV, "had purged," see PURIFICATION. (2) For the KJV rendering of the noun *katharismos*, "cleansing," "that he was purged," see CLEAN, C, No. 1.

PURIFICATION, PURIFY, PURIFYING

A. Nouns.

1. *katharismos* (καθαρισμός, 2512) is rendered "a cleansing" (akin to No. 4, above), Mark 1:44; Luke 5:14; in Heb. 1:3, RV, "purification."

2. *katharotēs* (καθαρότης, 2514), "cleansing," Heb. 9:13. See CLEAN, C, No. 2.

3. *hagnismos* (ἁγνισμός, 49) denotes "a ceremonial purification," Acts 21:26, for the circumstances of which with reference to the vow of a Nazirite (RV), see Num. 6:9-13.

B. Verbs.

1. *hagnizō* (ἁγνίζω, 48), akin to *hagnos*, "pure" (see CHASTE), "to purify, cleanse from defilement," is used of "purifying" (a) ceremonially, John 11:55; Acts 21:24, 26 (cf. No. 3 above); 24:18; (b) morally, the heart, Jas. 4:8; the soul, 1 Pet. 1:22; oneself, 1 John 3:3.

2. *katharizō* (καθαρίζω, 2511), "to cleanse, make free from admixture," is translated "to purify" in Acts 15:9, KJV (RV, "cleansing"); Titus 2:14; Heb. 9:23, KJV (RV, "cleansed"). See CLEAN, B, No. 1.

PURSUE

diōkō (διώκω, 1377), "to put to flight, pursue, persecute," is rendered "to pursue" in 2 Cor. 4:9, RV (KJV, "persecute"), and is used metaphorically of "seeking eagerly" after peace in 1 Pet. 3:11, RV (KJV, "ensue").

Q

QUAKE

1. *entromos* (ἔντρομος, 1790), an adjective signifying "trembling with fear" (*en*, "in," *tremō*, "to tremble"), is used with *eimi*, "to be," in Heb. 12:21 (some mss. have *ektromos*, with the same meaning), "I quake," lit., "I am trembling." It is used with *ginomai*,"to become," in Acts 7:32, "trembled," lit., "became trembling," and 16:29, RV, "trembling for fear" (KJV, "came trembling). See TREMBLE.

2. *seiō* (σείω, 4579), "did quake," Matt. 27:51, and 28:4, RV (KJV, "did shake"). See TREMBLE.

For **QUARREL** see COMPLAINT, No. 2, Mark 6:19, RV

QUARTER

pantothen (παντόθεν, 3840), "from all sides," is translated "from every quarter" in Mark 1:45.

Notes: (1) In Rev. 20:8, KJV, *gōnia*, "an angle, corner," is rendered "quarter" (RV, "corner"). (2) In Acts 16:3, KJV, *topois*, "parts" (RV) is translated "quarters." (3) In Acts 9:32 the phrase *dia pantōn*, lit., "throughout all," is rendered "throughout all parts," RV (*meros*, "a part," being understood), KJV, "throughout all *quarters*." (4) For "quarters" in Acts 28:7, KJV, see NEIGHBORHOOD.

QUEEN

basilissa (βασίλισσα, 938), the feminine of *basileus*, "a king," is used (a) of the "Queen of Sheba," Matt. 12:42; Luke 11:31; of "Candace," Acts 8:27; (b) metaphorically, of "Babylon," Rev. 18:7.

QUENCH, UNQUENCHABLE

A. Verb.

sbennumi (σβέννυμι, 4570) is used (a) of "quenching" fire or things on fire, Matt. 12:20, quoted from Isa. 42:3, figurative of the condition of the feeble; Heb. 11:34; in the passive voice, Matt. 25:8, of torches (see LAMP), RV, "are going out," lit., "are being quenched"; of the retributive doom hereafter of sin unrepented of and unremitted in this life, Mark 9:48 (in some mss. in vv. 44, 46); (b) metaphorically, of "quenching" the fire-tipped darts of the evil one, Eph. 6:16; of "quenching" the Spirit, by hindering His operations in oral testimony in the church gatherings of believers, 1 Thess. 5:19. "The peace, order, and edification of the saints were evidence of the ministry of the Spirit among them, 1 Cor. 14:26, 32, 33, 40, but if, through ignorance of His ways, or through failure to recognize, or refusal to submit to, them, or through impatience with the ignorance or self-will of others, the Spirit were quenched, these happy results would be absent. For there was always the danger that the impulses of the flesh might usurp the place of the energy of the Spirit in the assembly, and the endeavor to restrain this evil by natural means would have the effect of hindering His ministry also. Apparently then, this injunction was intended to warn believers against the substitution of a mechanical order for the restraints of the Spirit." Cf. Song of Sol. 8:7.

B. Adjective.

asbestos (ἄσβεστος, 762), "not quenched" (*a*, negative, and A), is used of the doom of persons described figuratively as "chaff," Matt. 3:12 and Luke 3:17, "unquenchable"; of the fire of Gehenna (see HELL), Mark 9:43, RV, "unquenchable fire" (in some mss. v. 45). In the Sept., Job 20:26.

For **QUICK,** see DISCERN, C, LIVE, No. 3, *Note*

QUICKEN

1. *zōopoieō* (ζωοποιέω, 2227), "to make alive": see LIFE, C.

2. *zōogoneō* (ζωογονέω, 2225), "to endue with life, produce alive, preserve alive": see LIVE, No. 6.

3. *suzōopoieō* (συζωοποιέω, 4806) or *sunzōopoieō*, "to quicken together with, make alive with" (*sun*, "with" and No. 1), is used in Eph. 2:5; Col. 2:13, of the spiritual life with Christ, imparted to believers at their conversion.

QUIET, QUIETNESS

A. Adjectives.

1. *ēremos* (ἤρεμος, 2263), "quiet, tranquil," occurs in 1 Tim. 2:2, RV, "tranquil" (KJV, "quiet"); it indicates tranquillity arising from without.

2. *hēsuchios* (ἡσύχιος, 2272) has much the same meaning as No. 1, but indicates "tranquillity arising from within," causing no disturbance to others. It is translated "quiet" in 1 Tim. 2:2, RV (KJV, "peaceable"); "quiet" in 1 Pet. 3:4, where it is associated with "meek," and is to characterize the spirit or disposition. See PEACEABLE.

B. Verbs.

1. *hēsuchazō* (ἡσυχάζω, 2270), akin to A, No. 2, "to be still, to live quietly."

2. *katastellō* (καταστέλλω, 2687) denotes to quiet: see APPEASE.

C. Nouns.

1. *eirēnē* (εἰρήνη, 1515), "peace," is translated "quietness" in Acts 24:2, KJV (RV, "peace"). See PEACE (e).

2. *hēsuchia* (ἡσυχία, 2271), akin to A, No. 2, and B. No. 1, denotes "quietness," 2 Thess. 3:12; it is so translated in the RV of 1 Tim. 2:11, 12 (KJV, "silence"); in Acts 22:2, RV, "(they were the more) quiet," KJV, "(they kept the more) silence," lit., "they kept quietness the more."

R

RABBI

rabbei (ῥαββεί) or *rabbi* (ῥαββί, 4461), from a word rab, primarily denoting "master" in contrast to a slave; this with the added pronominal suffix signified "my master" and was a title of respect by which teachers were addressed. The suffix soon lost its specific force, and in the NT the word is used as courteous title of address. It is applied to Christ in Matt. 26:25, 49; Mark 9:5; 11:21; 14:45; John 1:38 (where it is interpreted as *didaskalos*, "master," marg., "teacher" (see also "Rabboni" in John 20:16); v. 49; 3:2; 4:31; 6:25; 9:2; 11:8; to John the Baptist in John 3:26. In Matt. 23:7, 8 Christ forbids his disciples to covet or use it. In the latter verse it is again explained as *didaskalos*, "master" (some mss. have *kathegetes*, "a guide").

RABBONI

rabbounei (ῥαββουνεί, 4462) or *rabboni* (ῥαββονί, 4462), formed in a similar way to the above, was an Aramaic form of a title almost entirely applied to the president of the Sanhedrin, if such was a descendant of Hillel. It was even more respectful than Rabbi, and signified "My great master"; in its use in the NT the pronominal force of the suffix is apparently retained (contrast Rabbi above); it is found in Mark 10:51 in the best texts, RV, "Rabboni" (KJV, "Lord"), addressed to Christ by blind Bartimaeus, and in John 20:16 by Mary Magdalene, where it is interpreted by *didaskalos*, "Master" (marg., "Teacher").

For **RABBLE** see COURT, No. 1

RACA

raka (ῥακά, 4469) is an Aramaic word akin to the Heb. *rêq*, "empty," the first *a* being due to a Galilean change. In the KJV of 1611 it was spelled *racha*; in the edition of 1638, *raca*. It was a word of utter contempt, signifying "empty," intellectually rather than morally, "empty-headed," like Abimelech's hirelings, Judg. 9:4, and the "vain" man of Jas. 2:20. As condemned by Christ, Matt. 5:22, it was worse than being angry, inasmuch as an outrageous utterance is worse than a feeling unexpressed or somewhat controlled in expression; it does not indicate such a loss of self-control as the word rendered "fool," a godless, moral reprobate.

For **RACE (kindred)** see KIND

RACE (contest)

1. *agōn* (ἀγών, 73) is translated "race" in Heb. 12:1, one of the modes of athletic contest, this being the secondary meaning of the word. See CONFLICT.

2. *stadion* (στάδιον, 4712), "a stadium," denotes a "racecourse," 1 Cor. 9:24. The stadium (about 600 Greek feet or 1/8 of a Roman mile) was the length of the Olympic course.

Note: No. 1 signifies the "race" itself; No. 2 the "course."

RAGE, RAGING

A. Verb.

phruassō (φρυάσσω, 5433) was primarily used of "the snorting, neighing and prancing of horses"; hence, metaphorically, of "the haughtiness and insolence of men," Acts 4:25. In the Sept., Ps. 2:1.

B. Noun.

kludōn (κλύδων, 2830), "a billow, surge" (akin to *kluzō*, "to wash over," said of the sea; cf. *kludonizomai*, "to be tossed by the waves," Eph. 4:14), is translated "raging" in Luke 8:24; in Jas. 1:6, RV, "surge" (KJV, "wave").

Note: In Jude 13, KJV, the adjective *agrios*, "wild," is translated "raging" (RV, "wild").

RAIL, RAILER, RAILING

A. Verb.

blasphēmeō (βλασφημέω, 987), "to blaspheme, rail, revile" (for the meanings of which see BLASPHEME), is translated "to rail at, or on," in Matt. 27:39, RV (KJV, "reviled"); Mark 15:29; Luke 23:39; 2 Pet. 2:10, RV (KJV, "to speak evil of"); 2:12, RV (KJV, "speak evil of"). Cf. *loidoreo*, "to revile" (see REVILE), and B, No. 2 and C, No. 2.

B. Nouns.

1. *blasphēmia* (βλασφημία, 988) is translated "railings" in Matt. 15:19, RV; 1 Tim. 6:4, KJV and RV; "railing" in Mark 7:22, RV; Col. 3:8, RV; Jude 9, KJV and RV, lit., "judgment of railing"; in Eph. 4:31, RV (KJV, "evil speaking"). See BLASPHEMY.

2. *loidoria* (λοιδορία, 3059), "abuse, railing, reviling," is rendered "reviling" in the RV, 1 Pet. 3:9 (twice); in 1 Tim. 5:14, KJV marg., "for their reviling." See REVILE, C.

C. Adjectives.

1. *blasphēmos* (βλάσφημος, 989), akin to A, and B, No. 1; see BLASPHEME, C.

2. *loidoros* (λοίδορος, 3060), an adjective denoting "reviling, railing" (akin to B, No. 2), is used as a noun, "a railer," 1 Cor. 5:11. See REVILE.

RAIMENT

Note: For *himation*, rendered "raiment" in Matt. 17:2, KJV (RV, "garments"), so Matt. 27:31; Mark 9:3; Luke 23:34; John 19:24; Acts 22:20; Rev. 3:5, 18; 4:4; KJV and RV, Acts 18:6, see CLOTHING, No. 2. *Himatismos* is rendered "raiment" in Luke 9:29; *enduma* in Matt. 3:4; 6:25, 28; 28:3 and Luke 12:23.

RAINBOW

iris (ἶρις, 2463), whence Eng., "iris," the flower, describes the "rainbow" seen in the heavenly vision, "round about the throne, like an emerald to look upon," Rev. 4:3, emblematic of the fact that, in the exercise of God's absolute sovereignty and perfect counsels, He will remember His covenant concerning the earth (Gen. 9:9-17); in Rev. 10:1, "the rainbow," RV, the definite article suggests a connection with the scene in 4:3; here it rests upon the head of an angel who declares that "there shall be delay no longer" (v. 6, RV marg., the actual meaning); the mercy to be shown to the earth must be preceded by the execution of divine judgments upon the nations who defy God and His Christ. Cf. Ezek. 1:28.

RANSOM

1. *lutron* (λύτρον, 3083), lit., "a means of loosing" (from *luo*, "to loose"), occurs frequently in the Sept., where it is always used to signify "equivalence." Thus it is used of the "ransom" for a life, e.g., Exod. 21:30, of the redemption price of a slave, e.g., Lev. 19:20, of land, 25:24, of the price of a captive, Isa. 45:13. In the NT it occurs in Matt. 20:28 and Mark 10:45, where it is used of Christ's gift of Himself as "a ransom for many." Some interpreters have regarded the "ransom" price as being paid to Satan; others, to an impersonal power such as death, or evil, or "that ultimate necessity which has made the whole course of things what it has been." Such ideas are largely conjectural, the result of an attempt to press the details of certain Old Testament illustrations beyond the actual statements of New Testament doctrines.

That Christ gave up His life in expiatory sacrifice under God's judgment upon sin and thus provided a "ransom" whereby those who receive Him on this ground obtain deliverance from the penalty due to sin, is what Scripture teaches. What the Lord states in the two passages mentioned involves this essential character of His death. In these passages the preposition is *anti*, which has a vicarious significance, indicating that the "ransom" holds good for those who, accepting it as such, no longer remain in death since Christ suffered death in their stead. The change of preposition in 1 Tim. 2:6, where the word *antilutron*, a substitutionary "ransom," is used, is significant. There the preposition is *huper*, "on behalf of," and the statement is made that He "gave Himself a ransom for all," indicating that the "ransom" was provisionally universal, while being of a vicarious character. Thus the three passages consistently show that while the provision was universal, for Christ died for all men, yet it is actual for those only who accept God's conditions, and who are described in the Gospel statements as "the many." The giving of His life was the giving of His entire person, and while His death under divine judgment was alone expiatory, it cannot be dissociated from the character of His life which, being sinless, gave virtue to His death and was a testimony to the fact that His death must be of a vicarious nature.

2. *antilutron* (ἀντίλυτρον, 487), 1 Tim. 2:6. See under No 1.

For **RASH, RASHLY** see HEADSTRONG

RAVEN

korax (κόραξ, 2876), "a raven" (perhaps onomatopoeic, representing the sound), occurs in the plural in Luke 12:24. The Heb. *oreb* and the Arabic *ghurab* are from roots meaning "to be black"; the Arabic root also has the idea of leaving home. Hence the evil omen attached to the bird. It is the first bird mentioned in the Bible, Gen. 8:7. Christ used the "ravens" to illustrate and enforce the lesson of God's provision and care.

RAVENING

A. Adjective.

harpax (ἅρπαξ, 727), an adjective signifying "rapacious," is translated "ravening" (of wolves) in Matt. 7:15: see EXTORT, C.

B. Noun.

harpagē (ἁρπαγή, 724) is translated "ravening in Luke 11:39, KJV: see EXTORT, B, No. 1.

READ, READING

A. Verb.

anaginōskō (ἀναγινώσκω, 314), primarily, "to know certainly, to know again, recognize" (*ana*, "again," *ginōskō*, "to know"), is used of "reading" written characters, e.g., Matt. 12:3, 5; 21:16; 24:15; of the private "reading" of Scripture, Acts 8:28, 30, 32; of the public "reading" of Scripture, Luke 4:16; Acts 13:27; 15:21; 2 Cor. 3:15; Col. 4:16 (thrice); 1 Thess. 5:27; Rev. 1:3. In 2 Cor. 1:13 there is a purposive play upon words; firstly, "we write none other things unto you, than what ye read (*anaginōskō*)" signifies that there is no hidden or mysterious meaning in his epistles; whatever doubts may have arisen and been expressed in this respect, he means what he says; then follows the similar verb *epiginōskō*, "to acknowledge," "or even acknowledge, and I hope ye will acknowledge unto the end." The *paronomasia* can hardly be reproduced in English. Similarly, in 3:2 the verb *ginōskō*, "to know," and *anaginosko*, "to read," are put in that order, and metaphorically applied to the church at Corinth as being an epistle, a message to the world, written by the apostle and his fellow missionaries, through their ministry of the gospel and the consequent change in the lives of the converts, an epistle "known and read of all men." For other instances of *paronomasia* see, e.g., Rom. 12:3, *phroneō, huperphroneō, sōphroneō;* 1 Cor. 2:13, 14, *sunkrinō, anakrinō;* 2 Thess. 3:11, *ergazomai*, and *periergazomai;* 1 Cor. 7:31, *chraomai* and *katachraomai;* 11:31, *diakrinō* and *krinō;* 12:2, *agō* and *apagō;* Phil. 3:2, 3, *katatomē* and *peritomē.*

B. Noun.

anagnōsis (ἀνάγνωσις, 320) in nonbiblical Greek denoted "recognition" or "a survey" (the latter found in the papyri); then, "reading"; in the NT the public "reading" of Scripture, Acts 13:15; 2 Cor. 3:14; 1 Tim. 4:13, where the context makes clear that the reference is to the care required in reading the Scriptures to a company, a duty ever requiring the exhortation "take heed." Later, readers in churches were called *anagnōstai*. In the Sept, Neh. 8:8.

READINESS

1. *prothumia* (προθυμία, 4288), "eagerness, willingness, readiness" (*pro*, "forward," *thumos*, "mind, disposition," akin to *prothumos*, READY, A, No. 2), is translated "readiness of mind" in Acts 17:11, "readiness" in 2 Cor. 8:11; in v. 12, RV (KJV, "a willing mind"); in v. 19, RV "(our) readiness," KJV, "(your) ready mind"; in 9:2, RV, "readiness" (KJV, "forwardness of . . . mind."

2. *hetoimos* (ἕτοιμος, 2092), an adjective, is used with *echō*, "to have," and *en*, "in," idiomatically, as a noun in 2 Cor. 10:6, RV, "being in readiness" (KJV, "having in readiness"), of the apostle's aim for the church to be obedient to Christ.

REASON (Noun)

logos (λόγος, 3056), "a word," etc., has also the significance of "the inward thought itself, a reckoning, a regard, a reason," translated "reason" in Acts 18:14, in the phrase "reason would," *kata logon*, lit., "according to reason (I would bear with you)"; in 1 Pet. 3:15, "a reason (concerning the hope that is in you)." See WORD.

Note: In Acts 6:2, KJV, the adjective *arestos*, "pleasing, agreeable," is translated "reason" (RV, "fit," marg., "pleasing"). See FIT, No. 2.

REASON (Verb)

1. *dialogizomai* (διαλογίζομαι, 1260), "to bring together different reasons and reckon them up, to reason," is used in the NT (a) chiefly of thoughts and considerations which are more or less objectionable, e.g., of the disciples who "reasoned" together, through a mistaken view of Christ's teaching regarding leaven, Matt. 16:7, 8 and Mark 8:16, 17; of their "reasoning" as to who was the greatest among them, Mark 9:33, RV, "were ye reasoning," KJV, "ye disputed"; of the scribes and Pharisees in criticizing Christ's claim to forgive sins, Mark 2:6, 8 (twice) and Luke 5:21, 22; of the chief priests and elders in considering how to answer Christ's question regarding John's baptism, Matt. 21:25; Mark 11:31 (some mss. have *logizomai*, here, which is nowhere else rendered "to reason"); of the wicked husbandmen, and their purpose to murder the heir and seize his inheritance, Luke 20:14; of the rich man who "reasoned" within himself, RV (KJV, "thought"), as to where to bestow his fruits, Luke 12:17 (some mss. have it in John 11:50, the best have *logizomai*; (b) of considerations not objectionable, Luke 1:29, "cast in (her) mind"; 3:15, RV, and KJV, marg., "reasoned" (KJV, "mused").

2. *dialegomai* (διαλέγομαι, 1256), "to think different things with oneself, to ponder," then, "to dispute with others," is translated "to reason in Acts 17:2, KJV and RV; 17:17, RV; 18:4, 19, KJV and RV; 19:8, 9, RV; 24:25, KJV and RV; Heb. 12:5, RV, "reasoneth (with you)," KJV, "speaketh (unto you).

3. *sullogizomai* (συλλογίζομαι, 4817), "to compute" (*sun*, "with," and *logizomai*, cf. Eng., "syllogism"), also denotes "to reason," and is so rendered in Luke 20:5.

4. *suzēteō* (συζητέω, 4802), "to seek or examine together" (*sun*, "with," *zēteō*, "to seek"), "to discuss," is translated "reasoning" in Mark 12:28, KJV (RV, "questioning"); similarly in Luke 24:15.

REASONABLE

logikos (λογικός, 3050), pertaining to "the reasoning faculty, reasonable, rational," is used in Rom. 12:1, of the service (*latreia*) to be rendered by believers in presenting their bodies "a living sacrifice, holy, acceptable to God." The sacrifice is to be intelligent, in contrast to those offered by ritual and compulsion; the presentation is to be in accordance with the spiritual intelligence of those who are new creatures in Christ and are mindful of "the mercies of God." For the significance of the word in 1 Pet. 2:2, see under MILK.

REASONING

dialogismos (ἀΐδιος, 126), "a thought, reasoning, inward questioning" [akin to *dializomai*, see REASON (Verb), No. 1], is translated "reasoning" or "reasonings" in Luke 5:22, RV (KJV, "thoughts"); 9:46; v. 47, RV (KJV, "thoughts"); 24:38

(KJV, "thoughts"); Rom. 1:21 (KJV, "imaginations"); 1 Cor. 3:20 (KJV, "thoughts").

Note: In those mss. which contain Acts 28:29, occurs *suzētēsis*, "a disputation," which is translated "reasoning" (KJV).

REBUKE (Verb and Noun)

A. Verbs.

1. *epitimaō* (ἐπιτιμάω, 2008), primarily, "to put honor upon," then, "to adjudge," hence signifies "to rebuke." Except for 2 Tim. 4:2 and Jude 9, it is confined in the NT to the Synoptic Gospels, where it is frequently used of the Lord's rebukes to (a) evil spirits, e.g., Matt. 17:18; Mark 1:25; 9:25; Luke 4:35, 41; 9:42; (b) winds, Matt. 8:26; Mark 4:39; Luke 8:24; (c) fever, Luke 4:39; (d) disciples, Mark 8:33; Luke 9:55; contrast Luke 19:39. For rebukes by others see Matt. 16:22; 19:13; 20:31; Mark 8:32; 10:13; 10:48, RV, "rebuked" (KJV, "charged"); Luke 17:3; 18:15, 39; 23:40.

2. *elenchō* (ἐλέγχω, 1651), "to convict, refute, reprove," is translated "to rebuke" in the KJV of the following (the RV always has the verb "to reprove"): 1 Tim. 5:20; Titus 1:13; 2:15; Heb. 12:5; Rev. 3:19. See CONVICT, No. 1.

Note: While *epitimaō* signifies simply "a rebuke" which may be either undeserved, Matt. 16:22, or ineffectual, Luke 23:40, *elenchō* implies a "rebuke" which carries conviction.

3. *epiplēssō* (ἐπιπλήσσω, 1969), "to strike at" (*epi*, "upon" or "at," *plēssō*, "to strike, smite"), hence, "to rebuke," is used in the injunction against "rebuking" an elder, 1 Tim. 5:1.

Note: In Phil. 2:15, the best texts have *amōmos*, "without blemish" (*a*, negative, *mōmos*, "a blemish, a moral disgrace"), RV, "without blemish"; some mss. have *amōmētos* (*a*, negative, and *mōmaomai*, "to blame"), KJV, "without rebuke." Contrast *amemptos* in the same verse, "blameless on account of absence of inconsistency" or "ground of reproof," whereas *amōmos* indicates "absence of stain or blemish." We may have blemish, with freedom from blame.

B. Noun.

elenxis (ἔλεγξις, 1649), akin to A, No. 2, denotes "rebuke"; in 2 Pet. 2:16, it is used with *echō*, "to have," and translated "he was rebuked," lit., "he had rebuke." In the Sept., Job 21:4, "reproof"; 23:2, "pleading."

For **RECEIPT** see CUSTOM (Toll), No. 2

RECKON, RECKONING

1. *logizomai* (λογίζομαι, 3049) is properly used (a) of "numerical calculation," e.g., Luke 22:37; (b) metaphorically, "by a reckoning of characteristics or reasons, to take into account," Rom. 2:26, "shall … be reckoned," RV (KJV, "counted"), of "reckoning" uncircumcision for circumcision by God's estimate in contrast to that of the Jew regarding his own condition (v. 3); in 4:3, 5, 6, 9, 11, 22, 23, 24, of "reckoning" faith for righteousness, or "reckoning" righteousness to persons, in all of which the RV uses the verb "to reckon" instead of the KJV "to count or to impute"; in v. 4 the subject is treated by way of contrast between grace and debt, which latter involves the "reckoning" of a reward for works; what is owed as a debt cannot be "reckoned" as a favor, but the faith of Abraham and his spiritual children sets them outside the category of those who seek to be justified by self-effort, and, *vice versa*, the latter are excluded from the grace of righteousness bestowed on the sole condition of faith; so in Gal. 3:6 (RV, "was reckoned," KJV, "was accounted"); since Abraham, like all the natural descendants of Adam, was a sinner, he was destitute of righteousness in the sight of God; if, then, his relationship with God was to be rectified (i.e., if he was to be justified before God), the rectification could not be brought about by works of merit on his part; in Jas. 2:23, RV, "reckoned," the subject is viewed from a different standpoint (see under JUSTIFICATION, B, last four paragraphs); for other instances of "reckoning" in this respect see Rom. 9:8, RV, "are reckoned" (KJV, "are counted"); 2 Cor. 5:19, RV, "(not) reckoning (trespasses)," KJV, "imputing"; (c) "to consider, calculate," translated "to reckon" in Rom. 6:11; 8:36; 2 Cor. 10:11, RV, "let (such a one) reckon (this)"; (d) "to suppose, judge, deem," translated "to reckon" in Rom. 2:3, "reckonest thou (this)," RV (KJV, "thinkest"); 3:28 (KJV, "we conclude"); 8:18; 2 Cor. 11:5 (KJV, "I suppose); see COUNT, No. 3; (e) "to purpose, decide," 2 Cor. 10:2, RV, "count" (KJV, "think); see COUNT, No. 3.

2. *legō* (λέγω, 3004), "to say, speak," also has the meaning "to gather, reckon, account," used in this sense in Heb. 7:11, RV, "be reckoned" (KJV, "be called").

3. *sunairō* (συναίρω, 4868), "to take up together" (*sun*, "with," *airō*, "to take"), is used with the noun *logos*, "an account," signifying "to settle accounts," Matt. 18:23, RV, "make a reckoning" (KJV, "take account"); v. 24, KJV and RV, "to reckon" (*logos* being understood); 25:19, RV, "maketh a reckoning" (KJV, "reckoneth"). This phrase occurs not infrequently in the papyri in the sense of settling accounts (see Deissmann, *Light from the Ancient East*, 118). In the Sept. the verb occurs in its literal sense in Exod. 23:5, "thou shalt help to raise" (lit., "raise with").

RECLINE

anakeimai (ἀνακεῖμαι, 345), lit., and in classical usage, "to be laid up, laid," denotes, in the NT, "to recline at table"; it is translated "reclining" in John 13:23, RV (KJV, "leaning"); cf. *anapiptō* in v. 25, RV, "leaning back." See also v. 12, marg. See TABLE (AT THE).

For **RECOMMEND,** Acts 14:26; 15:40, KJV, see COMMEND, No. 2

RECONCILE, RECONCILIATION

A. Verbs.

1. *katallassō* (καταλλάσσω, 2644) properly denotes "to change, exchange" (especially of money); hence, of persons, "to change from enmity to friendship, to reconcile." With regard to the relationship between God and man, the use of this and connected words shows that primarily "reconciliation" is what God accomplishes, exercising His grace towards sinful man on the ground of the death of Christ in propitiatory sacrifice under the judgment due to sin, 2 Cor. 5:19, where both the verb and the noun are used (cf. No. 2, in Col. 1:21). By reason of this men in their sinful condition and alienation from God are invited to be "reconciled" to Him; that is to say, to change their attitude, and accept the provision God has made, whereby their sins can be remitted and they themselves be justified in His sight in Christ.

Rom. 5:10 expresses this in another way: "For if, while we were enemies, we were reconciled to God through the death of His Son ..."; that we were "enemies" not only expresses man's hostile attitude to God but signifies that until this change of attitude takes place men are under condemnation, exposed to God's wrath. The death of His Son is the means of the removal of this, and thus we "receive the reconciliation," v. 11, RV. This stresses the attitude of God's favor toward us. The KJV rendering "atonement" is incorrect. Atonement is the offering itself of Christ under divine judgment upon sin. We do not receive atonement. What we do receive is the result, namely, "reconciliation."

The removal of God's wrath does not contravene His immutability. He always acts according to His unchanging righteousness and lovingkindness, and it is because He changes not that His relative attitude does change towards those who change. All His acts show that He is Light and Love. Anger, where there is no personal element, is a sign of moral health if, and if only, it is accompanied by grief. There can be truest love along with righteous indignation, Mark 3:5, but love and enmity cannot exist together. It is important to distinguish "wrath" and "hostility." The change in God's relative attitude toward those who receive the "reconciliation" only proves His real unchangeableness. Not once is God said to be "reconciled." The enmity is alone on our part. It was we who needed to be "reconciled" to God, not God to us, and it is propitiation, which His righteousness and mercy have provided, that makes the "reconciliation" possible to those who receive it.

When the writers of the NT speak upon the subject of the wrath of God, "the hostility is represented not as on the part of God, but of man. And this is the reason why the apostle never uses *diallassō* [a word used only in Matt. 5:24, in the NT] in this connection, but always *katallassō*, because the former word denotes mutual concession after mutual hostility [frequently exemplified in the Sept.], an idea absent from *katallassō*" (Lightfoot, *Notes on the Epistles of Paul*, p. 288).

The subject finds its great unfolding in 2 Cor. 5:18-20, which states that God "reconciled us (believers) to Himself through Christ," and that "the ministry of reconciliation" consists in this, "that God was in Christ reconciling the world unto Himself." The insertion of a comma in the KJV after the word "Christ" is misleading; the doctrine stated here is not that God was in Christ (the unity of the Godhead is not here in view), but that what God has done in the matter of reconciliation He has done in Christ, and this is based upon the fact that "Him who knew no sin He made to be sin on our behalf; that we might become the righteousness of God in Him." On this ground the command to men is "be ye reconciled to God."

The verb is used elsewhere in 1 Cor. 7:11, of a woman returning to her husband.

2. *apokatallssō* (ἀποκαταλλάσσω, 604), "to reconcile completely" (*apo*, from, and No. 1), a stronger form of No. 1, "to change from one condition to another," so as to remove all enmity and leave no impediment to unity and peace, is used in Eph. 2:16, of the "reconciliation" of believing Jew and Gentile "in one body unto God through the Cross"; in Col. 1:21 not the union of Jew and Gentile is in view, but the change wrought in the individual believer from alienation and enmity, on account of evil works, to "reconciliation" with God; in v. 20 the word is used of the divine purpose to "reconcile" through Christ "all things unto Himself... whether things upon the earth, or things in the heavens," the basis of the change being the peace effected "through the blood of His Cross." It is the divine purpose, on the ground of the work of Christ accomplished on the cross, to bring the whole universe, except rebellious angels and unbelieving man, into full accord with the mind of God, Eph. 1:10. Things "under the earth," Phil. 2:10, are subdued, not "reconciled."

3. *diallassō* (διαλλάσσω, 1259), "to effect an alteration, to exchange," and hence, "to reconcile," in cases of mutual hostility yielding to mutual concession, and thus differing from No. 1 (under which see Lightfoot's remarks), is used in the passive voice in Matt. 5:24, which illustrates the point. There is no such idea as "making it up" where God and man are concerned.

B. Noun.

katallagē (καταλλαγή, 2643), akin to A, No. 1, primarily "an exchange," denotes "reconciliation," a change on the part of one party, induced by an action on the part of another; in the NT, the "reconciliation" of men to God by His grace and love in Christ. The word is used in Rom. 5:11 and 11:15. The occasioning cause of the world-wide proclamation of "reconciliation" through the gospel, was the casting away (partially and temporarily) of Israel. A new relationship Godward is offered to the Gentiles in the gospel. The word also occurs in 2 Cor. 5:18, 19, where "the ministry of reconciliation" and "the word of reconciliation" are not the ministry of teaching the doctrine of expiation, but that of beseeching men to be "reconciled" to God on the ground of what God has wrought in Christ. See No. 1, above.

Note: In the OT in some passages the KJV incorrectly has "reconciliation," the RV rightly changes the translation to "atonement," e.g., Lev. 8:15; Ezek. 45:20, RV, "make atonement for" (KJV, "reconcile").

For **RECONCILIATION (MAKE),** Heb. 2:17, KJV, see PROPITIATION

For **RECORD** (KJV) see TESTIFY, No. 3, TESTIMONY, No. 2

RECOVER

1. *sōzō* (σώζω, 4982), "to save," is sometimes used of "healing" or "restoration to health," the latter in John 11:12, RV, "he will recover," marg., "be saved" (KJV, "he shall do well"). See HEAL, PRESERVE, SAVE, WHOLE

2. *anansephō* (ἀνανήφω, 366), "to return to soberness," as from a state of delirium or drunkenness (*ana,* "back," or "again," *nēphō,* "to be sober, to be wary"), is used in 2 Tim. 2:26, "may recover themselves" (RV marg., "return to soberness," KJV marg., "awake"), said of those who, opposing the truth through accepting perversions of it, fall into the snare of the Devil, becoming intoxicated with error; for these "recovery" is possible only by "repentance unto the knowledge of the truth."

Notes: (1) For "recovering of sight," Luke 4:18, see SIGHT. (2) In Mark 16:18, the phrase *echō kalōs,* lit., "to have well," i.e., "to be well," is rendered "they shall recover."

REDEEM, REDEMPTION

A. Verbs.

1. *exagorazō* (ἐξαγοράζω, 1805), a strengthened form of *agorazō,* "to buy" (see BUY, No. 1), denotes "to buy out" (*ex* for *ek*), especially of purchasing a slave with a view to his freedom. It is used metaphorically (a) in Gal. 3:13 and 4:5, of the deliverance by Christ of Christian Jews from the Law and its curse; what is said of *lutron* (RANSOM, No. 1) is true of this verb and of *agorazō,* as to the death of Christ, that Scripture does not say to whom the price was paid; the various suggestions made are purely speculative; (b) in the middle voice, "to buy up for oneself," Eph. 5:16 and Col. 4:5, of "buying up the opportunity" (RV marg.; text, "redeeming the time," where "time" is *kairos,* "a season," a time in which something is seasonable), i.e., making the most of every opportunity, turning each to the best advantage since none can be recalled if missed.

Note: In Rev. 5:9; 14:3, 4, KJV, *agorazō,* "to purchase" (RV) is translated "redeemed."

2. *lutroō* (λυτρόω, 3084), "to release on receipt of ransom" (akin to *lutron,* "a ransom"), is used in the middle voice, signifying "to release by paying a ransom price, to redeem" (a) in the natural sense of delivering, Luke 24:21, of setting Israel free from the Roman yoke; (b) in a spiritual sense, Titus 2:14, of the work of Christ in "redeeming" men "from all iniquity" (*anomia,* "lawlessness," the bondage of self-will which rejects the will of God); 1 Pet. 1:18 (passive voice), "ye were redeemed," from a vain manner of life, i.e., from bondage to tradition. In both instances the death of Christ is stated as the means of "redemption."

Note: While both No. 1 and No. 2 are translated "to redeem," *exagorazō* does not signify the actual "redemption," but the price paid with a view to it, *lutroō* signifies the actual "deliverance," the setting at liberty.

B. Nouns.

1. *lutrōsis* (λύτρωσις, 3085), "a redemption" (akin to A, No. 2), is used (a) in the general sense of "deliverance," of the nation of Israel, Luke 1:68 RV, "wrought redemption"; 2:38; (b) of "the redemptive work" of Christ, Heb. 9:12, bringing deliverance through His death, from the guilt and power of sin. In the Sept., Lev. 25:29, 48; Num. 18:16; Judg. 1:15; Ps. 49:8; 111:9; 130:7; Isa. 63:4.

2. *apolutrōsis* (ἀπολύτρωσις, 629), a strengthened form of No. 1, lit., "a releasing, for (i.e., on payment of) a ransom." It is used of (a) "deliverance" from physical torture, Heb. 11:35, see DELIVER, B, No. 1; (b) the deliverance of the people of God at the coming of Christ with His glorified saints, "in a cloud with power and great glory," Luke 21:28, a "redemption" to be accomplished at the "outshining of His Parousia," 2 Thess. 2:8, i.e., at His second advent; (c) forgiveness and justification, "redemption" as the result of expiation, deliverance from the guilt of sins, Rom. 3:24, "through the redemption that is in Christ Jesus"; Eph. 1:7, defined as "the forgiveness of our trespasses," RV; so Col. 1:14, "the forgiveness of our sins," indicating both the liberation from the guilt and doom of sin and the introduction into a life of liberty, "newness of life" (Rom. 6:4); Heb. 9:15, "for the redemption of the transgressions that were under the first covenant," RV, here "redemption of" is equivalent to "redemption from," the genitive case being used of the object from which the "redemption" is

effected, not from the consequence of the transgressions, but from the transgressions themselves; (d) the deliverance of the believer from the presence and power of sin, and of his body from bondage to corruption, at the coming (the Parousia in its inception) of the Lord Jesus, Rom. 8:23; 1 Cor. 1:30; Eph. 1:4; 4:30. See also PROPITIATION.

For **REDOUND,** 2 Cor. 4:15 (RV, "abound"), see ABUNDANCE, B, No. 1 (c)

For **REFLECTING,** 2 Cor. 3:18, RV, see BEHOLD, No. 12

REFRAIN

1. *pauō* (παύω, 3973), "to stop," is used in the active voice in the sense of "making to cease, restraining" in 1 Pet. 3:10, of causing the tongue to refrain from evil.

2. *aphistēmi* (ἀφίστημι, 868), "to cause to depart," is used intransitively, in the sense of "departing from, refraining from," Acts 5:38.

REFRESH, REFRESHING

A. Verbs.

1. *anapauō* (ἀναπαύω, 373), "to give intermission from labor, to give rest, refresh" (*ana*, "back," *pauō*, "to cause to cease"), is translated "to refresh" in 1 Cor. 16:18; 2 Cor. 7:13; Philem. 7, 20. See REST.

2. *sunanapauomai* (συναναπαύομαι, 4875), "to lie down, to rest with" (*sun*, "with," and No. 1 in the middle voice), is used metaphorically of being "refreshed" in spirit with others, in Rom. 15:32, KJV, "may with (you) be refreshed" (RV, "... find rest"). In the Sept., Isa. 11:6.

3. *anapsuchō* (ἀναψύχω, 404), "to make cool, refresh" (*ana*, "back," *psuchō*, "to cool"), is used in 2 Tim. 1:16 (cf. B). In the papyri it is used of "taking relaxation."

Note: In Acts 27:3, the verb *tunchanō*, "to obtain or receive," with the object *epimeleia*, "care," is translated "to refresh himself" (RV, marg., "to receive attention," i.e., to enjoy the kind attention of his friends).

B. Noun.

anapsuxis (ἀνάψυξις, 403), "a refreshing" (akin to A, No. 3), occurs in Acts 3:19. In the Sept., Ex. 8:15. In the papyri it is used of "obtaining relief."

For **REFUGE** see FLEE, No. 3

REGARD

1. *blepō* (βλέπω, 991), "to behold, look, perceive, see," has the sense of "regarding" by way of partiality, in Matt. 22:16 and Mark 12:14. See BEHOLD, No. 2.

2. *entrepō* (ἐντρέπω, 1788), "to turn about" (*en*, "in," *trepō*, "to turn"), is metaphorically used of "putting to shame," e.g., 1 Cor. 4:14; in the middle voice, "to reverence, regard," translated "regard" in Luke 18:2, 4. See ASHAMED, REVERENCE, SHAME.

3. *phroneō* (φρονέω, 5426), "to think, set the mind on," implying moral interest and reflection, is translated "to regard" in Rom. 14:6 (twice); the second part in the KJV represents an interpolation and is not part of the original. The Scripture does not speak of not "regarding" a day. See MIND.

4. *epiblepō* (ἐπιβλέπω, 1914), "to look upon" (*epi*, "upon," and No. 1), in the NT "to look on with favor," is used in Luke 1:48, KJV, "hath regarded" (RV, "hath looked upon"); in Jas. 2:3, RV, "ye have regard to" (KJV, "ye have respect to). See LOOK, No. 6, RESPECT.

5. *oligōreō* (ὀλιγωρέω, 3643) denotes "to think little of" (*oligos*, "little," *ōra*, "care"), "to regard lightly," Heb. 12:5, RV (KJV, "despise"). See DESPISE, *Note* (3). In the Sept. Prov. 3:11.

6. *prosechō* (προσέχω, 4337), "to take or give heed," is translated "they had regard" in Acts 8:11, KJV (RV, "they gave heed). See ATTEND, No. 1.

7. *ameleō* (ἀμελέω, 272), "not to care," is translated "I regarded ... not" in Heb. 8:9. See NEGLECT.

Notes: (1) In Gal. 6:4, RV, *eis*, "into," is translated "in regard of (himself)," KJV, "in"; so in 2 Cor. 10:16; Eph. 5:32. (2) In Rom. 6:20, the dative case of *dikaiosunē*, "righteousness," signifies, not "from righteousness," KJV, but "in regard of righteousness," RV, lit., "free to righteousness"; i.e., righteousness laid no sort of bond upon them, they had no relation to it in any way. (3) In 2 Cor. 8:4 the accusative case of *charis* and *koinonia* is, in the best texts, used absolutely, i.e., not as the objects of an expressed verb; hence the RV, "in regard to" (KJV, "that we would receive," where the verb is the result of a supplementary gloss).

REGENERATION

palingenesia (παλιγγενεσία, 3824), "new birth" (*palin*, "again," *genesis*, "birth"), is used of "spiritual regeneration," Titus 3:5, involving the communication of a new life, the two operating powers to produce which are "the word of truth," Jas. 1:18; 1 Pet. 1:23, and the Holy Spirit, John 3:5, 6; the *loutron*, "the laver, the washing," is explained in Eph. 5:26, "having cleansed it by the washing (*loutron*) of water with the word."

The new birth and "regeneration" do not represent successive stages in spiritual experience, they refer to the same event but view it in different aspects. The new birth stresses the communication of spiritual life in contrast to antecedent spiritual death; "regeneration" stresses the inception of a new state of things in contrast with the old; hence the connection of the use of the word with its application to Israel, in Matt. 19:28. Some regard the *kai* in Titus 3:5 as epexegetic, "even"; but, as Scripture marks two distinct yet associated operating powers, there is not sufficient ground for this interpretation. See under EVEN.

In Matt. 19:28 the word is used, in the Lord's discourse, in the wider sense, of the "restoration of all things" (Acts 3:21, RV), when, as a result of the second advent of Christ, Jehovah "sets His King upon His holy hill of Zion" (Ps. 2:6), and Israel, now in apostasy, is restored to its destined status, in the recognition and under the benign sovereignty of its Messiah. Thereby will be accomplished the deliverance of the world from the power and deception of Satan and from the despotic and antichristian rulers of the nations. This restitution will not in the coming millennial age be universally a return to the pristine condition of Edenic innocence previous to the Fall, but it will fulfill the establishment of God's covenant with Abraham concerning his descendants, a veritable rebirth of the nation, involving the peace and prosperity of the Gentiles. That the worldwide subjection to the authority of Christ will not mean the entire banishment of evil, is clear from Rev. 20:7, 8. Only in the new heavens and earth, "wherein dwelleth righteousness," will sin and evil be entirely absent.

REGRET

A. Verb.

metamelomai (μεταμέλλομαι, 3338), "to regret, to repent one," is translated "to regret" in 2 Cor. 7:8, RV (twice), KJV, "repent." See REPENT.

B. Adjective.

ametamelētos (ἀμεταμέλητος, 278), "not repented of" (*a*, negative, and A), is translated "which bringeth no regret" in 2 Cor. 7:10, RV, said of repentance (KJV, "not to be repented of"); elsewhere, in Rom. 11:29. See REPENT.

For **REGULAR,** Acts 19:39, RV, see LAW, C, No. 2

REHEARSE

1. *anangellō* (ἀναγγέλλω, 312), "to bring back word" (*ana*, "back," *angellō*, "to announce"), is translated "to rehearse" in Acts 14:27; 15:4, RV. See ANNOUNCE.

2. *exēgeomai* (ἐξηγέομαι, 1834), primarily, "to lead, show the way," is used metaphorically with the meaning "to unfold, declare, narrate," and is translated "to rehearse" in the RV of Luke 24:35; Acts 10:8; 15:12, and 14, RV. See DECLARE, No. 8.

Note: In Acts 11:4, the KJV translates the middle voice of *archō*, "to begin," "rehearsed ... from the beginning," RV, "began, (and)."

REIGN (Verb and Noun)

1. *basileuō* (βασιλεύω, 936), "to reign," is used (I) literally, (a) of God, Rev. 11:17; 19:6, in each of which the aorist tense (in the latter, translated "reigneth") is "ingressive," stressing the point of entrance; (b) of Christ, Luke 1:33; 1 Cor. 15:25; Rev. 11:15; as rejected by the Jews, Luke 19:14, 27; (c) of the saints, hereafter, 1 Cor. 4:8 (2nd part), where the apostle, casting a reflection upon the untimely exercise of authority on the part of the church at Corinth, anticipates the due time for it in the future (see No. 2); Rev. 5:10; 20:4, where the aorist tense is not simply of a "point" character, but "constative," that is, regarding a whole action as having occurred, without distinguishing any steps in its progress (in this instance the aspect is future); v. 6; 22:5; (d) of earthly potentates, Matt. 2:22; 1 Tim. 6:15, where "kings" is, lit., "them that reign"; (II), metaphorically, (a) of believers, Rom. 5:17, where "shall reign in life" indicates the activity of life in fellowship with Christ in His sovereign power, reaching its fullness hereafter; 1 Cor. 4:8 (1st part), of the carnal pride that laid claim to a power not to be exercised until hereafter; (b) of divine grace, Rom. 5:21; (c) of sin, Rom. 5:21; 6:12; (d) of death, Rom. 5:14, 17.

2. *sunbasileuō* (συμβασιλεύω, 4821), "to reign together with" (*sun*, "with," and No. 1), is used of the future "reign" of believers together and with Christ in the kingdom of God in manifestation, 1 Cor. 4:8 (3rd part); of those who endure 2 Tim. 2:12. cf. Rev. 20:6.

Notes: (1) In Rom. 15:12, KJV, *archō*, "to rule" (RV, is translated "to reign." (2) In Rev. 17:18, *echō*, "to have," with *basileia*, "a kingdom," is translated "reigneth," lit., "hath a kingdom," suggestive of a distinction between the sovereignty of mystic Babylon and that of ordinary sovereigns.

(3) In Luke 3:1, *hēgemonia*, "rule," is rendered "reign."

REJECT

A. Verbs.

1. *apodokimazō* (ἀποδοκιμάζω, 593), "to reject" as the result of examination and disapproval (*apo*, "away from," *dokimazō*, "to approve"), is used (a) of the "rejection" of Christ by the elders and chief priests of the Jews, Matt. 21:42; Mark 8:31; 12:10; Luke 9:22; 20:17; 1 Pet. 2:4, 7 (KJV, "disallowed"); by the Jewish people, Luke 17:25; (b) of the "rejection" of Esau from inheriting "the blessing," Heb. 12:17. See DISALLOW. Cf. and contrast *exoutheneō*, Acts 4:11. See DESPISE.

2. *atheteō* (ἀθετέω, 114), properly, "to do away" with what has been laid down, to make *atheton* (i.e., "without place," *a*, negative, *tithēmi*, "to place"), hence, besides its meanings "to set aside, make void, nullify, disannul," signifies "to reject"; in Mark 6:26, regarding Herod's pledge to Salome, it almost certainly has the meaning "to break faith with" (cf. the Sept. of Jer. 12:6, and Lam. 1:2, "dealt treacherously"). Moulton and Milligan illustrate this meaning from the papyri. Field suggests "disappoint." In Mark 7:9 "ye reject (the commandment)" means "ye set aside"; in Luke 7:30, "ye

reject" may have the meaning of "nullifying or making void the counsel of God"; in Luke 10:16 (four times), "rejecteth," RV (KJV, "despiseth"); "rejecteth" in John 12:48; "reject" in 1 Cor. 1:19 (KJV, "bring to nothing"); 1 Thess. 4:8, "to despise," where the reference is to the charges in v. 2; in 1 Tim. 5:12 RV, "have rejected" (KJV, "have cast off"). See DESPISE, *Notes* (1).

3. *ekptuō* (ἐκπτύω, 1609), "to spit out" (*ek*, "out," and *ptuō*, "to spit"), i.e., "to abominate, loathe," is used in Gal. 4:14, "rejected" (marg., "spat out"), where the sentence is elliptical: "although my disease repelled you, you did not refuse to hear my message."

4. *paraiteomai* (παραιτέομαι, 3868), besides the meanings "to beg from another," Mark 15:6 (in the best texts); "to entreat that ... not," Heb. 12:19; "to beg off, ask to be excused," Luke 14:18, 19; 12:25, is translated to reject in Titus 3:10, KJV. See EXCUSE, INTREAT.

B. Adjectives.

1. *adokimos* (ἀδόκιμος, 96), "not standing the test," is translated "rejected" in 1 Cor. 9:27, RV; Heb. 6:8, KJV and RV. See REPROBATE.

2. *apoblētos* (ἀπόβλητος, 579), lit., "cast away" (*apo*, "from," *ballō*, "to throw"), occurs in 1 Tim. 4:4, RV, "rejected" (KJV, "refused").

REJOICE

1. *chairō* (χαίρω, 5463), "to rejoice," is most frequently so translated. As to this verb, the following are grounds and occasions for "rejoicing," on the part of believers: in the Lord, Phil. 3:1; 4:4; His incarnation, Luke 1:14; His power, Luke 13:17; His presence with the Father, John 14:28; His presence with them, John 16:22; 20:20; His ultimate triumph, 8:56; hearing the gospel, Acts 13:48; their salvation, Acts 8:39; receiving the Lord, Luke 19:6; their enrollment in Heaven, Luke 10:20; their liberty in Christ, Acts 15:31; their hope, Rom. 12:12 (cf. Rom. 5:2; Rev. 19:7); their prospect of reward, Matt. 5:12; the obedience and godly conduct of fellow believers, Rom. 16:19, RV, "I rejoice" (KJV, "I am glad"); 2 Cor. 7:7, 9; 13:9; Col. 2:5; 1 Thess. 3:9; 2 John 4; 3 John 3; the proclamation of Christ, Phil. 1:18; the gospel harvest, John 4:36; suffering with Christ, Acts 5:41; 1 Pet. 4:13; suffering in the cause of the gospel, 2 Cor. 13:9 (1st part); Phil. 2:17 (1st part); Col. 1:24; in persecutions, trials and afflictions, Matt. 5:12; Luke 6:23; 2 Cor. 6:10; the manifestation of grace, Acts 11:23; meeting with fellow believers, 1 Cor. 16:17, RV, "I rejoice"; Phil. 2:28; receiving tokens of love and fellowship, Phil. 4:10; the "rejoicing" of others, Rom. 12:15; 2 Cor. 7:13; learning of the well-being of others, 2 Cor. 7:16. See FAREWELL, GLAD, GREETING etc.

2. *sunchairō* (συγχαίρω, 4796), "to rejoice with" (*sun*, and No. 1), is used of "rejoicing" together in the recovery of what was lost, Luke 15:6, 9; in suffering in the cause of the gospel, Phil. 2:17 (2nd part), 18; in the joy of another, Luke 1:58; in the honor of fellow believers, 1 Cor. 12:26; in the triumph of the truth, 1 Cor. 13:6, RV, "rejoiceth with."

3. *agalliaō* (ἀγαλλιάω, 21), "to reioice greatly, to exult," is used, (I) in the active voice, of "rejoicing" in God, Luke 1:47; in faith in Christ, 1 Pet. 1:8, RV (middle voice in some mss.), "ye rejoice greatly"; in the event of the marriage of the Lamb, Rev. 19:7, "be exceeding glad," RV; (II), in the middle voice, (a) of "rejoicing" in persecutions, Matt. 5:12 (2nd part); in the light of testimony for God, John 5:35; in salvation received through the gospel, Acts 16:34, "he rejoiced greatly," RV; in salvation ready to be revealed, 1 Pet. 1:6; at the revelation of His glory, 1 Pet. 4:13, "with exeeding joy," lit., "ye may rejoice (see No. 1) exulting"; (b) of Christ's "rejoicing" (greatly) "in the Holy Spirit," Luke 10:21, RV; said of His praise, as foretold in Ps. 16:9, quoted in Acts 2:26 (which follows the Sept., "My tongue"); (c) of Abraham's "rejoicing," by faith, to see Christ's day, John 8:56.

4. *euphrainō* (εὐφραίνω, 2165), in the active voice, "to cheer, gladden" (*eu*, "well," *phrēn*, "the mind"), signifies in the passive voice "to rejoice, make merry"; it is translated "to rejoice" in Acts 2:26, RV, "was glad," KJV, "did ... rejoice," of the heart of Christ as foretold in Ps. 16:9 [cf. No. 3, II (b)]; in Acts 7:41, of Israel's idolatry; in Rom. 15:10 (quoted from the Sept. of Deut. 32:43, where it is a command to the Gentiles to "rejoice" with the Jews in their future deliverance by Christ from all their foes, at the establishment of the messianic kingdom) the apostle applies it to the effects of the gospel; in Gal. 4:27 (touching the barrenness of Sarah as referred to in Isa. 54:1, and there pointing to the ultimate restoration of Israel to God's favor, cf. 51:2), the word is applied to the effects of the gospel, in that the progeny of grace would greatly exceed the number of those who had acknowledged allegiance to the Law; grace and faith are fruitful, law and works are barren as a means of salvation; in Rev. 12:12, it is used in a call to the heavens to "rejoice" at the casting out of Satan and the inauguration of the Kingdom of God in manifestation and the authority of His Christ; in 18:20, of a call to heaven, saints, apostles, prophets, to "rejoice" in the destruction of Babylon. See GLAD, No. 3, MERRY, No. 1.

5. *kauchaomai* (καυχάομαι, 2744), "to boast, to glory," is rendered "to rejoice," (a) Rom. 5:2, in hope of the glory of God; (b) 5:3, RV (KJV "glory"), in tribulation; (c) 5:11, RV (KJV, "we joy"), in God; (d) Phil. 3:3, RV, "glory" (KJV, "rejoice") in Christ Jesus; (e) Jas. 1:9 (RV, "glory," KJV, "rejoice"), the brother of low degree in his high estate; the rich brother in being made low; (f) Jas. 4:16, of evil glorying. See GLORY (to boast).

Notes: (1) In Jas. 2:13, KJV, *katakauchaomai*, "to glory, boast against," is translated "rejoiceth against" (RV, "glorieth against"). See GLORY (to boast), A, No. 2. (2) The nouns *kauchēma, kauchēsis*, signifying "glorying, boasting," are always so rendered in the RV, where the KJV has "rejoicing," the former in 2 Cor. 1:14; Gal. 6:4; Phil. 1:26; 2:16; Heb. 3:6; the latter in 1 Cor. 15:31; 2 Cor. 1:12; 1 Thess. 2:19; Jas. 4:16. See GLORY, B, Nos. 1 and 2.

RELEASE

apoluō (ἀπολύω, 630), "to loose from," is translated "to release" in Matt. 18:27, RV (KJV, "loosed"); 27:15, 17, 21, 26; Mark 15:6, 9, 11, 15; Luke 6:37 (twice), RV (KJV, "forgive" and "ye shall be forgiven"); 23:16 (v. 17, in some mss.), 18, 20, 25; 23:22, RV (KJV, "let ... go"); John 18:39 (twice); 19:10; in 19:12, in the 1st part, KJV and RV; in the 2nd part, RV, "release" (KJV, "let ... go"); so in Acts 3:13. See DISMISS.

Note: For *aphesis*, "release," Luke 4:18, RV, see DELIVERANCE.

RELIEF

1. *diakonia* (διακονία, 1248), "ministry," is translated "relief" in Acts 11:29 [RV, marg., "for (*eis*) ministry"].

2. *anesis* (ἄνεσις, 425), "a loosening, relaxation" (akin to *aniēmi*, "to send away, let go, loosen"), is translated "relief" in 2 Cor. 2:13 and 7:5 (KJV, "rest"). See REST.

RELIEVE

eparkeō (ἐπαρκέω, 1884) signifies "to be strong enough for," and so either "to ward off," or "to aid, to relieve" (a strengthened form of *arkeo*, which has the same three meanings, *epi* being intensive); it is used in 1 Tim. 5:10, 16 (twice).

RELIGION

1. *thrēskeia* (θρησκεία, 2356) signifies "religion" in its external aspect (akin to *thrēskos*, see below), "religious worship," especially the ceremonial service of "religion"; it is used of the "religion" of the Jews, Acts 26:5; of the "worshiping" of angels, Col. 2:18, which they themselves repudiate (Rev. 22:8, 9); "there was an officious parade of humility in selecting these lower beings as intercessors rather than appealing directly to the Throne of Grace" (Lightfoot); in Jas. 1:26, 27 the writer purposely uses the word to set in contrast that which is unreal and deceptive, and the "pure religion" which consists in visiting "the fatherless and widows in their affliction," and in keeping oneself "unspotted from the world." He is "not herein affirming ... these offices to be the sum total, nor yet the great essentials, of true religion, but declares them to be the body, the *thrēskeia*, of which godliness, or the love of God, is the informing soul" (Trench).

2. *deisidaimonia* (δεισιδαιμονία, 1175) primarily denotes "fear of the gods" (from *deidō*, "to fear," *daimōn*, "a pagan deity," Eng., "demon"), regarded whether as a religious attitude, or, in its usual meaning, with a condemnatory or contemptuous significance, "superstition." That is how Festus regarded the Jews' "religion," Acts 25:19, KJV and RV marg., "superstition" (RV, "religion"). See RELIGIOUS, *Note* (1), and under SUPERSTITIOUS.

Notes: (1) *Thrēskeia* is external, *theosebeia* is the reverential worship of God (see GODLINESS), *eusebeia* is piety (see GODLINESS), *eulabeia* the devotedness arising from godly fear (see FEAR). (2) For "the Jews' religion," Gal. 1:13, 14, see JEWS, B.

RELIGIOUS

thrēskos (θρῆσκος, 2357), "religious, careful of the externals of divine service," akin to *threskeia* (see above), is used in Jas. 1:26.

Notes: (1) For *deisidaimōn*, Acts 17:22, RV, marg., "religious," see SUPERSTITIOUS. (2) For "religious (proselytes)," KJV in Acts 13:43, see DEVOUT, No. 3.

REMEMBER, REMEMBRANCE, REMINDED

A. Verbs.

1. *mimnēskō* (μιμνήσκω, 3403), from the older form *mnaomai*, in the active voice signifies "to remind"; in the middle voice, "to remind oneself of," hence, "to remember, to be mindful of"; the later form is found only in the present tense, in Heb. 2:6, "are mindful of," and 13:3, "remember"; the perfect tense in 1 Cor. 11:2 and in 2 Tim. 1:4 (RV, "remembering," KJV, "being mindful of"), is used with a present meaning. RV variations from the KJV are, in Luke 1:54, RV, "that He might remember" (KJV, "in remembrance of"); 2 Pet. 3:2, "remember" (KJV, "be mindful of"); Rev. 16:19 (passive voice), "was remembered" (KJV, "came in remembrance"). The passive voice is used also in Acts 10:31, KJV and RV, "are had in remembrance." See MINDFUL OF (TO BE).

2. *mnēmoneuō* (μνημονεύω, 3421) signifies "to call to mind, remember"; it is used absolutely in Mark 8:18; everywhere else it has an object, (a) persons, Luke 17:32; Gal. 2:10; 2 Tim. 2:8, where the RV rightly has "remember Jesus Christ, risen from the dead"; Paul was not reminding Timothy (nor did he need to) that Christ was raised from the dead (KJV), what was needful for him was to "remember" (to keep in mind) the One who rose, the Source and Supplier of all his requirements; (b) things, e.g., Matt. 16:9; John 15:20; 16:21; Acts 20:35; Col. 4:18; 1 Thess. 1:3; 2:9; Heb. 11:15, "had been mindful of"; 13:7; Rev. 18:5; (c) a clause, representing a circumstance, etc., John 16:4; Acts 20:31; Eph. 2:11; 2 Thess. 2:5;

Rev. 2:5; 3:3; in Heb. 11:22 it signifies "to make mention of." See MENTION.

3. *anamimnēskō* (ἀναμιμνήσκω, 363), *ana*, "back," and No. 1, signifies in the active voice "to remind, call to one's mind," 1 Cor. 4:17, "put (KJV, bring) ... into remembrance"; so 2 Tim. 1:6; in the passive voice, "to remember, call to (one's own) mind," Mark 11:21, "calling to remembrance"; 14:72, "called to mind"; 2 Cor. 7:15, "remembereth"; Heb. 10:32, "call to remembrance."

4. *hupomimnēskō* (ὑπομιμνήσκω, 5279) signifies "to cause one to remember, put one in mind of" (*hupō*, "under," often implying suggestion, and No. 1), John 14:26, "shall ... bring ... to (your) remembrance"; 2 Tim. 2:14, "put ... in remembrance"; Titus 3:1, "put ... in mind"; 3 John 10, RV, "I will bring to remembrance" (KJV, "I will remember"); Jude 5, "to put ... in remembrance." In Luke 22:61 it is used in the passive voice, "(Peter) remembered," lit., "was put in mind."

5. *epanamimnēskō* (ἐπαναμιμνήσκω, 1878), "to remind again" (*epi*, "upon," and No. 3), is used in Rom. 15:15, RV, "putting (you) again in remembrance," KJV, "putting (you) in mind." See MIND.

Note: In 1 Tim. 4:6, KJV, *hupotithēmi*, "to lay under, to suggest," is translated "put ... in remembrance" (RV, "put ... in mind"). See MIND.

B. Nouns.

1. *anamnēsis* (ἀνάμνησις, 364), "a remembrance" (*ana*, "up," or "again," and A, No. 1), is used (a) in Christ's command in the institution of the Lord's Supper, Luke 22:19; 1 Cor. 11:24, 25, not "in memory of" but in an affectionate calling of the Person Himself to mind; (b) of the "remembrance" of sins, Heb. 10:3, RV, "a remembrance" (KJV, "a remembrance again"; but the prefix *ana* does not here signify "again"); what is indicated, in regard to the sacrifices under the Law, is not simply an external bringing to "remembrance," but an awakening of mind. In the Sept., Lev. 24:7; Num. 10:10; Pss. 38 and 70, Titles.

2. *hupomnēsis* (ὑπόμνησις, 5280) denotes "a reminding, a reminder"; in 2 Tim. 1:5 it is used with *lambanō*, "to receive," lit., "having received a reminder," RV, "having been reminded" (KJV, "when I call to remembrance"); in 2 Pet. 1:13 and 3:1, "remembrance."

Note: A distinction has been drawn between Nos. 1 and 2, in that *anamnesis* indicates an unassisted recalling, *hupomnēsis*, a "remembrance" prompted by another.

3. *mneia* (μνεία, 3417) denotes "a remembrance," or "a mention." See MENTION.

4. *mnēmē* (μνήμη, 3420) denotes "a memory" (akin to *mnaomai*, A, No. 1), "remembrance, mention," 2 Pet. 1:15, "remembrance"; here, however, it is used with *poieo*, "to make" (middle voice), and some suggest that the meaning is "to make mention."

REMISSION, REMIT

A. Nouns.

1. *aphesis* (ἄφεσις, 859), "a dismissal, release" (from *aphiēmi*, B), is used of the forgiveness of sins and translated "remission" in Matt. 26:28; Mark 1:4; Luke 1:77; 3:3; 24:47; Acts 2:38; 5:31 (KJV, "forgiveness"); 10:43; 13:38, RV (KJV, "forgiveness"); 26:18 (ditto); Heb. 9:22; 10:18. See FORGIVE, B, and A, No. 1.

2. *paresis* (πάρεσις, 3929), "a passing by of debt or sin," Rom. 3:25, KJV, "remission" (RV and KJV marg., "passing over"). See PASSING OVER.

Note: No. 2 is a matter of forbearance, No. 1 a matter of grace.

B. Verb.

aphiēmi (ἀφίημι, 863), "to send away" (akin to A, No. 1), is translated "to remit" in John 20:23 (twice), KJV (RV, "to forgive"). Scripture makes clear that the Lord's words could not have been intended to bestow the exercise of absolution, which Scripture declares is the prerogative of God alone. There is no instance in the NT of this act on the part of the apostles. The words are to be understood in a "declarative" sense; the statement has regard to the effects of their ministry of the gospel, with its twofold effects of "remission" or retention. They could not, nor could anyone subsequently, forgive sins, any more than that Joseph actually restored the butler to his office and hanged the baker (Gen. 41:13), or any more than that the prophets actually accomplished things when they declared that they were about to be done (Jer. 1:10; Ezek. 43:3). See FORGIVE, No. 1.

REMNANT

1. *loipos* (λοιπός, 3062), an adjective (akin to *leipō*, "to leave") signifying "remaining," is used as a noun and translated "the rest" in the RV, where the KJV has "the remnant," Matt. 22:6; Rev. 11:13; 12:17; 19:21. See RESIDUE, REST (THE).

2. *leimma* (λεῖμμα, 3005), "that which is left" (akin to *leipo*, "to leave"), "a remnant," is used in Rom. 11:5, "there is a remnant," more lit., "there has come to be a remnant," i.e., there is a spiritual "remnant" saved by the gospel from the midst of apostate Israel. While in one sense there has been and is a considerable number, yet, compared with the whole nation, past and present, the "remnant" is small, and as such is an evidence of God's electing grace (see v. 4). In the Sept., 2 Kings 19:4.

3. *hupoleimma* (ὑπόλειμμα, 2640) (ὑπό, 5259, and λεῖμμα, 3005). *hupo*. "under." signifying "diminution," and No. 2, is used in Rom. 9:27: some mss. have *kataleimma*, which has

virtually the same meaning (*kata*, "down, behind"), "a remnant," where the contrast is drawn between the number of Israel as a whole, and the small number in it of those who are saved through the gospel. The quotation is chiefly from the Sept. of Isa. 10:22, 23, with a modification recalling Hosea 1:10, especially with regard to the word "number." The return of the "remnant" is indicated in the name "Shear-Jashub," see Isa. 7:3, marg. The primary reference was to the return of a remnant from captivity to their own land and to God Himself; here the application is to the effects of the gospel. There is stress on the word "remnant."

RENEW, RENEWING (Verb and Noun)

A. Verbs.

1. *anakainoō* (ἀνακαινόω, 341), "to make new" (*ana*, "back" or "again," *kainos*, "new," not recent but different), "to renew," is used in the passive voice in 2 Cor. 4:16, of the daily renewal of "the inward man" (in contrast to the physical frame), i.e., of the "renewal" of spiritual power; in Col. 3:10, of "the new man" (in contrast to the old unregenerate nature), which "is being renewed unto knowledge," RV (cf. No. 3 in Eph. 4:23), i.e., the true knowledge in Christ, as opposed to heretical teachings.

Note: This word has not been found elsewhere in Greek writings as yet, though No. 2 is, which would prevent the supposition that the apostle coined a new word.

2. *anakainizō* (ἀνακαινίζω, 340) is a variant form of No. 1, used in Heb. 6:6, of the impossibility of "renewing" to repentance those Jews who professedly adhered to the Christian faith, if, after their experiences of it (not actual possession of its regenerating effects), they apostatized into their former Judaism. In the Sept., 2 Chron. 15:8; Ps. 39:2; 103:5; 104:30; Lam. 5:21.

3. *ananeoō* (ἀνανεόω, 365), "to renew, make young" (*ana*, as in No. 1, and *neos*, "recent," not different), is used in Eph. 4:23, "be renewed (in the spirit of your mind)." The "renewal" here mentioned is not that of the mind itself in its natural powers of memory, judgment and perception, but "the spirit of the mind," which, under the controlling power of the indwelling Holy Spirit, directs its bent and energies Godward in the enjoyment of "fellowship with the Father and with His Son, Jesus Christ," and of the fulfillment of the will of God. The word is frequent in inscriptions and in the papyri.

B. Noun.

anakainosis (ἀνακαίνωσις, 342), akin to A, No. 1, "a renewal," is used in Rom. 12:2, "the renewing (of your mind)," i.e., the adjustment of the moral and spiritual vision and thinking to the mind of God, which is designed to have a transforming effect upon the life; in Titus 3:5, where "the renewing of the Holy Spirit" is not a fresh bestowment of the Spirit, but a revival of His power, developing the Christian life; this passage stresses the continual operation of the indwelling Spirit of God; the Romans passage stresses the willing response on the part of the believer.

RENOUNCE

1. *apeipon* (ἀπεῖπον, 550), lit., "to tell from" (*apo*, "from," *eipon*, an aorist form used to supply parts of *legō*, "to say"), signifies "to renounce," 2 Cor. 4:2 (middle voice), of disowning "the hidden things of shame." In the Sept. of 1 Kings 11:2 it signifies "to forbid," a meaning found in the papyri. The meaning "to renounce" may therefore carry with it the thought of forbidding the approach of the things disowned.

2. *apotassō* (ἀποτάσσω, 657), "to set apart, to appoint," a meaning found in the papyri (*apo*, from, *tassō*, "to arrange"), is used in the middle voice in the sense either of "taking leave of," e.g., Acts 18:18, or "forsaking," Luke 14:33, RV, "renounceth" (KJV "forsaketh"). See FORSAKE.

REPENT, REPENTANCE

A. Verbs.

1. *metanoeō* (μετανοέω, 3340), lit., "to perceive afterwards" (*meta*, "after," implying "change," *noeō*, "to perceive"; *nous*, "the mind, the seat of moral reflection"), in contrast to *pronoeō*, "to perceive beforehand," hence signifies "to change one's mind or purpose," always, in the NT, involving a change for the better, an amendment, and always, except in Luke 17:3, 4, of "repentance" from sin. The word is found in the Synoptic Gospels (in Luke, nine times), in Acts five times, in the Apocalypse twelve times, eight in the messages to the churches, 2:5 (twice), 16, 21 (twice), RV, "she willeth not to repent" (2nd part); 3:3, 19 (the only churches in those chapters which contain no exhortation in this respect are those at Smyrna and Philadelphia); elsewhere only in 2 Cor. 12:21. See also the general *Note* below.

2. *metamelomai* (μεταμέλλομαι, 3338), *meta*, as in No. 1, and *melō*, "to care for," is used in the passive voice with middle voice sense, signifying "to regret, to repent oneself," Matt. 21:29, RV, "repented himself"; v. 32, RV, "ye did (not) repent yourselves" (KJV, "ye repented not"); 27:3, "repented himself"; 2 Cor. 7:8 (twice), RV, "regret" in each case; Heb. 7:21, where alone in the NT it is said (negatively) of God.

B. Adjective.

ametamelētos (ἀμεταμέλητος, 278), "not repented of, unregretted" (*a*, negative, and a verbal adjective of A, No. 2), signifies "without change of purpose"; it is said (a) of God in regard to his "gifts and calling," Rom. 11:29; (b) of man, 2 Cor. 7:10, RV, "[repentance (*metanoia*, see C)] ... which bringeth no regret" (KJV, "not to be repented of"); the difference between *metanoia* and *metamelomai*, illustrated here, is briefly expressed in the contrast between "repentance" and "regret."

C. Noun.

metanoia (μετάνοια, 3341), "afterthought, change of mind, repentance," corresponds in meaning to A, No. 1, and is used of "repentance" from sin or evil, except in Heb. 12:17, where the word "repentance" seems to mean, not simply a change of Isaac's mind, but such a change as would reverse the effects of his own previous state of mind. Esau's birthright-bargain could not be recalled; it involved an irretrievable loss.

As regards "repentance" from sin, (a) the requirement by God on man's part is set forth, e.g., in Matt. 3:8; Luke 3:8; Acts 20:21; 26:20; (b) the mercy of God in giving "repentance" or leading men to it is set forth, e.g., in Acts 5:31; 11:18; Rom. 2:4; 2 Tim. 2:25. The most authentic mss. omit the word in Matt. 9:13 and Mark 2:17, as in the RV.

Note: In the OT, "repentance" with reference to sin is not so prominent as that change of mind or purpose, out of pity for those who have been affected by one's action, or in whom the results of the action have not fulfilled expectations, a "repentance" attributed both to God and to man, e.g., Gen. 6:6; Exod. 32:14 (that this does not imply anything contrary to God's immutability, but that the aspect of His mind is changed toward an object that has itself changed, see under RECONCILE).

In the NT the subject chiefly has reference to "repentance" from sin, and this change of mind involves both a turning from sin and a turning to God. The parable of the Prodigal Son is an outstanding illustration of this. Christ began His ministry with a call to "repentance," Matt. 4:17, but the call is addressed, not as in the OT to the nation, but to the individual. In the Gospel of John, as distinct from the Synoptic Gospels, referred to above, "repentance" is not mentioned, even in connection with John the Baptist's preaching; in John's gospel and 1st epistle the effects are stressed, e.g., in the new birth, and, generally, in the active turning from sin to God by the exercise of faith (John 3:3; 9:38; 1 John 1:9), as in the NT in general.

REPETITIONS (use vain)

battalogeō or *battologeō* (βαττολογέω, 945), "to repeat idly," is used in Matt. 6:7, "use (not) vain repetitions"; the meaning "to stammer" is scarcely to be associated with this word. The word is probably from an Aramaic phrase and onomatopoeic in character. The rendering of the Sinaitic Syriac is "Do not be saying *battalatha*, idle things," i.e., meaningless and mechanically repeated phrases, the reference being to pagan (not Jewish) modes of prayer. *Battalos*, "the Gabbler," was a nickname for Demosthenes, the great orator, assigned to him by his rivals.

REPORT (Noun and Verb)

A. Nouns.

1. *akoē* (ἀκοή, 189), "a hearing," is translated "report" in John 12:38 and Rom. 10:16, and in the RV of Matt. 4:24; 14:1; Mark 1:28. See HEARING, B, No. 1.

2. *euphēmia* (εὐφημία, 2162), "a good report, good reputation" (*eu*, "well," *phēmē* "a saying or report"), is used in 2 Cor. 6:8. Contrast No. 3.

3. *dusphēmia* (δυσφημία, 1426), "evilspeaking, defamation" (*dus-*, an inseparable prefix, the opposite to *eu*, "well," see No. 2), is used in 2 Cor. 6:8.

4. *logos* (λόγος, 3056), "a word," is translated "report," i.e., "a story, narrative"; in Luke 5:15 (KJV, "fame"); 7:17 (KJV, "rumor"); Acts 11:22 (KJV, "tidings"). See WORD.

Note: For *marturia*, rendered "report" in 1 Tim. 3:7, KJV, see TESTIMONY, WITNESS.

B. Adjective.

euphēmos (εὔφημος, 2163), akin to A, No. 2, primarily, "uttering words or sounds of good omen," then, "avoiding ill-omened words," and hence "fair-sounding," "of good report," is so rendered in Phil. 4:8.

C. Verbs.

1. *martureō* (μαρτυρέω, 3140), "to be a witness, bear witness, testify," signifies, in the passive voice, "to be well testified of, to have a good report," Acts 6:3, "of good (KJV, honest) report," lit., "being well testified of"; 10:22; 16:2; 22:12; 1 Tim. 5:10; in Heb. 11:2, 39, KJV, "obtained a good report" (RV, "had witness borne to them"); in 3 John 12, KJV "hath good report" (RV, "hath the witness"), lit., "witness hath been borne." See TESTIFY, WITNESS.

2. *apangellō* (ἀπαγγέλλω, 518), "to report" (*apo*, "from," *angellō*, "to give a message"), "announce, declare" (by a messenger, speaker, or writer), is translated "reported" in Acts 4:23; 16:36, RV (KJV, "told"); v. 38 (some mss. have No. 3; KJV, "told"); "report" in 1 Cor. 14:25, KJV (RV, "declaring"); 1 Thess. 1:9, RV, "report" (KJV, "shew"); so Acts 28:21. See DECLARE, No. 2.

3. *anangellō* (ἀναγγέλλω, 312), "to bring back word," in later Greek came to have the same meaning as No. 2, "to announce, declare"; it is translated "are reported" in 1 Pet. 1:12, KJV (RV, "have been announced"). See DECLARE, No. 1.

4. *akouō* (ἀκούω, 191), "to hear," is used in the passive voice, impersonally, in 1 Cor. 5:1, lit., "it is heard" or "there is heard," translated "it is reported." See HEAR.

5. *blasphemeō* (βλασφημέω, 987), "to speak slanderously, impiously, profanely" (*blaptō*, "to injure," and *phēmē*, "a

saying"), is translated "we be slanderously reported" in Rom. 3:8 (passive voice). See BLASPHEME, B.

Note: In Matt. 28:15, KJV, *diaphēmizō*, "to spread abroad" (*dia*, "throughout," *phēmē*, "a saying, report"), is translated "is commonly reported" (RV, "was spread abroad"). See BLAZE ABROAD.

REPROACH (Noun and Verb), REPROACHFULLY

A. Nouns.

1. *oneidismos* (ὀνειδισμός, 3680), "a reproach, defamation," is used in Rom. 15:3; 1 Tim. 3:7; Heb. 10:33; 11:26; 13:13.

2. *oneidos* (ὄνειδος, 3681), akin to No. 1, is used in Luke 1:25 in the concrete sense of "a matter of reproach, a disgrace." To have no children was, in the Jewish mind, more than a misfortune, it might carry the implication that this was a divine punishment for some secret sin. Cf. Gen. 30:1; 1 Sam. 1:6-10.

3. *atimia* (ἀτιμία, 819), "dishonor," is translated "reproach" in 2 Cor. 11:21, KJV (RV, "disparagement). See DISHONOR, SHAME, VILE.

Note: In 2 Cor. 12:10, KJV, *hubris*, "insolence injury," is translated "reproaches" (RV, "injuries"). See HARM.

B. Verbs.

1. *oneidizō* (ὀνειδίζω, 3679), akin to A, Nos. 1 and 2, signifies (a), in the active voice, "to reproach, upbraid," Matt. 5:11, RV, "shall reproach" (KJV, "shall revile"); 11:20, "to upbraid"; 27:44, RV, "cast ... reproach" [KJV, "cast ... in (His) teeth"]; Mark 15:32 RV, "reproached" (KJV, "reviled"); 16:14 "upbraided"; Luke 6:22 "shall reproach," Rom. 15:3; Jas. 1:5, "upbraideth"; (b) in the passive voice, "to suffer reproach, be reproached," 1 Tim. 4:10 (in some mss. in the 2nd part); 1 Pet. 4:14.

2. *hubrizō* (ὑβρίζω, 5195), akin to *hubris* (see A, Note), used transitively, denotes "to outrage, insult, treat insolently"; it is translated "Thou reproachest" in Luke 11:45. The word is much stronger than "to reproach"; the significance is "Thou insultest (even us)," i.e., who are superior to ordinary Pharisees. The lawyer's imputation was unjust; Christ's rebuke was not *hubris*, "insult." What He actually said was by way of "reproach" (*oneidizō*). See DESPITEFULLY.

Notes: (1) For *anepilēptos*, "without reproach," RV, in 1 Tim. 3:2; 5:7; 6:14, see BLAMELESS, B No. 5. (2) In 1 Tim. 5:14, KJV, *loidoria*, "reviling" (RV), used in the genitive case with *charin*, "in respect of," "for," is translated "reproachfully" (RV, "for reviling"). Cf. *loidoreō*, "to revile." See RAILING.

REPROBATE

adokimos (ἀδόκιμος, 96), signifying "not standing the test, rejected" (*a*, negative, *dokimos*, "approved"), was primarily applied to metals (cf. Isa. 1:22); it is used always in the NT in a passive sense, (a) of things, Heb. 6:8, "rejected," of land that bears thorns and thistles; (b) of persons, Rom. 1:28, of a "reprobate mind," a mind of which God cannot approve, and which must be rejected by Him, the effect of refusing "to have God in *their* knowledge"; in 1 Cor. 9:27 (for which see REJECT); 2 Cor. 13:5, 6, 7, where the RV rightly translates the adjective "reprobate" (KJV, "reprobates"), here the reference is to the great test as to whether Christ is in a person; in 2 Tim. 3:8 of hose "reprobate concerning the faith," i.e., men whose moral sense is perverted and whose minds are beclouded with their own speculations; in Titus 1:16, of the defiled, who are "unto every good work reprobate," i.e., if they are put to the test in regard to any good work (in contrast to their profession), they can only be rejected. In the Sept., Prov. 25:4; Isa. 1:22.

REPROOF, REPROVE

A. Noun.

elegmos (ἔλεγχος, 1650), "a reproof" (akin to B), is found in the best texts in 2 Tim. 3:16 (some mss. have *elenchos*, which denotes "a proof, proving, test," as in Heb. 11:1, "proving," RV marg., "test"). Cf. *elenxis*, "rebuke," 2 Pet. 2:16 (lit., "had rebuke").

B. Verb.

elenchō (ἐλέγχω, 1651), "to convict, rebuke, reprove," is translated "to reprove" in Luke 3:19; John 3:20, RV marg., "convicted"; the real meaning here is "exposed" (KJV marg., "discovered"); Eph. 5:11, 13, where "to expose" is again the significance; in John 16:8, KJV, "will reprove" (RV, "will convict"); in 1 Cor. 14:24, RV, "reproved" (KJV, "convinced"); in the following the RV has "to reprove," for KJV, "to rebuke," 1 Tim. 5:20; Titus 2:15; Heb. 12:5; Rev. 3:19; for synonymous words see CONVICT and REBUKE.

REPUTATION, REPUTE

dokeō (δοκέω, 1380) signifies (a) "to be of opinion" (akin to *doxa*, "an opinion"), "to suppose," e.g., Luke 12:51; 13:2; (b) "to seem, to be reputed"; in Gal. 2:2, RV, "who were of repute" (KJV, "which were of reputation"); in 2:6 (twice), and 9, RV, "were reputed" and "were of repute" (KJV, "seemed"); in each case the present participle of the verb with the article is used, lit., "(well) thought of" by them, persons held in consideration; in v. 6, RV, "(those) who were reputed to be somewhat" (KJV "who seemed to be somewhat"): so v. 9. where there is no irony [cf. the rendering "are accounted" in Mark 10:42 (i.e., not rulers nominally)], Paul recognized that James, Cephas, and John were, as they were "reputed" by the church at Jerusalem, its responsible guides; (c) impersonally, "to think, to seem good." See SEEM.

The first meaning, "to suppose," implies a subjective opinion based on thought; the second meaning, exemplified in the Galatians passages, expresses, from the standpoint of the observer, his own judgment about a matter (Trench, *Syn.*, Sec. LXXX).

Notes: (1) In Acts 5:34, KJV, *timios*, "honored, had in honor" (RV), is translated "had in reputation." (2) In Phil. 2:29, KJV, *entimos*, "honorable," with *echō*, "to have," i.e., "to hold in honor," is translated "hold ... in reputation" (RV, "hold ... in honor"). (3) For *kenoō*, in Phil. 2:7, KJV, "made (Himself) of no reputation," see EMPTY.

For **RESEMBLE,** Luke 13:18, KJV, see LIKEN, B, No. 1.

RESIDUE

kataloipos (κατάλοιπος, 2645), an adjective denoting "left remaining" (*kata*, "after, behind," *leipō*, "to leave"), akin to the verb in the *Note* above, is translated "residue" in Acts 15:17, from the Sept. of Amos 9:12.

Note: In Mark 16:13, KJV, the plural of *loipos*, "left," is translated "residue" (RV, "rest").

RESOLVE

ginōskō (γινώσκω, 1097), "to come to know, perceive, realize," is used in the 2nd aorist tense in Luke 16:4. "I am resolved," expressing the definiteness of the steward's realization, and his consequent determination of his course of action. See KNOW.

RESPECT (Noun and Verb)

A. Noun.

meros (μέρος, 3313), "a part," has occasionally the meaning of "a class" or "category," and, used in the dative case with *en*, "in," signifies "in respect of," 2 Cor. 3:10, "in (this) respect"; 9:3, RV, KJV, "in (this) behalf"; Col. 2:16, "in respect of (a feast day)."

B. Verbs.

1. *apoblepō* (ἀποβλέπω, 578), "to look away from all else at one object" (*apo*, "from"), hence, "to look steadfastly," is translated "he had respect" in Heb. 11:26, KJV (RV, "looked"). See LOOK.

2. *epiblepō* (ἐπιβλέπω, 1914), "to look upon" (*epi*), is translated "have respect" in Jas. 2:3 (RV "regard"); see LOOK, No. 6.

Notes: (1) The following prepositions are translated "in respect of": *peri*, "concerning," in John 16:8, RV; *epi*, "upon, over," in Heb. 11:4, RV; marg., "over (his gifts)"; *kata*, "in regard to," in Phil. 4:11. (2) For "respect of persons" and "respecter of persons" see PERSON.

REST (Noun and Verb)

A. Nouns.

1. *anapausis* (ἀνάπαυσις, 372), "cessation, refreshment, rest" (*ana*, "up," *pauō*, "to make to cease"), the constant word in the Sept. for the Sabbath "rest," is used in Matt. 11:29; here the contrast seems to be to the burdens imposed by the Pharisees. Christ's "rest" is not a "rest" from work, but in work, "not the rest of inactivity but of the harmonious working of all the faculties and affections—of will, heart, imagination, conscience—because each has found in God the ideal sphere for its satisfaction and development" (J. Patrick, in *Hastings Bib. Dic.*); it occurs also in Matt. 12:43; Luke 11:24; Rev. 4:8, RV, "(they have no) rest" [KJV, "(they) rest (not)"], where the noun is the object of the verb *echō*, "to have"; so in 14:11.

2. *katapausis* (κατάπαυσις, 2663), in classical Greek, denotes "a causing to cease" or "putting to rest"; in the NT, "rest, repose"; it is used (a) of God's "rest," Acts 7:49; Heb. 3:11, 18; 4:1, 3 (twice), RV (1st part), "that rest" (the KJV, "rest," is ambiguous), 5, 11; (b) in a general statement, applicable to God and man, 4:10.

3. *anesis* (ἄνεσις, 425) is translated "rest" in 2 Cor. 2:13, KJV (RV, "relief"); 7:5 (ditto); in 2 Thess. 1:7, the subject is not the "rest" to be granted to the saints, but the divine retribution on their persecutors; hence the phrase "and to you that are afflicted rest with us," is an incidental extension of the idea of recompense, and is to be read parenthetically. The time is not that at which the saints will be relieved of persecution, as in 1 Thess. 4:15-17, when the Parousia of Christ begins, but that at which the persecutors will be punished, namely, at the epiphany (or out-shining) of His Parousia (2 Thess. 2:8). For similar parentheses characteristic of epistolary writings see v. 10; 1 Thess. 1:6, 2:15, 16.

4. *sabbatismos* (σαββατισμός, 4520), "a Sabbath-keeping," is used in Heb. 4:9, RV, "a sabbath rest," KJV marg., "a keeping of a sabbath" (akin to *sabbatizō*, "to keep the Sabbath," used, e.g., in Exod. 16:30, not in the NT); here the sabbath-keeping is the perpetual sabbath "rest" to be enjoyed uninterruptedly by believers in their fellowship with the Father and the Son, in contrast to the weekly Sabbath under the Law. Because this sabbath "rest" is the "rest" of God Himself, 4:10, its full fruition is yet future, though believers now enter into it. In whatever way they enter into divine "rest," that which they enjoy is involved in an indissoluble relation with God.

5. *koimēsis* (κοίμησις, 2838), "a resting, reclining" (akin to *keimai*, "to lie"), is used in John 11:13, of natural sleep, translated "taking rest," RV.

Note: In Acts 9:31, KJV, *eirēnē*, "peace" (RV), is translated "rest."

B. Verbs.

1. *anapauō* (ἀναπαύω, 373), akin to A, No. 1, in the active voice, signifies "to give intermission from labor, to give rest, to refresh," Matt. 11:28; 1 Cor. 16:18, "have refreshed"; Philem. 20, "refresh"; passive voice, "to be rested, refreshed," 2 Cor. 7:13, "was refreshed"; Philem. 7, "are refreshed"; in the middle voice, "to take or enjoy rest," Matt. 26:45; Mark 6:31; 14:41; Luke 12:19, "take thine ease"; 1 Pet. 4:14; Rev. 6:11; 14:13. See REFRESH. In the papyri it is found as an agricultural term, e.g., of giving land "rest" by sowing light crops upon it. In inscriptions it is found on gravestones of Christians, followed by the date of death (Moulton and Milligan).

2. *katapauō* (καταπαύω, 2664), akin to A, No. 2, used transitively, signifies "to cause to cease, restrain," Acts 14:18; "to cause to rest," Heb. 4:8; intransitively, "to rest," Heb. 4:4, 10.

3. *episkēnoō* (ἐπισκηνόω, 1981), "to spread a tabernacle over" (*epi*, "upon," *skēnē*, "a tent"), is used metaphorically in 2 Cor. 12:9, "may rest upon (me)," RV, marg., "cover," "spread a tabernacle over."

4. *kataskēnoō* (κατασκηνόω, 2681), "to pitch one's tent, lodge," is translated "shall rest," in Acts 2:26, KJV (RV, "shall dwell").

5. *hēsuchazō* (ἡσυχάζω, 2270), "to be still, to rest from labor," is translated "they rested" in Luke 23:56. See PEACE (hold one's), No. 3.

6. *epanapauō* (ἐπαναπαύω, 1879), "to cause to rest," is used in the middle voice, metaphorically, signifying "to rest upon" (*epi*, "upon," and No. 1), in Luke 10:6 and Rom. 2:17.

Note: For "find rest" Rom. 15:32, RV, see REFRESH, No. 2.

REST (the)

1. *loipos* (λοιπός, 3062), "remaining" (for which see REMNANT), is frequently used to mean "the rest," and is generally so translated in the RV (KJV, "others" in Luke 8:10; Acts 28:9; Eph. 2:3; 1 Thess. 4:13; 5:6; 1 Tim. 5:20; KJV, "other" in Luke 18:11; Acts 17:9; Rom. 1:13; 2 Cor. 12:13; 13:2; Gal. 2:13; Phil. 1:13; 4:3); the neut. plur., lit., "remaining things," is used in Luke 12:26; 1 Cor. 11:34.

2. *epiloipos* (ἐπίλοιπος, 1954), signifying "still left, left over" (*epi*, "over," and No. 1), is used in the neuter with the article in 1 Pet. 4:2, "the rest (of your time)."

For **RESTITUTION** see RESTORATION

RESTORATION

apokatastasis (ἀποκατάστασις, 605), from *apo*, "back, again," *kathistemi*, "to set in order," is used in Acts 3:21, RV, "restoration" (KJV, "restitution"). See under REGENERATION, concerning Israel in its regenerated state hereafter. In the papyri it is used of a temple cell of a goddess, a "repair" of a public way, the "restoration" of estates to rightful owners, a "balancing" of accounts. Apart from papyri illustrations the word is found in an Egyptian reference to a consummating agreement of the world's cyclical periods, an idea somewhat similar to that in the Acts passage (Moulton and Milligan).

RESTORE

1. *apodidomi* (ἀποδίδωμι, 591), "to give back," is translated "I restore" in Luke 19:8. See DELIVER, A, No. 3.

2. *apokathistēmi* (ἀποκαθίστημι, 600), or the alternative form *apokathistanō* (ἀποκαθιστάνω, 600) is used (a) of "restoration" to a former condition of health Matt. 12:13; Mark 3:5; 8:25; Luke 6:10; (b) of the divine "restoration" of Israel and conditions affected by it, including the renewal of the covenant broken by them, Matt. 17:11; Mark 9:12; Acts 1:6; (c) of "giving" or "bringing" a person back, Heb. 13:19. In the papyri it is used of financial restitution, of making good the breaking of a stone by a workman by his substituting another, of the reclamation of land, etc. (Moulton and Milligan).

3. *katartizō* (καταρτίζω, 2675), "to mend, to furnish completely," is translated "restore" in Gal. 6:1, metaphorically, of the "restoration," by those who are spiritual, of one overtaken in a trespass, such a one being as a dislocated member of the spiritual body. The tense is the continuous present, suggesting the necessity for patience and perseverance in the process. See FIT, PERFECT.

RESTRAIN

1. *katapauō* (καταπαύω, 2664); See REST B, No. 2.

2. *katechō* (κατέχω, 2722), "to hold fast or down," is translated "restraineth" in 2 Thess. 2:6 and 7. In v. 6 lawlessness is spoken of as being "restrained" in its development: in v. 7 "one that restraineth" is, lit., "the restrainer" (the article with the present participle, "the restraining one"); this may refer to an individual, as in the similar construction in 1 Thess. 3:5, "the tempter" (cf. 1:10, lit., "the Deliverer"); or to a number of persons presenting the same characteristics, just as "the believer" stands for all believers, e.g., Rom. 9:33; 1 John 5:10. v. 6 speaks of a principle, v. 7 of the principle as embodied in a person or series of persons; cf. what is said of "the power" in Rom. 13:3, 4, a phrase representing all such rulers. Probably such powers, i.e., "constituted governments," are the "restraining" influence here intimated (specifications being designedly withheld). For an extended exposition see *Notes on Thessalonians*, by Hogg and Vine, pp. 254-261.

RESURRECTION

1. *anastasis* (ἀνάστασις, 386) denotes (I) "a raising up," or "rising" (*ana*, "up," and *histēmi*, "to cause to stand"), Luke 2:34, "the rising up"; the KJV "again" obscures the meaning; the Child would be like a stone against which many in Israel

would stumble while many others would find in its strength and firmness a means of their salvation and spiritual life; (II), of "resurrection" from the dead, (a) of Christ, Acts 1:22; 2:31; 4:33; Rom. 1:4; 6:5; Phil. 3:10; 1 Pet. 1:3; 3:21; by metonymy, of Christ as the Author of "resurrection," John 11:25; (b) of those who are Christ's at His Parousia (see COMING), Luke 14:14, "the resurrection of the just"; Luke 20:33, 35, 36; John 5:29 (1st part), "the resurrection of life"; 11:24; Acts 23:6; 24:15 (1st part); Rev. 20:5, "the first resurrection"; hence the insertion of "is" stands for the completion of this "resurrection," of which Christ was "the firstfruits"; 20:6; (c) of "the rest of the dead," after the Millennium (cf. Rev. 20:5); John 5:29 (2nd part), "the resurrection of judgment"; Acts 24:15 (2nd part), "of the unjust"; (d) of those who were raised in more immediate connection with Christ's "resurrection," and thus had part already in the first "resurrection," Acts 26:23 and Rom. 1:4 (in each of which "dead" is plural; see Matt. 27:52); (e) of the "resurrection" spoken of in general terms, Matt. 22:23; Mark 12:18; Luke 20:27; Acts 4:2; 17:18; 23:8; 24:21; 1 Cor. 15:12, 13; Heb. 6:2; (f) of those who were raised in OT times, to die again, Heb. 11:35 (1st part), lit., "out of resurrection."

2. *exanastasis* (ἐξανάστασις, 1815), *ek*, "from" or "out of," and No. 1, Phil. 3:11, followed by *ek*, lit., "the out-resurrection from among the dead."

3. *egersis* (ἔγερσις, 1454), "a rousing" (akin to *egeirō*, "to arouse, to raise"), is used of the "resurrection" of Christ, in Matt. 27:53.

REVEAL

1. *apokaluptō* (ἀποκαλύπτω, 601) signifies "to uncover, unveil" (*apo*, "from," *kaluptō*, "to cover"); both verbs are used in Matt. 10:26; in Luke 12:2, *apokalupōo* is set in contrast to *sunkaluptō*, "to cover up, cover completely." "The NT occurrences of this word fall under two heads, subjective and objective. The subjective use is that in which something is presented to the mind directly, as, (a) the meaning of the acts of God, Matt. 11:25; Luke 10:21; (b) the secret of the Person of the Lord Jesus, Matt. 16:17; John 12:38; (c) the character of God as Father, Matt. 11:27; Luke 10:22; (d) the will of God for the conduct of His children, Phil. 3:15; (e) the mind of God to the prophets of Israel, 1 Pet. 1:12, and of the Church, 1 Cor. 14:30; Eph. 3:5.

"The objective use is that in which something is presented to the senses, sight or hearing, as, referring to the past, (f) the truth declared to men in the gospel, Rom. 1:17; 1 Cor. 2:10; Gal. 3:23; (g) the Person of Christ to Paul on the way to Damascus, Gal. 1:16; (h) thoughts before hidden in the heart, Luke 2:35; referring to the future, (i) the coming in glory of the Lord Jesus, Luke 17:30; (j) the salvation and glory that await the believer, Rom. 8:18; 1 Pet. 1:5; 5:1; (k) the true value of service, 1 Cor. 3:13; (l) the wrath of God (at the Cross, against sin, and, at the revelation of the Lord Jesus, against the sinner), Rom. 1:18; (m) the Lawless One, 2 Thess. 2:3, 6, 8.

2. *chrēmatizō* (χρηματίζω, 5537), "to give divine admonition, instruction, revelation," is translated "it had been revealed," in Luke 2:26. See ADMONITION, B, No. 3, CALL.

REVELATION

apokalupsis (ἀποκάλυψις, 602), "an uncovering" (akin to *apokaluptō*; see above), "is used in the NT of (a) the drawing away by Christ of the veil of darkness covering the Gentiles, Luke 2:32; cf. Isa. 25:7; (b) 'the mystery,' the purpose of God in this age, Rom. 16:25; Eph. 3:3; (c) the communication of the knowledge of God to the soul, Eph. 1:17; (d) an expression of the mind of God for the instruction of the church, 1 Cor. 14:6, 26, for the instruction of the Apostle Paul, 2 Cor. 12:1, 7; Gal. 1:12, and for his guidance, Gal. 2:2; (e) the Lord Jesus Christ, to the saints at His Parousia, 1 Cor. 1:7, RV (KJV, 'coming'); 1 Pet. 1:7, RV (KJV, 'appearing'), 13; 4:13; (f) the Lord Jesus Christ when He comes to dispense the judgments of God, 2 Thess. 1:7; cf. Rom. 2:5; (g) the saints, to the creation, in association with Christ in His glorious reign, Rom. 8:19, RV, 'revealing' (KJV, 'manifestation'); (h) the symbolic forecast of the final judgments of God, Rev. 1:1 (hence the Greek title of the book, transliterated 'Apocalypse' and translated 'Revelation')." See APPEAR, COMING, LIGHTEN, B, Note, MANIFESTATION.

REVEL, REVELING

1. *truphē* (τρυφή, 5172), "luxuriousness, daintiness, reveling," is translated freely by the verb "to revel" in 2 Pet. 2:13, RV (KJV, "to riot"), lit., "counting reveling in the daytime a pleasure." In Luke 7:25 it is used with *en*, "in," and translated "delicately." See RIOT.

2. *kōmos* (κῶμος, 2970), "a revel, carousal," the concomitant and consequence of drunkenness, is used in the plural, Rom. 13:13, translated by the singular, RV, "reveling" (KJV, "rioting"); Gal. 5:21 and 1 Pet. 4:3, "revelings." See RIOT.

Note: For *entruphaō*, 2 Pet. 2:13, RV, "to revel," see SPORTING.

For **REVENGE and REVENGER** see AVENGE and AVENGER

REVERENCE (Noun and Verb)

A. Verbs.

1. *entrepō* (ἐντρέπω, 1788), lit., "to turn in" (i.e., upon oneself), "to put to shame," denotes, when used in the passive voice, "to feel respect for, to show deference to, to reverence," Matt. 21:37; Mark 12:6; Luke 20:13; Heb. 12:9. See ASHAMED, A, No. 4, REGARD.

2. *phobeō* (φοβέω, 5399), "to fear," is used in the passive voice in the NT; in Eph. 5:33 of reverential fear on the part of a wife for a husband, KJV, "reverence" (RV, "fear"). See FEAR, D, No. 1.

B. Noun

eulabeia (εὐλάβεια, 2124), "caution, reverence," is translated "reverence" in Heb. 12:28 (1st part in the best mss; some have *aidos*). See FEAR.

REVERENT

hieroprepēs (ἱεροπρεπής, 2412), "suited to a sacred character, reverend" (*hieros*, "sacred," *prepō*, "to be fitting"), is translated "reverent" in Titus 2:3, RV (KJV, "as becometh holiness"). See BECOME, B.

REVILE, REVILING, REVILER

A. Verbs.

1. *loidoreō* (λοιδορέω, 3058) denotes "to abuse, revile," John 9:28; Acts 23:4; 1 Cor. 4:12; 1 Pet. 2:23 (1st clause).

2. *oneidizō* (ὀνειδίζω, 3679), "to reproach, upbraid," is translated "to revile" in Matt. 5:11, KJV, and Mark 15:32 (RV, "reproach"). See REPROACH.

3. *blasphēmeō* (βλασφημέω, 987), "to speak profanely, rail at," is translated "reviled" in Matt. 27:39, KJV (RV, "railed on"); Luke 22:65, RV, "reviling" (KJV, "blasphemously").

4. *antiloidoreō* (ἀντιλοιδορέω, 486), "to revile back or again" (*anti*, and No. 1), is found in 1 Pet. 2:23 (2nd clause).

Note: For *epereazō*, 1 Pet. 3:16, RV, "revile," see ACCUSE, B, No. 3.

B. Adjective.

loidoros (λοίδορος, 3060), akin to A, No. 1, "abusive, railing, reviling," is used as a noun, 1 Cor. 5:11, RV, "a reviler" (KJV "a railer"); 6:10, "revilers." In the Sept., Prov. 25:24; 26:21; 27:15.

C. Noun.

loidoria (λοιδορία, 3059), akin to A, No. 1, and B, "abuse, railing," is used in 1 Tim. 5:14, RV, "for (*charin*, 'for the sake of') reviling" (KJV, "to speak reproachfully"—a paraphrase); 1 Pet. 3:9 (twice), RV, "reviling" (KJV, "railing"). See RAIL, B.

REVIVE

1. *anathallō* (ἀναθάλλω, 330), "to flourish anew" (*ana*, "again, anew," *thallō*, "to flourish or blossom"), hence, "to revive," is used metaphorically in Phil. 4:10, RV, "ye have revived (your thought for me)," KJV, "(your care of me) hath flourished again." In the Sept., Ps. 28:7; Ezek. 17:24; Hos. 8:9.

2. *anazaō* (ἀναζάω, 326), "to live again" (*ana*, "and" *zaō*, "to live"), "to regain life," is used of moral "revival," Luke 15:24, "is alive again"; (b) of sin, Rom. 7:9, "revived," lit., "lived again" i.e., it sprang into activity, manifesting the evil inherent in it; here sin is personified, by way of contrast to the man himself. Some mss. have it in Rom. 14:9, for *zaō*, as in the RV, which italicizes "*again*."

RICH, RICHES, RICHLY, RICH MAN

A. Adjective.

plousios (πλούσιος, 4145), akin to B, C, No. 1, "rich, wealthy," is used (I) literally, (a) adjectivally (with a noun expressed separately) in Matt. 27:57; Luke 12:16; 14:12; 16:1, 19; (without a noun), 18:23; 19:2; (b) as a noun, singular, a "rich" man (the noun not being expressed), Matt. 19:23, 24; Mark 10:25; 12:41; Luke 16:21, 22; 18:25; Jas. 1:10, 11, "the rich," "the rich (man)"; plural, Mark 12:41, lit., "rich (ones)"; Luke 6:24 (ditto); 21:1; 1 Tim. 6:17, "(them that are) rich," lit., "(the) rich"; Jas. 2:6, RV, "the rich"; 5:1, RV, "ye rich"; Rev. 6:15 and 13:16, RV, "the rich"; (II), metaphorically, of God, Eph. 2:4 ("in mercy"); of Christ, 2 Cor. 8:9; of believers, Jas. 2:5, RV, "(*to be*) rich (in faith)"; Rev. 2:9, of spiritual "enrichment" generally; 3:17, of a false sense of "enrichment."

B. Verbs.

1. *plouteō* (πλουτέω, 4147), "to be rich," in the aorist or point tense, "to become rich," is used (a) literally, Luke 1:53, "the rich," present participle, lit., "(ones or those) being rich"; 1 Tim. 6:9, 18; Rev. 18:3, 15, 19 (all three in the aorist tense); (b) metaphorically, of Christ, Rom. 10:12 (the passage stresses the fact that Christ is Lord; see v. 9, and the RV); of the "enrichment" of believers through His poverty, 2 Cor. 8:9 (the aorist tense expressing completeness, with permanent results); so in Rev. 3:18, where the spiritual "enrichment" is conditional upon righteousness of life and conduct (see GOLD, No. 2); of a false sense of "enrichment," 1 Cor. 4:8 (aorist), RV, "ye are become rich" (KJV, "ye are rich"); Rev. 3:17 (perfect tense, RV, "I ... have gotten riches," KJV, "I am ... increased with goods"), see GOODS, *Note* (3); of not being "rich" toward God, Luke 12:21.

2. *ploutizō* (πλουτίζω, 4148), "to make rich, enrich," is rendered "making (many) rich" in 2 Cor. 6:10 (metaphorical of "enriching" spiritually). See ENRICH.

C. Nouns

1. *ploutos* (πλοῦτος, 4149) is used in the singular (I) of material "riches," used evilly, Matt. 13:22: Mark 4:19; Luke 8:14; 1 Tim. 6:17; Jas. 5:2; Rev. 18:17; (II) of spiritual and moral "riches," (a) possessed by God and exercised towards men, Rom. 2:4, "of His goodness and forbearance and longsuffering"; 9:23 and Eph. 3:16, "of His glory" (i.e., of its manifestation in grace towards believers); Rom. 11:33, of His wisdom and knowledge; Eph. 1:7 and 2:7, "of His grace"; 1:18, "of the glory of His inheritance in the saints"; 3:8, "of Christ"; Phil. 4:19, "in glory in Christ Jesus," RV; Col. 1:27, "of the glory of this mystery ... Christ in you, the hope of glory"; (b) to be

ascribed to Christ, Rev. 5:12; (c) of the effects of the gospel upon the Gentiles, Rom. 11:12 (twice); (d) of the full assurance of understanding in regard to the mystery of God, even Christ, Col. 2:2, RV; (e) of the liberality of the churches of Macedonia, 2 Cor. 8:2 (where "the riches" stands for the spiritual and moral value of their liberality); (f) of "the reproach of Christ" in contrast to this world's treasures, Heb. 11:26.

2. *chrēma* (χρῆμα, 5536), "what one uses or needs" (*chraomai*, "to use"), "a matter, business," hence denotes "riches," Mark 10:23, 24; Luke 18:24; see MONEY, No. 2.

D. Adverb.

plousiōs (πλουσίως, 4146), "richly, abundantly," akin to A, is used in Col. 3:16; 1 Tim. 6:17; Titus 3:6, RV, "richly" (KJV, "abundantly"); 2 Pet. 1:11 (ditto).

RIGHT (opp. to left), RIGHT HAND, RIGHT SIDE

dexios (δεξιός, 1188), an adjective, used (a) of "the right" as opposite to the left, e.g., Matt. 5:29, 30; Rev. 10:5, RV, "right hand"; in connection with armor (figuratively), 2 Cor. 6:7; with *en*, followed by the dative plural, Mark 16:5; with *ek*, and the genitive plural, e.g., Matt. 25:33, 34; Luke 1:11; (b) of giving the "right hand" of fellowship, Gal. 2:9, betokening the public expression of approval by leaders at Jerusalem of the course pursued by Paul and Barnabas among the Gentiles; the act was often the sign of a pledge, e.g., 2 Kings 10:15; 1 Chron. 29:24, marg.; Ezra 10:19; Ezek. 17:18; figuratively, Lam. 5:6; it is often so used in the papyri; (c) metaphorically of "power" or "authority," Acts 2:33; with *ek*, signifying "on," followed by the genitive plural, Matt. 26:64; Mark 14:62; Heb. 1:13; (d) similarly of "a place of honor in the messianic kingdom," Matt. 20:21; Mark 10:37.

RIGHT (not wrong—Noun and Adjective), RIGHTLY

A. Noun.

exousia (ἐξουσία, 1849), "authority, power," is translated "right" in the RV, for KJV, "power," in John 1:12; Rom. 9:21; 1 Cor. 9:4, 5, 6, 12 (twice), 18; 2 Thess. 3:9, where the "right" is that of being maintained by those among whom the ministers of the gospel had labored, a "right" possessed in virtue of the "authority" given them by Christ, Heb. 13:10; Rev. 22:14.

Exousia first denotes "freedom to act" and then "authority for the action." This is first true of God, Acts 1:7. It was exercised by the Son of God, as from, and in conjunction with, the Father when the Lord was upon earth, in the days of His flesh, Matt. 9:6; John 10:18, as well as in resurrection, Matt. 28:18; John 17:2. All others hold their freedom to act from God (though some of them have abused it), whether angels, Eph. 1:21, or human potentates, Rom. 13:1. Satan offered to delegate his authority over earthly kingdoms to Christ, Luke 4:6, who, though conscious of His "right" to it, refused, awaiting the divinely appointed time. For various synonyms see DOMINION, No. 1, Note.

B. Adjectives.

1. *dikaios* (δίκαιος, 1342), "just, righteous, that which is in accordance with" *dikē*, "rule, right, justice," is translated "right" in Matt. 20:4; v. 7, KJV only (RV omits, according to the most authentic mss., the clause having been inserted from v. 4, to the detriment of the narrative); Luke 12:57; Acts 4:19; Eph. 6:1; Phil. 1:7, RV (KJV, "meet"); 2 Pet. 1:13 (KJV, "meet"). See JUST, RIGHTEOUS.

2. *euthus* (εὐθύς, 2117), "straight," hence, metaphorically, "right," is so rendered in Acts 8:21, of the heart; 13:10, of the ways of the Lord; 2 Pet. 2:15. See STRAIGHT.

C. Adverb.

orthōs (ὀρθῶς, 3723), "rightly" (akin to *orthos*, "straight, direct"), is translated "plain" in Mark 7:35; in Luke 7:43 and 20:21, "rightly"; in Luke 10:28, "right."

Note: For "right mind" see MIND, B, No. 5.

RIGHTEOUS, RIGHTEOUSLY

A. Adjective.

dikaios (δίκαιος, 1342) signifies "just," without prejudice or partiality, e.g., of the judgment of God, 2 Thess. 1:5, 6; of His judgments, Rev. 16:7; 19:2; of His character as Judge, 2 Tim. 4:8; Rev. 16:5; of His ways and doings, Rev. 15:3. See further under JUST, A, No. 1, RIGHT, B, No. 1.

In the following the RV substitutes "righteous" for the KJV "just"; Matt. 1:19; 13:49; 27:19, 24; Mark 6:20; Luke 2:25; 15:7; 20:20; 23:50; John 5:30; Acts 3:14; 7:52; 10:22; 22:14; Rom. 1:17; 7:12; Gal. 3:11; Heb. 10:38; Jas. 5:6; 1 Pet. 3:18; 2 Pet. 2:7; 1 John 1:9; Rev. 15:3.

B. Adverb.

dikaiōs (δικαίως, 1346) is translated "righteously" in 1 Cor. 15:34, RV "(awake up) righteously," KJV, "(awake to) righteousness"; 1 Thess. 2:10, RV (KJV, "justly"); Titus 2:12; 1 Pet. 2:23. See JUSTLY.

Notes: (1) In Rev. 22:11 the best texts have *dikaiosunē*, "righteousness," with *poieō*, "to do," RV, "let him do righteousness"; the KJV follows those which have the passive voice of *dikaioō* and renders it "let him be righteous," lit., "let him be made righteous." (2) *Dikaiokrisia*, "righteous judgment" (*dikaios*, and *krisis*), occurs in Rom. 2:5.

RIGHTEOUSNESS

1. *dikaiosune* (δικαιοσύνη, 1343) is "the character or quality of being right or just"; it was formerly spelled "rightwiseness," which clearly expresses the meaning. It is used to denote an attribute of God, e.g., Rom. 3:5, the context of which shows that "the righteousness of God" means essentially

the same as His faithfulness, or truthfulness, that which is consistent with His own nature and promises; Rom. 3:25, 26 speaks of His "righteousness" as exhibited in the death of Christ, which is sufficient to show men that God is neither indifferent to sin nor regards it lightly. On the contrary, it demonstrates that quality of holiness in Him which must find expression in His condemnation of sin.

"*Dikaiosunē* is found in the sayings of the Lord Jesus, (a) of whatever is right or just in itself, whatever conforms to the revealed will of God, Matt. 5:6, 10, 20; John 16:8, 10; (b) whatever has been appointed by God to be acknowledged and obeyed by man, Matt. 3:15; 21:32; (c) the sum total of the requirements of God, Matt. 6:33; (d) religious duties, Matt. 6:1 (distinguished as almsgiving, man's duty to his neighbor, vv. 2-4, prayer, his duty to God, vv. 5-15, fasting, the duty of self-control, vv. 16–18).

"In the preaching of the apostles recorded in Acts the word has the same general meaning. So also in Jas. 1:20, 3:18, in both Epp. of Peter, 1st John and the Revelation. In 2 Pet. 1:1, 'the righteousness of our God and Savior Jesus Christ,' is the righteous dealing of God with sin and with sinners on the ground of the death of Christ. 'Word of righteousness,' Heb. 5:13, is probably the gospel, and the Scriptures as containing the gospel, wherein is declared the righteousness of God in all its aspects.

"This meaning of *dikaiosune*, right action, is frequent also in Paul's writings, as in all five of its occurrences in Rom. 6; Eph. 6:14, etc. But for the most part he uses it of that gracious gift of God to men whereby all who believe on the Lord Jesus Christ are brought into right relationship with God. This righteousness is unattainable by obedience to any law, or by any merit of man's own, or any other condition than that of faith in Christ .... The man who trusts in Christ becomes 'the righteousness of God in Him,' 2 Cor. 5:21, i.e., becomes in Christ all that God requires a man to be, all that he could never be in himself Because Abraham accepted the Word of God, making it his own by that act of the mind and spirit which is called faith, and, as the sequel showed, submitting himself to its control, therefore God accepted him as one who fulfilled the whole of His requirements, Rom. 4:3 ....

"Righteousness is not said to be imputed to the believer save in the sense that faith is imputed ('reckoned' is the better word) for righteousness. It is clear that in Rom. 4:6, 11, 'righteousness reckoned' must be understood in the light of the context, 'faith reckoned for righteousness,' vv. 3, 5, 9, 22. 'For' in these places is *eis*, which does not mean 'instead of,' but 'with a view to.' The faith thus exercised brings the soul into vital union with God in Christ, and inevitably produces righteousness of life, that is, conformity to the will of God."

2. *dikaiōma* (δικαίωμα, 1345) is the concrete expression of "righteousness": see JUSTIFICATION, A, No. 2.

Note: In Heb. 1:8, KJV, *euthutēs*, "straightness, uprightness" (akin to *euthus*, "straight, right"), is translated "righteousness" (RV "uprightness"; KJV, marg., "rightness, or straightness").

RIOT, RIOTING, RIOTOUS, RIOTOUSLY

A. Nouns.

1. *asōtia* (ἀσωτία, 810), "prodigality, a wastefulness, profligacy" (*a*, negative, *sōzō*, "to save"), is rendered "riot" in Eph. 5:18, RV (KJV, "excess"); Titus 1:6 and 1 Pet. 4:4 (KJV and RV, "riot"). The corresponding verb is found in a papyrus writing, telling of "riotous living" (like the adverb *asōtōs*, see B). In the Sept., Prov. 28:7. Cf. the synonymous word *aselgeia* (under LASCIVIOUSNESS).

2. *kōmos* (κῶμος, 2970), "a revel," is rendered "rioting" in Rom. 13:13, KJV.

3. *truphē* (τρυφή, 5172), "luxuriousness," is rendered "riot" in 2 Pet. 2:13, KJV.

4. *stasis* (στάσις, 4714), primarily "a standing" (akin to *histēmi*, "to cause to ("stand"), then "an insurrection," is translated "riot" in Acts 19:40 RV (KJV, uproar). See DISSENSION, INSURRECTION, SEDITION, UPROAR.

B. Adverb.

asōtōs (ἀσώτως, 811), "wastefully" (akin to A, No. 1), is translated "with riotous living" in Luke 15:13; though the word does not necessarily signify "dissolutely," the parable narrative makes clear that this is the meaning here. In the Sept., Prov. 7:11.

Note: The verb *ekchunō*, a Hellenistic form of *ekcheō* (though the form actually used is the regular classical aorist passive of *ekcheō*), "to pour out, shed," is translated "ran riotously" in Jude 11, RV (KJV, "ran greedily").

RIPE (to be fully)

1. *akmazō* (ἀκμάζω, 187), "to be at the prime" (akin to *akmē*, "a point"), "to be ripe," is translated "are fully ripe" in Rev. 14:18.

2. *xerainō* (ξηραίνω, 3583), "to dry up, wither," is used of "ripened" crops in Rev. 14:15, RV, "overripe," KJV, "ripe" (marg., "dried"). See DRY, B, OVERRIPE, WITHER.

3. *paradidōmi* (παραδίδωμι, 3860), "to give over, commit, deliver," etc., also signifies "to permit"; in Mark 4:29, of the "ripe" condition of corn, RV, and KJV marg., "is ripe"; RV marg., "alloweth" (the nearest rendering); KJV, "is brought forth."

RIVER

potamos (ποταμός, 4215) denotes (a) "a stream," Luke 6:48, 49; (b) "a flood or floods," Matt. 7:25, 27; (c) "a river," natural, Matt. 3:6, RV; Mark 1:5; Acts 16:13; 2 Cor. 11:26, RV (KJV, "waters"); Rev. 8:10; 9:14; 16:4, 12; symbolical, Rev. 12:15 (1st part), RV, "river" (KJV, "flood"); so v. 16; 22:1, 2 (cf. Gen. 2:10; Ezek. 47); figuratively, John 7:38, "the effects of the operation of the Holy Spirit in and through the believer." See FLOOD, WATER.

Note: For *potamophorētos* in Rev. 12:15, see FLOOD, B.

For **ROBBERY** see PRIZE

ROCK

1. *petra* (πέτρα, 4073) denotes "a mass of rock," as distinct from *petros*, "a detached stone or boulder," or a stone that might be thrown or easily moved. For the nature of *petra*, see Matt. 7:24, 25; 27:51, 60; Mark 15:46; Luke 6:48 (twice), a type of a sure foundation (here the true reading is as in the RV, "because it had been well builded"); Rev. 6:15, 16 (cf. Isa. 2:19,ff.; Hos. 10:8); Luke 8:6, 13, used illustratively; 1 Cor. 10:4 (twice), figuratively, of Christ; in Rom. 9:33 and 1 Pet. 2:8, metaphorically, of Christ; in Matt. 16:18, metaphorically, of Christ and the testimony concerning Him; here the distinction between *petra*, concerning the Lord Himself, and *Petros*, the apostle, is clear (see above).

2. *spilas* (σπιλάς, 4694), "a rock or reef," over which the sea dashes, is used in Jude 12, "hidden rocks," RV, metaphorical of men whose conduct is a danger to others. A late meaning ascribed to it is that of "spots," (KJV), but that rendering seems to have been influenced by the parallel passage in 2 Pet. 2:13, where *spiloi*, "spots," occurs.

ROCKY

petrōdes (πετρώδης, 4075), "rock-like" (*petra*, "a rock," *eidos*, "a form, appearance"), is used of "rock" underlying shallow soil, Matt. 13:5, 20, RV, "the rocky places" (KJV, "stony places"); Mark 4:5, RV, "the rocky ground" (KJV, "stony ground"); v. 16, RV, "rocky places" (KJV, "stony ground").

Note: In Acts 27:29, KJV, the phrase *tracheis topoi*, lit., "rough places," is translated "rocks" (RV, "rocky ground").

ROMAN

rhōmaios (Ῥωμαῖος, 4514) occurs in John 11:48; Acts 2:10, RV, "from Rome" (KJV, "of Rome"); 16:21, 37, 38; 22:25, 26, 27, 29; 23:27; 25:16; 28:17. For a note on Roman citizenship see CITIZEN, No. 3.

ROYAL

1. *basileios* (βασίλειος, 934), from *basileus*, "a king," is used in 1 Pet. 2:9 of the priesthood consisting of all believers. Cf. Luke 7:25, for which see COURT, No. 3. In the Sept., Ex. 19:6; 23:22; Deut. 3:10.

2. *basilikos* (βασιλικός, 937), "belonging to a king," is translated "royal" in Acts 12:21; Jas. 2:8. See KING B, No. 2.

RUDIMENTS

stoicheion (στοιχεῖον, 4747), "one of a row or series," is translated "rudiments" in the RV of Gal. 4:3, 9; Heb. 5:12, and the KJV and RV of Col. 2:8, 20.

RUIN

1. *rhēgma* (ῥῆγμα, 4485), akin to *rhēgnumi*, "to break," denotes "a cleavage, fracture" (so in the Sept., e.g., 1 Kings 11:30, 31); by metonymy, that which is broken, "a ruin," Luke 6:49.

2. *katestrammena* (κατεστραμμένα, 2690), the neuter plural, perfect participle, passive, of *katastrephō*, "to overturn," is translated "ruins" in Acts 15:16. See OVERTHROW.

RULE (Noun and Verb)

A. Nouns.

1. *archē* (ἀρχή, 746), "a beginning," etc., denotes "rule," Luke 20:20, RV, "rule" (KJV, "power"); 1 Cor. 15:24; Eph. 1:21, RV, "rule" (KJV, "principality"). See BEGINNING, B.

2. *kanōn* (κανών, 2583) is translated "rule" in the KJV of 2 Cor. 10:13, 15; in Gal. 6:16, KJV and RV; in Phil. 3:16, KJV (RV, in italics): see PROVINCE, No. 2.

B. Verbs.

1. *archō* (ἄρχομαι, 756), (akin to A, No. 1), in the active voice denotes "to rule," Mark 10:42 and Rom. 15:12, RV, "to rule" (KJV, "to reign"). See BEGIN, A, No. 1.

2. *oikodespoteō* (οἰκοδεσποτέω, 3616), from *oikos*, "a house," and *despotēs*, "a master," signifies "to rule the household"; so the RV in 1 Tim. 5:14 (KJV, "guide the house"). See GUIDE, B, *Note* (1). Cf. *oikodespotēs*, "a householder."

3. *proistemi* (προΐστημι, 4291), lit., "to stand before," hence, "to lead, attend to" (indicating care and diligence), is translated "to rule" (middle voice), with reference to a local church, in Rom. 12:8; perfect active in 1 Tim. 5:17; with reference to a family, 1 Tim. 3:4 and 12 (middle voice); v. 5 (2nd aorist, active).

4. *hēgeomai* (ἡγέομαι, 2233), "to lead," is translated "to rule" in Heb. 13:7, 17, 24 (KJV marg., in the first two, "are the guides" and "guide."

5. *poimainō* (ποιμαίνω, 4165), "to act as a shepherd, tend flocks," is translated "to rule" in Rev. 2:27; 12:5; 19:15, all indicating that the governing power exercised by the Shepherd is to be of a firm character; in Matt. 2:6, KJV, "shall rule" (RV, "shall be shepherd of"). See FEED.

6. *brabeuō* (βραβεύω, 1018), properly, "to act as an umpire" (*brabeus*), hence, generally, "to arbitrate, decide," Col. 3:15, "rule" (RV, marg., "arbitrate"), representing "the peace of Christ" (RV) as deciding all matters in the hearts of believers; some regard the meaning as that of simply directing, controlling, "ruling." Cf. *katabrabeuō*.

RULER

1. *archōn* (ἄρχων, 758), "a ruler, chief, prince," is translated "rulers," e.g., in 1 Cor. 2:6, 8, RV (KJV, "princes"); "ruler," Rev. 1:5 (KJV, prince). See MAGISTRATE, PRINCE, No. 2.

2. *archē* (ἀρχή, 746), "a rule, sovereignty," is rendered "rulers" in Luke 12:11, RV (KJV, "magistrates"). See BEGINNING.

3. *kosmokratōr* (κοσμοκράτωρ, 2888) denotes "a ruler of this world" (contrast *pantokratōr*, "almighty"). In Greek literature, in Orphic hymns, etc., and in rabbinic writings, it signifies a "ruler" of the whole world, a world lord. In the NT it is used in Eph. 6:12, "the world rulers (of this darkness)," RV, KJV, "the rulers (of the darkness) of this world." The context ("not against flesh and blood") shows that not earthly potentates are indicated, but spirit powers, who, under the permissive will of God, and in consequence of human sin, exercise satanic and therefore antagonistic authority over the world in its present condition of spiritual darkness and alienation from God. The suggested rendering "the rulers of this dark world" is ambiguous and not phraseologically requisite. Cf. John 12:31; 14:30; 16:11; 2 Cor. 4:4.

4. *politarchēs* (πολιτάρχης, 4173), "a ruler of a city" (*polis*, "a city," *archō*, "to rule"), "a politarch," is used in Acts 17:6, 8, of the magistrates in Thessalonica, before whom the Jews, with a mob of market idlers, dragged Jason and other converts, under the charge of showing hospitality to Paul and Silas, and of treasonable designs against the emperor. Thessalonica was a "free" city and the citizens could choose their own politarchs. The accuracy of Luke has been vindicated by the use of the term, for while classical authors use the terms *poliarchos* and *politarchos* of similar "rulers," the form used by Luke is supported by inscriptions discovered at Thessalonica, one of which mentions Sosipater, Secundus, and Gaius among the politarchs, names occurring as those of Paul's companions. Prof. Burton of Chicago, in a paper on "The Politarchs," has recorded 17 inscriptions which attest their existence, thirteen of which belong to Macedonia and five presumably to Thessalonica itself, illustrating the influence of Rome in the municipal organization of the place.

5. *architriklinos* (ἀρχιτρίκλινος, 755) denotes "the superintendent of a banquet," whose duty lay in arranging the tables and food (*archē*, "ruler," *triklinos*, lit., "a room with three couches"), John 2:8, 9.

Notes: (1) In Mark 13:9 and Luke 21:12, KJV, *hēgemōn*, "a leader, a governor of a province," is translated "ruler" (RV, "governor"). See GOVERNOR, PRINCE, No. 3. (2) For ruler of the synagogue, see SYNAGOGUE. (3) In Matt. 24:45, KJV, *kathistēmi*, "to appoint," is translated "hath made ruler" (RV, "hath set"); so in v. 47; 25:21, 23; Luke 12:42, 44.

RUMOR

1. *akoē* (ἀκοή, 189), "a hearing," is translated "rumor" in Matt. 24:6; Mark 13:7. See HEARING, B, No. 1.

2. *ēchos* (ἦχος, 2279), "a noise, sound," is translated "rumor" in Luke 4:37, RV (KJV, "fame"). See SOUND.

Note: In Luke 7:17, KJV, *logos*, "a word," is translated "rumor" (RV, "report").

S

SABACHTHANI

sabachthani (σαβαχθανί, 4518), an Aramaic word signifying "Thou hast forsaken Me," is recorded as part of the utterance of Christ on the cross, Matt. 27:46; Mark 15:34, a quotation from Ps. 22:1. Recently proposed renderings which differ from those of the KJV and RV have not been sufficiently established to require acceptance.

SABAOTH

sabaōth (σαβαώθ, 4519) is the transliteration of a Hebrew word which denotes "hosts" or "armies," Rom. 9:29; Jas. 5:4. While the word "hosts" probably had special reference to angels, the title "the LORD of hosts" became used to designate Him as the One who is supreme over all the innumerable hosts of spiritual agencies, or of what are described as "the armies of heaven." Eventually it was used as equivalent to "the LORD all-sovereign." In the prophetical books of the OT the Sept. sometimes has *Kurios Sabaōth* as the equivalent of "the LORD of hosts," sometimes *Kurios Pantokratōr*, in Job, it uses *Pantokratōr* to render the Hebrew divine title *Shadday* (see ALMIGHTY).

SABBATH

1. *sabbaton* (σάββατον, 4521) or *sabbata:* the latter, the plural form, was transliterated from the Aramaic word, which was mistaken for a plural; hence the singular, *sabbaton*, was formed from it. The root means "to cease, desist" (Heb., *shābath*; cf. Arab., *sabata*, "to intercept, interrupt"); the doubled *b* has an intensive force, implying a complete cessation or a making to cease, probably the former. The idea is not that of relaxation or refreshment, but cessation from activity.

The observation of the seventh day of the week, enjoined upon Israel, was a sign between God and His earthly people, based upon the fact that after the six days of creative operations He rested, Exod. 31:16, 17, with 20:8-11. The OT regulations were developed and systematized to such an extent that they became a burden upon the people (who otherwise rejoiced in the rest provided) and a byword for absurd extravagance. Two treatises of the Mishna (the *Shābbath* and *'Ērūbin*) are entirely occupied with regulations for the observance; so with the discussions in the Gemara, on rabbinical opinions. The effect upon current opinion explains the antagonism roused by the Lord's cures wrought on the "Sabbath," e.g., Matt. 12:9-13; John 5:5-16, and explains the fact that on a "Sabbath" the sick were brought to be healed after sunset, e.g., Mark 1:32. According to rabbinical ideas, the disciples, by plucking ears of corn (Matt. 12:1; Mark 2:23), and rubbing them (Luke 6:1), broke the "sabbath" in two respects; for to pluck was to reap, and to rub was to thresh. The Lord's attitude towards the "sabbath" was by way of freeing it from these vexatious traditional accretions by which it was made an end in itself, instead of a means to an end (Mark 2:27).

In the Epistles the only direct mentions are in Col. 2:16, "a sabbath day," RV (which rightly has the singular, see 1st parag., above), where it is listed among things that were "a shadow of the things to come" (i.e., of the age introduced at Pentecost), and in Heb. 4:4-11, where the perpetual *sabbatismos* is appointed for believers (see REST); inferential references are in Rom. 14:5 and Gal. 4:9-11. For the first three centuries of the Christian era the first day of the week was never confounded with the "sabbath"; the confusion of the Jewish and Christian institutions was due to declension from apostolic teaching.

Notes: (1) In Matt. 12:1 and 11, where the plural is used, the KJV (as the RV) rightly has the singular, "the sabbath day"; in v. 5 the KJV has the plural (see above). Where the singular is used the RV omits the word "day," v. 2; 24:20; Mark 6:2; Luke 6:1 ("on a sabbath"); 14:3; John 9:14 ("it was the sabbath on the day when ..."). As to the use or omission of the article the omission does not always require the rendering "a sabbath"; it is absent, e.g., in Matt. 12:2. (2) In Acts 16:13, "on the sabbath day," is, lit., "on the day of the sabbath" (plural).

2. *prosabbaton* (προσάββατον, 4315) signifies "the day before the sabbath" (*pro*, "before," and No. 1), Mark 15:42; some mss. have *prin*, "before," with *sabbaton* separately).

SACKCLOTH

sakkos (σάκκος, 4526), "a warm material woven from goat's or camel's hair," and hence of a dark color, Rev. 6:12; Jerome renders it *saccus cilicinus* (being made from the hair of the black goat of Cilicia; the Romans called it *cilicium*); cf. Isa. 50:3; it was also used for saddlecloths, Josh. 9:4; also for making sacks, e.g., Gen. 42:25, and for garments worn as expressing mourning or penitence, Matt. 11:21; Luke 10:13, or for purposes of prophetic testimony, Rev. 11:3.

SACRED

hieros (ἱερός, 2413) denotes "consecrated to God," e.g., the Scriptures, 2 Tim. 3:15, RV, "sacred" (KJV "holy"); it is used as a noun in the neuter plural in 1 Cor. 9:13, RV, "sacred things" (KJV, "holy things"). The neuter singular, *hieron*, denotes "a temple." See TEMPLE. For a comparison of this and synonymous terms see HOLY, B, No. 1 (b) and *Note* (2).

SACRIFICE (Noun and Verb)

A. Noun.

thusia (θυσία, 2378) primarily denotes "the act of offering"; then, objectively, "that which is offered" (a) of idolatrous "sacrifice," Acts 7:41; (b) of animal or other "sacrifices," as offered under the Law, Matt. 9:13; 12:7; Mark 9:49; 12:33; Luke 2:24; 13:1; Acts 7:42; 1 Cor. 10:18; Heb. 5:1; 7:27 (RV, plural); 8:3; 9:9; 10:1, 5, 8 (RV, plural), 11; 11:4; (c) of Christ, in His "sacrifice" on the cross, Eph. 5:2; Heb. 9:23, where the plural antitypically comprehends the various forms of Levitical "sacrifices" in their typical character; 9:26; 10:12, 26; (d) metaphorically, (1) of the body of the believer, presented to God as a living "sacrifice," Rom. 12:1; (2) of faith, Phil. 2:17; (3) of material assistance rendered to servants of God, Phil. 4:18; (4) of praise, Heb, 13:15; (5) of doing good to others and communicating with their needs, Heb. 13:16; (6) of spiritual "sacrifices" in general, offered by believers as a holy priesthood, 1 Pet. 2:5.

B. Verb.

thuō (θύω, 2380) is used of "sacrificing by slaying a victim," (a) of the "sacrifice" of Christ, 1 Cor. 5:7, RV, "hath been sacrificed" (KJV, "is sacrificed"); (b) of the Passover "sacrifice," Mark 14:12, RV, "they sacrificed" (KJV, "they killed"); Luke 22:7, RV, "(must) be sacrificed," KJV, "(must) be killed"; (c) of idolatrous "sacrifices," Acts 14:13, 18; 1 Cor. 10:20 (twice). See KILL, No. 3.

Note: For *eidōlothutos*, "sacrificed to idols," see IDOLS (offered to), No. 1.

For **SAD** see COUNTENANCE

For **SADDUCEES** see under PHARISEES

SAFE, SAFELY, SAFETY

A. Adjective.

asphalēs (ἀσφαλής, 804), "certain, secure, safe" (from *a*, negative, and *sphallō*, "to trip up"), is translated "safe" in Phil. 3:1.

B. Nouns.

1. *asphaleia* (ἀσφάλεια, 803), "certainty, safety" (akin to A), is translated "safety" in Acts 5:23; 1 Thess. 5:3.

2. *sōtēria* (σωτηρία, 4991), "salvation," is translated "safety" in Acts 27:34, RV (KJV, "health"). See HEALTH, *Note*.

C. Adverb.

asphalōs (ἀσφαλῶς, 806), "safely" (akin to A, and B, No. 1), is so rendered in Mark 14:44 and Acts 16:23. See ASSURANCE, C. In the Sept., Gen. 34:25.

D. Verbs.

1. *diasōzō* (διασώζω, 1295), "to bring safely through danger," and, in the passive voice, "to come safe through" (*dia*, "through," *sōzō*, "to save"), is translated "bring safe" in Acts 23:24; "escaped safe" in 27:44. See ESCAPE, HEAL, SAVE, WHOLE.

2. *hugiainō* (ὑγιαίνω, 5198), "to be sound, healthy" (Eng., "hygiene," etc.), is translated "safe and sound" in Luke 15:27, lit., "being healthy. See HEALTH, SOUND, WHOLE.

SAINT(S)

hagios (ἅγιος, 40), for the meaning and use of which see HOLY, B, No. 1, is used as a noun in the singular in Phil. 4:21, where *pas*, "every," is used with it. In the plural, as used of believers, it designates all such and is not applied merely to persons of exceptional holiness, or to those who, having died, were characterized by exceptional acts of "saintliness." See especially 2 Thess. 1:10, where "His saints" are also described as "them that believed," i.e., the whole number of the redeemed. They are called "holy ones" in Jude 14, RV. For the term as applied to the Holy Spirit see HOLY SPIRIT. See also SANCTIFY.

Notes: (1) In Rev. 15:3 the RV follows those texts which have *aiōnōn*, "ages," and assigns the reading *ethnōn*, "nations," to the margin; the KJV translates those which have the inferior reading *hagiōn*, "saints," and puts "nations" and "ages" in the margin. (2) In Rev. 18:20, the best texts have *hagioi* and *apostoloi*, each with the article, each being preceeded by *kai*, "and," RV, "and ye saints, and ye apostles"; the KJV, "and ye holy apostles" follows those mss. from which the 2nd *kai* and the article are absent. (3) In Rev. 22:21, the RV follows those mss. which have *hagiōn*, with the article,"(with) the saints"; the KJV those which simply have *pantōn*, "all," but adds "you" (RV, marg., "with all").

SALT (Noun, Adjective and Verb), SALTNESS

A. Noun.

halas (ἅλς, 251), a late form of *hals* (found in some mss. in Mark 9:49), is used (a) literally in Matt. 5:13 (2nd part); Mark 9:50 (1st part, twice); Luke 14:34 (twice); (b) metaphorically, of "believers," Matt. 5:13 (1st part); of their "character and condition," Mark 9:50 (2nd part); of "wisdom" exhibited in their speech, Col.4:6.

Being possessed of purifying, perpetuating and antiseptic qualities, "salt" became emblematic of fidelity and friendship among eastern nations. To eat of a person's "salt" and so to share his hospitality is still regarded thus among the Arabs. So in Scripture, it is an emblem of the covenant between God and His people, Num. 18:19; 2 Chron. 13:5; so again when the Lord says "Have salt in yourselves, and be at peace one with another" (Mark 9:50). In the Lord's teaching it is also symbolic of that spiritual health and vigor essential to Christian virtue and counteractive of the corruption that is in the world, e.g., Matt. 5:13, see (b) above. Food is seasoned with "salt" (see B); every meal offering was to contain it, and it was to be offered with all offerings presented by Israelites, as emblematic of the holiness of Christ, and as betokening the reconciliation provided for man by God on the ground of the death of Christ, Lev. 2:13. To refuse God's provision in Christ and the efficacy of His expiatory sacrifice is to expose oneself to the doom of being "salted with fire," Mark 9:49.

While "salt" is used to fertilize soil, excess of it on the ground produces sterility (e.g., Deut. 29:23; Judg. 9:45; Jer. 17:6; Zeph. 2:9).

B. Verb.

halizō (ἁλίζω, 233), akin to A, signifies "to sprinkle" or "to season with salt," Matt. 5:13; Mark 9:49 (see under A). Cf. SAVOR, B.

C. Adjectives.

1. *halukos* (ἁλυκός, 252) occurs in Jas. 3:12, "salt (water)."

2. *analos* (ἄναλος, 358) denotes "saltless" (*a*, negative, *n*, euphonic, and A), insipid, Mark 9:50, "have lost its saltness," lit., "have become (*ginomai*) saltless (*analos*)"; cf. *mōrainō* in Luke 14:34.

For **SALUTATION and SALUTE** see GREET

SALVATION

A. Nouns.

1. *sōtēria* (σωτηρία, 4991) denotes "deliverance, preservation, salvation." "Salvation" is used in the NT (a) of material and temporal deliverance from danger and apprehension, (1) national, Luke 1:69, 71; Acts 7:25, RV marg., "salvation" (text, "deliverance"); (2) personal, as from the sea, Acts 27:34; RV, "safety" (KJV, "health"); prison, Phil. 1:19; the flood, Heb. 11:7; (b) of the spiritual and eternal deliverance granted immediately by God to those who accept His conditions of repentance and faith in the Lord Jesus, in whom alone it is to be obtained, Acts 4:12, and upon confession of Him as Lord, Rom. 10:10; for this purpose the gospel is the saving instrument, Rom. 1:16; Eph. 1:13 (see further under SAVE); (c) of the present experience of God's power to deliver from the bondage of sin, e.g., Phil. 2:12, where the special, though not the entire, reference is to the maintenance of peace and harmony; 1 Pet. 1:9; this present experience on the part of believers is virtually equivalent to sanctification; for this purpose, God is able to make them wise, 2 Tim. 3:15; they are not to neglect it, Heb. 2:3; (d) of the future deliverance of believers at the Parousia of Christ for His saints, a salvation which is the object of their confident hope, e.g., Rom. 13:11; 1 Thess. 5:8, and v. 9, where "salvation" is assured to them, as being deliverance from the wrath of God destined to be executed upon the ungodly at the end of this age (see 1 Thess. 1:10); 2 Thess. 2:13; Heb. 1:14; 9:28; 1 Pet. 1:5; 2 Pet. 3:15; (e) of the deliverance of the nation of Israel at the second advent of Christ at the time of "the epiphany (or shining forth) of His Parousia" (2 Thess. 2:8); Luke 1:71; Rev. 12:10; (f) inclusively, to sum up all the blessings bestowed by God on men in Christ through the Holy Spirit, e.g., 2 Cor. 6:2; Heb. 5:9; 1 Pet. 1:9, 10; Jude 3; (g) occasionally, as standing virtually for the Savior, e.g., Luke 19:9; cf. John 4:22 (see SAVIOR); (h) in ascriptions of praise to God, Rev. 7:10, and as that which it is His prerogative to bestow, 19:1 (RV).

2. *sōtērion* (σωτήριον, 4992), the neuter of the adjective (see B), is used as a noun in Luke 2:30; 3:6, in each of which it virtually stands for the Savior, as in No. 1 (g); in Acts 28:28, as in No. 1 (b); in Eph. 6:17, where the hope of "salvation" [see No. 1 (d)] is metaphorically described as "a helmet."

B. Adjective.

sōtērios (σωτήριος, 4992), "saving, bringing salvation," describes the grace of God, in Titus 2:11.

SANCTIFICATION, SANCTIFY

A. Noun.

hagiasmos (ἁγιασμός, 38), "sanctification," is used of (a) separation to God, 1 Cor. 1:30; 2 Thess. 2:13; 1 Pet. 1:2; (b) the course of life befitting those so separated, 1 Thess. 4:3, 4, 7; Rom. 6:19, 22; 1 Tim. 2:15; Heb. 12:14. "Sanctification is that relationship with God into which men enter by faith in Christ, Acts 26:18; 1 Cor. 6:11, and to which their sole title is the death of Christ, Eph. 5:25, 26; Col. 1:22; Heb. 10:10, 29; 13:12.

"Sanctification is also used in NT of the separation of the believer from evil things and ways. This sanctification is God's will for the believer, 1 Thess. 4:3, and His purpose in calling him by the gospel, v. 7; it must be learned from God, v. 4, as He teaches it by His Word, John 17:17, 19, cf. Ps. 17:4; 119:9, and it must be pursued by the believer, earnestly and undeviatingly, 1 Tim. 2:15; Heb. 12:14. For the holy character, *hagiōsunē*, 1 Thess. 3:13, is not vicarious, i.e., it cannot be transferred or imputed, it is an individual possession, built up, little by little, as the result of obedience to the Word of God, and of following the example of Christ, Matt. 11:29; John 13:15; Eph. 4:20; Phil. 2:5, in the power of the Holy Spirit, Rom. 8:13; Eph. 3:16.

"The Holy Spirit is the Agent in sanctification, Rom. 15:16; 2 Thess. 2:13; 1 Pet. 1:2; cf. 1 Cor. 6:11 .... The sanctification of the Spirit is associated with the choice, or election, of God; it is a Divine act preceding the acceptance of the Gospel by the individual."

For synonymous words see HOLINESS.

B. Verb.

hagiazō (ἁγιάζω, 37), "to sanctify," "is used of (a) the gold adorning the Temple and of the gift laid on the altar, Matt. 23:17, 19; (b) food, 1 Tim. 4:5; (c) the unbelieving spouse of a believer, 1 Cor. 7:14; (d) the ceremonial cleansing of the Israelites, Heb. 9:13; (e) the Father's Name, Luke 11:2; (f) the consecration of the Son by the Father, John 10:36; (g) the Lord Jesus devoting Himself to the redemption of His people, John 17:19; (h) the setting apart of the believer for God, Acts 20:32; cf. Rom. 15:16; (i) the effect on the believer of the Death of Christ, Heb. 10:10, said of God, and 2:11; 13:12, said of the Lord Jesus; (j) the separation of the believer from the world in his behavior— by the Father through the Word, John 17:17, 19; (k) the believer who turns away from such things as dishonor God and His gospel, 2 Tim. 2:21; (l) the acknowledgment of the Lordship of Christ, 1 Pet. 3:15.

"Since every believer is sanctified in Christ Jesus, 1 Cor. 1:2, cf. Heb. 10:10, a common NT designation of all believers is 'saints,' *hagioi*, i.e., 'sanctified' or 'holy ones.' Thus sainthood, or sanctification, is not an attainment, it is the state into which God, in grace, calls sinful men, and in which they begin their course as Christians, Col. 3:12; Heb. 3:1."

SANCTUARY

hagion (ἅγιον, 39), the neuter of the adjective *hagios*, "holy," is used of those structures which are set apart to God, (a) of "the tabernacle" in the wilderness, Heb. 9:1, RV, "its sanctuary, a *sanctuary* of this world" (KJV, "a worldly sanctuary"); in v. 2 the outer part is called "the Holy place," RV (KJV, "the sanctuary"); here the neuter plural *hagia* is used, as in v. 3.

Speaking of the absence of the article, Westcott says "The anarthrous form Agia (literally *Holies*) in this sense appears to be unique, as also ἅγια ἁγίων below, if indeed the reading is correct. Perhaps it is chosen to fix attention on the character of the sanctuary as in other cases. The plural suggests the idea of the sanctuary with all its parts: cf. Moulton-Winer, p. 220." In their margin, Westcott and Hort prefix the article *ta* to *hagia* in vv. 2 and 3. In v. 3 the inner part is called "the Holy of holies," RV (KJV, "the holiest of all"); in v. 8, "the holy place" (KJV, "the holiest of all"), lit., "(the way) of the holiest"; in v. 24 "a holy place," RV (KJV, "the holy places"), neuter plural; so in v. 25, "the holy place" (KJV and RV), and in 13:11, RV, "the holy place" (KJV, "the sanctuary"); in all these there is no separate word *topos*, "place," as of the Temple in Matt. 24:15; (b) of "Heaven itself," i.e., the immediate presence of God and His throne, Heb. 8:2, "the sanctuary" (RV, marg., "holy things"); the neut. plur. with the article points to the text as being right, in view of 9:24, 25 and 13:11 (see above), exegetically designated "the true tabernacle"; neut. plur. in 9:12, "the holy place"; so 10:19, RV (KJV, "the holiest"; there are no separate compartments in the antitypical and heavenly sanctuary), into which believers have "boldness to enter" by faith.

2. *naos* (ναός, 3485) is used of the inner part of the Temple in Jerusalem, in Matt. 23:35, RV, "sanctuary." See TEMPLE.

SATAN

satanas (Σατανᾶς, 4567), a Greek form derived from the Aramaic (Heb., *Sātān*), "an adversary," is used (a) of an angel of Jehovah in Num. 22:22 (the first occurrence of the Word in the OT); (b) of men, e.g., 1 Sam. 29:4; Ps. 38:20; 71:13; four in Ps. 109; (c) of "Satan," the Devil, some seventeen or eighteen times in the OT; in Zech. 3:1, where the name receives its interpretation, "to be (his) adversary," RV (see marg.; KJV, "to resist him").

In the NT the word is always used of "Satan," the adversary (a) of God and Christ, e.g., Matt. 4:10; 12:26; Mark 1:13; 3:23, 26; 4:15; Luke 4:8 (in some mss.); 11:18; 22:3; John 13:27; (b) of His people, e.g., Luke 22:31; Acts 5:3; Rom. 16:20; 1 Cor. 5:5; 7:5; 2 Cor. 2:11; 11:14; 12:7; 1 Thess. 2:18; 1 Tim. 1:20; 5:15; Rev. 2:9, 13 (twice), 24; 3:9; (c) of mankind, Luke 13:16; Acts 26:18; 2 Thess. 2:9; Rev. 12:9; 20:7.

His doom, sealed at the Cross, is foretold in its stages in Luke 10:18; Rev. 20:2, 10. Believers are assured of victory over him, Rom. 16:20.

The appellation was given by the Lord to Peter, as a "Satan-like" man, on the occasion when he endeavored to dissuade Him from death, Matt. 16:23; Mark 8:33.

"Satan" is not simply the personification of evil influences in the heart, for he tempted Christ, in whose heart no evil thought could ever have arisen (John 14:30; 2 Cor. 5:21; Heb. 4:15); moreover his personality is asserted in both the OT and the NT, and especially in the latter, whereas if the OT language was intended to be figurative, the NT would have made this evident. See DEVIL.

SATISFY

1. *chortazō* (χορτάζω, 5526), "to fill or satisfy with food," is translated "satisfy" in Mark 8:4, KJV (RV, "to fill").

2. *empiplēmi* or *emplethō* (ἐμπίπλημι, 1705), "to fill up, fill full, satisfy" (*en*, "in," *pimplēmi* or *plēthō*, "to fill"), is used metaphorically in Rom. 15:24, of taking one's fill of the

company of others, RV, "I shall have been satisfied" (KJV, "I be ... filled").

For **SATISFYING,** Col. 2:23, KJV, see INDULGENCE

SAVE, SAVING

A. Verbs.

1. *sōzō* (σώζω, 4982), "to save," is used (as with the noun *sōtēria*, "salvation") (a) of material and temporal deliverance from danger, suffering, etc., e.g., Matt. 8:25; Mark 13:20; Luke 23:35; John 12:27; 1 Tim. 2:15; 2 Tim. 4:18 (KJV, "preserve"); Jude 5; from sickness, Matt. 9:22, "made ... whole" (RV, marg., "saved"); so Mark 5:34; Luke 8:48; Jas. 5:15; (b) of the spiritual and eternal salvation granted immediately by God to those who believe on the Lord Jesus Christ, e.g., Acts 2:47, RV "(those that) were being saved"; 16:31; Rom. 8:24, RV, "were we saved"; Eph. 2:5, 8; 1 Tim. 2:4; 2 Tim. 1:9; Titus 3:5; of human agency in this, Rom. 11:14; 1 Cor. 7:16; 9:22; (c) of the present experiences of God's power to deliver from the bondage of sin, e.g., Matt. 1:21; Rom. 5:10; 1 Cor. 15:2; Heb. 7:25; Jas. 1:21; 1 Pet. 3:21; of human agency in this, 1 Tim. 4:16; (d) of the future deliverance of believers at the second coming of Christ for His saints, being deliverance from the wrath of God to be executed upon the ungodly at the close of this age and from eternal doom, e.g., Rom. 5:9; (e) of the deliverance of the nation of Israel at the second advent of Christ, e.g., Rom. 11:26; (f) inclusively for all the blessings bestowed by God on men in Christ, e.g., Luke 19:10; John 10:9; 1 Cor. 10:33; 1 Tim. 1:15; (g) of those who endure to the end of the time of the Great Tribulation, Matt. 10:22; Mark 13:13; (h) of the individual believer, who, though losing his reward at the judgment seat of Christ hereafter, will not lose his salvation, 1 Cor. 3:15; 5:5; (i) of the deliverance of the nations at the Millennium, Rev. 21:24 (in some mss.). See SALVATION.

2. *diasōzō* (διασώζω, 1295), "to bring safely through" (*dia*, "through," and No. 1), is used (a) of the healing of the sick by the Lord, Matt. 14:36, RV, "were made whole" (KJV adds "perfectly"); Luke 7:3; (b) of bringing "safe" to a destination, Acts 23:24; (c) of keeping a person "safe," 27:43; (d) of escaping through the perils of shipwreck, 27:44; 28:1, 4, passive voice; (e) through the Flood, 1 Pet. 3:20. See ESCAPE, WHOLE. *Note:* In 2 Pet. 2:5, KJV, *phulassō*, "to guard, keep, preserve," is translated "saved" (RV, "preserved"). In Luke 17:33 some mss. have *sozo* (KJV, "save"), for the RV. For "save alive," Luke 17:33, RV, see LIVE, No. 6.

B. Noun.

peripoiēsis (περιποίησις, 4047), (a) "preservation," (b) "acquiring or gaining something," is used in this latter sense in Heb. 10:39, translated "saving" (RV marg., "gaining"); the reference here is to salvation in its completeness. See POSSESSION.

Note: In Heb. 11:7 *sōtēria* is rendered saving. See SALVATION.

SAVING (Preposition)

parektos (παρεκτός, 3924), used as a preposition, denotes "saving," Matt. 5:32 (in some mss., 19:9).

Note: In Luke 4:27 and Rev. 2:17, KJV, *ei mē* (lit., "if not"), is translated "saving" (RV, "but only" and "but").

SAVIOR

sōtēr (σωτήρ, 4990), "a savior, deliverer, preserver," is used (a) of God, Luke 1:47; 1 Tim. 1:1; 2:3; 4:10 (in the sense of "preserver," since He gives "to all life and breath and all things"); Titus 1:3; 2:10; 3:4; Jude 25; (b) of Christ, Luke 2:11; John 4:42; Acts 5:31; 13:23 (of Israel); Eph. 5:23 (the sustainer and preserver of the church, His "body"); Phil. 3:20 (at His return to receive the Church to Himself); 2 Tim. 1:10 (with reference to His incarnation, "the days of His flesh"); Titus 1:4 (a title shared, in the context, with God the Father); 2:13, RV, "our great God and Savior Jesus Christ," the pronoun "our," at the beginning of the whole clause, includes all the titles; Titus 3:6; 2 Pet. 1:1, "our God and Savior Jesus Christ; RV, where the pronoun "our," coming immediately in connection with "God," involves the inclusion of both titles as referring to Christ, just as in the parallel in v. 11, "our Lord and Savior Jesus Christ" (KJV and RV); these passages are therefore a testimony to His deity; 2 Pet. 2:20; 3:2, 18; 1 John 4:14.

SAYING

1. *logos* (λόγος, 3056), "a word," as embodying a conception or idea, denotes among its various meanings, "a saying, statement or declaration," uttered (a) by God; RV, "word" or "words" (KJV, "saying"), e.g., in John 8:55; Rom. 3:4; Rev. 19:9; 22:6, 7, 9, 10; (b) by Christ, e.g., Mark 8:32; 9:10; 10:22; Luke 9:28; John 6:60; 21:23; the RV appropriately substitutes "word" or "words" for KJV, "saying" or "sayings," especially in John's gospel e.g. 7:36, 40; 8:51, 52; 10:19; 14:24; 15:20; 18:9, 32; 19:13; (c) by an angel, Luke 1:29; (d) by OT prophets, John 12:38 (RV, "word") Rom. 13:9 (ditto); 1 Cor. 15:54; (e) by the apostle Paul in the Pastoral Epp., 1 Tim. 1:15; 3:1; 4:9; 2 Tim. 2:11; Titus 3:8; (f) by other men, Mark 7:29; Acts 7:29; John 4:37 (in general). See WORD.

2. *rhēma* (ῥῆμα, 4487), "that which is said, a word," is rendered "saying" or "sayings" in Mark 9:32; Luke 1:65; 2:17, 50, 51; 7:1; 9:45 (twice); 18:34. See WORD.

Note: In Acts 14:18, "with these sayings" is lit., "saying (*legō*) these things." For *lalia*, "saying," John 4:42, KJV, see SPEECH, No. 2.

SCATTER

A. Verbs.

1. *skorpizō* (σκορπίζω, 4650) is used in Matt. 12:30; Luke 11:23; John 10:12; 16:32; 2 Cor. 9:9, RV. See DISPERSE, No. 2.

2. *diaskorpizō* (διασκορπίζω, 1287), "to scatter abroad," is rendered "to scatter" in Matt. 25:24, 26, RV (KJV, "strawed"); 26:31; Mark 14:27; Luke 1:51; John 11:52; Acts 5:37, RV. See DISPERSE, No. 3.

3. *diaspeirō* (διασπείρω, 1289), "to scatter abroad" (*dia*, "throughout," *speirō*, "to sow seed"), is used in Acts 8:1, 4; 11:19, all of the church in Jerusalem "scattered" through persecution; the word in general is suggestive of the effects of the "scattering" in the sowing of the spiritual seed of the Word of life. See DISPERSE, No. 4.

4. *rhiptō* (ῥίπτω, 4496), "to throw, cast, hurl, to be cast down, prostrate," is used in Matt. 9:36 of people who were "scattered" as sheep without a shepherd.

5. *likmaō* (λικμάω, 3039), "to winnow" (*likmos*, "a winnowing fan"), is rendered "will scatter ... as dust" in Matt. 21:44 and Luke 20:18, RV (KJV, "will grind ... to powder").

6. *dialuō* (διαλύω, 1262), "to dissolve," is translated "scattered" in Acts 5:36, KJV; see DISPERSE, No. 1.

B. Noun.

diaspora (διασπορά, 1290), "a dispersion," is rendered "scattered abroad" in Jas. 1:1, KJV; "scattered" in 1 Pet. 1:1, KJV; see DISPERSION, B.

SCHISM

schisma (σχίσμα, 4978), "a rent, division," is translated "schism" in 1 Cor. 12:25, metaphorically of the contrary condition to that which God has designed for a local church in "tempering the body together" (v. 24), the members having "the same care one for another" ("the same" being emphatic). See DIVISION, No. 3.

SCHOOL

scholē (σχολή, 4981) (whence Eng., "school") primarily denotes "leisure," then, "that for which leisure was employed, a disputation, lecture"; hence, by metonymy, "the place where lectures are delivered, a school," Acts 19:9.

For **SCHOOLMASTER,** Gal. 3:24, 25, see INSTRUCTOR, B, No. 1

SCIENCE

gnōsis (γνῶσις, 1108) is translated "science" in the KJV of 1 Tim. 6:20; the word simply means "knowledge" (RV), where the reference is to the teaching of the Gnostics (lit., "the knowers") "falsely called knowledge." Science in the modern sense of the word, viz., the investigation, discovery, and classification of secondary laws, is unknown in Scripture. See KNOW, C, No. 1.

SCOFF

ekmuktērizō (ἐκμυκτηρίζω, 1592), "to hold up the nose in derision at" (*ek*, "from," used intensively, *muktērizō*, "to mock"; from *muktēr*, "the nose"), is translated "scoffed at" in Luke 16:14, RV (KJV, "derided"), of the Pharisees in their derision of Christ on account of His teaching; in 23:35 (ditto), of the mockery of Christ on the cross by the rulers of the people. In the Sept., Ps. 2:4; 22:7; 35:16. For SCOFFERS, 2 Pet. 3:3, KJV, see MOCKER.

SCORCH, SCORCHING

A. Verb.

kaumatizō (καυματίζω, 2739), "to scorch" (from *kauma*, "heat"), is used (a) of seed that had not much earth, Matt. 13:6; Mark 4:6; (b) of men, stricken retributively by the sun's heat, Rev. 16:8, 9.

B. Noun.

kausōn (καύσων, 2742), "burning heat" (akin to *kaio*, "to burn"), is translated "scorching heat" in Matt. 20:12 (KJV, "heat"); Luke 12:55 (ditto); in Jas. 1:11, RV, "scorching wind" (KJV, "burning heat"), here the reference is to a hot wind from the east (cf. Job 1:19). See HEAT. In the Sept., Job 27:21; Jer. 18:17; 51:1; Ezek. 17:10; 19:12; Hos. 12:1; 13:15; Jonah 4:8.

For **SCORN** see LAUGH

SCOURGE (Noun and Verb)

A. Noun.

phragellion (φραγέλλιον, 5416), "a whip" (from Latin, *flagellum*), is used of the "scourge" of small cords which the Lord made and employed before cleansing the Temple, John 2:15. However He actually used it, the whip was in itself a sign of authority and judgment.

B. Verbs.

1. *phragelloō* (φραγελλόω, 5417) (akin to A: Latin, *flagellō;* Eng., "flagellate"), is the word used in Matt. 27:26, and Mark 15:15, of the "scourging" endured by Christ and administered by the order of Pilate. Under the Roman method of "scourging," the person was stripped and tied in a bending posture to a pillar, or stretched on a frame. The "scourge" was made of leather thongs, weighted with sharp pieces of bone or lead, which tore the flesh of both the back and the breast (cf. Ps. 22:17). Eusebius (*Chron.*) records his having witnessed the suffering of martyrs who died under this treatment.

Note: In John 19:1 the "scourging" of Christ is described by Verb No. 2, as also in His prophecy of His sufferings, Matt. 20:19; Mark 10:34; Luke 18:33. In Acts 22:25 the similar punishment about to be administered to Paul is described by Verb No. 3 (the "scourging" of Roman citizens was prohibited by the Porcian law of 197, B.C.).

2. *mastigoō* (μαστιγόω, 3146), akin to *mastix* (see below), is used (a) as mentioned under No. 1; (b) of Jewish "scourgings," Matt. 10:17 and 23:34; (c) metaphorically, in Heb. 12:6, of the "chastening" by the Lord administered in love to His spiritual sons.

Note: The Jewish method of "scourging," as described in the Mishna, was by the use of three thongs of leather, the offender receiving thirteen stripes on the bare breast and thirteen on each shoulder, the "forty stripes save one," as administered to Paul five times (2 Cor. 11:24). See also SCOURGINGS (below).

3. *mastizō* (μαστίζω, 3147), akin to No. 2, occurs in Acts 22:25 (see No. 1, above). In the Sept., Num. 22:25.

SCOURGING (-S)

mastix (μάστιξ, 3148), "a whip, scourge," is used (a) with the meaning "scourging," in Acts 22:24, of the Roman method (see above, B, No. 1, Note), (b) in Heb. 11:36, of the "sufferings" of saints in the OT times. Among the Hebrews the usual mode, legal and domestic, was that of beating with a rod (see 2 Cor. 11:25); (c) metaphorically, of "disease" or "suffering": see PLAGUE, No. 1.

SCRIBE (-S)

grammateus (γραμματεύς, 1122), from *gramma*, "a writing," denotes "a scribe, a man of letters, a teacher of the law"; the "scribes" are mentioned frequently in the Synoptists, especially in connection with the Pharisees, with whom they virtually formed one party (see Luke 5:21), sometimes with the chief priests, e.g., Matt. 2:4; Mark 8:31; 10:33; 11:18, 27; Luke 9:22. They are mentioned only once in John's gospel, 8:3, three times in the Acts, 4:5; 6:12; 23:9; elsewhere only in 1 Cor. 1:20, in the singular. They were considered naturally qualified to teach in the synagogues, Mark 1:22. They were ambitious of honor, e.g., Matt. 23:5–11, which they demanded especially from their pupils, and which was readily granted them, as well as by the people generally. Like Ezra (Ezra 7:12), the "scribes" were found originally among the priests and Levites. The priests being the official interpreters of the Law, the "scribes" ere long became an independent company; though they never held political power, they became leaders of the people.

Their functions regarding the Law were to teach it, develop it, and use it in connection with the Sanhedrin and various local courts. They also occupied themselves with the sacred writings both historical and didactic. They attached the utmost importance to ascetic elements, by which the nation was especially separated from the Gentiles. In their regime piety was reduced to external formalism. Only that was of value which was governed by external precept. Life under them became a burden; they themselves sought to evade certain of their own precepts, Matt. 23:16,ff.; Luke 11:46; by their traditions the Law, instead of being a help in moral and spiritual life, became an instrument for preventing true access to God, Luke 11:52. Hence the Lord's stern denunciations of them and the Pharisees (see PHARISEES).

Note: The word *grammateus* is used of the town "clerk" in Ephesus, Acts 19:35.

SCRIPTURE

1. *graphē* (γραφή, 1124), akin to *graphō*, "to write" (Eng., "graph," "graphic," etc.), primarily denotes "a drawing, painting"; then "a writing," (a) of the OT Scriptures, (1) in the plural, the whole, e.g., Matt. 21:42; 22:29; John 5:39; Acts 17:11; 18:24; Rom. 1:2, where "the prophets" comprises the OT writers in general; 15:4; 16:26, lit., "prophetic writings," expressing the character of all the Scriptures; (2) in the singular in reference to a particular passage, e.g., Mark 12:10; Luke 4:21; John 2:22; 10:35 (though applicable to all); 19:24, 28, 36, 37; 20:9; Acts 1:16; 8:32, 35; Rom. 4:3; 9:17; 10:11; 11:2; Gal. 3:8, 22; 4:30; 1 Tim. 5:18, where the 2nd quotation is from Luke 10:7, from which it may be inferred that the apostle included Luke's gospel as "Scripture" alike with Deuteronomy, from which the first quotation is taken; in reference to the whole, e.g. Jas. 4:5 (see RV, a separate rhetorical question from the one which follows); in 2 Pet. 1:20, "no prophecy of Scripture," a description of all, with special application to the OT in the next verse; (b) of the OT Scriptures (those accepted by the Jews as canonical) and all those of the NT which were to be accepted by Christians as authoritative, 2 Tim. 3:16; these latter were to be discriminated from the many forged epistles and other religious "writings" already produced and circulated in Timothy's time. Such discrimination would be directed by the fact that "every Scripture," characterized by inspiration of God, would be profitable for the purposes mentioned; so the RV. The KJV states truth concerning the completed canon of Scripture, but that was not complete when the apostle wrote to Timothy.

The Scriptures are frequently personified by the NT writers (as by the Jews, John 7:42), (a) as speaking with divine authority, e.g., John 19:37; Rom. 4:3; 9:17, where the Scripture is said to speak to Pharaoh, giving the message actually sent previously by God to him through Moses; Jas. 4:5 (see above); (b) as possessed of the sentient quality of foresight, and the active power of preaching, Gal. 3:8, where the Scripture mentioned was written more than four centuries after the words were spoken. The Scripture, in such a case, stands for its divine Author with an intimation that it remains perpetually characterized as the living voice of God. This divine agency is again illustrated in Gal. 3:22 (cf. v. 10 and Matt. 11:13).

2. *gramma* (γράμμα, 1121), "a letter of the alphabet," etc. is used of the Holy Scriptures in 2 Tim. 3:15. For the various uses of this word see LETTER.

SCROLL

biblion (βιβλίον, 975), the diminutive of *biblos*, "a book," is used in Rev. 6:14, of "a scroll," the rolling up of which illustrates the removal of the heaven. See BOOK, No. 2.

SEA

A. Nouns.

1. *thalassa* (θάλασσα, 2281) is used (a) chiefly literally, e.g., "the Red Sea," Acts 7:36; 1 Cor. 10:1; Heb. 11:29; the "sea" of Galilee or Tiberias, Matt. 4:18; 15:29; Mark 6:48, 49, where the acts of Christ testified to His deity; John 6:1; 21:1; in general, e.g., Luke 17:2; Acts 4:24; Rom. 9:27; Rev. 16:3; 18:17; 20:8, 13; 21:1; in combination with No. 2, Matt. 18:6; (b) metaphorically, of "the ungodly men" described in Jude 13 (cf. Isa. 57:20); (c) symbolically, in the apocalyptic vision of "a glassy sea like unto crystal," Rev. 4:6, emblematic of the fixed purity and holiness of all that appertains to the authority and judicial dealings of God; in 15:2, the same, "mingled with fire," and, standing by it (RV) or on it (KJV and RV marg.), those who had "come victorious from the beast" (ch. 13); of the wild and restless condition of nations, Rev. 13:1 (see 17:1, 15), where "he stood" (RV) refers to the dragon, not John (KJV); from the midst of this state arises the beast, symbolic of the final gentile power dominating the federated nations of the Roman world (see Dan., chs. 2, 7, etc.).

Note: For the change from "the sea" in Deut. 30:13, to "the abyss" in Rom. 10:7, see BOTTOM.

2. *pelagos* (πέλαγος, 3989), "the deep sea, the deep," is translated "the depth" in Matt. 18:6, and is used of the "Sea of Cilicia" in Acts 27:5. See DEPTH, No. 2. *Pelagos* signifies "the vast expanse of open water," *thalassa*, "the sea as contrasted with the land" (Trench, *Syn.*, Sec. XIII).

B. Adjectives.

1. *enalios* (ἐνάλιος, 1724), "in the sea," lit., "of, or belonging to, the salt water" (from *hals*, "salt"), occurs in Jas. 3:7.

2. *paralios* (παράλιος, 3882), "by the sea," Luke 6:17.

3. *parathalassios* (παραθαλάσσιος, 3864), "by the sea," Matt. 4:13.

4. *dithalassos* (διθάλασσος, 1337) primarily signifies "divided into two seas" (*dis*, "twice," and *thalassa*), then, "dividing the sea," as of a reef or rocky projection running out into the "sea," Acts 27:41.

SEAL (Noun and Verb)

A. Noun.

sphragis (σφραγίς, 4973) denotes (a) "a seal" or "signet," Rev. 7:2, "the seal of the living God," an emblem of ownership and security, here combined with that of destination (as in Ezek. 9:4), the persons to be "sealed" being secured from destruction and marked for reward; (b) "the impression" of a "seal" or signet, (1) literal, a "seal" on a book or roll, combining with the ideas of security and destination those of secrecy and postponement of disclosures, Rev. 5:1, 2, 5, 9; 6:1, 3, 5, 7, 9, 12; 8:1; (2) metaphorical, Rom. 4:11, said of "circumcision," as an authentication of the righteousness of Abraham's faith, and an external attestation of the covenant made with him by God; the rabbis called circumcision "the seal of Abraham"; in 1 Cor. 9:2, of converts as a "seal" or authentication of Paul's apostleship; in 2 Tim. 2:19, "the firm foundation of God standeth, having this seal, The Lord knoweth them that are His," RV, indicating ownership, authentication, security and destination, "and, Let every one that nameth the Name of the Lord depart from unrighteousness," indicating a ratification on the part of the believer of the determining counsel of God concerning him; Rev. 9:4 distinguishes those who will be found without the "seal" of God on their foreheads [see (a) above and B, No. 1].

B. Verbs.

1. *sphragizō* (σφραγίζω, 4972), "to seal" (akin to A), is used to indicate (a) security and permanency (attempted but impossible), Matt. 27:66; on the contrary, of the doom of Satan, fixed and certain, Rev. 20:3, RV, "sealed it over"; (b) in Rom. 15:28, "when ... I have ... sealed to them this fruit," the formal ratification of the ministry of the churches of the Gentiles in Greece and Galatia to needy saints in Judea, by Paul's faithful delivery of the gifts to them; this material help was the fruit of his spiritual ministry to the Gentiles, who on their part were bringing forth the fruit of their having shared with them in spiritual things; the metaphor stresses the sacred formalities of the transaction (Deissmann illustrates this from the papyri of Fayyum, in which the "sealing" of sacks guarantees the full complement of the contents); (c) secrecy and security and the postponement of disclosure, Rev. 10:4; in a negative command 22:10; (d) ownership and security, together with destination, Rev. 7:3, 4, 5 (as with the noun in v. 2; see A); the same three indications are conveyed in Eph. 1:13, in the metaphor of the "sealing" of believers by the gift of the Holy Spirit, upon believing (i.e., at the time of their regeneration, not after a lapse of time in their spiritual life, "having also believed"—not as KJV, "after that ye believed"—;the aorist participle marks the definiteness and completeness of the act of faith); the idea of destination is stressed by

the phrase "the Holy Spirit of promise" (see also v. 14); so 4:30, "ye were sealed unto the day of redemption"; so in 2 Cor. 1:22, where the middle voice intimates the special interest of the Sealer in His act; (e) authentication by the believer (by receiving the witness of the Son) of the fact that "God is true," John 3:33; authentication by God in sealing the Son as the Giver of eternal life (with perhaps a figurative allusion to the impress of a mark upon loaves), 6:27.

Note: In Rev. 7, after the 5th verse (first part) the original does not repeat the mention of the "sealing" except in v. 8 (last part) (hence the omission in the RV).

2. *katosphragizō* (κατασφραγίζω, 2696), No. 1, strengthened by *kata*, intensive, is used of the "book" seen in the vision in Rev. 5:1, RV, "close sealed (with seven seals)," the successive opening of which discloses the events destined to take place throughout the period covered by chapters 6 to 19. In the Sept., Job 9:7; 37:7.

SEARCH

1. *eraunao* (ἐραυνάω, 2045), or *ereunao* (ἐρευνάω, 2045), an earlier form, "to search, examine," is used (a) of God, as "searching" the heart, Rom. 8:27; (b) of Christ, similarly, Rev. 2:23; (c) of the Holy Spirit, as "searching" all things, 1 Cor. 2:10, acting in the spirit of the believer; (d) of the OT prophets, as "searching" their own writings concerning matters foretold of Christ, testified by the Spirit of Christ in them, 1 Pet. 1:11 (cf. No. 2); (e) of the Jews, as commanded by the Lord to "search" the Scriptures, John 5:39, KJV, and RV marg., "search," RV text, "ye search," either is possible grammatically; (f) of Nicodemus as commanded similarly by the chief priests and Pharisees, John 7:52.

2. *exeraunaō* (ἐξερευνάω, 1830), a strengthened form of No. 1 (*ek*, or *ex*, "out"), "to search out," is used in 1 Pet. 1:10, "searched diligently"; cf. No. 1 (d).

3. *exetazō* (ἐξετάζω, 1833), "to examine closely, inquire carefully" (from *etazō*, "to examine"), occurs in Matt. 2:8, RV, "search out"; so Matt. 10:11, RV: see INQUIRE, No. 4.

Note: For *anakrinō*, rendered "searched" in Acts 17:11, KJV, see EXAMINE.

For **SEARED** see BRANDED

SEAT (Noun and Verb)

A. Nouns.

1. *kathedra* (καθέδρα, 2515), from *kata*, "down," and *hedra*, "a seat," denotes "a seat" (Eng., "cathedral"), "a chair," Matt. 21:12; Mark 11:15; of teachers, Matt. 23:2.

2. *prōtokathedria* (πρωτοκαθεδρία, 4410), "the first seat," Matt. 23:6; Mark 12:39; Luke 11:43; 20:46; see CHIEF, No. 6. Cf. ROOM.

Note: For *thronos*, sometimes translated "seat" in the KJV, see THRONE.

B. Verb.

kathēmai (κάθημαι, 2521), "to sit, be seated," is translated "shall ... be seated" in Luke 22:69, RV; "is seated," Col. 3:1, RV (KJV, "shall ... sit" and "sitteth").

SECRET, SECRETLY

A. Adjectives.

1. *kruptos* (κρυπτός, 2927), "secret, hidden" (akin to *krupto*, "to hide"), Eng., "crypt," "cryptic," etc., is used as an adjective and rendered "secret" in Luke 8:17, KJV (RV, "hid"); in the neuter, with *en*, "in," as an adverbial phrase, "in secret," with the article, Matt. 6:4, 6 (twice in each v.), without the article, John 7:4, 10; 18:20; in the neuter plural, with the article, "the secrets (of men)," Rom. 2:16; of the heart, 1 Cor. 14:25; in Luke 11:33, KJV, "a secret place" (RV, "cellar"). See CELLAR, HIDDEN.

2. *apokruphos* (ἀπόκρυφος, 614) (whence "Apocrypha"), "hidden," is translated "kept secret" in Mark 4:22, KJV (RV, "made secret"); "secret" in Luke 8:17, RV (KJV, "hid"). See HIDE, B, No. 2.

3. *kruphaios* (κρυφαῖος, 2928d) occurs in the best mss. in Matt. 6:18 (twice; some have No. 1).

B. Adverbs.

1. *kruphē* (κρυφῇ, 2931), akin to A, No. 1, "secretly, in secret," is used in Eph. 5:12.

2. *lathra* (λάθρᾳ, 2977), akin to *lanthanō*, "to escape notice, be hidden," is translated "secretly" in John 11:28. See PRIVILY.

C. Verb.

kruptō (κρύπτω, 2928), "to hide," is translated "secretly" in John 19:38 [perfect participle, passive voice, lit., "(but) having been hidden"], referring to Nicodemus as having been a "secret" disciple of Christ; in Matt. 13:35, KJV, it is translated "kept secret" (RV, "hidden").

Notes: (1) For *tameion*, translated "secret chambers" in Matt. 24:26, see CHAMBER, No. 1. (2) For the KJV rendering of *sigao*, in Rom. 16:25, "kept secret," see PEACE (hold one's), No. 2, and SILENCE. (3) For "I have learned the secret, see LEARN, No. 4.

SECT

hairesis (αἵρεσις, 139), "a choosing," is translated "sect" throughout the Acts, except in 24:14, KJV, "heresy" (RV, "sect"); it properly denotes a predilection either for a particular truth, or for a perversion of one, generally with the expectation of personal advantage; hence, a division and the formation of a party or "sect" in contrast to the uniting power of "the truth," held *in toto;* "a sect" is a division developed and brought to an issue; the order "divisions, heresies" (marg. "parties") in "the works of the flesh" in Gal. 5:19-21 is suggestive of this. See HERESY.

SECURE (Verb)

perikratēs (περικρατής, 4031), an adjective, signifies "having full command of" (*peri*, "around, about," *krateō*, "to be strong, to rule"); it is used with *ginomai*, "to become," in Acts 27:16, RV, "to secure (the boat)," KJV, "to come by."

Note: In Matt. 28:14, KJV, *amerimnos*, "without anxiety," with *poieo*, "to make," is translated "we will ... secure (you)," RV, "we will ... rid (you) of care." The Eng. "secure" is derived from the Latin *se*, "free from," and *cura*, "care."

SECURITY

hikanos (ἱκανός, 2425), "sufficient," is used in its neuter form with the article, as a noun, in Acts 17:9, "(when they had taken) security," i.e., satisfaction, lit., "the sufficient." The use of *hikanos* in this construction is a Latinism in Greek. See Moulton, *Proleg.*, p. 20. Probably the bond given to the authorities by Jason and his friends included an undertaking that Paul would not return to Thessalonica. Any efforts to have the bond cancelled were unsuccessful; hence the reference to the hindrance by Satan (1 Thess. 2:18). See ABLE, C, No. 2.

SEDITION

A. Nouns.

1. *stasis* (στάσις, 4714), "a dissension, an insurrection," is translated "sedition" in Acts 24:5, KJV (KJV, "insurrections"). See DISSENSION, INSURRECTION.

2. *dichostasia* (διχοστασία, 1370), lit., "a standing apart" (*dicha*, "asunder, apart," *stasis*, "a standing"), hence "a dissension, division," is translated "seditions" in Gal. 5:20, KJV. See DIVISION, No. 2.

B. Verb.

anastatoō (ἀναστατόω, 387), "to excite, unsettle," or "to stir up to sedition," is so translated in Acts 21:38, RV (KJV, "madest an uproar"); in 17:6, "have turned (the world) upside down," i.e., "causing tumults"; in Gal. 5:12, RV, "unsettle" (KJV, "trouble"), i.e., by false teaching (here in the continuous present tense, lit., "those who are unsettling you"). The word was supposed not to have been used in profane authors. It has been found, however, in several of the papyri writings. See UNSETTLE.

SEDUCE, SEDUCING

A. Verbs.

1. *planaō* (πλανάω, 4105), "to cause to wander, lead astray," is translated "to seduce" in 1 John 2:26, KJV (RV, "lead ... astray"); in Rev. 2:20, "to seduce." See DECEIT, C, No. 6.

2. *apoplanaō* (ἀποπλανάω, 635) is translated "seduce" in Mark 13:22 (RV, "lead astray"); see LEAD, No. 13.

B. Adjective.

planos (πλάνος, 4108), akin to A, lit., "wandering," then, "deceiving," is translated "seducing in 1 Tim. 4:1. See DECEIVER, No. 1.

For **SEDUCERS** see IMPOSTORS

SEED

1. *sperma* (σπέρμα, 4690), akin to *speirō*, "to sow" (Eng., "sperm," "spermatic," etc.), has the following usages, (a) agricultural and botanical, e.g., Matt. 13:24, 27, 32 (for the KJV of vv. 19, 20, 22, 23, see SOW, as in the RV); 1 Cor. 15:38; 2 Cor. 9:10; (b) physiological, Heb. 11:11; (c) metaphorical and by metonymy for "offspring, posterity," (1) of natural offspring, e.g., Matt. 22:24, 25, RV, "seed" (KJV, "issue"); John 7:42; 8:33, 37; Acts 3:25; Rom. 1:3; 4:13, 16, 18; 9:7 (twice), 8, 29; 11:1; 2 Cor. 11:22; Heb. 2:16; 11:18; Rev. 12:17; Gal. 3:16, 19, 29; in the 16th v., "He saith not, And to seeds, as of many; but as of one, And to thy seed, which is Christ," quoted from the Sept. of Gen. 13:15 and 17:7, 8, there is especial stress on the word "seed," as referring to an individual (here, Christ) in fulfillment of the promises to Abraham—a unique use of the singular. While the plural form "seeds," neither in Hebrew nor in Greek, would have been natural any more than in English (it is not so used in Scripture of human offspring; its plural occurrence is in 1 Sam. 8:15, of crops), yet if the divine intention had been to refer to Abraham's natural descendants, another word could have been chosen in the plural, such as "children"; all such words were, however, set aside, "seed" being selected as one that could be used in the singular, with the purpose of showing that the "seed" was Messiah. Some of the rabbis had even regarded "seed," e.g., in Gen. 4:25 and Isa. 53:10, as referring to the Coming One. Descendants were given to Abraham by other than natural means, so that through him Messiah might come, and the point of the apostle's argument is that since the fulfillment of the promises of God is secured alone by Christ, they only who are "in Christ" can receive them; (2) of spiritual offspring, Rom. 4:16, 18; 9:8; here "the children of the promise are reckoned for a seed" points, firstly, to Isaac's birth as being not according to the ordinary course of nature but by divine promise, and, secondly, by analogy, to the fact that all believers are children of God by spiritual birth; Gal. 3:29.

As to 1 John 3:9, "his seed abideth in him," it is possible to understand this as meaning that children of God (His "seed") abide in Him, and do not go on doing (practicing) sin (the verb "to commit" does not represent the original in this passage). Alternatively, the "seed" signifies the principle of spiritual life as imparted to the believer, which abides in him without possibility of removal or extinction; the child of God remains eternally related to Christ, he who lives in sin has never become so related, he has not the principle of life in him. This meaning suits the context and the general tenor of the Epistle.

2. *sporos* (σπόρος, 4703), akin to No. 1, properly "a sowing," denotes "seed sown," (a) natural, Mark 4:26, 27; Luke 8:5, 11 (the natural being figuratively applied to the Word of God); 2 Cor. 9:10 (1st part); (b) metaphorically of material help to the needy, 2 Cor. 9:10 (2nd part), RV, "(your) seed for sowing" (KJV, "seed sown").

3. *spora* (σπορά, 4701), akin to No. 1, and like No. 2, "a sowing, seedtime," denotes "seed sown," 1 Pet. 1:23, of human offspring. In the Sept., 2 Kings 19:29.

SEEM

dokeō (δοκέω, 1380) denotes (a) "to be of opinion" (akin to *doxa*, "opinion"), e.g., Luke 8:18, RV, "thinketh" (KJV, "seemeth"); so 1 Cor. 3:18; to think, suppose, Jas. 1:26, RV, "thinketh himself (KJV, "seem"); (b) "to seem, to be reputed," e.g., Acts 17:18; 1 Cor. 11:16; 12:22; 2 Cor. 10:9; Heb. 4:1; 12:11; for Gal. 2:2, 6, 9, see REPUTE; (C) impersonally (1) to think, (2) to "seem" good, Luke 1:3; Acts 15:22, RV, "it seemed good" (KJV, "it pleased"); 15:25, 28 (v. 34 in some mss.); in Heb. 12:10, the neuter of the present participle is used with the article, lit., "the (thing) seeming good," RV, "(as) seemed good," KJV, "after (their own) pleasure."

Notes: In Matt. 11:26 and Luke 10:21, *eudokia*, "good pleasure, satisfaction" (*eu*, "well," and *dokeō*), is used with *ginomai*, "to become," and translated "it seemed good," KJV (RV, "it was well-pleasing"). (2) In Luke 24:11, KJV, *phainō*, "to appear" (passive voice), is translated "seemed" (RV, "appeared").

For **SEEMLY,** RV, see COMELINESS, B, and *Note* (2)

Note: In 1 Pet. 2:12, RV, *kalos*, "good, fair," is rendered "seemly."

For **SELF-CONDEMNED** see CONDEMN, C, No. 1

SELF-CONTROL (without)

akratēs (ἀκράτης, 193), "powerless" (*a*, negative, *kratos*, "strength"), is rendered "without self-control," in 2 Tim. 3:3, RV; see INCONTINENT.

SELF-WILLED

authadēs (αὐθάδης, 829), "self-pleasing" (*autos*, "self," *hēdomai*, "to please"), denotes one who, dominated by self-interest, and inconsiderate of others, arrogantly asserts his own will, "self-willed," Titus 1:7; 2 Pet. 2:10 (the opposite of *epieikses*, "gentle," e.g., 1 Tim. 3:3), "one so far overvaluing any determination at which he has himself once arrived that he will not be removed from it" (Trench, who compares and contrasts *philautos*, "loving self, selfish"; *Syn.* Sec. XCIII). In the Sept., Gen. 49:3, 7; Prov. 21:24.

SENATE

gerousia (γερουσία, 1087), "a council of elders" (from *geron*, "an old man," a term which early assumed a political sense among the Greeks, the notion of age being merged in that of dignity), is used in Acts 5:21, apparently epexegetically of the preceding word *sunedrion*, "council," the Sanhedrin.

SEND

1. *apostellō* (ἀποστέλλω, 649), lit., "to send forth" (*apo*, "from"), akin to *apostolos*, "an apostle," denotes (a) "to send on service, or with a commission." (1) of persons; Christ, sent by the Father, Matt. 10:40; 15:24; 21:37; Mark 9:37; 12:6; Luke 4:18, 43; 9:48; 10:16; John 3:17; 5:36, 38; 6:29, 57; 7:29; 8:42; 10:36; 11:42; 17:3, 8, 18 (1st part), 21, 23, 25; 20:21; Acts 3:20 (future); 3:26; 1 John 4:9, 10, 14; the Holy Spirit, Luke 24:49 (in some texts; see No. 3); 1 Pet. 1:12; Rev. 5:6; Moses, Acts 7:35; John the Baptist, John 1:6; 3:28; disciples and apostles, e.g., Matt. 10:16; Mark 11:1; Luke 22:8; John 4:38; 17:18 (2nd part); Acts 26:17; servants, e.g., Matt. 21:34; Luke 20:10; officers and officials, Mark 6:27; John 7:32; Acts 16:35; messengers, e.g., Acts 10:8, 17, 20; 15:27; evangelists, Rom. 10:15; angels, e.g., Matt. 24:31; Mark 13:27; Luke 1:19, 26; Heb. 1:14; Rev. 1:1; 22:6; demons, Mark 5:10; (2) of things, e.g., Matt. 21:3; Mark 4:29, RV, marg., "sendeth forth," text, "putteth forth" (KJV, "... in"); Acts 10:36; 11:30; 28:28; (b) "to send away, dismiss," e.g., Mark 8:26; 12:3; Luke 4:18, "to set (at liberty)." See *Note* below, No. 2.

2. *pempō* (πέμπω, 3992), "to send," is used (a) of persons: Christ, by the Father, Luke 20:13; John 4:34; 5:23, 24, 30, 37; 6:38, 39, (40), 44; 7:16, 18, 28, 33; 8:16, 18, 26, 29; 9:4; 12:44, 45, 49; 13:20 (2nd part); 14:24; 15:21; 16:5; Rom. 8:3; the Holy Spirit, John 14:26; 15:26; 16:7; Elijah, Luke 4:26; John the Baptist, John 1:33; disciples and apostles, e.g., Matt. 11:2; John 20:21; servants, e.g., Luke 20:11, 12; officials, Matt. 14:10; messengers, e.g., Acts 10:5, 32, 33; 15:22, 25; 2 Cor. 9:3, Eph. 6:22; Phil. 2:19, 23, 25; 1 Thess. 3:2, 5; Titus 3:12; a prisoner, Acts 25:25, 27; potentates, by God, 1 Pet. 2:14; an angel, Rev. 22:16, demons, Mark 5:12; (b) of things, Acts 11:29; Phil. 4:16;

2 Thess. 2:11; Rev. 1:11; 11:10; 14:15, 18, RV, "send forth" (KJV, "thrust in").

Notes: (1) *Pempō* is a more general term than *apostellō*; *apostellō* usually "suggests official or authoritative sending" (Thayer). A comparison of the usages mentioned above shows how nearly (in some cases practically quite) interchangeably they are used, and yet on close consideration the distinction just mentioned is discernible; in the Gospel of John, cf. *pempō* in 5:23, 24, 30, 37, *apostellō* in 5:33, 36, 38; *pempō* in 6:38, 39, 44, *apostellō* in 6:29, 57; the two are not used simply for the sake of variety of expression. *Pempō* is not used in the Lord's prayer in ch. 17, whereas *apostellō* is used six times.

(2) The "sending" of the Son by the Father was from the glory which He had with the Father into the world, by way of the Incarnation, not a "sending" out into the world after His birth, as if denoting His mission among and His manifestation to the people. "Hofmann, in support of his view that Jesus is called the Son of God only in virtue of His being born of man, vainly urges that the simple accusative after *apostellō* also denotes what the Person is or becomes by being sent. What he states is true but only when the name of the object spoken of is chosen to correspond with the purposed mission, as e.g., in Mark 1:2; Luke 14:32; 19:14. We can no more say, 'God sent Jesus that He should be His Son' than we can render 'he sent his servants,' Matt. 21:34, in this manner. That the Sonship of Christ is anterior to His mission to the world ... is clear from John 16:28; cf. especially also the double accusative in 1 John 4:14, 'the Father sent the Son the Savior of the world.' The expression that Jesus is sent by God denotes the mission which He has to fulfill and the authority which backs Him" (Cremer, *Lexicon of NT Greek*).

3. *exapostellō* (ἐξαποστέλλω, 1821) denotes (a) "to send forth": of the Son by God the Father, Gal. 4:4; of the Holy Spirit, 4:6; Luke 24:49 in the best texts (some have No. 1); an angel, Acts 12:11; the ancestors of Israel, Acts 7:12; Paul to the Gentiles, 22:21; of the word of salvation, 13:26 (some mss. have No. 1); (b) "to send away," Luke 1:53; 20:10, 11; Acts 9:30; 11:22; 17:14.

4. *anapempō* (ἀναπέμπω, 375) denotes (a) "to send up" (*ana*, "up," and No. 2), to a higher authority, Luke 23:7, 15; Acts 25:21 (in the best texts; some have No. 2); this meaning is confirmed by examples from the papyri (Moulton and Milligan), by Deissmann (*Bible Studies*, p. 229); see also Field, *Notes on the Trans. of the NT;* (b) "to send back," Luke 23:11; Philem. 12.

5. *ekpempō* (ἐκπέμπω, 1599) denotes "to send forth" (*ek*, "out of"), Acts 13:4, "being sent forth"; 17:10, "sent away."

6. *ballō* (βάλλω, 906), "to cast, throw," is translated "to send (peace)" in Matt. 10:34 (twice), (RV, marg., "cast").

7. *ekballō* (ἐκβάλλω, 1544), "to cast out," or "send out," is translated "sent out" in Mark 1:43, RV (KJV, "sent away"), and in KJV and RV in Jas. 2:25.

8. *apoluō* (ἀπολύω, 630), "to set free, to let go," is translated "to send away" in Matt. 14:15, 22, 23; Mark 6:36, 45; 8:3, 9; Luke 8:38; Acts 13:3, where the "sending" is not that of commissioning, but of letting go, intimating that they would gladly have retained them (contrast *ekpempō*, the act of commissioning by the Holy Spirit in v. 4).

9. *metapempō* (μεταπέμπω, 3343), "to send after or for, fetch" (*meta*, "after"), is used only in the Acts; in the middle voice, translated "to send for" in 10:22, 29 (2nd part: passive voice in the 1st part); 20:1, RV only (some texts have *proskaleō*); 24:24, 26; 25:3; in 10:5 and 11:13, RV, fetch.

10. *bruō* (βρύω, 1032), "to be full to bursting," was used of the earth in producing vegetation, of plants in putting forth buds; in Jas. 3:11 it is said of springs gushing with water, "(doth the fountain) send forth ...?"

11. *sunapostellō* (συναποστέλλω, 4882), "to send along with," is used in 2 Cor. 12:18. In the Sept., Ex. 33:2, 12.

12. *sunpempō* (συμπέμπω, 4842), "to send along with," is used in 2 Cor. 8:18, 22.

Notes: (1) In Matt. 13:36, KJV, *aphiēmi*, "to leave," is translated "He sent ... away" (RV, "He left"); so in Mark 4:36, KJV, "they had sent away," RV, "leaving." (2) In Mark 6:46, *apotassomai*, "to take leave of" (RV) is translated "He had sent ... away." (3) In John 13:16 *apostolos* is rendered "one (KJV, he) that is sent," RV marg., "an apostle." (4) *Paristēmi* is rendered "send" in Matt. 26:53, RV

For **SENSELESS** see FOOLISH, No. 4

SENSES

aisthētērion (αἰσθητήριον, 145), "sense, the faculty of perception, the organ of sense" (akin to *aisthanomai*, "to perceive"), is used in Heb. 5:14, "senses," the capacities for spiritual apprehension. In the Sept., Jer. 4:19, "(I am pained ... in the) sensitive powers (of my heart)."

For **SENSUAL** see NATURAL, A, No. 2

SENTENCE

A. Nouns.

1. *krima* (κρίμα, 2917), "a judgment," a decision passed on the faults of others, is used especially of God's judgment upon men, and translated "sentence" in 2 Pet. 2:3, RV (KJV, judgment). See JUDGMENT, No. 2.

2. *katadikē* (καταδική, 2613b), "a judicial sentence, condemnation," is translated "sentence" in Acts 25:15, RV (KJV, "judgment"); some mss. have *dikē*.

3. *apokrima* (ἀπόκριμα, 610) is translated "sentence" in 2 Cor. 1:9, KJV (RV, "answer"). See ANSWER, No. 2.

B. Verbs.

1. *krinō* (κρίνω, 2919), "to judge, to adjudge," is translated "(my) sentence is" in Acts 15:19, KJV, RV, "(my) judgment is," lit., "I (*ego*, emphatic) judge," introducing the substance or draft of a resolution. See JUDGE, B, No. 1.

2. *epikrinō* (ἐπικρίνω, 1948), "to give sentence," is used in Luke 23:24.

SEPARATE

A. Verbs.

1. *aphorizō* (ἀφορίζω, 873), "to mark off by bounds" (*apo*, "from," *horizō*, "to determine"; *horos*, "a limit"), "to separate," is used of "(a) the Divine action in setting men apart for the work of the gospel, Rom. 1:1; Gal. 1:15; (b) the Divine judgment upon men, Matt. 13:49; 25:32; (c) the separation of Christians from unbelievers, Acts 19:9; 2 Cor. 6:17; (d) the separation of believers by unbelievers, Luke 6:22; (e) the withdrawal of Christians from their brethren, Gal. 2:12. In (c) is described what the Christian must do, in (d) what he must be prepared to suffer, and in (e) what he must avoid."

2. *chōrizō* (χωρίζω, 5563), "to put asunder, separate," is translated "to separate" in Rom. 8:35, 39; in the middle voice, "to separate oneself, depart"; in the passive voice in Heb. 7:26, RV, "separated" (KJV, "separate"), the verb here relates to the resurrection of Christ, not, as KJV indicates, to the fact of His holiness in the days of His flesh; the list is progressive in this respect that the first three qualities apply to His sinlessness, the next to His resurrection, the last to His ascension.

3. *apodiorizō* (ἀποδιορίζω, 592), "to mark off" (*apo*, "from," *dia*, "asunder," *horizō*, "to limit"), hence denotes metaphorically to make "separations," Jude 19, RV (KJV, "separate themselves"), of persons who make divisions (in contrast with v. 20); there is no pronoun in the original representing "themselves."

B. Preposition.

chōris (χωρίς, 5565), "apart from, without" (cf. *aneu*, "without," a rarer word than this), is translated "separate from" in Eph. 2:12 (KJV, without). See BESIDE.

For **SEPARATIONS** see No. 3, above

SEPULCHRE

1. *taphos* (τάφος, 5028), akin to *thaptō*, "to bury," originally "a burial," then, "a place for burial, a tomb," occurs in Matt. 23:27; v. 29, RV (KJV, "tombs"); 27:61, 64, 66; 28:1; metaphorically, Rom. 3:13.

2 and 3. *mnēma* and *mnēmeion*: see GRAVE.

SERPENT

1. *ophis* (ὄφις, 3789): the characteristics of the "serpent" as alluded to in Scripture are mostly evil (though Matt. 10:16 refers to its caution in avoiding danger); its treachery, Gen. 49:17; 2 Cor. 11:3; its venom, Ps. 58:4; 1 Cor. 10:9; Rev. 9:19; its skulking, Job 26:13; its murderous proclivities, e.g., Ps. 58:4; Prov. 23:32; Eccl. 10:8, 11; Amos 5:19; Mark 16:18; Luke 10:19; the Lord used the word metaphorically of the scribes and Pharisees, Matt. 23:33 (cf. *echidna*, "viper," in Matt. 3:7; 12:34). The general aspects of its evil character are intimated in the Lord's rhetorical question in Matt. 7:10 and Luke 11:11. Its characteristics are concentrated in the archadversary of God and man, the Devil, metaphorically described as the serpent, 2 Cor. 11:3; Rev. 12:9, 14, 15; 20:2. The brazen "serpent" lifted up by Moses was symbolical of the means of salvation provided by God, in Christ and His vicarious death under the divine judgment upon sin, John 3:14. While the living "serpent" symbolizes sin in its origin, hatefulness, and deadly effect, the brazen "serpent" symbolized the bearing away of the curse and the judgment of sin; the metal was itself figurative of the righteousness of God's judgment.

2. *herpeton* (ἑρπετόν, 2062), "a creeping thing" (from *herpō*, "to creep"), "a reptile," is rendered "serpents" in Jas. 3:7, KJV (RV, "creeping things," as elsewhere). See CREEP, B.

SERVANT

A. Nouns.

1. *doulos* (δοῦλος, 1401), an adjective, signifying "in bondage," Rom. 6:19 (neuter plural, agreeing with *melē*, "members"), is used as a noun, and as the most common and general word for "servant," frequently indicating subjection without the idea of bondage; it is used (a) of natural conditions, e.g., Matt. 8:9; 1 Cor. 7:21, 22 (1st part); Eph. 6:5; Col. 4:1; 1 Tim. 6:1; frequently in the four Gospels; (b) metaphorically of spiritual, moral and ethical conditions: "servants" (1) of God, e.g., Acts 16:17; Titus 1:1; 1 Pet. 2:16; Rev. 7:3; 15:3; the perfect example being Christ Himself, Phil. 2:7; (2) of Christ, e.g., Rom. 1:1; 1 Cor. 7:22 (2nd part); Gal. 1:10; Eph. 6:6; Phil. 1:1; Col. 4:12; Jas. 1:1; 2 Pet. 1:1; Jude 1; (3) of sin, John 8:34 (RV, "bondservants"); Rom. 6:17, 20; (4) of corruption, 2 Pet. 2:19 (RV, "bondservants"); cf. the verb *douloō* (see B). See BONDMAN.

2. *diakonos* (διάκονος, 1249), for which see DEACON and *Note* there on synonymous words, is translated "servant" or "servants" in Matt. 22:13 (RV marg., "ministers"); 23:11 (RV marg., ditto); Mark 9:35, KJV (RV, "minister"); John 2:5, 9; 12:26; Rom. 16:1.

3. *pais* (παῖς, 3816), for which see CHILD, No. 4, also denotes "an attendant"; it is translated "servant" (a) of natural conditions, in Matt. 8:6, 8, 13; 14:2; Luke 7:7 ("menservants"

in 12:45); 15:26; (b) of spiritual relation to God, (1) of Israel, Luke 1:54; (2) of David, Luke 1:69; Acts 4:25; (3) of Christ, so declared by God the Father, Matt. 12:18; spoken of in prayer, Acts 4:27, 30, RV (KJV, "child"); the argument advanced by Dalman for the rendering "Child" in these passages, is not sufficiently valid as against the RV, "Servant" in Acts 4, and the KJV and RV in Matt. 12 (cf, e.g., the use of *pais* in the Sept. of Gen. 41:38; Jer. 36:24). The Matt. 12 passage by direct quotation, and the Acts 4 passages by implication, refer to the ideal "Servant of Jehovah" (Sept., *pais Kuriou*), of Isa. 42:1 and following passages, thus identifying the Servant with the Lord Jesus; for the same identification, cf. Acts 8:35.

4. *oiketēs* (οἰκέτης, 3610), "a house servant" (*oikeō*, "to dwell," *oikos*, "a house"), is translated "servant" in Luke 16:13 (RV marg., "household servant"); so Rom. 14:4 and 1 Pet. 2:18; in Acts 10:7, KJV and RV, "household servants."

5. *hupēretēs* (ὑπηρέτης, 5257), for which see MINISTER, No. 3, is translated "servants" in the KJV of Matt. 26:58; Mark 14:65 (RV, "officers"); in John 18:36, KJV and RV (RV, marg., "officers").

6. *therapēn* (θεράπων, 2324), akin to *therapeuē*, "to serve, to heal, an attendant, servant," is a term of dignity and freedom, used of Moses in Heb. 3:5.

7. *sundoulos* (σύνδουλος, 4889), "a fellow servant," is used (a) of natural conditions, Matt. 18:28, 29, 31, 33; 24:49; (b) of "servants" of the same divine Lord, Col. 1:7; 4:7; Rev. 6:11; of angels, Rev. 19:10; 22:9.

B. Verb.

douloō (δουλόω, 1402), "to enslave, to bring into bondage" (akin to A, No. 1), e.g., 1 Cor. 9:19, RV, "I brought (myself) under bondage (to all)," KJV, "I made myself servant," denotes in the passive voice, "to be brought into bondage, to become a slave or servant," rendered "ye became servants (of righteousness)" in Rom. 6:18; "being ... become servants (to God)," v. 22. See BONDAGE, B, No. 2.

SERVE

1. *diakoneō* (διακονέω, 1247), "to minister" (akin to *diakonos*, No. 2, above), "to render any kind of service," is translated "to serve," e.g., in Luke 10:40; 12:37; 17:8; 22:26, 27 (twice); see MINISTER, B, No. 1.

2. *douleuō* (δουλεύω, 1398), "to serve as a *doulos*" (No. 1, above), is used (a) of serving God (and the impossibility of serving mammon also), Matt. 6:24 and Luke 16:13; Rom. 7:6; in the gospel, Phil. 2:22; (b) Christ, Acts 20:19; Rom. 12:11; 14:18; 16:18; Eph. 6:7; Col. 3:24; (c) the law of God, Rom. 7:25; (d) one another, Gal. 5:13, RV, "be servants to" (KJV, "serve"); (e) a father, Luke 15:29 (with a suggestion of acting as a slave); (f) earthly masters, Matt. 6:24; Luke 16:13; 1 Tim. 6:2, RV, "serve"; (g) the younger by the elder, Rom. 9:12; (h) of being in bondage to a nation, Acts 7:7; Gal. 4:25, to the Romans, actually, though also spiritually to Judaizers; (i) to idols, Gal. 4:8, RV, "were in bondage" (KJV, "did service"); (j) to "the weak and beggarly rudiments," v. 9 (RV), "to be in bondage" (aorist tense in the best texts, suggesting "to enter into bondage"), i.e., to the religion of the Gentiles ("rudiments" being used in v. 3 of the religion of the Jews); (k) sin, Rom. 6:6, RV, "be in bondage" (KJV, "serve"); (l) "divers lusts and pleasures," Titus 3:3; (m) negatively, to any man—a proud and thoughtless denial by the Jews, John 8:33.

3. *latreuō* (λατρεύω, 3000), primarily "to work for hire" (akin to *latris*, "a hired servant"), signifies (1) to worship, (2) to "serve"; in the latter sense it is used of service (a) to God, Matt. 4:10; Luke 1:74 ("without fear"); 4:8; Acts 7:7; 24:14, RV, "serve" (KJV, "worship"); 26:7; 27:23; Rom. 1:9 ("with my spirit"); 2 Tim. 1:3; Heb. 9:14; 12:28, KJV, "we may serve," RV, "we may offer service"; Rev. 7:15; (b) to God and Christ ("the Lamb"), Rev. 22:3; (c) in the tabernacle, Heb. 8:5, RV; 13:10; (d) to "the host of heaven," Acts 7:42, RV, "to serve" (KJV, "to worship"); (e) to "the creature," instead of the Creator, Rom. 1:25, of idolatry: see WORSHIP.

Note: In Luke 2:37 the RV has "worshiping," for KJV, "served"; in Heb. 9:9, "the worshiper," for KJV, "that did the service."

4. *hupēreteō* (ὑπηρετέω, 5256), for which see MINISTER, B, No. 3, is translated "to serve" in Acts 13:36; there is a contrast intimated between the service of David, lasting for only a generation, and the eternal character of Christ's ministry as the One who not having seen corruption was raised from the dead.

SERVICE, SERVING

1. *diakonia* (διακονία, 1248) is rendered "service" in Rom. 15:31, KJV; "serving" in Luke 10:40. See MINISTRY, A, No. 1.

2. *leitourgia* (λειτουργία, 3009) is rendered "service" in 2 Cor. 9:12; Phil. 2:17, 30. See MINISTRY, A, No. 2.

3. *latreia* (λατρεία, 2999), akin to *latreuō* (see No. 3, above), primarily "hired service," is used (a) of the "service" *of God* in connection with the tabernacle, Rom. 9:4; Heb. 9:1, "divine service"; v. 6, plural, RV, "services" (KJV, "service," and, in italics, "of God"); (b) of the intelligent "service" of believers in presenting their bodies to God, a living sacrifice, Rom. 12:1, RV marg., "worship"; (c) of imagined "service" to God by persecutors of Christ's followers, John 16:2.

SETTER FORTH

katangeleus (καταγγελεύς, 2604), "a proclaimer, herald" (akin to *katangello*, "to proclaim"), is used in Acts 17:18, "a setter forth (of strange gods)." It is found in inscriptions in connection with proclamations made in public places.

SEVEN

hepta (ἑπτά, 2033), whence Eng. words beginning with "hept-," corresponds to the Heb. *sheba'* (which is akin to *sāba'*, signifying "to be full, abundant"), sometimes used as an expression of fullness, e.g., Ruth 4:15: it generally expresses completeness, and is used most frequently in the Apocalypse; it is not found in the Gospel of John, nor between the Acts and the Apocalypse, except in Heb. 11:30 (in Rom. 11:4 the numeral is *heptakischilioi*, "seven thousand"); in Matt. 22:26 it is translated "seventh" (marg., "seven").

Note: In 2 Pet. 2:5, RV, "Noah with seven others" is a translation into idiomatic English of the Greek idiom "Noah the eighth *person*" (so KJV, translating literally).

SEVENTH

hebdomos (ἕβδομος, 1442) occurs in John 4:52; Heb. 4:4 (twice); Jude 14; Rev. 8:1; 10:7; 11:15; 16:17; 21:20.

SEVEN TIMES

heptakis (ἑπτακίς, 2034) occurs in Matt. 18:21, 22; Luke 17:4 (twice).

SEVENTY

hebdomēkonta (ἑβδομήκοντα, 1440) occurs in Luke 10:1, 17; in Acts 7:14 it precedes *pente*, "five," lit., "seventy-five," rendered "threescore and fifteen"; in 23:23 it is translated "threescore and ten"; in 27:37 it precedes *hex*, "six," lit., "seventy-six," rendered "threescore and sixteen."

SEVENTY TIMES

hebdomēkontakis (ἑβδομηκοντακίς, 1441) occurs in Matt. 18:22, where it is followed by *hepta*, "seven," "seventy times seven"; RV marg. has "seventy times and seven," which many have regarded as the meaning; cf. Gen. 4:24 (Winer, in Winer-Moulton, *Gram.*, p. 314, remarks that while this would be the strict meaning, it "would not suit the passage"; his translator, W. F. Moulton, in a footnote, expresses the opinion that it would. So also J. H. Moulton, *Prol.*, p. 98, says: "A definite *allusion* to the Genesis story is highly probable: Jesus pointedly sets against the natural man's craving for seventy-sevenfold revenge the spiritual man's ambition to exercise the privilege of seventy-sevenfold forgiveness").

The Lord's reply "until seventy times seven" was indicative of completeness, the absence of any limit, and was designed to turn away Peter's mind from a merely numerical standard. God's forgiveness is limitless; so should man's be.

SEVER

1. *katargeō* (καταργέω, 2673), lit., "to reduce to inactivity" (see ABOLISH, where all the occurences are given), is rendered "ye are severed (from Christ)" in Gal. 5:4, RV; the aorist tense indicates that point of time at which there was an acceptance of the Judaistic doctrines; to those who accepted these Christ would be of no profit, they were as branches severed from the tree.

2. *aphorizō* (ἀφορίζω, 873), "to separate from," is used of the work of the angels at the end of this age, in "severing" the wicked from among the righteous, Matt. 13:49, a premillennial act quite distinct from the rapture of the Church as set forth in 1 Thess. 4.

SEVERITY

1. *apotomia* (ἀποτομία, 663), "steepness, sharpness" (*apo*, "off," *temnō*, "to cut"; *tomē*, "a cutting"), is used metaphorically in Rom. 11:22 (twice) of "the severity of God," which lies in His temporary retributive dealings with Israel. In the papyri it is used of exacting to the full the provisions of a statute. Cf. the adverb *apotomos*, "sharply" (which see).

2. *apheidia* (ἀφειδία, 857), primarily "extravagance" (*a*, negative, *pheidomai*, "to spare"), hence, "unsparing treatment, severity," is used in Col. 2:23, RV, "severity (to the body)," KJV, "neglecting of" (marg., "punishing, not sparing"); here it refers to ascetic discipline; it was often used among the Greeks of courageous exposure to hardship and danger.

SHADOW (Noun)

1. *skia* (σκία, 4639) is used (a) of "a shadow," caused by the interception of light, Mark 4:32; Acts 5:15; metaphorically of the darkness and spiritual death of ignorance, Matt. 4:16; Luke 1:79; (b) of "the image" or "outline" cast by an object, Col. 2:17, of ceremonies under the Law; of the tabernacle and its appurtenances and offerings, Heb. 8:5; of these as appointed under the Law, Heb. 10:1.

2. *aposkiasma* (ἀποσκίασμα, 644), "a shadow," is rendered "shadow that is cast" in Jas. 1:17, RV; the KJV makes no distinction between this and No. 1. The probable significance of this word is "overshadowing" or "shadowing-over" (which *apo* may indicate), and this with the genitive case of *tropē*, "turning," yields the meaning "shadowing-over of mutability" implying an alternation of "shadow" and light; of this there are two alternative explanations, namely, "overshadowing" (1) not caused by mutability in God, or (2) caused by change in others, i.e., "no changes in this lower world can cast a shadow on the unchanging Fount of light" [Mayor, who further remarks, "The meaning of the passage will then be, 'God is alike incapable of change (*parallagē*) and incapable of being changed by the action of others'"].

SHAME (Noun, and Verb)

A. Nouns.

1. *atimia* (ἀτιμία, 819) signifies (a) "shame, disgrace," Rom. 1:26, "vile (passions)," RV, lit., "(passions) of shame"; 1 Cor. 11:14; (b) "dishonor," e.g., 2 Tim. 2:20, where the idea

of disgrace or "shame" does not attach to the use of the word; the meaning is that while in a great house some vessels are designed for purposes of honor, others have no particular honor (*time*) attached to their use (the prefix a simply negatives the idea of honor). See DISHONOR.

2. *aischunē* (αἰσχύνη, 152): See ASHAMED, B, No. 1.

3. *entropē* (ἐντροπή, 1791), 1 Cor. 6:5 and 15:34. See ASHAMED, B, No. 2.

4. *aschēmosunē* (ἀσχημοσύνη, 808) denotes (a) "unseemliness," Rom. 1:27, RV (KJV, "that which is unseemly"); (b) "shame, nakedness," Rev. 16:15, a euphemism for No. 2.

B. Adjective.

aischros (αἰσχρός, 150), "base, shameful" (akin to *aischos*, "shame"), of that which is opposed to modesty or purity, is translated as a noun in 1 Cor. 11:6; 14:35, KJV (RV, "shameful"); Eph. 5:12; in Titus 1:11, "filthy (lucre)," lit., "shameful (gain)." See FILTHY.

C. Verbs.

1. *atimazō* (ἀτιμάζω, 818), "to dishonor, put to shame (akin to A, No. 1): see DISHONOR, C, No. 1.

2. *entrepō* (ἐντρέπω, 1788), lit., "to turn in upon, to put to shame" (akin to A, No. 3), is translated "to shame (you)" in 1 Cor. 4:14. See ASHAMED, A, No. 4.

3. *kataischunō* (καταισχύνω, 2617), "to put to shame" (*kata*, perhaps signifying "utterly"), is translated "ye ... shame (them)" in 1 Cor. 11:22, KJV, RV, "ye ... put (them) to shame." See ASHAMED, A, No. 3.

4. *paradeigmatizō* (παραδειγματίζω, 3856) signifies "to set forth as an example" (*para*, "beside," *deiknumi*, "to show"), and is used in Heb. 6:6 of those Jews, who, though attracted to, and closely associated with, the Christian faith, without having experienced more than a tasting of the heavenly gift and partaking of the Holy Ghost (not actually receiving Him), were tempted to apostatize to Judaism, and, thereby crucifying the Son of God a second time, would "put Him to an open shame." So were criminals exposed. In the Sept., Num. 25:4; Jer. 13:22; Ezek. 28:17.

SHAMEFASTNESS (*KJV*, SHAMEFACEDNESS)

aidōs (αἰδώς, 127), "a sense of shame, modesty," is used regarding the demeanor of women in the church, 1 Tim. 2:9 (some mss. have it in Heb. 12:28 for *deos*, "awe": here only in NT). "Shamefastness is that modesty which is 'fast' or rooted in the character ... The change to 'shamefacedness' is the more to be regretted because shamefacedness ... has come rather to describe an awkward diffidence, such as we sometimes call sheepishness" (Davies; *Bible English*, p. 12).

As to *aidōs* and *aischunē* (see ASHAMED, B, No. 1), *aidōs* is more objective, having regard to others; it is the stronger word. "Aidos would always restrain a good man from an unworthy act, *aischunē* would sometimes restrain a bad one" (Trench, *Syn.* Sec. XIX, XX).

SHAMEFULLY (ENTREAT)

Note: This forms part of the rendering of (a) *atimazō*, Mark 12:4, Luke 20:11, see DISHONOR, C, No. 1; (b) *hubrizō*, "to insult," Acts 14:5, RV; 1 Thess. 2:2, "were (RV, having been) shamefully entreated." See SPITEFULLY.

SHAPE

1. *eidos* (εἶδος, 1491), rendered "shape" in the KJV of Luke 3:22 and John 5:37: see FORM, No. 4.

2. *homoiōma* (ὁμοίωμα, 3667), rendered "shapes" in Rev. 9:7: see LIKENESS, No. 1.

For **SHARERS** (Heb. 2:14) see PARTAKE, B, No. 1.

SHEEP

1. *probaton* (πρόβατον, 4263), from *probainō*, "to go forward," i.e., of the movement of quadrupeds, was used among the Greeks of small cattle, sheep and goats; in the NT, of "sheep" only (a) naturally, e.g., Matt. 12:11, 12; (b) metaphorically, of those who belong to the Lord, the lost ones of the house of Israel, Matt. 10:6; of those who are under the care of the Good Shepherd, e.g., Matt. 26:31; John 10:1, lit., "the fold of the sheep," and vv. 2-27; 21:16, 17 in some texts; Heb. 13:20; of those who in a future day, at the introduction of the millennial kingdom, have shown kindness to His persecuted earthly people in their great tribulation, Matt. 25:33; of the clothing of false shepherds, Matt. 7:15; (c) figuratively, by way of simile, of Christ, Acts 8:32; of the disciples, e.g., Matt. 10:16; of true followers of Christ in general, Rom. 8:36; of the former wayward condition of those who had come under His Shepherd care, 1 Pet. 2:25; of the multitudes who sought the help of Christ in the days of His flesh, Matt. 9:36; Mark 6:34.

2. *probation* (προβάτιον, 4263a), a diminutive of No. 1, "a little sheep," is found in the best texts in John 21:16, 17 (some have No. 1); distinct from *arnia*, "lambs" (v. 15), but used as a term of endearment.

Note: For "keeping sheep," Luke 17:7, RV, see CATTLE.

SHEPHERD

poimēn (ποιμήν, 4166) is used (a) in its natural significance, Matt. 9:36; 25:32; Mark 6:34; Luke 2:8, 15, 18, 20; John 10:2, 12; (b) metaphorically of Christ, Matt. 26:31; Mark 14:27; John 10:11, 14, 16; Heb. 13:20; 1 Pet. 2:25; (c) metaphorically of those who act as pastors in the churches, Eph. 4:11. See PASTOR.

For **CHIEF SHEPHERD** see CHIEF, B, No. 3

SHEWBREAD

Note: The phrase rendered "the shewbread" is formed by the combination of the nouns *prothesis*, "a setting forth" (*pro*, "before," *tithēmi*, "to place") and *artos*, "a loaf" (in the plural), each with the article, Matt. 12:4; Mark 2:26 and Luke 6:4, lit., "the loaves of the setting forth"; in Heb. 9:2, lit., "the setting forth of the loaves." The corresponding OT phrases are lit., "bread of the face," Exod. 25:30, i.e., the presence, referring to the Presence of God (cf. Isa. 63:9 with Exod. 33:14, 15); "the bread of ordering," 1 Chron. 9:32, marg. In Num. 4:7 it is called "the continual bread"; in 1 Sam. 21:4, 6, "holy bread" (KJV, "hallowed"). In the Sept. of 1 Kings 7:48, it is called "the bread of the offering" (*prosphora*, "a bearing towards"). The twelve loaves, representing the tribes of Israel, were set in order every Sabbath day before the Lord, "on the behalf of the children," Lev. 24:8, RV (marg., and KJV, "from"), "an everlasting covenant." The loaves symbolized the fact that on the basis of the sacrificial atonement of the Cross, believers are accepted before God, and nourished by Him in the person of Christ. The showbread was partaken of by the priests, as representatives of the nation. Priesthood now being coextensive with all who belong to Christ, 1 Pet. 2:5, 9, He, the Living Bread, is the nourishment of all, and where He is, there, representatively, they are.

SHIELD

thureos (θυρεός, 2375) formerly meant "a stone for closing the entrance of a cave"; then, "a shield," large and oblong, protecting every part of the soldier; the word is used metaphorically of faith, Eph. 6:16, which the believer is to take up "in (*en* in the original) all" (all that has just been mentioned), i.e., as affecting the whole of his activities.

SHINE, SHINING

A. Verbs.

1. *phainō* (φαίνω, 5316), "to cause to appear," denotes, in the active voice, "to give light, shine," John 1:5; 5:35; in Matt. 24:27, passive voice; so Phil. 2:15, RV, "ye are seen" (for KJV, "ye shine"); 2 Pet. 1:19 (active); so 1 John 2:8, Rev. 1:16; in 8:12 and 18:23 (passive); 21:23 (active). See APPEAR.

2. *epiphainō* (ἐπιφαίνω, 2014), "to shine upon" (*epi*, "upon," and No. 1), is so translated in Luke 1:79, RV (KJV, "to give light"). See APPEAR, No. 2.

3. *lampō* (λάμπω, 2989), "to shine as a torch," occurs in Matt. 5:15, 16, 17:2; Luke 17:24; Acts 12:7; 2 Cor. 4:6 (twice).: see LIGHT, B, No. 3.

4. *stilbō* (στίλβω, 4744), "to shine, glisten," is used in Mark 9:3 of the garments of Christ at His transfiguration, RV, "glistering" KJV, "shining." Cf. *exastraptō*, "dazzling," in Luke 9:29, RV.

5. *eklampō* (ἐκλάμπω, 1584), "to shine forth" (*ek*, "out" and No. 3), is used in Matt. 13:43, of the future shining "forth" of the righteous "in the Kingdom of their Father."

6. *perilampō* (περιλάμπω, 4034), "to shine around" (*peri*, "around," and No. 3), is used in Luke 2:9, "shone round about," of the glory of the Lord; so in Acts 26:13, of the light from Heaven upon Saul of Tarsus.

7. *periastraptō* (περιαστράπτω, 4015), "to flash around, shine round about" (*peri*, and *astrapē*, "shining brightness"), is used in Acts 9:3 and 22:6 of the same circumstance as in 26:13 (No. 6).

8. *epiphauskō* (ἐπιφαύσκω, 2017), or *epiphauō* (ἐπιφαύω, 2017), "to shine forth," is used figuratively of Christ upon the slumbering believer who awakes and arises from among the dead, Eph. 5:14, RV, "shall shine upon thee" (KJV, "shall give thee light").

B. Noun.

astrapē (ἀστραπή, 796), denotes (a) "lightning," (b) "bright shining," of a lamp, Luke 11:36. See LIGHTNING. Cf. No. 7, above, and *Note* (1) below.

Notes: (1) In Luke 24:4, KJV, *astraptō*, "to lighten," is translated "shining" (RV, "dazzling"). (2) In 2 Cor. 4:4, KJV, *augazō*, "to shine forth," is translated "shine" (RV, "dawn").

For **OWNER OF THE SHIP** see OWNER, No. 2

For **SHIPMASTER** see MASTER, A, No. 7

For **SHOD** see BIND, No. 3

SHOE

hupodēmo (ὑπόδημα, 5266) denotes "a sole bound under the foot" (*hupō*, "under," *deō*, "to bind"; cf. *hupodeo*, "to bind under"), "a sandal," always translated "shoes," e.g., Matt. 3:11; 10:10; Mark 1:7.

SHOUT (Noun and Verb)

A. Noun.

keleusma (κέλευσμα, 2752), "a call, summons, shout of command" (akin to *keleuō*, "to command"), is used in 1 Thess. 4:16 of the "shout" with which (*en*, "in," denoting the attendant circumstances) the Lord will descend from heaven at the time of the rapture of the saints (those who have fallen asleep, and the living) to meet Him in the air. The "shout" is not here said to be His actual voice, though this indeed will be so (John 5:28). In the Sept., Prov. 30:27, "(the locusts … at the) word of command (march in rank)."

B. Verb.

epiphōneō (ἐπιφωνέω, 2019), "to call out" (*epi*, "upon," *phōneō*, "to utter a sound"), is translated "shouted" in Acts 12:22, RV (KJV, "gave a shout"). See CRY, B, No. 8.

SHOW (Noun)

logos (λόγος, 3056), "a word," is sometimes used of mere talk, the talk which one occasions; hence, "repute, reputation"; this seems to be the meaning in Col. 2:23, translated "a show (KJV 'show') of wisdom," i.e., "a reputation for wisdom," rather than "appearance, reason," etc. See WORD.

Note: In Luke 20:47, KJV, *prophasis*, "a pretense" (RV), is translated "show."

SHOW (make a)

1. *deigmatizō* (δειγματίζω, 1165), "to make a show of, expose," is used in Col. 2:15 of Christ's act regarding the principalities and powers, displaying them "as a victor displays his captives or trophies in a triumphal procession" (Lightfoot). Some regard the meaning as being that He showed the angelic beings in their true inferiority (see under TRIUMPH). For its other occurrence, Matt. 1:19, see EXAMPLE, B, No. 1.

2. *euprosōpeō* (εὐπροσωπέω, 2146) denotes "to look well, make a fair show" (*eu*, "well," *prosōpon*, "a face"), and is used in Gal. 6:12, "to make a fair show (in the flesh)," i.e., "to make a display of religious zeal." Deissmann illustrates the metaphorical use of this word from the papyri in *Light from the Ancient East*, p. 96.

Note: For *paratērēsis*, KJV marg. in Luke 17:20, "outward show," see OBSERVATION.

SHRINE

naos (ναός, 3485), "the inmost part of a temple, a shrine," is used in the plural in Acts 19:24, of the silver models of the pagan "shrine" in which the image of Diana (Greek Artemis) was preserved. The models were large or small, and were signs of wealth and devotion on the part of purchasers. The variety of forms connected with the embellishment of the image provided "no little business" for the silversmiths. See TEMPLE.

SHUDDER

phrissō (φρίσσω, 5425), primarily, "to be rough, to bristle," then, "to shiver, shudder, tremble," is said of demons, Jas. 2:19, RV, "shudder" (KJV, "tremble"). Cf. Matt. 8:29, indicating a cognizance of their appointed doom.

SICK, SICKLY, SICKNESS

A. Verbs.

1. *astheneō* (ἀσθενέω, 770), lit., "to be weak, feeble" (*a*, negative, *sthenos*, "strength"), is translated "to be sick," e.g., in Matt. 10:8, "(the) sick"; 25:36; v. 39 in the best texts (some have B, No. 1); Mark 6:56; Luke 4:40; 7:10 (RV omits the word); 9:2; John 4:46; 5:3, RV (KJV, "impotent folk"); v. 7; 6:2, RV (KJV, "were diseased"); 11:1-3, 6; Acts 9:37; 19:12; Phil. 2:26, 27; 2 Tim. 4:20; Jas. 5:14. See DISEASED, B, No. 1, and, especially, WEAK.

2. *kamnō* (κάμνω, 2577), primarily, "to work," hence, from the effect of constant work, "to be weary," Heb. 12:3, is rendered "(him) that is sick," in Jas. 5:15, RV, KJV "(the) sick." The choice of this verb instead of the repetition of No. 1 (v. 14, see above), is suggestive of the common accompaniment of "sickness," weariness of mind (which is the meaning of this verb), which not infrequently hinders physical recovery; hence this special cause is here intimated in the general idea of "sickness." In some mss. it occurs in Rev. 2:3. In the Sept., Job 10:1; 17:2.

3. *sunechō* (συνέχω, 4912), "to hold in, hold fast," is used, in the passive voice, of "being seized or afflicted by ills," Acts 28:8, "sick" (of the father of Publius, cf. Matt. 4:24; Luke 4:38, taken with). See CONSTRAIN, No. 3.

Notes: (1) *Noseō*, "to be sick," is used metaphorically of mental ailment, in 1 Tim. 6:4, "doting" (marg., "sick"). (2) The adverb *kakōs*, "evilly ill," with *echō*, "to hold, to have," is rendered "to be sick," in Matt. 4:24, RV, "that were sick"; 8:16; 9:12; 14:35 and Mark 1:32, RV (KJV, "diseased"); 1:34; 2:17; 6:55; Luke 5:31; 7:2. (3) For "sick of the palsy," Luke 5:24; Acts 9:33, see PALSY (SICK OF).

B. Adjectives.

1. *asthēnes* (ἀσθενής, 772), lit., "without strength," hence, "feeble, weak," is used of "bodily debility," Matt. 25:43 (for v. 39, see A, No. 1), 44; some texts have it in Luke 9:2 (the best omit it, the meaning being "to heal" in general); 10:9; Acts 5:15, 16; in 4:9 it is rendered "impotent. See FEEBLE, WEAK.

2. *arrhōstos* (ἄρρωστος, 732), "feeble, sickly" (*a*, negative, *rhōnnumi*, "to be strong"), is translated "sick" in Matt. 14:14; Mark 16:18; "sick folk" in Mark 6:5; "that were sick" in 6:13; "sickly" in 1 Cor. 11:30, here also of the physical state. In the Sept., 1 Kings 14:5; Mal. 1:8.

C. Nouns.

1. *astheneia* (ἀσθένεια, 769), "weakness, sickness" (akin to A, No. 1 and B, No. 1), is translated "sickness" in John 11:4. See DISEASE, No. 1, INFIRMITY, WEAKNESS.

2. *nosos* (νόσος, 3554): see DISEASE, No. 3.

SIDE

A. Noun.

pleura (πλευρά, 4125), "a side" (cf. Eng., "pleurisy"), is used of the "side" of Christ, into which the spear was thrust, John 19:34; 20:20, 25, 27 (some mss. have it in Matt. 27:49; see RV marg.); elsewhere, in Acts 12:7.

B. Adverb.

peran (πέραν, 4008), an adverb, signifying "beyond, on the other side," is used (a) as a preposition and translated "on the other side of," e.g., in Mark 5:1; Luke 8:22; John 6:1, RV;

6:22, 25; (b) as a noun with the article, e.g., Matt. 8:18, 28; 14:22; 16:5. See BEYOND, No. 2.

Notes: (1) In Luke 9:47, the preposition *para*, "by the side of," with the dative case of the pronoun *heautou*, is rendered "by His side," RV (KJV, "by Him"). (2) See also HIGHWAY, RIGHT.

SIGHT

A. Nouns.

1. *eidos* (εἶδος, 1491) is translated. "sight" in 2 Cor. 5:7; see APPEARANCE, No. 1.

2. *theōria* (θεωρία, 2335) denotes "a spectacle, a sight" (akin to *theoreō*, to gaze, behold"; see BEHOLD), in Luke 23:45.

3. *horama* (ὅραμα, 3705), "that which is seen" (akin to *horaō*, "to see"), besides its meaning, "a vision, appearance," denotes "a sight," in Acts 7:31. See VISION.

4. *ophthalmos* (ὀφθαλμός, 3788) "an eye" (Eng. "ophthalmic," etc.) in Acts 1:9 is translated "sight" (plur. lit., "eyes"). See EYE.

5. *anablepsis* (ἀνάβλεψις, 309) denotes "recovering of sight" (*ana*, "again," *blepō*, "to see"), Luke 4:18. In the Sept, Isa. 61:1. *Notes:* (1) For *horasis* (akin to No. 3), translated "in sight" in Rev. 4:3, KJV (RV, "to look upon"), see LOOK, B. (2) In Luke 7:21, the infinitive mood of *blepō*, "to see," is used as a noun, "(He bestowed, KJV, 'gave') sight." In Acts 9:9 it is used in the present participle with *mē*, "not," "without sight" (lit., "not seeing"). (3) In Heb. 12:21 *phantazomai*, "to make visible," is used in the present participle as a noun, with the article, "(the) sight." (4) In Luke 21:11, KJV, *phobētron* (or *phobēthron*), plur., is translated "fearful sights" (RV, "terrors").

B. Verb.

anablepō (ἀναβλέπω, 308), "to look up," also denotes "to receive or recover sight" (akin to A, No. 5), e.g., Matt. 11:5; 20:34; Mark 10:51, 52; Luke 18:41-43; John 9:11, 15, 18 (twice); Acts 9:12, 17, 18; 22:13.

SIGHT OF (in the)

1. *enōpion* (ἐνώπιον, 1799) is translated "in the sight of" in the RV (for KJV, "before") in Luke 12:6; 15:18; 16:15; Acts 7:46; 10:33; 19:19; 1 Tim. 5:4, 21; 2 Tim. 2:14; 4:1; Rev. 13:12. The RV is more appropriate in most passages, as giving the real significance of the word.

2. *katenōpion* (κατενώπιον, 2714) is translated "in the sight of" in 2 Cor. 2:17 (in some texts); Col. 1:22, KJV.

3. *emprosthen* (ἔμπροσθεν, 1715) is translated "in the sight of" in Matt. 11:26; Luke 10:21; 1 Thess. 1:3, KJV.

4. *enantion* (ἐναντίον, 1726) is translated "in the sight of" in Acts 7:10.

5. *enanti* (ἔναντι, 1725) is translated "in the sight of" in Acts 8:21, KJV.

6. *katenanti* (κατέναντι, 2713) is found in the best texts in 2 Cor. 12:19, "in the sight of," RV, and in 2:17.

SIGN

1. *semeion* (σημεῖον, 4592), "a sign, mark, indication, token," is used (a) of that which distinguished a person or thing from others, e.g., Matt. 26:48; Luke 2:12; Rom. 4:11; 2 Cor. 12:12 (1st part); 2 Thess. 3:17, "token," i.e., his autograph attesting the authenticity of his letters; (b) of a "sign" as a warning or admonition, e.g., Matt. 12:39, "the sign of (i.e., consisting of) the prophet Jonas"; 16:4; Luke 2:34; 11:29, 30; (c) of miraculous acts (1) as tokens of divine authority and power, e.g., Matt. 12:38, 39 (1st part); John 2:11, RV, "signs"; 3:2 (ditto); 4:54, "(the second) sign," RV; 10:41 (ditto); 20:30; in 1 Cor. 1:22, "the Jews ask for signs," RV, indicates that the Apostles were met with the same demand from Jews as Christ had been: "signs were vouchsafed in plenty, signs of God's power and love, but these were not the signs which they sought .... They wanted signs of an outward Messianic Kingdom, of temporal triumph, of material greatness for the chosen people .... With such cravings the Gospel of a 'crucified Messiah' was to them a stumblingblock indeed" (Lightfoot); 1 Cor. 14:22; (2) by demons, Rev. 16:14; (3) by false teachers or prophets, indications of assumed authority, e.g., Matt. 24:24; Mark 13:22; (4) by Satan through his special agents, 2 Thess. 2:9; Rev. 13:13, 14; 19:20; (d) of tokens portending future events, e. g., Matt. 24:3, where "the sign of the Son of Man" signifies, subjectively, that the Son of Man is Himself the "sign" of what He is about to do; Mark 13:4; Luke 21:7, 11, 25; Acts 2:19; Rev. 12:1, RV; 12:3, RV; 15:1.

"Signs" confirmatory of what God had accomplished in the atoning sacrifice of Christ, His resurrection and ascension, and of the sending of the Holy Spirit, were given to the Jews for their recognition, as at Pentecost, and supernatural acts by apostolic ministry, as well as by the supernatural operations in the churches, such as the gift of tongues and prophesyings; there is no record of the continuance of these latter after the circumstances recorded in Acts 19:1-20.

2. *parasēmos* (παράσημος, 3902), an adjective meaning "marked at the side" (*para*, "beside," *sēma*, "a mark"), is used in Acts 28:11 as a noun denoting the figurehead of a vessel.

SIGNS (to make)

enneuō (ἐννεύω, 1770), "to nod to" (*en*, "in," *neuō*, "to nod"), denotes "to make a sign to" in Luke 1:62. In the Sept., Prov. 6:13; 10:10.

Note: For *dianeuō*, Luke 1:22, RV, see BECKON, No. 2.

For **SIGNIFICATION,** 1 Cor. 14:10, see DUMB, No. 2

SIGNIFY

1. *sēmainō* (σημαίνω, 4591), "to give a sign, indicate" (*sēma*, "a sign": cf. SIGN, No. 1), "to signify," is so translated in John 12:33; 18:32; 21:19; Acts 11:28; 25:27; Rev. 1:1, where perhaps the suggestion is that of expressing by signs.

2. *dēloō* (δηλόω, 1213), "to make plain" (*dēlos*, "evident"), is translated "to signify" in 1 Cor. 1:11, RV, "it hath been signified" (KJV, "declared"); Heb. 9:8; 12:27; 1 Pet. 1:11, KJV (RV, "point unto"); 2 Pet. 1:14, RV, "signified" (KJV, "hath showed").

3. *emphanizō* (ἐμφανίζω, 1718), "to manifest, make known," is translated "signify" in Acts 23:15; v. 22, RV (KJV, "hath showed"). See APPEAR, No. 5.

Note: In Acts 21:26, KJV, *diangellō*, "to announce," is rendered "to signify" (RV, "declaring").

SILENCE

A. Noun.

sigē (σιγή, 4602) occurs in Acts 21:40; Rev. 8:1, where the "silence" is introductory to the judgments following the opening of the seventh seal.

Note: For *hēsuchia*, KJV, "silence," in Acts 22:2 and 1 Tim. 2:11, 12, see QUIETNESS.

B. Verbs.

1. *phimoō* (φιμόω, 5392), "to muzzle," is rendered "to put to silence" in Matt. 22:34; 1 Pet. 2:15. See PEACE (HOLD), SPEECHLESS.

2. *sigaō* (σιγάω, 4601), "to be silent": see PEACE (hold), No. 1.

For **SILENT,** Luke 1:20, RV, see DUMB, B

For **SILLY,** 2 Tim. 3:6, see WOMAN, No. 2

SILVER

A. Nouns.

1. *argurion* (ἀργύριον, 694) is rendered "silver" in Acts 3:6; 8:20, RV (KJV, "money"); 20:33; 1 Cor. 3:12 (metaphorical); 1 Pet. 1:18.

See MONEY.

2. *arguros* (ἄργυρος, 696), akin to *argos*, "shining," denotes "silver." In each occurrence in the NT it follows the mention of gold, Matt. 10:9; Acts 17:29; Jas. 5:3; Rev. 18:12.

B. Adjective.

argureos (ἀργύρεος, 693) signifies "made of silver," Acts 19:24; 2 Tim. 2:20; Rev. 9:20.

SIMILITUDE

Note: For *homoiōma*, rendered "similitude" in Rom. 5:14, KJV, see LIKENESS, No. 1. For *homoiotēs*, "similitude" in Heb. 7:15 KJV, see LIKE, C, *Note* (1), and LIKENESS, No. 3. For *homoiōsis*, "similitude" in Jas. 3:9, KJV, see LIKENESS, No. 2.

For **SIMPLE** see GUILELESS, No. 2, and HARMLESS

For **SIMPLICITY** see LIBERALITY

SIN (Noun and Verb)

A. Nouns.

1. *hamartia* (ἁμαρτία, 266) is, lit., "a missing of the mark," but this etymological meaning is largely lost sight of in the NT. It is the most comprehensive term for moral obliquity. It is used of "sin" as (a) a principle or source of action, or an inward element producing acts, e.g., Rom. 3:9; 5:12, 13, 20; 6:1, 2; 7:7 (abstract for concrete); 7:8 (twice), 9, 11, 13, "sin, that it might be shown to be sin," i.e., "sin became death to me, that it might be exposed in its heinous character": in the last clause, "sin might become exceeding sinful," i.e., through the holiness of the Law, the true nature of sin was designed to be manifested to the conscience;

(b) a governing principle or power, e.g., Rom. 6:6, "(the body) of sin," here "sin" is spoken of as an organized power, acting through the members of the body, though the seat of "sin" is in the will (the body is the organic instrument); in the next clause, and in other passages, as follows, this governing principle is personified, e.g., Rom. 5:21; 6:12, 14, 17; 7:11, 14, 17, 20, 23, 25; 8:2; 1 Cor. 15:56; Heb. 3:13; 11:25; 12:4; Jas. 1:15 (2nd part);

(c) a generic term (distinct from specific terms such as No. 2 yet sometimes inclusive of concrete wrong doing, e.g., John 8:21, 34, 46; 9:41; 15:22, 24; 19:11); in Rom. 8:3, "God, sending His own Son in the likeness of sinful flesh," lit., "flesh of sin," the flesh stands for the body, the instrument of indwelling "sin" [Christ, preexistently the Son of God, assumed human flesh, "of the substance of the Virgin Mary"; the reality of incarnation was His, without taint of sin (for *homoiōma*, "likeness," see LIKENESS)], and *as an offering* for sin," i.e., "a sin offering" (so the Sept., e.g., in Lev. 4:32; 5:6, 7, 8, 9), "condemned sin in the flesh," i.e., Christ, having taken human nature, "sin" apart (Heb. 4:15), and having lived a sinless life, died under the condemnation and judgment due to our "sin"; for the generic sense see further, e.g., Heb. 9:26; 10:6, 8, 18; 13:11; 1 John 1:7, 8; 3:4 (1st part; in the 2nd part, "sin" is defined as "lawlessness," RV), 8, 9; in these verses the KJV use of the verb to commit is misleading; not the committal of an act is in view, but a continuous course of "sin," as indicated by the RV, "doeth." The apostle's use of the present tense of *poieō*, "to do," virtually expresses the meaning of *prassō*, "to practice," which John does not use (it is not infrequent in this sense in Paul's Epp., e.g., Rom. 1:32, RV; 2:1; Gal. 5:21; Phil. 4:9); 1 Pet. 4:1 (singular in the best texts), lit., "has been made to cease from sin," i.e., as a result of suffering in the flesh, the mortifying of our members, and of obedience to a Savior who suffered in flesh. Such no longer lives in the flesh, "to the lusts of men, but to the will of God"; sometimes the word is used as virtually equivalent to a condition of "sin," e.g., John 1:29, "the sin (not sins) of the world"; 1 Cor. 15:17; or a course of "sin," characterized by continuous acts, e.g., 1 Thess. 2:16; in 1 John 5:16 (2nd part) the RV marg., is probably to be preferred, "there is sin unto death," not a special act of "sin," but the state or condition producing acts; in v. 17, "all unrighteousness is sin" is not a definition of "sin" (as in 3:4), it gives a specification of the term in its generic sense;

(d) a sinful deed, an act of "sin," e.g., Matt. 12:31; Acts 7:60; Jas. 1:15 (1st part); 2:9; 4:17; 5:15, 20; 1 John 5:16 (1st part).

Notes: (1) Christ is predicated as having been without "sin" in every respect, e.g., (a), (b), (c) above, 2 Cor. 5:21 (1st part); 1 John 3:5; John 14:30; (d) John 8:46; Heb. 4:15; 1 Pet. 2:22. (2) In Heb. 9:28 (2nd part) the reference is to a "sin" offering. (3) In 2 Cor. 5:21, "Him ... He made to be sin" indicates that God dealt with Him as He must deal with "sin," and that Christ fulfilled what was typified in the guilt offering. (4) For the phrase "man of sin" in 2 Thess. 2:3, see INIQUITY, No. 1.

2. *hamártēma* (ἁμάρτημα, 265), akin to No. 1, denotes "an act of disobedience to divine law" [as distinct from No. 1 (a), (b), (c)]; plural in Mark 3:28; Rom. 3:25; 2 Pet. 1:9, in some texts; sing. in Mark 3:29 (some mss. have *krisis*, KJV, "damnation"); 1 Cor. 6:18.

Notes: (1) For *paraptōma*, rendered "sins" in the KJV in Eph. 1:7; 2:5; Col. 2:13 (RV, "trespass"), see TRESPASS. In Jas. 5:16, the best texts have No. 1 (RV, "sins"). (2) For synonymous terms see DISOBEDIENCE, ERROR, FAULT, INIQUITY, TRANSGRESSION, UNGODLINESS.

B. Adjective.

anamartētos (ἀναμάρτητος, 361), "without sin" (*a*, negative, *n*, euphonic, and C, No. 1), is found in John 8:7. In the Sept., Deut. 29:19.

C. Verbs.

1. *hamartanō* (ἁμαρτάνω, 264), lit., "to miss the mark," is used in the NT (a) of "sinning" against God, (1) by angels, 2 Pet. 2:4; (2) by man, Matt. 27:4; Luke 15:18, 21 (heaven standing, by metonymy, for God); John 5:14; 8:11; 9:2, 3; Rom. 2:12 (twice); 3:23; 5:12, 14, 16; 6:15; 1 Cor. 7:28 (twice), 36; 15:34; Eph. 4:26; 1 Tim. 5:20; Titus 3:11; Heb. 3:17; 10:26; 1 John 1:10; in 2:1 (twice), the aorist tense in each place, referring to an act of "sin"; on the contrary, in 3:6 (twice), 8, 9, the present tense indicates, not the committal of an act, but the continuous practice of "sin" [see on A, No. 1 (c)]; in 5:16 (twice) the present tense indicates the condition resulting from an act, "unto death" signifying "tending towards death"; (b) against Christ, 1 Cor. 8:12; (c) against man, (1) a brother, Matt. 18:15, RV, "sin" (KJV, "trespass"); v. 21; Luke 17:3, 4, RV, "sin" (KJV, "trespass"); 1 Cor. 8:12; (2) in Luke 15:18, 21, against the father by the Prodigal Son, "in thy sight" being suggestive of befitting reverence; (d) against Jewish law, the Temple, and Caesar, Acts 25:8, RV, "sinned" (KJV, "offended"); (e) against one's own body, by fornication, 1 Cor. 6:18; (f) against earthly masters by servants, 1 Pet. 2:20, RV, "(when) ye sin (and are buffeted for it)," KJV, "(when ye be buffeted) for your faults," lit., "having sinned."

2. *proamartanō* (προαμαρτάνω, 4258), "to sin previously" (*pro*, "before," and No. 1), occurs in 2 Cor. 12:21; 13:2, RV in each place, "have sinned heretofore" (so KJV in the 2nd; in the 1st, "have sinned already").

SINCERE, SINCERELY, SINCERITY

A. Adjectives.

1. *adolos* (ἄδολος, 97), "guileless, pure," is translated "sincere" in 1 Pet. 2:2, KJV, "without guile," RV. See GUILELESS, No. 1.

2. *gnēsios* (γνήσιος, 1103), "true, genuine, sincere," is used in the neuter, as a noun, with the article, signifying "sincerity," 2 Cor. 8:8 (of love). See OWN, TRUE.

3. *eilikrinēs* (εἰλικρινής, 1506), see PURE, A, No. 3.

B. Adverb.

hagnōs (ἁγνῶς, 55) denotes "with pure motives," akin to words under PURE, A, No. 1, and B, Nos. 1 and 2, and is rendered "sincerely" in Phil. 1:17, RV (v. 16, KJV).

C. Noun.

eilikrinia (or —*eia*) (εἰλικρίνεια, 1505), akin to A, No. 3 denotes "sincerity, purity"; it is described metaphorically in 1 Cor. 5:8 as "unleavened (bread)"; in 2 Cor. 1:12, "sincerity (of God)," RV, KJV, "(godly) sincerity," it describes a quality possessed by God, as that which is to characterize the conduct of believers; in 2 Cor. 2:17 it is used of the rightful ministry of the Scriptures.

Notes: (1) For 2 Cor. 8:8, see A, No. 2. (2) In Eph. 6:24, KJV, *aphtharsia*, "incorruption," is translated "sincerity" (RV, "uncorruptness," KJV marg., "incorruption"); some inferior mss. have it in Titus 2:7, KJV; the RV follows those in which it is absent.

SINFUL

hamartōlos (ἁμαρτωλός, 268), an adjective, akin to *hamartanō*, "to sin," is used as an adjective, "sinful" in Mark 8:38; Luke 5:8; 19:7 (lit., "a sinful man"); 24:7; John 9:16, and 24 (lit., "a man sinful"); Rom. 7:13, for which see SIN, A, No. 1 (a). Elsewhere it is used as a noun: see SINNER. The noun is frequently found in a common phrase in sepulchral epitaphs in the S.W. of Asia Minor, with the threat against any desecrator of the tomb, "let him be as a sinner before the subterranean gods" (Moulton and Milligan).

Notes: (1) In Rom. 8:3, "sinful flesh" is, lit., "flesh of sin" (RV marg.): see SIN, No. 1 (c). (2) For the RV of Rom. 7:5, "sinful passions," see PASSION, No. 1.

SING, SINGING

1. *adō* (ᾄδω, 103) is used always of "praise to God," (a) intransitively, Eph. 5:19; Col. 3:16; (b) transitively, Rev. 5:9; 14:3; 15:3.

2. *psallō* (ψάλλω, 5567): see MELODY.

3. *humneō* (ὑμνέω, 5214): see HYMN, B.

SINGLE

haplous (ἁπλοῦς, 573), "simple, single," is used in a moral sense in Matt. 6:22 and Luke 11:34, said of the eye; "singleness" of purpose keeps us from the snare of having a double treasure and consequently a divided heart. The papyri provide instances of its use in other than the moral sense, e.g., of a marriage dowry, to be repaid pure and simple by a husband (Moulton and Milligan). In the Sept., Prov. 11:25.

SINK

1. *buthizo* (βυθίζω, 1036) is used literally in Luke 5:7.

2. *katapontizo* (καταποντίζω, 2670) is translated "to sink" in Matt. 14:30 (passive voice).

3. *tithemi* (τίθημι, 5087), "to put," is rendered "let ... sink" in Luke 9:44, RV ("let ... sink down," KJV). See APPOINT.

Note: In Acts 20:9 (2nd part), KJV, *katapbero*, "to bear down," is translated "he sunk down" (RV, "being borne down"); in the 1st part it is rendered "being fallen," KJV, "borne down," RV.

SINNER

hamartōlos (ἁμαρτωλός, 268), lit., "one who misses the mark" (a meaning not to be pressed), is an adjective, most frequently used as a noun (see SINFUL); it is the most usual term to describe the fallen condition of men; it is applicable to all men, Rom. 5:8, 19. In the Synoptic Gospels the word is used not infrequently, by the Pharisees, of publicans (tax collectors) and women of ill repute, e.g., "a woman which was in the city, a sinner," Luke 7:37; "a man that is a sinner," 19:7. In Gal. 2:15, in the clause "not sinners of the Gentiles," the apostle is taking the Judaizers on their own ground, ironically reminding them of their claim to moral superiority over Gentiles; he proceeds to show that the Jews are equally sinners with Gentiles.

Note: In Luke 13:4, KJV, *opheiletēs*, "a debtor," is translated "sinners" (RV, "offenders"; RV and KJV marg., "debtors").

SIR(-S)

1. *kurios* (κύριος, 2962): see LORD.

2. *anēr* (ἀνήρ, 435), "a man," is translated "sirs" in Acts 7:26; 14:15; 19:25; 27:10, 21, 25.

Note: In John 21:5 the KJV marg. has "sirs" for *paidia*, "children."

SISTER

adelphē (ἀδελφή, 79) is used (a) of natural relationship, e.g., Matt. 19:29; of the "sisters" of Christ, the children of Joseph and Mary after the virgin birth of Christ, e.g., Matt. 13:56; (b) of "spiritual kinship" with Christ, an affinity marked by the fulfillment of the will of the Father, Matt. 12:50; Mark 3:35; of spiritual relationship based upon faith in Christ, Rom. 16:1; 1 Cor. 7:15; 9:5, KJV and RV marg.; Jas. 2:15; Philem. 2, RV.

Note: In Col. 4:10, KJV, *anepsios* (cf. Lat., *nepos*, whence Eng., "nephew"), "a cousin" (so, RV), is translated "sister's son."

SKULL

kranion (κρανίον, 2898), Lat., *cranium* (akin to *kara*, "the head"), is used of the scene of the Crucifixion, Matt. 27:33; Mark 15:22; John 19:17; in Luke 23:33, RV, "(the place which is called) The skull," KJV, "Calvary" (from Latin *calvaria*, "a skull": marg., "the place of a skull"). The locality has been identified by the traces of the resemblance of the hill to a "skull." In the Sept., Judg. 9:53; 2 Kings 9:35.

For **SKY** see HEAVEN

SLANDERER

diabolos (διάβολος, 1228), an adjective, "slanderous, accusing falsely," is used as a noun, translated "slanderers" in 1 Tim. 3:11, where the reference is to those who are given to finding fault with the demeanor and conduct of others and spreading their innuendos and criticisms in the church; in 2 Tim. 3:3, RV (KJV, "false accusers"); Titus 2:3 (ditto): see ACCUSER, DEVIL.

For **SLANDEROUSLY** see REPORT, C, No. 5

SLAUGHTER

1. *sphagē* (σφαγή, 4967) is used in two quotations from the Sept., Acts 8:32 from Isa. 53:7, and Rom. 8:36 from Ps. 44:22; in the latter the quotation is set in a strain of triumph, the passage quoted being an utterance of sorrow. In Jas. 5:5 there is an allusion to Jer. 12:3, the luxurious rich, getting wealth by injustice, spending it on their pleasures, are "fattening themselves like sheep unconscious of their doom."

2. *kopē* (κοπή, 2871), "a stroke" (akin to *koptō*, "to strike, to cut"), signifies "a smiting in battle," in Heb. 7:1. In the Sept., Gen. 14:17; Deut. 28:25; Josh. 10:20.

3. *phonos* (φόνος, 5408), "a killing, murder," is rendered "slaughter" in Acts 9:1; see MURDER.

SLAVE

sōma (σῶμα, 4983), "a body," is translated "slaves" in Rev. 18:13 (RV and KJV marg., "bodies"), an intimation of the unrighteous control over the bodily activities of "slaves"; the next word "souls" stands for the whole being. See BODY.

For **SLAIN BEASTS** see BEAST, No. 5

For **SLEEP** see ASLEEP

SLEIGHT

kubia (or —*eia*) (κυβεία, 2940) denotes "dice playing" (from *kubos*, "a cube, a die as used in gaming"); hence, metaphorically, "trickery, sleight," Eph. 4:14. The Eng. word is connected with "sly" ("not with slight").

SLUMBER (Verb)

nustazō (νυστάζω, 3573) denotes "to nod in sleep" (akin to *neuo*, "to nod"), "fall asleep," and is used (a) of natural slumber, Matt. 25:5; (b) metaphorically in 2 Pet. 2:3, negatively, of the destruction awaiting false teachers.

SMELLING

osphrēsis (ὄσφρησις, 3750) denotes "the sense of smell," 1 Cor. 12:17, "smelling."

SMOOTH

leois (λεῖος, 3006), "smooth," occurs in Luke 3:5, figurative of the change in Israel from self-righteousness, pride and other forms of evil, to repentance, humility and submission. In the Sept., Gen. 27:11; 1 Sam. 17:40; Prov. 2:20; 12:13; 26:23; Isa. 40:4.

Note: Chrēstologia (*chrēstos*, "good," *legō*, "to speak") is rendered "smooth ... (speech)," in Rom. 16:18, RV (KJV, "good words").

SNARE

1. *pagis* (παγίς, 3803), "a trap, a snare" (akin to *pēgnumi*, "to fix," and *pagideuō*, "to ensnare," which see), is used metaphorically of (a) the allurements to evil by which the Devil "ensnares" one, 1 Tim. 3:7; 2 Tim. 2:26; (b) seductions to evil, which "ensnare" those who "desire to be rich," 1 Tim. 6:9; (c) the evil brought by Israel upon themselves by which the special privileges divinely granted them and centering in Christ, became a "snare" to them, their rejection of Christ and the Gospel being the retributive effect of their apostasy, Rom. 11:9; (d) of the sudden judgments of God to come upon those whose hearts are "overcharged with surfeiting, and drunkenness, and cares of this life," Luke 21:34 (v. 35 in KJV).

2. *brochos* (βρόχος, 1029), "a noose, slipknot, halter," is used metaphorically in 1 Cor. 7:35, "a snare" (RV, marg., "constraint," "noose"). In the Sept., Prov. 6:5; 7:21; 22:25.

SNATCH

harpazō (ἁρπάζω, 726), "to snatch," is translated "to snatch" in the RV only, in Matt. 13:19, KJV, "catcheth away"; John 10:12, KJV, "catcheth"; 10:28, 29, KJV, "pluck"; Jude 23, KJV, "pulling."

SOBER, SOBERLY, SOBERMINDED

A. Adjective.

sōphrōn (σώφρων, 4998) denotes "of sound mind" (*sōzō*, "to save," *phrēn*, "the mind"); hence, "self-controlled, soberminded," always rendered "sober-minded" in the RV; in 1 Tim. 3:2 and Titus 1:8, KJV, "sober"; in Titus 2:2, KJV, "temperate"; in 2:5, KJV, "discreet."

Note: For *nēphalios* (akin to B, No. 1), translated "sober" in 1 Tim. 3:11; Titus 2:2, see TEMPERATE.

B. Verbs.

1. *nēphō* (νήφω, 3525) signifies "to be free from the influence of intoxicants"; in the NT, metaphorically, it does not in itself imply watchfulness, but is used in association with it, 1 Thess. 5:6, 8; 2 Tim. 4:5; 1 Pet. 1:13; 4:7, RV (KJV, "watch"); 5:8. Cf. *eknēphō* and *ananēphō*, under AWAKE, No. 3 and *Note*.

2. *sōphroneō* (σωφρονέω, 4993), akin to A, is rendered "to think soberly," Rom. 12:3; "to be sober," 2 Cor. 5:13; "to be soberminded," Titus 2:6; in 1 Pet. 4:7, KJV "be ye sober" (RV, "of sound mind"); see MIND, B, No. 5.

3. *sōphronizō* (σωφρονίζω, 4994) denotes "to cause to be of sound mind, to recall to one's senses"; in Titus 2:4, RV, it is rendered "they may train" (KJV, "they may teach ... to be sober," marg., "wise"); "train" expresses the meaning more adequately; the training would involve the cultivation of sound judgment and prudence.

C. Adverb.

sōphronōs (σωφρόνως, 4996), akin to A and B, Nos. 2 and 3, "soberly," occurs in Titus 2:12; it suggests the exercise of that self-restraint that governs all passions and desires, enabling the believer to be conformed to the mind of Christ.

Note: For the phrase "to think soberly," see B, No. 2.

SOBERNESS, SOBRIETY

sōphrosunē (σωφροσύνη, 4997) denotes "soundness of mind" (see SOBER, A), Acts 26:25, "soberness"; 1 Tim. 2:9, 15, "sobriety"; "sound judgment" practically expresses the meaning; "it is that habitual inner self-government, with its constant rein on all the passions and desires, which would hinder the temptation to these from arising, or at all events from arising in such strength as would overbear the checks and barriers which *aidōs* (shamefastness) opposed to it" (Trench *Syn.* Sec. XX, end).

For **SOFT** see EFFEMINATE

For **SOFTLY** see BLOW (Verb), No. 2

SOJOURN, SOJOURNER, SOJOURNING

A. Verbs.

1. *paroikeō* (παροικέω, 3939) denotes "to dwell beside, among or by" (*para*, "beside," *oikeō*, "to dwell"); then, "to dwell in a place as a *paroikos*, a stranger" (see below), Luke 24:18, RV, "Dost thou (alone) sojourn ...?" [marg., "Dost thou sojourn (alone)" is preferable], KJV, "art thou (only) a stranger?" (*monos*, "alone," is an adjective, not an adverb); in Heb. 11:9, RV, "he became a sojourner" (KJV, "he sojourned"), the RV gives the force of the aorist tense.

2. *epidēmeo* (ἐπιδημέω, 1927) is rendered "to sojourn" in Acts 17:21, RV.

B. Adjectives.

1. *paroikos* (πάροικος, 3941), an adjective, akin to A, No. 1, lit., "dwelling near" (see above), then, "foreign, alien" (found with this meaning in inscriptions), hence, as a noun, "a sojourner," is used with *eimi*, "to be," in Acts 7:6, "should sojourn," lit., "should be a sojourner"; in 7:29, RV, "sojourner" (KJV, "stranger"); in Eph. 2:19, RV, "sojourners" (KJV, "foreigners"), the preceding word rendered "strangers" is *xenos;* in 1 Pet. 2:11, RV, ditto (KJV, "strangers").

2. *apodēmos* (ἀπόδημος, 590), "gone abroad" (*apo*, "from," *dēmos*, "people"), signifies "sojourning in another country," Mark 13:34, RV (KJV, "taking a far journey").

3. *parepidēmos* (παρεπίδημος, 3927), "sojourning in a strange place," is used as a noun, denoting "a sojourner, an exile," 1 Pet. 1:1, RV, "sojourners" (KJV, "strangers"). See PILGRIM.

C. Noun.

paroikia (παροικία, 3940), "a sojourning" (akin to A and B, Nos. 1), occurs in Acts 13:17, rendered "they sojourned," RV, KJV, "dwelt as strangers," lit., "in the sojourning"; in 1 Pet. 1:17, "sojourning."

For **SOLITARY,** Mark 1:35, KJV, see DESERT, B

SON

huios (υἱός, 5207) primarily signifies the relation of offspring to parent (see John 9:18-20; Gal. 4:30). It is often used metaphorically of prominent moral characteristics (see below). "It is used in the NT of (a) male offspring, Gal. 4:30; (b) legitimate, as opposed to illegitimate offspring, Heb. 12:8; (c) descendants, without reference to sex, Rom. 9:27; (d) friends attending a wedding, Matt. 9:15; (e) those who enjoy certain privileges, Acts 3:25; (f) those who act in a certain way, whether evil, Matt. 23:31, or good, Gal. 3:7; (g) those who manifest a certain character, whether evil, Acts 13:10; Eph. 2:2, or good, Luke 6:35; Acts 4:36; Rom. 8:14; (h) the destiny that corresponds with the character, whether evil, Matt. 23:15; John 17:12; 2 Thess. 2:3, or good, Luke 20:36; (i) the dignity of the relationship with God whereinto men are brought by the Holy Spirit when they believe on the Lord Jesus Christ, Rom. 8:19; Gal. 3:26 ....

"The Apostle John does not use *huios*, 'son,' of the believer, he reserves that title for the Lord; but he does use *teknon*, 'child,' as in his Gospel, 1:12; 1 John 3:1, 2; Rev. 21:7 (*huios*) is a quotation from 2 Sam. 7:14.

"The Lord Jesus used *huios* in a very significant way, as in Matt. 5:9, 'Blessed are the peacemakers, for they shall be called the sons of God,' and vv. 44, 45, 'Love your enemies, and pray for them that persecute you; that ye may be (become) sons of your Father which is in heaven.' The disciples were to do these things, not in order that they might become children of God, but that, being children (note 'your Father' throughout), they might make the fact manifest in their character, might 'become sons.' See also 2 Cor. 6:17, 18.

"As to moral characteristics, the following phrases are used: (a) sons of God, Matt. 5:9, 45; Luke 6:35; (b) sons of the light, Luke 16:8; John 12:36; (c) sons of the day, 1 Thess. 5:5; (d) sons of peace, Luke 10:6; (e) sons of this world, Luke 16:8; (f) sons of disobedience, Eph. 2:2; (g) sons of the evil one, Matt. 13:38, cf. 'of the Devil,' Acts 13:10; (h) son of perdition, John 17:12; 2 Thess. 2:3. It is also used to describe characteristics other than moral, as: (i) sons of the resurrection, Luke 20:36; (j) sons of the Kingdom, Matt. 8:12; 13:38; (k) sons of the bridechamber, Mark 2:19; (l) sons of exhortation, Acts 4:36; (m) sons of thunder, Boanerges, Mark 3:17." (From *Notes on Galatians*, by Hogg and Vine, pp. 167-69, and on Thessalonians, pp. 158-59)

Notes: (1) For the synonyms *teknon* and *teknion* see under CHILD. The difference between believers as "children of God" and as "sons of God" is brought out in Rom. 8:14-21. The Spirit bears witness with their spirit that they are "children of God," and, as such, they are His heirs and joint-heirs with Christ. This stresses the fact of their spiritual birth (vv. 16, 17). On the other hand, "as many as are led by the Spirit of God, these are sons of God," i.e., "these and no other." Their conduct gives evidence of the dignity of their relationship and their likeness to His character. (2) *Pais* is rendered "son" in John 4:51. For Acts 13:13, 26 see below.

The Son of God

In this title the word "Son" is used sometimes (a) of relationship, sometimes (b) of the expression of character. "Thus, e.g., when the disciples so addressed Him, Matt. 14:33; 16:16; John 1:49, when the centurion so spoke of Him, Matt. 27:54, they probably meant that (b) He was a manifestation of God in human form. But in such passages as Luke 1:32, 35; Acts 13:33, which refer to the humanity of the Lord Jesus, ... the word is used in sense (a).

"The Lord Jesus Himself used the full title on occasion, John 5:25; 9:35 [some mss. have 'the Son of Man'; see RV marg.]; 11:4, and on the more frequent occasions on which He spoke of Himself as 'the Son,' the words are to be understood as an abbreviation of 'the Son of God,' not of 'The Son of Man'; this latter He always expressed in full; see Luke 10:22; John 5:19, etc.

"John uses both the longer and shorter forms of the title in his Gospel, see 3:16-18; 20:31, e.g., and in his Epistles; cf. Rev. 2:18. So does the writer of Hebrews, 1:2; 4:14; 6:6, etc. An eternal relation subsisting between the Son and the Father in the Godhead is to be understood. That is to say, the Son of God, in His eternal relationship with the Father, is not so entitled because He at any time began to derive His being from the Father (in which case He could not be co-eternal with the Father), but because He is and ever has been the expression of what the Father is; cf. John 14:9, 'he that hath seen Me hath seen the Father.' The words of Heb. 1:3, 'Who being the effulgence of His (God's) glory, and the very image of His (God's) substance' are a definition of what is meant by 'Son of God.' Thus absolute Godhead, not Godhead in a secondary or derived sense, is intended in the title."

Other titles of Christ as the "Son of God" are: "His Son," 1 Thess. 1:10 (in Acts 13:13, 26, RV, *pais* is rendered "servant"); "His own Son," Rom. 8:32; "My beloved Son," Matt. 3:17; "His Only Begotten Son," John 3:16; "the Son of His love," Col. 1:13.

"The Son is the eternal object of the Father's love, John 17:24, and the sole Revealer of the Father's character, John 1:14; Heb. 1:3. The words, 'Father' and 'Son,' are never in the NT so used as to suggest that the Father existed before the Son; the Prologue to the Gospel according to John distinctly asserts that the Word existed 'in the beginning,' and that this Word is the Son, Who 'became flesh and dwelt among us.'"

In addressing the Father in His prayer in John 17 He says, "Thou lovedst Me before the foundation of the world." Accordingly in the timeless past the Father and the "Son" existed in that relationship, a relationship of love, as well as of absolute Deity. In this passage the "Son" gives evidence that there was no more powerful plea in the Father's estimation than that coeternal love existing between the Father and Himself.

The declaration "Thou art My Son, this day have I begotten Thee," Ps. 2:7, quoted in Acts 13:33; Heb. 1:5; 5:5, refers to the birth of Christ, not to His resurrection. In Acts 13:33 the verb "raise up" is used of the raising up of a person to occupy a special position in the nation, as of David in verse 22 (so of Christ as a Prophet in 3:22 and 7:37). The word "again" in the KJV in v. 33 represents nothing in the original. The RV rightly omits it. In v. 34 the statement as to the resurrection of Christ receives the greater stress in this respect through the emphatic contrast to that in v. 33 as to His being raised up in the nation, a stress imparted by the added words "from the dead." Accordingly v. 33 speaks of His incarnation, v. 34 of His resurrection.

In Heb. 1:5, that the declaration refers to the Birth is confirmed by the contrast in verse 6. Here the word "again" is rightly placed in the RV, "when He again bringeth in the Firstborn into the world." This points on to His second advent, which is set in contrast to His first advent, when God brought His Firstborn into the world the first time (see FIRSTBORN). (From *Notes on Galatians*, by Hogg and Vine, pp. 99-100)

So again in Heb. 5:5, where the High Priesthood of Christ is shown to fulfill all that was foreshadowed in the Levitical priesthood, the passage stresses the facts of His humanity, the days of His flesh, His perfect obedience and His sufferings.

Son of Man

In the NT this is a designation of Christ, almost entirely confined to the Gospels. Elsewhere it is found in Acts 7:56, the only occasion where a disciple applied it to the Lord and in Rev. 1:13; 14:14 (see below).

"Son of Man" is the title Christ used of Himself; John 12:34 is not an exception, for the quotation by the multitude was from His own statement. The title is found especially in the Synoptic Gospels. The occurrences in John's gospel, 1:51; 3:13, 14; 5:27; 6:27, 53, 62; 8:28 (9:35 in some texts); 12:23, 34 (twice); 13:31, are not parallel to those in the Synoptic Gospels. In the latter the use of the title falls into two groups, (a) those in which it refers to Christ's humanity, His earthly work, sufferings and death, e.g., Matt. 8:20; 11:19; 12:40; 26:2, 24; (b) those which refer to His glory in resurrection and to that of His future advent, e.g., Matt. 10:23; 13:41; 16:27, 28; 17:9; 24:27, 30 (twice), 37, 39, 44.

While it is a messianic title it is evident that the Lord applied it to Himself in a distinctive way, for it indicates more than Messiahship, even universal headship on the part of One who is Man. It therefore stresses His manhood, manhood of a unique order in comparison with all other men, for He is declared to be of heaven, 1 Cor. 15:47, and even while here below, was "the Son of Man, which is in Heaven," John 3:13. As the "Son of Man" He must be appropriated spiritually as a condition of possessing eternal life, John 6:53. In His death, as in His life, the glory of His Manhood was displayed in the absolute obedience and submission to the will of the Father (12:23; 13:31), and, in view of this, all judgment has been committed to Him, who will judge in full understanding experimentally of human conditions, sin apart, and will exercise the judgment as sharing the nature of those judged, John 5:22, 27. Not only is He man, but He is "Son of Man," not by human generation but, according to the Semitic usage of the expression, partaking of the characteristics (sin apart) of manhood belonging to the category of mankind. Twice in the Apocalypse, 1:13 and 14:14, He is described as "One like unto a Son of man," RV (KJV, "... the Son of Man"), cf. Dan. 7:13. He who was thus seen was indeed the "Son of Man," but the absence of the article in the original serves to stress what morally characterizes Him as such. Accordingly in these passages He is revealed, not as the Person known by the title, but as the One who is qualified to act as the Judge of all men. He is the same Person as in the days of His flesh, still continuing His humanity with His Deity. The phrase "like unto" serves to distinguish Him as there seen in His glory and majesty in contrast to the days of His humiliation.

SONG

ōdē (ᾠδή, 5603), "an ode, song," is always used in the NT (as in the Sept.), in praise of God or Christ; in Eph. 5:19 and Col. 3:16 the adjective "spiritual" is added, because the word in itself is generic and might be used of songs anything but spiritual; in Rev. 5:9 and 14:3 (1st part) the descriptive word is "new" (*kainos*, "new," in reference to character and form), a "song," the significance of which was confined to those mentioned (v. 3, and 2nd part); in 15:3 (twice), "the song of Moses ... and the song of the Lamb," the former as celebrating the deliverance of God's people by His power, the latter as celebrating redemption by atoning sacrifice.

For **SOON** see IMMEDIATELY, No. 1

SORCERER

1. *magos* (μάγος, 3097), (a) "one of a Median caste, a magician": see WISE; (b) "a wizard, sorcerer, a pretender to magic powers, a professor of the arts of witchcraft," Acts 13:6, 8, where Bar-Jesus was the Jewish name, Elymas, an Arabic word meaning "wise." Hence the name Magus, "the magician," originally applied to Persian priests. In the Sept., only in Dan. 2:2, 10, of the "enchanters," RV (KJV, "astrologers"), of Babylon. The superior Greek version of Daniel by Theodotion has it also at 1:20; 2:27; 4:7; 5:7, 11, 15.

2. *pharmakos* (φαρμακός, 5333), an adjective signifying "devoted to magical arts," is used as a noun, "a sorcerer," especially one who uses drugs, potions, spells, enchantments, Rev. 21:8, in the best texts (some have *pharmakeus*), and 22:15.

SORCERY

A. Nouns.

1. *pharmakia* (or *—eia*) (φαρμακεία, 5331) (Eng., "pharmacy," etc.) primarily signified "the use of medicine, drugs, spells"; then, "poisoning"; then, "sorcery," Gal. 5:20, RV, "sorcery" (KJV, "witchcraft"), mentioned as one of "the works of the flesh." See also Rev. 9:21; 18:23. In the Sept., Ex. 7:11, 22; 8:7, 18; Isa. 47:9, 12. In "sorcery," the use of drugs, whether simple or potent, was generally accompanied by incantations and appeals to occult powers, with the provision of various charms, amulets, etc., professedly designed to keep the applicant or patient from the attention and power of demons, but actually to impress the applicant with the mysterious resources and powers of the sorcerer.

2. *magia* (or *—eia*) (μαγεία, 3095), "the magic art," is used in the plural in Acts 8:11, "sorceries (see SORCERER, No. 1).

B. Verb.

mageuō (μαγεύω, 3096), akin to A, No. 2, "to practice magic," Acts 8:9, "used sorcery," is used as in A, No. 2, of Simon Magnus.

SORROW (Noun and Verb), SORROWFUL

A. Nouns.

1. *lupē* (λύπη, 3077), "grief, sorrow," is translated "sorrow" in Luke 22:45; John 16:6, 20-22; Rom. 9:2, RV (KJV, "heaviness"); 2 Cor. 2:1, RV; 2:3, 7; 7:10 (twice); Phil. 2:27 (twice). See GRIEF.

2. *odunē* (ὀδύνη, 3601), "pain, consuming grief, distress," whether of body or mind, is used of the latter, Rom. 9:2, RV, "pain"; 1 Tim. 6:10.

3. *ōdin* (ὠδίν, 5604), "a birth-pang, travail, pain," "sorrows," Matt. 24:8; Mark 13:8; see PAIN, A, No. 2.

4. *penthos* (πένθος, 3997), "mourning," "sorrow," Rev. 18:7 (twice); 21:4: see MOURN.

B. Verbs.

1. *lupeō* (λυπέω, 3076), akin to A, No. 1: see GRIEF, B, No. 1, SORRY, A (below).

2. *odunaō* (ὀδυνάω, 3600), "to cause pain" (akin to A, No. 2), is used in the middle voice in Luke 2:48; Acts 20:38: see ANGUISH, B, No. 3.

C. Adjectives.

1. *perilupos* (περίλυπος, 4036), "very sad, deeply grieved" (*peri*, intensive), is used in Matt. 26:38 and Mark 14:34, "exceeding sorrowful"; Mark 6:26; Luke 18:23 (v. 24 in some mss.).

2. *alupos* (ἀλυπότερος, 253) denotes "free from grief" (*a*, negative, *lupē*, "grief"), comparative degree in Phil. 2:28, "less sorrowful," their joy would mean the removal of a burden from his heart.

SORRY

A. Verb.

lupeō (λυπέω, 3076) is rendered "to be sorry" (passive voice) in Matt. 14:9, KJV (RV, "grieved"); 17:23; 18:31; 2 Cor. 2:2 [1st part, active voice, "make sorry" (as in 7:8, twice); 2nd part, passive]; 2:4, RV, "made sorry"; 9:9 and 11, RV, "ye were made sorry." See GRIEVE, B, No. 1.

B. Adjective.

perilupos (περίλυπος, 4036) is translated "exceeding sorry" in Mark 6:26: see SORROWFUL, C, No. 1.

SOUL

psuchē (ψυχή, 5590) denotes "the breath, the breath of life," then "the soul," in its various meanings. The NT uses "may be analyzed approximately as follows:

(a) the natural life of the body, Matt. 2:20; Luke 12:22; Acts 20:10; Rev. 8:9; 12:11; cf. Lev. 17:11; 2 Sam. 14:7; Esth. 8:11; (b) the immaterial, invisible part of man, Matt. 10:28; Acts 2:27; cf. 1 Kings 17:21; (c) the disembodied (or "unclothed" or "naked," 2 Cor. 5:3, 4) man, Rev. 6:9; (d) the seat of personality, Luke 9:24, explained as = "own self," v. 25; Heb. 6:19; 10:39; cf. Isa. 53:10 with 1 Tim. 2:6; (e) the seat of the sentient element in man, that by which he perceives, reflects, feels, desires, Matt. 11:29; Luke 1:46; 2:35; Acts 14:2, 22; cf. Ps. 84:2; 139:14; Isa. 26:9; (f) the seat of will and purpose, Matt. 22:37; Acts 4:32; Eph. 6:6; Phil. 1:27; Heb. 12:3; cf. Num. 21:4; Deut. 11:13; (g) the seat of appetite, Rev. 18:14; cf. Ps. 107:9; Prov. 6:30; Isa. 5:14 ("desire"); 29:8; (h) persons, individuals, Acts 2:41, 43; Rom. 2:9; Jas. 5:20; 1 Pet. 3:20; 2 Pet. 2:14; cf. Gen. 12:5; 14:21 ("persons"); Lev. 4:2 ('any one'); Ezek. 27:13; of dead bodies, Num. 6:6, lit., "dead soul"; and of animals, Lev. 24:18, lit., "soul for soul"; (i) the equivalent of the personal pronoun, used for emphasis and effect:—1st person, John 10:24 ("us"); Heb. 10:38; cf. Gen. 12:13; Num. 23:10; Jud. 16:30; Ps. 120:2 ("me"); 2nd person, 2 Cor. 12:15; Heb. 13:17; Jas. 1:21; 1 Pet. 1:9; 2:25; cf. Lev. 17:11; 26:15; 1 Sam. 1:26; 3rd person, 1 Pet. 4:19; 2 Pet. 2:8; cf. Exod. 30:12; Job 32:2, Heb. "soul," Sept. "self"; (j) an animate creature, human or other, 1 Cor. 15:45; Rev. 16:3; cf. Gen. 1:24; 2:7, 19; (k) "the inward man," the seat of the new life, Luke 21:19 (cf. Matt. 10:39); 1 Pet. 2:11; 3 John 2.

"With (j) compare *a-psuchos*, "soulless, inanimate," 1 Cor. 14:7.

"With (f) compare *di-psuchos*, "two-souled," Jas. 1:8; 4:8; *oligo psuchos*, "feeble-souled," 1 Thess. 5:14; *iso-psuchos*, "like-souled," Phil. 2:20; *sum-psuchos*, "joint-souled" ("with. one accord"), Phil. 2:2.

"The language of Heb. 4:12 suggests the extreme difficulty of distinguishing between the soul and the spirit, alike in their nature and in their activities. Generally speaking the spirit is the higher, the soul the lower element. The spirit may be recognized as the life principle bestowed on man by God, the soul as the resulting life constituted in the individual, the body being the material organism animated by soul and spirit....

"Body and soul are the constituents of the man according to Matt. 6:25; 10:28; Luke 12:20; Acts 20:10; body and spirit according to Luke 8:55; 1 Cor. 5:3; 7:34; Jas. 2:26. In Matt. 26:38 the emotions are associated with the soul, in John 13:21 with the spirit; cf. also Ps. 42:11 with 1 Kings 21:5. In Ps. 35:9 the soul rejoices in God, in Luke 1:47 the spirit.

"Apparently, then, the relationships may be thus summed up '*Soma*, body, and *pneuma*, spirit, may be separated, *pneuma* and *psuche*, soul, can only be distinguished' (Cremer)."

SOUND (Noun and Verb)

A. Nouns.

1. *phonē* (φωνή, 5456), most frequently "a voice," is translated "sound" in Matt. 24:31 (KJV marg., "voice"); John 3:8, KJV (RV, "voice"); so 1 Cor. 14:7 (1st part), 8; Rev. 1:15; 18:22 (2nd part, RV, "voice"); KJV and RV in 9:9 (twice); in Acts 2:6, RV, "(this) sound (was heard)," KJV, "(this) was noised abroad."

2. *ēchos* (ἦχος, 2279), "a noise, a sound of any sort" (Eng., "echo"), is translated "sound" in Acts 2:2; Heb. 12:19. See RUMOR.

3. *phthongos* (φθόγγος, 5353), akin to *phthengomai*, "to utter a voice," occurs in Rom. 10:18; 1 Cor. 14:7. In the Sept, Ps. 19:4.

B. Verbs.

1. *ēcheō* (ἠχέω, 2278), akin to A, No. 2, occurs in 1 Cor. 13:1, "sounding (brass)"; in some mss., Luke 21:25.

2. *exēcheō* (ἐξηχέοω, 1837), "to sound forth as a trumpet" or "thunder" (*ex*, "out," and No. 1), is used in 1 Thess. 1:8, "sounded forth," passive voice, lit., "has been sounded out." In the Sept., Joel 3:14.

3. *salpizō* (σαλπίζω, 4537), "to sound a trumpet" (*salpinx*), occurs in Matt. 6:2; 1 Cor. 15:52, "the trumpet shall sound"; Rev. 8:6-8, 10, 12, 13; 9:1, 13; 10:7; 11:15.

4. *bolizō* (βολίζω, 1001), "to heave the lead" (*bolis*, "that which is thrown or hurled," akin to *ballō*, "to throw"; sounding-lead), to take soundings, occurs in Acts 27:28 (twice).

Note: In Luke 1:44, KJV, *ginomai*, "to become," is rendered "sounded" (RV, "came").

SOUND (Adjective), BE SOUND

A. Adjective.

hugiēs (ὑγιής, 5199), "whole, healthy," is used metaphorically of "sound speech," Titus 2:8. See WHOLE.

B. Verb.

hugiainō (ὑγιαίνω, 5198), "to be healthy, sound in health" (Eng., "hygiene," etc.), translated "safe and sound" in Luke 15:27, is used metaphorically of doctrine, 1 Tim. 1:10; 2 Tim. 4:3; Titus 1:9; 2:1; of words, 1 Tim. 6:3, RV (KJV, "wholesome," RV marg., "healthful"); 2 Tim. 1:13; "in the faith," Titus 1:13 (RV marg., "healthy"); "in faith," Titus 2:2 (RV marg., ditto).

Note: For "sound mind" in 2 Tim. 1:7, KJV, see DISCIPLINE; in 1 Pet. 4:7 (KJV, "sober"), see MIND, B, No. 5.

SOUNDNESS

holoklēria (ὁλοκληρία, 3647), "completeness, soundness" (akin to *holokleros*, see ENTIRE), occurs in Acts 3:16. In the Sept., Isa. 1:6.

SOW (Verb), SOWER

speirō (σπείρω, 4687), "to sow seed," is used (1) literally, especially in the Synoptic Gospels; elsewhere, 1 Cor. 15:36, 37; 2 Cor. 9:10, "the sower," (2) metaphorically, (a) in proverbial sayings, e.g., Matt. 13:3, 4; Luke 19:21, 22; John 4:37; 2 Cor. 9:6; (b) in the interpretation of parables, e.g., Matt. 13:19-23 (in these vv., RV, "was sown," for KJV, "received seed"); (c) otherwise as follows: of "sowing" spiritual things in preaching and teaching, 1 Cor. 9:11; of the interment of the bodies of deceased believers, 1 Cor. 15:42-44; of ministering to the necessities of others in things temporal (the harvest being proportionate to the "sowing"), 2 Cor. 9:6, 10 (see above); of "sowing" to the flesh, Gal. 6:7, 8 ("that" in v. 7 is emphatic, "that and that only," what was actually "sown"); in v. 8, *eis*, "unto," signifies "in the interests of"; of the "fruit of righteousness" by peacemakers, Jas. 3:18.

SPEAKER (chief)

Note: In Acts 14:12 the verb *hēgeomai*, "to lead the way, be the chief," is used in the present participle with the article (together equivalent to a noun), followed by the genitive case of *logos*, "speech," with the article, the phrase being rendered "the chief speaker," lit., "the leader of the discourse." See CHIEF, C.

SPEAKING (evil, much)

polulogia (πολυλογία, 4180), "loquacity," "much speaking" (*polus*, "much," *logos*, "speech"), is used in Matt. 6:7. In the Sept., Prov. 10:19.

Note: For "evil speaking(s)," in Eph. 4:31, see RAILING. For "shameful speaking" see COMMUNICATION, B, *Note*.

SPECTACLE

theatron (θέατρον, 2302), akin to *theaomai*, "to behold," denotes (a) "a theater" (used also as a place of assembly), Acts 19:29, 31; (b) "a spectacle, a show," metaphorically in 1 Cor. 4:9. See THEATER.

SPEECH

1. *logos* (λόγος, 3056), akin to *legō* (SPEAK, No. 1), most frequently rendered "word" (for an analysis see WORD), signifies "speech," as follows: (a) "discourse," e.g., Luke 20:20, RV, "speech" (KJV, "words"); Acts 14:12 (see SPEAKER); 20:7; 1 Cor. 2:1, 4; 4:19, KJV (RV, "word"); 2 Cor. 10:10; (b) "the faculty of speech," e.g., 2 Cor. 11:6; (c) "the manner of speech," e.g., Matt. 5:37, RV, "speech" (KJV, "communication"); Col. 4:6; (d) "manner of instruction," Titus 2:8; 1 Cor. 14:9, RV (KJV, "words"); Eph. 4:29, RV (KJV, "communication"). See SAYING.

2. *lalia* (λαλιά, 2981), akin to *laleō* (SPEAK, No. 2), denotes "talk, speech," (a) of "a dialect," Matt. 26:73; Mark 14:70; (b) "utterances," John 4:42, RV, "speaking" (KJV, "saying"); 8:43.

3. *eulogia* (εὐλογία, 2129) has the meaning "fair speaking, flattering speech" in Rom. 16:18, RV, "fair speech" (KJV, "fair speeches"). See BLESSING, C, No. 1.

4. *chrēstologia* (χρηστολογία, 5542), which has a similar meaning to No. 3, occurs with it in Rom. 16:18 [RV, "smooth ... (speech)"]. See SMOOTH, *Note*.

Notes: (1) For "persuasiveness of speech," Col. 2:4, RV, see PERSUASIVE, B. (2) In Acts 14:11 "the speech of Lycaonia" translates the adverb *Lukaonisti*. Lycaonia was a large country in the center and south of the plateau of Asia Minor; the villages retained the native language, but cities like Lystra probably had a Seleucid tone in their laws and customs (Ramsay on Galatians).

SPEECHLESS

1. *eneos* (or *enneos*) (ἐνεός, 1769), "dumb, speechless," occurs in Acts 9:7. In the Sept., Prov. 17:28; Isa. 56:10.

2. *kōphos* (κωφός, 2974), which means either "deaf" or "dumb" (see DEAF), is translated "speechless" in Luke 1:22.

Note: For *phimoō*, translated "he was speechless" in Matt. 22:12, see SILENCE.

SPIRIT

pneuma (πνεῦμα, 4151) primarily denotes "the wind" (akin to *pneō*, "to breathe, blow"); also "breath"; then, especially "the spirit," which, like the wind, is invisible, immaterial and powerful. The NT uses of the word may be analyzed approximately as follows:

"(a) the wind, John 3:8 (where marg. is, perhaps, to be preferred); Heb. 1:7; cf. Amos 4:13, Sept.; (b) the breath, 2 Thess.

2:8; Rev. 11:11; 13:15; cf. Job 12:10, Sept.; (c) the immaterial, invisible part of man, Luke 8:55; Acts 7:59; 1 Cor. 5:5; Jas. 2:26; cf. Eccl. 12:7, Sept.; (d) the disembodied (or 'unclothed,' or 'naked,' 2 Cor. 5:3, 4) man, Luke 24:37, 39; Heb. 12:23; 1 Pet. 4:6; (e) the resurrection body, 1 Cor. 15:45; 1 Tim. 3:16; 1 Pet. 3:18; (f) the sentient element in man, that by which he perceives, reflects, feels, desires, Matt. 5:3; 26:41; Mark 2:8; Luke 1:47, 80; Acts 17:16; 20:22; 1 Cor. 2:11; 5:3, 4; 14:4, 15; 2 Cor. 7:1; cf. Gen. 26:35; Isa. 26:9; Ezek. 13:3; Dan. 7:15; (g) purpose, aim, 2 Cor. 12:18; Phil. 1:27; Eph. 4:23; Rev. 19:10; cf. Ezra 1:5; Ps. 78:8; Dan. 5:12; (h) the equivalent of the personal pronoun, used for emphasis and effect: 1st person, 1 Cor. 16:18; cf. Gen. 6:3; 2nd person, 2 Tim. 4:22; Philem. 25; cf. Ps. 139:7; 3rd person, 2 Cor. 7:13; cf. Isa. 40:13; (i) character, Luke 1:17; Rom. 1:4; cf. Num. 14:24; (j) moral qualities and activities: bad, as of bondage, as of a slave, Rom. 8:15; cf. Isa. 61:3; stupor, Rom. 11:8; cf. Isa. 29:10; timidity, 2 Tim. 1:7; cf. Josh. 5:1; good, as of adoption, i.e., liberty as of a son, Rom. 8:15; cf. Ps. 51:12; meekness, 1 Cor. 4:21; cf. Prov. 16:19; faith, 2 Cor. 4:13; quietness, 1 Pet. 3:4; cf. Prov. 14:29; (k) the Holy Spirit, e.g., Matt. 4:1 (see below); Luke 4:18; (l) 'the inward man' (an expression used only of the believer, Rom. 7:22; 2 Cor. 4:16; Eph. 3:16); the new life, Rom. 8:4-6, 10, 16; Heb. 12:9; cf. Ps. 51:10; (m) unclean spirits, demons, Matt. 8:16; Luke 4:33; 1 Pet. 3:19; cf. 1 Sam. 18:10; (n) angels, Heb. 1:14; cf. Acts 12:15; (o) divine gift for service, 1 Cor. 14:12, 32; (p) by metonymy, those who claim to be depositories of these gifts, 2 Thess. 2:2; 1 John 4:1-3; (q) the significance, as contrasted with the form, of words, or of a rite, John 6:63; Rom. 2:29; 7:6; 2 Cor. 3:6; (r) a vision, Rev. 1:10; 4:2; 17:3; 21:10."

Notes: (1) For *phantasma*, rendered "spirit," Matt. 14:26; Mark 6:49, KJV, see APPARITION. (2) For the distinction between "spirit" and "soul," see under SOUL, last three paragraphs.

The Holy Spirit

The "Holy Spirit" is spoken of under various titles in the NT ("Spirit" and "Ghost" are renderings of the same word, *pneuma;* the advantage of the rendering "Spirit" is that it can always be used, whereas "Ghost" always requires the word "Holy" prefixed.) In the following list the omission of the definite article marks its omission in the original (concerning this see below): "Spirit, Matt. 22:43; Eternal Spirit, Heb. 9:14; the Spirit, Matt. 4:1; Holy Spirit, Matt. 1:18; the Holy Spirit, Matt. 28:19; the Spirit, the Holy, Matt. 12:32; the Spirit of promise, the Holy, Eph. 1:13; Spirit of God, Rom. 8:9; Spirit of (the) living God, 2 Cor. 3:3; the Spirit of God, 1 Cor. 2:11; the Spirit of our God, 1 Cor. 6:11; the Spirit of God, the Holy, Eph. 4:30; the Spirit of glory and of God, 1 Pet. 4:14; the Spirit of Him that raised up Jesus from the dead (i.e., God), Rom. 8:11; the Spirit of your Father, Matt. 10:20; the Spirit of His Son, Gal. 4:6; Spirit of (the) Lord, Acts 8:39; the Spirit of (the) Lord, Acts 5:9; (the) Lord, (the) Spirit, 2 Cor. 3:18; the Spirit of Jesus, Acts 16:7; Spirit of Christ, Rom. 8:9; the Spirit of Jesus Christ, Phil. 1:19; Spirit of adoption, Rom. 8:15; the Spirit of truth, John 14:17; the Spirit of life, Rom. 8:2; the Spirit of grace, Heb. 10:29."

The use or absence of the article in the original where the "Holy Spirit" is spoken of cannot always be decided by grammatical rules, nor can the presence or absence of the article alone determine whether the reference is to the "Holy Spirit." Examples where the Person is meant when the article is absent are Matt. 22:43 (the article is used in Mark 12:36); Acts 4:25, RV (absent in some texts); 19:2, 6; Rom. 14:17; 1 Cor. 2:4; Gal. 5:25 (twice); 1 Pet. 1:2. Sometimes the absence is to be accounted for by the fact that *Pneuma* (like *Theos*) is substantially a proper name, e.g., in John 7:39. As a general rule the article is present where the subject of the teaching is the Personality of the Holy Spirit, e.g., John 14:26, where He is spoken of in distinction from the Father and the Son. See also 15:26 and cf. Luke 3:22.

In Gal. 3:3, in the phrase "having begun in the Spirit," it is difficult to say whether the reference is to the "Holy Spirit" or to the quickened spirit of the believer; that it possibly refers to the latter is not to be determined by the absence of the article, but by the contrast with "the flesh"; on the other hand, the contrast may be between the "Holy Spirit" who in the believer sets His seal on the perfect work of Christ, and the flesh which seeks to better itself by works of its own. There is no preposition before either noun, and if the reference is to the quickened spirit it cannot be dissociated from the operation of the "Holy Spirit." In Gal. 4:29 the phrase "after the Spirit" signifies "by supernatural power," in contrast to "after the flesh," i.e., "by natural power," and the reference must be to the "Holy Spirit"; so in 5:17.

The full title with the article before both *pneuma* and *hagios* (the "resumptive" use of the article), lit., "the Spirit the Holy," stresses the character of the Person, e.g., Matt. 12:32; Mark 3:29; 12:36; 13:11; Luke 2:26; 10:21 (RV); John 14:26; Acts 1:16; 5:3; 7:51; 10:44, 47; 13:2; 15:28; 19:6; 20:23, 28; 21:11; 28:25; Eph. 4:30; Heb. 3:7; 9:8; 10:15.

The Personality of the Spirit is emphasized at the expense of strict grammatical procedure in John 14:26; 15:26; 16:8, 13, 14, where the emphatic pronoun *ekeinos*, "He," is used of Him in the masculine, whereas the noun *pneuma* is neuter in Greek, while the corresponding word in Aramaic, the language in which our Lord probably spoke, is feminine (*rûchâ*, cf. Heb. *rûach*). The rendering "itself" in Rom. 8:16, 26, due to the Greek gender, is corrected to "Himself" in the RV.

The subject of the "Holy Spirit" in the NT may be considered as to His divine attributes; His distinct Personality in the Godhead; His operation in connection with the Lord Jesus in His birth, His life, His baptism, His death; His operations in the world; in the church; His having been sent at Pentecost by the Father and by Christ; His operations in the individual believer; in local churches; His operations in the production of Holy Scripture; His work in the world, etc.

SPIRITUAL

A. Adjective.

pneumatikos (πνευματικός, 4152) "always connotes the ideas of invisibility and of power. It does not occur in the Sept. nor in the Gospels; it is in fact an after-Pentecost word. In the NT it is used as follows: (a) the angelic hosts, lower than God but higher in the scale of being than man in his natural state, are 'spiritual hosts,' Eph. 6:12; (b) things that have their origin with God, and which, therefore, are in harmony with His character, as His law is, are 'spiritual,' Rom. 7:14; (c) 'spiritual' is prefixed to the material type in order to indicate that what the type sets forth, not the type itself, is intended, 1 Cor. 10:3, 4; (d) the purposes of God revealed in the gospel by the Holy Spirit, 1 Cor. 2:13a, and the words in which that revelation is expressed, are 'spiritual,' 13b, matching, or combining, spiritual things with spiritual words [or, alternatively, 'interpreting spiritual things to spiritual men,' see (e) below]; 'spiritual songs' are songs of which the burden is the things revealed by the Spirit, Eph. 5:19; Col. 3:16; 'spiritual wisdom and understanding' is wisdom in, and understanding of, those things, Col. 1:9; (e) men in Christ who walk so as to please God are 'spiritual,' Gal. 6:1; 1 Cor. 2:13b [but see (d) above], 15; 3:1; 14:37; (f) the whole company of those who believe in Christ is a 'spiritual house,' 1 Pet. 2:5a; (g) the blessings that accrue to regenerate men at this present time are called 'spiritualities,' Rom. 15:27; 1 Cor. 9:11; 'spiritual blessings,' Eph. 1:3; 'spiritual gifts,' Rom. 1:11; (h) the activities Godward of regenerate men are 'spiritual sacrifices,' 1 Pet. 2:5b; their appointed activities in the churches are also called 'spiritual gifts,' lit., 'spiritualities,' 1 Cor. 12:1; 14:1; (i) the resurrection body of the dead in Christ is 'spiritual,' i.e., such as is suited to the heavenly environment, 1 Cor. 15:44; (j) all that is produced and maintained among men by the operations of the Spirit of God is 'spiritual,' 1 Cor. 15:46 ….

"The spiritual man is one who walks by the Spirit both in the sense of Gal. 5:16 and in that of 5:25, and who himself manifests the fruit of the Spirit in his own ways ….

"According to the Scriptures, the 'spiritual' state of soul is normal for the believer, but to this state all believers do not attain, nor when it is attained is it always maintained. Thus the apostle, in 1 Cor. 3:1-3, suggests a contrast between this spiritual state and that of the babe in Christ, i.e., of the man who because of immaturity and inexperience has not yet reached spirituality, and that of the man who by permitting jealousy, and the strife to which jealousy always leads, has lost it. The spiritual state is reached by diligence in the Word of God and in prayer; it is maintained by obedience and self-judgment. Such as are led by the Spirit are spiritual, but, of course, spirituality is not a fixed or absolute condition, it admits of growth; indeed growth in 'the grace and knowledge of our Lord and Savior Jesus Christ,' 2 Pet. 3:18, is evidence of true spirituality."

B. Adverb.

pneumatikōs (πνευματικῶς, 4153), "spiritually," occurs in 1 Cor. 2:14, with the meaning as (j) above, and Rev. 11:8, with the meaning as in (c). Some mss. have it in 1 Cor. 2:13.

Notes: (1) In Rom. 8:6, the RV rightly renders the noun *pneuma* "(the mind) of the spirit," KJV, "spiritual (mind)." (2) In 1 Cor. 14:12 the plural of *pneuma*, "spirits," RV, marg., stands for "spiritual *gifts*" (text). (3) In 1 Pet. 2:2, the RV renders *logikos* "spiritual."

SPIT

1. *ptuō* (πτύω, 4429), "to spit," occurs in Mark 7:33; 8:23; John 9:6. In the Sept., Num. 12:14.

2. *emptuō* (ἐμπτύω, 1716), "to spit upon" (*en*, "in," and No. 1), occurs in Matt. 26:67; 27:30; Mark 10:34; 14:65; 15:19; Luke 18:32. In the Sept., Num. 12:14, in some texts; Deut. 25:9.

SPITEFULLY (ENTREAT)

hubrizō (ὑβρίζω, 5195), used transitively, denotes "to outrage, treat insolently"; "to entreat shamefully" in Matt. 22:6, RV (KJV, "spitefully"); so in Luke 18:32, RV; in Acts 14:5 (KJV, "use despitefully"); in 1 Thess. 2:2, KJV and RV; in Luke 11:45, "reproachest." See DESPITEFULLY, REPROACH, SHAMEFULLY.

SPORTING

entruphao (ἐντρυφάω, 1792) occurs in 2 Pet. 2:13 (RV, "revel").

SPRINKLE, SPRINKLING

A. Verb.

rhantizō (ῥαντίζω, 4472), "to sprinkle" (a later form of *rhainō*), is used in the active voice in Heb. 9:13, of "sprinkling" with blood the unclean, a token of the efficacy of the expiatory sacrifice of Christ, His blood signifying the giving up of His life in the shedding of His blood (cf. 9:22) under divine judgment upon sin (the voluntary act to be distinguished from that which took place after His death in the piercing of His side); so again in vv. 19, 21 (see B); in Heb. 10:22, passive voice, of the purging (on the ground of the same efficacy) of the hearts of believers from an evil conscience. This application of the blood of Christ is necessary for believers, in respect of their committal of sins, which on that ground receive forgiveness, 1 John 1:9. In Mark 7:4, the verb is found in the middle voice "in some ancient authorities" (RV marg.) instead of *baptizō*. In Rev. 19:13, the RV, "sprinkled" follows those texts which have *rhantizō* (marg., "some anc. auth. read 'dipped in.'" *baptō*; so Nestle's text). This requires mention as a variant text in Rev. 19:13 under DIP.

B. Nouns.

1. *rhantismos* (ῥαντισμός, 4473), "sprinkling," akin to A, is used of the "sprinkling" of the blood of Christ, in Heb. 12:24 and 1 Pet. 1:2, an allusion to the use of the blood of sacrifices, appointed for Israel, typical of the sacrifice of Christ (see under A).

2. *proschusis* (πρόσχυσις, 4378), "a pouring or sprinkling upon," occurs in Heb. 11:28, of the "sprinkling" of the blood of the Passover lamb.

SPY (Noun and Verb)

A. Nouns.

1. *enkathetos* (ἐγκάθετος, 1455), an adjective denoting "suborned to lie in wait" (*en*, "in," *kathiemi*, "to send down"), is used as a noun in Luke 20:20, "spies." In the Sept., Job. 19:12; 31:9.

2. *kataskopos* (κατάσκοπος, 2685) denotes "a spy" (*kata*, "down," signifying "closely," and *skopeō*, "to view"), Heb. 11:31.

B. Verb.

kataskopeō (κατασκοπέω, 2684), "to view closely" (akin to A, No. 2), "spy out, search out" with a view to overthrowing, is used in Gal. 2:4. In the Sept., 2 Sam. 10:3; 1 Chron. 19:3.

For **STAGGER** see WAVER

For **STALL** see MANGER

STAR

1. *astēr* (ἀστήρ, 792), "a star," Matt. 2:2–10; 24:29; Mark 13:25; 1 Cor. 15:41; Rev. 6:13; 8:10-12; 9:1; 12:1, 4, is used metaphorically, (a) of Christ, as "the morning star," figurative of the approach of the day when He will appear as the "sun of righteousness," to govern the earth in peace, an event to be preceded by the rapture of the Church, Rev. 2:28; 22:16, the promise of the former to the overcomer being suggestive of some special personal interest in Himself and His authority; (b) of the angels of the seven churches, Rev. 1:16, 20; 2:1; 3:1; (c) of certain false teachers, described as "wandering stars," Jude 13, as if the "stars," intended for light and guidance, became the means of deceit by irregular movements.

2. *astron* (ἄστρον, 798), practically the same as No. 1, is used (a) in the sing. in Acts 7:43, "the star of the god Rephan," RV, the symbol or "figure," probably of Saturn, worshiped as a god, apparently the same as Chiun in Amos 5:26 (Rephan being the Egyptian deity corresponding to Saturn, Chiun the Assyrian); (b) in the plur., Luke 21:25; Acts 27:20; Heb. 11:12.

For **STATE** see ESTATE, *Notes*

For **STATURE** see AGE, A, No. 3

For **STEADFAST** see STEDFAST

STEAL

kleptō (κλέπτω, 2813), "to steal," akin to *kleptēs*, "a thief" (cf. Eng., "kleptomania"), occurs in Matt. 6:19, 20; 19:18; 27:64; 28:13; Mark 10:19; Luke 18:20; John 10:10; Rom. 2:21 (twice); 13:9; Eph. 4:28 (twice).

STEDFAST, STEDFASTLY, STEDFASTNESS

A. Adjectives.

1. *bebaios* (βέβαιος, 949), "firm, secure" (akin to *baino*, "to go"), is translated "steadfast" in 2 Cor. 1:7; Heb. 2:2; 3:14, KJV (RV, "firm"); 6:19. See FORCE.

2. *hedraios* (ἑδραῖος, 1476) primarily denotes "seated" (*hedra*, "a seat"); hence, "steadfast," metaphorical of moral fixity, 1 Cor. 7:37; 15:58; Col. 1:23, RV (KJV, "settled").

3. *stereos* (στερεός, 4731), firm, is rendered "steadfast" in 1 Pet. 5:9.

B. Nouns.

1. *stereoma* (στερέωμα, 4733), primarily "a support, foundation," denotes "strength, steadfastness," Col. 2:5. In the Sept., in Gen. 1:6, and Ezek. 1:22, it is used of the firmament, which was believed to be a solid canopy. The corresponding Heb. word *raqia'* means "expanse," from *raqa'*, "to spread out."

2. *sterigmos* (στηριγμός, 4740), "a setting firmly, supporting," then "fixedness, steadfastness" (akin to *sterizo*, "to establish"), is used in 2 Pet. 3:17.

Note: For STEADFASTLY see BEHOLD, No. 10, LOOK, No. 15.

For **STEERSMAN** see GOVERNOR, B, *Note*

STERN

prumna (πρύμνα, 4403), the feminine form of the adjective *prumnos*, "hindmost," is rendered "stern" in Acts 27:29; and in the RV in v. 41 and Mark 4:38. See PART, A, *Note* (2).

STEWARD, STEWARDSHIP

A. Nouns.

1. *oikonomos* (οἰκονόμος, 3623) primarily denoted "the manager of a household or estate" (*oikos*, "a house," *nemō*, "to arrange"), "a steward" (such were usually slaves or freedmen), Luke 12:42; 16:1, 3, 8; 1 Cor. 4:2; Gal. 4:2, RV (KJV,

"governors"); in Rom. 16:23, the "treasurer (RV) of a city; it is used metaphorically, in the wider sense, of a "steward" in general, (a) of preachers of the gospel and teachers of the Word of God, 1 Cor. 4:1; (b) of elders or bishops in churches, Titus 1:7; (c) of believers generally, 1 Pet. 4:10.

2. *epitropos* (ἐπίτροπος, 2012) is rendered "steward" in Matt. 20:8; Luke 8:3: see GUARDIAN.

3. *oikonomia* (οἰκονομία, 3622) is rendered "stewardship" in Luke 16:2, 3, 4, and in the RV in 1 Cor. 9:17: see DISPENSATION.

B. Verb.

oikonomeō (οἰκονομέω, 3621), akin to A, Nos. 1 and 3, signifies "to be a house steward," Luke 16:2. In the Sept., Ps. 112:5.

STIFFNECKED

sklērotrachēlos (σκληροτράχηλος, 4644), from *sklēros*, "harsh, hard," *trachelos*, "a neck," is used metaphorically in Acts 7:51.

For **STING** see GOAD

STINK

ozō (ὄζω, 3605), "to emit a smell" (cf. Eng., "ozone"), occurs in John 11:39. In the Sept., Ex. 8:14.

STIR, STIR UP (Noun and Verb)

A. Noun.

tarachos (τάραχος, 5017), akin to *tarachē*, "trouble," and *tarassō*, "to trouble," is rendered "stir" in Acts 12:18; 19:23.

B. Verbs.

1. *anazopureō* (ἀναζωπυρέω, 329) denotes "to kindle afresh," or "keep in full flame" (*ana*, "up," or "again," *zoos*, "alive," *pur*, "fire"), and is used metaphorically in 2 Tim. 1:6, where "the gift of God" is regarded as a fire capable of dying out through neglect. The verb was in common use in the vernacular of the time.

2 *epegeirō* (ἐπεγείρω, 1892), "stirred up" in Acts 14:2.

3. *diegeirō* (διεγείρω, 1326), "stir up" in 2 Pet. 1:13; 3:1: see ARISE, No. 4.

4. *seiō* (σείω, 4579), "to move to and fro," is rendered "was stirred" in Matt. 21:10, RV (KJV, "was moved). See QUAKE.

5. *anaseiō* (ἀνασείω, 383) primarily denotes "to shake back or out, move to and fro"; then, "to stir up," used metaphorically in Mark 15:11, RV, "stirred ... up" (KJV, "moved"), and Luke 3:14; 23:5.

6. *saleuō* (σαλεύω, 4531), "stirred up" in Acts 17:13.

7. *parotrunō* (παροτρύνω, 3951), from *para*, used intensively, beyond measure, and *otrunō*, "to urge on, rouse," occurs in Acts 13:50, "stirred up."

8. *sunkineō* (συγκινέω, 4787), "to move together" (*sun*, "together," *kineō*, "to move"), "to stir up, excite," is used metaphorically in Acts 6:12.

9. *suncheō* (συγχέω, 4797), "to pour together," is used metaphorically in Acts 21:27, stirred up. See CONFOUND, B, No. 1.

10. *paroxunō* (παροξύνω, 3947), "stirred" in Acts 17:16: see PROVOKE, No. 2.

11. *erethizō* (ἐρεθίζω, 2042), "hath stirred" in 2 Cor. 9:2, RV. See PROVOKE, No. 3.

12. *anastatoō* (ἀναστατόω, 387), "to excite, unsettle" (akin to *anistēmi*, "to raise up," and *anastasis*, "a raising"), is used (a) of "stirring up" to sedition, and tumult, Acts 17:6, "turned ... upside down"; 21:38, RV, "stirred up to sedition," KJV, "madest an uproar"; (b) "to upset" by false teaching, Gal. 5:12, RV, "unsettle" (KJV, "trouble").

Note: In Acts 24:12, *poieō*, "to make," with *epistasis*, "a stopping" (in some texts *episustasis*), signifies "to collect" (a crowd), KJV, "raising up (the people)," RV, "stirring up (a crowd)."

For **STOCK** see KIND

STONE (Noun, Verb, and Adjective)

A. Nouns.

1. *lithos* (λίθος, 3037) is used (I) literally, of (a) the "stones" of the ground, e.g., Matt. 4:3, 6; 7:9; (b) "tombstones," e.g., Matt. 27:60, 66; (c) "building stones," e.g., Matt. 21:42; (d) "a millstone," Luke 17:2; cf. Rev. 18:21 (see MILLSTONE); (e) the "tables (or tablets)" of the Law, 2 Cor. 3:7; (f) "idol images," Acts 17:29; (g) the "treasures" of commercial Babylon, Rev. 18:12, 16; (II), metaphorically, of (a) Christ, Rom. 9:33; 1 Pet. 2:4, 6, 8; (b) believers, 1 Pet. 2:5; (c) spiritual edification by scriptural teaching, 1 Cor. 3:12; (d) the adornment of the foundations of the wall of the spiritual and heavenly Jerusalem, Rev. 21:19; (e) the adornment of the seven angels in Rev. 15:6, RV (so the best texts; some have *linon*, "linen," KJV); (f) the adornment of religious Babylon, Rev. 17:4; (III) figuratively, of Christ, Rev. 4:3; 21:11, where "light" stands for "Light-giver" (*phōstēr*).

2. *psēphos* (ψῆφος, 5586), "a smooth stone, a pebble," worn smooth as by water, or polished (akin to *psaō*, "to rub"), denotes (a) by metonymy, a vote (from the use of "pebbles" for this purpose; cf. *psēphizō*, "to count"), Acts 26:10, RV (KJV, "voice"); (b) a (white) "stone" to be given to the overcomer in the church at Pergamum, Rev. 2:17 (twice); a white "stone" was often used in the social life and judicial customs of the ancients; festal days were noted by a white "stone," days of calamity by a black; in the courts a white "stone" indicated acquittal, a black condemnation. A host's appreciation of a

special guest was indicated by a white "stone" with the name or a message written on it; this is probably the allusion here.

Note: In John 1:42 *petros* stands for the proper name, Peter, as the RV (KJV, "a stone"; marg., "Peter"); *petros* denotes "a piece of a rock, a detached stone or boulder," in contrast to *petra*, "a mass of rock." See ROCK.

B. Verbs.

1. *lithoboleō* (λιθοβολέω, 3036), "to pelt with stones" (A, No. 1, and *ballō*, "to throw"), "to stone to death," occurs in Matt. 21:35; 23:37; Luke 13:34 (John 8:5 in some mss.: see No. 2); Acts 7:58, 59; 14:5; Heb. 12:20.

2. *lithazō* (λιθάζω, 3034), "to stone," virtually equivalent to No. 1, but not stressing the casting, occurs in John 8:5 (in the most authentic mss.); 10:31-33; 11:8; Acts 5:26; 14:19; 2 Cor. 11:25; Heb. 11:37.

3. *katalithazō* (καταλιθάζω, 2642), an intensive form of No. 2, "to cast stones at," occurs in Luke 20:6.

C. Adjective.

lithinos (λίθινος, 3035), "of stone" (akin to A, No. 1), occurs in John 2:6; 2 Cor. 3:3; Rev. 9:20.

For **STONY** see ROCKY

For **STOREHOUSE, STORECHAMBER,** see CHAMBER

STRAIGHT

A. Adjectives.

1. *euthus* (εὐθύς, 2117), "direct, straight, right," is translated "straight," figuratively, of the paths of the Lord, Matt. 3:3; Mark 1:3; Luke 3:4; in v. 5 of the rectification of the crooked, with reference to moral transformation; in Acts 9:11, the name of a street in Damascus, still one of the principal thoroughfares. See RIGHT.

2. *orthos* (ὀρθός, 3717), used of height, denotes "upright," Acts 14:10; of line of direction, figuratively, said of paths of righteousness, Heb. 12:13.

B. Verbs.

1. *euthunō* (εὐθύνω, 2116), akin to A, No. 1, is used of the directing of a ship by the steersman, Jas. 3:4 (see GOVERNOR, B, *Note*); metaphorically, of making "straight" the way of the Lord, John 1:23.

2. *anorthoō* (ἀνορθόω, 461), "to set up, make straight."

For **STRAIGHTWAY** see IMMEDIATELY, No. 1

For the Adjective **STRAIT** see NARROW

STRANGE

A. Adjectives.

1. *xenos* (ξένος, 3581) denotes (a) "foreign, alien," Acts 17:18, of gods; Heb. 13:9, of doctrines; (b) "unusual," 1 Pet. 4:12, 2nd part, of the fiery trial of persecution (for 1st part, see B). See STRANGER.

2. *allotrios* (ἀλλότριος, 245) denotes (a) "belonging to another" (*allos*); (b) "alien, foreign, strange," Acts 7:6; Heb. 11:9, KJV, RV, "(a land) not his own." See ALIEN, STRANGER.

3. *paradoxos* (παράδοξος, 3861), "contrary to received opinion" (*para*, "beside," *doxa*, "opinion"; Eng. "paradox," "-ical"), is rendered "strange things" in Luke 5:26.

4. *exō* (ἔξω, 1854), outside, is rendered "strange" in Acts 26:11, KJV: see FOREIGN.

Note: In 1 Cor. 14:21 (1st part), RV, *heteroglōssos*, signifying "of a different tongue" (*heteros*, "another," *glōssa*, "a tongue") is translated "of strange (KJV, other) tongues."

B. Verb.

xenizō (ξενίζω, 3579) denotes "to think something strange," 1 Pet. 4:4, 12, passive voice, i.e., "they are surprised," and "be (not) surprised"; in Acts 17:20, the present participle, active, is rendered "strange," i.e., "surprising." See ENTERTAIN.

STRANGER

A. Adjectives (used as nouns).

1. *xenos* (ξένος, 3581), "strange" (see No. 1 above), denotes "a stranger, foreigner," Matt. 25:35, 38, 43, 44; 27:7; Acts 17:21; Eph. 2:12, 19; Heb. 11:13; 3 John 5.

2. *allotrios* (ἀλλότριος, 245), "strangers," Matt. 17:25, 26; John 10:5 (twice): see No. 2, above.

3. *allogenēs* (ἀλλογενής, 241) (*allos*, "another," *genos*, "a race") occurs in Luke 17:18, of a Samaritan. Moulton and Milligan illustrate the use of the word by the inscription on the Temple barrier, "let no foreigner enter within the screen and enclosure surrounding the sanctuary"; according to Mommsen this inscription was cut by the Romans: cf. PARTITION.

Notes: (1) For *paroikos*, in KJV, see SOJOURN, B, No. 1. For *parepidēmos*, in KJV, see PILGRIM. (2) The pronoun *heteros*, "other," is translated "strangers" in 1 Cor. 14:21 (2nd part), RV (KJV, "other"); cf. STRANGE, A, Note.

B. Verb.

xenodocheō (ξενοδοχέω, 3580), "to receive strangers" (*xenos*, No. 1, above, and *dechomai*, "to receive"), occurs in 1 Tim. 5:10, RV, "(if) she hath used hospitality to strangers," KJV, "(if) she have lodged strangers."

Note: For *epidēmeō*, in KJV, see SOJOURNER, A, No. 2. For *paroikeo*, in KJV, see SOJOURN, A, No. 1.

C. Noun.

philoxenia (φιλονεξία, 5381), "love of strangers," occurs in Rom. 12:13, "hospitality," and Heb. 13:2, RV, "to show love unto strangers," KJV, "to entertain strangers." See ENTERTAIN, Note.

Note: For *paroikia* in Acts 13:17, see SOJOURN, C.

STRENGTH, STRENGTHEN

A. Nouns.

1. *dunamis* (δύναμις, 1411) is rendered "strength" in the RV and KJV of Rev. 1:16; elsewhere the RV gives the word its more appropriate meaning "power," for KJV, "strength," 1 Cor. 15:56; 2 Cor. 1:8; 12:9; Heb. 11:11; Rev. 3:8; 12:10. See ABILITY, No. 1, POWER, No. 1.

2. *ischus* (ἰσχύς, 2479), "ability, strength," is rendered "strength" in Mark 12:30, 33; Luke 10:27; in Rev. 5:12, KJV (RV, "might"). See ABILITY, No. 2, MIGHT.

3. *krotos* (κράτος, 2904), "force, might," is rendered "strength" in Luke 1:51, RV and KJV; RV, "strength" (KJV,"power") in Eph. 1:19 and 6:10. See DOMINION, No. 1, POWER, No. 4.

Note: In Rev. 17:13, KJV, *exousia*, "freedom of action," is rendered "strength" (RV, "authority").

B. Verbs.

1. *dunamoō* (δυναμόω, 1412), "to strengthen," occurs in Col. 1:11, and in the best texts in Heb. 11:34, "were made strong" (some have No. 2); some have it in Eph. 6:10 (the best have No. 2). In the Sept., Ps. 52:7; 68:28; Eccl. 10:10; Dan. 9:27.

2. *endunamoō* (ἐνδυναμόω, 1743), "to make strong," is rendered "increased ... in strength" in Acts 9:22; "to strengthen" in Phil. 4:13; 2 Tim. 2:1, RV, "be strengthened"; 4:17. See STRONG, B.

3. *ischuō* (ἰσχύω, 2480), akin to A, No. 2, "to have strength," is so rendered in Mark 5:4, RV (KJV, "could"); in Luke 16:3, RV, "I have not strength to" (KJV, "I cannot").

4. *enischuō* (ἐνισχύω, 1765), akin to A, No. 2, a strengthened form of No. 3, is used in Luke 22:43 and Acts 9:19.

5. *krataioō* (κραταιόω, 2901), "to strengthen," is rendered "to be strengthened" in Eph. 3:16. See STRONG, B.

6. *sthenoō* (σθενόω, 4599), from *sthenos*, "strength," occurs in 1 Pet. 5:10, in a series of future tenses, according to the best texts, thus constituting divine promises.

Notes: (1) *Epistērizō* is found in some texts in Acts 18:23, KJV, "strengthening." See CONFIRM, A, No. 2. (2) For "without strength," Rom. 5:6, KJV, see WEAK.

STRICKEN (in years)

probainō (προβαίνω, 4260), "to go forward," is used metaphorically of age, in Luke 1:7, 18, with the phrases "in their (her) days," translated "well stricken in years" (see marg.); in 2:36, "of a great age" (marg., "advanced in many days"). See GO, No. 20.

STRIFE

1. *eris* (ἔρις, 2054), "strife, contention," is the expression of "enmity," Rom. 1:29, RV, "strife" (KJV, "debate"); 13:13; 1 Cor. 1:11, "contentions" (RV and KJV); 3:3; 2 Cor. 12:20, RV, "strife" (KJV, "debates"); Gal. 5:20, RV, "strife" (KJV, "variance"); Phil. 1:15; 1 Tim. 6:4; Titus 3:9, RV, "strifes" (KJV, "contentions"). See CONTENTION, A, No. 1.

2. *erithia* (or —*eia*) (ἐριθεία, 2052): see FACTION.

3. *antilogia* (ἀντιλογία, 485), "strife," Heb. 6:16, KJV.

4. *machē* (μάχη, 3163), "strifes," 2 Tim. 2:23: see FIGHTING, A.

5. *philoneikia* (φιλονεικία, 5379), "strife," Luke 22:24, KJV: see CONTENTION, A, No. 3.

6. *logomachia* (λογομαχία, 3055), "strife of words," 1 Tim. 6:4.

For **STRING** see BOND, No. 1

STRIP

ekduō (ἐκδύω, 1562), "to take off, strip off," is used especially of clothes, and rendered "to strip" in Matt. 27:28 (some mss. have *enduō*, "to clothe"), and Luke 10:30, to take off, Matt. 27:31; Mark 15:20; figuratively, 2 Cor. 5:4, "unclothed" (middle voice), of putting off the body at death (the believer's state of being unclothed does not refer to the body in the grave but to the spirit, which awaits the "body of glory" at the resurrection).

STRIPE

1. *mōlōps* (μώλωψ, 3468), "a bruise, a wound from a stripe," is used in 1 Pet. 2:24 (from the Sept. of Isa. 53:5), lit., in the original, "by whose bruise," not referring to Christ's scourging, but figurative of the stroke of divine judgment administered vicariously to Him on the cross (a comforting reminder to these Christian servants, who were not infrequently buffeted, v. 20, by their masters).

2. *plēgē* (πληγή, 4127), "a blow, stripe, wound" (akin to *plēssō*, "to strike," and *plēktēs*, "a striker"), is rendered "stripes" in Luke 12:48 (the noun is omitted in the original in v. 47 and the 2nd part of v. 48); Acts 16:23, 33; 2 Cor. 6:5; 11:23. See PLAGUE, WOUND.

STRIVE

1. *agōnizomai* (ἀγωνίζομαι, 75), "to contend" (Eng., "agonize"), is rendered "to strive" in Luke 13:24; 1 Cor. 9:25; Col. 1:29; 4:12, RV (KJV, "laboring fervently"). In 1 Tim. 4:10, the best texts have this verb (RV, "strive") for *oneidizomai*, "to suffer reproach," KJV; see FIGHT, B, No. 1.

2. *machomai* (μάχομαι, 3164), "to fight, to quarrel, dispute," is rendered "to strive" in John 6:52; Acts 7:26; 2 Tim. 2:24. See FIGHT, B, No. 3.

3. *diamachomai* (διαμάχομαι, 1264), "to struggle against" (*dia*, intensive, and No. 2), is used of "contending" in an argument, Acts 23:9, "strove."

4. *erizō* (ἐρίζω, 2051), "to wrangle, strive" (*eris*, "strife"), is used in Matt. 12:19.

5. *logomacheō* (λογομαχέω, 3054), "to strive about words" (*logos*, "a word," and No. 2), is used in 2 Tim. 2:14.

6. *antagōnizomai* (ἀνταγωνίζομαι, 464), "to struggle against" (*anti*), is used in Heb. 12:4, "striving against."

7. *sunagōnizomai* (συναγωνίζομαι, 4865), "to strive together with" (*sun*), is used in Rom. 15:30.

8. *sunathleō* (συναθλέω, 4866), "to strive together," Phil. 1:27: see LABOR, B, No. 3.

Notes: (1) In 2 Tim. 2:5, KJV, *athleō*, "to contend in games, wrestle" (*athlos*, "a contest"), is rendered "strive." See CONTEND. (2) For *philotimeornai*, Rom. 15:20, see AIM.

For **STRIVINGS,** Titus 3:9, KJV, see FIGHTING

STROLLING

perierchomai (περιέρχομαι, 4022), "to go about," as an itinerant (*peri*, "around," *erchomai*, "to go"), is used of certain Jews in Acts 19:13, RV, "strolling" (KJV, "vagabond"). See WANDER.

STRONG, STRONGER

A. Adjectives.

1. *dunatos* (δυνατός, 1415), "powerful, mighty," is translated "strong," in Rom. 15:1, where the "strong" are those referred to in ch. 14, in contrast to "the weak in faith," those who have scruples in regard to eating meat and the observance of days; 2 Cor. 12:10, where the strength lies in bearing sufferings in the realization that the endurance is for Christ's sake; 2 Cor. 13:9, where "ye are strong" implies the good spiritual condition which the apostle desires for the church at Corinth in having nothing requiring his exercise of discipline (contrast No. 2 in 1 Cor. 4:10). See ABLE, C, No. 1, MIGHTY, POWER.

2. *ichuros* (ἰσχυρός, 2478), "strong, mighty," is used of (a) persons: (1) God, Rev. 18:8; (2) angels, Rev. 5:2; 10:1; 18:21; (3) men, Matt. 12:29 (twice) and parallel passages; Heb. 11:34, KJV, "valiant" (RV, "mighty"); Rev. 6:15 (in the best texts; some have No. 1); 19:18, "mighty"; metaphorically, (4) the church at Corinth, 1 Cor. 4:10, where the apostle reproaches them ironically with their unspiritual and self-complacent condition; (5) of young men in Christ spiritually strong, through the Word of God, to overcome the evil one, 1 John 2:14; of (b) things: (1) wind, Matt. 14:30 (in some mss.), "boisterous"; (2) famine, Luke 15:14; (3) things in the mere human estimate, 1 Cor. 1:27; (4) Paul's letters, 2 Cor. 10 :10; (5) the Lord's crying and tears, Heb. 5:7; (6) consolation, 6:18; (7) the voice of an angel, Rev. 18:2 (in the best texts; some have *megas*, "great"); (8) Babylon, Rev. 18:10; (9) thunderings, Rev. 19:6. See BOISTEROUS, MIGHTY.

3. *ischuroteros* (ἰσχυρότερος, 2478), the comparative degree of No. 2, is used (a) of Christ, Matt. 3:11; Mark 1:7; Luke 3:16; (b) of "the weakness of God," as men without understanding regard it, 1 Cor. 1:25; (c) of a man of superior physical strength, Luke 11:22; (d) in 1 Cor. 10:22, in a rhetorical question, implying the impossibility of escaping the jealousy of God when it is kindled.

Note: For "strong delusion," 2 Thess. 2:11, KJV, see ERROR, No. 1.

B. Verbs.

1. *endunamoō* (ἐνδυναμόω, 1743), "to make strong" (*en*, "in," *dunamis*, "power"), "to strengthen," is rendered "waxed strong" in Rom. 4:20, RV (KJV, "was strong"); "be strong," Eph. 6:10; "were made strong," Heb. 11:34. See STRENGTH, B, No. 2.

2. *krataioō* (κραταιόω, 2901), "to strengthen" (akin to *kratos*, "strength"), is rendered (a) "to wax strong," Luke 1:80; 2:40; "be strong," 1 Cor. 16:13, lit., "be strengthened"; "to be strengthened," Eph. 3:16 (passive voice in each place). See STRENGTHEN.

STRONGHOLDS

ochurōma (ὀχύρωμα, 3794), "a stronghold, fortress" (akin to *ochuroō*, "to make firm"), is used metaphorically in 2 Cor. 10:4, of those things in which mere human confidence is imposed.

STUBBLE

kalamē (καλάμη, 2562), "a stalk of corn," denotes "straw" or "stubble"; in 1 Cor. 3:12, metaphorically of the effect of the most worthless form of unprofitable doctrine, in the lives and conduct of those in a church who are the subjects of such teaching; the teachings received and the persons who receive them are associated; the latter are "the doctrine exhibited in concrete form" (Lightfoot).

STUDY

Notes: For *philotimeomai*, "study," 1 Thess. 4:11, see AIM. For *spoudazo*, 2 Tim. 2:15, KJV, see DILIGENCE, B, No. 1.

For **STUFF,** Luke 17:31, KJV, see GOODS, No. 4

STUMBLE

1. *proskoptō* (προσκόπτω, 4350), "to strike against," is used of "stumbling," (a) physically, John 11:9, 10; (b) metaphorically, (1) of Israel in regard to Christ, whose Person, teaching, and atoning death, and the gospel relating thereto, were contrary to all their ideas as to the means of righteousness before

God, Rom. 9:32; 1 Pet. 2:8; (2) of a brother in the Lord in acting against the dictates of his conscience, Rom. 14:21. See BEAT, No. 6.

2. *ptaiō* (πταίω, 4417), "to cause to stumble," signifies, intransitively, "to stumble," used metaphorically in Rom. 11:11, in the sense (b) (1) in No. 1; with moral significance in Jas. 2:10 and 3:2 (twice), RV, "stumble" (KJV, "offend"); in 2 Pet. 1:10, RV, "stumble" (KJV, "fall").

For **STUMBLING, STUMBLING BLOCK, STUMBLING-STONE,** see OFFENSE, A, Nos. 1, 2, 3 ,and B

SUBJECT, SUBJECTION (Verb, Adjective, Noun)

A. Verb.

hupotassō (ὑποτάσσω, 5293), primarily a military term, "to rank under" (*hupo*, "under," *tassō*, "to arrange"), denotes (a) "to put in subjection, to subject," Rom. 8:20 (twice); in the following, the RV, has to subject for KJV, "to put under," 1 Cor. 15:27 (thrice), 28 (3rd clause); Eph. 1:22; Heb. 2:8 (4th clause); in 1 Cor. 15:28 (1st clause), for KJV "be subdued"; in Phil. 3:21, for KJV, "subdue"; in Heb. 2:5, KJV, "hath ... put in subjection"; (b) in the middle or passive voice, to subject oneself, to obey, be subject to, Luke 2:51; 10:17, 20; Rom. 8:7; 10:3, RV, "did (not) subject themselves" [KJV, "have (not) submitted themselves"]; 13:1, 5; 1 Cor. 14:34, RV, "be in subjection" (KJV, "be under obedience"); 15:28 (2nd clause); 16:16 RV, "be in subjection" (KJV, "submit, etc."); so Col. 3:18; Eph. 5:21, RV, "subjecting yourselves" (KJV, "submitting, etc."); v. 22, RV in italics, according to the best texts; v. 24, "is subject"; Titus 2:5, 9, RV, "be in subjection" (KJV, "be obedient"); 3:1, RV, "to be in subjection" (KJV, "to be subject"); Heb. 12:9, "be in subjection"; Jas. 4:7, RV, "be subject" (KJV, "submit yourselves"); so 1 Pet. 2:13; v. 18, RV, "be in subjection"; so 3:1, KJV and RV; v. 5, similarly; 3:22, "being made subject"; 5:5, RV, "be subject" (KJV, "submit yourselves"); in some texts in the 2nd part, as KJV. See OBEDIENT, SUBMIT.

Note: For *doulagōgeō*, 1 Cor. 9:27, KJV, bring into subjection, see BONDAGE, B, No. 3. For *anupotaktos*, "not subject," Heb. 2:8, see DISOBEDIENT, B, Note.

B. Adjective.

enochos (ἔνοχος, 1777), "held in, bound by," in Heb. 2:15, subject to: see DANGER, B, No. 1.

Note: For "subject to like passions," Jas. 5:17, KJV, see PASSION.

C. Noun.

hupotagē (ὑποταγή, 5292), "subjection," occurs in 2 Cor. 9:13; Gal. 2:5; 1 Tim. 2:11; 3:4.

SUBMIT

hupeikō (ὑπείκω, 5226), "to retire, withdraw" (*hupo*, under, *eiko*, "to yield"), hence, "to yield, submit," is used metaphorically in Heb. 13:17, of "submitting" to spiritual guides in the churches.

Note: For *hupotassō*, see SUBJECT, A.

SUBORN

hupoballō (ὑποβάλλω, 5260), "to throw or put under, to subject," denoted "to suggest, whisper, prompt"; hence, "to instigate," translated "suborned" in Acts 6:11. To "suborn" in the legal sense is to procure a person who will take a false oath. The idea of making suggestions is probably present in this use of the word.

SUBSTANCE

1. *ouisia* (οὐσία, 3776), derived from a present participial form of *eimi*, "to be," denotes "substance, property," Luke 15:12, 13, RV, "substance," KJV, "goods" and "substance."

2. *huparchonta* (ὑπάρχοντα, 5224), the neuter plural of the present participle of *huparchō*, "to be in existence," is used as a noun with the article, signifying one's "goods," and translated "substance" in Luke 8:3. See GOODS, POSSESS, A, No. 3.

3. *huparxis* (ὕπαρξις, 5223), existence (akin to No. 2), possession: see POSSESS, B, No. 4.

4. *hupostasis* (ὑπόστασις, 5287), for which see CONFIDENCE, A, No. 2, is translated substance" (a) in Heb. 1:3, of Christ as "the very image" of God's "substance"; here the word has the meaning of the real nature of that to which reference is made in contrast to the outward manifestation (see the preceding clause); it speaks of the divine essence of God existent and expressed in the revelation of His Son. The KJV, "person" is an anachronism; the word was not so rendered till the 4th cent. Most of the earlier Eng. versions have "substance"; (b) in Heb. 11:1 it has the meaning of "confidence, assurance" (RV), marg., "the giving substance to," KJV, "substance," something that could not equally be expressed by *elpis*, "hope."

SUBTLY

katasophizomai (κατασοφίζομαι, 2686), "to deal subtly" (from *kata*, "against, under," *sophos*, "wise, subtle," used in the Sept. in 2 Sam. 13:3, of Jonadab), occurs in Acts 7:19. In the Sept.. Ex. 1:10.

SUBTLETY

Note: For *dolos*, Matt. 26:4; Acts 13:10, see GUILE. For *panourgia*, 2 Cor. 11:3, see CRAFTINESS.

For **SUCCOR** see HELP, B, No. 4

SUCCORER

prostatis (προστάτις, 4368), a feminine form of *prostatēs*, denotes "a protectress, patroness"; it is used metaphorically of Phoebe in Rom. 16:2. It is a word of dignity, evidently chosen instead of others which might have been used (see, e.g., under HELPER), and indicates the high esteem with which she was regarded, as one who had been a protectress of many. *Prostatēs* was the title of a citizen in Athens, who had the responsibility of seeing to the welfare of resident aliens who were without civic rights. Among the Jews it signified a wealthy patron of the community.

SUCK (GIVE SUCK), SUCKLING

thēlazō (θηλάζω, 2337), from *thēlē*, "a breast," is used (a) of the mother, "to suckle," Matt. 24:19; Mark 13:17; Luke 21:23; in some texts in 23:29 (the best have *trephō*); (b) of the young, "to suck," Matt. 21:16, "sucklings"; Luke 11:27.

For **SUE** see LAW, B, No. 2

SUFFER

A. Verbs.

(a) *to permit*

1. *eaō* (ἐάω, 1439), "to let, permit," is translated "to suffer" in Matt. 24:43; Luke 4:41; 22:51; Acts 14:16; 16:7; 19:30; 28:4; 1 Cor. 10:13.

2. *proseaō* (προσεάω, 4330), "to permit further" (*pros*, and No. 1), occurs in Acts 27:7.

3. *epitrepō* (ἐπιτρέπω, 2010) is rendered "to suffer" in KJV and RV in Matt. 8:21; Mark 10:4; Luke 9:59; Acts 28:16; RV only, Luke 9:61 (KJV, "let"); KJV only, Acts 21:39; in some texts, Matt. 8:31, KJV only. See LIBERTY, C, Note, PERMIT.

4. *aphiēmi* (ἀφίημι, 863), "to send away," signifies "to permit, suffer," in Matt. 3:15 (twice); Matt. 19:14; 23:13; Mark 1:34; 5:19, 37; 10:14; 11:16; Luke 8:51; 12:39, KJV (RV, "left"); 18:16; John 12:7, RV, KJV and RV marg., "let (her) alone"; Rev. 11:9. See FORGIVE.

Notes: (1) In Acts 2:27 and 13:35, KJV, *didomi*, "to give" (RV), is rendered "to suffer." (2) In 1 Cor. 6:7, KJV, *apostereō*, in the passive voice, is rendered "*suffer yourselves to* be defrauded" (RV, "be defrauded"). (3) For *koluō* in Heb. 7:23, KJV, "were not suffered," see HINDER.

(b) *to endure suffering*

1. *anechō* (ἀνέχομαι, 430), in the middle voice, "to bear with," is rendered "to suffer" in Matt. 17:17 and parallel passages; KJV only, 1 Cor. 4:12 (RV, "endure"); 2 Cor. 11:19, 20 and Heb. 13:22 (RV, bear with). See ENDURE.

2. *paschō* (πάσχω, 3958), "to suffer," is used (I) of the "sufferings" of Christ (a) at the hands of men, e.g., Matt. 16:21; 17:12; 1 Pet. 2:23; (b) in His expiatory and vicarious sacrifice for sin, Heb. 9:26; 13:12; 1 Pet. 2:21; 3:18; 4:1; (c) including both (a) and (b), Luke 22:15; 24:26, 46; Acts 1:3, "passion"; 3:18; 17:3; Heb. 5:8; (d) by the antagonism of the evil one, Heb. 2:18; (II), of human "suffering" (a) of followers of Christ, Acts 9:16; 2 Cor. 1:6; Gal. 3:4; Phil. 1:29; 1 Thess. 2:14; 2 Thess. 1:5; 2 Tim. 1:12; 1 Pet. 3:14, 17; 5:10; Rev. 2:10; in identification with Christ in His crucifixion, as the spiritual ideal to be realized, 1 Pet. 4:1; in a wrong way, 4:15; (b) of others, physically, as the result of demoniacal power, Matt. 17:15, RV, "suffereth (grievously)," KJV, "is (sore) vexed"; cf. Mark 5:26; in a dream, Matt. 27:19; through maltreatment, Luke 13:2; 1 Pet. 2:19, 20; by a serpent (negatively), Acts 28:5, RV, "took" (KJV, "felt:" see FEEL, *Note*); (c) of the effect upon the whole body through the "suffering" of one member, 1 Cor. 12:26, with application to a church.

3. *propaschō* (προπάσχω, 4310), "to suffer before" (*pro*, and No. 2), occurs in 1 Thess. 2:2.

4. *sumpaschō* (συμπάσχω, 4841), "to suffer with" (*sun*, and No. 2), is used in Rom. 8:17 of "suffering" with Christ; in 1 Cor. 12:26 of joint "suffering" in the members of the body.

5. *hupechō* (ὑπέχω, 5254), "to hold under" (*hupo*, "under," *echo*, "to have or hold"), is used metaphorically in Jude 7 of "suffering" punishment. In the Sept., Ps. 89:50; Lam. 5:7.

6. *kakoucheō* (κακουχέω, 2558), "to illtreat" (*kakos*, "evil," and *echō*, "to have"), is used in the passive voice in Heb. 11:37, RV, "evil entreated" (KJV, "tormented"); in 13:3, RV, "are evil entreated" (KJV, "suffer adversity").

7. *sunkakoucheomai* (συγκακουχέομαι, 4778), "to endure adversity with," is used in Heb. 11:25 (*sun*, "with," and No. 6), RV, "to be evil entreated with," KJV, "to suffer affliction with."

8. *makrothumeō* (μακροθυμέω, 3114) is rendered "suffereth long" in 1 Cor. 13:4. See PATIENCE.

9. *adikeō* (ἀδικέω, 91), "to do wrong, injustice" (*a*, negative, *dikē*, "right"), is used in the passive voice in 2 Pet. 2:13, RV, "suffering wrong" (some texts have *komizō*, "to receive," KJV); there is a play upon words here which may be brought out thus, "being defrauded (of the wages of fraud)," a use of the verb illustrated in the papyri. See HURT.

Notes: (1) In 1 Cor. 9:12, KJV, *stegō*, "to bear up under," is translated "suffer" (RV, "bear"). (2) For *hupomenō*, rendered "to suffer" in 2 Tim. 2:12, see ENDURE, No. 2. (3) For "suffer hardship, suffer trouble," see HARDSHIP, Nos. 1 and 2. (4) For "suffer loss," 2 Cor. 7:9, RV, see LOSE, No. 2. (5) For "suffer persecution," see PERSECUTION. (6) For "suffereth violence," *biazō*, see FORCE, B, No. 1, VIOLENCE, B, No. 2. (7) In 2 Thess. 1:9, RV, *tinō*, "to pay a penalty," is rendered "shall suffer (punishment)."

B. Adjective.

pathētos (παθητός, 3805), akin to *paschō*, denotes "one who has suffered," or "subject to suffering," or "destined to suffer"; it is used in the last sense of the "suffering" of Christ, Acts 26:23.

SUFFERING

pathēma (πάθημα, 3804) is rendered "sufferings" in the RV (KJV, "afflictions") in 2 Tim. 3:11; Heb. 10:32; 1 Pet. 5:9; in Gal. 5:24, "passions (KJV, "affections"). See AFFLICTION, B, No. 3.

Note: For *kakopatheia*, Jas. 5:10, RV, "suffering," see AFFLICTION, B, No. 1.

SUM, SUM UP

anakephalaioō (ἀνακεφαλαιόω, 346), "to sum up, gather up" (*ana*, "up," *kephalē*, "a head"), "to present as a whole," is used in the passive voice in Rom. 13:9, RV, "summed up" (KJV, "briefly comprehended"), i.e., the one commandment expresses all that the Law enjoins, and to obey this one is to fulfil the Law (cf. Gal. 5:14); middle voice in Eph. 1:10, RV, "sum up" (KJV, "gather together"), of God's purpose to "sum up" all things in the heavens and on the earth in Christ, a consummation extending beyond the limits of the church, though the latter is to be a factor in its realization.

SUMPTUOUS, SUMPTUOUSLY

A. Adjective.

lampros (λαμπρός, 2986), "bright," is rendered "sumptuous" in Rev. 18:14, RV See BRIGHT, GOODLY, *Note.*

B. Adverb.

lamprōs (λαμπρῶς, 2988), the corresponding adverb, is used in Luke 16:19, "sumptuously."

SUN

hēlios (ἥλιος, 2246), whence Eng. prefix "helio—," is used (a) as a means of the natural benefits of light and heat, e.g., Matt. 5:45, and power, Rev. 1:16; (b) of its qualities of brightness and glory, e.g., Matt. 13:43; 17:2; Acts 26:13; 1 Cor. 15:41; Rev. 10:1; 12:1; (c) as a means of destruction, e.g., Matt. 13:6; Jas. 1:11; of physical misery, Rev. 7:16; (d) as a means of judgment, e.g., Matt. 24:29; Mark 13:24; Luke 21:25; 23:45; Acts 2:20; Rev. 6:12; 8:12; 9:2; 16:8.

Note: In Rev. 7:2 and 16:12, *anatolē*, "rising," used with *hēlios*, is translated "sunrising," RV (KJV, "east").

SUP

deipneō (δειπνέω, 1172), "to sup" (said of taking the chief meal of the day), occurs in Luke 17:8; 22:20 (in the best texts), lit., "(the) supping"; so 1 Cor. 11:25; metaphorically in Rev. 3:20, of spiritual communion between Christ and the faithful believer.

For **SUPERFLUITY** see ABUNDANCE, A, No. 2, B, No. 1

SUPERSCRIPTION

epigraphē (ἐπιγραφή, 1923), lit., "an overwriting" (*epi*, "over," *graphō*, "to write") (the meaning of the anglicized Latin word "superscription"), denotes "an inscription, a title." On Roman coins the emperor's name was inscribed, Matt. 22:20; Mark 12:16; Luke 20:24. In the Roman Empire, in the case of a criminal on his way to execution, a board on which was inscribed the cause of his condemnation, was carried before him or hung round his neck; the inscription was termed a "title" (*titlos*). The four Evangelists state that at the crucifixion of Christ the title was affixed to the cross, Mark (15:26), and Luke (23:38), call it a "superscription"; Mark says it was "written over" (*epigraphō*, the corresponding verb). Matthew calls it "His accusation"; John calls it "a title" (a technical term). The wording varies: the essential words are the same, and the variation serves to authenticate the narratives, showing that there was no consultation leading to an agreement as to the details. See further under TITLE.

For **SUPERSTITION** see RELIGION

SUPERSTITIOUS

deisidaimon (δεισιδαίμων, 1174), "reverent to the deity" (*deidō*, "to fear"; *daimōn*, "a demon," or "pagan god"), occurs in Acts 17:22 in the comparative degree, rendered "somewhat superstitious," RV (KJV, "too superstitious"), a meaning which the word sometimes has; others, according to its comparative form, advocate the meaning "more religious (than others)," "quite religious" (cf. the noun in 25:19). This is supported by Ramsay, who renders it "more than others respectful of what is divine"; so Deissmann in *Light from the Ancient East*, and others. It also agrees with the meaning found in Greek writers; the context too suggests that the adjective is used in a good sense; perhaps, after all with kindly ambiguity (Grimm-Thayer). An ancient epitaph has it in the sense of "reverent" (Moulton and Milligan).

SUPPER

deipnon (δεῖπνον, 1173) denotes "a supper" or "feast" (for an analysis of the uses see FEAST, No. 2). In John 13:2 the RV, following certain texts, has "during supper" (KJV, "supper being ended").

Note: For "supper" in Luke 22:20 see SUP.

SUPPLICATION

1. *deēsis* (δέησις, 1162) is always translated "supplication," or the plural, in the RV. See PRAYER, B, No. 3.

2. *hiketēria* (ἱκετηρία, 2428) is the feminine form of the adjective *hiketērios*, denoting "of a suppliant," and used as a noun, formerly "an olive branch" carried by a suppliant

(*hiketēs*), then later, "a supplication," used with No. 1 in Heb. 5:7. In the Sept., Job 40:22 (Eng. Vers. 41:3).

SUPREME

huperechō (ὑπερέχω, 5242), "to be superior, to excel," is translated "supreme" in 1 Pet. 2:13: see EXCEL, No. 3.

SURETY (Noun)

enguos (ἔγγυος, 1450) primarily signifies "bail," the bail who personally answers for anyone, whether with his life or his property (to be distinguished from *mesitēs*, "a mediator"); it is used in Heb. 7:22, "(by so much also hath Jesus become) the Surety (of a better covenant)," referring to the abiding and unchanging character of His Melchizedek priesthood, by reason of which His suretyship is established by God's oath (vv. 20, 21). As the Surety, He is the personal guarantee of the terms of the new and better covenant, secured on the ground of His perfect sacrifice (v. 27).

For **SURETY (of a)**, Acts 12:11, KJV, see TRUE, D, No. 1

SURFEITING

kraipalē (κραιπάλη, 2897) signifies "the giddiness and headache resulting from excessive wine-bibbing, a drunken nausea," "surfeiting," Luke 21:34. Trench (*Syn.* Sec. LXI) distinguishes this and the synonymous words, *methē*, "drunkenness," *oinophlugia*, "wine-bibbing" (KJV, "excess of wine," 1 Pet. 4:3), *kdomos*, "revelling."

For **SURGE**, Jas. 1:6, RV, see RAGE and WAVE

SURNAME

epikaleō (ἐπικαλέομαι, 1941), "to put a name upon" (*epi*, "upon," *kaleō*, "to call"), "to surname," is used in this sense in the passive voice, in some texts in Matt. 10:3 (it is absent in the best); in Luke 22:3, in some texts (the best have *kaleō*, "to call"); Acts 1:23; 4:36; 10:5, 18, 32; 11:13; 12:12, 25; in some texts, 15:22 (the best have *kaleō*).

Notes: (1) In Mark 3:16, 17, "He surnamed" is a translation of *epitithēmi*, "to put upon, to add to," with *onoma*, "a name," as the object. (2) In Acts 15:37, KJV, *kaleō*, "to call" (RV, "called"), is rendered "whose surname was." (3) The verb *eponomazō*, translated "bearest the name" in Rom. 2:17, RV, finds a literal correspondence in the word "surname" (*epi*, "upon," = *sur*), and had this significance in Classical Greek.

For **SURPASS**, 2 Cor. 3:10, see EXCEED, A, No. 1

For **SUSPENSE (hold in)** see DOUBT, No. 6

SWALLOW (Verb)

katapinō (καταπίνω, 2666), "to drink down" (*kata*, and *pinō*, "to drink"), "to swallow," is used with this meaning (a) physically, but figuratively, Matt. 23:24; Rev. 12:16; (b) metaphorically, in the passive voice, of death (by victory), 1 Cor. 15:54; of being overwhelmed by sorrow, 2 Cor. 2:7; of the mortal body (by life), 5:4. See DEVOUR, No. 3.

SWEAR, SWORN

omnumi (ὄμνυμι), or *omnuo* (ὀμνύω, 3660) is used of "affirming or denying by an oath," e.g., Matt. 26:74; Mark 6:23; Luke 1:73; Heb. 3:11, 18; 4:3; 7:21; accompanied by that by which one swears, e.g., Matt. 5:34, 36; 23:16; Heb. 6:13, 16; Jas. 5:12; Rev. 10:6. Cf. ADJURE.

Note: For "false swearers," 1 Tim. 1:10, see FORSWEAR.

SWELLING

1. *phusiōsis* (φυσίωσις, 5450) denotes "a pumng up, swelling with pride" (akin to *phusioo*, "to puff up"), 2 Cor. 12:20, "swellings."

2. *huperonkos* (ὑπέρογκος, 5246), an adjective denoting "of excessive weight or size," is used metaphorically in the sense of "immoderate," especially of arrogant speech, in the neuter plural, virtually as a noun, 2 Pet. 2:18; Jude 16, "great swelling words," doubtless with reference to gnostic phraseology.

SWINE

choiros (χοῖρος, 5519), "a swine," is used in the plural, in the Synoptic Gospels only, Matt. 7:6; 8:30, 31, 32; Mark 5:11, 13, 16; Luke 8:32, 33; Luke 15:15, 16. It does not occur in the OT.

SWORD

1. *machaira* (μάχαιρα, 3162), "a short sword or dagger" (distinct from No. 2), e.g., Matt. 26:47, 51, 52 and parallel passages; Luke 21:24; 22:38, possibly "a knife" (Field, *Notes on the Translation of the NT*); Heb. 4:12 (see TWO-EDGED); metaphorically and by metonymy, (a) for ordinary violence, or dissensions, that destroy peace, Matt. 10:34; (b) as the instrument of a magistrate or judge, e.g., Rom. 13:4; (c) of the Word of God, "the sword of the Spirit," probing the conscience, subduing the impulses to sin, Eph. 6:17.

2. *rhomphaia* (ῥομφαία, 4501), a word of somewhat doubtful origin, denoted "a Thracian weapon of large size," whether a sword or spear is not certain, but usually longer than No. 1; it occurs (a) literally in Rev. 6:8; (b) metaphorically, as the instrument of anguish, Luke 2:35; of judgment, Rev. 1:16; 2:12, 16; 19:15, 21, probably figurative of the Lord's judicial utterances.

SYCAMORE

sukomorea (συκομορέα, 4809) occurs in Luke 19:4. This tree is of the fig species, with leaves like the mulberry and fruit like the fig. It is somewhat less in height than the sycamine and spreads to cover an area from 60 to 80 feet in diameter. It is often planted by the roadside, and was suitable for the purpose of Zacchaeus. Seated on the lowest branch he was easily within speaking distance of Christ.

SYNAGOGUE

sunagōgē (συναγωγή, 4864), properly "a bringing together" (*sun*, "together," *agō*, "to bring"), denoted (a) "a gathering of things, a collection," then, of "persons, an assembling, of Jewish religious gatherings," e.g., Acts 9:2; an assembly of Christian Jews, Jas. 2:2, RV, "synagogue" (KJV, marg.; text, "assembly"); a company dominated by the power and activity of Satan, Rev. 2:9; 3:9; (b) by metonymy, "the building" in which the gathering is held, e.g. Matt. 6:2; Mark 1:21. The origin of the Jewish "synagogue" is probably to be assigned to the time of the Babylonian exile. Having no temple, the Jews assembled on the Sabbath to hear the Law read, and the practice continued in various buildings after the return. Cf. Ps. 74:8.

SYNAGOGUE (put out of the)

aposunagōgos (ἀποσυνάγωγος, 656), an adjective denoting "expelled from the congregation, excommunicated," is used (a) with *ginomai*, "to become, be made," John 9:22; 12:42; (b) with *poieō*, "to make," John 16:2. This excommunication involved prohibition not only from attendance at the "synagogue," but from all fellowship with Israelites.

SYNAGOGUE (ruler of the)

archisunagōgos (ἀρχισυνάγωγος, 752) denotes "the administrative official," with the duty of preserving order and inviting persons to read or speak in the assembly, Mark 5:22, 35, 36, 38; Luke 8:49; 13:14; Acts 13:15; "chief ruler" (KJV) in Acts 18:8, 17.

Note: In Luke 8:41, "ruler of the synagogue" represents *archon*, "ruler," followed by the genitive case of the article and *sunagōgē*.

SYROPHOENICIAN

surophoinikissa or *surophunissa* (Συροφοίνισσα, 4949) occurs in Mark 7:26 as the national name of a woman called "a Canaanitish woman" in Matt. 15:22, i.e., not a Jewess but a descendant of the early inhabitants of the coastland of Phoenicia. The word probably denoted a Syrian residing in Phoenicia proper. There is a tradition that the woman's name was Justa and her daughter Bernice (*Clementine Homilies*, ii:19; iii:73). In Acts 21:2, 3, the two parts of the term are used interchangeably.

T

TABERNACLE

1. *skēnē* (σκηνή, 4633), "a tent, booth, tabernacle," is used of (a) tents as dwellings, Matt. 17:4; Mark 9:5; Luke 9:33; Heb. 11:9, KJV, "tabernacles" (RV, "tents"); (b) the Mosaic tabernacle, Acts 7:44; Heb. 8:5; 9:1 (in some mss.); 9:8, 21, termed "the tent of meeting," RV (i.e., where the people were called to meet God), a preferable description to "the tabernacle of the congregation," as in the KJV in the OT; the outer part 9:2, 6; the inner sanctuary, 9:3; (c) the heavenly prototype, Heb. 8:2; 9:11; Rev. 13:6; 15:5; 21:3 (of its future descent); (d) the eternal abodes of the saints, Luke 16:9, RV, "tabernacles" (KJV, "habitations"); (e) the Temple in Jerusalem, as continuing the service of the tabernacle, Heb. 13:10; (f) the house of David, i.e., metaphorically of his people, Acts 15:16; (g) the portable shrine of the god Moloch, Acts 7:43.

2. *skēnos* (σκῆνος, 4636), the equivalent of No. 1, is used metaphorically of the body as the "tabernacle" of the soul, 2 Cor. 5:1, 4.

3. *skēnōma* (σκήνωμα, 4638) occurs in Acts 7:46; 2 Pet. 1:13, 14; see HABITATION, No. 6.

4. *skēnopēgia* (σκηνοπηγία, 4634), properly "the setting up of tents or dwellings" (No. 1, and *pēgnumi*, "to fix"), represents the word "tabernacles" in "the feast of tabernacles," John 7:2. This feast, one of the three Pilgrimage Feasts in Israel, is called "the feast of ingathering" in Exod. 23:16; 34:22; it took place at the end of the year, and all males were to attend at the "tabernacle" with their offerings. In Lev. 23:34; Deut. 16:13, 16; 31:10; 2 Chron. 8:13; Ezra 3:4 (cf. Neh. 8:14-18), it is called "the feast of tabernacles" (or "booths," *sukkōth*), and was appointed for seven days at Jerusalem from the 15th to the 22nd Tishri (approximately October), to remind the people that their fathers dwelt in these in the wilderness journeys. Cf. Num. 29:15-38, especially v. 35-38, for the regulations of the eighth or "last day, the great day of the feast" (John 7:37).

TABLE

1. *trapeza* (τράπεζα, 5132) is used of (a) "a dining table," Matt. 15:27; Mark 7:28; Luke 16:21; 22:21, 30; (b) "the table of shewbread," Heb. 9:2; (c) by metonymy, of "what is provided on the table" (the word being used of that with which it is associated), Acts 16:34; Rom. 11:9 (figurative of the special privileges granted to Israel and centering in Christ); 1 Cor. 10:21 (twice), "the Lord's table," denoting all that is provided for believers in Christ on the ground of His death (and thus expressing something more comprehensive than the Lord's Supper); "the table of demons," denoting all that is partaken of by idolaters as the result of the influence of demons in connection with their sacrifices; (d) "a moneychanger's table," Matt. 21:12; Mark 11:15; John 2:15; (e) "a bank," Luke 19:23 (cf. *trapezitēs*: see BANKERS); (f) by metonymy for "the distribution of money," Acts 6:2. See BANK.

2. *plax* (πλάξ, 4109) primarily denotes "anything flat and broad," hence, "a flat stone, a tablet," 2 Cor. 3:3 (twice); Heb. 9:4.

Note: Some texts have the word *klinē*, "a couch," in Mark 7:4 (KJV, "tables").

TABLE (at the)

anakeimai (ἀνακεῖμαι, 345), "to recline at a meal table," is rendered "sat at the table" in John 12:2, KJV, RV, "sat at meat" (some texts have *sunanakeimai*); "sat," of course does not express the actual attitude; in John 13:23, RV, "at the table reclining"; KJV, "leaning"; in 13:28, "at the table" (KJV and RV), lit., "of (those) reclining."

For **TABLET** see WRITING TABLET

For **TALES** see TALK

TALITHA

taleitha or *talitha* (ταλιθά, 5008), an Aramaic feminine meaning "maiden," Mark 5:41, has been variously transliterated in the NT Greek mss. *Koumi* or *Koum* (Heb. and Aram., *qûm*, "arise"), which follows, is interpreted by, "I say unto thee, arise." *Koum* is the better attested word; so in the Talmud, where this imperative occurs "seven times in one page" (Edersheim, *Life and Times of Jesus*, i, p. 631).

TALK (Noun and Verb)

A. Nouns.

1. *logos* (λόγος, 3056), a word, is translated "talk" in Matt. 22:15; Mark 12:13.

2. *leros* (λῆρος, 3026) denotes "foolish talk, nonsense," Luke 24:11, RV, "idle talk" (KJV, "idle tales").

B. Verbs.

1. *laleō* (λαλέω, 2980), "to speak, say," is always translated "to speak" in the RV, where the KJV renders it by "to talk," Matt. 12:46; Mark 6:50; Luke 24:32; John 4:27 (twice); 9:37; 14:30; Acts 26:31; Rev. 4:1; 17:1; 21:9, 15. The RV rendering is

preferable; the idea of "chat" or "chatter" is entirely foreign to the NT, and should never be regarded as the meaning in 1 Cor. 14:34, 35. See COMMUNE, *Note.*

2. *sullaleō* (συλλαλέω, 4814), "to speak with" (*sun*), is translated "to talk with," Matt. 17:3; Mark 9:4; Luke 9:30. See CONFER, No. 2.

3. *homileō* (ὁμιλέω, 3656), "to be in company with, consort with" (*homilos*, "a throng"; *homilia*, "company"), hence, "to converse with," is rendered "to talk with," Acts 20:11. See COMMUNE, No. 2.

4. *sunomileō* (συνομιλέω, 4926), "to converse, talk with," occurs in Acts 10:27.

TALKERS (vain)

mataiologos (ματαιολόγος, 3151), an adjective denoting "talking idly" (*mataios*, "vain, idle," *lego*, "to speak"), is used as a noun (plural) in Titus 1:10.

TALKING (vain, foolish)

1. *mataiologia* (ματαιολογία, 3150), a noun corresponding to the above, is used in 1 Tim. 1:6, RV, "vain talking" (KJV, "vain jangling").

2. *mōrologia* (μωρολογία, 3473), from *mōros*, "foolish, dull, stupid," and *legō*, is used in Eph. 5:4; it denotes more than mere idle "talk." Trench describes it as "that 'talk of fools' which is foolishness and sin together" (*Syn.* Sec. XXXIV).

TAME

damazō (δαμάζω, 1150), "to subdue, tame," is used (a) naturally in Mark 5:4 and Jas. 3:7 (twice); (b) metaphorically, of the tongue, in Jas. 3:8. In the Sept., Dan. 2:40.

TASTE

geuō (γεύω, 1089), "to make to taste," is used in the middle voice (γεύομαι, 1089), signifying "to taste" (a) naturally, Matt. 27:34; Luke 14:24; John 2:9; Col. 2:21; (b) metaphorically, of Christ's "tasting" death, implying His personal experience in voluntarily undergoing death, Heb. 2:9; of believers (negatively) as to "tasting" of death, Matt. 16:28; Mark 9:1; Luke 9:27; John 8:52; of "tasting" the heavenly gift (different from receiving it), Heb. 6:4; "the good word of God, and the powers of the age to come," 6:5; "that the Lord is gracious," 1 Pet. 2:3.

TATTLER

phluaros (φλύαρος, 5397), "babbling, garrulous" (from *phluō*, "to babble": cf. *phluareō*, "to prate against"), is translated "tattlers" in 1 Tim. 5:13.

TAUGHT (Adjective)

1. *didaktos* (διδακτός, 1318), primarily "what can be taught," then, "taught," is used (a) of persons, John 6:45; (b) of things, 1 Cor. 2:13 (twice), "(not in words which man's wisdom) teacheth, (but which the Spirit) teacheth," lit., "(not in words) taught (of man's wisdom, but) taught (of the Spirit)."

2. *theodidaktos* (θεοδίδακτος, 2312), "God-taught" (*Theos*, "God," and No. 1), occurs in 1 Thess. 4:9, lit., "God-taught (persons)"; while the missionaries had "taught" the converts to love one another, God had Himself been their Teacher. Cf. John 6:45 (see No. 1).

TEACH

A. Verbs.

1. *didaskō* (διδάσκω, 1321) is used (a) absolutely, "to give instruction," e.g., Matt. 4:23; 9:35; Rom. 12:7; 1 Cor. 4:17; 1 Tim. 2:12; 4:11; (b) transitively, with an object, whether persons, e.g., Matt. 5:2; 7:29, and frequently in the Gospels and Acts, or things "taught," e.g., Matt. 15:9; 22:16; Acts 15:35; 18:11; both persons and things, e.g., John 14:26; Rev. 2:14, 20.

2. *paideuō* (παιδεύω, 3811), "to instruct and train": see INSTRUCT, No. 2.

3. *katecheō* (κατηχέω, 2727), for which see INFORM, No. 2, INSTRUCT, No. 1, is rendered to teach" in 1 Cor. 14:19, KJV (RV, "instruct"); Gal. 6:6 (twice).

4. *heterodidaskaleō* (ἑτεροδιδασκαλέω, 2085), "to teach a different doctrine" (*heteros*, "different," to be distinguished from *allos*, "another of the same kind: see ANOTHER), is used in 1 Tim. 1:3; 6:3, RV, KJV, "teach (no) other doctrine" and "teach otherwise," of what is contrary to the faith.

Notes: (1) For *mathēteuō*, "to teach," in the KJV of Matt. 28:19; Acts 14:21, see DISCIPLE, B. (2) In Acts 16:21, KJV, *katangellō*, "to declare, preach," is rendered "teach" (RV, "set forth"). (3) For "teacheth" in 1 Cor. 2:13, see TAUGHT, No. 1 (b).

B. Adjective.

didaktikos (διδακτικός, 1317), "skilled in teaching" (akin to No. 1 above: Eng., "didactic"), is translated "apt to teach" in 1 Tim. 3:2; 2 Tim. 2:24.

TEACHER, FALSE TEACHERS

1. *didaskalos* (διδάσκαλος, 1320) is rendered "teacher" or "teachers" in Matt. 23:8, by Christ, of Himself; in John 3:2 of Christ; of Nicodemus in Israel, 3:10, RV; of "teachers" of the truth in the churches, Acts 13:1; 1 Cor. 12:28, 29; Eph. 4:11; Heb. 5:12; Jas. 3:1, RV; by Paul of his work among the churches, 1 Tim. 2:7; 2 Tim. 1:11; of "teachers," wrongfully chosen by those who have "itching ears," 2 Tim. 4:3. See MASTER, RABBI.

2. *kalodidaskalos* (καλοδιδάσκαλος, 2567) denotes "a teacher of what is good" (*kalos)*, Titus 2:3.

3. *pseudodidaskalos* (ψευδοδιδάσκαλος, 5572), "a false teacher," occurs in the plural in 2 Pet. 2:1.

For **TEACHING** (Noun) see DOCTRINE, Nos. 1 and 2

TEARS

dakruon (δάκρυον), or *dakru* (δάκρυ, 1144), akin to *dakruo*, "to weep," is used in the plural, Mark 9:24; Luke 7:38, 44 (with the sense of washing therewith the Lord's feet); Acts 20:19, 31; 2 Cor. 2:4; 2 Tim. 1:4; Heb. 5:7; 12:17; Rev. 7:17; 21:4.

TEDIOUS (to be)

enkopto (ἐγκόπτω, 1465), "to hinder," is rendered "to be tedious" in Acts 24:4, of detaining a person unnecessarily. See HINDER, No. 1.

TEMPER TOGETHER

sunkerannumi (συγκεράννυμι, 4786), "to mix or blend together," is used in 1 Cor. 12:24, of the combining of the members of the human body into an organic structure, as illustrative of the members of a local church (see v. 27, where there is no definite article in the original).

TEMPERANCE, TEMPERATE

A. Noun.

enkrateia (ἐγκράτεια, 1466), from *kratos*, "strength," occurs in Acts 24:25; Gal. 5:23; 2 Pet. 1:6 (twice), in all of which it is rendered "temperance"; the RV marg., "self-control" is the preferable rendering, as "temperance" is now limited to one form of self-control; the various powers bestowed by God upon man are capable of abuse; the right use demands the controlling power of the will under the operation of the Spirit of God; in Acts 24:25 the word follows "righteousness," which represents God's claims, self-control being man's response thereto; in 2 Pet. 1:6, it follows "knowledge," suggesting that what is learned requires to be put into practice.

B. Adjectives.

1. *enkratēs* (ἐγκρατής, 1468), akin to A, denotes "exercising self-control," rendered "temperate" in Titus 1:8.

2. *nēphalios* (νηφάλιος, 3524), for which see SOBER, is translated "temperate" in 1 Tim. 3:2, RV (KJV, "vigilant"); in 3:11 and Titus 2:2, RV (KJV, "sober").

Note: In Titus 2:2, KJV, *sōphrōn*, "sober," is rendered "temperate" (RV, "soberminded").

C. Verb.

enkrateuomai (ἐγκρατεύομαι, 1467), akin to A and B, No. 1, rendered "is temperate" in 1 Cor. 9:25, is used figuratively of the rigid selfcontrol practiced by athletes with a view to gaining the prize. See CONTINENCY.

TEMPEST

1. *thuella* (θύελλα, 2366), "a hurricane, cyclone, whirlwind" (akin to *thuo*, "to slay," and *thumos*, "wrath"), is used in Heb. 12:18. In the Sept., Ex. 10:22; Deut. 4:11; 5:22.

2. *seismos* (σεισμός, 4578), "a shaking" (Eng., "seismic," etc.), is used of a "tempest" in Matt. 8:24.

3. *cheimōn* (χειμών, 5494), "winter, a winter storm," hence, in general, "a tempest," is so rendered in Acts 27:20.

4. *lailaps* (λαῖλαψ, 2978), "a tempest," 2 Pet. 2:17, KJV.

Note: For "tossed with a tempest," Acts 27:18, KJV, see LABOR, B, No. 2.

TEMPESTUOUS

tuphōnikos (τυφωνικός, 5189), from *tuphōn*, "a hurricane, typhoon," is translated "tempestuous" in Acts 27:14.

TEMPLE

1. *hieron* (ἱερόν, 2411), the neuter of the adjective *hieros*, "sacred," is used as a noun denoting "a sacred place, a temple," that of Artemis (Diana), Acts 19:27; that in Jerusalem, Mark 11:11, signifying the entire building with its precincts, or some part thereof, as distinct from the *naos*, "the inner sanctuary" (see No. 2); apart from the Gospels and Acts, it is mentioned only in 1 Cor. 9:13. Christ taught in one of the courts, to which all the people had access. *Hieron* is never used figuratively. The Temple mentioned in the Gospels and Acts was begun by Herod in 20 B.C., and destroyed by the Romans in A.D. 70.

2. *naos* (ναός, 3485), "a shrine or sanctuary," was used (a) among the heathen, to denote the shrine containing the idol, Acts 17:24; 19:24 (in the latter, miniatures); (b) among the Jews, the sanctuary in the "Temple," into which only the priests could lawfully enter, e.g., Luke 1:9, 21, 22; Christ, as being of the tribe of Judah, and thus not being a priest while upon the earth (Heb. 7:13, 14; 8:4), did not enter the *naos*; for 2 Thess. 2:4 see *Note* (below); (c) by Christ metaphorically, of His own physical body, John 2:19, 21; (d) in apostolic teaching, metaphorically, (1) of the church, the mystical body of Christ, Eph. 2:21; (2) of a local church, 1 Cor. 3:16, 17; 2 Cor. 6:16; (3) of the present body of the individual believer, 1 Cor. 6:19; (4) of the "Temple" seen in visions in the Apocalypse, 3:12; 7:15; 11:19; 14:15, 17; 15:5, 6, 8; 16:1, 17; (5) of the Lord God Almighty and the Lamb, as the "Temple" of the new and heavenly Jerusalem, Rev. 21:22. See SANCTUARY and HOLY, B (b), par. 4.

Notes: (1) The "temple" mentioned in 2 Thess. 2:4 (*naos*), as the seat of the Man of Sin, has been regarded in different ways. The weight of Scripture evidence is in favor of the view that it refers to a literal "temple" in Jerusalem, to be reconstructed in the future (cf. Dan. 11:31 and 12:11, with Matt.

24:15). For a fuller examination of the passage, see *Notes on Thessalonians,* by Hogg and Vine, pp. 250-252. (2) For *oikos*, rendered "temple," Luke 11:51, KJV, see HOUSE, No. 1.

TEMPLE KEEPER

neōkoros (νεωκόρος, 3511), Acts 19:35, RV, and KJV marg., "temple keeper" (KJV, "worshiper"), is used in profane Greek of "one who has charge of a temple." Coin inscriptions show that it was an honorary title given to certain cities, especially in Asia Minor, where the cult of some god or of a deified human potentate had been established, here to Ephesus in respect of the goddess Artemis. Apparently the imperial cult also existed at Ephesus. Josephus applies the word to Jews as worshipers, but this is not the meaning in Acts 1:9.

TEMPORAL

proskairos (πρόσκαιρος, 4340), "for a season" (*pros*, "for," *kairos*, "a season"), is rendered "temporal" in 2 Cor. 4:18. See SEASON.

TEMPT

A. Verbs.

1. *peirazō* (πειράζω, 3985) signifies (1) "to try, attempt, assay" (see TRY); (2) "to test, try, prove," in a good sense, said of Christ and of believers, Heb. 2:18, where the context shows that the temptation was the cause of suffering to Him, and only suffering, not a drawing away to sin, so that believers have the sympathy of Christ as their High Priest in the suffering which sin occasions to those who are in the enjoyment of communion with God; so in the similar passage in 4:15; in all the temptations which Christ endured, there was nothing within Him that answered to sin. There was no sinful infirmity in Him. While He was truly man, and His divine nature was not in any way inconsistent with His Manhood, there was nothing in Him such as is produced in us by the sinful nature which belongs to us; in Heb. 11:37, of the testing of OT saints; in 1 Cor. 10:13, where the meaning has a wide scope, the verb is used of "testing" as permitted by God, and of the believer as one who should be in the realization of his own helplessness and his dependence upon God (see PROVE, TRY); in a bad sense, "to tempt" (a) of attempts to ensnare Christ in His speech, e.g., Matt. 16:1; 19:3; 22:18, 35, and parallel passages; John 8:6; (b) of temptations to sin, e.g., Gal. 6:1, where one who would restore an erring brother is not to act as his judge, but as being one with him in liability to sin, with the possibility of finding himself in similar circumstances, Jas. 1:13, 14 (see note below); of temptations mentioned as coming from the Devil, Matt. 4:1; and parallel passages; 1 Cor. 7:5; 1 Thess. 3:5 (see TEMPTER); (c) of trying or challenging God, Acts 15:10; 1 Cor. 10:9 (2nd part); Heb. 3:9; the Holy Spirit, Acts 5:9: cf. No. 2.

Note: "James 1:13-15 seems to contradict other statements of Scripture in two respects, saying (a) that 'God cannot be tempted with evil,' and (b) that 'He Himself tempteth no man.' But God tempted, or tried, Abraham, Heb. 11:17, and the Israelites tempted, or tried, God, 1 Cor. 10:9. v. 14, however, makes it plain that, whereas in these cases the temptation or trial, came from without, James refers to temptation, or trial, arising within, from uncontrolled appetites and from evil passions, cf. Mark 7:20-23. But though such temptation does not proceed from God, yet does God regard His people while they endure it, and by it tests and approves them."

2. *ekpeirazō* (ἐκπειράζω, 1598), an intensive form of the foregoing, is used in much the same way as No. 1 (2) (c), in Christ's quotation from Deut. 6:16, in reply to the Devil, Matt. 4:7; Luke 4:12; so in 1 Cor. 10:9, RV, "the Lord" (KJV, "Christ"); of the lawyer who "tempted" Christ, Luke 10:25. In the Sept., Deut. 6:16; 8:2, 16; Ps. 78:15. Cf. *dokimazō* (see PROVE).

B. Adjective.

apeirastos (ἀπείραστος, 551), "untempted, untried" (*a*, negative, and A, No. 1), occurs in Jas. 1:13, with *eimi*, "to be," "cannot be tempted," "untemptable" (Mayor).

TEMPTATION

peirasmos (πειρασμός, 3986), akin to A, above, is used of (1) "trials" with a beneficial purpose and effect, (a) of "trials" or "temptations," divinely permitted or sent, Luke 22:28; Acts 20:19; Jas. 1:2; 1 Pet. 1:6; 4:12, RV, "to prove," KJV, "to try"; 2 Pet. 2:9 (singular); Rev. 3:10, RV, "trial" (KJV, "temptation"); in Jas. 1:12, "temptation" apparently has meanings (1) and (2) combined (see below), and is used in the widest sense; (b) with a good or neutral significance, Gal. 4:14, of Paul's physical infirmity, "a temptation" to the Galatian converts, of such a kind as to arouse feelings of natural repugnance; (c) of "trials" of a varied character, Matt. 6:13 and Luke 11:4, where believers are commanded to pray not to be led into such by forces beyond their own control; Matt. 26:41; Mark 14:38; Luke 22:40, 46, where they are commanded to watch and pray against entering into "temptations" by their own carelessness or disobedience; in all such cases God provides "the way of escape," 1 Cor. 10:13 (where *peirasmos* occurs twice). (2) Of "trial" definitely designed to lead to wrong doing, "temptation," Luke 4:13; 8:13; 1 Tim. 6:9; (3) of "trying" or challenging God, by men, Heb. 3:8.

TEMPTER

Note: The present participle of *peirazō*, "to tempt," preceded by the article, lit., "the (one) tempting," is used as a noun, describing the Devil in this character, Matt. 4:3; 1 Thess. 3:5.

For **TEND,** John 21:16; 1 Pet. 5:2, RV, see FEED, No. 2

TENDER

hapalos (ἁπαλός, 527), "soft, tender," is used of the branch of a tree, Matt. 24:32; Mark 13:28.

Note: For Luke 1:78, "tender mercy"; Phil. 1:8; 2:1 "tender mercies," see BOWELS.

For **TENDERHEARTED** see PITIFUL, No. 2

TERRESTRIAL

epigeios (ἐπίγειος, 1919), "on earth, earthly" (*epi,* "on," *gē,* "the earth"), is rendered "terrestrial" in 1 Cor. 15:40 (twice), in contrast to *epouranios,* "heavenly." See EARTHLY, No. 2.

For **TERRIBLE,** Heb. 12:21, see FEARFUL, B, No. 1

TERRIFY

A. Verbs.

1. *ptoeō* (πτοέω, 4422), "to terrify," is used in the passive voice, Luke 21:9; 24:37.

2. *ekphobeō* (ἐκφοβέω, 1629), "to frighten away" (*ek,* "out," *phobos,* "fear"), occurs in 2 Cor. 10:9.

3. *pturō* (πτύρω, 4426), "to scare," Phil. 1:28: see AFFRIGHTED, B, No. 1.

B. Adjective.

emphobos (ἔμφοβος, 1719), "terrified," is so rendered in the RV of Acts 24:25. See TREMBLE.

TERROR

1. *phobos* (φόβος, 5401), "fear," is rendered "terror" in Rom. 13:3; in 2 Cor. 5:11 and 1 Pet. 3:14, KJV (RV, "fear"). See FEAR, No. 1.

2. *phobētron* (φόβητρον, 5400), "that which causes fright, a terror," is translated "terrors" in Luke 21:11, RV (KJV, "fearful sights"). See FEAR, A, *Note.* For *ptoēsis,* See AMAZEMENT.

For **TESTAMENT** see COVENANT

TESTATOR

diatithēmi (διατίθημι, 1303), "to arrange, dispose," is used only in the middle voice in the NT; in Heb. 9:16, 17, the present participle with the article, lit., "the (one) making a testament (or covenant)," virtually a noun, "the testator" (the covenanting one); it is used of "making a covenant" in 8:10 and 10:16 and Acts 3:25. In "covenant-making," the sacrifice of a victim was customary (Gen. 15:10; Jer. 34:18, 19). He who "made a covenant" did so at the cost of a life. While the terminology in Heb. 9:16, 17 has the appearance of being appropriate to the circumstances of making a will, there is excellent reason for adhering to the meaning "covenant-making." The rendering "the death of the testator" would make Christ a Testator, which He was not. He did not die simply that the terms of a testamentary disposition might be fulfilled for the heirs. Here He who is "the Mediator of a new covenant" (v. 15) is Himself the Victim whose death was necessary. The idea of "making a will" destroys the argument of v. 18. In spite of various advocacies of the idea of a will, the weight of evidence is confirmatory of what Hatch, in *Essays in Biblical Greek,* p. 48, says: "There can be little doubt that the word (*diathēkē*) must be invariably taken in this sense of 'covenant' in the NT, and especially in a book ... so impregnated with the language of the Sept. as the Epistle to the Hebrews" (see also Westcott, and W. F. Moulton). We may render somewhat literally thus: 'For where a covenant (is), a death (is) necessary to be brought in of the one covenanting; for a covenant over dead ones (victims) is sure, since never has it force when the one covenanting lives' [Christ being especially in view]. The writer is speaking from a Jewish point of view, not from that of the Greeks. "To adduce the fact that in the case of wills the death of the testator is the condition of validity, is, of course, no proof at all that a death is necessary to make a covenant valid .... To support his argument, proving the necessity of Christ's death, the writer adduces the general law that he who makes a covenant does so at the expense of life" (Marcus Dods). See APPOINT.

TESTIFY

1. *martureō* (μαρτυρέω, 3140), for which see WITNESS, is frequently rendered "to bear witness, to witness," in the RV, where KJV renders it "to testify," John 2:25; 3:11, 32; 5:39; 15:26; 21:24; 1 Cor. 15:15; Heb. 7:17; 11:4; 1 John 4:14; 5:9; 3 John 3. In the following, however, the RV, like the KJV, has the rendering "to testify," John 4:39, 44; 7:7; 13:21; Acts 26:5; Rev. 22:16, 18, 20.

2. *epimartureō* (ἐπιμαρτυρέω, 1957), "to bear witness to" (a strengthened form of No. 1), is rendered "testifying" in 1 Pet. 5:12.

3. *marturomai* (μαρτύρομαι, 3143), primarily, "to summon as witness," then, "to bear witness" (sometimes with the suggestion of solemn protestation), is rendered "to testify" in Acts 20:26, RV (KJV, "I take ... to record"); 26:22, in the best texts (some have No. 1), RV; Gal. 5:3; Eph. 4:17; 1 Thess. 2:11, in the best texts (some have No. 1), RV, "testifying" (KJV, "charged").

4. *diamarturomai* (διαμαρτύρομαι, 1263), "to testify or protest solemnly," an intensive form of No. 3, is translated "to testify" in Luke 16:28; Acts 2:40; 8:25; 10:42; 18:5; 20:21, 23, 24; 23:11; 28:23; 1 Thess. 4:6; Heb. 2:6; "to charge" in 1 Tim. 5:21; 2 Tim. 2:14; 4:8.

5. *promarturomai* (προμαρτύρομαι, 4303), "to testify beforehand," occurs in 1 Pet. 1:11, where the pronoun "it" should

be "He" (the "it" being due to the grammatically neuter form of *pneuma;* the personality of the Holy Spirit requires the masculine pronoun).

Note: In Rev. 22:18 some texts have *summartureō*, "to bear witness with." See WITNESS.

TESTIMONY

1. *marturion* (μαρτύριον, 3142), "a testimony, witness," is almost entirely translated "testimony" in both KJV and RV. The only place where both have "witness" is Acts 4:33. In Acts 7:44 and Jas. 5:3, the RV has "testimony" (KJV, "witness").

In 2 Thess. 1:10, "our testimony unto you," RV, refers to the fact that the missionaries, besides proclaiming the truths of the gospel, had borne witness to the power of these truths. *Kērugma*, "the thing preached, the message," is objective, having especially to do with the effect on the hearers; *marturion* is mainly subjective, having to do especially with the preacher's personal experience. In 1 Tim. 2:6 the RV is important, "the testimony (i.e., of the gospel) *to be borne* in its own times," i.e., in the times divinely appointed for it, namely, the present age, from Pentecost till the church is complete. In Rev. 15:5, in the phrase, "the temple of the tabernacle of the testimony in Heaven," the "testimony" is the witness to the rights of God, denied and refused on earth, but about to be vindicated by the exercise of the judgments under the pouring forth of the seven bowls or vials of divine retribution. See WITNESS.

2. *marturia* (μαρτυρία, 3141), "witness, evidence, testimony," is almost always rendered "witness" in the RV (for KJV, "testimony" in John 3:32, 33; 5:34; 8:17; 21:24, and always for KJV, "record," e.g., 1 John 5:10, 11), except in Acts 22:18 and in the Apocalypse, where both, with one exception, have "testimony," 1:2, 9; 6:9; 11:7; 12:11, 17; 19:10 (twice); 20:4 (KJV, "witness"). In 19:10, "the testimony of Jesus" is objective, the "testimony" or witness given to Him (cf. 1:2, 9; as to those who will bear it, see Rev. 12:17, RV). The statement "the testimony of Jesus is the spirit of prophecy," is to be understood in the light, e.g., of the "testimony" concerning Christ and Israel in the Psalms, which will be used by the godly Jewish remnant in the coming time of "Jacob's Trouble." All such "testimony" centers in and points to Christ. See WITNESS.

TETRARCH

A. Noun.

tetraarchēs (τετραάρχης, 5076), or *tetrarchēs* (τετράρχης, 5076) denotes "one of four rulers" (*tetra*, "four," *archē*, "rule"), properly, "the governor of the fourth part of a region"; hence, "a dependent princeling," or "any petty ruler" subordinate to kings or ethnarchs; in the NT, Herod Antipas, Matt. 14:1; Luke 3:19; 9:7; Acts 13:1.

B. Verb.

tetraarcheō (τετρααρχέω, 5075), or *tetrarcheō* (τετραρχέω, 5075), "to be a tetrarch," occurs in Luke 3:1 (thrice), of Herod Antipas, his brother Philip and Lysanias. Antipas and Philip each inherited a fourth part of his father's dominions. Inscriptions bear witness to the accuracy of Luke's details.

THANK, THANKS (Noun and Verb), THANKFUL, THANKFULNESS, THANKSGIVING, THANKWORTHY

A. Nouns.

1. *charis* (χάρις, 5485), for the meanings of which see GRACE, No. 1, is rendered "thank" in Luke 6:32, 33, 34; in 17:9, "doth he thank" is lit., "hath he thanks to"; it is rendered "thanks (be to God)" in Rom. 6:17, RV (KJV, "God be thanked"); "thanks" in 1 Cor. 15:57; in 1 Tim. 1:12 and 2 Tim. 1:3, "I thank" is, lit., "I have thanks"; "thankworthy," 1 Pet. 2:19, KJV (RV, "acceptable").

2. *eucharistia* (εὐχαριστία, 2169), *eu*, "well," *charizomai*, "to give freely" (Eng., "eucharist"), denotes (a) "gratitude," "thankfulness," Acts 24:3; (b) "giving of thanks, thanksgiving," 1 Cor. 14:16; 2 Cor. 4:15; 9:11, 12 (plur.); Eph. 5:4; Phil. 4:6; Col. 2:7; 4:2; 1 Thess. 3:9 ("thanks"); 1 Tim. 2:1 (plur.); 4:3, 4; Rev. 4:9, "thanks"; 7:12.

B. Verbs.

1. *eucharisteō* (εὐχαριστέω, 2168), akin to A, No. 2, "to give thanks," (a) is said of Christ, Matt. 15:36; 26:27; Mark 8:6; 14:23; Luke 22:17, 19; John 6:11, 23; 11:41; 1 Cor. 11:24; (b) of the Pharisee in Luke 18:11 in his selfcomplacent prayer; (c) is used by Paul at the beginning of all his epistles, except 2 Cor. (see, however, *eulogētos* in 1:3), Gal., 1 Tim., 2 Tim. (see, however, *charin echō*, 1:3), and Titus, (1) for his readers, Rom. 1:8; Eph. 1:16; Col. 1:3; 1 Thess. 1:2; 2 Thess. 1:3 (cf. 2:13); virtually so in Philem. 4; (2) for fellowship shown, Phil. 1:3; (3) for God's gifts to them, 1 Cor. 1:4; (d) is recorded (1) of Paul elsewhere, Acts 27:35; 28:15; Rom. 7:25; 1 Cor. 1:14; 14:18; (2) of Paul and others, Rom. 16:4; 1 Thess. 2:13; of himself, representatively, as a practice, 1 Cor. 10:30; (3) of others, Luke 17:16; Rom. 14:6 (twice); 1 Cor. 14:17; Rev. 11:17; (e) is used in admonitions to the saints, the Name of the Lord Jesus suggesting His character and example, Eph. 5:20; Col. 1:12; 3:17; 1 Thess. 5:18; (f) as the expression of a purpose, 2 Cor. 1:11, RV; (g) negatively of the ungodly, Rom. 1:21. "Thanksgiving" is the expression of joy Godward, and is therefore the fruit of the Spirit (Gal. 5:22); believers are encouraged to abound in it (e.g., Col. 2:7, and see C, below).

2. *exomologeō* (ἐξομολογέω, 1843), in the middle voice, signifies "to make acknowledgment," whether of sins (to confess), or in the honor of a person, as in Rom. 14:11; 15:9 (in

some mss. in Rev. 3:5); this is the significance in the Lord's address to the Father, "I thank (Thee)," in Matt. 11:25 and Luke 10:21, the meaning being "I make thankful confession" or "I make acknowledgment with praise." See CONFESS, No. 2, CONSENT, PROMISE.

3. *anthomologeomai* (ἀνθομολογέομαι, 437), "to acknowledge fully, to celebrate fully (*anti*) in praise with thanksgiving," is used of Anna in Luke 2:35. *Note:* For *homologeō*, rendered "giving thanks" in Heb. 13:15 (RV, "make confession"), See CONFESS, A, No. 1 (d).

C. Adjective.

eucharistos (εὐχάριστος, 2170), primarily, "gracious, agreeable" (as in the Sept., Prov. 11:16, of a wife, who brings glory to her husband), then "grateful, thankful," is so used in Col. 3:15.

THEATER

theatron (θέατρον, 2302), "a theater," was used also as "a place of assembly," Acts 19:29, 31; in 1 Cor. 4:9 it is used of "a show" or "spectacle." See SPECTACLE.

THEFT

1. *klopē* (κλοπή, 2829), akin to *kleptō*, "to steal," is used in the plural in Matt. 15:19; Mark 7:22.

2. *klemma* (κλέμμα, 2809), "a thing stolen," and so, "a theft," is used in the plural in Rev. 9:21. In the Sept., Gen. 31:39; Ex. 22:3, 4.

For **THICK** see GATHER, A, No. 8

THIEF, THIEVES

1. *kleptēs* (κλέπτης, 2812) is used (a) literally, Matt. 6:19, 20; 24:43; Luke 12:33, 39; John 10:1, 10; 12:6; 1 Cor. 6:10; 1 Pet. 4:15; (b) metaphorically of "false teachers," John 10:8; (c) figuratively, (1) of the personal coming of Christ, in a warning to a local church, with most of its members possessed of mere outward profession and defiled by the world, Rev. 3:3; in retributive intervention to overthrow the foes of God, 16:15; (2) of the Day of the Lord, in divine judgment upon the world, 2 Pet. 3:10 and 1 Thess. 5:2, 4; in v. 2, according to the order in the original "the word 'night' is not to be read with 'the day of the Lord,' but with 'thief,' i.e., there is no reference to the time of the coming, only to the manner of it. To avoid ambiguity the phrase may be paraphrased, 'so comes as a thief in the night comes.' The use of the present tense instead of the future emphasizes the certainty of the coming .... The unexpectedness of the coming of the thief, and the unpreparedness of those to whom he comes, are the essential elements in the figure; cf. the entirely different figure used in Matt. 25:1-13."

2. *lēstēs* (λῃστης, 3027) is frequently rendered "thieves" in the KJV, e.g., Matt. 21:13.

THIRD, THIRDLY

tritos (τρίτος, 5154) is used (a) as a noun, e.g., Luke 20:12, 31; in Rev. 8:7-12 and 9:15, 18, "the third part," lit., "the third"; (b) as an adverb, with the article, "the third time," e.g., Mark 14:41; John 21:17 (twice); without the article, lit., "a third time," e.g., John 21:14; 2 Cor. 12:14; 13:1; in enumerations, in Matt. 26:44, with *ek*, "from," lit., "from the third time" (the *ek* indicates the point of departure, especially in a succession of events, cf. John 9:24; 2 Pet. 2:8); absolutely, in the accusative neuter, in 1 Cor. 12:28, "thirdly"; (c) as an adjective (its primary use), e.g., in the phrase the third heaven, 2 Cor. 12:2 [cf. HEAVEN, A, No. 1 (c), PARADISE]; in the phrase "the third hour," Matt. 20:3; Mark 15:25; Acts 2:15 ("... of the day"); 23:23 ("... of the night"); in a phrase with *hemera*, "a day," "on the third day" (i.e., "the next day but one"), e.g., Matt. 16:21; Luke 24:46; Acts 10:40; in this connection the idiom "three days and three nights," Matt. 12:40, is explained by ref to 1 Sam. 30:12, 13, and Esth. 4:16 with 5:1; in Mark 9:31 and 10:34, the RV, "after three days," follows the texts which have this phrase, the KJV, "the third day," those which have the same phrase as in Matt. 16:21, etc.

THIRST (Noun and Verb), THIRSTY (to be), ATHIRST

A. Noun.

dipsos (δίψος, 1373), "thirst" (cf. Eng., "dipsomania"), occurs in 2 Cor. 11:27.

B. Verb.

dipsaō (διψάω, 1372) is used (a) in the natural sense, e.g., Matt. 25:35, 37, 42; in v. 44, "athirst" (lit., "thirsting"); John 4:13, 15; 19:28; Rom. 12:20; 1 Cor. 4:11; Rev. 7:16; (b) figuratively, of spiritual "thirst," Matt. 5:6; John 4:14; 6:35; 7:37; in Rev. 21:6 and 22:17, "that is athirst."

THORN, THORNS (of)

A. Nouns.

1. *akantha* (ἄκανθα, 173), "a brier, a thorn" (from *akē*, "a point"), is always used in the plural in the NT, Matt. 7:16 and parallel passage in Luke 6:44; Matt. 13:7 (twice), 22 and parallels in Mark and Luke; in Matt. 27:29 and John 19:2, of the crown of "thorns" placed on Christ's head (see also B) in mock imitation of the garlands worn by emperors. They were the effects of the divine curse on the ground (Gen. 3:18; contrast Isa. 55:13). The "thorns" of the crown plaited by the soldiers, are usually identified with those of the *Zizyphus spina Christi*, some 20 feet high or more, fringing the Jordan and abundant in Palestine; its twigs are flexible. Another species, however, the Arabian *qundaul*, crowns of which are plaited

and sold in Jerusalem as representatives of Christ's crown, seems likely to be the one referred to. The branches are easily woven and adapted to the torture intended. The word *akantha* occurs also in Heb. 6:8.

2. *skolops* (σκόλοψ, 4647) originally denoted "anything pointed," e.g., "a stake"; in Hellenistic vernacular, "a thorn" (so the Sept., in Num. 33:55; Ezek. 28:24; Hos. 2:6.), 2 Cor. 12:7, of the apostle's "thorn in the flesh"; his language indicates that it was physical, painful, humiliating; it was also the effect of divinely permitted Satanic antagonism; the verbs rendered "that I should (not) be exalted overmuch" (RV) and "to buffet" are in the present tense, signifying recurrent action, indicating a constantly repeated attack. Lightfoot interprets it as "a stake driven through the flesh," and Ramsay agrees with this. Most commentators adhere to the rendering "thorn." Field says "there is no doubt that the Alexandrine use of *skolops* for thorn is here intended, and that the ordinary meaning of 'stake' must be rejected." What is stressed is not the metaphorical size, but the acuteness of the suffering and its effects. Attempts to connect this with the circumstances of Acts 14:19 and Gal. 4:13 are speculative.

B. Adjective.

akanthinos (ἀκάνθινος, 174), "of thorns" (from A, No. 1), is used in Mark 15:17 and John 19:5. In the Sept., Isa. 34:13.

THOUGHT (Noun)

1. *epinoia* (ἐπίνοια, 1963), "a thought by way of a design" (akin to *epinoeō*, "to contrive," *epi*, intensive, *noeō*, "to consider"), is used in Acts 8:22. In the Sept.. Jer. 20:10.

2. *noēma* (νόημα, 3540), "a purpose, device of the mind" (akin to *noeō*, see No. 1), is rendered "thought" in 2 Cor. 10:5, "thoughts" in Phil. 4:7, RV: see DEVICE, No. 2.

3. *dianoēma* (διανόημα, 1270), "a thought," occurs in Luke 11:17, where the sense is that of "machinations."

4. *enthumēsis* (ἐνθύμησις, 1761), is translated "thoughts" in Matt. 9:4; 12:25; Heb. 4:12: see DEVICE, No. 1.

5. *logismos* (λογισμός, 3053) is translated "thoughts" in Rom. 2:15: see IMAGINATION, No. 1.

6. *dialogismos* (διαλογισμός, 1261), "reasoning," is translated "thoughts" in Matt. 15:19; Mark 7:21; Luke 2:35; 6:8; in 5:22, KJV, RV, "reasonings"; in 9:47, KJV, RV, "reasoning," and 24:38, KJV, RV, "reasonings"; so 1 Cor. 3:20; in Luke 9:46, KJV and RV, "reasoning"; "thoughts" in Jas. 2:4, KJV and RV. See IMAGINATION, REASONING.

THOUGHT (to take)

1. *merimnaō* (μεριμνάω, 3309) denotes "to be anxious, careful."

2. *promerimnaō* (προμεριμνάω, 4305), "to be anxious beforehand," occurs in Mark 13:11.

3. *pronoeō* (προνοέω, 4306), "to provide," is rendered "to take thought" in Rom. 12:17 and 2 Cor. 8:21. See PROVIDE.

THREATEN

1. *apeileō* (ἀπειλέω, 546) is used of Christ, negatively, in 1 Pet. 2:23; in the middle voice, Acts 4:17, where some texts have the noun *apeilē* in addition, hence the KJV, "let us straitly threaten," lit., "let us threaten ... with threatening (see THREATENING).

2. *prosapeileō* (προσαπειλέω, 4324), "to threaten further" (*pros*, and No. 1), occurs in the middle voice in Acts 4:21.

THREATENING

apeilē (ἀπειλή, 547), akin to *apeileō* (see above), occurs in Acts 4:29 (in some mss. v. 17); 9:1; Eph. 6:9.

THREE

treis (τρεῖς, 5140) is regarded by many as a number sometimes symbolically indicating fullness of testimony or manifestation, as in the three persons in the Godhead, cf. 1 Tim. 5:19; Heb. 10:28; the mention in 1 John 5:7 is in a verse which forms no part of the original; no Greek ms. earlier than the 14th century contained it; no version earlier than the 5th cent. in any other language contains it, nor is it quoted by any of the Greek or Latin "Fathers" in their writings on the Trinity. That there are those who bear witness in Heaven is not borne out by any other Scripture. It must be regarded as the interpolation of a copyist.

In Mark 9:31 and 10:34 the best texts have *meta treis hēmeras*, "after three days," which idiomatically expresses the same thing as *tē tritē hēmera*, "on the third day," which some texts have here, as, e.g., the phrase "the third day" in Matt. 17:23; 20:19; Luke 9:22; 18:33, where the repetition of the article lends stress to the number, lit., "the day the third"; 24:7, 46; Acts 10:40. For THREE TIMES see THRICE.

THRICE

tris (τρίς, 5151) occurs in Matt. 26:34, 75 and parallel passages; in Acts 10:16 and 11:10, preceded by *epi*, "up to"; 2 Cor. 11:25 (twice); 12:8.

THRONE

1. *thronos* (θρόνος, 2362), "a throne, a seat of authority," is used of the "throne" (a) of God, e.g., Heb. 4:16, "the throne of grace," i.e., from which grace proceeds; 8:1; 12:2; Rev. 1:4; 3:21 (2nd part); 4:2 (twice); 5:1; frequently in Rev.; in 20:12, in the best texts, "the throne" (some have *Theos*, "God," KJV); cf. 21:3; Matt. 5:34; 23:22; Acts 7:49; (b) of Christ, e.g. Heb. 1:8; Rev. 3:21 (1st part); 22:3; His seat of authority in the Millennium, Matt. 19:28 (1st part); (c) by metonymy for angelic powers, Col. 1:16; (d) of the Apostles in millennial authority, Matt. 19:28 (2nd part); Luke 22:30; (e) of the

elders in the heavenly vision, Rev. 4:4 (2nd and 3rd parts), RV, "thrones" (KJV, "seats"); so 11:16; (f) of David, Luke 1:32; Acts 2:30; (g) of Satan, Rev. 2:13, RV, "throne" (KJV, "seat"); (h) of "the beast," the final and federal head of the revived Roman Empire, Rev. 13:2; 16:10.

2. *bēma* (βῆμα, 968), for which see JUDGMENT SEAT, is used of the throne or tribunal of Herod, Acts 12:21.

THRUST

1. *ballo* (βάλλω, 906), for which cf. THROW, No. 1, is rendered "to thrust" in John 20:25, 27, KJV (RV, put); Acts 16:24, KJV (RV, "cast"); so Rev. 14:16, 19.

2. *ekballo* (ἐκβάλλω, 1544), "to cast out," is rendered "thrust ... out" in Luke 4:29, KJV (RV, "cast ... forth"); so 13:28 and Acts 16:37.

3. *apotheo* (ἀποπνίγω, 638), "to thrust away," is used in the middle voice, "to thrust away from oneself," and translated "thrust away" in Acts 7:27, 39; "thrust ... from," 13:46, RV (KJV, "put ... from"); "having thrust from them," 1 Tim. 1:19, RV (KJV, "having put away").

4. *katatoxeuo* (κατατοξεύω, 2700), "to strike down with an arrow, shoot dead," occurs in Heb. 12:20 in some mss. (in a quotation from Ex. 19:13, Sept.).

Notes: (1) In Matt. 11:23 and Luke 10:15 the best texts have *katabaino*, "to go down" (RV), instead of *katabibazo*, in the passive voice, "to be thrust down or brought down" (KJV). (2) In Acts 27:39, KJV, *exotheo*, "to drive out," is rendered "to thrust in," RV, "drive (the ship) upon (it [i.e., the beach])." (3) In Rev. 14:15, 18, KJV, *pempo*, to send (RV, "send forth"), is translated "thrust in."

THUNDER, THUNDERING

brontē (βροντή, 1027): in Mark 3:17 "sons of thunder" is the interpretation of Boanerges, the name applied by the Lord to James and John; their fiery disposition is seen in 9:38 and Luke 9:54; perhaps in the case of James it led to his execution. The name and its interpretation have caused much difficulty; some suggest the meaning "the twins." It is however most probably the equivalent of the Aramaic *bene regesh*, "sons of tumult"; the latter of the two words was no doubt used of "thunder" in Palestinian Aramaic; hence the meaning "the sons of thunder"; the cognate Hebrew word *ragash*, "to rage," is used in Ps. 2:1 and there only. In John 12:29 *bronte* is used with *ginomai*, "to take place," and rendered "it had thundered"; lit., "there was thunder"; elsewhere, Rev. 4:5; 6:1; 8:5; 10:3, 4; 11:19; 14:2; 16:18; 19:6.

TIDINGS

A. Noun.

phasis (φάσις, 5334), akin to *phēmi*, "to speak," denotes "information," especially against fraud or other delinquency, and is rendered "tidings" in Acts 21:31.

Note: In Acts 11:22, KJV, *logos*, "a word, a report" (RV), is rendered "tidings."

B. Verbs.

1. *euangelizō* (εὐαγγελίζω, 2097) is used of any message designed to cheer those who receive it; it is rendered "to bring, declare, preach," or "show good or glad tidings," e.g., Luke 1:19; 2:10; 3:18, RV; 4:43, RV; 7:22, RV; 8:1; Acts 8:12 and 10:36, RV; 14:15, RV; in 1 Thess. 3:6, "brought us glad (KJV, good) tidings"; in Heb. 4:2, RV, "we have had good tidings preached"; similarly, 4:6; in 1 Pet. 1:25 *rhēma*, "a word," is coupled with this verb, "the word of good tidings which was preached," RV (KJV, "the word which by the gospel is preached"). See PREACH, A, No. 1.

2. *anangellō* (ἀναγγέλλω, 312), "to announce, declare," is rendered "(no) tidings ... came," in Rom. 15:21, RV, KJV, "was (not) spoken of.

TIE

1. *deō* (δέω, 1210), "to bind," is rendered "to tie" in Matt. 21:2; Mark 11:2, 4; Luke 19:30. See BIND.

2. *proteinō* (προτείνω, 4385), "to stretch out or forth," is used of preparations for scourging, Acts 22:25, RV, "had tied (him) up" (KJV, "bound").

TIP

akron (ἄκρον, 206), "the top, an extremity," is translated "tip" in Luke 16:24. See END, C, *Note* (6), TOP.

TITHE (Verb)

1. *dekatoō* (δεκατόω, 1183), from *dekatos*, "tenth," in the active voice denotes "to take tithes of," Heb. 7:6, RV, "hath taken (KJV, received) tithes"; in the passive, "to pay tithes," 7:9, RV, "hath paid (KJV, 'payed') tithes." In the Sept., Neh. 10:37.

2. *apodekatoō* (ἀποδεκατόω, 586) denotes (a) "to tithe" (*apo*, "from," *dekatos*, "tenth"), Matt. 23:23 (KJV, "pay tithe of"); Luke 11:42; in Luke 18:12 (where the best texts have the alternative form *apodekateuō*), "I give tithes"; (b) "to exact tithes" from Heb. 7:5.

3. *apodekateuō* (ἀποδεκατόω, 586v), "to give tithes," in Luke 18:12 (some texts have No. 2).

Note: Heb. 7:4-9 shows the superiority of the Melchizedek priesthood to the Levitical, in that (1) Abraham, the ancestor of the Levites, paid "tithes" to Melchizedek (Gen. 14:20); (2) Melchizedek, whose genealogy is outside that of the Levites, took "tithes" of Abraham, the recipient himself of the divine promises; (3) whereas death is the natural lot of those who receive "tithes," the death of Melchizedek is not recorded; (4) the Levites who received "tithes" virtually paid them through Abraham to Melchizedek.

TITLE

titlos (τίτλος, 5102), from Latin *titulus*, is used of the inscription above the cross of Christ, John 19:19, 20. See SUPERSCRIPTION.

TOGETHER

1. *homou* (ὁμοῦ, 3674), used in connection with place, in John 21:2; Acts 2:1 (in the best texts), RV, "together" (KJV, "with one accord," translating the inferior reading *homothumadon:* see ACCORD, A), is used without the idea of place in John 4:36; 20:4.

2. *hama* (ἅμα, 260), "at once," is translated "together" in Rom. 3:12; 1 Thess. 4:17; 5:10.

Notes: (1) In 1 Thess. 5:11, KJV, *allēlous*, "one another" (RV), is rendered "yourselves together"; in Luke 23:12, KJV, *meta allēlōn*, lit., "with one another," is rendered "together" (RV, "with each other"); so in Luke 24:14, KJV, *pros allēlous*, RV, "with each other." (2) In the following, "together" translates the phrase *epi to auto*, lit., "to (upon, or for) the same," Matt. 22:34; Luke 17:35; Acts 1:15; 2:44 (3:1, in some texts); 4:26; 1 Cor. 7:5; 14:23, RV (3) In Acts 14:1, it translates *kata to auto*, "at the same"; it may mean "in the same way" (i.e., as they had entered the synagogue at Pisidian Antioch). (4) In many cases "together" forms part of another word.

TOIL (Verb and Noun)

A. Verbs.

1. *kopiaō* (κοπιάω, 2872), "to be weary, to labor," is rendered "to toil" in Matt. 6:28; Luke 5:5 (12:27), in some mss.); in 1 Cor. 4:12, RV (KJV, "we labor"). See LABOR

2. *basanizō* (βασανίζω, 928), primarily, "to rub on the touchstone, to put to the test," then, "to examine by torture" (*basanos*, "touchstone, torment"), hence denotes "to torture, torment, distress"; in the passive voice it is rendered "toiling" in Mark 6:48, KJV (RV, "distressed"). See PAIN, TORMENT, VEX.

B. Noun.

kopos (κόπος, 2873), "labor, trouble," is rendered "toil" in Rev. 2:2, RV (KJV, "labor"). See LABOR.

TOKEN

1. *semeion* (σημεῖον, 4592), "a sign, token or indication," is translated "token" in 2 Thess. 3:17, of writing of the closing salutations, the apostle using the pen himself instead of his amanuensis, his autograph attesting the authenticity of his Epistles. See MIRACLE, SIGN.

2. *sussēmon* (σύσσημον, 4953), "a fixed sign or signal, agreed upon with others" (*sun*, "with"), is used in Mark 14:44, "a token." In the Sept., Judg. 20:38, 40; Isa. 5:26; 49:22; 62:10.

3. *endeigma* (ἔνδειγμα, 1730), "a plain token, a proof" (akin to *endeiknumi*, "to point out, prove"), is used in 2 Thess. 1:5 "a manifest token," said of the patient endurance and faith of the persecuted saints at Thessalonica, affording proof to themselves of their new life, and a guarantee of the vindication by God of both Himself and them (see No. 4, *Note*).

4. *endeixis* (ἔνδειξις, 1732), "a pointing out, showing forth," is rendered "evident token" in Phil. 1:28. See DECLARE, B, PROOF. Cf. *apodeixis*, 1 Cor. 2:4.

Note: No. 4 refers to the act or process of proving, No. 3 to the thing proved. While the two passages, Phil. 1:28 and 2 Thess. 1:5, contain similar ideas, *endeigma* indicates the "token" as acknowledged by those referred to; *endeixis* points more especially to the inherent veracity of the "token."

TOLERABLE

anektos (ἀνεκτός, 414) (akin to *anechō*, in the middle voice, "to endure," see ENDURE, No. 5) is used in its comparative form, *anektoteros*, in Matt. 10:15; 11:22, 24; Luke 10:12, 14; some texts have it in Mark 6:11.

For **TOLL** see CUSTOM (TOLL)

TOMB

1. *mnēmeion* (μνημεῖον, 3419) is almost invariably rendered "tomb" or "tombs" in the RV, never "grave," sometimes "sepulchre"; in the KJV, "tomb" in Matt. 8:28; 27:60; Mark 5:2; 6:29. See GRAVE No. 1, SEPULCHRE.

2. *mnēma* (μνῆμα, 3418), rendered "tombs" in Mark 5:3, 5; Luke 8:27: see GRAVE, No. 2, SEPULCHRE.

3. *taphos* (τάφος, 5028), akin to *thaptō*, "to bury," is translated "tombs" in Matt. 23:29; elsewhere "sepulchre." See SEPULCHRE.

TONGUE (-S)

A. Nouns.

1. *glōssa* (γλῶσσα, 1100) is used of (1) the "tongues . . . like as of fire" which appeared at Pentecost; (2) "the tongue," as an organ of speech, e.g., Mark 7:33; Rom. 3:13; 14:11; 1 Cor. 14:9; Phil. 2:11; Jas. 1:26; 3:5, 6, 8; 1 Pet. 3:10; 1 John 3:18; Rev. 16:10; (3) (a) "a language," coupled with *phulē*, "a tribe," *laos*, "a people," *ethnos*, "a nation," seven times in the Apocalypse, 5:9; 7:9; 10:11; 11:9; 13:7; 14:6; 17:15; (b) "the supernatural gift of speaking in another language without its having been learnt"; in Acts 2:4-13 the circumstances are recorded from the viewpoint of the hearers; to those in whose language the

utterances were made it appeared as a supernatural phenomenon; to others, the stammering of drunkards; what was uttered was not addressed primarily to the audience but consisted in recounting "the mighty works of God"; cf. 2:46; in 1 Cor., chapters 12 and 14, the use of the gift of "tongues" is mentioned as exercised in the gatherings of local churches; 12:10 speaks of the gift in general terms, and couples with it that of "the interpretation of tongues"; chapt. 14 gives instruction concerning the use of the gift, the paramount object being the edification of the church; unless the "tongue" was interpreted the speaker would speak "not unto men, but unto God," v. 2; he would edify himself alone, v. 4, unless he interpreted, v. 5, in which case his interpretation would be of the same value as the superior gift of prophesying, as he would edify the church, vv. 4-6; he must pray that he may interpret, v. 13; if there were no interpreter, he must keep silence, v. 28, for all things were to be done "unto edifying," v. 26. "If I come ... speaking with tongues, what shall I profit you," says the apostle (expressing the great object in all oral ministry), "unless I speak to you either by way of revelation, or of knowledge, or of prophesying, or of teaching?" (v. 6). "Tongues" were for a sign, not to believers, but to unbelievers, v. 22, and especially to unbelieving Jews (see v. 21): cf. the passages in the Acts.

There is no evidence of the continuance of this gift after apostolic times nor indeed in the later times of the apostles themselves; this provides confirmation of the fulfillment in this way of 1 Cor. 13:8, that this gift would cease in the churches, just as would "prophecies" and "knowledge" in the sense of knowledge received by immediate supernatural power (cf. 14:6). The completion of the Holy Scriptures has provided the churches with all that is necessary for individual and collective guidance, instruction, and edification.

2. *dialektos* (διάλεκτος, 1258), "language" (Eng., "dialect"), is rendered "tongue" in the KJV of Acts 1:19; 2:6, 8; 21:40; 22:2; 26:14. See LANGUAGE.

B. Adjective.

heteroglōssos (ἑτερόγλωσσος, 2084) is rendered "strange tongues" in 1 Cor. 14:21, RV (*heteros*, "another of a different sort"—see ANOTHER—and A, No. 1), KJV, other tongues.

C. Adverb.

hebraisti (or *ebraisti*, Westcott and Hort) (Ἑβραϊστί, 1447) denotes (a) "in Hebrew," Rev. 9:11, RV (KJV, "in the Hebrew tongue"); so 16:16; (b) in the Aramaic vernacular of Palestine, John 5:2, KJV, "in the Hebrew tongue" (RV, "in Hebrew"); in 19:13, 17, KJV, "in the Hebrew" (RV, "in Hebrew"); in v. 20, KJV and RV, "in Hebrew"; in 20:16, RV only, "in Hebrew (Rabboni)."

Note: Cf. *Hellēnisti*, "in Greek," John 19:20, RV; Acts 21:37, "Greek."

TOP

A. Noun.

akron (ἄκρον, 206), for which see TIP, is used of Jacob's staff, Heb. 11:21.

B. Phrases.

Note: In Matt. 27:51 and Mark 15:38, *apo anōthen*, "from the top" (lit., "from above"), is used of the upper part of the Temple veil. In John 19:23, the different phrase *ek tōn anōthen* is used of the weaving of the Lord's garment (the *chitōn:* see CLOTHING), lit., "from the parts above."

TORCH

lampas (λαμπάς, 2985), "a torch," is used in the plur. and translated "torches" in John 18:3; in Rev. 8:10, RV, "torch" (KJV, "lamp"). See LAMP.

TORMENT (Noun and Verb)

A. Nouns.

1. *basanismos* (βασανισμός, 929), akin to *basanizō* (see TOIL, No. 2), is used of divine judgments in Rev. 9:5; 14:11; 18:7, 10, 15.

2. *basanos* (βάσανος, 931), primarily "a touchstone," employed in testing metals, hence, "torment," is used (a) of physical diseases, Matt. 4:24: (b) of a condition of retribution in Hades, Luke 16:23, 28.

Note: In 1 John 4:18, KJV, *kolasis*, "punishment" (RV), is rendered "torment." See PUNISHMENT, No. 3.

B. Verbs.

1. *basanizō* (βασανίζω, 928), for which see TOIL, No. 2, is translated "to torment," (a) of sickness, Matt. 8:6; (b) of the doom of evil spirits, Mark 5:7; Luke 8:28; (c) of retributive judgments upon impenitent mankind at the close of this age, Rev. 9:5; 11:10; (d) upon those who worship the Beast and his image and receive the mark of his name, 14:10; (e) of the doom of Satan and his agents, 20:10.

2. *kakoucheō* (κακουχέω, 2558), "to treat evilly," in the passive voice is translated "tormented" in Heb. 11:37, KJV (RV, "evil entreated"). See SUFFER, No. 6.

3. *odunaō* (ὀδυνάω, 3600), for which see ANGUISH, B, No. 3, in the passive voice is rendered "I am (thou art) tormented" in Luke 16:24, 25, KJV.

TORMENTOR

basanistēs (βασανιστής, 930), properly, "a torturer" (akin to *basanizo*, see TORMENT, B), "one who elicits information by torture," is used of jailors, Matt. 18:34.

TORTURE (Verb)

tumpanizō (τυμπανίζω, 5178) primarily denotes "to beat a drum" (*tumpanon*, "a kettledrum," Eng., "tympanal," "tympanitis," "tympanum"), hence, "to torture by beating, to beat to death," Heb. 11:35. In the Sept., 1 Sam. 21:13, "(David) drummed (upon the doors of the city)." The tympanum as an instrument of "torture" seems to have been a wheel-shaped frame upon which criminals were stretched and beaten with clubs or thongs.

TOUCH (Verb)

1. *haptō* (ἅπτω, 681), primarily, "to fasten to," hence, of fire, "to kindle," denotes, in the middle voice (a) "to touch," e.g., Matt. 8:3, 15; 9:20, 21, 29; (b) "to cling to, lay hold of," John 20:17; here the Lord's prohibition as to clinging to Him was indicative of the fact that communion with Him would, after His ascension, be by faith, through the Spirit; (c) "to have carnal intercourse with a woman," 1 Cor. 7:1; (d) "to have fellowship and association with unbelievers," 2 Cor. 6:17; (e) (negatively) "to adhere to certain Levitical and ceremonial ordinances," in order to avoid contracting external defilement, or to practice rigorous asceticism, all such abstentions being of "no value against the indulgence of the flesh," Col. 2:21, KJV (RV, "handle"); (f) "to assault," in order to sever the vital union between Christ and the believer, said of the attack of the Evil One, 1 John 5:18. See LIGHT.

2. *thinganō* (θιγγάνω, 2345), "to touch," a lighter term than No. 1, though Heb. 11:28 approximates to it, in expressing the action of the Destroyer of the Egyptian firstborn; in Heb. 12:20 it signifies "to touch," and is not to be interpreted by Ps. 104:32, "He toucheth (No. 1 in the Sept.) the hills and they smoke"; in Col. 2:21, RV (KJV, handle).

3. *prospsauō* (προσψαύω, 4379), "to touch upon, to touch slightly," occurs in Luke 11:46.

4. *psēlaphaō* (ψηλαφάω, 5584), "to feel, to handle," is rendered "that might be touched" in Heb. 12:18. See FEEL, No. 3.

5. *katagō* (κατάγω, 2609), to bring down, is used of bringing a ship to land in Acts 27:3.

6. *sumpatheo* (συμπαθέω, 4834), for which see COMPASSION, A, No. 3, is rendered "be touched with" in Heb. 4:15.

7. *paraballō* (παραβάλλω, 3846) is rendered "touched at" in Acts 20:15, RV.

TOWER

purgos (πύργος, 4444) is used of "a watchtower in a vineyard," Matt. 21:33; Mark 12:1; probably, too, in Luke 14:28 (cf. Isa. 5:2); in Luke 13:4, of the "tower in Siloam," the modern Silwan, which is built on a steep escarpment of rock.

TOWN CLERK

grammateus (γραμματεύς, 1122), "a writer, scribe," is used in Acts 19:35 of a state "clerk," an important official, variously designated, according to inscriptions found in Graeco-Asiatic cities. He was responsible for the form of decrees first approved by the Senate, then sent for approval in the popular assembly, in which he often presided. The decrees having been passed, he sealed them with the public seal in the presence of witnesses. Such an assembly frequently met in the theater. The Roman administration viewed any irregular or unruly assembly as a grave and even capital offense, as tending to strengthen among the people the consciousness of their power and the desire to exercise it. In the circumstances at Ephesus the town clerk feared that he might himself be held responsible for the irregular gathering. See SCRIBE.

TRACE

A. Verb.

parakoloutheō (παρακολουθέω, 3877), "to follow up," is used of investigating or "tracing" a course of events, Luke 1:3, where the writer, humbly differentiating himself from those who possessed an essential apostolic qualification, declares that he "traced the course of all things" (RV) about which he was writing (KJV, "having had ... understanding, etc.").

B. Adjective.

anexichniastos (ἀνεξιχνίαστος, 421) signifies "that cannot be traced out" (*a*, negative, *ex*, for *ek*, "out," *ichnos*, "a track"), is rendered "past tracing out" in Rom. 11:33, RV (KJV, "past finding out"); in Eph. 3:8, "unsearchable." See UNSEARCHABLE. In the Sept., Job 5:9; 9:10; 34:24.

TRADITION

paradosis (παράδοσις, 3862), "a handing down or on" (akin to *paradidōmi*, "to hand over, deliver"), denotes "a tradition," and hence, by metonymy, (a) "the teachings of the rabbis," interpretations of the Law, which was thereby made void in practice, Matt. 15:2, 3, 6; Mark 7:3, 5, 8, 9, 13; Gal. 1:14; Col. 2:8; (b) of "apostolic teaching," 1 Cor. 11:2, RV, "traditions" (KJV, "ordinances"), of instructions concerning the gatherings of believers (instructions of wider scope than ordinances in the limited sense); in 2 Thess. 2:15, of Christian doctrine in general, where the apostle's use of the word constitutes a denial that what he preached originated with himself, and a claim for its divine authority (cf. *paralambanō*, "to receive," 1 Cor. 11:23; 15:3); in 2 Thess. 3:6, it is used of instructions concerning everyday conduct.

For **TRAIN**, Titus 2:4, RV, see SOBER, B, No. 3

TRAITOR

prodotēs (προδότης, 4273) denotes "a betrayer, traitor"; the latter term is assigned to Judas, virtually as a title, in Luke 6:16; in 2 Tim. 3:4 it occurs in a list of evil characters, foretold as abounding in the last days. See BETRAY, B.

TRAMPLE

katapateō (καταπατέω, 2662), "to tread down, trample under foot," is rendered "trample in Matt. 7:6. See TREAD, No. 2.

TRANCE

ekstasis (ἔκστασις, 1611), for which see AMAZE, A, No. 1, denotes "a trance" in Acts 10:10; 11:5; 22:17, a condition in which ordinary consciousness and the perception of natural circumstances were withheld, and the soul was susceptible only to the vision imparted by God.

For **TRANQUIL**, 1 Tim. 2:2, RV, see QUIET, No. 1

For **TRANSFER** (in a figure) see FASHION, C, No. 1, and FIGURE, *Note* (2).

TRANSFIGURE

metamorphoō (μεταμορφόω, 3339), "to change into another form" (*meta*, implying change, and *morphē*, "form:" see FORM, No. 1), is used in the passive voice (a) of Christ's "transfiguration," Matt. 17:2; Mark 9:2; Luke (in 9:29) avoids this term, which might have suggested to gentile readers the metamorphoses of heathen gods, and uses the phrase *egeneto heteron*, "was altered," lit., "became (*ginomai*) different (*heteros*)"; (b) of believers, Rom. 12:2, "be ye transformed," the obligation being to undergo a complete change which, under the power of God, will find expression in character and conduct; *morphē* lays stress on the inward change, *schēma* (see the preceding verb in that verse, *suschēmatizo*) lays stress on the outward (see FASHION, No. 3, FORM, No. 2); the present continuous tenses indicate a process; 2 Cor. 3:18 describes believers as being "transformed (RV) into the same image" (i.e., of Christ in all His moral excellencies), the change being effected by the Holy Spirit.

TRANSFORM

1. *metamorphoō* (μεταμορφόω, 3339) is rendered "transformed" in Rom. 12:2: see TRANSFIGURE.

2. *metaschēmatizo* (μετασχηματίζω, 3345) in the passive voice is rendered "to be transformed" in the KJV of 2 Cor. 11:13, 14, 15: see FASHION, C, No. 1.

TRANSGRESS, TRANSGRESSION

A. Verbs.

1. *parabainō* (παραβαίνω, 3845), lit., "to go aside" (*para*), hence "to go beyond," is chiefly used metaphorically of "transgressing" the tradition of the elders, Matt. 15:2; the commandment of God, 15:3; in Acts 1:25, of Judas, KJV, "by transgression fell" (RV, "fell away"); in 2 John 9 some texts have this verb (KJV, "transgresseth"), the best have *proago* (see GO, No. 10).

2. *huperbainō* (ὑπερβαίνω, 5233), lit., "to go over" (*huper*), used metaphorically and rendered "transgress" in 1 Thess. 4:6 (KJV, "go beyond"), i.e., of "overstepping" the limits separating chastity from licentiousness, sanctification from sin..

3. *parerchomai* (παρέρχομαι, 3928), "to come by" (*para*, "by," *erchomai*, "to come"), "pass over," and hence, metaphorically, "to transgress," is so used in Luke 15:29.

B. Nouns.

1. *parabasis* (παράβασις, 3847), akin to A, No. 1, primarily "a going aside," then, "an overstepping," is used metaphorically to denote "transgression" (always of a breach of law): (a) of Adam, Rom. 5:14; (b) of Eve, 1 Tim. 2:14; (c) negatively, where there is no law, since "transgression" implies the violation of law, none having been enacted between Adam's "transgression" and those under the Law, Rom. 4:15; (d) of "transgressions" of the Law, Gal. 3:19, where the statement "it was added because of transgressions" is best understood according to Rom. 4:15; 5:13 and 5:20; the Law does not make men sinners, but makes them "transgressors"; hence sin becomes "exceeding sinful," Rom. 7:7, 13. Conscience thus had a standard external to itself; by the Law men are taught their inability to yield complete obedience to God, that thereby they may become convinced of their need of a Savior; in Rom. 2:23, RV, "transgression (of the Law)," KJV, "breaking (the Law)"; Heb. 2:2; 9:15.

2. *paranomia* (παρανομία, 3892), "lawbreaking" (*para*, "contrary to," *nomos*, "law"), is rendered "transgression" in 2 Pet. 2:16, RV (KJV, "iniquity").

Note: In 1 John 3:4 (1st part), KJV, *poieō*, "to do," with *anomia*, "lawlessness," is rendered "transgresseth … the law" (RV, "doeth … lawlessness"); in the 2nd part *anomia* alone is rendered "transgression of the law," KJV (RV, "lawlessness").

TRANSGRESSOR

1. *parabatēs* (παραβάτης, 3848), lit. and primarily, "one who stands beside," then, "one who oversteps the prescribed limit, a transgressor" (akin to *parabainō*, "to transgress," see above); so Rom. 2:25, RV (KJV, "a breaker"); v. 27, RV, "a transgressor" (KJV, "dost transgress"); Gal. 2:18; Jas. 2:9, 11.

Note: Hamartolōs, "a sinner, one who misses the mark," is applicable to all men without distinction; *parabatēs* stresses the positive side of sin, and is applicable to those who received the Law.

2. *anomos* (ἄνομος, 459), "without law" (*a-*, negative), is translated "transgressors" in Luke 22:37 (in some texts, Mark 15:28), in a quotation from Isa. 53:12. See LAW, C, No. 3, LAWLESS, A.

TRANSLATE, TRANSLATION

A. Verbs.

1. *methistēmi* (μεθίστημι, 3179), or *methistanō* (μεθιστάνω, 3179), "to change, remove" (*meta*, implying "change," *histēmi*, "to cause to stand"), is rendered "hath translated" in Col. 1:13.

2. *metatithēmi* (μετατίθημι, 3346), "to transfer to another place" (*meta*, see above, *tithēmi*, "to put"), is rendered "to translate" in Heb. 11:5 (twice).

B. Noun.

metathesis (μετάθεσις, 3331), "a change of position" (akin to A, No. 2), is rendered "translation" in Heb. 11:5.

For **TRANSPARENT**, Rev. 21:21, see DAWN, A, No. 2, *Note*

TRAP

thēra (θήρα, 2339) denotes "a hunting, chase," then, "a prey"; hence, figuratively, of "preparing destruction by a net or trap," Rom. 11:9.

TRAVAIL (Noun and Verb)

A. Nouns.

1. *mochthos* (μόχθος, 3449), "labor, involving painful effort," is rendered "travail" in 2 Cor. 11:27, RV (KJV, "painfulness"); in 1 Thess. 2:9 and 2 Thess. 3:8 it stresses the toil involved in the work.

2. *ōdin* (ὠδίν, 5604), a birth pang, "travail pain," is used illustratively in 1 Thess. 5:3 of the calamities which are to come upon men at the beginning of the Day of the Lord; the figure used suggests the inevitableness of the catastrophe. See PAIN, No. 2, SORROW.

B. Verbs.

1. *ōdinō* (ὠδίνω, 5605), akin to A, No. 2, is used negatively in Gal. 4:27, "(thou) that travailest (not)," quoted from Isa. 54:1; the apostle applies the circumstances of Sarah and Hagar (which doubtless Isaiah was recalling) to show that, whereas the promise by grace had temporarily been replaced by the works of the Law (see Gal. 3:17), this was now reversed, and, in the fulfillment of the promise to Abraham, the number of those saved by the gospel would far exceed those who owned allegiance to the Law. Isa. 54 has primary reference to the future prosperity of Israel restored to God's favor, but frequently the principles underlying events recorded in the OT extend beyond their immediate application.

In 4:19 the apostle uses it metaphorically of a second travailing on his part regarding the churches of Galatia; his first was for their deliverance from idolatry (v. 8), now it was for their deliverance from bondage to Judaism. There is no suggestion here of a second regeneration necessitated by defection. There is a hint of reproach, as if he was enquiring whether they had ever heard of a mother experiencing second birth pangs for her children.

In Rev. 12:2 the woman is figurative of Israel; the circumstances of her birth pangs are mentioned in Isa. 66:7 (see also Micah 5:2, 3). Historically the natural order is reversed. The Manchild, Christ, was brought forth at His first advent; the travail is destined to take place in "the time of Jacob's trouble," the "great tribulation," Matt. 24:21; Rev. 7:14. The object in 12:2 in referring to the birth of Christ is to connect Him with His earthly people Israel in their future time of trouble, from which the godly remnant, the nucleus of the restored nation, is to be delivered (Jer. 30:7).

2. *sunōdinō* (συνωδίνω, 4944), "to be in travail together," is used metaphorically in Rom. 8:22, of the whole creation.

3. *tiktō* (τίκτω, 5088), "to beget," is rendered "travail" in John 16:21.

For **TRAVEL** (companions in), Acts 19:29, and (TRAVEL WITH), 2 Cor. 8:19, see COMPANION, No. 1.

TREAD, TRODE, TRODDEN

1. *pateō* (πατέω, 3961) is used (a) intransitively and figuratively, of "treading" upon serpents, Luke 10:19; (b) transitively, of "treading" on, down or under, of the desecration of Jerusalem by its foes, Luke 21:24; Rev. 11:2; of the avenging, by the Lord in Person hereafter, of this desecration and of the persecution of the Jews, in divine retribution, metaphorically spoken of as the "treading" of the winepress of God's wrath, Rev. 14:20; 19:15 (cf. Isa. 63:2, 3).

2. *katapateō* (καταπατέω, 2662), "to tread down, trample under foot," is used (a) literally, Matt. 5:13; 7:6; Luke 8:5; 12:1; (b) metaphorically, of "treading under foot" the Son of God, Heb. 10:29, i.e., turning away from Him, to indulge in willful sin.

TREASURE (Noun and Verb)

A. Nouns.

1. *thēsauros* (θησαυρός, 2344) denotes (1) "a place of safe keeping" (possibly akin to *tithēmi*, "to put"), (a) "a casket," Matt. 2:11; (b) "a storehouse," Matt. 13:52; used metaphorically of the heart, Matt. 12:35, twice (RV, "out of his treasure"); Luke 6:45; (2) "a treasure," Matt. 6:19, 20, 21; 13:44; Luke 12:33, 34; Heb. 11:26; "treasure" (in heaven or the heavens),

Matt. 19:21; Mark 10:21; Luke 18:22; in these expressions (which are virtually equivalent to that in Matt. 6:1, "with your Father which is in Heaven") the promise does not simply refer to the present life, but looks likewise to the hereafter; in 2 Cor. 4:7 it is used of "the light of the knowledge of the glory of God in the face of Jesus Christ," descriptive of the gospel, as deposited in the earthen vessels of the persons who proclaim it (cf. v. 4); in Col. 2:3, of the wisdom and knowledge hidden in Christ.

2. *gaza* (γάζα, 1047), a Persian word, signifying "royal treasure," occurs in Acts 8:27.

B. Verb.

thēsaurizō (θησαυρίζω, 2343), akin to A, No. 1, is used metaphorically in Rom. 2:5 of "treasuring up wrath."

TREASURY

1. *gazophulakion* (γαζοφυλάκιον, 1049), from *gaza*, "a treasure," *phulakē*, "a guard," is used by Josephus for a special room in the women's court in the Temple in which gold and silver bullion was kept. This seems to be referred to in John 8:20; in Mark 12:41 (twice), 43 and Luke 21:1 it is used of the trumpet-shaped or ram's-horn-shaped chests, into which the temple offerings of the people were cast. There were 13 chests, six for such gifts in general, seven for distinct purposes.

2. *korbanas* (κορβᾶν, 2878), signifying "the place of gifts," denoted the Temple "treasury," Matt. 27:6. See CORBAN.

TREATISE

logos (λόγος, 3056), a word, denotes "a treatise or written narrative" in Acts 1:1. See WORD.

TREE

1. *dendron* (δένδρον, 1186), "a living, growing tree" (cf. Eng., "rhododendron," lit., "rose tree"), known by the fruit it produces, Matt. 12:33; Luke 6:44; certain qualities are mentioned in the NT; "a good tree," Matt. 7:17, 18; 12:33; Luke 6:43; "a corrupt tree" (ditto); in Jude 12, metaphorically, of evil teachers, "autumn trees (KJV, 'trees whose fruit withereth') without fruit, twice dead, plucked up by the roots," RV; in Luke 13:19 in some texts, "a great tree," KJV (RV, "a tree"); in Luke 21:29 "the fig tree" is illustrative of Israel, "all the trees" indicating gentile nations.

2. *xulon* (ξύλον, 3586), "wood, a piece of wood, anything made of wood," is used, with the rendering "tree," (a) in Luke 23:31, where "the green tree" refers either to Christ, figuratively of all His living power and excellencies, or to the life of the Jewish people while still inhabiting their land, in contrast to "the dry," a figure fulfilled in the horrors of the Roman massacre and devastation in A.D. 70 (cf. the Lord's parable in Luke 13:6–9; see Ezek. 20:47, and cf. 21:3); (b) of "the cross," the tree being the *stauros*, the upright pale or stake to which Romans nailed those who were thus to be executed, Acts 5:30; 10:39; 13:29; Gal. 3:13; 1 Pet. 2:24; (c) of "the tree of life," Rev. 2:7; 22:2 (twice), 14, 19, RV, KJV, "book."

TREMBLE, TREMBLING

A. Verbs.

1. *tremō* (τρέμω, 5141), "to tremble, especially with fear," is used in Mark 5:33; Luke 8:47 (Acts 9:6, in some mss.); 2 Pet. 2:10, RV, "they tremble (not)," KJV, "they are (not) afraid."

2. *seiō* (σείω, 4579), "to move to and fro, shake," is rendered "will I make to tremble" in Heb. 12:26, RV (KJV, "I shake"). See QUAKE.

Notes: (1) For *phrissō* in Jas. 2:19, KJV, "tremble," see SHUDDER. (2) For the adjective *entromos*, "trembling," Acts 7:32; 16:29, RV, "trembling for fear," see QUAKE, No. 1. (3) The adjective *emphobos*, used with *ginomai*, "to become," is rendered "trembled" in Acts 24:25 (RV, "was terrified"); in Luke 24:5, RV, "they were affrighted," KJV, "they were afraid." See AFFRIGHTED, A.

B. Noun.

tromos (τρόμος, 5156), "a trembling" (akin to A, No. 1), occurs in Mark 16:8, RV, "trembling (... had come upon them)"; 1 Cor. 2:3; 2 Cor. 7:15; Eph. 6:5; Phil. 2:12.

TRESPASS (Noun and Verb)

A. Noun.

paraptōma (παράπτωμα, 3900), primarily "a false step, a blunder" (akin to *parapiptō*, "to fall away," Heb. 6:6), lit., "a fall beside," used ethically, denotes "a trespass," a deviation, from uprightness and truth, Matt. 6:14, 15 (twice); 18:35, in some mss.; Mark 11:25, 26; in Romans the RV substitutes "trespass" and "trespasses" for KJV, "offense" and "offenses," 4:25, "for (i.e., because of) our trespasses"; 5:15 (twice), where the trespass is that of Adam (in contrast to the free gift of righteousness, v. 17, a contrast in the nature and the effects); 5:16, where "of many trespasses" expresses a contrast of quantity; the condemnation resulted from one "trespass," the free gift is "of (*ek*, expressing the origin, and throwing stress upon God's justifying grace in Christ) many trespasses"; v. 17, introducing a contrast between legal effects and those of divine grace; v. 18, where the RV, "through one trespass," is contrasted with "one act of righteousness"; this is important, the difference is not between one man's "trespass" and Christ's righteousness (as KJV), but between two acts, that of Adam's "trespass" and the vicarious death of Christ; v. 20 [cf. TRANSGRESSION, B, No. 1 (d)]; in 2 Cor. 5:19, KJV and RV, "trespasses"; in Eph. 1:7, RV, "trespasses" (KJV, "sins"); in 2:1, RV, "(dead through your) trespasses," KJV, "(dead in) trespasses"; 2:5, RV, "(dead through our) trespasses," KJV, "(dead in) sins"; so Col. 2:13 (1st part); in the 2nd part, KJV and RV, "trespasses."

In Gal. 6:1, RV, "(in any) trespass" (KJV, "fault"), the reference is to "the works of the flesh" (5:19), and the thought is that of the believer's being found off his guard, the "trespass" taking advantage of him; in Jas. 5:16, KJV, "faults" (RV, "sins" translates the word *hamartias*, which is found in the best texts), auricular confession to a priest is not in view here or anywhere else in Scripture; the command is comprehensive, and speaks either of the acknowledgment of sin where one has wronged another, or of the unburdening of a troubled conscience to a godly brother whose prayers will be efficacious, or of open confession before the church.

In Rom. 11:11, 12, the word is used of Israel's "fall," i.e., their deviation from obedience to God and from the fulfillment of His will (to be distinguished from the verb *ptaiō*, "fall," in the 1st part of v. 11, which indicates the impossibility of recovery).

B. Verb.

hamartanō (ἁμαρτάνω, 264), "to sin," is translated "to trespass," in the KJV of Matt. 18:15, and Luke 17:3, 4 (RV, "to sin").

Note: For the different meanings of words describing sin, see SIN. *Paraptōma*, and *hamartēma* ("a sinful deed") are closely associated, with regard to their primary meanings: *parabasis* seems to be a stronger term, as the breach of a known law (see TRANSGRESSION).

TRIAL

1. *dokimē* (δοκιμή, 1382), for which see EXPERIENCE, No. 2, is rendered "trial" in 2 Cor. 8:2, KJV (RV, "proof").

2. *peira* (πεῖρα, 3984), "a making trial, an experiment," is used with *lambanō*, "to receive or take," in Heb. 11:29, rendered "assaying," and v. 36, in the sense of "having experience of" (akin to *peiraō*, "to assay, to try"), "had trial." In the Sept., Deut. 28:56.

3. *peirasmos* (πειρασμός, 3986), akin to No. 2, is rendered "trials" in Acts 20:19, RV. See TEMPTATION.

4. *purōsis* (πύρωσις, 4451), akin to *puroō*, "to set on fire," signifies (a) "a burning"; (b) "a refining," metaphorically in 1 Pet. 4:12, "fiery trial," or rather "trial by fire," referring to the refining of gold (1:7). See BURNING.

Note: For *dokimion*, rendered "trial" in 1 Pet. 1:7, KJV, see PROOF, No. 2.

TRIBE (-S)

1. *phulē* (φυλή, 5443), "a company of people united by kinship or habitation, a clan, tribe," is used (a) of the peoples of the earth, Matt. 24:30; in the following the RV has "tribe(-s)" for KJV, "kindred(-s)," Rev. 1:7; 5:9; 7:9; 11:9; 13:7; 14:6; (b) of the "tribes" of Israel, Matt. 19:28; Luke 2:36; 22:30; Acts 13:21; Rom. 11:1; Phil. 3:5; Heb. 7:13, 14; Jas. 1:1; Rev. 5:5; 7:4-8; 21:12.

2. *dōdekaphulos* (δωδεκάφυλον, 1429), an adjective signifying "of twelve tribes" (*dōdeka*, "twelve," and No. 1), used as a noun in the neuter, occurs in Acts 26:7.

TRIBULATION

thlipsis (θλίψις, 2347), for which see AFFLICTION, B, No. 4, is translated "tribulation" in the RV (for KJV, "affliction") in Mark 4:17; 13:19; plural in 2 Thess. 1:4, KJV, "tribulations," RV, "afflictions"; in Acts 14:22 "many tribulations" (KJV, "much tribulation"); in Matt. 24:9, "unto tribulation" (KJV, "to be afflicted"); in 2 Cor. 1:4; 7:4; 2 Thess. 1:6, KJV, "tribulation" for RV, "affliction"; RV and KJV, "tribulation(-s)," e.g., in Rom. 2:9; 5:3 (twice); 8:35; 12:12; Eph. 3:13; Rev. 1:9; 2:9, 10, 22.

In Rev. 7:14, "the great tribulation," RV, lit., "the tribulation, the great one" (not as KJV, without the article), is not that in which all saints share; it indicates a definite period spoken of by the Lord in Matt. 24:21, 29; Mark 13:19, 24, where the time is mentioned as preceding His second advent, and as a period in which the Jewish nation, restored to Palestine in unbelief by gentile instrumentality, will suffer an unprecedented outburst of fury on the part of the antichristian powers confederate under the Man of Sin (2 Thess. 2:10-12; cf. Rev. 12:13-17); in this tribulation gentile witnesses for God will share (Rev. 7:9), but it will be distinctly "the time of Jacob's trouble" (Jer. 30:7); its beginning is signalized by the setting up of the "abomination of desolation" (Matt. 24:15; Mark 13:14, with Dan. 11:31; 12:11).

Note: For the verb *thlibō*, in the passive voice rendered "suffer tribulation" in 1 Thess. 3:4, KJV (RV, "suffer affliction"), see AFFLICT, No. 4.

TRIBUTE

1. *phoros* (φόρος, 5411), akin to *pherō*, "to bring," denotes "tribute" paid by a subjugated nation, Luke 20:22; 23:2; Rom. 13:6, 7.

2. *kensos* (κῆνσος, 2778), Lat. and Eng., "census," denotes "a poll tax," Matt. 17:25; 22:17, 19; Mark 12:14.

3. *didrachmon* (δίδραχμον, 1323), "the halfshekel," is rendered "tribute" in Matt. 17:24 (twice).

TRIUMPH

thriambeuō (θριαμβεύω, 2358) denotes (a) "to lead in triumph," used of a conqueror with reference to the vanquished, 2 Cor. 2:14. Theodoret paraphrases it "He leads us about here and there and displays us to all the world." This is in agreement with evidences from various sources. Those who are led are not captives exposed to humiliation, but are displayed as the glory and devoted subjects of Him who leads (see the context). This is so even if there is a reference to a Roman "triumph." On such occasions the general's sons, with various officers, rode behind his chariot (Livy, xlv. 40). But there is no necessary reference here to a Roman "triumph" (Field, in *Notes on the Trans. of the NT*). The main thought is that of the display, "in Christ" being the sphere; its evidences are the effects of gospel testimony.

In Col. 2:15 the circumstances and subjects are quite different, and relate to Christ's victory over spiritual foes at the time of His death; accordingly the reference may be to the triumphant display of the defeated.

For **TRODE** see TREAD

TROUBLE (Noun and Verb)

A. Noun.

thlipsis (θλίψις, 2347), for which see AFFLICTION, No. 4, and TRIBULATION, is rendered "trouble" in the KJV of 1 Cor. 7:28 (RV, "tribulation"); 2 Cor. 1:4 (2nd clause), 8 (RV, "affliction").

Note: In some mss. *tarachē*, "an agitation, disturbance, trouble," is found in Mark 13:8 (plur.) and John 5:4 (RV omits).

B. Verbs.

1. *tarossō* (ταράσσω, 5015), akin to *tarachē* (A, Note), is used (1) in a physical sense, John 5:7 (in some mss. v. 4), (2) metaphorically, (a) of the soul and spirit of the Lord, John 11:33, where the true rendering is "He troubled Himself"; (b) of the hearts of disciples, 14:1, 27; (c) of the minds of those in fear or perplexity, Matt. 2:3; 14:26; Mark 6:50; Luke 1:12; 24:38; 1 Pet. 3:14; (d) of subverting the souls of believers, by evil doctrine, Acts 15:24; Gal. 1:7; 5:10; (e) of stirring up a crowd, Acts 17:8; v. 13 in the best texts, "troubling (the multitudes)," RV.

2. *diatarassō* (διαταράσσω, 1298), "to agitate greatly" (*dia*, "throughout," and No. 1), is used of the Virgin Mary, Luke 1:29.

3. *ektarassō* (ἐκταράσσω, 1613), "to throw into great trouble, agitate," is used in Acts 16:20, "do exceedingly trouble (our city)." In the Sept., Ps. 18:4; 88:16.

4. *thlibō* (θλίβω, 2346), "to afflict," is rendered "to trouble" in the KJV, e.g., 2 Cor. 4:8 (RV, "pressed"); 7:5, but never in the RV: see AFFLICT, No. 4, PRESS, TRIBULATION.

5. *enochleō* (ἐνοχλέω, 1776), from *en*, "in," *ochlos*, "a throng, crowd," is used in Heb. 12:15 of a root of bitterness; in Luke 6:18 (in the best texts; some have *ochleō*), RV, "were troubled" (KJV, "were vexed").

6. *parenochleō* (παρενοχλέω, 3926), "to annoy concerning anything" (*para*, and No. 5), occurs in Acts 15:19, "we trouble (not them)."

7. *skullō* (σκύλλω, 4660), primarily "to flay," hence, "to vex, annoy" ("there was a time when the Greek, in thus speaking, compared his trouble to the pains of flaying alive," Moulton, *Proleg.*, p. 89), is used in the active voice in Mark 5:35; Luke 8:49; in the passive voice, Matt. 9:36, in the best texts, RV, "they were distressed" (some have *ekluō*, KJV, "they fainted"); in the middle voice, Luke 7:6, "trouble (not thyself)." The word is frequent in the papyri.

8. *anastatoō* (ἀναστατόω, 387) is rendered "trouble" in Gal. 5:12, KJV: see STIR, No. 12, UPROAR.

9. *thorubeō* (θορυβέω, 2350), akin to *thorubos*, "a tumult," in the middle voice, "to make an uproar," is rendered "trouble not yourselves" in Acts 20:10, KJV. See ADO, TUMULT.

10. *throeō* (θροέω, 2360), "to make an outcry" (*throos*, "a tumult"), is used in the passive voice, Matt. 24:6; Mark 13:7; Luke 24:37; 2 Thess. 2:2. In the Sept., Song of Sol. 5:4.

11. *thorubazō* (θορυβάζω, 2350a), "to disturb, to trouble" (akin to No. 9), is used in Luke 10:41, in the best texts (in some, *turbazō*, with the same meaning).

12. *adēmoneō* (ἀδημονέω, 85), "to be much troubled, distressed" (perhaps from *a*, negative, and *dēmōn*, "knowing," the compound therefore originally suggesting bewilderment), is translated "sore troubled" in Matt. 26:37 and Mark 14:33, RV (KJV, "very heavy"); so the RV in Phil. 2:26 (KJV, "full of heaviness"); Lightfoot renders it "distressed," a meaning borne out in the papyri. See HEAVY.

13. *diaponeō* (διαπονέω, 1278) denotes "to work out with toil," hence, "to be sore troubled"; so the RV in Acts 4:2 and 16:18 (KJV, "grieved"); Mark 14:4 in some texts.

Notes: (1) The noun *kopos*, "a striking, beating," then, "laborious toil, trouble," used with *parechō*, "to furnish, to supply," is rendered "to trouble" (lit., "to give trouble to"), in Matt. 26:10; Mark 14:6; Luke 11:7; 18:5; Gal. 6:17; the meaning is to embarrass a person by distracting his attention, or to give occasion for anxiety. In the last passage the apostle expresses his determination not to allow the Judaizing teachers to distract him any further. See LABOR, A, No. 1. (2) For "suffer trouble" in 2 Tim. 2:9, see HARDSHIP.

TROW

Note: Some mss. have *dokeō*, "to think," in Luke 17:9, KJV, "I trow (not)."

For **TRUCE BREAKERS** see IMPLACABLE

TRUE, TRULY, TRUTH

A. Adjectives.

1. *alēthēs* (ἀληθής, 227), primarily, "unconcealed, manifest" (*a*, negative, *lethō*, "to forget," = *lanthanō*, "to escape notice"), hence, actual, "true to fact," is used (a) of persons, "truthful," Matt. 22:16; Mark 12:14; John 3:33; 7:18; 8:26; Rom. 3:4; 2 Cor. 6:8; (b) of things, "true," conforming to reality, John 4:18, "truly," lit., "true"; 5:31, 32; in the best texts, 6:55

(twice), "indeed"; 8:13, 14 (v. 16 in some texts: see No. 2), 17; 10:41; 19:35; 21:24; Acts 12:9; Phil. 4:8; Titus 1:13; 1 Pet. 5:12; 2 Pet. 2:22; 1 John 2:8, 27; 3 John 1:2.

2. *alēthinos* (ἀληθινός, 228), akin to No. 1, denotes "true" in the sense of real, ideal, genuine; it is used (a) of God, John 7:28 (cf. No. 1 in 7:18, above); 17:3; 1 Thess. 1:9; Rev. 6:10; these declare that God fulfills the meaning of His Name; He is "very God," in distinction from all other gods, false gods (*alēthēs*, see John 3:33 in No. 1, signifies that He is veracious, "true" to His utterances, He cannot lie); (b) of Christ, John 1:9; 6:32; 15:1; 1 John 2:8; 5:20 (thrice); Rev. 3:7, 14; 19:11; His judgment, John 8:16 (in the best texts, instead of No. 1); (c) God's words, John 4:37; Rev. 19:9, 21:5; 22:6; the last three are equivalent to No. 1; (d) His ways, Rev. 15:3; (e) His judgments, Rev. 16:7; 19:2; (to His riches, Luke 16:11; (g) His worshipers, John 4:23; (h) their hearts, Heb. 10:22; (i) the witness of the apostle John, John 19:35; (j) the spiritual, antitypical tabernacle, Heb. 8:2; 9:24, not that the wilderness tabernacle was false, but that it was a weak and earthly copy of the heavenly.

Note: "*Alēthinos* is related to *alēthēs* as form to contents or substances; *alēthēs* denotes the reality of the thing, *alethinos* defines the relation of the conception to the thing to which it corresponds = genuine" (Cremer).

3. *gnēsios* (γνήσιος, 1103), primarily "lawfully begotten" (akin to *ginomai*, "to become"), hence, "true, genuine, sincere," is used in the apostle's exhortation to his "true yokefellow" in Phil. 4:3. See OWN, SINCERITY.

Note: In the KJV of 2 Cor. 1:18 and 1 Tim. 3:1, *pistos*, "faithful" (RV), is translated "true."

B. Verb.

alētheuō (ἀληθεύω, 226) signifies "to deal faithfully or truly with anyone" (cf. Gen. 42:16, Sept., "whether ye deal truly or no"), Eph. 4:15, "speaking the truth"; Gal. 3:16, "I tell (you) the truth," where probably the apostle is referring to the contents of his epistle.

C. Noun.

alētheia (ἀλήθεια, 225), "truth," is used (a) objectively, signifying "the reality lying at the basis of an appearance; the manifested, veritable essence of a matter" (Cremer), e.g., Rom. 9:1; 2 Cor. 11:10; especially of Christian doctrine, e.g., Gal. 2:5, where "the truth of the Gospel" denotes the "true" teaching of the Gospel, in contrast to perversions of it; Rom. 1:25, where "the truth of God" may be "the truth concerning God" or "God whose existence is a verity"; but in Rom. 15:8 "the truth of God" is indicative of His faithfulness in the fulfillment of His promises as exhibited in Christ; the word has an absolute force in John 14:6; 17:17; 18:37, 38; in Eph. 4:21, where the RV, "even as truth is in Jesus," gives the correct rendering, the meaning is not merely ethical "truth," but "truth" in all its fullness and scope, as embodied in Him; He was the perfect expression of the truth; this is virtually equivalent to His statement in John 14:6; (b) subjectively, "truthfulness," "truth," not merely verbal, but sincerity and integrity of character, John 8:44; 3 John 3, RV; (C) in phrases, e.g., "in truth" (*epi*, "on the basis of"), Mark 12:14; Luke 20:21; with *en*, "in," 2 Cor. 6:7; Col. 1:6; 1 Tim. 2:7, RV (KJV, "in ... verity"), 1 John 3:18; 2 John 1, 3, 4.

Note: In Matt. 15:27, KJV, *nai*, "yea" (RV), is translated "truth."

D. Adverbs.

1. *alēthos* (ἀληθῶς, 230), "truly, surely," is rendered "of a truth" in Matt. 14:33; 26:73 and Mark 14:70, RV, (KJV, "surely"); Luke 9:27; 12:44; 21:3; John 6:14; 7:40; 17:8, RV, "of a truth (KJV, surely); Acts 12:11, RV (KJV, "of a surety"); "in truth," 1 Thess. 2:13; "truly," Matt. 27:54; Mark 15:39.

2. *gnēsiōs* (γνησίως, 1104), "sincerely, honorably" (akin to A, No. 3), is rendered "truly" (marg., "genuinely") in Phil. 2:20 (KJV, "naturally").

Notes: (1) The particles *ara*, *men*, and *de* are sometimes rendered "truly" in the KJV, but are differently rendered in the RV. (2) In 1 Cor. 14:25, KJV, *ontos* (RV, "indeed") is rendered "of a truth. (3) In John 20:30, KJV, the particle *oun*, therefore (RV), is rendered "truly."

TRUMP, TRUMPET

A. Noun.

salpinx (σάλπιγξ, 4536) is used (1) of the natural instrument, 1 Cor. 14:8; (2) of the supernatural accompaniment of divine interpositions, (a) at Sinai, Heb. 12:19; (b) of the acts of angels at the second advent of Christ, Matt. 24:31; (c) of their acts in the period of divine judgments preceding this, Rev. 8:2, 6, 13; 9:14; (d) of a summons to John to the presence of God, Rev. 1:10; 4:1; (e) of the act of the Lord in raising from the dead the saints who have fallen asleep and changing the bodies of those who are living, at the Rapture of all to meet Him in the air, 1 Cor. 15:52, where "the last trump" is a military allusion, familiar to Greek readers, and has no connection with the series in Rev. 8:6 to 11:15; there is a possible allusion to Num. 10:2-6, with reference to the same event, 1 Thess. 4:16, "the (lit., a) trump of God" (the absence of the article suggests the meaning "a trumpet such as is used in God's service").

B. Verb.

salpizō (σαλπίζω, 4537), "to sound a trumpet," Matt. 6:2; as in (2) (c) above, Rev. 8:6, 7 8, 10, 12, 13; 9:1, 13; 10:7; 11:15; as in (2) (e) 1 Cor. 15:52.

TRUMPETER

salpistēs (σαλπιστής, 4538) occurs in Rev. 18:22.

TRUST (Noun and Verb)

A. Noun.

pepoithēsis (πεποίθησις, 4006) is rendered trust in 2 Cor. 3:4, KJV; see CONFIDENCE, No. 1.

B. Verbs.

1. *peithō* (πείθω, 3982), intransitively, in the perfect and pluperfect active, "to have confidence, trust," is rendered "to trust" in Matt. 27:43; Mark 10:24; Luke 11:22; 18:9; 2 Cor. 1:9; 10:7; Phil, 2:24; 3:4, KJV (RV, "to have confidence"); Heb. 2:13; in the present middle, Heb. 13:18, KJV (RV, "are persuaded"). See PERSUADE.

2. *pisteuō* (πιστεύω, 4100), "to entrust," or, in the passive voice, "to be entrusted with," is rendered "to commit to one's trust," in Luke 16:11; 1 Tim. 1:11; "to be put in trust with," 1 Thess. 2:4, KJV (RV, "to be intrusted").

Note: Wherever *elpizō*, "to hope," is translated "to trust" in the KJV, the RV substitutes "to hope." So *proelpizō*, "to hope before." See HOPE.

For **TRUTH** see TRUE

TRY, TRIED

1. *dokimazō* (δοκιμάζω, 1381) is rendered "to try" in the KJV in 1 Cor. 3:13; 1 Thess. 2:4; 1 Pet. 1:7; 1 John 4:1: see PROVE, No. 1.

2. *peirazō* (πειράζω, 3985) is rendered "to try" in Heb. 11:17; Rev. 2:2, 10; 3:10. In Acts 16:7 it is rendered "assayed"; in 24:6, RV, "assayed" (KJV, "hath gone about"): see GO, *Note* (2) (b). See EXAMINE, PROVE, TEMPT. Cf. *peiraō* in Acts 26:21, RV, "assayed" (KJV, "went about"); see GO, *Note* (2) (c).

Notes: (1) In Rev. 3:18, KJV, *puroō*, in the passive voice, "to be purified by fire" (RV, "refined"), is rendered "tried." (2) For *dokimion*, Jas. 1:3, KJV, "trying," see PROOF. (3) For *dokimos*, Jas. 1:12, KJV, "tried." (4) In 1 Pet. 4:12, KJV, the phrase *pros peirasmon*, lit., "for trial," i.e., "for testing," is rendered "to try (you)," RV, "to prove (you)."

TUMULT

1. *akatastasia* (ἀκαταστασία, 181) is rendered "tumults" in Luke 21:9, RV; 2 Cor. 6:5; 12:20. See CONFOUND, A, No. 1.

2. *thorubos* (θόρυβος, 2351), "a noise, uproar, tumult," is rendered "tumult" in Matt. 27:24 and Mark 5:38; in Matt. 26:5, RV (KJV, "uproar"), so in Mark 14:2; in Acts 20:1, "uproar," KJV and RV; in 24:18, "tumult"; in 21:34, KJV, "tumult" (RV, "uproar").

For **TURTLEDOVE** see DOVE

For **TUTOR** see GUARDIAN and INSTRUCTOR, No. 1.

TWELVE

dōdeka (δώδεκα, 1427) is used frequently in the Gospels for the twelve apostles, and in Acts 6:2; 1 Cor. 15:5; Rev. 21:14b; of the tribes of Israel, Matt. 19:28; Luke 22:30; Jas. 1:1; Rev. 21:12c (cf. 7:5-8; 12:1); in various details relating to the heavenly Jerusalem, Rev. 21:12-21; 22:2. The number in general is regarded as suggestive of divine administration.

TWINKLING

rhipē (ῥιπή, 4493), akin to *rhiptō*, "to hurl," was used of any rapid movement, e.g., the throw of a javelin, the rush of wind or flame; in 1 Cor. 15:52 of the "twinkling" of an eye.

TWO-EDGED

distomos (δίστομος, 1366), lit., "two-mouthed" (*dis*, and *stoma*, "a mouth"), was used of rivers and branching roads; in the NT of swords, Heb. 4:12; Rev. 1:16; 2:12, RV, "two-edged" (KJV, "with two edges"). In the Sept., Judg. 3:16; Ps. 149:6; Prov. 5:4.

U

For **UNAPPROACHABLE,** 1 Tim. 6:16, RV, see APPROACH, B

UNBELIEF

1. *apistia* (ἀπιστία, 570), "unbelief" 12 times, but see BELIEF, C, *Note* (2) for references.

2. *apeitheia* (ἀπείθεια, 543) is always rendered "disobedience" in the RV; in Rom. 11:30, 32 and Heb. 4:6, 11, KJV, "unbelief." See DISOBEDIENCE, A, No. 1.

UNBELIEVER

apistos (ἄπιστος, 571), an adjective, is used as a noun, rendered "unbeliever" in 2 Cor. 6:15 and 1 Tim. 5:8, RV; plural in 1 Cor. 6:6 and 2 Cor. 6:14; KJV only, Luke 12:46 (RV, "unfaithful"). See BELIEF, C, *Note* (3), FAITHLESS, INCREDIBLE.

UNBELIEVING

A. Adjective.

apistos (ἄπιστος, 571): see BELIEF, C, *Note* (3).

B. Verb.

apeitheō (ἀπειθέω, 544): see DISBELIEVE, DISOBEDIENT, C.

UNBLAMEABLE, UNBLAMEABLY

A. Adjectives.

1. *amemptos* (ἄμεμπτος, 273), "unblameable" (from *a*, negative, and *memphomai*, "to find fault"), is so rendered in 1 Thess. 3:13, i.e., "free from all valid charge." See BLAME, B, No. 3.

2. *amōmos* (ἄμωμος, 299): see BLEMISH, B.

B. Adverb.

amemptōs (ἀμέμπτως, 274) is used in 1 Thess. 2:10, "unblameably," signifying that no charge could be maintained, whatever charges might be made. See BLAME, C.

UNCERTAIN, UNCERTAINLY, UNCERTAINTY

A. Adjective.

adēlos (ἄδηλος, 82) denotes (a) "unseen"; with the article, translated "which appear not" (*a*, negative, *dēlos*, "evident"), Luke 11:44; (b) "uncertain, indistinct," 1 Cor. 14:8. In the Sept., Ps. 51:6.

B. Adverb.

adēlōs (ἀδήλως, 84), "uncertainly" (akin to A), occurs in 1 Cor. 9:26.

C. Noun.

adēlotēs (ἀδηλότης, 83), "uncertainty" (akin to A and B), occurs in 1 Tim. 6:17, "(the) uncertainty (of riches)," RV (the KJV translates it as an adjective, "uncertain"), i.e., riches the special character of which is their "uncertainty"; the Greek phrase is a rhetorical way of stressing the noun "riches"; when a genitive (here "of riches") precedes the governing noun (here "uncertainty") the genitive receives emphasis.

UNCHANGEABLE

aparabatos (ἀπαράβατος, 531) is used of the priesthood of Christ, in Heb. 7:24, "unchangeable," "unalterable, inviolable," RV, marg. (a meaning found in the papyri); the more literal meaning in KJV and RV margins, "that doth not pass from one to another," is not to be preferred. This active meaning is not only untenable, and contrary to the constant usage of the word, but does not adequately fit with either the preceding or the succeeding context.

For **UNCIRCUMCISED and UNCIRCUMCISION** see CIRCUMCISION

UNCLEAN

A. Adjectives.

1. *akathartos* (ἀκάθαρτος, 169), "unclean, impure" (*a*, negative, *kathairō*, "to purify"), is used (a) of "unclean" spirits, frequently in the Synoptists, not in John's gospel; in Acts 5:16; 8:7; Rev. 16:13; 18:2a (in the 2nd clause the birds are apparently figurative of destructive satanic agencies); (b) ceremonially, Acts 10:14, 28; 11:8; 1 Cor. 7:14; (c) morally, 2 Cor. 6:17, including (b), RV; "no unclean thing"; Eph. 5:5; Rev. 17:4, RV, "the unclean things" (KJV follows the text which have the noun *akathartēs*, "the filthiness").

2. *koinos* (κοινός, 2839), "common," is translated "unclean" in Rom. 14:14 (thrice); in Rev. 21:27, RV (KJV, "that defileth," follows the inferior texts which have the verb *koinoō*: see B). See COMMON, DEFILE, C, UNHOLY, No. 2.

B. Verb.

koinoō (κοινόω, 2840), to make *koinos*, "to defile," is translated "unclean" in Heb. 9:13, KJV, where the perfect participle, passive, is used with the article, hence the RV, "them that have been defiled." See DEFILE, A, No. 1.

C. Noun.

akatharsia (ἀκαθαρσία, 167), akin to A, No. 1, denotes "uncleanness," (a) physical, Matt. 23:27 (instances in the papyri speak of tenants keeping houses in good condition); (b) moral, Rom. 1:24; 6:19; 2 Cor. 12:21; Gal. 5:19; Eph. 4:19; 5:3; Col. 3:5; 1 Thess. 2:3 (suggestive of the fact that sensuality and evil doctrine are frequently associated); 4:7.

Note: In 2 Pet. 2:10, KJV, *miasmos*, "a defilement," is rendered "uncleanness"; see DEFILE, B, No. 2.

For **UNCLOTHED** see STRIP

UNCOMELY

aschēmōn (ἀσχήμων, 809), "shapeless" (*a*, negative, *schēma*, "a form"), the opposite of *euschēmōn*, "comely," is used in 1 Cor. 12:23. In the Sept., Gen. 34:7; Deut. 24:3.

Note: For the verb *aschēmoneō*, rendered "to behave oneself uncomely" in 1 Cor. 7:36, KJV, see BEHAVE, No. 4.

UNCONDEMNED

akatakritos (ἀκατάκριτος, 178), rendered "uncondemned" in Acts 16:37; 22:25 (*a*, negative, *katakrinō*, "to condemn"), properly means "without trial, not yet tried." Sir W. M. Ramsay points out that the apostle, in claiming his rights, would probably use the Roman phrase *re incognita*, i.e., "without investigating our case" (*The Cities of St. Paul*, p. 225).

For **UNCORRUPTIBLE** see CORRUPT, C, No. 2. For UNCORRUPTNESS, see CORRUPT, B, No. 4

UNDEFILED

amiantos (ἀμίαντος, 283), "undefiled, free from contamination" (*a*, negative, *miainō*, "to defile"), is used (a) of Christ, Heb. 7:26; (b) of pure religion, Jas. 1:27; (c) of the eternal inheritance of believers, 1 Pet. 1:4; (d) of the marriage bed as requiring to be free from unlawful sexual intercourse, Heb. 13:4.

UNDERSTANDING

A. Nouns.

1. *nous* (νοῦς, 3563), for which see MIND, No. 1, is translated "understanding" in Luke 24:45, KJV (RV, "mind"); 1 Cor. 14:14, 15 (twice), 19; Phil. 4:7; Rev. 13:18.

2. *sunesis* (σύνεσις, 4907), akin to *suniēmi*, "to set together, to understand," denotes (a) "the understanding, the mind or intelligence," Mark 12:33; (b) "understanding, reflective thought," Luke 2:47; 1 Cor. 1:19, RV, "prudence," Eph. 3:4, RV (KJV, "knowledge"); Col. 1:9; 2:2; 2 Tim. 2:7. See PRUDENCE, No. 2.

3. *dianoia* (διάνοια, 1271), for which see MIND, No. 2, is rendered "understanding" in Eph. 4:18; 1 John 5:20 (in some texts, Eph. 1:18, KJV, for *kardia*, "heart," RV).

B. Adjective.

asunetos (ἀσύνετος, 801), "without understanding or discernment" (*a*, negative, *sunetos*, "intelligent, understanding"), is translated "without understanding" in Matt. 15:16; Mark 7:18; Rom. 1:31; 10:19, RV, "void of understanding" (KJV, "foolish"); in Rom. 1:21, RV, "senseless" (KJV, "foolish").

Note: In 1 Cor. 14:20, KJV, *phrēn*, "the mind," is translated "understanding" (twice), RV, "mind."

For **UNEQUALLY** see YOKED

UNFAITHFUL

apistos (ἄπιστος, 571), "unbelieving, faithless," is translated "unfaithful" in Luke 12:46, RV (KJV, "unbelievers"). See BELIEF, C, *Note* (3), FAITHLESS, INCREDIBLE.

For **UNFEIGNED** see DISSIMULATION, C

For **UNFRUITFUL** see FRUIT, B, No. 2

UNGODLINESS, UNGODLY

A. Noun.

asebeia (ἀσέβεια, 763), "impiety, ungodliness," is used of (a) general impiety, Rom. 1:18; 11:26; 2 Tim. 2:16; Titus 2:12; (b) "ungodly" deeds, Jude 15, RV, "works of ungodliness"; (c) of lusts or desires after evil things, Jude 18. It is the opposite of *eusebeia*, "godliness."

Note: Anomia is disregard for, or defiance of, God's laws; *asebeia* is the same attitude towards God's Person.

B. Adjective.

asebēs (ἀσεβής, 765), "impious, ungodly" (akin to A), "without reverence for God," not merely irreligious, but acting in contravention of God's demands, Rom. 4:5; 5:6; 1 Tim. 1:9; 1 Pet. 4:18; 2 Pet. 2:5 (v. 6 in some mss.); 3:7; Jude 4, 15 (twice).

C. Verb.

asebeō (ἀσεβέω, 764), akin to A and B, signifies (a) "to be or live ungodly," 2 Pet. 2:6; (b) "to commit ungodly deeds," Jude 15.

UNHOLY

1. *anosios* (ἀνόσιος, 462), (*a*, negative, *n*, euphonic, *hosios*, "holy"), "unholy, profane," occurs in 1 Tim. 1:9; 2 Tim. 3:2. Cf. HOLY. In the Sept., Ezek. 22:9.

2. *koinon* (κοινός, 2839), the neut. of *koinos*, "common," is translated "an unholy thing" in Heb. 10:29. See COMMON, DEFILE, C, UNCLEAN, A, No. 2.

UNITY

henotēs (ἑνότης, 1775), from *hen*, the neuter of *heis*, "one." is used in Eph. 4:3, 13.

UNJUST

adikos (ἄδικος, 94), "not in conformity with *dikē*. 'right,'" is rendered "unjust" in the KJV and RV in Matt. 5:45; Luke 18:11; Acts 24:15; elsewhere for the KJV "unjust" the RV has "unrighteous. See UNRIGHTEOUS.

Note: For *adikeō*, "to be unrighteous," or "do unrighteousness," Rev. 22:11, RV, and *adikia*, "unrighteous," Luke 16:8 and 18:6, RV, see UNRIGHTEOUSNESS.

For **UNKNOWN** see IGNORANCE, B, No. 1, and KNOW, 13, No. 4

UNLAWFUL

athemitos (ἀθέμιτος, 111), a late form for *athemistos* (*themis*, "custom, right"; in classical Greek "divine law"), "contrary to what is right," is rendered "an unlawful thing" (neuter) in Acts 10:28; in 1 Pet. 4:3, "abominable."

Note: For 2 Pet. 2:8, KJV, see LAWLESS.

UNLEARNED

1. *agrammatos* (ἀγράμματος, 62), lit., "unlettered" (*grammata*, "letters": *graphō*, "to write") Acts 4:13, is explained by GrimmThayer as meaning "unversed in the learning of the Jewish schools"; in the papyri, however, it occurs very frequently in a formula used by one who signs for another who cannot write, which suggests that the rulers, elders and scribes regarded the apostles as "unlettered" (Moulton and Milligan).

2. *amathēs* (ἀμαθής, 261), "unlearned" *manthanō*, "to learn"), is translated "unlearned" in 2 Pet. 3:16, KJV (RV, "ignorant").

3. *apaideutos* (ἀπαίδευτος, 521), "unintructed" (*paideuō*, "to train, teach"), is translated "unlearned" in 2 Tim. 2:23, KJV (RV, "ignorant").

Note: For *idiōtēs*, rendered "unlearned" in 1 Cor. 14:16, 23, 24, see IGNORANT, No. 4.

For **UNLEAVENED** see BREAD, No. 2

UNLIFTED

anakaluptō (ἀνακαλύπτω, 343), "to uncover, unveil," used in 2 Cor. 3:14 with the negative *mē*, "not," is rendered "unlifted," RV, KJV, "untaken away" (a paraphrase rather than translation); the RV marg., "remaineth, it not being revealed that it is done away," is not to be preferred. The best rendering seems to be, "the veil remains unlifted (for it is in Christ that it is done away)." Judaism does not recognize the vanishing of the glory of the Law as a means of life, under God's grace in Christ. In 3:18 the RV, "unveiled (face)" (KJV, "open"), continues the metaphor of the veil (vv. 13-17), referring to hindrances to the perception of spiritual realities, hindrances removed in the unveiling.

UNLOOSE

luō (λύω, 3089), "to loose," is rendered "to unloose" in Mark 1:7; Luke 3:16; John 1:27; in Acts 13:25, RV: see LOOSE.

UNMARRIED

agamos (ἄγαμος, 22), *a*, negative, *gameō*, "to marry," occurs in 1 Cor. 7:8, 11, 32, 34.

UNMERCIFUL

aneleēmōn (ἀνελεήμων, 415), "without mercy" (*a*, negative, *n*, euphonic, *eleēmōn*, "merciful"), occurs in Rom. 1:31.

UNPREPARED

aparaskeuastos (ἀπαρασκεύαστος, 532), from *a*, negative, and *paraskeuazō* (see PREPARE, B, No. 4), occurs in 2 Cor. 9:4.

For **UNQUENCHABLE** see QUENCH

UNREASONABLE

1. *alogos* (ἄλογος, 249), "without reason, irrational," is rendered "unreasonable" in Acts 25:27. See BRUTE.

2. *atopos* (ἄτοπος, 824), lit., "out of place" (*topos*, "a place"), is translated "unreasonable" in 2 Thess. 3:2, where the meaning intended seems to be "perverse, truculent." See AMISS.

For **UNREBUKEABLE** see BLAME, B, No. 5

UNRIGHTEOUS

adikos (ἄδικος, 94), not conforming to *dikē*, "right," is translated "unrighteous" in Luke 16:10 (twice), RV, 11; Rom. 3:5; 1 Cor. 6:1, RV; 6:9; Heb. 6:10; 1 Pet. 3:18, RV; 2 Pet. 2:9, RV: see UNJUST.

UNRIGHTEOUSNESS

A. Noun.

adikia (ἀδικία, 93) denotes (a) "injustice," Luke 18:6, lit., "the judge of injustice"; Rom. 9:14; (b) "unrighteousness, iniquity," e.g., Luke 16:8, lit., "the steward of unrighteousness," RV marg., i.e., characterized by "unrighteousness"; Rom. 1:18, 29; 2:8; 3:5; 6:13; 1 Cor. 13:6, RV, "unrighteousness"; 2 Thess. 2:10, "[with all (lit., 'in every) deceit'] of unrighteousness," i.e., deceit such as "unrighteousness" uses, and that in every variety; Antichrist and his ministers will not be restrained by any scruple from words or deeds calculated to deceive; 2 Thess. 2:12, of those who have pleasure in it, not an intellectual but a moral evil; distaste for truth is the precursor of the rejection of it; 2 Tim. 2:19, RV; 1 John 1:9, which includes (c); (c) "a deed or deeds violating law and justice" (virtually the same as *adikēma*, "an unrighteous act"), e.g., Luke 13:27, "iniquity"; 2 Cor. 12:13, "wrong," the wrong of depriving another of what is his own, here ironically of a favor; Heb. 8:12, 1st clause, "iniquities," lit., "unrighteousnesses" (plural, not as KJV); 2 Pet. 2:13, 15, RV, "wrongdoing," KJV, "unrighteousness"; 1 John 5:17. See INIQUITY.

Notes: (1) In 2 Cor. 6:14, KJV, *anomia*, "lawlessness," is translated "unrighteousness" (RV, "iniquity"). (2) *Adikia* is the comprehensive term for wrong, or wrongdoing, as between persons; *anomia*, "lawlessness," is the rejection of divine law, or wrong committed against it.

B. Verb.

adikeō (ἀδικέω, 91), "to do wrong," is rendered in Rev. 22:11, RV, firstly, "he that is unrighteous," lit., "the doer of unrighteousness" (present participle of the verb, with the article), secondly, "let him do unrighteousness (still)," the retributive and permanent effect of a persistent course of unrighteous-doing (KJV, "he that is unjust, let him be unjust"). See HURT, OFFENDER, Note, WRONG.

For **UNRIPE, UNTIMELY,** see FIG, No. 2

UNRULY

1. *anupotaktos* (ἀνυπότακτος, 506), "not subject to rule" (*a*, negative, *n*, euphonic, *hupotassō*, "to put in subjection"), is used (a) of things, Heb. 2:8, RV, "not subject" (KJV, "not put under"); (b) of persons, "unruly," 1 Tim. 1:9, RV (KJV, "disobedient"); Titus 1:6, 10. See DISOBEDIENT, B, *Note.*

2. *ataktōs* (ἀτάκτως, 814) is rendered "unruly" in 1 Thess. 5:14, KJV (marg. and RV, "disorderly).

Note: In Jas. 3:8, some texts have *akataschetos*, "that cannot be restrained," KJV, "unruly"

UNSEARCHABLE

1. *anexeraunētos* (ἀνεξεραύνητος, 419), or *anexereunētos* (ἀνεξερεύνητος, 419), *a*, negative, *n*, euphonic, *ex* (*ek*), "out," *eraunaō*, "to search, examine," is used in Rom. 11:33, of the judgments of God.

2. *anexichniastos* (ἀνεξιχνίαστος, 421), with the same prefixes as in No. 1 and an adjectival form akin to *ichneuō*, "to trace out" (*ichnos*, "a footprint, a track"), is translated "unsearchable" in Eph. 3:8, of the riches of Christ; in Rom. 11:33, "past tracing out," of the ways of the Lord (cf. No. 1, in the same verse). The ways of God are the outworkings of His judgment. Of the two questions in v. 34, the first seems to have reference to No. 1, the second to No. 2. See TRACE.

UNSEEMLINESS, UNSEEMLY

aschēmosunē (ἀσχημοσύνη, 808), from *aschēmōn*, "unseemly," is rendered "unseemliness" in Rom. 1:27, RV: see SHAME, No. 4.

Note: For "behave ... unseemly" see BEHAVE, No. 4.

For **UNSETTLE,** Gal. 5:12, RV, see STIR, No. 12

For **UNSKILLFUL,** Heb. 5:13, see EXPERIENCE, No. 1

UNSPEAKABLE

1. *anekdiēgētos* (ἀνεκδιήγητος, 411) denotes "inexpressible" (*a*, negative, *n*, euphonic, *ekdiēgeomai*, "to declare, relate"), 2 Cor. 9:15, "unspeakable" (of the gift of God); regarding the various explanations of the gift, it seems most suitable to view it as the gift of His Son.

2. *aneklalētos* (ἀνεκλάλητος, 412) denotes "unable to be told out" (*eklaleō*, "to speak out"), 1 Pet. 1:8, of the believer joy.

3. *arrhētos* (ἄρρητος, 731), primarily, "unspoken" (*a*, negative, *rhetos*, "spoken"), denotes "unspeakable," 2 Cor. 12:4, of the words heard by Paul when caught up into paradise. The word is common in sacred inscriptions especially in connection with the Greek Mysteries; hence Moulton and Milligan suggest the meaning "words too sacred to be uttered."

UNSTABLE, UNSTEADFAST

1. *astēriktos* (ἀστήρικτος, 793), *a*, negative, *stērizō*, "to fix," is used in 2 Pet. 2:14; 3:16, KJV, "unstable," RV, "unsteadfast."

2. *akatastatos* (ἀκατάστατος, 182), from *kathistēmi*, "to set in order," is rendered "unstable" in Jas. 1:8.

For **UNTAKEN AWAY,** 2 Cor. 3:14, KJV, see UNLIFTED

UNTHANKFUL

acharistos (ἀχάριστος, 884) denotes "ungrateful, thankless" (*charis*, "thanks"), Luke 6:35; 2 Tim. 3:2.

For **UNTIMELY** see FIG, No. 2

For **UNTOWARD** see CROOKED

UNVEILED

akatakaluptos (ἀκατακάλυπτος, 177), "uncovered" (*a*, negative, *katakaluptō*, "to cover"), is used in 1 Cor. 11:5, 13, RV, "unveiled," with reference to the injunction forbidding women to be "unveiled" in a church gathering. Whatever the character of the covering, it is to be on her head as "a sign of authority" (v. 10), RV, the meaning of which is indicated in v. 3 in the matter of headships, and the reasons for which are given in vv. 7-9, and in the phrase "because of the angels," intimating their witness of, and interest in, that which betokens the headship of Christ. The injunctions were neither Jewish, which required men to be veiled in prayer, nor Greek, by which men and women were alike "unveiled." The apostle's instructions were "the commandment of the Lord" (14), and were for all the churches (vv. 33, 34).

Note: For the verb *anakaluptō*, rendered "unveiled" in 2 Cor. 3:18, RV, see UNLIFTED (2nd ref.).

UNWILLING

Note: "I am unwilling" is the RV rendering of *thelō*, "to will," with the negative *ou*, in 3 John 13 (KJV, "I will not").

UNWISE

1. *anoētos* (ἀνόητος, 453) is translated "unwise" in Rom. 1:14, KJV; see FOOLISH, No. 2.

2. *aphrōn* (ἄφρων, 878) is translated "unwise" in Eph. 5:17, KJV; see FOOLISH, No. 1.

3. *asophos* (ἄσοφος, 781), *a*, negative, is rendered "unwise" in Eph. 5:15, RV (KJV, "fools.)"

UNWORTHILY, UNWORTHY

A. Adverb.

anaxiōs (ἀναξίως, 371) is used in 1 Cor. 11:27, of partaking of the Lord's Supper "unworthily," i.e., treating it as a common meal, the bread and cup as common things, not apprehending their solemn symbolic import. In the best texts the word is not found in v. 29 (see RV).

B. Adjective.

anaxios (ἀνάξιος, 370), *a*, negative, *n*, euphonic, *axios*, "worthy," is used in 1 Cor. 6:2. In modern Greek it signifies "incapable."

Note: In Acts 13:46, "unworthy" represents the adjective *axios*, preceded by the negative *ouk*.

For **UPBRAID** see REPROACH, B, No. 1

For **UPPER** see CHAMBER

UPPERMOST

Note: In Luke 11:43 *protōkathedria*, "a chief seat," is translated "uppermost seats," KJV (RV, "chief seats"). In Matt. 23:6 and Mark 12:39, KJV, *protōklisia*, "a chief place," is translated "uppermost rooms" (RV, "chief place" and "chief places"). See CHIEF, B, Nos. 6 and 7.

For **UPRIGHT** see STRAIGHT, No. 2

UPRIGHTNESS

euthutēs (εὐθύτης, 2118), from *euthus*, "straight," is rendered "uprightness" in Heb. 1:8, RV, KJV, "righteousness," marg., "rightness," or, "straightness."

For **UPROAR** (Noun), *thorubos*, see TUMULT, and for *stasis* see RIOT

UPROAR (Verbs)

thorubeō (θορυβέω, 2350), used in the middle voice, denotes "to make a noise or uproar," or, transitively, in the active voice, "to trouble, throw into confusion," Acts 17:5. See ADO, TROUBLE.

Note: For *suncheō*, "to confuse," Acts 21:31 (KJV, "was in an uproar"), see CONFUSION; for *anastatoō*, Acts 21:38 (KJV, "madest an uproar"), see STIR UP.

URGE

Notes: (1) In Acts 13:50, KJV, *parotrunō*, "to urge on" (RV), is rendered "stirred up." (2) In Acts 13:43, *peithō*, "to persuade," is rendered "urged," RV (KJV, "persuaded"). (3) For *enechō*, rendered "to urge" in Luke 11:53, KJV, see ENTANGLE, No. 3.

USING

apochrēsis (ἀπόχρησις, 671), a strengthened form of *chrēsis*, "a using," and signifying "a misuse" (akin to *apochraomai*, "to use to the full, abuse"), is translated "using" in Col. 2:22; the clause may be rendered "by their using up." "The unusual word was chosen for its expressiveness; the *chrēsis* here was an *apochrēsis;* the things could not be used without rendering them unfit for further use" (Lightfoot).

USURY

Note: The RV, "interest," Matt. 25:27; Luke 19:23, is the preferable rendering of *tokos* here.

For **UTMOST PART** see END, A, No. 3

UTTERMOST

1. *pantelēs* (παντελής, 3838), the neuter of the adjective *pantelēs*, "complete, perfect," used with *eis to* ("unto the"), is translated "to the uttermost" in Heb. 7:25, where the meaning may be "finally"; in Luke 13:11 (negatively), "in no wise."

2. *telos* (τέλος, 5056), "an end," is rendered "the uttermost" in 1 Thess. 2:16, said of divine wrath upon the Jews, referring to the prophecy of Deut. 28:15-68; the nation as such, will yet, however, be delivered (Rom. 11:26; cf. Jer. 30:4-11). The full phrase is *eis telos*, "to the uttermost," which is probably the meaning in John 13:1, "to the end."

Notes: (1) For "uttermost (farthing)," Matt. 5:26, KJV, see LAST. (2) For "uttermost part (-s)," see END, A, No. 3 (a) and C (b).

V

For **VAGABOND** see STROLLING

For **VAIL** see VEIL

VAIN, IN VAIN, VAINLY

A. Adjectives.

1. *kenos* (κενός, 2756), "empty," with special reference to quality, is translated "vain" (as an adjective) in Acts 4:25; 1 Cor. 15:10, 14 (twice); Eph. 5:6; Col. 2:8; Jas. 2:20; in the following the neuter, *kenon*, follows the preposition *eis*, "in," and denotes "in vain," 2 Cor. 6:1; Gal. 2:2; Phil. 2:16 (twice); 1 Thess. 3:5. See EMPTY, B, where the applications are enumerated.

2. *mataios* (μάταιος, 3152), "void of result," is used of (a) idolatrous practices, Acts 14:15, RV, "vain things" (KJV, "vanities"); (b) the thoughts of the wise, 1 Cor. 3:20; (c) faith, if Christ is not risen, 1 Cor. 15:17; (d) questionings, strifes, etc., Titus 3:9; (e) religion, with an unbridled tongue, Jas. 1:26; (f) manner of life, 1 Pet. 1:18. For the contrast between No. 1 and No. 2 see EMPTY.

Note: For *mataiologoi*, Titus 1:10, see TALKERS (VAIN).

B. Verbs.

1. *mataioō* (ματαιόω, 3154), "to make vain, or foolish," corresponding in meaning to A, No. 2, occurs in Rom. 1:21, "became vain."

2. *kenoō* (κενόω, 2758), "to empty," corresponding to A, No. 1, is translated "should be in vain" in 2 Cor. 9:3, KJV. See EFFECT, EMPTY, VOID.

C. Adverbs.

1. *matēn* (μάτην, 3155), properly the accusative case of *matē*, "a fault, a folly," signifies "in vain, to no purpose," Matt. 15:9; Mark 7:7.

2. *dōrean* (δωρεάν, 1432), the accusative of *dōrea*, "a gift," is used adverbially, denoting (a) "freely" (see FREE, D); (b) "uselessly," "in vain," Gal. 2:21, KJV (RV, "for nought").

3. *eikē* (εἰκῆ, 1500) denotes (a) "without cause," "vainly," Col. 2:18; (b) "to no purpose," "in vain," Rom. 13:4; Gal. 3:4 (twice); 4:11.

VAINGLORY, VAINGLORIOUS

A. Nouns.

1. *kenodoxia* (κενοδοξία, 2754), from *kenos*, "vain, empty," *doxa*, "glory," is used in Phil. 2:3.

2. *alazoneia*, or *-ia* (ἀλαζονεία, 212) denotes "boastfulness, vaunting," translated "vainglory" in 1 John 2:16, RV (KlV, "pride"); in Jas. 4:16, RV, "vauntings" (KJV, "boastings"). Cf. *alazōn*, "a boaster."

B. Adjective.

kenodoxos (κενόδοξος, 2755), akin to A, No. 1, is rendered "vainglorious" in Gal. 5:26, RV (KJV, "desirous of vain glory").

For **VALIANT** see MIGHTY, B, No. 2, STRONG, No. 2 (a) (3)

VALUE

A. Verb.

diapherō (διαφέρω, 1308), used intransitively, means "to differ, to excel," hence "to be of more value," Matt. 6:26, RV, "are (not) ye of (much) more value" (KJV, "better"); 12:12 and Luke 12:24, ditto; Matt. 10:31; Luke 12:7. See BETTER (BE), EXCELLENT, PUBLISH, No. 2.

B. Noun.

time (τιμή, 5092) denotes "a valuing, a price, honor"; in Col. 2:23, RV, "(not of any) value (against the indulgence of the flesh)" [KJV, "(not in any) honor ..."], i.e., the ordinances enjoined by human tradition are not of any value to prevent (*pros*, "against"; cf. Acts 26:14) indulgence of the flesh. See HONOR, SUM.

VANISH, VANISHING

A. Verb.

aphanizō (ἀφανίζω, 853), "to render unseen," is translated "vanisheth away" in Jas. 4:14 (passive voice, lit., "is made to disappear"). See CONSUME, DISFIGURE, PERISH.

Note: In 1 Cor. 13:8, KJV, *katargeō*, "to abolish," is rendered "it shall vanish away" (RV, "... be done away"). See ABOLISH.

B. Noun.

aphanismos (ἀφανισμός, 854), *a*, negative, *phainō*, "to cause to appear" (akin to A), occurs in Heb. 8:13, RV, "(nigh unto) vanishing away"; the word is suggestive of abolition.

Note: In Luke 24:31, the adjective *aphantos* (akin to A and B), "invisible," used with *ginomai*, "to become," and followed by *apo*, "from," with the plural personal pronoun, is rendered "He vanished out of their sight" (KJV, marg., "He ceased to be seen of them"), lit., "He became invisible from them."

VANITY

mataiotēs (ματαιότης, 3153), "emptiness as to results," akin to *mataios* (see EMPTY, VAIN), is used (a) of the creation, Rom. 8:20, as failing of the results designed, owing to sin; (b) of the mind which governs the manner of life of the Gentiles, Eph. 4:17; (c) of the "great swelling *words*" of false teachers, 2 Pet. 2:18.

Note: For *mataios*, in the neut. plur. in Acts 14:15, "vanities," see VAIN, A, No. 2 (a).

VAPOR

atmis (ἀτμίς, 822) is used of "smoke," Acts 2:19; figuratively of human life, Jas. 4:14.

VARIANCE

dichazō (διχάζω, 1369), "to cut apart, divide in two," is used metaphorically in Matt. 10:35, "to set at variance."

Notes: (1) In Gal. 5:20, KJV, *eris*, "strife" (RV), is rendered "variance." (2) For *adiakritos*, Jas. 3:17, RV, "without variance" (marg., "doubtfulness, or partiality"), KJV, "without partiality" (marg., "without wrangling"), see PARTIAL.

VAUNT (ONESELF)

perpereuomai (περπερεύομαι, 4068), "to boast or vaunt oneself" (from *perperos*, "vainglorious, braggart," not in the NT), is used in 1 Cor. 13:4, negatively of love.

For **VAUNTINGS** see VAINGLORY

For **VEHEMENT** see DESIRE, A, No. 3

VEIL

1\. *katapetasma* (καταπέτασμα, 2665), lit., "that which is spread out" (*petannumi*) "before" (*kata*), hence, "a veil," is used (a) of the inner "veil" of the tabernacle, Heb. 6:19; 9:3; (b) of the corresponding "veil" in the Temple, Matt. 27:51; Mark 15:38; Luke 23:45; (c) metaphorically of the "flesh" of Christ, Heb. 10:20, i.e., His body which He gave up to be crucified, thus by His expiatory death providing a means of the spiritual access of believers, the "new and living way," into the presence of God.

2\. *kalumma* (κάλυμμα, 2571), "a covering," is used (a) of the "veil" which Moses put over his face when descending Mount Sinai, thus preventing Israel from beholding the glory, 2 Cor. 3:13; (b) metaphorically of the spiritually darkened vision suffered retributively by Israel, until the conversion of the nation to their Messiah takes place, vv. 14, 15, 16. See under UNLIFTED.

3\. *peribolaion* (περιβόλαιον, 4018), rendered "a veil" in the KJV marg. of 1 Cor. 11:15: see VESTURE.

VENGEANCE

ekdikēsis (ἐκδίκησις, 1557), lit., ("that which proceeds) out of justice," not, as often with human "vengeance," out of a sense of injury or merely out of a feeling of indignation. The word is most frequently used of divine "vengeance," e.g., Rom. 12:19; Heb. 10:30. For a complete list see AVENGE, B, No. 2. The judgments of God are holy and right (Rev. 16:7), and free from any element of self-gratification or vindictiveness.

Notes: (1) *Dikē*, "justice," is translated "vengeance" in the KJV of Acts 28:4 and Jude 7: see JUSTICE. (2) In Rom. 3:5, KJV, *orgē*, "wrath" (RV), is rendered "vengeance": see ANGER, WRATH.

For **VENOMOUS** see BEAST, No. 2

VERILY

1\. *alēthōs* (ἀληθῶς, 230), "truly" (akin to *alētheia*, "truth"), is translated "verily" in 1 John 2:5. See TRULY.

2\. *amēn* (ἀμήν, 281), the transliteration of a Heb. word = "truth," is usually translated "verily" in the four Gospels; in John's gospel the Lord introduces a solemn pronouncement by the repeated word "verily, verily" twenty-five times. See AMEN.

3\. *ontōs* (ὄντως, 3689), "really" (connected with *eimi*, "to be"), is rendered "verily" in Mark 11:32, RV, and Gal. 3:21.

Notes: (1) In Acts 16:37, *gar*, "for," is translated "verily." (2) In Heb. 2:16, *dēpou* (in some texts *dē pou*), a particle meaning "of course, we know," is rendered "verily." (3) In Luke 11:51, KJV, *nai*, "yea" (RV), is translated "verily." (4) The particle *men* is rendered "verily," e.g., in 1 Cor. 5:3; 14:17; Heb. 12:10; in the KJV, Heb. 3:5; 7:5, 18; 1 Pet. 1:20; in Acts 26:9 it is combined with *oun* ("therefore").

For **VERITY**, 1 Tim. 2:7, KJV, see TRUTH

VESSEL

1\. *skeuos* (σκεῦος, 4632) is used (a) of "a vessel or implement" of various kinds, Mark 11:16; Luke 8:16; John 19:29; Acts 10:11, 16; 11:5; 27:17 (a sail); Rom. 9:21; 2 Tim. 2:20; Heb. 9:21; Rev. 2:27; 18:12; (b) of "goods or household stuff," Matt. 12:29 and Mark 3:27, "goods"; Luke 17:31, RV, "goods" (KJV, "stuff"); (c) of "persons," (1) for the service of God, Acts 9:15, "a (chosen) vessel"; 2 Tim. 2:21, "a vessel (unto honor)"; (2) the "subjects" of divine wrath, Rom. 9:22; (3) the "subjects" of divine mercy, Rom. 9:23; (4) the human frame, 2 Cor. 4:7; perhaps 1 Thess. 4:4; (5) a husband and wife, 1 Pet. 3:7; of the wife, probably, 1 Thess. 4:4; while the exhortation to each one "to possess himself of his own vessel in sanctification and honor" is regarded by some as referring to the believer's body [cf. Rom. 6:13; 1 Cor. 9:27; see No. (4)], the view that the "vessel" signifies the wife, and that the reference is to the sanctified maintenance of the married state, is supported by the facts that in 1 Pet. 3:7 the same word *timē*, "honor," is used with regard to the wife, again in Heb. 13:4, *timios*, "honorable" (RV, "in honor") is used in regard to marriage; further, the preceding command in 1 Thess. 4 is against fornication, and the succeeding one (v. 6) is against adultery. In Ruth 4:10, Sept., *ktaomai*, "to possess," is used of a wife.

2. *angos* (ἄγγος, 30) denotes "a jar" or "pail," Matt. 13:48, in the best texts (some have No. 3). It is used, in an inscription, of a cinerary urn.

3. *angeion* (ἀγγεῖον, 30) denotes "a small vessel" (a diminutive of No. 2), e.g., for carrying oil, Matt. 25:4.

Note: For *phaulos*, Jas. 3:16, RV, see EVIL, A, No. 3.

VESTURE

1. *himation* (ἱμάτιον, 2440), "an outer garment," is rendered "vesture" in Rev. 19:13, 16, KJV (RV, "garment").

2. *himatismos* (ἱματισμός, 2441), used of "clothing in general," is translated "vesture" in Matt. 27:35, KJV, in a quotation from Ps. 22:18 (RV, following the better texts, omits the quotation); in John 19:24, KJV and RV; see CLOTHING, No. 4.

3. *peribolaion* (περιβόλαιον, 4018) is translated "vesture" in Heb. 1:12, KJV (RV, "mantle").

VEX

1. *ochleō* (ὀχλέω, 3791), "to disturb, trouble," is used in the passive voice, of being "troubled" by evil spirits, Acts 5:16.

2. *basanizō* (βασανίζω, 928), "to torment," is translated "vexed" in 2 Pet. 2:8. See TORMENT.

Notes: (1) In Luke 6:18, the best texts have *enochleō*, RV, "troubled." See TROUBLE, B, No. 5. (2) In 2 Pet. 2:7, KJV, *kataponeō*, "to wear down with toil," is translated "vexed." See DISTRESS, B, No. 4. (3) In Acts 12:1, KJV, *kakoō*, "to afflict" (RV), is translated "to vex." See AFFLICT, No. 1. (4) For Matt. 17:15, KJV, "vexed," see GRIEVOUSLY, B, *Note* (2).

For **VIAL** see BOWL

VICTORY, VICTORIOUS

A. Nouns.

1. *nikē* (νίκη, 3529), "victory," is used in 1 John 5:4.

2. *nikos* (νῖκος, 3534), a later form of No. 1, is used in Matt. 12:20; 1 Cor. 15:54, 55, 57.

B. Verb.

nikaō (νικάω, 3528), "to conquer, overcome," is translated "(them) that come victorious (from)" in Rev. 15:2, RV (KJV, "that had gotten the victory"). See CONQUER, OVERCOME, PREVAIL.

For **VIGILANT,** 1 Tim. 3:2, see TEMPERATE; 1 Pet. 5:8, see WATCHFUL

VILE

A. Noun.

atimia (ἀτιμία, 819), "dishonor," is translated "vile" in Rom. 1:26, RV, marg., "(passions) of dishonor." See DISHONOR.

B. Adjectives.

1. *rhuparos* (ῥυπαρός, 4508), "filthy dirty," is used (a) literally, of old shabby clothing, Jas. 2:2, "vile"; (b) metaphorically, of moral defilement, Rev. 22:11 (in the best texts). In the Sept., Zech. 3:3, 4.

2. *ponēros* (πονηρός, 4190), "evil," is translated "vile" in Acts 17:5, RV (KJV, "lewd"). See BAD, EVIL.

Note: For "vile" in the KJV of Phil. 3:21, see HUMILIATION.

VINE, VINTAGE

ampelos (ἄμπελος, 288) is used (a) lit., e.g., Matt. 26:29 and parallel passages; Jas. 3:12; (b) figuratively, (1) of Christ, John 15:1, 4, 5; (2) of His enemies, Rev. 14:18, 19, "the vine of the earth" (RV, "vintage" in v. 19), probably figurative of the remaining mass of apostate Christendom.

VINEGAR

oxos (ὄξος, 3690), akin to *oxus*, "sharp," denotes "sour wine," the ordinary drink of laborers and common soldiers; it is used in the four Gospels of the "vinegar" offered to the Lord at His crucifixion. In Matt. 27:34 the best texts have *oinos*, "wine" (RV). Some have *oxos* (KJV, "vinegar"), but Mark 15:23 (KJV and RV) confirms the RV in the passage in Matthew. This, which the soldiers offered before crucifying, was refused by Him, as it was designed to alleviate His sufferings; the "vinegar" is mentioned in Mark 15:36; so Luke 23:36, and John 19:29, 30. In the Sept., Num. 6:3; Ruth 2:14; Ps. 69:21; Prov. 25:20.

VINEYARD

ampelōn (ἀμπελών, 290) is used 22 times in the Synoptic Gospels; elsewhere in 1 Cor. 9:7.

VIOLENCE, VIOLENT, VIOLENTLY

A. Nouns.

1. *bia* (βία, 970) denotes "force, violence," said of men, Acts 5:26; 21:35; 24:7; of waves, 27:41.

2. *hormēma* (ὅρμημα, 3731), "a rush" (akin to *hormaō*, "to urge on, to rush"), is used of the fall of Babylon, Rev. 18:21, KJV, "violence," RV, "mighty fall."

3. *biastēs* (βιαστής, 973), "a forceful or violent man," is used in Matt. 11:12. See FORCE, B, No. 1, *Note*.

Note: In Heb. 11:34, KJV, *dunamis*, "power" (RV), is rendered "violence."

B. Verbs.

1. *diaseiō* (διασείω, 1286), "to shake violently," is used in Luke 3:14, "do violence," including intimidation. In the Sept., Job 4:14.

2. *biazō* (βιάζω, 971), in the passive voice, is rendered "suffereth violence" in Matt. 11:12; see FORCE, B, Nos. 1 and 2. Some, e.g., Cremer (*Lexicon*) and Dalman (*Words of Jesus*, pp. 139,ff.), hold that the reference is to the antagonism of the enemies of the kingdom, but Luke 16:16 (middle voice: RV, "entereth violently") indicates the meaning as referring to those who make an effort to enter the kingdom in spite of violent opposition: see PRESS, A, No. 3.

VIPER

echidna (ἔχιδνα, 2191) is probably a generic term for "poisonous snakes." It is rendered "viper" in the NT, (a) of the actual creature, Acts 28:3; (b) metaphorically in Matt. 3:7; 12:34; 23:33; Luke 3:7.

VIRGIN

parthenos (παρθένος, 3933) is used (a) of "the Virgin Mary," Matt. 1:23; Luke 1:27; (b) of the ten "virgins" in the parable, Matt. 25:1, 7, 11; (c) of the "daughters" of Philip the evangelist, Acts 21:9; (d) those concerning whom the apostle Paul gives instructions regarding marriage, 1 Cor. 7:25, 28, 34; in vv. 36, 37, 38, the subject passes to that of "virgin *daughters*" (RV), which almost certainly formed one of the subjects upon which the church at Corinth sent for instructions from the apostle; one difficulty was relative to the discredit which might be brought upon a father (or guardian), if he allowed his daughter or ward to grow old unmarried. The interpretation that this passage refers to a man and woman already in some kind of relation by way of a spiritual marriage and living together in a vow of virginity and celibacy, is untenable if only in view of the phraseology of the passage; (e) figuratively, of "a local church" in its relation to Christ, 2 Cor. 11:2; (f) metaphorically of "chaste persons," Rev. 14:4.

VIRGINITY

parthenia (παρθενία, 3932), akin to the above, occurs in Luke 2:36. In the Sept., Jer. 3:4.

VIRTUE

aretē (ἀρέτη, 703) properly denotes whatever procures preeminent estimation for a person or thing; hence, "intrinsic eminence, moral goodness, virtue," (a) of God, 1 Pet. 2:9, "excellencies" (KJV, "praises"); here the original and general sense seems to be blended with the impression made on others, i.e., renown, excellence or praise (Hort); in 2 Pet. 1:3, "(by His own glory and) virtue," RV (instrumental dative), i.e., the manifestation of His divine power; this significance is frequently illustrated in the papyri and was evidently common in current Greek speech; (b) of any particular moral excellence, Phil. 4:8; 2 Pet. 1:5 (twice), where virtue is enjoined as an essential quality in the exercise of faith, RV, "(in your faith supply) virtue."

Note: In the KJV of Mark 5:30; Luke 6:19; 8:46, *dunamis*, "power" (RV), is rendered "virtue."

VISIBLE

horatos (ὁρατός, 3707), from *horaō*, "to see," occurs in Col. 1:16.

VISION

1. *horama* (ὅραμα, 3705), "that which is seen" (*horaō*), denotes (a) "a spectacle, sight," Matt. 17:9; Acts 7:31 ("sight"); (b) "an appearance, vision," Acts 9:10 (v. 12 in some mss.): 10:3, 17, 19; 11:5; 12:9; 16:9, 10; 18:9.

2. *horasis* (ὅρασις, 3706), "sense of sight," is rendered "visions" in Acts 2:17; Rev. 9:17. See LOOK, B.

3. *optasia* (ὀπτασία, 3701) (a late form of *opsis*, "the act of seeing"), from *optanō*, "to see, a coming into view," denotes a "vision" in Luke 1:22; 24:23; Acts 26:19; 2 Cor. 12:1.

VISIT

1. *episkeptomai* (ἐπισκέπτομαι, 1980), primarily, "to inspect" (a late form of *episkopeō*, "to look upon, care for, exercise oversight"), signifies (a) "to visit" with help, of the act of God, Luke 1:68, 78; 7:16; Acts 15:14; Heb. 2:6; (b) "to visit" the sick and afflicted, Matt. 25:36, 43; Jas. 1:27; (c) "to go and see," "pay a visit to," Acts 7:23; 15:36; (d) "to look out" certain men for a purpose, Acts 6:3 See LOOK.

Note: In the Sept., "to visit with punishment," e.g., Ps. 89:32; Jer. 9:25.

2. *historeō* (ἱστορέω, 2477), from *histōr*, "one learned in anything," denotes "to visit" in order to become acquainted with, Gal. 1:18, RV, "visit" (KJV, "see"), RV marg., "become acquainted with."

3. *epipherō* (ἐπιφέρω, 2018) is rendered "visiteth (with wrath)" in Rom. 3:5, RV, KJV, "taketh (vengeance)."

VISITATION

episkopē (ἐπισκοπή, 1984), for which see BISHOP, No. 2, denotes "a visitation," whether in mercy, Luke 19:44, or in judgment, 1 Pet. 2:12.

For **VOCATION**, Eph. 4:1, see CALL, B

VOICE

phōnē (φωνή, 5456), "a sound," is used of the voice (a) of God, Matt. 3:17; John 5:37; 12:28, 30; Acts 7:31; 10:13, 15; 11:7, 9; Heb. 3:7, 15; 4:7; 12:19, 26; 2 Pet. 1:17, 18; Rev. 18:4; 21:3; (b) of Christ, (1) in the days of His flesh, Matt. 12:19 (negatively);

John 3:29; 5:25; 10:3, 4, 16, 27; 11:43; 18:37; (2) on the cross Matt. 27:46, and parallel passages; (3) from heaven, Acts 9:4, 7; 22:7, 9, 14; 26:14; Rev. 1:10, 12 (here, by metonymy, of the speaker), 15; 3:20; (4) at the resurrection "to life," John 5:28; 1 Thess. 4:16, where "the voice of the archangel" is, lit., "a voice of an archangel," and probably refers to the Lord's voice as being of an archangelic character; (5) at the resurrection to judgment, John 5:28 [not the same event as (4)]; (c) of human beings on earth, e.g., Matt. 2:18; 3:3; Luke 1:42, in some texts, KJV, "voice," and frequently in the Synoptists; (d) of angels, Rev. 5:11, and frequently in the Apocalypse; (e) of the redeemed in heaven, e.g., Rev. 6:10; 18:22; 19:1, 5; (f) of a pagan god, Acts 12:22; (g) of things, e.g., wind, John 3:8, RV, "voice" (KJV, "sound"). See SOUND.

Notes: (1) In Luke 1:42 (1st part), KJV, *anaphōneō*, "to lift up one's voice," is rendered "spake out," RV, "lifted up (her) voice." (2) In Acts 26:10, KJV, "I gave my voice" (RV, "... vote"): see STONE, No. 2.

VOID

1. *kenoō* (κενόω, 2758), "to empty, make of no effect," is rendered "to make void," in Rom. 4:14; 1 Cor. 1:17, RV; 9:15; 2 Cor. 9:3, RV. See EFFECT (of none), No. 3, EMPTY, VAIN, B, No. 2.

2. *atheteō* (ἀθετέω, 114) is rendered "to make void" in Gal. 2:21, RV (KJV, "frustrate"); 3:15, RV.

3. *akuroō* (ἀκυρόω, 208) is rendered "to make void" in Matt. 15:6; Mark 7:13, RV.

Notes: (1) In Rom. 3:31, KJV, *katargeō* is translated "to make void." See ABOLISH, EFFECT (of none), No. 2. (2) See also OFFENSE, UNDERSTANDING.

VOLUNTARY

Note: In Col. 2:18, *thelō* (for which see DESIRE, B, No. 6) is rendered "(in a) voluntary (humility)," present participle, i.e., "being a voluntary (in humility)," KJV marg., RV marg., "of his own mere will (by humility)," *en*, "in," being rendered as instrumental; what was of one's own mere will, with the speciousness of humility, would mean his being robbed of his prize.

For **VOTE**, Acts 26:10, RV, see STONE, No. 2

VOUCHSAFE

homologeō (ὁμολογέω, 3670), "to agree," is found in the best texts in Acts 7:17, and rendered "vouchsafed," RV, with reference to God's promise to Abraham; some mss. have *ōmosen*, "swore" (*omnumi*, "to swear"), as in KJV. See CONFESS, PROFESS, PROMISE THANKS, B, *Note.*

VOW

euchē (εὐχή, 2171) denotes also "a vow," Acts 18:18; 21:23, with reference to the "vow" of the Nazirite (wrongly spelt Nazarite), see Num. 6, RV; in Jas. 5:15, "prayer." See PRAYER.

WAGES

1. *opsōnion* (ὀψώνιον, 3800) denotes (a) "soldier's pay," Luke 3:14; 1 Cor. 9:7 ("charges"); (b) in general, "hire, wages of any sort," used metaphorically, Rom. 6:23, of sin; 2 Cor. 11:8, of material support which Paul received from some of the churches which he had established and to which he ministered in spiritual things; their support partly maintained him at Corinth, where he forebore to receive such assistance (vv. 9, 10).

2. *misthos* (μισθός, 3408), "hire," is rendered "wages" in John 4:36; in 2 Pet. 2:15, KJV (RV, hire).

WAIL, WAILING

Notes: (1) For *koptō*, rendered "to wail" in Rev. 1:7, KJV (RV, "shall mourn") and 18:9, RV, "wail" (KJV, "lament"), see BEWAIL. (2) For *pentheō*, rendered "to wail" in Rev. 18:15, 19, KJV, see MOURN. (3) For *klauthmos*, rendered "wailing" in Matt. 13:42, 50, KJV, see WEEP. (4) In Matt. 11:17 and Luke 7:32, KJV, *thrēneō*, "to wail" (RV), is rendered to mourn. See BEWAIL, *Note* (1), MOURN.

WAKE

grēgoreō (γρηγορέω, 1127), translated "wake" in 1 Thess. 5:10, is rendered "watch" in the RV marg., as in the text in v. 6, and the RV in the twenty-one other places in which it occurs in the NT (save 1 Pet. 5:8, "be watchful"). It is not used in the metaphorical sense of "to be alive"; here it is set in contrast with *katheudō*, "to sleep," which is never used by the apostle with the meaning "to be dead" (it has this meaning only in the case of Jairus' daughter). Accordingly the meaning here is that of vigilance and expectancy as contrasted with laxity and indifference. All believers will live together with Christ from the time of the Rapture described in ch. 4; for all have spiritual life now, though their spiritual condition and attainment vary considerably. Those who are lax and fail to be watchful will suffer loss (1 Cor. 3:15; 9:27; 2 Cor. 5:10, e.g.), but the apostle is not here dealing with that aspect of the subject. What he does make clear is that the Rapture of believers at the second coming of Christ will depend solely on the death of Christ for them, and not upon their spiritual condition. The Rapture is not a matter of reward, but of salvation. See WATCH.

WANDER

A. Verb.

planaō (πλανάω, 4105), for which see DECEIT, C, No. 6, is translated "to wander" in Heb. 11:38, passive voice, lit., "were made to wander."

Note: In the KJV of 1 Tim. 5:13 and Heb. 11:37, *perierchōmai*, "to go about or around," is translated "to wander about." See GO, No. 29.

B. Noun.

planētēs (πλανήτης, 4107), "a wanderer" (Eng., "planet"), is used metaphorically in Jude 13, of the evil teachers there mentioned as "wandering (stars)." In the Sept., Hos. 9:17.

WANTONNESS, WANTON, WANTONLY

A. Nouns.

1. *aselgeia* (ἀσέλγεια, 766), "lasciviousness, licentiousness," is rendered "wantonness" in 2 Pet. 2:18, KJV; see LASCIVIOUSNESS.

2. *strēnos* (στρῆνος, 4764), "insolent luxury," is rendered "wantonness" in Rev. 18:3, RV (marg., "luxury"; KJV, "delicacies," not a sufficiently strong rendering).

B. Verbs.

1. *strēniaō* (στρηνιάω, 4763), akin to A, No. 2, "to run riot," is rendered "waxed wanton" in Rev. 18:7, RV, and "lived wantonly" in v. 8. The root of the verb is seen in the Latin *strenuus*.

2. *katastrēniaō* (καταστρηνιάω, 2691), an intensive form of No. 1, "to wax wanton against," occurs in 1 Tim. 5:11.

WARN

1. *noutheteō* (νουθετέω, 3560), "to put in mind, warn," is translated "to warn" in the KJV, in the passages mentioned under ADMONISH, B, No. 1 (which see); the RV always translates this word by the verb "to admonish."

2. *hupodeiknumi* (ὑποδείκνυμι, 5263), primarily, "to show secretly" (*hupo*, "under," *deiknumi*, "to show"), hence, generally, "to teach, make known," is translated "to warn" in Matt. 3:7; Luke 3:7; 12:5, RV (KJV, "forewarn"). See FOREWARN, *Note.*

3. *chrēmatizō* (χρηματίζω, 5537), for which see ADMONISH, B, No. 3, is translated "to warn" in Matt. 2:12, 22; Acts 10:22; Heb. 8:5, RV (KJV, "admonished"); 11:7; 12:25, RV (KJV, "spake").

WASH

1. *niptō* (νίπτω, 3538) is chiefly used of "washing part of the body," John 13:5-6, 8 (twice, figuratively in 2nd clause), 12, 14 (twice); in 1 Tim. 5:10, including the figurative sense; in the middle voice, to wash oneself, Matt. 6:17; 15:2; Mark 7:3; John 9:7, 11, 15; 13:10. For the corresponding noun see BASON.

2. *aponiptō* (ἀπονίπτω, 633), "to wash off," is used in the middle voice, in Matt. 27:24.

3. *louō* (λούω, 3068) signifies "to bathe, to wash the body," (a) active voice, Acts 9:37; 16:33; (b) passive voice, John 13:10, RV, "bathed" (KJV, "washed"); Heb. 10:22, lit., "having been washed as to the body," metaphorical of the effect of the Word of God upon the activities of the believer; (c) middle voice, 2 Pet. 2:22. Some inferior mss. have it instead of *luō*, "to loose," in Rev. 1:5 (see RV).

4. *apolouō* (ἀπολούω, 628), "to wash off or away," is used in the middle voice, metaphorically, "to wash oneself," in Acts 22:16, where the command to Saul of Tarsus to "wash away" his sins indicates that by his public confession, he would testify to the removal of his sins, and to the complete change from his past life; this "washing away" was not in itself the actual remission of his sins, which had taken place at his conversion; the middle voice implies his own particular interest in the act (as with the preceding verb "baptize," lit., "baptize thyself," i.e., "get thyself baptized"); the aorist tenses mark the decisiveness of the acts; in 1 Cor. 6:11, lit., "ye washed yourselves clean"; here the middle voice (rendered in the Passive in KJV and RV, which do not distinguish between this and the next two passives; see RV marg.) again indicates that the converts at Corinth, by their obedience to the faith, voluntarily gave testimony to the complete spiritual change divinely wrought in them. In the Sept., Job 9:30.

5. *plunō* (πλύνω, 4150) is used of "washing inanimate objects," e.g., "nets," Luke 5:2 (some texts have *apoplunō*); of "garments," figuratively, Rev. 7:14; 22:14 (in the best texts; the KJV translates those which have the verb *poieō*, "to do," followed by *tas entolas autou*, "His commandments").

6. *rhantizō* (ῥαντίζω, 4472), "to sprinkle," is used in the middle voice in Mark 7:4, in some ancient texts, of the acts of the Pharisees in their assiduous attention to the cleansing of themselves after coming from the market place (some texts have *baptizō* here). See SPRINKLE.

7. *brechō* (βρέχω, 1026), "to wet," is translated "to wash" in Luke 7:38, 44, KJV; the RV, "to wet" and "hath wetted," gives the correct rendering.

8. *baptizō* (βαπτίζω, 907) is rendered "washed" in Luke 11:38. See BAPTIZE.

Note: With regard to Nos. 1, 3, 5, the Sept. of Lev. 15:11 contains all three with their distinguishing characteristics, No. 1 being used of the hands, No. 3 of the whole body, No. 5 of the garments.

WASHING

1. *baptismos* (βαπτισμός, 909) denotes "the act of washing, ablution," with special reference to purification, Mark 7:4 (in some texts, v. 8); Heb. 6:2, "baptisms"; 9:10, "washings." See BAPTISM.

2. *loutron* (λουτρόν, 3067), "a bath, a laver" (akin to *louō*, see above), is used metaphorically of the Word of God, as the instrument of spiritual cleansing, Eph. 5:26; in Titus 3:5, of "the washing of regeneration" (see REGENERATION). In the Sept., Song of Sol. 4:2; 6:6.

WASTE (Noun and Verb)

A. Noun.

apōleia (ἀπώλεια, 684), "destruction," is translated "waste" in Matt. 26:8; Mark 14:4. See DESTRUCTION, B, II, No. 1.

B. Verbs.

1. *diaskorpizō* (διασκορπίζω, 1287), "to scatter abroad," is used metaphorically of "squandering property," Luke 15:13; 16:1. See DISPERSE, SCATTER.

2. *portheō* (πορθέω, 4199), "to ravage," is rendered "wasted" in Gal. 1:13, KJV; see DESTROY, *Note,* HAVOC.

3. *lumainō* (λυμαίνω, 3075), "to outrage, maltreat," is used in the middle voice in Acts 8:3, of Saul's treatment of the church, RV, "laid waste" (KJV, "made havoc of").

WATCH (Noun and Verb), WATCHERS, WATCHFUL, WATCHINGS

A. Nouns.

1. *phulakē* (φυλακή, 5438) is used (a) with the meaning "a watch," actively, "a guarding," Luke 2:8, lit., "(keeping, *phulasso*) watches"; (b) of "the time during which guard was kept by night, a watch of the night," Matt. 14:25; 24:43; Mark 6:48; Luke 12:38. See CAGE, PRISON.

Note: Among the Jews the night was divided into three "watches" (see, e.g., Exod. 14:24; Judg. 7:19), and this continued on through Roman times. The Romans divided the night into four "watches"; this was recognized among the Jews (see Mark 13:35).

2. *koustodia* (κουστωδία, 2892), from Lat., *custodia* (cf. Eng., "custody"), is rendered "watch" in Matt. 27:65, 66 and 28:11, KJV: see GUARD.

3. *agrupnia* (ἀγρυπνία, 70), "sleeplessness" (akin to B, No. 4), is rendered "watchings" in 2 Cor. 6:5; 11:27.

B. Verbs.

1. *gregoreō* (γρηγορεύω, 1127), "to watch," is used (a) of "keeping awake," e.g., Matt. 24:43; 26:38, 40, 41; (b) of

"spiritual alertness," e.g., Acts 20:31; 1 Cor. 16:13; Col. 4:2; 1 Thess. 5:6, 10 (for which see WAKE); 1 Pet. 5:8, RV, "be watchful" (KJV, "be vigilant"); Rev. 3:2, 3; 16:15.

2. *tēreō* (τηρέω, 5083), "to keep," is rendered "to watch," of those who kept guard at the cross, Matt. 27:36, 54; 28:4, RV, "watchers" (KJV, "keepers"), lit., "the watching ones." See OBSERVE, PRESERVE.

3. *paratēreō* (παρατηρέω, 3906), "to observe," especially with sinister intent (*para*, "near," and No. 2), is rendered "to watch" in Mark 3:2; Luke 6:7; 14:1; 20:20; Acts 9:24. See OBSERVE.

4. *agrupneō* (ἀγρυπνέω, 69), "to be sleepless" (from *agreuō*, "to chase," and *hupnos*, "sleep"), is used metaphorically, "to be watchful," in Mark 13:33; Luke 21:36; Eph. 6:18; Heb. 13:17. The word expresses not mere wakefulness, but the "watchfulness" of those who are intent upon a thing.

5. *nēphō* (νήφω, 3525), "to abstain from wine," is used metaphorically of moral "alertness," and translated "to watch," in the KJV of 2 Tim. 4:5. See SOBER.

WATER (Noun and Verb), WATERING, WATERLESS

A. Noun.

hudōr (ὕδωρ, 5204), whence Eng. prefix, "hydro-," is used (a) of the natural element, frequently in the Gospels; in the plural especially in the Apocalypse; elsewhere, e.g., Heb. 9:19; Jas. 3:12; in 1 John 5:6, that Christ "came by water and blood," may refer either (1) to the elements that flowed from His side on the cross after His death, or, in view of the order of the words and the prepositions here used, (2) to His baptism in Jordan and His death on the cross. As to (1), the "water" would symbolize the moral and practical cleansing effected by the removal of defilement by our taking heed to the Word of God in heart, life and habit; cf. Lev. 14, as to the cleansing of the leper. As to (2), Jesus the Son of God came on His mission by, or through, "water" and blood, namely, at His baptism, when He publicly entered upon His mission and was declared to be the Son of God by the witness of the Father, and at the cross, when He publicly closed His witness; the apostle's statement thus counteracts the doctrine of the Gnostics that the divine *Logos* united Himself with the Man Jesus at His baptism, and left him at Gethsemane. On the contrary, He who was baptized and He who was crucified was the Son of God throughout in His combined deity and humanity.

The word "water" is used symbolically in John 3:5, either (1) of the Word of God, as in 1 Pet. 1:23 (cf. the symbolic use in Eph. 5:26), or, in view of the preposition *ek*, "out of," (2) of the truth conveyed by baptism, this being the expression, not the medium, the symbol, not the cause, of the believer's identification with Christ in His death, burial and resurrection. So the New Birth is, in one sense, the setting aside of all that the believer was according to the flesh, for it is evident that there must be an entirely new beginning. Some regard the *kai*, "and," in John 3:5, as epexegetic, = "even," in which case the "water" would be emblematic of the Spirit, as in John 7:38 (cf. 4:10, 14), but not in 1 John 5:8. where the Spirit and the "water" are distinguished. "The water of life," Rev. 21:6 and 22:1, 17, is emblematic of the maintenance of spiritual life in perpetuity. In Rev. 17:1 "the waters" are symbolic of nations, peoples, etc.

Note: For *potamos*, rendered "waters" in 2 Cor. 11:26, see RIVER.

B. Verb.

potizō (ποτίζω, 4222), "to give to drink," is used (a) naturally in Luke 13:15, "watering," with reference to animals; (b) figuratively, with reference to spiritual ministry to converts, 1 Cor. 3:6-8. See DRINK, B, No. 3.

Notes: (1) For *hudropoteō*, "to drink water," 1 Tim. 5:23, see DRINK, B, No. 5. (2) For the adjective *anudros*, "waterless" (RV), "without water," see DRY, No. 2.

WAVE

1. *kuma* (κῦμα, 2949), from *kuō*, "to be pregnant, to swell," is used (a) literally in the plural, Matt. 8:24; 14:24; Mark 4:37 (Acts 27:41, in some mss.); (b) figuratively, Jude 13.

2. *salos* (σάλος, 4535) denotes "a tossing," especially the rolling swell of the sea, Luke 21:25, KJV, "waves" (RV, "billows").

3. *kludōn* (κλύδων, 2830), "a billow," is translated "wave" in Jas. 1:6, KJV (RV, "surge"); in Luke 8:24 it is translated "raging (of the water)." See RAGE, B.

WAVER, WAVERING

A. Adjective.

aklinēs (ἀκλινής, 186), "without bending" (*a*, negative, *klinō*, "to bend"), occurs in Heb. 10:23, KJV, "without wavering," RV, "that it waver not."

B. Verb.

diakrinō (διακρίνω, 1252) is rendered "to waver" in Rom. 4:20, RV (KJV, "staggered"); in Jas. 1:6 (twice). See DOUBT, No. 3.

WAX

1. *prokoptō* (προκόπτω, 4298) is rendered "to wax" in 2 Tim. 3:13.

2. *ginomai* (γίνομαι, 1096), "to become," is translated "waxed" in Luke 13:19, KJV (RV, "became"); in Heb. 11:34, KJV and RV, "waxed."

Note: This verb forms part of the translation of certain tenses of other verbs; see, e.g., COLD, C, CONFIDENT, B, No.

1, CORRUPT, A, No. 2, OLD, D, No. 2, STRONG, B, No. 2, WANTON, B, Nos. 1 and 2, WEARY, No. 2, WROTH, No. 1.

WAY

1. *hodos* (ὁδός, 3598) denotes (a) "a natural path, road, way," frequent in the Synoptic Gospels; elsewhere, e.g., Acts 8:26; 1 Thess. 3:11; Jas. 2:25; Rev. 16:12; (b) "a traveler's way"; (c) metaphorically, of "a course of conduct," or "way of thinking," e.g., of righteousness, Matt. 21:32; 2 Pet. 2:21; of God, Matt. 22:16, and parallels, i.e., the "way" instructed and approved by God; so Acts 18:26 and Heb. 3:10, "My ways" (cf. Rev. 15:3); of the Lord, Acts 18:25; "that leadeth to destruction," Matt. 7:13; "... unto life," 7:14; of peace, Luke 1:79; Rom. 3:17; of Paul's "ways" in Christ, 1 Cor. 4:17 (plural); "more excellent" (of love), 1 Cor. 12:31; of truth, 2 Pet. 2:2; of the right "way," 2:15; of Balaam (*id.*), of Cain, Jude 11; of a "way" consisting in what is from God, e.g., of life, Acts 2:28 (plural); of salvation, Acts 16:17; personified, of Christ as the means of access to the Father, John 14:6; of the course followed and characterized by the followers of Christ, Acts 9:2; 19:9, 23; 24:22. See HIGHWAY.

Note: In Luke 5:19 and 19:4 the noun is not expressed in the original, but is understood.

2. *parodos* (πάροδος, 3938), "a passing or passage," is used with *en*, "in," 1 Cor. 16:7, "by the way" (lit, "in passing").

3. *tropos* (τρόπος, 5158), "a turning, a manner," is translated "way" in Rom. 3:2, "(every) way"; Phil. 1:18, "(in every) way."

Notes: (1) In Jas. 1:11, KJV, *poreia*, "a journey, a going," is rendered "ways" (RV, "goings"). (2) In Heb. 12:17, *topos*, "a place," is rendered in KJV marg., "way (to change his mind)." (3) In Luke 14:32, *porrō* is rendered "a great way off." (4) In Heb. 5:2, KJV, *planaō*, middle voice, "to wander," is rendered "(them) that are out of the way," RV, "(the) erring." (5) In Col. 2:14 and 2 Thess. 2:7, *ek mesou*, is translated "out of the way." (6) In John 10:1, the adverb *allachothen*, "from some other place" (from *allos*, "another"), is translated "some other way." (7) In 2 Pet. 3:1, the KJV translates *en* "by way of" ("by," RV). (8) In Gal. 2:5, the renderings "by," KJV, "in the way of," RV, serve to express the dative case of *hupotagē*, subjection. (9), For *propempō*, "to bring on one's way," Acts 15:3; 21:5, and the KJV of 2 Cor. 1:16 (RV, "to be set forward on my journey"). (10) *Aperchomai*, "to go away," is rendered "to go one's way," e.g., Matt. 13:25; 20:4; Mark 11:4; 12:12; Luke 19:32; John 11:46; Acts 9:17; Jas. 1:24. (11) In Luke 8:14, KJV, *poreuomai*, "to go on one's way" (RV), is rendered "go forth"; in 13:33, KJV, "walk" (RV, "go on my way"); in Matt. 24:1, KJV, it is rendered "departed" (RV, "was going on his way"). (12), In Acts 24:3, *pantē* is rendered "in all ways" (KJV, "always"). (13), In Rom. 3:12, KJV, *ekklinō*, "to turn aside" (RV), is rendered "are gone out of the way." (14), See also ESCAPE, B, LASCIVIOUS.

WEAK, WEAKENED, WEAKER, WEAKNESS

A. Adjectives.

1. *asthenēs* (ἀσθενής, 772), lit., "strengthless," is translated "weak," (a) of physical "weakness," Matt. 26:41; Mark 14:38; 1 Cor. 1:27; 4:10; 11:30 (a judgment upon spiritual laxity in a church); 2 Cor. 10:10; 1 Pet. 3:7 (comparative degree); (b) in the spiritual sense, said of the rudiments of Jewish religion, in their inability to justify anyone, Gal. 4:9; of the Law, Heb. 7:18; in Rom. 5:6, RV, "weak" (KJV, "without strength"), of the inability of man to accomplish his salvation; (c) morally or ethically, 1 Cor. 8:7, 10; 9:22; (d) rhetorically, of God's actions according to the human estimate, 1 Cor. 1:25, "weakness," lit., "the weak things of God." See FEEBLE, SICK.

2. *adunatos* (ἀδύνατος, 102), lit., "not powerful," is translated "weak" in Rom. 15:1, of the infirmities of those whose scruples arise through lack of faith (see 14:22, 23), in the same sense as No. 1 (c); the change in the adjective (cf. 14:1) is due to the contrast with *dunatoi*, the "strong," who have not been specifically mentioned as such in ch. 14.

B. Verb.

astheneō (ἀσθενέω, 770), "to lack strength," is used in much the same way as A, No. 1, and translated "being ... weak" in Rom. 4:19, KJV (RV, "being weakened"); 8:3; 14:1, 2 (in some texts, 1 Cor. 8:9); 2 Cor. 11:21, 29 (twice); 12:10; 13:3, 4, 9. See DISEASED, SICK.

C. Noun.

astheneia (ἀσθένεια, 769), for which see INFIRMITY, is rendered "weakness," of the body, 1 Cor. 2:3; 15:43; 2 Cor. 11:30, RV; 12:5 (plural, RV), 9, 1O, RV; Heb. 11:34; in 2 Cor. 13:4, "He was crucified through weakness" is said in respect of the physical sufferings to which Christ voluntarily submitted in giving Himself up to the death of the cross.

WEALTH

euporia (εὐπορία, 2142), primarily "facility" (*eu*, "well," *poros*, "a passage"), hence "plenty, wealth," occurs in Acts 19:25. Cf. *euporeō*, "to be well provided for, to prosper," Acts 11:29.

Note: In 1 Cor. 10:24, the KJV, "*wealth*," RV, "*good*," is, lit., "the (thing) of the other."

WEAPONS

hoplon (ὅπλον, 3696), always in the plur., is translated "weapons" in John 18:3 and 2 Cor. 10:4, the latter metaphorically of those used in spiritual warfare.

For **WEARINESS**, 2 Cor. 11:27, RV, see LABOR, No. 1

WEARY

1. *kopiaō* (κοπιάω, 2872), "to grow weary, be beaten out" (*kopos*, "a beating, toil"), is used of the Lord in John 4:6 (used in His own word "labor" in Matt. 11:28), in Rev. 2:3, RV. See LABOR, TOIL.

2. *kamnō* (κάμνω, 2577), "to be weary," is rendered "to wax weary" in Heb. 12:3, RV. See FAINT, No. 3, SICK.

3. *ekkakeō* (ἐκκακέω, 1573), or *enkakeō* (ἐγκακέω, 1573), for which see FAINT, No. 2, is rendered "to be weary" in Gal. 6:9; 2 Thess. 3:13.

For **WEDDING** see MARRIAGE

WEEK

sabbaton (σάββατον, 4521) is used (a) in the plural in the phrase "the first day of the week," Matt. 28:1; Mark 16:2, 9; Luke 24:1; John 20:1, 19; Acts 20:7; 1 Cor. 16:2; (b) in the singular, Luke 18:12, "twice in the week," lit., "twice of the sabbath," i.e., twice in the days after the sabbath. See SABBATH.

WEEP, WEEPING

A. Verbs.

1. *klaiō* (κλαίω, 2799) is used of "any loud expression of grief," especially in mourning for the dead, Matt. 2:18; Mark 5:38, 39; 16:10; Luke 7:13; 8:52 (twice); John 11:31, 33 (twice); 20:11 (twice), 13, 15; Acts 9:39; otherwise, e.g., in exhortations, Luke 23:28; Rom. 12:15; Jas. 4:9; 5:1; negatively, "weep not," Luke 7:13; 8:52; 23:28; Rev. 5:5 (cf. Acts 21:13); in 18:9, RV, "shall weep" (KJV, "bewail"). See BEWAIL.

2. *dakruō* (δακρύω, 1145), "to shed tears" (*dakruon*, "a tear"), is used only of the Lord Jesus, John 18:35.

Note: Other synonymom verbs are *thrēneō*, "to mourn," of formal lamentation: see BEWAIL, *Note* (1); *alalazō*, "to wail"; *stenazō*, "to groan" (*oduromai*, "to lament audibly," is not used in NT; see the noun *odurmos*, "mourning").

B. Noun.

klauthmos (κλαυθμός, 2805), akin to A, No. 1, denotes "weeping, crying," Matt. 2:18; 8:12; 13:42, 50, RV (KJV, "wailing"); 22:13; 24:51; 25:30; Luke 13:28; Acts 20:37.

WELCOME

1. *apodechomai* (ἀποδέχομαι, 588), "to receive gladly," is rendered "to welcome" in the RV of Luke 8:40; 9:11.

2. *hupolambanō* (ὑπολαμβάνω, 5274), "to take up, to entertain," is rendered "to welcome" in 3 John 8, RV, of a hearty "welcome" to servants of God.

WELL (Noun)

phrear (φρέαρ, 5421), "a pit," is translated a "well" in John 4:11, 12. See PIT.

Note: For *pēgē*, translated "well" in John 4:6 (twice), 14; 2 Pet. 2:17, see FOUNTAIN.

WELL (Adverb)

1. *kalōs* (καλῶς, 2573), "finely" (akin to *kalos*, "good, fair"), is usually translated "well," indicating what is done rightly, in the Epistles it is most frequent in 1 Tim. (3:4, 12, 13; 5:17); twice it is used as an exclamation of approval, Mark 12:32; Rom. 11:20; the comparative degree *kallion*, "very well," occurs in Acts 25:10. See GOOD, C, No. 1.

Note: The neuter form of the adjective *kalos*, with the article and the present participle of *poieō*, "to do," is translated "well-doing" in Gal. 6:9.

2. *eu* (εὖ, 2095), primarily the neuter of an old word, *eus*, "noble, good," is used (a) with verbs, e.g., Mark 14:7, "do (*poieō*) ... good"; Acts 15:29 (*prassō*); Eph. 6:3 (*ginomai*, "to be"); (b) in replies, "good," "well done," Matt. 25:21, 23; in Luke 19:17, *eu ge* (in the best texts). The word is the opposite of *kakōs*, "evilly." See GOOD, C, No. 2.

Notes: (1) In 2 Tim. 1:18, *beltion*, the neuter form of what is used as the comparative degree of *agathos*, "good," is used adverbially and translated "very well." (2) For John 2:10, "have well drunk" (RV, "freely"), see DRINK, B, No. 2. (3) *Hōs*, "as," with *kai*, "also (and)," is rendered "as well as" in Acts 10:47 (*kathōs* in some mss.) and 1 Cor. 9:5. (4) In Heb. 4:2 *kathaper*, "even as," with *kai*, is translated "as well as": see EVEN, No. 8.

WELL (do), WELL-DOING

A. Verbs.

1. *agathopoieō* (ἀγαθοποιέω, 15), "to do good" (*agathos*, "good," *poieō*, "to do"), is used (a) of such activity in general, 1 Pet. 2:15, "well-doing"; v. 20, "do well"; 3:6, 17; 3 John 11, "doeth good"; (b) of "acting for another's benefit," Mark 3:4; Luke 6:9, 33, 35.

2. *kalopoieō* (καλοποιέω, 2569), "to do well, excellently, act honorably" (*kalos*, "good," *poieō*, "to do"), occurs in 2 Thess. 3:13. The two parts of the word occur separately in Rom. 7:21; 2 Cor. 13:7; Gal. 6:9; Jas. 4:17.

Notes: (1) The distinction between Nos. 1 and 2 follows that between *agathos* and *kalos* (see GOOD). (2) In John 11:12, KJV, *sōzō* (passive voice, "to be saved"), is rendered "he shall do well" (RV, "he will recover").

B. Noun.

agathopoiia (ἀγαθοποιΐα, 16), "well-doing" (akin to A, No. 1), occurs in 1 Pet. 4:19.

C. Adjective.

agathopoios (ἀγαθοποιός, 17), "doing good, beneficent," is translated "them that do well" in 1 Pet. 2:14, lit., "well-doing (ones)."

For **WELL-BELOVED** see BELOVED

WELL-NIGH

Note: This forms part of the translation of *sumplēroō*, "to fulfill," in Luke 9:51, "were wellnigh" come, and *plēroō*, "to fulfill," in Acts 7:23, "was well-nigh ...," lit., "a time (of forty years) was fulfilled (to him)" (see FULFILL, A, No. 1).

WELL PLEASED

A. Noun.

eudokia (εὐδοκία, 2107), "good pleasure," occurs in the genitive case in Luke 2:14, lit., "(men) of good pleasure" (so RV marg.), RV, "(men) in whom He is well pleased" (the genitive is objective); the KJV, "good will (toward men)," follows the inferior texts which have the nominative. See DESIRE, PLEASURE, SEEM, WELL-PLEASING, WILL.

B. Verb.

eudokeō (εὐδοκέω, 2106), "to be well pleased": see PLEASE, A, No. 3, WILLING, B, No. 3.

WELL-PLEASING

A. Adjective.

euarestos (εὐάρεστος, 2101) is used in Rom. 12:1, 2, translated "acceptable (RV marg., "well-pleasing"); in the following the RV has "well-pleasing," Rom. 14:18; 2 Cor. 5:9; Eph. 5:10; in Phil. 4:18 and Col. 3:20 (RV and KJV); in Titus 2:9, RV, "well-pleasing" (KJV, "please ... well"); in Heb. 13:21, RV and KJV.

B. Verb.

euaresteō (εὐαρεστέω, 2100), akin to A, is rendered "to be well-pleasing" in Heb. 11:5, 6, RV (KJV, "please"); in Heb. 13:16, "is well pleased."

C. Noun.

eudokia (εὐδοκία, 2107), lit., "good pleasure," is rendered "well-pleasing" in Matt. 11:26 and Luke 10:21. See DESIRE, PLEASURE, SEEM, WELL PLEASED, WILL.

For **WET**, Luke 7:38, 44, RV, see WASH, No. 7

WHALE

kētos (κῆτος, 2785) denotes "a huge fish, a sea monster," Matt. 12:40. In the Sept., Gen. 1:21; Job 3:8; 9:13; 26:12; Jonah 1:17 (twice); 2:1, 10.

➔*WHAT*

Notes: (1) Most frequently this is a translation of some form of the relative pronoun *hos* or the interrogative *tis*. (2) Other words are (a) *hoios*, "of what kind," e.g., 2 Cor. 10:11, RV (KJV, "such as"); 1 Thess. 1:5, "what manner of men"; 2 Tim. 3:11 (twice), lit., "what sorts of things," "what sorts of persecutions"; (b) *poios*, "what sort of," e.g., Matt. 21:23, 24, 27; 24:42, 43; Luke 5:19; 6:32-34; 20:2, 8; 24:19; John 12:33, "what manner of"; so in 18:32; 21:19; Rom. 3:27; 1 Cor. 15:35; in Jas. 4:14, "what"; 1 Pet. 2:20 and Rev. 3:3 (ditto); 1 Pet. 1:11, "what manner of"; (c) *hopoios*, "what sort of," 1 Cor. 3:13; "what manner of," 1 Thess. 1:9; (d) *hosos*, "how great," Mark 6:30 (twice), RV, "whatsoever"; Acts 15:12; Rom. 3:19, "what things soever"; Jude 10 (1st part), "what soever things," RV; (2nd part) "what"; (e) *posos*, "how great, how much," 2 Cor. 7:11, "what (earnest care)," RV (*posos* here stands for the repeated words in the Eng. versions, the adjective not being repeated in the original); (f) *hostis*, "what (things)," Phil. 3:7; (g) in Matt. 26:40, *houtos*, "thus, so," is used as an exclamatory expression, translated "What" (in a word immediately addressed by the Lord to Peter), lit., "So"; (h) in 1 Cor. 6:16, 19, KJV, the particle *e*, "or" (RV), is rendered "What?"; in 1 Cor. 14:36, KJV and RV, "what?" (i) in 1 Cor. 11:22, *gar*, "in truth, indeed," has its exclamatory use "What?" (3) In John 5:19 "but what" translates a phrase, lit., "if not anything." (4) In Matt. 8:33 "what" is, lit., "the things" (neuter plural of the article).

WHISPERER, WHISPERING

1. *psithuristēs* (ψιθυριστής, 5588), "a whisperer," occurs in an evil sense in Rom. 1:29.

2. *psithurismos* (ψιθυρισμός, 5587), "a whispering," is used of "secret slander" in 2 Cor. 12:20. In the Sept., Eccl. 10:11, of "a murmured enchantment."

Note: Synonymous with No. 1 is *katalalos*, "a backbiter" (Rom. 1:30), the distinction being that this denotes one guilty of open calumny, *psithuristēs*, one who does it clandestinely.

WHITE (Adjective and Verb)

A. Adjective.

leukos (λευκός, 3022) is used of (a) clothing (sometimes in the sense of "bright"), Matt. 17:2; 28:3; Mark 9:3; 16:5; Luke 9:29; John 20:12; Acts 1:10; symbolically, Rev. 3:4, 5, 18; 4:4; 6:11; 7:9, 13; 19:14 (2nd part); (b) hair, Matt. 5:36; Christ's head and hair (in a vision; cf. Dan. 7:9), Rev. 1:14 (twice); ripened grain, John 4:35; a stone, Rev. 2:17, an expression of the Lord's special delight in the overcomer, the new name on it being indicative of a secret communication of love and joy; a horse (in a vision), 6:2; 19:11-14 (1st part); a cloud, 14:14; the throne of God, 20:11.

Note: Lampros, "bright, clear," is rendered "white" in Rev. 15:6, KJV, of "white (linen)" (RV, "bright," following those mss. which have *lithon* "stone"); in 19:8 (RV, "bright"). See BRIGHT, CLEAR, GOODLY, *Note*, GORGEOUS.

B. Verbs.

1. *leukainō* (λευκαίνω, 3021), "to whiten, make white" (akin to A), is used in Mark 9:3; figuratively in Rev. 7:14.

2. *koniaō* (κονιάω, 2867), from *konia*, "dust, lime," denotes "to whiten, whitewash," of tombs, Matt. 23:27; figuratively of a hypocrite, Acts 23:3. In the Sept., Deut. 27:2, 4; Prov. 21:9.

WHOLE (made), WHOLLY, WHOLESOME

A. Adjectives.

1. *holos* (ὅλος, 3650), for which see ALL, A, No. 3, signifies "whole," (a) with a noun, e.g., Matt. 5:29, 30; Mark 8:36; 15:1, 16, 33; Luke 11:36 (1st part), though *holon* may here be used adverbially with *photeinōn*, "wholly light" [as in the 2nd part, RV, "wholly (full of light)"]; John 11:50; 1 Cor. 12:17 (1st part); 1 John 2:2; 5:19; (b) absolutely, as a noun, e.g., Matt. 13:33; 1 Cor. 12:17 (2nd part).

2. *pas* (πᾶς, 3956), for which see ALL, A, No. 1, is sometimes translated "the whole" when used with the article, e.g., Matt. 8:32, 34; Rom. 8:22.

3. *hapas* (ἅπας, 537), for which see ALL, A, No. 2, is rendered "the whole," e.g., in Luke 19:37; 23:1.

4. *holoklēros* (ὁλόκληρος, 3648), from No. 1 and *klēros*, "a lot," is rendered "whole" in 1 Thess. 5:23: see ENTIRE

5. *hugiēs* (ὑγιής, 5199) (cf. Eng., "hygiene") is used especially in the Gospels of making sick folk "whole," Matt. 12:13; 15:31; Mark 3:5; 5:34; Luke 6:10; John 5:4, 6, 9, 11, 14, 15; 7:23; also Acts 4:10; of "sound (speech)," Titus 2:8. See SOUND.

6. *holotelēs* (ὁλοτελής, 3651), "wholly," 1 Thess. 5:23, is lit., "whole-complete" (A, No. 1, and *telos*, "an end"), i.e., "through and through"; the apostle's desire is that the sanctification of the believer may extend to every part of his being. The word is similar in meaning to No. 4; *holoklēros* draws attention to the person as a "whole," *holotelēs*, to the several parts which constitute him.

Note: In 1 Tim. 4:15, the sentence freely rendered "give thyself wholly to them" is, lit., "be in these (things)."

B. Verbs.

1. *hugiainō* (ὑγιαίνω, 5198), "to be in good health," akin to A, No. 5, is rendered "they that are whole" in Luke 5:31; "whole" in 7:10 (present participle); "wholesome" in 1 Tim. 6:3, KJV (RV, "sound"; marg., "healthful"). See HEALTH, SOUND.

2. *sōzō* (σώζω, 4982), "to save," is sometimes rendered "to make whole," and, in the passive voice, "to be made whole," or "to be whole," e.g., Matt. 9:21, 22 (twice), and parallel passages; Acts 4:9. See HEAL, SAVE.

3. *iaomai* (ἰάομαι, 2390), "to heal," is rendered "to make whole," Matt. 15:28; Acts 9:34, KJV (RV, "healeth"). See HEAL

4. *ischuō* (ἰσχύω, 2480), "to be strong," is rendered "they that are whole" in Matt. 9:12 and Mark 2:17. See ABLE, B, No. 4.

5. *diosōzō* (διασώζω, 1295), "to save thoroughly" (dia), is used in the passive voice and rendered "were made whole" in Matt. 14:36, RV (KJV, "were made perfectly whole"). See ESCAPE, HEAL, SAVE.

For **WHORE, WHOREMONGER** see FORNICATION, HARLOT

WICKED

1. *ponēros* (πονηρός, 4190), for which see BAD, No. 2, EVIL, A and B, No. 2, is translated "wicked" in the KJV and RV in Matt. 13:49; 18:32; 25:26; Luke 19:22; Acts 18:14; 1 Cor. 5:13; in the following the RV substitutes "evil" for KJV, "wicked": Matt. 12:45 (twice); 13:19; 16:4; Luke 11:26; Col. 1:21; 2 Thess. 3:2; and in the following, where Satan is mentioned as "the (or that) evil one": Matt. 13:38; Eph. 6:16; 1 John 2:13, 14; 3:12 (1st part); 5:18; in v. 19 for KJV, "wickedness"; he is so called also in KJV and RV in John 17:15; 2 Thess. 3:3; KJV only in Luke 11:4; in 3 John 10, KJV, the word is translated "malicious," RV, "wicked."

2. *athesmos* (ἄθεσμος, 113), "lawless" (*a*, negative, *thesmos*, "law, custom"), "wicked," occurs in 2 Pet. 2:7; 3:17. An instance of the use of the word is found in the papyri, where a father breaks off his daughter's engagement because he learnt that her fiance was giving himself over to lawless deeds (Moulton and Milligan, *Vocab.*).

Notes: (1) In Matt. 21:41, KJV, *kakos* (for which see BAD, No. 1, EVIL, A, No. 1), is translated "wicked" (RV, "miserable"). (2) In Acts 2:23 and 2 Thess. 2:8, KJV, *anomos*, "lawless" (RV), is translated "wicked."

WICKEDNESS

1. *ponēria* (πονηρία, 4189), akin to *poneros* (see above, No. 1), is always rendered "wickedness" save in Acts 3:26: see INIQUITY, No. 4.

2. *kakia* (κακία, 2549), "evil," is rendered "wickedness" in Acts 8:22; RV in Jas. 1:21, KJV, "naughtiness." See EVIL, B, No. 1, MALICE.

Notes: (1) For the KJV of 1 John 5:19 see WICKED, No. 1. (2) In Acts 25:5, KJV, the word *atopos* (RV, "amiss") is incorrectly rendered "wickedness."

WIDOW

chēra (χήρα, 5503), Matt. 28:13 (in some texts); Mark 12:40, 42, 43; Luke 2:37; 4:25, 26, lit., "a woman a widow"; 7:12; 18:3, 5; 20:47; 21:2, 3; Acts 6:1; 9:39, 41; 1 Tim. 5:3 (twice), 4, 5, 11, 16 (twice); Jas. 1:27; 1 Tim. 5:9 refers to elderly "widows" (not an ecclesiastical "order"), recognized, for relief or maintenance by the church (cf. vv. 3, 16), as those who had fulfilled the conditions mentioned; where relief could be ministered by those who had relatives that were "widows" (a likely circumstance in large families), the church was not to be responsible; there is an intimation of the tendency to shelve individual responsibility at the expense of church funds. In Rev. 18:7, it is used figuratively of a city forsaken.

WIFE, WIVES

1. *gunē* (γυνή, 1135) denotes (1) "a woman, married or unmarried" (see WOMAN); (2) "a wife," e.g., Matt. 1:20; 1 Cor. 7:3, 4; in 1 Tim. 3:11, RV, "women," the reference may be to the "wives" of deacons, as the KJV takes it.

2. *gunaikeios* (γυναικεῖος, 1134), an adjective denoting "womanly, female," is used as a noun in 1 Pet. 3:7, KJV, "wife," RV, "woman."

Note: In John 19:25 the article stands idiomatically for "the *wife* (of)"; in Matt. 1:6, the article is rendered "her *that had been the wife* (of)."

WIFE'S MOTHER

penthera (πενθερά, 3994) denotes "a mother-in-law," Matt. 8:14; 10:35; Mark 1:30; Luke 4:38; 12:53 (twice).

WILDERNESS

1. *erēmia* (ἐρημία, 2047), "an uninhabited place," is translated "wilderness" in the KJV of Matt. 15:33 and Mark 8:4 (RV, "a desert place"); RV and KJV, "wilderness" in 2 Cor. 11:26. See DESERT, A. (In the Sept., Isa. 60:20; Ezek. 35:4, 9.)

2. *erēmos* (ἔρημος, 2048), an adjective signifying "desolate, deserted, lonely," is used as a noun, and rendered "wilderness" 32 times in the KJV; in Matt. 24:26 and John 6:31, RV, "wilderness" (KJV, "desert"). For the RV, "deserts" in Luke 5:16 and 8:29 see DESERT, B.

WILES

methodia (μεθοδία, 3180), or *—eia* (μεθοδεία, 3180) denotes "craft, deceit" (*meta*, "after," *hodos*, "a way"), "a cunning device, a wile," and is translated "wiles (of error)" in Eph. 4:14, RV [KJV paraphrases it, "they lie in wait (to deceive)"], lit., "(with a view to) the craft (singular) of deceit"; in 6:11, "the wiles (plural) (of the Devil.)"

WILFULLY, WILLFULLY

A. Adverb.

hekousiōs (ἑκουσίως, 1596) denotes "voluntarily, willingly," Heb. 10:26, (of sinning) "willfully"; in 1 Pet. 5:2, "willingly" (of exercising oversight over the flock of God).

B. Verb.

thelō (θέλω, 2309), "to will," used in the present participle in 2 Pet. 3:5, is rendered "willfully (forget)" in the RV, KJV, "willingly (are ignorant of)," lit., "this escapes them (i.e., their notice) willing (i.e. of their own will)." See WILL, C, No. 1, WILLING, B, No. 1.

WILL, WOULD

A. Nouns.

1. *thelēma* (θέλημα, 2307) signifies (a) objectively, "that which is willed, of the will of God," e.g., Matt. 18:14; Mark 3:35, the fulfilling being a sign of spiritual relationship to the Lord, John 4:34; 5:30; 6:39, 40; Acts 13:22, plural, "my desires"; Rom. 2:18; 12:2, lit., "the will of God, the good and perfect and acceptable"; here the repeated article is probably resumptive, the adjectives describing the will, as in the Eng. versions; Gal. 1:4; Eph. 1:9; 5:17, "of the Lord"; Col. 1:9; 4:12; 1 Thess. 4:3; 5:18, where it means "the gracious design," rather than "the determined resolve"; 2 Tim. 2:26, which should read "which have been taken captive by him" [(*autou*), i.e., by the Devil; the RV, "by the Lord's servant" is an interpretation; it does not correspond to the Greek] unto His (*ekeinou*) will" (i.e., "God's will"; the different pronoun refers back to the subject of the sentence, viz., God); Heb. 10:10; Rev. 4:11, RV, "because of Thy will"; of human will, e.g., 1 Cor. 7:37; (b) subjectively, the "will" being spoken of as the emotion of being desirous, rather than as the thing "willed"; of the "will" of God, e.g., Rom. 1:10; 1 Cor. 1:1; 2 Cor. 1:1; 8:5; Eph. 1:1, 5, 11; Col. 1:1; 2 Tim. 1:1; Heb. 10:7, 9, 36; 1 John 2:17; 5:14; of human "will," e.g., John 1:13; Eph. 2:3, "the desires of the flesh"; 1 Pet. 4:3 (in some texts); 2 Pet. 1:21. See DESIRE, A, No. 5, PLEASURE, *Note* (1).

2. *thelēsis* (θέλησις, 2308) denotes "a willing, a wishing" [similar to No. 1 (b)], Heb. 2:4.

3. *boulēma* (βούλημα, 1013), "a deliberate design, that which is purposed," Rom. 9:19; 1 Pet. 4:3 (in the best texts).

4. *eudokia* (εὐδοκία, 2107) (*eu*, "well," *dokeō*, "to think") is rendered "good will" in Luke 2:14, KJV (see WELL PLEASED); Phil. 1:15: see DESIRE, PLEASURE, SEEM, WELL-PLEASING.

5. *eunoia* (εὔνοια, 2133), "good will" (*eu*, "well," *nous*, "the mind"), occurs in Eph. 6:7 (in some texts, 1 Cor. 7:3).

Notes: (1) In Acts 13:36, KJV, *boulē*, "counsel" (RV), is translated "will." (2) In Rev. 17:17, KJV, *gnōmē*, "an opinion," RV, "mind," is translated "will." (3) For "will-worship," Col. 2:23, see WORSHIP, B, No. 2.

B. Adjectives.

1. *hekōn* (ἑκών, 1635), "of free will, willingly," occurs in Rom. 8:20, RV, "of its own will" (KJV, "willingly"); 1 Cor. 9:17, RV, "of my own will" (KJV, "willingly"). In the Sept., Exod. 21:13; Job 36:19.

2. *akōn* (ἄκων, 210), *a*, negative, and No. 1, "unwillingly," occurs in 1 Cor. 9:17, RV, "not of mine own will" (KJV, "against my will"). In the Sept., Job 14:17.

C. Verbs.

When "will" is not part of the translation of the future tense of verbs, it represents one of the following:

1. *thelō* (θέλω, 2309), for the force of which see DESIRE, B, No. 6, usually expresses "desire" or "design"; it is most frequently translated by "will" or "would"; see especially Rom. 7:15, 16, 18-21. In 1 Tim. 2:4, RV, "willeth" signifies the gracious "desire" of God for all men to be saved; not all are "willing" to accept His condition, depriving themselves either by the selfestablished criterion of their perverted reason, or because of their self-indulgent preference for sin. In John 6:21, the KJV renders the verb "willingly" (RV, "they were willing"); in 2 Pet. 3:5, KJV, the present participle is translated "willingly" (RV, "wilfully").

The following are RV renderings for the KJV, "will": Matt. 16:24, 25, "would"; "wouldest," 19:21 and 20:21; "would," 20:26, 27; Mark 8:34, 35; 10:43, 44; "would fain," Luke 13:31; "would," John 6:67; "willeth," 7:17; in 8:44, "it is your will (to do)"; "wouldest," Rom. 13:3; "would," 1 Cor. 14:35 and 1 Pet. 3:10.

2. *boulomai* (βούλομαι, 1014), for the force of which see DESIRE, B, No. 7, usually expresses the deliberate exercise of volition more strongly than No. 1, and is rendered as follows in the RV, where the KJV has "will": Matt. 11:27 and Luke 10:22, "willeth"; Jas. 4:4, "would"; in Jas. 3:4, RV, "willeth" (KJV, "listeth"). In Jas. 1:18 the perfect participle is translated "of His own will," lit. "having willed."

3. *mellō* (μέλλω, 3195), "to be about to," is translated "will" in Matt. 2:13 and John 7:35 (twice); "wilt," John 14:22; "will," Acts 17:31; "wouldest," 23:20; "will," 27:10 and Rev. 3:16. See ABOUT, B.

WILLING (Adjective and Verb)

A. Adjectives.

1. *prothumos* (πρόθυμος, 4289) is rendered "willing" in Matt. 26:41; Mark 14:38, RV.

2. *hekousios* (ἑκούσιον, 1595), "willing," is used with *kata* in Philem. 14, lit., "according to willing," RV, "of free will" (KJV, "willingly").

B. Verbs.

1. *thelō* (θέλω, 2309) is rendered "ye were willing" in John 5:35. See WILL, C, No. 1.

2. *boulomai* (βούλομαι, 1014) is rendered "(if) Thou be willing" in Luke 22:42; in 2 Pet. 3:9, KJV (RV, wishing). See WILL, C, No. 2.

3. *eudokeō* (εὐδοκέω, 2106), "to be well pleased, to think it good," is rendered "we are willing" in 2 Cor. 5:8; in 1 Thess. 2:8, KJV, "we were willing" (RV, "we were well pleased"). See PLEASE, PLEASURE.

Notes: (1) In 2 Cor. 8:3, KJV, *authairetos*, "of one's own accord" (RV), is rendered "willing of themselves"; in v. 17, "of his own accord." See ACCORD. (2) For "willing to communicate," 1 Tim. 6:18, see COMMUNICATE, C.

For **WILLING MIND** see READINESS

WILLINGLY

Notes: (1) For *hekōn* see WILL, B, No. 1. (2) For *hekousiōs*, see WILLFULLY (3) For Philem. 14 see WILLING, A, No. 2. (4) For 2 Pet. 3:5 see WILL, C, No. 1.

For **WIN** see POSSESS, A, No. 2

WIND (Noun)

1. *anemos* (ἄνεμος, 417), besides its literal meaning, is used metaphorically in Eph. 4:14, of variable teaching. In Matt. 24:31 and Mark 13:27 the four "winds" stand for the four cardinal points of the compass; so in Rev. 7:1, "the four winds of the earth" (cf. Jer. 49:36; Dan. 7:2); the contexts indicate that these are connected with the execution of divine judgments. Deissmann (*Bible Studies*) and Moulton and Milligan (*Vocab.*) illustrate the phrase from the papyri.

2. *pnoē* (πνοή, 4157), "a blowing, blast" (akin to *pneō*, "to blow"), is used of the rushing wind at Pentecost, Acts 2:2. See BREATH.

3. *pneuma* (πνεῦμα, 4151) is translated "wind" in John 3:8 (RV, marg., "the Spirit breatheth," the probable meaning); in Heb. 1:7 the RV has "winds" for KJV, "spirits." See SPIRIT.

Note: For *pneō*, "to blow" ("wind" in Acts 27:40), see BLOW, No. 1.

WIND (Verb)

1. *deō* (δέω, 1210), "to bind," is translated "wound (it in linen clothes)," John 19:40, KJV, of the body of Christ (RV, "bound"). See BIND, No. 1, TIE.

2. *sustellō* (συστέλλω, 4958) is translated "wound ... up" in Acts 5:6 (RV, "wrapped ... round").

3. *eneileō* (ἐνειλέω, 1750), "to roll in, wind in," is used in Mark 15:46, of "winding" the cloth around the Lord's body, RV, "wound" (KJV, "wrapped").

WINE

1. *oinos* (οἶνος, 3631) is the general word for "wine." The mention of the bursting of the wineskins, Matt. 9:17; Mark 2:22; Luke 5:37, implies fermentation. See also Eph. 5:18 (cf. John 2:10; 1 Tim. 3:8; Titus 2:3). In Matt. 27:34, the RV has "wine" (KJV, "vinegar," translating the inferior reading *oxos*).

The drinking of "wine" could be a stumbling block and the apostle enjoins abstinence in this respect, as in others, so as to avoid giving an occasion of stumbling to a brother, Rom. 14:21. Contrast 1 Tim. 5:23, which has an entirely different connection. The word is used metaphorically (a) of the evils ministered to the nations by religious Babylon, 14:8; 17:2;

18:3; (b) of the contents of the cup of divine wrath upon the nations and Babylon, Rev. 14:10; 16:19; 19:15.

2. *gleukos* (γλεῦκος, 1098) denotes sweet "new wine," or must, Acts 2:13, where the accusation shows that it was intoxicant and must have been undergoing fermentation some time. In the Sept, Job 32:19.

Note: In instituting the Lord's Supper He speaks of the contents of the cup as the "fruit of the vine." So Mark 14:25.

WINEBIBBER

oinopotēs (οἰνοπότης, 3630), "a wine drinker" (*oinos*, and *potes*, "a drinker"), is used in Matt. 11:19; Luke 7:34. In the Sept., Prov. 23:20.

For **WINEBIBBINGS** see EXCESS, *Note* (2)

WIPE

1. *apomassō* (ἀπομάσσω, 631), "to wipe off, wipe clean" (*apo*, "from," masso, "to touch, handle"), is used in the middle voice, of "wiping" dust from the feet, Luke 10:11.

2. *ekmassō* (ἐκμάσσω, 1591), "to wipe out" (*ek*), "wipe dry," is used of "wiping" tears from Christ's feet, Luke 7:38, 44; John 11:2; 12:3; of Christ's "wiping" the disciples' feet, John 13:5.

3. *exaleiphō* (ἐξαλείφω, 1813), "to wipe out or away" (*ek*, or *ex*, "out," *aleiphō*, "to anoint"), is used metaphorically of "wiping" away tears from the eyes, Rev. 7:17; 21:4. See BLOT OUT.

WISDOM

1. *sophia* (σοφία, 4678) is used with reference to (a) God, Rom. 11:33; 1 Cor. 1:21, 24; 2:7; Eph. 3:10; Rev. 7:12; (b) Christ, Matt. 13:54; Mark 6:2; Luke 2:40, 52; 1 Cor. 1:30; Col. 2:3; Rev. 5:12; (c) "wisdom" personified, Matt. 11:19; Luke 7:35; 11:49; (d) human "wisdom" (1) in spiritual things, Luke 21:15; Acts 6:3, 10; 7:10; 1 Cor. 2:6 (1st part); 12:8; Eph. 1:8, 17; Col. 1:9, RV, "(spiritual) wisdom," 28; 3:16; 4:5; Jas. 1:5; 3:13, 17; 2 Pet. 3:15; Rev. 13:18; 17:9; (2) in the natural sphere, Matt. 12:42; Luke 11:31; Acts 7:22; 1 Cor. 1:17, 19, 20, 21 (twice), 22; 2:1, 4, 5, 6 (2nd part), 13; 3:19; 2 Cor. 1:12; Col. 2:23; (3) in its most debased form, Jas. 3:15, "earthly, sensual, devilish" (marg., "demoniacal").

2. *phronēsis* (φρόνησις, 5428), "understanding, prudence," i.e., a right use of *phrēn*, "the mind," is translated "wisdom" in Luke 1:17. See PRUDENCE.

Note: "While *sophia* is the insight into the true nature of things, *phronesis* is the ability to discern modes of action with a view to their results; while *sophia* is theoretical, *phronēsis* is practical" (Lightfoot). *Sunesis,* "understanding, intelligence," is the critical faculty; this and *phronēsis* are particular applications of *sophia*.

WISE, WISER, WISELY

A. Adjectives.

1. *sophos* (σοφός, 4680) is used of (a) God, Rom. 16:27; in 1 Tim. 1:17 and Jude 25 *sophos* is absent, in the best mss. (see the RV), the comparative degree, *sophōteros*, occurs in 1 Cor. 1:25, where "foolishness" is simply in the human estimate; (b) spiritual teachers in Israel, Matt. 23:34; (c) believers endowed with spiritual and practical wisdom, Rom. 16:19; 1 Cor. 3:10; 6:5; Eph. 5:15; Jas. 3:13; (d) Jewish teachers in the time of Christ, Matt. 11:25; Luke 10:21; (e) the naturally learned, Rom. 1:14, 22; 1 Cor. 1:19, 20, 26, 27; 3:15-20.

2. *phronimos* (φρόνιμος, 5429), "prudent, sensible, practically wise," Matt. 7:24; 10:16; 24:45; 25:2, 4, 8, 9; Luke 12:42; 16:8 (comparative degree, *phronimōteros*); 1 Cor. 10:15; in an evil sense, "wise (in your own conceits)," lit., "wise (in yourselves)," i.e., "judged by the standard of your self-complacency," Rom. 11:25; 12:16; ironically, 1 Cor. 4:10; 2 Cor. 11:19.

B. Noun.

magos (μάγος, 3097) denotes "a Magian," one of a sacred caste, originally Median, who apparently conformed to the Persian religion while retaining their old beliefs; it is used in the plural, Matt. 2:1, 7, 16 (twice), "wise men." See also SORCERER.

C. Verbs.

1. *sophizō* (σοφίζω, 4679) is rendered "to make wise" in 2 Tim. 3:15: see DEVISED.

2. *suniēmi* (συνίημι, 4920), or *suniō* (συνίω, 4920), "to perceive, understand," is used negatively in 2 Cor. 10:12, KJV, "are not wise" (RV, "are without understanding").

D. Adverb.

phronimōs (φρονίμως, 5430), "wisely" (akin to A, No. 2), occurs in Luke 16:8.

WISE (IN NO)

1. *ou mē* (οὐ μή, 3364), a double negative, expressing an emphatic negation, "by no means," is rendered "in no wise" in Matt. 10:42; Luke 18:17; John 6:37; Acts 13:41; Rev. 21:27.

2. *pantōs* (πάντως, 3843), "altogether, by all means," is used with the negative *ou* ("not") in Rom. 3:9, stating a complete denial, rendered "No, in no wise." See ALL.

3. *pantelēs* (παντελής, 3838), the neuter of *pantelēs*, is used with the negative *mē*, and with *eis to*, "unto the," in Luke 13:11, and translated "in no wise," lit., "not to the uttermost": see UTTERMOST, No. 1.

WIST

oida (οἶδα, 1492), "to know," in the pluperfect tense (with imperfect meaning) is rendered "wist" (the past tense of the verb "to wit": cf. WOT) in Mark 9:6; 14:40; Luke 2:49; John 5:13; Acts 12:9; 23:5. See KNOW, No. 2.

WIT (TO)

A. Adverb.

hōs (ὡς, 5613), a relative adverb signifying "as," or "how," is used in 2 Cor. 5:19 to introduce the statement "that God was . . . ," and rendered "to wit," lit., "how."

B. Verb.

gnōrizō (γνωρίζω, 1107), "to know, to make known," is rendered "we do (you) to wit" in 2 Cor. 8:1, KJV, RV, "we make known (to you)." See KNOW, No. 8.

Note: In Rom. 8:23 the italicized words "*to wit*" are added to specify the particular meaning of "adoption" there mentioned.

For **WITCHCRAFT** see SORCERY

WITHDRAW

1. *hupostellō* (ὑποστέλλω, 5288) is translated "withdraw" in Gal. 2:12.

2. *apospaō* (ἀποσπάω, 645), in the passive voice, is translated "was withdrawn" in Luke 22:41, KJV: see PART (Verb), No. 3.

3. *anachōreō* (ἀναχωρέω, 402) is translated "to withdraw" in the RV of Matt. 2:22 and John 6:15; RV and KJV in Matt. 12:15 and Mark 3:7.

4. *hupochōreō* (ὑποχωρέω, 5298), "to retire," is translated "withdrew Himself" in Luke 5:16; elsewhere in 9:10, RV, "withdrew apart" (KJV, "went aside"). See GO, No. 16.

5. *stellō* (στέλλω, 4724), "to bring together, gather up" (used of furling sails), hence, in the middle voice, signifies "to shrink from a person or thing," 2 Thess. 3:6, "withdraw"; elsewhere, 2 Cor. 8:20, "avoiding."

Note: In 1 Tim. 6:5, some texts have *aphistēmi*, rendered "withdraw thyself," KJV.

WITHER (away)

xērainō (ξηραίνω, 3583), "to dry up, parch, wither," is translated "to wither," (a) of plants, Matt. 13:6; 21:19, 20; Mark 4:6; 11:20, RV (KJV, "dried up"), 21; Luke 8:6; John 15:6; Jas. 1:11; 1 Pet. 1:24; (b) of members of the body, Mark 3:1, and, in some texts, 3. See DRY, B, OVERRIPE, RIPE.

Notes: (1) For the adjective *xēros*, "dry, withered," see DRY, A, No. 1. (2).

WITHHOLD

kōluō (κωλύω, 2967), "to hinder, restrain," is translated "withhold (not)" in Luke 6:29, RV, KJV, "forbid (not) to take." See FORBID, HINDER, KEEP, *Note* (7), SUFFER, WITHSTAND.

Note: For "withholdeth" in 2 Thess. 2:6 see RESTRAIN.

WITHSTAND

1. *kōluō* (κωλύω, 2967), "to hinder," is rendered "withstand" in Acts 11:17. See FORBID, HINDER.

2. *anthistēmi* (ἀνθίστημι, 436), "to set against," is translated "to withstand" in Acts 13:8 (middle voice); in the intransitive 2nd aorist, active voice, Eph. 6:13; 2 Tim. 3:8 (1st part; middle voice in 2nd part); 4:15.

WITNESS (Noun and Verb)

A. Nouns.

1. *martus* (μάρτυς, 3144) or *martur* (μάρτυρ, 3144) (whence Eng., "martyr," one who bears "witness" by his death) denotes "one who can or does aver what he has seen or heard or knows"; it is used (a) of God, Rom. 1:9; 2 Cor. 1:23; Phil. 1:8; 1 Thess. 2:5, 10 (2nd part); (b) of Christ, Rev. 1:5; 3:14; (c) of those who "witness" for Christ by their death, Acts 22:20; Rev. 2:13; Rev. 17:6; (d) of the interpreters of God's counsels, yet to "witness" in Jerusalem in the times of the Antichrist, Rev. 11:3; (e) in a forensic sense, Matt. 18:16; 26:65; Mark 14:63; Acts 6:13; 7:58; 2 Cor. 13:1; 1 Tim. 5:19; Heb. 10:28; (f) in a historical sense, Luke 11:48; 24:48; Acts 1:8, 22; 2:32; 3:15; 5:32; 10:39, 41; 13:31; 22:15; 26:16; 1 Thess. 2:10 (1st part); 1 Tim. 6:12; 2 Tim. 2:2; Heb. 12:1, "(a cloud) of witnesses," here of those mentioned in ch. 11, those whose lives and actions testified to the worth and effect of faith, and whose faith received "witness" in Scripture; 1 Pet. 5:1.

2. *marturia* (μαρτυρία, 3141), "testimony, a bearing witness," is translated "witness" in Mark 14:55, 56, 59; Luke 22:71; John 1:7, 19 (RV); 3:11, 32 and 33 (RV); 5:31, 32, 34 (RV), 36; RV in 8:13, 14, 17; 19:35; 21:24; KJV in Titus 1:13; KJV and RV in 1 John 5:9 (thrice), 10a; RV in 10b, 11; 3 John 12: see TESTIMONY, No. 2.

3. *marturion* (μαρτύριον, 3142), "testimony or witness as borne, a declaration of facts," is translated "witness" in Matt. 24:14, KJV; Acts 4:33; 7:44 (KJV); Jas. 5:3 (KJV): see TESTIMONY, No. 1.

4. *pseudomartus* or *-tur* (ψευδής, 5571) and ψευδής, 3144) denotes "a false witness," Matt. 26:60; 1 Cor. 15:15.

5. *pseudomarturia* (ψευδομαρτυρία, 5577), "false witness," occurs in Matt. 15:19; 26:59.

B. Verbs.

1. *martureō* (μαρτυρέω, 3140) denotes (I) "to be a *martus*" (see A, No. 1), or "to bear witness to," sometimes rendered "to testify" (see TESTIFY, No. 1); it is used of the witness (a) of God the Father to Christ, John 5:32, 37; 8:18 (2nd part); 1 John 5:9, 10; to others, Acts 13:22; 15:8; Heb. 11:2, 4 (twice), 5, 39; (b) of Christ, John 3:11, 32; 4:44; 5:31; 7:7; 8:13, 14, 18 (1st part); 13:21; 18:37; Acts 14:3; 1 Tim. 6:13; Rev. 22:18, 20; of the Holy Spirit, to Christ, John 15:26; Heb. 10:15; 1 John

5:7, 8, RV, which rightly omits the latter part of v. 7 (it was a marginal gloss which crept into the original text: see THREE); it finds no support in Scripture; (c) of the Scriptures, to Christ, John 5:39; Heb. 7:8, 17; (d) of the works of Christ, to Himself, and of the circumstances connected with His death, John 5:36; 10:25; 1 John 5:8; (e) of prophets and apostles, to the righteousness of God, Rom. 3:21; to Christ, John 1:7, 8, 15, 32, 34; 3:26; 5:33, RV; 15:27; 19:35; 21:24; Acts 10:43; 23:11; 1 Cor. 15:15; 1 John 1:2; 4:14; Rev. 1:2; to doctrine, Acts 26:22 (in some texts, so KJV; see No. 2); to the Word of God, Rev. 1:2; (f) of others, concerning Christ, Luke 4:22; John 4:39; 12:17; (g) of believers to one another, John 3:28; 2 Cor. 8:3; Gal. 4:15; Col. 4:13; 1 Thess. 2:11 (in some texts: see No. 2); 3 John 3, 6, 12 (2nd part); (h) of the apostle Paul concerning Israel, Rom. 10:2; (i) of an angel, to the churches, Rev. 22:16; (j) of unbelievers, concerning themselves, Matt. 23:31; concerning Christ, John 18:23; concerning others, John 2:25; Acts 22:5; 26:5; (II), "to give a good report, to approve of," Acts 6:3; 10:22; 16:2; 22:12; 1 Tim. 5:10; 3 John 12 (1st part); some would put Luke 4:22 here.

2. *marturomai* (μαρτύρομαι, 3143), strictly meaning "to summon as a witness," signifies "to affirm solemnly, adjure," and is used in the middle voice only, rendered "to testify" in Acts 20:26, RV (KJV, "I take ... to record"); 26:22, RV, in the best texts [see No. 1 (e)]; Gal. 5:3; Eph. 4:17; 1 Thess. 2:11, in the best texts [see No. 1 (g)].

3. *summartureō* (συμμαρτυρέω, 4828) denotes "to bear witness with" (*sun*), Rom. 2:15; 8:16; 9:1.

4. *sunepimartureō* (συνεπιμαρτυρέω, 4901) denotes "to join in bearing witness with others," Heb. 2:4.

5. *katamartureō* (καταμαρτυρέω, 2649) denotes "to witness against" (*kata*), Matt. 26:62; 27:13; Mark 14:60 (in some mss., 15:4, for *katēgoreō*, "to accuse," RV).

6. *pseudomartureō* (ψευδομαρτυρέω, 5576), "to bear false witness" (*pseudēs*, "false"), occurs in Matt. 19:18; Mark 10:19; 14:56, 57; Luke 18:20; in some texts, Rom. 13:9.

C. Adjective.

amarturos (ἀμάρτυρος, 267) denotes "without witness" (*a*, negative, and *martus*), Acts 14:17.

WOE

ouai (οὐαί, 3759), an interjection, is used (a) in denunciation, Matt. 11:21; 18:7 (twice); eight times in ch. 23; 24:19; 26:24; Mark 13:17; 14:21; Luke 6:24, 25 (twice), 26; 10:13; six times in ch. 11; 17:1; 21:23; 22:22; 1 Cor. 9:16; Jude 11; Rev. 8:13 (thrice); 12:12; as a noun, Rev. 9:12 (twice); 11:14 (twice); (b) in grief, "alas," Rev. 18:10, 16, 19 (twice in each).

WOLF

lukos (λύκος, 3074) occurs in Matt. 10:16; Luke 10:3; John 10:12 (twice); metaphorically, Matt. 7:15; Acts 20:29.

WOMAN

1. *gunē* (γυνή, 1135), for which see also WIFE, is used of a "woman" unmarried or married, e.g., Matt. 11:11; 14:21; Luke 4:26, of a "widow"; Rom. 7:2; in the vocative case, used in addressing a "woman," it is a term not of reproof or severity, but of endearment or respect, Matt. 15:28; John 2:4, where the Lord's words to His mother at the wedding in Cana, are neither rebuff nor rebuke. The question is, lit., "What to Me and to thee?" and the word "woman," the term of endearment, follows this. The meaning is "There is no obligation on Me or you, but love will supply the need." She confides in Him, He responds to her faith. There was lovingkindness in both hearts. His next words about "His hour" suit this; they were not unfamiliar to her. Cana is in the path to Calvary; Calvary was not yet, but it made the beginning of signs possible. See also 4:21; 19:26.

In Gal. 4:4 the phrase "born of a woman" is in accordance with the subject there, viz., the real humanity of the Lord Jesus; this the words attest. They declare the method of His incarnation and "suggest the means whereby that humanity was made free from the taint of sin consequent upon the Fall, viz., that He was not born through the natural process of ordinary generation, but was conceived by the power of the Holy Spirit ... To have written 'born of a virgin' would have carried the argument in a wrong direction ... Since that man is born of woman is a universal fact, the statement would be superfluous if the Lord Jesus were no more than man" (*Notes on Galatians*, by Hogg and Vine, pp. 184f.).

2. *gunaikarion* (γυναικάριον, 1133), a diminutive of No. 1, a "little woman," is used contemptuously in 2 Tim. 3:6, "a silly woman."

3. *presbuteros* (πρεσβύτερος, 4245), "elder, older," in the feminine plural, denotes "elder women" in 1 Tim. 5:2. See ELDER, A, No. 1.

4. *presbutis* (πρεσβῦτις, 4247), the feminine of *presbutes*, "aged," is used in the plural and translated "aged women" in Titus 2:3.

5. *thēleia* (θήλεια, 2338), the feminine of the adjective *thelus*, denotes "female," and is used as a noun, Rom. 1:26, 27. See FEMALE.

WOMB

1. *koilia* (κοιλία, 2836) denotes "the womb," Matt. 19:12; Luke 1:15, 41, 42, 44; 2:21; 11:27; 23:29; John 3:4; Acts 3:2; 14:8; Gal. 1:15. See BELLY, No. 1.

2. *gastēr* (γαστήρ, 1064), is rendered "womb" in Luke 1:31. See BELLY, No. 2.

3. *mētra* (μήτρα, 3388), the matrix (akin to meter "a mother"), occurs in Luke 2:23; Rom. 4:19.

WONDER (Noun and Verb)

A. Nouns.

1. *teras* (τέρας, 5059), "something strange," causing the beholder to marvel, is always used in the plural, always rendered "wonders," and generally follows *sēmeia*, "signs"; the opposite order occurs in Acts 2:22, 43; 6:8, RV; 7:36; in Acts 2:19 "wonders" occurs alone. A sign is intended to appeal to the understanding, a "wonder" appeals to the imagination, a power (*dunamis*) indicates its source as supernatural. "Wonders" are manifested as divine operations in thirteen occurrences (9 times in Acts); three times they are ascribed to the work of Satan through human agents, Matt. 24:24; Mark 13:22 and 2 Thess. 2:9.

2. *thambos* (θάμβος, 2285), "amazement," is rendered "wonder" in Acts 3:10. See AMAZE, A, No. 2.

Notes: (1) For *thauma*, "a wonder" (rendered "admiration" in Rev. 17:6, KJV), see MARVEL. (2) In Rev. 12:1, 3 and 13:13 *sēmeion*, "a sign," is translated in the KJV, "wonder(s)," RV, "sign(s)." (3) In Acts 3:11 *ekthambos* (*ek*, intensive, and No. 2) is translated "greatly wondering." (4) For *pseudos*, 2 Thess. 2:9, "lying wonders," see FALSE, B. Cf. AMAZE, B, Nos. 3 and 4.

B. Verb.

Note: For *thaumazō*, see MARVEL; for *existemi*, Acts 8:13, KJV, see AMAZE, B, No. 1.

WONDERFUL (THING, WORK)

Notes: (1) In Matt. 7:22, KJV, *dunamis* (in the plural) is rendered "wonderful works" (RV, "mighty works," marg., "powers"). See POWER. (2) In Acts 2:11, KJV, the adjective *megaleios*, "magnificent," in the neuter plural with the article, is rendered "the wonderful works" (RV, "the mighty works"). (3) In Matt. 21:15, the neuter plural of the adjective *thaumasios*, "wonderful," is used as a noun, "wonderful things," lit., "wonders."

WORD

1. *logos* (λόγος, 3056) denotes (I) "the expression of thought"—not the mere name of an object—(a) as embodying a conception or idea, e.g., Luke 7:7; 1 Cor. 14:9, 19; (b) a saying or statement, (1) by God, e.g., John 15:25; Rom. 9:9; 9:28, RV, "word" (KJV, "work"); Gal. 5:14; Heb. 4:12; (2) by Christ, e.g., Matt. 24:35 (plur.); John 2:22; 4:41; 14:23 (plur.); 15:20. In connection with (1) and (2) the phrase "the word of the Lord," i.e., the revealed will of God (very frequent in the OT), is used of a direct revelation given by Christ, 1 Thess. 4:15; of the gospel, Acts 8:25; 13:49; 15:35, 36; 16:32; 19:10; 1 Thess. 1:8; 2 Thess. 3:1; in this respect it is the message from the Lord, delivered with His authority and made effective by His power (cf. Acts 10:36); for other instances relating to the gospel see Acts 13:26; 14:3; 15:7; 1 Cor. 1:18, RV; 2 Cor. 2:17; 4:2; 5:19; 6:7; Gal. 6:6; Eph. 1:13; Phil. 2:16; Col. 1:5; Heb. 5:13; sometimes it is used as the sum of God's utterances, e.g., Mark 7:13; John 10:35; Rev. 1:2, 9; (c) discourse, speech, of instruction, etc., e.g., Acts 2:40; 1 Cor. 2:13; 12:8; 2 Cor. 1:18; 1 Thess. 1:5; 2 Thess. 2:15; Heb. 6:1, RV, marg.; doctrine, e.g., Matt. 13:20; Col. 3:16; 1 Tim. 4:6; 2 Tim. 1:13; Titus 1:9; 1 John 2:7;

(II) "The Personal Word," a title of the Son of God; this identification is substantiated by the statements of doctrine in John 1:1-18, declaring in verses 1 and 2 (1) His distinct and superfinite Personality, (2) His relation in the Godhead (*pros*, "with," not mere company, but the most intimate communion), (3) His deity; in v. 3 His creative power; in v. 14 His incarnation ("became flesh," expressing His voluntary act; not as KJV, "was made"), the reality and totality of His human nature, and His glory "as of the only begotten from the Father," RV (marg., "an only begotten from a father"), the absence of the article in each place lending stress to the nature and character of the relationship; His was the *shekinah* glory in open manifestation; v. 18 consummates the identification: "the only-begotten Son (RV marg., many ancient authorities read "God only begotten,"), which is in the bosom of the Father, He hath declared Him," thus fulfilling the significance of the title "*Logos*," the "Word," the personal manifestation, not of a part of the divine nature, but of the whole deity (see IMAGE).

The title is used also in 1 John 1, "the Word of life" combining the two declarations in John 1:1 and 4 and Rev. 19:13 (for 1 John 5:7 see THREE).

2. *rhēma* (ῥῆμα, 4487) denotes "that which is spoken, what is uttered in speech or writing"; in the singular, "a word," e.g., Matt. 12:36; 27:14; 2 Cor. 12:4; 13:1; Heb. 12:19; in the plural, speech, discourse, e.g., John 3:34; 8:20; Acts 2:14; 6:11, 13; 11:14; 13:42; 26:25; Rom. 10:18; 2 Pet. 3:2; Jude 17; it is used of the gospel in Rom. 10:8 (twice), 17, RV, "the word of Christ" (i.e., the "word" which preaches Christ); 10:18; 1 Pet. 1:25 (twice); of a statement, command, instruction, e.g., Matt. 26:75; Luke 1:37, RV, "(no) word (from God shall be void of power)," v. 38; Acts 11:16; Heb. 11:3.

The significance of *rhēma* (as distinct from *logos*) is exemplified in the injunction to take "the sword of the Spirit, which is the word of God," Eph. 6:17; here the reference is not to the whole Bible as such, but to the individual scripture which the Spirit brings to our remembrance for use in time of need, a prerequisite being the regular storing of the mind with Scripture.

Notes: (1) *Epos*, "a word," is used in a phrase in Heb. 7:9, lit., "(as to say) a word," RV, "(so to) say," KJV, "(as I may so) say"; *logos* is reasoned speech, *rhēma*, an utterance, *epos*, "the articulated expression of a thought" (AbbottSmith). (2) In Rom. 16:18, KJV, *chrēstologia*, "useful discourse" (*chrēstos*, "beneficial"), is rendered "good words" [RV, "smooth ... (speech)"]. (3) For *logikos*, 1 Pet. 2:2 (RV, "spiritual"), rendered "of the word," KJV, see MILK. (4) In Matt. 2:13, KJV, *eipon*, "to tell" (RV), is rendered "bring ... word." (5) For "enticing words," Col. 2:4, see ENTICE and PERSUASIVENESS. (6) For "strifes of words," 1 Tim. 6:4, KJV, and "strive ... about words," 2 Tim. 2:14, see STRIFE, STRIVE.

WORKING

1. *energeia* (ἐνέργεια, 1753) (Eng., "energy") is used (1) of the "power" of God, (a) in the resurrection of Christ, Eph. 1:19; Col. 2:12, RV, "working" (KJV, "operation"); (b) in the call and enduement of Paul, Eph. 3:7; Col. 1:29; (c) in His retributive dealings in sending "a working of error" (KJV, "strong delusion") upon those under the rule of the Man of Sin who receive not the love of the truth, but have pleasure in unrighteousness, 2 Thess. 2:11; (2) of the "power" of Christ (a) generally, Phil. 3:21; (b) in the church, individually, Eph. 4:16; (3) of the power of Satan in energizing the Man of Sin in his "parousia," 2 Thess. 2:9, "Coming."

2. *energēma* (ἐνέργημα, 1755), "what is wrought," the effect produced by No. 1, occurs in 1 Cor. 12:6, RV, "workings" (KJV, "operations"); v. 10.

WORLD

1. *kosmos* (κόσμος, 2889), primarily "order, arrangement, ornament, adornment" (1 Pet. 3:3, see ADORN, B), is used to denote (a) the "earth," e.g., Matt. 13:35; John 21:25; Acts 17:24; Rom. 1:20 (probably here the universe: it had this meaning among the Greeks, owing to the order observable in it); 1 Tim. 6:7; Heb. 4:3; 9:26; (b) the "earth" in contrast with Heaven, 1 John 3:17 (perhaps also Rom. 4:13); (c) by metonymy, the "human race, mankind," e.g., Matt. 5:14; John 1:9 [here "that cometh (RV, 'coming') into the world" is said of Christ, not of "every man"; by His coming into the world He was the light for all men]; v. 10; 3:16, 17 (thrice), 19; 4:42, and frequently in Rom., 1 Cor. and 1 John; (d) "Gentiles" as distinguished from Jews, e.g., Rom. 11:12, 15, where the meaning is that all who will may be reconciled (cf. 2 Cor. 5:19); (e) the "present condition of human affairs," in alienation from and opposition to God, e.g., John 7:7; 8:23; 14:30; 1 Cor. 2:12; Gal. 4:3; 6:14; Col. 2:8; Jas. 1:27; 1 John 4:5 (thrice); 5:19; (f) the "sum of temporal possessions," Matt. 16:26; 1 Cor. 7:31 (1st part); (g) metaphorically, of the "tongue" as "a world (of iniquity)," Jas. 3:6, expressive of magnitude and variety.

2. *aiōn* (αἰών, 165), "an age, a period of time," marked in the NT usage by spiritual or moral characteristics, is sometimes translated "world"; the RV marg. always has "age." The following are details concerning the world in this respect; its cares, Matt. 13:22; its sons, Luke 16:8; 20:34; its rulers, 1 Cor. 2:6, 8; its wisdom, 1 Cor. 1:20; 2:6; 3:18; its fashion, Rom. 12:2; its character, Gal. 1:4; its god, 2 Cor. 4:4. The phrase "the end of the world" should be rendered "the end of the age," in most places (see END, A, No. 2); in 1 Cor. 10:11, KJV, "the ends (*telē*) of the world," RV, "the ends of the ages," probably signifies the fulfillment of the divine purposes concerning the ages in regard to the church [this would come under END, A, No. 1, (c)]. In Heb. 11:3 [lit., "the ages (have been prepared)"] the word indicates all that the successive periods contain; cf. 1:2.

Aiōn is always to be distinguished from *kosmos*, even where the two seem to express the same idea, e.g., 1 Cor. 3:18, *aiōn*, v. 19, *kosmos;* the two are used together in Eph. 2:2, lit., "the age of this world." For a list of phrases containing *aiōn*, with their respective meanings, see EVER, B.

3. *oikoumenē* (οἰκουμένη, 3625), "the inhabited earth" (see EARTH, No. 2), is used (a) of the whole inhabited world, Matt. 24:14; Luke 4:5; 21:26; Rom. 10:18; Heb. 1:6; Rev. 3:10; 16:14; by metonymy, of its inhabitants, Acts 17:31; Rev. 12:9; (b) of the Roman Empire, the world as viewed by the writer or speaker, Luke 2:1; Acts 11:28; 24:5; by metonymy, of its inhabitants, Acts 17:6; 19:27; (c) the inhabited world in a coming age, Heb. 2:5.

Notes: (1) In Rev. 13:3, KJV, *gē*, "the earth" (RV), is translated "world." (2) For phrases containing *aiōnios*, e.g., Rom. 16:25; 2 Tim. 1:9; Titus 1:2, see ETERNAL, No. 2.

WORLDLY

kosmikos (κοσμικός, 2886), "pertaining to this world," is used (a) in Heb. 9:1, of the tabernacle, KJV, "worldly," RV, "of this world" (i.e., made of mundane materials, adapted to this visible world, local and transitory); (b) in Titus 2:12, ethically, of "worldly lusts," or desires.

For **WORLD RULERS,** Eph. 6:12, RV, see RULER, No. 3

WORSHIP (Verb and Noun), WORSHIPING

A. Verbs.

1. *proskuneō* (προσκυνέω, 4352), "to make obeisance, do reverence to" (from *pros*, "towards," and *kuneō*, "to kiss"), is the most frequent word rendered "to worship." It is used of an act of homage or reverence (a) to God, e.g., Matt. 4:10; John 4:21-24; 1 Cor. 14:25; Rev. 4:10; 5:14; 7:11; 11:16; 19:10 (2nd part) and 22:9; (b) to Christ, e.g., Matt. 2:2, 8, 11; 8:2; 9:18; 14:33; 15:25; 20:20; 28:9, 17; John 9:38; Heb. 1:6, in a quotation from the Sept. of Deut. 32:43, referring to Christ's second advent; (c) to a man, Matt. 18:26; (d) to the Dragon,

by men, Rev. 13:4; (e) to the Beast, his human instrument, Rev. 13:4, 8, 12; 14:9, 11; (f) the image of the Beast, 13:15; 14:11; 16:2; (g) to demons, Rev. 9:20; (h) to idols, Acts 7:43.

Note: As to Matt. 18:26, this is mentioned as follows, in the "List of readings and renderings preferred by the American Committee" (see RV *Classes of Passages*, IV): "At the word 'worship' in Matt. 2:2, etc., add the marginal note 'The Greek word denotes an act of reverence, whether paid to man (see chap. 18:26) or to God (see chap. 4:10).'" The Note to John 9:38 in the American Standard Version in this connection is most unsound; it implies that Christ was a creature. J. N. Darby renders the verb "do homage" [see the Revised Preface to the Second Edition (1871), of his *New Translation*].

2. *sebomai* (σέβομαι, 4576), "to revere," stressing the feeling of awe or devotion, is used of "worship" (a) to God, Matt. 15:9; Mark 7:7; Acts 16:14; 18:7, 13; (b) to a goddess, Acts 19:27. See DEVOUT, No. 3.

3. *sebazomai* (σεβάζομαι, 4573), akin to No. 2, "to honor religiously," is used in Rom. 1:25.

4. *latreuō* (λατρεύω, 3000), "to serve, to render religious service or homage," is translated "to worship" in Phil. 3:3, "(who) worship (by the Spirit of God)," RV, KJV, "(which) worship (God in the spirit)"; the RV renders it "to serve" (for KJV, "to worship") in Acts 7:42; 24:14; KJV and RV, "(the) worshipers" in Heb. 10:2, present participle, lit., "(the ones) worshiping." See SERVE.

5. *eusebeō* (εὐσεβέω, 2151), "to act piously towards," is translated "ye worship" in Acts 17:23. See PIETY (TO SHOW).

Notes: (1) The worship of God is nowhere defined in Scripture. A consideration of the above verbs shows that it is not confined to praise; broadly it may be regarded as the direct acknowledgement to God, of His nature, attributes, ways and claims, whether by the outgoing of the heart in praise and thanksgiving or by deed done in such acknowledgment. (2) In Acts 17:25 *therapeuō*, "to serve, do service to" (so RV), is rendered "is worshiped." See CURE, HEAL.

B. Nouns.

1. *sebasma* (σέβασμα, 4574) denotes "an object of worship" (akin to A, No. 3); Acts 17:23 (see DEVOTION); in 2 Thess. 2:4, "that is worshiped"; every object of "worship," whether the true God or pagan idols, will come under the ban of the Man of Sin.

2. *ethelothrēskeia* (or *-ia*) (ἐθελοθρησκεία, 1479), "will-worship" (*ethelō*, "to will," *thrēskeia*, "worship"), occurs in Col. 2:23, voluntarily adopted "worship," whether unbidden or forbidden, not that which is imposed by others, but which one affects.

3. *thrēskeia* (θρησκεία, 2356), for which see RELIGION, is translated "worshiping" in Col. 2:18.

Note: In Luke 14:10, KJV, *doxa*, "glory" (RV), is translated "worship."

WORSHIPER

1. *proskunētēs* (προσκυνητής, 4353), akin to *proskuneo* (see WORSHIP, A, No. 1), occurs in John 4:23.

2. *neōkoros* (νεωκόρος, 3511) is translated "worshiper" in Acts 19:35 KJV: see TEMPLE KEEPER.

3. *theosebēs* (θεοσεβής, 2318) denotes "reverencing God" (*theos*, "God," *sebomai*, see WORSHIP, A, No. 2), and is rendered "a worshiper of God" in John 9:35. Cf. *theosebeia*, "godliness," 1 Tim. 2:10.

Note: For Heb. 10:2, see WORSHIP, A, No. 4.

WORTHY, WORTHILY

A. Adjectives.

1. *axios* (ἄξιος, 514), "of weight, worth, worthy," is said of persons and their deeds: (a) in a good sense, e.g., Matt. 10:10, 11, 13 (twice), 37 (twice), 38; 22:8; Luke 7:4; 10:7; 15:19, 21; John 1:27; Acts 13:25; 1 Tim. 5:18; 6:1; Heb. 11:38; Rev. 3:4; 4:11; 5:2, 4, 9, 12; (b) in a bad sense, Luke 12:48; 23:15; Acts 23:29; 25:11, 25; 26:31; Rom. 1:32; Rev. 16:6.

2. *hikanos* (ἱκανός, 2425), "sufficient," is translated "worthy" in this sense in Matt. 3:11 (marg., "sufficient"); so 8:8; Mark 1:7; Luke 3:16; 7:6. See ABILITY, C, No. 2, etc.

3. *enochos* (ἔνοχος, 1777), "held in, bound by," is translated "worthy (of death)" in Matt. 26:66 and Mark 14:64, RV (marg., "liable to"; KJV, "guilty"). See DANGER.

Notes: (1) In Jas. 2:7, KJV, *kalos*, "good, fair," is translated "worthy" (RV, "honorable"). (2) For the KJV of Eph. 4:1; Col. 1:10; 1 Thess. 2:12, see C, below.

B. Verbs.

1. *axioo* (ἀξιόω, 515), "to think or count worthy," is used (1) of the estimation formed by God (a) favorably, 2 Thess. 1:11, "may count (you) worthy (of your calling)," suggestive of grace (it does not say "may make you worthy"); Heb. 3:3, "of more glory," of Christ in comparison with Moses; (b) unfavorably, 10:29, "of how much sorer punishment"; (2) by a centurion (negatively) concerning himself, Luke 7:7; (3) by a church, regarding its elders, 1 Tim. 5:17, where "honor" stands probably for "honorarium," i.e., "material support." See also DESIRE, B, No. 1 (Acts 28:22).

2. *kataxioō* (καταξιόω, 2661), a strengthened form of No. 1, occurs in Luke 20:35; 21:36, in some texts; Acts 5:41; 2 Thess. 1:5.

C. Adverb.

axiōs (ἀξίως, 516), "worthily," so translated in the RV [with one exception, see (c)], for KJV, "worthy" and other renderings, (a) "worthily of God," 1 Thess. 2:12, of the Christian walk as it should be; 3 John 6, RV, of assisting servants of

God in a way which reflects God's character and thoughts; (b) "worthily of the Lord," Col. 1:10; of the calling of believers, Eph. 4:1, in regard to their "walk" or manner of life; (c) "worthy of the gospel of Christ," Phil. 1:27, of a manner of life in accordance with what the gospel declares; (d) "worthily of the saints," RV, of receiving a fellow believer, Rom. 16:2, in such a manner as befits those who bear the name of "saints." Deissmann (*Bible Studies*, pp. 248ff.) shows from various inscriptions that the phrase "worthily of the god" was very popular at Pergamum.

For **WORTHY DEEDS,** Acts 24:2, KJV, see CORRECTION

WOT

Note: This form, the 1st person singular and the plural of the present tense of an AngloSaxon verb *witan*, "to see" or "to know" (for the past tense cf. WIST), is a rendering of (1) *oida*, "to know," in Acts 3:17; 7:40; Rom. 11:2 (see KNOW, No. 2); (2) *gnōrizō*, "to come to know," in Phil. 1:22 (see KNOW, No. 8).

WOUND (Noun and Verb)

A. Noun.

trauma (τραῦμα, 5134), "a wound," occurs in Luke 10:34.

Note: Plēgē, "a blow, a stroke," is used in Luke 10:30 with *epitithēmi* "to lay on," lit., "laid on blows," RV, "beat" (KJV, "wounded"). In Rev. 13:3, 12, *plēgē* is used with the genitive case of *thanatos*, "death," lit., "stroke of death," RV, "death stroke" (KJV, "deadly wound"); the rendering "wound" does not accurately give the meaning; in v. 14, with the genitive of *machaira*, "a sword," KJV, "wound" (RV, "stroke").

B. Verb.

traumaizō (τραυματίζω, 5135), "to wound" (from A), occurs in Luke 20:12 and Acts 19:16.

Note: In Rev. 13:3, KJV, *sphazō*, "to slay," is translated "wounded," RV, "smitten" (KJV and RV marg., "slain").

For **WOUND** (wrapped) see WIND (Verb)

WRANGLINGS

diaparatribē (διαπαρατριβή, 3859v), found in 1 Tim. 6:5, denotes "constant strife," "obstinate contests" (Ellicott), "mutual irritations" (Field), KJV, "perverse disputings" (marg., "gallings one of another"), RV "wranglings." Some texts have *paradiatribē*. The preposition *dia-* is used intensively, indicating thoroughness, completeness. The simple word *paratribē* (not found in the NT), denotes "hostility, enmity."

WRATH

1. *orgē* (ὀργή, 3709): see ANGER and *Notes* (1) and (2).

2. *thumos* (θυμός, 2372), "hot anger, passion," for which see ANGER, *Notes* (1) and (2), is translated "wrath" in Luke 4:28; Acts 19:28; Rom. 2:8, RV; Gal. 5:20; Eph. 4:31; Col. 3:8; Heb. 11:27; Rev. 12:12; 14:8, 10, 19; 15:1, 7; 16:1; 18:3; "wraths" in 2 Cor. 12:20; "fierceness" in Rev. 16:19; 19:15 (followed by No. 1).

3. *parorgismos* (παροργισμός, 3950) occurs in Eph. 4:26: see ANGER, A, *Note* (2).

Note: For the verb *parorgizō*, "to provoke to wrath," Eph. 6:4, KJV, see ANGER, B, No. 2.

WREST

strebloō (στρεβλόω, 4761), "to twist, to torture" (from *streblē*, "a winch" or "instrument of torture," and akin to *strephō*, "to turn"), is used metaphorically in 2 Pet. 3:16, of "wresting" the Scriptures on the part of the ignorant and unsteadfast. In the Sept., 2 Sam. 22:27.

WRESTLE, WRESTLING

palē (πάλη, 3823), "a wrestling" (akin to *pallō*, "to sway, vibrate"), is used figuratively in Eph. 6:12, of the spiritual conflict engaged in by believers, RV, "(our) wrestling," KJV, "(we) wrestle."

WRETCHED

talaipōros (ταλαίπωρος, 5005), "distressed, miserable, wretched," is used in Rom. 7:24 and Rev. 3:17. Cf. *talaipōria*, "misery," and *talaipōreō* (see AFFLICT).

WRINKLE

rhutis (ῥυτίς, 4512), from an obsolete verb *rhuō*, signifying "to draw together," occurs in Eph. 5:27, describing the flawlessness of the complete church, as the result of the love of Christ in giving Himself up for it, with the purpose of presenting it to Himself hereafter.

WRITE, WROTE, WRITTEN

A. Verbs.

1. *graphō* (γράφω, 1125) is used (a) of "forming letters" on a surface or writing material, John 8:6; Gal. 6:11, where the apostle speaks of his having "written" with large letters in his own hand, which not improbably means that at this point he took the pen from his amanuensis and finished the epistle himself; this is not negatived by the fact that the verb is in the aorist or past definite tense, lit., "I wrote," for in Greek idiom the writer of a letter put himself beside the reader and spoke of it as having been "written" in the past; in Eng. we should say "I am writing," taking our point of view from the time at which we are doing it; cf. Philem. 19 (this Ep. is undoubtedly a holograph), where again the equivalent English translation is in the present tense (see also Acts 15:23; Rom. 15:15); possibly the apostle, in Galatians, was referring to his having "written" the body of the epistle but the former alternative seems

the more likely; in 2 Thess. 3:17 he says that the closing salutation is written by his own hand and speaks of it as "the token in every epistle" which some understand as a purpose for the future rather than a custom; see, however, 1 Cor. 16:21 and Col. 4:18. The absence of the token from the other epistles of Paul can be explained differently, their authenticity not being dependent upon this; (b) "to commit to writing, to record," e.g., Luke 1:63; John 19:21, 22; it is used of Scripture as a standing authority, "it is written," e.g., Mark 1:2; Rom. 1:17 (cf. 2 Cor. 4:13); (c) of "writing directions or giving information," e.g., Rom. 10:5, "(Moses) writeth," RV (KJV, "describeth"); 15:15; 2 Cor. 7:12; (d) of "that which contained a record or message," e.g., Mark 10:4, 5; John 19:19; 21:25; Acts 23:25.

2. *epistellō* (ἐπιστέλλω, 1989) denotes "to send a message by letter, to write word" (*stellō*, "to send"; Eng., "epistle"), Acts 15:20; 21:25 (some mss. have *apostello*, "to send"); Heb. 13:22.

3. *prographō* (προγράφω, 4270) denotes "to write before," Rom. 15:4 (in the best texts; some have *graphō*); Eph. 3:3.

4. *engraphō* (ἐγγράφω, 1449) denotes "to write in," Luke 10:20; 2 Cor. 3:2, 3.

5. *epigraphō* (ἐπιγράφω, 1924) is rendered "to write over or upon" (*epi*) in Mark 15:26; figuratively, on the heart, Heb. 8:10; 10:16; on the gates of the heavenly Jerusalem, Rev. 21:12. See INSCRIPTION.

Note: In 2 Cor. 3:7 "written" is a translation of *en*, "in," with the dative plural of *gramma*, a letter, lit., "in letters."

B. Adjective.

graptos (γραπτός, 1123), from A, No. 1, "written," occurs in Rom. 2:15.

WRITING

gramma (γράμμα, 1121), from *graphō*, "to write," is rendered "writings" in John 5:47. See LETTER, No. 1.

Notes: (1) For *biblion*, "writing," KJV in Matt. 19:7, see BILL, No. 1. (2) In John 19:19, KJV, "the writing (was)" is a translation of the perfect participle, passive voice, of *graphō*, RV, "(there was) written."

WRITING TABLET (*KJV*, WRITING TABLE)

pinakidion (πινακίδιον, 4093) occurs in Luke 1:63, a diminutive of *pinakis*, "a tablet," which is a variant reading here.

WRONG, WRONGDOER, WRONGDOING

A. Nouns.

1. *adikia* (ἀδικία, 93), *a*, negative, *dikē*, "right," is translated "wrong" in 2 Pet. 2:13 (2nd part), 15, RV, "wrongdoing" (KJV, unrighteousness); in 2 Cor. 12:13, it is used ironically. See INIQUITY, UNJUST, UNRIGHTEOUSNESS.

2. *adikēma* (ἀδίκημα, 92) denotes "a misdeed, injury," in the concrete sense (in contrast to No. 1), Acts 18:14, "a matter of wrong"; 24:20, RV, "wrongdoing" (KJV, "evil doing"). See INIQUITY.

B. Verb.

adikeō (ἀδικέω, 91), "to do wrong," is used (a) intransitively, to act unrighteously, Acts 25:11, RV, "I am a wrongdoer" (KJV, "... an offender"); 1 Cor. 6:8; 2 Cor. 7:12 (1st part); Col. 3:25 (1st part); cf. Rev. 22:11 (see UNRIGHTEOUSNESS, B); (b) transitively, "to wrong," Matt. 20:13; Acts 7:24 (passive voice), 26, 27; 25:10; 2 Cor. 7:2, v. 12 (2nd part; passive voice); Gal. 4:12, "ye did (me no) wrong," anticipating a possible suggestion that his vigorous language was due to some personal grievance; the occasion referred to was that of his first visit; Col. 3:25 (2nd part), lit., "what he did wrong," which brings consequences both in this life and at the judgment seat of Christ; Philem. 18; 2 Pet. 2:13 (1st part); in the middle or passive voice, "to take or suffer wrong, to suffer (oneself) to be wronged," 1 Cor. 6:7. See HURT, OFFENDER, UNJUST.

WRONGFULLY

adikōs (ἀδίκως, 95), akin to the above, occurs in 1 Pet. 2:19.

Note: For "exact wrongfully," Luke 3:14, RV, see ACCUSE, B, No. 5.

WROTH (be)

1. *orgizō* (ὀργίζω, 3710), always in the middle or passive voice in the NT, is rendered "was (were) wroth" in Matt. 18:34; 22:7; Rev. 11:18, RV, (KJV, were angry); 12:17, RV, "waxed wroth." See ANGER, B, No. 1.

2. *thumoō* (θυμόω, 2373) signifies "to be very angry" (from *thumos*, "wrath, hot anger"), "to be stirred into passion," Matt. 2:16, of Herod (passive voice).

3. *cholaō* (χολάω, 5520), primarily, "to be melancholy" (*cholē*, "gall"), signifies "to be angry." John 7:23, RV, "are ye wroth" (KJV, "... angry").

Y

YIELD

1. *didōmi* (δίδωμι, 1325), "to give," is translated "to yield," i.e., "to produce," in Matt. 13:8, RV (KJV, "brought forth"); Mark 4:7, 8. See GIVE.

2. *apodidōmi* (ἀποδίδωμι, 591), "to give up or back," is translated "to yield" in Heb. 12:11; Rev. 22:2 (in each case, of bearing fruit). See DELIVER, A, No. 3, etc.

3. *paristēmi* (παρίστημι, 3936), or *paristanō* (παρίστανω, 3936), "to present," is translated "to yield" in Rom. 6:13 (twice), 16, 19 (twice), RV, "to present," in each place. See COMMEND, etc.

4. *poieō* (ποιέω, 4160), "to make, to do," is translated "yield" in Jas. 3:12.

5. *aphiēmi* (ἀφίημι, 863), "to send away," is translated "yielded up (His spirit)" in Matt. 27:50 (cf. *paratithēmi*, "I commend," Luke 23:46, and *paradidōmi*, "He gave up," John 19:30). See FORGIVE, etc.

6. *peithō* (πείθω, 3982), "to persuade," in the passive voice, "to be persuaded," is translated "do (not) thou yield," Acts 23:21. See PERSUADE.

Note: In Acts 5:10, KJV, *ekpsuchō*, "to breathe one's last, expire" (*ek*, "out," *psuchē*, "the life"), is translated "yielded up (RV, "gave up") the ghost."

YOKE, YOKED

A. Nouns.

1. *zugos* (ζυγός, 2218), "a yoke," serving to couple two things together, is used (1) metaphorically, (a) of submission to authority, Matt. 11:29, 30, of Christ's "yoke," not simply imparted by Him but shared with Him; (b) of bondage, Acts 15:10 and Gal. 5:1, of bondage to the Law as a supposed means of salvation; (c) of bond service to masters, 1 Tim. 6:1; (2) to denote "a balance," Rev. 6:5. See BALANCE.

2. *zeugos* (ζεῦγος, 2201), "a pair of animals," Luke 14:19.

B. Verb.

heterozugeō (ἑτεροζυγέω, 2086), "to be unequally yoked" (*heteros*, "another of a different sort," and A, No. 1), is used metaphorically in 2 Cor. 6:14.

YOKEFELLOW

sunzugos or *suzugos* (σύζυγος, 4805), an adjective denoting "yoked together," is used as a noun in Phil. 4:3, "a yokefellow, fellow laborer"; probably here it is a proper name, Synzygus, addressed as "true," or "genuine" (*gnēsios*), i.e., "properly so-called."

YOUNG, YOUNG (children, daughter, man, men, woman, women)

1. *neōteros* (νεώτερος, 3501), the comparative degree of *neos*, "new, youthful," is translated "young" in John 21:18; in the plural, Acts 5:6, "young men" (marg., "younger"); Titus 2:6, KJV, RV, "younger men." See YOUNGER.

2. *neos* (νέος, 3501), in the feminine plural, denotes "young women," Titus 2:4.

3. *neanias* (νεανίας, 3494), "a young man," occurs in Acts 7:58; 20:9; 23:17, 18 (in some texts).

4. *neaniskos* (νεανίσκος, 3495), a diminutive of No. 3, "a youth, a young man," occurs in Matt. 19:20, 22; Mark 14:51 (1st part; RV omits in 2nd part); 16:5; Luke 7:14; Acts 2:17; 5:10 (i.e., attendants); 23:18 (in the best texts), 22; 1 John 2:13, 14, of the second branch of the spiritual family.

5. *nossos* (νοσσός, 3502), or *neossos* (νεοσσός, 3502), "a young bird" (akin to No. 2), is translated "young" in Luke 2:24. Cf. *nossia*, "a brood," Luke 13:34, and the noun *nossion*, used in the neuter plural, *nossia*, in Matt. 23:37, "chickens"; *nossion* is the diminutive of *nossos*.

Notes: (1) In Acts 20:12, KJV, *pais*, a "lad" (RV), is translated "young man." (2) In Mark 7:25, KJV, *thugatrion*, a diminutive of *thugatēr*, "a daughter," is rendered "young (RV, 'little') daughter." (3) In Mark 10:13, KJV, *paidion*, in the neuter plural, is rendered "young (RV, 'little') children." (4) In Acts 7:19, KJV, *brephos*, in the neuter plural, is rendered "young children," RV, "babes." See BABE, No. 1.

YOUNGER

1. *neōteros* (νεώτερος, 3501), for which see No. 1, above, occurs in Luke 15:12, 13; 22:26; 1 Tim. 5:1 ("younger men"); 5:2, feminine; v. 11, "younger (widows)"; v. 14, "younger (*widows*)," RV, marg. and KJV, "younger (women)" (see WIDOW); 1 Pet. 5:5. For Titus 2:6 see YOUNG, No. 1.

2. *elassōn* (ἐλάσσων, 1640) is rendered "younger" in Rom. 9:12.

YOUTH

neotēs (νεότης, 3503), from *neos*, "new," occurs in Mark 10:20; Luke 18:21; Acts 26:4; 1 Tim. 4:12 (in some mss., Matt. 19:20).

YOUTHFUL

neōterikos (νεωτερικός, 3512), from *neōteros*, the comparative degree of *neos*, "new," is used especially of qualities, of lusts, 2 Tim. 2:22.

Z

ZEAL

zēlos (ζῆλος, 2205) denotes "zeal" in the following passages: John 2:17, with objective genitive, i.e., "zeal for Thine house"; so in Rom. 10:2, "a zeal for God"; in 2 Cor. 7:7, RV, "(your) zeal (for me)," KJV, "(your) fervent mind (toward me)"; used absolutely in 7:11; 9:2; Phil. 3:6 (in Col. 4:13 in some texts; the best have *ponos*, labor, RV). See ENVY, *Note*, FERVENT, C, *Note* (2), INDIGNATION, A, *Note* (3), JEALOUSY.

ZEALOUS

A. Noun.

zēlōtēs (ζηλωτής, 2207) is used adjectivally, of "being zealous" (a) "of the Law," Acts 21:20; (b) "toward God," lit., "of God," 22:3, RV, "for God"; (c) "of spiritual gifts," 1 Cor. 14:12, i.e., for exercise of spiritual gifts (lit., "of spirits," but not to be interpreted literally); (d) "for (KJV, 'of') the traditions of my fathers," Gal. 1:14, of Paul's loyalty to Judaism before his conversion; (e) "of good works," Titus 2:14.

The word is, lit., "a zealot," i.e., "an uncompromising partisan." The "Zealots" was a name applied to an extreme section of the Pharisees, bitterly antagonistic to the Romans. Josephus (*Antiq.* xviii. 1. 1, 6; *B.J.* ii. 8. 1) refers to them as the "fourth sect of Jewish philosophy" (i.e., in addition to the Pharisees, Sadducees, and Essenes), founded by Judas of Galilee (cf. Acts 5:37). After his rebellion in A.D. 6, the Zealots nursed the fires of revolt, which, bursting out afresh in A.D. 66, led to the destruction of Jerusalem in 70. To this sect Simon, one of the apostles, had belonged, Luke 6:15; Acts 1:13. The equivalent Hebrew and Aramaic term was "Cananaean" (Matt. 10:4); this is not connected with Canaan, as the KJV "Canaanite" would suggest, but is derived from Heb. *qannâ*, "jealous."

B. Verbs.

1. *zēloō* (ζηλόω, 2206), "to be jealous," also signifies "to seek or desire eagerly"; in Gal. 4:17, RV, "they zealously seek (you)," in the sense of taking a very warm interest in, so in v. 18, passive voice, "to be zealously sought" (KJV, "to be zealously affected"), i.e., to be the object of warm interest on the part of others; some texts have this verb in Rev. 3:19 (see No. 2). See AFFECT, *Note,* COVET, DESIRE, ENVY, JEALOUS.

2. *zēleuō*, a late and rare form of No. 1, is found in the best texts in Rev. 3:19, "be zealous."

Note: For *spoudazō*, Gal. 2:10, RV, see DILIGENT, B, No. 1.

1. Exegesis should create more questions

CIS: Isolate keys or clues + follow them to logical end

Notes

passage   noun   verb   key words   parsing the passage

subj

obj.

Ephesians : Paul
Grace
workmanship

object
subject
use
changes over time

Nominative

Luke 19:9

Notes

Notes

Notes

Notes

Notes

Notes

Notes

Notes

Notes

Notes

Notes